CONSTITUTIONAL LAW

THIRTY-NINTH EDITION

STEVEN L. EMANUEL

Founder & Editor-in-Chief, *Emanuel Law Outlines* and
Emanuel Bar Review
Harvard Law School, J.D. 1976
Member (ret.), NY, CT, MD and VA bars

The *Emanuel® Law Outlines* Series

ASPEN
PUBLISHING

To contact Customer Service, e-mail customer.service@aspenpublishing.com, call 1-800-950-5259, or mail correspondence to:

> Aspen Publishing
> Attn: Order Department
> PO Box 990
> Frederick, MD 21705

Printed in the United States of America.

1 2 3 4 5 6 7 8 9 0

ISBN   978-1-5438-4738-3

This book is intended as a general review of a legal subject. It is not intended as a source for advice for the solution of legal matters or problems. For advice on legal matters, the reader should consult an attorney.

About Aspen Publishing

Aspen Publishing is a leading provider of educational content and digital learning solutions to law schools in the U.S. and around the world. Aspen provides best-in-class solutions for legal education through authoritative textbooks, written by renowned authors, and breakthrough products such as Connected eBooks, Connected Quizzing, and PracticePerfect.

The Aspen Casebook Series (famously known among law faculty and students as the "red and black" casebooks) encompasses hundreds of highly regarded textbooks in more than eighty disciplines, from large enrollment courses, such as Torts and Contracts to emerging electives such as Sustainability and the Law of Policing. Study aids such as the *Examples & Explanations* and the *Emanuel Law Outlines* series, both highly popular collections, help law students master complex subject matter.

Major products, programs, and initiatives include:

- **Connected eBooks** are enhanced digital textbooks and study aids that come with a suite of online content and learning tools designed to maximize student success. Designed in collaboration with hundreds of faculty and students, the Connected eBook is a significant leap forward in the legal education learning tools available to students.

- **Connected Quizzing** is an easy-to-use formative assessment tool that tests law students' understanding and provides timely feedback to improve learning outcomes. Delivered through CasebookConnect.com, the learning platform already used by students to access their Aspen casebooks, Connected Quizzing is simple to implement and integrates seamlessly with law school course curricula.

- **PracticePerfect** is a visually engaging, interactive study aid to explain commonly encountered legal doctrines through easy-to-understand animated videos, illustrative examples, and numerous practice questions. Developed by a team of experts, PracticePerfect is the ideal study companion for today's law students.

- The **Aspen Learning Library** enables law schools to provide their students with access to the most popular study aids on the market across all of their courses. Available through an annual subscription, the online library consists of study aids in e-book, audio, and video formats with full text search, note-taking, and highlighting capabilities.

- Aspen's **Digital Bookshelf** is an institutional-level online education bookshelf, consolidating everything students and professors need to ensure success. This program ensures that every student has access to affordable course materials from day one.

- **Leading Edge** is a community centered on thinking differently about Legal Education and putting those thoughts into actionable strategies. At the core of the program is the Leading Edge Conference, an annual gathering of legal education thought leaders looking to pool ideas and identify promising directions of exploration.

Dedication

To Jeffrey Howard Emanuel,

No longer even close to being
the littlest Emanuel

Abbreviations Used in Text

CASEBOOKS

Chemerinsky Csbk (6e) — Erwin Chemerinsky, *Constitutional Law* Casebook (Wolters Kluwer, 6th Ed. 2020)

L,K,&C — Lockhart, Kamisar, Choper, Shiffrin & Fallon, *Constitutional Law — Cases, Comments, Questions* (West Publ., 8th Ed., 1996)

S,S,S,T&K — Stone, Seidman, Sunstein, Tushnet & Karlan, *Constitutional Law* (Wolters Kluwer, 8th Ed., 2018)

Sullivan & Gunther — Kathleen Sullivan & Gerald Gunther, *Constitutional Law* (West Academic, 19th Ed., 2016). (Where earlier editions are referenced, the edition number is indicated.)

HORNBOOKS AND OTHER AUTHORITIES

Chemerinsky Hnbk (6e) — Erwin Chemerinsky, *Constitutional Law: Principles and Policies* Treatise (Wolters Kluwer, 6th Ed. 2019)

Chemerinsky Hnbk (5e) — Erwin Chemerinsky, *Constitutional Law: Principles and Policies* Treatise (Wolters Kluwer, 5th Ed. 2017)

Ely — John Ely, *Democracy and Distrust* (Harvard Univ. Press, 1980)

Engdahl — David Engdahl, *Constitutional Power: Federal and State* (West Publ., Nutshell Series, 1974)

N&R — Nowak & Rotunda, *Constitutional Law* (West Publ., 5th Ed., 1995)

Schwartz — Bernard Schwartz, *Constitutional Law: A Textbook* (MacMillan Publ., 2nd Ed., 1979)

Tribe — Lawrence Tribe, *American Constitutional Law* (Foundation Press, 2nd Ed., 1988)

SUMMARY OF CONTENTS

Table of Contents ix

Preface xxiii

Casebook Correlation Chart xxv

Capsule Summary C-1

1. INTRODUCTION 1

2. THE SUPREME COURT'S AUTHORITY 5

3. FEDERALISM AND FEDERAL POWER GENERALLY 15

4. THE FEDERAL COMMERCE POWER 21

5. OTHER NATIONAL POWERS 57

6. TWO LIMITS ON STATE POWER: THE DORMANT COMMERCE CLAUSE
   AND CONGRESSIONAL ACTION. 73

7. INTERGOVERNMENTAL IMMUNITIES AND INTERSTATE RELATIONS . . 101

8. SEPARATION OF POWERS 111

9. DUE PROCESS OF LAW 161

10. EQUAL PROTECTION 241

11. MISCELLANEOUS CLAUSES: 14TH AM. PRIVILEGES OR IMMUNITIES;
    TAKING; CONTRACT; RIGHT TO BEAR ARMS; EX POST FACTO;
    BILLS OF ATTAINDER. 397

12. STATE ACTION 431

13. CONGRESSIONAL ENFORCEMENT OF CIVIL RIGHTS 451

14. FREEDOM OF EXPRESSION 475

15. FREEDOM OF RELIGION 659

16. JUSTICIABILITY 729

Table of Cases 775

Subject Matter Index 783

TABLE OF CONTENTS

Preface xxiii

Casebook Correlation Chart xxv

Capsule Summary C-1

Chapter 1

INTRODUCTION

I.   ROADMAP OF CONSTITUTIONAL LAW 1

II. THREE STANDARDS OF REVIEW 2

Chapter 2

THE SUPREME COURT'S AUTHORITY

I.   REVIEW OF ACTS OF CONGRESS (*MARBURY v. MADISON*) 5

II. REVIEW OF STATE COURT DECISIONS 7
   A. General principles of review 7
   B. *Martin v. Hunter's Lessee* 8
   C. Independent and adequate state grounds 8

III. CONGRESS' CONTROL OF FEDERAL COURT JURISDICTION 10
   A. The problem generally 10
   B. *McCardle* case 10
   C. Limits on congressional power 11
   D. Modern congressional controls on federal jurisdiction 12

IV. THE SUPREME COURT'S JURISDICTION TODAY 12

Quiz Yourself on
THE SUPREME COURT'S AUTHORITY (ENTIRE CHAPTER) 13

Exam Tips on
THE SUPREME COURT'S AUTHORITY 14

Chapter 3

FEDERALISM AND FEDERAL POWER GENERALLY

I.   THE CONCEPT OF FEDERALISM 15
   A. Nature of federalism 15
   B. Federal government has limited powers 15
   C. Specific powers 16

II. *McCULLOCH v. MARYLAND* 17

    A. Doctrine of implied powers 17

    B. *McCulloch* **and the "Necessary and Proper" Clause** 17

    Quiz Yourself on
    FEDERALISM AND FEDERAL POWER (ENTIRE CHAPTER)............. 19

    Exam Tips on
    FEDERALISM AND FEDERAL POWER GENERALLY 20

Chapter 4

THE FEDERAL COMMERCE POWER

I. THE COMMERCE CLAUSE GENERALLY 21

    A. Introduction 21

    B. Limitation on states vs. limitation on Congress 21

    C. Chronological approach 21

II. CASES PRIOR TO 1933 22

III. COURT BARRIERS TO THE NEW DEAL 25

    A. The New Deal threatened 25

    B. The *Schechter Poultry* **("Sick Chicken") case** 25

    C. The *Carter Coal* **case** 25

    D. The Court-packing plan 26

IV. THE POST-NEW-DEAL TREND 26

V. SOME MODERN LIMITS ON THE COMMERCE POWER 31

    A. Some limits still exist 31

    B. Can't ban "guns near schools" (*U.S. v. Lopez*) 31

    C. Violence against women (*Morrison*) 34

    D. Regulation of non-commercial activity as part of broader regulatory scheme 35

    E. Forcing someone to buy a product (*N.F.I.B. v. Sebelius*) 37

    F. Summary of the modern limits on the Commerce power 44

    G. Summary of modern view 45

VI. THE TENTH AMENDMENT AS A LIMIT ON CONGRESS' POWER .. 46

    Quiz Yourself on
    THE FEDERAL COMMERCE POWER (ENTIRE CHAPTER) 52

    Exam Tips on
    THE FEDERAL COMMERCE POWER................................. 55

Chapter 5

OTHER NATIONAL POWERS

I. THE TAXING POWER 57
   A. Several provisions on tax 57
   B. Special rules on taxes 58
   C. Regulatory effect 58

II. THE SPENDING POWER 62
   A. The spending power generally 62
   B. Not limited to enumerated powers 62
   C. Achievement of otherwise disallowed objectives 63
   D. Spending program can't "coerce" the states (*N.F.I.B.* case) 63
   E. "General welfare" still required 67

III. THE WAR, TREATY AND FOREIGN AFFAIRS POWERS 67

IV. OTHER POWERS 69

Quiz Yourself on
OTHER NATIONAL POWERS (ENTIRE CHAPTER) 70

Exam Tips on
OTHER NATIONAL POWERS 72

Chapter 6

TWO LIMITS ON STATE POWER: THE DORMANT COMMERCE CLAUSE AND CONGRESSIONAL ACTION

I. THE DORMANT COMMERCE CLAUSE — REGULATION 74
   A. Negative implications of federal power 74
   B. Negative implications of the Commerce Clause 74
   C. Traditional approach 74
   D. Early interpretations 75
   E. Rise of the "local" vs. "national" distinction 76
   F. Modern approach 76
   G. Application of the test 77
   H. Regulation of transportation 79
   I. State barriers to incoming trade 81
   J. State barriers to outgoing trade 84
   K. Local-processing requirements 85
   L. Environmental regulation 87
   M. State as purchaser or subsidizer 89

II. STATE TAXATION OF INTERSTATE COMMERCE 90

    III. CONGRESSIONAL ACTION — PREEMPTION AND CONSENT 92

        Quiz Yourself on
        TWO LIMITS ON STATE POWER (ENTIRE CHAPTER). 96

        Exam Tips on
        TWO LIMITS ON STATE POWER 98

Chapter 7

INTERGOVERNMENTAL IMMUNITIES & INTERSTATE RELATIONS

    I. TAX IMMUNITIES 101

    II. FEDERAL IMMUNITY FROM STATE REGULATION 103

    III. STATE IMMUNITY FROM FEDERAL REGULATION 103

    IV. INTERSTATE RELATIONSHIPS 103

        Quiz Yourself on
        INTERGOVERNMENTAL IMMUNITIES & INTERSTATE RELATIONS
        (ENTIRE CHAPTER). 107

        Exam Tips on
        INTERGOVERNMENTAL IMMUNITIES AND
        INTERSTATE RELATIONS. 108

Chapter 8

SEPARATION OF POWERS

    I. DOMESTIC POLICY AND THE SEPARATION OF POWERS 112
        A. General problem 112
        B. No right to "make laws" 112
        C. President's veto power 113

    II. THE PROHIBITION OF EXCESSIVE DELEGATION BY
         CONGRESS TO THE EXECUTIVE BRANCH 116

    III. FOREIGN AFFAIRS AND THE WAR POWERS 119
        A. Special presidential role in foreign affairs 119
        B. The war powers 121
        C. National security and entry into the U.S. 124
            1. Deference to Congress and the Executive Branch 124
            2. The travel ban case (*Trump v. Hawaii*) 124

    IV. APPOINTMENT AND REMOVAL OF EXECUTIVE PERSONNEL
         (INCLUDING IMPEACHMENT) 126
        A. The President's power of appointment, generally 126

B. Distinguishing between "principal" and "inferior" officers 126

C. Appointing "inferior "officers 127

D. Dividing line between "principal" and "inferior" officers in more detail. 128

E. No appointments by Congress 130

F. Dividing line between "officer" and non-officer 131

G. The President's Recess Appointments power 133

H. The President's right to remove appointees 135

I. Removal by Congress 142

J. Impeachment 143

V. LEGISLATIVE AND EXECUTIVE IMMUNITY 144

Quiz Yourself on
SEPARATION OF POWERS (ENTIRE CHAPTER) 151

Exam Tips on
SEPARATION OF POWERS 158

Chapter 9

DUE PROCESS OF LAW

I. THE BILL OF RIGHTS AND THE STATES 163

A. The Bill of Rights generally 163

B. Enactment of the Civil War Amendments 163

C. Due process of law and "incorporation" 164

D. The Fifth Amendment's Due Process Clause 166

II. SUBSTANTIVE DUE PROCESS — BEFORE 1934 166

III. SUBSTANTIVE DUE PROCESS — THE MODERN APPROACH
TO ECONOMIC AND SOCIAL-WELFARE REGULATION 170

Quiz Yourself on
SUBSTANTIVE DUE PROCESS — ECONOMIC AND SOCIAL-WELFARE
REGULATION 172

IV. SUBSTANTIVE DUE PROCESS — PROTECTION OF FUNDAMENTAL
RIGHTS GENERALLY 173

A. Overview 173

B. The early non-economic cases 174

C. Birth control (the *Griswold* case) 175

D. Post-*Griswold* contraceptive law 176

V. SUBSTANTIVE DUE PROCESS — REGULATION OF ABORTION ... 177

A. Abortion generally 177

B. *Roe v. Wade* 177

C. The modification of *Roe* by *Casey* 179

D. The meaning of "undue burden" (*Whole Woman's Health
v. Hellerstedt*) 183

E. The future of state efforts to regulate abortions 190

F. Cases on third-party consent, public funding and rules on particular
abortion methods 192

G. Consent 192

H. Public funding of abortions 194

I. Types of abortion allowable 194

VI. OTHER SUBSTANTIVE DUE PROCESS ISSUES:
CONTRACEPTION, CHILD REARING, THE RIGHT TO MARRY,
SEXUAL EXPRESSION, AND THE "RIGHT TO DIE" 196

A. Post-*Roe* regulation of contraception (*Carey* case) 196

B. Family relations 197

C. Sexuality, including homosexuality 202

D. The "right to die" 205

E. Other assorted autonomy issues 210

F. No right to be protected from privately-imposed harm 211

Quiz Yourself on
SUBSTANTIVE DUE PROCESS — PROTECTION OF NON-ECONOMIC
RIGHTS 213

VII. PROCEDURAL DUE PROCESS 219

A. Introduction 219

B. "Liberty" and "property" before 1970 220

C. Growth in the '70s of "entitlements" 221

D. Narrowing of "entitlements" theory 221

E. The tenure cases (*Roth* and *Perry*) 221

F. Breadth of injury is weighed 223

G. Freedom from arbitrary procedures 223

H. Narrowing of protected "liberty" interests 223

I. Rights of students 223

J. What process is due 223

Quiz Yourself on
PROCEDURAL DUE PROCESS 233

Exam Tips on
DUE PROCESS OF LAW 235

Chapter 10

EQUAL PROTECTION

I. INTRODUCTION 243

**II. ECONOMIC AND SOCIAL LAWS —
THE "MERE-RATIONALITY" STANDARD** 248
   A. Deferential review 248
   B. Broad reading of "legitimate public objective" 248
   C. "One step at a time" approach 249
   D. Determining a statute's "purpose" 249
   E. Legal disabilities motivated by "animus" towards unpopular groups . 251
   F. Highly deferential standard 252
   G. Summary of Court's approach 254

Quiz Yourself on
EQUAL PROTECTION — ECONOMIC & SOCIAL LAWS 254

III. SUSPECT CLASSIFICATIONS, ESPECIALLY RACE 256
   A. Suspect classes generally 256
   B. Groups covered 256
   C. "Purposeful" discrimination 257
   D. Other requirements for strict scrutiny 262
   E. How strict is "strict scrutiny" 263
   F. Segregation and its remedies 267

IV. AFFIRMATIVE ACTION AND "BENIGN" DISCRIMINATION 274
   A. "Benign" discrimination generally 274
   B. Benign use of sex classes 275
   C. Race 278
   D. Desegregation 281
   E. Preferential admissions to universities 281
   **F. Admissions to public secondary schools by race-conscious
      pupil-assignments (the *Parents Involved* case)** 294
   G. Minority set-asides by states and cities 301
   H. Set-asides by Congress 306
   I. Hiring, lay-offs, and promotions 308
   J. Drawing of election districts on race-conscious grounds .. 312
   K. Harm to members of minority 316
   L. Law enforcement, prison administration and military operations 317
   M. Popular votes to repeal affirmative action 318

V. CLASSIFICATIONS BASED ON SEX 319
   A. Introduction 319
   B. Traditional deference by Court 320
   C. Stricter review 320
   D. Middle-level review not always fatal 322
   E. Stereotypical thinking rejected 324
   F. Remedial statutes 328
   G. Discriminatory purpose required 329

    H. "As applied" challenges 331

    Quiz Yourself on
    EQUAL PROTECTION — SUSPECT CLASSES, AFFIRMATIVE ACTION
    AND CLASSIFICATIONS BASED ON SEX 331

  VI.   CLASSIFICATIONS BASED ON ALIENAGE 340

  VII. ILLEGITIMACY 346

  VIII. MENTAL RETARDATION AND MENTAL ILLNESS 347

  IX.   GENERAL PRINCIPLES OF MIDDLE-LEVEL SCRUTINY 349

    Quiz Yourself on
    EQUAL PROTECTION — ALIENAGE AND ILLEGITIMACY 350

  X.   UNEQUAL TREATMENT OF GAYS, AND THE BANNING OF
      SAME-SEX MARRIAGE 352
    A. Issues generally 352
    B. Singling out of gays because of animus (*Romer v. Evans*) 354
    C. The federal Defense of Marriage Act struck down (*Windsor*) 355
    D. States must allow same-sex marriage (*Obergefell*) 356

  XI. FUNDAMENTAL RIGHTS 364
    A. Introduction 364
    B. Education 365
    C. Marriage as fundamental right 367
    D. Adult sexual relations 367
    E. Voting rights 368
    F. Access to the ballot 375
    G. Access to courts 378
    H. The right to travel 381
    I. Wealth classifications 383

    Quiz Yourself on
    EQUAL PROTECTION — UNEQUAL TREATMENT OF GAYS;
    FUNDAMENTAL RIGHTS 385

    Exam Tips on
    EQUAL PROTECTION 390

Chapter 11

MISCELLANEOUS CLAUSES: 14TH AM. PRIVILEGES OR IMMUNITIES; TAKING; CONTRACT; RIGHT TO BEAR ARMS; EX POST FACTO; BILLS OF ATTAINDER

  I.   THE 14TH AMENDMENT'S PRIVILEGES OR IMMUNITIES
    CLAUSE 398

II. THE "TAKING" CLAUSE 400

   A. The Taking Clause generally 400

   B. The taking/regulation distinction, generally 400

   C. Denial of all economically viable use of land 402

   D. "Prevention of harm" or "noxious use" rationale 403

   E. Zoning, environmental and landmark-preservation rationales 404

   F. Physical occupation 405

   G. Subsequent owner who takes with notice of restriction 407

   H. Dedications, and the requirement of a tight means-end fit 407

   I. Requirement of "public" use 411

III. THE "CONTRACT" CLAUSE 413

IV. THE SECOND AMENDMENT "RIGHT TO BEAR ARMS" 417

V. EX POST FACTO LAWS 423

VI. BILLS OF ATTAINDER 424

Quiz Yourself on
MISCELLANEOUS CLAUSES (ENTIRE CHAPTER) 425

Exam Tips on
MISCELLANEOUS CLAUSES 429

Chapter 12

STATE ACTION

I. INTRODUCTION 431

II. THE "PUBLIC FUNCTION" APPROACH 435

   A. The "public function" approach generally 435

   B. The *White Primary* Cases 435

   C. Company towns and shopping centers 435

   D. Parks and recreation 437

   E. The requirement of state "exclusivity" 437

   F. Future of "public function" doctrine 438

III. "NEXUS" — THE SIGNIFICANCE OF STATE INVOLVEMENT 438

   A. The "nexus" theory generally 438

   B. "Commandment" 439

   C. "Encouragement" by the state 441

   D. "Symbiosis" between state and private actor 442

   E. Involvement or "entanglement" by state 443

Quiz Yourself on
STATE ACTION (ENTIRE CHAPTER) 446

Exam Tips on
STATE ACTION 448

Chapter 13

CONGRESSIONAL ENFORCEMENT OF CIVIL RIGHTS

I.   **INTRODUCTION** 451

II. **CONGRESS' POWER TO REACH PRIVATE CONDUCT** 453

III. **CONGRESS' POWER TO REMEDY VIOLATIONS OF THE
     CIVIL WAR AMENDMENTS** 458
     A. General problem 458
     B. Congress' broad "remedial" powers 459
     C. The Voting Rights Act 460

IV. **CONGRESS' POWER TO REDEFINE THE MEANING AND
     SCOPE OF CONSTITUTIONAL GUARANTEES** 464

V.   **CONGRESS' POWER TO ABROGATE THE ELEVENTH
     AMENDMENT, AND THUS AUTHORIZE PRIVATE DAMAGE
     SUITS AGAINST THE STATES FOR DISCRIMINATION** 467

Quiz Yourself on
CONGRESSIONAL ENFORCEMENT OF CIVIL RIGHTS
(ENTIRE CHAPTER). 472

Exam Tips on
CONGRESSIONAL ENFORCEMENT OF CIVIL RIGHTS 473

Chapter 14

FREEDOM OF EXPRESSION

I.   **GENERAL THEMES** 477
     A. Text of First Amendment 477
     B. Two broad classes 477
     C. Analysis of "track one" cases ("content-based" regulation) 479
     D. Analysis of "track two" cases ("non-content-based" regulation) 488
     E. Regulation of "pure conduct" 488

II. **ADVOCACY OF ILLEGAL CONDUCT** 489

III. **OVERBREADTH AND VAGUENESS** 498

Quiz Yourself on
FREEDOM OF EXPRESSION — GENERAL THEMES; ADVOCACY OF
ILLEGAL CONDUCT; OVERBREADTH AND VAGUENESS 502

IV. REGULATION OF CONTEXT — "TIME, PLACE AND MANNER" .. 506
    A. Context regulations generally 506
    B. Requirement that means be "narrowly tailored" to the objective 508
    C. "Leave open alternative channels" requirement 510
    D. Licensing 510
    E. Intrusive speakers vs. right to be left alone 512
    F. Canvassing and soliciting 513
    G. Protest and persuasion on public property outside of abortion clinics . 515
    H. The hostile audience and "fighting words" 516
    I. Offensive words and the sensitive audience 519
    J. Regulation of "hate speech" 523
    K. All speech not necessarily created equal (the disfavoring of indecent speech) 527
    L. Regulation of indecency in media 529
    M. The public forum 532
    N. Right of access to private places 541

V. SYMBOLIC EXPRESSION 542

    Quiz Yourself on
    "TIME, PLACE AND MANNER" RESTRICTIONS;
    SYMBOLIC EXPRESSION.. 547

VI. DEFAMATION, INTENTIONAL INFLICTION OF EMOTIONAL DISTRESS, AND THE BANNING OF "FALSE SPEECH" 552
    A. Regulation of defamatory and other false speech 552
    B. Initially no protection 552
    C. *New York Times v. Sullivan* 552
    D. Extension to "public figures" 553
    E. Private figures 554
    F. Non-media defendants 555
    G. Statements of no "public interest" 556
    H. Statements of opinion 556
    I. Intentional infliction of emotional distress 556
    J. False statements of fact outside the defamation context 557

VII. OBSCENITY 559
    A. Generally unprotected 559
    B. *Miller* 561
    C. Private possession by adults 562
    D. Protection of children 562
    E. Protection of animals, and the "animal crush video" issue 563
    F. Other issues 564

VIII. COMMERCIAL SPEECH 565

A. Overview 565

B. The *Virginia Pharmacy* revolution 565

C. Regulation of lawyers 567

D. Commercial speech doctrine curtailed (*Central Hudson Gas*) 568

E. Advertising of lawful but harmful products 570

F. Current status 571

G. Constitutionally-protected products 573

Quiz Yourself on
DEFAMATION, OBSCENITY AND COMMERCIAL SPEECH 573

IX. REGULATION IN THE CONTEXT OF POLITICAL CAMPAIGNS 576

A. Money in political campaigns, generally 576

B. *Buckley v. Valeo* 576

C. Limits on aggregate contributions by an individual (*McCutcheon*) 580

D. "Soft money" and pre-election "issue ads" (*McConnell, Wisconsin Right to Life* and *Citizens United*) 582

E. Campaign spending by political parties 588

F. How low can limits be set 588

G. Corporate and judicial expression during campaigns 589

X. SOME SPECIAL CONTEXTS 591

A. Scope 591

B. Schools 592

C. Furnishing of legal services by lay groups 599

D. Government as speaker or as funder of speech 600

XI. THE FREEDOM OF ASSOCIATION, THE RIGHT NOT TO
    SPEAK OR ASSOCIATE, AND THE DENIAL OF PUBLIC JOBS
    OR BENEFITS 605

A. Freedom of association generally 605

B. Right not to associate, generally 606

C. Right to avoid compulsory financial support 607

D. Veto on unwanted participants 609

E. Right to exclude from membership in group 610

F. Illegal membership 611

G. Denial of public job or benefit 611

H. Compulsory disclosure (*Americans for Prosperity v. Bonta*) 615

I. The bar membership cases 620

J. The "right not to speak" 621

XII. UNCONSTITUTIONAL CONDITIONS 623

XIII. SPECIAL PROBLEMS CONCERNING THE MEDIA 626

A. Summary of issues 626

B. Special role for the press 626

C. **Prior restraints** 628

D. **Governmental demands for information held by press** 633

E. **Disclosure of confidential or illegally-obtained information** 636

F. **Right of access to government-held information** 638

G. **Regulation of broadcast media** 639

Quiz Yourself on
REGULATION IN POLITICAL CAMPAIGNS; SPECIAL CONTEXTS;
FREEDOM OF ASSOCIATION; DENIAL OF PUBLIC JOBS OR BENEFITS;
SPECIAL PROBLEMS OF THE MEDIA 641

Exam Tips on
FREEDOM OF EXPRESSION 648

Chapter 15

FREEDOM OF RELIGION

I. **INTRODUCTION** 660

II. **THE ESTABLISHMENT CLAUSE** 661

   A. **Background** 661

   B. **Religion and the public schools** 662

   C. **Sunday closing laws** 667

   D. **Property-tax exemptions for churches** 667

   E. **Military and prison chaplains** 668

   F. **Helping religious groups spread their message** 668

   G. **The "excessive entanglement prong"** 669

   H. **Entanglement by church involvement in government affairs** 671

   I. **Ceremonies, displays and monuments — generally** 671

   J. **Ceremonies** 671

   K. **Displays and monuments with religious themes** 672

   L. **The Ten Commandments cases** 673

   M. **The Christian cross case (*Amer. Legion*)** 674

   N. **Financial aid to religious schools** 677

   O. **No intentional preference for one sect over others** 680

III. **THE FREE EXERCISE CLAUSE** 688

   A. **Introduction** 688

   B. **Intent to disfavor religious practice** 688

   C. **Incidental burdensome effect, and required accommodations** 698

   D. **The 1990 "generally-applicable rule" case (*Employment Div. v. Smith*)** 700

   E. **Post-*Smith* law generally** 701

   F. **The meaning of "generally applicable"** 701

   G. **Strict scrutiny under *Smith*, and the "most favored nation" rule** . . . 712

   H. **Anti-discrimination laws, and a group's right to pick its "ministers"** . . 713

I. Possible overruling of *Smith* 713
J. Public health regulations 715
K. What constitutes a "religious belief" 715

Quiz Yourself on
FREEDOM OF RELIGION (ENTIRE CHAPTER) 716

Exam Tips on
FREEDOM OF RELIGION 724

Chapter 16

JUSTICIABILITY

I. INTRODUCTION 729

II. ADVISORY OPINIONS 730

III. STANDING 731
A. Nature of "standing" generally 731
B. Federal taxpayer and citizen suits 733
C. Standing not based on taxpayer or citizen status 735
D. The "injury in fact" requirement 735
E. Harm suffered by many 737
F. Causation 738
G. Special deference when plaintiff is a state acting for its citizens 740
H. Third-party standing 741
I. "Prudential" standing 743

IV. MOOTNESS 743

V. RIPENESS 744

VI. THE 11TH AMENDMENT, AND SUITS AGAINST STATES 746

VII. POLITICAL QUESTIONS 750

Quiz Yourself on
JUSTICIABILITY (ENTIRE CHAPTER) 765

Exam Tips on
JUSTICIABILITY 770

TABLE OF CASES 775

SUBJECT MATTER INDEX 783

Preface

Thank you for buying this book.

This new edition includes full coverage of the Supreme Court's term that ended in July 2021, the first term after Justice Barrett replaced the late Justice Ginsburg. The edition features extensive coverage of several major Supreme Court decisions from that term, including:

❏ *Cedar Point Nursery v. Hassid*, a *Takings Clause* case in which the Court held that if government requires a landowner to submit to a *physical occupation*, that occupation will normally be a *compensable* taking, even if the occupation is a *temporary* and/or *intermittent* one.

❏ *Mahanoy Area School District v. B.L.*, a *free-speech* case in which the Court held that when a *public-high-school student* expresses herself *off-campus* (and not as part of a school-sponsored activity), school authorities have a *weaker interest* in regulating that speech than where the speech occurs *on*-campus.

❏ *Americans for Prosperity Foundation v. Bonta,* a *freedom-of-association* case in which the Court held that when government requires a group to *disclose who its members are*, the disclosure scheme will be subjected to *"exacting scrutiny,"* under which government will have the burden of proving that the disclosure requirement was *"narrowly tailored"* to the achievement of an important governmental interest.

❏ Two *free-exercise-of-religion* cases posing the issue of when a law is a *"generally-applicable"* one, and thus one from which government need not *give an exemption* to those claiming that requiring them to obey the law would infringe their religious beliefs. The two cases — *Fulton v. City of Philadelphia* and *Tandon v. Newsom* — show that if government grants exemptions from a law to those pursuing some *secular* activity, government's refusal to grant a similar exemption to one pursuing a comparable *religious* activity is likely to make the law *not* a "generally applicable" one, in which case the refusal will be *strictly scrutinized* and probably struck down.

Here are some of this book's special features:

▨ **"Casebook Correlation Chart"** — This chart, located just after this Preface, correlates each section of the main Outline with the pages covering the same topic in the four leading Constitutional Law casebooks.

▨ **"Capsule Summary"** — This is a 128-page summary of the key concepts of Constitutional Law, specially designed for use in the last week or so before your final exam.

▨ **"Quiz Yourself"** — Either at the end of the chapter or after major sections of a chapter I give you short-answer questions so that you can exercise your analytical muscles. There are over 100 of these questions, each written by me.

▨ **"Exam Tips"** — These alert you to the issues that repeatedly pop up on actual Constitutional Law exams, and to the fact patterns commonly used to test those issues. I created these Tips by looking at literally hundreds of multiple-choice and essay questions asked by law professors and bar examiners. You'd be surprised at how predictable the issues and fact patterns chosen by professors really are!

I intend for you to use this book both throughout the semester and for exam preparation. Here are some suggestions about how to use it:

1. The book seems (and is) *big*. But don't panic. The actual text includes over 75 pages of *Quiz Yourself* short-answer questions and answers, plus lots of *Exam Tips*. Anyway, you don't have to read everything in the book — there are lots of special features that you may or may not decide to take advantage of.

2. During the semester, use the book in preparing each night for the next day's class. To do this, first read your casebook. Then, use the *Casebook Correlation Chart* to get an idea of what part of the outline to read. Reading the outline will give you a sense of how the particular cases you've just read in your casebook fit into the overall structure of the subject. You may want to use a yellow highlighter to mark key portions of the *Emanuel*®.

3. If you make your own outline for the course, use the *Emanuel*® to give you a structure, and to supply black letter principles. You may want to rely especially on the *Capsule Summary* for this purpose. You are hereby authorized to copy small portions of the *Emanuel*® into your own outline, provided that your outline will be used only by you or your study group, and provided that you are the owner of the *Emanuel*®.

4. When you first start studying for exams, read the *Capsule Summary* to get an overview. This will probably take you about one day.

5. Either during exam study or earlier in the semester, do some or all of the *Quiz Yourself* short-answer questions. You can find these quickly by looking for *Quiz Yourself* entries in the Table of Contents. When you do these questions: (1) record your short "answer" on the small blank line provided after the question, but also: (2) try to write out a "mini essay" on a separate piece of paper or on your computer. Remember that the only way to get good at writing essays is to write essays.

6. Three or four days before the exam, review the *Exam Tips* that appear at the end of each chapter. You may want to combine this step with step **5**, so that you use the Tips to help you spot the issues in the short-answer questions. You'll also probably want to follow up from many of the Tips to the main Outline's discussion of the topic.

7. The night before the exam: (1) do some *Quiz Yourself* questions, just to get your thinking and writing juices flowing, and (2) re-scan the *Exam Tips* (spending about 2-3 hours).

My deepest thanks go to my editorial colleagues, Barbara Lasoff and Barbara Roth, who have helped greatly to assure the quality of this edition. Warm thanks also to the excellent publishing team at Aspen Publishing, Nicole Pinard, Joe Terry and Natalie Danner, who have been highly supportive of the *Emanuel Law Outlines, CrunchTime* and *Law in a Flash* series that I've created.

Good luck in your ConLaw course. If you'd like any other Aspen publication, you can find it at your bookstore or at **www.AspenPublishing.com**. If you'd like to contact me, you can email me at **semanuel@westnet.com**.

Steve Emanuel

Larchmont NY

November 2021

CASEBOOK CORRELATION CHART

(**Note:** general sections of the outline are omitted from this chart. **NC** = not directly covered by this casebook.)

Emanuel's Constitutional Law Outline *(by chapter and section heading)*	Feldman & Sullivan **Constitutional Law** (20th ed. 2019)	Stone, Seidman, Sunstein, Tushnet & Karlan **Constitutional Law** (8th ed. 2018)	Varat, Amar & Caminker **Constitutional Law** (16th ed. 2021)	Chemerinsky, **Constitutional Law** (6th ed. 2020)
CHAPTER 2 **THE SUPREME COURT'S AUTHORITY**				
I. Review of Acts of Congress (*Marbury v. Madison*)	1-16	25-39	29-41	1-9
II. Review of State Court Decisions	16-20	39-49	51-62	10-11
III. Congress' Control of Federal Court Jurisdiction	30-34	73-85	41-48	32-39
IV. The Supreme Court's Jurisdiction Today	NC	171-174	NC	NC
CHAPTER 3 **FEDERALISM AND FEDERAL POWER GENERALLY**				
I. The Concept of Federalism	75-76	175-196	115-120	119-120, 130-155
II. *McCulloch v. Maryland*	77-91	56-69	120-136	120-130
CHAPTER 4 **THE FEDERAL COMMERCE POWER**				
I. The Commerce Clause Gen'ly	113-114	196-197	136-148	155-156, 159-167
II. Cases Prior to 1933	114-122	197-202	148-152	156-166
III. Court Barriers to the New Deal	122-128	202-210	152-153	161-162
IV. The Post-New-Deal Trend	128-139	210-220	153-161	167-179
V. Some Modern Limits	139-167	220-254	161-199	179-215
V. The Tenth Amendment as a Limit on Congress' Power	167-183	356-375	235-261	216-240
CHAPTER 5 **OTHER NATIONAL POWERS**				
I. The Taxing Power	191-200	308-314	199-207	240-243
II. The Spending Power	200-219	314-331	207-217	243-248
III. The War, Treaty, and Foreign Affairs Powers	333-390, 392-393	331-334	217-228	NC
CHAPTER 6 **TWO LIMITS ON STATE POWER: THE DORMANT COMMERCE CLAUSE AND CONGRESSIONAL ACTION**				
I. The Dormant Commerce Clause — Regulation	221-271	254-293	280-322	444-480, 483-489
II. State Taxation of Interstate Commerce	290-294	294-296	270-280	NC
III. Congressional Action — Preemption and Consent	278-287	296-305	329-349	420-444, 480-483

CASEBOOK CORRELATION CHART (continued)

Emanuel's Constitutional Law Outline *(by chapter and section heading)*	Feldman & Sullivan **Constitutional Law** (20th ed. 2019)	Stone, Seidman, Sunstein, Tushnet & Karlan **Constitutional Law** (8th ed. 2018)	Varat, Amar & Caminker **Constitutional Law** (16th ed. 2021)	Chemerinsky, **Constitutional Law** (6th ed. 2020)
CHAPTER 7				
INTERGOVERNMENTAL IMMUNITIES AND INTERSTATE RELATIONS				
I. **Tax Immunities**	293-294	NC	NC	NC
II. **Federal Immunity from State Regulation**	294	NC	NC	NC
III. **State Immunity from Federal Regulation**	294	NC	235-261	NC
IV. **Interstate Relationships**	295	NC	NC	489-501
CHAPTER 8				
SEPARATION OF POWERS				
I. **Domestic Policy and the Separation of Powers**	297-315	377-392, 433-457	351-356, 379-394	275-328
II. **Prohibition on Excessive Delegation by Congress**	390-393	433-437	386-387	292-304
III. **Foreign Affairs and the War Powers**	315-390	392-421	356-378	339-395
IV. **Appointment and Removal of Executive Personnel (Including Impeachment)**	404-441	429-433, 457-463	394-415	328-339
V. **Legislative and Executive Immunity**	424-441	421-429	415-433	406-417
CHAPTER 9				
DUE PROCESS OF LAW				
I. **The Bill of Rights and the States**	443-484	736-746	437-497	504-532
II. **Substantive Due Process — Before 1934**	485-499	746-761	499-509	581-599
III. **Substantive Due Process — The Modern Approach to Economic and Social-Welfare Regulation**	500-509	761-769	509-521	599-618
IV. **Substantive Due Process — Protection of Fundamental Rights Generally**	509-520	825-836	574-582, 625	950-961
V. **Substantive Due Process — Regulation of Abortion**	520-546	836-887	625-675	961-1015
VI. **Other Substantive Due Process Issues: Contraception, Child Rearing, The Right to Marry, Sexual Expression and the "Right to Die"**				
Family Relations	547-553	918-922	582-594	929-950
Sexuality, Incl. Homosexuality	553-592	887-918	594-613, 675-684	1030-1042
The Right to Die	592-604	922-928	684-696	1015-1030
Rights of the Mentally Retarded	NC	NC	917-923	NC
VII. **Procedural Due Process**	604-610	928-952	1088-1125	1128-1176

CASEBOOK CORRELATION CHART (continued)

Emanuel's Constitutional Law Outline *(by chapter and section heading)*	Feldman & Sullivan **Constitutional Law** (20th ed. 2019)	Stone, Seidman, Sunstein, Tushnet & Karlan **Constitutional Law** (8th ed. 2018)	Varat, Amar & Caminker **Constitutional Law** (16th ed. 2021)	Chemerinsky, **Constitutional Law** (6th ed. 2020)
CHAPTER 10 **EQUAL PROTECTION**				
I. Introduction	645-646	NC	711-717	683-689
II. Economic and Social Laws — The "Mere-Rationality" Test	646-656	509-530	717-732, 923-930	689-711
III. Suspect Classifications, Especially Race	656-691	465-509, 530-578	732-768, 804-825	711-803
IV. Affirmative Action and "Benign" Discrimination	691-755	578-637	777-901, 1175-1177	803-836
V. Classifications Based on Sex	755-793	637-678	768-804	836-876
VI. Classifications Based on Alienage	794-798	696-706	901-910	876-891
VII. Illegitimacy	NC	716	910-916	891-894
VIII. Mental Retardation and Mental Illness	798-803	516-518, 713-716	917-923	898-899
IX. General Principles of Middle-Level Scrutiny	755-761	NC	NC	NC
X. Unequal Treatment of Gays, and the Banning of Same-Sex Marriage	553-592, 793	678-696, 897-918	923-940	911-929
XI. Fundamental Rights	805-851	706-713, 769-825	941-1085	899-900, 1046-1128
CHAPTER 11 **MISCELLANEOUS CLAUSES**				
I. The 14th Amendment's Privileges or Immunities Clause	457-464	728-736	455-458	506-514, 1046-1052
II. The "Taking Clause"	611-636	965-1008	533-574	631-682
III. The "Contract Clause"	636-643	952-965	521-533	618-631
IV. The Second Amendment "Right to Bear Arms"	472-484	50-53, 738-746	697-709	13-32
V. *Ex Post Facto* Laws	444, 485-489	69-70	NC	NC
VI. Bills of Attainder	444	NC	NC	NC
CHAPTER 12 **STATE ACTION**				
I. Introduction	853-856	1529-1530	1127-1133	532-536
II. The "Public Function" Approach	856-863	1533-1542, 1572-1583	1134-1141	538-553
III. "Nexus" — The Significance of State Involvement	863-877	1542-1571	1141-1175	553-578
CHAPTER 13 **CONGRESSIONAL ENFORCEMENT OF CIVIL RIGHTS**				
II. Congress' Power to Reach Private Conduct	878-888	353-356, 1530-1533	1182-1194	248-253
III.- V. Congress' Power to Remedy Violations of the Civil War Amendments & to Redefine the Scope of Const'l Guarantees	888-929	334-353	1194-1241	253-274

CASEBOOK CORRELATION CHART (continued)

Emanuel's Constitutional Law Outline *(by chapter and section heading)*	Feldman & Sullivan **Constitutional Law** (20th ed. 2019)	Stone, Seidman, Sunstein, Tushnet & Karlan **Constitutional Law** (8th ed. 2018)	Varat, Amar & Caminker **Constitutional Law** (16th ed. 2021)	Chemerinsky, **Constitutional Law** (6th ed. 2020)
CHAPTER 14 **FREEDOM OF EXPRESSION**				
I. General Themes	931-946	1009-1020	1245-1252, 1514-1518	1177-1229, 1266-1294
II. Advocacy of Illegal Conduct	946-1002	1020-1067	1252-1296	1308-1341
III. Overbreadth and Vagueness	1347-1365	1097-1103	1296-1307	1229-1237
IV. Regulation of Context — "Time, Place and Manner"	1159-1176, 1195-1347	1067-1084, 1195-1398	1389-1412, 1459-1514, 1572-1579	1341-1365, 1391-1419, 1531-1605
V. Symbolic Expression	1003-1055, 1176-1195	1317-1341	1585-1596	1481-1531
VI. Defamation, Intentional Infliction of Emotional Distress, Banning of False Speech	1006-1033	1113-1145	1315-1343, 1446-1458	1455-1481
VII. Obscenity	1055-1099	1163-1195	1343-1388	1365-1391
VIII. Commercial Speech	1132-1157	1145-1163	1412-1446	1419-1455
IX. Regulation in the Context of Political Campaigns	1460-1513	1352-1399	1646-1715	1491-1531
X. Some Special Contexts	1290-1315	1298-1317, 1339-141	1520-1579	1294-1308, 1582-1597
XI. Freedom of Association, Right Not to Speak or Associate, and Denial of Public Jobs or Benefits	1418-1460	1341-1352, 1397-1399	1597-1645, 1716-1732	1605-1635
XII. Unconstitutional Conditions	1326-1328, 1338-1347	1303, 1308-1314	1541-1546, 1580-1583	1294-1306
XIII. Special Problems Concerning the Media	1513-1556	1084-1096, 1103-1112, 1399-1430	1733-1761	1238-1265, 1635-1664
CHAPTER 15 **FREEDOM OF RELIGION**				
II. The Establishment Clause	1615-1695	1448-1493	1763-1856	1717-1822
III. The Free Exercise Clause	1570-1615	1493-1527	1856-1907	1675-1717
CHAPTER 16 **JUSTICIABILITY**				
II. Advisory Opinions	35-38	87-88	63-68	41-44
III. Standing	38-57	89-137	68-93	45-79
IV. Mootness	58	170-171	93-96	85-90
V. Ripeness	58-59	170-171	96-100	79-85
VI. The 11th Amendment, and Suits Against States	183-190	346-353	261-268	NC
VII. Political Questions	59-74	137-169	100-112	90-118

CAPSULE SUMMARY

This Capsule Summary is intended for review at the end of the semester. Reading it is not a substitute for mastering the material in the main outline. Numbers in brackets refer to the pages in the main outline where the topic is discussed. The order of topics is occasionally somewhat different from that in the main outline.

CHAPTER 1

INTRODUCTION

I. THREE STANDARDS OF REVIEW

A. Three standards: There are three key *standards of review* which reappear constantly throughout Constitutional Law. When a court reviews the constitutionality of government action, it is likely to be choosing from among one of these three standards of review: (1) the *mere-rationality* standard; (2) the *strict scrutiny* standard; and (3) the *middle-level review* standard. [2]

1. **Mere-rationality standard:** Of the three standards, the easiest one to satisfy is the *"mere-rationality"* standard. When the court applies this "mere-rationality" standard, the court will *uphold* the governmental action so long as two requirements are met:

    a. **Legitimate state objective:** First, the government must be pursuing a *legitimate governmental objective*. This is a very broad concept — practically any type of health, safety or "general welfare" goal will be found to be "legitimate."

    b. **Rational relation:** Second, there has to be a *"minimally rational relation"* between the means chosen by the government and the state objective. This requirement, too, is extremely easy to satisfy: only if the government has acted in a completely *"arbitrary and irrational"* way will this rational link between means and end not be found.

2. **Strict scrutiny:** At the other end of the spectrum, the standard that is hardest to satisfy is the *"strict scrutiny"* standard of review. This standard will only be satisfied if the governmental act satisfies two very tough requirements:

    a. **Compelling objective:** First, the *objective* being pursued by the government must be *"compelling"* (not just "legitimate," as for the "mere-rationality" standard); and

    b. **Necessary means:** Second, the *means* chosen by the government must be *"necessary"* to achieve that compelling end. In other words, the "fit" between the means and the end must be extremely tight. (It's not enough that there's a "rational relation" between the means and the end, which is enough under the "mere-rationality" standard.)

        i. **No less restrictive alternatives:** In practice, this requirement that the means be "necessary" means that there must not be any *less restrictive* means that would accomplish the government's objective just as well.

3. **Middle-level review:** In between these two review standards is so-called *"middle-level"* review.

    a. **"Important" objective:** Here, the governmental objective has to be *"important"* (half way between "legitimate" and "compelling").

  b. "Substantially related" means: And, the means chosen by the government must be *"substantially related"* to the important government objective. (This "substantially related" standard is half way between "rationally related" and "necessary").

B. Consequences of choice: The court's choice of one of these standards of review has two important consequences: [2]

  1. Burden of persuasion: First, the choice will make a big difference as to who has the *burden of persuasion*.

    a. Mere-rationality standard: Where the governmental action is subject to the "mere-rationality" standard, the *individual* who is attacking the government action will generally bear the burden of persuading the court that the action is unconstitutional.

    b. Strict scrutiny: By contrast, if the court applies "strict scrutiny," then the *governmental body* whose act is being attacked has the burden of persuading the court that its action is constitutional.

    c. Middle-level review: Where "middle level" scrutiny is used, it's not certain how the court will assign the burden of persuasion, but the burden will usually be placed on the government.

  2. Effect on outcome: Second, the choice of review standard has a very powerful effect on the *actual outcome*. Where the "mere-rationality" standard is applied, the governmental action will *almost always be upheld*. Where "strict scrutiny" is used, the governmental action will *almost always be struck down*. (For instance, the Supreme Court applies strict scrutiny to any classification based on race, and has upheld only one such strictly scrutinized racial classification in the last 50 years.) Where middle-level scrutiny is used, there's roughly a 50-50 chance that the governmental action will be struck down.

    a. Exam Tip: So when you're writing an exam answer, you've got to concentrate exceptionally hard on choosing the correct standard of review. Once you've determined that a particular standard would be applied, then you might as well go further and make a prediction about the outcome: if you've decided that "mere-rationality" review applies, you might write something like, "Therefore, the court will almost certainly uphold the governmental action." If you've chosen strict scrutiny, you should write something like, "Therefore, the governmental action is very likely to be struck down."

C. When used: Here is a quick overview of the entire body of Constitutional Law, to see where each of these review standards gets used: [3]

  1. Mere-rationality standard: Here are the main places where the "mere-rationality" standard gets applied (and therefore, the places where it's very hard for the person attacking the governmental action to get it struck down on constitutional grounds):

    a. Dormant Commerce Clause: First, the "mere-rationality" test is the main test to determine whether a state regulation that affects interstate commerce violates the *"dormant Commerce Clause."* The state regulation has to pursue a legitimate state end, and be rationally related to that end. (But there's a second test which we'll review in greater detail later: the state's interest in enforcing its regulation must also outweigh any *burden* imposed on interstate commerce, and any discrimination against interstate commerce.)

    b. Substantive due process: Next comes *substantive due process*. So long as no "fundamental right" is affected, the test for determining whether a governmental act violates substantive due process is, again, the "mere-rationality" standard. In other words, if the state is pursuing a legitimate objective, and using means that are rationally related to that objective, the state will not be found to have violated the substantive Due Process Clause. So the vast bulk of *eco-*

nomic regulations (since these don't affect fundamental rights) will be tested by the mere-rationality standard and almost certainly upheld.

c. **Equal protection:** Then, we move on to the *equal protection* area. Here, "mere-rationality" review is used so long as: (1) *no suspect* or *quasi-suspect classification* is being used; and (2) *no fundamental right* is being impaired. This still leaves us with a large number of classifications which will be judged based on the mere-rationality standard, including: (1) almost all economic regulations; (2) some classifications based on alienage; and (3) rights that are not "fundamental" even though they are very important, such as food, housing, and free public education. In all of these areas, the classification will be reviewed under the "mere-rationality" standard, and will therefore almost certainly be upheld.

d. **Contracts Clause:** Lastly, we find "mere-rationality" review in some aspects of the *"Obligation of Contracts"* Clause.

2. **Strict scrutiny:** Here are the various contexts in which the court applies *strict scrutiny*: [4]

a. **Substantive due process/fundamental rights:** First, where a governmental action affects *fundamental rights*, and the plaintiff claims that his *substantive due process* rights are being violated, the court will use strict scrutiny. So when the state impairs rights falling in the *"privacy"* cluster of marriage, child-bearing, and child-rearing, the court will use strict scrutiny (and will therefore probably invalidate the governmental restriction). For instance, government restrictions that impair the right to use contraceptives receive this kind of strict scrutiny.

b. **Equal protection review:** Next, the court uses strict scrutiny to review a claim that a classification violates the plaintiff's *equal protection* rights, if the classification relates either to a *suspect classification* or a *fundamental right*. "Suspect classifications" include *race*, *national origin*, and (sometimes) *alienage*. "Fundamental rights" for this purpose include the right to *vote*, to be a *candidate*, to have access to the *courts*, and to *travel interstate*. So classifications that either involve any of these suspect classifications or impair any of these fundamental rights will be strictly scrutinized and will probably be struck down.

c. **Freedom of expression:** Next, we move to the area of *freedom of expression*. If the government is impairing free expression in a *content-based way*, then the court will use strict scrutiny and will almost certainly strike down the regulation. In other words, if the government is restricting some speech but not others, based on the *content of the messages*, then this suppression of expression will only be allowed if necessary to achieve a compelling purpose (a standard which is rarely found to be satisfied in the First Amendment area). Similarly, any interference with the right of *free association* will be strictly scrutinized.

d. **Freedom of religion/Free Exercise Clause:** Lastly, the court will use strict scrutiny to evaluate any impairment with a person's *free exercise* of religion. Even if the government does *not intend* to impair a person's free exercise of his religion, if it substantially burdens his exercise of religion the government will have to give him an *exemption* from the otherwise-applicable regulation unless denial of an exemption is necessary to achieve a compelling governmental interest.

3. **Middle-level review:** Finally, here are the relatively small number of contexts in which the court uses middle-level review: [4]

a. **Equal protection/semi-suspect:** First, middle-level review will be used to judge an *equal protection* claim, where the classification being challenged involves a *semi-suspect* trait. The two traits which are considered semi-suspect for this purpose are: (1) *gender*; and (2) *illegitimacy*. So any government classification based on gender or illegitimacy will have to be "substantially related" to the achievement of some "important" governmental interest.

   b. Contracts Clause: Second, certain conduct attacked under the Obligation of Contracts Clause will be judged by the middle-level standard of review.

   c. Free expression/non-content-based: Finally, in the First Amendment area we use a standard similar (though not identical) to the middle-level review standard to judge government action that impairs expression, but does so in a ***non-content-based*** manner. This is true, for instance, of any content-neutral ***"time, place and manner"*** regulation.

CHAPTER 2
THE SUPREME COURT'S AUTHORITY AND THE FEDERAL JUDICIAL POWER

I. THE SUPREME COURT'S AUTHORITY AND THE FEDERAL JUDICIAL POWER

A. *Marbury* principle: Under *Marbury v. Madison*, it is the Supreme Court, not Congress, which has the authority and duty to declare a congressional statute unconstitutional if the Court thinks it violates the Constitution. [5-7]

B. Supreme Court review of state court decision: The Supreme Court may review state court opinions, but only to the extent that the decision was decided ***based on federal law.*** [7-10]

   1. "Independent and adequate state grounds": Even if there is a federal question in the state court case, the Supreme Court may not review the case if there is an ***"independent and adequate"*** state ground for the state court's decision. That is, if the same result would be reached even had the state court made a different decision on the federal question, the Supreme Court may not decide the case. This is because its opinion would in effect be an "advisory" one. [8]

      a. Violations of state and federal constitutions: If a state action violates the ***same clause*** of both state and federal constitutions (e.g., the Equal Protection Clause of each), the state court decision may or may not be based on an "independent" state ground. If the state court is saying, "This state action would violate our state constitution whether or not it violated the federal constitution," that's "independent." But if the state court is saying, "Based on our reading of the constitutional provision (which we think has the same meaning under both the state and federal constitutions), this state action violates both constitutions," this is ***not*** "independent," so the Supreme Court may review the state court decision. [9]

   2. Review limited to decisions of highest state court: Federal statutes limit Supreme Court review to decisions of the ***highest state court available***. But this does not mean that the top-ranking state court must have ruled on the ***merits*** of the case in order for the Supreme Court to review it. All that is required is that the case be heard by the highest state court ***available*** to the petitioner, which might be an intermediate appellate court.

C. Federal judicial power: Article III, Section 2 sets out the federal judicial power. This includes, among other things: (a) cases arising under the ***Constitution*** or the ***"laws of the U.S."*** (i.e., cases posing a "federal question"); (b) cases of ***admiralty***; (c) cases between ***two or more states***; (d) cases between ***citizens of different states***; and (e) cases between a state or its citizens and a ***foreign country or foreign citizen***. Note that this does ***not*** include cases where both parties are citizens (i.e., residents) of the same state, and no federal question is raised. [10]

II. CONGRESS' CONTROL OF FEDERAL JUDICIAL POWER

A. Congress' power to decide: ***Congress*** has the general power to ***decide what types of cases the***

Supreme Court may hear, so long as it doesn't expand the Supreme Court's jurisdiction beyond the federal judicial power (as listed in the prior paragraph). [*Ex parte McCardle*] [10-12]

B. Lower courts: Congress also may decide what *lower federal courts* there should be, and what cases they may hear. Again, the outer bound of this power is that Congress can't allow the federal courts to hear a case that is not within the federal judicial power. [12]

> **Example 1:** Congress may cut back the jurisdiction of the lower federal courts pretty much whenever and however it wishes. Thus Congress could constitutionally eliminate diversity jurisdiction (i.e., suits between citizens of different states), even though such suits are clearly listed in the Constitution as being within the federal judicial power.

> **Example 2:** But Congress could not give the lower federal courts jurisdiction over cases between two citizens of the same state, where no federal issue is posed. The handling of such a case by the federal courts would simply go beyond the federal judicial power as recited in the Constitution.

CHAPTER 3
FEDERALISM AND FEDERAL POWER GENERALLY

I. THE CONCEPT OF FEDERALISM

A. The federalist system: We have a *"federalist"* system. In other words, the national government and the state governments co-exist. Therefore, you always have to watch whether some power being asserted by the federal government is in fact allowed under the Constitution, and you must also watch whether some power asserted by the states is limited in favor of federal power. [15]

B. Federal government has limited powers: The most important principle in this whole area is that the federal government is one of *limited, enumerated powers*. In other words, the three federal branches (Congress, the executive branch, and the federal courts) can only assert powers *specifically granted* to them by the United States Constitution. (This is very different from what our Constitution says about the powers of *state* governments: state governments can do whatever they want as far as the U.S. Constitution is concerned, unless what they are doing is *expressly forbidden* by the Constitution.) [15]

1. **No general police power:** The most dramatic illustration of this state/federal difference is the general *"police power."* Each state has a general police power, i.e., the ability to regulate solely on the basis that the regulation would enhance the welfare of the citizenry. But there is *no general federal police power*, i.e., no right of the federal government to regulate for the health, safety or general welfare of the citizenry. Instead, each act of federal legislation or regulation must come within one of the very specific, enumerated powers (e.g., the Commerce Clause, the power to tax and spend, etc.).

   a. **Tax and spend for general welfare:** Congress *does* have the right to "lay and collect taxes … to pay the debts and provide for the … general welfare of the United States. … " (Article I, Section 8.) But the phrase "provide for the … general welfare" in this sentence modifies "lay and collect taxes … to pay the debts. … " In other words, the power to tax and spend is subject to the requirement that the general welfare be served; there is no *independent* federal power to provide for the general welfare.

C. "Necessary and Proper" Clause: In addition to the very specific powers given to Congress by the Constitution, Congress is given the power to "make all laws which shall be *necessary and proper* for carrying into execution" the specific powers.

1. **Rational-relation test:** The "Necessary and Proper" Clause is easy for Congress to satisfy: if Congress is seeking an *objective* that is within the specifically enumerated powers, then Congress can use *any means* that is: (1) *rationally related* to the objective Congress is trying to achieve; and (2) is not specifically forbidden by the Constitution. [17]

   a. **Broad reading given to Clause:** Congress gives a very *broad and deferential reading* to Congress' powers under the Clause. [19]

D. **Can't violate specific constitutional provision:** Even where congressional action appears to fall within a specific grant of power, the federal action may not, of course, violate some *other* specific constitutional guarantee. In other words, congressional (or other federal) action must satisfy *two* tests to be constitutional: (1) it must fall within some specific grant of power under the Constitution; and (2) it must not violate any specific constitutional provision. [16]

CHAPTERS 4, 5 AND 8

POWERS OF THE FEDERAL GOVERNMENT; THE SEPARATION OF POWERS

I. POWERS OF THE THREE FEDERAL BRANCHES

A. **Powers of the three branches:** Here is a summary of the powers of the *three branches* of the federal government:

1. **Congress:** Here are the main powers given to Congress [16]:

   a. **Interstate commerce:** Congress has the power to *regulate interstate commerce*, as well as foreign commerce.

   b. **Taxing and spending:** Congress has the power to *tax* and the power to *spend*.

   c. **DC:** Congress can regulate the *District of Columbia*.

   d. **Federal property:** Congress has power to regulate and dispose of *federal property.*

   e. **War and defense:** Congress can *declare war*, and can establish and fund the armed forces.

   f. **Enforcement of Civil War amendments:** Congress can *enforce* the *post-Civil War amendments*. (For instance, under its power to enforce the Thirteenth Amendment's abolition of slavery, Congress can ban even private intrastate non-commercial conduct.)

2. **President:** Here are the main powers of the President:

   a. **Execution of laws:** The President holds the *"executive power."* That is, he *carries out* the laws made by Congress. It is his obligation to make sure the laws are "faithfully executed."

   b. **Commander in Chief:** He is *Commander in Chief* of the armed forces. So he directs and leads our armed forces (but he cannot declare war — only Congress can do this).

   c. **Treaty and foreign affairs:** The President can make *treaties* with foreign nations (but only if two-thirds of the Senate approves). He appoints *ambassadors.* Also, he effectively controls our *foreign policy* — some of this power over foreign policy stems from his right to appoint ambassadors, but much is simply *implied* from the nation's need to speak with a single voice in foreign affairs (so that congressional involvement in the details of foreign affairs will generally not be appropriate).

   d. **Appointment of federal officers:** The President appoints all *federal officers*. These include *cabinet members*, *federal judges* and *ambassadors*. (But the Senate must approve all such federal officers by majority vote.) As to *"inferior* [federal] officers," it's up to Congress to decide whether these should be appointed by the President, by the Judicial Branch, or by the "heads of departments" (i.e., cabinet members). (But Congress can't make these lower-level appointments itself; it may merely decide who *can* make these appointments.)

e. **Pardons:** The President can issue *pardons*, but only for federal offenses. (Also, he can't pardon anyone who has been impeached and convicted.)

f. **Veto:** The President may *veto* any law passed by both houses (though this veto may be *overridden* by a 2-3's majority of each house). If the President doesn't veto the bill within 10 days after receiving it, it becomes law (unless Congress has adjourned by the 10th day after it sent him the bill — this is the so-called "pocket veto").

3. **Judiciary:** The federal *judiciary* may decide "cases" or "controversies" that fall within the federal judicial power. See the section on "Federal Judicial Power" in the chapter called "The Supreme Court's Authority and the Federal Judicial Power," above.

II. THE FEDERAL COMMERCE POWER

A. **Summary:** Probably Congress' most important power is the power to *"regulate Commerce …* among the several states." (Art. I, §8.) This is the "Commerce power." [21]

> **Exam Tip:** Any time you have a test question in which Congress is doing something, first ask yourself, "Can what Congress is doing be justified as an exercise of the commerce power?" Most of the time the answer will be "yes."

B. **Summary of modern view:** There seem to be *four broad categories* of activities which Congress can constitutionally regulate under the Commerce power:

1. **Channels:** First, Congress can regulate the use of the *"channels"* of interstate commerce. Thus Congress can regulate in a way that is reasonably related to highways, waterways, and air traffic. Presumably Congress can do so even though the activity in question in the particular case is completely intrastate. [45]

2. **Instrumentalities:** Second, Congress can regulate the *"instrumentalities"* of interstate commerce, even though the particular activities being regulated are completely intrastate. This category refers to people, machines, and other "things" used in carrying out commerce. [45]

> **Example:** Probably Congress could say that every truck must have a specific safety device, even if the particular truck in question was made and used exclusively within a single state.

3. **Articles moving in interstate commerce:** Third, Congress can regulate *articles moving* in interstate commerce. [45]

> **Example:** The states and private parties keep information about the identities of drivers. Since this information gets exchanged across state lines (e.g., from states to companies that want to sell cars), the information is an article in interstate commerce and Congress may regulate how it's used. [*Reno v. Condon*]

4. **"Substantially affecting" commerce:** Finally, the biggest (and most interesting) category is that Congress may regulate those activities having a *"substantial effect"* on interstate commerce. [*U.S. v. Lopez*] As to this category, the following rules now seem to apply: [45]

a. **Activity is commercial:** If the activity itself is arguably *"commercial,"* then it doesn't seem to matter whether the *particular instance* of the activity directly affects interstate commerce, as long as the instance is part of a general class of activities that, *collectively,* substantially affect interstate commerce. So even purely intrastate activities can be regulated if they're directly "commercial." This is especially true where Congress regulates the intrastate commercial activities as part of a ***broad scheme*** to regulate interstate commerce in the same activity. [45]

Example: In the federal Controlled Substances Act (CSA), Congress outlaws all distribution and possession of marijuana. California then makes it legal under state law for a Californian to cultivate marijuana for her own personal medicinal use. The U.S. seeks to prevent P, a Californian, from taking advantage of this state-law loophole. P asserts that the application of the CSA to bar P from personally cultivating marijuana for her own personal medical use is beyond Congress' Commerce powers.

Held, Congress' Commerce powers extend to this regulation of P's own cultivation and use. Marijuana is a commercial commodity, and the CSA is regulating interstate commerce in that commodity. Congress reasonably feared that if it exempted personal — and thus "intrastate" — cultivation and use of marijuana for medical purposes, some of the marijuana so cultivated would be illegally drawn into the interstate market, jeopardizing Congress' overall scheme of banning the drug. So the private cultivation of marijuana by people like P, even though purely an intrastate activity, falls within Congress' Commerce power. [*Gonzales v. Raich*] [35]

b. **Activity is not commercial:** But if the activity itself is ***not "commercial,"*** then there will apparently have to be a ***pretty obvious connection*** between the activity and interstate commerce. [46]

Example 1: Congress makes it a federal crime to possess a firearm in or near a school. The act applies even if the particular gun never moved in (or affected) interstate commerce. *Held*, in enacting this statute Congress went beyond its Commerce power. To fall within the Commerce power, the activity being regulated must have a "substantial effect" on interstate commerce. The link between gun-possession in a school and interstate commerce is too tenuous to qualify as a "substantial effect," because if it did, there would be essentially no limit to Congress' Commerce power. [*U.S. v. Lopez*]

Example 2: Congress says that any woman who is the victim of a violent gender-based crime may bring a civil suit against the perpetrator in federal court. *Held*, Congress went beyond its Commerce power. Although it may be true that some women's fear of gender-based violence dissuades them from working or traveling interstate, gender-based violence is not itself a commercial activity, and the connection between gender-based violence and interstate commerce is too attenuated for the violence to have a "substantial effect" on commerce. [*U.S. v. Morrison*]

   i. **Jurisdictional hook:** But where the congressional act applies only to particular activities each of which has a direct link to interstate commerce, then the act will probably be within the Commerce power. Thus the use of a ***"jurisdictional hook"*** will probably suffice. (*Example*: Suppose the statute in *Lopez* by its terms applied only to in-school gun possession if the ***particular gun had previously moved in interstate commerce.*** This would be enough of a connection to interstate commerce to qualify.) [45]

c. **Little deference to Congress:** The Court ***won't*** give much ***deference*** (as it used to) to the fact that Congress ***believed*** that the activity has the requisite "substantial effect" on interstate commerce. The Court will basically decide this issue for itself, from scratch. It certainly will no longer be enough that Congress had a ***"rational basis"*** for believing that the requisite effect existed — the effect must *in fact* exist to the Court's own independent satisfaction. [*Lopez*] [46]

d. Traditional domain of states: If what's being regulated is an activity the regulation of which has *traditionally* been the *domain of the states*, and as to which the states have expertise, the Court is less likely to find that Congress is acting within its Commerce power. Thus *education*, *family law* and *general criminal law* are areas where the court is likely to be especially suspicious of congressional "interference." [46]

e. Forcing someone to buy or sell a product: Congress may not use its Commerce powers to require that a person *not presently in the marketplace* for a particular type of product to *buy that product*. That's true even if many individuals' combined failure to purchase the product significantly affects interstate commerce in the product. [*Nat'l Fed. of Indep. Bus. v. Sebelius* (2012)] [37]

  i. Health insurance: So, for instance, Congress can't use its Commerce powers to require otherwise-uninsured citizens to *purchase health insurance* or pay a penalty, even though the uninsureds' failure to have insurance has a substantial effect on the interstate health-insurance market by making everyone else's insurance costs higher. [*N.F.I.B. v. Sebelius, supra*]

  Example: Congress, in an attempt to greatly broaden the availability of health-care insurance, enacts the 2010 Affordable Care Act ("ACA"). Under the ACA, Congress imposes an "individual mandate," under which most uninsured individuals are required to buy a specified level of health insurance or else make a "shared-responsibility payment" to the Internal Revenue Service, which the ACA refers to as a "penalty." (The payment to the IRS is typically much less than the cost of qualifying insurance.) In Congress' view, the individual mandate and the shared-responsibility payment system fall within the Commerce power, because these measures are simply a means of regulating how and when people will pay (via insurance) for a product (health care) that they would inevitably consume even without regulation. Twenty-six states claim that the mandate goes beyond the Commerce power.

  Held, 5-4, for the state plaintiffs on this point: the individual mandate is not authorized by the Commerce power. The Commerce Clause allows Congress to regulate **"existing commercial activity."** But it does not allow Congress to "compel[] individuals to *become* active in commerce by purchasing a product, on the ground that their failure to do so affects interstate commerce." Allowing Congress to regulate based on the effect of *inaction* on commerce "would bring countless decisions an individual could potentially make within the scope of federal regulation[.]" For instance, many Americans do not eat a balanced diet, and therefore become obese. Obese people have higher health costs, which are borne in part by other Americans. Under Congress' theory, therefore, "Congress could address the diet problem by ordering everyone to buy vegetables." But giving Congress the power to "regulate what we do not do [would] fundamentally chang[e] the relation between the citizen and the Federal Government," in a way the drafters of the Commerce power never intended. [*N.F.I.B. v. Sebelius, supra*] [37]

  Note: But by a different 5-4 majority, the Court in *N.F.I.B.* sustained the individual mandate as an exercise of Congress *taxing* power. See *infra*, p. C-11.

C. The Tenth Amendment as a limit on Congress' power: The *Tenth Amendment* provides that "the powers not delegated to the United States by the Constitution, nor prohibited by it to the States, are reserved to the States respectively, or to the People." This Amendment today seems to place a small but possibly significant limit on Congress' ability to use its commerce power to *regulate the states*. [46-52]

  1. Generally-applicable law: If Congress passes a *generally applicable law*, the fact that the regulation *affects the states* has virtually no practical significance, and the Tenth Amendment never comes into play. If the regulation would be valid if applied to a private party, it is also valid as to the state. [48]

> **Example:** Congress passes minimum-wage and overtime provisions, which are made applicable to all businesses of a certain size. The statute contains no exemption for employees of state-owned mass transit systems. *Held*, the regulation even of state employees here is a constitutional exercise of the commerce power, and is not forbidden by the Tenth Amendment. [*Garcia v. San Antonio Metropolitan Transit Authority*]

2. **Use of state's law-making mechanisms:** But the Tenth Amendment *does* prevent Congress from interfering in certain ways with a state's *law-making processes*. Congress may not simply "*commandeer* the legislative processes of the states by directly *compelling them to enact and enforce a federal regulatory program.*" [*New York v. United States*] [48-52] This is the *"anti-commandeering"* principle.

> **Example:** Congress provides that each state must arrange for the disposal of toxic waste generated within its borders, or else be deemed to "take title" to the waste and thereby become liable for tort damages stemming from it. *Held*, the congressional scheme violates the Tenth Amendment's anti-commandeering principle. That is, Congress may not force a state to enact or enforce a federal regulatory program, and this is in effect what Congress has tried to do here. *New York v. United States, supra.*

a. **Administrative actions:** Similarly, the anti-commandeering principle forbids Congress to compel a state or local government's *executive branch* to perform functions, even ones that are easy-to-do and involve no discretion.

> **Example:** Congress can't order local sheriffs to perform background checks on applicants for handgun permits. [*Printz v. U.S.*] [50]

b. **Can't order state to refrain from legislating:** Just as the anti-commandeering principle prevents Congress from forcing states to act *affirmatively* by enacting or enforcing laws (see *N.Y. v. U.S.* and *Printz v. U.S. supra*), so that principle bars Congress from ordering a state *not* to legislate. For instance, Congress *may not prohibit a state from repealing an existing law.* [*Murphy v. NCAA*] (2018)] [51]

III. THE TAXING AND SPENDING POWERS

A. **Taxing power:** Congress has the power to "*lay and collect taxes.*" (Art. I, §8.) This is an independent source of congressional power, so it can be used to reach conduct that might be beyond the other sources of congressional power, like the Commerce Clause. [57]

1. **Regulation:** Congress can probably *regulate* under the guise of taxing, so long as there's some real revenue produced. [58-62]

2. **Limits on taxing power:** There are a few *limits* which the Constitution places upon the taxing power:

a. **Direct taxes:** "Direct taxes" must be allocated among the states in proportion to population. This provision is of little practical importance today.

b. **Customs duties and excise taxes must be uniform:** All *customs duties* and *excise taxes* must be *uniform* throughout the United States. (*Example:* Congress may not place a $.10 per-gallon federal excise tax on gasoline sales that take place in New Jersey, and a $.15 per-gallon tax on those that take place in Oklahoma.) [58]

c. **No export taxes:** Congress may not tax any *exports* from any state. (*Example:* Congress may not place a tax on all computers which are exported from any state to foreign countries.) [58]

3. Effect of calling a measure a "penalty": The fact that Congress labels a measure as a *"penalty"* does *not* prevent the measure from being upheld as a valid tax, as long as the measure actually functions in a way that resembles a tax. [*N.F.I.B. v. Sebelius* (2012)] [59]

> **Example:** As described *supra*, C-9, in the 2010 Affordable Care Act ("ACA"), Congress requires most individuals to purchase health insurance (this requirement being called the "individual mandate"). If a covered person doesn't make the required insurance purchase, she must pay the IRS at tax-filing time a *"shared-responsibility payment,"* a payment that the Act repeatedly characterizes as a *"penalty"* rather than as a tax. If a person doesn't make the shared-responsibility payment, the IRS can use some of its standard tax-collection methods, but cannot bring a *criminal prosecution*.
>
> *Held*, by a 5-4 vote, the individual mandate and shared-responsibility payment scheme is a valid exercise of Congress' taxing power. If a federal statute would be unconstitutional unless found to be a valid tax, the Court will treat it as a tax as long as that interpretation is a "fairly possible" one. The process here "yields the essential feature of any tax: it *produces at least some revenue* for the Government." And the fact that Congress called this a "penalty" rather than a "tax" is not dispositive, because the Court will look at the reality of how the scheme operates, not the label used by Congress. Here, the payment to the IRS would typically be far less than the price of insurance, making it look more like a tax (which a rational person might voluntarily choose to pay instead of buying insurance) than a penalty for unlawful conduct. [*N.F.I.B. v. Sebelius*, *supra*] [59]

B. Spending power: Congress also has the power to "pay the debts and provide for the common defense and general welfare of the United States." (Art. I, §8.) This is the *"spending"* power. [62]

1. Independent power: This is an independent power, just like the Commerce power. So Congress could spend to achieve a purely local benefit, even one that it couldn't achieve by regulating under the Commerce power.

2. Use of conditions: Congress may generally place *conditions* upon use of its spending power, even if the congressional purpose is in effect to regulate. Conditions placed upon the doling out of federal funds are usually justified under the "Necessary and Proper" Clause (which lets Congress use any means to seek an objective falling within the specifically-enumerated powers, as long as the means is rationally related to the objective, and is not specifically forbidden by the Constitution). [62]

> **Example:** Suppose Congress makes available to the states certain funds that are to be used for improving the states' highway systems. Congress provides, however, a state will lose 5% of these funds unless the state passes a statute imposing a speed limit of no higher than 55 mph on all state roads. Even without reference to the Commerce Clause, this is a valid use of congressional power. That's because by the combination of the spending power and the "Necessary and Proper" Clause, Congress is permitted to impose conditions (even ones motivated solely by regulatory objectives) on the use of federal funds. [*South Dakota v. Dole*] [63]

a. Conditions can't amount to "coercion": But there is a *limit* to how much pressure Congress can bring to bear on the states when it sets conditions on a new program that relies on the spending power. Pressure that amounts to *"coercion"* will cause the new program to go beyond the spending power.

i. Loss of pre-existing federal funding: So far, this "coercion" problem has arisen only where Congress tells the states that if they don't agree to participate in a new federally-funded program, they will lose *major federal funding* associated with an independent *pre-existing program*. In this situation, the Court will ask whether Congress has left the states *"no real option but to acquiesce"* in the new program and its conditions. If the answer is "yes," the Court will conclude that Congress has coerced the states, and that this coercion ***goes beyond the scope of Congress' spending power.*** (Only one case — set forth in the following Example — has found that Congress used such unconstitutional coercion.)

Example: Every state has for decades participated in Medicaid, a federal-state program under which the states provide health care for certain classes of poor people, and Congress pays most of the costs. In the 2010 Affordable Care Act (ACA), Congress dramatically expands the Medicaid program by means of the "Medicaid Expansion." Under the Medic-aid Expansion, each participating state must now give Medicaid coverage to ***every adult under 65*** with income up to 133% of the federal poverty level (whereas far fewer people have been covered by most states under the pre-Expansion version of Medicaid). Congress promises to pay all or nearly all of the costs (depending on the year) of the Expansion. If a state declines to participate in the Expansion, it will lose ***all*** Medicaid funding, not just the "extra" funding to cover the newly-eligible recipients. Twenty-six states claim that the threatened loss of all existing Medicaid funding is so coercive that the Medicaid Expansion goes beyond Congress' spending power.

Held (by a 7-2 vote), for the plaintiff states. Congress is entitled to impose conditions on the use of money it provides to states. But the Court will give closer scrutiny to those situations in which Congress, in connection with ***one*** federally-financed program, imposes conditions that take the form of threats to terminate a state's participation in ***another*** significant federally-funded program. Here, Congress has held "a gun to the head" of the states: a state that rejects the Medicaid Expansion (essentially a new program) will lose all funding for "old" Medicaid, typically over 10% of the state's overall budget. This is "economic dragooning that leaves the states with ***no real option but to acquiesce"*** in the Medicaid Expansion. Such compulsion goes beyond Congress' spending power.[1] [*N.F.I.B. v. Sebelius* (2012)] (other aspects of which are discussed *supra*, C-9 and C-11). [63]

C. **"General Welfare" Clause:** Although, as noted above, Congress can "provide for the common defense and general welfare of the United States," the reference to "general welfare" does ***not*** confer any independent source of congressional power. In other words, no statute is valid solely because Congress is trying to bring about the "general welfare." Instead, the phrase "for the general welfare" describes the circumstances under which Congress may use its "taxing and spending" power. So if Congress is ***regulating*** (rather than taxing and spending), it must find a specific grant of power (like the Commerce Clause), and it's not enough that the regulation will promote the general welfare. [62]

IV.   THE SEPARATION OF POWERS

A. **Separation of powers generally:** Let's now review some of the major practical consequences that come from the fact that each federal branch gets its own set of powers. These practical consequences are collectively referred to as ***"separation of powers"*** problems. [112-119]

B. **Limits on Congress's delegation of law-making power to the executive branch:** An important category of separation-of-powers problems involves the boundary between ***Congress's*** core power (the power to ***legislate***, i.e., to "make the laws") and the core power of the ***President*** and the executive branch (the power to "execute" the laws, i.e., to carry them out). And within this category, the most important issue concerns the limits on the Congress's power to ***delegate to the President*** (and to the ***executive branch*** that the President controls) ***Congress's law-making powers.*** [116-118]

---

1. But the Court held that the rest of the ACA could be ***severed*** from the unconstitutional condition. So each state got to choose whether to participate in the Medicaid Expansion, or instead just keep its pre-existing Medicaid rights and funding. [67]

1. **Grant of "legislative powers" to Congress:** Recall that ***all the "legislative powers"*** of the federal government are entrusted by the Constitution solely to ***Congress***. Art. I, § 1.

2. **President and agencies can't "make the laws":** This exclusive grant of lawmaking power to Congress means that the ***President cannot make the laws*** — all he or she can do is to ***carry out the laws*** made by Congress. And the grant means that the many ***federal agencies and commissions*** that are part of the executive branch similarly cannot make laws — they can only administer Congress-made laws. [116]

   a. **Rise of federal agencies:** But during the last century or so, Congress has increasingly ***delegated*** its law-making powers to these administrative agencies and commissions. Congress has done this by giving the agencies the power to promulgate ***administrative "rules"*** that have the ***force of law.*** [116]

      i. **Rationale:** Why has Congress done this? Because, as the Supreme Court has put it, "[I]n our increasingly complex society, ... Congress ***simply cannot do its job*** absent an ability to ***delegate power under broad general directives.***" *Mistretta v. U.S.* (1989). [117]

3. **Possibility of "excessive delegation":** Given that only Congress can "make" laws, it's easy to imagine a situation in which Congress so completely delegates to an executive-branch agency or commission the authority to make "rules" that are like "laws" that the Supreme Court would find a violation of separation-of-powers principles.

   a. ***Schechter Poultry* case:** Very occasionally (and not recently), the Supreme Court has held that Congress has, indeed, ***excessively, and unconstitutionally, delegated too much authority*** to the executive branch without giving that branch adequate guidance about how to use the authority. But the last time the Court so held was in *Schechter Poultry Corp. v. U.S.* (1935) [117]

4. **Modern "intelligible principle" standard:** The Court's test for measuring whether a delegation is constitutional is in theory the so-called ***"intelligible principle" test***, which says that delegation is constitutional if, but only if, Congress has ***supplied an "intelligible principle"*** to guide the person or agency to whom Congress has delegated rule-making authority. [118]

   a. **Never found to be violated:** But in the many post-1935 cases in which the Supreme Court has heard challenges to congressional statutes delegating legislative power to federal agencies, the Court has ***never once struck down a statute*** as an unconstitutional delegation. All delegations, including those ***without any meaningful criteria,*** have been upheld. [*Gundy v. U.S.* (2019)] [117-118]

C. **Limits on the powers of the President:** Let's concentrate now on several aspects of how the Constitution's separation-of-powers principles ***limit the powers of the President***.

   1. **President can't make the laws:** As we just saw in the special context of delegation of rule-making power by Congress to the President, a key separation-of-powers principle is that the ***President cannot make the laws***. All he or she can do is to ***carry out the laws*** made by Congress. [112]

      Example: During the Korean War, Pres. Truman wants to avert a strike in the nation's steel mills. He therefore issues an "executive order" directing the Secretary of Commerce to seize the mills and operate them under federal direction. The President does not ask Congress to approve the seizure. *Held*, the seizure order is an unconstitutional exercise of the lawmaking authority reserved to Congress. [*Youngstown Sheet & Tube v. Sawyer*]

   2. **Line Item Veto:** The principle that the President can't make the laws means that the President can't be given a ***"line item veto."*** That is, if Congress tries to give the President the right to veto individual portions of a statute (e.g., particular expenditures), this will violate the Presentment Clause. (The Presentment Clause says that bills are enacted into law by being passed by both

Houses, then being presented to the President and signed by him.) [*Clinton v. City of New York*] [114]

3. **Congress' acquiescence:** But the scope of the President's powers may be at least somewhat expanded by ***Congress' acquiescence*** to his exercise of the power. This congressional acquiescence will never be ***dispositive***, but in a close case, the fact that Congress acquiesced in the President's conduct may be enough to tip the balance, and to convince the Court that the President is merely carrying out the laws rather than making them. [113]

4. **Implied powers:** Recall that Congress' powers are somewhat expanded by the "Necessary & Proper" clause — Congress can pass any laws reasonably related to the exercise of any enumerated power. There's no comparable "Necessary & Proper" clause for the President. But the effect is the same, because of the inherent vagueness of the phrase "shall take care that the laws be faithfully executed..." The Constitution does specifically enumerate some of the President's powers (e.g., the pardon power, the commander-in-chief power, etc.), but this specific list is not supposed to be exclusive. Instead of giving a complete list of the President's powers (as is done for Congress), the Constitution gives the President this general "executive" or "law carrying out" power.

   a. **Consequence:** Consequently, so long as the President's act seems reasonably related to carrying out the laws made by Congress, the Court won't strike that act merely because it doesn't fall within any narrow, enumerated Presidential power. (*Example:* Nothing in the Constitution expressly gives the President prosecutorial discretion [the power to decide whom to prosecute], yet he clearly has this power, because it's part of the broader job of "carrying out the law.")

5. **War powers:**   Separation-of-powers issues often arise when the President's ***war-related powers*** are at stake.

   a. **Can't declare war:**   The President is the Commander-in-Chief of the armed forces. But ***only Congress, not the President, can declare war.*** The President can commit our armed forces to repel a sudden attack, but he cannot fight a long-term engagement without a congressional declaration of war. [121]

6. **Treaties and executive agreements:**   As noted, the President has the power to enter into a ***treaty*** with foreign nations, but only if two-thirds of the Senate approves. Additionally, the Court has held that the Constitution implicitly gives the President, as an adjunct of his foreign affairs power, the right to enter into an ***"executive agreement"*** with a foreign nation, without first getting express congressional consent. [68]

D. **National security and the entry of foreigners into the U.S.:**   The   President   and   Congress (together, the "political branches") — ***not*** the judiciary — have the principal role in matters of ***national security and the entry of foreigners into the U.S.*** Therefore, the courts will show ***extreme deference*** to the political branches' judgment in these matters. Thus the courts will usually apply easy-to-satisfy ***"mere-rationality"*** standard to review the constitutionality of any federal statute or executive order in these areas, even though the courts would likely use heightened scrutiny to review a similar measure in the *domestic* arena.

1. **Sustained despite evidence of religious bias:**   Thus even if the President's statements in support of limits on the entry of foreign nationals from certain countries indicate that the President is acting largely out of ***bias towards a particular religious group,*** the Court will apparently sustain the measure so long as it's ***rationally related to the achievement of a national security interest.***

   Example: President Trump issues a "Proclamation" (a type of executive order) greatly restricting entry to the U.S. by citizens of eight countries, most of which are majority-Muslim (e.g., Iran, Iraq, Libya, and Syria). There is evidence that this "travel ban" was motivated in part by the President's bias against foreigners who are Muslim.

Held (by a 5-4 vote), the ban does not violate any provision of the Constitution, and is therefore valid. The admission and exclusion of foreign nationals is "largely immune from judicial control." The Court will therefore apply an easy-to-satisfy "rational basis review" to the travel ban, under which the ban will be upheld so long as it is "plausibly related to the Government's stated objective." Since the travel ban plausibly advances the government's stated interest in protecting the country against the entry of foreign nationals who may be terrorists, the Court will uphold the ban even though there may also be evidence that the ban was motivated in part by religious bias. [*Trump v. Hawaii*] [124-126]

E. Appointment of executive personnel: The President, not Congress, is given the power to *appoint federal executive officers*. This is the *"Appointments" Clause.* [126-135]

1. **Text of Clause:** If we ignore the Clause's treatment of the power to make treaties, here's how the Clause reads:

> [The President] ... shall **[1]** *nominate,* and by and with the *Advice and Consent of the Senate,* shall *appoint Ambassadors,* other *public Ministers* and Consuls, *Judges* of the supreme Court, and *all other Officers of the United States,* whose Appointments are not herein otherwise provided for, and which shall be established by Law: but **[2]** *the Congress may by Law* vest the *Appointment of such inferior Officers,* as they think proper, in *the President alone, in the Courts of Law, or in the Heads of Departments.*

(I have added the "[1]" and "[2]" markers, so that in our discussions below I can refer separately to each of these two main provisions.) [126]

2. **Summary of the Clause:** As we'll see in more detail below (in Pars. 4 and 6), the Appointments Clause is interpreted to *create two different classes* of "federal officers":

❏ **Top-level ("principal") officers:** Under what I've marked above as prong [1] of the Clause, *top-level* "officers of the United States" are *appointed by the President*, *subject to Senate approval*; and

❏ **Inferior officers:** Under prong [2] of the Clause, "*inferior*" officers are to be appointed by *whichever group* (the President, the Judicial Branch or the "Heads of Departments") *Congress specifies*. [126]

3. **Congress can't appoint federal officers:** A major consequence of the Appointments Clause is that *Congress may not appoint "federal officers,"* whether the officer is a "principal" one or an "inferior" one. See Par. 7 below.

4. **Distinguishing between "principal" and "inferior" officers:** We'll discuss the dividing line between "principal" and "inferior" officers in greater detail in Par. 6 below.

a. **Two categories:** But for now, here's a high-level overview of how the two categories are defined:

i. **Who are "principal" officers:** "*Principal*" officers of the U.S. are people who *have no boss* except for the President. *Members of the Cabinet, heads* of *federal agencies,* federal *judges,* and *ambassadors* are the main examples of principal federal officers.

ii. **Who are "inferior" officers:** All officers who are *not* "principal" officers of the U.S. are automatically "*inferior*" officers. Therefore, any officer who *has a boss other than the President* is an inferior officer. People *who work in federal agencies* but who are not the head of the agency are typically inferior officers, if they are officers at all. (As to the dividing line between "officers" and non-officers, see Par. 8 below.) [127]

b. How the two types differ: A key reason why it's important to determine whether any given federal officer is a "principal" one or instead an "inferior" one is that the Appointments Clause makes the process for *appointing* the two types of officers dramatically different:

    i. Appointing "principal" (top-level) officers: In the case of *"principal"* officers of the United States (i.e., *top-level* officers), the **President nominates a candidate.** But the Appointments Clause says that the nomination cannot take effect until the Senate has given its *"Advice and Consent"* (i.e., has "*confirmed*") the nomination. That approval must be by an **ordinary majority** of those Senators voting. [127]

        (1) Congress relatively powerless: An important aspect of this system for appointing principal officers is that Congress *may not take away or limit* the President's power to appoint (i.e., nominate) a principal officer.

    ii. Appointing "inferior" (lower-level) officers: But Congress *does* have the right to circumscribe the President's power to appoint "*inferior*" federal officers. The Appointments Clause specifies several methods for making these appointments. The portion of the Clause marked as prong [2] in Par. 1 *supra* says that "Congress may by Law vest the Appointment of such *inferior* Officers, as they think proper, in the **President alone**, in the **Courts of Law**, or in the **Heads of Departments**." For more about these methods, see Par. 5 immediately below. [127]

5. Appointing "inferior "officers: Here's a bit more detail about the various ways an *inferior* officer can be appointed, according to the Appointments Clause.

    a. Limits on Congress: First, Congress has *no* power of its own to *appoint inferior officers,* at least those who are to work in the Executive or Judicial Branches. In other words, whereas the Senate can at least veto any Presidential appointment of a *principal* officer (by refusing to "Advise and Consent" to the appointment), neither the House nor Senate has the power to appoint (or to veto the appointment of) an *inferior* Executive Branch officer. [127]

    b. Three possible appointers: But Congress *does* have a limited power to **choose the class of persons who are to appoint** any given type of inferior officer. This power comes from the final portion of the Appointments Clause:

        ". . . but Congress may by Law vest the Appointment of such *inferior* Officers, as they think proper, in the **President alone**, in the **Courts of Law**, or in the **Heads of Departments**."

    Thus Congress has the right to choose, on a position-by-position basis, to confer the power of appointment on *any* of the following groups (but *only* on those groups):

        [1] the **President**;

        [2] members of the **federal judiciary**; or

        [3] the **"heads of departments"** (e.g., Cabinet members). [128]

Example 1: Congress creates the post of Deputy Secretary of State, and says that the person occupying this post must be appointed by the Secretary of State. There is no constitutional problem with this statute, since (1) the Secretary of State is a Cabinet member and is thus automatically a "Head of Department"; and (2) the Deputy Secretary is an "inferior" federal officer, who Congress may therefore say (by authority of the final portion of the Appointments Clause) is to be appointed by the head of the department in which the Deputy will serve. [128]

Example 2: Congress creates the post of *Assistant* Deputy Secretary of State, and specifies that the power to appoint a person to hold this post shall be held by the Deputy Secretary of State. This statute *is* a violation of the final portion of the Appointments Clause, assuming that the post is senior enough that the person who holds it exercises "significant authority."[2] Although Congress can limit the President's power to make appointment of an inferior federal officer, Congress must give this appointment power to one of the following: the President, members of the federal judiciary, or a "Head of Department" (typically, a Cabinet member). The Deputy Secretary of State does not fall into any of these three categories, so Congress can't constitutionally grant her the power to appoint an inferior federal officer. [128]

6. **Dividing line between "principal" and "inferior" officers in more detail:** As we saw earlier, a "principal" officer of the U.S. is one who *has no "boss" except the President*; and any officer of the U.S. who has a boss other than the President is an "inferior" officer. But what exactly is the definition of a *"boss"* for these purposes? The Supreme Court has never given a precise definition that can be applied to all scenarios involving those who supervise U.S. Executive-Branch officers.

   a. **"Administrative law judges" (the *Arthrex* case):** But there *is* one category of Executive-Branch officer as to which the Supreme Court *has* had occasion to analyze this "who is a boss?" issue: so-called *"administrative law judges,"* who are employed by various federal agencies to conduct "hearings" in specialized federally-regulated areas like patent law and the military criminal-justice system. [128]

      i. **Summary of rule:** Here's the rule announced by the Supreme Court to determine whether a given administrative law judge has a "boss" for purposes of the Appointments Clause: In cases where an administrative law judge of some sort makes a decision following a "hearing," the officer is a *"principal"* officer (i.e., has no boss) if, and only if, the decision is *"final"* in the sense that it is *not reviewable* by any member of the Executive Branch. Conversely, if the decisions by an administrative law judge *are reviewable/modifiable by an Executive Branch member,* then the judge is an *"inferior"* officer (i.e., has a boss), and can therefore legally be appointed by the *head of the "department"* in which the judge works. [*U.S. v. Arthrex*] [130]

7. **No appointments by Congress:** As we've seen, a key aspect of the Appointments Clause is that *Congress itself may not make any appointments* of federal officials, whether "principal" or "inferior." The most it may do (and only in the case of inferior officers) is to prescribe the *procedures* by which the President, department heads or members of the Judicial Branch shall make appointments. These "procedures" may, however, include fairly detailed *qualifications* regarding *age*, *experience*, etc.

   a. **Supporting employees appointable by Congress:** On the other hand, Congress may *make its own appointments* of persons who *will help Congress perform its "legislative" duties* (as opposed to duties associated with the Executive or Judicial Branches). As the Supreme Court has put it, the Appointments Clause does not apply where Congress wants to designate people who will help Congress exercise "powers ... essentially of an *investigative and informative* nature." *Buckley v. Valeo*, discussed *infra*, p. C-18. [130]

   Example: Suppose the Senate Banking Committee is considering reforming the nation's banking system. The Committee has the power to appoint staff members to investigate possible changes that Congress might make to that system. Because these staff members will be working on what's essentially a "legislative" matter, the Appointments Clause doesn't apply, so Congress may appoint whomever it wishes, with no participation from the Judicial or Executive Branches. [131]

---

2. See *infra*, p. C-18, Sub-Par. 8(b,) establishing "significant authority" as the standard for determining whether a person is an inferior federal officer at all, as opposed to a rank-and-file federal employee who is not even an inferior officer.

8. **Dividing line between "officer" and non-officer:** Let's now examine another dividing line, the one between all federal "*officers*" (whether principal or inferior) on the one hand, and all non-officer "*employees*" of the federal government on the other.

   a. **Why it matters:** Here's why this dividing line matters: *Mere "employees"* of the Executive Branch — i.e., workers who are *not powerful enough to qualify as at least "inferior officers"* — are *not required* to be appointed in compliance with the Appointments Clause at all. By contrast, "inferior officers" *are* required to be appointed in compliance with that Clause. Therefore, if an appointee is an "inferior officer of the U.S.," that person *may not be appointed by a federal employee* (or group of employees) who is *not* a Head of Department. [131]

   b. **"Significant authority" standard (*Buckley v. Valeo*):** So where is the *dividing line* between the least-powerful "*inferior officer*" and the most-powerful *non-officer employee*? The Supreme Court has given the following limited, semi-cryptic, guidance: federal "officers" (as opposed to mere federal "employees") are persons who *"exercise significant authority"* under federal law. [*Buckley v. Valeo*] [131]

   c. **ALJs have "significant authority":** What, then, does *"significant authority"* mean? The one area in which the Supreme Court has discussed the detailed meaning of this phrase is that *administrative law judges* (ALJs) for the Securities and Exchange Commission (SEC) *have* such authority, and thus must be appointed by a Head of Department (which in the case of the SEC means by the Commission itself, not by Commission staff members). [*Lucia v. SEC*] [133]

      Example: The SEC brings civil charges against P for violating securities laws. The case is heard in a "hearing" by an ALJ, Judge Elliot, who was appointed by an SEC official rather than by majority vote of the Commissioners themselves. Each SEC ALJ is given a set of powers to use in hearings that is comparable to the powers of a federal trial judge (e.g., power to take testimony, to rule on motions and evidentiary objections, to make findings of fact, and to issue a proposed "opinion" that will resolve the case unless the full Commission votes to reject the opinion, something that rarely occurs). Elliot conducts the hearing and finds that P has broken SEC rules. P appeals, saying that Elliot exercised "significant authority," and therefore was not properly appointed to his ALJ post given that he wasn't appointed by the Commission itself.

      Held, for P: SEC ALJs like Judge Elliot, because they hold nearly all the tools of federal trial judges, have "substantial authority." Therefore, Judge Elliot was an "inferior officer" (not just a garden-variety SEC employee). As such, he needed to have been appointed by a "Head of Department" (i.e., by the whole Commission); without such an appointment his hearing of P's case was constitutionally invalid. [*Lucia v. SEC, supra.*] [132-133]

9. **President's Recess Appointments power:** If a *vacancy* in a post requiring Senate confirmation *arises* when *Congress is not in session*, so that Congress is *not available* to confirm the President's choice of replacement, Art. II, §2, cl. 3 applies. That clause gives the President, *acting alone*, the power "to *fill up all Vacancies* that may happen *during the Recess of the Senate*, by granting Commissions which shall *expire at the End of their next Session."* This is the so-called *"Recess Appointments" Clause.* [134]

   Example: Suppose the Secretary of State dies suddenly in early December of 2014, at a time when the old Congress has ended, and the new Congress hasn't yet been sworn in (which won't happen until early January, 2015). There is therefore no Senate in session that can "advise and consent" on any replacement nominee. The President may immediately after the prior Secretary's death use his Recess Appointments power to appoint a temporary Secretary, who will serve even without Senate approval until the end of the *next* session of Congress (an end that will occur in December 2016).

   a. Intra-session appointments: The Recess Appointment Clause's use of the phrase "the recess" includes not only the single long *"inter-session"* recess by the Senate (i.e., the one between the end of the first session in December of odd-numbered years and the start of the second in the following January), but also any *"intra-session recess* of substantial length." [*N.L.R.B. v. Noel Canning*] [134]

   Example: The second session of Congress starts on Jan. 3, 2012. Congress goes on recess on Jan. 4. Even though this is an "intra-session" recess, if it lasts a "substantial length" of time (usually 10 days or more, as discussed below), the President may use his Recess Appointments power during that recess. [Cf. *Noel Canning*]

   i. Minimum length: There is a *minimum length* that an intra-session recess must have in order to trigger the recess power, according to the Supreme Court: any recess of *10 days or more is sufficiently long*, but any recess *less than 10 days* will be *presumed to be too short* to fall within the Clause. [*Noel Canning*] [134]

   (1) Emergency: However, in a truly *emergency* situation ("a national catastrophe, for instance, that renders the Senate unavailable but calls for an urgent response"), the Court may find that the presumption that a 10-day recess is the shortest allowable has been rebutted. [*Noel Canning*]

   ii. Vacancy need not arise during the recess: A vacancy will still be deemed to "happen" during recess (so that it qualifies under the Clause) even though the prior occupant *leaves the post while the Senate is still in session*, as long as the Senate has gone into recess by the time the President makes the new appointment. (That's what has happened historically in the vast majority of cases where the President has purported to exercise the recess power.) [*Noel Canning*]

F. Removal of federal officers: The power to *remove* federal officers similarly rests mainly with the *President*.

   1. General rule: The general rule (subject to exceptions discussed below) is that the President *may remove* any presidential or executive-branch appointee *without cause*.

   a. High-level ("principal") federal officers: Thus Congress may not limit in any way the President's right to remove a *high-level* ("principal") appointee with pure executive-branch powers, such as a *Cabinet member* or *ambassador*. [141]

   Example: The President may remove the Secretary of State)at any time, without cause. Congress may not limit this right by saying, for instance, "The President may remove the Secretary of State only for good cause." [142]

   Note: But Congress has more power to limit the President's power to remove federal officers who head *"independent"* federal agencies possessing mostly judicial or legislative powers. See Par. 2, *infra*, C-20.

   i. Lower-level ("inferior") officers: The above rule — that Congress may not prevent the President from removing without cause a presidential or executive-branch appointee having executive-branch powers — applies *only* to *high-level* ("principal") federal officers, not to lower-level ("inferior") ones. In the case of an *"inferior"* federal officer (i.e., one who *has a boss*, such as someone who reports to the head of a cabinet department), Congress *may* say that the President or the executive branch may remove the officer — whether or not she heads an executive branch agency — only for cause. [141]

Example: Congress may say that an independent counsel who is to investigate possible executive-branch wrongdoing — an "inferior" executive officer — may only be removed by the executive branch for "good cause" or other inability to perform his duties. [*Morrison v. Olson*]) [141]

2. **Quasi-legislative and quasi-judicial officers:**   The rule discussed in Par. 1 above — that Congress may not limit the President's right to remove, even without cause, a high-level presidential or executive-branch appointee with executive-branch powers — does *not* apply to appointees who *head certain federal agencies* that have a significant *quasi-judicial* or *quasi-legislative* role. Congress may *limit* or even completely *block* the President's right to removel such agency heads. [135]

   a. **"Independent" federal agencies:**   This special rule applies to the heads of so-called "*independent*" federal agencies, i.e., agencies that *don't mainly carry out the President's policies* (as, say, cabinet members do), but instead make significant rules governing the actions of *persons outside the executive branch*, such as private citizens. It's important that these agencies be *insulated from interference by the President.* Therefore, the Court has held, Congress *may* under Article I limit the President from removing the heads of such agencies unless he has *just cause* for the firing. [136]

   Example: Congress creates the Federal Trade Commission, an administrative agency whose function is to administer a federal statute designed to guard against certain types of unfair competition. Congress provides that Commissioners will be appointed for fixed terms by the President (with the advice and consent of the Senate), and that the President may remove a Commissioner before the expiration of his fixed term only for cause. The President (Franklin Roosevelt) contends that the statute improperly interferes with what he says is his constitutional right to remove a Commissioner even without cause.

   Held, against the President. The FTC is an independent body designed to act quasi-legislatively and quasi-judicially; it is not part of the executive branch. To perform its functions properly, it must be free from executive-branch interference. Therefore, Congress was constitutionally entitled to maintain the Commission's independence by insisting that the President may remove a Commissioner only for cause. [*Humphrey's Executor v. U.S.*] [136]

   i. **Agencies with executive powers and one-member heads don't qualify:**   But this special rule illustrated by *Humphrey's Executor* — allowing Congress to prevent the President from removing the heads of "independent" agencies or commissions except for cause — applies *only* if the structure and powers of the agency or commission satisfy *two stringent requirements:*

   [1] First, the powers of the independent agency or commission *must not include significant executive powers.* Thus the agency's powers must be *primarily legislative and/ or judicial*, and must *not involve a significant power to enforce existing laws*; and …

   [2] Second, the agency or commission must be *governed by a multi-member board* rather than by a *single director.*

   [*Seila Law v. Consumer Fin. Prot. Bureau* (2020) [136]

   ii. **Two levels of protection not allowed:**   As we just saw in (i) above, the special rule that Congress may limit the President's power to prevent the President from removing the heads of "independent" agencies or commissions except for cause applies only if the body meets two stringent requirements. Furthermore, even if the agency or commission *does* meet these two requirements, there's yet *another* restriction on Congress' power to protect the body's leadership: Congress *can't* confer on the agency's leadership *two levels* of only-for-good-cause protection from Presidential or executive-branch removal. [140]

Example: Congress may say that the Chairman of the Federal Election Commission (an independent agency) may be removed by the President only for cause. But Congress *may not* then *also* say, "there shall be a Deputy FEC Commissioner, who may be removed by the Chairman only for cause." Such a provision would unduly limit the President's ability to discharge his power to appoint federal officers. [*Free Enterprise Fund v. Public Co. Accounting Oversight Bd.*] [140]

3. **Impeachment:** Separately, Congress may directly remove any federal executive officer by *impeachment*, a power discussed immediately below.

G. **Impeachment:** Congress can remove any "officer" of the U.S. (President, Vice President, Cabinet members, federal judges, etc.) by *impeachment*. The House must vote by a *majority* to impeach (which is like an indictment). Then, the Senate conducts the trial; a two-thirds vote of the Senators present is required to convict. Conviction can be for treason, bribery, and other "high crimes and misdemeanors."

1. **Meaning of "high crimes and misdemeanors":** Probably only *serious* crimes, and *serious* non-criminal abuses of power, fall within the phrase "high crimes and misdemeanors." But the Supreme Court has never had occasion to determine this (and probably never will, since the Court has generally treated issues about impeachment as being non-justiciable political questions). [143]

H. **Removal of federal judges:** Federal *judges* cannot be removed by *either* Congress or the President. Article III provides that federal judges shall hold their office *during "good behavior."* This has been held to mean that so long as a judge does not act improperly, she may not be removed from office. The only way to remove a sitting federal judge is by formal *impeachment* proceedings, as noted above.

1. **Non-Article III judges:** However, the above "life tenure" rule applies only to garden-variety federal judges who hold their positions directly under *Article III*. Congress is always free to establish what are essentially *administrative* judgeships, and as to these, lifetime tenure is not constitutionally required.

V. LEGISLATIVE AND EXECUTIVE IMMUNITY

A. **Speech and Debate Clause:** Members of Congress are given a quite broad *immunity* by the ***"Speech and Debate" Clause:*** "For any speech or debate in either house, [members of Congress] shall not be questioned in any other place." This clause shields members of Congress from: (1) civil or criminal suits relating to their legislative actions; and (2) grand jury investigations relating to those actions. [145]

B. **Executive immunity:** The Speech and Debate Clause has no counterpart in the Constitution giving any sort of immunity to members of the *executive* branch. However, as a common-law matter, the federal courts have recognized certain types of executive immunity.

1. **Judicial process, including subpoenas to produce documents:** The President and other members of the executive branch *do not have general immunity* from *judicial process*, such as *subpoenas to produce documents.*

a. **Federal-court subpoenas:** Thus, Presidents do not have general or absolute immunity from subpoenas *issued by federal courts.*

Example: During Watergate, the Watergate Special Prosecutor secures a federal-court subpoena directing Pres. Nixon to produce tape recordings of Oval Office meetings. Nixon moves to quash the subpoena, claiming that the Constitution provides an absolute privilege of confidentiality to all presidential communications. *Held* (unanimously), claim rejected: Presidents are subject to subpoenas issued by federal courts. [*U.S. v. Nixon.*] [145]

   b.   State-court subpoenas: The same rule applies to subpoenas issued in state-court proceedings: the President ***does not have absolute immunity from state-court subpoenas.***

   Example: The office of the New York State district attorney for Manhattan begins a grand jury investigation of whether business transactions by various individuals linked to a sitting President, Donald Trump, have violated state law. The grand jury serves a subpoena *duces tecum* on Trump's personal accounting firm, directing it to produce financial records relating to Trump and his businesses, starting before Trump ran for office. Trump sues to quash the subpoena, arguing that a sitting President should have absolute immunity from subpoenas issued as part of state criminal proceedings, because forcing a President to comply with such subpoenas will allow state officials to harass the President, and will inevitably divert him from performance of his constitutionally-mandated duties.

   Held (7-2), the President's claim of absolute immunity is ***rejected***. Any danger of harassment posed by state-grand-jury subpoenas can be eliminated by enforcing existing rules prohibiting grand juries from engaging in "arbitrary fishing expeditions" or from initiating investigations out of "malice or an intent to harm." Furthermore, a state grand jury subpoena seeking a President's private papers is ***not*** required to satisfy a ***"heightened need standard"*** as Trump has argued. (But Presidents still have the right to "challenge specific subpoenas as impeding their Article II functions.") [*Trump v. Vance* (2020)] [145]

2.   Civil liability of President for official acts: But the President ***does*** have ***absolute immunity*** from being held ***civilly liability*** for his ***official acts.*** [146]

Example: P sues Pres. Nixon (D), as well as several Nixon Administration officials, for violating his First Amendment and statutory rights. P claims that he was fired from his Defense Department job in retaliation for testimony in which he criticized military cost overruns.

Held, for Nixon. The President is entitled to ***absolute immunity*** from civil damage actions for all acts within the ***"outer perimeter"*** of his authority. Since the President has authority to prescribe the manner in which the business of the armed forces will be conducted, including the authority to dismiss personnel, Nixon is immune from liability for the firing of Fitzgerald ***even if he caused it maliciously or in an illegal manner***. [*Nixon v. Fitzgerald.*] [146-146]

   a.   Civil liability of presidential assistants: Do presidential ***assistants*** get a similar absolute immunity from civil suits for their official acts? The brief answer is ***"no."*** [*Harlow v. Fitzgerald*] [147]

      i.   Qualified immunity granted: But presidential assistants do get fairly broad ***"qualified immunity"*** from civil suits for their official acts. Essentially, a presidential assistant has immunity from civil suit for conduct arising out of her ***performance of her office***, except where the official has violated a ***"clearly established"*** right.

      Example: Suppose a cabinet official fires a subordinate on the grounds that the subordinate is openly gay. Suppose further that at the time of the firing, there is no clearly established law about whether the federal government may fire a person for being gay.

      Even if, immediately after the firing, the Supreme Court decides that such firings are illegal, the cabinet official will have qualified immunity. That immunity will protect the official here, because, at the moment of the firing, the official was not violating a "clearly established" right. [147]

3.   No presidential immunity for non-official acts: *Nixon v. Fitzgerald, supra,* only establishes absolute immunity for ***official*** presidential acts, i.e., those that are within the "outer perimeter" of the President's job. There is ***no immunity — not even qualified immunity —*** for acts that the President takes that are completely ***unrelated to the carrying out of his job***. [147]

Example: P (Paula Jones) brings a private damages suit against President Clinton, filed while Clinton is in office. Jones claims that while she was employed by the state of Arkansas and Clinton was Governor of Arkansas, Clinton made illegal sexual advances to her. Clinton argues that a President should have "temporary immunity" — to last while he is in office — against virtually all civil litigation arising out of events that occurred before he took office.

Held (unanimously) for P. There is no policy reason supporting even temporary immunity for unofficial acts. The rationale for immunity for *official* acts of the President and other officials is that such immunity enables them to perform their designated functions effectively **without fear** that a particular decision may expose them to civil liability. This rationale does not apply to the President's *unofficial* acts, a category that includes any acts he took before he became President. [*Clinton v. Jones*] [147]

4. **Criminal prosecution:** Members of the executive branch have **no** general executive immunity, either of a common-law or constitutional nature, from **criminal** prosecution.

   a. **Delay in the case of the President:** However, at least in the case of the **President**, there's a strong argument that the Constitution's provision of impeachment as the means of removal bars any criminal prosecution of a President until **after he or she has been removed from office.**

      i. **Justice Department view:** This is the position of the U.S. Justice Department. Since 2000, the Department's official policy has been that no criminal prosecution of a President may be begun until he has left office, because "[t]he indictment or criminal prosecution of a **sitting President** would **unconstitutionally undermine the capacity of the executive branch to perform its constitutionally assigned functions**."

   b. **People other than the President:** In the case of the Vice-President and other principal federal officers besides the President, criminal prosecution prior to impeachment seems to be **permissible**. For instance, Nixon's Vice-President, Spiro Agnew, was indicted by a federal grand jury on bribery and tax evasion charges prior to his resignation. (But the Supreme Court never passed on whether the Constitution prohibited such prosecution of a sitting Vice President.)

5. **Subpoenas by Congress (*Trump v. Mazars*):** As we saw earlier (see *Trump v. Vance, supra*, p. C-21), the President does not receive any special protection from *court*-issued subpoenas to produce documents. But the same is **not** true of **"legislative subpoenas,"** that is, subpoenas **by Congress** for presidential documents. Before courts enforce congressional demands for presidential records, they must make a **"careful analysis"** that weighs Congress' interest in enacting legislation against the "unique position" of the President. [*Trump v. Mazars USA* (2020)] [148]

   a. **Factors in "careful analysis":** Congressional subpoenas for the President's records pose separation-of-powers issues, because such subpoenas "unavoidably **pit the political branches against one another**." [*Trump v. Mazars, supra*.] Therefore, a court's "careful analysis" of such subpoenas must apply the following principles:

      (1) the subpoena should be quashed if **other sources could provide** Congress the information it needs;

      (2) the subpoena must be **"no broader than reasonably necessary"** to support Congress's legislative objective;

      (3) the court must scrutinize the strength of the evidence offered by Congress of the **legislative purpose** for which it's seeking the documents — the more **"detailed and substantial"** this evidence, the **better**; and

      (4) the court must carefully assess **"the burdens imposed on the President"** by the subpoena, keeping in mind that where it's *Congress* (not a court) that's issuing the subpoena, the constitutional dangers are greater, because the subpoenas "stem from a **rival political**

branch*" that has "*incentives* to use subpoenas for **institutional advantage."**

[*Trump v. Mazars USA, supra.*]

C. Executive privilege: Presidents have a **qualified** right to refuse to disclose confidential information relating to their performance of their duties. This is called "***executive privilege***." [149-151]

> **1. Outweighed:** Since the privilege is qualified, it may be outweighed by other compelling governmental interests. For instance, the need for the President's evidence in a **criminal trial** will generally outweigh the President's vague need to keep information confidential. [*U.S. v. Nixon, supra,* C-21]. [149-151]

CHAPTER 6

TWO LIMITS ON STATE POWER: THE DORMANT COMMERCE CLAUSE AND CONGRESSIONAL ACTION

I. THE DORMANT COMMERCE CLAUSE

A. Dormant Commerce Clause generally: The ***mere existence*** of the federal commerce power ***restricts the states*** from ***discriminating against***, or ***unduly burdening***, interstate commerce. This restriction is called the ***"dormant Commerce Clause."*** [74]

> **1. Three part test:** A state regulation which affects interstate commerce must satisfy **each** of the following three requirements in order to avoid violating the dormant Commerce Clause:
>
>> **a.** The regulation must pursue a ***legitimate state end***;
>>
>> **b.** The regulation must be ***rationally related*** to that legitimate state end; and
>>
>> **c.** The regulatory **burden** imposed by the state on interstate commerce must be **outweighed** by the state's interest in enforcing its regulation.
>>
>> **d. Summary:** So to summarize this test, it's both a ***"mere-rationality"*** test (in that the regulation must be rationally related to fulfilling a legitimate state end) plus a separate **balancing test** (in that the benefits to the state from the regulation must outweigh the burdens on interstate commerce). [76]
>
> **2. Discrimination against out-of-staters:** Above all else, be on the lookout for ***intentional discrimination against out-of-staters***. If the state is promoting its residents' ***own economic interests***, this will not be a legitimate state objective, so the regulation will virtually automatically violate the Commerce Clause. [77]
>
>> **Example:** The state of Tennessee says that any individual who applies for a license to operate a liquor store in the state must have resided in the state for the prior two years.
>>
>> *Held*, this two-year residency requirement violates the dormant Commerce Clause. If a state law discriminates against out-of-state goods or nonresident economic actors, the law can be sustained only on a showing that it is ***"narrowly tailored to advanc[e] a legitimate local purpose."*** The two-year requirement here "blatantly favors the State's residents and has little relationship to public health and safety." Therefore, it isn't narrowly tailored to any legitimate local purpose, making it an unconstitutional violation of the dormant Commerce Clause. [*Tenn. Wine & Spirits Ret. Ass'n v. Thomas*] [77-78]
>
> **3. Health/safety/welfare regulations:** Regulations that are truly addressed to the state's **health, safety and welfare** objectives are usually "legitimate." (But again, this cannot be used as a smoke-screen for protecting residents' own economic interests at the expense of out-of-staters.)

4. **Balancing test:** When you perform the balancing part of the test (to see whether the benefits to the state from its regulation outweigh the unintentional burdens to commerce), pay special attention to whether there are *less restrictive means* available to the state: if the state could accomplish its objective as well (or even almost as well) while burdening commerce less, then it probably has to do so. [78]

> **Example**: Wisconsin can't ban all out of state milk, even to promote the legitimate objective of avoiding adulterated milk — this is because the less restrictive means of conducting regular health inspections would accomplish the state's safety goal just as well. [*Dean Milk Co. v. Madison*]

   a. **Lack of uniformity:** A measure that leads to a *lack of uniformity* is likely to constitute a big burden on interstate commerce. For instance, if various states' regulations are *in conflict*, the Court will probably strike the minority regulation, on the grounds that it creates a lack of uniformity that substantially burdens commerce without a sufficiently great corresponding benefit to the state.

5. **Some contexts:** The most standard illustrations of forbidden protectionism are where the state says, *"You can't bring your goods into our state,"* or *"You can't take goods out of our state into your state."* Here are some other contexts where dormant Commerce Clause analysis may be important:

   a. **Embargo of natural resources:** Laws that prevent *scarce natural resources* from moving out of the state where they are found are closely scrutinized. Often, this is just protectionism (e.g., a state charges higher taxes on oil destined for out-of-state than for in-state use.) But even if the state's interest is *conservation* or *ecology*, the measure will probably be struck down if *less-discriminatory alternatives* are available. [85]

   b. **Environmental regulations:** Similarly, the states may not *protect their environment* at the expense of their neighbors, unless there is no less-discriminatory way to achieve the same result. (*Example:* New Jersey prohibits the importing of most solid or liquid waste into the state. *Held*, this violates the Commerce Clause. Even if the state's purpose was to protect the state's environment or its inhabitants' health and safety, the state may not accomplish these objectives by discriminating against out-of-staters. [*Philadelphia v. New Jersey*]) [87-89]

   c. **"Do the work in our state":** Statutes that pressure out-of-state businesses to *perform certain operations* within the state are likely to be found violative of the dormant Commerce Clause. Such statutes will probably be found to unduly burden interstate commerce. [85-86]

6. **Discrimination by city against out-of-towners:** The dormant Commerce Clause also prevents a *city or county* from protecting its own local economic interests by discriminating against both out-of-state and out-of-town (but in-state) producers.

> **Example:** Michigan allows each county to decide that it will not allow solid wastes generated outside the county to be disposed of in the county. County X responds by barring both non-Michigan waste and waste generated in Michigan by counties other than X. *Held*, this scheme violates the dormant Commerce Clause because it is an attempt to protect local interests against non-local interests. The regulation is not saved merely because it discriminates against in-state but out-of-county waste producers as well as out-of-state producers. [*Fort Gratiot Sanitary Landfill v. Mich. Dept. of Nat. Res.*] [83]

7. **Market participant exception:** But there is one key *exception* to the dormant Commerce Clause rules: if the state acts as a *market participant*, it *may* favor local over out-of-state interests. (*Example:* South Dakota owns a cement plant. It favors in-state customers during shortages. *Held*, this does not violate the Commerce Clause, because the state is acting as a market participant. [*Reeves v. Stake*]) [89-90]

B. State taxation of interstate commerce: Just as state regulation may be found to unduly burden (or discriminate against) interstate commerce, so state ***taxation*** may be found to unduly burden or discriminate against interstate commerce, and thus violate the Commerce Clause. To strike a state tax as violative of the Commerce Clause, the challenger must generally show either: [90-92]

   1. Discrimination: That the state is ***discriminating*** against interstate commerce, by taxing in a way that unjustifiably benefits local commerce at the expense of out-of-state commerce. [91]

   2. Burdensome: Or, that the state's taxing scheme (perhaps taken in conjunction with other states' taxing schemes) unfairly ***burdens*** interstate commerce even though it doesn't discriminate.

      a. Sales and use taxes: Most litigation about whether state tax schemes unduly burden interstate commerce involves the right of a state or local government to require "out-of-state" vendors to collect ***sales and use taxes*** on shipments sent to an in-state recipient. Here are the basic rules:

         [1] **"Substantial nexus":** In order for a state or local government to impose sales-tax-collection obligations on out-of-state vendors without the tax scheme being found to be an undue burden on commerce, there must be a ***"substantial nexus"*** between the vendor and the taxing state.

         [2] **"Physical presence" test overruled:** On the other hand, as the result of a 2018 decision, states ***may now tax out-of-state firms, including Internet-only firms, even if the firm has no in-state physical presence.*** [*South Dakota v. Wayfair* (2018)]. [92]

II. CONGRESSIONAL ACTION — PREEMPTION AND CONSENT

A. Federal preemption generally: The discussion above relates only to the "dormant" Commerce Clause, i.e., the situation in which Congress has not attempted to ***exercise*** its commerce power in a particular area. Now, we consider what happens when Congress *does* take action in a particular area of commerce.

   1. Supremacy Clause: If there is a ***conflict*** between ***federal law and state law***, the ***state law is simply invalid***. The ***Supremacy Clause*** of the Constitution (Article VI Clause 2) says that "This Constitution, and the Laws of the United States which shall be made in Pursuance thereof … shall be the supreme Law of the Land. … " So if federal and state law conflict, the Supremacy Clause means that ***state law must yield to federal law***. In that event, federal law is said to have "***preempted***" state law. [92]

   2. Express vs implied preemption: Federal preemption of state law falls into two main categories: ***"express"*** preemption and ***"implied"*** preemption [92]:

      [1] *Express* preemption occurs when a federal law ***specifically*** (i.e., "expressly") says that it preempts state or local law.

      [2] *Implied* preemption occurs when Congress does *not* expressly state that it intends to preempt state or local law, but ***manifests an intent*** to do so.

B. Express preemption: Congress sometimes, in enacting a statute, takes the trouble to state explicitly that the statute is intended to preempt some area of state or local law. That is, Congress says, "In the area of [X], the only governing law shall be federal law." This is ***"express preemption."*** As long as the federal statute is validly enacted (e.g., it falls within one of Congress' enumerated powers, such as the commerce power), any state or local law that falls ***within the zone*** intended by Congress to be ***exclusively federal*** will be ***invalid*** under the Supremacy Clause. [93]

> **Example:** The federal Employee Retirement Income Security Act (ERISA) says that it "supersede[s] any and all State laws insofar as they ... relate to any employee benefit plan[.]" If a state purports to regulate some aspect of an employee benefit plan, the state regulation will be valid as a violation of the Supremacy Cause. That's true even though the state regulation may be perfectly consistent with ERISA.

C. Implied preemption: Most preemption cases involve *"implied preemption,"* i.e., situations in which Congress has not explicitly said that it intends to preempt state or local law, but in which the *structure or purpose* of the congressional action suggests that Congress intended to displace non-federal law.

There are *two main types* of implied preemption:

[1] *"field* preemption" and

[2] *"conflicts* preemption"

[*Gade v. National Solid Wastes Management*] [93]

1. "Field preemption": *"Field preemption"* occurs "where the scheme of federal regulation is *so pervasive* as to make reasonable the inference that Congress *left no room* for the states to supplement it." *Gade, supra.* In other words, field preemption occurs where Congress has indicated that it intends to *"occupy the entire field"* in question. [93]

> **Example:** In 1940, Congress passes the Alien Registration Act, which requires aliens 14 and over to register with the federal Immigration and Naturalization Service, be finger-printed, and obey other restrictions. The prior year, Pennsylvania passed a state alien registration act which required all aliens to register with a state agency, and to receive and carry a state-issued alien identification card.
>
> *Held*, the state alien registration law is preempted by the federal one. The federal government's special role in immigration and foreign relations, and Congress' decision to enact a single integrated system for alien registration, make it clear that Congress intended to displace any state requirements that aliens register. [*Hines v. Davidowitz*]

a. Congressional intent is paramount: In field preemption, as with other preemption categories, the issue is always one of *congressional intent.* [93]

i. Broad federal coverage of area: Where the existing federal regulatory scheme is *broad*, and *covers most of the subject area*, the Court is much more likely to find federal field-preemption than where the federal scheme is less comprehensive.

ii. Field traditionally left to states: Subject matter areas *traditionally left to the states* are *less likely* to be found to be the subject of federal field-preemption. This means that if the subject area is usually viewed as *"local"* rather than "national," preemption is unlikely to be found. This is especially true in cases involving *health* and *safety* regulations.

iii. National matters: Conversely, areas *traditionally left to federal control*, such as foreign relations, bankruptcy, patent and trademark, admiralty, immigration, etc., will normally be found to be federally preempted. Registration of aliens, at issue in *Hines*, *supra*, is an illustration.

2. "Conflicts preemption": *"Conflicts preemption"* applies to two situations: first, where compliance with both federal and state regulations is a *physical impossibility*; and second, where state law is inconsistent with the *purposes and objectives* of federal law.

a. Direct physical conflict: Occasionally, federal and state regulations are drafted in such a way that it is *physically impossible for a person to obey the federal and state regulations simultaneously.* When this happens, the state regulation is of course invalid. *Labelling regulations* sometimes fall into this category. [94]

> **Example:** Wisconsin's syrup-labeling rules are written in such a way that if out-of-state syrup is labeled so as to comply with the federal Food and Drug Act, the syrup will be mislabeled under Wisconsin law. *Held*, the Wisconsin regulations are invalid under the Supremacy Clause. [*McDermott v. Wisconsin*]

b. Conflict in purposes: Alternatively, a regulatory scheme imposed by a state may be inconsistent with the *purposes* of a federal regulation. Here, too, the issue is always: what was the *intent* of Congress? [95] [*Pacific Gas & Electric Co. v. State Energy Comm'n*] [95]

D. Federal consent to state laws: May Congress affirmatively *consent* to state action which would otherwise be an unconstitutional violation of the Commerce Clause?

1. Generally allowable: The answer is *"yes"*: Congress *may affirmatively consent to state interference with interstate commerce.* [95]

INTERGOVERNMENTAL IMMUNITIES; INTERSTATE RELATIONS

I. TAX AND REGULATORY IMMUNITIES

A. Several types of immunities: There are several kinds of *immunities* produced by our federalist system: [101]

1. Federal immunity from state taxation: The federal government is immune from being *taxed by the states*. [101]

a. "Legal incidence" standard: This immunity applies only if the *"legal incidence"* of the tax — not just the practical burden — falls on the federal government. [102]

> **Example:** Suppose a private contractor doing work for the federal government under a cost-plus contract is required to pay a state tax. The fact that the burden of this tax will be passed on to the federal government under the contract won't be enough to trigger the immunity. This is so because on these facts, the "legal incidence" of the tax is not on the U.S.

2. State immunity from federal taxation: The *states* have *partial immunity* from federal taxation. What this means is that the federal government can't tax property used in or income from a state's performance of its *basic governmental functions.* (*Example:* The federal government probably can't put a property tax on a state's public parks.) [102]

3. Federal immunity from state regulation: The federal government is essentially free from *state regulatory interference*. (*Example:* A state cannot set the laws for conduct on a military post located within the state, unless Congress consents.) [103]

a. Federal contractors: State regulation of a federal *contractor* (one performing a contract on behalf of the federal government) may also violate the federal immunity from state regulation. However, as in the state taxation context, the states have greater leeway to regulate federal contractors than to regulate the federal government directly. In general, a state may regulate federal contractors as long as the regulation does not interfere with *federal purposes* or *poli-*

cies. For instance, a state regulation that has the effect of ***increasing the cost*** borne by the federal government under the contract might be invalid as a violation of this immunity.

4. **State immunity from federal regulation:** The converse immunity, immunity of the ***states*** from ***federal*** regulation, exists only in a very theoretical way. In general, federal regulation of the states is valid. However, if a federal regulatory scheme had the effect of preventing the states from exercising their ***core functions***, this might be found to be a violation of the Tenth Amendment. [103]

II. THE INTERSTATE PRIVILEGES AND IMMUNITIES CLAUSE

A. **Interstate Privileges and Immunities:** Article IV of the Constitution says that "the Citizens of each State shall be entitled to all Privileges and Immunities of Citizens in the several States." This is the ***"interstate" Privileges and Immunities Clause.*** (Be sure you distinguish this from the Privileges or Immunities Clause of the Fourteenth Amendment, which prevents a state from denying certain rights of "national citizenship" (like the right to travel).) [104]

1. **Standard:** The interstate Privileges and Immunities Clause prevents a state from ***discriminating against non-residents***. But it only operates with respect to rights that are ***fundamental*** to ***national unity***. [104]

   a. **What rights are fundamental:** The rights that are "fundamental in the national unity" are all related to ***commerce***. Thus the right to ***be employed***, the right to ***practice one's profession***, and the right to ***engage in business*** are all fundamental, and are therefore protected by the interstate Privileges and Immunities Clause.

      Example: Alaska requires that Alaskan residents be given an absolute preference over non-residents for all jobs on the Alaska oil pipeline. *Held*, since access to employment is a right fundamental to national unity, Alaska's decision to prefer its own citizens over out-of-staters impairs the out-of-staters' rights under the interstate Privileges and Immunities Clause, and is invalid. [*Hicklin v. Orbeck*, the "Alaska Hire" case] [104]

2. **Two-prong test:** Even if a state does impair an out-of-stater's exercise of a right fundamental to national unity, the state impairment is not necessarily invalid. But the state will lose unless it satisfies a two-pronged test:

   a. **"Peculiar source of evil":** First, the state must show that out-of-staters are a ***"peculiar source of the evil"*** the statute was enacted to rectify. [104]

   b. **Substantial relation to state objective:** Second, the state must show that its solution (the discriminatory statute) is ***"substantially related"*** to this "peculiar evil" the out-of-staters represent. Generally, to meet this prong the state must show that there are no ***less discriminatory alternatives*** that would adequately address the problem. (For instance, in *Alaska Hire*, had Alaska been able to show that there was no other way to combat unemployment than to absolutely prefer in-staters, it would have met this prong.) [105]

3. **No "market participant" exception:** Recall that a state is immune from Commerce Clause violations if it's acting as a ***market participant***. But there's ***no*** such market participant exception for the Privileges & Immunties Clause. (Thus even if, in the *Alaska Hire* case, Alaska had been hiring the workers itself, its absolute preference for residents would have violated the clause.) [105-106]

4. **Distinguished from Equal Protection:** When a non-resident is discriminated against, he may also have an Equal Protection claim. But there are two key differences:

   a. **Aliens and corporations:** The Equal Protection Clause can apply to ***corporations*** and to ***aliens***; the Privileges & Immunities Clause can't. [106]

  b. Strict scrutiny: Conversely, the level of scrutiny given to the state's action is much tougher under Privileges & Immunities Clause than under Equal Protection Clause. Under Equal Protection, non-residency isn't a suspect classification, and therefore the discrimination must just meet the "mere-rationality" standard. Under the Privileges & Immunities Clause, by contrast, the statute must survive what amounts to ***strict scrutiny*** — the non-residents must be a "peculiar source of the evil," and there must not be less-discriminatory alternatives available. [106]

  c. Tactical tip: Wherever possible, couch the attack as Privileges & Immunities, rather than Equal Protection, since the level of scrutiny usually makes a dispositive difference.

CHAPTER 9

THE DUE PROCESS CLAUSE

I. INTRODUCTION

  A. Two major principles: For the rest of this outline, we'll be talking about rights guaranteed to individuals by the Constitution. Before we get into the individual rights, there are two general principles that are crucial to remember: [163]

  1. Protected against the government: First, practically all of the individual rights conferred by the Constitution upon individuals ***protect only against government action***. They do ***not*** protect a person against acts by other private individuals. (*Example:* Suppose P is a woman who's two months pregnant, and none of the private hospitals in her state will perform an abortion. P's substantive due process right to an abortion has not been violated, because the government has not interfered with that right.)

    Note: The only exception to the "government action only" rule is the Thirteenth Amendment's ban on slavery, which *does* apply to private conduct.

  2. Not directly applicable to states: The other general principle to remember is the central role of the Fourteenth Amendment's ***Due Process*** Clause. Many of the important individual guarantees are given by the Bill of Rights (the first ten amendments). For instance, the First Amendment rights of free expression and freedom of religion fall into this category. But the Bill of Rights does ***not directly*** apply to the states. However, the Fourteenth Amendment's Due Process Clause (which does apply to the states) has been interpreted to make nearly all of the Bill of Rights guarantees applicable to the states — these individual guarantees are "incorporated" into the Bill of Rights. "Incorporation" is discussed further below.

II. THE 14TH AMENDMENT GENERALLY

  A. Text of 14th Amendment: Section 1 of the 14th Amendment provides, in full, that: "All persons born or naturalized in the United States, and subject to the jurisdiction hereof, are citizens of the United States and of the State wherein they reside. No State shall make or enforce any law which shall abridge the privileges or immunities of citizens of the United States; nor shall any State deprive any person of life, liberty, or property, without due process of law; nor deny to any person within its jurisdiction the equal protection of the laws." [163]

  1. Three rights: So in one sentence we have three major rights: (1) the right to due process; (2) the right to equal protection; and (3) the right to the privileges or immunities of national citizenship.

  B. The Bill of Rights and the states: One of the major functions of the 14th Amendment's Due Process Clause is to make the ***Bill of Rights*** — that is, the first 10 amendments — applicable to the states. [163]

1. **Not directly applicable to states:** The Bill of Rights is not *directly* applicable to the States. The Supreme Court held early on (in 1833) that the Bill of Rights limited only the federal government, not state or municipal governments. [163]

2. **Effect of due process clause:** But enactment of the 14th Amendment in 1868 effectively changed this. The 14th Amendment directly imposes on the states (and local governments as well) the requirement that they not deprive anyone of "life, liberty or property" without due process. Nearly all the guarantees of the Bill of Rights have been interpreted by the Supreme Court as being so important that if a state denies these rights, it has in effect taken away an aspect of "liberty."

3. **Application of Bill of Rights to states:** The Supreme Court has never said that due process requires the states to honor the Bill of Rights as a whole. Instead, the Court uses an approach called *"selective incorporation."* Under this approach, each right in the Bill of Rights is examined to see whether it is of *"fundamental"* importance. If so, that right is "selectively incorporated" into the meaning of "due process" under the 14th Amendment, and is thus made binding on the states. [164-166]

4. **Nearly all rights incorporated:** By now, nearly *all rights contained in the Bill of Rights* have been incorporated, one by one, into the meaning of "due process" (and thus made applicable to the states). [164] There are now only two major Bill of Rights guarantees that have *not* yet been incorporated:

   a. **Grand jury:** The 5th Amendment's right not to be subject to a criminal trial without a *grand jury indictment* (so that a state may begin proceedings by an "information," as some states do); and

   b. **Right to jury in civil cases:** The 7th Amendment's right to a *jury trial* in *civil* cases. [165]

5. **"Jot-for-jot" incorporation:** Once a given Bill of Rights guarantee is made applicable to the states, the *scope* of that guarantee is interpreted the *same way* for the states as for the federal government. The Court has rejected "the notion that the 14th Amendment applies to the states only a 'watered-down' ... version of the individual guarantees of the Bill of Rights." [*Malloy v. Hogan*] [165-166]

   Example: The 4th Amendment right not to be subject to an unreasonable search or seizure is interpreted the same way whether the case involves federal or state police — thus if on a given set of facts the FBI would be found to have violated the 4th Amendment, so would local police.

C. **The federal Due Process Clause:** We'll generally be discussing the *14th* Amendment's due process clause, which binds the states. But keep in mind that there is also a due process clause in the *5th* Amendment, that is binding on the *federal* government. Both clauses have been interpreted the same way, so that any state action that would be forbidden by the 14th Amendment Due Process Clause is also forbidden to the federal government via the 5th Amendment Due Process Clause. (For instance, exactly the same limits apply to federal and state regulations that impair the right to have an abortion.)[166]

III. SUBSTANTIVE DUE PROCESS — ECONOMIC AND SOCIAL WELFARE REGULATION

A. **Substantive due process generally:** There are two quite different functions that the Due Process Clause serves. Most obviously, it imposes certain *procedural* requirements on governments when they impair life, liberty, or property. (We'll be talking about this "procedural due process" area below.) But the Due Process Clause also limits the *substantive power* of the states to regulate certain areas of human life. This "substantive" component of the Due Process Clause derives mainly from the interpretation of the term *"liberty"* — certain types of state limits on human conduct have been held to so unreasonably interfere with important human rights that they amount to an unreasonable (and unconstitutional) denial of "liberty." [166]

> **Exam Tip:** Any time your fact pattern suggests that a state or federal government is *taking away* some thing or value that could be considered "life," "liberty," or "property," then entirely apart from the issue of whether the government has used proper procedures, you must ask the question: Has the government by carrying out this taking violated the individual's *substantive* interest in life, liberty, or property?

1. **Non-fundamental rights:** There's an absolutely critical distinction that you must make right at the outset, when you're analyzing a substantive due process problem. That's the distinction between *fundamental* and *non-fundamental* rights. If a right or value is found to be "non-fundamental," then the state action that impairs that right only has to meet the easy *"mere-rationality"* test. In other words, it just has to be the case that the state is pursuing a *legitimate governmental objective*, and is doing so with a means that is *rationally related* to that objective.

    a. **Economic regulation:** Nearly all *economic* regulation (and most *"social welfare"* regulation) will turn out to implicate only non-fundamental rights, and will almost certainly be upheld under this easy-to-satisfy mere-rationality standard. So anytime you can't find a fundamental right being impaired, you should presume that the measure does not violate substantive due process.

2. **Fundamental rights:** But if a state or federal government is impairing a *"fundamental"* right, then it's a different ball game entirely: here, the court uses *strict scrutiny*. Only if the governmental action is *"necessary"* to achieve a *"compelling"* governmental objective, will the government avoid violating substantive due process.

3. **Significance of distinction:** So 95% of the battle in analyzing a substantive due process problem is deciding whether the right in question is "fundamental" or not. Once you know that, you pretty much know how the case will come out — if the right is not "fundamental," there's almost certainly no substantive due process problem; if the right *is* fundamental, then strict scrutiny will almost certainly result in the measure being invalidated. So as you prepare for your exam, it's worth devoting some significant mental effort to remembering which rights are fundamental.

B. **Economic and social-welfare regulation:** It is very easy for state *economic regulation* to survive substantive due process attacks. *Since 1937, the Court has not struck down an economic regulation for violating substantive due process.* [171]

1. **Two requirements:** Today, an economic statute has to meet only two easily-satisfied requirements to be in conformity with substantive due process [171]:

    a. **Legitimate state objective:** The state must be pursuing a *legitimate state objective*. But virtually any health, safety or "general welfare" goal comes within the state's *"police power"* and is thus "legitimate."

    b. **Minimally rationally related:** Second, there must be a *"minimally rational relation"* between the means chosen by the legislature and the state objective. To put it another way, the Court will presume that the statute is constitutional unless the legislature has acted in a completely *"arbitrary and irrational"* way.

2. **Other (non-economic) non-fundamental rights:** Outside the economic area, the same rule applies as long as no *fundamental right* is being affected: the state must merely be pursuing a legitimate state objective by rational means. So most *"social welfare"* legislation merely has to meet this very easy standard. We discuss below what rights are "fundamental" — in summary, these rights relate to sex, marriage (both opposite-sex and same-sex), child-bearing and child-rear-

ing, all components of the general "right to privacy." (By contrast, practically no economic rights are "fundamental" — the sole exception may be the right to practice a profession or calling, and even this is not certain.)

    a. **General rule:** For now, the important thing to remember is that if the right does ***not*** fall within this grouping of "fundamental" rights, the state must ***merely act rationally*** in pursuit of ***some health, safety or other "general welfare" goal.*** [172]

        Example: New York sets up a prescription drug reporting scheme, whereby the names and addresses of all patients who receive prescriptions for certain drugs must be reported by doctors, and are placed on a central computer. Some individuals claim that this regulation infringes on their right to avoid government collection of private matters. *Held,* the statute does infringe on a patient's right to keep prescription information secret. But this right is not "fundamental." Therefore, the statute will be sustained as long as the state is acting in pursuit of a legitimate state objective, and has chosen a rational means. Here, these requirements are satisfied. [*Whalen v. Roe*]

    b. **Regulation struck down even though right is non-fundamental:** Where the right being regulated is non-fundamental, and the review is therefore mere-rationality, the regulation will usually, *but not always*, be sustained. Some regulations — especially those found to be motivated by ***public hostility to unpopular minorities*** — are found to be so irrational that they cannot pass even mere-rationality review.

        i. **Sexual expression:** For instance, regulations that ***interfere with sexual expression***, though given mere-rationality review, may be ***struck down*** as totally irrational.

        Example: Laws criminalizing sodomy, enforced principally against gays, have been struck down as failing the rational-relation test, on the theory that they demean homosexuals and interfere with their autonomy, in a way that the Court has deemed "illegitimate." [*Lawrence v. Texas*] [204]

IV. SUBSTANTIVE DUE PROCESS — PROTECTION OF FUNDAMENTAL RIGHTS GENERALLY

A. **Fundamental rights generally:** The rest of our discussion of substantive due process will be solely about rights that are either ***fundamental***, or that are otherwise subjected to ***more searching judicial*** review than the easy-to-satisfy mere-rationality standard used for garden-variety economic and social-welfare legislation as described on pp. C-31 to C-33 above. [173]

    1. **Strict scrutiny:** If a state or federal regulation is impairing a fundamental right, the court ***strictly scrutinizes*** the regulation. Here is what it means in practical terms for the Court to apply strict scrutiny to a state or federal regulation that impairs a fundamental right:

        [1] the ***objective*** being pursued by the state must be ***"compelling"*** (not just "legitimate" as for a non-fundamental right); and

        [2] the ***means*** chosen by the state must be ***"necessary"*** to achieve that compelling end. In other words, there must not be any ***less restrictive means*** that would do the job just as well (if there were, then the means actually chosen wouldn't be "necessary"). [173]

    a. **Burden of proof:** When strict scrutiny is used, there is an important impact on ***who bears the burden of persuasion***. In the usual case in which strict scrutiny is not being used, the person attacking the statute has the burden of showing that the state is pursuing an illegitimate objective, or that the state has chosen a means that is not rationally related to its objective. But if strict scrutiny is used because a "fundamental" right is involved, the burden of proof shifts:

now, it's up to the state to show that it's pursuing a compelling objective, and that the means it chose are "necessary" to achieve that objective.

2. **Rights governed:** The only rights that have been recognized as "fundamental" for substantive due process purposes are ones related to the loose category *"right to privacy."* Sometimes this area is said to involve the "right to *autonomy*" — what we're really talking about is usually a person's right to *make his own decisions* about *highly personal matters*. This right of privacy or autonomy derives indirectly from several Bill of Rights guarantees, which collectively create a *"penumbra"* or *"zone"* of privacy. [173]

    a. **List:** The list of rights or interests falling within this "right to privacy" or "right to autonomy" include actually just a few related areas: *marriage (both opposite-sex* and *same-sex)*, *child-bearing*, and *child-rearing*. So anytime you're looking at a particularly narrow interest and you have to decide whether it's "fundamental," first ask yourself, "Does it fall within the areas of marriage, child-bearing, or child-rearing?" If not, it's probably not "fundamental."

        i.   **Illustrations:** So the right to *use birth control*, to *live together with your family*, to *direct the upbringing* and *education* of your children, to *marry* — these are some (probably most) of the specific interests that are "fundamental."

        ii. **Non-illustrations:** By contrast, an interest that does not fall within one of these areas probably is not fundamental — for instance, an adult's interest in having consensual sex outside of marriage seems not to be "fundamental." (The right to *abortion* used to be "fundamental," but now seems to be only "quasi-fundamental" after *Planned Parenthood v. Casey*.)

B. **Birth control:** Individuals' interest in *using birth control* is "fundamental." So whether a person is married or single, he or she has a fundamental interest in contraception, and the state cannot impair that interest without satisfying strict scrutiny. (*Example:* Planned Parenthood cannot be prohibited from supplying condoms or diaphragms to single or married adults who want them. [*Griswold v. Connecticut*]) [175-176]

    1. **Minors:** We still don't know whether *minors* have a fundamental right to contraception. If this comes up on your exam, just say that there is plausible logic behind viewing a minor's interest in contraception as being either "fundamental" or "non-fundamental." [197]

V. SUBSTANTIVE DUE PROCESS — REGULATION OF ABORTION

A. **Abortion generally:** The right of *abortion* is the primary example of a right protected by courts' use of a more-than-ordinarily-demanding substantive due process review. [177-196] Here is what seems to be the status of this right today:

    1. **Summary of the right today:** A woman has a constitutionally-protected privacy interest in choosing to have an abortion *before viability* (generally about 23 weeks after the woman's last period). However, the state has a somewhat countervailing interest in promoting other legitimate state interests, including the *health and safety of the pregnant woman* who is seeking a pre-viability abortion. This conflict seems to yield the following results:

        a. **No right to ban:** The state does not have the right to *ban* all pre-viability abortions. Also, the state may not even forbid all pre-viability abortions except those necessary to save the life or health of the mother. [177]

        b. **Not a fundamental right that will be strictly scrutinized:** Abortion is *not a fundamental right*, and restrictions on it will not *be strictly scrutinized*. This represents a huge departure from the law as it stood under *Roe v. Wade*, the 1973 decision that recognized a pregnant woman's right to abortion as a form of the *right of privacy*. [182]

    i.   **Undue burden standard:** But the Court's use of the ***"undue burden"*** standard (see below) in reviewing abortion regulations seems to amount to treating the right to abortion as a ***"quasi-fundamental"*** right. That is, governmental restrictions that significantly interfere with women's access to pre-viability abortions must survive a judicial review that is at least somewhat more stringent than the easy-to-satisfy "mere-rationality" standard (discussed *supra*, p. C-31). We don't have a precise answer to *how much* stricter than ordinary mere-rationality review the undue-burden standard is, but it's clear that the standard is at least *somewhat* harder for the government to satisfy.

   c.   **The state's right to regulate abortions:** As the result of the two most important post-*Roe* abortion cases, the state can ***regulate*** the abortion process as long as the state follows these two principles:

     ❑   The regulation pursues a ***legitimate state interest***; and (most importantly) ...

     ❑   The regulation ***does not place an "undue burden"*** on the woman's right to ***obtain an abortion before the fetus has attained viability*** (defined as the ability to survive outside the womb).

     See *Whole Woman's Health v. Hellerstedt* (2016) and *Planned Parenthood of Southeastern Pennsylvania v. Casey* (1992). [179-188]

2.   **Legitimate state interest:** If the regulation substantially impairs access to pre-viability abortion, the state interest being pursued will have to be at least ***"legitimate."*** It may also turn out (this is not yet clear from the Court's decisions) that the state interest must be of ***more-than-trivial significance***.

   a.   **Moral disapproval of abortion:** One governmental interest that the present Court views as *not* being "legitimate" for this purpose is a desire to reduce the number of abortions on account of the legislature's ***moral disapproval of abortion.***

   b.   **Woman's health:** Conversely, the state's interest in protecting the mental or physical ***health of the woman*** seeking or undergoing an abortion ***is*** a legitimate, and potentially sufficiently-weighty, interest (so long as the resulting burden on abortion rights is not "undue," a requirement analyzed immediately below).

3.   **What is an "undue burden":** As noted, the regulation ***must not place an "undue burden"*** on the woman's right to obtain a pre-viability abortion. Here's an alternative formulation of this idea that the Court has given: a regulation constitutes an "undue burden" if it "places a ***substantial obstacle*** in the path of women seeking a pre-viability abortion." [*Hellerstedt*] (Observe that this "substantial obstacle" formulation doesn't say much more than the "undue burden" formulation — neither gives a court much help in *determining* whether a particular abortion regulation is or isn't constitutional.)

   a.   **Balance burdens against benefits:** Whether the "burden" is "undue" depends not only on the size of the burden, but also on the size of the countervailing ***"benefits"*** conferred by the regulation. It appears (from *Hellerstedt*) that a reviewing court is to ***weigh*** or ***balance*** the burdens imposed by the regulation against whatever benefits the state is claiming the regulation confers. So far, the only type of benefit from abortion regulations that the Court has recognized as being legitimate is the ***protection of the physical or mental health*** of the woman seeking a pre-viability abortion. [184-187]

   b.   **Must "actually advance" woman's health:** The state will have to show that the regulation in question ***actually advances the health*** of women seeking abortions. (If the regulation does not in fact confer any actual benefits to women's health, then any significant burden will, as a logical matter, outweigh the non-existent benefits.) In other words, it's not enough that the legislature "finds" or "concludes" or "asserts" that its regulation furthers women's health; some "actual" health benefit is required. [185-186]

4. **Particular types of restrictions:** Here are several types of restrictions, and how the Court has ruled on the constitutionality of each.

    a. **"Must have hospital admitting-privileges" rule struck down:** States have sometimes imposed a *"hospital admitting privileges"* requirement on physicians who perform abortions. One such requirement was struck down in *Hellerstedt*. [186]

        Example: Texas says that no doctor may perform any kind of abortion unless the doctor has admitting privileges at a hospital no more than 30 miles from the location at which the doctor is going to perform the abortion. Texas defends the requirement on the grounds that if something goes medically wrong during the procedure, having a prearranged method of rapidly admitting the woman to a nearby hospital is needed to protect her health.

        Held: this requirement imposes an unconstitutional "undue burden." Abortions are so safe that this requirement produces no incremental benefit to the woman's health. That's especially true since the requirement would only help for medical emergencies occurring on the *same day* as the abortion, and the few emergencies that occur almost always happen on a later day. [*Hellerstedt*]

    b. **"Must meet ambulatory surgery center standards" rule struck down:** States have sometimes imposed elaborate physical-plant, staffing and other operational requirements on abortion facilities, in effect requiring them to conform to the *standards of hospitals or outpatient surgery centers.* Again, one such requirement, making every abortion facility conform to the state's requirements for *"ambulatory surgery centers,"* was struck down in *Hellerstedt*. [186-187]

    c. **Ban on partial-birth method:** Various states, as well as Congress, have tried to ban the *"partial-birth"* method of abortion. The Court has **upheld** a ban on this method imposed by Congress. [194-196]

        Example: Congress makes it a crime to carry out a "partial birth abortion," defined as a two-step procedure in which the physician (1) causes a still-living fetus to be delivered until either its entire head, or in a breech delivery its feet up past its naval, are outside the mother's body; and then (2) commits an "overt act" (e.g., evacuation of skull contents) with the purpose of killing the partly-delivered fetus. The Ps attack the statute "on its face" (i.e., they claim that in *all* instances the statute is unconstitutional).

        Held, the Ps lose; the statute is not unconstitutional on its face, because it does not necessarily impose an undue burden on women's right to control their reproductive destiny. Congress has an interest in protecting the mental health of pregnant women. But if there should arise a future case involving a particular woman whose health would be placed in jeopardy by the ban, a reviewing court could still strike the ban "as applied" to that woman. [*Gonzales v. Carhart*] [194]

    d. **Consent by third parties:** States have sometimes tried to condition a woman's right to abortion on the *consent of a third party*, such as a husband or (in the case of a minor) a parent.

        i. **Husband:** It's clear that the states may not give a pregnant woman's *spouse* an absolute veto right over the woman's abortion decision. [*Planned Parenthood of Missouri v. Danforth*] In fact, a state may not even require that the woman's spouse be *notified* of the woman's intent to get an abortion. [*Planned Parenthood v. Casey*] [192]

     ii. **Parents of woman who is a minor:** Where a *minor* is found to be *insufficiently mature or emancipated* to make the abortion decision for herself, the state *may require parental consent.*

        (1) Informed consent by parents: When the state requires parental consent, the state may insist that the consent be *"informed."* So the state may insist that the parent listen to a presentation by the doctor about the alternatives to abortion, about the probable gestational age of the daughter's fetus, about the availability of state-printed literature, etc. [192]

        (2) Court hearing: If the state *does* require parental consent, it must also give the girl an opportunity to *persuade a court* that, although she is not sufficiently mature or emancipated to make the decision for herself, an abortion is nonetheless *in her best interests.* If she does make such a showing, *the court must override* the parental veto. This procedure is sometimes called a *"judicial bypass."* [193]

        (3) Emancipation or maturity: Also, the state must provide for an *individualized judicial hearing* in which the girl may persuade the court that she is in fact sufficiently *mature* or *emancipated* that she is able to make this decision for herself. If the court concludes that she is mature or emancipated, it must allow the operation whether or not the court feels it is in the girl's best interest. [193]

    e. **Prohibitions on public funding:** Some cases have involved government's *refusal to pay* for abortions, or government's discrimination against abortion by refusing to pay while paying for other types of health services. [194-194] The Court has *sustained* virtually all such government actions.

       Example: A state may pay for the expenses of *childbirth*, while *refusing to pay the expenses of abortion,* even where the abortion is necessary for the health or life of the mother. [*Harris v. McRae*] [194]

  5. **Future of *Roe v. Wade*:** As of this writing (late November 2021), the post-Ginsburg Court seems to be about to decide *whether Roe v. Wade* should *remain good law.* The Court has agreed to hear oral argument in December 2021 in a constitutional challenge to a highly-restrictive anti-abortion statute enacted by *Mississippi.* [*Dobbs v. Jackson Women's Health Organization*, scheduled for oral argument on Dec. 1, 2021.]

    a. **Mississippi statute:** That Mississippi statute bans most abortions *after 15 weeks.* Recall that *Roe* forbids states from banning pre-viability abortions, and viability doesn't generally occur until around 23 weeks (see *supra*, p. C-34). Therefore, when the Court decides *Dobbs*, it's hard to see how the Court can avoid holding Mississippi's ban on abortions occurring between 15 weeks and 23 weeks to be unconstitutional, unless the Court *overrules Roe's key holding* that abortions may not be forbidden (though they may be regulated) prior to viability.

VI. OTHER SUBSTANTIVE DUE PROCESS ISSUES: CONTRACEPTION, CHILD REARING, THE RIGHT TO MARRY, SEXUAL EXPRESSION, AND THE "RIGHT TO DIE"

  A. **Family relations:** Whenever the state interferes with a person's decision about how to live his *family life* and *raise his children*, you should be on the lookout to see whether a fundamental right is being interfered with. [197-202]

    1. **Right to live together:** For instance, *relatives* have a fundamental right to *live together*. [197]

Example: A city may not enact a zoning ordinance that prevents first cousins from living together, because the right of members of a family — even a non-nuclear family — to live together is "fundamental," and any state interference with that right will be strictly scrutinized. [*Moore v. East Cleveland*]

Note: What the Court was protecting in *Moore* was clearly the right of *families* to live together, not the more general right to live with whomever one wants outside of ties of blood and marriage. Thus the Court had previously held [*Belle Terre v. Borass*] that unrelated people had no "fundamental right" to live together, and in *Moore* the Court pointed out that families' rights to live together were different, and much stronger.

2. **Upbringing and education:** Similarly, a parent's right to direct the **upbringing** and **education** of his children is "fundamental."

    Example 1: The state may not require parents to send their children to public schools. Parents have a fundamental right to determine how their children will be educated. [*Pierce v. Soc. of Sisters*] [174]

    Example 2: A parent has a fundamental interest in deciding who will spend time with the child. Therefore, the state may not award visitation rights to a child's grandparents over the objection of the child's fit custodial parent, unless the state first gives "special weight" to the parent's wishes. [*Troxel v. Granville*]

    a. **Right to continue parenting:** There's also probably a fundamental right to *continue parenting* — so the state can't take away your child just because it thinks a foster home would be "better" for the child. (Even if there's child abuse, the parent still has a fundamental right to parent, but here the state's interest in protecting the child would be "compelling," so putting the child in foster care would probably satisfy strict scrutiny.)

    b. **No relationship:** If a parent has *never married* the other parent, and has never *developed a relationship* with the child (e.g., they have never lived together), then there is probably *not* a fundamental right to continue to be a parent. (So the state may, for instance, deny the non-custodial unwed parent who has never participated in the child's upbringing the right to block an adoption of the child. [*Quilloin v. Walcott*] [201]

3. **Right to marry:** The *right to marry* is viewed by the Supreme Court as being "fundamental"; substantial interferences with that right will therefore not be sustained merely because they are "rational." This principle now (since 2015) applies to *both opposite-sex* and *same-sex* marriage.

    a. **Opposite-sex couples:** Since the 1970s, the Court has held that the *right to marry* a *person of the opposite sex* is fundamental, so any regulation substantially interfering with this right will have to pass strict scrutiny. [199]

    Example: A state forbids anyone from remarrying unless he is current on all support payments from his prior marriage. *Held,* such a prohibition directly interferes with the fundamental right of marriage, and must therefore be strictly scrutinized. Here, the state's interest (ensuring that spousal and child support is paid) may be compelling, but the means chosen (denial of all right to marry) is not a "necessary" means of achieving that interest, since less restrictive methods are available. [*Zablocki v. Redhail*] [199]

    b. **Same-sex marriage:** *Same-sex couples,* too, have a fundamental due-process liberty interest in being permitted to marry, as the result of a key 5-4 decision in 2015. Therefore, all states must issue such licenses. [***Obergefell v. Hodges*** (2015) (also decided on equal protection grounds, as further discussed *infra*, p. C-59).] [199]

    i. **No level of scrutiny specified:** Curiously, the majority opinion in *Obergefell* doesn't say what *level of scrutiny* is appropriate for judicial review of laws abridging this recently-recognized right that's fundamental for due process purposes.

        (1) **Something more than mere-rationality review:** It's pretty clear that *Obergefell* doesn't apply typical easy-to-satisfy *"mere-rationality" review*, of the sort applied to regulations that do not substantially interfere with any fundamental right. But the opinion doesn't say *how much more stringent* than mere-rationality the standard for review is to be. So the answer may turn out to be anywhere from *strict scrutiny* (so that the regulation will be struck down unless "necessary" to achieve a "compelling" state interest) down to *"mere-rationality with bite"* (which might mean something not-very-demanding like "pretty tightly linked to a significant governmental objective"). [201]

B. **Sexuality, including homosexuality:** A person's *sexual conduct* — apart from any issues of procreation or family life — receives substantive due process protection.

    1. **Laws against homosexual sodomy:** Thus the Court has *struck down* all state laws that *criminalize homosexual sodomy*, on the grounds that such laws *"demean the lives of homosexual persons,"* and thereby violate their substantive due process rights. [*Lawrence v. Texas*] In *Lawrence*, the Court said that same-sex couples have "the full right to engage in their [homosexual] conduct without intervention of the government." [204]

    2. **Other forms of adult sexuality:** While *Lawrence* directly holds only that states may not criminalize private *homosexual* conduct between consulting adults, the expansive language used by the majority suggests that the Court is willing to recognize a fairly broad autonomy/liberty interest in *private consensual adult sexual conduct* generally. [202]

        Example: Suppose a state criminally prosecuted persons who commit "adultery," defined as sex between a married person (let's call her or him "D") and another (one) person who is not D's spouse. It seems clear that enforcement of such a law would violate D's substantive-due-process right to sexual autonomy, at least if D and the other person were both adult humans not closely related to each other (i.e., not a statutory rape, incest, bestiality or "polyamatory" situation).

        a. **Standard of review not clear:** However, *Lawrence* (and the Court's other precedents, like the same-sex marriage decision in *Obergefell, supra*) don't always make it clear **what standard of review** the Court would use to examine a broad restriction on adult sexual conduct like the one in the above example. So the Court might use a standard as forgiving as "mere-rationality with bite." But whatever the standard used, it's unlikely that the broad anti-adultery statute in the above example would survive.

C. **The "right to die," and the right to decline unwanted medical procedures:** The law of "right to die" and "right to pull the plug" is developing. Here's what we know already:

    1. **Can't be forced to undergo unwanted procedures:** A competent adult has a 14th Amendment liberty interest in *not being forced to undergo unwanted medical procedures*, including artificial life-sustaining measures. It's not clear whether this is a "fundamental" interest. (*Example:* P, dying of stomach cancer, has a liberty interest in refusing to let the hospital feed him through a feeding tube.) [205]

    2. **State's interest in preserving life:** The state has an important *countervailing interest in preserving life.*

    3. **"Clear and convincing evidence" standard:** In the case of a now-incompetent patient, the state's interest in preserving life entitles it to say that it won't allow the "plug" to be "pulled" unless there is *"clear and convincing evidence"* that the patient would have voluntarily declined the life-sustaining measures. [*Cruzan v. Missouri*] [206]

> **Example:** P is comatose, hospitalized, being fed through a tube, and kept breathing through a respirator. P's parents want the hospital to discontinue the tube-feeding and respirator. *Held*, the state may insist that if the parents can't show "clear and convincing evidence" that during her conscious life P showed a desire not to be kept alive by such artificial measures, the measures must be continued. [*Cruzan, supra*]

4. **No "right to commit suicide":** Terminally-ill patients do *not* have a general liberty interest in *"committing suicide."* Nor do they have the constitutional right to *recruit a third person* to help them commit suicide. [*Washington v. Glucksberg*] [207-209]

> **Example:** A state may make it a felony for a physician to knowingly prescribe a fatal dose of drugs for the purpose of helping the patient commit suicide.

D. **Other possible places:** Here are a couple of other areas where there might be a fundamental right.

1. **Reading:** You probably have a fundamental right to *read what you want*. (*Example*: A state cannot forbid you from reading pornography in the privacy of your own home, even though it can make it criminal for someone to sell you that pornography.) [*Stanley v. Georgia*] [210]

2. **Physical appearance:** You may have a fundamental right to control your *personal appearance*. (*Example:* If the public school which you are required to attend forces you to cut your hair to a length of no more two inches for boys and four inches for girls, this might violate a "fundamental right." But this is not clear.) [205]

E. **Final word:** Deciding whether the right in question is "fundamental" is, as noted, the key to substantive due process analysis. But it's not the end of the story. Even if you decide that the right is "fundamental" you've still got to carry out the strict scrutiny analysis: it might turn out that the state's countervailing interest is indeed "compelling" and the means chosen is "necessary" to achieve that interest. (*Example:* A state has a compelling interest in taking a child away from an abusive parent and putting him into foster care.)

1. **Non-fundamental:** Conversely, even if the right is not "fundamental," you've still got to apply the "mere-rationality" standard, and you might decide that the state is being so completely irrational that the state action is a violation of substantive due process anyway.

VII. PROCEDURAL DUE PROCESS

A. **Introduction:** We turn now to the other main aspect of the 14th Amendment's Due Process Clause: this is the requirement that the state act with adequate or fair *procedures* when it deprives a person of life, liberty or property. Here, the emphasis is on the particular case presented by the particular person — has the government handled his particular situation fairly? Our discussion is divided into two main questions: (1) has the individual's life, liberty or property been "taken"?; and, if so, (2) what process was "due" him prior to this taking?

1. **Life, liberty or property:** The most important single thing to remember about procedural due process is that there cannot be a procedural due process problem unless government is taking a person's *life*, *liberty* or *property*. In other words, there is *no general interest in having the government behave with fair procedures*.

> **Example:** A city hires for an opening on its police force. The city can be as arbitrary and random as it wants, because as we'll see, an applicant for a job has no liberty or property interest in obtaining the job. Therefore, the city doesn't have to give the applicant a hearing, a state-

ment of reasons why she didn't get the job, a systematic test of her credentials, or any other aspect of procedural fairness. [219]

2. **Distinction between substance and procedure:** Always distinguish between "substantive" due process and "procedural" due process. Procedural due process applies only where *individual determinations* are being made.

> **Example:** Suppose a state passes a law that says that no person with child support may marry. This statute raises an issue of substantive due process — unless this means of enforcing child support payments is necessary to achieve a compelling state interest, the state may not use that method at all, against anyone. Separately, even if this "ban on marriage" could pass this substantive due process hurdle (which it apparently can't, based on past Supreme Court cases like *Zablocki v. Redhail*) the state still must use *adequate procedures* before enforcing the ban *against a particular person.*
>
> For instance, the state must probably provide a person with *notice* that the ban will be applied, and a *hearing* at which he can show that the ban shouldn't apply to him because (for instance) he's fully paid up. The obligation to use fair procedures always applies *"one case at a time,"* and governs the application of government action to a particular person in a particular situation.

B. **Liberty:** Remember that *"liberty"* is one of the things the government cannot take without procedural due process. What *is* "liberty" for due process purposes? [220]

1. **Physical liberty:** First, we have the interest in *"physical"* liberty. This liberty interest is violated if you are *imprisoned*, or even if you are placed in some other situation where you do not have physical freedom of movement (e.g., juvenile and/or civil commitment).

2. **Intangible rights:** Also, a person has a liberty interest in being able to do certain intangible things not related to physical freedom of movement. There's no complete catalog of what interests fall within this "intangible" aspect of liberty. Here are some examples, however:

   [1] the right to *drive*;

   [2] the right to *practice one's profession*; and

   [3] the right to *raise one's family*.

   But one's interest in having a *good reputation* is not "liberty" (so the state can call you a crook without giving you due process — see *Paul v. Davis*). [223]

C. **Property:** The government also can't take *"property"* without procedural due process. Here are the things that may be "property" for procedural due process purposes: [220]

1. **Conventional property:** First, of course, we have "conventional" property (i.e., personal and real property). Thus the government cannot impose a monetary fine against a person, or declare a person's car forfeited, without complying with procedural due process.

   a. **Debt collection:** Certain kinds of *debt collection* devices involve "property." For instance, if the state lets private creditors *attach* a person's bank account prior to trial (which means that the owner can't get at the funds), even that temporary blockage is a "taking" of property. Similarly, if the state lets a private creditor *garnish* a person's wages, that's a taking of property. On the other hand, if the state simply passes a law that lets creditors use *self-help* to repossess goods, there's no governmental taking of property when the creditor repossesses. (The due process requirement applies only where it is *government* that does, or at least is involved in, the taking of liberty or property.)

2. **Government benefits:** *Government benefits* may or may not constitute "property" rights. Generally, if one is just *applying* for benefits and hasn't yet been receiving them, one does *not* have a

property interest in those benefits. (*Example:* If P applies for welfare, and has never gotten it before, the government does not have to comply with procedural due process when it turns P down. Therefore, the government doesn't have to give P a statement of reasons, a hearing, etc.)

    a. Already getting benefits: But if a person has *already been getting the benefits*, it's probably the case that he's got a property interest in *continuing* to get them, so that the government cannot *terminate* those benefits without giving him procedural due process. [*Goldberg v. Kelly*] [221] (But state law can change even this — for instance, if the state statute governing welfare benefits says that "benefits may be cut off at any time," you probably don't have a property interest in continuing to get those benefits, so you have no claim to due process.)

3. Government employment: A government *job* is similar to government benefits.

    a. Applicant: If you're just *applying* for the job, you clearly do *not* have a property interest in it.

    b. Already have job: If you already have the job, then the court looks to *state law* to determine whether you had a property interest in the job.

        i. Ordinarily at-will: Ordinarily, under state law a job is *terminable at will*; if so, the job-holder has no property right to it, so he may be fired without due process. [222]

        ii. Legitimate claim of entitlement: If either a statute or the public employer's *practices* give a person a *"legitimate claim of entitlement"* to keep the job, then she's got a property interest. (*Example*: If a public university follows the publicized custom of never firing anybody from a non-tenured position without cause except on one year's notice, then a non-tenured teacher has a property right to hold his non-tenured job for a year following notice. [*Perry v. Sindermann*]) [222]

D. Process required: If a person's interest in property or liberty is being impaired, then she is entitled to due process. But *what procedures* does the person get? There is no simple answer. [223]

1. Traditional civil litigation: When a person's property is at stake in a traditional *civil lawsuit*, the range of procedural protections required by due process is broad. The litigant probably has a due process right to a *hearing*, the right to *call witnesses*, the right to *counsel*, and the right to a *fair and objective trial*. [225]

    a. Punitive damages: In some circumstances the award of *punitive damages* may violate the defendant's due process rights. [225]

        i. Ratio of actual to punitive: A punitive damages award will violate due process if it is *"grossly excessive."* [*BMW of North America v. Gore*]

        (1) Ratio of punitive to compensatory: One of the most important factors in whether an award of punitive damages is grossly excessive is the *ratio* of the *punitive damages* to the *actual damages.* A punitive award that is *more than nine times* the compensatory award probably won't satisfy due process. [State *Farm Mut. v. Campbell*]

        ii. Reprehensibility: Another of the key factors in the due process analysis is the *reprehensibility* of the defendant's conduct — the more reprehensible the conduct, the higher the amount of punitive damages that may be awarded without violating due process.

        iii. Conduct vis a vis strangers to the litigation: Only the defendant's conduct *towards the plaintiff*, not its conduct towards *strangers to the litigation,* may be taken into account by the jury in setting the amount of punitive damages. [*Philip Morris USA v. Williams*]

    b. Judicial bias: A litigant also has a procedural due process right to be free of a *large risk of bias on the part of the judge hearing the case.* [226-227]

i.   **Standard:** Removal of the judge is required where "a person with a personal stake in a particular case had a ***significant and disproportionate influence in placing the judge on the case*** by ***raising funds or directing the judge's election campaign*** when the case was pending or imminent." [*Caperton v. A.T. Massey Coal Co.*]

ii. **Campaign contributions:**   So in states that ***elect judges***, ***large judicial campaign contributions*** by one party in a pending case can give the other party a procedural due process right to have the judge in question ***removed from the case***. [*Caperton, supra*]

2.   **Criminal defendants and prisoners:** ***Criminal defendants*** receive the broadest procedural due process protections during the course of their trial (e.g., right to counsel, right to present witnesses, right to confront opposing witnesses, etc.). [227-230]

a.   **Convicted prisoners:**   Once the criminal defendant has been ***convicted***, he gets dramatically ***less*** procedural due process protection. Thus prison officials who give extra punishment to a prisoner or change his terms of confinement won't commit a substantive due process violation, and don't need to observe procedural due process protections during their decision-making process, so long as their action doesn't "impose[] ***atypical and significant hardship*** on the inmate in relation to the ***ordinary incidents of prison life***." [*Sandin v. Conner*] [228]

   Example: A prisoner who is charged with disobeying prison regulations is not entitled by due process to *present witnesses* during the disciplinary hearing, even if the hearing leads to his being put in solitary confinement for 30 days. [*Sandin*]

   i.   **Access to DNA testing:**   A prisoner has no independent liberty interest in being given access to ***DNA evidence to prove his innocence***. [*District Attorney's Office for the Third Judicial District v. Osborne*] [229-230]

3.   **Non-judicial proceeding:**   Where the property or liberty interest is being impaired in something ***other*** than a judicial proceeding, the state does ***not*** have to give the individual the full range of procedural safeguards that would be needed for a court proceeding. Instead, for any particular procedural safeguard that the plaintiff says she should get (e.g., the right to a hearing), the court conducts a ***balancing*** test: the strength of the plaintiff's interest in receiving the procedural safeguard is weighed against the government's interest in avoiding extra burdens. [*Mathews v. Eldridge*] [224-225]

   Examples: If *A* has been receiving welfare benefits, these benefits may not be terminated without giving *A* an evidentiary hearing, because a wrongful termination of welfare benefits, even temporarily, is likely to lead to extreme hardship, without a large countervailing benefit to the government. [*Goldberg v. Kelly*]

   By contrast, a tenured employee who is being fired from a government job gets fewer procedural safeguards — he gets notice of the charges and an opportunity to present some evidence, but not a full adversarial evidentiary hearing with right to counsel; this is because the government's interest in being able to fire unsatisfactory employees quickly is factored into the balance. [*Cleveland Board of Ed. v. Loudermill*]

a.   **School suspensions:**   Where a ***public-school student*** is ***suspended*** for disciplinary reasons for more than a trivial period, due process requires that he be given at least ***oral notice*** of the charges against him and, if he denies them, an ***explanation of the evidence*** the authorities have and an ***opportunity to present his side of the story***. [*Goss v. Lopez*] But the student is ***not*** constitutionally entitled to ***written notice, a formal hearing***, the right to have ***counsel present***, or the right to ***call and examine witnesses***. [233]

CHAPTER 10

EQUAL PROTECTION

I. EQUAL PROTECTION GENERALLY

A. Text of clause: The Equal Protection Clause is part of the 14th Amendment. It provides that "[n]o state shall make or enforce any law which shall ... deny to any person within its jurisdiction the equal protection of the laws." [243]

1. General usage: The Clause, like all parts of the 13th, 14th and 15th Amendments, was enacted shortly after the Civil War, and its primary goal was to attain free and equal treatment for ex-slaves. But it has always been interpreted as imposing a *general* restraint on the governmental use of classifications, not just classifications based on race but also those based on sex, alienage, illegitimacy, wealth, or any other characteristic.

2. State and federal: The direct text of the Clause, of course, applies only to state governments. But the federal government is also bound by the same rules of equal protection — this happens by the indirect means of the Fifth Amendment's Due Process Clause. So if a given action would be a violation of Equal Protection for a state, that same action would be unconstitutional if done by the federal government (though in this situation, if you wanted to be scrupulously correct, you would call it a violation of the Fifth Amendment's Due Process Clause). [243]

    a. Government action only: The Equal Protection Clause, and the Fifth Amendment's Due Process Clause, apply *only to government action*, not to action by private citizens. This is commonly referred to as the requirement of *"state action,"* and is discussed further below.

        Example: D, a large private university, refuses to admit African American students. No government participates in this decision. The university's conduct cannot be a violation of the Equal Protection Clause, because there is no "state action."

3. Making of classes: The Equal Protection Clause is only implicated where the government *makes a classification*. It's not implicated where the government merely decides which of two classes a particular person falls into. (For instance, if Congress says that you don't receive Social Security if you work more than 1,000 hours per year, then it's made a classification that distinguishes between those who work more than 1,000 hours and those who work less — this classification can be attacked under the Equal Protection Clause. But an administrative determination that a particular person did or did not work 1,000 hours is not a classification, and cannot be attacked under the Equal Protection Clause, only the Due Process Clause.) [243]

4. "As applied" vs. "facial": Here is some nomenclature: If P attacks a classification that is clearly written into the statute or regulation, he is claiming that Equal Protection is violated by the statute or regulation *"on its face."* If P's claim is that the statute does not make a classification on its face, but is being *administered* in a purposefully discriminatory way, then he is claiming that the statute or regulation is a violation of equal protection *"as applied."* (*Example:* A statute that says "you must be a citizen to vote" creates a classification scheme "on its face" — citizens vs. non-citizens. But if P claims that in actual administration, blacks are required to prove citizenship but whites are not, then his equal protection claim would be on the statute "as applied.")

    a. Same standards for both: Either kind of attack — facial or "as applied," — may be made. Both follow essentially the same principles. For instance, if no suspect classification or fundamental right is involved, the classification scheme will violate the Equal Protection Clause if it's not rationally related to a legitimate state objective, whether the scheme is on the face of the statute or merely in the way the statute is applied.

5. **What the Clause guarantees:** The Clause in essence guarantees that *people who are similarly situated will be treated similarly.* [244]

> **Example:** Consider racial segregation in the public schools. Such segregation gives a different treatment to two groups that are similarly situated, African Americans and whites. Therefore, it violates the Equal Protection rights of African Americans. (Of course, this reflects a judgment that there are no meaningful differences between blacks and whites that relate to public education. If the issue were, say, compulsory medical screening for sickle cell anemia, blacks and whites might not be similarly situated.)

   a. **Dissimilar:** The Equal Protection Clause also guarantees that people who are *not* similarly situated will not be treated similarly. But this aspect is rarely of practical importance, because courts are rarely convinced that differences in situation require differences in treatment by the government.

6. **Three levels of review:** Recall that in our discussion of substantive due process, we saw that depending on the circumstances, one of two sharply different standards of review of governmental action was used, the easy "rational relation" test or the very demanding "strict scrutiny" standard. In the Equal Protection context, we have two tests that are virtually the same as these two, plus a third "middle level" of scrutiny. Let's consider each of the three types of review: [247]

   a. **Ordinary "mere-rationality" review:** The easiest-to-satisfy standard of review applies to statutes that:

      [1] are *not based on a "suspect classification"*;

      [2] do not involve a *"quasi-suspect"* category that the Court has implicitly recognized (principally gender and illegitimacy); and

      [3] don't impair a *"fundamental right."*

      This is the so-called *"mere-rationality"* standard. Almost every *economic regulation* will be reviewed under this easy-to-satisfy standard. (This is similar to the ease with which economic regulation passes muster under the substantive due process clause.) Under this easiest "mere-rationality" standard, the Court asks only "whether it is conceivable that the classification bears a rational relationship to an end of government which is not prohibited by the Constitution." [247]

      i. **Standard summarized:** So where "mere-rationality" review is applied, the classification must satisfy *two easy tests:*

         [1] government must be pursuing a *legitimate governmental objective*; and

         [2] there must be a *rational relation* between the classification and that objective.

         Furthermore, it's not necessary that the court believe that these two requirements are satisfied; it's enough that the court concludes that it's *"conceivable"* that they're satisfied.

   b. **Strict scrutiny:** At the other end of the spectrum, the Court will give *"strict scrutiny"* to any statute which is based on a *"suspect classification"* or which impairs a *"fundamental right."* (We'll be discussing below the meaning of these two terms, "suspect classification" and "fundamental right.") A classification based on *race* is a classic example of a "suspect class"; the right to *vote* is an example of a fundamental right. [248]

      i. **Standard:** Where strict scrutiny is invoked, the classification will be upheld only if it is *necessary* to promote a *compelling* governmental interest. Thus not only must the objective be an extremely important one, but the "fit" between the means and the end must be extremely tight. This strict scrutiny test is the same as for substantive due process when a "fundamental right" (e.g., the right to privacy) is involved.

C
A
P
S
U
L
E

S
U
M
M
A
R
Y

    c. **Middle-level review:** In a few contexts, the Court uses a ***middle level*** of scrutiny, more probing than "mere-rationality" review but less demanding than "strict scrutiny." This middle level is mainly used for cases involving classifications based on ***gender*** and ***illegitimacy***. [248]

        i. **Standard:** This middle-level test is usually stated as follows: the means chosen by the legislature (i.e., the classification) must be ***substantially related*** to an ***important governmental objective***. So the legislative objective must be ***"important"*** (but not necessarily "compelling," as for strict scrutiny), and means and end must be ***"substantially related"*** (easier to satisfy than the almost perfect "necessary" fit between means and end in strict scrutiny situations).

  7. **Importance:** Con Law essay exams very frequently test the Equal Protection Clause because: (1) it's open-ended, so it applies to a lot of different situations; (2) there are often no clear right or wrong answers under it, so it gives the student a good chance to show how well she can articulate arguments on either side; and (3) it's one of the two or three most important single limitations on what government can do to individuals.

    a. **Test tip:** Therefore, any time you're asked to give an opinion about whether a particular governmental action is constitutional, make sure to check for an equal protection violation.

II. ECONOMIC AND SOCIAL LAWS — THE "MERE-RATIONALITY" STANDARD OF REVIEW

A. **Non-suspect, non-fundamental rights (economic and social legislation):** First, let's examine the treatment of classifications that do ***not*** involve either a ***suspect class*** or a ***fundamental right***. Most ***economic*** and ***social-welfare*** legislation falls into this category. [248]

  1. **Mere-rationality standard:** Here, as noted, courts use the "mere-rationality" standard. In other words, as long as there is some ***rational relation*** between the classification drawn by the legislature and some ***legitimate legislative objective***, the classification scheme will not violate the Equal Protection Clause. [248]

> **Example:** Suppose the Muni City Council, in order to cope with a budget deficit, increases the fares on all city-operated buses from $1 to $2. Statistical evidence shows that 80% of people who ride the Muni bus system on a typical day have incomes below the city-wide median. At the same time the City Council increases the bus fares, it refuses to raise the annual automobile inspection fee; car owners on average have higher-than-median incomes. P, a bus passenger, sues Muni, arguing that it is a violation of his equal protection rights for the city to increase bus fares for the poor while not increasing inspection fees for the affluent.
>
> A court would apply the "mere-rationality" standard to this regulation, because poverty is not a suspect class, and no fundamental right is at issue here. Since the City Council could rationally have believed that Muni's deficit would be better handled by raising bus fares, and because the Council could rationally have decided to tackle its deficit problem one phase at a time, the constitutional challenge will almost certainly lose.

    a. **Need not be actual objective:** One thing this "mere-rationality" standard means is that the "legitimate government objective" part of the test is satisfied even if the statute's defenders come up with merely a ***"hypothetical"*** objective that the legislature "might have" been pursuing. The government does not have to show that the objective it's pointing to was the one that ***actually motivated*** the legislature. [250-251]

    b. **No empirical link:** Also, there does not have to in fact be even a "rational relation" between the means chosen and the end — all that's required is that the legislature ***"could have rationally believed"*** that there was a link between the means and the end.

 c. **Loose fit:** Finally, a very ***loose fit*** between means and end will still be O.K.

2. **Conclusion:** Therefore, if you decide that a particular government classification does not involve a suspect category or a fundamental right, and should thus be subjected to "mere-rationality" review, you should almost always conclude that the classification survives equal protection attack. (But see the discussion of "mere-rationality with bite" immediately below, for an important exception to this rule.)

3. **Review "with bite" for laws motived by "animus" towards the unpopular:** But if the Court finds that a law has been motivated solely by ***"animus"*** or ***"hostility"*** towards a ***politically-unpopular group***, the Court has generally been willing to ***strike down*** such legislation even though only "mere-rationality" review is supposedly being used. In so doing, the Court has said that the ***desire to harm an unpopular group*** cannot be a ***"legitimate governmental objective."*** These cases are frequently described as involving mere-rationality review ***"with bite,"*** i.e., review without the customary ***extreme deference*** to the legislature that made the challenged classification. [251]

 a. **"Hippies"** For instance, where the Court found that a federal statute involving food stamps was motivated solely by congressional animus against "hippies," it invalidated the statute. [*U.S. Dep't of Agric. v. Moreno*] [251]

 b. **Discrimination against gays:** Similarly, the Court has been quick to find that legislation disadvantaging ***gays*** was motivated solely by "animus," and to strike down such legislation even while purporting to use mere-rationality review.

  Example: Colorado amends its constitution to prohibit any state or local law that protects homosexuals against discrimination on the basis of their sexual orientation or conduct. *Held*, this amendment violates gays' equal protection rights — it's not even minimally rational, and is motivated solely by animus towards gays. [*Romer v. Evans*] [354]

4. **Non-suspect classes:** Here is a partial list of classifications that have been held ***not*** to involve a suspect or quasi-suspect class:

 a. **Age:** Classifications based on ***age***.

  Example: Suppose that a state requires all state troopers over 50 to retire, in order preserve a physically fit police force. Because age is not a suspect or quasi-suspect classification, the "mere-rationality" test will be used. Because there is some slight overall relation between age and fitness, this requirement is satisfied, so the retirement rule does not violate equal protection. [*Mass. Board of Retirement v. Murgia*] [253]

 b. **Wealth:** Classifications based upon ***wealth***.

  Example: Suppose that a state provides that no low-income housing project may be built in any community unless a majority of the voters approve it in a popular referendum. A resident who would like to live in the low-income housing that would be built if allowed challenges the statute on equal protection grounds.

  Even if P shows that the statute was motivated by a desire to discriminate against the poor, P's constitutional challenge will probably fail. Because wealth is not a suspect or quasi-suspect class, the court will use "mere-rationality" review, and will uphold the statute if it finds that the legislature could reasonably have believed that its statute might help achieve some legitimate state objective, perhaps letting communities avoid the greater governmental cost that arguably accompanies concentrations of low-income residents.

 c. **Mental condition:** Classifications based upon ***mental illness*** or ***mental retardation***.

  Example: A city makes it harder for group homes for the mentally retarded to achieve zoning permission than for other group living arrangements to do so. This classification, based upon mental status, will not be treated as suspect or quasi-suspect, and will thus be subject only to "mere-rationality" review. (However, such a zoning procedure was found to violate even "mere-rationality," in *City of Cleburne v. Cleburne Living Center*.)

d. **Sexual orientation:** Classifications based on *sexual orientation.* Thus governments, at least historically, have faced only mere-rationality review when they have treated *homosexuals* differently from heterosexuals. (But as noted *supra*, the Court now seems to apply mere-rationality review *"with bite"* to what it perceives as anti-gay legislation, even though gays still don't have suspect or semi-suspect status. [252])

III. SUSPECT CLASSIFICATIONS, ESPECIALLY RACE

A. **Suspect classifications:** At the other end of the spectrum, we apply *strict scrutiny* for any classification that involves a *"suspect class."* [256]

1. **Race and national origin:** There are only three suspect classes generally recognized by the Supreme Court: (1) *race*; (2) *national origin*; and (3) for some purposes, *alienage*. So be on the lookout for a classification based on race, national origin, or alienage. For other classifications, you can safely assume that these are not suspect. [256]

2. **Purposeful:** One of the most important things to remember about strict scrutiny of suspect classifications is that this strict scrutiny will only be applied where the differential treatment of the class is *intentional* on the part of the government. If the government enacts a statute or regulation that merely has the unintended incidental *effect* of burdening, say, African Americans worse than whites, the court will *not* use strict scrutiny. [*Washington v. Davis*] *This is probably the most frequently-tested aspect of suspect classifications.* [257-259]

    Example: Suppose a city gives a standardized test to all applicants for the local police force. The city and the test designers do not intend to make it harder for African Americans than for whites to pass the test. But it turns out that a lot fewer African Americans pass than whites, even though the applicant pools otherwise seem identical. This differential will not trigger strict scrutiny, because the government did not intend to treat African Americans differently from whites.

    a. **Circumstantial evidence:** However, remember that an intent to classify based on a suspect class can be proven by *circumstantial*, not just direct, evidence.

    Example: Suppose a particular police force picks new officers based on a personal interview conducted by the police chief, and over five years it turns out that only 1% of African American applicants receive jobs but 25% of whites do (and there is no apparent objective difference in the black versus white applicant pools). This statistical disparity could furnish circumstantial evidence of purposeful discrimination, which would then allow a court to apply strict scrutiny to the selection procedures.

3. **Invidious:** In addition to the requirement that the discrimination be "purposeful," it must also be *"invidious,"* i.e., based on prejudice or tending to denigrate the disfavored class. This requirement is what has caused race, national origin, and (for some purposes) alienage to be the only suspect classes — these involve the only minorities against whom *popular prejudice is sufficiently deep.* [262]

    a. **Rationale:** Why do we give especially close scrutiny to governmental action that disadvantages very unpopular minorities? Because ordinarily, groups will protect themselves through use of the *political process*, but: (1) these particular groups don't usually have very much political power, because the past discrimination against them has included keeping them out of the voting system; and (2) even if the minority votes in proportion to its numbers, the majority is very likely to vote as a block against it, because of the minority's extreme unpopularity.

b. **"Discrete and insular" minority:** A famous phrase to express this concept, from a footnote in a Supreme Court opinion, is ***"discrete and insular minorities"*** — discrete and insular minorities are ones that are so disfavored and out of the political mainstream that the courts must make extra efforts to protect them, because the political system won't. [262]

c. **Traits showing suspectness:** Here are some traits which probably make it more likely that a court will find that a particular class is suspect:

   i. **Immutability:** If the class is based on an ***immutable*** or unchangeable trait, this makes a finding of suspectness more likely. Race and national origin qualify; wealth does not. The idea seems to be that if you can't change the trait, it's especially unfair to have it be the basis of discrimination. [262]

   ii. **Stereotypes:** If the class or trait is one as to which there's a prevalence of false and disparaging ***stereotypes***, this makes a finding of suspectness more likely. Again, race, national origin and alienage seem to qualify, at least somewhat better than, say, wealth. [262]

   iii. **Political powerlessness:** If the class is ***politically powerless***, or has been subjected to ***widespread discrimination*** (especially official discrimination) historically, this makes it more likely to be suspect.

d. **"Separate but equal" as invidious:** Even if a classification involves a group that has frequently been discriminated against, the classification's defenders may argue that their particular use of the classification is not "invidious" because it's not intended to disadvantage the class. ***Affirmative action*** is one example where this argument might be raised. Another context in which the requirement that the discrimination be "invidious" arises is the ***"separate but equal"*** situation; in this context, the defenders of the classification claim that although both classes are treated differently, the unpopular class is being treated no "worse." In general, the Court now seems to hold that discrimination based on race or national origin is ***"per se" invidious***; for instance, the argument that the races are being treated "separately but equally" will almost never serve as a successful defense to an Equal Protection problem. [265]

   Example: Virginia forbids interracial marriage. It claims that blacks aren't disfavored, because whites are blocked from marrying blacks just as much as blacks are blocked from marrying whites. *Held*, the statute's legislative history shows that it was enacted to protect the "racial purity" of whites, so the classification is invidious and violates Equal Protection. [*Loving v. Virginia*]

4. **Strict equals fatal:** Once the court does decide that a suspect classification is involved, and that strict scrutiny must be used, that scrutiny is almost always ***fatal*** to the classification scheme. For instance, no purposeful racial or ethnic classification has survived strict scrutiny since 1944. [263]

a. **"Necessary" prong:** Sometimes, this is because the state cannot show that it is pursuing a "compelling" objective. But more often, it's because the means chosen is not shown to be ***"necessary"*** to achieve that compelling objective. A means is only "necessary" for achieving the particular objective if there are ***no less discriminatory alternatives*** that will accomplish the goal as well, or almost as well.

   Example: Suppose Pearl Harbor occurred today, and the U.S. government once again put any citizen of Japanese ancestry into an internment camp. Presumably this would not be a "necessary" means of dealing with the danger of treason and sabotage, because less discriminatory alternatives like frequent document inspections and/or loyalty oaths would be almost as effective as virtual imprisonment.

5. **Some examples:** Here are two contexts in which claims have been made (and in most instances accepted) that a suspect class has been intentionally discriminated against in violation of Equal Protection:

a. **Child custody and adoption:** Some notion of "racial compatibility" or "racial purity" may motivate state officials to differentiate based on race in *child custody* and *adoption* proceedings. In general, the practical rule is that the state may not impose flat rules that handle child custody and adoption differently based solely on the race of the child and parents. [266]

> **Example:** Mother and Father are divorced, and Mother is given custody of Child. All are white. Mother then marries Husband, who is African American. The family court transfers custody to Father, on the grounds that Child will be socially stigmatized if she grows up in an interracial family. *Held*, this custody decision can't survive strict scrutiny — government may not bow to private racial prejudices. [*Palmore v. Sidoti*]

b. **Political process:** Actions taken by government that relate to the *political process*, and that are intended to disadvantage racial or ethnic minorities, often run afoul of Equal Protection. [266]

> **Example:** A state requires that in every election, each candidate's race must appear on the ballot. *Held*, this violates Equal Protection because it was motivated by a desire to keep African Americans out of office. [*Anderson v. Martin*]

6. **Segregation:** The clearest example of a classification involving a suspect class and thus requiring strict scrutiny is *segregation*, the maintenance of physical separation between the races.

a. **General rule:** Official, intentional segregation based on race or national origin is a violation of the Equal Protection Clause. As the result of *Brown v. Board of Education*, even if the government were to maintain truly "separate but equal" facilities (in the sense that, say, a school for blacks had as nice a building, as qualified teachers, etc., as a school for whites), the intentional maintenance of separate facilities *per se* violates the Equal Protection Clause. [267-270]

b. **Education and housing:** The two areas where official segregation is most often found are *education* and *housing.*

   i. **Education:** Thus if a school board establishes attendance zones for the purpose of making one school heavily African American and/or Hispanic, and another school heavily white, this would violate Equal Protection.

   ii. **Housing:** Similarly, government may not intentionally segregate in housing. For example, it's a violation of Equal Protection for a city to do its *zoning* in such a way that all *government-subsidized housing* is built in the heavily black part of town, if the intent of this zoning practice is to maintain racial segregation.

c. **Must be *de jure*:** But it's critical to remember that there is a violation of equal protection only where the segregation is the result of *intentional government action*. In other words, the segregation must be *"de jure,"* not merely *"de facto."* [270]

> **Example:** School district lines are drawn by officials who have no desire to separate students based on race. Over time, due to housing choices made by private individuals, one district becomes fully African American, and the other all-white. Even though the schools are no longer racially balanced, there has been no equal protection violation, because there was no act of intentional separation on the part of the government. *Cf. Bd. of Ed. v. Dowell.* [271]

d. Wide remedies: If a court finds that there has been intentional segregation, it has a wide range of *remedies* to choose from. For instance, it can bus students to a non-neighborhood school, or order the redrawing of district boundaries. But whatever remedy the court chooses, the remedy must *stop* once the effects of the original intentional discrimination have been eradicated. (Then, if because of housing patterns or other non-government action, the schools become resegregated, the court may *not* reinstitute its remedies.)

IV. RACE-CONSCIOUS AFFIRMATIVE ACTION

A. Race-conscious affirmative action: You're more likely to get an exam question about race-conscious *affirmative action* than about official discrimination against racial minorities. If you see a question in which government is trying to help racial or ethnic minorities by giving them some sort of preference, you should immediately think "equal protection" and you should think "strict scrutiny." [275]

1. Public entity: Be sure to remember that there can only be a violation of equal protection if there's *state action*, that is, action by the federal government or by a state or municipality. In general, the use of affirmative action by private entities does *not* raise any constitutional issue (except perhaps where a judge orders a private employer to implement a race-conscious plan). But any time you have a fact pattern in which a police department, school district, public university, or other governmental entity seems to be intentionally preferring one racial group over another, that's when you know you have a potential equal protection problem.

2. Strict scrutiny: It is now the case that *any affirmative action program that classifies on the basis of race will be strictly scrutinized.* [*Richmond v. Croson*] So a race-conscious affirmative action plan, whether it's in the area of employment, college admissions, voting rights or anywhere else, must be adopted for the purpose of furthering some "compelling" governmental interest, and the racial classification must be "necessary" to achieve that compelling governmental interest. [278]

> **a. Past discrimination:** Since a race-conscious affirmative action plan will have to be in pursuit of a "compelling" governmental interest, probably the only interests that are likely to qualify are:
>
> [1] the *government's* interest in *redressing past discrimination*; and
>
> [2] a public *university's* interest in *student-body diversity*.
>
> So if the government is merely trying to get a *racially-balanced workforce*, to make African Americans *more economically successful*, or any other objective that is not closely tied to one of these two objectives, you should immediately be able to say, "The government interest is not compelling, and the measure flunks the strict scrutiny test." [278-279]

> **b. Clear evidence:** Even if the government *is* trying to redress past discrimination, there's got to be *clear evidence* that this discrimination in fact occurred.

> > **i. Societal discrimination:** Redressing past discrimination "*by society* as a whole" will *not* suffice. There must be past discrimination closely related to the problem, typically discrimination *by government*. [279]

> **c. Quotas:** One device that is especially vulnerable to Equal Protection attack is the racially-based *quota*. A racially-based quota is an inflexible number of admissions slots, dollar amounts, or other "goodies" set aside for minorities. For instance, it's a quota if the state says that 1/2 of all new hires in the police department must be African American, or if it says that 20% of all seats in the public university's law school class will be set aside for African Americans and Hispanics. Probably *virtually all racially-based quotas will be struck down even*

where the government is trying to eradicate the effects of past discrimination — the Court will probably say that a quota is not "necessary" to remedy discrimination, because more flexible "goals" can do the job. [280]

    d. Congress: It doesn't make any (or at least much) difference that the affirmation action program was enacted by *Congress* rather than by a state or local government. Here, too, the Court will apply strict scrutiny if the program is race-conscious. [*Adarand Constructors, Inc. v. Pena*]

        i. Possibly greater deference: However, the Court might give slightly greater *deference* to a congressional finding that official discrimination had existed in a particular domain, or that a particular race-conscious remedy was required, than it would to a comparable finding by a state or local government. (We don't know yet whether this greater deference would occur.)

B. Preferential admissions in higher education: Any scheme which gives a preference to one racial group for *admission* to a *public university* must be *strictly scrutinized*. However, such preferences will not necessarily be *invalidated* as the result of this strict scrutiny.

    1. Main principles: Here are what seem to be the main principles governing affirmative action in public-university admissions, as the result of two 2003 cases involving the University of Michigan and decisions case involving the University of Texas (one from 2013 and one from 2016): [281]

        [a] Public universities and colleges *may explicitly consider minority racial status* as a factor that increases the odds of admission, so as to promote the compelling goal of *"education diversity."*

        [b] These institutions *may not award "points" for minority status*, or otherwise pursue *mechanical quota-like schemes,* and must instead evaluate each candidate as part of a *"holistic" review* that treats race as *merely one factor among others.*

        [c] Even when an institution uses a non-quota "holistic" race-conscious method, that method must *survive strict scrutiny*. That is, the method may be used *only* if the institution carries the burden of showing that *no workable race-neutral alternatives* would achieve the educational benefits of diversity *as well or almost as well* as the race-conscious method being used.

        [d] Despite the need for strict scrutiny of race-conscious admissions schemes, such schemes can *survive* that scrutiny.

        [e] The *only* governmental objective that has ever been recognized by the Supreme Court as *"compelling"* (and thus as sufficient to survive strict scrutiny) is the interest in obtaining the *"educational benefits"* of *a diverse student body.* An interest in having the racial or ethnic breakdown of the student body merely *resemble the demography* of, say, the state in which the university is located, is *not* by itself a compelling objective. But achieving a *"critical mass"* of students from each of various otherwise-under-represented racial minorities, so as to foster *educational benefits* like the *breaking down of racial stereotypes, is* part of what is needed for these educational benefits to accrue.

    2. Two illustrations: Here are two illustrations of how the Court reviews race-conscious university admissions policies. These are taken from the facts of two of the Court's most important decisions (one upholding the plan in question, and the other striking down the plan).

        a. Illustration of valid plan: The following case illustrates principles [a], [c], [d] and [e] above (plan is *upheld* despite strict scrutiny, because it pursues the compelling goal of educational diversity, and does so in a sufficiently narrowly-tailored way):

Example (valid plan): The University of Texas (UT) chooses undergraduate applicants this way: (1) 75% of the slots are allocated on a (supposedly) race-neutral basis, under which any student in the top 10% of her high-school graduating class is guaranteed a slot (the "Top Ten Percent Plan"); and (2) the remaining 25% of the slots are allocated based on a "Holistic Review" method, under which race is expressly considered, but only as one factor among many. UT has previously used a non-race-conscious version of Holistic Review, but after five or so years the percentage of blacks and Hispanics in the entering class has stagnated at numbers far below what UT believes are needed to have a "critical mass" of each group on campus. (Achieving a "critical mass" of under-represented viewpoints is how UT specifically defines its compelling goal of achieving "educational diversity.") For instance, in the year just before adoption of the race-conscious version, 80% of classes with more than five students have either zero or one black student, leading many black students to feel racially isolated in class. UT adds the race-conscious aspect to Holistic Review instead of, for instance, expanding the Top Ten Percent Plan as the basis for selecting the entire incoming class.

Held (by a 4-3 vote), the UT plan does *not* violate the equal protection rights of white applicants, even though the plan is expressly race-conscious. The educational benefits UT has sought from a diverse student body (which it lists as promoting of "cross-racial understanding," preparing of its student body for a diverse workforce, and cultivating of a "set of leaders with legitimacy in the eyes of the citizenry") constitute a compelling governmental goal. And UT has carried its heavy burden of showing a "narrow tailoring" between the method it has chosen (adding a race-conscious component to the Holistic Review as to 25% of the class) and this compelling goal. UT has shown that it adequately considered race-neutral alternatives, and reasonably rejected each as not workable. For instance, it properly rejected expanding the Top Ten Percent Plan to choose the entire class, because (1) such a Plan depends heavily on the racially-segregated nature of the state's public schools, and so is not truly race-neutral; and (2) such class-rank-based plans in general create "perverse incentives," such as encouraging parents to keep their children in low-performing segregated schools, and possibly weakening the academic excellence of the student body. Also, UT's use of race-consciousness as only "one factor among many," and for selection of only 25% of the entering class, help make the Plan narrowly-tailored. [*Fisher II*] [289-291]

b. **Illustration of invalid plan:** The following case illustrates principles [b] and [c] above (plan is *invalidated* after strict scrutiny; although it pursues the compelling goal of educational diversity, it does not do so in a sufficiently narrowly-tailored way, because it is a mechanical approach resembling a quota):

Example (invalid plan): The University of Michigan undergraduate college awards pre-measured "points" to applicants for various attributes (e.g., up to 5 points for being an outstanding artist or student leader). Every black or Hispanic applicant automatically gets 20 points for diversity. 100 points are needed for admission. The extra 20 points for minority-group status has the effect that virtually every minimally-qualified black or Hispanic applicant is admitted, whereas many well-qualified non-minority applicants are rejected.

Held (by 6-3), this form of affirmative action is unconstitutional, because it is not narrowly-tailored to the achievement of the compelling interest in student-body diversity. The scheme here is a mechanical one that is equivalent to a quota, not an individualized-evaluation scheme. And the fact that "near-misses" can be flagged for individualized review does not save the scheme. [*Gratz v. Bollinger*] [285]

C. **Other affirmative action contexts:**

1. **Admissions to public schools by race-conscious means:** *No individual student's race may be considered in making that student's public high-school or elementary school assignment,* if the

district is not combating prior official segregation. ***Parents Involved in Community Schools v. Seattle School District No. 1*** (2007). [294]

> **Example:** The Seattle school system adopts a "tiebreaker" plan for allocating spaces to incoming ninth graders who want to attend certain racially-imbalanced oversubscribed high schools. One of the tiebreakers is that as between a white and nonwhite student seeking admission to the same oversubscribed high school, the one who will lessen the target school's degree of racial imbalance (compared with district-wide percentages) will get the slot.
>
> *Held,* the race-conscious plan here must be strictly scrutinized, and will be struck down. Five members of the Court believe that it is not narrowly-tailored to meet any governmental objective. The decisive fifth member of the Court (Kennedy) believes that reducing school-by-school racial imbalance and increasing diversity in the student population are compelling governmental interests, but that the plan here — based on labeling each student as "white" or "non-white" — is not necessary to achieve those interests, because the district has not shown that methods not involving the "crude" binary racial classification of each students (e.g., race-conscious drawing of school-attendance zones) cannot adequately achieve these same objectives. *Parents Involved in Community Schools v. Seattle School District No. 1, supra.*

2. **Minority set-asides:** *Minority set-asides,* by which some percentage of publicly-funded contracts are reserved for minority-owned businesses, will be subjected to scrutiny and generally struck down. That's true whether the set-aside is enacted by Congress or by a state/local government. [301-308]

3. **Employment:** Whenever a public *employer* gives an intentional preference to one racial group, strict scrutiny will probably be called for. [308]

   a. **Layoffs:** If the employer intentionally prefers blacks over whites when it administers *layoffs,* that preference will almost certainly be unconstitutional. [*Wygant v. Jackson Bd. of Ed.*] [311]

   b. **Hiring:** A racial preference in *hiring* is almost as hard to justify (though it might pass muster if that particular public employer had clearly discriminated against African Americans in the past, and there seemed to be no way short of a racial preference in hiring to redress that past discrimination).

   c. **Promotions:** A race-based scheme of awarding *promotions* to cure past discrimination (so that African Americans eventually get promoted to the levels that they would have been at had there not been any discrimination in the first place) is the easiest to justify, since it damages the expectations of whites the least. But even this will have to satisfy strict scrutiny. [311]

4. **Drawing of election districts (racial gerrymanders):** A *voter* who thinks she has been disadvantaged by the drawing of *electoral districts* in an *intentionally race-conscious way* may bring an equal protection suit against the government body that drew the district lines. Such *"racial-gerrymander"* cases have often proved to be *winnable* by the plaintiff voters.

   a. **Race as predominant factor:** If the court concludes that *race* was the *predominant factor* in how the electoral district lines were drawn, the court will *strictly scrutinize* the lines, and probably strike them down. [312]

      i. **Strict scrutiny:** Legislatures may *"take account"* of race in drawing district lines (just as they take account of ethnic groups, precinct lines, and many other factors). But they *may not make race the predominant factor,* unless they can show that using race in this way satisfies strict scrutiny. That is, the line-drawers must bear a very heavy burden: they must show that using race as the predominant fact is *necessary to achieve a compelling governmental interest* (e.g., eradication of prior official voting-rights discrimination). [*Miller v. Johnson*] [314]

C
A
P
S
U
L
E

S
U
M
M
A
R
Y

(1) Maximizing the number of "majority black" districts: The desire to create the ***maximum number of "majority black" districts*** is ***not*** by itself a "compelling" interest. [*Miller v. Johnson*] [314]

ii. **Partisan gerrymanders:** Be sure to distinguish between racial gerrymanders and ***"partisan gerrymanders,"*** in which one political party enacts a gerrymander that intentionally dilutes the voting power of members of the other political party. Federal-court suits challenging non-racially-inspired partisan gerrymanders are ***non-justiciable,*** as the result of an important 2019 Supreme Court decision, *Rucho v. Common Cause* (discussed *infra*, p. C-128).

5. **Law enforcement and other operational areas:** Even where government's own ***operational needs*** are arguably aided by a race-conscious policy, the Court will strictly scrutinize this use of race. Thus race-conscious government decisions in such operational areas as ***law enforcement, prison administration*** and the ***military*** will be strictly scrutinized.

Example: A state prison system racially segregates new prisoners in cell assignments, believing that this cuts down on gang-related violence. *Held*, the race-conscious policy must be strictly scrutinized, even though the state believes that its policy does not prefer one race over another. [*Johnson v. California*] [317]

D. **Popular votes to repeal affirmative action:** What happens if some unit of government ***voluntarily adopts*** a constitutionally-permissible affirmative action approach to some problem, and the electorate responds by ***voting to overturn the plan*** and to make it much ***harder to institute*** this sort of affirmative action in the future? Does the electorate's use of its voting power to abolish previously-instituted affirmative action ***itself constitute the denial of equal protection*** to members of minority groups that would in theory have benefited from the affirmative action? The answer will generally be ***"no,"*** as the result of *Schuette v. Coaltion to Defend Affirmative Action (BAMN)* (2014). [318-319]

1. **Result of *Schuette*:** *Schuette* means that voters are generally ***free to repeal an affirmative action plan***, and to ***change the political process*** in a way that intentionally makes it harder for affirmative action to be instituted in the future.

V. MIDDLE-LEVEL REVIEW (GENDER, ILLEGITIMACY AND ALIENAGE)

A. **Middle-level review generally:** A few types of classifications are subjected to "middle-level" review, easier to satisfy than strict scrutiny but tougher than "mere-rationality" review. [320]

1. **Standard:** Where we apply the middle-level standard, the government objective must be ***"important,"*** and the means must be ***"substantially related"*** to that objective.

a. **No hypothetical objective:** One important respect in which mid-level review differs from "mere-rationality" review concerns the state ***objectives*** that the Court will consider. Recall that in the case of the easy "mere-rationality" review, the Court will consider virtually ***any objective that might have conceivably motivated*** the legislature, regardless of whether there's any evidence that that objective was in fact in the legislature's mind. But with "intermediate-level" review, the Court will ***not*** hypothesize objectives; it will consider only those objectives that are shown to have ***actually motivated the legislature.***

2. **What classes:** There are two main types of classifications that get middle-level review: (1) ***gender***; and (2) ***illegitimacy***. We also consider ***alienage*** here, because it has aspects of both strict scrutiny and mere-rationality review, so it's kind of a hybrid.

B. Gender: The most important single rule to remember in the entire area of middle-level scrutiny is that *sex-based classifications get middle-level review*. [*Craig v. Boren*] So if government intentionally classifies on the basis of sex, it's got to show that it's pursuing an important objective, and that the sex-based classification scheme is substantially related to that objective. [320-322]

> **Example:** City sets the mandatory retirement age for male public school teachers at 65, and for female teachers at 62. Because this classification is based upon gender, it must satisfy middle-level review: City must show that its sex-based classification is substantially related to the achievement of an important governmental objective. In this case, it is unlikely that City can make this showing.

1. **Benign as well as invidious:** The same standard of review is used whether the sex-based classification is *"invidious"* (intended to harm women) or *"benign"* (intended to help women, or even intended to redress past discrimination against them). [262]

2. **Male or female plaintiff:** This means that where government classifies based on sex, the scheme can be attacked either by a *male* or by a *female*, and either gender will get the benefit of mid-level review.

   > **Example:** Oklahoma forbids the sale of low-alcohol beer to males under the age of 21, and to females under the age of 18. *Held*, this statute violates the equal protection rights of males aged 18 to 20, because it is not substantially related to the achievement of important governmental objectives. [*Craig v. Boren*] [321-322]

3. **Purpose:** Sex-based classifications will only be subjected to middle-level review if the legislature has *intentionally* discriminated against one sex in favor of the other. (This is similar to the requirement for strict scrutiny in race-based cases.) If, as the result of some governmental act, one sex happens to suffer an *unintended burden* greater than the other sex suffers, that's not enough for mid-level review.

   > **Example:** Massachusetts gives an absolute preference to veterans for civil service jobs. It happens that 98% of veterans are male. *Held*, this preference does not have to satisfy mid-level review because the unfavorable impact on women was not intended by the legislature. Therefore, the preference does not violate equal protection, since it satisfies the easier "mere-rationality" standard. [*Personnel Admin. of Mass. v. Feeney*]

4. **Stereotypes:** Be on the lookout for *stereotypes*: if the legislature has made a sex-based classification that seems to reinforce stereotypes about the "proper place" of women, it probably cannot survive middle-level review.

   > **Example:** Virginia maintains Virginia Military Institute as an all-male college, because of the state's view that only men can handle the school's harsh, militaristic method of producing "citizen soldiers." *Held*, this sex-based scheme does not satisfy mid-level review, because it stems from traditional ways of thinking about gender roles; there are clearly *some* women who are qualified for and would benefit from the VMI approach, and these women may not be deprived of the opportunity to attend VMI. [*U.S. v. Virginia*]) [324-326]

5. **"Exceedingly persuasive justification":** Although the Supreme Court still gives gender-based classifications only mid-level, not strict, scrutiny, the Court now applies that scrutiny in a very tough way. The Court now says that it will require an *"exceedingly persuasive justification"* for any gender-based classification, and will review it with *"skeptical scrutiny."* [*U.S. v. Virginia, supra.*] [320]

C. Illegitimacy: Classifications disadvantaging *illegitimate children* are "semi-suspect" and therefore get middle-level review. [346]

1. **Claims can't be flatly barred:** Therefore, the state can't simply bar unacknowledged illegitimate children from bringing wrongful death actions, from having any chance to inherit, etc. Such children must be given at least *some reasonable opportunity* to obtain a *judicial declaration of paternity* (e.g., in a suit brought by their mother). Once they obtain such a declaration, they must be *treated equivalently to children born legitimate.*

   Example: Pennsylvania passes a statute of limitations saying that no action for child support may be brought on behalf of an out-of-wedlock child unless the action is brought before the child turns 6. *Held*, the statute violates the child's equal protection rights. Since the classification is based on out-of-wedlock status, it will be upheld only if it is substantially related to an important governmental objective. Concededly, Pennsylvania has an interest in avoiding the litigation of stale or fraudulent claims. But the 6-year statute of limitations is not "substantially related" to the achievement of that interest. [*Clark v. Jeter*]

D. **Alienage:** Alienage might be thought of as a "semi-suspect" category. In fact, though, alienage classifications, depending on the circumstances, will be subjected either to *strict scrutiny* or to *mere-rationality* review (so there's only middle-level review as a kind of "average").

   1. **Distinguished from national origin:** Be careful to distinguish "alienage" from "national origin": if a person is discriminated against because he is *not yet a United States citizen,* that's "alienage" discrimination. If, on the other hand, he's discriminated against because he is a naturalized citizen who originally came from Mexico (or whose ancestors came from Mexico), that's discrimination based on "national origin." Remember that national origin always triggers strict scrutiny, whereas alienage does not necessarily do so.

   2. **General rule:** Subject to one large exception covered below, discrimination against aliens is subject to *strict scrutiny*. [341]

      Example 1: A state cannot deny welfare benefits to aliens, because such a classification based on alienage cannot be shown to be necessary to the achievement of a compelling state interest. [*Graham v. Richardson*]

      Example 2: A state cannot prevent resident aliens from practicing law, because such a classification cannot survive strict scrutiny. [*In re Griffiths*]

   3. **"Representative government" exception:** But the major exception is that strict scrutiny does not apply where the discrimination against aliens relates to a *"function at the heart of representative government."* Basically, this means that if the alien is applying for a *government job*, and the performance of this job is *closely tied in with politics, justice or public policy*, we use only *"mere-rationality"* review. So government may discriminate against aliens with respect to posts like *state trooper, public school teacher*, or *probation officer*. See, e.g., [*Ambach v. Norwick*]. [342]

      a. **Low-level government jobs:** But don't make the mistake of thinking that because what's involved is a government job, strict scrutiny automatically fails to apply. If the job is *not* closely tied in with politics, justice or public policy — something that is true of most *low-level jobs* — then strict scrutiny applies.

         Example: Strict scrutiny would almost certainly be applied to a city ordinance that said that no resident alien may work for the city government as a sanitation worker.

   4. **Education of illegal aliens:** A last quirky rule in the area of alienage is that if a state denies *free public education* to *illegal aliens*, this will be subjected to intermediate-level review, and probably struck down. [*Plyler v. Doe*] (But this comes from a combination of the fact that the plaintiffs were aliens and also that they were children. If a state discriminates against *adult* illegal aliens, we don't know whether something higher than middle-level review will be applied.) [343-346]

E. Other unpopular groups: Discrimination against *other unpopular groups* might conceivably be subjected to middle-level review. For instance, discrimination against the *elderly* or the *disabled* might possibly trigger mid-level review, but the Court has not addressed this question. (This would be a good gray area for an exam question — you could argue both the pros and the cons of applying mid-level review to these unpopular, frequently-discriminated-against groups.)

F. Congressional affirmative action plans: Finally, remember that there's one other area where the Court uses mid-level review: affirmative action programs established by *Congress*.

VI. UNEQUAL TREATMENT OF GAYS, INCLUDING THE BANNING OF SAME-SEX MARRIAGE

A. Sexual orientation classifications generally: The Court has decided *four cases* since 1996 in which legislatures classified based on *sexual orientation*. Three of the four have been in major part equal protection cases.

　　1. Gay plaintiffs win all four: The gay *plaintiffs prevailed* in their constitutional challenge in all three of these equal protection cases (as well as in the one substantive due process case, *Lawrence v. Texas*, *supra*, p. C-39). All four of the majority opinions were written by Justice Kennedy (who was, interestingly, appointed by Ronald Reagan, a Republican).

　　2. Summary of the state of the law: Here's a summary of where these four gay-rights decisions have left the law of gays' equal protection rights:

　　　❑ **Right to same-sex marriage:** Same-sex couples have a *fundamental right to be married.* Therefore, states must *issue marriage licenses* to gay couples, and states (as well as the federal government) must *recognize* same-sex marriages entered into in other jurisdictions.

　　　❑ **No "semi-suspect" status:** The Court has *not* so far *treated* classifications based on sexual orientation as having official *"semi-suspect"* or *"suspect"* status. So when the Court hears a challenge to a classification based on sexual orientation and not involving a fundamental right, the Court seems to use some form of easy-to-satisfy *"mere-rationality"* review, not mid-level review (which is given to semi-suspect classifications, like gender) or strict scrutiny (given to suspect classifications, like race and ethnicity).

　　　❑ **Mere-rationality "with bite":** However, in cases *not* involving a fundamental right,[3] although the Court appears to apply mere-rationality review, it has in fact given *much less deference* to the legislature's sexual-orientation-based classification system than is typically applied in mere-rationality cases. The level of review used can fairly be described as "mere rationality *with bite.*"

　　　❑ **Animus towards unpopular minority:** In these four decisions, the majority has often (1) noted that legislative classifications based on sexual orientation have historically been *based solely on animus towards a disfavored minority*, and (2) concluded that such animus *cannot be a "legitimate governmental interest."* Therefore, the Court has typically reasoned, the classification system *fails even mere-rationality review* because of the lack of a legitimate governmental interest.

B. Singling out of gays because of animus: In the first of the four "pro-gay" decisions mentioned above, in 1996 the Court *struck down* a Colorado state-constitutional amendment that would have *pre-*

---

3. As noted, the *right to marriage* is now deemed fundamental for equal protection purposes, so the text of this paragraph does not apply to the claim that states violate the Constitution when they refuse to allow same-sex marriage.

vented the state or any of its cities from giving certain protections to gays or lesbians. The Court found that the measure flunked even "mere-rationality" review. [*Romer v. Evans*] [354]

1. **Rationale:** The majority concluded that the Colorado amendment was "inexplicable by anything but *animus toward the class that it affects*" (gays and lesbians). And, the majority said, "a *bare ... desire to harm a politically unpopular group cannot constitute a legitimate governmental interest.*" The lack of a legitimate governmental objective meant that the amendment was a violation of equal protection, even though the Court used only mere-rationality review.

C. **Same-sex marriage:** The most important and controversial area concerning the constitutional rights of gay people has been the area of *same-sex marriage*. As the result of the Court's 2015 decision in *Obergefell v. Hodges*, gay and lesbian couples have a *constitutional right to enter into same-sex marriages*.

1. *Windsor* **case:** Before the 2015 *Obergefell* decision, the Court had already decided by a 5-4 vote in 2013 that *when a same-sex couple has been married under the law of a state*, the federal government *may not treat the couple any differently* than it would treat a *heterosexual couple* married under that same state's law. [*U.S. v. Windsor* (2013)] [355]

2. **States must allow same-sex marriage (*Obergefell*):** In *Obergefell*, the Court recognized a *constitutionally-guaranteed right to same-sex marriage*. The Court held by a 5-4 vote that *all states* must: (1) *issue marriage licenses to same-sex couples*; and (2) *recognize all same-sex marriages entered into in other states*. [356]

   a. **Based on both equal protection and due process:** *Obergefell* holds that state laws banning same-sex marriages violate *both the equal protection* and the *substantive due process rights of gay and lesbian couples* who wish to marry. [356]

   b. **Kennedy's majority opinion:** Justice Kennedy wrote the Court's opinion, as he had written each of the Court's three major prior opinions gradually enhancing the constitutional rights of gays and lesbians. [357]

      i. **Marriage as fundamental for equal protection analysis:** Kennedy concluded that marriage should be considered a "fundamental right" both for *equal protection purposes* and for substantive due process purposes. In earlier cases, the Court had found *opposite-sex marriage to be a "fundamental" right* (at least for substantive due process purposes). Kennedy concluded in *Obergefell* that the factors making marriage fundamental *apply equally to the same-sex marriage context.*

      ii. **No review standard mentioned:** Kennedy's opinion did not say *what standard of review* he was applying in his equal protection analysis. [358]

         (1) **More than "mere rationality":** It's pretty clear from the result in *Obergefell* that the standard Kennedy applied was *not* the typical easy-to-satisfy *"mere-rationality"* standard, used in reviewing run-of-the-mill economic and social-welfare legislation. (See *supra*, p. C-46.) But it's unclear whether he used *"strict scrutiny"* (like that used concerning classifications based on race or ethnicity), *"intermediate review"* (like the standard used for classifications based on gender), or what might be called *"mere-rationality with bite"* (as the Court seems to have used in some other gay-rights cases).

   c. **Dissents:** Each of the four Justices in the minority — Roberts, Scalia, Alito and Thomas — wrote a separate dissent. The dissents all sounded one major theme: that the decision on whether to allow same-sex marriages should be *left to the elected legislatures of each state*, not to nine unelected members of the Supreme Court. [356]

   d. **Significance of case:** Here are the most significant principles that *Obergefell* establishes:

i.   **Fundamental right for equal protection purposes:** Government distinctions treating same-sex couples less favorably with respect to access to marriage than opposite-sex couples will be deemed interferences with the fundamental right of marriage *under the Equal Protection Clause*. So government regulations that intentionally make it harder for same-sex couples to marry than for opposite-sex couples will be more rigorously reviewed by the courts (though as noted we don't yet know what precise standard of review will be used, just that something more rigorous than ordinary mere-rationality review will be employed). [360]

ii. **Federal, state and local governments:** The fundamental status of the right to same-sex marriage is binding on *all levels of government,* federal, state and local.

iii. **Right to a marriage license:** Since all states authorize marriages to take place between opposite-sex couples that meet certain requirements (e.g., age and residency), all states must similarly *authorize marriages between same-sex couples meeting those same requirements.*

iv. **Right to same consequences once married:** Post-*Obergefell*, no level of government may give same-sex married couples *significantly less favorable benefits* or other treatment as the result of being married than government gives to opposite-sex married couples. [360]

Example: When the wife in an opposite-sex marriage gives birth to a child conceived by anonymous sperm donation, state law says that the husband shall be listed on the child's birth certificate. But when one woman in a same-sex marriage gives birth to a child conceived by anonymous sperm donation, the state refuses to list that woman's wife as the other parent. *Held*, the state has violated *Obergefell*. The listing of both members of a married couple on the birth certificate to any child born during the marriage is one of those "benefits linked to marriage" that the state has chosen to confer on opposite-sex couples; therefore, it must give that same benefit to same-sex couples as it gives to opposite-sex couples. [*Pavan v. Smith* (2017)]. [361]

(1) **Divorce, adoption, taxation, etc:** It follows from *Obergefell* and *Pavan* that a state may not treat same-sex married couples less favorably than opposite-sex couples with respect to *divorce*, *child custody*, *adoption*, *state income and estate taxation*, or any other aspect of law that derives from a couple's status of being married.

Example: Suppose state X limits the class of people who can *adopt* any given child to (1) opposite-sex married couples and (2) one single individual. Pre-*Obergefell*, this rule would prevent both members of a same-sex married couple from adopting the same child. (Then, if the adopting parent died, the other would have no legal rights regarding the child.)

Post-*Obergefell*, not only must State X permit a same-sex couple to marry, but it must then permit the two spouses to adopt the same child if it would permit both members of an opposite-sex couple to adopt a given child. [361]

e.   **Open questions:** Here are a couple of the important questions left open by *Obergefell*:

i.   **Strict scrutiny of interferences with fundamental right to marriage?** As noted, we don't know what *standard of review* the Court will apply to regulations that substantially interfere with the newly-recognized fundamental right to marriage. This could turn out to be anything from strict scrutiny down to "mere rationality with bite." [361]

ii. **Suspect status of anti-gay laws outside of the marriage context:** Another category of questions left open by *Obergefell* concerns government's right to treat gays and lesbians less favorably than straight people *outside of the right-to-marry context.*

(1) **Not necessarily a suspect or semi-suspect class:** The majority gives no hint that homosexual orientation outside of the marriage context is to be treated as constituting a *"suspect class" or "semi-suspect class,"* the way the Court treats classifications based on race (a suspect class; see *supra*, p. C-48) or gender (a semi-suspect class; see *supra,* p. C-56).

(2) **Disfavoring of gays possibly allowable outside of marriage context:** If it turns out that unfavorable classifications based on sexual orientation outside of the marriage context are not deemed suspect or semi-suspect (and assuming no fundamental right is at issue), gays may get only the *relatively minimal protection conferred by mere-rationality review*, which usually doesn't lead to a striking down of the classification.

Example: It's not clear whether government rules on adoption, child custody and visitation, or other family-law issues may intentionally treat gay people less favorably, where the context does not involve marriage. [362]

iii. **Free speech rights of opponents to same-sex marriage:** A state's ability to protect same-sex married couples against *discrimination* by private businesses can conflict with the First Amendment *free-speech rights* of a business operator to oppose same-sex marriage. At least where a married same-sex couple requests goods or services that are to be *customized* by the supplier to meet the specific needs of the same-sex wedding ceremony, the supplier's free-speech right to avoid delivering a message with which she disagrees may be found to *override* the state's *Obergefell*-derived right to *prohibit discrimination* against same-sex couples. [363]

VII. FUNDAMENTAL RIGHTS

A. **Fundamental rights generally:** Now, let's look at the second way strict scrutiny can be triggered in equal protection cases: there will be strict scrutiny not only when a "suspect classification" is used, but also when a *"fundamental right"* is burdened by the classification the government has selected. Whenever a classification burdens a "fundamental right" or "fundamental interest," the classification will be subjected to strict scrutiny *even though the people who are burdened are not members of a suspect class*. [364]

1. **"Fundamental" defined:** "Fundamental" means something absolutely different in this Equal Protection context than it means in the Substantive Due Process context. Remember that in due process, the fundamental rights are ones related to privacy. Here, the fundamental rights are related to a variety of interests protected by the Constitution, some of which have nothing to do with privacy. [364]

2. **List:** The short list of rights that are "fundamental" for equal protection strict scrutiny purposes is as follows: (1) the right to *marry* (even for same-sex couples); (2) the right to *vote*; (3) maybe the right to be a *political candidate*; (4) the right to have access to the *courts* for certain kinds of proceedings; and (5) the right to *migrate interstate.* [346]

B. **Marriage as fundamental right:** The Court has recognized *marriage* as a fundamental right for equal protection (as well as substantive due process) purposes.

1. **Marriage by parent who is in default on child support:** For example, the Court has held that the right to marry is sufficiently fundamental that it is a violation of equal protection for a state to

deny a marriage license to a parent who is in default *on making court-ordered child-support pay-ments*. [*Zablocki v. Redhail*]

2. **Same-sex marriage:**   Similarly, the right to marry is sufficiently fundamental that states may not deny marriage licenses to *same-sex couples.* [*Obergefell v. Hodges* (2015), discussed further *supra*, p. C-59)]

C. **Adult sexual relations:**   The Court has not so far recognized any forms of *adult sexual relations* (at least outside of marriage) as being fundamental rights for equal protection purposes.

1. **Unusually-rigorous review:**   But recall that in *Lawrence v. Texas* (*supra,* p. C-39), the Court struck down a statute *criminalizing gay sodomy.* The *Lawrence Court's* use of *unusually-rigorous* mere-rationality review suggests that a majority of the Court may well come to view adult sexual expression — whether same-sex or different-sex — as effectively being of more-than-usual impor-tance (perhaps *"quasi-fundamental"*) for both substantive-due process and equal-protection pur-poses.

2. **Same-sex intimacy:**   Also, language in the majority opinion in the same-sex-marriage case of *Obergefell v. Hodges* (*supra*, p. C-59) suggests that *sexual intimacy* is part of the package of val-ues that makes *marriage* a fundamental right for both same-sex and opposite-sex couples. If the freedom to pursue intimacy is part of what makes *marriage* a fundamental right, perhaps the right to pursue adult sexual intimacy even *outside* of marriage will ultimately be classified as fundamen-tal too.

D. **Voting rights:**   For some purposes, the Court seems to treat the *right to vote* in state and federal elec-tions as being fundamental. But the case law on how extensively the states may regulate this right, without abridging any fundamental aspect of the right, is confusing.

1. **No explicit limits on states' power to regulate state and local elections:**   The Constitution does not place any *explicit limits* on the power of states to *control state and local elections.* So the states may exercise substantial control over the right to vote in such elections.

   a. **Reasonable age and citizenship requirements:** Thus the states may require that voters be of *reasonable age*, and that they be *citizens and residents* of the state. [368]

      i. **Federal elections:**   In fact, the Constitution indirectly gives the states the right to set voter qualifications not just for state elections but for *federal* ones. That's because the Constitution says that voters for House and Senate elections must have the same qualifica-tions as such voters need for voting in elections for their own state legislature, unless Con-gress provides otherwise. (But Congress has no such right of override of qualifications for *state* elections, so that state power there is exclusive.) [368]

2. **Voting as fundamental right:**   Yet, because voting is integrally related to protecting various con-stitutional rights, the Court has sometimes labeled the right to vote in state and local (as well as federal) elections as *"fundamental."*

   a. **Strict scrutiny:**   Consequently, the Supreme Court has — but only in some circumstances — subjected laws that impair some group's right to vote to *strict scrutiny.* [368-375]

3. **The "related to voter qualifications" issue:**   In deciding whether to use strict scrutiny, the Court seems to place great weight on whether the voting regulation is *reasonably related to determining voter qualifications.*

   a. **If not reasonably related to voter qualifications:** If the Court decides that the regulation is *not* reasonably related to determining voter qualifications, then the Court *uses strict scrutiny*, and will probably strike down the regulation.

b. If reasonably related to voter qualifications: If, on the other hand, the Court decides that the regulation *is* reasonably related to determining voter qualifications, then the Court generally does *not* use strict scrutiny. Instead, it uses some less stringent review method (typically, an intermediate-level *balancing test*), and is likely to *uphold* the measure.

4. **Not reasonably related to voter qualifications:** Here are various types of regulations that the Court has found to be *not reasonably related to determining voter qualifications*, and as to which it has therefore *applied strict scrutiny.* [369-371]

   a. Poll tax: *Poll taxes* are not reasonably related to determining voter qualifications. Therefore, a poll tax, no matter how minor, creates an inequality in the right to vote that must be strictly scrutinized, and struck down as an Equal Protection violation. [*Harper v. Virginia Bd. of Elections*]

   b. Ballot restricted to "interested voters": The requirement that voters *own property* or otherwise have some *"special interest"* is ordinarily not related to voter qualifications, and is thus usually given strict scrutiny. [*Kramer v. Union Free School District No. 15*]

      i. Exception for "special purpose" body: However, if the Court finds that the governmental unit for which elections are being held has a *limited purpose* which *disproportionately affects* only one group, the franchise may be limited to that group. Thus *"special purpose bodies"* may restrict the vote to persons who are directly affected by the body's activities.

      Example: Votes for a special-purpose *"water storage district"* can be limited to landowners, and can be on a "one acre, one vote" basis. [*Ball v. James*]

   c. Duration-of-residence requirements: A requirement that voters have *resided within the state* for *more than a certain time* prior to Election Day are strictly scrutinized, if the requirement goes beyond what's reasonably required to ensure that the voter really is a local resident.

      Example: A state limits the right to vote to people who have resided in the state for at least one year before the election. *Held*, the requirement will be strictly scrutinized and struck down. Such a duration-of-residence requirement violates both the voter's fundamental right to vote and his right to travel. [*Dunn v. Blumstein*]

      i. Fifty-day statutes: But *shorter* residency requirements (e.g., 50 days) have been *upheld*, on the theory that these are merely methods of ensuring that the person *really is a resident.*

5. **Reasonably related to voter qualifications:** If the Court finds that the regulation *is reasonably related to voter qualifications*, the Court reviews it by a *less-than-strict-scrutiny* standard (some form of *intermediate-level* review). [371-373]

   a. Voter identification requirements: For example, a state requirement that every voter *present a photo ID* has been *upheld* under this non-strict-scrutiny standard, as a means of protecting the "integrity and reliability of the electoral process." [*Crawford v. Marion County Election Board* (2008)]

   b. Denial of vote to felons: Many states deny the vote to *felons*, even ones who have served their sentence and finished any parole. Such disenfranchisement has been *upheld.* [*Richardson v. Ramirez*].

   c. Burden on right to vote by limiting voter's choices: Where state regulation of voting merely has the effect of *"burdening"* the right to vote, by *limiting the voter's choices*, the Court does *not* use strict scrutiny, and merely balances the degree of burden against the magnitude of the state's interest.

Example: A state may completely ban all ***write-in votes***. So long as the state gives candidates reasonable access to the ballot (thus preserving each voter's interest in having a reasonable choice of candidates), the state is not required to protect each voter's interest in being able to vote for any candidate of his choosing. [*Burdick v. Takushi*]

E. Ballot access: The right to be a ***political candidate***, and to have your name on the ballot, seems to be "quasi-fundamental." [375]

  1. Two invalid restrictions: The two kinds of ballot restrictions that the Supreme Court does seem to give strict or almost strict scrutiny to are:

    a. Unfair to new parties: Restrictions that are unfair to ***new, not-yet-established political parties***. (*Example:* A rule saying that a minor party can get its candidate on the ballot only if it presents signatures from 15% of the voters, holds a formal primary, and has an elaborate party structure, violates Equal Protection. [*Williams v. Rhodes*]) [376]

    b. Based on wealth: Ballot access limits that are based on ***wealth***. (*Example:* A $700 candidate filing fee, which the state refuses to waive for an indigent candidate, violates Equal Protection. [*Lubin v. Panish*])

  2. Candidate eligibility rules: But reasonable rules concerning the eligibility of the individual candidate, that don't fall into either of these two categories — unfair to new parties, or based on wealth — seem to be generally ***upheld*** by the Court. Thus a state may set a ***minimum age***, or may require that the candidate have ***resided for a certain period of time*** in the state or district where he is seeking office.

F. Court access: Access to the ***courts*** is sometimes a "fundamental right," so that if the right is burdened by a state-imposed classification, that classification will sometimes be closely scrutinized. Basically, what it comes down to is that if the state imposes a ***fee*** that the rich can pay but the poor cannot, and the access relates to a ***criminal*** case, strict scrutiny will be used. (*Example:* The state cannot charge an indigent for his trial transcript in a criminal case. [*Griffin v. Illinois*] Similarly, the state must provide him with free counsel on appeal.) [378-379]

  1. Civil litigation: When ***civil*** litigation is involved, access to the courts is usually ***not*** fundamental. Only for various family-law proceedings (e.g., ***divorce, paternity suits, termination of parental rights)*** is the state barred from charging fees. [*Boddie v. Connecticut*] [380]

G. Right to travel: The so-called ***"right to travel"*** is generally a "fundamental" right. This term "right to travel" is misleading — it's really the right to ***change one's state of residence or employment.*** So any time the state imposes a classification that burdens one's right to change her state of residence or employment, that classification will be strictly scrutinized. [381-383]

  1. Duration of residence: This mainly means that if the state imposes a substantial ***waiting period*** on newly-arrived residents, before they can receive some ***vital governmental benefit***, this will be strictly scrutinized.

    Example: Pennsylvania denies welfare benefits to any resident who has not resided in the state for at least a year. *Held*, this one-year waiting period impairs the "fundamental right of interstate movement" so it must be strictly scrutinized, and in fact invalidated. [*Shapiro v. Thompson*]. [381-382]

  2. Vital government benefit: But the key phrase here is ***"vital government benefit"*** — if the benefit is ***not*** vital, then the state may impose a substantial waiting period. (*Example:* A one-year waiting period before a student can qualify for low in-state tuition at the public university probably does not burden a fundamental right, and thus does not need to be strictly scrutinized.)

H. Necessities: The right to ***"necessities"*** is ***not*** fundamental. So if the state distributes necessities in a way that treats different people differently (or if it distributes the money to be used to buy these things differentially), there will be no strict scrutiny because there is no fundamental right. [384]

1. **Education:** For instance, one does not have a fundamental right to a ***public school education***. Therefore, the state may allow or even foster inequalities in the distribution of that public school education, without violating any fundamental right, and thus without having to pass strict scrutiny. [*San Antonio School Dist. v. Rodriguez*] [365-367]

    Example: The Ps claim that Texas' system of financing public education violates equal protection, because districts with a high property tax base per pupil consistently spend more on education than those with a low base are able to do.

    Held, education is not a fundamental right. Therefore, Texas' scheme merely has to undergo "rational relation" review. Because the use of property taxes to finance education is a rational way of achieving the legitimate state goal of giving each local school district a large measure of control over the education its residents get, this "mere-rationality" standard is satisfied. *San Antonio School Dist. v. Rodriguez, supra.*

    a. **Complete deprivation:** Actually, it's still possible that a ***complete deprivation*** of public education might be held to be a violation of a "fundamental" right. If a state simply refused to give any public education *at all* to some groups of residents, this might be such a large deprivation that it would amount to a violation of a fundamental right, and thus be subject to strict scrutiny. [366]

2. **Food, shelter, or medical care:** There is no fundamental right to the material ***"necessities of life."*** Thus ***food***, ***shelter***, and ***medical care*** are not "fundamental" for equal protection purposes. Therefore, the state may distribute these things unevenly. Similarly, the state may give some people but not others money for these things without having to survive strict scrutiny. (*Example:* The state can give a smaller per capita welfare payment to big families than small families, without having the scheme subjected to strict scrutiny. This is because the food and shelter for which the payments are used are not "fundamental rights." [*Dandridge v. Williams*]) [384]

CHAPTER 11
MISCELLANEOUS CLAUSES

I. FOURTEENTH AMENDMENT PRIVILEGES OR IMMUNITIES

A. **Privileges or Immunities Clause Generally:** The Fourteenth Amendment has its own "Privileges or Immunities" Clause: "No state shall make or enforce any law which shall abridge the privileges or immunities of citizens of the United States." [398]

1. **National rights only:** But this clause is very narrowly interpreted: it only protects the individual from state interference with his rights of ***"national"*** citizenship. The most important of these rights of "national" citizenship are: (1) the right to ***travel from state to state*** (which as we saw is also protected by the Equal Protection Clause); and (2) the right to ***vote in national elections***.

2. **Right to change state of residence:** The clause is most relevant where a state treats ***newly-arrived residents less favorably*** than those who have resided in-state for a longer time: this violates the "right to travel," protected by the clause. (*Example:* If a state gives newly-arrived residents lower welfare payments than ones who have been residents longer, this is a violation of the "right to travel" protected by the 14th Amendment P&I clause. [*Saenz v. Roe*]) [399]

3. **Strict scrutiny:** The Court gives ***strict scrutiny*** to state laws that interfere with the rights of national citizenship. [*Saenz v. Roe*]

II. THE "TAKING" CLAUSE

A. The "Taking" Clause Generally: The Fifth Amendment contains the "Taking" Clause: "*[N]or shall private property be taken for public use, without just compensation.*"

1. **General meaning:** The gist of the Taking Clause is that the government may take private property under its "power of eminent domain," but if it does take private property, it must *pay a fair price*. This is true even if the property is taken to serve a compelling governmental interest. [400]

2. **Taking vs. regulation:** The government (whether it's federal or state) must pay for any property that it "takes." On the other hand, if it merely *"regulates"* property under its police power, then it does not need to pay (even if the owner's use of his property, or its value, is substantially diminished). [400-411]

   a. **Land use regulations:** Usually the problem of distinguishing between a compensable "taking" and a non-compensable "regulation" occurs in the context of *land-use regulation*.

   b. **Guidelines:** Here are some guidelines about when a land-use regulation will avoid being a taking:

      i. **No denial of economically viable use:** A land-use regulation must not "deny an owner *economically viable use* of his land," or it will be considered a taking. However, few land use regulations are likely to be found to deny the owner all economically viable use of his land. For instance, if a particular 3-story building is made a landmark, the fact that the owner can't tear down the building to build a skyscraper doesn't deprive him of "all economically viable use." But if the state were to *permanently* deny the owner the right to *build any dwelling* on the land, this *would* probably constitute a denial of all economically viable use. [402]

      Example: The state of South Carolina, in order to protect against coastal erosion, prohibits landowners from building any permanent habitable structure at all on certain parcels. P owns 2 vacant parcels (for which he paid $1 million), on which the building ban applies. *Held*, by the Supreme Court, if this regulation indeed prevents P from making any "economically viable use" of the parcels (something for the state court to decide on remand), there has been a "taking" for which the state must pay compensation, even if the state was just trying to protect the health and safety of its citizens. [*Lucas v. South Carolina Coastal Council*] [402]

      Note 1: Most zoning, environmental laws and landmark-preservation laws will satisfy this don't-deny-all-economically-viable-uses rule, and will thus *not* be takings, merely non-compensable regulations.

      Note 2: If a land-use law merely *temporarily* prevents all economically viable use of a parcel, this will not necessarily constitute a taking — *all surrounding circumstances* must be considered to determine whether the interference with use is significant enough to constitute a taking. For instance, a 2- or 3-year *moratorium on development* of a particular parcel, until a permanent land-use scheme can be enacted by government, might not constitute a taking even though for that period an affected owner can't make any economically viable use of her parcel. [*Tahoe-Sierra Preservation Council v. Tahoe Regional Planning Agency*] [402-403]

      ii. **Diminution in value:** The more drastic the *reduction in value* of the owner's property, the more likely a taking is to be found. But a very drastic diminution in value (almost certainly much more than 50%) is required. [401]

iii. **Landmark:** *Landmark preservation schemes*, just like zoning and environmental regulations, will rarely be found to constitute a taking. This is especially true where the designation of a particular building to landmark status occurs as part of a *comprehensive* citywide preservation scheme.

   Example: New York City designates Grand Central Station as a landmark, as part of a citywide preservation system. *Held*, the City didn't carry out a taking when it imposed this designation. That's true even though the designation prevented the owner from constructing a 55-story office building above the Terminal. [*Penn Central v. New York City*]) [404]

3. **Physical occupation:** Where government makes a *physical occupation* of private property, that occupation is treated as an automatic "*per se*" taking, for which the government must pay compensation *no matter how minor* the occupation's *economic impact* on the landowner.

   a. **Where occupation is permanent and continuous:** This rule that a physical occupation amounts to a *per se* compensable taking has long been clear in those situations in which the occupation is essentially a *permanent and continuous* one.

   b. **Temporary occupation:** But since 2021, this same principle — that a physical occupation commanded by government *automatically* amounts to a compensable taking — normally applies even where the occupation is a *temporary* and/or *intermittent one*. [*Cedar Point Nursery v. Hassid* (2021)] [406-407]

   Example: A California labor regulation requires agricultural employers to allow labor unions to come onto the work site and meet with workers there for up to 120 days per year. On each of those days, the employer must allow access for an hour before work, an hour after work, and an hour during the lunch break. P, an agricultural employer, claims that the regulation imposes a taking on it, for which the Takings Clause requires compensation.

   Held (by a 6-3 vote), for P. The regulation imposes on P a compulsory "physical appropriation" that constitutes a *per se* taking of P's property, no matter how small an economic harm the appropriation causes to the value of the land. And a physical appropriation constitutes a *per se* taking even where (as here) the appropriation is *intermittent* rather than permanent. [*Cedar Point Nursery v. Hassid, supra.*] [406-407]

4. **Requirement of "public" use:** The Taking Clause says that private property shall not be taken *"for public use"* unless just compensation is paid. This language has been interpreted by the Supreme Court as prohibiting the taking of private property for *private use, even if just compensation is made.* Thus the government cannot simply take private property from one person, and give it to another, without any public purpose.

   a. **"Public use" construed broadly:** However, the Supreme Court has construed the requirement of a "public use" quite *broadly*. Here are two principles illustrating just how broadly the Court stretches the phrase:

   ❑ So long as the state's use of its eminent domain power is "*rationally related* to a *conceivable public purpose*," the public use requirement is satisfied. *Hawaii Housing Authority v. Midkiff.* [411]

   ❑ The property *need not be open to the general public after the taking*. Therefore, the fact that the property is *turned over to some private user* does not prevent the use from being a public one as long as the public can be expected to derive some benefit (e.g., economic development) from the use. [411]

   Example: The City of New London, as part of an economic-development plan for the City's waterfront area, condemns 15 houses owned by the Ps. The properties are not blighted. The plan contemplates turning the properties over to private developers. The Ps claim that this is not a "public use," and thus violates their rights under the Fifth Amendment even if "just compensation" is paid.

Held, for the City. Even though the properties are being turned over to private developers (not made available to the public), and even though the properties were not blighted, this is still a "public use" as the term is used in the Fifth Amendment. [*Kelo v. New London*] [412]

III. THE "CONTRACT" CLAUSE

A. The "Contract" Clause: The so-called "Contract" Clause (Art. I, §10) provides that "no state shall … pass any … law impairing the obligation of contracts." The clause effectively applies to both federal and state governments. The Clause has a different meaning depending on whether the government is impairing its own contracts or contracts between private parties. [413]

    1. Public contracts: If the state is trying to escape from its ***own financial obligations***, then the Court will ***closely scrutinize*** this attempt. Here, the state attempt to "weasel" will be struck down unless the modification is "***reasonable*** and ***necessary*** to support an ***important*** public purpose" (basically ***middle-level review***). [413]

    2. Private contracts: But when the state is re-writing contracts made by ***private parties***, the judicial review is not so stringent. Here, even a ***substantial*** modification to contracts between private parties will be allowed so long as the state is acting "***reasonably***" in pursuit of a "legitimate public purpose." So we apply what is basically "mere-rationality" review in this situation. (*Example:* If a state's economy is in shambles with widespread home mortgage foreclosures, the state probably may temporarily order a lower interest rate on home mortgages, or impose a moratorium on mortgage repayments, without violating the Contract Clause.) [414-416]

        a. Incidental effect on contracts: Even this "mere-rationality" standard applies only where the state takes an action that is ***specifically directed*** at contractual obligations. If the state applies a "***generally applicable rule of conduct***" that has the ***incidental by-product*** of impairing contractual obligations, the Contract Clause ***does not apply at all***. [417]

        Example: Suppose Manco, a manufacturing company located outside the state of Texahoma, contracts with Disposal Corp., which operates a toxic waste disposal facility within Texahoma. The contract runs through the year 2100, and allows Manco to deliver up to 1,000 tons of toxic waste per year to the dump. The Texahoma legislature then enacts a statute that, effective immediately, prohibits anyone from disposing of any additional toxic wastes within the state. Even though this enactment has an effect on the Manco-Disposal contract, it does not trigger Contract Clause review at all, because the statute affects contracts as an incidental by-product, rather than being specifically directed at contractual obligations.

IV. THE SECOND AMENDMENT "RIGHT TO BEAR ARMS"

A. Text of the Amendment: The Second Amendment provides: "A well regulated Militia, being necessary to the security of a free State, the right of the people to ***keep and bear Arms***, shall ***not be infringed***." [417]

B. Applicable to private individuals: The ***Amendment*** confers on ***private individuals*** a right to keep basic firearms, including handguns, ***at home for self-defense***. [*District of Columbia v. Heller* (2008)] [417]

    Example: Washington D.C. makes it a crime to keep any type of handgun at home. It also makes it a crime to keep a non-gun (e.g., a rifle) at home unless the weapon is kept unloaded and inoperable (e.g., by a trigger lock). *Held*, both provisions violate the Second Amendment right of private individuals to keep at home operable firearms of the type that were kept by private citizens for self-defense in 1791. [*Heller, supra.*] [417-421]

1. **Applies to states and cities:** The Second Amendment *applies the same way to state and local governments* as to the federal government. [*McDonald v. City of Chicago*] [421]

    a. **Selectively incorporated:** This result is due to the Supreme Court's conclusion in *McDonald* that the Second Amendment should be deemed to be *selectively incorporated* into the 14th Amendment's *Due Process Clause*, and thereby made applicable to the states. (The Court believed that the right to bear arms in self-defense is *"fundamental to our scheme of ordered liberty,"* the test for whether any Bill of Rights guarantee should be deemed incorporated into the 14th Amendment guarantee of due process and thus made applicable to the states.) [421]

2. **Review standard to be used:** It's unclear what *standard* the court will use for reviewing governmental restrictions that impair Second Amendment rights (*Heller* and *McDonald* didn't decide this). The most likely outcome is that *mid-level review*, under which the question is whether the means chosen by government is *"substantially related"* to the achievement of an *"important"* governmental interest, will ultimately be used. [422]

3. **Some regulation allowed:** It seems likely that despite the broad reading of the Second Amendment in *Heller* and *McDonald* , all governments will be allowed to exercise *substantial regulation of gun possession.* So, for example:

    a. **Licensing requirements:** *Licensing requirements* will probably *not* be found to violate the Second Amendment as long as the procedures for obtaining a license are not unreasonably burdensome, and are directed towards keeping guns out of the hands of people who do not have a Second Amendment right to possess them. [422]

        Example: Licensing requirements that deny gun permits to felons and the mentally ill — and that give government a reasonable amount of time to check whether the applicant falls into these categories — are probably valid even after *Heller* and *McDonald*.

    b. **Concealed-carry permits:** Similarly, the Amendment will probably be found not to prohibit governments from banning the *carrying of concealed weapons in public places.* [422]

    c. **Modern weapons:** Probably the Amendment won't be found to block governments from banning the possession of *modern weapons* that are much more *advanced and dangerous* than those existing in 1791. So *machine guns, assault rifles* and *sawed-off shotguns* probably may still be banned. [422]

V. *EX POST FACTO* LAWS

A. **Constitutional prohibition:** Article I prohibits both state and federal governments from passing any "ex post facto" law. An *ex post facto* law is a law which has a *retroactive punitive effect*. So government may not *impose a punishment* for conduct which, at the time it occurred, was *not punishable*. Also, government may not *increase* the punishment for an offense over what was on the books at the time of the act. [423]

> **Example:** On June 1, Joe smokes a cigarette in a public building. On June 10, the state legislature makes it a crime, for the first time, to smoke in a public building. Because of the ban on *ex post facto* laws, Joe cannot be convicted of the June 1 smoking, since it was not a crime at the time he did it. The same would be true if the legislature on June 15 increased the penalty for such smoking over what it was on June 1.

1. **Criminal only:** The ban on *ex post facto* laws applies only to measures that are *"criminal"* or *"penal,"* not to those that are civil. Basically, this means that only measures calling for *imprisonment* will come within the *ex post facto* ban (so a measure that imposes, say, *disbarment*, or one that imposes *deportation*, can be made retroactive, since these sanctions are civil). See, e.g., *Galvan v. Press*.

VI. BILLS OF ATTAINDER

A. **Generally:** Art. I prohibits both the federal government and the states from passing any *"bill of attainder."* A bill of attainder is a legislative act which "applies either to named individuals or to easily ascertainable members of a group in such a way as to *punish* them without a *judicial trial*." (*Example:* Congress prohibits the payment of salaries to three named federal agency employees, on the grounds that they are engaged in subversive activities. This is an invalid bill of attainder, since it applies to named or easily-identified individuals, and punishes them without a judicial trial. [*U.S. v. Lovett*]) [424]

CHAPTERS 12 AND 13

THE "STATE ACTION" REQUIREMENT; CONGRESSIONAL ENFORCEMENT OF CIVIL RIGHTS

I. STATE ACTION

A. **State action generally:** Virtually all of the rights and liberties guaranteed by the Constitution to individuals are protected only against interference by the government. We summarize this rule by referring to the requirement of *"state action."* But sometimes, even a *private individual's act* will be found to be "state action" that must comply with the Constitution. There are two main doctrines that may lead a private act to be classified as state action; if *either* of these doctrines applies, then the private action is "state action" even if the other doctrine would not apply. The two doctrines are the *"public function"* doctrine and the *"state involvement"* doctrine. [431-434]

B. **"Public function" doctrine:** Under the *"public function"* approach to state action, if a private individual (or group) is entrusted by the state to perform functions that are *governmental in nature*, the private individual becomes an *agent of the state*, and his acts constitute state action. [435-438]

1. **Carrying out of primary elections:** The *electoral process* is a "public function," and is thus state action. Therefore, the carrying out of *primary elections* is state action, even if the acts are directly carried out by "private" political parties.

   Example: A state convention of Democrats (in essence, a "private" political party) rules that only whites may vote in the Texas Democratic Primary. *Held*, this racial restriction is "state action," and therefore violates the 15th Amendment. The primary is an integral part of the election scheme, and the running of elections is traditionally a "public function," so the running of the primary is state action even though it is directly carried out by private groups. [*Smith v. Allwright*]) [435]

2. **Company town:** Similarly, operation of a *"company town"* is a "public function," and thus is state action, because towns have traditionally been operated by the government. [435-436]

   a. **Shopping centers not a public function:** But operation of a *shopping center* is *not* the equivalent of operating a company town, so a person does not have any First Amendment rights in the shopping center. [*Hudgens v. NLRB*] [436]

3. **Parks:** Operation of a *park* has traditionally been a governmental function, so generally the operation of a park will constitute "state action" under the "public function" doctrine. Therefore, even

if the park is being operated by private persons, it must still obey constitutional constraints (e.g., it can't be operated for whites only). [*Evans v. Newton*]. [437]

4. **The "exclusively public" requirement:** For the public-function doctrine to apply, it's **not enough** that the function is one that, historically, has **"usually"** been performed by government. Rather, the function must be one that has traditionally been **"exclusively"** a public function. [*Manhattan Community Access Corp. v. Halleck*] [437-438]

C. **"State involvement" doctrine:** Even if the private individual is not doing something that's traditionally a "public function," his conduct may constitute state action if the state is **heavily involved** in his activities. This is the **"state involvement"** branch of state-action doctrine. Here are some of the ways in which the state and private actor can be so closely involved that the private person's acts become state action: [438]

1. **Commandment:** The state may become responsible for the private party's actions because it **commanded**, i.e., required, the private party to act in that way. (*Example:* The state enforces a private agreement among neighbors that none will sell his house to a black. Because the state has lent its state judicial enforcement mechanism to this otherwise private contract, the combination of enforcement and private discrimination violates equal protection. [*Shelley v. Kraemer*] [439-441]

2. **Encouragement:** If the state **"encourages"** the private party's actions, then the private action will be converted into state action. (*Example:* The voters of California amend their constitution to prohibit the state government from interfering with any private individual's right to discriminate when he sells or leases residential real estate. This amendment immediately results in the repeal of two state Fair Housing statutes. *Held,* this state-constitutional amendment amounts to governmental "encouragement" of private discrimination. Therefore, the resulting private discrimination will be imputed to the state, and the state constitutional provision violates the 14th Amendment. [*Reitman v. Mulkey*]) [441]

3. **Symbiosis:** There is state action if there exists between the state and private actor a **"symbiotic"** relationship, i.e., a relation between the two that is **mutually beneficial**.

   Example: A Wilmington, Delaware city agency owns and runs a parking garage complex. The agency gives a 20 year lease to a privately-operated restaurant located in the complex. The restaurant refuses to serve African Americans. *Held,* African Americans who are refused service have had their equal protection rights violated. The relation between the restaurant and the publicly-run garage was so close and symbiotic — the garage wouldn't have been able to operate viably without rents from the restaurant — that the restaurant's actions must be imputed to the state, and therefore constitute state action. [*Burton v. Wilmington Parking Authority*] [442-442]

4. **Entanglement or entwinement:** State action may arise from the fact that the state is so **"entangled"** or **"entwined"** with a private actor that even though the state might not directly benefit from the private actor's conduct, the conduct will still be treated as state action. This is true where the state and the private party **act together** to carry out the action being challenged. [443-445]

   Example: A state allows a private litigant — either a civil litigant or a defendant in a criminal case — to use peremptory challenges to exclude jurors on racial grounds. This conduct constitutes state action, and therefore violates the Equal Protection Clause. [*Edmondson v. Leesville Concrete Co.*; *Georgia v. McCollum*] [444]

   a. **Mere acquiescence not enough:** But if the state merely **acquiesces** in the private party's discrimination, this won't be enough of a state involvement to convert the private actor's conduct into state action. [445]

Example: The state regulates all utilities. A private utility cuts off plaintiff's service without notice or a hearing, and this fact is known to the state, which does not object. *Held*, the utility's conduct was not state action, because the state merely acquiesced in that conduct, rather than actively participating in it. [*Jackson v. Metropolitan Edison Co.*]

b. Licensing: Similarly, the fact that the state has *licensed* a private person is generally not enough to convert the private person's conduct into state action. [443-443]

Example: A private club refuses to serve African Americans. Even though the state has given the club one of a limited number of liquor licenses, this act of licensing is not enough to turn the club's action into state action. [*Moose Lodge v. Irvis*]

II. CONGRESSIONAL ENFORCEMENT OF CIVIL RIGHTS

A. Congressional enforcement of civil rights: Congress has special powers to enforce the post-Civil War amendments, i.e., the Thirteenth, Fourteenth, and Fifteenth Amendments. [451-453]

  1. 13th Amendment: The Thirteenth Amendment *abolishes "slavery"* and *"involuntary servitude."*

  2. 14th Amendment: The Fourteenth Amendment requires the states to give *"due process," "equal protection,"* and *"privileges and immunities."*

  3. 15th Amendment: The Fifteenth Amendment bars the states from denying *voting rights* on the basis of race, color or previous condition of servitude.

B. Congress' power to reach private conduct: The special enforcement powers let Congress reach a lot of *private conduct* that it could not reach by means of any other congressional power. [453-458]

  1. 14th and 15th Amendments: When Congress enforces the Fourteenth and Fifteenth Amendments, it has some, but not unlimited, power to reach private conduct. So Congress could, for instance, make it a crime for somebody to *interfere with a state official* who is trying to guarantee another person's equal protection rights or voting rights. (*Example:* Congress can make it a crime for D to prevent a school principal from allowing African Americans to enroll in an all white school.) [453-456]

   a. Can't reach purely private discrimination: But Congress under the Fourteenth Amendment *cannot* simply make it a crime for one private person to practice ordinary racial discrimination against another. [453] (Congress would instead have to use its power to regulate interstate commerce; this is the basis on which the 1964 Civil Rights Act, forbidding racial discrimination in places of public accommodation, was upheld. [*Katzenbach v. McClung*])

  2. 13th Amendment: But the *13th* Amendment is different. §1 of the 13th Amendment provides that "neither slavery nor involuntary servitude, except as a punishment for crime … shall exist within the United States." §2 gives Congress the power to "enforce this [amendment] by appropriate legislation." The 13th Amendment, unlike the 14th and 15th, is *not explicitly limited to governmental action.* Indeed, that's the most important thing to remember about the 13th Amendment, and its principal use today — it's practically the only clause in the entire Constitution that prevents one private citizen from doing something to another. So the 13th Amendment gives Congress important authority to reach certain private conduct that it couldn't reach through the 14th and 15th Amendments. [456-458]

   a. "Badges of slavery": If the 13th Amendment only meant that Congress could take special action to ensure that slavery itself, in its most literal sense, shall be wiped out, the Amendment wouldn't be of much practical use today. But instead, the Supreme Court has held that the Amendment allows Congress also to stamp out the *"badges and incidents"* of slavery. In fact,

Congress has the power to determine what the "badges and incidents of slavery" are, so long as it acts rationally — once Congress defines these "badges and incidents," it can then forbid them. [456-458]

> **Example:** In 1866, Congress passes a statute, 42 U.S.C. §1982, which provides that "all citizens of the United States shall have the same right, in every state and Territory, as is enjoyed by white citizens thereof to inherit, purchase, lease, sell, hold and convey real and personal property." In a modern case, the Ps argue that the statute prevents D (a private developer) from refusing to sell them a house solely because they are African American.
>
> *Held*, this statute applies to block discrimination by D, a private citizen. Furthermore, the statute is constitutional under the 13th Amendment. §2 of the 13th Amendment, which gives Congress enforcement powers under that amendment, gives Congress the power to make a rational determination of *what the badges and incidents of slavery are*. Here, Congress could have rationally concluded that barriers to enjoyment of real estate, and discrimination in housing, are relics of slavery. [*Jones v. Alfred H. Mayer Co.*] [456-458]

    b. Ancestry, ethnic discrimination: As we've just seen, the 13th Amendment clearly lets Congress prevent private discrimination against African Americans, on the grounds that it's a "badge or incident" of slavery. *All other racial minorities are also protected* — Congress could probably even bar private racial discrimination against *whites* based on the 13th Amendment (though the Court has never explicitly decided this). But it's not clear whether private discrimination based on *non-racial grounds* (e.g., *ancestry*, *ethnic background*, religion, sex, etc.) can be barred by Congress acting pursuant to the 13th Amendment. [457]

    c. Must have statute: The application of the 13th Amendment to a broad range of "badges and incidents of slavery" applies only where Congress has used its *enforcement* powers by passing a *statute* that relies on the Amendment. If private citizen *A* discriminates against *B* on the basis of race, but the type of discrimination is not one that Congress has outlawed, then the 13th Amendment's "naked" or "self-executing" scope *won't* be enough to reach that discrimination. Probably actual *peonage* — the keeping of a person as a slave — is the only type of private racial discrimination that is directly barred by the 13th Amendment in the absence of a congressional statute. [457]

C. Congress' remedial powers: The Thirteenth, Fourteenth and Fifteenth Amendments all have specific provisions giving Congress the power to *"enforce"* that amendment. See, e.g., §5 of the Fourteenth Amendment, giving Congress the power to enforce the amendment *"by appropriate legislation."*

    1. Remedial powers: Under this enforcement power, Congress may *prohibit* certain actions that *don't directly violate* these amendments, if it reasonably believes that these actions would or might *lead* to violations of the amendments. That is, Congress has *broad "remedial" or "prophylactic" powers.* [464]

    Example: Congress may use its 15th Amendment remedial powers to forbid, in the Voting Rights Act (further discussed below), any voter literacy test or character test in states with a history of voting rights violations. That's true even though such tests aren't themselves necessarily unconstitutional — Congress' 15th Amendment remedial powers are triggered by Congress's reasonable fears that such tests *may lead* to violations of the 15th Amendment. [*South Carolina v. Katzenbach*]

    2. Reference to "Necessary and Proper" clause: Congress' power to enforce the Civil War Amendments is to be judged generally by reference to the *"Necessary and Proper"* clause (*supra*, p. C-5). That is, as long as the *means* chosen by Congress are *"rationally related"* to achieving an objective that one of these Amendments is designed to fulfill, Congress has not exceeded its enforcement authority. (But as we'll see below, there is one important limitation on this principle, the special "congruent and proportional" standard for judging Congress's exercise of its Fourteenth Amendment enforcement powers; see *City of Boerne v. Flores, infra*, p. C-75.)

    a. Easy "rationally related" review standard: This easy-to-satisfy "rationally related" standard means that if Congress reasonably fears that the *effect* of a state law will include interferences with a right guaranteed by one of these three Amendments, Congress can prohibit the state law from being enforced. That's true even if it's clear that the members of the state legislature did not, when they enacted the law, have a *purpose* of promoting violations of any of the Amendments. [459]

    3. Obligation to rely on current data (*Shelby County v. Holder*): Cases like *South Carolina v. Katzenbach, supra*, giving a broad reading to Congress' remedial powers under the Fifteenth Amendment, were decided when massive official racial discrimination against minority voters in many southern states — and Congress' response — were both relatively *recent* phenomena. But recent decades have seen large reductions in such overt racial discrimination in voting. So the question arises, may Congress continue to single out for more-burdensome federal regulation of voting practices certain states based solely on these states' 1960s and 1970s histories of official racial discrimination in voting?

    The answer is *"no."* If in the present era Congress wants to use its Fifteenth Amendment enforcement powers to prevent future violations of the Amendment — rather than punish past violations — Congress must *adjust the measures it uses* to reflect *current rather than historical voting circumstances*. [*Shelby County v. Holder* (2013)] [461-464]

III. CONGRESS' POWER TO REDEFINE THE MEANING AND SCOPE OF CONSTITUTIONAL GUARANTEES

A. Congressional power to redefine the scope of constitutional rights: Congress does *not* have the power to *redefine the scope* of the rights protected by the Civil War amendments in a way that is different from the way the Supreme Court would define their scope. [464]

    1. No power to redefine scope: This is true whether Congress is trying to *expand* or *contract* the right.

        Example: The Supreme Court issues a decision defining the First Amendment Establishment Clause more narrowly than the Court had previously defined that clause. Congress doesn't like this decision. It therefore passes the "Religious Freedom Restoration Act," which in effect says that all state and local governments must refrain from any action that would have violated the Establishment Clause under the earlier, now-overruled, cases. *Held*, Congress has no power to either expand or contract the scope of constitutional rights, so the Act is an unconstitutional exercise of congressional power. [*Boerne v. Flores*] [464-466]

IV. CONGRESS' POWER TO ABROGATE THE ELEVENTH AMENDMENT AND THUS AUTHORIZE DAMAGE SUITS AGAINST THE STATES FOR DISCRIMINATION

A. Private money-damage suits against states for discrimination: Congress often prohibits a certain type of discrimination, and then attempts to make *state and local governments*, not just private individuals, obey the prohibition. Sometimes, Congress goes even further, and attempts to *give private individuals the right to bring private actions* for *money damages* against a *state or local government* that commits the prohibited discrimination.

1. **Significance of Eleventh Amendment:** But because of the existence of the ***Eleventh Amendment***, it will often turn out that Congress ***has overstepped its boundaries*** by such an attempt to let private individuals sue state and local governments for discrimination.

2. **The Eleventh Amendment:** The Eleventh Amendment says, in brief, that the ***states are immune*** from being sued for ***money damages by private citizens in federal court***. We discuss the Amendment in much greater detail below (see p. C-125).

    a. **Abrogation of amendment:** It's always been clear, however, that Congress has in some circumstances the power to ***abrogate*** the states' Eleventh Amendment immunity from private suits. But the Court's view of how and when Congress can do so has changed over the years.

    b. **Use of Commerce powers:** Originally, nearly everyone thought that Congress could use its extremely broad ***Commerce Clause*** powers to abrogate the states' Eleventh Amendment immunity. That is, it was thought that Congress could ***ban a particular type of discrimination*** by use of its Commerce powers, and under those same powers (i) require the states to comply with the ban, and (ii) ***strip their Eleventh Amendment immunity*** so that private citizens could sue the state for violation of the federal ban.

        i. **Use of Commerce powers disallowed:** But in *Seminole Tribe of Florida v. Florida* (discussed in more detail *infra*, p. C-126), the Court held that the Commerce powers ***cannot*** serve as the basis for a congressional abrogation of the Eleventh Amendment, and thus as the basis for letting private individuals sue a state for damages for violating a federal ban on some sort of discrimination.

        ii. **Use of Civil-War-Amendment powers:** On the other hand, it's always been clear that Congress ***may*** rely on its ***Civil-War-Amendment remedial powers*** as the source of authority for a general anti-discrimination statute. And under those powers (unlike the Commerce power), Congress can not only ban discrimination that would violate the Civil War amendments, but can subject state governments to the ban, and ***abrogate the states' Eleventh Amendment immunity***, so as to let private victims sue a discriminating state for damages.

            (1) **Restrictions:** But as we'll discuss immediately below (in Par. (B)), the Court has placed a special "congruent and proportional" restriction on Congress' powers to enforce the Civil War amendments. This restriction, when coupled with the above-described ban on Congress' use of its Commerce powers to abrogate states' Eleventh Amendment immunity, significantly limits Congress' ability to let private citizens sue state governments for discrimination.

B. **"Congruent and proportional":** When Congress purports to use its enforcement powers to prohibit acts that it fears might lead to constitutional violations, Congress' action must be ***"congruent and proportional"*** to the threatened violation. If not, the congressional action is ***invalid*** under the enforcement powers. [*Boerne v. Flores*] [466-466]

1. **Significance:** The most important consequence of this principle is that if Congress wants to let private individuals ***sue the states*** in federal district court for money ***damages*** for state violations of a federal anti-discrimination statute, two conditions must be satisfied:

    [1] Congress must ordinarily have before it evidence of ***widespread past constitutional violations by the states*** of the sort that Congress is trying to prevent; and

    [2] the ***remedy*** picked by Congress must be ***"congruent and proportional"*** to the state violations that Congress is trying to prevent.

    Otherwise, Congress' action cannot be justified by its Civil-War-Amendments enforcement powers. And only those powers (not, say, the Commerce power) are sufficient to let Congress overcome states' ***Eleventh Amendment immunity from private federal-court damage suits.*** [466-468]

> **Example:** In the Age Discrimination in Employment Act (ADEA) Congress makes the states, when they act as employers, obey the same age-discrimination rules as private employers. And Congress authorizes state employees to sue the states in federal court for money damages for ADEA violations committed by the state. Congress says it has acted under authority of its 14th Amendment §5 remedial powers, to prevent violations by the states of older state employees' equal protection rights.
>
> *Held*, Congress went beyond the scope of its §5 remedial powers, because there was no evidence that the states routinely violated older workers' equal protection rights. Therefore, Congress' regulation was not a "congruent and proportional" response to any threatened constitutional violations, making the regulation not authorized under Congress' §5 remedial powers. Consequently, the states are free to assert their Eleventh Amendment immunity from private damage suits (which immunity can properly be overcome only by Congress' use of its §5 remedial powers, not by its use of other powers like the Commerce power). [*Kimel v. Fla. Bd. of Regents*] [468-469]

a. **Area receiving heightened scrutiny:** But if the federal statute that creates the right of the plaintiff to sue a state for damages deals with an area that involves ***either a suspect or semi-suspect class or a fundamental right, Congress has more freedom.*** Since the Court applies some form of ***heightened scrutiny*** to these areas, the Court will be much more likely to find that Congress' decision to allow a damages suit ***meets the "congruent and proportional" requirement*** and is thus constitutional. [470-470]

> **Example:** Title II of the Americans with Disabilities Act (ADA) requires states (as well as private citizens) to accommodate disabled persons' access to certain public facilities, including courthouses. The Ps are paraplegics who seek damages from the state of Tennessee because they do not have adequate access to court services. (One P, for instance, has been required to crawl up stairs to answer criminal charges, because the county courthouse has no elevator.)
>
> *Held*, for the Ps. Congress has power to allow damages for violations of ADA Title II, at least in the court-access area. The right of access to courts is subject to ***"more searching judicial review"*** than the rational-relation review used in ADA Title I disability-discrimination-in-*employment* cases (as to which the Court has held that Congress does *not* have power to subject the states to money-damage awards, because of lack of evidence that the states as employers have systematically discriminated against disabled employees). [*Tennessee v. Lane*]

b. **Right to prohibit direct constitutional violations:** Also, if the state conduct that the plaintiff is complaining of was an ***actual violation*** by the state of the plaintiff's ***constitutional rights,*** Congress can grant the plaintiff the right to recover damages against the state in federal court without worrying about whether the federal statute is congruent-and-proportional to the overall pattern of constitutional violations that Congress was trying to prevent. [*U.S. v. Georgia*] [471]

CHAPTER 14

FREEDOM OF EXPRESSION

I. GENERAL THEMES

A. **Text of First Amendment:** The First Amendment provides, in part, that "Congress shall make no law ... abridging the ***freedom of speech***, or of the press; or the right of the people peaceably to assemble, and to petition the Government for a redress of grievances." [477]

1. **Related rights:** There are thus several distinct rights which may be grouped under the category "freedom of expression": freedom of *speech*, of the *press*, of *assembly*, and of *petition*. Additionally, there is a well-recognized "freedom of *association*" which, although it is not specifically mentioned in the First Amendment, is derived from individuals' rights of speech and assembly.

B. Two broad classes: Whenever you consider governmental action that seems to infringe upon the freedom of expression, there's one key question that you must always ask before you ask anything else. That question is, "Is this governmental action intentionally '*content-based*' or '*content-neutral*'?" If the action is "content-based," the government's action will generally be subjected to strict scrutiny, and the action will rarely be sustained. On the other hand, if the action is "content-neutral," the government's action is subjected to a much less demanding standard, and is thus much more likely to be upheld. [477-479]

1. **Classifying:** A governmental action that burdens a person's expression is "content-based" if the government is aiming at the *"communicative impact"* of the expression. By contrast, if the government is aiming at something other than the communicative impact of the expression, the government action is "content-neutral," even though it may have the *effect* of burdening the expression.

> **Example 1 (content-based):** Under Maryland tort law, if a speaker (D) intentionally makes outrageous statements attacking another person (P), P may be able to recover against D for intentional infliction of emotional distress (IIED). In a federal-court diversity case based on Maryland tort law, a jury grants P (the father of a Marine killed in Iraq) a civil judgment for IIED against the Ds, who are members of a church that thinks God punishes the U.S. military for tolerating homosexuality. The IIED consists of the Ds' having carried, during and nearby the Marine's funeral, picket signs attributing the Marine's death to God's desire to punish the military for not rooting out homosexuality.
>
> Maryland's common law of IIED is "content based." That's because the "outrageousness" of the Ds' messages on the picket signs results solely from the content of those messages. [*Snyder v. Phelps*] [520]

> **Example 2 (content-neutral):** A city forbids the distribution of all single-page leaflets, because it wishes to prevent littering. This ban is "content-neutral" — the government is banning all leaflets, regardless of their content or even the topic they cover, and the harm sought to be avoided (littering) would exist to the same extent regardless of the message in the leaflets. Therefore, the government action is subject to less rigid review — more or less "intermediate level review" (though it was still struck down on these facts). [*Schneider v. State*] [479]

a. **Tip:** Here's a tip to help you decide whether a given governmental action is content-based or not: would the harm the government is trying to prevent exist to the same degree if the listeners/readers *didn't understand English*? If the answer is "no," the action is probably content-based.

> **Example:** Suppose a funeral attendee in *Snyder v. Phelps* (Example 1 *supra*) didn't speak English. He wouldn't suffer the harm the state was trying to prevent — being emotionally harmed by the statements on the picketers' signs — even if he saw or read the signs, so it's clearly the content of the communication that the state is objecting to. But in the case of the ban on littering, even a whole city of non-English-speakers would suffer the same harm — littered streets — so the ban is content-neutral.

b. **Motive counts:** When a court decides whether a regulation is content-based or content-neutral, *motives* count for everything — the question is what the state really *intends* to do. If the court believes that the state intends to inhibit certain speech because of its message, the court will treat the statute as content-based (and strictly scrutinize it) even though it is neutral on its face.

C. Analysis of content-based government action: Once we've determined that a particular government action impairing expression is "content-based," we then have to determine whether the expression falls within a category that is **protected** by the First Amendment.

  1. Unprotected category: If the speech falls into certain pre-defined **unprotected categories**, then the government can basically **ban that expression completely** based on its content, without any interference at all from the First Amendment. [486]

  a. List of categories: Here is a list of these unprotected categories, as the Supreme Court has recognized them: [489]

  [1] **"Incitement."** This category includes advocacy of **imminent lawless behavior**, as well as the utterance of **"fighting words,"** i.e., words that are likely to precipitate an immediate physical conflict;

  [2] **Obscenity**;

  [3] **Misleading or deceptive speech (i.e., fraud)**;

  [4] Speech **integral to criminal conduct**, such as speech that is part of a **conspiracy** to commit a crime or speech **proposing an illegal transaction**; and

  [5] **Defamation**.

  b. Not totally unprotected: But even speech falling within an "unprotected category" receives one small First Amendment protection: government must regulate in a basically **viewpoint-neutral** way. That is, it can exclude certain subjects entirely, but it can't single out certain viewpoints for less favorable treatment. [486]

  Example: The state may ban all "fighting words." But it may not choose to ban just those fighting words directed at the listener's race, religion, or other enumerated traits. [*R.A.V. v. City of St. Paul*]

  2. Protected category: All expression not falling into one of these five pre-defined categories is "protected." If expression is protected, then any government ban or restriction on it based on its content will be **presumed to be unconstitutional**. The Court will subject any content-based regulation of protected speech to **strict scrutiny** — the regulation will be sustained only if it (1) serves a **compelling governmental objective**; and (2) is **"necessary,"** i.e., drawn as **narrowly as possible** to achieve that objective (since a broader-than-needed restriction wouldn't be a "necessary" means). [479]

  Example: A District of Columbia statute bans the display of any sign within 500 feet of a foreign embassy, if the sign would bring the foreign government into "public odium [or] disrepute." *Held*, this regulation is content-based, since a sign is prohibited or not prohibited based on what the sign says. Therefore, the regulation must be strictly scrutinized, and cannot be upheld. Even if the government's interest in protecting the dignity of foreign diplomats is compelling — which it may or may not be — the statute is not "necessary" to achieve that interest, since a narrower statute that only banned the intimidation, coercion or threatening of diplomats would do the trick. [*Boos v. Barry*] [480-481]

  a. Singling out of particular "messages" based on message-content: When government singles out a particular **"message"** for disfavor, based on the message's content, that's obviously a form of "viewpoint based" regulation, making the regulation "content based" and thus triggering strict scrutiny.

b. Bans on discussing "either side" of issues are "viewpoint based": But a statute will *also* be held to be viewpoint based even if the statute singles out a ***whole category*** of speech, ***not just a particular "point of view,"*** for negative treatment based on the speech's message content. Thus a regulation that restricts people from making arguments in favor of ***either side*** of a contested issue (e.g., abortion rights) will nonetheless be treated as viewpoint based (and therefore content based). [*Matal v. Tam* (2017)] [481-482]

3. Distinctions based on message versus ones based on subject matter: Most of the content-based regulations we've discussed above have involved government's singling out of *viewpoints*. But there's another type of content-based regulation, which consists of restrictions on *"topics"* or *"subject matter."* And these types of restrictions, too, pose such serious First Amendment issues that the Supreme Court strictly scrutinizes them. [483]

a. Combined rules on modes and topics: Such "topic-specific" restrictions virtually never occur in the form of a government ban on *all* discussion of a topic. Instead, they occur as a more limited restriction, on only the use of a particular ***medium or mode of expression*** to discuss a ***particular topic.*** [483]

b. Signage regulation, generally: A common scenario in which government might try to regulate a combination of a particular mode of expression and a particular topic — without any apparent intent to favor particular messages — is by regulation of ***signage.*** Most cities tightly regulate how and when ***signs may be posted by private citizens*** — these regulations typically require private signs to be no more than some stated ***maximum size***, be posted for no more than a ***certain duration***, be limited to a certain ***number*** or to certain ***places***, etc. [483]

i. Regulations apply differently depending on subject matter: Frequently, even where a city doesn't intend to disfavor any particular message, the city divides signs into ***multiple categories***, and treats certain categories as meriting fewer restrictions than others, perhaps for reasons as innocuous as preventing "visual litter." Such category-based regulation schemes are likely to ***violate the First Amendment.*** [483]

Example: The Town of Gilbert, Arizona, imposes different requirements for different categories of signs. For temporary signs giving directions to an event such as a church service, the Town requires that the signs be relatively small, number no more than four on a single property; and be put up no more than 12 hours before the event and taken down within an hour afterwards. By contrast, political campaign signs may be larger, are not limited in number, and need not be taken down until 15 days following the election. The Ps, a church and its members, put up signs announcing services, and are cited for not taking them down within the allowed 12 hours. The Ps sue, claiming that the Town has engaged in content-based regulation that cannot survive the required strict scrutiny.

Held, for the Ps. A regulation need not single out particular viewpoints in order to be deemed content-based — even a regulation of speech that draws a distinction based upon the speech's ***"particular subject matter"*** or its particular ***"function or purpose"*** is content-based, and must be strictly scrutinized. So the Town's differing treatment of temporary directional signs versus, say, political campaign signs, is content-based and must be strictly scrutinized.

Even if the two governmental interests cited by the Town in support of its regulation (preserving the Town's aesthetic appeal, and maintaining traffic safety) are "compelling," the distinctions used by the Town are not necessary to achieve those objectives. That's because the distinctions are "underinclusive"; for instance, the Town can't claim that putting strict limits on temporary directional signs is necessary to beautify the Town, while at the same time allowing unlimited numbers of, say, campaign signs that pose the same problem. [*Reed v. Town of Gilbert* (2015)] [483]

D. Analyzing content-neutral regulations: Now, let's go back to the beginning, and assume that the government restriction is *content-neutral*.

   1. Three-part test: Here, we have a *three-part test* that the government must satisfy before its regulation will be sustained if that regulation substantially impairs expression [488-488]:

   a. Significant governmental interest: First, the regulation must serve a *significant governmental interest.*

   b. Narrowly tailored: Second, the regulation must be *narrowly tailored* to serve that governmental interest. So if there's a somewhat *less restrictive* way to accomplish the same result, the government must use that less-intrusive way. (*Example:* Preventing littering is a significant governmental interest. But the government can't completely ban the distribution of handbills to avoid littering, because the littering problem could be solved by the less restrictive method of simply punishing those who drop a handbill on the street. [*Schneider v. State*])

   c. Alternative channels: Finally, the state must *"leave open alternative channels"* for communicating the information. (*Example:* Suppose a city wants to ban all billboards. If a political advertiser can show that there's no other low-cost way to get his message across to local motorists, this billboard ban might run afoul of the "alternative channels" requirement.)

   2. Mid-level review: This three-part test basically boils down to *mid-level* review for content-neutral restrictions that significantly impair expression (as opposed to strict scrutiny for content-based restrictions).

E. Overbreadth: The doctrine of *overbreadth* is very important in determining whether a governmental regulation of speech violates the First Amendment. A statute is *"overbroad"* if it bans speech which could constitutionally be forbidden but *also bans speech which is protected* by the First Amendment. [498-501]

   1. Standing: To see why the overbreadth doctrine is important, let's first consider how a litigant attacks the constitutionality of a statute *outside* the First Amendment area. Here, the litigant can only get a statute declared unconstitutional if he can show that it's unconstitutional in its *application to him*.

   a. Lets P assert third-party rights: But the overbreadth doctrine lets a litigant prevail if he can show that the statute, applied according to its terms, would violate the First Amendment rights of *persons not now before the court*. So overbreadth is really an exception to the usual rule of *"standing"* — under the usual standing rules, a person is not normally allowed to assert the constitutional rights of others, only his own.

   2. "Substantial" overbreadth: In cases where the statute is aimed at *conduct* that has expressive content (rather than aimed against pure speech), the overbreadth doctrine will only be applied if the overbreadth would be *"substantial."* In other words, the potential unconstitutional applications of the statute must be reasonably *numerous* compared with the constitutional applications. [500-501]

F. Vagueness: There is a second important First Amendment doctrine: *vagueness*. A statute is unconstitutionally vague if the conduct forbidden by it is so *unclearly defined* that a reasonable person would have to *guess at its meaning*. [501]

   1. Distinguish from overbreadth: Be careful to *distinguish vagueness from overbreadth:* they both leave the citizen uncertain about which applications of a statute may constitutionally be imposed. But in overbreadth, the uncertainty is hidden or "latent," and in vagueness the uncertainty is easily apparent. [501]

Example: Statute I prohibits anyone from "burning a U.S. flag as a symbol of opposition to organized government." Statute II prohibits anyone from "burning a U.S. flag for any purpose whatsoever." Statute I is probably unconstitutionally vague, because there's no way to tell what the statute means by "symbols of opposition to organized government." Statutue II is unconstitutionally overbroad — it's obviously not vague, since it's perfectly clear that it bans *all* flag burning. But since by its terms it appears to apply to constitutionally-protected conduct (e.g., burning that's intended as a political expression), and since there's no easy way to separate out the constitutional from unconstitutional applications, it's overbroad.

II. ADVOCACY OF ILLEGAL CONDUCT

A. **Advocacy of illegal conduct:**   Remember that one of our "unprotected categories" is the ***advocacy of imminent illegal conduct***. The government can ban speech that advocates crime or the use of force if (but only if) it shows that two requirements are met:

[1] The advocacy must be ***intended*** to incite or produce "imminent lawless action"; and

[2] The advocacy must in fact be ***likely*** to incite or produce that imminent lawless action.

[*Brandenburg v. Ohio* (1969)] [495]

1. **Mere membership not enough:** M*ere knowing membership* in a group — even a very dangerous and subversive group — cannot be forbidden. Membership in a group can be punished only if the member is an *active* (not passive) member who ***specifically intends to further the organization's illegal ends***. [*Scales v. U.S.* (1961)] [496]

   a. **Active support by intangible means:** On the other hand, the government *can* constitutionally prohibit virtually any kind of ***active support*** of an illegal organization, even support that is intended to further the organization's *legal* aims. [497]

   Example: Congress makes it a crime to provide "material support" to a designated foreign terrorist organization, and defines "material support" broadly to include such things as training the group's members to use legal methods of accomplishing their objectives. *Held*, Congress did not violate the First Amendment — even support of a terrorist organization's *legitimate* aims can be harmful (e.g., by "free[ing] up other resources within the organization that may be put to violent ends, and "lend[ing] legitimacy" to the group). Therefore, government may forbid such support. [*Holder v. Humanitarian Law Project* [497]]

III. TIME, PLACE AND MANNER REGULATIONS

A. **Time, place and manner generally:** Let's now focus on regulations covering the ***"time, place and manner"*** of expression. This is probably the area of Freedom of Expression on which you are most likely to be tested, since these kinds of regulations are quite often found in real life. When we give you the rules for analyzing "time, place and manner" restrictions below, assume that the speech that is being restricted is taking place in a ***public forum***. (If it's not, then the government has a somewhat easier time of getting its regulation sustained; we'll be talking about these non-public forum situations later.) [506]

1. **Three-part test:** A "time, place and manner" regulation of public-forum speech has to pass a ***three-part test*** to avoid being a violation of the First Amendment [507]:

   a. **Content-neutral:** First, it has to be ***content-neutral***. In other words, the government can't really be trying to regulate content under the guise of regulating "time, place and manner."

Example: City enacts an ordinance allowing parades or demonstrations "to protest governmental policies" to be conducted only between 10 a.m. and 4 p.m. No such restrictions are placed on other kinds of parades or demonstrations. Even though this restriction is ostensibly merely a "time, place and manner" restriction, it violates the requirement of content-neutrality, because the restriction applies to some expressive conduct but not others, based on the content of the speech.

   b. **Narrowly tailored for significant governmental interest:** Second, it's got to be ***narrowly tailored*** to serve a ***significant governmental interest***. (We saw this above when we were talking more generally about the analysis of all content-neutral restrictions on speech.) This basically means that not only must the government be pursuing an important interest, but there must not be some significantly ***less intrusive*** way that government could achieve its objective.

   Example: Suppose the government wants to prevent littering on the streets. Even though prevention of littering is an important governmental objective, the government may not simply ban all distribution of handbills, because there is a significantly less restrictive means of achieving this objective — a direct ban on littering — so the ban on handbills is not "narrowly tailored" to achieving the anti-littering objective.

   c. **Alternative channels:** Finally, the state must "leave open ***alternative channels***" for communicating the information.

   Example: City is a medium-sized city, with six public parks and many streets. City enacts an ordinance stating that any parade or demonstration, no matter what the content of the message, shall take place only in Central Park or on Main Street. City argues that its limited budget for police security, and the greater ease of handling crowds in these two places than in other places, justify the ordinance. Even though this time, place and manner restriction is apparently content-neutral and is arguably narrowly tailored for a significant governmental interest, it probably violates the "leave open alternative channels" requirement because it puts off limits for parades and demonstrations the vast majority of locations within City.

2. **Application to conduct:** These rules on when the state may regulate the "time, place and manner" of expression apply where what is being regulated is pure speech. But much more importantly, these rules apply where the state is regulating ***"conduct"*** that has an expressive component. ***So the state can never defend on the grounds that "We're not regulating speech, we're just regulating conduct."*** [509]

   Example: It's "conduct" to hand out handbills, or to form a crowd that marches down the street as part of a political demonstration. But since both of these activities have a major expressive component, the state cannot restrict the conduct unless its satisfies the three-part test described above, i.e., the restriction is content-neutral, it's narrowly tailored to achieve a significant governmental interest, and it leaves open alternative channels.

3. **"Facial" vs. "as applied":** A "time, place and manner" regulation, like any other regulation impinging upon First Amendment rights, may be attacked as being either invalid ***"on its face"*** or invalid ***"as applied."*** Thus even a time, place and manner restriction that has been very carefully worded to as to satisfy all three requirements listed above may become unconstitutional ***as applied to a particular plaintiff***. [499]

   Example: A City ordinance provides that any parade or demonstration participated in by more than five people shall be held only after the purchase of a permit, which shall be issued by the City Manager for free to any applicant upon two days notice. The City Manager normally issues such permits without inquiring into the nature of the demonstration planned by the applicant. P, who is known locally as an agitator who opposes the current city government, applies for a permit. The City Manager denies the permit, saying, "I don't like the rabble rousing you've been doing."

Even though the ordinance on its face is probably a valid time, place and manner restriction, the application of the ordinance to P's own permit request ("as applied to P") violates P's First Amendment rights, because that application is not being carried out in a content-neutral manner. P's "as applied" attack will succeed.

4. **Meaning of "narrowly tailored":** When content-neutral time, place and manner regulations are being litigated, the key issue tends to be whether the regulation is sufficiently *narrowly tailored* to achieve the significant government interest. The "narrowly tailored" requirement means that the law *must not "burden substantially more speech than is necessary* to further the government's legitimate interests." [*McCullen v. Coakley*] [508-508]

> **Example:** A North Carolina law makes it a felony for any registered sex offender to use any "commercial social networking Web site." The definition is broad enough to place off-limits to sex offenders highly popular sites like Facebook, LinkedIn and Twitter.
>
> *Held*, the statute is invalid because the state has not carried its burden of showing that it is narrowly tailored to fulfillment of the important goal of preventing child abuse. The speech restrictions imposed by the statute are extreme, given the importance of social media sites. And the state hasn't shown that a ban forbidding a narrower range of online conduct wouldn't suffice to protect against sexual abuse of minors. But a *narrower set* of restrictions would likely be constitutional (e.g., prohibiting a sex offender from *contacting a minor* or from using a website to *gather information about a minor).* [*Packingham v. North Carolina*] [508]

B. **Licensing:** Be especially skeptical of governmental attempts to require a *license* or *permit* before expressive conduct takes place. [510-512]

1. **Content-neutral:** Obviously, any permit requirement must be applied in a *content-neutral* way. (*Example:* Local officials give permits for speeches made for purposes of raising money for non-controversial charities, but decline to give permits for demonstrations to protest the racism of local officials. The requirement of content-neutrality in the licensing scheme is not being satisfied, and the scheme will be automatically struck down.) [511]

2. **No excess discretion:** Also, the licensing scheme must set forth the grounds for denying a permit *narrowly* and *specifically*, so that the discretion of local officials will be curtailed. (*Example*: A municipal ordinance cannot require a permit for every newspaper vending machine where the permit is to be granted on "terms and conditions deemed necessary by the mayor" — the grounds for denying a permit must be set forth much more specifically, to curb the official's discretion. [*Lakewood v. Plain Dealer Publ. Co.*]) [511]

3. **Narrow means-end tailoring:** Finally, the permit *mechanism* must be *closely tailored* to the *objective* that the government is trying to achieve.

4. **Reasonable means of maintaining order:** But if these three requirements — content-neutral application, limited administrative discretion and close means-end fit — are satisfied, the permit requirement will be *upheld* if it is a *reasonable means of ensuring that public order is maintained.* [511]

> **Example:** A requirement that a permit be obtained before a large group of people may march would probably be upheld as a reasonable way of maintaining order, if the requirement is applied in a content-neutral way and is drafted so as to apply without exception to *all* large marches.

5. **Right to ignore requirement:** Assuming that a permit requirement is unconstitutional, must the speaker apply, be rejected, and then sue? Or may he simply speak without the permit, and then

raise the unconstitutionality as a defense to a criminal charge for violating the permit requirement? The answer depends on whether the permit is unconstitutional on its face or merely as applied. [512]

    a. Facially invalid: If the permit requirement is unconstitutional *on its face*, the speaker is *not* required to apply for a permit. He may decline to apply, speak, and then defend (and avoid conviction) on the grounds of the permit requirement's unconstitutionality.

    b. As applied: But where the permit requirement is not facially invalid, but only unconstitutional *as applied to the speaker*, the speaker generally does *not* have the right to ignore the requirement — he must apply for the permit and then seek prompt judicial review, rather than speaking and raising the unconstitutionality-as-applied as a defense. (However, an exception to this rule exists where the applicant shows that *sufficiently prompt judicial review* of the denial was *not available*.)

C. Right to be left alone: People have no strong *right to be left alone*, and the government therefore can't regulate broadly to protect that right. As a general rule, it's *up to the unwilling listener* (or viewer) *to avoid the undesired expression.* [512]

    Example: A city can't make it a misdemeanor to walk up and down the street handing advertising brochures to people without the recipient's express consent. (It's up to the recipient to decline the handbill.)

    1. Captive audience: But if the audience is *"captive"* (unable to avert their eyes and ears), this makes it *more likely* that a fair degree of content-neutral regulation *will be allowed*. (However, the fact that the audience is captive is just one factor in measuring the strength of the state interest in regulating.) [513]

    2. Protests outside of abortion clinics: Opponents of legalized abortion frequently seek to *picket* on public streets and sidewalks around the entrance to *abortion clinics*, and from there attempt to *persuade* women approaching the clinic entrance that they should reconsider getting abortions. In general, the Supreme Court has been quite *protective of the free-speech rights of abortion protesters* in this public-forum scenario, in the face of government regulations that claim to protect the interest of clinic patrons to be free of unwanted communications. [515]

        a. Summary: Thus the Court has *struck down* government attempts to establish sizable *"buffer zones"* around clinic entrances, within which no sort of speech is permitted. And the Court has done this even where it is convinced that government is attempting to act in a content-neutral way (by proscribing *all* speech, regardless of the viewpoint expressed, in the buffer zone). [515] [*McCullen v. Coakley* (2014)] [515]

D. Canvassing: A speaker's right to *canvass*, that is, to go around ringing doorbells or giving out handbills, similarly receives substantial protection. [513]

    1. Homeowner can say "no": The individual listener (e.g., the homeowner), is always free to say, "No, I don't want to speak to you about becoming (say), a Jehovah's Witness." The city can then make it a crime for the speaker to persist.

    2. City can't give blanket prohibition: But the *government* cannot say "No" *in advance* on behalf of its homeowners or other listeners. [514]

        Example: A city passes an ordinance providing that "All doorbell ringing for the purpose of handing out handbills is hereby forbidden." *Held*, such an ordinance violates the First Amendment, even if (as the city claims) it is a content-neutral ordinance designed to protect unwilling listeners, such as those who work nights and sleep days. The most the city can do is to provide that once the individual homeowner makes it clear he doesn't want to be spoken to, the speaker must honor that request. [*Martin v. Struthers*]

3. **Time, place & manner:** But the authorities may impose "time, place & manner" limits on canvassing, if these limits: (1) are content-neutral; (2) serve a significant governmental interest; and (3) leave open adequate other channels for communication.

> **Example:** A town might prohibit canvassing after 6:00 PM, if its policy is truly content-neutral (e.g., it wasn't enacted for the purpose of silencing Jehovah's Witnesses), was enacted to protect homeowners' night-time tranquility, and allows solicitation to take place at other times.

E. **Fighting words:** One of the other "unprotected categories" consists of *"fighting words."* "Fighting words" are words which are likely to make the person to whom they are addressed commit an *act of violence*, probably against the speaker. Expression that falls within the "fighting words" category can be flatly banned or punished by the state. [*Chaplinsky v. New Hampshire*] [516-518]

> **Example**: D picks out one member of his audience and calls him a liar, racist and crook. D can be arrested for this speech, because these are words which might well provoke a reasonable person to whom they are addressed into physically attacking D.

1. **Limits:** But the "fighting words" doctrine is tightly limited:

   a. **Anger not enough:** It's not enough that the speaker has made the crowd angry; they must be so angry that they are *likely to fight*. [517]

   b. **Crowd control:** The police must *control* the angry crowd instead of arresting the speaker if they've got the physical ability to do so. (In other words, the police can't grant the hostile crowd a "heckler's veto.") [517]

   c. **Dislike of speaker's identity:** The doctrine doesn't apply where it's the mere *identity* or *lawful acts* of the speaker, rather than his threatening words, that moves the crowd to anger. (*Example*: If D is a black civil rights worker speaking in a small southern town with a history of racial violence, the fact that members of the audience are ready to attack D because they hate all black civil rights activists will not suffice to make D's speech "fighting words" — here the anger is not really coming from the speaker's particular threatening words, but from his identity and his lawful advocacy of change.) [517]

F. **Offensive language:** Language that is *"offensive"* is nonetheless protected by the First Amendment. [519-522]

1. **Profanity:** This means that even language that is *profane* may not be banned from public places. (*Example*: D wears a jacket saying "Fuck the Draft" in the L.A. County Courthouse. D cannot be convicted for breaching the peace. The state may not ban language merely because it is "offensive," even if profane. [*Cohen v. Calif.*]) [519-520]

   a. **Sexually-oriented non-obscene language:** This protection of "offensive" material also means that messages or images that are *sexually-oriented* but not obscene are, similarly, protected.

   > **Example:** Congress bans the use of the Internet to display any "indecent" language or images which may be accessed by minors. *Held*, this statute is unconstitutional, because it restricts the First Amendment rights of adults to receive indecent-but-not-obscene material. [*Reno v. ACLU*] [529]

2. **Racial or religious hatred:** Similarly, this means that messages preaching *racial or religious hatred* are protected (at least if they don't incite imminent violence or come within the "fighting words" doctrine). (*Example*: A member of the American Nazi Party tells a predominantly-Jewish audience, "Jews are the scum of the earth and should be eliminated." D cannot be punished for, or even restricted from, saying these words.) [522]

3.   **Limits:**   But offensive language *can* be prohibited or punished if: (1) the audience is a *"captive"* one (e.g., the speech occurs on a city bus or subway); or (2) the language is *"obscene,"* under the formal legal definition of this term (lewd and without socially redeeming value).

G.   **Regulation of "hate speech":**   Government efforts to regulate *"hate speech"* — for instance, speech attacking racial minorities, women, homosexuals, or other traditionally disfavored groups — may run afoul of the First Amendment for being content-based. [523-527]

1.   **Three rules:** Here are the general rules about how a state may go about banning hate speech:

❏   **General ban:** A ban on speech or conduct intended or likely to incite anger or violence based solely on *particular listed topics or motives* — such as race, color, religion or gender hatred — is *impermissibly content-based.* That's true even if all the speech/conduct banned falls within an *"unprotected"* category such as, here, *"fighting words."* [*R.A.V. v. St. Paul*] [523]

Example: City bans only those "fighting words" that evoke hatred or conflict based on race, ethnicity or gender (not fighting words based on, say, the listeners' political affiliation). This enactment is content-based, in that it selects speech for proscription based on its content. Therefore, the statute will be strictly scrutinized, and struck down for not being sufficiently narrowly-tailored to achieve the compelling state interest in avoiding dangerous physical conflict. (However, a state could ban *all* fighting words — it just can't select fighting words based only on certain types of hatred.) [*R.A.V.*] [523]

❏   **Worst examples:** However, a state *may* impose a content-based ban on *particular instances* of unprotected speech if the ban forbids *only the very worst examples* illustrating *the very reason the particular class of speech is unprotected.*

Example: The state may choose to criminalize just the very most dangerous "fighting words," just the very most obscene obscene images, etc. [*R.A.V.*]

❏   **Penalty-enhancement statutes:** Also, a state may identify particular generally-applicable criminal proscriptions, and may then choose to punish *more severely* those criminal acts that happen to be motivated by hate than those not motivated by hate. This is called the *"penalty enhancement"* approach. [*Wisconsin v. Mitchell*] [526]

Example: For instance, from within the overall class of acts that constitute arson (all of which are defined as crimes), the state may punish arson more seriously if it's motivated by bias against particular groups.

❏   **All intimidating acts:** Finally, a state may select a particular type of expressive act (e.g., cross-burning), and punish *all instances* where that act is done with a purpose of *intimidating or threatening* someone, even though the state doesn't punish other types of intimidating or threatening acts. [*Virginia v. Black*] [526]

Example: A state may choose to ban all cross-burnings that are done with intent to intimidate another. That's true even if the state chooses not to criminalize other types of expressive activity that are done with intent to intimidate another (e.g., burning that other in effigy).

H.   **Injunctions against expressive conduct:** Where the restriction on expression is in the form of an *injunction* issued by a judge, there is a special standard of review. When a court issues an injunction that serves as a kind of "time, place and manner" restriction, the injunction will be subjected to slightly *more stringent* review than would a generally-applicable statute or regulation with the same substance: the injunction must *"burden no more speech than necessary* to serve a significant governmental interest." [*Madsen v. Women's Health Center, Inc.*] [527]

I.   **The public forum:**   Let's turn now to the concept of the *"public forum."* [532-541]

1. **Rules:** Here are the rules concerning when the fact that speech occurs in a public forum makes a difference, and how: [532]

    a. **Content-based:** If a regulation is ***content-based***, it makes no difference whether the expression is or is not in a public forum: strict scrutiny will be given to the regulation, and it will almost never be upheld.

    b. **Neutral "time, place & manner":** It's where a regulation is ***content-neutral*** that the existence of a public forum makes a difference; especially regulations on "time, place & manner" are less likely to be upheld where the expression takes place in a public forum. [532]

        i.   **Non-public forum:** When expression takes place in a ***non-public forum***, the regulation merely has to be ***rationally related*** to some ***legitimate governmental objective***, as long as equally effective alternative channels for the expression are available.

        ii. **Public forum:** When the expression takes place in a ***public forum***, by contrast, the regulation has to be ***narrowly drawn*** to achieve a ***significant governmental interest*** (roughly *intermediate-level* review). It is necessary, but not sufficient, that the government also leaves alternative channels available. [532]

        Example 1 (public forum speech): A city says, "No political campaign messages may be presented in handbills distributed on city streets." Since this rule impairs communications in a public forum (city streets), the city will have to show that its ordinance is necessary to achieve a significant governmental interest, which it probably can't do (anti-littering won't be enough, for instance). The city can't say, "Well, TV or radio ads will let the same message be given" — the existence of alternative channels for the communication is necessary, but is not enough, when the expression takes place in a public forum.

        Example 2 (non-public forum speech): A city says, "No privately-owned billboard may be larger than 300 square feet." Therefore, as long as adequate alternative channels are available (which they probably are, e.g., smaller signs, or radio & TV ads), the city only has to show that its regulation is rationally related to some legitimate governmental objective. The city can probably meet this burden (e.g., by pointing to the objective of beautifying the city).

2. **What are public forums:** What places, then, are public forums?

    a. **"True" or "traditional" public forums:** First, there are ***"true"*** or ***"traditional"*** public forums. These are areas that are public forums by custom and tradition, not by virtue of any particular government policy. The classic examples are: (1) ***streets;*** (2) ***sidewalks;*** and (3) ***parks***. [534]

    b. **"Designated" public forums:** There's a second type of public forum: places that the government has ***decided to open up*** to a broad range of expressive conduct.

        Some possible examples:

        [1] places where ***government meetings*** take place that the government has decided to open to the public at large (e.g., a school board meeting held in a school auditorium);

        [2] places that government has decided may be ***used by a broad range of people or groups*** (e.g., school classrooms after hours, under a policy that lets pretty much any group use them, or a municipal theater that any group may rent).

        These are called ***"designated"*** public forums. [535]

        i. **Same rules:** The ***same rules*** apply to designated public forums as apply to true public forums, except that government can ***change its mind*** and remove the designation (in which case the place becomes a non-public forum that can be subjected to much broader viewpoint-neutral regulation, as described below).

c. **Non-public-forums:** Still other public places are not at all associated with expression traditionally, so they can be treated as ***non-public forums*** (also sometimes called ***"limited public forums"***).

    i. **Illustrations of non-public-forums:** Here are some illustrations of facilities that, even though they are owned by the government, are not public forums: ***airport terminals***, ***jails***, ***military bases***, the insides of ***courthouses***, and ***governmental workplaces***. [539-541]

    ii. **Rules for non-public forums:** In a non-public forum, the government regulation just has to be:

        [1] ***reasonable*** in light of the ***purpose served*** by the forum; and

        [2] ***viewpoint neutral.***

    [*Int'l Soc. for Krishna Consciousness, Inc. v. Lee* (1992)] [537]

    iii. **Reasonableness:** The above requirement of ***"reasonableness"*** has relatively little bite here, as in the due process and equal protection areas. Government may limit speech in the non-public forum even if ***less restrictive alternatives are readily available***, and even if the restriction chosen is not the ***"most reasonable."*** [537]

        (1) **All expression banned:** Often, even a regulation that completely ***bans*** expression in a particular non-public forum will be found to satisfy this "mere-rationality" test. Or, the government can choose entirely to forbid discussion of ***certain subjects*** (but ***can't*** forbid just certain ***viewpoints***).

        Example: A publicly-owned airport terminal is not a public forum. Therefore, the government may ban face-to-face solicitation of funds in the terminal, because such a ban is rationally related to the legitimate governmental objectives of reducing congestion and combating fraud. (However, a total ban even on literature distribution will not be upheld, because this ban does not even satisfy the "mere-rationality" standard.) [*Int'l Soc. for Krishna Consciousness v. Lee*]

    iv. **Viewpoint neutrality:** But the requirement of ***viewpoint neutrality*** has a real impact in these non-public-forum cases. The government can restrict speech across the board in these forums, but it can't restrict speech by ***preferring some messages or perspectives over others.*** [537]

        (1) **Can't bar religious viewpoint, even if it involves worship:** The requirement of viewpoint-neutrality for non-public forums means that when a school district allows after-hours use of ***school facilities*** by various (even though not all) community groups, ***religious groups*** must be given ***equal access***. [537]

        Example: A school district allows an elementary school to be used after hours by any community group that wishes to put on a program about current affairs. However, the district says that "programs of primarily religious content" are excluded. The Good Christians Club wants to hold a discussion of how practicing Christians should view recent events in the Middle East, to be followed by a prayer for peace in that region.

        Held, for the Club. The district's program is a non-public forum (or as the Court calls it, a "limited public forum"). Since the program proposed by the Club concerns the appropriate topic (current affairs), the school district cannot exclude it on the grounds of its religious orientation, because that would be illegal viewpoint-discrimination. [Cf. *Good News Club v. Milford Central School*] [537]

J. **Access to private property:** In general, a speaker does not have any First Amendment right of ***access*** to another person's ***private property*** to deliver his message.

1. **Shopping centers:** Most significantly, a person does not have a First Amendment right to speak in *shopping centers*. [*Hudgens v. NLRB*] (*Example:* State trespass laws may be used to prevent a person from conducting an anti-war demonstration or a religious proselytizing campaign at her local privately-owned shopping center.) [541]

IV. REGULATION OF SYMBOLIC EXPRESSION

A. **Symbolic expression:** Let's consider *"symbolic expression,"* i.e., expression that consists solely of *non-verbal* actions. [542-546]

1. **Standard:** We use essentially the same rules to analyze restrictions on symbolic expression as we do for restrictions that apply to verbal speech, or to verbal speech coupled with conduct. Thus: (1) any attempt by government to restrict symbolic expression because of the *content* of the message will be strictly scrutinized and almost certainly struck down; (2) any restriction on the *time, place or manner* of symbolic expression will have to be *narrowly tailored* to a *significant governmental objective* and will have to *leave open alternative channels*. [542]

   Example: The Ds (high school students) wear armbands to school, in the face of a school policy forbidding students from wearing such armbands. Because school officials were motivated by a desire to suppress particular messages — anti-war messages — the ban must be strictly scrutinized, and is struck down. [*Tinker v. Des Moines Schl. Dist.*] [543]

2. **Flag desecration:** The most interesting example of government regulation of symbolic expression is *flag desecration* statutes. The main thing to remember is that if a statute bans flag desecration or mutilation, and either on the statute's face or as it is applied, the statute is directed only at particular *messages*, it will be invalid. (*Examples:* Both the Texas and federal flag burning statutes have been struck down by the Supreme Court. In the case of the federal statute, the Court concluded that Congress was trying to preserve the flag as a "symbol of national unity." The statute was therefore content-based, so the Court struck it down. [*U.S. v. Eichman*]) [546]

V. DEFAMATION, INTENTIONAL INFLICTION OF EMOTIONAL DISTRESS, AND THE BANNING OF "FALSE SPEECH"

A. **Defamation:** The First Amendment places limits on the extent to which a plaintiff may recover tort damages for *defamation.* [552]

1. *New York Times v. Sullivan* **test:** Most importantly, under the rule of *New York Times v. Sullivan*, 376 U.S. 254 (1964), where P is a *public official*, he may only win a defamation suit against D for a statement relating to P's official conduct if P can prove that D's statement was made either "with *knowledge* that it was false" or with *"reckless disregard"* of whether it was true or false. These two mental states are usually collectively referred to as the *"actual malice"* requirement. [552-554]

   Example: The *New York Times* runs an ad saying that P — the Montgomery, Alabama police commissioner — has terrorized Dr. Martin Luther King by repeatedly arresting him. Even if these statements are false, P cannot recover for libel unless he can show that the *Times* knew its statements were false or acted with reckless disregard of whether the statements were true or false. [*N.Y. Times v. Sullivan, supra*].

2. **Public figures:** This rule of *Times v. Sullivan* — that P can only recover for defamation if he shows intentional falsity or recklessness about truth — applies not only to public "officials" but also to public *"figures."* Thus a well known college football coach, and a prominent retired Army

general, were public figures who had to show that the defendant acted with actual malice. [*Assoc. Press v. Walker*] [553]

    a. Partial public figure: Someone who voluntarily ***injects himself*** into a public controversy will be a public figure for ***just that controversy*** — thus an anti-abortion activist might be a public figure for any news story concerning abortion, but not for stories about, say, his private life unrelated to abortion.

    b. Involuntary public figure: Also, some people may be *"involuntary"* public figures. (*Example:* A ***criminal defendant*** is an involuntary public figure, so he cannot sue or recover for a news report about his crime or trial unless he shows actual malice.)

3. Private figure: If the plaintiff is a *"private"* (rather than "public") figure, he does ***not*** have to meet the *New York Times v. Sullivan* "actual malice" rule. [*Gertz v. Robert Welch, Inc.*]. On the other hand, the First Amendment requires that he show at least ***negligence*** by the defendant — the states may not impose strict liability for defamation, even for a private-figure plaintiff. *Id.* [554]

    a. No punitive damages: Also, a private-figure plaintiff who shows only negligence cannot recover ***punitive*** damages — he must show actual malice to get punitive damages. *Id.*

4. Falsity: The First Amendment also probably requires that the defamation plaintiff (whether or not she is a public figure) must show that the statement was ***false***.

B. Intentional infliction of emotional distress: The *Times v. Sullivan* rule applies to actions for intentional infliction of ***emotional distress*** as well as ones for defamation. Thus a public-figure plaintiff cannot recover for any intentional infliction of emotional distress unless he shows that the defendant acted with actual malice. [556]

> **Example:** *Hustler Magazine* satirizes religious leader Jerry Falwell as a drunken hypocrite who has sex with his mother. *Held*, Falwell cannot recover for intentional infliction of emotional distress unless he shows that *Hustler* made a false statement with knowledge of falsity or with reckless disregard of falsity. [*Hustler Magazine v. Falwell*] [556]

C. Forbidding other types of false speech: Defamation necessarily involves speech that is false. And as we've seen, in most instances government may ban (or allow damages for) defamatory speech, in part because the falsity of the speech makes it less valuable. This raises the question, can government ***categorically forbid factually-false statements***, even ones that are *not* defamatory? Could a state, for instance, ***make it a crime to "tell a lie"?***

1. Can't forbid all false speech: The brief answer is *"no."* Except for a few narrow ***pre-defined sub-categories*** (defamation, fraud, and perjury, for instance), as to which there is a long-standing consensus that the type of false speech in question is especially likely to cause severe harm, government ***may not forbid statements merely on the grounds that they are factually false.***

    a. Lying about military honors: For instance, the Court has held that Congress' decision to make it a crime for a person to falsely state he has won certain ***military medals*** violates the First Amendment. [*U.S. v. Alvarez* (2012)] [558]

VI. OBSCENITY

A. Obscenity: Another of our "unprotected categories" is ***obscenity***. Expression that is obscene is simply ***unprotected*** by the First Amendment, so the states can ban it, punish it, or do whatever else they want without worrying about the First Amendment. [559-565]

B. Three-part test: For a work to be "obscene," all three parts of the following test must be met [561]:

1. **Prurient interest:** First, the average person, applying today's community standards, must find that the work as a whole appeals to the *"prurient"* interest;

2. **Sexual conduct:** Second, the work must depict or describe in a "patently offensive way" particular types of *sexual conduct* defined by state law; and

3. **Lacks value:** Finally, the work taken as a whole, must lack "serious literary, artistic, political or scientific value."

[*Miller v. Calif.*]

C. **Significance:** So something will not be "obscene" unless it depicts or describes *"hard core sex."* (For instance, mere *nudity*, by itself, is not obscene.) [561]

D. **Materials addressed to minors:** It will be much easier for the state to keep erotic materials out of the hands of *minors*. Probably even minors have some First Amendment interest in receiving sexually explicit materials, but this is typically *outweighed* by the state's compelling interest in protecting minors against such material. So the distribution of non-obscene but sexually explicit materials may basically be forbidden to minors (provided that the regulations do not substantially impair the access of adults to these materials). [562]

1. **Adult's rights impaired:** But if a measure aimed at minors *does* substantially impair the access of adults to material that's "indecent" but not obscene, the measure will be struck down. (*Example:* If Congress outright bans all "indecent" material on the Internet (as it has done), out of a fear that the material will be seen by minors, the measure will be found to violate the First Amendment rights of adults. [*Reno v. ACLU*]) [529]

E. **Private possession by adults:** The mere *private possession* of obscene material by an adult may *not* be made criminal. [*Stanley v. Georgia*] [562]

> **Example:** While police are lawfully arresting D at his house on a robbery charge, they spot obscene magazines on his shelf. D may not be criminally charged with possession of pornography, because one has both a First Amendment right and a privacy right to see or read what one wants in the privacy of one's own home.

1. **Child pornography:** However, the states *may* criminalize even private possession of *child pornography*. [*Osborne v. Ohio*] [563]

2. **No right to supply to consenting adults:** Also, the state may punish a person who *supplies* pornography even to consenting adults. In other words, there is a right to *have* pornography for one's own home use, but not a right to supply it to others for their home use. [562]

VII. COMMERCIAL SPEECH

A. **Commercial speech generally:** Speech that is *"commercial"* — that is, speech advertising a product or proposing some commercial transaction — gets First Amendment protection. But this protection is in some ways *more limited* than the protection given to non-commercial (e.g., political) speech.[565]

1. **Truthful speech:** *Truthful* commercial speech gets a pretty fair degree of First Amendment protection. The government may restrict truthful commercial speech only if the regulation meets the three following requirements:

[1] it *directly advances* ...

[2] a *substantial governmental interest* ...

[3] in a way that is *"no more extensive than necessary"* to achieve the government's objective.

[*Central Hudson Gas v. Public Serv. Comm.* (1980)]

So basically, the court will apply ***mid-level review*** to government restrictions based on the content of commercial speech (whereas it applies ***strict scrutiny*** to content-based restrictions on non-commercial speech). [572]

> **Example:** Virginia forbids a pharmacist from advertising his prices for prescription drugs. Virginia must show that it is pursuing a "substantial" governmental interest, and that materially-less-restrictive alternatives are not available. Here, the state's desire to prevent price-cutting that will lead to shoddy service is not strong enough to qualify as "substantial," so the measure must be struck down on First Amendment grounds. [*Virginia Pharmacy Board v. Virginia Consumer Council*] [565-566]

a. **"Consume less" objective will fail:** The three-part mid-level review described above is often used to strike down advertising regulations that are premised on the government's argument that if advertising of the legal-but-harmful product is limited, people will ***consume less*** of the item. The limitation will usually flunk requirement [3] above (that the limitations be ***"no more extensive than necessary"*** to achieve the government's objectives), because government will almost always be free to ***increase taxes*** on the item, to ***regulate how and where it can be sold***, or to conduct an ***educational campaign*** showing its dangers — and any of these methods would likely be less restrictive than an advertising ban, while still reducing consumption of the harmful product. [570]

> **Example:** Rhode Island prohibits all advertising of liquor prices, except for price tags displayed with the merchandise and not visible from the street. The state defends the prohibition on the grounds that forbidding price advertising will lower liquor consumption, in accordance with the state's goal of "temperance."
>
> *Held*, the prohibition violates the First Amendment, because it fails the 3-part *Central Hudson Gas* test. For instance, that test requires that a regulation of commercial speech be "no more extensive than necessary." The ban here fails this requirement because the state could have limited alcohol consumption by less restrictive means, such as increased taxation, caps on per capita purchases, or educational campaigns. [*44 Liquormart v. Rhode Island*] [570]

b. **Protect minors:** Similarly, if the government's principal justification for the regulation is to prevent ***minors*** from gaining access to, or being enticed by, the "vice" product, government will have to ***tailor its methods very tightly*** so that there is no undue interference with the rights of ***adults*** to obtain or learn about the product. [571-573]

> **Example:** Massachusetts dramatically restricts the advertising of smokeless tobacco and cigars (e.g., by forbidding billboards). The state defends on the grounds that this limit will protect minors from being attracted to the product.
>
> *Held*, the regulations violate the free-speech rights of the tobacco industry and its adult customers. "No matter how laudable the state's interest in preventing minors' access to tobacco products, the state may not regulate advertising in a way that interferes materially with the legitimate rights of the tobacco industry, and its ***adult customers***, to exchange truthful information." [*Lorillard Tobacco Co. v. Reilly*] [571]

2. **False, deceptive or illegal:** But the principles discussed above assume that the commercial speech — even if it concerns a harmful product — is ***truthful***. ***False or deceptive*** commercial speech may be ***forbidden*** by the government.

a. **Integral to criminal conduct:** This stems from the more general rule that speech that is ***"integral to criminal conduct"*** is not protected at all (i.e., that such speech constitutes an "unprotected category"). [571]

    i. **Proposing an illegal transaction:** Similarly, commercial speech that ***proposes an illegal transaction*** (e.g., a help-wanted ad that indicates a preference for white males, in violation of anti-discrimination laws) doesn't receive any First Amendment protection.

    ii. **Conspiracy:** And commercially-oriented speech that is part of a ***conspiracy*** to commit a crime ("We hereby agree to rob the First National Bank") may likewise be punished, because such speech is unprotected.

B. Lawyers: The qualified First Amendment protection given to commercial speech means that ***lawyers*** have a limited right to advertise. Thus a state may not ban all advertising by lawyers or even ban advertising directed to a particular problem. See, e.g., *Bates v. State Bar of Ariz.* (Thus a lawyer can advertise, "If you've been injured by a Dalkon shield, I may be able to help you.") [567]

    1. In-person solicitation: On the other hand, the states may ban certain types of ***in-person solicitation*** by lawyers seeking clients (e.g., solicitation of accident victims in person by tort lawyers who want to obtain a contingent-fee agreement. [*Ohralik v. Ohio St. Bar Ass'n.*]) [567]

    2. Direct mail: Similarly, the states may ban lawyers from ***direct-mail*** solicitation of accident victims, at least for a 30-day period following the accident. [*Florida Bar v. Went For It*]

VIII. REGULATION IN THE CONTEXT OF POLITICAL CAMPAIGNS

A. Campaign spending, generally: The state or federal governments can regulate ***campaign spending*** to some extent, but other campaign regulations would violate the First Amendment. [576-591]

B. Contributions: ***Contributions*** made by individuals or groups to a single candidate or political party may be somewhat ***limited***.

    Example: Congress may constitutionally prevent anyone from contributing more than $1,000 to a single candidate for federal office, in order to curb actual or apparent corruption. [*Buckley v. Valeo*] [576]

    1. Lower limit: But the limit on single-donor-single-candidate contributions may not be made ***so low*** that it substantially interferes with candidates' and parties' ability to ***run a competitive election campaign.***

        Example: Vermont prevents any individual or political party from contributing more than $400 to the campaign of any candidate for governor during any two-year period. Held, this limit is so low that it violates the free speech and free association rights of individuals and parties (though no majority of the Court can agree on the precise test for "how low is too low"). *Randall v. Sorrell.* [579]

    2. Aggregate limits struck down: Whereas limits on the amount of contributions by one donor to one candidate or party so far remain constitutional under *Buckley, supra,* limits on the ***aggregate amount*** of contributions by a donor to *all* candidates, parties or PACs are ***not***. [*McCutcheon v. FEC*] [580-582]

C. Expenditures: Furthermore, a person or entity's ***independent*** campaign-related ***expenditures*** (whether he's a candidate or not) may ***not*** be limited at all.

    Example 1: A candidate may not be prevented from spending as much of his own money on getting elected as he wishes. [*Buckley v. Valeo; Randall v. Sorrell*]

    Example 2: Similarly, private citizen X may spend as much money to try to get Y elected as he wishes, as long as X spends the money in a truly independent manner rather than contributing it to Y or coordinating with Y on how it should be spent. [*Buckley v. Valeo*] [577]

1. **Corporations' expenditures:** *Corporations* (and probably *unions*) can spend *limitless sums* from their general treasuries to advocate or advertise for or against particular candidates, as long as the spending is "*independent*," i.e., not coordinated with the candidate.

    a. **Rationale:** That's because the First Amendment does not permit corporations to be *treated less favorably than individuals,* and individuals are entitled, under *Buckley, supra,* to make unlimited independent expenditures to get others elected. [*Citizens United v. FEC*] [586-587].

D. **Corporate and judicial expression during campaigns:** We look now at two special questions involving regulation of campaign *speech* (as opposed to campaign spending, covered above):

    [1] to what extent may political expression be regulated on account of the fact that the speaker is a *business* or *corporation*?; and

    [2] in places where *judges* must run for electoral office, what restrictions may be placed upon the candidates' *campaign speech*, and on their efforts to communicate in order to *raise campaign funds*?

    1. **Corporate political expression:** On the first issue, campaign-related speech by *businesses* and *corporations*, the Court has held that political expression may not be denied First Amendment protection merely because its source is a *corporation* rather than an individual. *Citizens United, supra,* makes it clear that independent political expression by a *business or corporation* cannot be *treated any less favorably* than such expression by an *individual*.

    2. **Campaign speech in judicial elections:** Most states select *judges* by *elections*, rather than appointment. In these states, there is a risk that candidates for judgeships will, in order to get elected, say things or do things that may conflict with a judge's ethical obligations once elected.

        a. **Split decisions:** In a pair of cases, the Supreme Court has approved relatively modest government regulation of campaign speech (and campaign fundraising) by judicial candidates against First Amendment attack, but has struck down more extensive regulations.

            i. **Ban on discussion of "legal or political issues":** In the earlier case, the Court struck down by 5-4 a Minnesota rule that a candidate for judicial office may not "*announce his or her views on disputed legal or political issues.*" The majority conceded that if a judicial candidate is permitted to make her views known on issues that may come before her court, the *due process rights* of later litigants might well be abridged. But, the majority said, the First Amendment does not permit a state to combat this problem by maintaining judicial elections and then "*preventing candidates from discussing what the elections are about.*" [*Republican Party of Minn. v. White* (2002)] [589]

            ii. **Ban on direct solicitation of contributions (*Williams-Yulee* case):** But in a more recent case, the Court *upheld,* by a different 5-4 configuration, a more limited rule than the Minnesota rule invalidated in *White*: a Florida rule that prohibited judicial candidates from *personally soliciting campaign contributions.* [*Williams-Yulee v. Florida Bar* (2015)] [590]

IX. SOME SPECIAL CONTEXTS

A. **Public school students:** Students in *public schools* have a limited right of free speech. The student's right to speak freely has to be *balanced* against the administration's right to carry out its educational mission and to maintain discipline. [592]

    1. **Non-allowable regulation:** School officials may *not* suppress students' speech merely because the officials *disagree* with that speech on *ideological or political grounds*.

        Example: Recall the *Tinker* case, *supra*, p. C-89: The Ds (high school students) wear black arm-bands to school to express their opposition to the War in Vietnam. School policy forbids students from wearing such armbands. The policy was adopted because of school officials' desire to suppress particular messages, namely anti-war messages. *Held*, because the policy was not content-netural, it must be strictly scrutinized, and is struck down. [*Tinker v. Des Moines Schl Dist.*]

2. **Allowable regulation:** But public school districts are ***permitted*** to impose *some* types of regulation of student speech, typically ones that are content-neutral, and that are motivated by the district's desire to further the schools' special educational objectives. For instance, here are two scenarios in which school authorities are free to limit student speech:

    [1] **School discipline:** First, where the limit is needed in order to ***maintain school discipline*** and fulfill the school's ***educational mission***. For instance, a school may ban profanity or lewd speech. [593]

    Example: P, a high school student, gives a speech at a high school assembly that school officials find to be lewd. The speech, made in support of a candidate for a student government office, contains an elaborate sexual metaphor (e.g., "Jeff Kuhlman is a man who takes his point and pounds it in. … He doesn't attack things in spurts — he drives hard, pushing and pushing until finally — he succeeds."). The officials suspend P, and remove him from the list of candidates for commencement speaker. P sues the school district for violating his freedom of speech.

    Held, for the school district: the district did not violate P's right to free speech. A student's right to free expression must be "balanced against society's countervailing interest in ***teaching students the boundaries of socially appropriate behavior.***" Here, the school's interest in prohibiting "vulgar and lewd speech" outweighed whatever First Amendment interests P might have had, especially since the school imposed the discipline in a way that was "unrelated to any political viewpoint," i.e., it acted in a ***content-neutral way***. [*Bethel School District No. 403 v. Fraser*] [594]

    [2] **Advocacy of illegality:** Second, where the speech ***advocates illegality***, at least in the special case of ***drug use***. Thus schools may ban the ***advocacy of illegal drug use,*** even where the advocacy does not pose an immediate threat to discipline or to the school's educational mission. [*Morse v. Frederick*] [595]

    a. **Off-campus speech:** So far, we've been assuming that the student speech occurred either ***on campus*** or during the course of a ***school-sponsored off-campus activity.*** But how much speech-regulation may the school impose when the speech in question ***takes place off-campus,*** and the student is ***not speaking as part of a school-sponsored event?***

        i. **Rules of thumb:** Here are some rules of thumb for handling scenarios involving off-campus-speech that's not part of a school-sponsored event:

            [1] The fact that the speech occurs off-campus and not as part of a school event ***does not completely prevent*** the school from ***regulating*** the content or manner of the speech; but …

            [2] The school's authority to regulate is ***generally much weaker*** than it is where the speech occurs on-campus or as part of a school-sponsored off-campus activity; and …

            [3] Unless the speech falls within a few special categories (e.g., harassment, fighting words, obscenity, or significant disruption of school activities), the speech receives ***at least as much constitutional protection*** as if it had occurred ***on-campus*** or during the course of a school-sponsored off-campus activity. [595]

        ii. **Scenarios where school's regulatory interest is significant:** Here are some scenarios in which the Court has said the school's "regulatory interests" ***remain significant*** even though the speech takes place off-campus:

❏ "serious or severe ***bullying or harassment*** targeting ***particular individuals***";

❏ "***threats*** aimed at ***teachers or other students***";

❏ the "***failure to follow rules*** concerning ***lessons***, the ***writing of papers***, the ***use of computers***, or participation in other ***online school activities***";

❏ "breaches of ***school security devices***, including ***material maintained within school computers***."

See *Mahanoy Area School District v. B.L.* (2021) (discussed further below). [595-599]

iii. Illustrative case: The points mentioned in Sub-paragraphs (i) and (ii) above come from a 2021 case, the first case in which the Court has analyzed schools' regulatory powers over off-campus speech that is not part of a school-sponsored event. That case is *Mahanoy Area School District v. B.L.*, discussed in the following Example:

Example: P is a student at D, a public high school. P tries out for the varsity cheerleading squad but is rejected and instead offered a spot on the junior varsity. When she gets this news, she and a friend go to a local convenience store on a Saturday, from which P uses her smartphone to post two photos on Snapchat. Snapchat allows her to send these photos so that they can be viewed by her Snapchat "friends" (of which she has about 250), but will vanish after 24 hours. One of the photos shows P and her friend with their middle fingers raised; the caption reads, "Fuck school fuck softball fuck cheer fuck everything." One of P's Snapshot friends, a member of the cheerleading squad, takes screenshots of the photos before they vanish, and shows them to her mother, a cheerleading coach. The cheerleading coaches, together with the principal, decide that because the posts use profanity in connection with a school extracurricular activity, the posts violate team and school rules. P apologizes, but the coaches nonetheless suspend her from the junior varsity cheerleading squad for the upcoming year. P sues D, alleging that D has violated her First Amendment right of free speech.

Held (by a 8-1 vote), for P. Off-campus speech has several features that diminish the strength of a school's interest in regulating student speech. For instance, when a school regulates off-campus speech together with on-campus speech, the school is regulating "all the speech a student utters during the full 24-hour day"; therefore, the courts must be quite skeptical of the school's efforts to regulate the off-campus speech, since those efforts "may mean the student cannot engage in that kind of speech at all." Similarly, the school usually does not stand "*in loco parentis*" as to off-campus speech that doesn't occur during an extracurricular activity; this, too, weakens the school's interest in regulation.

Here, the school district was pursuing some important interests, but those interests are weaker than the district claims. For instance, the district had an interest in "teaching good manners" and "punishing the use of vulgar language," but the district didn't show that it made any *general* effort to "prevent students from using vulgarity outside the classroom." Similarly, the district had an interest in "prevent[ing] disruption" of a "school-sponsored extracurricular activity"; but the district did not show that P's conduct had caused a ***"substantial"*** disruption of any school activity. In sum, the district's interference with P's speech went beyond what was required for the district to achieve its legitimate educational objectives, and thereby violated P's First Amendment freedom of expression. [***Mahanoy Area School District v. B.L.*** (2021)] [595-599]

B. Group activity: The rights of a ***group*** to engage in ***joint expressive activity*** get special First Amendment protection, generally called the ***"freedom of association."*** (*Example*: Groups have the right to get together to bring law suits, or to conduct non-violent economic boycotts. Therefore, they cannot be prevented from doing these things by state rules against fomenting litigation or conducting boycotts. [*NAACP v. Button*]) [600]

C.   Government as speaker or as funder of speech: So far, we've looked only at the role of government as the regulator of speech by non-government actors. But sometimes, *government itself wishes to speak*. And sometimes, government wishes to give *financial support* to certain speech by others. In the former situation, government has a broad right to act in a non-viewpoint-neutral way; in the latter situation, the rules are more complex. [600]

1.   Government as speaker: When government wishes to *be a speaker itself*, it is pretty clear that government may *say essentially what it wants*, and is not subject to any real rule of viewpoint neutrality. [600]

> **Example:** Government can pay for ads attacking smoking as a health hazard, without having to pay for opponents' ads saying that the dangers of smoking are overrated.

2.   Government as funder of third-party speech: If government *funds speech by third parties*, may government be non-viewpoint-neutral, by funding only those viewpoints of which it approves? The answer is heavily dependent on the *details* of the government funding.

> **a.   Use of agents to deliver government's message:** Government *may* use content-based criteria when government is selecting third parties who will serve as the *government's agents* in *spreading the government's own message*. [601]

> > **Example:** The federal government funds certain family-planning "projects" (essentially, clinics) that are operated by private parties. The program's regulations say that while a person (e.g., a doctor) is working in such a clinic, that person may not discuss the possibility of an abortion with a pregnant clinic patient.

> > *Held*, this limitation of private speech does not violate the First Amendment. When the government appropriates public funds to promote a particular policy of its own, it is *entitled to say what it wishes*. [*Rust v. Sullivan* (as summarized later in *Rosenberger v. Rector & Visitors of the Univ. of Va.*)] [601]

> **b.   No forbidding of some topics or messages for disfavor:** On the other hand, if government decides to *fund* (or *allow* on government property) *some expressions of private citizens' own views*, government must generally *behave not only in a content-neutral but also a subject-neutral way.* That is, government cannot (1) decide that it's going to subsidize (or allow on public property) private messages on various topics, but then (2) decline to fund (or decide to exclude from the discussion) a few *disfavored topics or messages*. [601-601]

> > **i.   Religion:** For example, government cannot decide to fund a broad range of expressive activities and then exclude expressive activities that are *mainly religious.*

> > **Example:** The University of Virginia (a public university) funds certain student publications, by paying for their printing costs. The University disqualifies from this funding any primarily-religious publication.

> > *Held*, this exclusion violates the free speech rights of student religious organizations. If the University were disseminating only its own messages, it would not have to fund opposing viewpoints. But once it chooses to fund some *third-party viewpoints* (i.e., some student-run publications), it may not choose which ones to fund based on the viewpoint of the speaker. [*Rosenberger v. Rector & Visitors of the Univ. of Va.*] [602]

> **c.   Unconstitutional conditions:** Similarly, where government decides to award public funding for a privately-run program the doctrine of *"unconstitutional conditions"* may prevent government from conditioning the funding on the recipient's agreement to (i) give up its right to

speak on certain topics, or (ii) deliver certain messages with which recipient doesn't agree. See our discussion of this doctrine *infra*, p. C-103.

3. **Blurry line between government speech and government-facilitated private speech:**　The ***boundary line*** between government speech (where government does not have to be content-netural) and government-facilitated private speech (where government must be content-neutral) can sometimes be ***blurry***.

   a. **Acceptance of privately-donated monument:**　One context in which it can be hard to say whether the government is the speaker arises when government accepts and permanently displays a ***privately-donated monument***. Here, the court has held that government is probably ***acting as a speaker***, in which case it is free to ***reject other similar donations*** of property bearing messages with which government does not agree. [*Pleasant Grove City v. Summum*] [603]

   b. **Specialty license plates:**　Another context in which it may be unclear whether government is the speaker involves ***state-issued specialty license plates***, which allow vehicle owners to pay the state extra to display certain pre-approved ***slogans or images***. In such a case, the Court found the message on such a plate to be a ***form of government speech***, thereby entitling the state to ***reject messages it found offensive***. [*Walker v. Tex. Div., Sons of Conf. Vets., Inc.*] [603]

X. FREEDOM OF ASSOCIATION, THE RIGHT NOT TO SPEAK OR ASSOCIATE, AND THE DENIAL OF PUBLIC JOBS OR BENEFITS

A. **Freedom of association generally:**　First Amendment case law recognizes the concept of ***"freedom of association."*** In general, the idea is that if an individual has a First Amendment right to engage in a particular expressive activity, then a ***group*** has a "freedom of association" right to engage in that same activity as a group. [605]

1. **Strict scrutiny:** Government is not absolutely forbidden to impair the freedom of association, just as it is not absolutely forbidden to interfere with freedom of speech. However, before the government may significantly interfere with protected associational activity, two showings must be made: (1) that the governmental interest being pursued is a ***compelling*** one; and (2) that that interest cannot be achieved by means ***less restrictive*** of the freedom of association. In other words, ***strict scrutiny*** is normally applied to restrictions that significantly interfere with freedom of association. [605]

B. **Right not to associate, generally:**　The Court has also recognized, in effect, a right ***not*** to associate. That is, an individual has a general First Amendment right ***not to be compelled by the government to associate with, or support, the speech or expressive activities of persons or groups of which the individual does not approve.***

1. **Some contexts:** Here's a preview of some of the major contexts in which this "right not to associate" comes into play, each of which will be discussed more fully below: [606]

   a. **Right not to give financial support:**　A person has a free-association right not to be ***compelled to give financial support*** to an organization whose message the person disagrees with. See Paragraph (C), p. C-99 below.

   b. **Veto on unwanted participants:**　A group has a free-association right not to be ***forced to accept a participant in an event*** if that person's participation would interfere with the group's expressive activities. See Paragraph (D) below, p. C-99.

   c. **Veto on unwanted members:** Similarly, a group has a free-association right not to be forced to allow ***unwanted members*** into the group. See Paragraph (E) below, p. C-99.

   d. **Right not to have membership in group be illegal:** A person has a free-association right not to have the government *criminalize membership in the group.* See Paragraph (F) below, p. C-100.

   e. **Right to public jobs and benefits:** A person normally has a free-association right not to have a *public-sector job,* or a *license or benefit issued by the government,* be denied because of the person's protected associational activities. See Paragraph (G) below, p. C-100.

C. Right to avoid compulsory financial support: The "right not to associate" includes a person's right not to be compelled to *give financial support to organizations or activities* where the money will be used to *disseminate messages with which the person disagrees.* [607]

   1. **Applies to union's cost of collective bargaining:** This right to avoid compulsory financial support means that the states may not pass laws *forcing public employees to pay dues to a union* that represents them. That is, government employees who choose not to join the union that represents them have a *First Amendment right to refuse to contribute even one dollar towards the costs of collective bargaining.* And that's true even though under federal law, once a union is designated for a workplace, that union bargains for *all* employees in the workplace, not just the union members. [*Janus v. AFSCME* (2018)] [607-608]

D. Veto on unwanted participants: Another aspect of the "right not to associate" is that a group has a First Amendment right *not to be forced to accept participants whose presence would interfere with the group's expressive activities.* [609]

   1. **Parade:** For instance, private parties who conduct a *parade* may exclude unwanted members — or at least unwanted messages — from the parade.

      Example: Massachusetts uses a state anti-discrimination law to try to require a private group that conducts a St. Patrick's Day parade in Boston to include gay and lesbian marchers marching under their own banner. *Held,* the state may not require the group to include such marchers. A parade inevitably has expressive content, and gays marching under a banner would be sending a message (presumably a message supporting gay rights and gay lifestyles) that the parade organizers have a right to refuse to endorse. [*Hurley v. Irish-American Gay, Lesbian, and Bisexual Group of Boston*] [609]

   2. **Must affect group's own message:** But the right of a group not to be forced to accept co-participants of whose message the group disapproves applies *only* where the *group's own "message" would be affected by the unwanted participation.* [609]

      Example: In the "Solomon Amendment," Congress says that any university may receive certain federal funding only if all parts of the university, including its law school, give the same on-campus access to military recruiters as to recruiters from other employers. Some law schools argue that since the military discriminates against gays, the Amendment, by forcing the schools to serve as hosts for on-campus military recruiting, is unconstitutionally forcing the schools to support an anti-gay message they abhor, analogous to the forced-association unconstitutionally forced on the parade organizers in *Hurley, supra.*

      Held, the Amendment does not violate the law schools' freedom of association or expression. Unlike a parade organizer's choice of parade contingents, nothing about on-campus recruiting suggests that the law schools agree with any speech by recruiters. [*Rumsfeld v. FAIR*] [609-610]

E. Right to exclude from membership in group: Just as the "right not to associate" means that a group may veto the participation of unwanted outsiders in the group's activities (see Par. (D) above), this right also means that an association has a First Amendment interest in *not being forced to accept unwanted members.*

Example: A state anti-discrimination law bars the Boy Scouts from excluding gays as members. Dale, an Eagle Scout who is openly gay, seeks to rejoin the Scouts as an "adult member." *Held*, for the Scouts: because opposition to homosexuality is part of the Scouts' "expressive message," the Scouts' freedom of association is violated by the law forbidding the group to exclude gays as members. [*Boy Scouts of America v. Dale*] [610]

F. **Illegal membership:** The freedom of association means that *mere membership in a group or association may not be made illegal*. Membership in a group may only be made part of an offense if: (1) the group is *actively engaged in unlawful activity*, or *incites others* to *imminent lawless action*; and (2) the individual *knows* of the group's illegal activity, and specifically intends to further the group's illegal goals. (*Example*: Congress cannot make it a crime simply to be a member of the American Communist Party. On the other hand, Congress can make it a crime to be a member of a party that advocates imminent overthrow of the government, if the member knows that the party so advocates and the member intends to help bring about that overthrow.) [611]

G. **Denial of public benefit or job:** Freedom of expression also prevents the government from *denying a public benefit or job* based on a person's association. [611-615]

1. **Non-illegal activities:** If a person's activities with a group could not be made *illegal*, then those activities may generally not be made the basis for denying the person the government job or benefit.

   Example 1: A state may not refuse to hire a person as a teacher merely because he is a member of the American Communist Party, since the state could not make it illegal to be a member of the ACP.

   Example 2: At a time when Republicans are in power, a state may not refuse to hire Democrats for non-policy-making jobs like police officer or clerk. [*Rutan v. Republican Party of Illinois*]

2. **No right/privilege distinction:** There is no constitutional distinction between a *"right"* and a *"privilege."* Even if, say, a particular public benefit or job is defined by the state to be a "privilege," the state may not deny that job or benefit on the basis of the applicant's constitutionally-protected membership in a group or organization. [611]

3. **Loyalty oath:** Government may generally not require an applicant to sign a *loyalty oath*, unless the things that the applicant is promising in the loyalty oath not to do are things which, if he did them, would be grounds for punishing him or denying him the job. (*Example*: You cannot be required to sign a loyalty oath that you are not a member of the Communist Party in order to get a teaching job. But you can be required to sign an oath that you will not advocate the forcible overthrow of our government.) [612]

4. **Compulsory disclosure:** Similarly, the government may not force you to *disclose* your membership activities (or require a group to disclose who its members are), unless it could make that membership illegal. (*Example*: The state cannot require the Communist Party to furnish a list of its members.) [615-620]

5. **Some exceptions:** There are some *exceptions* to the general rule that associational activities that couldn't be outlawed directly also can't be made the basis for public hiring or benefits decisions. In general, these exceptions are for conduct which, although it includes protected expression, directly (and negatively) relates to *performance of the job*.

   a. **Partisan political activities:** For instance, civil servants can constitutionally be forced to choose between their jobs and engaging in *partisan political activities*, since there's a very strong government interest in making sure that civil servants can do their jobs without being coerced into campaigning for or contributing to their elected bosses. [*CSC v. Letter Carriers*]

C
A
P
S
U
L
E

S
U
M
M
A
R
Y

b. **Patronage hirings:** Similarly, some public jobs may be awarded as *patronage appointments*, ones the performance of which is *reasonably related to a person's politics*. [612]

> **Example:** Even though I have a First Amendment right to be a Democrat, the Republican Congressman representing my district doesn't violate my rights when, on the basis of my political beliefs, he declines to hire me as, say, a speech writer, a high advisor, or some other post with a *heavy political content*.
>
> On the other hand, if I'm a Democrat, and there's a Republican governor in power, he can't block me from getting a government job as a clerk or secretary or police officer — the old fashioned "patronage" system whereby all public jobs could be restricted to supporters of the party in power has been outlawed as a violation of freedom of association, and only jobs with a heavy political content, like speech writer, say, or Chief of Staff, can be based on party membership.

c. **Speech critical of superiors or otherwise inappropriate:** An employee gets limited protection for speech or associational activities that are *critical of superiors*, or that the employer believes are *inappropriate for the workplace*. Where such speech involves a matter of *"public concern,"* the court will *balance* the speech rights of the employee and the government's interest as employer in promoting efficiency on the job. [*Connick v. Myers*] [613]

> **Example:** P, a government clerical worker, hears that John Hinckley has tried to shoot Pres. Reagan, and says, "If they go for him again, I hope they get him." P is fired for the remark. *Held*, for P. This remark was intended as political commentary and was thus on a matter of "public concern," so P could not be fired unless the remark heavily affected P's job performance, which it did not. [*Rankin v. McPherson*]

   i. **Not a matter of public concern:** But where the speech does *not* involve a matter of public concern, *Connick* and *Rankin*, *supra*, do *not* apply, and the court gives great *deference* to the employer's judgment.

   ii. **Must not be part of employee's job function:** Also, even the limited protection given to employee speech on matters of public concern doesn't apply where the speech occurs as *part of the employee's job functions* — here, the employee gets no First Amendment protection at all, no matter how important the issue on which the employee is speaking.

> **Example:** P, a supervising lawyer in a District Attorney's Office (D), is called on to investigate whether an affidavit prepared by a deputy sheriff to obtain a search warrant was properly done. P writes a memo to his supervisor concluding that the affidavit was improperly done. The supervisor retaliates against him for what he says in the memo.
>
> *Held*, for D. "[W]hen public employees make statements *pursuant to their official duties*, the employees are *not speaking as citizens* for First Amendment purposes, and *the Constitution does not insulate their communications from employer discipline.*" Here, because P's investigation and the ensuing memorandum were part of his job responsibilities, D had the right to regulate the content and manner of P's speech. [*Garcetti v. Ceballos*] [614]

H. Compulsory disclosure : When the government requires a group, such as a charity or a political party, to *disclose who its members or contributors are*, the disclosure requirement may be an unconstitutional interference with the group's associational freedoms.

1. **"Exacting scrutiny" is used:** Such a government-mandated disclosure requirement will be subjected to *"exacting scrutiny,"* essentially a form of *intermediate-level review*. Under this standard, the disclosure being compelled must be *"narrowly tailored* to the government's asserted interest," though *not* necessarily the *"least restrictive means"* of achieving that end." [*Americans for Prosperity Foundation v. Bonta* (2021)] [615-620]

Example: California says that any tax-exempt charity that solicits contributions in-state must, after it files a "Form 990" with the federal IRS (showing the names and addresses of every major donor), also file a copy of the form with the office of the state's Attorney General ("A.G."). The A.G. defends the Form 990 disclosure requirement as a means of furthering the state's interest in preventing "charitable fraud and self-dealing." Even without this automatic "up-front" disclosure scheme, the A.G.would be free to subpoena the Form 990 from any particular charity the A.G. wanted to investigate; but, the A.G. says, collecting all Form 990s up front improves the efficiency of the office's regulatory efforts.

The Ps (two charities) sue the A.G.'s office, arguing that by requiring them to file their Form 990s, the state is violating each charity's (and the charity's donors') First Amendment freedom of association. The Ps contend that the disclosure requirement makes it harder for them to fund-raise, by subjecting their donors to the risk of reprisals and harassment from the public if the information is leaked by the A.G.'s office to the public (which the A.G. promises won't happen, but which has happened by accident in the past). The Ps claim that the disclosure requirement is not only a violation of freedom of association "as applied" to each P and its donors, but is also invalid "on its face," i.e., that it cannot constitutionally be applied to *any* charity.

Held (by a 6-3 vote), for the Ps. The California disclosure scheme must be subjected to "exacting scrutiny," and cannot survive that scrutiny. When exacting scrutiny applies, the means chosen must be "narrowly tailored" to the governmental interest. Here, there is a "dramatic mismatch" between the A.G.'s interest in combating fraud and the broad disclosure regime being used. For instance, narrow tailoring would have required the A.G.'s office to have considered (which it didn't) the use of selective subpoenas or letters announcing an audit instead of broad up-front collection of donor information from every charity; that's true even if up-front collection would be somewhat easier for the office administratively.

In fact, the scheme is invalid *on its face* (i.e., it cannot be applied to *any* charity). When a law substantially impairs First Amendment freedoms, the law may be struck down as "overbroad" (a form of facial invalidation) if "a substantial number of its applications are unconstitutional, judged in relation to the statute's plainly legitimate sweep." That's the case here, because the "risk of a *chilling effect* on association is enough" for facial invalidity, because "First Amendment freedoms need breathing space to survive." [*Americans for Prosperity Foundation v. Bonta, supra.*] [615-620]

I. **The "right not to speak":** The "right not to associate" is closely related to the *"right not to speak,"* which we'll focus on now. Part of a person's freedom of expression is the *right not to be forced* by the government to *express a message* that the person does not wish to express. [621]

   1. **Pledge of allegiance:** For instance, a state law requiring all public school students to *salute and pledge allegiance to the U.S. flag* violates some students' freedom of expression, by compelling them to utter a message with which they disagree. [*West Virginia State Board of Educ. v. Barnette*] [621]

   2. **"Live free or die" on license:** Similarly, the state of New Hampshire may not criminally punish vehicle owners who cover up the *state motto "Live Free or Die"* on their state-issued *license plates,* if the motto is at odds with the owner's moral or religious beliefs. [*Wooley v. Maynard*] [621]

   3. **Required notices in "crisis pregnancy centers":** A business operator's "right not to speak" even includes the right not to be required to *post government-drafted notices* that deliver a message with whose content the operator disagrees. [*National Institute of Family and Life Advocates v. Becerra* (2018)] [621]

Example: California requires "crisis pregnancy centers" — which try to persuade pregnant women not to get an abortion — to post a notice informing patients of the availability of public family-planning services including abortions. Several such centers (the Ps) seek an injunction against the post-the-notice requirement.

Held, for the Ps. The Ps will probably be able to prove at trial that their free-speech rights have been unconstitutionally restricted. The notice the Ps are being required to post is a "content-based regulation of speech," in that the state is "alter[ing] the content of [the Ps'] speech." Therefore, the requirement must be subjected to at least "intermediate scrutiny," which it cannot survive (because it's "wildly underinclusive," in that it exempts many similar types of clinics from a similar requirement). [*National Institute, supra*] [621]

XI. UNCONSTITUTIONAL CONDITIONS

A. **Unconstitutional conditions generally:** Suppose that before government gives a particular *benefit* — such as housing, employment, funding for an activity, or a license — government imposes a *condition*. That is, government says that the recipient must, in exchange for the benefit, agree to *waive her freedom of expression* or other constitutional right. The Court *sometimes* invokes the doctrine of *"unconstitutional conditions"* in order to strike down the condition. [623]

1. **Statement of doctrine:** When the doctrine applies, it holds that government *may not grant a benefit on the condition that the beneficiary surrender a constitutional right*, even if the government may *withhold that benefit altogether*. The idea behind the doctrine is that what the government may not do *directly*, it may not do *indirectly* either. [623]

   Example: Suppose that the Republican-controlled legislature of a state passes a statute saying that no one may get or keep a job working for the state — no matter how low-level the position or what the requirements of the position are — unless the person signs a pledge not to criticize any elected Republican official during the employment.

   The Supreme Court would undoubtedly invoke the doctrine of unconstitutional conditions to strike down this statute as a violation of state employees' and applicants' freedom of expression. Government obviously couldn't directly forbid citizens from criticizing politicians, and letting the state condition a government benefit (state employment) on the waiver of this right would amount to letting the state do indirectly what it could not to directly.

2. **Guiding principles:** The Court seems to apply the unconstitutional conditions doctrine somewhat inconsistently. But here are a couple of principles that seem to explain the outcome in most of the Court's unconstitutional-condition cases. [624-626]

   [1] **Government uses agents to deliver government's own speech:** Since government is *permitted* to say pretty much whatever it wants *when the government is itself the speaker,* government is also free to *pay agents* to deliver the government's message, and to *condition that payment* on the agent's willingness to *waive his otherwise-protected right* to engage in speech that would contradict or garble the government message the agent is being paid to deliver. [624]

      Example: A state government engages (and pays) P, a celebrity, to make public speeches as part of the government's campaign to have the federal constitution amended so as to limit the scope of abortion rights under *Roe v. Wade*. Government *may*, as a condition to engaging P, insist that P agree that during the course of the campaign, P will not publicly state that P is in favor of a woman's right to choose an abortion as presently construed by the Supreme Court.

   [2] **Limits on use of government's payments:** Government is also free to set up *"subsidy programs,"* under which government funds private groups to help the groups carry out some func-

tion. And when government does this, it is free to *refuse* to allow *the subsidy dollars to be used for particular activities opposed by government*, including otherwise-constitutionally-protected activities like *speaking* on certain topics, *performing abortions*, or lobbying legislators. [624]

> **Example:** Congress provides federal grants to help private groups operate family-planning clinics. When a special-purpose "project" is set up to receive such a grant and operate a clinic, the project's founders are required to prohibit the project's employees (while on the job) from advocating for, or counseling about, abortion.
>
> *Held*, the condition is not an unconstitutional condition, and does not violate the First Amendment rights of the group that runs the project. "[T]he Government is not denying a benefit to anyone, but is instead simply insisting that *public funds be spent for the purposes* for which they were authorized." (The way the statute is written, a group that runs the project/clinic and receives the funds for it can continue to engage in abortion advocacy or counseling; the group simply is required to conduct those activities through a program or project that is separate from the project [the clinic] receiving the government funds.) [*Rust v. Sullivan.*] [625]

XII. SPECIAL PROBLEMS OF THE MEDIA

A. The media (and its special problems): Here is a brief review of some special problems related to the *media*: [626-641]

1. Prior restraint: In general, the government will not be able to obtain a *prior restraint* against broadcasters or publishers. In other words, only in exceptionally rare circumstances may the government obtain an *injunction* against the printing or airing of a story, and the government will almost never be allowed to require that a publisher or broadcaster obtain a *permit* before it runs a story. [628-631]

> **Example**: The *New York Times* may not constitutionally be enjoined from publishing part of the Pentagon Papers, even though these government-prepared materials might contain information that is useful to our enemies or that would embarrass the U.S. [*N.Y. Times v. U.S.*]

a. Gag order: This means that a judge may generally not impose a *gag order* on the media ordering it not to disclose a certain fact about a pending trial. [631-633]

i. Participants: But the judge may usually order the *participants* not to speak to the press. For instance, a state may prevent a lawyer from making any statement which would have a "substantial likelihood of materially prejudicing" a trial or other court proceeding. [*Gentile v. State Bar of Nevada*] [633]

2. Subpoenas by government: The press does not get any special protection from government demands that the press *furnish information* which other citizens would have to furnish. In particular, if a reporter has information that is of interest to a *grand jury*, the reporter may be required by subpoena to disclose that information to the grand jury even though this would cause him to violate a promise of confidentiality to a source. [*Branzburg v. Hayes*] (But the state is always free to enact a "shield law" making such subpoenas illegal under some or all circumstances.) [633-636]

3. Right of access: The press does not get any general *right of access* to information held by the government. [638-639]

a. Right to attend trials: However, the media does have a constitutionally protected right to *attend criminal trials*. This right is not absolute — the government can close the media (and the public) out of a trial if it shows that there is an "overriding" government interest being served by a closed trial, and that that interest cannot be served by less restrictive means. [*Richmond Newspapers v. Virginia*] [638]

    i. **Showing rarely made:** But this showing will rarely be made, so that as a practical matter the press is usually entitled to attend a criminal trial. (*Example:* A state statute automatically bars the press from hearing any trial testimony by a minor who was allegedly the victim of a sex crime. *Held*, the statute unduly interferes with the public's right of access to criminal trials. [*Globe Newspapers v. Sup. Ct.*])

    ii. **Other proceedings:** Probably the media also has a qualified constitutional right to attend other proceedings, like *civil trials* and *pre-trial proceedings*. [*Gannett Co. v. DePasquale*]. [638]

4. **Disclosure of confidential or illegally-obtained information:** Government may generally *not* prohibit the media from disclosing information that goverment believes ought to be *secret*. If a media member *lawfully* obtains information about a matter of public significance, government may punish disclosure of the information only if government has "a *need* of the *highest order*," which it will rarely be found to have. [*Smith v. Daily Mail*] [636-637]

    Example: A broadcaster may not be held civilly liable for *publishing the name of a rape victim*, if the broadcaster learns the name from reading a publicly-filed indictment. [*Cox Broadcasting v. Cohn*]

    a. **Where publisher has acted illegally:** If the *publisher itself* has *acted illegally* in obtaining the information, then government *may make it a crime* to punish the information, no matter how newsworthy it is. (*Example:* A newspaper reporter breaks into a private home to steal an audiotape, then publishes a transcript of the tape. The newspaper may constitutionally be punished for the publication.)

    b. **Where private party has acted illegally but publisher has not:** On the other hand, the fact that the secret information was originally *obtained illegally* by a person *acting independently* of the eventual publisher is *not* enough to allow publication to be made criminal, at least where the material has significant newsworthiness.

    Example: X, a private individual acting alone, intercepts and tapes a cellphone conversation between the Ps (two teachers' union officials) who are discussing their upcoming negotiation with a school board. The interception violates federal wiretapping laws. X anonymously mails the tape to a radio station, which broadcasts it. The Ps sue the station. *Held*, the station may not constitutionally be held liable for damages to the officials, because the station did not participate in the illegality, and the strong First Amendment interest in disseminating this newsworthy material outweighs the admittedly strong interest in safeguarding cellphone conversations. [*Bartnicki v. Vopper*] [637]

CHAPTER 15

FREEDOM OF RELIGION

I. INTRODUCTION

A. **Two clauses:** There are two quite distinct clauses in the First Amendment pertaining to religion.[660]

    1. **Establishment Clause:** First, we have the *Establishment* Clause. That clause prohibits any law "respecting an establishment of religion." The main purpose of the Establishment Clause is to prevent government from *endorsing* or *supporting* religion.

2. **Free Exercise:** The second clause is the *Free Exercise* Clause. That clause bars any law "prohibiting the free exercise of religion." The main purpose of the Free Exercise Clause is to prevent the government from **outlawing** or seriously **burdening** a person's pursuit of whatever religion (and whatever religious practices) he chooses.

B. **Applicable to states:** Both the Establishment and the Free Exercise Clauses by their terms only restrict legislative action by **Congress**. However, both clauses have been interpreted to apply also to the **states**, by means of the Fourteenth Amendment's due process clause. Therefore, you don't have to worry whether the government action in question is federal or state — the same standards apply to each. [660]

C. **Conflict:** Occasionally, the Establishment and Free Exercises Clauses seem to **conflict** on particular facts. That is, a religious group may be asking for some government benefit; if the benefit is given, there may be an Establishment Clause problem. Yet if the benefit is not given, this may be a burdening of religion. When the two clauses seem to conflict, the **Free Exercise** Clause dominates. In other words, if a particular benefit or accommodation to religion is arguably required by the Free Exercise Clause, then when government grants that accommodation or benefit it is not violating the Establishment Clause.

> **Example:** A public university makes meeting rooms available to all sorts of student groups. If the university allows religious groups to use the room, there might be an Establishment Clause problem. But if it doesn't allow religious groups to use the rooms, while allowing non-religious groups to do so, there might be a Free Exercise Clause problem. Consequently, it will not be an Establishment Clause violation for the university to allow the religious groups to use the rooms. [660]

II. THE ESTABLISHMENT CLAUSE

A. **General rule:** The overall purpose of the Establishment Clause is to put a **wall between church and state**. In other words, the government must stay out of the business of religion, and religious groups must to some extent stay out of the business of government. [661-662]

1. **Some examples:** Here are some things that would clearly be forbidden by the Establishment clause:

   a. **Official church:** Congress cannot establish an "official religion of the United States." In fact, Congress probably couldn't even declare that "the American people believe in God," because the Establishment Clause means that government may not prefer or endorse religion over non-religion.

   b. **Go to church:** The government cannot force people to worship. In fact, the state can't even intentionally **encourage** people to worship — for example, it cannot decide that it wants to promote church attendance, and then give people a special tax deduction that applies to church donations but not to other charitable donations. (But it could, as Congress does, give a *general* tax deduction for charitable contributions, and let contributions to churches be eligible. This would be allowable because the government is treating religion the same as non-religion, not preferring religion over non-religion.)

   c. **Preference of one religion over another:** The government cannot intentionally **prefer one religion over another religion.** For instance, a state may not decide that since Christians are in the majority, it will allow tax deductions for contribution to Christian churches but not for contributions made, say, to synagogues.

   d. **Participate:** Government may not actively **participate** in religious affairs, or allow religious organizations to have a special participation in government affairs. For instance, Congress probably could not constitutionally use public officials and public polling places to run an election to determine the next head of the American Presbyterian Church — this would be an undue governmental entanglement in religious affairs.

B. Three-part test: Officially, the modern Court applies a *three-fold test* to determine whether governmental action violates the Establishment Clause. This is the "*Lemon*" test, from *Lemon v. Kurtzman*. Under this test, only if the action satisfies *each* of the following conditions will it be *valid*:

[1] Secular purpose: The government action must have a *secular purpose*;

[2] Effect: The action's principal or *primary effect* must neither *advance* nor *inhibit* religion; and

[3] Entanglement: The action must not foster an *excessive government entanglement* with religion. [661]

1. Present Court's discontent with *Lemon*: But there are some strong clues that a majority of the present Court is so *unhappy* with the *Lemon* test that the Court may *abandon it*, or at least *curtail the situations* in which it is used. [661]

a. Abandoned for religious-symbol displays on public land: For instance, as the result of a 2019 case, the Court now seems to have *abandoned* the use of *Lemon* for cases involving the *display of religious symbols on public property.* See *American Legion v. American Humanist Assoc., infra*, p. C-109.

C. Religion and the public schools: If the government tries to introduce religion into the *public schools*, it is probably violating the Establishment Clause. [662-666]

1. Instruction: Thus the government may, of course, not conduct religious instruction in the public schools. In fact, it can't even allow privately-employed religious teachers to conduct classes on the public schools' premises during school hours. [662-663]

a. Accommodation: However, it's probably allowable for the government to allow students to *leave school early* to attend religious instruction somewhere else. It's also probably acceptable for government to let religious groups have access to school facilities, as long as non-religious groups are given equal access. Remember our example of the university that lets all kinds of student groups, including religious groups, use meeting rooms — that's permissible.

2. Prayer reading: The official *reading of prayers* in the public schools will virtually always be unconstitutional. See, e.g., *Engel v. Vitale*. That is, it will almost always turn out to be the case that either the sole purpose, or the primary effect, of the prayer reading is to advance religion. [663-664]

a. Moment of silence: Even the setting aside of a *"moment of silence"* at the beginning of the school day will generally violate the Establishment Clause, since a moment-of-silence statute will usually turn out to have been solely motivated by the legislators' intent to advance religion, or will at least have the primary effect of advancing religion. (But this will always turn on the actual purpose and effect of the particular statute — there's no absolute *per se* rule against moments of silence. [*Wallace v. Jaffree*] [663]

b. Prayer reading at graduation: Similarly, the school may not conduct a prayer as part of a *graduation ceremony*, at least where school officials can fairly be said to be sponsoring the religious message. [*Lee v. Weisman*] [664-664]

c. Student-selected speakers don't solve problem: The school can't easily get around prayer-reading problems by having the student body *elect a student speaker,* and then having that speaker decide whether to give a prayer. As long as the school's process can be reasonably viewed as supporting school prayer, the fact that a student-body election intervenes is irrelevant. [*Santa Fe Indep. Sch. Dist. v. Doe*] [664]

3. **Curriculum:** The state may not design or modify the *curriculum* of its schools in order to further religion at the expense of non-religion, or to further one set of religious beliefs over others. (*Example*: A state may not forbid the teaching of evolution. [*Epperson v. Ark.*] Similarly, it probably may not demand that "creationism" be taught in addition to evolution, since "creationism" is mainly a religious doctrine the teaching of which would have the primary effect of advancing religion. [*Edwards v. Aguillard*]) [665-666]

4. **Equal treatment of religion and non-religion:** But it's not a violation of the Establishment Clause for government to treat religion and non-religion *equally* in the schools (and government may in fact be *required* to do this because of free-speech principles). (*Example*: If a public university funds non-religiously-oriented student publications, it must fund an evangelical Christian publication on the same terms. [*Rosenberger v. Univ. of Virginia.*])

D. **Sunday closing laws:** Laws requiring *merchants* to be *closed on Sundays* generally do *not* violate the Establishment Clause. The reason is that these "blue laws" have a primarily secular effect and purpose — they permit everyone (Christian, non-Christian and atheist alike) to have a uniform day of rest. [*McGowan v. Md.*] [667-667]

E. **Ceremonies, displays and monuments:** Any time your exam question involves a religiously-oriented *ceremony*, *display or monument*, there may be an Establishment Clause violation if government either seems to be *sponsoring it,* or is allowing it to *occur on public property.* [671-680]

1. **Ceremonies mentioning God:** First, consider government-led *ceremonies* referring to God or other religious themes. In this context, the fact that God is *referred to* in a ceremony put on by the government will usually *not* cause the ceremony to violate the Establishment Clause.

   a. **Chaplain at sessions of legislature:** For instance, the practice of opening each daily session of a state *legislature* with a *prayer* by a state-paid chaplain does *not violate* the Establishment Clause. [*Marsh v. Chambers*] [671]

   b. **Chaplain at meetings of town board:** Similarly, it's not an Establishment Clause violation if each week a different member of the clergy offers a prayer before the opening of a *town board's meeting*, as long the practice does not disparage other religions or coerce members of the public into praying. [*Town of Greece v. Galloway*] [671]

2. **Displays and monuments with religious themes:** The Establishment Clause may be violated when the government either erects, or makes its property available for private groups to erect, some sort of *display*, *monument* or *presentation* that involves religious themes. [672-673]

   a. **Illustrations:** Here are some of the types of religiously-themed displays or monuments located on public land whose Establishment Clause status has come before the Court:

      ❏ A display of the *Ten Commandments*;

      ❏ A Christmas-time *nativity scene*;

      ❏ A war memorial featuring a *Christian cross*.

   b. **The endorsement test:** In this area, the Court's test usually seems to be: Would a *reasonable observer* seeing the display or monument conclude that the government was either *endorsing religion in general*, or *endorsing a particular religion*? If the answer to either part of the question is "*yes*," the display or monument violates the Establishment Clause. If the answer is "*no*," it does not. [672]

      i. **Context:** This means that the constitutionality of a given Ten Commandments display, nativity scene, monument featuring a cross, etc., will be a *question of fact.* The most important single factor seems to be the *context* in which the religious symbol is displayed. [672]

(1) Presented by itself: If the religious symbol is presented *by itself* in what is clearly a space reserved by the government for its own property and its own messages, the Court is likely to conclude that a "reasonable observer" would believe that the government *was* endorsing the religious message.

(2) Presented near other, non-religious, symbols: Conversely, the presence of *other non-religious symbols nearby*, or the existence of a *sign* indicating that the display was furnished by private parties without governmental approval, or evidence that the religious material was provided for its historical rather than religious value — any of these factors may well be enough to lead a reasonable observer to the conclusion that government was *not* endorsing religion.

ii. **Intent:** Government's *intent or motive* in establishing (or making its property available for) the display or monument is also of vital importance. If the court believes that the government's principal purpose in establishing the display or monument was to *promote or endorse religion* (or some particular religion), this fact by itself will probably lead to a finding of unconstitutionality. [673]

iii. **Passage of time coupled with additional significance:** Lastly, even if, at the time the display or monument was created, a court would have found that government was endorsing the religious message (leading to a conclusion that the Establishment Clause was violated), the sheer *passage of time* — during which the item acquires *additional non-religious, purely cultural, significance* — may well lead a court considering the matter now to find that no ongoing violation of the Clause exists. [673]

Example: In 1918, a private group in a Maryland county erects a 32-foot-high plain white cross ("the Cross") as a memorial to the county's soldiers who have recently died in WWI. In 1961, a state government commission (the "Commission") acquires the monument, and public funds are thereafter used to maintain it. By the time an Establishment Clause challenge is filed in 2014, the monument sits on public land (owned by the Commission) at the center of a busy intersection.

Held, maintenance of the Cross is not an Establishment Clause violation, on account of various factors. An important factor is that even though this monument's "original purpose" was "infused with religion," the *passage of time* has *changed the monument's meaning to the community,* which has come to view it as a secular monument to the county's fallen soldiers. Another factor is that if a court were to order this long-standing monument to be removed now for Establishment Clause reasons, the removal would "strike many as *aggressively hostile to religion.*" Therefore, the monument may remain, even though it might have violated the Establishment Clause when it was first erected. [*American Legion v. American Humanist Assoc.* (2019)] [674]

iv. ***Lemon* three-part test not used:** As the result of *American Legion, supra,* the Court has now *rejected* the use of the three-part *Lemon v. Kurtzman* test (*supra*, p. C-107) in cases where an Establishment Clause challenge is brought against the maintenance of religious symbols or monuments on government property. Instead, the factors discussed in Pars. (i) through (iii) above are applied, and this will often lead to the challenge being *rejected.* [675-676]

F. **Financial aid to religious schools:** Whenever your fact patterns shows that the government is giving some sort of *financial aid* to religious schools, consider the possibility that the program violates the Establishment Clause. [677-680]

1. **General principles:** In general, here are some things to look for when you analyze aid to religious schools:

    a. **Benefit to all students:** A government program that benefits ***all students***, at public, private non-parochial and parochial schools alike, is much more likely to pass muster than aid which goes overwhelmingly to parochial-school students;

    b. **Colleges:** Aid to religious ***colleges*** is easier to justify than aid to high schools or, especially, elementary schools; and

    c. **Aid to parents:** Aid given to ***parents*** in a way that permits them to choose what school to use the aid at is more likely to be sustained than aid given directly to the ***school.***

2. Transportation: Programs by which parents may have their children ***transported*** free to religious schools are probably constitutional, as long as the transport program also covers public and private non-parochial students. [*Everson v. Bd. of Ed.*] [678]

3. Textbooks and equipment: Similarly, ***textbooks*** and ***equipment*** (e.g., computers) may be loaned to parochial school students as long as loans on the same basis are made to public school and private non-parochial students. But only books and materials that are ***strictly secular*** may be used (e.g., Bibles can't be lent out). [*Bd. of Ed. v. Allen; Mitchell v. Helms*] [678]

4. Teachers: The state ***may*** send ***public school teachers*** into parochial schools, even to teach basic academic subjects, as long as what's taught is free of: (1) religious content and (2) influence from the parochial school's administration. [*Agostini v. Felton*] [679]

5. Tuition vouchers: The state may give ***tuition vouchers*** to parents to enable them to pay religious-school tuition, if the vouchers may also be used in non-religious private schools. That's true even if the tuition is used to cover the costs of educating the children in core religious doctrine, and even if the benefits overwhelmingly go to the parents of religious school students. [*Zelman v. Simmons-Harris*] [679-680]

    a. **Free Exercise violation:** In fact, if the state's program gives tuition assistance to private-school students and their parents generally, it's likely to be a ***Free Exercise violation*** for the state to ***exclude parochial-school students*** from the program. And that's true even if the state has a deep and long-standing interest in maintaining the separation of church and state. See *Espinoza v. Montana Dept. of Revenue, infra,* C-114.

G. No preference for one sect over others: Just as the Establishment Clause is violated when government prefers religion over non-religion, so it is violated when the government ***favors a particular sect over other sects***, or over non-religious interests. As the Court has put it, "[t]he clearest command of the Establishment Clause is that ***one religious denomination cannot be officially preferred over another."*** [*Larson v. Valente*] [680]

1. Strict scrutiny: In fact, if the Court is convinced that government is intentionally preferring some sect(s) over others (rather than aiding religion generally), the Court will ***apply strict scrutiny:*** the preference will be struck down unless it is "justified by a ***compelling governmental interest*** and ... ***closely fitted to further that interest."*** *Larson, supra.*

    Example: The state of Minnesota modifies a tax exemption given to all religious organizations so that it now applies only to the benefit of those religious organizations that receive more than half of their total contributions from members; this is the "50% Rule." (The state says that the Rule is designed to guard against groups that conduct abusive in-person solicitation of non-members.) The "Moonies," a Christian sect that widely solicits funds in public places, claim that the Rule violates the group's rights under the Establishment Clause.

    Held, for the Moonies. Given that the 50% Rule on its face prefers some religious groups over others, the Court will automatically strictly scrutinize the Rule, and uphold it only if it is "justified by a compelling governmental interest and ... closely fitted to further that interest." Here, even if the state's asserted interest in combating solicitation abuse is compelling, the

50% Rule is not "closely fitted" to furthering that interest, since nothing in the record suggests that the likelihood of solicitation abuse is closely related to the ratio of member contributions to total contributions. *Larson, supra.* [681-681]

2. **Intentional "accommodation" of a religion:**   The principle that government may not intentionally prefer one religion over another, or one sect over another, applies even if government thinks that it's merely trying to **"accommodate"** a particular religion.

   Example: The New York legislature creates a special school district whose residents consist solely of members of a particular orthodox Jewish sect, the Satmar Hassidim. The purpose and effect of the special district is to let the Satmars get public funding for a public school in their village to educate their handicapped children. *Held,* the district violates the Establishment Clause, because it was created in a way that singled out the Satmars for a special preference not made available to other groups (and also because it amounted to a delegation of state authority to a group chosen according to a religious criterion). [*Bd. of Educ. of Kiryas Joel Village v. Grumet*] [681-682]

3. **Unintended effect:**   But a regulation that has the *incidental unintended effect* of helping one religion or sect more than another, or hurting one more than another, does not generally violate the Establishment Clause.

4. **Preference of religion over non-religion:**   In theory, government can't even "accommodate" *religion generally*, by giving religious groups in general a preference over other types of groups or persons. But in practice, the Court is *less likely to object* to a special accommodation of religion generally than to an accommodation of a particular sect.

   Example: In a federal statute, the Religious Land Use and Institutionalized Persons Act (RLUIPA), the federal government orders prison officials to go out of their way to accommodate the religious needs of all prisoners (e.g., by giving them opportunities for group worship and the right to adhere to the dress mandates of their religion). *Held,* even though comparable accommodations are not given to similar needs/desires that are not mandated by religious belief, RLUIPA (at least on its face) does not violate the Establishment Clause. [*Cutter v. Wilkinson*] [682]

5. **National security, and the entry of foreigners into the U.S. (*Trump v. Hawaii*):**   The rule that governmental actions that are motivated by a desire to prefer one sect over another will be strictly scrutinized is subject to an important *exception*: when the preference occurs in the context of the federal government's authority to protect national security by determining **which non-U.S. nationals may enter the country,** the courts will use only *mere-rationality review*, not strict scrutiny. [*Trump v. Hawaii*] [683]

   Example: President Trump issues a "Proclamation," (a/k/a a "travel ban") which greatly restricts entry into the U.S. by nationals of eight countries, six of which have majority-Muslim populations. The Proclamation is "facially neutral" with respect to religion; it recites that it's designed to protect against entry by nationals from countries that the federal government has determined to have inadequate procedures for vetting their citizens against terrorist leanings. Before and after issuing the Proclamation, Mr. Trump makes numerous comments suggesting that the reason for having a travel ban is to block entry of Muslims into the U.S. to reduce the likelihood of terror attacks (e.g., as a candidate, he says, "Islam hates us. . . . [W]e can't allow people coming into this country who have this hatred of the United States . . . [a]nd of people that are not Muslim."). The Ps (the state of Hawaii and some of its citizens) seek an injunction against the travel ban. They assert that the ban violates the Establishment Clause, in that it is a "religious gerrymander," intentionally devised to apply mainly to countries with majority-Muslim populations, and reflecting the President's animus towards Muslims. The lower courts grant the injunction.

Held, for the Trump Administration: the Ps are unlikely to win at trial, so the injunction is dissolved. The Constitution is structured so that the power to make decisions about foreigners' entry to the U.S. — like most matters of national security — is held by Congress and the executive branch, "largely immune from judicial control." Therefore, the President's actions in this area will be subject only to an easy-to-satisfy *"rational-basis review,"* under which the Court will uphold the action so long as it is "plausibly related" to achieving a legitimate objective, in this case, protecting the country from terrorism by improving pre-entry vetting processes. Here, this standard is satisfied, in part because the ban's details were worked out in a *"worldwide review process* ... by multiple Cabinet officials and their agencies," making those details rationally related to the anti-terrorism objective. [*Trump v. Hawaii, supra*] [683-688]

Note: The *Trump v. Hawaii* decision seems to say that in the area of national security, the Court will uphold the government action long as that action is rationally related to the achievement of a plausible and legitimate national-security interest; any evidence that government in fact acted based mostly based on bias against a religious group will essentially be *ignored*. [687-688]

H. The "excessive entanglement prong": Don't forget the third prong of the test for Establishment Clause violations: governmental action must not give rise to *excessive entanglement* on the part of government in the affairs of religion, or vice versa.

1. The "ministerial exception" from government regulation: For instance, governmental regulation that has the effect of interfering with a religious group's determination of *who is qualified to convey the group's message* and/or *carry out its mission* is likely to violate the Establishment Clause. Thus religious groups are entitled to a *"ministerial exception,"* under which the group's choice of *who may be a minister or leader* will be essentially *immune from regulation*, such as *anti-discrimination* laws. [669-670]

   a. Discretion in defining "minister": The religious group must be given *extremely wide discretion* in *determining who is a "minister"* for the group. Indeed, it's not really accurate to refer to the exception as one for "ministers" — it's more accurate to say that the exception applies to any employee whom the institution regards as *"educating students in the [institution's] faith."* [*Our Lady of Guadalupe School v. Morrissey-Berru* (2020)] [669-670]

   Example: The Ps are two fifth-grade teachers at Catholic elementary schools; each of these schools is a defendant (a "D"). Each of the Ps sues her school for violating generally-applicable employment laws (in one case it's an age discrimination claim, and the other is a disability-discrimination claim). The Ds defend by arguing that (1) each D has the right to determine whether a particular employee is a "minister"; (2) each D has correctly determined that the P is a minister, even though neither of the Ps is an ordained minister and both teach primarily secular subjects; (3) since each P is a minister, the Ds are entitled (under both the Free Exercise and the Establishment Clause) to an exemption from the otherwise-applicable anti-discrimination laws.

   Held (by a 7-2 vote), for the Ds. Both Ps were correctly classified as "ministers," and are therefore not protected by anti-discrimination-in-employment laws. It doesn't matter that neither school gave the employee the title "minister." Nor does it necessarily matter that the employee did not have formal religious training, especially in the case of elementary school teaching. Instead, "what matters ... is *what an employee does*[.]" A religious school is entitled to apply the ministerial exception to a teacher if at the core of the teacher's mission is *"educating young people in their faith,"* and *"training them to live their faith[.]"*

Both of the Ps easily meet this standard, because both teachers "prayed with their students, attended Mass with the students, and prepared the children for their participation in other religious activities." [*Our Lady of Guadalupe, supra.*] [669-670]

III. THE FREE EXERCISE CLAUSE

A. **Free Exercise generally:** Let's now turn to the second clause relating to religion, the Free Exercise Clause. Under this clause, the government is barred from making any law "prohibiting the free exercise" of religion. The Free Exercise Clause prevents the government from getting in the way of people's ability to practice their religions. [688]

   1. **Conduct vs. belief:** The Free Exercise Clause of course prevents the government from unduly burdening a person's abstract "beliefs." (*Example:* Congress cannot ban the religion of voodooism merely because it disapproves of voodooism or thinks that voodooism is irrational.) But the Clause also relates to *conduct*.

      a. **Non-religious objectives:** Free Exercise problems most typically arise when government, acting in pursuit of *non-religious objectives*, either: (1) forbids or burdens conduct which happens to be *required* by someone's religious belief; or conversely, (2) compels or encourages conduct which happens to be *forbidden* by someone's religious beliefs.

B. **Intentional vs. unintentional burdens:** The Free Exercise Clause is much more likely to prevent the government from interfering with religion when the government does so *intentionally* (i.e., with knowledge or intent that a religious practice is being burdened) than when it does so *unintentionally*.

   1. **Intentional burden:** If the interference with religion is *intentional* on government's part, then in most contexts the interference is subjected to *strict scrutiny*, which it will usually not survive. [688]

   2. **Unintentional burden:** If government *unintentionally burdens* religion, it's much harder for a religious person or group to demonstrate a Free Exercise violation. The Free Exercise Clause does not relieve a person of the obligation to comply with a *valid and neutral law* of *general applicability* even though the law forbids (or requires) conduct that his religion requires (or forbids).

Below, we consider the "intentional" and "unintentional" cases in turn.

C. **Three categories of intentional discrimination vs religion:** Within the *"intentional discrimination against religion"* branch of Free Exercise case law, let's divide government actions relating to religion into *three different categories* for analysis:

   [1] **Prohibition or punishment:** As category [1], we have cases in which government actively *prohibits or punishes* a private person's religiously-motivated actions, under circumstances in which the government seems to be acting based on a *desire to discriminate* against a particular religion or against religion generally. In this category, *strict scrutiny* will certainly be applied.

      Example: A city council enacts an ordinance making it illegal to carry out animal sacrifices. The council is shown to have been motivated by prejudice against a particular locally-unpopular religious sect that had been engaging in such sacrifices. The court will surely give the ordinance strict scrutiny, and will strike it down. (Cf. *Church of the Lukumi Babalu Aye,* [p. 690], where the Supreme Court strictly scrutinized, and *struck down,* such a prohibition.)

      a. **Hostility during adjudication:** Category [1] also encompasses scenarios in which government behaves with hostility to religion generally (or to a particular religious group) during the course of *adjudicating* whether a person is *entitled to an accommodation* on religious grounds. (As to accommodation requests generally, see C-114 below.) [*Masterpiece Cakeshop, Ltd. v. Colorado Civ. Rights Comm'n,* (2018)] [691]

[2] Pool of discretionary benefits denied for "essentially religious" uses: As category [2], we have cases in which government does both of the following: (a) uses its discretion to furnish a benefit to a *class* of individuals, and (b) tells recipients that they may not use the benefit towards any *"essentially religious endeavor,"* like *training for the ministry.* In this situation, the Court will apparently *not* apply strict scrutiny, and will conclude that the carve-out for "essentially religious" uses does not violate the recipient's Free Exercise rights. [*Locke v. Davey*] [689]

[3] Denial of generally-available benefit: Finally, Category [3] consists of cases in which government makes a benefit *generally available to citizens*, except that government intentionally makes the benefit *unavailable* to those who want to use it *in connection with activities run by a religious institution even though those activities are not themselves religiously-oriented.* As in Category [1] cases, the Supreme Court will *apply strict scrutiny* to the governmental action, and will almost certainly *strike down* the action as a violation of the Free Exercise Clause. [694]

> **Example:** The Montana Legislature sets up a program in which donors who fund scholarships for use at private schools are given dollar-for-dollar tax credits for their donations. The program allows the scholarships to be used at any "qualifying" private school in the state, a term that encompasses virtually any private school, religious or not. After the program is enacted, 94% of the scholarship dollars are used at private schools operated by religious groups. However, the Montana State Constitution contains a provision prohibiting any use of public funds to aid any school controlled by any "church, sect, or denomination" (the "no-aid" provision). In order to prevent the scholarship program from violating the no-aid provision, the state Department of Revenue enacts an administrative rule ("Rule 1") barring the use of the scholarships at any private school operated by a religious group. The Ps — three mothers who want to use the scholarships at a church-run school — sue, claiming that Rule 1's religious-school carveout violates their and their children's Free Exercise rights.
>
> *Held*, for the Ps. The state-constitutional no-aid provision, as applied to invalidate the scholarship program, violates the Ps' Free Exercise rights. "[D]isqualifying *otherwise eligible recipients from a public benefit* 'solely *because of their religious character'* imposes 'a *penalty on the free exercise of religion.'* " The no-aid provision as applied here *constitutes "status-based discrimination,"* thereby triggering *"the strictest scrutiny."* The state court's use of the provision to exclude religious schools can survive this scrutiny only if the state can show that the provision (1) "advance[s] *'interests of the highest order'"* and (2) is *"narrowly tailored* in pursuit of those interests." The no-aid provision as applied here *flunks both prongs of strict scrutiny.* [*Espinoza v. Montana Dept. of Revenue* (2020)] [695-697]

D. Unintentional burdening of religious practices: Where government *unintentionally burdens* a religious practice by enacting a *generally-applicable* rule, it is very difficult for the affected individual whose religious practice has been burdened to obtain an *exemption* from the rule on free exercise grounds.

1. Rule since 1990 (*Employment Div. v. Smith*): In this situation, a 1990 decision changed the law. In that decision, the Court held that the right of free exercise does not relieve a person of the obligation to comply with a *valid and neutral law* of *general applicability,* even though the law forbids (or requires) conduct that his religion requires (or forbids). [*Employment Division v. Smith*]. [700]

Example: Oregon makes it a crime to possess the drug peyote, and refuses to give an exemption to Native Americans whose use of the drug is a central part of their religious rites. The Native Americans assert that their rights under the Free Exercise Clause require the state to give them an exemption from the rule, unless the state can show that denial of an exemption is necessary for the achievement of a compelling state objective.

Held, for the state. Oregon may refuse an exemption. And it may do so without application of strict scrutiny by the court, indeed, without the court's doing any balancing of the strength of the state's interest in its prohibition against the burden on the individual's religious beliefs. "[T]he right of free exercise does not relieve an individual of the obligation to comply with a *valid and neutral law* of *general applicability* on the ground that the law proscribes (or prescribes) conduct that his religion prescribes (or proscribes)." [*Employment Division v. Smith, supra.*] [700]

    a. **A few exceptions may remain:** Before the 1990 *Smith* decision, the Court sometimes held that where a generally-applicable law significantly impaired a person's religious practice, the government had to *grant the person an exemption* from obeying the law, unless the government proved that the law was the *least restrictive means* of accomplishing whatever compelling objective the state was pursuing (a strict scrutiny standard). A few of these decisions are still on the books, and might well *come out the same way today*, notwithstanding *Smith*.

        i. **Compulsory schooling:** For instance, before deciding *Smith*, the Court required a state to give an exemption from a requirement that all students under a certain age *attend school,* in the case described in the following Example. [699-699]

        Example: Wisconsin requires all youths to attend school until the age of 16. This is a generally-applicable law, i.e., one not intended to disfavor religion. The Ps, parents of a group of 14- and 15-year-old Amish students, argue that the Free Exercise Clause requires that these students be exempted from the law. The Ps show that a core belief of their religion is that members should be informally taught at home to earn their living through farming and other rural activities.

        Held, for the Ps. Given the Ps' religious beliefs about at-home schooling, the Free Exercise Clause required the state to exempt the Ps' 14- and 15-year-old Amish children from the schooling requirement. The state's interest in education can be adequately served by the less-restrictive means of allowing home-schooling of this particular group of children. [*Wisconsin v. Yoder*, a pre-*Smith* decision from 1972.] [699-699]

2. **The meaning of "generally-applicable law" under *Smith*:** As we've seen, in order for a government regulation that burdens the free exercise of religion to nonetheless be enforceable under *Smith*, the regulation must be a *"law of general applicability."* What kind of laws will be found to *flunk* this generally-applicable requirement?

    a. **Two categories:** There seem to be *two main categories* that will cause a law to be found not generally-applicable:

    [1] **Individualized exemptions:** First, where government has allowed *"individualized exemptions"* to the law's requirements, i.e., exemptions based on the circumstances of the particular person seeking the exemption; and

    [2] **Comparable secular activity:** Second, where government has *exempted an entire category of secular activities* from the law's application, if that category is found to pose dangers or problems that are *"comparable"* to dangers/problems posed by the religious activity that has not been granted an exemption.

[701] We'll consider each of these categories separately. Category [1] is discussed in Sub-par. (b) immediately below; category [2] is discussed in Sub-par. (c) starting on p. C-116 *infra*.

b. Individualized exemptions (*Fulton v. Philadelphia*): *Smith* says (in passing) that a law that has the unintended effect of burdening religious expression will be deemed ***not*** to be "generally applicable" — and thus not eligible for the favorable-to-government status conferred by *Smith* — if the law contains a mechanism for ***recognizing "individualized exemptions"*** to the law. A 2021 decision, ***Fulton v. City of Philadelphia***, discussed in the following Example, shows how this works: there, the fact that the law in question authorized government to make individualized exemptions from the law's requirements caused *Smith* not to apply, with the result that the Court ***strictly scrutinized*** the law as a burden on religious expression, and unanimously struck it down. [702-706]

> **Example:** The City of Philadelphia uses a roster of private social-services agencies to help the City place children into foster homes. Each participating agency maintains a list of potential foster homes, which it sends to the City's Department of Human Services. When the Department determines that a child cannot remain with her family, it picks from these lists whatever family it regards as the most suitable, and contracts for support services from the agency that listed that family. In a change of policy, the Department begins to require each agency on its roster to agree that the agency will not reject a family as a prospective foster family based on the family's "sexual orientation." One agency that has long been on the City's roster, P (Catholic Social Services or "CSS"), tells the Department that for religious reasons, CSS has a policy — founded in Catholic doctrine — that CSS may not assist same-sex married couples in becoming foster parents (but CSS also tells the Department that CSS will be happy to refer such couples to other placement agencies). When the Department responds by refusing to contract with CSS for further placements, CSS sues the Department, asserting that the latter's refusal to exempt CSS from the no-discrimination policy violates CSS' Free Exercise rights.
>
> The Department defends by saying that its no-discrimination rule is a "generally-applicable" rule under *Smith*. But it turns out that the standard foster-care contract between the Department and each private agency contains a provision, "Section 3.21," giving the Commissioner of the Department the power to grant, in the Commissioner's ***"sole discretion,"*** an ***"individual exemption"*** to the non-discrimination rule as to any given placement. CSS argues that Section 3.21 prevents the Department's no-discrimination-against-same-sex-couples rule from being "generally applicable."
>
> *Held*, for CSS: the Department's decision to allow the Commissioner discretion to grant ***individualized exemptions*** to the no-discrimination rule indeed prevents the Department's rule from being a "generally applicable" law. Therefore, *Smith* does not apply. And since *Smith* doesn't apply, then because the Department's rule imposes (even unintentionally) a significant burden on P's religious exercise, the rule must be ***subjected to strict scrutiny.*** Strict scrutiny in this context means that unless the government can bear the burden of showing that its ability to achieve a compelling objective would be ***significantly impaired*** by ***granting an exemption*** to the applicant, the government ***must grant the exemption.*** Here, the Department has not carried its burden of showing why granting CSS a limited exemption (under which CSS would refer to a different agency any same-sex couples seeking to be foster parents) would significantly impair the government's admittedly-compelling interest in finding foster homes for as many children as possible. [***Fulton v. City of Philadelphia*** (2021)] [702-706]

c. Categorical exemptions for secular activities (*Tandon v. Newsom*): Even where a law does ***not*** give officials discretion to carve out an "individualized" exemption to cover a person's specific situation (the scenario covered in Sub-par. (b) immediately above), if the law provides for one or more ***"categorical" (non-discretionary) exemptions***, the existence of such an exemption may, similarly, prevent the law from qualifying for *Smith*'s pro-government treatment. A 2021 case, ***Tandon v. Newsom***, described in the following Example, demonstrates how this can work.

Tandon says that the existence of even a ***single "categorical" exemption*** — one that is not discretionary, and ***automatically covers all situations*** within a particular category — will prevent the law from meeting the generally-applicable requirement of *Smith* if the exemption is ***for a secular activity*** posing dangers/problems that the Court finds to be ***"comparable"*** to those posed by the non-exempt religious exercise in question. [707]

Example: California attempts to reduce the spread of COVID-19 by restricting various activities that it thinks will amplify the contagion. In particular, it bans all in-home gatherings of more than three households, whether the gathering is for religious or for secular purposes, and whether it is indoors or outdoors (e.g., in a backyard). But the state does *not* impose a "no more than three households" restriction on certain activities occurring inside *commercial premises* (as opposed to inside a home). For instance, hair salons and retail stores are among the types of commercial premises that are permitted to host more than three households at a time.

The Ps are two individuals who argue that the restriction prevents them from hosting Bible studies and communal worship services in their homes if more than two other families will attend. The Ps, seeking an injunction against the three-household limit, contend that (1) since California permits some indoor commercial "personal care" businesses (e.g., hair salons) to operate without a maximum-number-of-households limitation, the restriction on in-home gatherings is not a "generally applicable" one as required for protection under *Smith;* and (2) the restriction must therefore be strictly scrutinized, and struck down.

Held (in a 5-4 unsigned opinion), for the Ps: because the restriction allows some comparable secular activities to be held in homes without reference to the number of households present, the restriction's number-of-household limits on religious activities causes the restriction to fail to be "generally applicable." Whether two activities are comparable for Free Exercise Clause purposes is to be judged by comparing the ***risks the two activities pose,*** not by, say, comparing the reasons for which the people do the activity. Here, the state has failed to show that if in-home gatherings are subjected to the same COVID-limiting measures as in-commercial-premises gatherings (e.g., masks or social distancing), the former will pose greater COVID-spreading danger than the latter. Therefore, the two types of activities are "comparable." Consequently, the state's refusal to grant the same categorical exemption for in-home religious gatherings as for secular in-commercial-premises gatherings must be strictly scrutinized (and struck down because it's not sufficiently narrowly-tailored to survive that scrutiny). [***Tandon v. Newsom*** (2021)] [707-711]

i. **"Most favored nation" principle:** We can sensibly call *Tandon*'s category-based approach — under which government's decision to deny a regulatory exemption for a religious activity will be strictly scrutinized if government gives an exemption for a "comparable" secular activity — a ***"most favored nation"*** (or ***"MFN"***) approach. [712]

    (1) ***Smith*'s reach is greatly narrowed:** The MFN approach dramatically ***narrows the reach*** of *Smith*: government's decision to give a categorical (non-discretionary) regulatory exemption to cover a secular activity *automatically* prevents the exemption scheme from being "generally applicable" — and thus triggers strict scrutiny of government's refusal to give a similar categorical exemption to cover a religious activity — if the court finds that the religious and secular activities would pose "comparable" dangers if the same exemption were given to each. [712]

        Example: Suppose that in *Tandon*, to fight COVID California had (1) forbidden more than three households from gathering in *any* type of commercial premises, except that in the one narrow case of grocery stores, the state said that up to 20 households could gather as long as all persons wore masks and socially-distanced themselves; and (2) also forbidden more than three households from gathering (even if masked and socially-distanced) in any *home* for any reason, including religious worship.

If the *Tandon* 5-Justice majority opinion really meant to apply literally what we're calling the MFN approach, then unless the state carried the burden of proving that despite similar risk-reduction measures, in-home religious gatherings with 4 to 19 households would still pose materially more COVID risk than 4-to-19-household grocery-store visits, the state's decision to treat the two differently would have to be strictly scrutinized (and almost certainly struck down as insufficiently narrowly-tailored). And that result would follow even though all *non-grocery-store commercial-premises gatherings* were subjected to the *same* number-of-household limits as in-home worship gatherings were. [712]

3. **Possible overruling of *Smith*:** Several present members of the Supreme Court have **criticized** the 1990 decision in *Employment Division v. Smith*. *Smith* will likely be **overruled** if and when a suitable case comes before the Court. [713]

   a. **Most common criticism:** The most common criticism of *Smith* is that it reduces the Free Exercise Clause to **nothing more than an anti-discrimination principle**, rather than an **independent source of protection** against laws that place an **unintended but substantial burden on religious practices.** [714]

   b. **Five potential votes to overrule *Smith*:** *Smith* remains the law as of this writing (late 2021). But **five members** of the present Court are now on record as either calling for the overruling of *Smith*, or as at least being seriously open to that possibility. [714]

4. **Anti-discrimination laws, and a group's right to pick its "ministers":** There's one last major limit to the reach of *Smith*: the rule of that case does **not** apply when the government regulation, even though neutral and generally-applicable on its face, would have the effect of **interfering with the internal decision-making of a religious group** regarding who will be entrusted to further the group's **core faith and mission**. See *Our Lady of Guadalupe School v. Morrissey-Berru* (2020), discussed *supra*, p. C-112 (state's anti-discrimination laws violate both the Establishment Clause and the Free Exercise Clause rights of church-run schools to choose which teachers will spread the church's core faith and mission). [669-670]

E. **Conscientious objection:** It's not clear whether Congress **must** (as it does) give an exemption for military service for **conscientious objectors** (i.e., those who believe that all war is evil). [715]

   1. **Selective c.o.'s:** But it's clear that Congress need not give an exemption to "selective" c.o.'s (i.e., those who do not believe that all war is evil, but who believe that the particular war in which they are being asked to fight is evil). [*Gillette v. U.S.*]

F. **Public health:** Government may have to sacrifice its interest in the **health** of its citizenry, if individuals' religious dictates so require. [715]

   1. **Competent adult:** Where the case involves a **competent adult**, and only that adult's own health is at stake, government may probably not force treatment on the individual over his religious objection. (*Example:* A state probably can't force a Jehovah's Witness to accept a blood transfusion or other life-saving medical care over that person's religious objections.)

   2. **Child:** However, where the patient is a **child** whose parents object on religious grounds, the state may probably compel the treatment.

   3. **Danger to others:** Also, if the case involves not only a health danger to the person asserting a religious belief, but also a health danger to **others**, then government probably does not have to give

an exemption. (*Example:* P may be forced to undergo a vaccination over his religious objections. [*Jacobsen v. Mass.*])

G. What constitutes a religious belief: Only *bona fide* "religious beliefs" are protected by the Free Exercise Clause. But "religious beliefs" are defined very ***broadly***. [715]

   1. Non-theistic: For instance, ***non-theistic*** beliefs are protected. That is, the belief need not recognize the existence of a supreme being. (*Example:* Public officials cannot be forced to take an oath in which they say that they believe that God exists. [*Torcaso v. Watkins*])

   2. Unorganized religions: Similarly, ***unorganized*** or obscure religions get the same protection as the major religions. In fact, even if a person's religious beliefs are followed ***only by him***, he's still entitled to free exercise protection.

   3. Sincerity: A court will not sustain a free exercise claim unless it is convinced that the religious belief is ***"genuine"*** or ***"sincere."*** (The fact that the belief or practice has been observed by a religious group for a long period of time may be considered in measuring sincerity. But the converse — absence of a long-standing practice — does not mean that the belief is insincere.)

      a. Unreasonableness: The court will ***not*** consider whether the belief is "true" or ***"reasonable."*** Even a very "unreasonable" belief (that is, a belief that most people might consider unreasonable) is not deprived of protection, so long as it is ***genuine***. [*U.S. v. Ballard*] (*Example:* The practice of voodoo, including sticking pins into dolls representing one's enemies, might be considered by most of us to be "unreasonable." But as long as such a practice is part of a person's genuine set of beliefs and religious practices, it will not be deprived of protection merely because most find it unreasonable.)

CHAPTER 16

JUSTICIABILITY

I. JUSTICIABILITY GENERALLY

A. List: In order for a case to be heard by the federal courts, the plaintiff must get past a series of procedural obstacles which we collectively call requirements for ***"justiciability"***: (1) the case must not require the giving of an ***advisory opinion***; (2) the plaintiff must have ***standing***; (3) the case must not be ***moot***; (4) the case must be ***ripe*** for decision; and (5) the case must not involve a non-justiciable ***political question***. [730]

II. ADVISORY OPINIONS

A. Constitutional "case or controversy" requirement: Article III, Section 2 of the Constitution gives the federal courts jurisdiction only over "cases" and "controversies." The federal courts are therefore prevented from issuing opinions on ***abstract*** or ***hypothetical*** questions. This means that the federal courts may not give ***"advisory opinions."*** In other words, the federal courts may not render opinions which answer a legal question when no party is before the court who has suffered or faces specific injury. [730]

   Example: Suppose that both houses of Congress approve a bill, but the President has doubts about the bill's constitutionality. The President may ***not*** go to a federal court and ask the federal court whether the bill is constitutional, so that he may decide whether to veto it. If the federal court were to give its opinion about whether the bill was constitutional, at a time when no party who had been or might soon be injured by the unconstitutionality was before the court, this would be an "advisory opinion" that would violate the constitutional "case or controversy" requirement.

1. **Declaratory judgments sometimes allowed:** But *declaratory judgments* are sometimes allowed, and are not forbidden by the rule against advisory opinions. A declaratory judgment is a judicial decision in which the court is not requested to award damages or an injunction, but is instead requested to state what the legal effect would be of proposed conduct by one or both of the parties. [731]

   a. **Requirements:** But the plaintiff is not entitled to get a declaratory judgment on just any question about what the legal consequence of the particular conduct would be. If the declaratory judgment action raises only questions that are very *hypothetical* or *abstract*, the federal court is likely to conclude that what's sought here is an illegal advisory opinion, because no specific, concrete controversy exists.

III. STANDING

A. **Function of a standing requirement:** Probably the most important rule about when the federal courts may hear a case is that they may do so only when the plaintiff has *"standing"* to assert his claim. By this, we mean that the plaintiff must have a significant *stake* in the controversy. [731-733]

> **Example:** Suppose that during the Vietnam War, P, a federal taxpayer, becomes convinced that, since Congress has never formally declared war, P's tax dollars are being used to support an unconstitutional war. If P were to sue the federal government in federal court to have the war effort enjoined on this ground, the court would not hear his claim — he would be found to lack "standing," since (as we'll see in detail later) a person whose only connection with the controversy is that he is a taxpayer will almost never be deemed to have standing to claim that tax dollars are being used illegally.

B. **Requirement of "injury in fact":** The key concept behind the law of standing is simple: the litigant must show that he has suffered an *"injury in fact."* At its broadest level, the standing requirement means that the plaintiff must show that *he has himself been injured* in some way by the conduct that he complains of. [732]

C. **Who is kept out:** The standing rules tend to keep two main types of cases *out* of the federal courts: [732]

   1. **Non-individuated harm:** First, we have cases in which the harm suffered by the plaintiff is *no different* from that suffered by very large numbers of people not before the court. (*Example:* Suppose P's only connection with the suit is that he is a federal "citizen" or a "taxpayer" who is injured the same as any other citizen or taxpayer by the fact that the government is spending tax dollars illegally or otherwise violating some law. P does not have standing.)

   2. **Third parties' rights:** Second, we have cases where the rights claimed to be violated are not the rights of the plaintiff, but instead the rights of *third parties* who are not before the court. (But there are some important exceptions to the general rule that the plaintiff can't complain of government actions that violate someone else's rights.)

D. **Taxpayer and citizen suits:** Here is the single most important context in which standing problems arise: suits that are brought by federal *"citizens"* or *"taxpayers"* arguing that their general rights as citizens or taxpayers are violated by governmental action. [733-734]

   1. **Taxpayer suits:** Suppose that the plaintiff contends that: (1) he is a federal *taxpayer*; and (2) his tax dollars are being spent by the government in some illegal way. May the plaintiff pursue this suit in federal court? In general, the answer will be, *"no."* The fact that a person's federal taxes are

used to fund an unconstitutional or illegal government program is simply not a sufficient connection with the governmental action to confer standing on the plaintiff. [*Frothingham v. Mellon*]

   a. One exception: There is one very narrow exception: a federal taxpayer has standing to sue to overturn a ***congressional tax or spending program*** that violates the ***Establishment Clause***. [*Flast v. Cohen*] [733]

      i. Tightly limited: But this "*Flast* exception" is extremely ***tightly limited:*** it applies only to *congressional* spending that violates the Establishment Clause, not even to *executive-branch* spending that might violate the Clause. [*Hein v. Freedom from Religion Foundation*] [734]

   b. State taxpayers: A *state* taxpayer, like a federal taxpayer, does ***not*** have federal-court standing to litigate the legality of the state's expenditures. [*DaimlerChrysler Corp. v. Cuno*]

   c. Municipal taxpayer: But a ***municipal*** taxpayer definitely *does* have standing to litigate the legality of his city's expenditures. [734]

2. Citizen suits: Suppose now that plaintiff argues that he is a federal ***"citizen,"*** and that as such he has the right to have his government act in accordance with the Constitution. Assume that P has no direct connection with the governmental act he's complaining about (he's merely claiming that, like every other citizen, he has the right to have the federal government obey the Constitution). In this "citizen suit" situation, P will ***not have standing***. The Court has always held that one federal citizen's interest in lawful government is no different from the interest of any other citizen, and that an individual litigant relying on citizenship has not shown the ***"individualized"*** injury-in-fact that is required for standing. [734]

E. Cases not based on taxpayer or citizen status: Now suppose that the plaintiff is not arguing that his standing derives from his status as citizen or taxpayer. In other words, we're now talking about the vast bulk of ordinary law suits. [735-740]

1. Three requirements: Here, there are three standing requirements that the plaintiff must meet: (1) he must show that he has suffered (or is likely to suffer) an ***"injury in fact"***; (2) the injury he is suffering must be ***concrete*** and ***"individuated"***; and (3) the action being challenged must be the ***"cause in fact"*** of the injury. [735]

2. "Injury in fact": The plaintiff must show that he either ***has suffered***, or ***will probably suffer***, some concrete ***"injury in fact."*** [735]

   a. Non-economic harm: This "injury in fact" requirement is pretty loosely applied. For instance, the harm does not have to be *economic* in nature.

   Example: A group of people who use a national forest claim that the construction of a recreation area in the forest will violate federal laws. To get standing, the plaintiffs point to the injury to their "esthetic and environmental well-being" which would result from the construction. *Held*, this esthetic and environmental injury satisfies the "injury in fact" requirement, even though the harm is non-economic and very intangible. [*Sierra Club v. Morton*] [735]

   b. Imminent harm: If P has not ***already*** suffered the injury in fact, he must show that the future injury is not only probable but ***"concrete"*** and ***"imminent."*** Thus if the threatened harm is too ***far in the future***, or its eventual occurrence is too ***"speculative,"*** the "actual or imminent" element will not be satisfied, and standing will not be found.

   Example: The Ps challenge a federal regulatory action that they say will endanger certain species abroad. The Ps say that they have in the past, and will in the future, travel abroad to visit the habitats of these species. *Held*, the Ps lack standing, because the lack of specific information about their future plans means the harm to them is not sufficiently concrete or imminent. [*Lujan v. Defenders of Wildlife*] [735]

    i. **"Certainly impending":** In at least one case, the Court has said that the threatened harm has to be ***"certainly impending."*** [*Clapper v. Amnesty Int'l USA* (2013)] The Court's use of this term in *Clapper* seems to mean that if the harm hasn't already occurred, not only must it be the case that if the harm occurs, it will occur soon (the requirement of "imminence"), but also that the occurrence of the harm in the near future is ***very probable.*** [736]

  c. **Individual threatened with enforcement of law:** A common issue is whether a person who ***reasonably fears that a statute will be enforced against him*** if he takes a contemplated action has suffered an actual/imminent injury even though the individual ***hasn't yet taken*** that action. In this situation, P will be deemed to meet the injury-in-fact requirement as long as (1) he alleges that he ***intends to engage*** in an arguably-protected act that is forbidden by the statute; and (2) there exists a ***"credible threat"*** that if P takes the act, he'll be prosecuted. [*Susan B. Anthony List v. Driehaus*] [737]

3. **Remedy:** In addition to showing an "injury in fact," P must show that the injury would be ***remedied*** by a favorable court decision. [735]

    Example: The various plaintiffs claim to have been injured by the zoning rules of Penfield, New York. They claim that these rules were imposed for the purpose of excluding the building of low- and moderate-income housing in the town. Certain Ps (the only ones we'll discuss here) are low- and moderate-income individuals who have never lived in Penfield, but who allege that they sought housing there and would have moved there had affordable housing been available.

    Held, these Ps lack standing for several reasons. One reason is that these Ps fail the ***"redressability"*** requirement: they can't show that if the court awarded the relief being sought — a striking down of the zoning rules — the desired moderate-income projects will in fact likely be built. Therefore, they can't show that a favorable decision would redress (make better) the harm the Ps complain about. [*Warth v. Seldin*] [739]

4. **Individuated harm:** The harm that has been or will be suffered by the plaintiff has to be ***"individuated."*** That is, it can't be the same harm as suffered by every citizen, or every taxpayer.

  a. **Large number:** But the harm may still be found to be "individuated" even though there are a ***large number*** of people suffering the harm. [737]

    i. **Same harm:** But remember that if the harm complained of by the plaintiff is truly the same harm as suffered by every citizen or every taxpayer in the country, the harm will not be sufficiently "individuated," and the plaintiffs won't have standing.

  b. **Organizations and associations:** What about ***organizations and associations*** — does the organization itself have to suffer the harm, or can it merely assert that its ***members*** will suffer or have suffered the required harm? In general, the answer is that organizations and associations ***will be able to sue*** on behalf of their members. However:

    [1] the members have to be people who would have ***standing in their own right*** (so that an organization of citizens or taxpayers could not complain of harm that is suffered by all citizens or taxpayers);

    [2] the interests being asserted by the organization in the lawsuit must be ***related to the organization's purpose*** (so that an environmental group could probably not try to pursue its members' interests in, say, an effective criminal justice system); and

    [3] the case cannot be one which requires the ***participation of individual members.*** [738]

[*Hunt v. Wash. Apple Advt'g. Comm.*]. These three requirements are pretty liberally applied.

5. **Causation:** Finally, the action that the plaintiff is complaining about must be the ***"cause in fact"*** of his injury. Actually, this causation requirement breaks down into two sub-requirements:

[1] P has to show that the challenged action was a ***"but for"*** cause of his injury, that is, that the injury would not have occurred unless the challenged action had taken place; and

[2] P must show that a favorable decision in the suit will probably ***redress*** the injury to him. [738]

F. **Third-party standing:** One of the key functions of the standing doctrine is that this is how courts apply the general rule that a litigant normally may ***not assert the constitutional rights of persons not before the court***. (This principle is sometimes called the rule against use of "constitutional *jus tertii*," — *jus tertii* means "rights of third persons" in Latin.) [741]

> **Example:** Zoning laws enacted by the city of Penfield, N.Y., intentionally exclude the building of low-income housing. The Ps are residents of nearby Rochester, who claim that because Penfield has refused to allow low- and middle-income housing, the taxes of these Rochester residents have risen, since Rochester has to subsidize or build more low-income housing than it would have to build than had Penfield not practiced exclusionary zoning.
>
> *Held*, these Rochester residents lack standing. It is true that their higher taxes are an "injury in fact" to them. But Penfield's zoning laws do not apply to these Rochester residents, and therefore do not violate *their* rights. And the Rochester residents may not claim that the rights of ***other people not before the court*** have been violated (e.g., people who would have moved to Penfield had exclusionary zoning not been practiced). [*Warth v. Seldin*]) [741]

1. **Not constitutionally required:** This rule against the assertion of third-party rights is ***not*** mandated by the Article III "case or controversy" requirement. In other words, it is not a rule imposed by the Constitution on the federal courts; instead, it is a rule of ***"prudence,"*** a policy decision adopted by the Supreme Court. [741]

2. **Exceptions:** Since the rule against asserting third-party rights is not required by the Constitution, the Supreme Court is free to make whatever ***exceptions*** it wishes to the doctrine. Here are the four major exceptions the Court has recognized:

[1] **Third party unlikely to be able to sue:** First, a person may assert the rights of a third party not before the court ***if the third party would face substantial obstacles to asserting his or her own rights.*** But the exception applies only if there's reason to believe that the advocate will ***effectively represent*** the interests of the third party. [741]

[2] **Close relationship between P and the third party:** Second, a litigant may assert the rights of someone not before the court where there is a ***close relationship between the advocate and the third party.*** Generally, this happens because the litigant is ***part of the third party's constitutionally protected activity.*** [741]

> **Example:** A state requires doctors who perform abortions to have admitting privileges at a local hospital. Doctor X sues the state, arguing that this requirement is an unconstitutional "undue burden" on the rights of her patients (not before the court) who want abortions.
>
> The court will allow X to assert these patients' rights. The case qualifies under both exception [1] above (since the patients would face obstacles going to court themselves, given the time constraints); and exception [2] (since there is a close relationship between X and her patients, and X is "part" of each patient's constitutionally-protected activity in having an abortion). [*June Medical Services v Russo*] [742]

[3] **First Amendment "overbreadth" doctrine:** Third is the doctrine known as the ***First Amendment "overbreadth" doctrine.*** Recall (*supra*, C-80) that by the overbreadth doctrine, a party to whom a criminal statute clearly (and constitutionally) applies may be per-

mitted to argue that the statute as drafted would criminalize some types of *expressive conduct* that, if engaged in by third parties not before the court, would be protected by those parties' First Amendment rights. We allow overbreadth in the *First Amendment area* but not elsewhere because statutes that purport to restrict expression in an overbroad manner will have a *"chilling effect"* on citizens' general willingness to exercise their freedom of speech.

[4] **Associations:** Fourth, an *association* will normally be allowed to raise the rights of its *members*. For instance, if a group of people would be injured by damage to the air they breathe and the water they drink, an organization of which they are members (e.g., the Sierra Club) would typically be allowed to sue on their behalf. [743]

IV. MOOTNESS

A. General rule: A case may not be heard by the federal courts if it is *"moot."* A case is moot if it raised a live controversy at the time the complaint was filed, but *events occurring after the filing* have deprived the litigant of an ongoing stake in the controversy. [743]

> **Example:** P sues D, a state university, claiming that the university's law school admissions program is racially discriminatory. P is permitted to attend the law school while the case is being litigated. By the time the case arrives at the Supreme Court for review, P is in his final year of law school, and the university says that he will be allowed to graduate regardless of how the case is decided. *Held*, the case is moot. Therefore, the appeal will not be decided. [*DeFunis v. Odegaard*]

1. Constitutional basis for: Apparently the rule that the federal courts may not decide "moot" cases is *required* by the Constitution. That is, deciding a case when the parties no longer have a live controversy would amount to issuing an advisory opinion, in violation of Article III's "case or controversy" requirement.

B. Exceptions: Nonetheless, the courts recognize a few situations where a case that would appear to be "moot" will nonetheless be heard. [744]

1. "Capable of repetition, yet evading review": For instance, a case will not be treated as moot if the issue it raises is *"capable of repetition, yet evading review."* This "capable of repetition, yet evading review" doctrine takes care of situations in which, if the case were to be declared moot, a *different person* might be injured in the *same way* by the same defendant, and his claim, too, would be mooted before review could be had. [744]

> **Example:** P, a pregnant woman, attacks the constitutionality of Texas' anti-abortion law. She brings the suit as a class action, in which she is the named plaintiff and other pregnant women who want abortions are unnamed members. By the time the case reaches the Supreme Court, P is no longer pregnant.
>
> *Held*, the case should not be dismissed as moot. A pregnancy will almost always be over before the usual appellate process is complete. Therefore, if the Court insisted that the named plaintiff who starts the suit must still be pregnant by the time the suit gets to the Supreme Court, no plaintiff could ever get to that Court. So the constitutionality of the Texas anti-abortion law is "capable of repetition, yet evading review." [*Roe v. Wade*]

2. Voluntary cessation by defendant: The case will generally not be treated as moot if the defendant *voluntarily ceases* the conduct that the plaintiff is complaining about. So if the plaintiff is seeking an injunction, the defendant can't usually get the case dismissed on mootness grounds merely by saying that he has voluntarily stopped the conduct that the plaintiff is trying to get an injunction against — unless the defendant shows that there is no reasonable likelihood that he will return to his old ways, the court will let the action go forward. [744]

3. **Collateral consequences:** Finally, a case will not be moot even if it is mostly decided, if there are still *collateral consequences* that might be adverse to the defendant. For instance, suppose that a criminal defendant has already served his sentence by the time his attack on the constitutionality of his conviction comes before the federal court. The case will not be moot, because there will probably be future collateral consequences to the defendant from his conviction (e.g., he will lose the right to vote, his reputation or employability will be damaged, etc.). [744]

V. RIPENESS

A. **Ripeness problem generally:** You can think of the problem of ripeness as being the opposite of mootness. A case is moot, as we've just seen, because it *no longer* involves an actual controversy. By contrast, a case is not yet ripe (and therefore not yet decidable by a federal court) if it has *not yet become sufficiently concrete* to be easily adjudicated. [744]

   Example: The Hatch Act prohibits federal executive-branch employees from getting involved in "political management or … political campaigns." The plaintiffs are federal civil servants who want to attack the constitutionality of the Hatch Act. The plaintiffs claim that they want to engage in prohibited political activities. But they concede that they have not yet engaged in such activities.

   　Held, the plaintiffs' claims are not yet ripe. The problem is not that the Ps have not yet violated the statute. Rather, the problem is that the plaintiffs have not been adequately specific about the *precise acts* that they wish to carry out. (If the Ps would specify in detail what they want to do, their suit might not be unripe even though they haven't yet violated the act.) [*United Public Workers v. Mitchell*] [745]

B. **Uncertain enforcement of criminal statute:** One common ripeness problem arises where the plaintiff attacks the constitutionality of a statute and says that he has violated the statute, but it is clear that the statute is *rarely enforced* and probably will not be enforced in this particular situation. Here, the rules are pretty blurry — suffice it to say that if the court believes that it is *very unlikely* that the statute will be enforced against the plaintiff either for the activity he has already done or similar activity he is likely to do in the future, the court will probably treat the case as being not ripe.

   Example: Connecticut forbids the distribution of contraceptives. Two married couples and a physician challenge the law's constitutionality, and allege that they have violated the law. *Held*, the case is not ripe, because the statute has been on the books for 80 years with only one reported prosecution, so there does not exist the required "clear" threat that the plaintiffs will be prosecuted. [*Poe v. Ullman*] [745]

1. **Specific threatened harm required:** But for a case to be ripe, it is not necessary that the litigant have *already suffered* harm. It will be enough that there is a *reasonable probability* of harm. However, the anticipated harm has to be fairly *specific*. [745]

VI. THE ELEVENTH AMENDMENT AND SUITS AGAINST STATES

A. **The Eleventh Amendment generally:** The *Eleventh Amendment* bars any federal suit "against any one of the *states* by citizens of another state, or by citizens or subjects of any foreign state." [746]

1. **Damage suits against states:** The Eleventh Amendment has been held to bar most types of *damage suits* against a state.

   a. **Plaintiff not a citizen of defendant state:** By its own terms, the Amendment clearly applies to suits against a state brought by citizens of a *different state* or by foreigners. (*Examples:* A citizen of Missouri may not bring a damage suit against the state of Illinois. Nor may a British subject bring a damage suit against the state of Illinois.)

   b. **Suit by citizen of defendant state:** The Eleventh Amendment has been *interpreted* to apply also to bar a damage suit where the plaintiff is a *citizen of the defendant state*. [*Hans v. Louisiana*] (*Example:* Suppose P is an employee of the Delmarva state legislature. He is then fired, in apparent violation of his employment contract. P brings a suit for contract damages against Delmarva, in federal court. This suit would be a violation of the Eleventh Amendment, as broadly interpreted by the Supreme Court.)

2. **Suits by states or federal government:** The Eleventh Amendment does *not* bar federal suits brought by *one state* against another state, or by the *federal government* against a state.

3. **No counties or cities protected:** Only the *state itself*, not its *subdivisions*, such as *counties* or *cities*, is protected by the Eleventh Amendment. (*Example:* P, a county worker, is fired. He brings a federal suit for damages against the county. Since the suit is not against the state *per se*, the Eleventh Amendment does not apply, even though the county is in essence a subdivision of the state.)

4. **No bar against injunctions:** The Eleventh Amendment essentially bars only suits for *damages*. That is, it does not bar most suits for *injunctions*. For instance, if a private litigant sues a state official to enjoin him from taking acts which would violate the plaintiff's *constitutional* or *federal-law* rights, the Eleventh Amendment does not apply and the suit may proceed. [*Ex parte Young*]

5. **Congress can't override:** *Congress* generally *can't change* the "no federal-court suits against the states" principle behind the Eleventh Amendment, even if it wants to and expressly says it's doing so. [*Seminole Tribe v. Florida*] [748-749]

   Example: Congress passes a statute saying any state *can* be sued in federal court by private citizens for violating, say, federal patent or environmental laws. This statute won't have any effect — a federal court still can't hear a private suit against a state for damages for violating the federal law. [*Florida Prepaid v. Coll. Sav. Bank*] [749]

   a. **Exception for remedial powers:** But there's an *exception* — if Congress is acting properly pursuant to its *remedial powers* under the Thirteenth, Fourteenth or Fifteenth Amendments, it *may abrogate* the states' Eleventh Amendment immunity.

B. **States' sovereign immunity:** The states have a constitutionally-guaranteed *sovereign immunity* from certain proceedings brought by private parties.

1. **Suit in states' own courts:** Thus the states have constitutional sovereign immunity from private damage suits brought against the state in the *state's own courts*. This is true even if the suit is based on a *congressionally-granted federal right*. [749]

   Example: Congress passes a valid statute saying that state employees must receive premium pay for overtime just as private-sector employees do. Employees of Maine sue the state in Maine courts on this right. *Held*, the Constitution's structure incorporates the doctrine of sovereign immunity, and that doctrine allows Maine to avoid hearing the employees' suit, even if Congress has expressly said that the states must hear such suits. [*Alden v. Maine*] [749]

2. **Proceeding before federal administrative agency:** Similarly, the states have sovereign immunity from being required to respond to a private complaint before a *federal administrative agency*. [*Federal Maritime Comm. v. So. Car. St. Ports Auth.*] [750]

VII. POLITICAL QUESTIONS

A. **The doctrine generally:** The final aspect of justiciability is the requirement is that the case not involve the decision of a *"political question."* This rule is even more vague than the other justiciability rules we've talked about already. The doctrine does *not* mean that federal courts will not decide a case that involves politics. It doesn't even mean that courts will refuse to decide cases where political issues are right at the heart of the controversy. Instead, the court will decline to hear a case on political question grounds only if it thinks that the doctrine of *separation of powers* requires this, or if it thinks that deciding the case would be unwise as a policy matter. [750]

1. **Two of the factors used:** Two of the factors that seem to be very important in whether a case will be found to involve a non-justiciable political question are:

   a. **Commitment to another branch:** First, the fact that the case presents an issue which has been committed by the Constitution to *another branch of the federal government*, i.e., to Congress or to the President instead of the courts.

   b. **Lack of standards:** Second, the fact that there are no manageable *standards* by which a court could resolve the issue.

B. **"Commitment to other branches" strand:** The courts will refuse to decide a case on political-question grounds if the case raises an issue the determination of which is clearly committed by the Constitution to *another branch of the federal government*. [751-753]

   Example: D, a federal judge, claims that the Senate has used improper procedures in convicting him following his impeachment, because the case was heard before a committee of Senators rather than the full Senate (though the full Senate voted, after receiving a transcript of the committee proceedings). D claims that this violates the Impeachment Clause, which says that "the Senate shall have sole Power to try all Impeachments." *Held*, the case presents a nonjusticiable political question, because the Constitution has given the Senate, not the courts, the power to decide what constitutes a "trial." [*Nixon v. U.S.*]

   1. **Other impeachment issues:** The same principle probably applies to *all* aspects of the impeachment process. Thus if the House voted to impeach the President and the Senate voted to convict, the Supreme Court would probably refuse to review either of these decisions on "commitment to other branches" political-question grounds (so that if the President tried to get the Supreme Court to hear his argument that the crime for which he was impeached and convicted was not within the constitutionally-defined category of "high crimes and misdemeanors," the Court would probably refuse to consider the merits of this argument).

   2. **Rare:** It is quite rare for a case to be declined on the grounds that it involves a question committed to some other branch of government.

C. **"Lack of judicially manageable standards":** The second major factor that may lead the court to decide that there is a non-justiciable political question, is that there are no *manageable standards* by which the courts can resolve the issue. [753]

   Example: Article IV, Section 4 provides that "the United States shall guarantee to every state in this union a republican form of government." Some unhappy Rhode Island citizens stage a rebellion. Ultimately, various Rhode Islanders ask the federal courts to decide which of two competing factions is the lawful government of the state. *Held*, the Court cannot decide this question, because it presents a political question. There are no criteria by which a court could determine whether a particular "government" was "Republican." [*Luther v. Borden*]

D. **Reapportionment -- the one person, one vote rule:** Let's now look in some detail at the federal cases on *legislative reapportionment*, and the issue of *how nearly equal the populations* of the individual districts must be. [754-756]

   1. **One person, one vote rule:** The landmark case of *Baker v. Carr*, and cases following it, establish the so-called *"one person, one vote"* principle: any governmental body, whether it's a federal one (like congressional districts) or a state one (like a state legislature) must be apportioned on a *population* basis, so that *all voters have essentially the same voting power.* If a governmental electoral scheme does not comply with this "one person, one vote" principle, it violates the *equal protection*

rights of the under-represented voters. [*Reynolds v. Sims*] [754-755]

    a.   **Justiciable:** Such cases raising the "one person, one vote" argument are *justiciable*. The Court has rejected the argument that these cases raise non-justiciable political questions. [*Baker v. Carr*] [754]

    b.   **Both houses of state legislature:** One of the consequences of the "one person, one vote" principle is that if a state has a bicameral (two-house) legislature, *both* houses must be elected based on population. Thus, paradoxically, the U.S. Constitution prohibits a state from having one body that awards seats without reference to population (e.g., a house that gives the same number of votes to each county), even though the U.S. Senate is built upon exactly this kind of non-population-based scheme!

  2.   **How much equality is required:** The rules for *how much equality is required* vary depending on whether we're talking about a congressional districting scheme or, instead, a state or local districting scheme. [756]

    a.   **Congressional:** For *congressional districts*, the districts have to be *almost precisely equal.* Even a scheme where one congressional district within a state was only 1% more populous than another has been struck down. States must make a "good-faith effort to achieve *precise mathematical equality*" in the drawing of congressional districts. [*Kirkpatrick v. Preisler*]

    b.   **State and local:** *Much greater deviation* from mathematical equality is allowed where what is being apportioned is *state legislatures* or *local governmental bodies*. So for example, a *10%* or smaller deviation between the voting power of a voter in one district versus a voter in another will generally be *upheld*. [*White v. Regester*] Even greater disparities will be allowed if there are good reasons for them. (For instance, suppose a state wants not to have to redraw its county boundaries, and wants to have each county elect its own representative to the state Assembly. This desire to "respect pre-existing political boundaries" will probably justify, say, a 15% or even 20% disparity in per-person voting power.)

E.   **Reapportionment — partisan gerrymanders:** The "one person, one vote" rule discussed above says nothing about *how the district lines are to be drawn.* The district-line-drawing problem arises when a state uses *"gerrymanders,"* including one particular type, the *"partisan gerrymander."*

  1.   **"Gerrymander" defined:** In a gerrymander, the *strength of a disfavored voting bloc* is *curtailed* by restricting its members to carefully- and artificially-constructed districts. There are *two quite different forms* of gerrymandering, only one of which poses major issues of justiciability.

    a.   **Racial gerrymanders:** First, there are *"racial gerrymanders,"* in which the people drawing the district lines act with the predominant purpose of boosting or curtailing the voting strength of a *particular racial group*. Racial gerrymanders *are* justiciable, and they will often be struck down on equal protection grounds. See *supra*, p. C-54.

    b.   **Partisan gerrymanders:** Second, there are *"partisan gerrymanders,"* in which district lines are drawn for the purpose of curtailing the voting strength of a *particular political group*, typically members of a particular *political party.*

  2.   **Partisan gerrymanders are non-justiciable:** As the result of a key 2019 decision, *suits attacking partisan gerrymanders* are *always non-justiciable.* [*Rucho v. Common Cause* (2019)] [757-764]

    a.   **Significance:** *Rucho* means that no matter how severely a gerrymander *dilutes the effective voting power* of members of a particular party (or ideology), and no matter how clear it is that the party whose members have sponsored the plan in the state legislature acted with the *primary intent* of bringing about that dilution, there is *no possible federal-court remedy available* to any group or person whose vote has been diluted. [764]

CHAPTER 1

INTRODUCTION

I. ROADMAP OF CONSTITUTIONAL LAW

A. Roadmap: Here is a very brief "roadmap" of Constitutional Law:

1. **Federalism:** First, we'll be covering various aspects of *"federalism."* Federalism means that the federal and state governments co-exist. Some of the main principles stemming from federalism are:

   a. **Limited, enumerated powers:** The powers of the federal government are *limited* to those that are *enumerated* in the Constitution. [Chap. 3]

   b. **Separation of powers:** Each of the three branches of the federal government (Congress, the President and the Judiciary) has its own enumerated powers, and one branch may not take actions reserved by the Constitution to one of the other branches. This is the doctrine of *"separation of powers."* [Chap. 8]

   c. **Congress' Commerce power:** The most important power given to Congress is the power to regulate *"commerce."* [Chap. 4]

2. **Dormant Commerce Clause:** Under the *"Dormant* Commerce Clause," the mere existence of the federal commerce power *restricts the states* from *discriminating against*, or unduly *burdening*, *interstate commerce*. [Chap. 6]

3. **Due Process Clause:** The *"Due Process Clause"* of the 14th Amendment has two different types of effects [Chap. 9]:

   a. **Substantive due process:** It limits the *"substantive"* power of the government to regulate certain areas of human life (e.g., child-bearing);

   b. **Procedural due process:** It imposes certain *"procedural"* requirements on government when it takes an individual's *"life, liberty or property."* (*Example:* Before government can take away your food stamps, it must give you a hearing.)

4. **Equal Protection Clause:** The *"Equal Protection Clause"* of the 14th Amendment prevents government from making certain types of *"classifications,"* mainly ones that unfairly treat similarly-situated people differently. (*Example:* The Equal Protection Clause is what prohibits governments from running racially segregated schools.) [Chap. 10]

5. **Freedom of Expression:** The First Amendment protects *"speech"* against government interference. This includes the freedom of individuals to engage in *political protest,* the freedom of the *press* to publish, the freedom of individuals to *"associate"* with whomever they wish, and more. As you might expect, this "freedom" is far from absolute — often, government will be able to restrict free expression in some way or another (e.g., by requiring a permit before a large political demonstration takes place, or by prohibiting someone from advocating that a crime be committed). [Chap. 14]

6. **Freedom of Religion:** The First Amendment also protects *"freedom of religion."* There are two distinct clauses in the First Amendment dealing with religion [Chap. 15]:

   a. **Establishment Clause:** The *"Establishment"* Clause prevents government from "establishing" an official religion. That is, government may not *endorse* or *support* religion generally, or a particular religion.

b. Free Exercise Clause: The *"Free Exercise"* Clause prevents government from *out-lawing* or seriously *burdening* a person's pursuit of whatever religion (and whatever religious practices) he chooses.

II. THREE STANDARDS OF REVIEW

A. Three standards: There are three key *standards of review* which reappear constantly throughout Constitutional Law. When a court reviews the constitutionality of government action, it is likely to be choosing from among one of these three standards of review: (1) the *mere-rationality* standard; (2) the *strict scrutiny* standard; and (3) *mid-level review.*

1. Mere-rationality standard: Of the three standards, the easiest one to satisfy is the *"mere-rationality"* standard. When the court applies this "mere-rationality" standard, the court will *uphold* the governmental action so long as two requirements are met:

a. Legitimate state objective: First, the government must be pursuing a *legitimate governmental objective*. This is a very broad concept — practically any type of health, safety or "general welfare" goal will be found to be "legitimate."

b. Rational relation: Second, there has to be a *"minimally rational relation"* between the means chosen by the government and the state objective. This requirement, too, is extremely easy to satisfy: only if the government has acted in a completely *"arbitrary and irrational"* way will this rational link between means and end not be found.

2. Strict scrutiny: At the other end of the spectrum, the standard that is hardest to satisfy is the *"strict scrutiny"* standard of review. This standard will only be satisfied if the governmental act satisfies two very tough requirements:

a. Compelling objective: First, the *objective* being pursued by the government must be *"compelling"* (not just "legitimate," as for the "mere-rationality" standard); and

b. Necessary means: Second, the *means* chosen by the government must be *"necessary"* to achieve that compelling end. In other words, the "fit" between the means and the end must be extremely tight. (It's not enough that there's a "rational relation" between the means and the end, which is enough under the "mere-rationality" standard.)

i. No less restrictive alternatives: In practice, this requirement that the means be "necessary" means that there must not be any *less restrictive* means that would accomplish the government's objective just as well.

3. Mid-level review: In between these two standards is so-called *"mid-level"* review.

a. "Important" objective: Here, the governmental objective has to be *"important"* (half way between "legitimate" and "compelling").

b. "Substantially related" means: And, the means chosen by the government must be *"substantially related"* to the important government objective. (This "substantially related" standard is halfway between "rationally related" and "necessary.")

B. Consequences of choice: The court's choice of one of these standards of review has two important consequences:

1. **Burden of persuasion:** First, the choice will make a big difference as to who has the *burden of persuasion*.

    a. **Mere-rationality standard:** Where the governmental action is subject to the *"mere-rationality"* standard, the *individual* who is attacking the government action will generally bear the burden of persuading the court that the action is unconstitutional.

    b. **Strict scrutiny:** By contrast, if the court applies *"strict scrutiny,"* then the *governmental body* whose act is being attacked has the burden of persuading the court that its action is constitutional.

    c. **Middle-level review:** Where *"middle level"* scrutiny is used, it's not certain how the court will assign the burden of persuasion, but the burden will usually be placed on the government.

2. **Effect on outcome:** Second, the choice of review standard has a very powerful effect on the *actual outcome*. Where the "mere-rationality" standard is applied, the governmental action will *almost always be upheld*. Where "strict scrutiny" is used, the governmental action will *almost always be struck down*. Where middle-level scrutiny is used, there's roughly a 50-50 chance that the governmental action will be struck down.

C. **When used:** Here is a quick overview of the entire body of Constitutional Law, to see where each of these review standards gets used:

1. **Mere-rationality standard:** Here are the main places where the "mere-rationality" standard gets applied (and therefore, the places where it's very hard for the person attacking the governmental action to get it struck down on constitutional grounds):

    a. **Dormant Commerce Clause:** First, the "mere-rationality" standard is the main test used to determine whether a state regulation that affects interstate commerce violates the *"Dormant Commerce Clause."* The state regulation has to pursue a legitimate state end, and be rationally related to that end. (But there's a second test, too: the state's interest in enforcing its regulation must also outweigh any *burden* imposed on interstate commerce, and any discrimination against interstate commerce.)

    b. **Substantive due process:** Next comes *substantive due process*. So long as no "fundamental right" is affected, the test for determining whether a governmental act violates substantive due process is, again, "mere rationality." In other words, if the state is pursuing a legitimate objective, and using means that are rationally related to that objective, the state will not be found to have violated the substantive Due Process Clause. So the vast bulk of *economic regulations* (since these don't affect fundamental rights) will be tested by the mere-rationality standard and almost certainly upheld.

    c. **Equal protection:** Then, we move on to the *equal protection* area. Here, "mere-rationality" review is used so long as: (1) *no suspect* or *quasi-suspect classification* is being used; and (2) *no fundamental right* is being impaired. This still leaves us with a large number of classifications which will be judged based on the mere-rationality standard, including: (1) almost all economic regulations; (2) some classifications based on alienage; and (3) rights that are not "fundamental" even though they are very important, such as food, housing, and free public education. In all of these areas, the classification will be reviewed under the "mere-rationality" standard, and will therefore almost certainly be upheld.

    d. **Contracts Clause:** Lastly, we find "mere-rationality" review in some aspects of the

"Obligation of Contracts" Clause.

2. **Strict scrutiny:** Here are the various contexts in which the Court applies *strict scrutiny*:

   a. **Substantive due process/fundamental rights:** First, where a governmental action affects *fundamental rights*, and the plaintiff claims that his *substantive due process* rights are being violated, the Court will use strict scrutiny. So when the state impairs rights falling in the *"privacy"* cluster of marriage, child-bearing, and child-rearing, the Court will use strict scrutiny (and will therefore probably invalidate the governmental restriction). For instance, government restrictions that impair the right to use contraceptives receive this kind of strict scrutiny.

   b. **Equal protection review:** Next, the Court uses strict scrutiny to review a claim that a classification violates the plaintiff's *equal protection* rights, if the classification relates either to a *suspect classification* or a *fundamental right*. "Suspect classifications" include *race*, *national origin*, and (sometimes) *alienage*. "Fundamental rights" for this purpose include the right to *marry*, to *vote*, to have access to the *courts*, and to *travel interstate*. So classifications that either involve any of these suspect classifications or impair any of these fundamental rights will be strictly scrutinized and will probably be struck down.

   c. **Freedom of expression:** Next, we move to the area of *freedom of expression*. If the government is impairing free expression in a *content-based way*, then the court will use strict scrutiny and will almost certainly strike down the regulation. In other words, if the government is restricting some speech but not others, based on the *content of the messages*, then this suppression of expression will only be allowed if necessary to achieve a compelling purpose (a standard which is rarely found to be satisfied in the First Amendment area).

   d. **Freedom of religion/Free Exercise Clause:** Lastly, the court will use strict scrutiny to evaluate any impairment with a person's *free exercise* of religion. Even if the government does *not intend* to impair a person's free exercise of his religion, if it substantially burdens his exercise of religion, the government will have to give him an *exemption* from the otherwise-applicable regulation unless denial of an exemption is necessary to achieve a compelling governmental interest.

3. **Mid-level review:** Finally, here are the relatively small number of contexts in which the court uses mid-level review:

   a. **Equal protection/semi-suspect:** First, mid-level review will be used to judge an *equal protection* claim, where the classification being challenged involves a *semi-suspect* trait. The two traits which are considered semi-suspect are: (1) *gender*; and (2) *illegitimacy*. So any government classification based on gender or illegitimacy will have to be "substantially related" to the achievement of some "important" interest.

   b. **Contracts Clause:** Second, certain conduct attacked under the Obligation of Contracts Clause will be judged by the middle-level standard of review.

   c. **Free expression/non-content-based:** Finally, in the First Amendment area we use a standard similar (though not identical) to the middle-level review standard to judge government action that impairs expression, but does so in a *non-content-based* manner. This is true, for instance, of any content-neutral *"time, place and manner"* regulation.

CHAPTER 2

THE SUPREME COURT'S AUTHORITY

ChapterScope

This Chapter examines several aspects of the Supreme Court's authority.

- **Supreme Court review:** It is the ***Supreme Court, not Congress,*** which has the authority and duty to review the ***constitutionality*** of statutes passed by Congress, and to invalidate the statute if it violates the Constitution.

- **Review of state court decisions:** The Supreme Court may review state court decisions, but only to the extent that the decision was based on ***federal law***.

  - ❏ **"Independent and adequate state grounds":** Even if there ***is*** a federal question in a state court case, the Supreme Court may not review the case if there was an ***"independent and adequate" state ground*** for the state court's decision. (That is, if the same result would be reached even if the state court had made a different decision on the federal question, the Supreme Court may not decide the case.)

- **Federal judicial power:** The federal judicial power is set forth in Art. III, Section 2 of the U.S. Constitution. The federal judicial power includes (a partial listing):

  - ❏ cases arising under the ***Constitution*** or under ***federal statutes***;

  - ❏ cases of ***admiralty***;

  - ❏ cases between ***two or more states***;

  - ❏ cases between citizens of ***different states***; and

  - ❏ cases between a state or its citizens and a ***foreign country*** or ***foreign citizens***.

  The federal judicial power does ***not*** include cases where both parties are citizens (i.e., residents) of the same state, and no federal question is raised.

- **Congress' control of federal judicial power:** Congress has some meaningful control over the federal judicial power:

  - ❏ **Control of Supreme Court docket:** Congress has the general power to decide ***what types*** of cases the ***Supreme Court*** may hear, so long as it doesn't expand the Court's jurisdiction beyond the federal judicial power summarized above.

  - ❏ **Lower courts:** Congress may also decide what lower ***federal courts*** there should be, and what cases they may hear.

I. REVIEW OF ACTS OF CONGRESS (*MARBURY v. MADISON*)

    A. The *Marbury* case itself: Which branch of the federal government shall have the ***final say in interpreting the Constitution***? That is the principal question resolved by Chief Justice John

Marshall's opinion in ***Marbury v. Madison***, 1 Cranch 137 (1803), perhaps the cornerstone of American constitutional law.

1. **Historical background of *Marbury*:** The background of the case was a political struggle between John Adams and the Federalists, and his successor Thomas Jefferson and the Republicans. Just before leaving office, Adams appointed a number of new judges, including several justices of the peace for the District of Columbia. Commissions for these justices of the peace had been signed by Adams, but not yet delivered by the time he left office. The Jefferson Administration then refused to honor the appointments for which commissions had not actually been delivered prior to the end of Adams' term.

2. **Subject of suit:** Several of the would-be justices of the peace, including William Marbury, brought suit directly in the Supreme Court. They sought a writ of mandamus compelling Jefferson's Secretary of State (James Madison) to deliver their commissions.

3. **Marshall's decision:** Justice Marshall's opinion dealt with a number of issues, of which only the last gives the case its present significance.

   a. **Right to commission:** First, Marshall decided that Marbury and the other justices did indeed become entitled to their commissions once these had been signed by the President (and sealed by the Secretary of State, who was none other than Marshall himself!) Marshall could have short-circuited the whole problem by ruling that delivery was required for validity, but he did not take this route.

   b. **Remedy:** Secondly, Marshall had to decide whether Madison's failure to deliver the commissions entitled the plaintiffs to some sort of remedy. Marshall distinguished between political acts, which are not reviewable by the courts, and acts specifically required by law, which are reviewable. The refusal to deliver the commissions, Marshall ruled, fell into this latter category.

   c. **Mandamus not allowed:** Lastly, Marshall had to decide whether the particular remedy sought by the plaintiffs, an application for a writ of mandamus directly to the Supreme Court, could be granted.

      i. **Judiciary Act allows:** The then-effective Judiciary Act provided that the Supreme Court would have jurisdiction "to issue … writs of mandamus … [to] persons holding office under the authority of the United States." Thus the Act itself explicitly authorized the relief being sought by the plaintiffs.

      ii. **At odds with Constitution:** However, Marshall concluded, this grant of jurisdiction was in conflict with Article III, §2, of the Constitution, which grants the Supreme Court original jurisdiction only "[i]n all Cases affecting Ambassadors, other public Ministers and Consuls, and those in which a State shall be Party." Since issuance of mandamus is not among the types of cases as to which original jurisdiction is conferred on the Supreme Court, Marshall held, the congressional statute was at odds with the Constitution.

   d. **Supremacy of Constitution:** This brought Marshall to the holding for which *Marbury v. Madison* is principally known today. If the Supreme Court identifies a ***conflict*** between a constitutional provision and a congressional statute, ***the Court has the authority (and the duty) to declare the statute unconstitutional and to refuse to enforce it***. Therefore, Marshall concluded, the requested writ of mandamus could not be issued. In reaching this conclusion, Marshall made two interlocking arguments:

i. **Constitution is paramount:** First, the very purpose of a written constitution is to establish a fundamental and paramount law. It follows from this that any act of the legislature repugnant to the Constitution must be void.

ii. **Who interprets:** Second, "[i]t is emphatically the ***province and duty of the judicial department to say what the law is***." That is, it is the ***court, not the legislature***, which must make the determination whether, in a particular case, an act of Congress is in conflict with the Constitution. To deny the permissibility of judicial review of the constitutionality of a congressional statute would be to say that the courts "must close their eyes on the constitution, and see only the law. This doctrine would subvert the very foundation of all written constitutions."

4. **Criticism of *Marbury*:** Because of its key importance, *Marbury v. Madison* has been subject to a huge amount of analysis and criticism. Only one of these lines of criticism is of interest to us here.

   a. **Who determines constitutionality:** Most critics are willing to concede Step One of the two arguments above, i.e., that the Constitution is superior to statutes and that where there is a conflict, the Constitution must be respected. But Step Two is what all the shouting is about: ***the critics argue that nowhere in the Constitution is it stated that the courts, not Congress, ought to decide whether a given statute does in fact conflict with the Constitution.***

      i. **Congress could decide:** Thus it is possible to imagine a system in which we would still have our written Constitution, acknowledged to be the supreme law of the land, but in which *Congress* (not the courts) would have the final say in interpreting that Constitution. See Tribe, p. 25.

      ii. **Assumption, not conclusion:** Many commentators believe that this criticism is well-taken, at least in the sense that the Constitution nowhere states that courts are to have the last say on whether a conflict between statute and Constitution exists. However, one answer to the critics is to say that Marshall was making an ***assumption***, rather than a deduction, when he stated that courts have the ultimate right to interpret constitutionality. That is, the Constitution can be classified as being "indeterminate" as to who has the final say. When viewed in this way (which is Tribe's approach; *id.*), Marshall's assumption is at least as reasonable as the contrary one (that Congress, not the courts, should decide constitutionality) — this contrary assumption is also nowhere to be found in the Constitution.

      iii. **Judicial independence:** Furthermore, if one is merely trying to decide which assumption to make, there are some practical reasons why judicial interpretation, rather than legislative interpretation, might be a better means of construing the Constitution. Federal judges are appointed for life, and are thus free of day-to-day political pressures. Since Congress generally responds to the ***majority's*** will, and since one of the key functions of the Constitution is to protect the rights of ***minorities***, the relatively apolitical judiciary will interpret the Constitution in a way more sensitive to this minority-protection goal.

II. REVIEW OF STATE COURT DECISIONS

A. **General principles of review:** When the Supreme Court reviews the judgment of a state court, it is of course exercising its appellate, rather than its original, jurisdiction. Article III,

§2, provides that the Supreme Court's appellate jurisdiction may be regulated and limited as Congress shall provide. (See *infra*, p. 10.) Since the original Judiciary Act was enacted in 1789, the Supreme Court's appellate review of state court judgments has always been limited to the *federal questions* decided by the state courts. Tribe, p. 162.

1. **No review of state law issues:** Thus the Supreme Court may determine whether a state court has reached a decision that is not in conformity with the Constitution; but it may *not review state court decisions that merely adjudicate questions of state law*. How the Court determines whether a state court decision is limited to state law questions is a problem discussed more extensively below; the main point is that the Supreme Court's review of state court judgments is limited to *questions of federal law.*

B. *Martin v. Hunter's Lessee:*   Recall that in *Marbury v. Madison*, the Court held that it had the power to review acts of Congress for constitutionality. In the later case of ***Martin v. Hunter's Lessee***, 1 Wheat. 304 (1816), the Court confronted the similar, and perhaps even more important question, of whether the Supreme Court is constitutionally authorized to review the constitutionality of *state court decisions.*

    1. **Virginia's argument:**   *Martin* involved the issue of whether a particular Virginia statute conflicted with a federal treaty. The Virginia courts took the position that if litigation commenced in state courts, then it was up to the state court to say whether the state action violated the federal constitution, and the U.S. Supreme Court had no right to review whatever conclusion the state court reached.

    2. **Supreme Court's holding:**   The Supreme Court flatly rejected the Virginia courts' view, and held that the Court could *review the constitutionality of a decision by a state's highest court*. There were two principal strands to the Court's opinion, which was written by Justice Story:

        a. **Sovereignty argument rejected:**   First, the Virginia court's assertion that it was "sovereign" was rejected, on the grounds that the federal Constitution cut back upon state sovereignty in numerous respects. There was no reason to presume that state judiciaries were immune from this set of limitations.

        b. **Uniformity:**   Secondly, Story wrote, there is a need for *uniformity* in decisions throughout the nation interpreting the Constitution. "[I]f there were no revising authority to control these jarring and discordant judgments, and harmonize them into uniformity, the laws, the treaties and the constitution of the United States would be different in different states. ... "

    3. *Cohens v. Virginia:*   *Martin v. Hunter's Lessee* dealt with Supreme Court review of state *civil* cases. The Supreme Court's right to review state *criminal cases* for constitutionality was similarly upheld, in ***Cohens v. Virginia***, 6 Wheat. 264 (1821).

C. **Independent and adequate state grounds:**   The federal judicial power extends, by Article III, §2, to "all Cases, in Law and Equity, arising under this Constitution, the Laws of the United States, and Treaties. ... " On its face, this language seems to allow for Supreme Court review of state court decisions in any case where a federal question was involved, regardless of how the state court disposed of that federal question. Also, nothing in this clause seems to prevent the Supreme Court from reviewing all of the issues raised in any case, so long as a federal question is present.

1. **Statutory basis:** However, as noted, the Supreme Court's appellate jurisdiction exists only as provided by Congress. The limitations presently in force are discussed *infra*, p. 12. For the moment, it is sufficient to note that the mere fact that a federal question is involved in a case is ***not sufficient*** to entitle the Supreme Court to review it. Furthermore, even if the Supreme Court is entitled to review a case, it will generally adjudicate ***only the federal issues***. (Tribe, at p. 163, suggests that if Congress attempted to give the Supreme Court the right to issue on matters of state law decisions which would be binding under the Supremacy Clause, this would be an interference with state sovereignty violative of the Tenth Amendment.)

2. **Independent and adequate state ground:** Suppose that a state supreme court upholds a state statute against a federal constitutional attack. This would seem to be by itself enough to bring the case within the Supreme Court's congressionally-granted appellate jurisdiction (see *infra*, p. 10). But another doctrine, that of the *"**independent and adequate state ground**,"* may nonetheless prevent the Supreme Court from reviewing the constitutionality of the state statute.

   a. **How doctrine works:** The federal judiciary may decide only those cases presenting a "justiciable" controversy; one consequence is that the Supreme Court ***may not render an advisory opinion***. (See *infra*, p. 730.) Suppose now that the state supreme court decision rested upon two grounds, each of which would have been sufficient to produce the same result: (1) a determination that the state statute does not violate the federal Constitution; and (2) a determination that, even if the state statute being attacked were invalid, the party attacking it would lose the case anyway. In this situation, a Supreme Court determination that the state statute violated the U.S. Constitution would have ***no effect*** upon the ultimate outcome of the case (since the party attacking the statute would lose anyway); therefore the Court's opinion would, in effect, be advisory. For this reason, the Supreme Court has repeatedly held that it will not review a state court decision otherwise falling within its appellate jurisdiction if that state decision rests upon an "independent and adequate state ground."

3. **State substantive law:** Sometimes, the state ground may be ***substantive***. For instance, the state court may hold that a state statute ***violates both the state and federal constitutions***. However, the holding that the state constitution is violated may be achieved in one of two ways: (1) the state court may have independently interpreted the state constitutional provision, without relying directly on federal cases construing the federal constitutional provision; or (2) the state court may have interpreted the state constitutional provision as being ***co-extensive*** with the comparable federal constitutional provision, and then attempted to follow the relevant federal case law. In the latter situation, the Supreme Court may find that an independent and adequate state ground really ***did not exist***.

4. **State rules of procedure:** In the "substantive state law" situation discussed immediately above, it is generally clear that the state ground is "adequate," and the real issue is whether it is "independent" of the federal ground. But the state ground may, by contrast, be *"**procedural.**"* That is, because of some state procedural rule, the state court may simply fail to reach a federal issue. In this situation, the state procedural rule is clearly independent of the federal question, but it is not necessarily *"**adequate.**"*

   a. **Meaning of "adequacy":** The mere fact that the state court itself recites that state procedural grounds bar consideration of the federal claim does not automatically render those grounds "adequate." Instead, the Supreme Court will review the procedural grounds. In several different types of situations, the Supreme Court is likely to hold that the state procedural grounds are ***not "adequate,"*** and therefore do not foreclose Supreme Court review of the federal issues:

    i. **"Fundamental fairness":** Most importantly, a state procedural rule must at least meet the requirement of "***fundamental fairness***." This is a requirement imposed on the states by the Fourteenth Amendment Due Process Clause (see *infra*, p. 161).

    b. **Narrow review:** But modern cases indicate that the present Supreme Court will seek to ***respect***, rather than disregard, state procedural rules wherever possible. For instance, the Court has held that in a federal *habeas corpus* proceeding (a collateral attack, brought in federal district court, upon a prior state criminal conviction), state procedural rules will be given serious respect.

III. CONGRESS' CONTROL OF FEDERAL COURT JURISDICTION

    A. **The problem generally:** To what extent may Congress ***curtail the jurisdiction*** of the Supreme Court, or of the lower federal courts? If one looks solely at Article III, the only direct grant of jurisdiction to any particular court is that the Supreme Court shall have original jurisdiction in cases involving ambassadors, ministers and consuls, and cases in which a state is a party.

    1. **Limits indicated by Article III:** Article III itself suggests that Congress may place certain limits both on the Supreme Court's appellate jurisdiction and on the jurisdiction of the lower federal courts. First, Article III, §2 states that in all cases not falling within the Supreme Court's original jurisdiction (but falling within the federal judicial power), the Supreme Court shall have "appellate Jurisdiction both as to Law and Fact, ***with such Exceptions, and under such Regulations as the Congress shall make.***" Similarly, the lower federal courts do not even exist until Congress creates them; Article III, §1, provides that federal judicial power shall vest in the Supreme Court and "in such inferior Courts as the Congress may from time to time ordain and establish."

    B. ***McCardle*** **case:** The Supreme Court has confirmed that Congress does indeed have at least some power to control the boundaries of the Supreme Court's appellate jurisdiction. The principal case so holding is ***Ex parte McCardle***, 74 U.S. 506 (1869).

    1. **Facts of *McCardle*:** McCardle was imprisoned by a military government imposed by Congress as part of post-Civil War Reconstruction. He brought a *habeas corpus* action in federal circuit court, charging that the Reconstruction Acts under which he was imprisoned were unconstitutional. The circuit court rejected his claim, and he then appealed under an 1867 congressional statute, authorizing the grant of *habeas corpus* by federal circuit courts and also authorizing appeal to the Supreme Court in such cases.

    2. **Congress restricts appeal:** After the Supreme Court heard arguments in the *McCardle* case, but before it handed down its decision, Congress passed a law repealing the portion of the 1867 Act which allowed appeals to the Supreme Court. (Congress did this out of fear that the Court would hold in *McCardle* that the Reconstruction Acts were unconstitutional.) Thus Congress purported to deprive the Supreme Court of its right to decide the

McCardle case and any other *habeas corpus* case coming to it by appeal from the circuit courts.

3. **Holding:**   The Supreme Court **upheld** Congress' restriction of the Court's jurisdiction. The opinion noted that the appellate jurisdiction of the Supreme Court is conferred "with such exceptions and under such regulations as Congress shall make." The limitation enacted by Congress here was such an exception. Therefore, the Court concluded, it had no jurisdiction to decide the case.

4. **Limited withdrawal:**   Observe that in the statute involved in *McCardle*, Congress was not completely withdrawing the Supreme Court's right to hear *habeas corpus* cases. Rather, it was withdrawing that right only where the Supreme Court got the case by appeal from the lower courts; under the jurisdictional statutes of the time, an ***original petition*** for *habeas corpus* could be commenced in the Supreme Court itself. See Schwartz, p. 21. Furthermore, even if only the lower courts had jurisdiction, this would still not be leaving the litigant without the possibility of federal *habeas corpus* relief; the lower court decision would simply be final.

    a. **Limited significance:**   Thus *McCardle* does not by any means stand for the proposition that Congress may strip the federal courts in their entirety of the right to issue *habeas corpus* relief; such congressional action would probably be a violation of prisoners' Fourteenth Amendment right to due process.

5. **Neutral:**   Also, note that the congressional statute in *McCardle* operated in a ***neutral manner***. That is, appeal to the Supreme Court was not allowed either to the government or to a private party; thus in a future case, it might be the government which suffered because of the statute. The fact that the congressional restriction of jurisdiction would not always favor the same side makes that curtailment less objectionable constitutionally. See N&R, p. 34.

C. **Limits on congressional power:**   But Congress ***does not have unlimited power*** to tamper with the Supreme Court's appellate jurisdiction.

1. ***Klein case:***   An important Supreme Court case from the same era as *McCardle* shows that there are some limitations to Congress' power to modify the Supreme Court's appellate jurisdiction. ***U.S. v. Klein***, 80 U.S. 128 (1872).

    a. **Facts of *Klein*:**   Klein sued in the Court of Claims under a federal statute allowing citizens who had abandoned property to federal troops during the Civil War to recover compensation for it, if they could satisfy a loyalty requirement. Klein won in the Court of Claims, on the strength of earlier cases holding that a general presidential pardon satisfied the statutory requirement that the claimant not have been a supporter of the Confederacy. Before the government's appeal was heard in the Supreme Court, Congress passed a new statute providing that a presidential pardon would show the opposite (that the claimant *had* supported the Confederacy); the statute also provided that the Court of Claims and the Supreme Court were both without jurisdiction to decide cases where a pardon had been granted.

    b. **Statute struck down:**   The Supreme Court in *Klein* struck down the statute as ***unconstitutional***, on the grounds that it violated the separation of powers and invaded the judicial function. The Court argued that this was not a valid and *bona fide* denial of appellate jurisdiction in a ***whole class*** of cases; instead, it was merely a "means to an end," i.e., a way "to deny to pardons granted by the President the effect which this Court had adjudged them to have."

    c. Standard set by *Klein*: Thus *Klein* seems to stand for the proposition that "[A]ny jurisdictional limitation must be ***neutral***; that is, Congress may not decide the merits of a case under the guise of limiting jurisdiction." N&R, p. 36.

  2. Practical limitation: Observe that there is also a ***practical*** limitation upon Congress' ability to cut back on the appellate jurisdiction of the Supreme Court. If Congress is motivated by hostility to a particular Court decision, then it might be defeating its own purpose by restricting the Court's subsequent ability to hear similar cases — the adverse precedent will be ***left on the books***. Furthermore, without Supreme Court jurisdiction in an area, the individual courts of appeals will be left to go their own ways, destroying national uniformity of the law in that area. See Sullivan & Gunther, p. 83.

D. Modern congressional controls on federal jurisdiction: In the twentieth century, Congress has acted to cut back on lower federal court and Supreme Court jurisdiction in a number of special situations. None of these curtailments has been found to be unconstitutional.

  1. Forum left open: When Congress has acted to restrict the jurisdiction of either the Supreme Court or the lower federal courts, it has generally ***not entirely deprived litigants*** of a judicial remedy. For instance, often the ***state courts*** are left with jurisdiction. But if Congress curtailed federal jurisdiction in such a way that a litigant was completely deprived of the right to have his case heard in ***any court***, the congressional scheme would probably be unconstitutional; thus Congress could probably not deprive the federal courts of the right to hear a certain type of case falling within the federal courts' exclusive jurisdiction (e.g., bankruptcy cases).

IV. THE SUPREME COURT'S JURISDICTION TODAY

A. Limited scope of discussion: A full discussion of the jurisdiction of the Supreme Court is beyond the scope of this outline. We will discuss mainly how the Court selects its docket.

B. *Certiorari*: Until recent decades, there were two ways a case could get to the Supreme Court: "appeal" and "*certiorari*." If a case fell within the Court's appeals jurisdiction, in theory the Court had to hear the case and decide it (though it often did so by means of a "summary disposition," which had almost no precedential value because it did not involve an opinion). But in 1988, Congress virtually eliminated the Court's appeals jurisdiction. Therefore, nearly all cases now come to the Court by ***"writ of certiorari."***

  1. Grounds for grant of *certiorari*: The Court's decision on whether to grant *certiorari* is ***completely discretionary***. Since *certiorari* is now the sole means by which cases get to the Court, this means that the Court has ***full control*** over what cases it will hear and decide.

    a. Rules: However, the Court's decision whether to grant *certiorari* is not completely unguided. The Court has adopted formal Court Rules, which list several types of reasons which may lead the Court to grant *certiorari*. These include: (1) a ***conflict*** between ***different federal courts of appeal*** (e.g., the Second Circuit disagrees with the Ninth Circuit); (2) a conflict between the ***highest courts of two states***, or between a state's highest court and a federal court of appeals; (3) a state court or federal court of appeals decision on an ***important question*** which has not yet been settled by the

Supreme Court. See Supreme Court Rule 17(1). In all of these situations, the issue triggering the decision to grant *certiorari* will of course be one of *federal* law.

2. **Four votes needed:** The votes of *four* of the nine Justices are needed to grant *certiorari*.

    a. **Denial not precedent:** A *denial* of *certiorari* is *not a decision on the merits*, and is therefore *not a precedent* which may be cited in other cases.

Quiz Yourself on
THE SUPREME COURT'S AUTHORITY *(ENTIRE CHAPTER)*

1. The Constitution of the state of Ames contains a due process clause whose language is identical to the Due Process Clause of the U.S. Constitution's Fourteenth Amendment. Tom was a teacher in the Town of Aaron, in Ames. Because Tom's status was that of "probationary teacher," the custom in Aaron was that Tom could be fired at the end of any school year without cause. Tom was fired without cause. He sued Aaron in Ames state court. His suit was premised on the argument that his firing violated the Ames due process clause, in that he was not given a hearing before being fired. The Ames state court agreed, and the highest appeals court in Ames affirmed. Now, the Town of Aaron has appealed the case to the U.S. Supreme Court. May the U.S. Supreme Court hear the case? Give your reasons. _____

2. Same basic fact pattern as prior question. Now, however, assume that Tom in his Ames state court litigation asserted that his firing violated both the Ames constitution's due process clause and the federal Due Process Clause. The state trial court agreed with Tom that both constitutional provisions were violated, and the Ames Supreme Court affirmed the trial court decision in all respects. The trial court's decision on the state-constitution issue was based solely upon the court's reading of prior Ames state court decisions that in turn relied upon the intent of Ames voters in adopting the Ames due process clause. The portion of the decision relating to the federal constitution relied on U.S. Supreme Court cases construing the federal Due Process Clause. May the U.S. Supreme Court review the decision of the Ames Supreme Court? _____

3. Congress, in an effort to streamline the federal judiciary, passes a statute eliminating diversity jurisdiction (i.e., jurisdiction over cases brought by a citizen of one state against a citizen of another state). The legislation would prevent diversity suits from being brought in federal district court, so that they would have to be brought in state court. (The legislation does not directly change the Supreme Court's appellate jurisdiction, so that the Supreme Court can continue to review the judgments of state courts, including state court suits that turn on a federal question.) Is the congressional legislation constitutional? _____

Answers

1. **No, because the case does not involve a federal question.** The federal judicial power extends, by Article III, Section 2, to cases arising under the U.S. Constitution and federal laws. That power does not extend to cases decided solely on state-law grounds. Here, although the Ames due process clause may have mirrored the language of the U.S. Constitution's Due Process Clause, the state decision was solely based on the Ames courts' interpretation of the Ames constitution. Since no federal issue was involved, the Supreme Court has no jurisdiction (whether by appeal or by certiorari).

2. **No.** In contrast to the prior question, here at least a decision on an issue of federal law (the meaning of the U.S. Constitution) was part of the state court decision. However, the federal judicial power does not extend to Supreme Court review of any state court case for which there is an *"independent and adequate state ground."* Because Tom's firing would be unlawful even without any finding that the federal Consti-

tution had been violated (since the state constitution was found to have been violated as well), an independent and adequate state ground exists here. (If the Ames state court decision on the meaning of the Ames constitution's due process provision had derived in part from the court's belief that the clause should mean the same thing as it means in the federal Constitution, the state ground would not be truly "independent." But the facts make it clear that the finding on the meaning of the state constitution here derived solely from Ames state-law sources.)

3. Yes. The Constitution gives Congress full control over the jurisdiction of the lower federal courts. In fact, these lower federal courts do not even exist until Congress creates them; Article III, Section 1 grants the federal judicial power to the Supreme Court and to "such inferior courts as Congress may from time to time ordain and establish." This language has been interpreted to mean that Congress may also define the cases that may be heard by the lower federal courts, and that Congress may do this by refusing to let the lower federal courts hear cases that fall within the general federal judicial power (e.g., cases between citizens of different states).

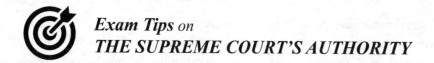

Exam Tips on
THE SUPREME COURT'S AUTHORITY

If the facts describe a lawsuit that takes place in federal court (or a state-court lawsuit that is eventually heard by the U.S. Supreme Court) be alert to *limits* on the *federal judicial power:*

☛ If the facts involve a state-court suit that is heard by the *Supreme Court* on *certiorari*, be sure that the state-court decision was *based on federal law*.

☞ Be alert to the possible existence of an *independent and adequate state ground*. That is, if the state court decided some issue of state law in a way that would have been enough to dispose of the case, there is no federal issue that is vital to the case, and the Supreme Court may not decide the federal issue. In particular, be alert for fact patterns where a *state* and *federal constitutional provision* cover the *same territory* — the state court might have decided the state issue as solely a matter of state law, in which case there would be no federal issue necessary to the case.

☛ If a fact pattern involves an attempt by *Congress* to *limit the power* of either the Supreme Court or the lower federal courts, the main things to remember are:

☞ Congress can within limits *cut back* on the kinds of cases the Supreme Court may hear, but cannot *expand* the case load beyond the categories set forth as the federal judicial power in the Constitution; and

☞ Congress may cut back, perhaps even completely eliminate, the *lower federal courts*; as with the Supreme Court, Congress may not *expand* the lower courts' dockets beyond the bounds of the constitutional federal judicial power.

CHAPTER 3

FEDERALISM AND FEDERAL POWER GENERALLY

ChapterScope

In this brief Chapter, we examine the following concepts:

■ **Federal system:** The U.S. has a *federal* system. The national government, and the government of each of the states, coexist.

■ **Federal government has limited powers:** The federal government is one of *limited, enumerated,* powers. That is, the three branches of the federal government may only assert those powers *specifically granted* by the U.S. Constitution.

❑ **"Necessary and Proper" Clause:** However, Congress does have the power to make all laws that are *"necessary and proper"* for carrying out its enumerated powers. So if Congress is seeking an *objective* that falls within the specifically enumerated powers, Congress may use *any means* that is *rationally related* to the objective being sought, and that is not specifically forbidden by the Constitution.

I. THE CONCEPT OF FEDERALISM

A. Nature of federalism: The United States has a *federalist* system. That is, the national government, and the government of each of the states, coexist. This chapter, and the several that follow, are devoted to the implications of this fact. Thus we will be examining the limits on federal power imposed in favor of state power, and conversely the limits on state power in favor of federal power.

B. Federal government has limited powers: The fundamental attribute of federal power under the U.S. Constitution is that the federal government is one of *limited, enumerated, powers*. That is, the three branches of the federal government can only assert those powers *specifically granted by the U.S. Constitution.*

1. **Comparison with state power:** This limited-power concept should be contrasted with the nature of state power. The power of state governments might be called "inherent" — a state government, at least as far as the federal Constitution is concerned, holds a general "police power", i.e., the power to protect the health, safety or general welfare of state residents. An action by a state government is *valid* under federal law unless it violates some *specific limitation* imposed by the U.S. Constitution. A federal action, by contrast, *must fall within one of the enumerated powers* listed in the Constitution.

   a. **No general police power:** In other words, there is *no general federal police power*, i.e., no right of the federal government to regulate for the health, safety or general welfare of the citizenry. Instead, each act of federal legislation or regulation must come within one of the very specific, enumerated powers (e.g., the Commerce Clause, the power to tax and spend, etc.).

i. **Tax and spend for general welfare:** Congress *does* have the right to "lay and collect taxes ... to pay the debts and provide for the ... general welfare of the United States. ... " (Article I, Section 8.) But the phrase "provide for the ... general welfare" in this sentence modifies "lay and collect taxes ... to pay the debts. ... " Thus the power to tax and spend is subject to the requirement that the general welfare be served; there is no *independent* federal power to provide for the general welfare.

2. **Review of government action:** Thus for an action by the federal government to be valid, it must meet *two* distinct requirements: (1) it must fall within one of the powers *specifically enumerated* within the Constitution as being given to the federal government; *and* (2) it must *not violate any particular limitation* on federal power given in the Constitution (e.g., the limitations contained in the Bill of Rights).

C. **Specific powers:** The principal grant of specific federal powers is in Article I, §8. That section contains 18 clauses which grant power to *Congress*. (Grants of power to the judicial and executive branches are contained in other parts of the Constitution.)

1. **Congressional powers:** Among the more important powers given to the Congress by Article I, §8, are the power to:

a. lay and collect *taxes*;

b. provide for the *defense* of the country;

c. *borrow money* on the credit of the U.S.;

d. *regulate commerce* with foreign nations, and *among the* several states;

e. regulate *immigration* and *bankruptcy*;

f. establish *post offices*;

g. control the issuance of *patents* and *copyrights*;

h. *declare war*;

i. pass all laws needed to govern the *District of Columbia* and federal *military enclaves* (e.g., military bases); and

j. "make all Laws which shall be *necessary and proper* for *carrying into Execution* the foregoing Powers, and all other Powers vested by this Constitution in the Government of the United States. ... " This is the so-called "*necessary and proper*" clause.

2. **Other sources:** Other parts of the Constitution provide additional grants of power to the various branches of the federal government. Article II defines the powers and duties of the President. Article III confers the federal judicial power (and also gives Congress power to control Supreme Court jurisdiction). Other grants of power are scattered throughout the document (e.g., Article IV, §3 gives Congress power over U.S. territories and federal property). Finally, many of the *amendments* specifically give Congress the power to enact supporting legislation (e.g., §5 of the Fourteenth Amendment). See N&R, p. 128.

3. **Foreign affairs power:** One exception has been recognized to the general rule that only enumerated powers may be exercised by the federal government. Nothing in the Constitution explicitly gives the federal government the power to regulate *foreign affairs* (though Article I, §8, gives Congress the right to "regulate Commerce with foreign Nations"). The federal government's right to conduct foreign affairs is generally considered to be implied

by the nature of the federal union, and by the impracticability of having each of the several states conduct its own foreign policy. N&R, pp. 133-34.

II. *McCULLOCH v. MARYLAND*

A. **Doctrine of implied powers:** Although the federal government may act only where it is affirmatively authorized to do so by the Constitution, the authorization does not have to be ***explicit***. That is, by the doctrine of "***implied powers***," the federal government (especially Congress) may validly exercise power that is ***ancillary*** to one of the powers explicitly listed in the Constitution, so long as this ancillary power does not conflict with specific constitutional prohibitions (e.g., those of the Bill of Rights). See Tribe, p. 301.

B. ***McCulloch* and the "Necessary and Proper" Clause:** This notion of implied powers is itself explicitly stated in the ***"Necessary and Proper"*** Clause of Art. I, §8: Congress may "make all Laws which shall be necessary and proper for carrying into Execution" the specific legislative powers granted by Art. I, §8, or by other parts of the Constitution. The first case to make an important interpretation of "Necessary and Proper" was the landmark case of ***McCulloch v. Maryland***, 17 U.S. 316 (1819).

1. **Setting of *McCulloch*:** Congress chartered the second Bank of the United States in 1816. The Bank was designed to regulate the currency and help solve national economic problems. However, it soon encountered substantial political opposition, mostly as the result of the Panic of 1818 and corruption within the various branches of the Bank. As a result, a number of states enacted anti-Bank measures.

   a. **The Maryland Act:** One of these anti-Bank statutes, enacted by Maryland, was at the center of the *McCulloch* dispute. Maryland imposed a tax upon all banks operating in the state that were not chartered by the state. The measure was intended to discriminate against the national Bank, and its Maryland branch. The state then brought suit against the Bank and its cashier (McCulloch) to collect the tax. The Supreme Court held the tax constitutionally invalid in *McCulloch*.

2. **Structure of opinion:** The opinion, one of the most significant ever written by Marshall, had two main portions: (1) a determination that the chartering of the Bank was within the constitutionally-vested power of the federal government; and (2) a finding that since the Bank was constitutionally chartered, Maryland's tax upon it was unconstitutional. At this juncture, we examine only the first of these two parts; the second is discussed *infra*, p. 101.

3. **Constitutionality of the Bank:** In concluding that the Bank was constitutionally chartered, Marshall first disposed of Maryland's argument that the powers of the national government were delegated to it by the states, and that these powers must be exercised in subordination to the states. Marshall concluded that the powers come ***directly from the people***, not from the states *qua* states.

4. **Grant need not be explicit:** Marshall then turned to the issue of whether the constitutional grant of the particular power (here, the power to charter a bank or a corporation) was required to be made ***explicitly*** in the Constitution. Marshall concluded that particular powers could be ***implied*** from the explicit grant of other powers: "A constitution, to contain an accurate detail of all the subdivisions of which its great powers will admit, and of all the means by which they may be carried into execution, would partake of the prolixity

of a legal code, and could scarcely be embraced by the human mind. ... *[W]e must never forget that it is a constitution we are expounding.*"

a. Corporation allowed: More specifically, Marshall found that Congress had the power to create a corporation (in this case, the Bank), if this was incidental to the carrying out of one of the constitutionally-enumerated powers, such as the power to *raise revenue*.

b. "Necessary and Proper" Clause: Marshall relied upon the "Necessary and Proper" Clause as a justification for Congress' right to create a bank or corporation even though such a power was not specifically granted in the Constitution. In perhaps the most significant part of the opinion, he *rejected* the contention that "necessary" meant "absolutely necessary" or "indispensable." Instead, he stated that: "let the end be legitimate, let it be within the scope of the constitution, and all means which are *appropriate*, which are *plainly adapted* to that end, which are not prohibited, [and which are consistent] with the letter and spirit of the constitution, are constitutional."

   i. Summary: Thus so long as the means is *rationally related* to a constitutionally-specified object, the means is also constitutional (assuming that it does not violate any specific prohibition, such as those from the Bill of Rights).

c. Support for conclusion: To support his liberal interpretation of "necessary and proper," Marshall pointed to a number of situations where Congress' power to carry out constitutionally-specified objectives had been liberally interpreted. For instance, the Constitution does not contain any specific grant of the power to *punish* the violation of federal laws, yet this power had always been inferred. Similarly, the power "to establish post offices and post roads" had been substantially expanded, to include the federal prohibition on mail theft. Yet these exercises of power could not be termed "indispensable" to a carrying out of the constitutionally-specified ends.

d. Separation of powers rationale: Marshall also based his opinion upon *separation-of-powers* principles: An examination by the judicial branch into the "degree of necessity" justifying a statute would be an invasion of Congress' domain. Thus Marshall felt that the Supreme Court should strike down a law as being beyond the powers of Congress only where it was *quite clear* that no constitutionally-specified object was being pursued; in any closer case, the final decision should be left to Congress, not the courts.

5. Conclusion: Marshall thus concluded that the act chartering the national bank was valid, because it bore a reasonable relationship to various constitutionally-enumerated powers of the government (e.g., the power to collect taxes, to borrow money, to regulate commerce, etc.).

a. Maryland tax invalid: Marshall then went on to find the Maryland tax invalid, because it interfered with the exercise of a valid federal activity. See *infra*, p. 102, for a discussion of this part of the opinion.

6. "Rational relation" test still in force: The standard set forth in *McCulloch* is *still in force* today. Courts interpreting the *Necessary and Proper Clause* will uphold a congressional action so long as Congress has employed a means which is not prohibited by the Constitution and which is *rationally related* to objectives that are themselves within constitutionally-enumerated powers.

a. **Motive irrelevant:** As a corollary, the Court will show great *deference* to Congress, and will generally *not* inquire into the legislators' *motives*. Thus as long as the legislation is rationally related to *one* constitutionally-enumerated motive which Congress was or might have been pursuing, the fact that other ends not within the enumerated powers of Congress might also be achieved does not invalidate the power. Tribe, pp. 302-03.

b. **Broad reading given to Clause:** The *broad and deferential reading* that the Court continues to give to the Necessary and Proper Clause is illustrated by 2010 case, *U.S. v. Comstock*, 130 S.Ct. 1949 (2010), set out in the following example.

Example: Congress passes a statute authorizing the Department of Justice to civilly commit certain federal prisoners at the end of their prison sentences. The statute applies where the prisoner has previously committed or tried to commit sexual violence or child molestation, currently suffers from a serious mental illness, and is as a result sexually dangerous to others. The Department must prove these elements to a federal judge by clear and convincing evidence. Once the Department makes this proof, it must then either persuade a state to take custody of the prisoner or keep the prisoner in a federal treatment facility until he is no longer dangerous. The plaintiffs (prisoners whom the Department is trying to civilly commit after their sentences) argue that the statute is beyond the federal government's powers.

Held, for the federal government: the commitment statute is justified by the Necessary and Proper Clause. The Clause grants Congress "*broad authority* to enact federal legislation" (citing *McCulloch*). In deciding whether the Clause grants authority in a particular situation, "we look to see whether the statute constitutes a means that is *rationally related* to the implementation of a constitutionally enumerated power." Furthermore, Congress is to be given a "*large discretion*" in choosing the *particular means* to carry out a given enumerated power. Here, Congress has a long-recognized power to define federal crimes, and to run a prison system to incarcerate those who commit such crimes. Allowing the Federal Bureau of Prisons to maintain custody of prisoners who would be dangerous to others if released is a rational method of carrying out the federal power to incarcerate those who commit federal crimes. *U.S. v. Comstock*, 130 S.Ct. 1949 (2010).

Quiz Yourself on

FEDERALISM AND FEDERAL POWER *(ENTIRE CHAPTER)*

4. Congress, pursuant to its power to establish and regulate copyrights, has decided that there is far too much counterfeiting of copyrighted musical recordings. Therefore, Congress has passed a statute making it a felony, punishable by up to five years in prison, to give a "bootlegged" (i.e., not authorized by the copyright owner) CD or MP3 recording to any other person, even if it is the donor's neighbor or relative, and even though no compensation is charged. Dennis, charged with a violation of this statute, asserts that it is unconstitutional because it is beyond the scope of Congress' authority. Should the Court agree with Dennis' assertion, and why? _____

Answer

4. No, because the statute is valid under the "Necessary and Proper" Clause. *McCulloch v. Maryland*, 17 U.S. 316 (1819), establishes that when Congress is acting in pursuit of a constitutionally-specified objective, the means chosen merely has to be *rationally related* to the objective, not "necessary" to the objective's attainment. Here, Congress is exercising its enumerated power to regulate copyrights. Congress could rationally have believed that even non-profit-motivated transfers of copyright-violating recordings contribute to the general decline of copyright protection, and that felony punishment for such transfers is a reasonable way of combatting the problem. The Court will show great deference to Congress' choice of the means to attain constitutionally-enumerated objectives, so the statute here will certainly be sustained.

Exam Tips on
FEDERALISM AND FEDERAL POWER GENERALLY

Issues covered by this Chapter are often hidden in a fact pattern. Here are some things to watch out for:

☛ Most importantly, any time your fact pattern tells you that Congress (or, for that matter, the executive or judicial branch) is doing something, be sure that the action taken falls within one of the *enumerated* powers.

☛ Remember that there is *no general federal police power*.

   ☞ It's true that Congress has the power to *tax* and *spend* for the "general welfare." But Congress *doesn't* have a general power to *legislate* for the "general welfare."

   ☞ Therefore, if your fact pattern indicates that Congress is *regulating* rather than taxing or spending, it is not enough that Congress is acting for the "general welfare"; it must be regulating pursuant to some other enumerated power, typically the commerce power or the post-Civil War amendments.

☛ Once you identify an enumerated power that might be relied upon by Congress, invoke the "Necessary and Proper" Clause. Under this clause, Congress may use *any means* that is: (1) *rationally related* to the exercise of the enumerated power; and (2) not specifically *forbidden* by the Constitution.

   ☞ Remember that the Clause is *very broadly construed*, to give Congress *lots of authority* to choose the means with which to carry out an enumerated power. So if in your fact pattern Congress seems to be trying to exercise some valid source of power, resolve in favor of Congress any doubts about the validity of the particular method Congress has chosen. Perhaps cite to *U.S. v. Comstock* (holding that Congress can civilly commit dangerous prisoners at the end of their prison terms, as a Necessary and Proper means of enforcing Congress' power to pass and enforce federal criminal statutes).

CHAPTER 4

THE FEDERAL COMMERCE POWER

ChapterScope

This Chapter examines Congress' power to "regulate commerce … among the several states." This is the "commerce power." The most important concepts in this Chapter are:

- **Test for commerce power:** A particular congressional act comes within Congress' commerce power if both of the following are true:

  - ❑ **Substantially affects commerce:** The activity being regulated *substantially affects commerce*; and

  - ❑ **Reasonable means:** The *means* chosen by Congress is *"reasonably related"* to Congress' objective in regulating.

- **Conclusion:** Where Congress thinks that what it is doing falls within its commerce power, the Court rarely disagrees, especially where the activity being regulated is itself "commercial."

- **The Tenth Amendment as a limit on Congress' power:** The *Tenth Amendment* ("the powers not delegated to the United States by the Constitution, nor prohibited by it to the States, are reserved to the States respectively, or to the People") occasionally limits Congress' ability to use its commerce power to *regulate the states*.

I. THE COMMERCE CLAUSE GENERALLY

A. **Introduction:** Article I, §8 of the Constitution gives Congress the power "to regulate Commerce with foreign Nations, and among the several States, and with the Indian Tribes."

   1. **Foreign and Indian regulation:** Congress' power to regulate foreign trade and trade with Indian tribes is not of great interest to us here. It is sufficient to note that since the adoption of the Constitution, the Supreme Court has always recognized full power on Congress' part to regulate these matters, since there is no countervailing interest in them on the part of the states. See N&R, pp. 133-134.

   2. **Commerce among the states:** Congress' power to regulate commerce *among the states*, by contrast, is of paramount importance — it is upon the commerce power that many, perhaps most, congressional activities are based.

B. **Limitation on states vs. limitation on Congress:** The Commerce Clause serves two distinct functions: (1) it acts as a *source of congressional authority*; and (2) it acts, implicitly, as a *limitation* on *state legislative power*. In this chapter, we examine the commerce power solely as a source of congressional authority; its function as a limitation on state power is treated in a separate chapter beginning *infra*, p. 73.

C. **Chronological approach:** Our approach to the federal commerce power will be a chronological one, so that development of the power may be clearly seen. Our discussion begins with the landmark commerce-power case of *Gibbons v. Ogden*, proceeds through the late nineteenth and early twentieth century cases, details the broadening scope of the commerce power beginning in 1937, and then covers some post-1995 cases limiting that scope.

II. CASES PRIOR TO 1933

A. The groundwork — *Gibbons v. Ogden*: The first major case construing the Commerce Clause was a Marshall opinion, ***Gibbons v. Ogden***, 9 Wheat. 1 (1824). Although the *Gibbons* opinion contained some discussion of the Commerce Clause as a limitation upon state powers, its principal interest is for its broad-sweeping view of ***congressional power*** under that clause.

    1. Facts of *Gibbons*: Ogden acquired, by grant from the New York legislature, monopoly rights to operate steamboats between New York and New Jersey. Gibbons began operating steamboats between New York and New Jersey, in violation of Ogden's monopoly; Gibbons' boats were licensed, however, under a federal statute. Ogden obtained an injunction in a New York court ordering Gibbons to stop operating his boats in New York waters.

    2. Holding: When the case came to the Supreme Court, Justice Marshall found the injunction against Gibbons invalid, on the ground that it was based upon a monopoly that conflicted with a valid federal statute, and thus violated the Supremacy Clause.

    3. Broad view of commerce power: In reaching this conclusion, Marshall took a broad view of Congress' powers under the Commerce Clause. Under that clause, he said, Congress could legislate with respect to ***all*** "commerce which concerns more States than one." "Commerce," he concluded, included not only buying and selling, but ***all "commercial intercourse."***

        a. May affect intrastate matters: Ogden apparently argued that insofar as his New York-granted monopoly affected his rights in New York waters, this monopoly was superior to any federal rights regarding those New York waters. But Marshall answered that the congressional power to regulate interstate commerce included the ability to ***affect matters occurring within a state***, so long as the activity had some commercial connection with another state. Thus federal law could affect New York waters, if voyages beginning in New York ended in New Jersey. (But Marshall conceded that "[t]he completely internal commerce of a State … may be considered as reserved for the State itself.")

        b. May be used to "utmost extent": In the most important portion of his opinion, Marshall stated that ***no area of interstate commerce is reserved for state control***. That is, the mere existence of the states does not by itself act as a limit upon Congress' power to govern commercial matters that affect more than one state: "This power, like all others vested in Congress, is complete in itself, may be exercised to its utmost extent, and acknowledges no limitations, other than are prescribed in the constitution."

            i. Tenth Amendment no bar: Thus Marshall implicitly rejected the argument that the Tenth Amendment (which provides that "[t]he powers not delegated to the United States by the Constitution, nor prohibited by it to the States, are reserved to the States respectively … ") acts as an independent limit on Congress' power to regulate interstate commerce.

    4. Limits on state power: The other portion of Marshall's opinion in *Gibbons* dealt with New York's right to grant a monopoly, and with whether this monopoly was invalid under the Supremacy Clause. This aspect of the opinion is discussed in the treatment of limitations on state power, *infra*, p. 75.

B. Inactive: From *Gibbons* until the late nineteenth century, the Supreme Court had practically no occasion to consider Congress' powers under the Commerce Clause. It was not until enactment of the Interstate Commerce Act (in 1887) and the Sherman Antitrust Act (in 1890) that Congress' powers under the Commerce Clause were again seriously scrutinized by the Court. When this scrutiny did occur, the result was much more hostile to congressional power than it was in the Marshall *Gibbons* approach.

    1. Economic regulation vs. police power: Between about 1880 and 1937, the Supreme Court reviewed (and frequently struck down) two different types of congressional legislation premised upon the commerce power: (1) economic regulatory laws; and (2) "police power" regulations, i.e., those directed at moral or general welfare issues. We consider each of these areas in turn.

C. Economic regulation: The Supreme Court's review of *economic regulatory laws* from about 1880 to 1937 was characterized by what has been called a "*dual federalism*" approach. That is, the Court felt that there were areas of economic life which, under the Tenth Amendment, were to be *left to state regulation*, and other areas of activity which were properly the preserve of the federal government. These two areas were viewed as being essentially *non-overlapping* — either an area was proper for state regulation, or for congressional regulation, but not for both.

    1. "Substantial economic effects": During this period from 1880 to 1937, congressional regulation was found to fall within the Commerce power so long as the activities being regulated had a "*substantial economic effect*" upon interstate commerce. See, e.g., *Houston E. & W. Texas Railway Co. v. U.S.*, 234 U.S. 342 (1914), the so-called Shreveport Rate Case.

D. "Police power" regulations and the commerce-prohibiting technique: In cases like the Shreveport Rate Case, *supra*, Congress attempted to regulate local activities directly. But Congress also developed a separate technique; instead of regulating intrastate activities directly, Congress used the technique of *prohibiting interstate transport* of certain items or persons. This "commerce-prohibiting" technique was used not only for pure economic regulatory matters, but also for "*police power*" or "*moral*" regulation. During the first two decades of the twentieth century, the Court was substantially more sympathetic to this "commerce-prohibiting/police power" technique than to direct regulation of intrastate affairs.

    1. The Lottery Case: For instance, when Congress passed the Federal Lottery Act, which prohibited the interstate shipment of *lottery tickets*, the Court upheld the statute in *Champion v. Ames* ("*The Lottery Case*"), 188 U.S. 321 (1903). The majority opinion began with the assumption that lotteries were clearly an "evil" which it was desirable for Congress to regulate; since Congress regulated only the interstate shipment of these evil articles, it could not be said to be interfering with intrastate matters reserved for state control. (But a four-Justice dissent contended that only commerce itself could be regulated, and that lottery tickets were not "articles of commerce.")

    2. Regulation of intrastate affairs: Once it became apparent that the Court looked favorably upon the commerce-prohibiting technique as a means of asserting national police power, Congress took a significant additional step: it began to regulate *intrastate* activities as a *means of enforcing* bans on interstate transport. Even this extension was generally favorably viewed by the Supreme Court.

> **Example:** Congress passed the Pure Food and Drug Act of 1906. Acting under the Act, federal officials seized a shipment of adulterated eggs after they had arrived in the state of their destination. The right to seize adulterated eggs once they had arrived at their destination was "certainly appropriate to the right to bar them from interstate commerce, and completes its purpose, which is not to merely prevent the physical movement of adulterated articles, but the use of them. … " *Hipolite Egg Co. v. U.S.,* 220 U.S. 45 (1911).

3. **The Child Labor Case:**   But the Supreme Court was more hostile to congressional interference with the *employer-employee relationship*. The Justices were particularly unwilling to allow congressional legislation which was pro-labor, and which the Justices saw as being an unwarranted interference with the free-market system. This was most dramatically illustrated in the so-called Child Labor Case, *Hammer v. Dagenhart*, 247 U.S. 251 (1918).

   a. **Holding in case:**   In that case, the Court voted, 5-to-4, to strike down a federal statute which prohibited the interstate transport of articles produced by companies which employed children younger than certain ages or under certain conditions.

   b. **Rationale:**   The majority distinguished this statute from other police power/commerce-prohibiting statutes which the Court had upheld; in those cases, the Court argued, the interstate transportation being prohibited was *part of the very evil* sought to be prohibited (e.g., the prohibition on the interstate shipment of lottery tickets, where the tickets themselves were viewed as evil). Here, by contrast, the goods shipped in interstate commerce were themselves harmless; it was only the employment of child labor which was an evil, and this employment was not directly related to interstate commerce.

      i. **Powers reserved to states:**   The majority reasoned further that if a prohibition on interstate commerce were permitted in this situation, all manufacturing intended for interstate shipment would be brought under federal control, destroying what the majority said was the Constitution's reservation of the "power of the States over local matters," made clear by the Tenth Amendment.

   c. **Holmes' dissent:**   But it was the classic dissent by Justice Holmes that in the long run became the more significant opinion in *Hammer*. Holmes argued that so long as the congressional regulation falls within power specifically given to the Congress (here, the power to regulate interstate commerce), the fact that it *has a collateral effect upon local activities* otherwise left to state control *does not render the statute unconstitutional.*

      i. **Tenth Amendment of no force:**   Thus Holmes' dissent implicitly rejected the Tenth Amendment as a source of limitations on federal authority — so long as congressional action technically comes within a constitutionally-enumerated power, it is valid *no matter how substantially* it impairs the states' ability to regulate what would otherwise be local affairs. This highly restrictive view of the Tenth Amendment became the *majority view* beginning in 1937, and has endured to the present. See *infra*, pp. 46-52.

III. COURT BARRIERS TO THE NEW DEAL

A. The New Deal threatened: After Congress and President Roosevelt began implementing the New Deal in 1933, the Supreme Court took an increasingly narrow view of congressional power under the Commerce Clause. Within a few years, it became apparent that a majority of the Court would strike down congressional regulation of any area which the majority felt was reserved by the Tenth Amendment to state control.

B. The *Schechter Poultry* ("Sick Chicken") case: The decision which caused the greatest public uproar during the New Deal was *Schechter Poultry Corp. v. U.S.*, 295 U.S. 495 (1935), the "Sick Chicken" case. At issue in the case was the validity of the National Industrial Recovery Act (NIRA). The NIRA authorized the President to adopt "codes of fair competition" for various trades or industries; the codes regulated such items as minimum wages and prices, maximum hours, collective bargaining, etc. See Sullivan & Gunther, p. 135.

1. **Facts of *Schechter*:** The *Schechter* case involved the conviction of Schechter Poultry Corp. on charges of violating the wage and hour provisions of the New York Metropolitan Area Live Poultry Industry Fair Competition Code. Although the vast majority of poultry sold in New York came from other states, Schechter itself bought within New York City, and resold its stock *exclusively to local dealers*.

2. **Act held unconstitutional:** The Supreme Court held the NIRA *unconstitutional* as applied to *Schechter*.

   a. **Not in "current of commerce":** Schechter's activities were not within the "current" or "stream" of commerce, because the interstate transactions ended when the shipments reached Schechter's New York City slaughter-houses (unlike the cattle in the *Swift* case, which were ultimately reshipped out of state after being slaughtered).

   b. **Not "affecting commerce":** Nor was the "affecting commerce" rationale applicable; what was required was a *direct*, not indirect, effect on commerce. Although Schechter's wage and price policies might have forced interstate competitors to lower their own prices, this impact was much too indirect to allow for congressional control.

C. The *Carter Coal* case: The facts of *Schechter* made it a particularly weak case for the government, so the decision was not as damaging as was popularly perceived. A much more significant blow to the New Deal was delivered in *Carter v. Carter Coal Co.*, 298 U.S. 238 (1936). That case was a challenge to the Bituminous Coal Conservation Act of 1935, which *set maximum hours and minimum wages for workers in coal mines*.

1. **Held unconstitutional:** The Court found the Act not to be a valid use of the commerce power. The Court distinguished between "production" and "commerce." Production, which was what was being regulated here, was a "purely local activity," even though the materials produced would nearly all ultimately be sold in interstate commerce. Nor did the production "directly affect" interstate commerce; the issue was not the *extent* of the effect produced on interstate commerce, but the existence or nonexistence of a *direct logical relation* between the production and the interstate commerce.

   a. **Local evil:** Furthermore, the Court held, the issue was the link between the employer-employee relationship (the precise matter being regulated) and interstate commerce; it could not be said that this relationship had a sufficiently direct effect upon interstate commerce. Also, the employer-employee relationship was a "local relation," and whatever evils currently characterized that relationship in the coal industries were all "*local evils* over which the federal government has no legislative control."

D. The Court-packing plan: The *Carter* decision was a body-blow to the New Deal, since it implied that all attempts to deal with what the Court perceived as "local problems," including probably all employer-employee problems, would be struck down. President Roosevelt waited until after the 1937 election to launch a counterattack. When he did so, it was principally in the form of the infamous *Court-packing plan.*

    1. How the plan was to work: Roosevelt's proposal sought congressional authority for him to appoint an additional federal judge for each judge who was 70 years old and had served on a court for at least 10 years. The plan was to apply to all levels of the federal judiciary, and provided for a maximum of 15 members on the Supreme Court, i.e., an additional six Justices. (Not by coincidence, there were six Supreme Court Justices over the age of 70 in 1937. See Sullivan & Gunther, p. 140.)

    2. Plan defeated: The plan stirred enormous political controversy. Those opposed to it contended that "its practical operation would be to make the Constitution what the executive or legislative branches of the Government choose to say it is — an interpretation to be changed with each change of administration." (Senate Judiciary Committee Report, June 14, 1937, in Sullivan & Gunther, p. 141.) The plan was ultimately defeated, in mid-1937.

        a. Practical effect: However, by that time the Supreme Court had materially "reformed" itself. The retirement of Justice Van Devanter was enough to form a new majority, and the Court decided the important *NLRB v. Jones & Laughlin* case (*infra*, p. 26) in favor of the validity of the NLRA; all this occurred while the debate on the Court-packing plan was still in progress. Thus President Roosevelt made a plausible claim to have lost the battle but won the war.

IV. THE POST-NEW-DEAL TREND

    A. The post-New-Deal trend generally: Beginning with the Court's 1937 decision in *NLRB v. Jones & Laughlin Steel Corp.* (discussed shortly below), the Court began to show a vastly greater *deference* to Congress' use of its Commerce power. Under these post-1937 cases, the Court will uphold laws based on the Commerce power if the Court is convinced that what is being regulated is economic activity, and that the activity *"substantially affects"* interstate commerce.

        1. Three theories: The Court gradually expanded the reach of the Commerce power by recognizing three theories upon which a commerce-based regulation may be premised: (1) an expanded *"substantial economic effect"* theory; (2) a *"cumulative effect"* theory; and (3) an expanded *"commerce-prohibiting" protective* technique. We consider each of these in turn, after which we consider the special case of use of the Commerce power to regulate *civil rights* (*infra*, p. 29).

            a. Some limits remain: But there remain some important *limits* on the Commerce power, as the result of several post-1995 Supreme Court decisions, which are discussed beginning *infra*, p. 31.

    B. Expanded "substantial economic effect": Recall that in pre-1937 cases, the Court had insisted upon a "direct" and "logical" relationship between the intrastate activity being regulated and interstate commerce. But beginning in *NLRB v. Jones & Laughlin Steel Corp.*, 301

U.S. 1 (1937), the Court substantially loosened the nexus required between the intrastate activity being regulated and interstate commerce.

1. **Facts of *Jones & Laughlin*:** The *Jones & Laughlin* case tested the constitutionality of the National Labor Relations Act of 1935 (NLRA). The case involved the NLRB's attempt to prevent Jones & Laughlin (a large integrated steel producer) from engaging in "unfair labor practices" by the discriminatory firing of employees for union activity.

2. **NLRA upheld:** In *Jones & Laughlin*, a majority of the Court held that the NLRA, as applied to Jones & Laughlin, lay within the commerce power. The Court noted that while Jones & Laughlin manufactured iron and steel only in Pennsylvania, it owned mines in two other states, operated steamships on the Great Lakes, held warehouses in four states, and sent 75% of its product out of Pennsylvania.

   a. **Conclusion:** Because of this multi-state network of operations, the Court concluded, a labor stoppage of the Pennsylvania intrastate manufacturing operations would have a ***substantial effect on interstate commerce***. Therefore, labor relations at the Pennsylvania plants could constitutionally be regulated by Congress.

   b. **Tenth Amendment rejected as limitation:** The Court implied, though it did not expressly state, that the Tenth Amendment would no longer act as an independent limitation on federal commerce-clause powers.

3. **Practical consequence:** *Jones & Laughlin* made it irrelevant whether the activity being regulated occurred before, during or after the interstate movement. Today, so long as the regulated activity has a ***"substantial economic effect"*** upon interstate commerce, that activity may occur substantially before the interstate movement (e.g., steel production in the *Jones & Laughlin* case, where the steel might not have been shipped out of state for months after its production) or even long ***after*** the interstate commerce. See Tribe, p. 309.

C. **The "cumulative effect" theory:** The second major expansion of Commerce Clause power might be termed the *"cumulative effect"* theory. That theory provides that Congress may regulate not only acts which ***taken alone*** would have a substantial economic effect on interstate commerce, but also an entire ***class*** of acts, if the class has a substantial economic effect (even though one act within it might have virtually no interstate impact at all). As a result of this "cumulative effect" principle, it is not only the type of regulation sustained in *Jones & Laughlin* (regulation of a large steel producer, where that producer's labor problems would ***by themselves*** have a substantial effect on interstate commerce) which may be regulated. See Tribe, pp. 310-11.

1. ***Wickard v. Filburn:*** The case which established this "cumulative effect" principle was ***Wickard v. Filburn***, 317 U.S. 111 (1942). This case (the facts of which are almost like a law school examination question in their far-fetchedness), is probably the ***furthest*** the Court has ever gone in sustaining Commerce-Clause powers, at least in the economic, as opposed to "police power," area.

   a. **Facts of *Wickard*:** *Wickard* involved the Agricultural Adjustment Act of 1938, which permitted the Secretary of Agriculture to set quotas for the raising of wheat on every farm in the country. The Act allowed not only the setting of quotas on wheat that would be sold interstate and intrastate, but also quotas on wheat which would be ***consumed on the very farm where it was raised***. Wheat raised in excess of the quota was subject to a per-bushel penalty.

  i. **Home consumption:** Filburn, the plaintiff in *Wickard*, owned a small farm in Ohio. He challenged the government's right to set a quota on the wheat which he raised and consumed on his own farm, on the grounds that this was a purely local activity beyond the scope of federal control.

 b. **Statute upheld:** But a unanimous Court (whose composition had changed radically from the days of the *Carter Coal* case just six years before) **upheld** the Act, even as it applied to home-consumed wheat. The Court reasoned as follows:

  i. **Consumption has market effect:** First, the consumption of home-grown wheat is a large and variable factor in the economics of the wheat market. The more wheat that is consumed on the farm where it is grown, the less wheat that is bought in commerce (i.e., from other farmers), whether interstate or not.

  ii. **Cumulative effect:** Plaintiff's own effect on the market, by his decision to consume wheat grown himself, might be trivial. But this decision, "taken together with that of *many others similarly situated*, is far from trivial. ... " That is, home-grown wheat "supplies a need of the man who grew it which would otherwise be reflected by purchases in the open market," and the home-grown wheat thus "competes with wheat in commerce." Protection of the interstate commercial trade in wheat clearly falls within the commerce power, and the regulation of home-grown wheat is *reasonably related to protecting that commerce.*

 c. **Still good law:** *Wickard* is *still good law*. In a 2005 case, the Court relied extensively on *Wickard* to hold that Congress had the power to forbid cultivation and consumption of home-grown marijuana for medical purposes. In that case, *Gonzales v. Raich*, 545 U.S. 1 (2005), the Court said that "*Wickard* ... establishes that Congress can regulate purely intrastate activity that is not itself 'commercial,' in that it is not produced for sale, if it concludes that failure to regulate that class of activity would undercut the regulation of the interstate market in that commodity." The case is discussed further *infra*, p. 35.

D. **The commerce-prohibiting technique (police power regulations):** Recall that apart from the "affecting commerce" line of cases, another pre-1933 line of cases dealt (ambiguously) with Congress' right to use *prohibitions* on the *interstate transportation* of items or people in furtherance of "*police power*" or "*general welfare*" regulations. This commerce-prohibiting technique, like the "affecting commerce" principle, was substantially broadened shortly after 1937.

 1. *Darby* **reverses** *Hammer:* Recall that in the *Child Labor Case*, *Hammer v. Dagenhart* (*supra*, p. 24), the Court held that Congress could not prohibit the interstate sale of the products of child labor. *Hammer* was flatly overruled in **U.S. v. Darby**, 312 U.S. 100 (1941).

 a. **Minimum wage regulations upheld:** In *Darby*, the Court unanimously upheld the Fair Labor Standards Act of 1938, which set minimum wages and maximum hours for employees engaged in the production of goods for interstate commerce. The Act not only prohibited the shipment in interstate commerce of goods made by employees employed for more than the maximum hours or not paid the prevailing rates, but it also made it a federal crime to employ workmen in the production of goods "for interstate commerce" at other than the prescribed rates and hours.

b. Direct ban upheld: The Court first upheld the direct ban on interstate shipments; it disposed of the argument that manufacturing conditions are left for exclusive state control, by stating that "[t]he power of Congress over interstate commerce [can] neither be enlarged nor diminished by the exercise or non-exercise of state power. ... The [Tenth Amendment] states but a truism that all is retained which has not been surrendered."

    i. Tenth Amendment irrelevant: Thus the Tenth Amendment will *no longer act as an independent limitation on congressional authority over interstate commerce*. (See *infra*, pp. 46-52 for a summary of the present status of the Tenth Amendment.) As the result of *Darby*, Congress is completely free to impose whatever conditions it wishes upon the privilege of engaging in an activity that substantially affects interstate commerce, so long as the conditions themselves violate no independent constitutional prohibition (e.g., the Equal Protection Clause of the Fourteenth Amendment). See Tribe, pp. 311-312.

c. Motive irrelevant: The Court also disavowed any interest in Congress' *motive*: "The motive and purpose of a regulation of interstate commerce are matters for the legislative judgment upon the exercise of which the Constitution places no restriction and over which the courts are given no control."

    i. Present rule: The irrelevance of motive remains a feature of Commerce Clause, and most other sorts, of constitutional analysis. (But motive may be relevant where a preferred right, such as the right of free expression or freedom from racial discrimination, is concerned. See, e.g., pp. 257 and 477 *infra*.)

d. Reasonable means to achieve end: Finally, the Court in *Darby* upheld the portion of the Act making it a crime to employ workers engaged in interstate commerce in violation of the wage/hour provisions.

    i. Rationale: Given Congress' right to impose direct prohibitions or conditions on interstate commerce, Congress "may choose the *means reasonably adapted to the attainment of the permitted end*, even though they involve control of intrastate activities." Thus the outright criminalization of employer conduct was a reasonable means of *implementing* the prohibition on interstate shipments.

    ii. Bootstrap: This portion of the *Darby* opinion has been referred to as a "super-bootstrap suggestion"; see Gunther & Sullivan (13th Ed.), pp. 195-96. If it is taken seriously, it means that Congress may attack any problem (even one of overwhelmingly local concern) by prohibiting all interstate activity associated in any way with it; then, the local activity itself could be prohibited as a means of implementing the ban on interstate transactions.

E. Civil rights legislation: A key use of the federal Commerce power has been in *civil rights* legislation. Thus Title II of the 1964 Civil Rights Act bans discrimination in places of public accommodation. This ban applies against all but the very most localized, small hotels or restaurants. It does this by covering any establishment that *serves interstate travelers,* or (in the case of a restaurant) that buys *food,* a substantial portion of which "has *moved in commerce.*"

1. **The Court decisions:**   Any doubts about the constitutionality of the 1964 Act were put to rest by two 1964 Supreme Court decisions upholding it. Both, but especially the second discussed below, involved what might be termed "local" enterprises.

   a. *Heart of Atlanta* **case:**   In *Heart of Atlanta Motel v. U.S.*, 379 U.S. 241 (1964), the plaintiff was a motel located in downtown Atlanta, which refused to rent rooms to blacks.

      i. **Contacts with interstate travel:**   The motel was near two interstate highways, derived 75% of its occupancy from out-of-state guests, and solicited business in national media.

      ii. **Holding:**   The Supreme Court held that the motel could constitutionally be reached by the Civil Rights Act, under the Commerce Clause. The Court took note of Congress' findings that racial discrimination discouraged travel on the part of a substantial portion of the black community, and that such discrimination could therefore be regulated by Congress in the aggregate. Furthermore, the Court held, "[t]he power of Congress to *promote interstate commerce* also includes the power to *regulate the local incidents thereof*, including *local activities* in both the States of origin and destination, which *might have a substantial and harmful effect upon that commerce*." The Court quoted a prior decision, to the effect that "if it is *interstate commerce that feels the pinch*, it does not matter *how local the operation that applies the squeeze*."

      iii. **Police-powers motive acceptable:**   Nor was the Court troubled by the fact that Congress' *motive* for this legislation was not purely economic, but rather, principally moral and social.

   b. *Katzenbach v. McClung:*   The other early Civil Rights Act case, *Katzenbach v. McClung*, 379 U.S. 294 (1964), demonstrates even more clearly the Court's approval of the use of the Commerce Clause to reach what seemed to be overwhelmingly local activities.

      i. **Facts:**   *Katzenbach* involved a Birmingham, Alabama restaurant called Ollie's Barbecue. The restaurant was relatively far from any interstate highway or train or bus station, and there was no evidence that an appreciable part of its business was in serving out of state travellers. However, 46% of the food purchased by the restaurant during the previous year had been bought from a supplier who had bought it from out of state. (Recall that the Civil Rights Act applies to any restaurant a substantial portion of whose food has moved in commerce.)

      ii. **Application of Act upheld:**   The Court *upheld* the Act as applied to the restaurant. As in the *Heart of Atlanta* case, the Court observed that unavailability of accommodations dissuaded blacks from travelling in interstate commerce. The Court returned to the *Wickard v. Filburn* rationale: even though Ollie's itself was small, and the value of food it purchased from out of state had only an insignificant effect on commerce, the restaurant's discriminatory conduct was representative of a great deal of similar conduct throughout the country, and *this conduct in the aggregate* clearly had an effect on interstate commerce. Therefore, Congress was *entitled to regulate the individual case.*

V. SOME MODERN LIMITS ON THE COMMERCE POWER

A. Some limits still exist: But some important *limits* still exist on Congress' Commerce powers, as the result of several major decisions since 1995. Here's a brief summary of these key limiting decisions:

❏ **"Substantial" effect required:** It is not enough that the activity being regulated merely *"affects"* interstate commerce. Instead, the activity must *"substantially* affect" interstate commerce. So, for instance, Congress can't prohibit possession of guns near schools, because the effect on Commerce of such possession is not substantial enough. (See *U.S. v. Lopez, infra*, p. 31.)

❏ **"Non-economic" activities:** The Court will be more skeptical of Commerce-based regulation if the activity being regulated is essentially *non-economic*. So, for instance, Congress can't allow women who are the victims of gender-motivated violent crimes to bring federal civil-court suits, because gender-motivated violent crime against women is essentially a non-economic activity. (See *U.S. v. Morrison, infra*, p. 34.)

❏ **Forced entry into market:** Congress may not use its Commerce power to compel someone who is *not already active* in a commercial market to *enter that market by purchasing a product*. For instance, Congress can't use its Commerce power to force individuals to *buy health insurance* (or pay a penalty if they don't), even though the collective decisions of many people not to buy insurance substantially affect the interstate market for health care. (See *N.F.I.B. v. Sebelius, infra*, p. 37.)

We review these key post-1995 cases below. We also review one post-1995 case that went the other way, in which Congress' use of its Commerce power to regulate some very local transactions (growing marijuana for one's personal purposes) was *sustained*, on the grounds that without such regulation, an entire nationwide scheme for regulating interstate commerce would be jeopardized; see *Gonzales v. Raich, infra*, p. 35.

B. Can't ban "guns near schools" (*U.S. v. Lopez*): The case holding that the effect on interstate commerce from the activity being regulated must be *"substantial"* was *U.S. v. Lopez*, 514 U.S. 549 (1995). There, the Court for the first time in 60 years *invalidated a federal statute on the grounds that it was beyond Congress' Commerce power*.

1. **Gun-Free Schools:** The statute was the Gun-Free School Zones Act of 1990, in which Congress made it a federal crime "for any individual knowingly to possess a firearm at a place that the individual knows, or has reasonable cause to believe, is a school zone."

   a. **Little connection to commerce:** The statute clearly had less explicit connection to interstate commerce than most federal statutes premised on the Commerce power. For instance:

   i. **No findings:** The statute did not include explicit findings by Congress that the activity being regulated (possession of guns in schools) affected commerce.

   ii. **No jurisdictional nexus:** Perhaps more important, the statute *did not include a "jurisdictional nexus."* For instance, Congress could have made it a crime only to possess a gun that had moved in (or otherwise affected) interstate commerce. (Congress often uses this "jurisdictional" approach to carry out the "commerce-prohibiting" technique; see, for instance, the 1964 Civil Rights Act, discussed *supra,* p. 29, regulating restaurants that buy food a substantial part of which has moved in interstate commerce.) But this isn't what Congress did here — instead it ***banned even possession of a gun that had never traveled in, or even affected, interstate commerce.***

2. **Statute struck down:** By a 5-4 vote, the Court ***struck down*** the statute. The majority opinion was by Chief Justice Rehnquist, joined by Justices O'Connor, Scalia, Kennedy and Thomas.

   a. **"Substantial" effect required on Commerce:** The majority opinion first resolved a prior uncertainty, by holding that it is not enough that the activity being regulated merely "affects" interstate commerce. Instead, the activity must "***substantially*** affect" interstate commerce.

   b. **Requisite effect not present:** Then, the majority concluded that the possession of guns in schools had not been demonstrated to "substantially affect" commerce.

      i.   **Not commercial:** The majority seemed to think that it was important that the particular activity being regulated — possession of guns in schools — ***was not itself a "commercial" activity.*** The majority distinguished *Wickard v. Filburn, supra,* p. 27 (which it called "perhaps the most far reaching example of Commerce Clause authority over intrastate activity. … ") from the activity at issue here, saying that *Wickard* "involved economic activity in a way that the possession of a gun in a school zone does not." Also, unlike the wheat-growing regulation in *Wickard,* the regulation here was not part of a "larger regulation of economic activity, in which the regulatory scheme could be undercut unless the intrastate activity were regulated."

      ii. **Government's argument:** The federal government, in defending the statute, had argued that gun possession in schools *does* have a "substantial effect" on commerce. The government asserted the following syllogism: (1) possession of a firearm in a school may result in violent crime; and (2) violent crime affects the functioning of the national economy in several ways (e.g., (a) the costs of crime are insured against, and thus spread across state lines because of the interstate nature of the insurance market; (b) violent crime reduces individuals' willingness to travel to areas of the country they believe are unsafe; and (c) violent crime in the schools reduces the schools' ability to educate their students, who thus become less economically-productive).

      iii. **Argument rejected:** But the majority rejected this argument, essentially because it ***proved too much.*** For instance, under the "economic productivity" argument, "Congress could regulate any activity that it found was related to the economic productivity of individual citizens: family law (including marriage, divorce, and child custody), for example." In general, under the government's approach, "[I]t is difficult to perceive ***any limitation on federal power,*** even in areas such as criminal law enforcement or education where States historically have been sovereign. Thus, if we were to accept the Government's arguments, we are hard-pressed to posit any activity that Congress is without power to regulate."

      iv. **Parade of horribles:** The majority went on to describe some of the types of federal regulation that would fall within the Commerce power, if the government's approach were accepted: "Congress could mandate a ***federal curriculum*** for local elementary and secondary schools because what is taught in local schools has a significant 'effect on classroom learning,' and that, in turn, has a substantial effect on interstate commerce." Similarly, "Congress could ... look at *child rearing* as 'fall[ing] on the commercial side of the line', because it provides a 'valuable service — namely, to equip [children] with the skills they need to survive in ... the workplace.'" Such results would make the Commerce power limitless.

    v. **Summary:** In summary, the majority said, "To uphold the Government's contentions here, we would have to pile inference upon inference in a manner that would bid fair to convert congressional authority under the Commerce Clause to a *general police power* of the sort retained by the States." Prior cases may have extended the Commerce power to great lengths, "but we decline here to proceed any further." To uphold the act here "would require us to conclude ... that there never will be a distinction between what is truly national and what is truly local...."

3. Dissent: There were four dissenters (Stevens, Souter, Breyer and Ginsburg), who wrote three separate opinions. The principal one was by Justice Breyer, in which all three of the other dissenters joined.

    a. **"Rational basis" test:** For Breyer, the test was "whether Congress could have had a *rational basis* for finding a significant (or substantial) connection between gun-related school violence and interstate commerce." (The majority had not mentioned "rational basis" — to the majority, the question was whether there actually *was* a substantial connection, not merely whether Congress could rationally have believed that there was.) With the issue formulated this way, Breyer had no trouble concluding that the answer was yes.

        i. **Government's arguments accepted:** Breyer accepted the government's arguments on this point. There was ample evidence available to Congress that gun-related violence in the schools interfered with the quality of education. And there was also extensive evidence that education was intimately tied to the economic viability of not only individuals but whole areas (since "many firms base their location decisions upon the presence, or absence, of a workforce with a basic education").

    b. **Majority's view rejected:** Breyer vehemently objected to the majority's approach.

        i. **Contrary to case law:** First, Breyer found that approach contrary to modern cases upholding congressional action regulating activities that (in his opinion) had less connection with interstate commerce than the guns-in-schools at issue here. For instance, he thought that a single instance of racial discrimination at a local restaurant, found regulable in *Katzenbach v. McClung, supra*, p. 30, had no greater connection with interstate commerce than the instance of gun possession being regulated here.

        ii. **Commercial/non-commercial distinction rejected:** Second, Breyer rejected the majority's distinction between "commercial" and "non-commercial" transactions, believing that the line would prove hard to draw. He also thought that the majority drew the line in the wrong place here — if the majority was holding that education as a whole was a non-commercial activity, the majority was mistaken because

"Congress ... could rationally conclude that schools fall on the commercial side of the line."

C. Violence against women (*Morrison*):   The second major case limiting Congress' Commerce powers was *U.S. v. Morrison,* 529 U.S. 598 (2000). *Morrison* suggests that whenever Congress tries to regulate conduct that is ***essentially non-commercial,*** the Court will be quick to say that the regulation goes beyond the Commerce power.   Just as *Lopez* held that Congress can't ban gun possession in schools, *Morrison* says that Congress ***can't broadly regulate violence against women,*** because such violence is essentially non-commercial.

1. **Facts:** In *Morrison*, Congress was concerned that the states' judicial systems were not taking gender-motivated violence against women sufficiently seriously. Congress therefore passed the Violence Against Women Act of 1994, 42 U.S.C. § 13981. The Act announced that all persons within the U.S. "shall have the right to be free from crimes of violence motivated by gender." To enforce that right, the Act then said that a woman who was a victim of such a gender-motivated violent crime could bring a civil suit against the perpetrator in federal court. A female student at Virginia Tech who said she had been raped by two members of the school's football team sued them under the Act. They defended by arguing that the act was beyond Congress' powers, including its Commerce power.

2. **Holding:** By the same 5-4 split as in *Lopez*, the Court agreed with the defendants that the Act was beyond Congress' Commerce power. The majority opinion by Chief Justice Rehnquist relied principally on the fact that the activity being regulated was essentially ***non-economic***: "Gender-motivated crimes of violence are not, in any sense of the phrase, economic activity.   While we need not adopt a categorical rule against aggregating the effects of any noneconomic activity ... Thus far in our Nation's history our cases have upheld Commerce Clause regulation of intrastate activity only where that activity is economic in nature."

   a. **Congressional findings not enough:** Rehnquist conceded that here, unlike in *Lopez*, there were ***detailed findings*** by Congress detailing the effect of the conduct being regulated on interstate commerce; for instance, Congress had found that gender-motivated violence deterred potential victims from traveling interstate or from being employed in interstate businesses. However, Rehnquist seemed to give virtually no deference to these findings, because they made for too attenuated a causal chain: "If accepted [this] reasoning would ***allow Congress to regulate any crime*** as long as the nationwide, aggregated impact of that crime has substantial effects on employment, production, transit, or consumption.   Indeed, if Congress may regulate gender-motivated violence, it would be able to ***regulate murder or any other type of violence***. ..."

   b. **Local vs. national distinction:** Rehnquist concluded by relying on the ***distinction between local and national activities:*** "The Constitution requires a distinction between what is truly national and what is truly local ... The regulation and punishment of intrastate violence that is not directed at the instrumentalities, channels, or goods involved in interstate commerce has always been the province of the States."

3. **Dissent:** Four Justices dissented, in separate dissents by Justices Souter and Breyer. The dissenters were especially critical of the majority's rejection of Congress' factual findings.

   a. **Economic / non-economic distinction criticized:** The dissenters also criticized the majority's view that where an activity is basically non-commercial its aggregate affects on commerce cannot suffice. Justice Breyer contended that ***the economic/non-***

economic distinction would be a hard one to implement reliably. (E.g., "Would evidence that desire for economic domination underlies many brutal crimes against women save the present statute?") He also argued that there was no reason for attaching such importance to that distinction in situations where non-commercial local activities have a large *effect* on interstate commerce. (E.g., "If chemical emanations through indirect environmental change cause identical, severe commercial harm outside a State, why should it matter whether local factories or home fireplaces release them?")

D. Regulation of non-commercial activity as part of broader regulatory scheme: Not every post-1995 Commerce decision has gone against Congress. When Congress is engaged in a *broad regulation of a commercial activity*, even after *Lopez* and *Morrison* the Court has allowed Congress to regulate *purely non-commercial and intrastate instances of that activity,* if it *reasonably believes that failure to regulate these instances would jeopardize the success of the overall regulatory scheme.* Thus in *Gonzales v. Raich*, 545 U.S. 1 (2005), the Court concluded by 6-3 that Congress, as part of its overall ban on the cultivation and sale of marijuana, could forbid even the purely *intrastate and noncommercial cultivation* of *marijuana* for *medical purposes.*

1. **Facts:** Congress had since the 1970s classified marijuana as a Schedule 1 drug (drugs with high potential for abuse and lack of any accepted medical use), and had made it a crime to manufacture distribute or possess any Schedule I drug. Congress did so in the Controlled Substances Act (CSA). California then, in 1996, by means of a voter-approved Proposition, established an exemption from criminal prosecution for physicians who recommended marijuana to a patient for medical purposes, as well as for patients and primary caregivers who possessed or cultivated marijuana for medicinal purposes with the recommendation or approval of a physician. (Eight other states also authorized use of marijuana for medicinal purposes.)

   a. **How suit arose:** The two plaintiffs in *Raich* were California residents who suffered from very serious medical ailments that they sought to treat with marijuana. (One of them, Monson, grew her own marijuana, which was confiscated by federal Drug Enforcement Administration agents.) The plaintiffs then sued for an injunction barring the enforcement of the CSA against them, on the theory that Congress did not have the power, under the Commerce Clause or any other grant of authority, to regulate the interstate, noncommercial cultivation and possession of marijuana for personal medical purposes. The Ninth Circuit agreed with the plaintiffs, on the basis of *Lopez* and *Morrison*.

2. **Plaintiffs lose by 6-3:** By a 6-3 vote, the Court held against the Ps in *Raich*, concluding that Congress' Commerce clause powers gave it the right to regulate *even the purely intrastate and noncommercial cultivation of marijuana.* The majority opinion was by Justice Stevens.

   a. **Reliance on *Wickard*:** Stevens relied heavily on *Wickard v. Filburn* (*supra*, p. 27), the home-grown wheat case. There, the Court had concluded that when Congress was attempting to regulate the production (and thus pricing) of wheat that moved in interstate commerce, Congress could also regulate farmer Filburn's cultivation of 12 acres of wheat for consumption on his own farm. Stevens asserted that *Wickard* "thus establishes that Congress *can regulate purely intrastate activity that is not itself 'commer-*

cial,' in that it is not produced for sale, if it concludes that *failure to regulate that class of activity would undercut the regulation of the interstate market in that commodity."*

    i.   **Application to facts:** Stevens believed that this *Wickard* principle easily fit the facts of the marijuana cultivation here. "Like the farmer in *Wickard*, [plaintiffs] are cultivating, for home consumption, a fungible commodity for which there is an established, albeit illegal, interstate market." And, just as Congress in *Wickard* rationally feared that "when viewed in the aggregate, leaving home-consumed wheat outside the regulatory scheme would have a substantial influence on price and market conditions," so, here, Congress had "a rational basis for concluding that leaving home-consumed marijuana outside federal control would similarly affect price and market conditions." That is, Congress, in passing the CSA, rationally believed that if cultivation of home-grown marijuana were permitted for medicinal consumption, the high demand in the interstate market would *draw that home-grown marijuana into the interstate market*, frustrating Congress' purpose of banning interstate commerce in marijuana.

    ii.   ***Lopez* and *Morrison* distinguished:** Stevens distinguished *Lopez* and *Morrison*. In those two cases, the parties making the "no congressional authority" argument asserted that a particular statute or provision fell outside Congress' commerce power *in its entirety*. For instance, in *Lopez*, the Gun-Free School Zones Act *did not regulate any economic activity at all,* and did not contain any requirement that possession of a gun have any connection to past or future commercial activity. Here, by contrast, Congress' regulation of marijuana grown for home consumption was merely one of many *"essential part[s] of a larger regulation of economic activity*, in which the regulatory scheme could be undercut unless the interstate activity were regulated" (quoting language from *Lopez*).

    iii.   **"Economic activity":** Indeed, for Stevens, the activities regulated by the CSA, unlike those regulated in *Lopez* (gun possession near schools) and *Morrison* (violence against women), were *"quintessentially economic."* "Economics," he noted, refers to the "production, distribution and consumption of commodities." Since the CSA regulated the "production, distribution, and consumption of commodities for which there was an established, and lucrative, interstate market[,]" and since the Court had long recognized that prohibiting the *intrastate* manufacture or possession of an article of commerce was a rational means of regulating interstate commerce in that product, the intrastate regulation here easily fell within Congress' commerce powers.

  b. **Scalia's concurrence:** Justice Scalia concurred. Unlike the majority, he relied on the *necessary and proper clause* (*supra*, p. 17): he believed that Congress could regulate even noneconomic local activity that did not "substantially affect" interstate commerce, if "that regulation is a *necessary part of a more general regulation of interstate commerce."* Since Congress could reasonably conclude that its objective of barring marijuana from the interstate market might be undercut if local growing for medical purposes was allowed, a ban on that local activity was necessary to the success of the overall regulatory scheme.

    c. **Dissent:** Justice O'Connor, joined by Chief Justice Rehnquist and (for the most part) by Justice Thomas, ***dissented*** in *Raich*. She objected that the majority's approach "allows Congress to regulate intrastate activity without check, so long as there is some implication by legislative design that regulating intrastate activity is essential ... to the interstate regulatory scheme." She believed that the majority's method reduced *Lopez* to "nothing more than a ***drafting guide:*** Congress should have described the relevant crime [in *Lopez*] as 'transfer or possession of a firearm anywhere in the nation' — thus including commercial and noncommercial activity ... Had it done so ... we would have sustained its authority to regulate possession of firearms in school zones."

        i. **"Separate class of activity" approach:** Instead, O'Connor would have treated the possession and use of homegrown marijuana for medical purposes as being a ***separate class of activity*** that had not been shown to have even "a discernible, let alone substantial, impact on the national illicit drug market." Consequently, she would have distinguished that marijuana use from the wheat being consumed in *Wickard*, and would have found it to be beyond Congress' commerce powers.

E. **Forcing someone to buy a product (*N.F.I.B. v. Sebelius*):** Suppose Congress decides to use its powers under the Commerce Clause to require that a person ***buy some good or service***. It's clear that Congress can regulate individual existing intrastate activities (like a farmer growing wheat for his own consumption in *Wickard*, *supra*, p. 27), if such intrastate activities, taken in the aggregate, have a substantial effect on interstate commerce. But suppose Congress instead says, in effect, "The decisions of many individuals ***not*** to purchase a product, taken in the aggregate, have a substantial ***negative effect*** on the interstate market for that product; therefore, we are going to use our Commerce power to ***require individuals to buy that product,*** even individuals who are not now, and have never been, in the market for that product." Can Congress do this?

In the most significant and controversial Commerce power case since at least the 1930s, the Supreme Court decided by a 5-4 vote in 2012 that the answer is ***"no":*** Congress may ***not*** use its Commerce power to "compe[l] individuals to ***become active in commerce by purchasing a product,***" even if the individuals' combined failure to do significantly affects interstate commerce. The case was ***N.F.I.B. v. Sebelius,*** 132 S.Ct. 2566 (2012), striking down Congress' use of its Commerce power to force individuals to ***buy health insurance or else pay a penalty***.

    1. **Adoption of the ACA:** Congress passed an elaborate ***health-care reform statute*** in 2010 called the Patient Protection and Affordable Care Act (which we'll call the ***"Affordable Care Act"*** or ***"ACA"***). The ACA was adopted on almost straight party lines, with the vast majority of Democrats (and the Obama administration) in favor, and nearly all Republicans opposed. The Act was a broad-sweeping attempt to dramatically reduce the number of Americans without health insurance.

        a. **The "individual mandate" to purchase insurance:** Until the ACA, Congress had never tried to use its Commerce powers to compel an individual to ***buy a good or service.*** But in one of many provisions of the ACA, Congress set a "minimum coverage provision," by which most healthy individuals were ***required to purchase health insurance***, even if they had previously chosen to "self-insure," i.e., to go without health insurance entirely in the hope of being able to get any needed care for free, or pay for it out of their own pockets at the time of need. The Affordable Care Act referred to this requirement that most healthy individuals must buy insurance as the *"individual mandate."* An individual who was subject to the mandate and did not buy the required insurance was required to pay to the Internal Revenue Service (IRS) what the ACA called a *"shared-responsibility payment,"* which was also frequently referred to in the statute as a *"penalty."*

b. Motivation: Congress reasoned that under the pre-ACA system, healthy individuals had been permitted to self-insure (and wait to get sick), and thereby *made insurance more expensive for everyone else*. It had never been thought practical to force the uninsured to pay *at the time they got sick and needed care* — many simply wouldn't have the money for treatment, and would be left to die. Therefore, federal and state laws, as well as professional obligations, had long required hospitals and doctors to treat uninsured patients for free in emergencies. The substantial cost of this uncompensated care had then traditionally been *added onto everyone else's health-care bill,* so that employers who bought insurance for their employees, and individuals who bought their own health insurance, had to pay considerably more (an estimated $1,000 per family per year) than if everyone had insurance. The uninsured were thus, in Congress' view, *"free riders"* who received unpaid care at the expense of everyone else.

    i. The "guaranteed issue" and "community rating" provisions: The ACA was not just an attempt to deal with the traditional cost of free-riding by the uninsured. The Act was an ambitious attempt to create a system of *near-universal health-care insurance.* Two of the most significant ways by which the ACA attempted to broaden the availability of health insurance were by:

        [1] banning insurance companies from *denying coverage to sick people* (the *"guaranteed issue"* provision); and

        [2] banning insurers from *charging sick people more* than healthy people (the *"community rating"* provision).

    Congress feared that these two new provisions would make the free-rider problem much worse: If Congress did not somehow induce the large numbers of healthy (and cheap-to-insure) people who had been self-insuring to start buying insurance, adding the guaranteed-isue and community-rating provisions would cause rates for everyone else to grow even higher — the insurers would have to start covering lots of much sicker people than before, at the same prices as the non-sick, creating a spiral in which insurers either had to raise prices for everyone, lose money, or drop out of the market.

    ii. Ban on "free riders": So the individual mandate was seen by Congress as the only way to fulfill the ACA's overall goal of broadening health-care availability. There would be no more "free riders": those who had previously gone without health insurance would either have to buy insurance, or else make the shared-responsibility payments. And these payments would be pooled and used to cover part of the cost of otherwise-uncompensated care for the remaining uninsured.

c. No desire to tax: Congress could clearly have accomplished much the same result by using its tax-and-spend power to impose a "tax" on anyone who did not buy insurance.[1] But Congress apparently did not want to be seen to be creating a new tax, so the bill never referred to the shared-responsibility payment scheme as being a tax.

d. **Commerce-regulation rationale:** Therefore, instead of relying explicitly on its power to tax, Congress asserted that the individual mandate and the shared-responsibility payment system together represented a proper exercise of the Commerce power. Congress reasoned that everyone will ultimately need, and consume, health care; even the youngest and healthiest person might well have a health emergency tomorrow, in which case he would receive care without it being practical to charge him at the time of the emergency. Therefore, in Congress' view, the individual mandate and the shared-responsibility payment system were simply a means of regulating ***how and when people would pay*** (via insurance) for a product (health care) that they would ***inevitably consume*** even without regulation.

2. **Attacked by states:** Twenty-six states (nearly all with Republican governors), as well as many other plaintiffs including the National Federation of Independent Business (N.F.I.B.), immediately brought suits challenging the ACA's constitutionality. Although these suits focused on various provisions, their principal thrust was against the individual mandate — the plaintiffs contended that forcing people to enter a market to buy a product (health insurance) that they didn't want went beyond the Commerce power.

3. **Majority strikes down Commerce rationale:** Five members of the Court ***agreed with the plaintiffs*** on this argument: the individual mandate ***went beyond Congress' Commerce powers.*** The principal opinion on this point was by Chief Justice Roberts. No other justice formally joined his opinion on the Commerce issue, but the four other conservative members (Scalia, Kennedy, Thomas and Alito) agreed with him that the mandate was not authorized by the Commerce power.[2] We concentrate here on Roberts' opinion, in part because it is the one to which the dissent by Justice Ginsburg (see *infra*, p. 41) was mostly addressed.

   a. **Novelty:** Roberts began by noting that Congress had never before attempted to rely on the Commerce power "to ***compel individuals not engaged in commerce to purchase an unwanted product.***" He conceded that "Legislative novelty is not necessarily fatal; there is a first time for everything." But, he said, "sometimes 'the most telling indication of [a] severe constitutional problem ... is the lack of historical precedent[.]'"

   b. **Must regulate "activity":** Roberts then got to the gist of his argument: "The power to *regulate* [emphasis in original] commerce ***presupposes the existence of commercial activity to be regulated.***"

      i. **"Superfluous powers" argument:** If the power to "regulate" something included the power to ***create*** it, he said, "many of the provisions in the Constitution would be ***superfluous***." For instance, the Constitution gives Congress the power to "coin money," and also the power to "regulate the Value thereof." If the power to regulate the value of money included the power to bring the subject of

---

1. Indeed, by a separate 5-4 vote within *N.F.I.B.*, the Supreme Court saved the bulk of the ACA by holding that what Congress called a "penalty" for those who did not buy the required insurance was in fact a constitutional use of the tax-and-spend power. See *infra*, p. 59.

2. The opinion by Scalia, Kennedy, Thomas and Alito is referred to by some other members of the Court as a ***"joint dissent"***; it is signed by all four, with no principal author. It's a "dissent" as to the overall result in the case, because these four Justices rejected the argument that the individual mandate was justified under the tax-and-spend power (see *infra*, p. 61); they would have struck down the entire ACA. But the arguments in the joint dissent about why the mandate doesn't fall within the Commerce power largely parallel Roberts' arguments.

the regulation (money) into existence, the power to create money would have been superfluous.

ii.   **Regulating "activity":** Similarly, Roberts argued, the Court's cases describing the Commerce power "uniformly describe the power as reaching *'activity.'*" The individual mandate, by contrast, "does not regulate *existing commercial activity*. It instead compels individuals to *become* active in commerce by purchasing a product, on the ground that their failure to do so affects interstate commerce."

iii.   **Unwarranted expansion of Congress' powers:**   Interpreting the Commerce power to permit Congress to "regulate individuals precisely *because* they are doing nothing" would, he said, *"open a new and potentially vast domain to congressional authority."* "Every day individuals *do not do an infinite number of things."* Allowing Congress to regulate based on the effect of inaction on commerce "would bring countless decisions an individual could potentially make within the scope of federal regulation[.]"

iv.   ***Wickard* example:**   Roberts pointed to the facts of *Wickard v. Filburn* (the wheat-growing case, *supra*, p. 27) as an example of how the government's theory would expand the scope of permissible regulation. *Wickard* justified regulating the farmer's growing of wheat for home consumption on the ground that his growing allowed him to avoid purchasing wheat in the market, and that this decision to grow his own wheat, when aggregated with the similar decisions of others, would have a substantial effect on the interstate market for wheat. But, Roberts argued, "price can be supported by *increasing demand* as well as by decreasing supply. The aggregated decisions of some consumers *not to purchase wheat* have a *substantial effect on the price of wheat,* just as decisions not to purchase health insurance have on the price of insurance." By the government's theory, "Congress can therefore *command that those not buying wheat do so,* just as it argues here that it may command that those not buying health insurance do so."

v.   **The "broccoli" argument:** During the public debate on the individual mandate, and in the oral argument before the Court, opponents of the mandate's constitutionality had made frequent use of the so-called *"broccoli"* hypothetical: if Congress could force people to buy health insurance because lack of widespread health insurance is bad for the nation, Congress could attack the country's dietary and obesity problems, and associated health costs, by forcing everyone to *"buy broccoli."*

   (1)   **"Vegetables":** Roberts essentially adopted the broccoli argument, though he made it a touch more generic. "Many Americans do not eat a balanced diet," and therefore become obese. Obese people have higher health costs, which are borne in part by other Americans, "just as the uninsured shift costs to the insured." Under the government's theory, therefore, *"Congress could address the diet problem by ordering everyone to buy vegetables."*

vi.   **Fundamental change:** But, he said, "That is not the country the framers of our Constitution envisioned." Congress already has vast power to regulate much of what people do. Under the government's theory, Congress would have "the same license to regulate what we do *not do, fundamentally changing the relation* between the citizen and the Federal Government."

vii. **The "mere financing" argument:** The federal government had argued that this was *not* in fact a situation where people were being forced to *become active* in a market in which they did not otherwise participate. The government contended that because sickness and injury are unpredictable but unavoidable, "the uninsured as a class are *active in the market for health care*, which they *regularly seek and obtain*." The individual mandate therefore "merely regulates *how individuals finance and pay* for that active participation," by requiring them to buy insurance instead of self-insuring.

(1) **Argument rejected:** But Roberts rejected this "mere financing" argument. "An individual who bought a car two years ago and may buy another in the future is not 'active in the car market' in any pertinent sense." The individual mandate primarily affects "healthy, often young adults who are less likely to need significant health-care and have other priorities for spending their money ... If the individual mandate is targeted at a class, it is a class whose commercial *inactivity rather than activity* is its defining feature."

(2) **Can't anticipate future activity to regulate it now:** Roberts conceded that prior Commerce Clause cases had allowed Congress to *anticipate* the effects of existing local economic activity on interstate commerce. "But we have never permitted Congress to *anticipate that [economic] activity itself* in order to regulate individuals not currently engaged in commerce. ... Everyone will likely participate in the markets for food, clothing, transportation, shelter, or energy; that does not authorize Congress to direct them to purchase particular products in those or other markets today. The Commerce Clause is *not a general license to regulate an individual from cradle to grave*, simply because he will predictably engage in particular transactions."

viii. **Necessary and Proper Clause:** The government had also argued that even if the Commerce power was not enough, standing alone, to justify the individual mandate, the *Necessary and Proper Clause* supplied any additional needed authority. If the guaranteed-issue and community-rating insurance reforms were to be carried out, the individual mandate was a necessary and proper means of doing so, the government contended.

(1) **Roberts disagreees:** But Roberts again disagreeed, taking a much *narrower* view of the Necessary and Proper clause than the government. Quoting *McCulloch v. Maryland* (*supra*, p. 17), he said that the Necessary and Proper Clause only gives Congress the power to enact provisions "*incidental* to the [enumerated] power," and does not authorize the exercise of any "*great substantive and independent power[s]*" beyond the enumerated ones. What Congress was doing here with the individual mandate, he said, was *not "incidental"* to the exercise of the commerce power, and would "work a *substantial expansion* of federal authority." Therefore, even if the individual mandate was "necessary" to the ACA's insurance reforms, it was *not a "proper" means* of making those reforms effective.

4. **Dissent disagrees on Commerce power:** Four Justices sharply *dissented* from Roberts' conclusion that the individual mandate did not fall within Congress' Commerce powers.

The opinion on this point was by Justice Ginsburg, who was joined by Justices Sotomayor, Breyer and Kagan. The Ginsburg opinion was only a partial dissent (since these four joined with Roberts to uphold the individual mandate under the power to *tax*; see *infra*, p. 60). But the opinion was a vigorous dissent to every aspect of Roberts' treatment of the Commerce Clause issue.

a. **Uninsured are still "active" consumers:** First, Ginsburg rejected Roberts' core assertion that most uninsured were "inactive" in the market for health care. She cited statistics showing that more than 60% of those without insurance visit a hospital or doctor's office each year, and 90% do so within five years. Furthermore, Congress had *no way to distinguish* between uninsured persons who would soon need emergency health care and those who would not. "No one knows when an emergency will occur, yet emergencies involving the uninsured arise daily." Therefore, Congress was entitled to require all persons to have insurance, because (quoting a prior Commerce Clause case) "When it is necessary in order to prevent an evil to make the law embrace *more than the precise thing to be prevented* [Congress] may do so."

b. **Right to anticipate future conduct:** Ginsburg also disagreed with Roberts' assertion that the Court's precedents did not support the proposition that "Congress may dictate the conduct of an individual today because of prophesied future activity." She pointed to *Wickard* (p. 27) as a counter-example: Congress had said that the farmer in *Wickard* could be prevented from growing too much wheat for home consumption today, because if he did so (and others did likewise), this wheat might *in the future* overhang the market and depress interstate prices.

c. **Health care market is different:** Roberts had asserted that the fact that a person might some day need health care didn't make him "active" in the health-care market, any more than the fact that he might buy a car some day made him active in the car market. But Ginsburg believed that *health care was a special case.* Roberts' analogy between health care and, say, car sales was inapt, because "The inevitable yet unpredictable need for medical care, and the guarantee that *emergency care will be provided* when required are *conditions nonexistent in other markets."* Although a consumer *might* some day buy a car (or a piece of broccoli), there is no guarantee that she ever will. And if she ever does want a car or broccoli, "she will be obliged to *pay at the counter* before receiving the vehicle or nourishment. She will *get no free ride or food at the expense of another consumer forced to pay an inflated price."*

    i. **No worry about later expansion:** Therefore, Ginsburg said, these special features of the health-care market meant that there was no reason to worry that upholding the individual mandate would logically force the Court to later concede to Congress the Commerce-based power to require the purchase of other products and services.

d. **Just a payment mechanism:** Ginsburg also rejected Roberts' characterization of the mandate as "compel[ling] individuals ... to *purchase an unwanted product.*" Since virtually everyone would consume health care, Congress was not "mandating purchase of a discrete, unwanted product." All that Congress was doing was merely "*defining the terms on which individuals pay for an interstate good they consume:* Persons subject to the mandate must now pay for medical care *in advance* (instead of at the point of service) and *through insurance* (instead of out-of-pocket)." She concluded that "establishing payment terms for goods in or affecting interstate commerce is *quintessential economic regulation.*"

e. **Active/inactive distinction:** Ginsburg also dismissed the significance Roberts attached to the *"active"/"inactive"* distinction. Most actions can be *restated as corresponding inactions* with the same effect. She offered the present case as an example: "An individual who opts not to purchase insurance from a private insurer can be seen as *actively selecting another form of insurance: self-insurance.*" Thus the individual mandate could be described as "regulating activity in the self-insurance market." Similarly, in the *Wickard* wheat-growing case, the statute could be described either as targeting *activity* (the growing of too much wheat) or *inactivity* (the farmer's failure to purchase wheat in the marketplace).

f. **Necessary and Proper Clause:** Finally, Ginsburg disagreed with Roberts' assertion that the *Necessary and Proper Clause* did not augment Congress' Commerce powers regarding the individual mandate. She didn't see why requiring individuals to choose between buying health insurance or paying a penalty was any more far-reaching than other implied powers that the Court had found to be justified by the Necessary and Proper Clause. For instance, the Court had used the Clause as the basis for implying a congressional power to enact criminal laws, to impose civil imprisonment, and to create a national bank. She predicted that Roberts' distinction between an "independent power" (not authorized by the N&P Clause) and a "derivative" one (authorized), or between a "substantive" power and an "incidental" one, would prove hard for judges to administer. Roberts was in effect instructing the lower courts, she said, that "You will know it when you see it."

5. **Significance:** So *N.F.I.B.* seems to establish several important limitations on the Commerce power:

❏ Most significantly, "The power to regulate commerce *presupposes the existence of commercial activity* to be regulated." So if the person being regulated is *not already engaged in commercial activity* of the relevant sort (she doesn't have to necessarily be involved in *interstate* commercial activity, but has to be engaged in at least a local version of the commercial activity), Congress cannot require the person to *become* commercially active. And that's true even if the failure of large numbers of people to become commercially active causes, in the aggregate, a *significant (and harmful) effect on interstate commerce*.

❏ As a corollary, Congress cannot force a person who is not already engaged in commerce *"to purchase an unwanted product."*

❏ Even if the person being regulated is likely — or even near-certain — to *become active* in the relevant market *at some time in the future*, that's *not enough* to justify regulating the person now. So even conceding that the vast majority of individuals will at some point use health care (and Roberts did seem to concede this point), that's not grounds for requiring the purchase of health insurance *now*.

a. **Practical impact may be small:** But the practical impact of these limits may well prove small. After all, Congress had never before used its Commerce power in what the Court characterized as an attempt to force people into a commercial market in which they were not already participating. So it's hard to see how this new "can't force someone to enter a market" doctrine is likely to cramp Congress' style very much going forward.

    i.   **Tax-and-spend:**   Furthermore, the individual mandate itself turned out to be sustainable under the ***tax-and-spend*** power. (See *infra*, p. 59.) So if Congress wants to induce people to take Action X (even if X is the purchase of an unwanted product by someone not already participating in the relevant market), all Congress has to do is to impose a non-punitive "tax" on not taking Action X. To take what Justice Ginsburg refers to as the "broccoli horrible," apparently Congress is still free to impose a tax on anyone who can't prove that she purchased a specified amount of broccoli during the year, as long as the tax is small enough that a rational consumer might elect to pay the tax rather buy the broccoli.

F. **Summary of the modern limits on the Commerce power:**   So the major post-1995 Commerce power cases for the most part — but not always — *limit* Congress' authority:

    [1] Where a consumer wants to ***"make or grow his own product"*** and the product has a somewhat ***commercial nature***, Congress can regulate or prohibit his activities, even though the consumer is acting in an entirely ***intrastate manner***, and it is only the adding together of many such purely intrastate activities that produces a cumulative effect on interstate commerce. So cases like *Wickard v. Filburn* (Congress can tightly regulate how a farmer may grow his own crops, because if it can't, the whole agricultural regulation system will fall apart) and *Gonzales v. Raich* (Congress can make it a crime for a private citizen to grow her own marijuana, because if she can't be forbidden from growing it, Congress won't be able to effectively regulate interstate marijuana sales either) reflect a broad reading of Congress' Commerce powers.

But ...

    [2] Where Congress wants to regulate an activity that is essentially ***not a commercial activity***, Congress can quickly go ***beyond*** its Commerce power, and into the realm of attempting an unconstitutional exercise of power to ***"regulate for the general federal welfare."*** Cases like *Lopez* (Congress can't forbid the possession of guns near schools) and *Morrison* (Congress can't make it a crime to use violence against women) reflect a narrow reading of Congress' Commerce powers applicable to those instances where what is being regulated is ***not really economic activity at all.***

and ...

    [3] where Congress wants to take an individual who is ***not currently participating in a particular marketplace at all***, and wants to insist that the individual ***purchase a good or service in that marketplace***, Congress may not use its Commerce power to do so. That's the result of *N.F.I.B. v. Sebelius*, where Congress' Commerce powers were held not sufficient to allow Congress to force individuals to ***buy health insurance***, even though the failure of many individuals to buy such insurance might substantially (and negatively) affect the clearly-commercial interstate market for health care.

Here are some additional rules of thumb that come out of these opposing lines of post-1995 cases:

    a. **Effect must be "significant":** The activity being regulated must be one that ***"significantly"*** affects commerce — an ***incidental effect*** on commerce is ***not*** enough.

b. Findings: The fact that Congress has made particular *findings* that an activity substantially affects interstate commerce may make some difference, but is unlikely to be dispositive very often. So legislative findings will at most tip a *close case* over the line into the "regulable" category.

c. Jurisdictional hooks: Where Congress drafts the statute in a way that requires a *"jurisdictional hook"* between the particular activity and commerce, the act is still quite likely to be found within the Commerce power.

Example: Suppose Congress makes it a crime to possess near a school a gun that *moved in interstate commerce* at some point in its career (and Congress doesn't purport to criminalize possession of a gun made and used within a single state up to the point of the arrest). There's a very good chance the statute would be upheld.

G. Summary of modern view: In closing, let's summarize the *four broad categories* of activities that, even after the post-1995 limiting cases, Congress can still constitutionally regulate:

1. Channels: First, Congress can regulate the use of the *"channels"* of interstate commerce. Thus Congress can regulate in a way that is reasonably related to highways, waterways, and air traffic. Presumably Congress can do so even though the activity in question in the particular case is quite intrastate.

2. Instrumentalities: Second, Congress can regulate the *"instrumentalities"* of interstate commerce, "even though the threat may come only from intrastate activities." *Lopez.* This category refers to people, machines, and other "things" used in carrying out commerce. So, for instance, presumably Congress could say that every truck must have a specific safety device, even if the particular truck in question was made and used exclusively within a single state.

3. Articles moving in interstate commerce: Third, Congress can regulate *articles moving* in interstate commerce. For instance, in *Reno v. Condon*, 528 U.S. 141 (2000), the Court said that computerized information about motorists was an "article of commerce" whose release into the "interstate stream of business" made the information an appropriate subject for congressional regulation. (Apparently this would have been so even if the information did not "substantially affect" commerce, as described in the next paragraph.)

4. "Substantially affecting" commerce: Finally, the biggest (and most interesting) category is that Congress may regulate those activities having a *"substantial effect"* on interstate commerce. *Lopez.* As to this category, the following rules now seem to apply:

a. Real bite: The requirement of a "substantial" effect has *real bite*.

i. Activity is commercial: If the activity itself is arguably *"commercial,"* then it doesn't seem to matter whether the *particular instance* of the activity directly affects interstate commerce, as long as the instance is part of a general class of activities that, collectively, substantially affect interstate commerce. Thus in the *Gonzales v. Raich* type of situation — P's own marijuana-growing activities are in a sense "commercial," but are entirely intrastate; however, when aggregated with all other local medicinal-marijuana-growing activities P's activities might undermine Congress' interstate-regulatory scheme — Congress can regulate even the solely-intrastate events.

      ii. **Activity is not commercial:** But if the activity itself is ***not "commercial,"*** then there will apparently have to be a ***pretty obvious connection*** between the activity and interstate commerce. This is the main legacy of *Lopez* (can't make schools a gun-free zone) and *Morrison* (can't criminalize all violence against women).

      iii. **Must already be an "activity":** Only ***pre-existing*** commercial ***"activity"*** may be regulated; Congress may not require persons who are not presently "active" in a commercial market to become active by buying or selling; see Par. (d), "Activity/inactivity distinction" below.

    b. **Little deference to Congress:** The Court ***won't*** give much ***deference*** to the fact that Congress ***believed*** that the activity has the requisite "substantial effect" on interstate commerce. The Court will basically decide this issue for itself, from scratch. It certainly will no longer be enough that Congress had a ***"rational basis"*** for believing that the requisite effect existed — the effect must *in fact* exist to the Court's own independent satisfaction.

    c. **Traditional domain of states:** If what's being regulated is an activity the regulation of which has ***traditionally*** been the ***domain of the states***, and as to which the states have expertise, the Court is less likely to find that Congress is acting within its Commerce power. Thus ***education***, ***family law*** and ***general criminal law*** are areas where the Court is likely to be especially suspicious of congressional "interference."

    d. **Activity/inactivity distinction:** Congress may not use its Commerce powers to say to a person who is ***not presently active in a market*** (i.e., not presently trying to buy, sell or use a product in the relevant market) that the person must ***do a transaction in that market or else pay a penalty***. So, for instance, *N.F.I.B. v. Sebelius* (*supra*, p. 37) says that Congress' Commerce powers don't allow it to tell individuals who are presently without health insurance that they must ***buy such insurance or else pay a financial penalty to the IRS***. So Congress ***can regulate*** pre-existing ***"activity,"*** but not pre-existing ***"inactivity."***

VI. THE TENTH AMENDMENT AS A LIMIT ON CONGRESS' POWER

  A. **Apparent irrelevance of Tenth Amendment:** For nearly 40 years following the *Carter Coal* decision (*supra*, p. 25), the Supreme Court did not invalidate a single federal statute on the grounds that it violated state or local government sovereignty. This sustained stretch led most observers to conclude that the Tenth Amendment was completely dead as an independent check upon federal power under the Commerce Clause.

  B. **Once again irrelevant:** As of this writing, it does indeed seem to be the case that the Tenth Amendment places relatively few practical limitations upon the exercise of federal power under the Commerce Clause. However, for the period 1976-85, the Supreme Court treated the Tenth Amendment as imposing an important limit on federal power — this Amendment was held to bar the federal government from doing anything that would impair the states' ability to perform their "traditional functions." Then, in 1985, the line of cases establishing this limit was ***flatly overruled*** by the Supreme Court, in one of the most amazing reversals of doctrine in modern Supreme Court history.[3] Before the 1985 reversal can be understood, some understanding of the prior line of cases is needed.

    1. *National League of Cities:* Like a bolt out of the blue, the Supreme Court in 1976 gave the Tenth Amendment practical significance in ***National League of Cities v. Usery***, 426

U.S. 833 (1976). In that case, the Court held that the Tenth Amendment barred Congress from making federal minimum-wage and overtime rules applicable to state and municipal employees. The vote was 5-4.

a. Rationale: The five-justice majority conceded that the minimum-wage/overtime rules, as applied to state employees, clearly affected commerce. Thus these wage/hour regulations could unquestionably be constitutionally applied to private employers, under the commerce power. But when these wage/hour rules were applied to state employees, they violated the independent requirement, imposed by the Tenth Amendment, that "Congress may not exercise power in a fashion that *impairs the States' integrity* or their *ability to function effectively in the federal system*." The wage/hour rules violated this requirement in two ways.

i. Cost: First, the wage/hour provisions impaired the states' ability to function effectively purely as a matter of *cost*: compliance would have cost the states and their municipal subdivisions substantial sums.

ii. Removal of discretion: Secondly, the new rules stripped the states of their discretion to decide how they wished to allocate a fixed pool of funds available for salaries.

b. Summary: Thus if the wage/hour rules were allowed to stand, the majority reasoned, Congress would have the right to make "fundamental employment decisions" regarding state employees, and "there would be little left of the States' 'separate and independent existence.' "

C. Overruling of *National League of Cities*: *National League of Cities* was on tenuous ground from the day it was decided. The fifth vote came from Justice Blackmun, who stated in his concurrence that he was "not untroubled by certain possible implications of the Court's opinion." All it took to overturn the decision in *National League of Cities* was for Justice Blackmun to abandon his never-passionate attachment to the principle of that case. In *Garcia v. San Antonio Metropolitan Transit Authority*, 469 U.S. 528 (1985), he joined with the four Justices who had dissented in *National League of Cities* (Brennan, White, Marshall and Stevens) to repudiate that case. By a 5-4 majority, the Court stated that *National League of Cities* "is *overruled*."

1. Question raised: The issue in *Garcia* was whether the minimum-wage and overtime provisions of the federal Fair Labor Standards Act (the same statute at issue in *National League of Cities*) should apply to employees of a municipally-owned and-operated *mass-transit system*.

2. Court's answer: The Court's answer was "*yes*," these provisions *could* constitutionally be applied to the municipal transit systems.

a. Difficulty of line-drawing: The majority opinion, by Justice Blackmun, contended that the 8-year period following *National League of Cities* had shown that it was "difficult, if not impossible, to identify an organizing principle" that would *distinguish*

---

3. Then, this reversal was partially "re-reversed," in several cases from the 1990s that established that Congress cannot directly command the states to enact or enforce federal policies; see *New York v. U.S.* (p. 48) and *Printz* v. U.S. (p. 50).

between those functions that *are* "traditional governmental functions" and those that are *not*.

    b. The problem of subjectivity: An additional, but related, problem was that the *National League of Cities* approach inevitably **led to judicial subjectivity**. "Any rule of state immunity that looks to the 'traditional,' 'integral,' or 'necessary' nature of governmental functions inevitably **invites an unelected federal judiciary to make decisions about which state policies it favors and which ones it dislikes.**"

    c. Procedural safeguards: Yet, the *Garcia* majority insisted, its rejection of *National League of Cities* did *not* mean that there are *no* limitations upon the federal government's right to use its delegated powers to impair state sovereignty. However, state sovereign interests are protected by **"procedural safeguards inherent in the structure of the federal system,"** not by "judicially created limitations on federal power."

        i. Examples of structural protection: For instance, the majority said, the requirement that each state have two Senators, the fact that the states are given general control over electoral qualifications for federal elections, and the fact that the states have a special role in presidential elections by means of the electoral college, are all indications that the **structure of the federal government** has been constitutionally arranged so as to protect state sovereignty.

  3. Dissent: The four **dissenters** in *Garcia* asserted that the majority approach "effectively **reduces the Tenth Amendment** to **meaningless rhetoric** when Congress acts pursuant to the Commerce Clause."

D. Significance of case: *Garcia* seems to mean that once Congress, acting pursuant to its Commerce power, regulates the states, the fact that it is a state being regulated **has virtually no practical significance — if the regulation would be valid if applied to a private party, it is also valid as to the state.**

  1. Later cases cut back: But several post-*Garcia* cases have **cut back** the apparently-broad scope of *Garcia*. *New York v. United States* (discussed immediately *infra*) and *Printz v. U.S.* (*infra*, p. 50) both place limits on the extent to which Congress can force state or local governments to **make or enforce laws**. And *Alden v. Maine* (*infra*, p. 749) blocks Congress from forcing the states to **hear damage suits** against themselves in **state courts**, even on federally-created claims. So the principle that there are some limits to the ways Congress can regulate a state remains alive after *Garcia*.

E. Use of state's lawmaking mechanisms: One aspect of state sovereignty is a state's ability to **make and apply law**, through legislative, judicial, and administrative functions. Even after *Garcia*, there are limits to Congress' right to interfere with these state legislative or executive processes, and Congress will violate the Tenth Amendment if it exceeds those limits. In a pair of cases, the Court has held that the federal government may not: (1) compel a state to **enact** or enforce a particular **law** or type of law; or (2) compel state/local officials to perform federally-specified **administrative** tasks. Holding (1) occurred in *New York v. United States*, 505 U.S. 144 (1992). Holding (2) occurred in *Printz v. U.S.*, 521 U.S. 898 (1997).

  1. Waste disposal case: *New York v. United States*, *supra*, dramatically illustrates the principle that Congress may not simply force a state to **enact a certain statute** or to **regulate** in a certain manner.

a. **Regulatory scheme:** Congress enacted the Low-Level Radioactive Waste Policy Amendments Act of 1985. The Act attempted to force each state to make its own arrangements for disposing (either in-state or out-of-state) of the low-level radioactive waste generated in that state. The Act tried to do this with several types of incentives. Most significant was the *"take title"* incentive, whereby any state which did not arrange for disposal of its waste would be required to "take title" to the waste (upon request by the waste generator), and would be liable for damages in connection with disposal of this waste.

b. **New York attacks statute:** New York, unlike most states, made little progress in solving its waste disposal problems, because local residents of each community where the state proposed to put disposal sites fiercely objected. New York then sued the federal government, arguing that the "take title" provision violated the Tenth Amendment, by effectively forcing the state to regulate in a particular area.

c. **Tenth Amendment found violated:** A majority of the Court agreed that the "take title" provision violated the Tenth Amendment: Congress may not simply *"commandee[r] the legislative processes of the States* by directly *compelling them to enact and enforce* a federal regulatory program."

    i. **Explanation:** New York was being put to the choice of two "unconstitutionally coercive regulatory techniques": it could either choose to regulate on its own by making arrangements for disposal of waste generated inside the state, or be forced to indemnify waste-generators against tort damages. Because Congress could not employ either of these methods alone, it could not escape the problem by giving the state a choice between the two.

d. **Dissent:** Three members of the Court (White, joined by Blackmun and Stevens) dissented. White argued that this was not an instance where Congress was forcing its will upon the states. Rather, he said, Congress had responded to a request by many of the states to ratify a compromise worked out among themselves, so that the waste-disposal problem could be solved. "The Court's refusal to force New York to accept responsibility for its own problem inevitably means that some other State's sovereignty will be impinged by it being forced, for public health reasons, to accept New York's low-level radioactive waste. I do not understand the principle of federalism to impede the National Government from acting as referee among the States to prohibit one from bullying another."

e. **Alternative methods:** Is Congress powerless to make each state deal with its radioactive waste (or any other specific problem)? Probably not. Justice White's dissent suggests several methods that are apparently still open to Congress, notwithstanding *N.Y. v. U.S.*

    i. **Spending power:** First, Congress clearly may *supply funds* to the states for the purpose of solving the problem, and then *condition* the receipt of these funds on the states' agreeing to Congress' proposed methods for solving the problem.

    ii. **Threat of regulation:** Second, Congress could *directly regulate* the conduct in question, and could therefore take the less drastic step of telling the states that this direct regulation will follow if the states do not take care of the problems themselves. (For instance, Congress' commerce power would entitle it to say, "No state may ship radioactive waste outside of its own border." Congress could therefore say, as a lesser exercise of this power, "Any state which does not make its own arrangements for disposing of waste, whether in-state or out-of-state, shall be required to keep its waste within its own borders.")

  iii. **Summary:** In summary, Congress may have to be a little more clever about how it accomplishes its regulatory purposes — and it will not be able to escape the ***"political heat"*** for unpopular decisions by forcing state officials to make those decisions. But Congress, by careful use of its enumerated powers (including the spending and Commerce powers) can achieve practically any regulatory end it wants without running afoul of the Tenth Amendment.

2. **No commandeering of executive branch:** *N.Y. v. U.S.* limits Congress' power to "commandeer the *legislative* processes of the States[.]" In a post-*N.Y.* case, the Court has held that Congress may, similarly, not compel a state or local government's **executive** branch to perform functions. And that's true even if the functions are fairly ministerial and easy-to-perform, and even if the compulsion is only temporary. ***Printz v. U.S.***, 521 U.S. 898 (1997).

  a. **Brady bill's provision:** In 1993, Congress enacted the "Brady Bill," aimed at controlling the flow of guns. As a temporary 5-year measure, the law ***ordered local law enforcement officials*** to ***conduct background checks*** on prospective purchasers, until a national computerized system for doing these checks could be phased in. Printz, a county sheriff in Montana, objected to the background-check requirement and sued. He argued that under *New York v. U.S.*, Congress could not force him to conduct background checks on the federal government's behalf.

  b. **Decision:** By a 5-4 margin, the Court agreed with the plaintiff. Justice Scalia's majority opinion noted that in *N.Y. v. U.S.*, the Court had said that the federal government "may not compel the States to enact or administer a federal regulatory program." Scalia then concluded that the background-check portion of the Brady bill violated this prohibition.

    i. **Rationale:** Scalia ***rejected*** the dissent's distinction between compelling a state to ***make policy*** (such as the compelled enactment of a regulatory scheme, like the "take title" scheme at issue in *N.Y. v. U.S.*) and compelling state executive-branch officers to perform ***ministerial tasks*** (such as the background checks at issue here). Even if no policy-making was involved here, this did not prevent Congress' action from being an intolerable incursion into state sovereignty.

  c. **Dissents:** Four Justices dissented in *Printz*.

    i. **Justice Stevens' dissent:** The main dissent was by Justice Stevens. He first pointed out that the federal commerce power gave Congress the authority to regulate handguns. He then concluded that this being so, the ***"necessary and proper" clause*** gave Congress the right to implement its regulation by temporarily requiring local police officers to perform the ministerial step of identifying persons who should not be entrusted with handguns.

  d. **Control over purse strings:** Again (as in *N.Y. v. U.S.*) presumably Congress could ***get around the problem*** by conditioning the state's or local government's ***receipt of federal funds*** on its officials' willingness to do the federal bidding. Only compulsion, not a voluntary *quid pro quo*, seems foreclosed by the majority's analysis.

3. **Prohibition on state's right to legislate (*Murphy v. NCAA*):** *N.Y. v. U.S.* and *Printz v. U.S.* invalidated efforts by Congress to commandeer the states' functions by forcing them to **perform affirmative acts,** such as by ordering a state to enact a statute. But as a 2018 case shows, the anti-commandeering principle also applies to invalidate congressional efforts to **prevent a state from legislating,** such as where Congress tries to prohibit a state from **repealing an existing law.** In that case, **Murphy v. National Collegiate Athletic Ass'n,** 138 S.Ct. 1461 (2018), the Court struck down on anti-commandeering grounds a federal statute that effectively said to the states, "If you currently forbid certain types of sports gambling, you are **forbidden to repeal** that prohibition."

   a. **PASPA statute:** In 1992, Congress passed the Professional and Amateur Sports Protection Act (PASPA), which made it unlawful for a state to "authorize" sports gambling.[4] New Jersey already prohibited sports gambling as of the time PASPA was enacted, so PASPA had no immediate effect on the state's actions. But in 2014, the state enacted a statute that purported to partially **repeal the state's total ban on sports gambling,** by allowing sports betting at horse racing tracks and Atlantic City casinos.

   b. **Attacked by NCAA:** The NCAA and several professional sports leagues, which had long opposed gambling on the sports they supervised, sued New Jersey in federal court, claiming that the statute violated PASPA. The state defended on the theory that PASPA was unconstitutional because it violated the anti-commandeering principle; the state asserted that this principle forbade not only congressional action that commanded a state to *enact* law, but also congressional action that *prohibited* a state from enacting law (in this case, prohibiting the state from repealing a law already on its books).

   c. **Supreme Court agrees:** The Supreme Court **agreed with New Jersey** that PASPA **violated the anti-commandeering principle.** In fact, no justice disagreed with this aspect of the Court's ruling. Justice Alito's opinion **rejected** the plaintiffs' argument that the anti-commandeering principle applies only when Congress **affirmatively commands a state to enact law**, not when Congress prohibits a state from enacting law.

      i. **"Ready to stop legislators from voting":** Alito wrote that Congress' prohibition of state authorization of sports gambling violated the anti-commandeering rule because it "unequivocally **dictates what a state legislature may and may not do.**"

      ii. **Rationale:** Alito noted that a key function of the anti-commandeering principle is to **protect state sovereignty.** That being so, he said, a conclusion that the no-commandeering principle should apply to a command that a state enact a law, but not to a command that the state **not enact** a law, would be to make an "empty" distinction — the effect on state sovereignty would be the same in the two situations.

   d. **Significance:** So the principle that the Congress (or indeed any part of the federal government) may not, in effect, tell state legislatures what they must do, is now extended to also **block Congress from telling a state legislature what it may _not_ do**.

4. **Significance of the three cases:** The trio of *New York v. U.S.*, *Printz* and *Murphy* stand for the propositions that Congress may **not** (1) **force a state to legislate or regulate in a**

---

4. The statute contained a couple of exemptions covering states and cities that already allowed sports betting, but New Jersey did not qualify for the exemption (as Nevada, for example, did).

certain way; or (2) require state ***executive-branch*** personnel to perform (or not to perform) even ***ministerial functions***.

    a. Distinguished from *Garcia* situation: How does the rationale of these cases fit in with the rationale of *Garcia* (*supra*, p. 47)? *Garcia* seems to apply mainly to ***generally applicable*** federal lawmaking; that case holds that where Congress passes a generally applicable law (e.g., a minimum wage law that applies to ***all*** or nearly all businesses), the Tenth Amendment does not entitle a state's own operations to an ***exemption***, merely because it is a state that is being regulated along with all the other private entities.

        i. Singling out of states: But where the federal government tries to force a state or local government to ***enact (or not enact) legislation*** or ***regulation***, or tries to force state or local ***officials*** to perform (or not perform) particular governmental functions, this is not part of a generally-applicable federal scheme, and is instead ***directed specifically at the state's basic exercise of sovereignty:*** the state's right to carry out the business of government. The federal government may not single out the states in this coercive way, *N.Y. v. U.S., Printz* and *Murphy* say.

Quiz Yourself on

THE FEDERAL COMMERCE POWER *(ENTIRE CHAPTER)*

5. Congress makes it a federal felony for any individual to place a bet with another individual on a sporting event, or to propose such a bet. The statute is written broadly, so as to cover two friends who bet with each other primarily for purposes of friendship rather than profit. The House and Senate Committee Reports on the bill show that Congress believed that ostensibly "friendly" betting creates a climate that is tolerant of gambling, which in turn increases the interstate gambling profits of organized crime, a multi-million dollar nationwide problem. Devon is charged with violating the statute by placing a bet on the Super Bowl with her best friend, Elaine. They made the bet face to face within a single state.

    (a) If Devon challenges the constitutionality of the statute on the grounds that it goes beyond Congress' enumerated powers, what enumerated power should the prosecutors point to in defending the statute's constitutionality? _____

    (b) Is the statute in fact constitutional? State your reasons. _____

6. By 2020, the federal government is paying approximately 50% of total health-care costs for the nation out of general revenues. Congress, concerned that Americans are living increasingly sedentary, unhealthy and medically-costly lifestyles, enacts the Walk to Fitness Act of 2020 ("WFA"). The WFA provides that each American over the age of 16 must purchase and use a specified government-manufactured pedometer, which when attached to the hip measures how many miles the wearer walks each day. The pedometer is sold to the public at a price of $20 (which provides a small profit to the government, made possible by the huge volumes expected to be sold). Another provision of the WFA says that after the end of each year, the device-wearer shall print out the total miles registered on the device during the prior year, and enclose the printout with his tax return. Anyone whose age-adjusted total annual mileage walked does not reach a pre-specified threshold (e.g., 150 miles for a young adult) must pay a "penalty" of $200, payable to the IRS together with the person's taxes. Exemptions are given for those whose doctor certifies that the person is not medically capable of walking the threshold amount. Congress defends the constitutionality of the WFA on the grounds that the pedometer program encourages fitness, and that fitter people will cause the nation's ever-increasing health-care bill to decline, leading to a substantial lowering of costs billed in the interstate market for health-care services. Therefore, Congress asserts, the WFA is valid as a regulation of commerce.

Is the WFA a proper exercise of the Congress' Commerce power? _____

7. After several years of rising unemployment nationally, and falling wage levels, Congress passes a statute prohibiting the employment of any person under the age of 19. Congress' intent is to keep teenagers in high school or college, where they may or may not learn something but will at least not be competing with adults for jobs, thus allowing wage rates to rise. The state of Alahoma employs many 17- and 18-year-olds, for such posts as cleaners in state parks and apprentice state troopers. Alahoma estimates that its total payroll costs will rise by 8% if it is required to obey the new federal statute (which by its terms applies to government as well as private-sector employees).

(a) Assuming that the federal statute falls within Congress' power to regulate commerce, what is the strongest argument that Alahoma can make as to why the Constitution requires that the state's own hiring be exempted from the statute? _____

(b) Will this argument succeed? _____

8. Congress has concluded that cigarette smoking raises the nation's annual health-care budget 15% above what it would otherwise be. Congress has therefore enacted a statute that requires each state to: (1) place a tax of at least 10% on the sale of cigarettes (in addition to existing federal cigarette taxes); (2) compile a registry of every premises in the state where cigarettes are sold, and audit those premises quarterly to make sure they're collecting the tax; (3) modify its health-care financing scheme so that the state does not pay any hospital or doctor for the costs of treating any condition found to be caused by cigarette smoking; and (4) modify its tort law so as to treat cigarettes as a "defective product" for which strict liability is allowed under state tort law. Congress does not allocate any funds for the carrying out of these objectives. It provides that if a state is found not to be in compliance one year after enactment of the act, the federal district courts for that state shall have authority to direct the legislature and agencies of the state to comply, and to hold state officials in contempt if they do not comply.

(a) If you are given the job of arguing on behalf of a state that this provision is an unconstitutional infringement of your state's sovereignty, what constitutional provision should you point to? _____

(b) Will your argument succeed? _____

(c) If you are charged with improving the likelihood that the federal scheme will pass muster, what fundamental change will you urge to be made in that scheme? _____

Answers

5. (a) **Congress' power to regulate commerce.**

(b) **Probably, but this is no longer as certain as it once was.** Before the 1995 decision in *U.S. v. Lopez*, it was enough that there was a "rational basis" for Congress' belief that a regulated activity "affects" interstate commerce. But *Lopez* establishes that the activity which Congress is regulating must *in fact* have a **"substantial effect"** on interstate commerce.

Where an activity is "commercial," the Court still seems willing to find regulation of it to be within Congress' commerce power even if the particular act is wholly intrastate, as long as the act is part of a **class** of activities which, collectively, substantially affect interstate commerce. See, e.g., *Wickard v. Filburn* (farmer's growing of wheat for family use only can be regulated, because the cumulative effect of all such intrastate wheat-growing decisions significantly affects the interstate price of wheat). The bet here seems to qualify — the bet is probably itself a "commercial" transaction (i.e., one primarily motivated by the desire to make a profit), and private bets taken as a group probably have a substantial effect on interstate commerce (e.g., they are often made over interstate phone lines, they contribute to the use of interstate "handicapping" services and interstate money transfers, etc.). Once the Court finds that the activity substantially affects commerce, the Court requires only that the means selected by Congress be "rationally related" to the objective being sought. Here, prohibition of the damaging activity — friendly sports betting — would certainly seem to be a reasonable means of combatting that activity. The scenario seems a lot like that in *Gonzales v. Raich*, where the Court held that Congress could regulate a purely intrastate but commercially-oriented activity regarding a commodity (personal cultivation of marijuana for one's own medicinal uses) because such regulation was reasonably tied in to Congress' regulation of the interstate commercial aspects of that same commodity.

6. **No.** *N.F.I.B. v. Sebelius*, *supra*, p. 37 (the health-insurance case) establishes that five members of the Court believe that Congress' Commerce powers do not allow Congress "to ***compel individuals not engaged in commerce to purchase an unwanted product.***" The case also says that "the power to regulate ***presupposes the existence of commercial activity to be regulated***." Since the WFA requires people who are not in the market for a pedometer to buy one, it seems to run afoul of these principles: these individuals are "not engaged in commerce" (at least, commerce of the relevant sort: purchase of walking-measurement devices), and at least some don't want to purchase the pedometer. So it's hard to see how the Commerce power can extend to this compulsory-purchase program. That's true even though Congress is probably correct in reasoning that if everyone either bought and used the device, or paid the penalty, the interstate market for health-care expenditures would be substantially affected.

7. **(a) The Tenth Amendment.** That Amendment provides that "the powers not delegated to the United States by the Constitution, nor prohibited by it to the States, are reserved to the States respectively, or to the People." Alahoma could make a plausible argument that Congress, by precisely detailing whom the state may hire, has interfered with the sovereignty reserved to the state by the Tenth Amendment.

(b) No, probably. At one time, Alahoma would probably have succeeded with this argument, because of *National League of Cities v. Usery*, which held that the Tenth Amendment prevented Congress from regulating the states in a way that might impair their "ability to function effectively in the federal system"; state employees were exempted from federal wage/hour regulations on this theory. But *National League of Cities* was overruled in *Garcia v. San Antonio Metropolitan Transit Authority*. *Garcia* seems to mean that when Congress, acting pursuant to its commerce power, regulates the states as part of a ***generally applicable regulatory scheme,*** the fact that it is a state being regulated has no practical significance — if the regulation would be valid where applied to a private party, it is also valid as to the state. Consequently, since Congress would almost certainly have the power to set a minimum age for employment in the private sector (on the theory that this directly affects commerce, because of its effect on unemployment and wage limits), the state is not entitled to an exemption.

8. **(a) The Tenth Amendment.**

(b) Yes. The Tenth Amendment does not have very huge scope in light of *Garcia* (see previous question), but it has *some*. In particular, Congress may not simply ***"commandee[r] the legislative processes of the States by directly compelling them to enact and enforce a regulatory program."*** *New York v. U.S.* Thus in *New York v. U.S.*, *supra*, the Court held that Congress could not force states to regulate nuclear waste.

So, here, the Court would almost certainly conclude that Congress may not force a state to enact a specific regulatory framework for dealing with the cigarette/health-care problem. Nor may Congress force state official to carry out administrative tasks (such as the audits of cigarette vendors here); see *Printz* and *Mack*. Congress is always free to regulate health care directly, but it may not thrust onto the states the job of doing this.

(c) Supply federal funds, and make the loss of those funds the only penalty for failure to comply. Congress is always free to use its power to tax and spend for the general welfare in order to carry out a regulatory scheme. Furthermore, it may do this by giving an incentive to the states to get them to do the regulating. See, e.g., *South Dakota v. Dole* (Congress may induce states to prevent underage drinking by withholding 5% of federal highway funds from states that don't prohibit drivers under age 21 from drinking). So long as the only penalty is "mild encouragement" via a loss of funds that are related to the new congressional program, there should not be a constitutional problem. However, Congress cannot cut off major funding for a pre-existing program that has no relation to the regulatory scheme desired by Congress; thus Congress probably couldn't cut off, say, *all educational funding* to states that refuse to enact the cigarette/health-care scheme. That's because when financial inducements are combined with conditions, in a way that is "so coercive as to pass the point at which 'pressure turns into **compulsion**'," and that leaves the states with "no real option but to acquiesce," the scheme goes beyond the spending power. See *N.F.I.B. v. Sebelius, infra*, p. 63. Assuming that federal educational funding is so great a portion of the average state's budget that most states couldn't afford to refuse to enact the cigarette/health-care regulation, the scheme would be found to go beyond the spending power under *N.F.I.B.*

Exam Tips on
THE FEDERAL COMMERCE POWER

Any time your fact pattern involves an action by Congress, you've got to keep the Commerce Clause in mind. In particular:

☞ Whenever you've got to decide whether a congressional statute falls within an enumerated power, **check the Commerce Clause first**. It encompasses a broader variety of congressional action than any other congressional power.

☞ Remember that the Court takes a fairly **deferential** view on the issue of whether a particular action falls within the commerce power. So long as a regulated activity **"substantially affects"** interstate commerce, the regulation will be found to fall within the commerce power.

  ☞ For instance, even if a particular commercial activity being regulated seems to take place solely **intrastate**, the Court will usually find that when all similar activities are considered as a **class**, they have a cumulative effect on interstate commerce. (*Example:* Remember *Gonzales v. Raich*, where the Court upheld Congress' right to ban intrastate cultivation of marijuana for one's own medicinal use because exemption of such cultivation might damage Congress' scheme banning interstate marijuana distribution.)

  ☞ Also, remember that Congress may ban or regulate interstate transport as a way of dealing with local problems.

☞ However, look out for congressional regulation of activities that are ***not really commercial***. Here, there's a much better chance that the Court will find that the activity does ***not*** substantially affect interstate commerce. Cite to *U.S. v. Lopez* in this situation.

Examples of attempts to regulate activities that probably ***don't substantially affect interstate commerce***, so that the regulation is probably ***invalid***:

❏ Congress prescribes the curriculum public schools must use.

❏ Congress makes it a federal crime to commit a gender-based violent crime against a woman (see *U.S. v. Morrison*).

❏ Congress bans marriage under the age of 18.

☞ But if there's a "jurisdictional hook" — like a ban only on those machine guns that passed in interstate commerce — the regulation is probably O.K.

☛ Be alert for fact patterns where Congress purports to tell a person who is not presently in the market for a particular product that they ***must purchase that product.*** This type of command probably goes beyond Congress' Commerce powers. The result in *N.F.I.B. v. Sebelius* — where Congress was found not to have the Commerce power to require most individuals to ***buy health insurance even if they don't want to*** — is an example of the kind of fact pattern you may get on an exam. Point out that under *N.F.I.B.*, even the fact that millions of individuals' decision not to buy a product substantially (and negatively) affects the interstate market for that product isn't enough to make Congress' decision to require the purchase a proper exercise of the Commerce power.

☛ Be alert for fact patterns where Congress is regulating ***the states***. Such regulation raises a ***Tenth Amendment*** issue:

☞ So long as Congress has merely passed a ***generally applicable*** law, this law can apply to the states just as it does to private individuals, and there is no Tenth Amendment violation. (*Example:* Minimum wage laws may be applied to state workers just as to private workers.)

☞ But Congress may not directly ***compel the states to enact or enforce a federal regulatory program.*** [*New York v. United States; Printz*] This is the ***"anti-commandeering"*** rule. When Congress commandeers the state's lawmaking or enforcement mechanism, it violates the Tenth Amendment. (But Congress may single out the states for regulation when the states are acting as market participants. [*Reno v. Condon*])

☞ The anti-commandeering principle also applies to invalidate congressional efforts to ***prevent a state from legislating,*** such as where Congress tries to prohibit a state from ***repealing an existing law.*** [*Murphy v. NCAA* (2018)]

CHAPTER 5

OTHER NATIONAL POWERS

ChapterScope

The previous Chapter covered the Commerce Clause, clearly the most important source of federal power. This Chapter considers other sources of federal authority:

■ **Taxing power:** Under the *"taxing* power," Congress is given a far-reaching ability to tax in order to raise revenue.

    ❏ **Taxation as regulation:** Congress may also *regulate* via taxation.

■ **Spending power:** Under the *"spending* power," Congress may "provide for the common Defense and general Welfare of the United States. ... "

    ❏ **Conditional spending:** Congress may place *conditions* on its spending power as a kind of regulation. This is true even if Congress could not regulate in an area directly (because the area regulated would be of such completely local concern that the commerce power would not be triggered). Conditions placed upon the doling out of federal funds are usually justified under the "Necessary and Proper" Clause.

    ❏ **"General Welfare" Clause:** There is *no* independent congressional power to pursue the *"general welfare."* The only relevance of general welfare is that Congress when it taxes and spends must be pursuing the general welfare (a requirement that has very little independent significance today).

■ **War power:** Congress is given the power to *declare war*, and to tax and spend for national defense.

■ **DC:** Congress can regulate the *District of Columbia*.

■ **Federal property:** Congress can regulate and dispose of *federal property* (e.g., federal parks).

■ **Enforcement of Civil War amendments:** Congress can *enforce* the *post-Civil War amendments* (13th, 14th and 15th).

I. THE TAXING POWER

A. **Several provisions on tax:** Several constitutional clauses relate to the power of the federal government to *tax*. The basic power is given in Article I, §8: "The Congress shall have Power To lay and collect Taxes, Duties, Imposts and Excises. ... "

    1. **Independent federal power:** This power to tax is an *independent source* of federal authority. That is, Congress may tax activities or property that it might not be authorized to regulate directly under any of the enumerated regulatory powers (e.g., the Commerce Clause). Tribe, p. 318.

        Example: Congress could enact a national marriage tax, which would be payable by any couple getting married. Marriage is an area which may be beyond direct federal legislative regulation (unless some tie-in to interstate commerce were devised), but the power to tax stands on its own and does not derive from the commerce power or any other power.

B. Special rules on taxes: In addition to the general enabling provision just discussed, the Constitution imposes several specific limits and rules on the taxing power. These are as follows:

1. **Uniform indirect taxes:** Article I, §8 requires that "all Duties, Imposts and Excises shall be uniform throughout the United States. … " This requirement merely means that the tax structure may not discriminate among the states; it does not matter that specific individuals are not taxed uniformly. Tribe, p. 318. The requirement applies to "indirect" taxes, that is, ones which tax an activity (e.g., the carrying on of a business) rather than taxing property.

2. **Apportionment of direct taxes:** A more specific, and burdensome, requirement is imposed with respect to so-called "direct" taxes. Article I, §2 provides that "direct Taxes shall be apportioned among the several States which may be included within this Union, according to their respective Numbers. … " Thus direct taxes must be arranged in such a way that the revenue produced by them comes from each state in proportion to its share of the nation's overall population.

    a. **"Direct" defined:** There has been substantial dispute over the years about what exactly is a "direct" tax. In general, taxes on *real property* are virtually the only kind of tax likely to be imposed today that would be considered "direct." Provisions of the 1894 Income Tax Act were held to be direct (and therefore invalid because not apportioned by population) since they taxed income from real estate and personal property. However, the Sixteenth Amendment, passed in 1913, provides that "Congress shall have power to lay and collect taxes on incomes, from whatever source derived, without apportionment among the several States. … " This Amendment has essentially put to rest the need to distinguish between "direct" and "indirect" taxes.

3. **No duty on exports:** The final tax-related rule imposed by the Constitution is that no *duty* may be imposed on *exports*. Article I, §9.

C. Regulatory effect: Nearly any measure enacted in the form of a tax will have at least an incidental *regulatory effect*. For instance, if an excise tax on cigarettes is enacted, people may smoke, on average, fewer cigarettes. If the regulatory impact of the tax is one which could be *achieved directly*, by use of one of the other enumerated powers (e.g., the Commerce Clause), the fact that the tax has this regulatory effect is not of constitutional significance.

1. **Disguised regulation:** If, however, the regulatory effect is one which could ***not*** have been achieved directly (e.g., the subject matter is so purely local that it could not be reached under the Commerce Clause, and there is no other enumerated power which applies), then it is possible that the tax may be stricken as an ***invalid disguised regulation.***

    a. **Health Care case:** But in the most famous case on this point, *N.F.I.B. v. Sebelius*, 132 S.Ct. 2566 (2012), the Court did not strike the measure in question as a disguised regulation. Instead, the Court held by 5-4 that the "individual mandate" provision in the 2010 Affordable Care Act — requiring most individuals to buy health insurance or pay a "penalty" — was a valid tax, even though it was essentially regulatory and was found not to fall within Congress' Commerce powers. The tax aspect of the case is discussed *infra*, p. 59.

2. **Modern rules:** The "tax vs. regulation" issue has become somewhat less important in recent years, because almost anything that's even plausibly characterizable as a tax seems to be upheld as one, no matter how great Congress' regulatory motive seems to be. The following rules now seem to apply:

[1] A tax that produces **substantial revenue** will almost certainly be **sustained**, and the Court will not inquire into Congress' principal **motive** (e.g., to regulate) in enacting it;

[2] **Regulatory provisions** that accompany the tax are valid if they bear **some reasonable relation** to the tax's enforcement, an easy-to-satisfy test;

[3] A tax that regulates directly through its **rate structure** is valid. (*Example:* A tax of 1/4 cent per pound on white margarine versus 10 cents per pound on yellow margarine, designed to encourage people to use white margine, is valid.)

[4] Even if Congress calls a measure a **"penalty"** rather than a "tax," if the scheme behaves somewhat like a tax (e.g., it raises material revenue, and doesn't make the activity being taxed flatly "against the law"), it can be sustained as an exercise of the taxing power (see *N.F.I.B. v. Sebelius*, immediately below).

3. **Effect of calling a measure a "penalty" (the Affordable Care case):** The fact that Congress labels a measure as a **"penalty"** does **not** prevent the measure from being upheld as a valid tax, as long as the measure actually functions in a way that resembles a tax. That's the result of probably the most famous case ever on the taxing power, **N.F.I.B. v. Sebelius,** 132 S.Ct. 2566 (2012), involving a federal statute designed to dramatically extend the scope of health insurance (the Affordable Care Act). There, by a 5-4 vote, the Court **upheld** the "individual mandate" portion of the Affordable Care Act as a tax, after finding by a different 5-4 majority that the mandate was not within Congress' Commerce powers (see *supra*, p. 37).

a. **Facts of *N.F.I.B.*:** In the 2010 Affordable Care Act ("ACA" or "Act"), Congress required most individuals to purchase health insurance, even if they had previously chosen to "self-insure." The Act called this requirement the **"individual mandate."** Covered persons (a group that included nearly all individuals and families having income beyond a certain modest threshold) had to fulfill the individual mandate by **buying health insurance coverage** meeting certain minimum standards. And if a covered person didn't make the purchase, she had to pay to the Internal Revenue Service (IRS) what the Act called a **"shared-responsibility payment,"** a payment that the Act characterized as a **"penalty"** rather than as a tax.

i. **Administered by the IRS:** The ACA said that covered individuals **"shall"** maintain health insurance, a term that made it sound as though the government was **commanding** that people buy insurance. But if a covered person didn't do so, the only consequence was that he had to make an **additional payment to the IRS** when paying his taxes.

(1) **Enforcement mechanism:** In those cases where a covered person did not buy insurance and did not initially make the required shared-responsibility payment, the ACA made the general statement that the payment was to be "assessed and collected [by the IRS] in the same manner" as tax penalties. But the ACA's detailed provisions cut back on the IRS' collection powers consid-

erably: the IRS was barred from using several of its normal enforcement tools, such as *criminal prosecutions*. So the IRS' collection powers were materially weaker than in the case of non-payment of standard taxes.

ii. **Government argument:** The federal government would have preferred to see the statute upheld as a valid exercise of Congress' Commerce power. (For this aspect of the case, in which the government was unsuccessful, see p. 37.) But as a fall-back, the Obama administration argued (as the Court characterized the argument) that the individual mandate simply "made going without insurance *just another thing the Government taxes,* like buying gasoline or earning income." Therefore, the government said, the mandate was valid as an exercise of Congress' power to tax and spend for the general welfare.

b. **Found to be a tax:**   Five members of the Court (Roberts plus the four liberals, Ginsburg, Sotomayor, Breyer and Kagan) *agreed* with this Government position: *the individual mandate was a valid exercise of Congress' taxing power.* The main opinion on this point was by Chief Justice Roberts; the other four members of the majority concurred in the result but didn't formally join Roberts' opinion on this point.

i. **A "fairly possible" interpretation:** Roberts conceded that viewing the individual mandate as a tax (rather than as an attempt by Congress to use its Commerce power) was *not the "most natural interpretation"* of the statute — the mandate "reads more naturally as a command to buy insurance than as a tax." But that didn't matter, he said; the only issue was whether interpreting the mandate as a tax was a *"fairly possible"* interpretation. In order to *save a statute from unconstitutionality*, the Court should resort to *"every reasonable construction."* Granting the statute "the full measure of *deference* owed to federal statutes," the mandate could be read as a valid tax, Roberts said.

ii. **"Looks like a tax":**   Roberts noted that the shared-responsibility payment *"looks like a tax* in many respects."* For instance, those required to pay it were to pay it to the Treasury with their tax returns. And, he said, the process "yields the essential feature of any tax: it *produces at least some revenue* for the Government." Indeed, the Congressional Budget Office had projected that the scheme would raise about $4 billion per year by 2017.

iii. **"Penalty" not dispositive:** Roberts conceded that the ACA itself repeatedly described the payment as a *"penalty,"* not a "tax." But, he said, Congress' *choice of label was not determinative* on whether the payment could be viewed as an exercise of the taxing power. Rather, the Court had historically used a *"functional approach"* to deciding whether a payment system fell within Congress' power to tax. There were several factors that convinced him that the way the shared-responsibility payment functioned entitled it to be viewed as a tax. Two of these were as follows:

❑ First, the *small size of the burden* on the "taxpayer" cut in favor of viewing the payment as a tax. Roberts believed that the smaller the burden, the stronger the case for regarding the charge as a tax rather than a penalty. In the ACA, the *size of the payment, relative to the underlying transaction, was very small.* For most people who went without health insurance, the payment would be *far less than the price of insurance*, and was guaranteed to never be more. Even someone with an annual income of $100,000 would pay only about $200 per month, compared with an estimated monthly cost for qualifying health insurance of $400.

❏ Second, the *mechanisms used to collect* the payments, and the language used in the Act to *describe the group* subjected to the payment requirements, similarly suggested that this was in essence a tax, not a punishment. The IRS was permitted to use only its regular collection efforts, not the "means most suggestive of a punitive sanction, such as *criminal prosecution.*" The language of the statute did not classify failure to buy insurance as *"unlawful."* And Congress expected that four million people per year would choose to pay the IRS rather than buy insurance; the fact that Congress seemed to view this as "tolerable" suggested that Congress "did not think it was creating four million *outlaws.*"

In summary, despite Congress' decision to call the shared-responsibility payments a "penalty," the actual way the payment system was designed justified a finding that it fell within Congress' power to tax-and-spend, if the alternative was to find the mandate unconstitutional.

c. **Dissent on the tax issue:**   Four members of the Court *dissented* from the conclusion that the shared-responsibility payment was a valid exercise of Congress' taxing power. In a "joint dissent" with no principal author, Justices Scalia, Kennedy, Thomas and Alito argued that while Congress *could* have used its taxing power to enact the payment system, it had *not in fact used* that power. Consequently, the joint dissenters said, Congress had acted unconstitutionally (since the four dissenters joined with Roberts in finding that the scheme was beyond the Commerce power as well; see *supra*, p. 39).

d. **Significance:** The tax portion of *N.F.I.B.* certainly seems to make it easier for Congress to rely on its taxing power even when, for political purposes, the legislators don't want to admit that what they are doing is passing a tax. Even if Congress labels a required payment as a *"penalty,"* the payment will apparently fall within the tax-and-spend power as long as Congress obeys a few simple and painless formalities, like:

❏ setting the penalty *low enough* relative to the estimated profitability of the underlying conduct that a rational person might *voluntarily choose to pay* the penalty rather than perform (or refrain from) the act that Congress is trying to encourage or discourage;

❏ not calling individual actions that trigger the payment *"unlawful,"* or allowing them to be *prosecuted* as crimes;

❏ *using the IRS* as the means of collecting the payments.

i. **Extended regulatory power:**   In theory, Congress ought to be able to use the "penalty" technique approved in *N.F.I.B.* to stretch its regulatory powers far beyond what the Commerce power has been held to allow. Take, for instance, the prohibition on possession of guns near schools, struck down in *Lopez* (*supra*, p. 31) as going beyond the Commerce power; Congress could presumably do a pretty good job of discouraging such possession (though not criminalizing it) by imposing a $2,000 "penalty" on possessing a gun near a school, and having the IRS collect the penalty as part of the general tax-collection process.

II. THE SPENDING POWER

A. The spending power generally: Article I, §8, gives Congress the power "[t]o lay and collect Taxes … to pay the Debts and provide for the common Defence and general Welfare of the United States. … " The power to spend is thus linked to the power to tax — money may be raised by taxation, and then spent "for the common Defence and general Welfare of the United States."

B. Not limited to enumerated powers: Prior to 1937, it was not clear whether Congress could spend for whatever purpose it wished (so long as the "general welfare" was being served), or whether Congress could only spend in order to carry out one of the other enumerated powers listed in Article I, §8. Then, in *U.S. v. Butler*, 297 U.S. 1 (1936), the Court held that *no such limitation exists* — the spending (and taxing) powers are themselves enumerated powers, so Congress may spend (or tax) to achieve the general welfare, even though no other enumerated power is being furthered.

1. **Facts of *Butler*:**   *Butler* involved the validity of the Agricultural Adjustment Act of 1933, a New Deal measure which sought to raise farm prices by cutting back agricultural production. The scheme was to be carried out by authorizing the Secretary of Agriculture to contract with farmers to reduce their acreage under cultivation in return for benefit payments; the payments were in turn to be made from a fund generated by the imposition of a "processing tax" on the processing of the commodity.

2. **Separate spending power:**   The Court first concluded that the power to "tax and spend for the general welfare" existed as a power *separate and distinct* from the other powers enumerated in Article I, §8. Thus the taxing-and-spending power stood on equal footing with, say, the power to regulate interstate commerce. By this standard, there was no difficulty with the Agricultural Adjustment Act.

3. **Not usable for regulation:**   But the Court rejected the contention that Congress had an independent power to "provide for the general welfare" apart from the power to tax and spend. Thus Congress *may not regulate in a particular area merely on the ground that it is thereby providing for the general welfare*; it is only *taxing and spending* which may be done "for the general welfare." Otherwise, the Court noted, the federal government would be one of "general and unlimited powers," rather than enumerated and limited ones.

4. **Can't regulate for general welfare:**   The most important principle for which *U.S. v. Butler* stands today is that Congress has *no power* to *regulate* for the purpose of providing for the *"general welfare."* Congress may *spend* for the general welfare, it may *tax* for the general welfare, but it may not regulate for the general welfare. (For this reason, a congressional regulatory scheme has to be justified as a reasonable means of carrying out *some other enumerated power*, typically the commerce power. See *supra*, p. 21.)

5. **Other constitutional provisions as limits:**   A federal spending program may still be found invalid because it runs afoul of other, specific, federal constitutional provisions protecting individuals. For instance, Congress could not violate the Due Process Clause of the Fifth Amendment, even as part of an otherwise-valid spending program in furtherance of the "general welfare."

C. Achievement of otherwise disallowed objectives: Suppose that Congress could not achieve objective X by direct regulation, since that would lie beyond its enumerated powers. May Congress use its *conditional* spending power to achieve that result *indirectly*, say by depriving the states of money if *they* do not achieve the regulatory result? The answer is, "*yes*," so long as (1) the action by the state does not violate the constitutional rights of any individual; and (2) Congress has not "coerced" or "unduly influenced" the state into taking the deal (a limit discussed *infra*, p. 63).

1. Illustration of general rule: The 1987 case described in the following example is the leading illustration of the general principle that Congress can use its conditional spending power to achieve a result that would be beyond Congress' direct regulatory powers.

> **Example:** Congress, in order to prevent drivers under the age of 21 from drinking, withholds 5% of a state's federal highway funds from any state that doesn't pass a law forbidding individuals younger than 21 from purchasing or possessing in public any alcoholic beverage. South Dakota attacks the statute on the grounds that this condition interferes with its own exclusive powers under both the Tenth and Twenty-First Amendments.
>
> *Held*, the statute is valid. Even if, *arguendo*, direct congressional setting of the drinking age for the entire country would be unconstitutional, Congress' indirect use of its conditional spending power to achieve the same results is permissible. If, by the use of that conditional spending power, Congress induced the states to pass laws that would *themselves* violate the constitutional rights of individuals, that congressional action would be unconstitutional. But that didn't happen here. Also, if the financial inducement offered by Congress was "so coercive as to pass the point at which '*pressure turns into compulsion*,' " the inducement would so undermine state sovereignty as to go beyond the spending power. But here, Congress has told the states that they will lose only "a relatively small percentage" of their highway funds (5% in South Dakota's case) if they don't comply, and that "relatively mild encouragement" leaves the states free to refuse, "not merely in theory but in fact." Therefore, the inducement was not impermissibly coercive. *South Dakota v. Dole*, 483 U.S. 203 (1987).

D. Spending program can't "coerce" the states (*N.F.I.B.* case): The modern Supreme Court has often worried that the federal government may become *so powerful* that state decision-making power will be diminished and the basic two-government federalist system will be eviscerated. In the *Dole* decision, *supra*, you can see this fear reflected in the Court's statement that a financial inducement so large that it would constitute invalid "compulsion" of the states would undermine state sovereignty and thus be invalid under the Spending Clause. The Court eventually decided in 2012 that such impermissible compulsion had occurred in the form of Congress' decision to make a major change to the *Medicaid* program; the Court concluded that Congress had attached such stringent conditions to large grants it made to states that the set-up unduly *"coerced"* the States, and thus went beyond the spending power.

This result came in the same health-care decision that we've already reviewed in two other contexts (see *supra*, p. 37 and 58), *N.F.I.B. v. Sebelius*, 132 S.Ct. 2566 (2012). The case represents the *first time* the Court has ever overturned an exercise of Congress' spending power as *unconstitutionally coercive*.

1. **Facts:** As we've seen, in the 2010 Affordable Care Act (ACA), Congress took many coordinated steps to expand the availability of health care. One of the biggest steps was to restructure and broaden the Medicaid program.

   a. **Nature of Medicaid:** Under the Medicaid program as it has long existed, Congress *gives major funding to states to help pay for the medical care of various categories of poor people*, such as pregnant women, families with young children, and the disabled. The program is essentially administered by the states, but a majority of the money spent comes from the federal government. The states have always been free to participate or not participate in Medicaid; but if they choose to participate (as every state has done since 1982), they must obey various federally-mandated rules about whom to cover and what services are to be provided.

   b. **The ACA's expansion:** The ACA dramatically broadened the number and types of individuals to whom the states had to give Medicaid. (We'll call this the "Medicaid Expansion.") For instance, the Medicaid Expansion said that states must give Medicaid coverage to *every adult under 65* with income up to 133% of the federal poverty level. Pre-ACA, many states, acting with congressional consent, did not cover childless adults at all, and set a much lower income limit for covering families with children. (For instance, in the case of unemployed parents, pre-ACA the average state covered only the very poorest, those who made less than 37% of the federal poverty level.)

   c. **Funding:** For the early years of the Expansion (from 2014 through 2016), Congress committed to paying *100% of the costs* of covering these newly-eligible recipients. After 2016, the federal payment level would gradually decline, but would still cover 90% of the costs.

   d. **"All or nothing":** The key feature of the Medicaid Expansion — the feature that led 26 states to bring their constitutional challenge — was that if a state declined to participate in the Expansion, *it would lose __all__ Medicaid funding*, not just the "extra" funding to cover the newly-eligible recipients. Medicaid spending accounts for over 20% of the average state's total budget, and pre-Expansion, federal funds covered 50% to 83% of those costs. So an average state that declined to agree to the Expansion would lose, in addition to the funds to cover the Expansion itself, *more than 10% of its total budget.*[1] And such a state would then be left to find some other, completely non-federally-funded, way to afford health-care coverage for their poorest citizens, or leave them without coverage.

2. **The challenge:** The 26 states that challenged the ACA argued that Congress' "take all or none" approach to the Medicaid Expansion was *so coercive* that it violated the basic principle established in earlier cases under the Tenth Amendment (see, e.g., *New York v. U.S.*, p. 48) holding that "the Federal Government may not *compel the states* to *enact or administer a federal regulatory program.*"

3. **Held unconstitutional:** By a 7-2 vote, the Court *agreed* with the plaintiffs: requiring a state to choose between accepting the Medicaid Expansion and losing all Medicaid funds

---

1. This was the estimate of Chief Justice Roberts. By the estimate of the "joint dissent," see *infra*, p. 66, the loss would be even greater: states that lost all Medicaid would lose federal payments equal to 22% of all combined state expenditures, not counting the federal Expansion funds.

was *so coercive* that it *exceeded Congress' authority under the Spending Clause.* The main opinion so holding was by Chief Justice Roberts, who was joined, perhaps surprisingly, by Justices Breyer and Kagan. The four-person "joint dissent" (by Justices Scalia, Kennedy, Thomas and Alito) did not officially join this part of Roberts' opinion for reasons that are unclear, but they agreed with Roberts that the scheme was an unconstitutionally coercive violation of the spending power.

a. **"Appropriate conditions"**: Roberts agreed that Congress could normally "attach appropriate conditions" to federal taxing and spending programs, in order to preserve its control over the use of federal funds. In the usual case, if a state didn't like the conditions that Congress was attaching, the state as an "independent sovereign" was free to simply decline the funds.

b. **Threats to terminate "other significant grants"**: But, Roberts said, the Court's precedents gave much closer scrutiny to those situations in which Congress, in connection with *one* federally-financed program, imposed conditions that took the form of "threats to *terminate other significant independent grants.*" In that situation, the conditions "are properly viewed as a means of *pressuring the states* to accept policy changes." And if the financial inducements are "so coercive as to pass the point at which *'pressure turns into compulsion'* " (citing a 1937 case, *Steward Machine Co. v. Davis*), Congress will be found to have exceeded its spending powers.

   i. The *Dole* drinking-age case: Roberts apparently could not find any case in which the Court had concluded that such impermissible compulsion had actually occurred. But he contrasted the conditions that Congress had imposed in the ADA with the conditions imposed in the only major case since 1937 in which the compulsion issue had arisen, *South Dakota v. Dole*, 483 U.S. 203 (1987) (*supra*, p. 63).

   (1) **The condition in *Dole***: In *Dole*, Congress had threatened to withhold 5% of federal highway funding (a long pre-existing program) payable to any state, if the state did not raise its drinking age to 21. South Carolina claimed that this was unconstitutional coercion.

   (2) **Court disagrees**: But the *Dole* Court disagreed, on the grounds that Congress was offering only *"relatively mild encouragement* to the States"; for instance, the funds at stake amounted to less than one half of one percent of South Dakota's budget at the time. Therefore, whether to accept the drinking age change remained the prerogative of each state "not merely in theory but in fact."

   ii. A **"gun to the head"**: The conditions governing the Medicaid Expansion here, by contrast, were *dramatically more coercive*, Roberts said. In contrast to the "relatively mild encouragement" that Congress had given the states in *Dole*, here Congress' financial "inducement" was in reality *"a gun to the head."* A state that rejected the Medicaid expansion would lose the whole federally-funded portion of its entire Medicaid program, amounting to a loss of over 10% of a typical state's overall budget. This was "economic dragooning that leaves the states with *no real option but to acquiesce* in the Medicaid [E]xpansion."

   iii. **Far side of the persuasion/coercion line**: Roberts concluded that Congress had simply *"conscript[ed] state [agencies] into the national bureaucratic army,"* something that prior cases (decided under the Tenth Amendment) had said was forbidden under our federalist system.

c. Severability: So under Roberts' basic ruling (with which six other Justices agreed), Congress had acted unconstitutionally by threatening to withhold "regular" Medicaid funds from the state as a penalty for refusing to agree to the Medicaid Expansion. But what should be the *consequences* of this finding of unconstitutionality? Could the rest of the ACA (and the Medicaid Expansion itself) be *"severed"* from the unconstitutional penalty, and thus survive? Roberts concluded that the answer was *"yes."*[2]

   i. Congress' presumed intent: The issue came down to *congressional intent:* would Congress have wanted the rest of the ACA to stand if it had known that the Court would hold that Congress didn't have the power to withhold all Medicaid funds from any state that declined the Medicaid Expansion? Roberts concluded that the answer was *"yes."* It was not even clear to Roberts that any state *would* actually reject the Expansion, given the very high level of federal funding for it. But even if Congress knew that some states would reject the Expansion, Roberts saw no reason to believe that Congress would have wanted that state-by-state freedom to decline the Expansion to trigger a complete collapse of the ACA.

4. Two dissenters would allow total withholding: Justice Ginsburg, joined only by Justice Sotomayor on this point, *dissented* from Roberts' conclusion that withholding all Medicaid funding from states that declined the Medicaid Expansion was so coercive that it went beyond Congress' spending powers. Ginsburg asserted that Congress' general right to attach conditions to federal funding would have permitted it to *cancel the entire Medicaid program*, and then *replace it with a new Medicaid* that included the Expansion; in that event, it was clear to her that Congress could require the states to choose between taking the entire newly-constituted Medicaid package or none of it.

5. Four "joint dissenters" say entire ACA should fall: At the other end of the spectrum, the four conservative justices who made up the *"joint dissent"* argued that severance of the Medicaid Expansion should not be allowed: the ACA should instead be found *"invalid in its entirety."* The joint dissenters not only agreed with the majority view that the compulsory Medicaid Expansion was unconstitutional, they believed that the individual mandate, too, was unconstitutional (see *supra*, p. 39). Given the centrality of these two provisions to the overall structure of the ACA, the joint dissenters believed that leaving the numerous other provisions of the ACA[3] in place amounted to "a vast judicial overreaching." The Court was creating, they said, "a debilitated, inoperable version of healthcare regulation that Congress did not enact and the public does not expect."

---

2. On this "severance" issue, Roberts spoke for a bare five-Justice majority: his overall opinion about the Medical Expansion was joined by Justices Breyer and Kagan. And Ginsburg and Sotomayor, though they disagreed with Roberts' conclusion that the loss-of-all-Medicaid-funds penalty was unconstitutional, agreed that the rest of the ACA, including the rest of the Expansion, could be severed so that the remainder survived. (The four members of the "joint dissent," by contrast, believed that severance was improper, and that the entire ACA therefore could not stand; see *infra*, p. 66.)

3. These other provisions included, for instance, the community-rating and guaranteed-issue requirements for insurance companies (see *supra*, p. 38), a penalty on larger employers who did not furnish health insurance to their employees, and the establishment of state-administered and federally-subsidized "insurance exchanges" in which people could buy individual health insurance.

6. **Consequence of severance for ACA:** As a consequence of the 5-4 lineup on the severance issue, the ***entire ACA stayed in force as drafted***, with the sole exception of the federal government's right to cut off the full Medicaid funding of any state that declines to participate in the Medicaid Expansion. If a state declined the Medicaid Expansion, that state would ***keep its "regular" Medicaid funding***, and would be allowed to continue covering whatever classes of citizens it would have covered had the ACA not been enacted.

   a. **Relatively small effect:** As of this writing (early October, 2020), 38 states, plus Washington D.C., had elected to adopt the Medicaid expansion, and 12 states had not. https://www.kff.org/medicaid/issue-brief/status-of-state-medicaid-expansion-decisions-interactive-map. So the Court's decision in *N.F.I.B. v. Sibelius* to strike the part of the ACA witholding all Medicaid funds from states that didn't participate in the Medicaid Expansion has turned out to have a relatively small, though not trivial, impact.

7. **Macro significance:** On the more macro level, *N.F.I.B.* illustrates a ***limit on the spending power:*** Congress' freedom to attach conditions to federal spending does not extend to a situation in which the ***conditions are so "coercive" that the states are left with "no real option but to acquiesce"*** (i.e., situations in which Congress can fairly be described as ***holding a "gun to the head"*** of the states). The principles of state sovereignty prevent Congress from ***"conscript[ing] state [agencies] into the national bureaucratic army,"*** as the majority concluded had occurred in *N.F.I.B.*

   a. **Alteration of pre-existing program:** The Court will apparently be more likely to find such impermissible coercion when Congress dramatically alters a major ***pre-existing*** federally-funded program, than where Congress creates and funds a new program essentially from scratch, and imposes tough conditions on state participation in such a way that the conditions relate solely to the new program.

E. **"General welfare" still required:** A federal spending program must advance the "general welfare." However, the Court gives great deference to Congress' judgment that a spending program will indeed advance the general welfare. Therefore, this requirement seems to have almost ***no bite*** at present.

III. THE WAR, TREATY AND FOREIGN AFFAIRS POWERS

A. **War power:** Congress is given the power to ***declare war***, and to ***tax and spend for national defense***. Also, it is explicitly given the right to "raise and support Armies" and to provide and maintain a navy. All of these powers are given by Article I, §8. The President, by contrast, is made the Commander in Chief of the Armed Forces. (Article II, §2.) Thus Congress and the President in effect split the war powers.

1. **Separation of powers:** This division raises important questions of the separation of powers. (E.g., may the President commit armed forces to battle without express congressional authorization?) However, these questions are deferred until a separate chapter on separation of powers, *infra*, p. 111.

2. **Federalism:** The war powers raise important issues regarding *federalism*.

   a. **Economic regulation:** These issues of federalism have principally arisen in a context of ***economic regulations*** promulgated during wartime. The right to promulgate such regulations as an adjunct to the war powers was broadly construed by the Supreme Court in *Woods v. Miller Co.*, 333 U.S. 138 (1948).

    i. ***Woods* case:** *Woods* involved the constitutionality of the Housing and Rent Act of 1947, by which Congress sought to impose rent controls because of the post-war housing shortage. The Court held that even though actual combat had terminated, a state of war still technically existed. Furthermore, the shortage directly resulted from the war; therefore, Congress could act to combat the shortage, under its power to take all "necessary and proper" steps to enforce an enumerated power (the power to declare war).

  3. **Impact on private citizens:** The war powers sometimes permit Congress to *regulate private behavior* without the need to rely on broad powers like the commerce or the taxing-and-spending powers. Indeed, when Congress does purport to act under its war powers, the Supreme Court will give the resulting action maximum judicial *deference*, and will be extremely reluctant to hold that the congressional action is unconstitutional.

     Example: In *Rumsfeld v. FAIR*, 547 U.S. 47 (2006), the Court upheld the constitutionality of the "Solomon Amendment," under which Congress said that any university could receive certain federal funding only if all parts of the university, including its law school, gave the same on-campus access to military recruiters as to other recruiters. A group of law schools argued that the Solomon Amendment infringed their First Amendment rights by forcing the schools to accommodate the anti-gay message of military recruiters. At the outset of its opinion, a unanimous court noted that Congress' war powers "include[] the authority to *require campus access for military recruiters.*" That is, as an adjunct to its war powers Congress could simply have required every law school and university to host military recruiters, without giving the schools the choice between giving access or foregoing the funding. In the course of finding that the Solomon Amendment was constitutional, the Court noted that *"judicial deference [to Congress] is at its apogee when Congress legislates under its authority to raise and support armies."*

B. **The treaty power:** Like the war powers, the *treaty power* is divided between two branches of the federal government. The President may make a treaty, but it must be ratified by two-thirds of the Senate. Article II, §2.

  1. **Equivalent of federal statute:** A validly-ratified treaty is the rough equivalent of a *federal statute*. Thus when a conflict arises between a valid treaty and a valid congressional statute, *whichever was enacted later* controls, under the rule that "the last expression of the sovereign will must control." See Tribe, p. 226.

  2. **Independent source of authority:** The power to ratify treaties is in effect an enumerated legislative power, just like the specific powers listed in Article I, §8. Thus even though a subject area might not otherwise be within congressional control, if it falls within the scope of an otherwise valid treaty, it will be valid as a "necessary and proper means" of exercising the treaty power. It will also be binding on the states, under the Supremacy Clause.

  3. **May not violate constitutional guarantees:** A treaty may not violate any distinct constitutional prohibitions or guarantees (e.g., the Bill of Rights). See, e.g., *Reid v. Covert*, 354 U.S. 1 (1957), holding that "no agreement with a foreign nation can confer power on the

Congress, or on any other branch of Government, which is free from the restraints of the Constitution."

4. **Executive agreements:** The Constitution's only reference to international agreements is to the treaty power, the exercise of which, as noted, requires ratification by the Senate. However, the Constitution does not explicitly prohibit the President from entering into international agreements without Senate consent, and Presidents have traditionally frequently done so. These unratified agreements are usually called *"executive agreements."*

   a. **Status of executive agreements:** The precise status of such agreements is unclear. It seems settled that they are not *per se* unconstitutional; for instance, if such an agreement is enacted within the scope of an enumerated presidential power, it will surely be upheld. Thus Tribe (pp. 170-71) cites the example of an armistice agreement justified by use of the President's commander-in-chief power.

   b. **Cannot override congressional act:** An executive agreement, unlike a treaty, *cannot override* a prior act of Congress. Tribe, p. 171.

   c. **Superior to state law:** But such an agreement, like a treaty, will have *priority over conflicting state laws*, because the Constitution as a general principle vests all control over international affairs in the federal government. *Id.*

C. **Power over foreign affairs:** Neither Congress nor any other branch of the federal government is explicitly given power over *"foreign affairs"* as such. However, the Supreme Court has always recognized that Congress and the executive branch have power over foreign affairs, even where no enumerated power is applicable. That is, the Court has recognized a "general constitutional principle" that foreign affairs are the proper province of the federal government. Support for this proposition comes from several constitutionally-imposed limitations on state interference with foreign affairs (e.g., the bans on states' making of treaties, and on their laying of import or export duties, both imposed by Article I, §10).

   1. **State action improper:** Thus "all state action, whether or not consistent with current federal foreign policy, that has significant impact on the conduct of American diplomacy is *void* as an unconstitutional infringement upon an exclusively federal sphere of responsibility." Tribe, p. 230.

IV. OTHER POWERS

A. **Other federal powers:** It is not profitable to examine in detail all of the constitutionally-enumerated sources of federal authority. However, a brief listing of some of the other sources of federal authority is as follows:

B. **Congressional powers:** Some of the powers given to *Congress* are:

   1. **Money:** To *coin money*, and to regulate its value (Art. I, §8);

   2. **Bankruptcy:** To establish laws governing *bankruptcy (id.)*;

   3. **Post offices:** To establish *post offices (id.)*;

   4. **Copyrights and patents:** To control the issuance of *copyrights* and *patents (id.)*;

   5. **Federal property:** To govern the District of Columbia, and all other *federal properties (id.)*;

   6. **Immigration and naturalization:** To control *naturalization* (and implicitly, *immigra-*

tion) of aliens *(id.)*;

7. **Civil War Amendments:** To enforce, "by appropriate legislation," the Thirteenth, Fourteenth and Fifteenth Amendments (all arising out of the Civil War). See *infra*, p. 451.

8. **Constitutional amendments:** To *propose*, by a two-thirds vote, a *constitutional amendment* for ratification by three-fourths of the states (Art. V). (The holding of a constitutional convention is an alternative, but one which has never been used since the Constitution's original ratification.)

C. **Powers of the executive:** The powers of the *executive branch* will not be reviewed here. However, some of these powers are discussed in the treatment of separation of powers, beginning *infra*, p. 112. See also the discussion of the President's role in the treaty-making process, *supra*, p. 68.

D. **Judicial powers:** The powers of the federal *judiciary* are spelled out in Article III, §2. These powers, discussion of which is generally reserved for the course in federal courts, include the power to decide:

1. cases *arising under the Constitution or under federal* laws;

2. cases involving *ambassadors* and other diplomats;

3. cases involving *admiralty* and *maritime* issues;

4. cases in which the *U.S. is a party*;

5. cases *between two or more states*, between *a state and* citizens of another state, or between *citizens of different states*; and

6. cases between *a state or its citizens and foreign states* or citizens.

> **Note:** Observe that although all of these types of cases fall within the federal courts' constitutionally-vested power, Congress has the right to "regulate" the jurisdiction of the lower federal courts, and to make "exceptions" to that jurisdiction. This has resulted in a substantial curtailment of the theoretically-available powers of the federal judiciary, as a practical matter. This area is more extensively discussed *supra*, pp. 10-12.

Quiz Yourself on

OTHER NATIONAL POWERS *(ENTIRE CHAPTER)*

9. Congress has decided that breast implants, even of the less-dangerous saline variety, are undesirable. Congress has therefore placed a tax of $2,000 on any breast implant, to be paid by the surgeon at the time of implantation. The legislative history of the statute shows that Congress' principal purpose was to discourage the use of such implants, and that Congress did not believe the measure would produce very much revenue. In its first year, the Act produced collections of about $1 million. Doc, a surgeon specializing in implants, sues to have the statute declared unconstitutional on the grounds that it is beyond the powers of Congress. Is Doc's suit likely to succeed? If so, state why. _____

10. Congress, after concluding that the states have lagged behind in educating school children to be tolerant towards homosexuals, enacts a program providing a small subsidy to any public elementary school that conducts a program teaching a better understanding of, and tolerance of, gay people.

    (a) Putting aside the commerce power, what constitutional provision best supplies constitutional authority for this statute? _____

(b) A parent whose child is about to receive such instruction sues to have the provision found unconstitutional, on the grounds that it encourages homosexuality and thus detracts from the general welfare of the nation. Assuming that the federal court hearing the case concludes that the measure will probably make the nation worse off than it was before, will this constitutional attack on the statute succeed? _____

11. Congress, alarmed about the dramatic rise in teenage pregnancies, passes the Underage Procreation Act of 2021. That Act requires any person under the age of 17 to obtain a federal permit before becoming pregnant. The permit is granted to any woman who shows that she has received one hour of counselling about the dangers of teen pregnancy from a state-licensed social worker. Violators are to be fined. A 16-year-old woman who wishes to become pregnant files suit to attack the statute's constitutionality on the grounds that it is beyond Congress' enumerated powers. The federal government defends the statute on the grounds that it is a proper exercise of Congress' power to regulate for the "general welfare." Will the plaintiff's attack on the statute succeed? (Ignore any issues relating to a woman's constitutional right to privacy or right to become pregnant. Assume that the Court decides that nothing in the activity being regulated affects interstate commerce.) _____

Answers

9. **No.** The fact that the principal purpose of a tax is regulatory rather than revenue-raising does not pose a constitutional problem today. So long as the tax produces at least non-trivial revenue, and does not run afoul of any explicit constitutional limitation on the taxing power (e.g., the prohibition on export duties in Art. I, Section 9), the tax will be found to be within Congress' general power to "lay and collect taxes. … " Art. I, Section 8.

10. **(a) The spending power.** Art. I, Section 8 gives Congress power to "lay and collect Taxes … to pay the Debts and provide for the … general Welfare of the United States. … " This language includes the "spending" power, although the word "spend" is not used.

   (b) No. It is true that the spending power of Art. 1, Section 8 is phrased specifically in terms of providing for the "general welfare" of the nation. However, the requirement that a federal spending program be for the "general welfare" has almost no bite at present — certainly, the Court is not entitled to substitute its own judgment of what would be "best" in lieu of Congress'.

11. **Yes.** There is *no federal "police power."* That is, Congress does not have the right to *regulate "for the general welfare."* Congress' only powers regarding the general welfare are the right to tax and to spend to achieve that welfare. Since nothing in the statute provides for either a tax or an expenditure, the statute is not supported by the taxing and spending power or any other enumerated power. Normally, a federal regulatory scheme could be supported by the commerce power (since the Court takes an extremely expansive view of what activity can be found to "affect commerce"), but the facts tell us to ignore the commerce power here.

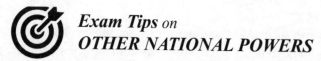

Exam Tips on
OTHER NATIONAL POWERS

Here are some of the ways issues discussed in this Chapter can appear on exams:

☛ Professors sometimes test on the blurry line between *taxing* and *regulation*. Your fact pattern might give you a *tax* that is principally for *regulatory purposes*. If so, you can rely on the taxation power as an independent source of congressional power (distinct from the Commerce Clause, for instance) — so long as the tax produces at least a non-trivial amount of revenue, and its regulatory scheme seems *rationally related* to the collection of the tax itself, it's a valid exercise of the tax power.

    ☞ To determine whether a revenue-raising device is a "tax," the Court now does a *"functional"* analysis: if the measure *behaves like a tax* (most importantly, it raises some *material revenue*), it doesn't matter than Congress has labelled it a *"penalty."* Cite *N.F.I.B. v. Sebelius* on this point.

       ☞ But to be a valid "tax," the measure must probably not make the activity being regulated a *"crime"* or *"offense,"* and the money collected must be small enough that a rational person might choose to pay the "tax" rather than committing the act that Congress is trying to encourage (e.g., buying health insurance).

       Example: In the Affordable Care Act, Congress said that anyone who didn't buy health insurance (at a typical cost for a high-income person of $400 per month) had to pay the IRS a "penalty" (which for a high-income person would be about $200 per month). Since the ACA didn't make non-purchase a serious offense (e.g., there were no criminal penalties for not buying and not paying the penalty), and since the "penalty" was much smaller than the cost of the actual insurance, the penalty was found valid as an exercise of the Taxing power. *N.F.I.B. v. Sebelius*.

☛ Occasionally, you will be tested on the procedural requirements for a *treaty*. Remember that the President may propose a treaty, but it does not become effective until *ratified* by two-thirds of the Senate.

    ☞ Also, keep in mind that even where the President cannot get a treaty ratified, the President may create an international agreement as an *"Executive Agreement."* (An Executive Agreement is essentially an agreement entered into between the President and some other country but not ratified by the Senate.) An Executive Agreement can't override a prior act of Congress, but is superior to state law.

☛ Be on the lookout for questions involving congressional regulation of the *District of Columbia*. Congress has a special enumerated power to govern the District of Columbia, so it may regulate there in purely local matters (which would not fall, say, within the commerce power).

☛ Similarly, remember that Congress can govern all *federal property*. Fact patterns frequently involve national parks, national monuments, military bases, and other types of federal property. In all of these areas, Congress has complete regulatory power, so you do not need to worry about whether the activity being regulated falls within the commerce power or any other general congressional power.

TWO LIMITS ON STATE POWER: THE DORMANT COMMERCE CLAUSE AND CONGRESSIONAL ACTION

ChapterScope

This Chapter examines two federalism-based limits on state and local power: (1) the so-called "dormant" Commerce Clause; and (2) ways in which Congress may block the states from legislating in particular areas. The most important concepts in this Chapter are:

■ **Dormant Commerce Clause:** The *mere existence* of the federal commerce power *restricts the states* from *discriminating against*, or *unduly burdening*, interstate commerce. This restriction is called the "dormant Commerce Clause."

❑ **Three part test:** A state regulation which affects interstate commerce must satisfy *each* of the following three requirements in order to avoid violating the dormant Commerce Clause:

❑ The regulation must pursue a *legitimate state end;*

❑ The regulation must be *rationally related* to that legitimate state end; and

❑ The regulatory *burden* imposed by the state on interstate commerce must be *outweighed* by the state's interest in enforcing its regulation.

❑ **Intentional discrimination:** Courts especially frown on *intentional discrimination* against out-of-staters. If the state is promoting its residents' own economic interests, this will not be a legitimate state objective, so the regulation will almost always be found to violate the Commerce Clause.

❑ **Market participant exception:** There is one key *exception* to the dormant Commerce Clause rules: if the state acts as a *market participant*, it *may* favor local over out-of-state interests.

■ **Preemption:** Congress can *preempt* the states from affecting commerce. There are two ways it can do this:

❑ **Conflict:** First, the congressional statute and the state action may be in *actual conflict*. If so, the state regulation is automatically invalid.

❑ **Federal occupation of field:** Congress may also pre-empt state regulation not because there is an actual conflict between what Congress does and what the states do, but because Congress is found to have made the decision to *occupy the entire field*.

❑ **Consent by Congress:** Conversely, Congress may *consent* to state action that would otherwise violate the Commerce Clause. Congress may even allow a state to discriminate against out-of-staters.

■ **The Supremacy Clause:** Under the *"Supremacy Clause"* of the Constitution, the Constitution and federal laws *take priority* over any conflicting state law.

I.   THE DORMANT COMMERCE CLAUSE — REGULATION

A. **Negative implications of federal power:**   Prior chapters of this book have been devoted to limitations on the federal powers. We turn now to limitations on *state power* embodied in the Constitution.

   1. **Express limits:**   Some limitations on state action are explicitly set forth in the Constitution; for instance, Article I, §9 flatly prohibits any state from imposing an export duty.

   2. **Implied limits:**   With respect to most areas in which the Constitution gives the federal government authority, however, that document does not say anything about whether the states may exercise similar power in the area. For instance, does the Constitution's grant to Congress of the power to issue patents mean that a state cannot give a different kind of protection to inventors?

      a. **No general rule:**   The "negative implications" to be drawn from a constitutional grant of power to Congress have generally been resolved by the Supreme Court on an *area-by-area basis.* Thus a finding of no preemption in the patent context would not necessarily mean the same finding in, say, the bankruptcy area.

B. **Negative implications of the Commerce Clause:**   There is only one power whose grant in the Constitution has given rise to substantial litigation concerning states' powers: this is the Commerce Clause. The issue which has been posed over and over again in the so-called *"dormant* Commerce Clause" cases is: Does the mere fact that the Constitution gives Congress the power to regulate interstate commerce *prevent a state* from taking a particular action which affects interstate commerce, assuming that Congress has not actually exercised its power in the subject area in question (so that no Supremacy-Clause questions are involved)? In other words, the controversy in the dormant Commerce Clause cases focuses not on what Congress *has* done, but on what it *might* have done.

   1. **No simple test:**   As we shall see, no easy answer or test for solving this question has been devised.

C. **Traditional approach:**   The early Supreme Court could have adopted either of two extreme views on the significance of the dormant Commerce Clause for state regulation.

   1. **Great freedom to states:**   It could have held that where Congress has remained silent as to a particular subject matter, the states are completely free to regulate, no matter what the burden on or discrimination against interstate commerce.

   2. **Exclusive federal terrain:**   Alternatively, the Court could have held that Congress' power to regulate interstate commerce is *exclusive*, so that even if Congress has chosen not to act in a certain area affecting interstate commerce, the states are not entitled to act.

   3. **Middle ground:**   But rather than adopting either of these two extreme positions, the Court has always chosen something of a *middle ground*, though the precise nature of that middle position has varied through the years. Essentially, the Court's approach has always been to *weigh* the *state interest in regulating its local affairs* against the *national interest* in *uniformity* and in an *integrated national economy.*

   4. **Congress has ultimate say:**   Because the limitations on state authority imposed by the dormant Commerce Clause are not explicitly stated in the Constitution, but are rather

derived by negative implication, limitations on state commerce-related conduct imposed by the Court *may always be reversed by Congress.*

a. **States given greater freedom:** Thus if the Court holds that a particular type of state action unduly burdens interstate commerce, Congress may pass a law explicitly allowing the state to interfere with commerce in this manner.

b. **Stricter standard:** Conversely, if the Court holds that a particular type of state action, although it affects interstate commerce, does not burden it unduly, Congress may reverse this ruling either by stating that it intends to *preempt the entire field* to which the state regulation relates, or by passing a statute which *explicitly conflicts* with the state rule.

c. **Summary of Court's role:** To put it another way, the Supreme Court's role in this area is limited to *interpreting congressional silence.* See Tribe, p. 404.

D. **Early interpretations:** From its earliest days, the Supreme Court has given great weight to the purposes behind the Commerce Clause: the creation and nurturing of a *common market* among the states, and the *abolition of trade barriers.*

1. **Failure of Articles of Confederation:** The pre-Constitution *Articles of Confederation* had failed largely because the states fought destructive *trade wars* against each other. Tribe, p. 404. These trade wars arose principally from the fact that state governments were too responsive to local economic interests — each state government tended to pursue the interests of its own constituents, at the expense of citizens of other states. *Id.*

2. **Prevention of economic balkanization:** Therefore, under the Constitution, the power of the federal judiciary, interpreting the Commerce Clause, had to be used to prevent this *"economic balkanization."*

3. **Congress' silence:** Also, the Supreme Court has always well recognized that the fact that Congress has not chosen to speak out in a particular area does not mean that it tacitly approves of state regulation of that area. Congress is simply too busy, with too many pressing matters on its legislative docket, for there to be any assurance that state regulations which burden or discriminate against interstate commerce will be overturned by congressional action. Tribe, p. 402. Therefore, the Supreme Court has always been intensely conscious of its own obligation to *keep the channels of interstate commerce free of state-originated impediments.*

4. *Gibbons v. Ogden:* The first Supreme Court case interpreting the meaning of congressional silence in a commerce context was *Gibbons v. Ogden*, 22 U.S. (9 Wheat.) 1 (1824). Other aspects of this case, the opinion in which was written by Chief Justice Marshall, are discussed *supra*, p. 22.

a. **Factual summary:** To summarize briefly the facts, New York had granted an exclusive steamboat operating license which was ultimately owned by Ogden. Gibbons obtained a federal license to operate his vessel between New York and New Jersey, but was enjoined by the New York courts from sailing it in New York waters because of Ogden's monopoly. Gibbons argued that the New York monopoly violated the federal commerce power.

b. **Holding:** After giving a broad definition of "commerce" (see *supra*, p. 22), Marshall went on to hold that the New York monopoly was invalid because it *conflicted with the federal commerce power*. He took two steps to reach this conclusion:

    i.   **Meaning of congressional silence:**   Gibbons' counsel had argued that the federal commerce power was *exclusive*; that is, that the states had no right to take any action which affected interstate commerce. Marshall conceded that there was "great force" in this argument, and that he was "not satisfied that it has been refuted." However, he avoided an explicit ruling on the argument, and assumed, without deciding, that the states could regulate commerce in a particular way if there was no actual conflict between the state regulation and an act of Congress.

    ii.   **Actual conflict:**   But then, Marshall found that there was indeed an *actual conflict* between New York's action and a law of Congress: the federal licensing law, in Marshall's view, conflicted with the New York monopoly, and the New York monopoly had to fall under the *Supremacy Clause.*

    iii.   **Effect of silence not adjudicated:**   Thus Marshall never made any dispositive holding in *Gibbons* about the effect of congressional silence on the States' regulatory powers.

E. Rise of the "local" vs. "national" distinction: Beginning in 1851, the Court embarked on a new way of looking at the dormant Commerce Clause problem, a view which continues to have great significance at present: the Court began to focus on *whether the subject matter being regulated was "local" or "national."*

    1.   **The *Cooley* decision:** That new focus started in ***Cooley v. Board of Wardens of the Port of Philadelphia***, 53 U.S. (12 How.) 299 (1851), where the Court affirmed a Pennsylvania law that required ships entering or leaving the port of Philadelphia to hire a local pilot.

        a.   **"Local" vs. "national" problem:**   The Court refused to hold either that Congress had an exclusive right to make regulations affecting interstate commerce, or that the states had a complete right to regulate interstate commerce in areas where Congress had remained silent. Instead, it held, *some but not all* state regulation affecting interstate commerce was permissible. The states were free to regulate those aspects of interstate commerce that were of *such a local nature as to require different treatment from state to state*. But the states could not regulate aspects of interstate commerce which, because of their nature, required a *uniform national treatment* (which only Congress could provide).

        b.   **Application to facts of *Cooley*:**   On the facts of *Cooley* itself, the Court found Pennsylvania's regulation was permissible, because pilotage in local harbors was a subject appropriate for local control (at least if that local control did not conflict with an explicit congressional action). In reaching this conclusion, the Court relied on a congressional statute adopted many years previously allowing pilotage to be regulated by the states.

        c.   **Legacy of *Cooley*:**   From the 1851 decision in *Cooley* to the present, the basic policy behind that decision has remained in effect; the dormant Commerce Clause blocks *some but not all* state regulations which affect interstate commerce. The resolution of particular cases turns, roughly speaking, on a balancing between the state interest in regulating local affairs and the national interest in uniformity. Tribe, p. 407.

F. Modern approach: The distinction between "direct" and "indirect" effects upon interstate commerce has proven to be no more satisfactory than the "effect on commerce" vs. "police power" distinction. In recent years, the Supreme Court has shifted to a more complex series of tests. A state regulation which affects interstate commerce must meet *each* of the following requirements in order to be upheld:

1. the regulation must pursue a *legitimate state end;*

2. the regulation must be *rationally related* to that legitimate end; and

3. the regulatory *burden* imposed by the state on interstate commerce, and any *discrimination* against interstate commerce, must be *outweighed* by the state's interest in enforcing its regulation. See Tribe, p. 408.

G. Application of the test: While these three requirements are somewhat vague, and the Court has tended to decide dormant Commerce Clause cases on very much of a case-by-case basis, there are at least some general observations that can be made about how the Court will apply each of the three tests:

    1. Meaning of "legitimate state end": The Court has sharply distinguished between measures that are designed for promotion of health, safety and welfare objectives, on the one hand, and those that are designed for furtherance of *economic benefits*, on the other.

        a. Health, safety and welfare: If the state is acting to further *health, safety or "general welfare" objectives*, the Court is quite likely to hold that these objectives constitute "*legitimate* state ends." The states are said to be using their *"police powers,"* which the Court has regarded as a proper source of state regulatory authority since the early 1800s. (However, the Court will not accept at face value a state's contention that it is acting for these purposes, if there is substantial evidence that the state's real purpose is for economic advantage.)

        b. Economic advantage: But the Court is *much more skeptical* of a state regulatory scheme where the state's objective is to promote the *economic interests* of its *own residents*. Protection of a state's economic interests is generally *not considered to be a legitimate state objective*, where pursuit of that objective materially affects interstate commerce.

            i. Need to resist state-by-state protectionism: As the Court said recently, "the proposition that the Commerce Clause by its own force *restricts state protectionism* is *deeply rooted in our case law.*" *Tenn. Wine & Spirits Ret. Ass'n v. Thomas*, 139 S.Ct. 2449 (2019).

            Example: The state of Tennessee says that individuals and businesses who seek to obtain or renew a license to operate a liquor store must meet various demanding duration-of-residency requirements. For instance, any individual who applies for an initial license must have resided in the state for the prior two years.

            Held, this two-year residency requirement violates the dormant Commerce Clause. Under the Court's cases in this area, "if a state law discriminates against out-of-state goods or nonresident economic actors, the law can be sustained only on a showing that it is *narrowly tailored to 'advanc[e] a legitimate local purpose.'* " The two-year requirement here "blatantly favors the State's residents and has little relationship to public health and safety," so it is an unconstitutional violation of the dormant Commerce Clause. *Tenn. Wine & Spirits Ret. Ass'n v. Thomas, supra*.[1]

2. **Rational means to end:** The second requirement, that the means used have a *rational relation* to the (legitimate) end, usually has *less "bite"* than the first requirement. The Court has been fairly careful not to substitute its judgment for that of the legislature in determining whether the regulation is a good way of attaining the end. A mere "rational relation" between means and end is *all* that is required; it is *not* required that the means used be the *best* way of achieving that end, or the way which least affects interstate commerce.

   a. **Deference to legislative fact finding:** In judging whether there is a requisite "rational relation," the Court will also give *due deference to any "facts" found by the state legislature*; that is, the Court will not conduct its own *de novo* inquiry into the facts.

   b. **Similarity to review of Congress' actions:** In general, the Court's role is similar to the one it follows when evaluating whether an act of Congress falls within the commerce power (*supra*, p. 26).

3. **Balancing test:** Once the first two tests (legitimate end, and rationally-related means) have been met, the Court generally performs a rough *"balancing" test*, but one skewed towards a finding of constitutionality. "Where the statute regulates even-handedly to effectuate a legitimate local public interest, and its effects on interstate commerce are only incidental, it will be upheld unless the burden imposed on such commerce is *clearly excessive* in relation to the putative local benefits." *Pike v. Bruce Church, Inc.*, 397 U.S. 137 (1970). Thus in the case of legislation that is non-discriminatory (even if somewhat burdensome to interstate commerce), the state regulation achieves a *presumption of constitutionality*. But this presumption can be overcome by a *clear showing* that the national interest in uniformity or in free commerce outweighs the state benefit.

   a. **Less-restrictive alternatives:** In performing this balancing test, the Court has sometimes considered not only the objectives which the state is pursuing, but also the *necessity of the means* which the state has used to achieve this objective: if the objective could have been achieved by means *less burdensome* (or less discriminatory) to interstate commerce, the Court is more likely to find that the national interest in free commerce outweighs the state's interest. See Tribe, pp. 426-27.

      i. *Dean Milk* **case:** For instance, in *Dean Milk Co. v. City of Madison*, 340 U.S. 349 (1951) (discussed *infra*, p. 82), local regulations preventing importation of milk were struck down. Even though the state's objective (protection of residents against adulterated milk) was permissible, and the regulatory scheme (prohibiting importation so that only regularly-inspected local plants could sell milk) was rationally related to that objective, the safety objective could have been achieved by

---

1. The Court also held in *Tenn. Wine & Spirits* that the residency requirement's constitutionality was not saved by § 2 of the Twenty-first Amendment. Section 1 of that Amendment *repealed Prohibition.* But § 2 gave each state the power to prohibit shipments of liquor into the state; the section does this by saying that "The transportation or importation into any State, Territory, or possession of the United States for delivery or use therein of intoxicating liquors, *in violation of the laws thereof*, is hereby prohibited." The Court held in *Tenn. Wine & Spirits* that although § 2 restored to the states their general pre-Prohibition power to regulate alcohol, the section did not authorize a state to regulate alcohol via a law whose *"predominant effect … is protectionism,* not the protection of public health or safety[.]"] The two-year residency requirement, the Court said, was an obviously protectionist measure, and was thus not saved by § 2.

less burdensome means (e.g., sending of inspectors to out-of-state pasteurization plants to make quality checks, at the out-of-state producers' expense).

4. **Scope of following discussion:** The remainder of our treatment of state regulation and the dormant Commerce Clause is organized according to the type of regulation being pursued by the state. We break our dicussion down into five major subject areas:

[1] regulation of *transportation* (Par. H);

[2] regulation of *incoming trade* (Par. I);

[3] regulation of *outgoing trade* (including exportation of *scarce resources*) (Par. J);

[4] attempts to compel out-of-staters to *perform business activities within the state* (Par. K); and

[5] regulation of the *environment* (Par. L).

H. Regulation of transportation: When states have regulated the *instrumentalities* of interstate commerce (generally, *railroads* and *highways*), they have usually done so in the name of public safety objectives, rather than to benefit local economic interests. Therefore, the existence of a legitimate state objective is generally not in doubt, and the Supreme Court's scrutiny of such measures has usually focused on the second and third of the tests listed above (i.e., rational relation between the means and the safety objective, and balancing benefit to the state against burden on commerce).

1. **Absence of discrimination as factor:** The Court has been much more likely to find that a transportation regulation does not violate the dormant Commerce Clause where the evidence is that it is *not discriminatory* against interstate commerce, either in *intent* or in *effect*. That is, even though the measure may create burdens on interstate commerce, if *similar burdens are created on intrastate activities*, the Court is likely to take the position that in-state political processes supply a sufficient check against abuse.

   a. ***Barnwell* case:** For instance, in *South Carolina State Highway Dept. v. Barnwell Bros., Inc.,* 303 U.S. 177 (1938), South Carolina prohibited the use on state highways of trucks wider than 90 inches or weighing more than 20,000 pounds. There was clear evidence that the vast majority of trucks used in interstate commerce exceeded one or both of these limitations, so the regulation clearly burdened interstate commerce.

      i. **Measure upheld in *Barnwell*:** Yet the Supreme Court, in an opinion by Justice (later Chief Justice) Stone, *upheld the regulation* against Commerce Clause attack. The Court stressed that the regulations were *applicable to interstate and intrastate traffic alike*, and "[t]he fact that they affect alike shippers in interstate and intrastate commerce in large number within as well as without the state is a *safeguard against their abuse.* … "

2. **Balancing test:** Even where a transportation regulation pursues a legitimate state objective (e.g., public safety) in a rational manner, the Court will usually apply a *balancing test*, weighing the benefit to the state from the regulation against the burdens it places on interstate commerce. However, the Court has been reluctant to substitute its judgment for that of state legislatures; therefore, it has usually tried to perform this "balancing" in a way that is fairly deferential to state policies.

a. Slight safety improvement: Thus the balance has generally been struck in favor of interstate commerce interests and against state safety interests only where the regulation's contribution to safety is *so marginal* or *so speculative* that there is little doubt in the Court's mind that the safety interest is outweighed by the burdens on commerce.

3. **Look for discrimination before doing balancing test:** A plaintiff attacking a transportation regulation on Commerce Clause grounds has a far greater chance of prevailing by showing *discrimination* against out-of-staters than by showing merely that the scheme's burdens outweigh its benefits. It seems probable that a majority of the present Supreme Court is now *unwilling* to use balancing, and will automatically *uphold* a transportation regulation, if the safety interests asserted by the state are more than "slight" or "problematic." Conversely, the Supreme Court remains very quick to strike down any transportation regulation that seems to the Court to be motivated by *discriminatory* or protectionist impulses. See, e.g., *Kassel v. Consolidated Freightways Corp.*, 450 U.S. 662 (1981) (Iowa statute prohibiting 65-foot-long trucks is struck down, but at most four members of the Court seem to use a balancing test, and the remainder decide the case based on whether there is a clear discriminatory purpose).

4. **Cumulative and contradictory burdens:** A particular regulation, even though it may seem to be non-discriminatory and non-burdensome when viewed in isolation, may be part of a discriminatory or burdensome *mass* of regulations imposed by *many states*. This may occur either because many states impose regulations that *contradict* each other, or even because many states impose regulations that are not contradictory, but that become burdensome if compliance with all is required. Such a set of multiple regulations is by nature discriminatory in effect against interstate commerce, since only those enterprises that do business in many states will suffer from this problem. The problem is especially likely to occur in the case of regulation of interstate transport.

a. **Actual conflict:** When an actual *conflict* between the regulations of two or more states is shown, the Court is likely to strike down at least one of the conflicting rules, on the grounds that the need for *national uniformity* outweighs the individual state's interest in regulating its own highways, railroads, etc.

Example: An Illinois statute requires trucks operating in that state to be equipped with contoured rear-fender mudguards. At least 45 other states which have mudguard requirements permit a straight, rather than contoured, mudguard, and one state (Arkansas) explicitly requires a straight mudguard. Thus a particular truck could not be operated in both Arkansas and Illinois (at least without re-welding a new mudguard onto it each time).

Held, the Illinois statute violates the dormant Commerce Clause. "This is one of those cases — few in number — where local safety measures that are nondiscriminatory place an unconstitutional burden on interstate commerce." If the Illinois mudguard were so clearly superior in safety to the straight mudguard, it might be the straight-mudguard regulations which would have to give way; but the safety advantage of the Illinois curved mudguard is far from clear. Therefore, it is Illinois which must conform. *Bibb v. Navajo Freight Lines, Inc.*, 359 U.S. 520 (1959).

b. **Cumulative burden:** *Bibb* involved, at least in part, an actual conflict between the regulations of two states. But even where no actual conflict exists, it may be the case that the differing regulations of two or more states may place a large *cumulative bur-*

den on interstate commerce. In this situation, the Court is likely to strike down one or more of the measures.

> **Example:** Suppose that many states each impose different limits on the length of trains. The train-length limits are not contradictory; a railroad can simply follow the shortest limit, and thus operate in all states with the same length trains. However, such national compliance with the rule of the most restrictive state would probably be held to be a violation of the Commerce Clause, because it gives the most restrictive state authority beyond its own borders. See *Southern Pacific Co. v. Arizona*, 325 U.S. 761 (1945), so holding.

5. **Discriminatory intent or effect:** It is vital to remember that, in any regulation of transportation (or other aspect of commerce), the existence of an *intent to discriminate* against interstate commerce, or even an unintended discriminatory effect, will make it dramatically more likely that the Court will strike the measure as violating the dormant Commerce Clause. See, e.g., *Kassel v. Consolidated Freightways Corp., supra* p. 80.

I. **State barriers to incoming trade:** Many cases have involved state regulations which, either intentionally or otherwise, place *barriers upon the importing of goods into the state*. As a general rule, the test to which these regulations will be subjected depends on the nature of the state interest being served:

1. **Protection of economy:** If the purpose of the regulation is to *protect in-state producers* from competing out-of-state commodities, or otherwise to *strengthen the local economy*, the Court will generally *strike the measure*, without even inquiring whether the benefit to the state outweighs the national interest in free commerce. N&R, pp. 295-296. Protection of local economic interest is thus viewed as an "illegitimate" aim, so that Test One of the three tests described *supra*, p. 76, is failed, and the inquiry goes no further.

> **Example:** Recall *Tenn. Wine & Spirits* (*supra*, pp. 77-78), where the Court struck down Tennessee's requirement that no one can obtain a license to operate a liquor store unless she has resided in the state for two years. The Court found that the residency requirement "blatantly favors the State's residents," and had "little relationship to public health and safety." That was enough to lead the Court to strike the statute on dormant Commerce Clause grounds without even reaching the step of balancing the benefits of the regulation against the burdens it placed on interstate commerce.

   a. **Small size of discrimination irrelevant:** Even if the discrimination against out-of-state commodities is *small*, the Court will strike it down if it is motivated by a desire to protect in-state interests — the *mere fact* of discrimination, not the *magnitude* of it, is what counts.

2. **Health and safety regulations:** If, however, the state is in good faith pursuing *health* or *safety* objectives, then the Court will generally balance the benefit to the state against the burdens to interstate commerce. In conducting this balancing test, the degree to which the regulation has a discriminatory effect (even though an unintended one), and the extent to which less burdensome or less discriminatory alternatives are available, will be considered. *Id.* at 231.

3. ***Baldwin* case:** The classic illustration of an impermissible protection of local economic interests at the expense of interstate commerce is *Baldwin v. G.A.F. Seelig, Inc.*, 294 U.S. 511 (1935).

a. **Facts of *Baldwin*:**   *Baldwin* involved a New York attempt to set minimum prices to be paid by New York milk dealers to New York milk producers. The statute also ***prohibited retail sales in New York of out-of-state milk***, if the milk had been ***purchased at a lower price than the one set for purchases within New York***. The avowed purpose of the statute was to ***make sure that New York's farmers could earn an adequate income.***

b. **Act stricken:**   The act was held unconstitutional by the Supreme Court, in an opinion by Justice Cardozo. The statute "set a barrier to traffic between one state and another as effective as if custom duties, equal to the price differential, had been laid upon the [goods]."

   i. **Danger of interstate rivalries:**   Cardozo's opinion observed that "[i]f New York, in order to promote the economic welfare of her farmers, may guard them against competition with the cheaper prices of Vermont, the door has been opened to rivalries and reprisals that were meant to be averted by subjecting commerce between the states to the power of the nation. … [The Constitution] was framed upon the theory that ***the peoples of the several states must sink or swim together***[.]*"*

4. **Valid health objective not sufficient:**   The New York regulation in *Baldwin, supra,* was clearly designed to foster the purely economic interests of New York residents. The Court is at least somewhat more sympathetic where the state regulation of incoming goods, while it burdens interstate commerce, is in good faith designed to protect the ***safety or health*** of residents. But even in the case of such safety or health regulations, the Court will either implicitly or explicitly perform a "***balancing test***," weighing the state's interest in its regulatory scheme against the national interest in unburdened, free-flowing interstate commerce. A crucial part of this balancing is often whether there are ***less burdensome alternatives*** which the state might have adopted.

a. **The *Dean Milk* case:**   Thus in ***Dean Milk Co. v. Madison***, 340 U.S. 349 (1951), the city of Madison, Wisconsin made it unlawful to sell any milk that had not been processed and bottled within five miles of the city. The city claimed (perhaps correctly) that the measure was not intended to discriminate against out-of-state milk producers, but was rather designed to permit inspection of pasteurization quality control so as to guard against adulterated milk. The regulation was attacked by an Illinois corporation which distributed milk in both Illinois and Wisconsin.

b. **Statute stricken:**   The Supreme Court agreed that the Madison regulation ***unduly burdened interstate commerce.*** The Court conceded that the regulation might have been motivated by *bona fide* safety and health concerns. But the regulation nonetheless discriminated against interstate commerce (in the sense of a discriminatory ***effect***). Nor did the fact that companies within Wisconsin, but more than five miles from Madison, were also discriminated against save the regulation from unduly burdening commerce, in the Court's view.

c. **Reasonable non-discriminatory alternatives:**   The real crux of the Court's holding in *Dean Milk* was that ***reasonable non-discriminatory alternatives***, which would have protected the local interest in unadulterated milk, ***could have been implemented.*** For instance, Madison could have sent its inspectors to out-of-state plants, and could have passed the cost onto the producers. Alternatively, Madison could have agreed to be bound by the standards of neighboring areas, provided that those standards were at least as high as Madison's own.

5. **Intentional discrimination (the *Washington Apple* case):** Although the Court has occasionally stricken barriers to incoming trade that are not enacted for discriminatory purposes (e.g., the *Dean Milk* case), the Court is, as noted, much more likely to strike down a statute whose clear purpose is to *favor local economic interests* by discriminating against out-of-state interests. This is what really happened, for instance, in *Hunt v. Washington Apple Advertising Commission*, 432 U.S. 333 (1977).

   a. **Facts of *Hunt*:** North Carolina required that all closed containers of apples shipped into or sold within the state bear the applicable U.S. grade or no grade at all. A group of Washington state apple growers attacked the North Carolina statute, since it prohibited the display in North Carolina of Washington's stringently-policed apple grades. The Washington manufacturers had to either obliterate the printed labels on containers shipped to North Carolina, or repack apples bound for North Carolina in special containers.

   b. **Holding:** The Court found that the North Carolina statute unconstitutionally burdened interstate commerce. More significantly, it also *discriminated* against Washington growers, since it raised the costs of doing business for Washington producers but not North Carolina ones; Washington growers had to repack their apples or obliterate their labels, whereas North Carolina growers were unaffected. Furthermore, whereas North Carolina had no grading requirements at all, Washington state had very strict ones; the North Carolina statute hurt Washington by stripping from it the competitive advantages it had earned through its rigorous and well-known inspection and grading system.

      i. **Intentional:** The Court attached substantial weight to the fact that the North Carolina scheme was apparently *intentionally* discriminatory. There was evidence that it was the North Carolina apple growers who were responsible for the passage of the statute. Also, the state's declared purpose for the statute (to safeguard consumers against fraud) was suspect, since: (1) the statute applied only to the labels of closed shipping containers, and retail sales are generally not made while the apples are still in their shipping containers; and (2) the state permitted the sale of apples with no grading at all.

6. **Discrimination by city against out-of-towners:** Suppose a *city* or *county* tries to protect its own local economic interests by discriminating not only against out-of-*state* producers, but also out-of-town producers in the *same state*. Is it open to the city/county to argue, "The fact that we discriminate against other in-state but non-local producers shows we're not discriminating against interstate commerce"? The short answer is *"no"*: if the locality is protecting its own local interests at the expense of out-of-staters, the protectionism is not saved by the fact that it also comes at the expense of in-staters who are not local.

7. **Facially neutral statutes and the meaning of "discrimination" (*Exxon v. Maryland*):** A statute which is evenhanded on its face may nonetheless turn out to be *disproportionately burdensome* to some or all out-of-state businesses. Where this disproportionate impact is truly *accidental*, and does not directly derive from the fact that the burdened firms are out-of-staters, the Court will normally *uphold* the statute. This is what happened in *Exxon Corp. v. Governor of Maryland*, 437 U.S. 117 (1978).

   a.   Facts of *Exxon* case: Maryland passed a law prohibiting oil producers or refiners from operating retail gas stations in Maryland. The law was enacted because of evidence that gas stations operated by producers and refiners had received preferential treatment during the 1973 oil shortage. Since no gas is produced or refined in Maryland, the rule against vertically-integrated operations *affected out-of-state companies exclusively.* Conversely, the vast majority (but not all) of the non-integrated retailers, who were not harmed and were probably helped by the statute, were in-state business people.

   i.   Statute attacked: Exxon and several other out-of-state integrated oil companies sued. They made two arguments based on the dormant Commerce Clause: (1) that the measure impermissibly discriminated against interstate commerce; and (2) that the measure unduly burdened such commerce.

   b.   Statute upheld: The Court *upheld* the statute against both of these attacks.

   i.   No discrimination: First, the opinion (by Justice Stevens) held that the statute *did not discriminate* against interstate commerce. Most significantly, not all out-of-state companies were affected by the statute; Sears Roebuck, for instance, was an out-of-state company which was selling gas at retail within Maryland, yet was not involved in refining it and was therefore not affected by the statute. The mere fact that the entire burden of the statute fell on *some* out-of-state companies was insufficient to establish that "interstate commerce" was discriminated against.

   ii.   Not burdened: Similarly, the Court found that the statute *did not impermissibly burden* interstate commerce. The opinion conceded that the statute might cause sales volume to shift from refiner-operated stations to independent dealers. But, the Court held, the Commerce Clause "protects the interstate market, not particular interstate firms, from prohibitive or burdensome regulation." Furthermore, the Court noted, in all probability the same percentage of gasoline would come from out-of-state suppliers after the statute as before it (i.e., 100% that the flow of goods in the interstate market would not be decreased.

8.   Personal mobility: Commerce Clause analysis has also been used to strike down state limits on *individuals'* ability to *migrate* from state to state. Thus in *Edwards v. California*, 314 U.S. 160 (1941), the Court invalidated a law making it a misdemeanor to bring into California an indigent non-resident. (The law was aimed at stemming the flow of "Okies" during the Dust Bowl years.) A majority found that the law was an unconstitutional burden on commerce. (Four Justices concurred, but on the basis of the Privileges or Immunities Clause of the Fourteenth Amendment, discussed *infra*, p. 398.)

J.   State barriers to outgoing trade: Another important group of Commerce Clause cases involves attempts by a state to regulate or restrict the *export* to other states of agricultural products, scarce natural resources, or other commodities. The cases in this area are hard to reconcile. However, the following general observations may be made:

1.   "Local" vs. "national" subject: The *Cooley* distinction (*supra*, p. 76) between subject areas of primarily *"local"* concern and "national" concern continues to be of importance in the export area. If the subject matter being regulated is of *primarily local concern*, and the effect on interstate commerce is *incidental*, the regulation is fairly likely to be sustained, even if it is motivated by local economic concerns rather than public safety and health purposes. However, all of this assumes that the regulation does *not discriminate*, in either purpose or effect, against interstate commerce (although it may burden that commerce).

2. **Discrimination important:** The presence or absence of ***discrimination*** continues to be an important factor in the outgoing trade cases, as in the other areas we have already examined. If the burden of a particular regulation falls on in-state and out-of-state persons alike, the Court is much more likely to sustain it than if the burden falls more heavily on out-of-staters (whether by design or by accident). This is especially true where the state interest being pursued is an ***economic,*** rather than public health or safety, one.

3. **Embargo of natural resources:** The most significant, and troublesome, of the barrier-to-outgoing-trade cases are those in which a state attempts to ***prevent exportation of scarce natural resources***, either to keep them from being used at all right now, or to restrict their use to in-state residents.

   a. **Strict scrutiny approach:** Courts give relatively ***strict scrutiny*** to measures which, whether by design or by accident, keep such scarce resources from moving interstate. This strict review is often imposed even where the state's interest is a valid conservation or ecological one, rather than a crude desire to keep economic benefits in-state.

   b. **Less discriminatory alternatives:** A key feature of this stricter scrutiny is that the regulation will generally be upheld only if ***less-discriminatory alternatives*** for achieving the state's interest are unavailable.

      Example: Oklahoma bars the export for sale of any minnows which are procured from the natural waters of the state. (The statute does not apply to hatchery-bred minnows.)

      Held, the statute violates the Commerce Clause. The statute discriminates on its face against out-of-state commerce. Therefore, the burden falls on Oklahoma to justify it under a balancing test, and the state must show that non-discriminatory alternatives are not adequate to preserve the state interest. Here, regardless of the unquestioned validity of the state's interest in conservation and protection of wild animals, no attempt to use non-discriminatory measures was made. (For instance, the state could have set limits on the number of minnows which could be taken by any dealer, rather than completely prohibiting export of minnows, and placing no restrictions at all on capture of minnows for in-state sale.) *Hughes v. Oklahoma*, 441 U.S. 322 (1979).

K. **Local-processing requirements:** The Supreme Court has been especially suspicious of state regulations which pressure out-of-state businesses to ***perform certain operations*** within the state. Most often, these regulations require that agricultural products or natural resources produced in the state also be ***processed*** in the state.

   Example: Arizona requires that all Arizona cantaloupes be packed in Arizona. The regulation is applied to prevent a California company from shipping uncrated cantaloupes from its Arizona ranch to its California packing plant. The purpose of the requirement is to enhance the reputation of (and demand for) Arizona's cantaloupes, which are of high quality.

   Held, statute invalid. The state's interest in enhancing the reputation of Arizona cantaloupes is legitimate (though tenuous). However, this interest is clearly outweighed by the national interest in unencumbered commerce. "[T]he Court has viewed with particular suspicion state statutes requiring business operations to be performed in the home State that could more efficiently be performed elsewhere. Even where the State is pursuing a clearly legitimate local interest, this particular burden on commerce has been declared to be virtually *per se* illegal." *Pike v. Bruce Church, Inc.*, 397 U.S. 137 (1970).

1. **Local processing of garbage:** A state or local government may not even require that its own **garbage** be **locally processed**, as a result of *C & A Carbone, Inc. v. Clarkstown*, 511 U.S. 383 (1994). Such a local-processing requirement discriminates against firms that could have done the processing out-of-state.

   a. **Facts:** In *Carbone*, the town of Clarkstown enacted a "flow control" ordinance. The practical effect of the ordinance was to require that any trash generated in the town be taken to a particular "waste transfer station," which charged a tonnage fee for all trash it processed.

      i. **How it came about:** The town had been required by the state to set up the waste transfer station. Instead of building the station itself, the town induced a local entrepreneur to build it, and promised the entrepreneur a certain volume of trash to process. The town then required residents to take their trash there, as a means of delivering the guaranteed volume.

   b. **Holding:** The Court held that the flow control ordinance violated the Commerce Clause. The majority described the ordinance as a "local processing ordinance," whose purpose and effect was to hoard trash processing jobs (and the income from those jobs) within the town. The ordinance thus discriminated against interstate commerce — it deprived out-of-state firms of the opportunity to do the processing. As a discriminatory "protectionist" statute, the ordinance was virtually *per se* invalid.

      i. **Consequence to in-staters irrelevant:** To the majority, it did not matter that lots of *in-state* trash processors were also deprived of the ability to process Clarkstown's trash. A government-authorized monopoly was no less discriminatory against out-of-state commerce than would be a more typical ordinance protecting all local producers against all out-of-state producers, such as the ordinance struck down in *Pike, supra*.

   c. *Carbone* **not applicable where government owns the facility:** But *Carbone* does **not** apply where government awards a monopoly to a **government-owned facility** rather than the type of privately-owned facility at issue in *Carbone*. See *United Haulers Ass'n v. Oneida-Herkimer Solid Waste Management Auth.*, 550 U.S. 330 (2007).

      i. **Facts of *United Haulers*:** *United Haulers* involved a flow-control ordinance virtually indistinguishable from the one in *Carbone*, except that the garbage-transfer station that all residents were required to use was owned by a **public agency** rather than a private company as in *Carbone*. The government monopoly resulted in residents' being required to pay higher fees for trash removal.

      ii. **Preference upheld:** A majority of the court believed that this distinction between private and public ownership of the transfer station made a critical difference – unlike in *Carbone*, the majority in *United Haulers* concluded that the counties' "all trash must be brought to our facility" ordinance did not discriminate against interstate commerce, and did not violate the dormant commerce clause. The majority thought that the public/private distinction was constitutionally significant for two reasons:

❏ First, regulations by which government takes a monopoly on the performance of an activity — especially in an area where the function has been a "traditionally government activity" — raise *fewer fears of protectionism* than where government favors a local privately-owned business. For one thing, any higher costs from the government-owned monopoly are "likely to fall upon the very people who voted for the [monopoly-causing] laws," whereas in the usual discrimination-in-favor-of-local-businesses scenario much of the burden of the regulation falls on out-of-staters who cannot vote.

❏ Second, if the traditional strict scrutiny were applied to government regulations that conferred a monopoly on government, the result would be an "unprecedented and unbounded *interference by the courts* with state and local government." Local voters here chose the government to be the exclusive provider of waste management services, and the dormant commerce clause should not be used as a "roving license for federal courts to decide what activities are appropriate for state and local government to undertake, and what activities must be the province of private market competition."

iii. **Significance:** So *Carbone* remains in force — and bars government from preferring a local privately-owned business over out-of-staters, at least with respect to trash processing – but under *United Haulers* government is *permitted to go into the waste management business itself and then to require that all citizens use the government-owned facility.*

L. **Environmental regulation:** States' attempts to *control their environment* have sometimes been attacked as violative of the Commerce Clause. As the result of a case on garbage disposal, it appears that the Court will now strictly scrutinize any discriminatory or protectionist state action, even if it was enacted in furtherance of environmental or other *non-economic* motives. Only if *no less-discriminatory alternatives* are available will the Court uphold such a statute.

1. **Summary:** To put it another way, a state may no longer maintain or improve its environment at the expense of its neighbors' environmental or economic interests, unless no reasonable alternative is available.

2. **The *New Jersey Garbage* Case:** The garbage disposal case was *City of Philadelphia v. New Jersey*, 437 U.S. 617 (1978). The case involved a New Jersey statute prohibiting the importing of most solid or liquid waste into the state. The law was enacted in response to the use of New Jersey landfills for disposal of waste from cities in Pennsylvania and New York. Several New Jersey operators and out-of-state users of the landfill sites (including Philadelphia) sued to have the statute invalidated on the ground that it discriminated against interstate commerce.

a. **Statute stricken:** The Supreme Court (by a 7-2 vote) struck the statute as violative of the Commerce Clause. The majority opinion, by Justice Stewart, concluded that the law was "basically a protectionist measure," rather than a way of resolving legitimate local concerns.

    i. **Purpose unclear:** The opinion declined to decide whether the main purpose of the statute was to protect the state's environment and its inhabitants' health and safety (as New Jersey claimed) or to stabilize the costs of waste disposal for New Jersey residents at the expense of out-of-state interests (as the plaintiffs claimed).

    ii. **Discriminatory means:** It was unnecessary to decide this issue because "the evil of protectionism can reside in ***legislative means*** as well as legislative ends." Since New Jersey had chosen a discriminatory means of furthering its objectives (whatever those objectives were), it was a protectionist measure. That is, "it imposes on out-of-state commercial interests the full burden of conserving the State's remaining landfill space. … [It is an] attempt by one State to isolate itself from a problem common to many by erecting a barrier against the movement of interstate trade."

b. **Per se rule of invalidity:** In striking the statute, the Court suggested, though it did not explicitly state, that the same ***"virtually per se rule of invalidity"*** which had previously been applied in cases of protectionism should be extended to non-economic regulations such as the one at hand. See 92 HARV. L. REV. 57.

c. **Quarantine laws distinguished:** The Court's opinion attempted to distinguish ***quarantine*** laws (i.e., laws preventing the importation of diseased or otherwise dangerous livestock or goods into a state), which had often been upheld by the Court. Such quarantine laws banned the importation of materials which, ***at the moment of importation***, were hazardous. Here, by contrast, the solid waste whose importation was prohibited by New Jersey endangered health (if at all) only when buried in landfill sites, by which time there was no valid reason to differentiate between out-of-state and domestic garbage. *Id.* at 54.

d. **Dissent:** A two-Justice dissent, authored by Justice Rehnquist, contended that the quarantine law cases supported the New Jersey law. He saw no reason why New Jersey "may ban the importation of items whose movement risks contagion, but cannot ban the importation of items which, although they may be transported into the State without undue hazard, will then simply pile up in an ever increasing danger to the public's health and safety." The dissent found it reasonable for New Jersey to guard against a worsening of its own waste disposal problem by banning the addition of out-of-state waste.

3. **Taxation of out-of-state waste:** Some states have responded to the *Philadelphia* case by trying to ***tax*** out-of-state waste rather than forbidding it. If the state really taxes out-of-state and in-state waste ***equally***, then there is probably no violation of the Commerce Clause. But the Court is extremely vigilant to ensure that any such taxing scheme is ***not discriminatory***. For instance, a state may not impose a flat ***per-ton*** tax on out-of-state waste, and then claim that this tax "compensates" for general income-tax revenues that are collected from in-staters and used to defray the cost of in-state waste. See *Oregon Waste Systems, Inc. v. Dep't of Environmental Quality*, 511 U.S. 93 (1994).

4. **Non-protectionist legislation:** Although ecological legislation which is purposefully discriminatory appears to be virtually "*per se* invalid" under the *Philadelphia* case, this is not true for environmental acts which merely ***burden*** (without discriminating against) interstate commerce. For instance, the Supreme Court sustained a state law which banned non-returnable milk containers made of plastic (but permitted non-returnable milk containers made of other substances, principally cardboard cartons), in ***Minnesota v. Clover Leaf Creamery Co.***, 449 U.S. 456 (1981).

   a.   **Burden on out-of-state firms:**   The Court sustained the statute even though the plastic used for milk cartons was made solely by non-Minnesota firms, whereas pulpwood, used for making the cardboard containers, was a major Minnesota product. The Court concluded that the statute was not simple "protectionist" legislation camouflaged in a recitation of environmental purposes.

M. **State as purchaser or subsidizer:**   All of the cases considered so far involved state action that was purely regulatory. But suppose the state acts as a ***market participant***, spending money to run a proprietary enterprise, or to subsidize private businesses. Is the state barred from discriminating against interstate commerce, or unduly burdening it, as it would be if its actions were solely regulatory? Where the state acts as a market participant, dormant Commerce Clause analysis will ***not*** be applied, and the state may favor local citizens over out-of-state economic interests.

   Example 1: Maryland, in an effort to rid the state of abandoned cars, purchases crushed auto hulks at an above-market price. The state refuses to buy hulks from out-of-state sellers. *Held,* Maryland did not violate the Commerce Clause. The Commerce Clause simply does not apply when a state, in its role as participant in a market, favors its own citizens. *Hughes v. Alexandria Scrap Corp.*, 426 U.S. 794 (1976).

   Example 2: A state-owned cement plant favors in-state customers in times of shortage. *Held*, this preference does not violate the Commerce Clause. When states act as proprietors, they are free of dormant Commerce Clause limitations. *Reeves v. Stake*, 447 U.S. 429 (1980).

   1.   **Summary of market-participant exception:** So the *"market participant"* exception to the dormant Commerce Clause is pretty ***narrow***: it applies only where state or local government, acting as a market participant, ***chooses to deal with in-staters rather than out-of-staters in direct transactions.*** So a government-owned entity may ***prefer in-state buyers*** when government sells, ***may prefer in-state sellers*** when government buys, and the like.

      a.   **Does not affect state's acts as regulator:** Importantly, the market-participant exception does ***not*** permit the state to ***regulate*** in a way that discriminates against out-of-staters, even if the state is *also* acting as market participant.

         i.   **Effect on "downstream" participants:**   For example, the market-participant exception does not apply where the state tries to use its market clout to regulate transactions ***involving parties that are not dealing directly*** with the state-owned market-participant entity. Thus a state market-participant cannot, for instance, try to regulate *"downstream"* from its own transactions, by saying to its customers, "We'll sell to you [or buy from you] only if you, in turn, discriminate against out-of-staters."

         Example: Alaska sells timber from state-owned lands at below-market prices. The state requires each buyer to promise that it will process the timber inside Alaska before the timber is exported. A non-Alaska firm with no Alaska processing facilities attacks the local-processing rule as violative of the dormant Commerce

Clause. The state defends on the grounds that it is a "market participant" that is merely selling a commodity it owns.

Held, for the plaintiff. The market-participant exception does not apply here, for several reasons. One reason is that the exception will apply only where the effects of the state's terms are *limited to the particular market in which the state is participating*, not to a broader one. Here, the state is trying to engage in "downstream regulation" of the timber-processing market (i.e., trying to affect the conduct of parties with whom the state is not dealing directly), and the market-participant exception does not apply to immunize that downstream regulation from dormant Commerce Clause attack. *South-Central Timber Development, Inc. v. Wunnicke*, 467 U.S. 82 (1984).

2. **Privileges and Immunities attack:** In any case in which out-of-staters are discriminated against by the state acting as a "market participant," the state's actions may be vulnerable to an attack based on the ***Privileges and Immunities Clause*** of Article IV ("The Citizens of each State shall be entitled to all the Privileges and Immunities of Citizens in the several States.") The Supreme Court has held that there is no "market participant" exception to the Privileges and Immunities Clause. See *United Building and Construction Trades Council v. Camden*, *infra*, p. 105, holding that this Clause might be violated by an ordinance providing that at least 40% of any workforce on a city-funded construction project must consist of city residents.

II. STATE TAXATION OF INTERSTATE COMMERCE

A. **Compared with regulation:** Just as state regulation may violate the dormant Commerce Clause, so may certain types of state *taxation*. This is most likely to happen where a state tries to tax operations of a business that operates in more than one state. Many of the same issues are involved in the two situations; for instance, a tax may be stricken on the grounds that it discriminates against interstate commerce, or on the grounds that an interstate business is being subjected to unfair cumulative taxation.

B. **Limited scope:** The Supreme Court has decided literally hundreds of state taxation cases involving the Commerce Clause, and most of the decisions are confusing and hard to reconcile. No attempt will be made here to give full treatment to this subject area. Instead, a few of the general principles which the Court has applied will be discussed.

C. **General principles:** For a multi-state company to succeed in a challenge to a particular state tax, it will generally have to make one of the three following showings: (1) that the company's business activity does not have a ***sufficient connection*** with the taxing state; (2) that the tax ***discriminates against interstate commerce***; or (3) that the tax has led to an unfair ***cumulative burden*** (e.g., it is not fairly apportioned as between the company's in-state and out-of-state activities, or it is unrelated to services rendered by the taxing state).

D. **Minimum contacts:** Not only because of the Commerce Clause, but also because of the ***Due Process Clause*** of the Fourteenth Amendment, a non-domiciliary company may not be taxed *at all* unless there are "***minimum contacts***" between the company and the taxing state. This is a threshold matter, which must be resolved even before examining whether the particular tax involved is equitable.

E. No discrimination: The state may not tax in a way which ***discriminates*** against interstate commerce, i.e., in a way which unjustifiably benefits local commerce at the expense of out-of-state commerce. Tribe, pp. 453-54.

F. Cumulative burden: Even non-discriminatory taxes may nonetheless violate the dormant Commerce Clause if the taxpaying company can show that the taxing scheme ***unduly burdens*** interstate commerce.

1. **Sales and use taxes:** Most litigation about whether state tax schemes unduly burden interstate commerce has focused on the right of a state or local government to require "out-of-state" vendors to collect ***sales and use taxes*** on shipments sent to an in-state recipient. So it's on sales and use taxes that we'll concentrate here.

2. **Thousands of jurisdictions:** Not just every state, but also every one of the thousand counties and cities in the U.S., has the power to impose a sales tax and to define its own rates, exemptions, record-keeping requirements, etc. That being so, a scheme that allowed each of these jurisdictions to force each vendor anywhere in the U.S. to collect taxes whenever it makes even a small sale to a resident ofd the jurisdiction could "entangle interstate business in a ***virtual welter of complicated obligations*** to local jurisdictions[.]" *National Bellas Hess, Inc. v. Dep't of Rev.*, 386 U.S. 753 (1967). Therefore, the Court has long held that some relationships between a vendor and a jurisdiction are simply so small that it would place an undue burden on interstate commerce to allow the jurisdiction to tax sales by that vendor.

3. **Rise of Internet:** Starting in the 1960s the Supreme Court relied on the dormant commerce clause to exempt from state sales taxes any vendor without a physical presence in the state. But as the volume of ***Internet commerce*** ballooned over the last few decades, the Supreme Court has changed course, and now holds that it does ***not*** necessarily unduly burden commerce for state and local governments to tax totally-out-of-state vendors on their shipments into the state.

4. **The requirement of a "substantial nexus":** The Supreme Court has long held — and still holds — that in order for a state or local government to impose sales-tax-collection obligations on out-of-state vendors without the tax scheme being found to be an undue burden on commerce, there must be a ***"substantial nexus"*** between the vendor and the taxing state.

   a. **The bright-line "physical presence" rule:** Until 2018, the Supreme Court applied a ***bright line rule*** for determining whether a vendor had the requisite ***"substantial nexus"*** with a taxing state: the firm would not be deemed to have the required substantial nexus unless it had a ***"physical presence"*** in the state. As the Court explained the idea in *Quill Corp v. No. Dokota*, 504 U.S. 298 (1992), the physical-presence test meant that "***vendors whose only connection with customers in the [taxing] State is by common carrier or the United States mail***" were automatically ***deemed not to have a substantial nexus*** with the state, and were thus ***immune from sales-tax collection obligations.***

   b. **Rise of Internet sales:** In the decades after the 1992 *Quill* decision, the explosive growth of ***Internet commerce*** meant that the "safe harbor" granted by the physical-presence test ***shielded an ever-increasing portion of the nation's retail sales from state (and local) taxation*** — no matter how large an Internet company was, the company could sell limitless quantities of goods to a state's residents without any obligation to collect sales taxes, as long as the company had no store, office, salesperson, or other physical presence in the state. Both brick-and-mortar retailers and revenue-starved states bitterly complained about the unfairness of this regime.

c. Physical-presence test overruled (*South Dakota v. Wayfair*): Finally, in an important 2018 decision, the Supreme Court — by a 5-4 vote — *reversed the physical-presence test* of *Quill*. The case was ***South Dakota v. Wayfair, Inc.***, 138 S.Ct. 2080 (2018).

  i. Facts of *Wayfair*: *Wayfair* involved a South Dakota statute that required any firm that made retail sales of goods and services in the state to collect and remit sales tax, *even if the firm lacked a physical presence in the state.* However, small sellers with no physical presence in the state — defined as firms that neither delivered more than $100,000 of goods or services annually into the state nor made 200 or more separate annual transactions involving deliveries into the state — were *exempted* from the statute.

  ii. Majority reverses the physical-presence rule: In an opinion by Justice Kennedy, a five-justice majority *overruled* the *Quill* physical-presence safe harbor, and thus effectively upheld the South Dakota statute. The majority reasoned that the physical-presence rule created *"market distortions"* that unfairly favored "remote sellers" at the expense of local brick-and-mortar sellers. The result was a system that was *"unfair and unjust* to those *competitors* [with physical presence] who must remit the tax; to the *consumers* who pay the tax; and to the *States* that seek fair enforcement of the sales tax[.]"

d. Effect: The effect of the *Wayfair* decision is that states *may now tax out-of-state firms, including Internet-only firms, even if the firm has no in-state physical presence.* But the *substantial-nexus requirement is still in place*; thus a firm whose in-state sales and activities are so minimal that they don't constitute a substantial nexus with the state still cannot be taxed.

III.   CONGRESSIONAL ACTION — PREEMPTION AND CONSENT

A. Federal preemption generally: The aspect of the Commerce Clause that we have been examining thus far in this chapter is its "dormant" aspect, i.e., its force as a negative implication where Congress has not acted. A different, but surprisingly similar, set of problems is presented when Congress (or any branch of the federal government) *does exercise its power*: To what extent does this exercise of valid federal power restrict what the states may do?

1. Supremacy Clause: If there is a conflict between federal law and state law, the resolution is clear: the *state law is simply invalid*. The *Supremacy Clause* of Article VI provides that in case of a conflict, state law must yield to federal law. Federal law is said to have "*preempted*" state law.

2. Express vs implied preemption: Federal preemption of state law is usually described as falling into two main categories: *"express"* preemption and *"implied"* preemption:

  ❏ *Express* preemption occurs when a federal law *specifically* (i.e., "expressly") says that it preempts state or local law. Chemerinsky Hnbk (5e), p. 434.

  ❏ *Implied* preemption occurs when Congress does *not* expressly state that it intends to preempt state or local law, but *manifests an intent* to do so. *Id.*

After a brief discussion of express preemption, we'll spend most of our time on implied preemption, which is by far the more complicated of the two categories.

B. Express preemption: Congress sometimes, in enacting a statute, takes the trouble to state explicitly that the statute is intended to preempt some area of state or local law. That is, Congress says, "In the area of [X], the only governing law shall be federal law." This is *"express preemption."* As long as the federal statute is validly enacted (e.g., it falls within one of Congress' enumerated powers, such as the commerce power), any state or local law that falls *within the zone* intended by Congress to be *exclusively federal* will be invalid under the Supremacy Clause.

> **Example:** The federal Employee Retirement Income Security Act (ERISA) says that it "supersede[s] any and all State laws insofar as they ... relate to any employee benefit plan[.]" 29 U.S.C. §1144(a). If a state purports to regulate some aspect of an employee benefit plan, the state regulation will be valid as a violation of the Supremacy Cause. That's true even though the state regulation may be perfectly consistent with ERISA.

C. Implied preemption: Most preemption cases involve *"implied preemption,"* i.e., situations in which Congress has not explicitly said that it intends to preempt state or local law, but in which the *structure or purpose* of the congressional action suggests that Congress intended to displace non-federal law.

The Supreme Court has identified *two main types* of implied preemption:

❏ *"field* preemption" and

❏ *"conflicts* preemption"

See *Gade v. National Solid Wastes Management*, 505 U.S. 88 (1992).

We'll look at each type of implied preemption separately.

1. "Field preemption": *"Field preemption"* occurs "where the scheme of federal regulation is *so pervasive* as to make reasonable the inference that Congress *left no room* for the states to supplement it." *Gade, supra.* In other words, field preemption occurs where Congress has indicated that it intends to *"occupy the entire field"* in question.

> **Example:** In 1940, Congress passes the Alien Registration Act, which requires aliens 14 and over to register with the federal Immigration and Naturalization Service, be finger-printed, and obey other restrictions. The prior year, Pennsylvania passed a state alien registration act which required all aliens to register with a state agency, and to receive and carry a state-issued alien identification card.
>
> *Held*, the state alien registration law is preempted by the federal one. The federal government's special role in immigration and foreign relations, and Congress' decision to enact a "single integrated and all-embracing system" for alien registration, make it clear that Congress intended to displace any state requirements that aliens register. *Hines v. Davidowitz*, 312 U.S. 52 (1941).

a. Congressional intent is paramount: In field-preemption, as with other preemption categories, the issue is always one of *congressional intent*; Congress could, if it wished, enact one narrow regulation in a broad subject area, yet evince a clear intent to preempt the entire subject area against state regulation. But Congress rarely makes its intent so clear, and the Court must work by inference. Supreme Court decisions indicate that Congress will be deemed to have preempted an area only where either its *intent* is *unmistakable*, or where "the *nature* of the regulated subject matter permits no other conclusion. ... " *Florida Lime & Avocado Growers v. Paul*, 373 U.S. 132 (1963).

i.   **Broad federal coverage of area:** Where the existing federal regulatory scheme is *broad*, and *covers most of the subject area*, the Court is much more likely to find federal field-preemption than where the federal scheme is less comprehensive. Tribe, p. 497.

ii. **Field traditionally left to states:** Subject matter areas *traditionally left to the states* are *less likely* to be found to be the subject of federal field-preemption. This means that if the subject area is usually viewed as "*local*" rather than "national," preemption is unlikely to be found. This is especially true in cases involving *health* and *safety* regulations.

iii. **National matters:** Conversely, areas *traditionally left to federal control*, such as foreign relations, bankruptcy, patent and trademark, admiralty, immigration, etc., will normally be found to be federally preempted. Registration of aliens, at issue in *Hines, supra*, is an illustration.

iv. **Federal licensing scheme:** The fact that the federal government has enacted a *licensing scheme* for a particular aspect of interstate commerce usually does *not* automatically mean that state regulation of that aspect of commerce is preempted. The Court will look to the goals of the federal and state policies to see if there is a true conflict.

Example: Congress extensively regulates the nuclear power industry, through power delegated to the Nuclear Regulatory Commission (NRC), which licenses and inspects all nuclear power plants. California passes a law conditioning the construction of any new nuclear plant in the state upon a finding by a state agency that when the plant produces nuclear waste, there will be "adequate storage facilities and means of disposal" for that waste. A utility claims that Congress, by enacting its federal licensing scheme, has shown an intent to preempt the entire field of nuclear regulation.

Held, California's regulation is valid. The federal system of licensing and inspecting nuclear plants was set up solely to deal with *safety* issues, and with the construction and operation of nuclear plants. Since California asserts (and the Court accepts) that its statute was aimed at the *economic* problems of storing and disposing of waste, not safety problems, the California statute does not come within the area preempted by Congress. (But if California placed a moratorium on nuclear construction because of safety concerns, or sought to regulate the way in which nuclear plants are constructed and operated, these actions *would* fall within the area preempted by Congress.) Nor does the California regulation conflict with federal objectives, an aspect of the case discussed *infra*, pp. 95-95. *Pacific Gas & Electric Co. v. State Energy Comm'n*, 461 U.S. 190 (1983).

2. **"Conflicts preemption":** *"Conflicts preemption"* has been described by the Supreme Court as applying to two situations: first, "where compliance with both federal and state

regulations is a ***physical impossibility***"; and second, "where state law stands as an obstacle to the accomplishment and execution of the ***full purposes and objectives*** of Congress." *Gade, supra.* Let's talk about each of these two conflicts-preemption scenarios.

a. **Direct physical conflict:** Occasionally, federal and state regulations are drafted in such a way that it is ***physically impossible for a person to obey the federal and state regulations simultaneously.*** When this happens, the state regulation is of course invalid. ***Labelling regulations*** sometimes fall into this category.

   Example: Wisconsin's syrup-labeling rules are written in such a way that that if out-of-state syrup is labeled so as to comply with the federal Food and Drug Act, the syrup will be mislabeled under Wisconsin law. *Held*, the Wisconsin regulations are invalid under the Supremacy Clause. *McDermott v. Wisconsin*, 228 U.S. 115 (1913).

b. **Conflict in purposes:** Alternatively, a regulatory scheme imposed by a state may be inconsistent with the ***purposes*** of a federal regulation. Here, too, the issue is always: what was the ***intent*** of Congress?

   Example: Consider the facts of *Pacific Gas, supra,* where California passed a law conditioning the construction of any new nuclear plant in the state upon a finding by a state agency that there would be "adequate storage facilities and means of disposal" for that waste. Does the state scheme conflict with the purposes of the federal nuclear-power regulatory system, in which Congress showed a desire to promote adoption of nuclear power?

   Held, "no" — the California waste-disposal requirement does not conflict with federal purposes. While it is true that Congress showed a desire to promote the spread of nuclear power, the history of the legislation demonstrates that Congress only wanted to do this if and where nuclear power could be used safely. Therefore, allowing states to require adequate storage and disposal of hazardous waste does not conflict with the purposes behind the federal regulatory scheme. *Pacific Gas & Electric Co. v. State Energy Comm'n*, 461 U.S. 190 (1983).

D. **Easier to win on express than implied preemption:** On average, it is ***easier*** for a litigant seeking preemption to win on an ***express***-preemption theory than on an implied-preemption one.

1. **Summary:** That is, on average it will be easier for a litigant to persuade the court that where Congress has expressly preempted some types of state regulation the preemption should be found to extend to the situation at issue, than to persuade the court that although Congress has remained silent on the preemption issue implied preemption should be found.

E. **Federal consent to state laws:** We turn now to an obverse problem: To what extent may Congress affirmatively ***consent*** to state action which would otherwise be an unconstitutional violation of the Commerce Clause?

1. **Generally allowable:** Early decisions, including *Cooley v. Board of Wardens, supra,* p. 50, suggested that Congress did ***not*** have the power to consent to what would otherwise be state encroachments on the congressional commerce power. But the more modern view is that Congress ***may affirmatively consent to state interference with interstate commerce***. See Tribe, pp. 524-25; N&R, pp. 286-287.

     a. **Rationale:** One rationale for giving Congress the right to give such consent is that the ban on state interference with interstate commerce stems from the danger that each local part of the national economy will protect its own interests at the expense of the other parts; when Congress acts, by contrast, it is the "whole" rather than any individual part which is consenting to the interference with commerce, so that all affected parties are presumably represented in the political process. See N&R, pp. 281-282.

  2. **Discrimination:** Thus the Court has allowed Congress to ***authorize a state to discriminate overtly against out-of-state corporations.*** For instance, Congress has authorized each state to ***regulate insurance*** in a way that intentionally ***discriminates against out-of-state insurers.*** See *Prudential Insurance Co. v. Benjamin,* 328 U.S. 408 (1946).

Quiz Yourself on
TWO LIMITS ON STATE POWER *(ENTIRE CHAPTER)*

12. The City of Fairhaven is located in the state of North Texarkansas. The border with the neighboring state of South Texarkansas is three miles south of the Fairhaven city limits. After a serious outbreak of food poisoning, traced to improperly butchered meat, the Fairhaven City Council passed an ordinance forbidding the sale within Fairhaven of any meat not killed at a slaughterhouse inspected by the Fairhaven Department of Sanitation. All evidence suggests that the Fairhaven ordinance was in fact motivated solely by health and safety objectives, not by any desire to favor local producers. Fairhaven Sanitation inspectors survey all slaughterhouses within a 70-mile radius of the city, but do not attempt to cross the boundary to inspect South Texarkansas slaughterhouses. South Texarkansas, at the state level, conducts its own inspections of slaughterhouses for sanitation, using standards that are closely similar to those used by the Fairhaven inspectors.

    Chopem, the owner of a butcher shop in Fairhaven, sells meat purchased from a slaughterhouse in South Texarkansas. Chopem was charged with selling meat that had not been slaughtered in a Fairhaven-inspected slaughterhouse. Chopem would like to get the charges dismissed on the grounds that the statute, as applied here, violates the U.S. Constitution.

    (a) What is the strongest argument that Chopem can make for the unconstitutionality of the Fairhaven ordinance? _____

    (b) Will this constitutional attack succeed? State your reasons. _____

13. The state of New Wales has a single nuclear power plant. Because the power plant has been in operation for over 20 years, it is now time for the plutonium used in the plant to be disposed of. The safest and cheapest way to do this is to bury it in a lead-enclosed structure 200 feet below the surface. Because residents of the state are worried that their state will become a "toxic dumping ground" if strict measures are not taken, the New Wales state legislature has enacted the following statute: "No plutonium imported into this state after 1994 may be buried anywhere within the confines of this state." The effect of this statute is to permit the state's existing utility to make a one-time disposal of its pre-1994 plutonium by the burial method described above. The owners of a nuclear reactor located in South Brunswick, the state directly east of New Wales, have attacked the new statute on the grounds that it violates the Commerce Clause because it prevents them from shipping their spent plutonium into New Wales and burying it there. Assume that Congress has not spoken on the issue of nuclear-waste disposal at all. Should the court hearing this action agree with the plaintiff? _____

14. The state of Rouge decided to build a new and large state office building. Quarries in Rouge had for years produced fine granite. However, in recent years, the in-state granite industry had begun to suffer because of high costs. In an effort to give a shot in the arm to the local industry, the Rouge legislature provided that all granite used in the new building should be purchased from in-state granite producers, even though the price would inevitably be higher than if the materials were bought from out-of-staters. A granite producer in a neighboring state has sued Rouge in federal District Court, asserting that Rouge's preference for in-staters violates the Commerce Clause. Should the court agree with the plaintiff's argument?

_____

15. The state of Sylvan, in order to raise money to repair its existing highways and build new ones, has imposed a flat "axle tax" on any truck travelling more than 100 miles on Sylvan highways during any calendar year. The tax is $200 per axle. (The typical truck has two axles.) If all trucks were required to pay their fair share of maintaining the state's highways, the fairly-allocated cost for a truck driven full time (at least 20,000 miles per year) within the state would be approximately $500 per year. Trucker is a trucking company located in a state adjacent to Sylvan. Trucker's one truck drives about 200 miles a year in Sylvan, carrying goods into and out of the state.

   (a) What is Trucker's best argument for attacking the constitutionality of the taxing scheme as applied to it? _____

   (b) Will this attack succeed? _____

16. Same facts as Question 13 (on plutonium disposal). Now, assume that Congress has passed the following statute: "Any state may define the circumstances, if any, under which nuclear waste products [defined to include plutonium] may be buried or otherwise disposed of within the confines of that state." If the New Wales statute is attacked on the grounds that it violates the dormant Commerce Clause, should the Court find the statute invalid? _____

Answers

12. (a) That the ordinance unreasonably burdens interstate commerce.

(b) Yes. The dormant Commerce Clause prevents a state or local government from placing **undue burdens** on interstate commerce. Most violations of the dormant Commerce Clause occur when government acts in a "protectionist" manner, i.e., with an intent to favor the economic interests of local residents over out-of-staters. But even a non-protectionist "neutral" regulation will be found to violate the dormant Commerce Clause if it amounts to an **unreasonable burden** on commerce. This can be true, for instance, of regulations that are enacted for the good-faith purpose of protecting the safety or health of local residents. The Court performs a "balancing test," weighing the state or local government's interest in its regulatory scheme against the national interest in unburdened free-flowing interstate commerce. A major part of this balancing is whether there were **less burdensome alternatives** which the government might have adopted.

Here, since South Texarkansas conducts a similar inspection, Fairhaven could simply have accepted the results of South Texarkansas's inspection without materially compromising its own health standards. Therefore, the Fairhaven ordinance will probably be found to have been an "unreasonable" burden on commerce. See *Dean Milk Co. v. Madison*. (The fact that Fairhaven is a municipality rather than a state, and its ordinance might have discriminated against out-of-town but in-state slaughterhouses, i.e., those beyond the 70-mile inspection radius, does not save the ordinance from a dormant Commerce Clause attack.)

13. Yes. Any state or local action that is taken for a ***protectionist purpose*** — that is, for the purpose of preferring in-state economic interests over out-of-state interests — will be ***strictly scrutinized***. This is true even where the measure is taken for what are basically environmental or other non-economic motives. Thus in *City of Philadelphia v. New Jersey* (a garbage disposal case), the Court held that one state could not ban the importation of another's garbage, unless there were no less-discriminatory alternatives. Here, New Wales is clearly preferring local nuclear plant operators to out-of-state operators. New Wales clearly has a less-discriminatory alternative (allow importation, and simply limit the total amount of plutonium that may be buried in the state), so the measure would almost certainly be struck down.

14. No. Ordinarily, if a state prefers the economic interests of in-staters over out-of-staters, we have a classic violation of the Commerce Clause. But there is an important exception: where the state acts as a ***market participant***, spending its money to acquire goods or services, dormant Commerce Clause analysis is not applied, and the state may favor local interests over out-of-staters. Here, Rouge is clearly spending its own money, so it is free to limit that money to acquisitions from in-state producers. See, e.g., *Hughes v. Alexandria Scrap Corp.*; *Reeves v. Stake*.

15. (a) That the tax operates as an undue burden on interstate commerce.

(b) Yes, probably. A state may impose a tax that operates "on" interstate commerce. That is, an interstate business may be required to pay to a state the business' fair share of services supplied by that state to the business' operations in the state. So Trucker can be required to pay its fair share of the construction costs of highways it uses. But in determining whether the tax is fair, the Court requires "internal consistency." That is, the Court determines what would happen if all states taxed interstate operators the same way the state in question is doing; if this "all states" approach would produce a tax that is out of all proportion to the fair value of state services supplied to the payor, the tax is likely to be struck down as unreasonable. Here, each trucker who comes into the state for more than a trivial distance is required to pay the same amount as a truck that drives full time on Sylvan's roads, an approach that would make interstate trucking impossibly expensive if applied by all other states. See *American Trucking Assoc. v. Scheiner*, 483 U.S. 260 (1987), striking down such a flat "axle tax."

16. No. Dormant Commerce Clause analysis is only to be performed when Congress has not expressly allowed the type of discrimination against out-of-staters in question. Here, by the federal statute, Congress has in effect allowed a state to prefer its own citizens over out-of-staters.

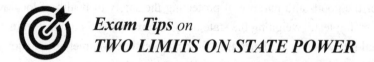

Exam Tips on
TWO LIMITS ON STATE POWER

Issues involving the dormant Commerce Clause and congressional pre-emption can often be well-hidden in a fact pattern; you must be especially vigilant to spot these issues. Here are some particular things to look for:

☛ Remember that one main branch of dormant Commerce Clause analysis is the ***"burden"*** branch: if a state's regulations would burden interstate commerce, the regulation will be struck down unless the burdens are ***outweighed*** by the state's interest in enforcing its regulation. Thus you must use a ***balancing test*** to evaluate "burden" problems. Also:

☞ Look for *conflicts* between the laws of two or more states. The existence of conflicting regulations is likely to be an undue burden on commerce, since a business operating in multiple states would find it difficult or impossible to comply with all of the conflicting regulations.

☞ Be on the lookout for regulations affecting *transportation*, especially *trucking*. These are classic scenarios where the states have differing regulations and commerce is directly affected because goods have to pass from state to state.

☞ Remember that you must do a "burden" analysis even where the state seems totally *even-handed*, and is not showing any protectionism.

  ☞ A common instance of state regulations that are even-handed but nonetheless unduly burdensome are *health* and *safety* regulations. If the state (or local government) insists on performing its own inspection of goods that are imported from elsewhere, this is likely to be an undue burden on commerce even if the state is truly pursuing health and safety rather than protectionism.

☛ Remember that the other main branch of dormant Commerce Clause analysis is the *"protectionist"* branch — if the state is intentionally *discriminating* against out-of-staters, in order to promote its residents' *own economic interests*, this is not a legitimate state objective, so the regulation will almost *automatically* violate the Commerce Clause.

Here are some ways to spot protectionism:

☞ Look for rules *restricting* the *export* of *"good stuff"* produced inside the state. This is especially likely where *natural resources* are the "good stuff" (e.g., a rule saying, "No more than x% of coal mined from the state may be exported").

☞ Look for rules barring the *import* of *"bad stuff"* (e.g., "No out-of-state garbage or toxic waste may be buried in our state").

☞ Look for rules that make it harder for out-of-staters to *work in*, or *do business in*, the state, such as *residency requirements* (e.g., "You can't get a license to operate a liquor store in our state unless you've been a resident of the state for at least two years.").

☛ Remember that the dormant Commerce Clause does not apply at all where the state is a *market participant*. Therefore, be on the lookout for instances where the state is *operating a factory*, *purchasing goods*, or otherwise *directly engaging in commercial transactions* for its own account (as opposed to regulating the transactions done by private parties).

☛ Don't forget that *local ordinances*, not just state rules, can violate the dormant Commerce Clause. This is true even where the ordinance discriminates against out-of-town in-staters as well as out-of-staters.

☛ Remember that *taxes* can be a violation of the dormant Commerce Clause (DCC) just as readily as regulations can be. We have the same two branches of analysis for taxes:

☞ Thus if the state is *discriminating* against interstate commerce by taxing it less favorably than in-staters, this will be a DCC violation.

☞ Alternatively, a tax scheme will violate the DCC if the scheme unfairly *burdens* commerce even though it doesn't discriminate against out-of-staters on its face. One common type of illustration: the state puts a *flat tax* on some activity, regardless of its degree of connection with the state. (*Example:* The state puts a flat annual tax on all trucks entering the state even occasionally, which has the effect of taxing out-of-state trucks much more heavily per mile than in-state trucks.) In considering the burden, consider whatever the fact pattern tells you about the tax policies of *other states* — inconsistencies can make the whole scheme burdensome even though each state's scheme is not burdensome when viewed in isolation.

☛ Separately, be on the lookout for *federal preemption* problems. Remember that this is an aspect of the Supremacy Clause; if Congress (or a federal agency acting under Congress' direction) has acted in a particular respect or occupied a particular domain, the states are often precluded from regulating.

    ☞ Be on the lookout for a fact pattern telling you that there are federal and state statutes dealing with the *same subject area*. This is a clue to preemption problems.

    ☞ First, check for *"express"* preemption: if Congress has explicitly said that the states may not regulate in a particular area, then any state regulation in that area is invalid under the Supremacy Clause, even if the state regulation seems to be consistent with the federal regulation.

    ☞ Next, check for *"implied"* preemption. This can come in either of two flavors: *"conflicts preemption"* and *"field preemption."*

        ☞ *Conflicts preemption* has two flavors, too, *"direct"* and *"indirect."* First, check for a *direct conflict*. If a person or business *could not simultaneously obey both* the state and federal regulation, then obviously the state regulation must fall. Most fact patterns are *not* of this "direct conflict" type, however.

        ☞ Next, check for an *indirect conflict*, mainly a conflict due to inconsistencies in the *purposes* of the two regulations. For instance, you may see a fact pattern where there are federal and state statutes dealing with the same activity, and the state statute is *more stringent* than the federal statute. Obviously, a person can obey both (simply by obeying the more stringent state statute). Here, ask yourself whether Congress meant to say, "We're setting a minimum standard, and we'll let the states be more stringent," or meant to say instead, "We're regulating this way, and we don't want states interfering with our scheme by being more stringent." In the latter situation, the state regulation conflicts with the purposes of the federal regulation, so the state regulation is invalid. Remember that it is always a question of *what Congress intended*.

    ☞ Finally, be on the lookout for *"field preemption."* That is, look for a federal statutory scheme that seems to deal with an *entire broad area*. Where Congress has acted in this way, this may represent Congress' intent to *"occupy the whole field,"* in which case even a state regulation dealing with an aspect of the problem that is not addressed in the federal regulatory scheme may be pre-empted. Commonly, this happens in fact patterns involving *nuclear power* and *immigration* — the existence of a broad federal regulatory scheme in these areas may well prevent the states from enacting even non-conflicting regulations dealing with these subjects.

INTERGOVERNMENTAL IMMUNITIES AND INTERSTATE RELATIONS

ChapterScope

This Chapter, like the ones before it, examines several aspects of federal-state relationships and interstate relationships. As before, the emphasis is on federalism, and the limits it places both on state and federal power. The most important concepts in this Chapter are:

■ **Several types of immunities:** There are several types of *immunities* produced by our federalist system. The most important are:

❏ **Federal immunity from state taxation:** The *federal* government is immune from being *taxed by the states*.

❏ **State immunity from federal tax:** The *states* have *partial immunity* from *federal* taxes.

❏ **Federal immunity from state regulation:** The federal government is essentially free from *state regulatory interference.*

❏ **State immunity from federal regulation:** The states generally are *not* immune from federal regulation. However, if a federal regulatory scheme had the effect of preventing the states from exercising their *core functions*, this might be found to be a violation of the Tenth Amendment.

■ **Interstate privileges and immunities:** The *"Privileges and Immunities"* Clause of Article IV says that "the Citizens of each State shall be entitled to all Privileges and Immunities of Citizens in the several States." This clause means that a state may not *discriminate against non-residents*.

❏ **Rights fundamental to national unity:** But this clause only operates with respect to rights that are *fundamental* to *national unity*. Thus only rights related to *commerce* are covered: the right to *be employed*, the right to *practice one's profession*, and the right to *engage in business* are the prime examples.

I. TAX IMMUNITIES

A. Federal and state immunity: It has long been established that the federal government is *immune* from taxation by any state, unless Congress has consented to such taxation. Likewise, it has always been accepted that a *state*, at least in the performance of its *essential government functions*, is *immune from federal taxation*. However, the scope of this state immunity has been significantly narrowed in recent years. Although the rules in the federal immunity and state immunity situations are similar, there are enough differences to warrant separate treatment of the two.

B. Federal immunity from state taxation: The principle that the federal government is *immune from taxation by any state* derives from *McCulloch v. Maryland*, 4 Wheat. 316 (1819) (discussed *supra*, pp. 17-19).

1. **Holding of *McCulloch*:** Recall that *McCulloch* held that the Bank of the U.S. was immune from a Maryland tax against it. This conclusion was essentially the result of this syllogism: (1) the power to tax is the power to destroy; (2) if state taxation were permitted to destroy or harm the Bank, the federal government's exercise of its powers under the Constitution (especially the "Necessary and Proper" and Spending Clauses) would be thwarted; and (3) the Constitution must be preserved against such state interference.

2. **Broad rationale:** More generally, the theory behind federal immunity from state taxation is that a government may not tax those it does not represent, so that a state may not tax the entire nation. See Tribe, p. 512.

3. **Modern "legal incidence" test:** Federal immunity from state taxation exists only in those situations where the "*legal incidence*" of the tax is on the United States (or upon one of its instrumentalities, such as a federally-sponsored entity like a VA hospital).

    a. **Meaning of "legal incidence":** "Legal incidence" means "*obligation to pay*," not "economic burden." Thus if a private contractor or other non-government entity is required to pay the state tax, the fact that the burden of this tax might be *passed on* to the government is *not enough* to confer tax immunity. Only where the government entity is *directly required to make the payment* will there be federal immunity from state taxation.

    b. **Employees not immune:** *Employees* of the federal government are *not* immune from state taxation. See *Graves v. New York ex rel. O'Keefe*, 306 U.S. 466 (1939).

4. **Congressional control:** Congress may, whenever it wishes, explicitly *confer additional immunity* from state taxation upon other persons or entities.

5. **Congressional waiver:** Conversely, Congress may *waive* its constitutionally-derived immunity whenever it sees fit.

C. **State immunity from federal taxation:** Similar, though not identical, principles control the *immunity of states* from *federal* taxation. The federal government may not tax in a way which would "interfere unduly with the State's performance of its sovereign functions of government." *New York v. United States*, 326 U.S. 572 (1946) (Stone, C.J., concurring).

1. **Source of limitation:** The Constitution nowhere explicitly provides that the states shall be immune from federal taxation of essential government functions. Rather, the state immunity is implied from the *Tenth Amendment's* preservation of state autonomy.

2. **Essential functions:** Thus the federal government may generally not impose a significant tax on property used in or income received from a state's performance of its *basic governmental functions*. For instance, it is doubtful that the federal government may include a state's *public schools* or *public parks* within a general property tax, or its revenues from state taxes within a general federal income tax. See *New York v. United States*, *supra* (Stone, C.J., concurring).

3. **Non-essential function:** But where a state government engages in a function that is not at the core of traditional governmental functions, the federal government may tax that function as part of a non-discriminatory, generally-applicable tax.

4. **Employees not covered:** As in the case of state taxation of the federal government, state *employees*, and other persons doing business with the state, will generally *not be immune* from federal taxation.

II. FEDERAL IMMUNITY FROM STATE REGULATION

A. Federal immunity from regulation: The freedom of the federal government from state regulation is governed by principles similar to those in the taxation context. That is, the federal government is essentially *immune from state regulatory interference*.

> **Example:** Suppose a state attempts to apply its criminal code to actions that take place on a U.S. military base located within the state. Such a state regulation of the federal government would be found unconstitutional, assuming that Congress did not consent to it.

B. Sources of immunity: This federal immunity from state regulation, like federal immunity from state taxation, derives from *McCulloch v. Maryland* (*supra*, p. 17). The theory is that a government may not control those whom it does not represent; thus a state may not control the entire nation. See Tribe, p. 512.

1. Who is covered: Generally, only the United States and its instrumentalities will be free of state regulation. However, sometimes a federal employee will be free of state regulation while acting in the course of his federal duties. See, e.g., *Johnson v. Maryland*, 254 U.S. 51 (1920), reversing the conviction of a post office employee for driving a truck without a state license.

2. Congress' consent: Again, keep in mind that Congress is always free to *consent* to state regulation of federal instrumentalities. This is frequently done, for instance, with respect to the law governing *military posts* and other federal enclaves. Thus Congress has made the changing body of state criminal law applicable to federal enclaves; the Court found this to be constitutional in *U.S. v. Sharpnack*, 355 U.S. 286 (1958).

III. STATE IMMUNITY FROM FEDERAL REGULATION

A. Exits only theoretically: The immunity of the *states* from *federal* regulation exists only in a very theoretical way. In general, federal regulation of the states is *valid*.

1. Interference with core functions: However, if a federal regulatory scheme had the effect of preventing the states from exercising their *core functions*, this might be found to be a violation of the *Tenth Amendment*.

> **Example:** Suppose Congress enacted a statute that said, "No state may have its own criminal code, and the only crimes that may be defined in the United States are those defined in the federal criminal code." The Supreme Court might well hold that this federal regulation so interfered with a traditional state core function — enactment and enforcement of a criminal code — that the Tenth Amendment was violated.

> **Note:** The Tenth Amendment, and the limited extent to which it may prevent the federal government from regulating the states, is discussed *supra*, pp. 46-52. See especially *Garcia v. San Antonio Metropolitan Transit Authority*, *supra*, p. 47.

IV. INTERSTATE RELATIONSHIPS

A. Interstate relationships generally: We now examine two aspects of *interstate* relationships: (1) the Privileges and Immunities Clause; and (2) interstate collaboration, including compacts.

B. The Privileges and Immunities Clause: Article IV, §2, cl. 1 of the Constitution provides: "The Citizens of each State shall be entitled to all Privileges and Immunities of Citizens in the several States." (We'll call this the "P&I" Clause to save space.)

1. Function: This *interstate* P&I Clause (to be distinguished from the Privileges <u>or</u> Immunities Clause of §1 of the Fourteenth Amendment) *prevents states from discriminating against out-of-state individuals*. As the Supreme Court has put it, the clause "was designed to insure to a citizen of State A who ventures into State B the same privileges which the citizens of State B enjoy." *Toomer v. Witsell*, 334 U.S. 385 (1948). Like the Commerce Clause, the interstate P&I Clause is an attempt to "help fuse into one Nation a collection of independent, sovereign States." *Id.*

2. "Citizenship" vs. "residence":   The P&I Clause speaks of "citizens" of other states. But as a practical matter, discrimination against non-*residents* is what is barred.

    a. Corporations and aliens not protected: The one practical effect of the use of the word "citizens" within the Clause is that *corporations* and *aliens* are not protected by the Clause. (In contrast, observe that both corporations and aliens are protected by the Equal Protection and Due Process Clauses of the Fourteenth Amendment.)

3. Test for P&I violation: Even where a state does discriminate against out-of-staters, it is relatively hard for the out-of-staters to establish a violation of the P&I Clause.

    a. Only "fundamental rights" covered: First, only rights that are *"fundamental to national unity"* are covered. The rights that meet this "fundamental to national unity" standard are all related to *commerce*.

        i. Examples: The right to be *employed*, the right to *practice one's profession*, and the right to *engage in business* are all fundamental, and are therefore protected.

        Example: Alaska requires that Alaskan residents be given an absolute preference over non-residents for all jobs on the Alaska oil pipeline. *Held*, the preference violates the P&I Clause. Access to employment is a right fundamental to national unity. Since the statute cannot survive the two-part standard applicable to discrimination against out-of-staters (described below), the preference is invalid. *Hicklin v. Orbeck* (the *"Alaska Hire"* case), 437 U.S. 518 (1978).

        ii. Recreational use: Conversely, *non-economic* rights are generally *not* "fundamental to national unity," and thus not protected by the P&I Clause. For example, the right to engage in *recreational* activities is not protected by the clause.

        Example: Montana allows Montana residents to purchase a license for hunting elk and other animals for $30, while non-residents are charged $225. *Held*, this scheme does not violate the P&I Clause, because the right to recreation is not a right that is fundamental to national unity. *Baldwin v. Montana Fish and Game Comm'n*, 436 U.S. 371 (1978).

    b. Two-part test: Once the Court concludes that a "fundamental right" *is* at stake, then the Court applies a *two-part test* to determine whether the discrimination against non-residents is acceptable. The plaintiff (who is attacking the discrimination against out-of-staters) will win if *either* of the following is shown:

        i. "Peculiar source of evil":   First, the discrimination will violate the P&I Clause unless non-residents are a *"peculiar source of the evil"* which the law was enacted to remedy.

Example: In the "Alaska Hire" case, *supra*, Alaska argued that its employment preference for residents was a reasonable response to high unemployment rates. But the Court held that the state had not shown that the non-residents were a "peculiar source of the evil" (unemployment), because much of the unemployment came from the fact that too many residents were untrained or lived too far from job opportunities, and the influx of out-of-staters seeking jobs was just a small part of the problem.

ii. **"Substantial relationship" test:** Second, the plaintiff will win if the discrimination against non-residents *does not bear a "substantial relationship" to the problem* the statute is attempting to solve.

Example: In "Alaska Hire" this prong was not satisfied, either — a blanket and absolute preference for all qualified residents over all non-residents was not *sufficiently "closely tailored"* to the unemployment problem. (In other words, if there is a *less discriminatory alternative* that would solve the problem, the requisite "substantial relationship" between the discrimination against out-of-staters and the problem will not be found to exist.)

Note: Once a "right fundamental to national unity" is shown to be at stake, the Supreme Court uses something close to *strict scrutiny*: the burden is on the state to show both that non-residents are a peculiar source of the evil, and that the discrimination bears a substantial relationship to the problem being solved.

4. **Practice of law:** The right to *practice law* is a sufficiently important and "fundamental" right that this privilege may not be limited to state residents. Thus in *Supreme Court of New Hampshire v. Piper*, 470 U.S. 274 (1985), the Supreme Court held that New Hampshire could not restrict the right to practice to those who resided within the state.

5. **No "market participant" exception for state:** Recall that where a state is acting as a *"market participant,"* it is not subject to the Commerce Clause's prohibition on discrimination against interstate commerce. (See *supra*, p. 89.) It can plausibly be argued that a similar "market participant" exception should exist to render the P&I Clause inapplicable where the state discriminates against out-of-state residents for *government jobs*. However, the Court has held that there is *no "market participant" exception to the P&I Clause*. The Court reached this conclusion in ruling that the clause applied to a Camden, New Jersey ordinance which required that at least 40% of the workforce on any construction project funded by the city must reside in the city. (The Court did not hold that the ordinance violated the clause; it remanded for a determination on this issue.) *United Building and Construction Trades Council v. Camden*, 465 U.S. 208 (1984).

a. **Grounds for distinction:** The majority reasoned that the rationale for a "market participant" exemption in the privileges and immunities context was not nearly as strong as in the Commerce Clause context. The Commerce Clause deals only with regulation, and a state acting as "market participant" is simply not regulating. But the P&I Clause bars *any* type of state conduct, regulatory or otherwise, which discriminates against out-of-staters on matters of fundamental concern.

b. **Factor to be considered:** Nonetheless, the Court indicated, the fact that the discriminatory conduct consists of the state's expenditure of its own funds is *a non-disposi-*

tive factor which militates in favor of upholding the action against a privileges and immunities attack.

   c. **Discrimination against municipal residence barred:**   The Supreme Court broke other major new ground in the *Camden* case: it held that the P&I Clause bars discrimination based on *municipal residence*, just as it bars such discrimination based on state residence. The Court conceded that a regulation that discriminates against out-of-towners burdens some in-staters as well as out-of-staters. But it reasoned that *in-staters* "at least have a *chance to remedy at the polls any discrimination against them.* Out-of-state citizens have no similar opportunity," so that there is a violation of the P&I Clause as to them.

   d. **"Substantial reason" may justify:**   The Court emphasized in *Camden* that the ban on discrimination against out-of-staters is *not absolute*; all that is required is that there be a *tight fit* between the particular discrimination used and a significant evil that the state is combating.

   e. **Local residence requirements generally:**   Thus after *Camden*, municipalities may still be able to require that all or a specified portion of their employees live within the city limits. Such provisions will be subjected to privileges and immunities scrutiny, but if the city can show that out-of-towners are a peculiar source of the significant evil at which the discriminatory measure is aimed, the measure will still be upheld.

      i. **Illustration:** For instance, if a city can show that a particular spending program was created *for the purpose* of *reducing local unemployment* (e.g., a program giving summer jobs to inner-city youths) a ban on those not living within the city limits, including those living out-of-state, would probably survive privileges and immunities attack.

6. **Distinguished from equal protection:**   Where a nonresident is discriminated against, the case may be actionable under the *Equal Protection Clause* as well as under the P&I Clause. There are two principal differences between these two types of claims:

   a. **Aliens and corporations:**   First, as noted, an *alien* or *corporation* may not take advantage of the P&I Clause, but may take advantage of the Equal Protection Clause.

   b. **Not suspect classification:**   Secondly, nonresidency (unlike alienage) has never been held by the Court to be a *"suspect classification"* for equal protection purposes. Therefore, a state scheme which discriminates against nonresidents is not subject to *strict* equal protection scrutiny, and must just meet the "mere-rationality" standard. (See *infra*, p. 247.)

      i. **Strict scrutiny:**   Where a privileges and immunities attack is lodged, by contrast (assuming that a right fundamental to national unity is involved), the functional equivalent of *strict scrutiny* is given, since nonresidents must be shown to be a "peculiar source" of the evil, and there must be a relatively close fit between the evil and the state's solution to it.

C. **Interstate compacts:**   No state may enter into any "treaty, alliance, or confederation. ... " Article I, §10, cl. 1. However, by negative implication, Clause 3 of that same section allows certain interstate agreements: "No state shall, *without the consent of Congress* ... enter into any agreement or compact with another state or with a foreign power. ... " Such *"interstate compacts"* are a frequently-used device for insuring cooperation among two or more states.

1. **When congressional consent necessary:** Despite the literal wording of Clause 3 (quoted above), *not every agreement between states requires congressional consent*. Rather, congressional consent is required only where the interstate combination tends to *increase the political power of a State*, thereby "encroach[ing] upon the just supremacy of the United States. ... " *Virginia v. Tennessee*, 148 U.S. 503 (1893).

   a. **Illustrations:** Thus if two states were to agree that one would cede part of its territory to the other, this agreement would probably require congressional consent, since it would increase the power of the latter in the House. But a reciprocal tax agreement (whereby each consenting state would agree not to tax residents of other states) would not affect the national government, and would not require congressional consent.

Quiz Yourself on

INTERGOVERNMENTAL IMMUNITIES & INTERSTATE RELATIONS
(ENTIRE CHAPTER)

17. Arms Co. is a government military contractor. Its sole business is to manufacture M-16 rifles, all of which are then sold by it to the U.S. government. Arms Co.'s contract with the U.S. government is of a "cost plus fixed fee" variety. Okra, the state in which Arms Co. is located, has enacted a generally-applicable sales tax on all wholesale sales of tangible property made within the state. Okra applies this tax to Arms Co., with the result that Arms Co. must pay a tax of 8% on all goods bought by it for use in the manufacture of the M-16 rifle. The net effect of this tax is to increase by 4% the price paid by the U.S. government to Arms Co. for each M-16 rifle.

    (a) If Arms Co. wishes to attack the constitutionality of the Okra sales tax as applied to its purchase of materials for use in the M-16, what is its best argument? _____

    (b) Will this argument succeed? _____

18. The state of River provides that no physician may practice within the state unless that physician resides in the state. The state has enacted this rule because its legislators believed (with at least some rationality) that doctors are frequently called upon to give emergency service after hours, and doctors who live out-of-state will be, on the whole, less able to do this than those who live in-state. Doc, a person who has satisfied all other requirements for a license to practice in River (e.g., passage of the national medical boards), lives in the neighboring state of Lake.

    (a) If Doc wishes to challenge River's residency requirement on constitutional grounds, what is his best argument? _____

    (b) Will this argument probably succeed? _____

Answers

17. (a) That the tax violates the federal immunity from state taxation.

(b) No. It's true that the federal government is itself immune from taxation by any state. But this immunity generally does not extend to federal government *employees* or to *contractors* who work for the federal government. And it doesn't matter that the "economic incidence" of the tax falls on the federal government — as long as it is not the federal government itself that is being *directly obliged* to pay the tax, the fact that the economic burden of the tax may fall on the federal government is irrelevant.

18. (a) That the requirement violates the Privileges and Immunities Clause of Article IV.

(b) Yes. Art. IV, Section 2, provides that "the Citizens of each State shall be entitled to all Privileges and Immunities of Citizens in the several States." This Clause prevents states from discriminating against out-of-state individuals. It applies only to rights that are "fundamental to national unity." The right to practice one's profession has been found to be such a right. Once such a "fundamental right" is shown to be at stake, then the defenders of the statute will lose unless they show that non-residents are a "peculiar source of the evil" which the law was enacted to remedy, and that there are no less discriminatory alternatives that would satisfactorily solve the problem.

Here, the unavailability of physicians after-hours may be an important problem, but it is unlikely the state can show that non-residents are a "peculiar source of the evil" (since resident physicians will also frequently be unavailable after hours). Furthermore, it is highly unlikely that there are no less discriminatory alternatives (e.g., requiring that each physician be reachable after hours). Therefore, the statute will almost certainly be found to violate at least one of the two required tests, and will thus be struck down. See *Supreme Court of New Hampshire v. Piper*, holding that a state requirement that lawyers practicing within the state reside within it violated the P&I Clause.

Exam Tips on
INTERGOVERNMENTAL IMMUNITIES AND INTERSTATE RELATIONS

Here are things to watch for in connection with the two main topics from this Chapter, intergovernmental immunities and Art. IV's Privileges and Immunities Clause:

☞ If your fact pattern shows that a *federal tax* is being applied directly to an activity conducted by a *state government*, consider whether the limited state immunity from federal taxation is being violated.

    ☞ Typical fact patterns raising this issue are: the federal government requires every user, including states, to pay a fee for *federally-sponsored services* (e.g., a tax on airplanes to support the air traffic controller system), or the federal government applies a *general tax* on certain *wages* (e.g., a payroll tax applicable to state as well as private-sector employees).

    ☞ Remember the general rule: the only real state immunity from federal taxation is that the federal government may not tax in a way which *substantially interferes* with a state's performance of its *basic governmental functions*.

        ☞ Thus if the federal government is taxing a state's public parks or schools, you might have a violation of the state immunity.

        ☞ But in the vast majority of situations, including virtually all situations where the federal tax is a *generally applicable* tax, there will be *no* interference with basic governmental functions and thus no violation of state immunity. (*Example*: The federal government can tax all airplanes, including state-operated ones.)

☞ Conversely, any time you spot a *state tax* that is applied to an activity somehow connected with the ***federal government***, consider whether this violates the ***federal immunity from state taxation:***

☞ The federal government is certainly immune from **direct** taxation by any state. For instance, if your fact pattern involves a state or local property tax on, say, a post office, that's a clear violation.

☞ But most exam fact patterns do *not* involve a "direct" tax on a federal instrumentality. Instead, the state taxes a ***private party***, in a way that (arguably) increases the federal government's costs. The classic illustration is a tax on the operations of a ***contractor*** who is performing tasks for the federal government on a cost-plus basis. Here, the rule is that it doesn't matter whether the economic burden is passed onto the federal government; as long as the ***"legal incidence"*** of the tax is ***not*** on the federal government, there is ***no violation*** of the federal immunity. (*Example:* A state may impose a sales tax on materials used by a contractor who is building a post office for the U.S. on a cost-plus basis, since the legal incidence of the tax is not on the federal government.)

☛ Similarly, be on the lookout for state ***regulations*** that affect the federal government. Such a fact pattern may indicate a violation of the federal immunity from state regulation.

☞ Typically, federal immunity from state regulation arises where the states are attempting to regulate a ***federal enclave***, such as a post office or military post. Even if the state is regulating in a generally-applicable way, federal enclaves are ***immune*** from this regulation unless Congress has expressly consented to it. (*Example:* A state may not impose its criminal code on a military base, unless Congress consents.)

☛ If your facts show that the ***federal government*** is ***regulating a state***, consider whether the state immunity from federal regulation is being violated.

☞ Here, you should almost always conclude that the state immunity is ***not*** being violated. State immunity from federal regulation is exceptionally narrow. Only if a federal regulation prevents a state from exercising its ***core functions*** will there be a violation. (If you do find a violation, it is essentially a violation of the Tenth Amendment.) It is unlikely you will see a fact pattern where the federal regulatory interference with state functioning is so great that this test is satisfied.

☛ Issues involving Article IV's ***Privileges and Immunities Clause*** are easily hidden.

☞ You should be looking for fact patterns where there is ***discrimination*** against ***out-of-staters***. When you see such discrimination, your first instinct will be to see if there is a violation of the dormant Commerce Clause, and you will also want to examine the possibility of an equal protection violation. But don't forget to check for an Article IV P&I violation, since where that clause applies, the standard of review is very tough.

☞ When you do see a state discriminating against out-of-staters, remember that Article IV P&I applies ***only*** to rights that are ***"fundamental to national unity."*** Essentially, the only rights covered are rights related to ***commerce***.

☞ In general, for the "fundamental to national unity" standard to be satisfied, your fact pattern will usually involve an individual who is a ***U.S. citizen***, ***resides out of state***, and is either ***totally blocked*** from following his ***chosen profession or job*** in the state, or is subjected to a *higher license fee* than is charged to in-staters. (*Example:* A state law preventing citizens of other states from practicing law or medicine in the state would involve a right "fundamental to national unity," and would in fact violate the Article IV P&I Clause.)

☞ If you conclude that the right in question *is* fundamental to national unity, then be sure to articulate the correct *standard of review*. Something akin to *strict scrutiny* is used: the state *loses* unless it can prove *both* that: (1) non-residents are a *"peculiar source of the evil"* which the discrimination against out-of-staters is attempting to remedy; and (2) the discrimination bears a *"substantial relationship"* to the problem the discriminatory statute is attempting to solve. Usually, you should conclude that the state has *failed* to satisfy one or both of these tests (especially number (1)).

☞ There is one context in which you should always conclude that a right "fundamental to national unity" is *not* involved: where what is involved is the pursuit of *recreation*. Thus your fact pattern will frequently involve an out-of-stater's right to *hunt*, *fish*, use tennis courts, etc.; typically the out-of-stater will either be entirely blocked from doing these things, or charged a much higher *fee* than in-staters. Even if the ban on out-of-staters is total, you should still conclude that Article IV's P&I is *not* violated, because commerce is not involved and thus there is no right fundamental to national unity. (But if the out-of-stater wants to hunt, fish, etc. as a *professional* who will earn his living that way, then this analysis probably will not apply, and the P&I Clause will apply.)

☞ When you spot discrimination against out-of-staters that seems to trigger the Article IV P&I Clause, you typically will want to compare the application of the P&I Clause with the Equal Protection Clause. Keep in mind the important differences between how these two clauses apply to discrimination against out-of-staters:

  ☞ *Aliens* and *corporations* do *not* get to use the Article IV P&I Clause (since it applies only to "national citizenship," and neither aliens nor corporations are "United States citizens").

  ☞ On the other hand, once the P&I Clause does apply, something like *strict scrutiny* is applied, and the out-of-stater will almost always win. By contrast, under Equal Protection Clause analysis, non-residency is *not* a suspect classification, so a state can usually discriminate against out-of-staters without violating the Equal Protection Clause as long as the state regulation is rationally related to a legitimate state objective. Often, the state will be able to satisfy this easy standard.

☞ Be sure to specify that it is the *Article IV* P&I Clause, *not* the Fourteenth Amendment "P-or-I" Clause that you're talking about. The Fourteenth Amendment P-or-I Clause is extremely limited, and is virtually never used. Especially on multiple choice questions, be careful not to pick a response stating that the challenged action is a violation of "the Fourteenth Amendment's Privileges and Immunities Clause" — professors love to slip this in as a trick (wrong) answer.

CHAPTER 8

SEPARATION OF POWERS

ChapterScope

A prior Chapter (*supra*, p. 15) summarized the general boundaries of the powers of the three federal branches. Here, we examine closely certain *conflicts* between branches, especially between the Executive and Legislative Branches. Here are the most important concepts in this Chapter:

■ **President/Congress boundary line:** Many separation-of-powers conflicts involve the boundary line between the President (Executive Branch) and Congress (Legislative Branch). Here are some of the more important principles concerning this boundary line:

❑ **President can't make the laws:** The President cannot make the laws. All he can do is to *carry out the laws* made by Congress.

❑ **Declaration of War:** Only *Congress*, not the President, can *declare war*.

❑ **Appointments:** The President, not Congress, has the power to *appoint* federal executive officers.

❑ **Removal by Congress:** Just as Congress may not directly appoint federal executive officers, it may not *remove* an executive officer, except by the special process of *impeachment*.

❑ **Removal of federal judges:** Federal *judges* cannot be removed by *either* Congress or the President.

■ **Other issues:** The other main separation-of-powers area involves issues of *immunity* and *executive privilege*:

❑ **"Speech and Debate" Clause:** Members of Congress are given a quite broad immunity by the *"Speech and Debate"* Clause. This clause shields members of Congress from: (1) civil or criminal suits relating to their legislative actions; and (2) grand jury investigations relating to those actions.

❑ **Executive immunity:** Courts recognize an implied *executive* immunity from civil actions.

❑ **Absolute for President:** The President has *absolute* immunity from civil liability for his official acts.

❑ **Qualified for others:** All other federal officials, including presidential assistants, receive only *qualified* civil immunity.

❑ **Executive privilege:** Presidents have a qualified right to refuse to disclose *confidential information* relating to the performance of their duties. This is called *"executive privilege."*

❑ **Outweighed:** Since the privilege is qualified, it may be outweighed by other compelling governmental interests (e.g., the need for the President's evidence in a criminal trial).

I.   DOMESTIC POLICY AND THE SEPARATION OF POWERS

A. **General problem:**   There are a few powers which are explicitly granted by the Constitution to the President. These are enumerated in Article II, §2, and will not be listed here. They include, for instance, the President's status as Commander-in-Chief of the armed forces and his treaty-making power.

1. **Implied powers:**   But unlike the Congress, whose powers are much more closely delineated (by Article I, §8), much of the President's power, in both the domestic and foreign spheres, is *implied*. This process of implication has been derived mostly from Article II, §1, which provides, in relevant part, "The executive Power shall be vested in a President. … " If the Supreme Court concludes that a presidential action is properly regarded as being part of the "executive" (rather than judicial or legislative) sphere, that action will not be rendered unconstitutional merely by the fact that it does not fall within any specific constitutionally-enumerated power. See Tribe, pp. 210-211.

B. **No right to "make laws":**   Despite its willingness to infer the existence of broad presidential authority, the Supreme Court has adhered to one over-arching limitation on presidential power: *The President may not make laws*; he may only *carry them out*. The best-known case evidencing this limitation is *Youngstown Sheet & Tube Co. v. Sawyer*, 343 U.S. 579 (1952) (the *Steel Seizure Case*).

1. **Facts of *Youngstown Sheet:***   During the Korean War, President Truman sought to avert a strike in the nation's steel mills. He therefore issued an executive order directing his Secretary of Commerce to seize the mills and operate them under federal direction. Congressional approval of the seizure order was not requested. The steel companies sought an injunction to prevent the seizure.

2. **Supreme Court strikes down seizure:**   The Court *struck down the seizure order*, concluding that it was an unconstitutional exercise of the lawmaking authority reserved to Congress. Although the decision was 6-3, four of the six Justices on the majority side wrote separate concurring opinions, making it difficult to summarize the "doctrine" of the case.

a. **Black's opinion:**   Justice Black's opinion for the Court flatly stated that the President's seizure order, coming as it did without the consent of Congress, was a clear usurpation of congressional lawmaking power. The order could not be justified under the "Commander-in-Chief" power; the taking of private property in order to keep labor disputes from stopping production of war materiel was too far removed from the actual "theater of war" in which the President had the right to set policy. Nor could the seizure be justified under the President's power to see that the laws are faithfully executed — the very language of the clause shows that the President must merely carry out the laws, not make them.

b. **Concurring opinions:**   But the four concurring opinions, unlike Justice Black's opinion for the Court, attached principal importance to the fact that Congress had previously, and repeatedly, *explicitly rejected* plant seizure as a means of handling labor disputes. *Justice Jackson's concurrence*, the best known of the four, contended that the President's powers "are not fixed but *fluctuate*, depending on their disjunction or conjunction with those of Congress." He conceived of three categories:

[1] where the President acts pursuant to express or implied *authorization* of Congress, in which case his authority is at its *maximum*;

[2] where the President acts in the *absence* of either a congressional *grant or denial* of authority, in which case "there is a zone of twilight in which he and Congress may have *concurrent* authority, or in which its distribution is uncertain"; and

[3] where the President acts in *contradiction* to the express or implied will of Congress; in this case, his power is *"at its lowest ebb."* Jackson felt that the steel seizure fell into this third category, and that it could therefore not be constitutionally justified.

   c. **Dissent:** Three Justices dissented in *Youngstown Sheet & Tube*. They contended that temporary seizure was justified because of the emergency nature of the situation, and in order to preserve temporarily the *status quo* until Congress could act.

3. **Implied acquiescence by Congress:** Congress may sometimes be found to have *impliedly acquiesced* in the President's exercise of power in a certain area. Where such acquiescence exists, this fact may be enough to tip the balance in favor of a finding that the President acted within the scope of his constitutional authority.

   a. ***Dames & Moore* case:** The Court relied on such a theory of implied congressional acquiescence when it upheld President Carter's power to take certain actions for the purpose of obtaining the release of American hostages from Iran, in ***Dames & Moore v. Regan***, 453 U.S. 654 (1981).

      i. **Facts:** As part of the settlement of the hostage situation, President Carter took a number of actions affecting the claims of American creditors against Iran. The action which posed the most difficult constitutional issue was his *suspension* of all contractual claims against Iran then pending in American courts; such claims were to be later arbitrated by an international tribunal.

      ii. **Suspension upheld:** The Court found that the claims suspension was *within* the President's constitutional authority. While Congress had never explicitly delegated to the President the power to suspend such claims, it had *implicitly authorized* that practice by a long history of *acquiescing* in similar presidential conduct. (For instance, Congress had implicitly approved the use of executive agreements between the President and foreign powers to *settle* claims.)

      iii. **Not dispositive:** In any event, the fact that Congress has impliedly consented to Presidential action will almost certainly not *by itself* bring the action within the scope of his constitutional authority; it will merely be a *factor* in the analysis of close cases. In *Dames & Moore*, the President's general executive authority in foreign policy matters (and perhaps his Commander-in-Chief powers) were probably also part of the equation.

C. President's veto power: Article I, §7, gives the President the power to *veto* any bill passed by Congress. If the measure is vetoed, the veto can be overridden (and the measure enacted into law) only by a *two-thirds vote* in each house. There are several major separation-of-powers issues concerning the presidential veto power: (1) To what extent does the President have the ability to make a "pocket veto"? (2) Can the President constitutionally be given a "line-item veto"? and (3) To what extent does the so-called "legislative veto" violate the President's veto power?

1. **The "pocket veto":** Article I, §7 provides that ordinarily, if the President fails within ten days either to sign a bill or to veto it and return it to the house in which it originated (so that a possible override attempt can be made), the bill becomes law. However, that section also provides that if Congress by its *adjournment* has *prevented* return of the vetoed legislation, the statute cannot go into effect unless the President signs it. In this situation, the President is given an *absolute* veto power (i.e., one which cannot be overridden); this is known as a *"pocket veto."*

2. **The "line item" veto:** Nearly every President since Grant has coveted the *"line item veto."* This is the ability to *veto a particular part of a bill* — typically, a *single item of spending* — rather than the entire bill. In 1997, President Clinton became the first U.S. President to receive essentially this power from Congress. However, the Supreme Court quickly ruled that the line item veto as implemented by Congress violated the Presentment clause of the Constitution, in *Clinton v. City of New York*, 524 U.S. 417 (1998).

   a. **How the line-item veto worked:** The Line Item Veto Act gave the President the power to *"cancel"* any of several types of provisions contained in new statutes enacted by Congress, including any "item of new direct spending" and any "limited tax benefit." The Act allowed the President to sign an entire multiple-provision bill into law, and then to "cancel" any individual spending or limited-tax-benefit item he wished, if that he did so within five days after enactment. The only way Congress could then restore the vetoed item was to re-enact it as a separate "disapproval bill," which the President could again veto.

   b. **Majority strikes down:** By a 6-3 vote, the court found that the Line Item Veto Act *violated the Presentment clause,* Art. I, §7, cl. 2. The majority opinion was by Justice Stevens.

      i. **The Presentment clause:** The Presentment clause provides that after a bill has passed both houses of Congress, but before it has become a law, *it must be presented to the President*; if he approves it, "he shall sign it, but if not he shall return it, with his objections to that house in which it shall have originated, who shall . . . proceed to reconsider it." (The President's "return" of the bill is what is commonly known as a *presidential "veto."*)

      ii. **Violates Presentment clause:** The majority concluded that the Line Item Veto Act failed to follow the Presentment clause's method of enacting or repealing statutes. The process laid down in that clause was, the majority concluded, the *only* way authorized in the Constitution to enact or repeal a bill. The Act failed to follow this procedure in at least two ways: (1) the President's "return" of the bill (his veto of it) occurred *after* the bill had been signed into law, rather than before, as the Presentment clause requires; and (2) the cancellation could apply to only *part* of the bill, whereas the Presentment clause requires veto of the *entire* bill.

   c. **Dissent:** Three Justices — Breyer, O'Connor and Scalia — dissented in *Clinton v. New York*. The dissenters rejected the majority's core assertion that the Line Item Veto Act enabled the President to repeal or amend statutes. The President's use of his power to cancel a spending item was *not a repeal or amendment of a statute*, they said — the statute itself would remain fully in force following the President's "cancellation" action. Instead, Congress had merely given the President the *discretion to spend or* *not spend an appropriated item*, something it had done many times in the past without problems.

3. **The legislative veto:** The so-called "*legislative veto*" is a device which enables Congress to monitor actions by the Executive Branch, including federal administrative agencies. Typically, such a legislative veto provision is included as part of a congressional statute delegating certain powers to federal agencies. If, after an agency takes a certain action (usually, issuance of a regulation), Congress disagrees, the veto provision in the original bill allows one or both houses to cancel that administrative action by means of a *resolution*. The resolution is not presented to the President (as a statute must be), and he does not receive the opportunity to veto it.

   a. **Veto ruled unconstitutional:** In one of the most important constitutional law decisions of the 1980's, the Supreme Court held that a typical one-house legislative veto was **unconstitutional**, because it violated both the President's veto power and the bicameral structure of Congress. *Immigration and Naturalization Service (INS) v. Chadha*, 462 U.S. 919 (1983).

      i. **Facts:** Article I, §8 of the Constitution gives Congress the right to establish rules of naturalization and, by implication, immigration. Congress has always possessed, and has frequently exercised, the power to allow an alien who would otherwise be deportable under existing immigration rules to remain in the country; typically, this has been done by means of a *"private bill"* applicable to one or a few particular aliens.

         (1) **Congress' solution:** In an effort to relieve itself of the burdens of considering numerous private bills, Congress delegated to the Attorney General, in the Immigration and Nationality Act, the authority to suspend deportation of aliens in certain situations. However, in order to retain some control over this delegated power, Congress reserved to itself a legislative veto over each decision by the Attorney General suspending deportation. The veto could be exercised by a resolution passed by *either* house within a certain time after the Attorney General's decision to suspend deportation. Chadha, the plaintiff, was one of several aliens as to whom the House of Representatives used its veto power to reverse the Attorney General's suspension of deportation.

      ii. **Veto provision stricken:** The Supreme Court *struck down* this legislative veto as a violation of two distinct constitutional requirements. First, the veto violated the *Presentment Clause* (Art. I, §7, cl. 2), which requires that every bill be presented to the President for his signature, so that he may have the opportunity to veto it. Secondly, this particular veto provision, since it could be exercised by a *single house*, violated the *bicameral* requirement of Article I, §§1 and 7, by which both houses must pass a bill before it can become law.

      iii. **Essentially legislative act:** The real issue in the case was whether the House's issuance of the legislative veto here itself constituted the exercise of *legislative power*. Not all acts by a house fall into this category, and only the ones that do, require presentment and bicameral approval. However, in the Court's view the overruling of the Attorney General's decision on a deportation matter did constitute the exercise of legislative power, since it had the "purpose and effect of *alter-*

ing the legal rights, duties and relations of persons … outside the legislative branch."

iv. **Consequence:**   Consequently, Congress could reverse the Attorney General's decision on a deportation matter only by *passing a law*, in the constitutionally-pre-scribed manner (passage by both houses, presentment to the President and either signature by him or the overriding of his veto). The fact that the legislative veto mechanism may be a more "efficient" means of controlling administrative action was irrelevant.

b. **Dissent:**   Two Justices, White and Rehnquist, dissented in *Chadha*. The main dissent was by Justice White, who argued that a house's use of the legislative veto was simply not the functional equivalent of passing a law. The legislative veto "no more allows one House of Congress to make law than does the presidential veto confer such power upon the President."

c. **Significance:**   *Chadha* thus makes the one-house legislative veto completely unus-able. If the House or Senate wants to reserve power to *undo the action of an adminis-trative agency*, both houses will have to pass the same bill and present it to the President for a possible veto.

d. **Two-house veto provisions:**   In the vast majority of instances, legislative veto clauses allowing a veto only where *both houses* act concurrently are *just as unconsti-tutional* as a single-house veto provision, since both types of clauses *deprive the Pres-ident of his veto power*.

II.   THE PROHIBITION OF EXCESSIVE DELEGATION BY CONGRESS TO THE EXECUTIVE BRANCH

A. **The problem generally:**   Article I, § 1, of the Constitution vests all of the *"legislative pow-ers"* enumerated in the Constitution to Congress. But during the last century or so, Congress has increasingly *delegated* its legislative power to *administrative agencies*, most of which are part of the Executive Branch. Chemerinsky Csbk (6e), p. 292. And some instances of this del-egation by Congress have been *so broad* that they could conceivably be found to violate Arti-cle I's grant of *exclusive* legislative power to that branch.

1. **Rise of federal agencies:**   In fact, the powers now exercised by federal agencies often go beyond the purely legislative. Thus major federal agencies like the Securities and Exchange Commission (SEC), the Environmental Protection Agency (EPA) and the Fed-eral Communications Commission (FCC) now exercise *"all of the powers of government: legislative, executive, and judicial." Id*. That is:

   [1] **Legislative power:** The agencies have *legislative power*, because Congress has given them "the authority to *promulgate rules* that have the force of law." *Id.*

   [2] **Executive power:** The agencies have *executive power*, because "they are respon-sible *for bringing enforcement actions* against those who violate the relevant fed-eral laws and regulations." *Id.*

   [3] **Judicial power:** Lastly, they often have *judicial power*, because "they *employ administrative law judges who hear cases brought by agency officials* against

those accused of violating the agencies regulation." *Id.*

2. **Constitutional issue:** But the Constitution does not even *mention* administrative agencies, which barely existed when the Constitution was written in 1787. So the question arises, Should the Constitution, including its concept of separation of powers, be interpreted to *place limits* on the extent to which federal agencies may exercise the three forms of federal power discussed above? The most serious aspect of this question – and the one we'll be concerned with here – is, What limits, if any, are there on the extent to which Congress may properly delegate *its legislative powers to the Executive Branch*, including to federal agencies that are effectively part of that branch?

3. **Practical need for broad agency powers:** Before we take a detailed look at this question, consider this: If the Supreme Court were to significantly limit Congress' authority to make *broad delegations* of its legislative powers to federal agencies, *the modern "administrative state" might become impossible.* As the Court has said, "[I]n our increasingly complex society, ... Congress *simply cannot do its job* absent an ability to *delegate power under broad general directives.*" *Mistretta v. U.S.*, 488 U.S. 361 (1989).

B. **Broad delegation always accepted in the modern era:** Because of the need for administrative agencies to help regulate the complexities of modern American life, the Court has, for over 80 years, placed *"very few, if any, constitutional restraints* on Congress's power to delegate." S,S,S,T&K (8e), p. 434. In fact, since 1936, *"[N]ot a single federal law has been declared an impermissible delegation of legislative power* by the Supreme Court." Chemerinsky Csbk (6e), p. 295.

1. **The nondelegation doctrine:** But prior to 1936, the Court took a different view, under which what the Court considered to be unguided instances of delegation by Congress were occasionally found to violate Article I's grant of exclusive legislative power to that body. In this pre-1936 period, the Court announced what is sometimes called the *"nondelegation doctrine,"* which says that Congress may not delegate its legislative powers to another branch without providing adequate guidance on how the power is to be exercised.

a. *Schechter Poultry* **case:** Thus in a 1935 decision, the Court struck down a delegation of power to the Executive Branch, reasoning that "Congress is not permitted to *abdicate or to transfer to others the essential legislative function* with which it is thus vested[.]" *Schechter Poultry Corp. v. U.S.*, 295 U.S. 495 (1935).[1]

   i. **Facts:** In *Schechter Poultry*, Congress passed a statute, the National Industrial Recovery Act (NIRA), that purported to give the President the authority to approve and enforce certain *codes of "fair competition"* drawn up by various industry groups.

   ii. **Delegation struck down:** The Court *struck down* on excessive-delegation grounds the portion of the NIRA (§ 3) that authorized these industry codes. Section 3, the Court said, did not *supply any actual standards* for any industry. The provision merely said that the codes must *pursue the general aims* of industry rehabilitation and expansion. The delegation of code-promulgation to the President was thus *"virtually unfettered,"* making the delegation "utterly inconsistent with the constitutional prerogatives and duties of Congress."

---

1. The separate Commerce Clause aspect of this case is discussed *supra*, p. 25.

2. **Requirement of an "intelligible principle":** The Court's test for measuring whether a delegation is constitutional has in theory **remained in force** since the *Schechter* era. That test is the so-called ***"intelligible principle" test***: the delegation is constitutional if, but only if, Congress has "la[id] down … an ***intelligible principle*** to which the person or body authorized [to take action] is ***directed to conform***[.]" *J. W. Hampton, Jr. & Co., v. U.S.*, 276 U.S. 394 (1928).

C. **Possible rise of greater limits on delegation (*Gundy*):** It remains the case, as of this writing (November 2021), that no congressional grant of legislative authority to the Executive Branch has been struck down by the Supreme Court on excessive-delegation grounds since 1935. But a 2019 case shows that the Supreme Court may well be on the verge of ending its uncritical acceptance of all delegations by Congress, and ***putting real bite*** back into the nondelegation doctrine. In that case, ***Gundy v. U.S.***, 139 S.Ct. 2116 (2019), the Court, by a 5-3 vote, reached the standard modern-era conclusion that no unconstitutional delegation had occurred. But there was ***no majority opinion,*** just a four-justice plurality[2] concluding that the delegation here was not unconstitutional.

1. **Facts and issue:** The detailed facts of *Gundy* are not worth going into here, but here's a brief summary. Congress passed a statute — the Sex Offender Registration and Notification Act (SORNA) — requiring sex offenders to register with their local communities. The issue was whether Congress had delegated too broadly when it delegated to the U.S. Attorney General (part of the Executive Branch, of course) the power to ***draft rules*** governing whether, when and how certain of these offenders were required to register under SORNA.

2. **Kagan's plurality view:** Justice Kagan, writing for the four-justice plurality, said that Congress had given adequate guidance to the Attorney General. She said that if SORNA's delegation was unconstitutional, then ***"most of Government is unconstitutional*** — dependent as Congress is on the ***need to give discretion to executive officials*** to ***implement its programs."***

   a. **Ginsburg replaced:** Since *Gundy*, Justice Ginsburg, one of the four in the plurality, has been replaced by Justice Barrett; I discuss the implications of this switch below.

3. **Dissent by 3 members:** Justice Gorsuch (joined by Roberts and Thomas) ***dissented*** in *Gundy*. The dissent argued that the ***"intelligible principle" test*** (*supra*, p. 118), as it had been applied by the Court in recent decades, "has ***no basis in the original meaning*** of the Constitution [or] in history[.]" Gorsuch thought that the Court should be asking "Did Congress, and not the Executive Branch, ***make the policy judgments?"*** Only if the answer was ***yes*** (which was not the case in SORNA, he said) "can we fairly say that a statute contains the ***kind of intelligible principle the Constitution demands."***

   a. **Possible rejection of modern approach:** Justice Alito indicated in a concurrence in *Gundy* that he, too, was dissatisfied with the modern loose approach. Neither Justices Kavanaugh nor Barrett took part in *Gundy*; there are indications that neither likes the modern loose approach. Therefore, there's a good chance that five or six members of the present Court (the three dissenters in *Gundy* plus Alito, Kavanaugh and/or Barrett)

---

2. Justice Alito, concurring, contributed the fifth vote for the proposition that no unconstitutional delegation should be found to have occurred if the modern approach to delegation was used. But as we'll see in a moment, he said he was dissatisfied with that approach.

are now ready to *reject the modern approach,* and require Congress to *give far more guidance* to the Executive Branch when delegating legislative (rule-making) powers.

III. FOREIGN AFFAIRS AND THE WAR POWERS

A. Special presidential role in foreign affairs: The Constitution gives the President substantially greater authority with respect to *foreign affairs* than with respect to domestic ones. Article II, §2, explicitly enumerates a number of powers given to him in this area (e.g., the Commander-in-Chief power, the treaty-making power and the right to appoint ambassadors). But even more generally, the need to present a clear and unified face to the world dictates that the President bear a special role in implementing the nation's foreign policy.

1. ***Curtiss-Wright* case:** This special role was emphasized in **U.S. v. Curtiss-Wright Export Corp.**, 299 U.S. 304 (1936). In *Curtiss-Wright*, a joint resolution of Congress authorized the President to *ban the sale of arms to countries engaged in a particular conflict.* President Roosevelt proclaimed such an embargo, and Curtiss-Wright was charged with conspiring to sell arms to Bolivia, one of the countries to which the embargo extended. Curtiss-Wright challenged the joint resolution as being an unconstitutionally broad *delegation* of legislative power to the President.

   a. **Upheld by Supreme Court:** The Supreme Court *upheld* the resolution, and the resulting presidential embargo. The Court stressed the "very delicate, plenary and exclusive power of the President as the sole organ of the federal government in the field of international relations. ... " The need for negotiation, plus the President's special access to sources of information, required "a degree of discretion and freedom from statutory restriction which would not be admissible were domestic affairs alone involved." Here, for instance, the President would be better able than Congress to determine whether Bolivia was in fact engaged in the conflict. Thus the delegation to the President was not unconstitutionally broad, regardless of whether such delegation would be permissible with respect to a domestic issue (a question which the Court did not decide).

   b. **In accord with Congress' intent:** Observe that the presidential embargo in *Curtiss-Wright* was *in accord with congressional intent*; in fact, the very point of the defendant's argument was that there was excessive *harmony* between Congress and the President (i.e., excessive delegation). If, however, the President acted in an area where Congress had been *silent*, or where Congress had manifested a *contrary intent*, the President's power to make international policy would presumably be less broad. This is certainly the theory behind Justice Jackson's concurrence in the *Youngstown Sheet & Tube* case (*supra*, pp. 112-113).

   c. **Delegation problems generally:** The *Curtiss-Wright* case was really about the proper limits of delegation of power by Congress to the President. A full discussion of delegation doctrine is more properly made in the course on Administrative Law. However, the following general propositions can be stated:

      i. **International vs. domestic:** Broader delegation of lawmaking power by Congress to the President will be tolerated in the area of international affairs than in the domestic area; this is the explicit holding of *Curtiss-Wright*; and

ii. Delegation rules relaxed: Even in the domestic area, the limits on delegation by Congress to the President or to administrative agencies have been substantially relaxed since the late 1930's. In general, the more precise the *standards* laid down by Congress to guide the Executive Branch or administrative agencies, the less likely it is that excessive delegation will be found.

2. Executive agreements: Recall that by Article II, §2, the President may enter into treaties only upon a two-thirds vote of the Senate. Presidents have often used the device of the *"executive agreement"* to avoid the need for Senate ratification. This device presents some separation-of-powers difficulties, which are discussed briefly *supra*, p. 69.

3. Recognition of foreign governments (the *Zivitofsky* case): One aspect of the President's special authority regarding foreign affairs is that the President holds the *sole power* to *recognize foreign governments.* The Court so held in a conflict between Congress and President Obama touching on whether Jerusalem should be considered part of Israel. In that case, ***Zivotofsky v. Kerry***, 135 S.Ct. 2076 (2015), the Court held that Congress acted unconstitutionally when it attempted to require the State Department to give any American citizen born in Jerusalem the right to have the Department list "Israel" as the citizen's birthplace.

a. Facts: In 2002, Congress passed a law, which we'll call "§214(d)," instructing the State Department to list a U.S. citizen's "place of birth" as "Israel" in passports, if the person was born in Jerusalem and he or his guardian requested this designation. The legislative history of §214(d) made it clear that the statute was an attempt by Congress to take a pro-Israel stand on the hotly-contested issue of whether Israel should be viewed as having sovereignty over Jerusalem, as it has long contended. The two Presidents who served during the years between passage of the law and the Court's decision — Bush and Obama — both ordered the State Department to refuse to honor such requests, on the grounds that the law interfered with the President's constitutional authority to conduct the nation's foreign affairs.

b. President wins: By a 6-3 vote, the Court held §214(d) to be an unconstitutional infringement by Congress of the President's exclusive power to choose whether to recognize a foreign government. The opinion was by Justice Kennedy,[3] who reasoned as follows:

i. Power of recognition: First, Kennedy said, the Constitution implicitly gives the President the power of *"recognition,"* i.e., the power to *say which regime is the effective government of a foreign state.* It's true that the Constitution does not expressly mention "recognition" as a Presidential power. But other powers expressly given to the President in Article II — like the power to "receive Ambassadors and other public Ministers," to nominate American ambassadors (though subject to Senate confirmation), and to negotiate treaties (though again subject to Senate approval) — make it a "logical and proper conference," Kennedy said, that the President has the "power to recognize other nations."

---

3. Only four other judges — the liberal bloc of Ginsburg, Breyer, Kagan and Sotomayor — joined Kennedy's reasoning. The sixth vote came from Justice Thomas, who concurred in the result, but under a slightly different rationale.

ii. Rationale: Furthermore, Kennedy wrote, "the Nation must have a *single policy* regarding which governments are legitimate in the eyes of the United States and which are not ... Recognition is a topic on which the Nation must *'speak ... with one voice.'* That voice *must be the President's."*

c. Dissent: There were two dissenting opinions in *Zivitofsky*, by Chief Justice Roberts and Justice Scalia (each of which was joined by Alito). The dissenters thought that the drafters of the Constitution probably intended the recognition power to be *shared* between the President and Congress, not to be the President's exclusively. But in any event, the dissenters were confident that §214(d) *did not abridge* whatever recognition power the President possessed.

B. The war powers: The Constitution gives both Congress and the President special powers with respect to *war*:

❑ *Congress* is given the power to "*declare War* ... and make Rules concerning *Captures on Land and Water."* Art. I, § 8, cl. 11. Congress is also given the power to "*raise and support Armies*" (*id.*, cl. 12); to "define and punish ... Offences against the Law of Nations," (*id.*, cl. 10), and to "make Rules for the Government and Regulation of the *land and naval Forces*" (*id.*, cl. 14).

❑ On the other hand, the *President* is made the "*Commander in Chief*" of the *armed forces.* Art. II, § 2, cl. 1. (Also, more generally, "the *executive Power*" is "vested" in the President. Id., § 1.)

So the basic idea is that Congress declares war and maintains the armed forces, but the President, by use of his Commander-in-Chief power executive powers, carries out any war that is so declared.

We consider here two areas in which the division of war powers between Congress and the President has raised important separation-of-powers questions: (1) the President's right to *commit our armed forces abroad* without congressional approval; and (2) the President's right to *detain and try enemy combatants* who have been captured.

1. Commitment of the armed forces abroad: The extent to which the President may use his Commander-in-Chief powers to *commit the use of American armed forces abroad*, without a congressional declaration of war, has sparked great controversy during the last two decades.

a. Courts silent: Although the President has committed American armed forces to military action without a declaration of war at numerous times during our history, the courts have rarely passed on the constitutionality of such action. Generally, Congress has tacitly acquiesced in such action, so that no litigation has arisen.

b. Sudden attack: It is settled that the President may commit our armed forces to *repel a sudden attack* upon the United States itself.

c. Attack on allies: It is not clear whether the President may commit forces, without congressional approval, where it is an *ally* of the U.S., rather than the U.S. itself, that is attacked.

d. Preemptive strike: Similarly, the President's right to order a *preemptive strike* in anticipation of an enemy attack is unclear. Since in this situation there would probably not be time for Congress to consider the wisdom of military action, a presidentially-ordered preemptive strike would be likely to be found constitutional.

e. **Delegation by Congress:** Congress sometimes *delegates* to the President in advance the discretion to commit the armed forces. The best known example of this is the Gulf of Tonkin Resolution, enacted by Congress in 1964 during the early stages of the Vietnam War. The Resolution stated that "[t]he United States is … prepared, *as the President determines*, to take all necessary steps, including the use of armed force, to assist any member or protocol state" of SEATO.

   i. **Possibly overbroad delegation:** But such a vague delegation of Congress' war-making powers is arguably *unconstitutionally broad.*

2. **Habeas corpus, and the rights of enemy combatants to it (*Boumediene*):** The post-9/11 war on terror has caused the Supreme Court to focus on the separation-of-powers implications of the *"writ of habeas corpus."* As we'll see below (p. 123), in a 2008 case, *Boumediene v. Bush*, the Court, relying on separation-of-powers principles, concluded that non-citizens detained as enemy combatants at Guantanamo Bay, Cuba, had the constitutional right to use the habeas process to challenge in federal district court the lawfulness of their imprisonment.

   a. **Nature of the habeas writ:** For centuries, Anglo-American law has generally entitled prisoners to use the "writ of habeas corpus." In American law, the right of habeas corpus is basically the right of a state or federal prisoner to go to a federal district court and argue that the prisoner is being held in violation of the federal Constitution or federal law. "Habeas corpus" is Latin for "You have the body," and the idea is that the prisoner can force the "jailer" (i.e., the governmental body that is imprisoning the prisoner) to *justify* to the federal judge hearing the habeas petition *why the imprisonment is proper.*

      i. **Suspension Clause:** The right to bring a habeas corpus petition is granted by the Constitution. This occurs by means of Art. I, § 9, cl. 2 (the *"Suspension Clause"*), which says that "The privilege of the Writ of Habeas Corpus shall not be suspended, unless when in Cases of Rebellion or Invasion the public Safety may require it." Under post-Civil War Supreme Court cases, the right applies to *both state and federal prisoners.*

      ii. **Federal judge can order release:** If a prisoner properly brings a habeas proceeding, the federal judge is authorized to conduct her own factual inquiry into the case. Then, if the judge concludes that the prisoner is indeed being held in violation of the federal Constitution or federal law, the judge has the power to order the prisoner released.

   b. **Applicability to enemy combatants:** Prior to 9/11, it had never been clear whether a *non-U.S. citizen* held by U.S. military authorities as an enemy combatant was entitled to bring a federal habeas corpus proceeding, in which the prisoner could have a federal district judge review the legality of his detention.

      i. **Combatant Status Review Tribunals:** Beginning soon after 9/11, the U.S. military detained hundreds of non-U.S. citizens (aliens) in combat areas like Afghanistan and Bosnia. U.S. forces designated many of these as *"enemy combatants,"* and brought them to the U.S. base at Guantanamo Bay, Cuba, where they were held, sometimes for years. At Guantanamo, the Defense Department conducts *Combatant Status Review Tribunals (CSRTs)* to determine whether each detainee was properly classified as an enemy combatant. In the CSRTs, detainees have limited rights compared with the rights they would have if subjected to a traditional U.S. criminal trial — for instance, they do not have the right to counsel, they do not have the right to full knowledge of the charges against them, and hearsay evidence is fully admissible against them.

ii. **Congress agrees:** In two post-9/11 statutes, Congress agreed with the George W. Bush administration's view that enemy combatants held at Guantanamo should not have habeas rights.

(1) **The DTA:** First, in the Detainee Treatment Act of 2005 (*DTA*), Congress said that no court would have jurisdiction to hear an application for habeas corpus brought by any alien detained by the military at Guantanamo. Instead, the sole jurisdiction given power to review (not by habeas corpus) any decision by a CSRT that a prisoner was indeed an enemy combatant was the federal Court of Appeals for the District of Columbia. And the D.C. Court of Appeals was *limited in the facts that it could consider* on the appeal — for instance, it *could not consider newly-discovered evidence* that the prisoner was not in fact an enemy combatant, as the court could presumably have done in a true habeas proceeding.

(2) **The MCA:** Then, in the Military Commissions Act of 2006 (*MCA*), Congress said that these jurisdiction-stripping provisions of the DTA were to be applied not just prospectively, but also to cases that were already "in the pipeline" when the DTA was enacted.

c. **The *Boumediene* case:** Several Guantanamo prisoners were able to get to the Supreme Court on two issues regarding the DTA's and MCA's jurisdiction-stripping rules: (1) Did a foreign national held at Guantanamo — which is not officially U.S. territory — have the constitutional right to bring a habeas petition? and (2) if so, did the procedures specified by Congress in the DTA and the MCA violate the prisoners' habeas rights? In *Boumediene v. Bush*, 128 S.Ct. 2229 (2008), by a 5-4 vote, the Court answered *"yes"* to both of these questions. Consequently, all prisoners held as enemy combatants at Guantanamo — and probably held at other foreign military bases that are under the full control of U.S. authorities — *have the right to challenge the legality of their detention in federal district court.*

i. **Majority opinion:** Justice Kennedy allied with the four liberal members of the court (Stevens, Souter, Breyer and Ginsburg) to form a majority that found for the prisoners. Kennedy's majority opinion concluded that the MCA's stripping of federal-court jurisdiction over cases brought by foreign nationals detained at Guantánamo *violated the Suspension Clause.* To reach that conclusion, he took several steps:

(1) **"No sovereignty over the territory" argument:** The Bush administration argued that because Guantanamo is not officially U.S. territory (it's leased from Cuba), the constitutional right of habeas does not extend to detentions there. But Kennedy concluded that, since the U.S. has "complete jurisdiction

and control over the base," the country ***"maintains de facto sovereignty*** over this territory." He continued, "in every practical sense Guantanamo is ***not abroad***; it is within the ***constant jurisdiction*** of the United States"; therefore, ***habeas rights apply as if the prison were on U.S. soil.***

    (2) Not a substitute: Kennedy then addressed the issue of whether the procedures here violated the Suspension Clause. For there not to be a violation, the federal court review of the results of the CSRT proceeding would have to represent an adequate substitute for habeas corpus. But under the DTA, the reviewing court (the D.C. Court of Appeals) was ***not permitted to consider any evidence outside the CSRT record*** (e.g., ***newly-discovered*** evidence). This lack of authority to consider anything beyond the CSRT record meant that the D.C. Circuit review was ***not an "adequate substitute"*** for habeas corpus, making the review procedures a violation of the Suspension Clause.

C. National security and entry into the U.S.: Article I, § 8 of the Constitution gives Congress the power "to establish an uniform Rule of ***Naturalization.***"[4] The Constitution does not expressly mention two related areas: (1) ***immigration*** and (2) the ***national security*** implications of allowing foreigners to enter the U.S. as non-immigrants (e.g., on temporary visas such as student and work visas). But the Supreme Court, partly in reliance on the Constitution's explicit grant to Congress of the power over naturalization, has long given significant ***deference*** to ***Congress and the Executive Branch*** in these areas of ***immigration*** and ***entry of foreigners.***

    1. Deference to Congress and the Executive Branch: In particular, the Court has held that:

        [1] When Congress acts in these two areas, the Court should be quick to conclude that Congress has intended that federal law ***preempt the entire field,*** thereby ***displacing state law;***[5] and

        [2] Also in these two areas, the Constitution implicitly grants primary federal authority to the ***two "political branches"*** (Congress and the Executive Branch), so that the Judicial Branch should give ***extra deference*** to these branches when deciding constitutional issues.[6]

    2. The travel ban case (*Trump v. Hawaii*): A 2018 decision dramatically illustrates the great deference the Court will give to Congress' and the President's judgment in matters relating to foreigners' entry to the U.S. In ***Trump v. Hawaii***, 128 S.Ct. 2392 (2018), the Court ***upheld*** by a 5-4 vote President Trump's ***"travel ban,"*** an executive order restricting

---

4. "Naturalization" refers to the process by which a person who is not a U.S. citizen gains citizenship.

5. See, e.g., *Hines v. Davidowitz*, *supra*, p. 93, where the Court held that the federal government's special role in immigration and foreign relations, when coupled with Congress' decision to enact a comprehensive system for alien registration, made it clear that Congress intended to displace any *state* requirement that aliens register.

6. See, e.g., *Fiallo v. Bell*, 430 U.S. 787 (1977), saying that admission and exclusion of foreign nationals is a "fundamental sovereign attribute exercised by the Government's political departments largely immune from judicial control." As we'll see (*infra*, p. 125), the Court cited this passage approvingly in *Trump v. Hawaii*, discussed immediately below.

entry to the U.S. by citizens of eight countries, most of which were majority-Muslim. The Court applied the easy-to-satisfy *"mere-rationality"* standard to review the measure, in contrast to the much stricter standard it would probably use in reviewing a comparable domestic measure.

a. **The travel ban:** The ban was a presidential Proclamation greatly *restricting entry into the U.S.* by nationals of eight countries, six of which had majority-majority populations.[7]

b. **The challenge:** The Proclamation was challenged by the state of Hawaii and several Hawaiian citizens affected by it. The plaintiffs sought a preliminary injunction on the grounds that the Proclamation violated both (1) federal statutory provisions, including one prohibiting race and religious discrimination in the issuance of visas and (2) the First Amendment Establishment Clause's prohibition on religious discrimination.

   i. **Plaintiffs win below:** The district court found in favor of the plaintiffs, and enjoined the federal government from putting the injunction into effect; the Ninth Circuit affirmed.

c. **Special role for Congress and the Executive Branch:** But at the Supreme Court, a majority of the Court saw things differently: five Justices voted to dissolve the injunction, after concluding that once a trial on the merits was held, the Proclamation would likely be found to be both authorized by statute and *constitutional*.

   In reaching this conclusion, the majority relied heavily on the *special role given by the Constitution to the President and Congress* in matters relating to *foreign policy, national security, and immigration*. In an opinion by Chief Justice Roberts, the majority said that "the admission and exclusion of foreign nationals is a *'fundamental sovereign attribute* exercised by the Government's *political departments* [i.e., Congress and the Executive Branch], *largely immune from judicial control.'*" (quoting the earlier case of *Fiallo v. Bell*, 430 U.S. 787 (1977)).

   i. **Relations with foreign powers:** This relative immunity from judicial scrutiny is appropriate, Roberts said, because such decisions regarding admission of foreigners often *"implicate relations with foreign powers[.]"* Furthermore, he said, tight judicial review of "matters of entry and national security" might "inhibit the *flexibility* of the President to *respond to changing world conditions*[.]"

   ii. **"Rational basis" review:** Roberts wrote that the deference due to the political branches required that the Court apply an easy-to-satisfy *"rational basis review"* to the Proclamation. That is, he said, the entry policy would be upheld so long as it was *"plausibly related to the Government's stated objective to protect the country and improve vetting processes."* And, he noted, "the Court *hardly ever strikes down* a policy as *illegitimate* under rational basis scrutiny."

d. **Policy passes the review:** Given Roberts' decision to apply the rational-basis standard, he found it easy to conclude that the entry policy passed muster. For more about Roberts' reasoning on this point, see *infra*, p. 685.

---

7. For more about the Proclamation, see our discussion of the Establishment Clause issue in the case, *infra*, p. 683.

    e. Significance: *Hawaii v. Trump* illustrates that in matters relating to ***national security***, including the screening of foreign nationals for entry into the country, the Court will grant ***extreme deference*** to the Executive Branch's assertion that it is acting for valid security reasons, not out of religious animus. Whereas in a domestic context the Court will strictly scrutinize government action for any hint of intent to discriminate against one religion or religions generally,[8] in the national-security context the Court will apparently apply the easy-to-satisfy rational-basis standard.

IV. APPOINTMENT AND REMOVAL OF EXECUTIVE PERSONNEL (INCLUDING IMPEACHMENT)

    A. The President's power of appointment, generally: An important aspect of how the Constitution implements the Separation of Powers is the way that document controls (1) ***who*** has power to appoint *"federal officers"* who are ***part of the Executive Branch***; and (2) the ***process*** by which such officers are to be appointed and/or replaced.

    These rules are laid out in the ***"Appointments" Clause***, Article II, §2. If we ignore the Clause's treatment of the power to make treaties, here's how the Clause reads:

> [The President] ... shall [1] ***nominate***, and by and with the ***Advice and Consent of the Senate***, shall ***appoint Ambassadors***, other ***public Ministers*** and Consuls, ***Judges*** of the supreme Court, and ***all other Officers of the United States***, whose Appointments are not herein otherwise provided for, and which shall be established by Law: but [2] ***the Congress may by Law*** vest the ***Appointment of such inferior Officers***, as they think proper, in ***the President alone, in the Courts of Law, or in the Heads of Departments.***

    (I have added the "[1]" and "[2]" markers, so that in our discussions below I can refer separately to each of these two main provisions.)

    1. Summary of the Clause: As we'll see in more detail below (in Par. B), the Appointments Clause is interpreted to ***create two different classes*** of "federal officers":

        ❏ **Top-level ("principal") officers:** Under what I've marked above as prong [1] of the Clause, ***top-level*** "officers of the United States" are ***appointed by the President, subject to Senate approval***; and

        ❏ **Inferior officers:** Under prong [2] of the Clause, *"inferior"* officers are to be appointed by ***whichever group*** (the President, the judicial branch or the "Heads of Departments") ***Congress specifies***.

    2. Congress can't appoint federal officers: A major consequence of the Appointments Clause is that ***Congress may not appoint "federal officers,"*** whether the officer is a "principal" one or an "inferior" one. See Par. E below.

    B. Distinguishing between "principal" and "inferior" officers: We'll discuss the dividing line between "principal" and "inferior" officers in greater detail in Par. D below.

    1. Two categories: But for now, here's a high-level overview of how the two categories are defined:

---

8. See, e.g., *Masterpiece Cakeshop*, *infra*, p. 691, for an example of rigorous scrutiny for anti-religious bias on the part of government.

a. **Who are "principal" officers:** *"Principal"* officers of the U.S. are people who *have no boss* except for the President. *Members of the Cabinet, heads* of *federal agencies,* federal *judges,* and *ambassadors* are the main examples of principal federal officers.

b. **Who are "inferior" officers:** All officers who are *not* "principal" officers of the U.S. are automatically *"inferior"* officers. Therefore, any officer who *has a boss other than the President* is an inferior officer. People *who work in federal agencies* but who are not the head of the agency are typically inferior officers, if they are officers at all. (As to the dividing line between "officers" and non-officers, see Par. F on p. 131.)

2. **How the two types differ:** A key reason why it's important to determine whether any given federal officer is a "principal" one or instead an "inferior" one is that the Appointments Clause makes the process for *appointing* the two types of officers dramatically different. Here's how the appointment process *differs* as between principal officers and inferior ones:

   a. **Appointing "principal" (top-level) officers:** In the case of *"principal"* officers of the United States (i.e., *top-level* officers), the *President nominates a candidate.* But the Appointments Clause says that the nomination cannot take effect until the Senate has given its *"Advice and Consent"* to (i.e., has *"confirmed"*) the nomination. That approval must be by an *ordinary majority* of those Senators voting.

      i. **Congress relatively powerless:** An important aspect of this system for appointing principal officers is that *Congress may not take away or limit* the President's power to appoint (i.e., nominate) a principal officer.

   b. **Appointing "inferior" (lower-level) officers:** In contrast to the President's absolute right to choose whom he wants to nominate as a principal officer, Congress *does* have the right to circumscribe the President's power to appoint *"inferior"* federal officers. The Appointments Clause specifies several methods for making these appointments. The portion of the Clause marked as prong [2] in Par. A on p. 126 *supra* says that "Congress may by Law vest the Appointment of such *inferior* Officers, as they think proper, in the *President alone,* in the *Courts of Law,* or in the *Heads of Departments.*" For more about these methods, see Par. C immediately below.

C. **Appointing "inferior "officers:** Let's look now in a bit more detail at the various ways an *inferior* officer can be appointed, according to the Appointments Clause.

1. **Limits on Congress:** First, Congress has *no* power of its own to appoint inferior officers, at least those who are to work in the Executive or Judicial branches. In other words, whereas the Senate can at least veto any Presidential appoinment of a principal officer (by refusing to "Advise and Consent" to the appointment), neither the House nor Senate has the power to appoint (or to veto the appointment of) an inferior Executive Branch officer.

2. **Three possible appointers:** But Congress *does* have a limited power to *choose the class of persons who are to appoint* any given type of inferior officer. This power comes from the final portion of the Appointments Clause:

   ". . . but Congress may by Law vest the Appointment of such *inferior* Officers, as they think proper, in the *President alone,* in the *Courts of Law*, or in the *Heads of Departments*."

Thus Congress has the right to choose, on a position-by-position basis, to confer the power of appointment on *any* of the following groups (but *only* on those groups):

[1] the *President*;

[2] members of the *federal judiciary*; or

[3] the *"heads of departments"* (e.g., Cabinet members).

Example 1: Congress creates the post of Deputy Secretary of State, and says that the person occupying this post must be appointed by the Secretary of State. There is no constitutional problem with this statute, since (1) the Secretary of State is a cabinet member and is thus automatically a "Head of Department"; and (2) the Deputy Secretary is an "inferior" federal officer, who Congress may therefore say (by authority of the final portion of the Appointments Clause) is to be appointed by the head of the department in which the Deputy will serve.

Example 2: Congress creates the post of *Assistant* Deputy Secretary of State, and specifies that the power to appoint a person to hold this post shall be held by the Deputy Secretary of State. This statute *is* a violation of the final portion of the Appointments Clause, assuming that the Assistant Deputy post is senior enough that the person who holds it exercises "significant authority."[9] Although Congress can limit the President's power to make appointment of an inferior federal officer, Congress must give this appointment power to one of the following: the President, member(s) of the federal judiciary, or a "Head of Department" (typically, a Cabinet member). The Deputy Secretary of State does not fall into any of these three categories, so Congress can't constitutionally grant her the power to appoint an inferior federal officer such as the Assistant Deputy.

D. **Dividing line between "principal" and "inferior" officers in more detail:** As we saw earlier, a "principal" officer of the U.S. is one who *has no "boss" except the President*; and any officer of the U.S. who has a boss other than the President is an "inferior" officer. But what exactly is the definition of a *"boss"* for these purposes? The Supreme Court has never given a precise definition that can be applied to all scenarios involving those who supervise U.S. Executive-Branch officers.

1. **"Administrative law judges" (the *Arthrex* case):** But there *is* one category of Executive-Branch officer as to which the Supreme Court *has* had occasion to analyze this "who is a boss?" issue: so-called *"administrative law judges,"* who are employed by various federal agencies to conduct "hearings" in specialized federally-regulated areas like patent law or the military criminal-justice system.

   A 2021 decision involving administrative judges in the *patent* area, *U.S. v. Arthrex*, 141 S.Ct. 1970 (June 21, 2021), contains the Court's most recent analysis of how the courts are to determine whether an administrative law judge does or doesn't have a boss other than the President.

   a. **Nature of "Administrative Patent Judges":** *Arthrex* required the Court to decide whether specialized *"Administrative Patent Judges"* ("APJs") are "principal" officers or instead "inferior" officers. The court decided that *APJs are principal officers.* To follow the Court's reasoning, you'll need some details about an APJ's duties.

---

9. See *infra*, p. *Buckley v. Valeo*, *infra*, p. 131, saying that the standard for determining whether a person is an inferior federal officer, as opposed to a rank-and-file federal employee who is not even an inferior officer, is whether the person holds "significant authority."

❏ **PTABs review patents for validity:** Patents are issued by a federal agency called the "Patent and Trademark Office" ("PTO"). After a patent has been issued by the PTO, the validity of the patent may be challenged by a third party before an "executive tribunal" within the PTO called a "Patent Trial and Appeal Board" (or "***PTAB***").

❏ **APJs:** When a PTAB hears a third-party challenge to a particular patent, the PTAB is a panel consisting of at least three members. Most often, the PTAB consist of APJs, of whom there are more than 200. APJs are appointed by the Secretary of Commerce (the cabinet officer who has responsibility for the PTO).

❏ **Director of the PTO:** The PTO is headed by a "***Director***," to whom Congress has given various supervisory powers. One of the Director's powers is the right to ***appoint the three members of the particular PTAB*** that is to hear a third-party challenge to a patent.

❏ **Not reviewable by the Executive Branch:** A third-party's challenge to a patent — brought before the PTAB — takes place in a "hearing" that is similar in most respects to a civil lawsuit. After the hearing, the PTAB issues a written decision. What's most important for understanding the *Arthrex* decision is that, according to the relevant statute by which Congress established the PTAB structure, ***neither*** the PTO's ***Director***, nor ***anyone else in the Executive Branch***, has the ***power to modify or cancel*** a PTAB decision.[10]

b. **How *Arthrex* arose:** A company named Arthrex, Inc. challenged the validity of another company's patent in a proceeding before a PTAB. The PTAB decided the challenge adversely to Arthrex. Arthrex then claimed on appeal that the manner in which the APJs on the PTAB had been appointed violated the Appointments Clause.

In brief, here was Arthrex's argument: (1) By function, the APJs were principal officers, who must therefore have been appointed by the President and approved by the Senate. (2) But Congress had misclassified the APJs, by providing that they could be appointed by a "Head of Department" (the Secretary of Commerce), thereby treating them as inferior officers. (3) Therefore, the APJs who formed the PTAB panel that decided Arthrex's challenge had not been constitutionally appointed.

c. **Court agrees:** By a 5-4 vote, the Court ***agreed with Arthrex***: the powers given by Congress to the APJs were sufficiently broad that the ***APJs were "principal officers"*** under the Appointments Clause. Therefore, their appointment by a cabinet head (the Secretary of Commerce) rather than by the President with Senate approval, ***was unconstitutional.*** The Court's opinion on this point was by Chief Justice Roberts.

i. **Rationale:** Prior case law had made it clear that officers who perform "adjudications" are inferior officers if and only if their ***decisions*** in adjudications are ***subject to "review by a superior executive officer."*** Here, under the structure set up by Congress, APJs had the "power to render a final decision," without any review by either their "nominal superior" (the Director of the PTO) nor any other "principal

---

10. The PTAB's decision can be appealed to a special federal Court of Appeals for the Federal Circuit. But no one in the *Executive Branch* can review the PTAB's decision, a fact that as we'll see means that the APJs making up a PTAB are principal officers of the U.S.

officer in the Executive Branch" (e.g., the Secretary of Commerce, who was the head of the "department" in which they worked). Therefore, the APJs were "principal" officers, who as such had to be appointed by the President.

ii. **Summary of rule:**   Therefore, Roberts wrote, in cases where a hearing officer — an "administrative law judge" of some sort — makes a decision following adjudications, the officer would be a ***"principal"*** officer if (and only if) the decision was ***"final"*** in the sense that it was ***not reviewable*** by any member of the Executive Branch. (That lack of reviewability is what made the APJs in *Arthrex* functionally principal officers who had to be appointed by the President and confirmed by the Senate.) If, however, Congress said that decisions by an administrative law judge ***would be reviewable/modifiable by an Executive Branch member*** — which is what happened in *Arthrex* and is actually the more common scenario in Executive Branch agencies today — then the judge would be an ***"inferior"*** officer, who could therefore legally be appointed by the ***head of the "department"*** in which the judge works. So, Roberts concluded, the statute by which Congress provided for the appointment and functions of APJs violated the Appointments Clause.

iii. **The remedy:**   By the way, the Court in *Arthrex* was badly split about the proper ***remedy*** for Congress' constitutional error in granting principal-type powers to APJs while not requiring these officers to be appointed by the President with Senate consent. A different 5-4 majority[11] decided that the appropriate remedy was to re-interpret the statute by which Congress set up the PTAB structure as ***not containing the provision forbidding the Director from reviewing PTAB decisions.*** This majority (still speaking through the opinion by Roberts) therefore ***remanded*** the case to the Director of the PTO,[12] with instructions that he decide whether to review the decision against Arthrex.

   (1) **Rationale:**   Since it was the power to issue non-reviewable decisions that made the APJs in *Arthrex* "principal" rather than "inferior" officers, the re-interpretation ***transformed them back into inferior officers***, who under the Appointments Clause could be validly appointed by a department head rather than by the President.

E. **No appointments by Congress:**   A key aspect of the Appointments Clause is that ***Congress itself may not make any appointments*** of federal officials, ***whether "principal" or "inferior."*** The most it may do (and only in the case of inferior officers) is to prescribe the ***procedures*** by which the President, department heads or members of the Judicial Branch shall make appointments. These "procedures" may, however, include fairly detailed ***qualifications*** regarding ***age***, ***experience***, etc. N&R, p. 272.

1. **Supporting employees appointable by Congress:**   On the other hand, Congress may ***make its own appointments*** of persons who ***will help Congress perform its "legislative" duties*** (as opposed to duties associated with the Executive or Judicial Branches). As the Supreme Court has put it, the Appointments Clause does not apply where Congress wants to designate people who will help Congress exercise "powers ... essentially of an ***investigative and informative*** nature." *Buckley v. Valeo*, discussed *infra*, p. 131.

---

11. Different, that is, from the majority that held that the APJs had the powers of principal officers.

12. The remand was actually to the "Acting Director" at this point.

Example: Suppose the Senate Banking Committee is considering reforming the nation's banking system. In that case, the Committee would have the power to appoint staff members to investigate possible changes that Congress might make to that system. Because these staff members will be working on what's essentially a "legislative" matter, the Appointments Clause doesn't apply, so Congress is free to appoint whomever it wishes, with no participation from the Judicial or Executive Branches.

F. Dividing line between "officer" and non-officer: Let's now examine another dividing line, the one between all federal "*officers*" (whether principal or inferior) on the one hand, and all non-officer "*employees*" of the federal government on the other.

1. **Why it matters:** Here's why this dividing line matters: *Mere "employees"* of the Executive Branch — i.e., workers who are *not powerful enough to qualify as at least "inferior officers"* — are *not required* to be appointed in compliance with the Appointments Clause at all. By contrast, "inferior officers" *are* required to be appointed in compliance with that Clause. Therefore, if an appointee *is* an "inferior officer of the U.S.," that person *may not be appointed by a federal employee* (or group of employees) who is *not* a Head of Department.

   Example: Recall Example 2 on p. 128: The issue there was whether Congress could say that an "Assistant Deputy Secretary of State" may be appointed by the "Deputy Secretary of State." Let's assume that the Assistant Deputy is given enough authority to be classified as an inferior federal officer rather than an ordinary federal employee. In that scenario, the Appointments Clause says that the Deputy Secretary of State cannot be given authority under to make the appointment — the only person in the State Department who could make this appointment is the "Head of [a] Department," i.e., the Secretary of State.

   Now, however, let's assume that our "Assistant Deputy Secretary of State" is given so little authority that she is properly classified as an *ordinary federal employee* rather than an "inferior federal officer." In this case, it's perfectly fine for Congress to allow the Deputy Secretary of State to appoint the Assistant Deputy. That's so because the Appointments Clause does not apply to the appointment of mere federal employees (i.e., those who are not "officers" of either type). Consequently, Congress may authorize anyone in the Executive Branch (not just a "Head of Department") to make this low-level appointment.

2. **"Significant authority" standard (*Buckley v. Valeo*):** So where is the *dividing line* between the least-powerful "*inferior officer*" and the most-powerful *non-officer employee*? The Supreme Court has given the following limited, semi-cryptic, guidance: federal "officers" (as opposed to mere federal "employees") are persons who *"exercise significant authority* pursuant to the laws of the United States." *Buckley v. Valeo*, 424 U.S. 1 (1976).

   a. **Facts of *Buckley*:** *Buckley* involved the constitutionality of the *Federal Election Commission* (the "FEC" or the "Commission"), which Congress set up when it enacted a statute called the Federal Election Campaign Act (the "FECA"). Congress provided that the Commision would have six members, of which four were to be appointed by members of Congress (two by the President *pro tem* of the Senate and two by the Speaker of the House). One issue in *Buckley* was whether the four members appointed by members of Congress were or weren't federal "officers." The Court's answer would depend on exactly what powers the Commission (and thus each Commissioner) had been given by Congress.

    i.   Wide powers: Congress gave the FEC broad powers to enforce the FECA, including (1) the power to ***bring civil actions against violators***; and (2) the power to ***enact administrative rules*** by which the Commission would administer the FECA.

b.   "Significant authority" test: The *Buckley* Court decided to use the "significant authority" standard to determine whether the Commissioners were federal officers. It then applied that standard to conclude that the Commissioners *were* federal officers. Here is the reasoning by which the Court did this:

[1] The powers (summarized in (a)(i) above) held by the Commissioners were ***"executive"*** (not "legislative") in nature.

[2] In performing those tasks, the Commissioners were inevitably exercising ***"significant authority"*** (of an executive nature), making the Commissioners "***officers*** of the U.S." rather than mere federal "employees."[13]

[3] As "officers of the U.S.," the Commissioners had to be appointed ***pursuant to the Appointments Clause.***

[4] ***Neither prong*** of the Appointments Clause[14] allows ***members of Congress*** to ***appoint officers of the U.S.*** Therefore, the four Commissioners who were purportedly appointed by members of Congress (two by the President *pro tem* of the Senate and two by the Speaker of the House) had ***not been constitutionally appointed***.

[5] Consequently, the Commission could not exercise any of these executive powers until Congress rewrote the FECA to ensure that all Commissioners would be appointed by a method that would satisfy the appropriate prong of the Appointments Clause.

c.   Applied to SEC administrative law judges (*Lucia v. SEC*): As we've just seen, *Buckley v. Valeo* establishes that the dividing line between an inferior "officer" of the U.S. on the one hand, and a mere federal "employee" on the other, is that the ***"officer"*** is a person who ***exercises "significant authority"*** (of an executive nature), and the "employee" is one who ***does not.***

Post-*Buckley*, the Court has never stated any broadly-applicable rule for determining when a person has "significant authority" sufficient to be at least an inferior federal officer rather than a mere federal employee. However, in a 2018 case, ***Lucia v. SEC***, 138 S.Ct. 2044 (2018), the Court, without giving a broadly-applicable definition, held that one category of federal employee — ***administrative law judges ("ALJs")*** working for the Securities and Exchange Commission (SEC) — definitely have "significant authority."

    i.   Must be appointed by the Commission: As we'll see in a moment, this conclusion in *Lucia* that SEC ALJs have significant authority meant that each ALJ is at least an inferior ***officer***, not a ***mere employee***. Therefore, the Appointments Clause controlled how each ALJ must be appointed: the ALJ ***had to be appointed by a "Department Head"*** (in this case, the Court treated the Commissioners voting as a

---

13. The Court didn't decide (because it didn't need to decide) whether the Commissioners were "principal" officers or "inferior" officers.

14. "Prong" refers to my markings "[1]" and "[2]" in the text of the Clause in Par. A on p. 126 *supra*.

body as being a Department Head), not by any non-Department Head working for the SEC.

    ii. Powers of SEC ALJs: To understand the *Lucia* decision, you'll need to understand some details about the powers Congress gave to ALJs. The federal securities laws authorize the SEC to enforce those laws by bringing administrative proceedings. Those laws do this by allowing the Commission to employ "administrative law judges" (ALJs), who conduct "hearings" to determine whether a person has violated the securities laws. The ALJs have powers fairly similar to those of, say, federal district court judges, including the power to take testimony, to conduct trials, to rule on motions and evidentiary objections, to issue proposed findings of fact, and to issue a proposed opinion at the end of the hearing. In other words, the ALJ can conduct **what is pretty much a civil "trial"** of alleged securities violators, subject to the Commission's right to review and reject the resulting opinion.

    iii. Lucia's challenge: The SEC brought an enforcement action against Lucia, an action that was heard by an ALJ, Judge Elliot. Judge Elliot had been appointed not by the Commission itself, but by members of the Commission's staff. When the judge wrote a proposed opinion finding that Lucia had violated securities laws, Lucia asserted that the opinion was invalid because Elliot was an "inferior officer," who could therefore not constitutionally have been appointed except by a Head of Department (i.e., by vote of the Commission itself).[15]

  d. Lucia wins: The Supreme Court **agreed with Lucia.** The Court concluded that because SEC ALJs have "all the authority needed to **ensure fair and orderly adversarial hearings** — indeed, nearly all the tools of federal trial judges," the ALJs have "substantial authority." And because they have substantial authority, that makes them "inferior officers," as Lucia claimed. Therefore, Judge Elliot needed to have been appointed by a "Head of Department" (i.e., by the whole Commission); without such an appointment his hearing of Lucia's case was constitutionally invalid.

  e. Significance: There are other U.S. cabinet departments and independent agencies that use administrative law judges who are given similar powers to "try cases." At least where the package of powers given to the ALJ is comparable to the package given to SEC ALJs, *Lucia* means that these judges will have to be appointed by the President or by the relevant Commissioners, cabinet department heads or agency heads.[16]

G. The President's Recess Appointments power: Recall that under the Appointments Clause, although the President has the power to nominate "principal officers" (i.e., top-level officers), the nomination cannot **take effect** except "by and with the **advice and consent of the Senate.**" In other words, the Senate must by majority vote **approve** the President's nominees for top-

---

    15. The Supreme Court treated the Commission the way it has treated any other independent federal agency, as itself being a "Head of Department." Therefore, if Judge Elliot had been appointed directly by the Commission (i.e., by a majority vote of the Commissioners), rather than by the Commission's staff members, his appointment would have been unquestionably *proper* under the Appointments Clause even though he was found to be an "inferior officer" as opposed to a garden-variety federal employee.

    16. For another case resolving the status of certain administrative law judges, see the *Arthrex* decision (*supra*, p. 128), where the issue was whether "Administrative Patent Judges," who try certain patent cases, have been given sufficiently extensive powers that they are "principal" rather than merely "inferior" federal officers.

level federal positions. But what happens if a ***vacancy arises*** when ***Congress is not in session*** — is the nation to be without anyone to serve in the vacated position?

1. **The "Recess Appointments" Clause:** The Constitution attempts to deal with this scenario by means of a clause that immediately follows the Appointments Clause. Art. II, §2, cl. 3, the so-called "***Recess Appointments" Clause***, gives the President, ***acting alone***, the power to:

    > ***fill up all Vacancies*** that may happen ***during the Recess of the Senate***, by granting Commissions which shall ***expire at the End of their next Session.***

    Example: Suppose the Secretary of State dies suddenly in early December of 2018, at a time when the old Congress has ended, and the new Congress hasn't yet been sworn in (which won't happen until early January, 2019). There is therefore no Senate in session that can "advise and consent" to any replacement nominee proposed by the President. It would be potentially catastrophic for the nation to be without a Secretary of State for over a month.

    Therefore, immediately following the prior Secretary's death, the President may use his Recess Appointments power to appoint a temporary Secretary of State, who will serve even without Senate approval until the end of the *next* session of Congress (an end that will occur in December 20<u>20</u>).

    a. **Intra-session appointments:** Note that the Recess Appointment Clause, as quoted above, uses the phrase "the Recess of the Senate." There are two different types of "gaps" that the Clause refers to by using the term "recess":

    [1] There is the single long "***inter-session***" recess by the Senate (i.e., the one between the end of the first session in December of odd-numbered years and the start of the second session in the following January of the even-numbered year).

    [2] But there is also a type of gap that's called an "***intra-session***" recess.

    > **Example of "intra-session" recess:** Suppose the second session of the 11th Congress started on Jan. 3, 2018, a Tuesday. Also, suppose Congress met on Jan. 4 (Wednesday), then went on recess for Jan. 5 (Thursday) and Jan. 6 (Friday). The Jan. 5-to-Jan. 6 recess would be an "***intra session***" recess.

2. **The *Noel Canning* case:** In a 2014 case, the Supreme Court laid out some rules for determining how and when the President may use the Recess Appointment Clause. The case was ***National Labor Relations Board v. Noel Canning***, 134 S.Ct. 2550 (2014). Here are the two main rules established in *Noel Canning*:

    a. **Minimum length:** Where the recess is an "***intra-session***" rather than "inter-session" one, there is a ***minimum length*** that the recess must have in order to trigger the recess-appointment power: any recess of ***10 days or more is sufficiently long***, but any recess ***less than 10 days*** will be ***presumed to be too short*** to fall within the Clause. Here's an example, drawn from the actual facts of *Noel Canning*.

    > **Example:** In December, 2011, at the end of President Obama's third year in office, the Senate adopts a resolution that it will take a series of brief recesses beginning the next day. Under the resolution, between the start of the holiday season on December 17, 2011 and the resumption of "ordinary business" on Jan. 23, 2012, the only Senate activity will be a series of what the resolution

calls *"pro forma sessions,"* to occur every Tuesday and Friday. (These are called *"pro forma"* sessions because, the resolution announces, "no business" will be "transacted" during them.) The second session of the 112th Congress begins on Jan. 3, 2012, a Tuesday. On Jan. 4 (Wednesday), Obama appoints three people to fill vacancies on the N.L.R.B., vacancies that had existed since before the start of the holiday season. The issue arises: are these Jan. 4 appointments, made during the intra-session recess that lasted from Jan. 4 through 5, valid under the Recess Appointment Clause?

Held, they are *not* valid. Intra-recess appointments are not *per se* invalid; but any recess of **less than 10 days** is presumptively **too short** to trigger the Recess Appointment Clause, in light of historical practice. *N.L.R.B. v. Noel Canning, supra.*

Note: However, in a truly **emergency** situation ("a national catastrophe, for instance, that renders the Senate unavailable but calls for an urgent response"), the Court may find that the presumption that a 10-day recess is the shortest allowable has been rebutted. *Noel Canning, supra.*

b. Vacancy need not arise during the recess: A vacancy will be deemed to "happen" during recess (so that it qualifies under the Clause) even though the prior occupant **leaves the post while the Senate is still in session**, as long as the Senate has gone into recess by the time the President makes the new appointment. (That's what has happened historically in the vast majority of cases where the President has purported to exercise the recess power.)

Example: On the facts of *Noel Canning*, assume that the three vacancies on the N.L.R.B. all occurred while the Senate was in session during November, 2011. Assume further that President Obama appointed three replacements during a 12-day intra-session recess that occurred in early January from Jan. 10 to Jan. 21. Are the appointments valid under the Recess Appointment Clause?

Yes, these appointments are valid, because they occurred during a 10-day-or-longer intra-session recess. The fact that the vacancies initially occurred while the Senate was in session (not in recess) doesn't matter. *Noel Canning, supra.*

H. The President's right to remove appointees: Let's now leave the constitutional rules for making appointments, and turn to the opposite issue, the power to **remove** appointees from office. Apart from setting out the process for impeachment, *infra*, p. 143, the Constitution does not state whether and when the President, Congress, or both, may **remove** federal appointees and employees. (Article III, §1, does provide that federal judges may not be removed except for misconduct.) Accordingly, it has been left to the Supreme Court to determine the extent of the President's right to make such removals.

1. Quasi-legislative and quasi-judicial officers: Where a federal appointee holds a **quasi-judicial** or **quasi-legislative** role, under certain circumstances Congress may **limit** or even completely **block** the President's right of removal.

a. "Independent" federal agencies: This special rule applies to so-called "**independent**" federal agencies, i.e., agencies that **don't** mainly **carry out the President's poli-**

cies (as, say, cabinet members do), but instead make significant rules governing the actions of *persons outside the Executive Branch*, such as private citizens. (The NLRB, the board whose powers were at issue in *Noel Canning, supra*, is an illustration of such an independent agency.) It's important that these agencies be *insulated from interference by the President.* Therefore, the Court has held, Congress may under Article I limit the President from removing such agency heads unless he has *just cause* for the firing. Chemerinsky Hnbk (5e), p. 351, § 4.2.

Example: Congress creates the Federal Trade Commission, an administrative agency whose function is to administer a federal statute designed to guard against certain types of unfair competition. Congress provides that Commissioners will be appointed for fixed terms by the President (with the advice and consent of the Senate), and that the President may remove a Commissioner before the expiration of his fixed term only for cause. The President (Franklin Roosevelt) contends that the statute improperly interferes with what he says is his constitutional right to remove a Commissioner even without cause.

Held, against the President. The FTC is an independent body designed to act quasi-legislatively and quasi-judicially. It is not part of the Executive Branch. To perform its functions properly, it must be free from Executive-Branch interference. Therefore, Congress was constitutionally entitled to maintain the Commission's independence by insisting that the President may remove a Commissioner only for cause. *Humphrey's Executor v. U.S.*, 295 U.S. 602 (1935).

b. **Other agencies:** In addition to the Federal Trade Commission (at issue in *Humphrey's Executor*), examples of independent federal agencies with multi-member heads and without significant executive powers include the *Securities and Exchange Commission*, the *Federal Communications Commission*, and the *Federal Reserve*. Cf. Chemerinsky Hnbk (5e), § 4.2, p. 351. So Congress does not violate separation-of-powers principles by saying that the head(s) of one of these agencies (e.g., a Commissioner of the FCC, or the head of the Federal Reserve) may not be removed by the President except for good cause.

c. **Rule that agencies with executive powers and single-member heads don't qualify for an exception (*Seila Law*):** But as the result of a 2020 decision, the special rule allowing Congress to prevent the President from removing the heads of quasi-legislative or quasi-judicial agencies or commissions except for cause is subject to two important *limitations*:

[1] The powers of the agency or commission *must not include significant executive powers.* Thus the agency's powers must be *primarily legislative and/or judicial*, and must not involve a significant power to enforce existing laws; and …

[2] the agency or commission must be *governed by a multi-member board* rather than by a *single director.*

The 2020 decision that announced these rules was *Seila Law v. Consumer Fin. Prot. Bureau,* 140 S.Ct. 2183 (2020).

i. **Facts of *Seila Law*:** The *Seila Law* case involved the constitutionality of the removal process for the Director of a federal agency created by Congress in 2010, the *Consumer Financial Protection Bureau (CFPB).* The CFPB is an independent federal regulator within the Federal Reserve System. The agency is responsible for enforcing a large body of financial consumer protection laws, embodied in 18 different statutes, including major ones like the Fair Debt Collection Practices Act and the Truth in Lending Act. The agency's extensive *enforcement powers* include the authority to issue subpoenas, to prosecute civil actions in federal court, and to seek and collect restitution and civil penalties for violations of federal consumer financial loss. But the agency also has significant quasi-judicial powers, including the authority to conduct administrative proceedings via "hearing officers"; the proceedings can result in "legal and equitable relief."

(1) Structure of traditional independent agencies: As we noted above, various "independent agencies" have long existed, "independent" in the sense that they have been intentionally designed to be largely free of political influence by the President. The Federal Trade Commission (FTC), the Securities and Exchange Commission (SEC) and the Federal Reserve System are examples. All of these traditional independent agencies are headed by *multi-member boards*, and Congress has tried to make each independent from the Executive Branch in part by denying the President to remove a board member before the expiration of the member's fixed term except "for cause." As we just saw, in *Humphrey's Executor v. U.S.*, 295 U.S. 602 (1935), the Court held that the structure of the New Deal version of the FTC was constitutional even though Congress stripped the President of his power to remove a Commissioner except for cause.

(2) Single Director at head of CFPB: But Congress imposed a different structure when it created the CFPB: rather than putting a multi-member board or commission in charge, Congress put the agency *under the leadership of a single Director.* The Director serves a fixed term of five years, during which the President may remove her only for cause (defined as "inefficiency, neglect of duty, or malfeasance in office").

ii. **The claim by Sheila Law:** Seila Law, which challenged the constitutionality of the CFPB's structure, refused to comply with a subpoena from the agency, arguing that the agency's structure – in particular, the fact that the President could not remove the Director except for cause – violated the Constitution's separation-of-power principles.

iii. **The holding:** The Supreme Court, by a 5-4 vote, *agreed with Seila Law* that the agency's structure *violated the separation of powers*. The majority opinion, by Chief Justice Roberts, reached this conclusion by taking four main steps:

[1] Roberts noted that as a *general rule*, the Court had long held that separation-of-powers principles required that the President's power to *remove federal officers* who assist with the carrying out of Executive Branch duties *not be restricted.*

[2] He then noted that the Court had recognized only *two exceptions* to this general rule. One (recognized in *Humphrey's Executor*) upheld the structure of the New-Deal version of the FTC, whereby Congress deprived the President of power to remove any Commissioner before the expiration of the Commissioner's fixed term, except for cause. The other (recognized in *Morrison v. Olson*, discussed *infra*, p. 141), upheld a statute allowing the Attorney General to bring about the *appointment of a special prosecutor* in certain cumstances, who could then be removed (by the Attorney General) only for cause.

[3] But Roberts concluded that the CFPB's structure *did not fit into either of these exceptions*. (We consider his analysis of the reasons for this conclusion in Sub-pars. (iv) and (v) below.)

[4] Roberts then decided that there was no good reason to *extend* either of these exceptions to fit the CFPB's structure. (We'll review this reasoning in Sub-par. (vi) below.)

iv. Why the *Humphrey's Executor* exception didn't apply: As to why the CFPB's structure did not fall within the exception that *Humphrey's Executor* carved out to validate the for-cause-only removal protections in the FTC's structure, Roberts found two differences between the two agencies, either of which, he said, sufficed to make the exception *inapplicable* to the CFPB situation.

(1) Multi-member board vs. single Director: First, the FTC was *headed by a multi-member body* (a 5-member Board), rather than a *single Director* as in the CFPB situation.

(2) Executive functions: Second, the FTC did not have *"executive powers,"* whereas the CFPB did. The Court in *Humphrey's Executor* had viewed the FTC's Board as it stood then as having *no "executive powers."* By contrast, Roberts said, Congress had given the CFPB's Director *extensive executive powers,* including the power to enforce agency regulations by seeking "daunting monetary penalties against private parties," a *"quintessentially executive power"* not considered in the *Humphrey's* case.

v. Why the *Morrison* exception did not apply: Next, Roberts explained why the other traditional exception to the general rule forbidding Congress from restricting the President's power to remove agency heads — the exception recognized in *Morrison v. Olson* (*infra*, p. 141) — similarly did not apply to the CFPB structure. *Morrison* involved an "independent counsel" appointed by a special court (that court being the "Special Division") to investigate and prosecute certain alleged crimes by high governmental officials.

(1) Importance of maintaining independence: Because of the importance of maintaining the independent counsel's independence from Executive Branch interference, the *Morrison* Court found, it was not unconstitutional for Congress to specify that once an independent counsel was appointed by the Special Division, she could be removed only by the Attorney General, and only for good cause.

(2) "Inferior" vs "principal" officer: But Roberts thought there was a *key distinction* between the independent-counsel position in *Morrison* and the CFPB's Director position in *Seila Law*. *Morrison* had determined that the independent counsel was an *"inferior"* federal officer, rather than a *"principal"* one.[17] By contrast, Roberts wrote, everyone agreed that *the CFPB Director is a principal, not inferior, officer.*[18] Since the *Morrison* exception applied only to inferior officers, it did not apply to the CFPB Director.

---

17. For the distinction between "principal" and "inferior" federal officers, see p. 128 *supra*.

vi. No extension to this "new situation": Finally, Roberts concluded that the Court *should not extend these two limited exceptions* to cover the *"new situation"* posed by the CFPB, namely "an independent agency led by a single Director and vested with significant executive power."

vii. No severance: But in a crucial passage of Roberts' opinion for the Court, he held that the unconstitutional limit on the Director's removability was *severable* from the rest of the statute. He concluded that Congress had clearly shown that if the removability aspect was found unconstitutional, Congress would *prefer to have the rest of the statute* establishing the agency *continue in force.*

(1) Result: Given this decision on severance, *Seila Law* brings about only a *limited change* in how the CFPB operates:

[1] the agency *continues in force* exactly as authorized by Congress;

[2] the single Director continues to have the *same powers* as before the finding of unconstitutionality; but ...

[3] *Seila Law* means that the President now has *the power to remove the Director for any reason or no reason*, not just "for cause."

viii. Dissent: In an opinion by Justice Kagan, the four liberal members of the Court *dissented* from the majority's basic holding in *Seila Law* that Congress had acted constitutionally when it said that the President could remove the Director for cause.[19]

(1) Inconsistent with precedent: In Kagan's view, the majority's holding was inconsistent with *long-standing precedent.* The Court had long allowed Congress and the President, working together, to "create *zones of administrative independence* by limiting the President's power to remove agency heads." The Federal Reserve Board, the FTC, the National Labor Relations Board, all were among agencies whose enabling statutes allowed the President to remove their directors only for cause, and whose structure the Court had approved.

(2) Rejects the majority's "rule" with "exceptions": Kagan took sharp issue with the majority's assertion that there was a "general rule" regarding limits on the President's power to remove directors coupled with two "exceptions" (one based on *Humphrey's Executor* and the other on *Morrison v. Olson*) to that rule. The "exceptions" relied on by the majority were, she said, *"made up for the occasion – gerrymandered* so the CFBP falls outside them."

d. The two-level-of-protection problem: The Roberts Court has been quick to find that Congress has unduly limited the President's right to remove persons who head, or in

---

18. The Director is a principal officer, Roberts said, because she has "the authority to *bring the coercive power of the state to bear on millions of private citizens and businesses*, imposing even billion-dollar penalties through administrative adjudications and civil actions."

19. The dissenters concurred in the judgment; they did so because, given the majority's holding that the limits on the President's removal powers were unconstitutional (a holding they disagreed with), the dissenters agreed that the proper remedy was to sever the offending provision and to allow the rest of the statute creating the agency to remain in force.

some cases merely work in, administrative agencies. And that's true even where the Court agrees that Congress rationally concluded that the agency should be relatively independent of politically-motivated presidential interference. *Seila Law v. Consumer Fin. Prot. Bureau, supra*, is one example of the Roberts Court's pro-presidential-power approach to limits on the President's removal powers.

Another example came in a 2010 case involving presidential removal of *inferior* officers of an independent federal agency. In that case, ***Free Enterprise Fund v. Public Company Accounting Oversight Board***, 561 U.S. 477 (2010), the conservative wing of the Court held, by a 5-4 vote, that Congress ***could not set up a two-level scheme in which:***

[1] the President was prevented from removing the ***heads*** of an independent agency except for cause, and

[2] those agency heads were in turn prevented from removing, except for cause, an ***inferior federal officer*** that they had appointed.

The two levels of good-cause protection together were found to constitute a violation of the separation-of-powers principle that the executive power is held by the President only.

i.   **Facts:** After many accounting scandals, Congress set up the Public Company Accounting Oversight Board (PCAOB) to regulate most accounting firms. The members of the PCAOB were to be appointed by vote of the Securities Exchange Commission. The SEC is an independent federal agency, whose members are appointed by the President but can be removed by him only for cause.[20] In setting up the PCAOB, Congress said that Board members, in turn, could only be removed during their terms by a vote of the SEC commissioners, again only for cause.

(1) **PCAOB were inferior officers:** Members of the PCAOB were (the Supreme Court decided), federal officers, because they had significant authority under federal law. They were "inferior" federal officers, not principal officers, because they were subject to supervision not directly by the President, but by someone appointed by the President (namely, the SEC Commissioners). So the question in the suit was, can the President's ability to remove an ***inferior federal officer*** be limited by ***multiple layers*** of good-cause protection?

ii.   **Violation of separation-of-powers:** Five members of the Court, led by Chief Justice Roberts, answered ***"no"***: this type of "multilevel protection" from removal ***violated Article II's vesting of the executive power in the President.***

(1) **Rationale:** Roberts reasoned that in the usual case where Congress gives a department head (e.g., a cabinet member) the power to appoint an inferior officer, then even if the inferior officer could only be removed for cause, the President could at least express unhappiness with the inferior officer by removing

---

20. The SEC members were all principal federal officers, but it was permissible, under the principle of *Humphrey's Executor, supra*, p. 157, for Congress to limit the President's power to remove them to the good-cause-shown situation, because the agency was headed by a multi-member body, and was an independent quasi-legislative agency with little executive authority.

the department head who appointed her. But here, the two levels of good-cause protection (SEC Commissioners who could not be removed by the President except for cause, and an inferior officer appointed by those Commissioners who, similarly, could only be removed by them for cause) ***"subverts the President's ability to ensure that the laws are faithfully executed[.]"***

2. **Purely executive officers:** Paragraph 1 above mainly covered removal of federal officers whose role is *quasi-judicial* or *quasi-legislative*, such as heads of certain "independent" federal regulatory agencies.[21] But what about officers whose authority is mainly *executive*: may Congress limit the President's right to remove such officers?

   a. **Inferior officers:** As the result of a 1988 case, the answer seems to be that, at least in the case of *"inferior"* (lower-level) officers, Congress *may* limit the President's right to remove such an officer as long as the removal restrictions are ***not "of such a nature that they impede the President's ability to perform his constitutional duty. ... "*** *Morrison v. Olson*, 487 U.S. 654 (1988). Typically, Congress' decision to prevent the President from removing the inferior executive officer without cause (while allowing him to remove for cause) won't result in such an impairment, and thus won't be unconstitutional. The facts of *Morrison* illustrate this result.

      i. **Facts:** The statute in *Morrison* required the Attorney General ("A.G.") to investigate any allegations of wrongdoing against certain high level members of the Executive Branch (including members of the Cabinet), and to apply to a special federal court (the "Special Division") for the appointment of an ***independent counsel*** if the A.G. found "reasonable grounds to believe that further investigation or prosecution is warranted." Once the independent counsel was appointed, she could only be removed by the A.G., and only ***"for good cause***, physical disability, mental incapacity, or any other condition that ***substantially impairs the performance*** of [her] duties."

      ii. **Holding:** By a 7-1 vote, the Court held that ***neither*** the removal provisions nor the statute taken as a whole so restricted the President's powers as to violate the separation-of-powers principle. Because the A.G. could terminate the independent counsel for "good cause," the Executive Branch "retains ample authority to assure that the counsel is competently performing her statutory responsibilities[.]"

   b. **Top-level officers:** The principle we just reviewed, that Congress may constitutionally prevent the President from removing executive federal officers without cause, applies ***only where what's involved is limits on the President's power to remove "inferior" federal officers*** (*supra*, p. 127), ***not to remove "principal" officers***, like heads of Cabinet departments. That is, even post-*Morrison*, the Roberts Court has kept in force the long-established view that Congress ***may not place any limits at all on the President's right to remove Cabinet heads or other principal officers***. (Recall that the *Morrison* Court determined that the special prosecutor was an "inferior" officer rather than a "principal" officer.)

---

21. But *Seila Law*, *supra*, p. 136, although it's a case we covered in Par. 1, involved a federal agency that had *both* quasi-judicial and executive functions.

i. **Cabinet officers:** In the case of heads of Cabinet departments, it's always been clear – not just since the Roberts Court – that Congress may not limit the President's right of removal.

Example: Suppose that Congress passes a statute saying, "No Secretary of State may, once appointed by the President and confirmed by the Senate, be removed by the President during the Secretary's first year in office, except either on consent of the Senate or for good cause shown." While such a statute would likely be constitutional if applied to an *inferior* federal officer (like the special prosecutor in *Morrison*), it is clearly **unconstitutional** when applied to a Cabinet head like the Secretary of State. That's because the removal restriction would impede the President's ability to perform his constitutional duty of running the Executive Branch.

ii. **Single-director agency heads:** But in the case of *independent agencies and commissions* (as opposed to Cabinet departments), it has not always been clear whether or how Congress may limit the President's power to remove these bodies' leader(s). But since a 2020 decision by the Roberts Court, it's now the case that even if Congress wants an agency to be "independent,"[22] Congress **may not impose a "for good cause only" limit** on the President's power to remove a single-person director of the agency if that director is a "*principal*" federal officer. In other words, separation-of-powers principles require that **the President must be free to fire a federal agency director for any or no reason,** if:

[1] the agency is **headed by a single director** who is a federal officer **with no "boss"** other than the President (that's the definition of a "*principal*" federal officer); *and*

[2] the agency has **significant executive powers**.

(1) *Seila Law* **case:** This rule follows directly from the 2020 decision in *Seila Law v. Consumer Fin. Prot. Bureau, supra*, p. 136.

I. **Removal by Congress:** Now that we've completed our review of the constitutionality of congressionally-imposed limits on the *President*'s power to remove presidential appointees, let's take a quick look at the converse problem: May Congress *reserve to itself* the power to remove a federal officer who holds Executive-Branch authority? The brief answer to this question is "*no*." See *Bowsher v. Synar*, 478 U.S. 714 (1986).

1. **Facts:** *Bowsher* involved the Gramm-Rudman Act, in which Congress attempted to reduce federal budget deficits by instituting a procedure under which automatic spending cuts would be made in certain circumstances. The Act gave a key role in carrying out these automatic-cut provisions to the *Comptroller General* of the U.S.

    a. **Right to remove Comptroller:** By separate, much older, legislation, Congress had reserved to itself the right to remove the Comptroller General from office for five specified reasons.

2. **Statute struck down:** By a 7-2 vote, the Court struck down the automatic-reduction provisions of the Act. To reach this result, the Court concluded that (1) the Comptroller, if he

---

22. "Independent" in this context means an agency that Congress believes should be free from political influence from the Executive Branch.

did what the Act told him to do, would be exercising Executive-Branch powers; but (2) Congress' retention of the right to remove the Comptroller for certain specified types of cause *converted him into an agent of Congress, so that he could no longer exercise these executive powers* due to separation-of-powers principles.

3. **Constitutional significance:** So *Bowsher* establishes that ***Congress may not reserve the right to remove an executive officer even for cause***, at least where the definition of "cause" is fairly ***broad*** (e.g., "inefficiency," "neglect of duty," or "malfeasance," three of the causes listed in the Act).

   a. **Narrower grounds:** Apparently the retention of ***narrower grounds*** for removal of an executive officer (e.g., "permanent disability" or "commission of a felony or conduct involving moral turpitude," two other grounds for removal of a Comptroller to which the Court seemed not to object) will *not* be unconstitutional. Furthermore, nothing in the decision seems to have any impact on Congress' right to remove an executive officer by ***impeachment*** (see *infra*, immediately below).

J. **Impeachment:** The standards for ***impeachment*** are set forth in Article II, §4 of the Constitution: "[t]he President, Vice President and all civil Officers of the United States, shall be removed from Office on Impeachment for, and Conviction of, Treason, Bribery, or other ***high Crimes and Misdemeanors***."

   1. **Procedure for impeachment:** The term "impeachment" itself refers to the decision by the ***House of Representatives*** to subject the President, or other federal official, to a trial in the Senate. See Art. I, §2, Cl. 5. A House vote to impeach is thus similar to a grand jury indictment; it is not a conviction, but merely the necessary pre-condition to a trial.

      a. **Trial in Senate:** If the House votes (by a ***majority*** vote) to impeach, the trial itself occurs in the Senate, and a ***two-thirds vote*** of those Senators present is required to convict. Art. I, §3, Cl. 6. In the case of impeachment of a President, the Chief Justice presides over the trial.

   2. **Sparingly used:** The impeachment power has been sparingly used throughout our nation's history. Only four Presidents, Andrew Johnson, Richard Nixon, Bill Clinton and Donald Trump, have been the subject of serious impeachment efforts. Presidents Johnson, Clinton and Trump were impeached by the House, and escaped conviction in the Senate. President Nixon resigned after three articles of impeachment had been voted against him by the House Judiciary Committee, but before the full House could vote on the impeachment issue.

   3. **Meaning of "high crimes and misdemeanors":** Because the constitutional phrase "high Crimes and Misdemeanors" is inevitably somewhat vague, its meaning has been subject to great dispute.

      a. **Serious crimes:** Some have argued that only "serious indictable crimes" may serve as the basis for impeachment. See Gunther & Sullivan (13th Ed.), pp. 411-12.

      b. **Abuse of power:** Others have contended that any serious ***abuse of the powers*** of the presidency may serve as the basis for a President's impeachment, even if the offense would not be a crime.

      c. **Majority view:** Many commentators reject the Nixon view that only crimes may be impeachable. However, they also reject the view that *any* crime is necessarily an impeachable offense.

Example: Suppose the President deliberately and maliciously decided to weaken our national defenses. This would probably not violate any criminal statute, but it should be considered grounds for impeachment. Tribe, p. 294.

Example: During President Clinton's impeachment, his defenders made a plausible argument that the minor crime of perjury in a civil deposition, at least where it concerned a peripheral matter (whether President Clinton had had sex with someone not a party to the litigation, Monica Lewinsky) should not be treated as an impeachable offense. The Senate, by voting to acquit him despite relatively clear evidence that perjury occurred, seems to have accepted this argument.

4. **Effect of resignation:** The fact that a federal officer has *resigned* does not bar the use of subsequent impeachment proceedings against him. The same is true of a *pardon*: thus the pardon of President Nixon by his successor, Gerald Ford, would not have prevented the use of impeachment proceedings against Nixon.

5. **Criminal liability:** The Constitution explicitly provides that an impeachment conviction has no immediate effect other than to remove the officer from office (and to disqualify him from holding any other federal office). Art. I, §3, Cl. 7. But that same Clause provides that "the Party convicted shall nevertheless be liable and subject to Indictment, Trial, Judgment, and Punishment, according to Law." Consequently, following the impeachment conviction a *criminal prosecution* may be brought against the impeached officer, based on the same set of facts as the impeachment. A criminal conviction in this situation does not constitute double jeopardy. Tribe, p. 296.

   a. **No pardon power:** Furthermore, a criminal conviction following an impeachment cannot be avoided by use of the pardon power. Art. II, §2, Cl. 1 gives the President the power to grant pardons "except in Cases of Impeachment." Thus had President Nixon been convicted by the Senate, Gerald Ford would not have been able to pardon him from criminal liability (at least with respect to offenses of which he was convicted in the Senate).

6. **Reviewability by Court:** Once the Senate has convicted in an impeachment trial, it is not clear whether the *Supreme Court* may review the conviction. There are no Supreme Court precedents on point.

   a. **Pros and cons:** The traditional view is that an impeachment conviction presents a *non-justiciable political question*. The contrary view is that the Supreme Court may review an impeachment conviction to determine at least some issues, for instance, whether an adequate definition of "high Crimes and Misdemeanors" was applied. The traditional view is probably the correct one, in light of *Nixon v. U.S.*, 506 U.S. 224 (1993) (involving a different Nixon, Walter Nixon, a federal judge) — the Court held there that the question of what procedures validly constitute a "trial" of an impeachment case by the Senate was a non-justiciable political question. See *infra* p. 752.

V.   LEGISLATIVE AND EXECUTIVE IMMUNITY

A. **Scope of discussion:** We examine now several facets of *immunity* held by the various branches of the federal government. In particular, we examine: (1) Congress' immunity from civil and criminal suits and from grand jury investigations; (2) the civil and criminal immunity of the Executive Branch; and (3) the doctrine of "executive privilege," and the related issue of protection of state secrets.

B. Congress and the Speech and Debate Clause: Article I, §6, provides that "for any Speech or Debate in either House, [members of Congress] shall not be questioned in any other Place." In general terms, this so-called Speech and Debate Clause shields members of Congress from: (1) *civil or criminal suits* relating to their *legislative actions*; and (2) *grand jury investigations* relating to those actions.

1. Rationale: The Speech and Debate Clause serves important separation-of-powers functions: for instance, it protects members of Congress against executive officials (e.g., Justice Department officials) who might seek unduly to influence congressional conduct by conducting criminal prosecutions or grand jury investigations. More generally, it serves the related function of assuring that members of Congress are not distracted from their duties by being called into court to defend their actions. See Tribe, p. 370.

C. Executive immunity: The Speech and Debate Clause has no counterpart in the Constitution giving any sort of immunity to members of the *Executive* Branch. However, as a common-law matter, the federal courts have recognized certain types of executive immunity.

1. Judicial process, including subpoenas to produce documents: The President and other members of the Executive Branch *do not have general immunity* from *judicial process*, such as *subpoenas to produce documents.*

a. Federal-court subpoenas (the *Nixon* case): The first modern case establishing that the President does not have absolute immunity from subpoenas was *U.S. v. Nixon*, 418 U.S. 683 (1974), the famous *"Watergate Tapes" case*, discussed extensively *infra*, pp. 149-151, in the context of executive privilege. There, the Watergate Special Prosecutor secured a federal-court subpoena directing Nixon to *produce tape recordings of Oval Office meetings.* Nixon moved to quash the subpoena, on the grounds that the Constitution provides an absolute privilege of confidentiality to all presidential communications. But the Supreme Court *rejected* this argument, unanimously holding that *Presidents are subject to subpoenas issued by federal courts.*

b. State-court subpoenas (*Trump v. Vance*): As noted, *U.S. v. Nixon* involved a subpoena to a President issued by a *federal* court; the case thus left open the possibility that the President might still be found to have absolute immunity to subpoenas from a *state court*. But a 2020 case involving records relating to President Trump shows that the fact that the subpoena is issued in a state-court proceeding *makes no constitutional difference* – the President *does not have absolute immunity from state-court subpoenas* any more than from ones issued by a federal court. The case was *Trump v. Vance*, 140 S.Ct. 2412 (2020).

i. Facts: The *Vance* case began when the office of Vance, the New York State district attorney for Manhattan, began a grand jury investigation of whether business transactions by various individuals had violated state law. Vance's office, on behalf of the grand jury, in 2018 served a subpoena *duces tecum* on President Trump's personal accounting firm, Mazars USA, directing Mazars to produce financial records, dating from 2011 and later, relating to Trump and his businesses.

(1) Trump's motion to quash: The President moved to quash the subpoena. He conceded that Presidents do not have constitutional immunity from *federal* criminal subpoenas. But he argued that the opposite was true of subpoenas issued as part of state criminal proceedings; as to these, he contended, a sitting President *enjoys absolute immunity.* His main argument was that forcing a President to comply with subpoenas issued in state criminal proceedings would inevitably divert him from performance of his duties.

ii. **7-2 victory for the prosecution:** By a 7-2 vote, the Court, in an opinion by Chief Justice Roberts, *rejected* Trump's contention that he had absolute immunity from state-court criminal subpoenas. Roberts was not convinced by any of Trump's multiple arguments about why subpoenas arising from *state* criminal proceedings posed a greater threat to the Constitution than those from federal proceedings.

(1) **Right to argue about the effect of the particular subpoena:** But Roberts noted that the only thing the majority was deciding was that Presidents *do not have either absolute immunity* or the benefit of a *heightened standard of need*. Mr. Trump and other Presidents would still have the right to "challenge *specific subpoenas* as impeding their Article II functions."

iii. **Just five votes for Roberts' reasoning:** Despite the 7-2 vote in *Vance*, only a *bare five-justice majority* agreed with both major aspects of Roberts' reasoning, that the President is neither absolutely immune from state criminal subpoenas seeking his private papers, nor entitled to a heightened standard of need.[23]

(1) **Four Justices disagree:** Each of the other four Justices (Thomas, Alito, Kavanaugh and Gorsuch) thought either that the President should be *absolutely immune* from state criminal document subpoenas, or that at the very least, the state prosecutor should have to meet a *heightened standard of need* for the materials.

2. **Civil liability of President for official acts:** In contrast to the President's lack of absolute immunity from judicial subpoenas, the President *does* have *absolute immunity* from *civil liability* for his *official acts*, as the result of *Nixon v. Fitzgerald*, 457 U.S. 731 (1982), a 5-4 decision.

a. **Facts:** Fitzgerald, the plaintiff, contended that he had been fired from his Defense Department job in retaliation for testimony in which he had criticized military cost overruns. His suit charged Nixon and several Nixon Administration officials with violating his First Amendment and statutory rights.

b. **Holding:** In an opinion by Justice Powell, the Court held that the President is entitled to *absolute immunity* from civil damage actions for all acts within the "*outer perimeter*" of his authority. Since the President has authority to prescribe the manner in which the business of the armed forces will be conducted, including the authority to dismiss personnel, Nixon was immune from liability for the firing of Fitzgerald *even if he caused it maliciously or in an illegal manner*.

c. **Dissent:** Four members of the Court dissented vigorously. The principal dissent, by Justice White, contended that there was no reason to depart from the usual rule that absolute immunity "attaches to particular functions — not to particular offices." The

---

23. Roberts' reasoning was fully joined only by the Court's four liberal members, Ginsburg, Breyer, Sotomayor and Kagan.

majority's approach, White argued, *"places the President above the law* [and] is a reversion to the old notion that the King can do no wrong."

3. **Civil immunity of presidential assistants:** Do presidential *assistants* get a similar absolute immunity from civil suits for their official acts? The brief answer is *"no." Harlow v. Fitzgerald*, 457 U.S. 731 (1982), a companion case to *Nixon v. Fitzgerald*.

    a. **Qualified immunity granted:** But presidential assistants do get fairly broad *"qualified* immunity." Essentially, a presidential assistant has immunity from civil suit for conduct arising out of her performance of her office, except where the official has violated a *"clearly established"* right.

    Example: Suppose a cabinet official fires a subordinate, on the grounds that the subordinate is openly gay. Suppose further that at the time of the firing, there is no clearly established law about whether the federal government may fire a person for being gay. Even if, immediately after the firing, the Supreme Court decides that such firings are illegal, the cabinet official will benefit from his qualified immunity. This is because, at the moment of the firing, he was not violating a "clearly established" right.

4. **No presidential immunity for non-official acts:** *Fitzgerald* only established immunity for *official* presidential acts, i.e., those that are within the "outer perimeter" of the President's job. There is *no immunity* — not even qualified immunity — for acts that the President takes that are completely *unrelated to the carrying out of his job*. This was the holding of *Clinton v. Jones*, 520 U.S. 681 (1997).

    a. **Paula Jones case:** *Clinton v. Jones* involved a private damages suit by Paula Jones against President Clinton, filed while Clinton was in office. Jones claimed that while she was employed by the state of Arkansas and Clinton was Governor of Arkansas, Clinton made illegal sexual advances to her. Clinton argued that a President should have "temporary immunity" — to last while he is in office — against virtually all civil litigation arising out of events that occurred before he took office.

    b. **Claim rejected:** But the Court unanimously *rejected* this claim. The Court noted that the rationale for immunity for *official* acts of the President and other officials was that such immunity "serves the public interest in enabling such officials to perform their designated functions effectively *without fear* that a particular decision may give rise to personal liability." This rationale did not apply to the President's unofficial acts, including any acts he took before he became President. Therefore, there was no policy reason for allowing even temporary immunity for unofficial acts.

5. **Criminal prosecution:** There is *no* executive immunity, either of a common-law or constitutional nature, from *criminal* prosecution. Tribe, p. 268.

    a. **Delay:** However, a strong argument may be made that, at least in the case of the President, the Constitution's provision of impeachment as the means of removing federal officers bars any criminal prosecution of such officials until *after they have been removed from office.* In the case of the President, Tribe, writing in 1988, said that "[t]he question must be regarded as an open one." Tribe, p. 269. Official Justice Department policy remains that no criminal prosecution of the President may be begun until he has left office. [24]

        i. **People other than the President:** In the case of the Vice-President and other principal federal officers other than the President, criminal prosecution prior to impeachment seems to be ***permissible***. For instance, Vice-President Agnew was indicted by a federal grand jury on bribery and tax evasion charges prior to his resignation, although the Supreme Court did not pass on the "no prosecution prior to impeachment" argument. *Id.*

6. **Subpoenas by Congress (*Trump v. Mazars*):** We saw earlier, in *Trump v. Vance* (*supra*, p. 145) that the President does not receive absolute immunity – or even the benefit of a heightened standard of need – from ***court-issued subpoenas*** to produce documents. But the same is ***not*** true of ***"legislative subpoenas,"*** that is, subpoenas ***by Congress*** for presidential documents. In a second 2020 case involving President Trump's personal records, the Court held that before enforcing congressional demands for such records, a court must make a ***"careful analysis"*** that weighs Congress' interest in enacting legislation against the "unique position" of the President. The case was ***Trump v. Mazars USA***, 140 S.Ct. 2019 (2020), decided the same day as *Vance*, and decided by the same 7-2 vote as that case. As in *Vance*, the majority opinion was by Chief Justice Roberts.

   a. **Facts:** *Mazars* involved subpoenas by three different committees of the Democratic-controlled House of Representatives seeking a wide range of financial records relating to Mr. Trump, his family and his businesses; the records were held by Trump's accounting firm (Mazars) and by two commercial banks.

   The committees said they wanted the records to advance various legislative purposes, among them (1) closing loopholes that had permitted ***"illicit money***, including from ***Russian oligarchs"*** to flow into the U.S.; (2) preventing ***"money laundering*** and the financing of terrorism"; and (3) examining alleged ***Russian attempts to influence the 2016 election***,

   b. **The suit:** Trump, backed by the Solicitor General, brought separate federal-court suits in New York and Washington D.C. to quash these subpoenas. Trump and the Solicitor made the broad claim that when Congress subpoenas a President's records, separation-of-powers principles dictate that Congress should have to show that the information is ***"demonstrably critical"*** to its legislative purposes.[25] The House countered with an equally broad but opposing view, that when Congress subpoenas a President's personal (i.e., non-government-job-related) records, the requests should be treated like ***ordinary congressional subpoenas*** not involving a President, so long as the records relate to a "valid legislative purpose." The two suits were heard together at the Supreme Court.

---

24. A U.S. Justice Department Memorandum Opinion issued in October, 2000, says that "The indictment or criminal prosecution of a ***sitting President*** would ***unconstitutionally undermine the capacity of the executive branch to perform its constitutionally assigned functions***." This Opinion is still in force as of this writing (early October, 2020). When special counsel Robert Mueller issued his 2019 *Report on Russian Interference in the 2016 Presidential Election*, the Report relied on the Opinion's existence as its reason for declining to express a conclusion about whether President Trump committed any crimes relating to Russian interference. (Mueller thought it would be unfair to label the President as a law-breaker unless and until he could properly be charged.) See https://www.vox.com/2019/7/24/20708393/robert-mueller-report-trump-olc-justice-department-indictment-charge-sitting-president.

25. Trump and the Solicitor General did ***not*** argue that the records were protected by ***executive privilege***, an argument that President Nixon had made, unsuccessfully, in the Watergate Tapes case (see *infra*, p. 149).

c. **Court chooses a middle standard:** Roberts' majority opinion steered a *middle course* between these two positions: When courts assess whether a congressional subpoena directed at the President's personal information sufficiently furthers a "legitimate task" of Congress, they must perform "a *careful analysis* that takes adequate account of the *separation of powers principles* at stake, including both the *significant legislative interests of Congress* and the *'unique position' of the President.*"

This "careful analysis" should include these elements, he said:

[1] **Availability of alternate sources:** First, courts should carefully assess whether the legislative purpose asserted by Congress "warrants the *significant step* of involving the President and his papers." This will not be the case if *"other sources could provide* Congress the information it needs."

[2] **No broader than necessary:** Second, to minimize inter-branch conflicts, the courts should "should insist on a subpoena *no broader than reasonably necessary* to support Congress's legislative objective."

[3] **Strength of evidence about the legislative purpose:** Third, courts should focus carefully on "the *nature of the evidence offered* by Congress" to establish that the subpoena advances a *valid legislative purpose*; "[t]he more *detailed and substantial* the evidence of Congress's legislative purpose, the better."

[4] **Burden on the President:** Finally, courts should "be careful to *assess the burdens imposed on the President"* by the subpoena. When subpoenas are issued by *courts*, Roberts said, the burdens on the President's time and attention generally don't "cross constitutional lines." But where it's *Congress* that's issuing the subpoena, the constitutional dangers are *greater*, because the subpoenas "stem from a *rival political branch* that has an ongoing relationship with the President and *incentives* to use subpoenas for *institutional advantage.*"

i. **Remand:** Roberts concluded that the lower courts in the congressional cases had *not "taken adequate account"* of these *"special concerns regarding the separation of powers."* Therefore, he remanded the two cases to the lower courts for an additional review based on these concerns.

ii. **Dissent:** The same two Justices, Thomas and Alito, *dissented* in *Mazars* as in *Vance*.

D. **"Executive privilege":** Several Presidents have invoked what they described as the doctrine of "*executive privilege*" to justify their refusal to *disclose information* which they claimed to be confidential. The only Supreme Court case to give any definitive scope to the doctrine was *U.S. v. Nixon*, 418 U.S. 683 (1974), the famous "Watergate Tapes" case. In *Nixon*, the Court recognized in general terms a constitutionally-based doctrine of executive privilege, but held that the privilege was only a *qualified* one, which was *overcome* on the facts of *Nixon* by the *needs of a pending criminal investigation.*

1. **Facts:** In March of 1974, a federal grand jury indicted seven Nixon aides on charges of conspiracy to obstruct justice and other Watergate-related offenses. The President was named as an unindicted co-conspirator. The Watergate Special Prosecutor then persuaded the federal trial court to issue a subpoena *duces tecum* to the President requiring him to produce various tapes and documents relating to certain meetings involving the President;

these documents and tapes were to be used during the trial of the indictments. The President released transcripts of some of the tapes, but **refused to produce the tapes themselves,** and moved to quash the subpoena. The trial court rejected the President's claim of privilege, and the matter was heard by the Supreme Court on an expedited basis.

2. **Holding:** Although the Supreme Court upheld the general doctrine of executive privilege, the Court held that in this case, **the privilege did not apply,** and ordered the President to comply with the subpoena.

   a. **Court, not President, decides:** First, the Court rejected the President's claim that "the separation of powers doctrine precludes judicial review of a President's claim of privilege." The Court quoted Justice Marshall's statement, in *Marbury v. Madison* (*supra*, p. 7) that it is the duty of the Judicial Branch to "say what the law is." Thus the **Court**, not the President, must evaluate claims of presidential privilege.

   b. **Privilege exists:** The Court then held that there was indeed a privilege for **"confidentiality of Presidential communications in the exercise of Article II powers. ... "** The Court observed that the privilege of confidentiality "can be said to derive from the **supremacy of each branch within its own assigned area of constitutional duties."**

   c. **Privilege only qualified:** However, the Court **rejected** the President's claim that the executive privilege was an **absolute** one. At least where the claim of privilege was (as in the present case) a **general** one, and not related to a particular need to protect "military, diplomatic, or sensitive national security secrets," the privilege was merely a **qualified** one. As such, it was **outweighed** by the need to **develop all relevant facts in a criminal trial.**

   d. **Duty of trial court:** The President was therefore ordered to deliver the subpoenaed tapes and documents to the federal district court. However, the district court was ordered to perform a close *in camera* (i.e., non-public) examination of all of the materials. Statements that were both admissible and relevant to the criminal prosecution were to be isolated, and all other statements were to be disregarded and kept secret.

3. **Scope of *Nixon* holding:** The precise scope of the *Nixon* Court's holding is unclear.

   a. **Status in criminal proceedings:** Where, as in the *Nixon* case itself, the presumptively privileged material is sought by the **prosecution** for use in a criminal case, the Court's opinion seems to mean that the qualified privilege will always be outweighed by the needs of the criminal justice system (at least if military, diplomatic or national security secrets are not involved).

   b. **Criminal defendant:** Where privileged information is sought by a **defendant** in a criminal proceeding (rather than by the prosecution, as in *Nixon*), the reasons for overriding the claim of privilege seem to be even more compelling.

   c. **Congressional inquiries:** One area left untouched by the *Nixon* Court was the conflict between a presidential claim of privilege and the needs of a **congressional inquiry**. For the most recent Supreme Court ruling on a conflict between a congressional demand for presidential documents and a President's resistance to the demand, see the discussion of *Trump v. Mazars USA*, *supra*, p. 148. (That case did not involve a President's claim of executive privilege, solely a claim of immunity; but the Court's opinion shows that when the party seeking presidential documents is Congress rather than the courts, additional separation-of-powers concerns require that Congress' need for the documents be *carefully scrutinized*.)

d. Assertion by non-incumbents: *U.S. v. Nixon* involved an assertion of executive privilege by the *incumbent* President. In a subsequent case, also related to Richard Nixon, the Court held that the qualified privilege could *also* be asserted by a *non-incumbent*. In *Nixon v. Administrator of General Services*, 433 U.S. 425 (1977), the Court held that Nixon, now out of office, could assert executive privilege with respect to his presidential papers, which were to be entrusted to succeeding administrations for archiving under congressionally-prescribed guidelines.

i. Privilege not violated: However, the Court held that the guidelines, at least insofar as they permitted an Executive Branch employee to screen the materials and return items of a personal nature to the ex-President, ***did not violate*** his executive privilege. The Court's decision was influenced in part by the fact that neither of the two succeeding administrations supported Nixon's claim of privilege, thus suggesting that the functioning of the Executive Branch was not threatened by the archiving and screening process.

Quiz Yourself on
SEPARATION OF POWERS (ENTIRE CHAPTER)

19. Congress passes the Personal Communications Services Act of 2020. The PCSA authorizes the FCC to award to private applicants, based on competitive bid, various pieces of radio spectrum for use in a new method of providing cellular phone service. The PCSA provides that any spectrum award by the FCC shall become permanently effective 90 days after it is first made, unless Congress has within the 90-day period enacted a Joint Resolution cancelling the particular award. According to the statute, such a Joint Resolution is to take effect immediately, without further action by any government official. The FCC then awards a particular spectrum license to Comm Co. Sixty days after this award, Congress passes a Joint Resolution purporting to cancel the award to Comm Co.

(a) If Comm Co. wishes to attack the constitutionality of the Joint Resolution stripping it of its license, what is the best argument it can make? _____

(b) Will this constitutional attack succeed? _____

20. To combat the over-prescription of opioid-based medications, Congress passes the Opioid Over-prescription Act of 2020 (the "OOA" or the "Act"). The OOA establishes a new federal agency, the Narcotics Prescription Agency ("NPA"), whose director is to be appointed by the President, subject to Senate confirmation. The Act directs the NPA to "enact and enforce rules governing when and how health-care professionals may prescribe medications containing opioids." The Act says that these rules are to be issued "for the purpose of curbing the over-prescription of medicines containing opioids," but gives no further guidance to the agency about the content of the rules. Lastly, the Act provides that the willful violation of any of the rules shall constitute a federal felony.

The NPA then promulgates a rule prohibiting any health-care provider from prescribing more than 130 Mg of morphine per day for any patient. Doc, a physician, is charged in federal district court with the crime of issuing a prescription to Vic for 200 Mg per day, and is convicted. He appeals to the Court of Appeals, raising only the argument that his conviction must be reversed because the OOA is "void as a standardless and thus unconstitutionally-broad delegation by Congress to the NPA of Congress's legislative powers." Should the Court of Appeals affirm or overturn Doc's conviction, and why?

———————————

21. The Caribbean island of Grenoble is a small but strategically important ally of the United States. Grenoble holds a popular election, but the military refuses to allow the democratically elected President to take office. The military then begins to seize the property of American businesses located in Grenoble. The President of the U.S., concerned that U.S. strategic interests are endangered, and invoking his powers as Commander in Chief, sends 20,000 U.S. troops onto the island. This action is taken after the President confers with congressional leaders, but with no other congressional action. With Congress still inactive, fighting continues for six months, due to the Grenoble military's well-entrenched status. A member of Congress, Senator Piper, then brings suit for a declaratory judgment that the President has acted unlawfully in using U.S. forces in this manner.

(a) What is the best argument that Senator Piper can make against the constitutionality of the President's actions? _____

(b) Will Piper's attack succeed? Assume there's no existing relevant federal legislation. _____

22. Congress recently passed the "Credit Card Consumer Protection Act" (the "Act"), which imposed new limits on how credit card issuers may extend consumer credit. The Act also created a new federal agency, the Consumer Credit Card Protection Agency (the "Agency"). The Act gives the Agency cabinet-level status, in part by creating the post of "Director" of the Agency, who must be nominated by the President and confirmed by the Senate. The Act also specifies that the Agency may bring administrative actions against credit card companies for violations of the Act; these actions may be resolved via "hearings" conducted by "administrative law judges" (ALJs) employed by the Agency. The Act says that ALJs conducting such hearings shall have powers comparable to those of a federal district judge hearing a federal civil case. Finally, the Act creates the post of Deputy Secretary (who is to be appointed by, and reports to, the Director), and gives the Deputy Secretary the authority to appoint Agency ALJs. A duly-appointed Deputy Secretary of the Agency recently appointed various ALJs, including Judge Jones.

The Agency brought an administrative action against Credit Co., a credit card issuer. The case was heard by Judge Jones, who found that Credit Co. violated the Act. The Agency then, by taking no further action, allowed Judge Jones' decision to become final, and Credit Co. was required to pay a fine. Now, Credit Co. would like to get Judge Jones' finding and consequent fine thrown out, preferably on federal constitutional grounds. The company hires you to represent it.

(a) What is the best argument can you make about why the finding and fine violate the U.S. Constitution? _____

(b) Will the argument you make in part (a) succeed, and why? _____

23. Congress, concerned that colleges were taking unfair economic advantage of intercollegiate athletes, enacted the Intercollegiate Sports Regulation Act (the "ISRA"). The ISRA established a new federal agency, the "Intercollegiate Sports Regulatory Bureau" (the "ISRB" or the "Bureau"). In the ISRA, Congress specified that every student given a scholarship to participate as a member of an NCAA Division I athletic team should be deemed to be an "employee" for purposes of the federal Fair Labor Standards Act ("FLSA"). (The FLSA sets minimum wages, overtime pay, and other labor standards.) According to the ISRA, the ISRB is to be led by a "Director," who is nominated by the President and approved by the Senate. Because Congress wanted the ISRB to function independently of Executive-Branch interference, Congress specified in the ISRA that the Director would receive a six-year term, during which the President may remove him or her only for "inefficiency, neglect of duty, or malfeasance in office." Congress also provided that the Director is to be assisted by an Assistant Director, who can be removed by the President without cause. Lastly, Congress specified that in the event any portion of the statute were found to be unconstitutional, the remainder of the statute "shall not be affected" by the finding of unconstitutionality.

The ISRA gives the Bureau various powers, some essentially "legislative" and others "executive." The legislative powers include the power to issue regulations defining who is a Division I athlete. The executive powers include the power to sue any college or university in federal court to obtain a civil judgment on behalf of a scholarship athlete for wages that should have been paid to the athlete and were not. The ISRA says that such a suit must be signed by the Director or Assistant Director before being filed. In an ISRA complaint signed by the Bureau's Director, the Bureau has just sued Powerhouse University in federal court, seeking damages from the University for not paying its student-athletes as employees. Powerhouse has asked you for advice about whether there are any constitutional defenses it might plausibly raise to this suit.

(a) What is the strongest constitutionally-based defense that Powerhouse can raise? _____

(b) Putting aside any issue as to the proper remedy, is the defense you raise in part (a) likely to be found correct on the merits? _____

(c) For this part (c) only, assume that your answer to Part (b) is "yes"; assume also that the complaint against Powerhouse is amended, with the amended complaint signed by the Assistant Director. May the case go forward? _____

24. Congress has established the Federal Truck Safety Board (FTSB). In the statute setting up the FTSB, Congress has provided that the Director of the FTSB shall be appointed by the President, without the need for House or Senate confirmation. The enabling legislation also provides that at any time, without cause, the House and Senate, acting together in the form of a Joint Resolution, may remove the Director. The Director is given certain powers, including the ability to issue an order suspending certain types of truck traffic if the Director concludes that the suspension is needed to protect the safety of interstate commerce.

In the 30 years since the FTSB was set up, Congress has played no role in the appointment or removal of the FTSB's Director. The incumbent, Derrick, was appointed 10 years ago. Recently, there have been a rash of accidents on the highway involving trucks of more than six feet in width. Derrick has decided that such wide trucks are dangerous, and has, therefore, issued an order suspending any truck of that width or greater from moving on the federal highways across a state border. Truck Co., owner of many extra-wide trucks, wishes to challenge the constitutionality of Derrick's action.

(a) What is the best grounds on which Truck Co. can challenge the constitutionality of Derrick's order? _____

(b) Will this attack succeed? _____

25. Jessica was the White House Press Secretary. After she had served for one year, the President summarily fired her, without giving any reasons. Jessica sued the President for damages in federal court, alleging that he fired her in violation of a federal statute, Title VII. Jessica's claim is that the President made sexual advances to her, and fired her in retaliation for her refusal to entertain those advances. (Title VII does indeed prohibit sexual harassment of the sort charged here.) The President has moved to dismiss the suit on the broad grounds that he has absolute immunity from civil liability for any official act done by him

during his term of office, and that the court must dismiss the case without considering whether the allegations are true or false. Should the President's motion be granted? _____

26. Ronald Dumpster, the presidential nominee of the Plutocrat Party, was elected President of the U.S. in the 2020 election. Soon after his inauguration, press reports appeared suggesting that around 2017, when Dumpster was mayor of Cap City in the state of Corruption, he may have solicited and/or received bribes from Tornado Corp, a real estate developer seeking approval to build a large project in Cap City. It was common knowledge that while mayor, Dumpster had kept bank accounts at a Cap City branch of Banco. In late 2021, at a time when the House of Representatives was controlled by the Plutocrats' opposition (the Radical Party), the House Banking Committee issued a subpoena *duces tecum* to Banco for its records from 2016 through 2018 of any account associated with Dumpster. At about the same time, a Corruption state prosecutor, Radical Party member Rudy Spritzer, called a state criminal grand jury to investigate these bribery allegations. That grand jury issued, at Spritzer's request, a subpoena *duces tecum* to Banco for Banco's records of any Dumpster-associated accounts for the same period. Dumpster's personal lawyer brought separate federal-court suits seeking to quash both the House subpoena and the Spritzer subpoena, each on the grounds that Dumpster, as a sitting President, has absolute immunity from such subpoenas. Lawyers for the House and for Spritzer's office have opposed the suits, claiming that the President has no immunity – absolute or qualified – that would protect the records.

(a) (i) In the House suit, what is the farthest-reaching type of immunity – absolute or qualified – that the judge hearing this suit may properly conclude that Dumpster has? _____ (ii) What standard should that judge apply in deciding whether Dumpster has the type of immunity you listed in part (a)(i)? _____

(b) (i) In the Spritzer suit, what is the farthest-reaching type of immunity – absolute or qualified – that the judge hearing this suit may properly conclude that Dumpster has? _____ (ii) Does Spritzer need to make a showing of greater need for the subpoenaed records than he would have had to make in support of a subpoena by him of comparable bank records pertaining to a private individual? _____

─────────

Answers

19. (a) That the Resolution violates the Presentment Clause, by which the President is given the opportunity to veto any bill.

(b) Yes. The scheme described here is a classic two-house ***"legislative veto,"*** under which Congress attempts to keep oversight over administrative action by reserving the power to cancel that administrative action by means of a Resolution. The scheme here, insofar as it calls for the Joint Resolution to take effect immediately, deprives the President of his opportunity to veto any bill. Therefore, the scheme is invalid. See *INS v. Chadha* (The theory behind the invalidity of the legislative veto is that the Resolution is itself the exercise of legislative power, so it must be carried out by the same procedures as for any other legislative act, i.e., passage by a majority of each house and presentment to the President for his signature.)

20. The court should affirm the conviction, because the Act's delegation of power to the NPA here is constitutionally proper. The facts here are fairly similar to those in *Gundy v. U.S.* (2019), where Congress enacted a statute (SORNA) that delegated to the Attorney General the job of drafting rules governing whether, how, and when certain convicted sex offenders would have to register with their local communities. In *Gundy*, D, an offender who was convicted for not having registered as required by these rules, claimed that SORNA was an instance of standardless and therefore overly broad delegation. But the Court disagreed and affirmed D's conviction. (Though the vote in *Gundy* to affirm was 5-3, there was no majority opinion.) A plurality in *Gundy* said that since Congress had laid down an ***"intelligible principle"*** to guide the Attorney General in her rule-making, the delegation to the A.G. "falls well within permissible bonds." Since *Gundy* indicates that this easy-to-satisfy "intelligible principle" standard remains the only constitutional requirement that a delegation by Congress to the Executive Branch must meet, that's the standard the Court of Appeals must apply to the delegation in this question. And since the instruction the OOA here gives to the NPA – that the NPA should promulgate rules "for the purpose of curbing the over-prescription of medicines containing opioids" – seems to contain as much of an intelligible principle as the instruction upheld in *Gundy*, the outcome in *Gundy* indicates that the OOA's delegation to the NPA is equally valid.

But, as I note on p. 118 *supra* in the discussion of *Gundy*, the next time a delegation issue comes before the present Supreme Court, a majority may well **overrule Gundy** in favor of a more-stringent anti-delegation standard. However, note that the question here asks you what the *Court of Appeals – not* the Supreme Court – should do. Since the Court of Appeals must follow established law until that law is overruled, and since the "intelligible-principal" is still established law after *Gundy*, the Court of Appeals must affirm based on that easy-to-satisfy standard.

21. **(a) That it violates Congress' sole power to declare war.**

(b) Yes, probably. It is true that Article II, Section 2, explicitly grants the President the power of Commander in Chief of the U.S. Armed Forces. However, the President must use this power subject to oversight by Congress. In particular, the power to "declare war" is given solely to Congress, in Art. I, Section 8. While the President may, without a declaration of war, probably commit our troops to repel an immediate emergency, it is very unlikely that the President may wage a prolonged ground war, without a declaration of war, especially where the United States has not been directly attacked.

22. **(a) That Judge Jones' appointment as ALJ did not satisfy the Appointments Clause.** In *Lucia v. SEC* (2018), the Supreme Court held that an ALJ conducting enforcement hearings for the SEC had ***"significant authority"*** under federal law, and was therefore an ***"inferior officer"*** (not a garden-variety federal employee) as that term is used in the Appointments Clause. Consequently, the Court in *Lucia* said, the ALJ had to be appointed by a "Head of Department" (which in the case of the SEC meant appointed by direct vote of the Commissioners) rather than by a non-Department-Head federal employee working for that Department. Since the ALJ there had not been appointed directly by the Commission, he did not have the constitutional authority that he needed to have in order to conduct the enforcement hearing from which the plaintiff (Lucia) was appealing.

(b) Yes, because Judge Jones was not properly appointed to the role (ALJ) that he purported to occupy. It follows from *Lucia, supra*, that when an ALJ holds enforcement hearings in which he exercises a suite of powers comparable to those of federal district court judges, the ALJ is exercising "significant authority" under federal law, and is thus acting as an "inferior officer" under the Constitution. Here, the fact pattern tells us that Agency ALJs have the same broad set of powers as the ALJ in *Lucia* did; therefore, Judge Jones, like the ALJ in *Lucia*, exercised "significant authority" when he decided Credit Co.'s case, and thus acted as an "inferior officer" under the Constitution. Judge Jones was consequently required to have been appointed by no one lower than a "Head of Department." In the case of an independent federal agency — as in the case of a cabinet department — the only person deemed to be the "Head of Department" is the person in charge, i.e., the highest-level person in the agency, one who was appointed by the President. Here, that person is the Secretary. Since Jones was not appointed by the Secretary, but rather by a Deputy Secretary who in turn reported to the Secretary, Jones' appointment did not satisfy this requirement. As in *Lucia*, the consequence of this procedural irregularity is that any hearing conducted by Jones in which he exercised this "significant authority" was constitutionally unauthorized, and must be nullified.

23. **(a) That because the Director is a "principal federal officer," and the Bureau has significant executive powers, Congress was not empowered to say that the President can remove the Director only for cause.**

(b) Yes. It's always been the case that *Congress may not place any limits at all* on the President's power to *remove Cabinet heads or other "principal officers" of agencies that have significant "executive powers."* However, Congress *is* constitutionally permitted to assure the *independence of agencies that are essentially legislative or judicial* (even if they have minor executive powers); Congress may do this by providing that the President may not remove the leaders of such an agency except for cause. *Humphrey's Executor.* But as a result of a 2020 decision, *Seila Law v. Consumer Fin. Prot. Bureau,* Congress may limit the President's removal power in this way only if two conditions are satisfied: (1) the agency *does not have significant "executive powers"* (just legislative or judicial ones); and (2) the agency is *governed by a multi-member board* rather than by a single director. If either of these conditions is not satisfied, then separation-of-powers principles dictate (*Seila Law* says) that the President must be left with the power to remove the agency's leader(s) without cause.

Here, the ISRB's structure fails to satisfy *either* of these conditions: (1) the Bureau's ability to sue universities who violate the statute – a manifestation of the power to enforce the law – shows that the Bureau has significant executive powers; and (2) the Bureau is headed by a single Director, not by a multi-member board or commission. Therefore, according to *Seila Law,* the *Humphrey's Executor* exception allowing Congress to limit the President's removal power *does not apply.* Rather, the situation is governed by the general separation-of-powers principle that the President must be left with the power to remove any principal federal officer(s) at any time for any or no reason. Since the Director of the Bureau is a "principal" federal officer rather than an "inferior" officer (that's so because he/she has no boss except the President), the President-may-remove-only-for-cause aspect of the ISRA is unconstitutional. Consequently, the defense articulated in part (a) is correct on the merits.

(c) Yes, because the constitutional flaw in the Bureau's structure is severable from the rest of the statute. Whenever a court concludes that an individual provision in a statute is unconstitutional, the court must then decide whether that provision is *"severable"* from the rest of the statute. To answer, the court must ask two sub-questions: (i) does the court believe that Congress would have wanted the rest of the statute to be enforced despite the unconstitutionality of the provision?; and (ii) are the surviving provisions capable of "functioning independently" of the now-stricken provision? If the answer to *both* questions is "yes," the court must apply the statute as best it can without the unconstitutional provision. (Otherwise, the court must treat the entire statute as invalid.)

Here, as to sub-question (i), there is no doubt about what Congress would have wanted, because the statute contains an express instruction that in the event any portion of the statute is found to be unconstitutional, the remainder of the statute *"shall not be affected"* by the finding of unconstitutionality. (By the way, this is exactly the same severability language that Congress used in the statute creating the agency at issue in *Seila Law,* where the Supreme Court found that the unconstitutional provision was severable from the rest of the statute.) As to sub-question (ii), notice that the statute says that the Assistant Director is removable by the President without cause; since the A.D. has signed the amended complaint, it's clear that in this set of circumstances, letting the suit continue based on the A.D.'s signature would allow the statute to "function independently" after severance of the offending "Director may only be removed for cause" provision. Therefore, the suit as amended can continue (as happened in *Seila Law* as well).

24. **(a) That by retaining the right to remove Derrick, Congress has improperly vested executive functions in its own agent.**

    (b) Yes, probably. Congress and its agents can only exercise "legislative power," not "executive power." The FTSB Director's powers are clearly executive — the Director is carrying out the laws (by determining what is required for safety) rather than "formulating" the laws. Congress, by retaining the right to remove the Director without cause, converted the post of Director into an agent of Congress, thus in effect taking executive powers onto itself. Therefore, Derrick is not permitted to exercise his statutory powers, including issuance of the order. See *Bowsher v. Synar*, striking down certain powers of the Comptroller General on the similar analysis that Congress improperly converted him into an agent of Congress by retaining the power to remove him.

25. **Yes.** The President does indeed have absolute immunity from civil liability for his official acts. See *Nixon v. Fitzgerald*. This immunity applies even if the official act was done illegally or maliciously. If the President did in fact fire Jessica for the reasons she states, the President has clearly violated Title VII, which bans various forms of sexual discrimination, including sexual harassment. However, since the President was clearly acting within the "outer perimeter" of his duties as President (that is, when he fired his Press Secretary he was clearly acting within the bounds of his presidential authority), the illegality of his actions is irrelevant for civil damage purposes. (Observe that if the conduct charged here had been carried out by any other federal government official, the immunity would have merely been a "qualified" one, since the conduct charged here violated a "clearly established" right. See *Harlow v. Fitzgerald*.)

26. **(a)(i) Qualified**.

    (a)(ii) A "middle" standard, one that is more demanding than the easy-to-satisfy standard applicable to ordinary congressional subpoenas not involving a President (which just have to relate to a "valid legislative purpose"), but that is **less demanding than the hard-to-satisfy standard urged by President Trump in comparable litigation** (which would have required the House to show that the information was "demonstrably critical" to the House's legislative purposes). The Court announced this standard in *Trump v. Mazars USA*, a 2020 decision involving subpoenas to President Trump's bank demanding his pre-presidential banking records, where the subpoenas were issued by House Committees investigating Russian interference with the 2016 election and other topics. Under this middle standard, the court must take account of separation-of-powers issues, by assessing (1) whether *other sources* could provide Congress the information it needs; (2) whether the subpoena is *"no broader than reasonably necessary"* to support Congress' legislative objective; and (3) whether the *evidence* offered by Congress as to its *legislative purpose* is *sufficiently strong* (where the "more detailed and substantial" the evidence of purpose is, the stronger Congress' position will be).

    (b)(i) Qualified. In *Trump v. Vance*, a 2020 suit involving a New York State criminal grand jury's subpoena for President Trump's bank records in a setting like that of our question here, the Court *rejected Mr. Trump's claim* that he had *absolute* immunity from such a subpoena, and said that his immunity was merely a *"qualified"* one.

    (b)(ii) No. In the *Vance* case, the Court rejected President Trump's argument that Vance (the state D.A. seeking to enforce the grand jury's subpoena) should have to satisfy a "heightened need" standard. Whereas Trump argued that Vance should have to show that the evidence was "essential," the Court held that all Vance had to show was that the evidence being sought was *"material,"* the standard used to evaluate subpoenas issued by state courts for records of *ordinary persons* being investigated. But according to the *Vance* decision, if the President were able to show that the subpoena was issued to "manipulate" him, or that its enforcement would impair his ability to perform his constitutional duties, then the subpoena could be quashed.

In our case, nothing in the facts suggests that President Dumpster can show either that the Spritzer subpoena was issued for the purpose of manipulating him, or that compliance would impair Dumpster's ability to perform his constitutional duties. (As to the burden from compliance, keep in mind that the records are being held by ***third parties***, a fact that makes compliance with the subpoena much less likely to impair Dumpster's performance of his duties than if the records were held by Dumpster himself.)

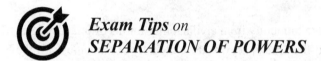

Exam Tips *on* SEPARATION OF POWERS

Separation-of-powers problems are usually pretty easy to spot. The harder part, usually, is to say something intelligent about how the issue should be resolved, since the law in this area is very hazy. Here are some particular things to watch for:

☞ If you see a question in which ***Congress delegates*** to a federal agency or other part of the Executive Branch the authority to ***make rules*** to implement a statute, consider whether Congress has violated separation-of-powers principles by ***giving up too much discretion***.

   ☞ At present, the test is the easy-to-satisfy ***"intelligible principle"*** standard – the delegation is valid as long as Congress supplies an intelligible principle to guide the person or agency to whom Congress has delegated rule-making authority. Remember that ***no delegation since 1935 has been held to violate*** this test (but you might indicate that the present Court seems ready to put some teeth back into this standard).

☞ Whenever your fact pattern indicates that the President is issuing an ***"executive order,"*** consider whether this may amount to the ***making of law*** rather than the mere carrying out of law. If so, the President is probably treading on Congress' domain. (But remember that if Congress acquiesces, even implicitly, to the President's exercise of power, then the problem disappears. See, e.g., *Dames & Moore v. Regan.*)

☞ Always remember that "legislation" cannot go into effect unless the President has been given the opportunity to ***veto*** the bill. Therefore, if your fact pattern has Congress do something by a one-house or concurrent ***resolution***, determine whether what Congress is doing amounts to lawmaking; if so, the action is unlawful. (See, e.g., *INS v. Chadha*, the "legislative veto" case.)

☞ One of the most common separation-of-powers issues involves the President's power as Commander in Chief to ***commit the use of American armed forces abroad***. The general rule, of course, is that only Congress, not the President, may declare war.

   ☞ However, the President may commit our armed forces even without a declaration of war in order to ***repel a sudden attack***, and probably to defend an ally with whom we have a treaty.

☞ Any time your fact pattern involves the ***appointment*** or the ***firing*** of a ***federal official***, be alert to possible separation-of-powers problems.

☞ The President, not Congress, has the *power to appoint* federal officers. Federal officers include ambassadors, federal judges, Cabinet members, agency heads, etc.

❑ When the President appoints a *"principal"* officer of the United States (i.e., a *top-level* officer), the appointment does not take effect until the Senate *"advises and consents,"* i.e., approves. This applies to *members of the Cabinet, ambassadors* and *federal judges.*

❑ Congress cannot appoint *"inferior"* federal officers either. But it can decide *which of three players* (the President, the federal judiciary, and the *"heads of departments,"* i.e., Cabinet members) may appoint any given inferior officer.

     ☞ An *"inferior federal officer"* is defined as one that has *"substantial authority"* even though she is not a "principal" (i.e., top-level) officer. *Administrative law judges* usually meet this definition. Be on the lookout for situations in which an inferior federal officer is being *appointed* — unless the appointment is made by the President or the judiciary, the *appointer* must be a *"Head of Department"* (cabinet-level official or agency-head), not someone below that rank. (Cite to *Lucia v. SEC* on this point.)

☞ The most frequently-tested area involving appointment of federal officers involves *removal* of officers once they have been appointed.

     ☞ Congress may *not* itself ever remove a federal officer, *except by impeachment.* But Congress *may limit the President's right to remove* a federal official, in two special cases: (1) leaders of *"independent"* agencies without major Executive-Branch powers (so long as the agency has a multi-member board rather than a single director), and (2) leaders of agencies with major executive powers but where the leader is an *"inferior" federal officer* (one who has a boss other than the President).

         Example of (1): Because the Federal Trade Commission is an "independent" agency with mostly legislative and judicial powers (not powers to enforce the law), and because the agency is led by a multi-member Commission, Congress may say that the President can remove a Commissioner only for cause. [Cite to *Humphrey's Executor* and *Seila Law.*]

         Example of (2): Congress may say that no Special Prosecutor (appointed to investigate certain Justice Department activities) may be removed by the President except for cause, because the S.P. is an "inferior" officer (one who reports to someone other than the President, namely, to the Attorney General). [Cite to *Morrison v. Olson.*]

❑ Congress may *not* limit the President's right to fire *high-level purely-Executive-Branch officers* (e.g., *Cabinet members*).

         Example: Congress may not pass a law stating, "The Secretary of State shall have a fixed term of at least four years, and may not be sooner removed by the President without cause." That would violate the separation-of-powers, since it would seriously impair the President's power to carry out his own responsibilities as head of the Executive Branch.

☞ *Impeachment* is occasionally tested.

 ☞ Keep in mind the procedural rules: by majority vote, the House decides whether to "impeach" (which is like an indictment). Then, the Senate conducts a trial, at which a *two-thirds vote* is necessary for conviction.

 ☞ Your fact pattern may involve the issue of whether the President or another federal official may only be removed for crimes, or may also be removed for non-criminal "abuses of power." The constitutional phrase is "high crimes and misdemeanors," but it is not clear what this means.

☞ Issues relating to *immunity* of the various branches are sometimes tested:

 ☞ If a *member of Congress* is sued (either civilly or criminally), or called before a grand jury, be alert to the possibility that the member may be protected by the *"Speech or Debate"* Clause, which is basically a form of immunity.

 ☞ The *President* and other *Executive-Branch members* have certain types of immunity, either absolute or qualified depending on the situation.

  ☞ The President and other Executive-Branch members do *not* have absolute immunity from *subpoenas issued by courts*, whether in federal-court proceedings or state-court proceedings. This includes subpoenas for *documents*.[Cite to *Trump v. Vance*.]

 ☞ But the President *does* have *absolute* immunity from being *held civilly liable for his official acts.*

  Example: P, an inspector in the State Department, is fired by the President for what P says is the President's fear that P will accuse the President of a crime (but for what the President says is P's "sloppy work"). P sues the President for civil damages. As long as the President has acted within the "outer perimeter" of his authority (which seems to be the case here, since the firing relates to P's work), the President has absolute immunity, and the case must be dismissed. [Cite to *Nixon v. Fitzgerald*.]

  ☞ But members of the Executive Branch *other than* the President get only *qualified* immunity from civil suits. (Focus on whether the right violated by the official was "clearly established" at the time he acted; if it was, he can be liable, if not, he'll be immune.)

 ☞ Remember that there is *no* Executive immunity from *criminal* prosecutions.

☞ If your fact pattern involves a President or other Executive Branch member who wants to *decline to disclose* material, consider the possibility that the doctrine of *"executive privilege"* may apply. If you discuss the doctrine, remember that the privilege is merely a *qualified* one, which can be outweighed by other interests (e.g., the need to develop all facts at a criminal trial). Also, mention that claims of executive privilege are justiciable — that is, the Court will typically decide these claims, rather than avoiding them as non-justiciable political questions.

CHAPTER 9

DUE PROCESS OF LAW

ChapterScope

This Chapter examines principally the Due Process Clause of the *Fourteenth* Amendment, which imposes the obligation of due process on the states. As you read, keep in mind that there is also a *Fifth* Amendment Due Process Clause, which applies only to the federal government; in general, anything that the Fourteenth Amendment Due Process Clause would require the states to do, the Fifth Amendment Due Process Clause requires the federal government to do. Here are the key concepts in this Chapter:

- **Due Process Clause generally:** The Fourteenth Amendment provides (in part) that "no state shall make or enforce any law which shall ... deprive any person of *life*, *liberty*, or *property*, without due process of law. ... " This is the Fourteenth Amendment's Due Process Clause.

- **The Bill of Rights and the states:** One of the major functions of the Fourteenth Amendment's Due Process Clause is to make the *Bill of Rights* — that is, the first ten amendments — applicable to the states.

  ❏ **Not directly applicable to states:** The Bill of Rights is not *directly* applicable to the states — the Bill of Rights as originally drafted limited only the *federal* government, not state or municipal governments.

  ❏ **Application of Bill of Rights to states:** But the Fourteenth Amendment, enacted in 1868, essentially changed this rule. That amendment requires that the states not deprive anyone of "life, liberty or property" without due process. Nearly all the guarantees of the Bill of Rights have been interpreted by the Supreme Court as being so important that if a state denies these rights, it has in effect taken away an aspect of "liberty."

  ❏ **Selective incorporation:** The Supreme Court has never said that due process requires the states to honor the Bill of Rights as a whole. Instead, the Court uses an approach called *"selective incorporation."* Under this approach, each right in the Bill of Rights is examined to see whether it is of "fundamental" importance. If so, that right is "selectively incorporated" into the meaning of "due process" under the Fourteenth Amendment, and is thus made binding on the states.

    ❏ **Nearly all rights incorporated:** By now, virtually *all rights* contained in the Bill of Rights have been incorporated, one by one, into the meaning of "due process."

    ❏ **"Jot-for-jot" incorporation:** Once a given Bill of Rights guarantee is made applicable to the states, the *scope* of that guarantee is interpreted the *same way* for the states as for the federal government.

- **Substantive due process generally:** One function of the Due Process Clause is to limit the *substantive power* of the states to regulate certain areas of human life. That is, certain types of state limits on human conduct are held to so unreasonably interfere with important human rights that they amount to an unconstitutional denial of "liberty." This use of due process analysis is called "substantive due process" analysis.

❏ **Non-fundamental rights:** In doing substantive due process analysis, courts distinguish between *fundamental* and *non-fundamental* rights. If a right or value is found to be "non-fundamental," then the state action that impairs that right only has to meet the easy "mere-rationality" test. That is, the state must merely be pursuing a *legitimate governmental objective*, and be doing so with a means that is *rationally related* to that objective.

  ❏ **Economic regulation:** Nearly all *economic* regulation (and most *"social welfare"* regulations) implicates only non-fundamental rights, and is thus usually upheld under this easy "mere-rationality" standard.

❏ **Fundamental rights:** But if a state or federal government is impairing a *"fundamental"* right, then the Court uses *strict scrutiny*: only if the governmental action is *"necessary"* to achieve a *"compelling"* governmental objective, will the government avoid violating substantive due process.

❏ **Significance of distinction:** The single most important thing to do when analyzing a substantive due process problem is thus to determine whether the right in question is "fundamental." If the right is not fundamental, there's almost certainly no substantive due process problem. If the right *is* fundamental, then strict scrutiny will almost certainly result in the measure's being invalidated.

■ **Economic and social-welfare regulation:** It is very easy for state *economic* and *social-welfare* regulation to survive substantive due process attack. The state must merely be pursuing a legitimate state objective by rational means. Virtually every state enactment that does not implicate a fundamental right will be upheld under this standard.

■ **Fundamental rights generally:** If a state or federal regulation *does* impair a fundamental right, then the Court *strictly scrutinizes* the regulation.

  ❏ **Test used:** Here is the test used by courts applying strict scrutiny where a state or federal regulation impairs a fundamental right: (1) the objective being pursued by the state must be *"compelling"*; and (2) the means chosen must be *"necessary"* to achieve that compelling end. In other words, there must not be any *less restrictive means* that would do the job just as well.

  ❏ **Rights governed:** The only rights that are "fundamental" for substantive due process purposes are ones related to the *"right of privacy"* or *"right of autonomy"*:

    ❏ **Birth control:** Individuals' interest in *using birth control* is "fundamental." So the state can't impair that interest without satisfying strict scrutiny.

    ❏ **Abortion:** Similarly, *abortion* is a right protected by substantive due process. (However, the state has a somewhat countervailing interest in protecting "potential life," so that not all restrictions on the right of abortion will be subjected to strict scrutiny.)

    ❏ **Family relations:** A person's decisions about how to live her *family life* and *raise her children* are also usually "fundamental." Thus the right of relatives to *live together*, a parent's right to direct the *upbringing* and *education* of his children, and the right to *marry* are all fundamental. Therefore, these rights can be impaired only if the state can pass strict scrutiny.

■ **Procedural due process:** The Due Process Clause protects not only "substantive" rights as discussed above, it also requires that the state act with adequate or fair *procedures* when it deprives a person of life, liberty or property.

❏ **Life, liberty or property:** There cannot be a procedural due process problem unless the government is taking a person's *life, liberty or property*. There is *no general interest* in having the government behave with fair procedures.

❏ **Property:** Most procedural due process problems involve the issue of whether the thing being taken constitutes "property."

❏ **Government benefits:** *Government benefits* may or may not constitute "property" rights. Generally, if one is just *applying* for benefits, one does *not* have a property interest in those benefits. But if a person has *already been getting* the benefits, usually he's got a property interest in *continuing* to get them, so the government cannot *terminate* those benefits without giving him procedural due process. The same analysis generally applies to government *jobs*: if you're just applying for the job, you don't have a property interest in it, but if you already have the job, then you may have a property interest, which entitles you to fair procedures before the job can be taken away.

❏ **Process required:** Once you determine that a person's interest in property or liberty is being impaired, you have to determine exactly *what procedures* the person is entitled to get.

❏ **Balancing test:** The court conducts a *balancing* test to determine the required procedures — the strength of the plaintiff's interest in receiving a particular procedural safeguard is weighed against the government's interest in avoiding extra burdens from having to give that safeguard.

I. THE BILL OF RIGHTS AND THE STATES

A. **The Bill of Rights generally:** The first ten amendments to the Constitution, all adopted in 1791, are commonly called the *Bill of Rights*. Their principal purpose is to protect the individual against various sorts of interference by the federal government.

1. **Not applicable to the states:** The Supreme Court decided fairly early that the guarantees of the Bill of Rights *were not directly binding upon state governments*. In *Barron v. The Mayor and City Council of Baltimore*, 32 U.S. (7 Pet.) 243 (1833), an opinion by John Marshall, the Court reasoned that "[h]ad the framers of [the Bill of Rights] Amendments intended them to be limitations on the powers of the state governments, they would have … expressed that intention … in plain and intelligible language." This conclusion has generally been accepted as being historically justified.

B. **Enactment of the Civil War Amendments:** The relative lack of constitutional restrictions on relations between state governments and individuals was drastically changed by the enactment of the three *post-Civil War Amendments*, the Thirteenth, Fourteenth and Fifteenth. Each of these three was enacted for the purpose of barring discrimination *by states* against individuals, especially blacks.

1. **Fourteenth Amendment:** Of greatest interest to us here is the *Fourteenth Amendment*, especially §1. §1 provides, in full, as follows:

"All persons born or naturalized in the United States, and subject to the jurisdiction thereof, are citizens of the United States and of the State wherein they reside. *No State* shall make or enforce any law which shall abridge the privileges or immunities of citizens of the United States; *nor shall any State deprive any person of life, liberty, or property, without due process of law; nor deny to any person* within its jurisdiction *the equal protection of the laws*."

C. **Due process of law and "incorporation":** Shortly after the Fourteenth Amendment was enacted, the Supreme Court seems to have implicitly rejected the notion that that Amendment automatically made applicable to the states all of the Bill of Rights guarantees (which had previously been binding solely on the federal government). See Gunther & Sullivan (13th Ed.), p. 431. But exactly what effect the Fourteenth Amendment had on the states' obligation to honor the Bill of Rights remained quite unsettled until well into this century. Most of the litigation on this issue has involved the *criminal procedure* aspects of the Bill of Rights.

1. **Two contrasting views:** There have been two main contrasting views espoused by members of the Court on this issue: the "*selective incorporation*" or "fundamental rights" approach, and the "*total incorporation*" approach. The former has always held a majority on the Court, but proponents of the latter view have triumphed in practice, although not in doctrine.

2. **"Selective incorporation" or "fundamental rights" view:** The "*selective incorporation*" approach denies that the entire Bill of Rights is made applicable to the states via the Fourteenth Amendment. Instead, the term "liberty" as used in that Amendment is to be interpreted by judges without regard to the Bill of Rights. Only those aspects of liberty that are in some sense "*fundamental*" are protected by the Fourteenth Amendment against state interference. (That is, those parts of the Bill of Rights which are of fundamental importance are "selectively incorporated" into the Fourteenth Amendment.) For this reason, the selective incorporation approach is sometimes called the "*fundamental rights*" approach.

3. **"Total incorporation" view:** The contrary view, that *all* of the guarantees specified in the Bill of Rights are made applicable to the states by the Fourteenth Amendment's Due Process Clause, is usually referred to as the "*total incorporation*" view.

4. **Modern approach:** As noted, the *selective incorporation/fundamental rights approach has always held a majority* on the Court. The Court today incorporates into the Fourteenth Amendment any guarantee which is "fundamental in the context of the [judicial] processes *maintained by the American states*." *Duncan v. Louisiana*, 391 U.S. 145 (1968).

    a. **Right to jury trial:** Thus in *Duncan*, the Court held that the Fourteenth Amendment guaranteed the right to a jury trial in state criminal prosecutions for which the potential sentence was two years in jail. A criminal process which was fair and equitable but used no juries was easy to imagine, the Court noted, but in the American scheme, where the jury is extensively used, and very serious punishments are generally imposed only after a right to a jury trial, the jury plays a fundamental role which the Fourteenth Amendment must safeguard.

    b. **Nearly all guarantees incorporated:** Although the Court has continued to adhere, in theory at least, to the selective incorporation/fundamental rights approach, the Warren Court sped up the process by which individual Bill of Rights guarantees were incorporated into the Fourteenth Amendment. Today, *virtually the entire Bill of*

Rights has been selectively incorporated into the Fourteenth Amendment (and thereby made applicable to the states), one guarantee at a time.

i. **Exception:** The only important Bill of Rights guarantee that has ***not*** been incorporated into the Fourteenth Amendment is the Fifth Amendment's prohibition of ***criminal trials*** without a ***grand jury indictment.*** [1]

ii. **Recent add-ons to the selectively-incorporated list:** Here are the three Bill of Rights guarantees that have been most recently added to the long list of rights that have been selectively-incorporated:

(1) **Second Amendment's right to bear arms:** The ***Second Amendment*** right of individuals to ***keep weapons for self-defense*** has been selectively incorporated, and thus made applicable to the states. See *McDonald v. City of Chicago*, 561 U.S. 742 (2010) (discussed *infra*, p. 438).

(2) **Eighth Amendment's ban on "excessive fines":** The ***Eighth Amendment's*** ban on ***"excessive fines"*** has also been selectively incorporated, and thus made applicable to the states. That Amendment (with the Excessive Fines clause highlighted) reads as follows: "Excessive bail shall not be required, ***nor excessive fines imposed***, nor cruel and unusual punishments inflicted." The incorporation of the Excessive Fines clause came in *Timbs v. Indiana*, 139 S.Ct. 682 (2019).

(3) **Jury verdict unanimity:** The Sixth Amendment's ***right to a jury trial*** for serious crimes has always been understood to require a ***unanimous verdict*** in *federal* trials. Then, in *Ramos v. Louisiana*, 140 S.Ct. 1390 (2020), the Court decided that the Sixth Amendment's right to a unanimous jury verdict for serious crimes also applies to *state* trials.

c. **"Jot-for-jot" or "bag and baggage" incorporation:** Once the Court determines that a particular Bill of Rights guarantee is incorporated into the Fourteenth Amendment, is the ***scope*** of that guarantee the same when applied to the states as when applied to the federal government? Some members of the Court, at various times, have argued that the answer should be "no." But a majority of the Court has always believed that once a particular guarantee is applied to the states, its ***contours should be the same*** as in its federal application. This majority view has sometimes been characterized (by those not holding it) as the ***"jot-for-jot"*** or ***"bag and baggage"*** approach to incorporation. See the dissent in *Crist v. Bretz*, 437 U.S. 28 (1978).

i. **Illustration:** An example of the prevailing "jot-for-jot" approach is *Malloy v. Hogan*, 378 U.S. 1 (1964): "[T]he prohibition of unreasonable searches and seizures of the Fourth Amendment ... and the right to counsel guaranteed by the Sixth Amendment are ... to be enforced against the states under the Fourteenth Amendment according to the ***same standards*** that protect those personal rights against federal encroachment. ... The Court has rejected the notion that the Fourteenth Amendment applies to the states only a ***'watered-down' subjective version***

---

1. The Third Amendment right not to have ***soldiers quartered*** in one's home has also never been incorporated. This is probably because the issue has never reached the Court; if it did, the Court "surely would find this provision applies to the states." Chemerinsky Csbk (6e), p. 531.

of the individual guarantees of the Bill of Rights."

D. The Fifth Amendment's Due Process Clause: Throughout this chapter, we'll be referring almost exclusively to the Due Process Clause of the *Fourteenth* Amendment. But there is another Due Process Clause: the *Fifth* Amendment states that "No person shall be ... deprived of life, liberty, or property, without due process of law..."

1. **Binding on federal government:** The Fifth Amendment, since it is part of the Bill of Rights, **binds the federal government.** Observe that the language of the Fifth Amendment's Due Process Clause is virtually identical to that of the Fourteenth Amendment's Due Process Clause, except as to which government is bound.

2. **Same interpretation:** Court decisions have interpreted the two clauses *identically*. That is, if a given type of conduct would be a due process violation when carried out by a state, it's equally forbidden to the federal government. It's important, however, to state which Amendment is triggered: the Fourteenth Amendment governs state action and the Fifth Amendment governs federal action.

II. SUBSTANTIVE DUE PROCESS — BEFORE 1934

A. Introduction: The Due Process Clause of the Fourteenth Amendment reads as follows: "Nor shall any State deprive any person of life, liberty, or property, without due process of law[.]"

If this language is analyzed literally, it sounds like a limitation that relates solely to *procedures*. However, the clause came to be interpreted as a limitation upon the *substantive power* of state legislatures to regulate various areas of economic and non-economic life.

1. **Meaning of "liberty":** Courts' willingness to review (and often invalidate) the substance of state legislation has taken place principally through interpretation of the term *"liberty,"* as used in the Due Process Clause. For instance, if a given state regulation is found to be an undue interference with a private person's "freedom of contract," or with his "right to privacy," the regulation is stricken as a taking of "liberty" without due process of law.

2. **Substantive due process:** The doctrine relying on the Fourteenth Amendment to invalidate a substantive state regulation is commonly called the *"substantive due process"* doctrine.

3. **Growth, abandonment and rebirth:** The present section of this outline, and the two which follow it, trace: (1) the rise of substantive due process from the late nineteenth century until the 1930s; (2) the doctrine's abandonment (at least with respect to economic regulation) in the late 1930s; and (3) its fairly dramatic rebirth as a means for vindicating a broad range of *non-economic* interests (especially the so-called *"right to privacy"*).

B. Early history of substantive due process: When the Fourteenth Amendment was first enacted, it was not clear whether it would be found to limit states' substantive, as opposed to procedural, powers.

1. *Slaughterhouse Cases*: In fact, in a case decided shortly after the Fourteenth Amendment was enacted, the Court seemed reluctant to conclude that that Amendment might limit states' powers. In the *Slaughterhouse Cases*, 83 U.S. (16 Wall.) 36 (1873), the Court had to decide whether Louisiana could give a monopoly on New Orleans-area slaughterhouses to a particular company. The Court held that this monopoly did *not* violate the Due Pro-

cess Clause. Although one of the dissenters argued that a statute prohibiting a large group of citizens from pursuing a lawful employment deprived them of both liberty and property without due process of law, the majority curtly rejected this contention, apparently on the theory that the Due Process Clause protects only against procedural unfairness.

2. **Rise of substantive due process:**   But within just a few years after the 1873 *Slaughterhouse* decision, public pressure on the Court to review the *substance* of state economic regulation proved compelling.

    a. **Increasing scrutiny:**   This pressure on the Court to review state economic regulations for substantive due process violations began to take its toll. For instance, in two important post-*Slaughterhouse Cases* decisions, the Supreme Court sustained state regulations, but indicated its willingness to engage in substantive review in some circumstances.

        i. **Regulation of "private" contracts:**   Thus in *Munn v. Illinois*, 94 U.S. 113 (1877), the Court deferred to the legislature's judgment as to an issue which the Court found to be "public" rather than "private" (the rates charged by grain elevators); but the Court indicated that in "mere private contracts," the judiciary would determine what regulations were "reasonable."

        ii. **Violations of "fundamental law":**   And in *Mugler v. Kansas*, 123 U.S. 623 (1887), even though the Court sustained a state ban on alcoholic beverages, the opinion indicated that legislation would be valid under the states' "police powers" only if it truly related to protection of the public health, safety or morals, and only if it did not violate "rights secured by the *fundamental law.*"

3. **Liberty of contract:**   Then, in 1897, the Court finally used substantive due process review to *invalidate a state statute.* In *Allgeyer v. Louisiana*, 165 U.S. 578 (1897), the Court struck down a Louisiana statute which prohibited anyone from obtaining insurance on Louisiana property from any company not licensed in Louisiana.

    a. **Rationale:**   The Court held that the statute violated the Fourteenth Amendment's Due Process Clause because it prevented the defendant (who had bought insurance from an out-of-state firm) from exercising his *freedom of contract*. The guarantee of "liberty" in the Fourteenth Amendment, the Court stated, protected not only physical liberty, but also such intangibles as the right to live and work where one wishes, to earn one's livelihood "by any lawful calling," and to enter any contracts necessary to accomplish any of these goals. While the state's police power might allow it to prohibit certain activities or contracts, that power did not extend to barring contracts, like this one, that were both made, and to be performed, outside of the state.

C. *Lochner* **and its aftermath:**   The 40 years after *Allgeyer* saw an enormous Supreme Court trend towards striking down state legislation on due process and similar constitutional grounds. Between 1899 and 1937, 159 Supreme Court decisions (not counting civil rights cases) held state statutes unconstitutional under the Due Process and Equal Protection Clauses; another 25 were struck down under the Due Process Clause coupled with some other constitutional provision. L,K&C, p. 439.

1. **The *Lochner* case itself:**   The best known, and from today's perspective most infamous, of these cases was *Lochner v. New York,* 198 U.S. 45 (1905). In *Lochner*, the Court struck down as an abridgment of *"liberty of contract,"* and therefore a violation of due process, a

New York law which *limited the hours which a bakery employee could work* to 10 per day and 60 per week.

a. **Two defenses of statute:**   New York defended its law on two grounds: (1) that it was a valid labor law; and (2) that it protected the health and safety of the workers.

b. **Not valid labor law:**   The Court quickly rejected the labor law justification for the statute. The police power extended only to protection of the "public welfare." The readjustment of bargaining power between bakery employees and their employers, the Court implied, was not of sufficiently public (as opposed to private) concern, especially in view of the law's infringement of the "liberty of contract." (The Court suggested that if bakers were not as intelligent as other workers, or for some reason needed unusual protection, the statute might be valid as a labor law; but the Court found no reason to believe that bakers as a class needed such special protection.)

c. **Not safety or health measure:**   Nor did the Court accept the "health and safety" rationale advanced for the statute. The Court did not find bakers to be an especially endangered group (as it had found miners to be in a case a few years previously). And long working hours did not affect the *public* health and safety by making the baked goods less fit to eat. In any event, the Court indicated, any interest the state had in guarding the wholesomeness of the baked goods could be satisfied by measures which *interfered less with freedom of contract*, e.g., inspecting premises, requiring that washrooms be furnished, etc.

d. **Legislature's motives suspected:**   The *Lochner* majority clearly disbelieved that the legislature had in fact acted in part for safety and health reasons. The law's natural effect was to regulate labor conditions, not to protect anyone's health and safety. The Court thus implied that only the legislature's *actual motive*, not a hypothetical motive, would be looked to in evaluating a statute subjected to substantive due process attack.

e. **No deference to legislative fact finding:**   Another key element of the *Lochner* Court's holding was its *refusal to defer to legislative findings of fact*. The Court insisted on reaching its own conclusions on the factual issue of whether the health and safety of bakers, or of the bread-eating public, needed special protection. For instance, the Court stated that "[i]n our judgment it is not possible in fact to discover the connection between the number of hours a baker may work in the bakery and the healthful quality of the bread made by the workman."

f. **Dissent:**   Four Justices dissented in *Lochner*.

   i.   **Harlan's dissent:**   One dissent, authored by Justice Harlan, argued that there was enough evidence that the statute would promote the health and safety of bakers that the legislature's judgment on this issue should have been accepted.

   ii. **Holmes' dissent:**   The other dissent, a very famous one by Justice *Holmes*, contended that the *Court had no right to impose its own views about correct economic theory on legislatures.* He made one of the most famous remarks in constitutional law: "The Fourteenth Amendment does not enact Mr. Herbert Spencer's social statics," a reference to a then popular "social Darwinism"/"laissez faire" theory.

   (1) **No economic theory embedded in Constitution:**   Holmes went on to say that "[a] constitution is *not intended to embody a particular economic theory,*

whether of paternalism and the organic relation of the citizens of the state or of laissez faire." "Liberty," as the term is used in the Fourteenth Amendment, should be found to be violated only when "a rational and fair man necessarily would admit that the statute ... would *infringe fundamental principles* as they had been understood by the traditions of our people and our law." By that test, Holmes contended, the statute was valid.

g. **Analysis of *Lochner* test:** Observe that the *Lochner* majority's test was an extremely stringent one in at least two respects:

   i. **Close fit:** First, it required a *very close "fit"* between the statute and its objectives. In the majority's words, there had to be a "real and substantial" relationship between the statute and the goals which it was to serve. This tight fit was absent in *Lochner* because bakers could have been protected by less restrictive measures, e.g., more frequent inspections, required bathrooms, etc.

   ii. **Limited objectives:** Second, only certain legislative *objectives* were acceptable. Regulation of health and safety was permissible, but *readjustment of economic power* or economic resources was *not*. Thus to the extent that the New York law in *Lochner* was merely a "labor law" which readjusted bargaining power, rather than a true health regulation, it served an impermissible objective. See Tribe, pp. 570-74.

h. **Relation to fundamental interests:** Even today, *strict due process scrutiny* is used by the Court where a *"fundamental interest"* is at stake. Perhaps the *Lochner* Court's mistake was in treating *"freedom of contract"* as a *"fundamental interest,"* so that the counterbalancing state interest had to be subjected to strict-scrutiny rather than minimal-rationality review. Gunther & Sullivan (13th Ed.), pp. 466-67.

2. **Other decisions of the *Lochner* era:** The period from about 1900 to 1937 was characterized, as noted, by widespread invalidation of economic legislation on substantive due process grounds. But not every statute directly affecting economic rights was overturned.

   a. **Maximum hours:** Consider laws setting maximum work hours, for instance. The *Lochner* case, of course, invalidated maximum-hour statutes as they pertained to bakers. But the Court was willing to allow such laws where it found that the benefited class for some reason *needed special protection*, beyond that given to workers in general.

      i. **Women:** Thus in *Muller v. Oregon*, 208 U.S. 412 (1908), the Court sustained a law barring the employment of *women* in a factory or laundry for more than ten hours in a day; the decision viewed women as members of a weaker class "disadvantage[d] in the struggle for subsistence," and therefore needing special protection.

         (1) **"Brandeis brief" technique:** By the way, *Muller* saw the first successful use of the "Brandeis brief" technique by a litigant. This type of brief (named after then-lawyer Louis Brandeis, who used it in *Muller*) contained *extensive documentation* to demonstrate the requisite link between the legislative end and the means used to achieve it (e.g., in *Muller*, the special weaknesses and needs of women, and the extra protection which a ten-hour maximum work day would give them).

b. Minimum wages: On the other hand, the Supreme Court in the *Lochner* era struck down a **minimum wage** law for women. *Adkins v. Children's Hospital*, 261 U.S. 525 (1923). The Court did this even though it had previously accepted maximum-hour laws for women (in *Muller, supra*). Again, the rationale was "freedom of contract," and again, Justice Holmes dissented.

III. SUBSTANTIVE DUE PROCESS — THE MODERN APPROACH TO ECONOMIC AND SOCIAL-WELFARE REGULATION

A. Initial decline of Lochnerism: *Lochner*, and the judicial philosophy behind it, were subjected to intense criticism in the three decades which followed that case. In addition to this criticism, the election of Franklin Roosevelt, and his New Deal programs, convinced many people of the need for aggressive legislative programs to ensure the nation's economic survival. Such large-scale government intervention in economic affairs was clearly at odds with the *Lochner* "freedom of contract" philosophy.

1. **Shift in Court personnel:**   Turnover in the Court's personnel, together with Roosevelt's threat to "pack the Court" with additional Justices, contributed to a philosophical shift towards greater deference to legislative intervention in economic affairs. See Tribe, p. 449.

2. *Nebbia* **case:**   The decline of Lochnerism was presaged by *Nebbia v. New York*, 291 U.S. 502 (1934), where the Court sustained a New York regulatory scheme for fixing milk prices. The Court did not explicitly reject the *Lochner* philosophy. However, the majority noted that due process required only that "[t]he law shall not be unreasonable, arbitrary or capricious, and that the means selected shall have a real and substantial relation to the object sought to be attained … " A state was free "to adopt whatever economic policy may reasonably be deemed to promote public welfare, and to enforce that policy by legislation adapted to its purpose."

   a. Significance: *Nebbia's* requirement of a substantial means-end relationship was essentially the test of *Lochner*. But the *Nebbia* Court was clearly determined not to impose upon legislatures its own views about correct economic policy, as the *Lochner* Court had done.

3. *West Coast Hotel Co. v. Parrish:*   But it was not until several years after *Nebbia* that the Supreme Court explicitly overruled one of the major *Lochner*-era precedents. This occurred in *West Coast Hotel v. Parrish*, 300 U.S. 379 (1937), where the Court upheld a state minimum wage law for women, and thereby explicitly overruled the *Adkins* case (*supra*, 170).

   a. Rationale: The Court mentioned the state's interest in protecting the health of women. But it gave substantial weight to the state's interest in redressing women's **inferior bargaining power** as well. The Court conceded that the minimum wage law interfered with "freedom of contract," but unlike *Adkins* (or *Lochner*), the decision concluded that a readjustment of economic bargaining power in order to enable workers to obtain a living wage was a legitimate limitation on that freedom of contract.

B. Judicial abdication in economic cases: *Nebbia* explicitly (and *West Coast Hotel* implicitly) preserved the requirement of a "real and substantial relation" between an economic regulation and a legitimate state objective. But cases following *West Coast Hotel* virtually abandoned even this degree of scrutiny between means and ends in economic cases.

1. *Carolene Products:* The year after *West Coast Hotel*, the Court made it clear that a *presumption of constitutionality* would be applied in the case of an economic regulation subjected to due process attack. In *U.S. v. Carolene Products Co.*, 304 U.S. 144 (1938), the Court sustained against a due process attack a federal prohibition on the interstate shipment of "filled" milk, i.e., skimmed milk mixed with non-milk fats.

   a. **Rationale:** The Court noted that Congress had acted upon findings of fact (e.g., committee reports) showing a public health danger from the filled milk. But even in the absence of explicit legislative findings, the Court held, "[t]he existence of facts supporting the legislative judgment is to be *presumed*, for regulatory legislation affecting ordinary commercial transactions is not to be pronounced unconstitutional unless ... [the legislation fails to] rest[] upon *some rational basis* within the knowledge and experience of the legislators." This test might be characterized as a *"minimum rationality"* standard, coupled with a *presumption of constitutionality*.

2. **Lessening of scrutiny:** But even the relatively mild scrutiny of *Carolene Products* was *abandoned* by the Supreme Court in subsequent economic regulation cases.

   a. **Hypothetical reasons to support act:** For instance, the Court has frequently been willing to *hypothesize* reasons which would support the legislature's action, even though there is *no evidence* whatsoever that these reasons *in fact motivated* the lawmakers.

      Example: An Oklahoma statute prevents opticians from fitting eyeglass lenses into frames (even old lenses into new frames) without a prescription from an ophthalmologist or optometrist. *Held*, the statute is constitutional, because it is a rational health measure. The legislature *"might have concluded"* that in some instances prescriptions are necessary to permit accurate fitting. *Williamson v. Lee Optical Co.*, 348 U.S. 483 (1955).

      i. **Consequence:** A consequence of the Court's tendency to hypothesize reasons in support of economic legislation is that one who attacks such legislation has the *burden of rebutting* not only reasons given by the legislature, but also *all reasons which the legislature "might have" considered*. Some of these hypothetical reasons may not even surface until the Court writes its opinion, making the job of attacking such legislation difficult indeed. See N&R, p. 388.

C. **Summary of modern approach:** In summary, the modern Court has *withdrawn almost completely from the business of reviewing state legislative economic regulation for substantive due process violations*. Not since 1937 has the Court struck down an economic regulation for violating substantive due process, and the present members of the Court all seem in agreement with this withdrawal.

1. **"Minimum rationality" standard:** Assuming that the objective being pursued by the legislature in an economic regulation falls within the state's "police power" (now extremely broadly defined to include virtually any health, safety or "general welfare" goal), all that is required is that there be a *minimally rational relation* between the means chosen and the end being pursued. This easy-to-satisfy standard is frequently called the *"mere-rationality"* standard, and that's the term we'll use here.

a. **"Arbitrary and irrational":** As the Supreme Court has sometimes phrased the standard, a regulation will be presumed to be constitutional unless government has acted in an "***arbitrary and irrational***" way. *Duke Power v. Carolina Environmental Study Group, Inc.*, 438 U.S. 59 (1978).

2. **"Social welfare" legislation:** The highly deferential mere-rationality standard applies not only in the case of economic regulation, but also in the case of "***social welfare***" legislation, so long as "fundamental" constitutional rights are not impinged. See, e.g., *Whalen v. Roe*, 429 U.S. 589 (1977), where the Court sustained New York's maintenance of a computerized data base of users of certain prescription drugs; the scheme was held to be an "orderly and rational legislative decision," and therefore not violative of substantive due process.

    a. **Distinguished from "fundamental" rights:** But where a law in the economic or "social welfare" area impinges on something the Court has found to be a "***fundamental right***," a substantially higher level of scrutiny is applied. The most important fundamental right, at least in substantive due process cases, has turned out to be the broadly-defined "***right of privacy***"; see infra, p. 173.

Quiz Yourself on

SUBSTANTIVE DUE PROCESS — ECONOMIC AND SOCIAL-WELFARE REGULATION

27. The legislature of the state of Utopia was worried about the large number of consumers being abused by the harassing tactics of debt collectors. A committee of the legislature investigated, and discovered that the vast majority of complaints involved debt collection techniques used by non-lawyers. Therefore (and at the urging of the state Bar Association), the Utopia legislature passed a statute providing that no person not admitted to the Bar of the State of Utopia may engage in the business of collecting debts owed by consumers. Kneecap, a non-lawyer debt collector, wishes to challenge the statute's constitutionality.

    (a) Putting aside any possible First Amendment issues, what right held by Kneecap is most likely to have been violated by the Utopia statute? _____

    (b) With respect to the right you listed in your response to (a), what is the standard for determining whether the right has been violated? _____

    (c) Will Kneecap's attack on the statute succeed? _____

Answer

27. **(a) Kneecap's substantive due process rights have been violated.**

(b) Whether the statute bore a rational relation to a legitimate state objective.

(c) No. Where a state statute regulates a purely economic matter, and does not involve any fundamental right, all that is required is that the means chosen be rationally related to a legitimate governmental objective. Here, the objective of reducing the harassment of consumer debtors falls within the state's police power, and is clearly "legitimate." The relation between the means chosen (ban on all non-lawyer collections) and achievement of the objective of reducing harassment is tenuous. But so long as the legislature could rationally have **believed** that non-lawyers were worse offenders on average than lawyers, the requisite "rational relation" between means and end is satisfied. In fact, for over 50 years, no state economic regulation has been overturned for substantive due process purposes, assuming an absence of a fundamental right. (The right to engage in the business of debt collection will almost certainly be held not to be "fundamental," a status limited in substantive due process cases to the "right to privacy," i.e., the areas of sex, marriage, child-bearing and child-rearing.)

IV. SUBSTANTIVE DUE PROCESS — PROTECTION OF NON-ECONOMIC AND FUNDAMENTAL RIGHTS GENERALLY

A. **Overview:** We turn now to those cases, mostly modern, in which the Supreme Court has in effect given substantive due process protection for certain *non-economic* rights. In contrast with the economic rights area, where the Supreme Court has virtually abstained from meaningful due process review since the late 1930s (see *supra*, p. 171), the Court has been surprisingly willing, during the last fifteen or so years, to strike down legislation which it finds to violate important non-economic interests.

1. **"Two-tier" scrutiny:** This dichotomy stems from the fact that the Court has applied *two* (or more) different *standards of review* in substantive due process cases. In the case of economic rights, the Court has required merely that there be a *rational relation* between the statute and a legitimate state objective. But where the Court finds that a *"fundamental right"* is impaired by a statute, it has applied a scrutiny that is stricter in two respects:

   a. the state's *objective* must be *"compelling,"* not merely "legitimate"; and

   b. the *relation* between that objective and the means (i.e., the means-end "fit") must be very close, so that the means can be said to be *"necessary"* to achieve the end.

2. **Comparison with equal protection:** This two-tier scrutiny is used in very much the same way in *equal protection* cases; differential treatment of groups will be sustained if it is rationally related to a legitimate state goal, unless either the classification impairs a "fundamental right," or the classification itself is found to be "suspect." See *infra*, p. 247.

3. **Which rights are "fundamental":** In the substantive due process area, the rights which the Supreme Court has found to be *"fundamental"* have tended to be in the related areas of *sex, marriage, child-bearing* and *child-rearing*.

   a. **Right to "privacy":** Generally, the Court has treated most of the interests it has found to be fundamental as falling within the broad category of the *"right to privacy."* However, as will be seen below, the Court's use of the term "privacy" often differs substantially from what we normally consider this term to mean. In many instances (e.g., the child-bearing situation), a more descriptive term might be the right to *"personal autonomy."*

4. **Significance of two tiers:** The significance of the Court's decision to place a particular "right" into the "fundamental" or "non-fundamental" side of the line is even greater than might at first be supposed.

   a. **Non-fundamental right:** Where the right is found not to be fundamental, so that a "legitimate" state objective, and a rational relation between the means chosen and that objective, are all that is required, the Court's deference to the legislative judgment is so extreme that there is *virtually no scrutiny at all*. As noted, for instance, in the economic area no statute has been invalidated on substantive due process grounds in over 50 years.

b. Fundamental right: By contrast, if the right is found to be fundamental, the scrutiny is so strict that few statutes impairing it can meet the double test of showing that the state's objective is "compelling," and that it cannot be achieved in a less burdensome way.

c. Significance: Thus the Court's decision on "fundamentalness" tends to be *virtually dispositive* of whether the statute is sustained or invalidated.

5. Relevance of "liberty": In some of the cases discussed below, the Supreme Court does not expressly state that it is using the doctrine of substantive due process. Nonetheless, these cases are usually treated as being, at bottom, substantive due process holdings. This is so because these decisions are properly viewed as holding that the right in question (whatever it is) is part of the *"liberty"* guaranteed against state action by the Fourteenth Amendment. For instance, Justice Stewart's concurrence in *Roe v. Wade, infra,* p. 177, stated that the prior *Griswold* decision (striking down state barriers to birth control by married couples) "can be rationally understood only as a holding that the Connecticut statute substantively invaded the 'liberty' that is protected by the Due Process Clause of the Fourteenth Amendment."

6. Scope of following discussion: Most of the discussion which follows is concerned with two principal areas: *birth control* and *abortion* (*infra,* pp. 175 and 177, respectively). Then, aspects of family relations (*infra,* p. 197) and other privacy/autonomy-related issues (including sexuality, *infra,* p. 202) are treated. We then conclude with a more complete discussion of the process by which the Court deems a particular right to be fundamental or non-fundamental (*infra,* p. 213).

B. The early non-economic cases: Although vindication of non-economic rights by use of the substantive due process doctrine has become of great practical importance only in recent years, several much older cases make similar use of the doctrine. The best known are *Meyer v. Nebraska,* 262 U.S. 390 (1923) and *Pierce v. Society of Sisters,* 268 U.S. 510 (1925).

1. *Meyer:* In *Meyer,* the Supreme Court struck down a state law which prohibited the *teaching of foreign languages* to young children. The Court held that the term "liberty," as used in the Fourteenth Amendment, included many non-economic, but nonetheless important, rights; the right of teachers to teach, and that of students to *acquire knowledge,* were among these. The Court applied what appears to have been a "mere-rationality" test (rather than any kind of strict scrutiny), but nonetheless concluded that the statute was "without reasonable relation to any end within the competency of the State."

2. *Pierce:* In *Pierce,* the Court struck down a state statute requiring children to attend public schools, and thus preventing them from attending private and parochial ones. This decision rested on the "liberty of parents and guardians to *direct the upbringing and education of children* under their control." The Court denied the power of the state to "standardize its children" by forcing them to accept only public instruction.

3. *Skinner:* A third case was decided on equal protection grounds, but was motivated by substantive-due-process-like concerns. In *Skinner v. Oklahoma,* 316 U.S. 535 (1942), the Court invalidated an Oklahoma statute which provided for compulsory sterilization of persons convicted three times of felonies showing "moral turpitude," but which did not apply to such "white-collar" crimes as embezzlement. The Court objected to the discrimination between, say, grand larceny and embezzlement, but it emphasized that its reason for strictly scrutinizing the discrimination was that "marriage and procreation are fundamental to the very existence and survival of the race."

a. **Probable modern view:** If a statute like the one in *Skinner* arose today, it would almost certainly be struck down on substantive due process/"right of privacy" grounds, even without regard to equal protection. Given the Supreme Court's acceptance of the fundamental importance of procreation in *Griswold* (birth control) and *Roe v. Wade* (abortion), it is almost inconceivable that the state would be permitted to sterilize any group (with the possible exception of convicted rapists).

   i. **Sterilization of mental defectives:** A law allowing involuntary sterilization of institutionalized *mental defectives* would also almost surely be struck down today. Yet such a statute was upheld, in one of the less glorious moments of the Supreme Court, in *Buck v. Bell*, 274 U.S. 200 (1927); Justice Holmes justified the statute with the remark that "three generations of imbeciles are enough."

C. Birth control (the *Griswold* case): The first major modern-era case which used a substantive-due-process-like approach to protect a fundamental right was *Griswold v. Connecticut*, 381 U.S. 479 (1965), the famous *contraceptives* case.

1. **Facts of *Griswold*:** The statute at issue in *Griswold* was a Connecticut law which forbade the use of contraceptives (and made this use a criminal offense); the statute also forbade the aiding or counseling of others in their use. The defendants were the director of the local Planned Parenthood Association and its medical director. They were convicted of counseling *married persons* in the use of contraceptives. No users, married or single, were charged in the case.

2. **Majority strikes statute:** The Court, by a 7-2 vote, *struck down* the statute. The majority opinion, authored by Justice Douglas, declined to make explicit use of the substantive due process doctrine. Instead, the opinion found that several of the Bill of Rights guarantees protect individuals' *privacy interest* and create a *"penumbra"* or *"zone"* of *privacy*. The Court then concluded that the right of married persons to use contraceptives fell within this penumbra.

   a. **Examples:** Thus the Court claimed that the First Amendment, by its explicit protection of the freedoms of speech and of the press, has "emanations" which create a "penumbra"; it is this penumbra which protects, for instance, the freedom of association, a freedom not explicitly mentioned in the Constitution. Similarly, the Court found, the Fourth Amendment's ban on unreasonable searches has a penumbra which protects privacy interests, as do the Third, Fifth and Ninth Amendments. Collectively, these Amendments establish a zone in which "privacy is protected from governmental intrusion."

   b. **Why statute was invalid:** Douglas' majority opinion did not specify exactly how the Connecticut ban on contraceptives violated this penumbra of privacy. But a good part of the rationale seemed to have to do with the privacy implications of *proof* in prosecutions. Thus the Court asked: "Would we allow the police to *search the sacred precincts of marital bedrooms for telltale signs of the use of contraceptives?*" Douglas concluded that "[t]he very idea is repulsive to the notions of privacy surrounding the marriage relationship."

3. **Concurrences:**   There were three separate concurring opinions in *Griswold*. We'll comment briefly on two of those concurrences, by Justices Goldberg and Harlan.

   a. **Goldberg's "fundamental rights" view:**   Justice Goldberg believed that the Fourteenth Amendment Due Process Clause protected all "fundamental" rights, whether or not these were explicitly listed in the Bill of Rights. Goldberg believed that the right of "marital privacy" was among such fundamental rights; he concluded that the statute unconstitutionally violated that right, because the contraceptive ban was not necessary for the fulfilling of a "compelling" state objective.

   b. **Harlan "ordered liberty" approach:**   Justice Harlan's concurrence was essentially in accord with Justice Goldberg's. As he had done several times before, he argued that the Fourteenth Amendment Due Process Clause does not merely incorporate the specific Bill of Rights guarantees, but instead "stands ... on its own bottom," to protect those basic values "implicit in the concept of ordered liberty." He then relied on his prior dissent in *Poe v. Ullman*, 367 U.S. 497 (1961), which had contended that the same Connecticut statute violated the due process interest in marital privacy.

      i. **No protection outside of marriage:**   Harlan's *Griswold/Poe* opinions stopped carefully short of finding a general right to privacy for sexual relations. He explicitly rejected the idea that adultery, homosexuality, fornication and incest were protected by the same right to privacy.

4. **Dissent:**   Justices Black and Stewart each wrote a separate dissent. Black reiterated his familiar argument that only those rights explicitly protected by a specific Bill of Rights (or other constitutional) provision were protected by the Fourteenth Amendment; he felt that no "right of privacy," in the broad and general way the majority used that term, was protected by any specific provision. Justice Stewart similarly failed to find a right of privacy in any specific guarantee, and also rejected the Goldberg Ninth Amendment rationale (claiming that it limited only the powers of the federal government).

   a. **Stewart reverses view:**   But Justice Stewart, as noted *infra*, p. 178, ultimately changed his view of *Griswold*, and concluded that the statute was properly invalidated as a substantive invasion of the Fourteenth Amendment Due Process Clause's "liberty" interest.

D. **Post-*Griswold* contraceptive law:**   Developments since *Griswold* make it clear that that case ultimately means much more than that married persons may not be prevented from using birth control — it means that ***no person***, single or married, may be prohibited from using contraception, or otherwise be subjected to undue interference with ***decisions on procreation***. As the Court said in a post-*Griswold* case, "[r]ead in light of its progeny, the teaching of *Griswold* is that the Constitution protects individual decisions in matters of child-bearing from unjustified intrusion by the state." *Carey v. Population Services Int'l*, discussed *infra*, p. 196.

   1. ***Eisenstadt v. Baird:***   Much of the expansion of the meaning of *Griswold* came in ***Eisenstadt v. Baird***, 405 U.S. 438 (1972), where the Court invalidated a statute which, by permitting contraceptives to be distributed only by registered physicians and pharmacists, and ***only to married persons***, ***discriminated against the unmarried***.

      a. **Rationale:**   In striking down the statute, the majority invoked equal protection as well as substantive due process grounds. The Court observed that "[w]hatever the rights of the individual to access to contraceptives may be, the rights must be the same for the unmarried and the married alike. … If the right of privacy means anything, it is the right of the *individual*, married or single, to be free from unwarranted government intrusion into matters so fundamentally affecting a person as the decision whether to bear or beget a child." (Emphasis in original.)

2. **Private place no longer required:** What might be called the right of *"reproductive autonomy"* (see Tribe, p. 1339), protected by both *Griswold* and *Eisenstadt*, now exists *even in non-private situations*. In the post-*Eisenstadt* case of *Carey v. Population Services Int'l* (discussed further *infra*, p. 196), the Court noted that the constitutionally-protected privacy interest in, *inter alia*, procreation and child-rearing "is not just concerned with a particular place, but with a protected intimate relationship. Such protected privacy extends to the doctor's office, the hospital, the hotel room or as otherwise required to safeguard the right to intimacy involved."

3. **Non-marital relationships:** Just as *Eisenstadt* broadened at least the contraceptive aspect of privacy to non-married couples, the Supreme Court has begun to recognize *a general right of privacy in sexual or procreational matters* outside the bounds of marriage. For instance, in *Lawrence v. Texas, infra*, p. 202, the Court held that state bans on sodomy violate the substantive due process rights of homosexuals, because there is "an autonomy of self that includes ... certain intimate conduct."

V. SUBSTANTIVE DUE PROCESS — REGULATION OF ABORTION

A. **Abortion generally:** The right of privacy which the Court found to exist in *Griswold* has been extended to the *abortion* context. The case recognizing that the right of privacy limits a legislature's freedom to proscribe or regulate abortion was the landmark case of *Roe v. Wade*, 410 U.S. 113 (1973). That case has since been interpreted and modified in a long line of decisions, the most recent of which is the 2016 decision in *Whole Woman's Health v. Hellerstedt* (*infra*, pp. 183-190). We will first review *Roe v. Wade*, then the various post-*Roe* cases on government's right to regulate the abortion process.

B. *Roe v. Wade:* In *Roe v. Wade*, 410 U.S. 113 (1973), the Court held that a woman's right to privacy is a *"fundamental" right* under the Fourteenth Amendment. Therefore, the legislature has only a limited right to regulate — and may not completely proscribe — abortions. The actual result of the case was to invalidate, on privacy grounds, Texas' nearly-complete ban on abortions.

1. **Precise holding in *Roe*:** The actual holding of *Roe* was remarkably specific, almost legislative. In an opinion by Justice Blackmun, the Court divided pregnancy into three *trimesters*, and prescribed a different rule for each:

   a. **First trimester:** During the first trimester, a state *may not ban, or even closely regulate, abortions*. The decision to have an abortion, and the manner in which it is to be carried out, are to be left to the pregnant woman and her physician.

      i. **Rationale:** The Court's rationale for this approach was that at present, the mortality rate for mothers having abortions during the first trimester is lower than the rate for full-term pregnancies. Therefore, the state has no valid (or at least no compelling) interest in protecting the mother's health by banning or closely regulating abortions during this period. (But the state may require that abortions be performed only by licensed physicians.)

b. Second trimester: During the second trimester, the state may protect its interest in the ***mother's health***, by regulating the abortion procedure in ways that are "reasonably related" to her health. Such regulation might include, for instance, a requirement that the operation take place in a hospital rather than a clinic. (The Court implied that during this second trimester, the risk of maternal death through abortion was higher than that in full-term pregnancies.)

    i. No protection of fetus: But the state may protect only the mother's health, ***not the fetus' life***, during this period. Therefore, a flat ban on second trimester abortions is not permitted. Nor may the state regulate in ways that protect the fetus rather than the mother's health.

c. Third trimester: At the beginning of the third trimester, the Court stated, the fetus typically becomes "***viable***." (Today, viability is generally estimated to occur about ***23 weeks*** after the woman's last period). That is, it has a "capability of meaningful life outside the mother's womb." Therefore, after viability the state has a "***compelling***" interest in protecting the fetus. It may therefore regulate, or ***even proscribe***, abortion. However, abortion ***must be permitted*** where it is necessary to preserve the ***life or the health*** of the mother.

2. Rationale of *Roe*: The *Roe* decision was premised upon the ***right of privacy***. The Court pointed to *Griswold*, as well as to other privacy-derived holdings (e.g., *Pierce v. Society of Sisters* and *Meyer v. Nebraska*, both *supra*, p. 174, recognizing freedom in child-rearing and education). This right of privacy, which the Court found to be part of the "liberty" guaranteed by the Fourteenth Amendment, was "broad enough to encompass a woman's decision whether or not to terminate her pregnancy."

a. Standard of review: In fact, the Court held, a woman's interest in deciding this issue herself was a "***fundamental***" one, which could only be outweighed if: (1) there was a "***compelling state interest***" in barring or restricting abortion; and (2) the state statute was "***narrowly drawn***" so that it fulfilled only that legitimate state interest.

b. Countervailing state interest: The Court found that the state had two interests which, in particular circumstances, might be compelling: protecting the health of the mother, and protecting the viability of the fetus. The former would only be compelling after the first trimester (when the abortion-related dangers outweigh the live-birth-related ones); the latter only applied during the last trimester, when the fetus was viable. From these two postulates the Court drew its three-part rule, summarized above.

    i. Fetus not person: The Court explicitly rejected the argument that the state had a compelling interest, even before viability, in ***protecting the fetus as a "person"*** as that term is used in the Fourteenth Amendment. The Court reached this conclusion largely on historical grounds.

3. Concurrences: There were two concurrences in *Roe*, by Justices Stewart and Douglas.

a. Stewart's concurrence: The Stewart concurrence reversed that Justice's dissenting position in *Griswold*, and accepted both *Griswold* and *Roe* as substantive due process cases; these and other decisions "make clear that freedom of personal choice in matters of marriage and family life is one of the liberties protected by the Due Process Clause of the Fourteenth Amendment."

   b. **Douglas' concurrence:** Justice Douglas wrote that the Fourteenth Amendment protected "freedom of choice in the basic decisions of one's life respecting marriage, divorce, procreation, contraception, and the education and upbringing of children." Douglas conceded that this freedom of choice was subject to regulation where there was a compelling state interest, but found that Texas' nearly-complete proscription of abortion in *Roe* went beyond such state interest.

4. **Dissent:** Justices White and Rehnquist wrote separate dissents.

   a. **White's dissent:** Justice White objected to what he called the Court's imposition of its own value scheme, preferring the "convenience, whim or caprice of the putative mother [over] the life or potential life of the fetus" prior to viability. He thought that the relative weights which should be assigned to these two interests should be left to "the people and to the political processes."

   b. **Rehnquist's dissent:** Justice Rehnquist argued that only a *"mere-rationality"* test, not a strict scrutiny one, should be applied; in his view, at least some of the abortion prohibitions and regulations forbidden by the majority could meet this minimum rationality standard. Also, he criticized the majority's three-part result as being "judicial legislation."

C. **The modification of *Roe* by *Casey*:** *Roe* has been ***partially overruled***. This occurred in one of the Court's two most important[2] post-*Roe* abortion decision, ***Planned Parenthood of Southeastern Pennsylvania v. Casey***, 505 U.S. 833 (1992). In *Casey*, a majority of the Court declined to overrule *Roe v. Wade* explicitly. However, important aspects of *Roe* — including abortion's status as a *"fundamental right,"* the state's almost complete inability to ***regulate first-trimester abortions***, and in fact the whole ***trimester framework*** of *Roe* — were all ***overturned***. As a result of *Casey*, the states ***may restrict abortion*** so long as they do not place ***"undue burdens"*** on the woman's right to choose.

1. **Pennsylvania statute:** At issue in *Casey* was a Pennsylvania statute which placed a number of significant restrictions on abortion, such as a requirement that the woman ***wait for 24 hours*** after receiving from a doctor certain information about abortion, and a requirement that a married woman ***notify her husband*** of her intent to abort. Several of these restrictions were clearly unconstitutional judged by the standards of the Court's post-*Roe* decisions.

2. **Three blocs:** There were three distinct voting blocs in *Casey*. First, two traditionally "liberal" Justices — Stevens and Blackmun (the author of *Roe*) — voted to reaffirm *Roe* completely. Second, a four-Justice "conservative" bloc — Chief Justice Rehnquist, and Justices White, Scalia and Thomas — voted to overturn *Roe* completely. The "swing" votes were supplied by a middle-of-the-road bloc consisting of Justices O'Connor, Souter and Kennedy, who voted to reaffirm the "central principle" of *Roe v. Wade*, but to allow state regulation that did not "unduly burden" the woman's freedom to choose. Thus the Court decided by 5-4 to maintain *Roe v. Wade* as precedent, but by 7-2 to allow states to regulate more strictly than *Roe* and its progeny had allowed.

3. **The joint opinion:** The three "centrist" Justices — O'Connor, Souter and Kennedy — formed a ***plurality*** opinion, which spoke for the Court on all points. The plurality opinion

---

2. The other key post-*Roe* abortion decision is *Whole Woman's Health v. Hellerstedt*, 579 U.S. __ (2016), discussed *infra*, p. 183.

was written by all three Justices *jointly*, rather than by a single Justice with others joining in the opinion. We will refer to this plurality opinion as the *"joint opinion."* The joint opinion was ultimately adopted by a *majority* of the Court more than two decades later, in *Whole Woman's Health v. Hellerstedt* (*infra*, p. 183), so that opinion is worthy of special attention.

a. ***Roe* reaffirmed:**   The joint opinion began by stating broadly that it was *reaffirming* the *"essential holding* of *Roe v. Wade*." The opinion saw this "essential holding" as having three parts: (1) a recognition of "the right of the woman to choose to have an abortion before viability and to obtain it without undue interference from the state"; (2) a confirmation of the State's power to restrict abortions after fetal viability, if the law contains exceptions for pregnancies endangering the woman's life or health; and (3) a recognition of the state's "legitimate interests from the outset of the pregnancy in protecting the health of the woman and the life of the fetus[.]"

b. **The "undue burden" standard:**   But what the joint opinion gave, it partly took away. Two aspects of *Roe* and the cases interpreting it should be *abandoned*, the three Justices held: the *"trimester framework"* of *Roe*, and (at least implicitly) the principle that any pre-viability abortion regulation must survive *strict scrutiny*.

   i. **Trimester approach rejected:**   The joint opinion noted that *Roe* used a trimester approach to govern abortion regulations: almost no regulation at all was permitted during the first trimester of pregnancy; regulations designed to protect the woman's health (but not to further the state's interest in potential life) were permitted during the second trimester; during the third trimester, because the fetus was now viable, the state could prohibit abortion as long as the life or health of the mother was not at stake. But the joint opinion did not agree that the trimester approach was a necessary method of safeguarding a woman's right to choose. The biggest vice of the trimester approach was that it *"undervalues the State's interest in potential life,"* because it completely ignores that interest during the first two trimesters.

   ii. **The "undue burden" standard:**   In place of the trimester approach, the joint opinion articulated a new *"undue burden"* standard: "Only where state regulation imposes an undue burden on a woman's ability to make [the decision whether to abort] does the power of the State *reach into the heart of liberty protected* by the Due Process Clause." A state regulation will constitute an "undue burden" if the regulation "has the purpose or effect of placing a *substantial obstacle* in the path of a woman seeking an abortion of a nonviable fetus."

      (1) **Furthering health or safety of woman:** Under the "undue burden" standard, if state regulations merely "create a *structural mechanism*" by which the state may "express profound respect for the life of the unborn," and do not place a substantial obstacle in the woman's path, the regulations will be *upheld*. Similarly, the state may regulate to further the *health or safety of the woman*, as long as the regulation does not unduly burden the right to abortion.

      (2) **Post-viability:** *After viability*, the joint opinion said, the state may proscribe all abortions not needed to protect the health or the life of the mother (a holding that does not represent any change from *Roe* or later cases).

iii. Fundamental rights and strict scrutiny: The joint opinion implicitly rejected *Roe*'s view that the right to abortion is a "fundamental" right, and *Roe*'s concomitant rule that every pre-viability restriction on this fundamental right must survive **strict scrutiny**. The opinion did not discuss either the "fundamental rights" or "strict scrutiny" issue, but it is clear that the opinion did not in fact apply strict scrutiny to the Pennsylvania statute (and applied the "undue burden" test instead). So we must assume that **abortion is no longer a fundamental right**, and restrictions on it are **no longer to be strictly scrutinized**.

c. Application to Pennsylvania statute: The joint opinion then applied its new "undue burden" analysis to the Pennsylvania statute. All but one of the Pennsylvania restrictions were **upheld** as not being unduly burdensome:

i. Informed consent: The Pennsylvania statute contained an elaborate **"informed consent"** requirement, both aspects of which the joint opinion **upheld**.

(1) 24 hour waiting period: First, at least **24 hours** before performing an abortion, a physician was required to inform the woman of the nature of the procedure, the health risks of both abortion and childbirth, and the "probable gestational age of the unborn child." (The waiting period was subject to an exception for "medical emergencies," defined as situations where an immediate abortion is required to avert serious risk of death or major bodily impairment to the woman.)

(2) Non-abortion alternatives: Second, either a physician or a qualified non-physician had to **inform** the woman of the **availability of state-printed materials** describing the fetus and providing information about non-abortion alternatives (e.g., adoption, child support, etc.).

(3) No undue burden found: The joint opinion found that these two informed consent requirements **did not "unduly burden"** the woman's right to choose to abort. The closer question came as to the 24-hour waiting period; here, the joint opinion relied mainly on the absence of any strong findings by the district court that the increased costs and potential delays which might stem from this waiting period were truly "substantial" obstacles.

ii. Spousal notification: But the joint opinion **struck down** the Pennsylvania statute's **"spousal notification"** provision. Under that provision, a married woman could not receive an abortion without signing a statement that she had notified her spouse that she was about to undergo the procedure. The provision contained several exceptions, including one for the situation where the pregnancy was the result of spousal **sexual assault** (provided that the assault was reported to the police within 90 days), and one applicable if the woman believed that notifying her husband would cause him or someone else to inflict **bodily injury** upon her.

(1) Struck down as undue burden: The joint opinion found that this spousal notification requirement was a **substantial obstacle** to abortion for some women: many fear that they will be **psychologically abused** by the husband, or that he will abuse their **children** (neither situation was covered by an exception in the notification requirement); others may fail to be able to use the exception for sexual assaults because they will be terrified to report the episode to the police, as was required for the use of that exception.

iii. **Parental consent:**   The joint opinion ***upheld*** the statute's ***parental consent*** provision, by which except in medical emergencies, an unemancipated young woman under 18 may not obtain an abortion unless she and one of her parents provides informed consent. The statute allowed for a "judicial bypass," by which a court could authorize performance of the abortion without parental consent, if the judge determined that the young woman had given informed consent and that an abortion would be in her best interest.

   (1) **Rationale for upholding:** The three Justices had little trouble upholding this provision, because it matched other "parental consent with possibility of judicial bypass" provisions that the Court had previously upheld (see the cases summarized *infra*, pp. 192-193).

4. **The Stevens and Blackmun opinions:**   Justices Stevens and Blackmun each wrote a separate opinion, concurring in part and dissenting in part. Each agreed that *Roe v. Wade* should be maintained as precedent, but each disagreed with the plurality as to how tightly the states may regulate abortion, and each believed that some of the Pennsylvania regulations upheld by the plurality were unconstitutional.

5. **Dissents:**   There were four ***dissenters*** in *Casey*. Chief Justice Rehnquist wrote one dissent, in which Justices White, Scalia and Thomas joined. Justice Scalia wrote another dissent, in which Rehnquist, White and Thomas joined.

   a. **Rehnquist dissent:** Rehnquist's dissent argued that the joint opinion "retains the outer shell of *Roe v. Wade* … but beats a wholesale retreat from the substance of that case." By contrast, he said, he and the other dissenters "believe that *Roe* was wrongly decided, and that it can and should be overruled[.]" The dissenters would have upheld ***all*** the challenged provisions of the Pennsylvania statute.

      i. **Not a fundamental right:**   To Rehnquist, the right to terminate a pregnancy was not, and should not have ever been declared to be, ***"fundamental."*** Abortion was quite different from marriage, procreation and contraception (other rights found to be "fundamental"), because it involved the termination of life and was thus a unique situation.

      ii. **Application to statute:**   Given Rehnquist's belief that the regulations merely needed to be "rationally related to a legitimate state interest," it was not surprising that he found them all to be valid. For instance, the spousal notice requirement was a "rational attempt by the State to improve truthful communication between spouses and encourage collaborative decision making, and thereby fosters marital integrity."

   b. **Scalia's dissent:**   Justice Scalia's dissent said that the right to terminate an unwanted pregnancy was simply not a liberty interest protected in any way by the U.S. Constitution. "I reach [this conclusion] for the same reason I reach the conclusion that ***bigamy*** is not constitutionally protected — because of two simple facts: (1) the constitution says absolutely nothing about it, and (2) the long-standing traditions of American society have permitted it to be legally proscribed."

D. The meaning of "undue burden" (*Whole Woman's Health v. Hellerstedt*): From the 1992 decision in *Casey* until 2016, the Court rarely considered whether particular regulations governing abortions did or did not constitute an "undue burden" on women's reproductive rights.

1. ***Whole Woman's Health v. Hellerstedt* puts teeth into "undue burden":** Then, in the most important abortion case since *Casey*, the Court in 2016 for the first time interpreted the *Casey* "undue burden" standard in a way that *placed meaningful limits* on the extent to which government may enact regulations having either the purpose or effect of putting substantial obstacles in the way of women who want to get a pre-viability abortion. That case, ***Whole Woman's Health v. Hellerstedt***, 579 U.S. 582 (2016), struck down by a 5-3 vote a pair of Texas regulations that severely limited *which doctors and abortion clinics could perform abortions* in the state.

2. **Facts of *Hellerstedt*:** In 2013, Texas passed a statute, H.B. 2, that imposed severe new restrictions on both abortion clinics and on doctors who perform abortions.

   a. **The two provisions:** There were two provisions whose constitutionality was at issue in the litigation:

      [1] **Admitting-privileges rule:** The first, called the *"admitting-privileges requirement,"* said that no doctor could perform or induce any kind of abortion in the state unless the doctor had *admitting privileges at a hospital no more than 30 miles from the location* at which the doctor was going to perform or induce the abortion.

      [2] **Surgical-center rule:** The second, called the *"surgical-center requirement,"* set minimum standards that any *"abortion facility"* (i.e., the office in which the abortion was to be performed) had to meet. Abortion facilities were required to meet the same standards as any *"ambulatory surgery center"* had to meet. Ambulatory surgical centers (which as the name implies are places where "surgery" is performed) had to satisfy demanding standards regarding building dimensions, number of nurses on duty, size of operating rooms, etc., which collectively cost large sums.

   b. **Trial court strikes down:** A group of abortion providers sued the state in federal court, contending that both the admitting-privileges requirement and the surgical-center requirement violated *Casey*'s prohibition on the imposition of "undue burdens" on abortion.

      i. **Trial and result:** After a four-day bench trial, the District Court agreed that each requirement imposed an undue burden on the right of at least some women to receive abortions in Texas.

      ii. **Reduction in number of clinics:** The court found that where before the passage of H.B. 2 there were more than 40 licensed abortion facilities in Texas, this number had dropped by almost half when the admitting-privileges requirement went into effect, and would drop by more than another half as soon as the surgical-center requirement began to be enforced (an event that was stayed by commencement of the suit). The court concluded that with both requirements in force, there would be only seven or eight abortion facilities left in the state (all in the Houston, Austin, San Antonio and Dallas/Fort Worth metropolitan areas); the judge projected that 1.3 million women of reproductive age would live more than 100 miles from the nearest abortion provider, and that 750,000 of these would be more than 200 miles away. The court found that the requirements would "erect a particularly high barrier for poorer, rural, or disadvantaged women."

    iii. Conclusion: In light of these findings, the judge concluded that the two restrictions imposed a "substantial obstacle" on women's exercise of their right to previability abortion. Consequently, the judge ***enjoined***, as to the entire state, the operation of both requirements.

  c. Court of Appeals reverses: The Court of Appeals *reversed* the District Court on the merits, concluding that with minor exceptions neither of the restrictions in H.B. 2 constituted an "undue burden." Therefore, the Court of Appeals dissolved the injunction except as applied to one particular abortion facility, in McAllen, Texas.

3. Breyer's opinion strikes the law: The Supreme Court, by a 5-3 vote,[3] *reversed* the Court of Appeals, and instead agreed with the District Court that both restrictions placed an undue burden in the path of large numbers of women who wished to undergo abortions in Texas. The majority opinion was by Justice Breyer (joined by Justices Kennedy, Ginsburg, Sotomayor and Kagan). Justices Alito, Thomas and Roberts dissented.

  a. Kennedy as swing vote: The *"swing vote"* turned out to be that of Justice Kennedy, as was so often the case. Kennedy joined the four liberals, casting the fifth vote to hold that Texas' restrictions *were* "undue burdens."

  b. Each part places an "undue burden": Breyer's opinion began by stating the Court's conclusion: Neither of the two restrictions ***"confers medical benefits sufficient to justify the burdens*** upon access that each imposes." He continued, "Each places a substantial obstacle in the path of women seeking a previability abortion, each constitutes an undue burden on abortion access [citing *Casey*] . . . and each violates the Federal Constitution."

  c. Balance benefits against burdens: Breyer described how a court reviewing an abortion restriction should go about deciding whether the restriction posed an "undue burden" or "substantial obstacle: courts must ***"consider the burdens*** a law imposes on abortion access ***together with the benefits*** those laws confer." And later in his opinion, he was even more explicit: the trial court, he said, had appropriately ***"weighed the asserted benefits against the burdens."*** In other words, to determine whether the burdens that a regulation places on abortions are "undue," the court is to *weigh* or *balance* those burdens against whatever benefits the state is claiming to be achieving.

    i. Limited deference to legislature: Breyer then tackled the related issue of *who was to decide* what (and how large) the "benefits" of the restrictions were: the *legislature* enacting the restriction, or the *court* reviewing that restriction?

      (1) What legislatures claim: Texas, in defending the suit, said that its legislature had designed the restrictions to protect the ***health of women seeking abortions*** — the legislature wanted to ensure that if something went medically wrong during the procedure, ***emergency help would be available*** either at the

---

3. At the time of the decision, the Court had only eight members, due to Justice Scalia's death in January, 2016, and Congress' failure to confirm a successor.

clinic itself (due to the surgical-center requirement) or at the hospital to which the woman would be transfered (due to the admitting-privileges requirement).

(2) Fifth Circuit requires deference to legislature: The Fifth Circuit had resolved this "who should decide?" sub-issue in favor of the legislature rather than the court system, in part because *"medical uncertainty underlying a statute is for resolution by legislatures*, not the courts."

(3) Breyer rejects this deference: But Breyer rejected the Fifth Circuit's wide deference to the legislature's factual conclusions about health benefits. That court said that the District Court had "substitute[d] its own judgment for that of the legislature." But Breyer disagreed: the District Court merely (and properly) *"considered the evidence in the record* — including expert evidence, presented in stipulations, depositions and testimony," and had then *correctly "weighed the asserted benefits against the burdens."*

(4) Absence of legislative findings: Furthermore, Breyer noted, the Texas statute here did not *"set forth any legislative findings."* Therefore, it was especially "consistent with this Court's case law" for the trial court to "give significant weight to *evidence in the judicial record.*"

ii. **Analysis of admitting-privileges requirement:** Breyer then turned to the task of carrying out this *weighing of burdens against benefits* as to the two Texas restrictions, beginning with the admitting-privileges requirement.

(1) Change from prior law: In doing this balancing, Breyer took care to compare the effect of that requirement against Texas' *pre-H.B. 2 regulations.* Even before H.B. 2, Texas had had regulations in place to deal with the possibility that a patient receiving an abortion might develop complications requiring hospitalization; these regulations had required that an abortion-provider *either* herself have admitting privileges at a "local" hospital, *or* "have a working arrangement with a physician(s) who has [such] privileges," so as to "ensure the necessary backup for medical complications." H.B. 2 merely *tightened* these pre-existing regulations, by saying it was no longer enough for the physician to have a working arrangement with a different doctor who had local admitting privileges, and by specifying that the "local" hospital had to be one "not further than 30 miles" away from where the procedure was being done.

(2) Weighed against prior law: Breyer then summarized the District Court's factual findings concerning the requirement. For instance, the trial judge found that even before H.B. 2's passage, "abortion in Texas was *extremely safe* with particularly low rates of serious complications and virtually no deaths occurring on account of the procedure."

(3) "No significant problems" that were helped: Because abortions in Texas prior to H.B. 2 were already "extremely safe" with regard to complications requiring immediate hospitalization, the District Court had concluded that the new admitting-privileges requirement *did not help to cure any significant health-related problem.* Breyer agreed, concluding that the new law *did not advance Texas' "legitimate interest in protecting women's health."*

(4) Closure of half of all clinics: On the "burden" side of the balance, Breyer concluded, there was ample evidence in the trial record that the admitting-privileges requirement *placed significant burdens* on patients' ability to obtain abortions. Between the passage of H.B. 2 and the effective date of the admitting-privileges requirement, the number of abortion clinics in the state had *dropped in half*, from 40 to about 20. And there was strong reason to believe that the admitting-privileges requirement was the *cause* of the closures.

(5) Consequence of closure: The large number of clinic closures made getting an abortion *significantly more difficult for many pregnant women* in Texas. Breyer pointed to record evidence that the closures meant "fewer doctors, longer waiting times, and increased crowding." And this burden was to be "viewed in light of the *virtual absence of any health benefit*" from the restriction. Therefore, he said, the record "adequately supports" the district court's finding that the restriction constituted an "undue burden."

iii. **Analysis of surgical-center requirement:** Breyer then conducted a similar benefits-versus-burdens analysis of the other Texas requirement, the *surgical-center requirement*. As noted, this provision required every abortion facility to meet the complex standards for *"ambulatory surgical centers."* As with the admitting-privileges requirement, Breyer concluded that the requirement imposed large obstacles to abortion, while *doing virtually nothing to improve patient health or safety.*

(1) Already safe: Breyer reasoned that the surgical-center requirement failed to improve patient safety for the same reason as the admitting-privileges requirement did: Texas abortions, under the pre-H.B. 2 regulatory scheme, were *already so safe* that requiring abortion facilities to meet the ambulatory-surgery requirements would not meaningfully add to patient safety.

(2) Safer than other procedures not subject to the requirement: Indeed, Breyer said, abortions were demonstrably safer than *other types of outpatient procedures* to which Texas did *not* apply its surgical-center requirements. For instance, Texas allowed a midwife to oversee *childbirth* in the patient's own home, yet nationwide, childbirth was 14 times more likely than abortion to result in death.

(3) Burdens are substantial: On the other side of the balance, imposing the surgical-center requirements on abortion facilities would *place a "substantial obstacle"* in the path of women seeking abortion. The parties had stipulated that enforcement of the surgical-center requirement (when added to the already-in-force admitting-requirement) would reduce the number of abortion facilities in the state to *seven or eight*, all located in either Houston, Austin, San Antonio or Dallas/Fort Worth. And there was expert testimony that to meet the demand, the number of abortions that these surviving clinics would have to provide annually would rise from 14,000 to 60,000-70,000, a *five-fold increase* compared with the number these facilities had handled before H.B. 2.

(4) "Undue burden": Therefore, Breyer concluded, the District Court had correctly concluded that the surgical-center requirement, like the admitting-privileges one, "provides few, if any health benefits for women, poses a substantial obstacle to women seeking abortions, and constitutes an 'undue burden' on their constitutional right to do so."

4. **Ginsburg's concurrence:** Justice Ginsburg wrote a brief concurrence in *Hellerstedt*.

   a. **Criticism of "TRAP" laws:** Ginsburg's concurrence made the first mention in a Supreme Court opinion of a phrase that pro-choice groups had been using to refer to state laws that single out abortion providers for special medical regulation: *"Targeted Regulation of Abortion Providers"* (or "TRAP") laws. As Ginsburg put it, "So long as this Court adheres to *Roe v. Wade* [and *Casey*] ... Targeted Regulation of Abortion Providers laws like H.B. 2 that 'do little or nothing for health, but rather *strew impediments to abortion*,' ... *cannot survive judicial inspection*."

5. **Dissents:** There were three *dissenters* in *Hellerstedt*. Justice Thomas wrote a dissent that no other Justice joined. Justice Alito wrote a longer one, in which both of the other dissenters, Chief Justice Roberts and Thomas, joined.[4]

   a. **Thomas' dissent:** Thomas' dissent was the only one to focus on the merits of the majority's conclusion that the Texas restrictions were an "undue burden" on the right to abortion.

      i. **Imposes strict scrutiny:** Thomas complained that the majority had unjustifiably *"radically rewrit[ten]* the undue-burden test" in several ways. For instance, he said, the majority had overruled a "central aspect of *Casey*" by requiring laws to have *"more than a rational basis* even if they do not substantially impede access to abortion." In his view, the majority's version of the undue burden test "looks far less like our post-*Casey* precedents and far more like the *strict-scrutiny standard* that *Casey* rejected, under which only the most compelling rationales justified restrictions on abortion."

      ii. **Creates a "preferred constitutional right":** Thomas also complained that the majority had "transformed judicially created rights like the right to abortion into *preferred constitutional rights*[.]" This was wrong, he said: "our Constitution renounces the notion that some constitutional rights are more equal than others."

6. **Degree of scrutiny of legislature's conclusion about burdens and benefits:** An important question *Hellerstedt* raises but doesn't resolve is this: what *degree of scrutiny* should courts give to the legislature's judgment that the regulation will not place a "substantial obstacle" in the path of women seeking abortions?

   a. **Majority silent:** Breyer's majority opinion in *Hellerstedt* doesn't really say. But that opinion does say that the Court of Appeals below was "wrong to equate the judicial review applicable to the regulation of a constitutionally protected personal liberty with the *less strict review applicable* where, for example, *economic legislation is at issue."* So Breyer seems to be saying at the very least that regulations placing a substantial obstacle in the way of pre-viability abortions must be subjected to a review that is *stricter than that applied to economic legislation*.

---

4. Because Alito's dissent focused on procedural issues like standing, we don't discuss it.

    i. Contrast to economic regulations: As we've seen earlier in this chapter (p. 171), when a court is evaluating garden-variety economic (or social) regulations not involving special "personal liberty" interests, ***very deferential review*** occurs, often referred to as ***"mere-rationality"*** review.

    ii. What standard beyond mere-rationality: Although Breyer is clearly saying that in the case of regulations significantly interfering with pre-viability abortions the standard of review is at least somewhat stricter than mere-rationality review, he doesn't specify ***what*** that more stringent standard is. Thus we don't know whether the review standard is "mid-level review" (of the sort used in equal protection cases for classifications based on gender; see *infra*, p. 320), "strict scrutiny" (used in equal protection for classifications based on suspect classifications like race or classifications that impair a fundamental right; *supra*, p. 256), or something else.

7. Reaffirmed in *June Medical* case: *Hellerstedt* remains good law as of this writing (late November, 2021). In ***June Medical Services v. Russo***, 140 S.Ct. 2103 (2020), the Court struck down, by a 5-4 vote, a Louisiana statute that, like the Texas statute in *Hellerstedt*, required doctors performing abortions to have admitting privileges at local hospitals. The five justices who voted to strike the Louisiana statute thought that it was virtually identical to the Texas statute.

    a. Roberts supplies fifth vote: Changes in the Court's composition between the 5-3 decision in *Hellerstedt* and the decision in *June Medical* – the ascension of Gorsuch and Kavanaugh and the departure of Kennedy – put the outcome in *June Medical* in doubt.

    b. Breyer's opinion for the Court: There was no majority opinion in *June Medical*. Justice Breyer wrote for a four-member plurality, joined by the Court's other three liberal members (Ginsburg, Kagan and Sotomayor).

        i. Roberts' rationale: The fifth vote needed to invalidate the statute came from Chief Justice Roberts, who had voted the other way (in dissent) in *Hellerstedt*. Roberts concurred only in the result in *June Medical*, not the reasoning of the four-member plurality. He said that he continued to believe that *Hellerstedt* was wrongly decided. But he concluded that, given the virtually identical nature of the two statutes, the doctrine of *stare decisis* required the Court to "treat like cases alike" unless there were "special circumstances" present. Roberts did not believe that such circumstances existed here.

    c. Future of *Hellerstedt*: The futures of both *Hellerstedt* and *June Medical* are questionable. Shortly after the June, 2020, decision in *June Medical*, Justice Ginsburg, a member of the 4-Justice plurality who had voted to strike the Louisiana statute there, died. She was replaced by Justice Barrett. Given Barrett's apparent hostility to the Court's abortion-rights precedents, it would not be too surprising if, in a later case involving a similar admitting-privileges requirement, she were to join the four conservatives who dissented in *June Medical*. If that happened, *Hellerstedt* would not survive even if Roberts continued to honor that decision on account of *stare decisis*. Indeed, even *Roe* itself may not survive in the present Court; see the paragraph immediately following this one for details

d. Two cases challenging *Hellerstedt* and *Roe* itself: As of this writing (late November, 2021), the post-Ginsburg Court seems to be about to decide whether *Hellerstedt* — and indeed, ***Roe v. Wade itself*** — should ***remain good law.*** The Court is in the process of hearing oral arguments in the last two months of 2021 in separate constitutional challenges to two highly-restrictive state anti-abortion statutes, one enacted by ***Mississippi*** and the other by ***Texas.***

i. Mississippi statute: Of these, the more direct threat to *Roe v. Wade* is the one involving a 2018 ***Mississippi*** statute. That statute bans most abortions ***after 15 weeks.*** Recall that *Roe* forbids states from banning pre-viability abortions, and viability doesn't generally occur until around 23 weeks (see *supra*, p. 178). There-fore, it's hard to see how the Court can avoid holding Mississippi's ban on abor-tions occurring between 15 weeks and 23 weeks to be unconstitutional, unless the Court ***overrules Roe's key holding*** that abortions may not be forbidden (though they may be regulated) prior to viability. The Mississippi case is *Dobbs v. Jackson Women's Health Organization*, and is scheduled for oral argument on Dec. 1, 2021.

ii. Texas statute: The other challenge before the Court is to a ***Texas*** statute, ***"S.B. 8,"*** which is probably the ***most restrictive abortion statute in the country.*** S.B. 8 bans nearly all abortions after ***six weeks of pregnancy*** (a time by which many women ***don't even realize they are pregnant***), and ***makes no exceptions for preg-nancies that result from incest or rape.*** The Court heard oral argument on the statute's constitutionality[5] in early November, 2021, but had not ruled by the time this book went to press in late November.

(1) No enforcement by government officials: However, the Court is apparently ***not*** going to decide the substantive issue of whether the S.B. 8's near-total ban on abortion is constitutional (i.e., whether *Roe v. Wade* should be overruled). Rather, the Court will decide the constitutionality of a unique feature of S.B. 8, which is that the statute ***may not be enforced by any government official*** (e.g., a prosecutor), but only by ***ordinary citizens serving as civil plaintiffs.*** The statute permits citizen-plaintiffs to sue clinics and others (but not patients) who provide, or even pay for or drive a patient to, an abortion that the statute makes illegal. The statute awards a citizen-plaintiff a ***minimum of $10,000 for each abortion*** they show to be illegal.

(2) Purpose of provision: It's clear that this "citizen-plaintiffs-only" provision was designed to ***prevent the usual method*** of contesting the constitutionality of an abortion restriction; that method is for a pregnant woman or abortion provider to sue — typically in federal court — the ***state official(s)*** charged with enforcing the statute. Texas's position is that because no state official can enforce the statute, any challenge to the constitutionality of the statute's under-

---

5. There are actually two suits before the Court attacking the Texas statute's constitutionality on which the Court has already heard oral arguments. One suit, *U.S. v. Texas,* has been brought by the Biden administration against the state. The other is *Whole Woman's Health v. Jackson,* brought against Texas by an organization that wants to provide abortions in the state. As discussed in the main text, both suits are before the Supreme Court only on a standing issue.

lying abortion ban cannot occur except in the context of a suit brought by a *bona fide* citizen-plaintiff against an abortion-provider under the statute, in which the defendant provider would raise the statute's unconstitutionality as a defense. (Neither of the two suits before the Supreme Court involves a citizen plaintiff, and there has been no such citizen-plaintiff suit as of this writing.)

    (3) Ruling on standing: In the November, 2021 oral argument, a majority of the Justices seemed to be leaning towards ruling against Texas on the standing issue, i.e., towards holding that would-be abortion providers would have standing to contest S.B. 8's constitutionality by bringing their own suit against Texas in federal district court. If a majority does so rule on the standing issue, the constitutionality of the underlying abortion ban would presumably not be presented to the Supreme Court until after the Court had already ruled on the constitutionality of the Mississippi statute (*supra*).

E. The future of state efforts to regulate abortions: Now that we have discussed the full range of Supreme Court abortion cases from *Roe v. Wade* through *Casey* and up to *Hellerstedt/June Medical*, here is a summary of current constitutional limits on the power of governments to restrict or regulate abortions:

1. The "undue burden" standard survives: The principal standard for judging the constitutionality of abortion regulations is the ***"undue burden"*** standard. That is, if the regulation is found to pose an "undue burden" on pregnant women's ability to get pre-viability abortions, the regulation is ***unconstitutional***, even if it is rationally related to the achievement of a legitimate state objective.

    a. Effect of *Hellerstedt*: As the result of the 2016 decision in *Hellerstedt* (*supra*, p. 183), a majority of the present Court has adopted this undue burden test (which previously had only been adopted by a plurality, in the 1992 *Casey* joint opinion). Here's how the *Hellerstedt* majority phrased the test: "There exists an 'undue burden' on a woman's right to decide to have an abortion, and consequently a provision of law is constitutionally invalid, ***if the 'purpose or effect'*** of the provision 'is to ***place a substantial obstacle*** in the path of a woman seeking an abortion ***before the fetus attains viability.***'" (The interior single-quotes show the *Hellerstedt* majority's use of phrases from the *Casey* joint opinion.)

    b. Purpose or effect: Notice that under *Hellerstedt*'s formulation, there are ***two different ways*** a regulation can be an "undue burden" on right to a pre-viability abortion: ***either*** by having the ***"effect"*** of imposing a "substantial obstacle" to the exercise of the right, ***or*** by having the ***"purpose"*** (on the part of the legislature that enacted the regulation) of imposing such a substantial obstacle.

2. "Undue" burden depends on comparing benefits vs. burdens: A regulation won't be struck down under *Hellerstedt* merely because it places *some* burdens on the availability of abortions: the burden on abortions must be found by the court to be ***"undue."*** And *Hellerstedt* doesn't say much about how the reviewing court is to determine whether the burden is "undue." But *Hellerstedt* gives a few clues about how this is to be done:

    a. Weighing benefits against burdens: Whether the "burden" is "undue" depends not only on the size of the burden, but also on the size of the countervailing ***"benefits"*** conferred by the regulation.

b. **Review is somewhat stricter than "mere rationality":** When the reviewing court is deciding whether the burdens caused by the regulation are "undue," it's unclear what *standard of review* the court is to use. But as I describe more fully above (*supra*, p. 187), it's pretty clear that the review is to be *more stringent* than the easy-to-satisfy "mere-rationality" standard used in ordinary cases not involving specially-protected constitutional interests.

c. **Little deference to legislative factfinding:** The reviewing court is required to pay some, but not necessarily very much, *deference to any factual findings made by the legislature* regarding the types and magnitudes of the burdens and benefits stemming from the regulation. Here's what *Hellerstedt* has to say on the topic: the reviewing court "retains an *independent constitutional duty to review factual findings* where constitutional rights are at stake," and at least as to medical issues that are unsettled, *"uncritical deference"* to the factual findings of the legislature is "inappropriate." (For more about this, see *supra*, p. 185.)

3. **Possible legislative responses:** Just because the Texas statute in *Hellerstedt* — and the matching Louisiana one in *June Medical* — were completely struck down, these results don't mean that other states that legislate in an attempt to discourage or restrict abortions will similarly fail.

a. **Some other potential restrictions:** Here are some additional abortion restrictions that have been proposed, and in some cases enacted; we will have to see whether these can survive the fairly demanding judicial review that *Hellerstedt* and *June Medical* seem to require.

❑ Provisions requiring that the woman be given *extensive warnings* before an abortion is performed, including detailed descriptions of how the procedure will be performed or what its consequences will be.

❑ Mandatory *ultrasound examinations* for women who are proposing to have an abortion, with the woman required to look at the fetus in the film. Again, this might be justified on the theory that the state is entitled to guard against the woman's later change of heart and consequent emotional distress.

❑ *Waiting periods* before an abortion can be performed, again on the "prevent later emotional distress" theory.

❑ *Mandatory reporting* by abortion clinics, or *emergency rooms*, of *medical complications* from abortions. This might help abortion opponents to amass data contradicting *Hellerstedt*'s conclusion that there is no medical need for abortion physicians to have local-hospital admitting privileges.

❑ Prohibitions on abortion decisions that the woman makes on the basis of the fetus' *race, sex, or genetic anomaly.*

❑ Requirements that there be *cremations* or *burials* for all fetal or embryo remains from abortions.

❑ Bans on particular abortion *methods*, including the use of *abortion-causing drugs.* (A legislature could point to possible side effects from the drugs.)

Note: See also pp. 189-190 *supra*, for a discussion of the draconian time limits that Texas and Mississippi have imposed, in cases that are before the Supreme Court in its 2021-22 term.

F. Cases on third-party consent, public funding and rules on particular abortion methods: Beyond the cases we've already discussed, the most important post-*Roe* cases about the constitutionality of abortion-related restrictions have centered on several areas:

> [1] requirements that ***persons other than the pregnant woman consent*** to the operation before it may be performed;
>
> [2] limits on ***public funding*** of abortions; and
>
> [3] bans on particular ***types*** of abortion ***methods***.

We discuss the cases on third-party consent in Par. G below; the ones on public funding of abortions in Par. H; and the ones on restrictions applicable to particular abortion procedures in Par. I.

1. Caution: In reading the following discussion of these issues, consider that most of these cases were decided before *Planned Parenthood v. Casey*'s adoption of the undue-burden standard, and *all* were decided before the 2016 *Hellerstedt* decision, which put real teeth into that standard. Therefore, any given case might well be decided differently today.

G. Consent: A number of states have enacted statutes that impose requirements that ***third persons consent*** to a woman's decision to get an abortion, or that require ***notice*** to third persons. The Supreme Court has decided a number of major cases in this area.

1. No absolute veto allowed (*Danforth*): The first, and most important, of these cases was ***Planned Parenthood of Missouri v. Danforth***, 428 U.S. 52 (1976), where the Supreme Court barred the states from giving a pregnant woman's ***spouse*** or parents, in most instances, an ***absolute right to veto*** the woman's decision to obtain an abortion.

> **a. Statute invalidated:** The statute struck down in *Danforth* barred abortions unless the operation was consented to by the woman's ***spouse*** or (if she was unmarried and under 18) by her parents.
>
> **b. Husband's consent:** The Court flatly ***rejected*** the requirement of consent by the husband. Both parents have rights at stake, but since the woman is more directly affected by the pregnancy, the Court concluded, she should have the deciding vote. Also, since the state itself cannot proscribe abortions during the early stages of pregnancy, it cannot delegate this power to the husband by allowing him to veto the procedure.
>
> > **i. Effect of *Casey*:** The principal holding in *Danforth* — that the states may not give a pregnant woman's spouse an absolute veto right over the woman's abortion decision — seems still to be good law. In *Planned Parenthood v. Casey, supra*, p. 179, the Court struck down a requirement that the woman's spouse be ***notified*** of the woman's intent to get an abortion. Even this lesser requirement of notice (as distinguished from consent, at issue in *Danforth*) was found to be an "undue burden" upon abortion, and this restriction was, indeed, the only restriction that the Court struck down in *Casey*. So it's quite clear that the state may not require spousal consent.

2. Parental consent reexamined: In numerous cases decided in the last several decades, the Court has reexamined the circumstances under which the state may require ***parental***

consent before allowing a *minor* to procure an abortion. See *Bellotti v. Baird*, 443 U.S. 622 (1979); *Akron v. Akron Center for Reproductive Health*, 462 U.S. 416 (1983); *Planned Parenthood v. Casey* (*supra*, p. 179). These cases have established the following rules to govern consent for minors' abortions:

a. **No automatic right to abortion:** Where a minor is found to be *insufficiently mature or emancipated* to make the abortion decision for herself, the state *may require parental consent.*

   i. **Informed consent by parents:** When the state requires parental consent, it may insist that that consent be *"informed."* More precisely, the state may insist that the parent listen to a presentation by the doctor about the alternatives to abortion, about the probable gestational age of the daughter's fetus, about the availability of state-printed literature, etc. Also, the state may apparently insist that this parental informed consent take place as part of an *in-person* visit by the parent to the facility where the abortion will be performed, and may insist that at least 24 hours elapse between the visit and the procedure. See *Planned Parenthood v. Casey*, *supra*, p. 179.

b. **Court hearing:** If the state *does* require parental consent, it must also give the girl an opportunity to *persuade a court* that, although she is not sufficiently mature or emancipated to make the decision for herself, an abortion is nonetheless *in her best interests*. If she does make such a showing, the court must override the parental veto. This procedure is sometimes called a *"judicial bypass."*

   i. **Consent of both parents:** If the state supplies the "judicial bypass," it may require the consent of *both* parents where the girl does not use the bypass. This is true *even if one parent does not live with the girl.*

   ii. **Emancipation or maturity:** Also, the state must provide for an *individualized judicial hearing* in which the girl may persuade the court that she is in fact sufficiently *mature* or *emancipated* that she is able to make this decision for herself. If the court concludes that she is mature or emancipated, it must allow the operation whether or not the court feels it is in the girl's best interest.

3. **Notice and consultation (*H.L. v. Matheson*):** Some states, seeing their ability to require parental consent in minor-abortion cases curtailed by *Danforth* and *Bellotti*, took a different route: they required that *notice* be given to the parents before an operation is performed on a minor. Most of these statutes have the express purpose of promoting "consultation" between the minor and her parents (even if the statute does not purport to give the parents veto power over the minor's decision to obtain the abortion). In *H.L. v. Matheson*, 450 U.S. 398 (1981), the Court *upheld* such a notice requirement, when applied to a young woman who is *neither emancipated* (i.e., living on her own) *nor mature enough* to make the abortion decision herself.

a. **Equivalent to consent:** Post-*Matheson* cases suggest, though they do not explicitly hold, that requiring *notice* to parents is constitutionally the equivalent of requiring *consent* by the parents.

   i. **Need for judicial bypass:** Therefore, it's probably the case that under *Casey* and *Hellerstedt*, a state may require parental notice and consultation only if the state *supplies a judicial bypass*, similar to the bypass required to be made available if the girl wants to avoid a parental refusal to give *consent*. Also, it seems likely that parental notice may not be required if the girl is mature or emancipated.

H. Public funding of abortions: While *Roe v. Wade* held that the decision on whether or not to procure an abortion (at least before viability) belongs solely to the woman, not to the legislature, this line of reasoning was not followed by the Court in its decisions on whether *public funding* of abortions is required. In two post-*Roe* decisions, the Court held that the government may pay for the expenses of childbirth, yet refuse to pay the expenses of abortion: (1) where the abortion is non-therapeutic (i.e., not necessary for the health of the mother); and (2) even where the abortion *is* necessary for the health, or even the life, of the mother. In a third post-*Roe* case, the Court held that the state may prohibit the use of any *public facility* or public staff to perform abortions.

1. **Non-therapeutic abortions (the *Maher* case):**   In 1977, the Court held that the states may refuse to provide Medicaid funding for *non-therapeutic* abortions, i.e., those where the operation is not necessary to protect the mother's life or health. Although the Court simultaneously decided three cases relating to this issue, the most important is *Maher v. Roe*, 432 U.S. 464 (1977). In *Maher*, the Court held by a 6-3 vote that Connecticut could constitutionally refuse to give Medicaid financing for non-therapeutic abortions, *even though it gave Medicaid financing for the expenses of ordinary childbirth*.

2. **Funding of medically-necessary abortions (*Harris v. McRae*):**   Then, the Court had to face an arguably tougher question: may the states or federal government refuse to fund *medically-necessary* abortions? Here, too, the Court answered *"yes,"* in *Harris v. McRae*, 448 U.S. 297 (1980).

3. **Use of public facilities and staff (*Webster*):**   *Maher* and *Harris* both stand for the proposition that the government need not give assistance to women desiring to exercise their constitutional right to an abortion. A later case carries this principle even further: in *Webster v. Reproductive Health Services*, 492 U.S. 490 (1989), the Court held that a state may prohibit all use of *public facilities* and *publicly-employed staff* in abortions.

   a. **Rationale:**   In *Webster*, the five-Justice majority believed that this no-public-facilities-or-staff rule was constitutional on the rationale that the state's refusal to allow public employees or public hospitals to participate in abortions "leaves a pregnant woman with the same choices as if the State had chosen not to operate any public hospitals at all," so that the state can't be said to have interfered with her reproductive autonomy.

4. **Abortion counseling:**   A final case in this sequence on public-funding of abortions goes even further: the government may, as a condition of funding family-planning clinics, insist that the doctor or other professional *not recommend abortion*, and *not refer clinic patients to an abortion provider*. *Rust v. Sullivan*, 500 U.S. 173 (1991).

I. Types of abortion allowable: A state's restrictions on the *types* of abortion that may be used, or the *procedures* surrounding the performance of abortions, may run afoul of women's constitutional right to have access to pre-viability abortions.

1. **The "partial birth" abortion method:**   The most significant case about the regulation of particular abortion *methods* is one in which the Court by a 5-4 vote *upheld* a federal statute banning the *"partial birth"* abortion method. *Gonzales v. Carhart*, 550 U.S. 124 (2007).

a. **Congress enacts a ban:** Congress enacted this federal ban in response to a decision made seven years previously in *Stenberg v. Carhart*, 530 U.S. 914 (2000), where the Court had struck down (also by a 5-4 vote) a similar Nebraska ban on partial-birth abortions. Between the *Stenberg* and *Conzales* decisions, Justice O'Connor, who had been part of the majority that invalidated the ban in *Stenberg*, had retired, and had been replaced by Justice Alito. That change in Court personnel seems to have made a decisive difference in *Gonzales*.[6]

b. **Definition of the forbidden type of abortion:** Congress made it a crime to carry out an abortion by a procedure that the *Gonzales* Court referred to as an "intact D&E." Congress defined the crime of performing a *"partial-birth abortion"* (the term used in the statute itself) as occurring only when the physician takes *two separate intentional steps*:

❏ First, the physician causes a still-living fetus to begin to be *delivered* until either (a) in a head-first delivery, the *entire head* of the fetus is outside the mother's body; or (b) in the case of a breech delivery, any part of the fetus' *body past its naval* is outside the mother's body; and

❏ Second, the physician performs an *"overt act"* on the partially-delivered fetus for the purpose of killing it. (The overt act must be something other than the mere completion of the delivery — typically, the overt act consists of the physician's use of scissors to make an opening at the base of the fetus's skull, through which a surgical catheter evacuates the skull contents.)

i. **Does not cover standard D&E procedure:** The federal statute, by requiring *two steps* before a prohibited abortion would be deemed to have occurred — a partial live birth followed by a *later overt act* of killing — made it pretty clear that the standard *constitutionally-protected* late-term D&E procedure (in which the fetus is killed inside the uterus, and then individual parts are separated and removed one at a time) was *not covered by the statute.*

c. **Protection of mother's health:** The federal statute *did not contain an exception* allowing the partial-birth procedure where it was necessary to *protect the mother's health* (though there *was* an exception to protect the mother's *life*).

d. **Attack on statute:** The suits in *Gonzales*[7] were *"facial attacks"* rather than "as applied" ones — that is, the plaintiffs were claiming that *all* applications of the statute should be ruled unconstitutional, whether or not application of the statute to the plaintiff's own behavior or proposed behavior would be unconstitutional. (See p. 243 for a discussion of the facial / as-applied distinction.)[8]

e. **Supreme Court upholds the statute:** The Supreme Court concluded by a 5-4 vote that the federal statute was *not invalid on its face.* The majority opinion was by Justice

---

6. However, the federal ban (enacted in response to *Stenberg*) was slightly less draconian than the Nebraska ban that had been struck down in *Stenberg*. The majority and dissenters in *Gonzales* sharply disagreed about how significant these differences were.

7. The case consisted of two separate suits that were consolidated before the Supreme Court.

8. The suit in *Stenberg*, too, had been a facial attack, and had led to a ruling by the Supreme Court that the Nebraska statute could not be enforced against *anyone*.

Kennedy, who served as the swing vote as he often did, and who as a dissenter in *Stenberg* had contended that the Nebraska statute was constitutional too. Kennedy's opinion (which was joined by Roberts, Scalia, Thomas and Alito) ***did not overrule Stenberg***, and instead ***distinguished*** it.

 i. Not an undue burden: Kennedy concluded that the statute ***did not impose an undue burden*** on a woman's right to control her reproductive destiny. In reaching this conclusion, he seemed to endorse legislative goals and methods that no prior post-*Roe* decision had approved:

  ❑ Citing *Casey*, Kennedy said that Congress was free to legislate to "show its ***profound respect for the life within the woman,***" and to further government's "legitimate interest in ***regulating the medical profession*** in order to ***promote respect for life***, including ***life of the unborn.***"

  ❑ Kennedy then said that the ban here would ***fulfill this legitimate interest*** without constituting an ***undue burden*** on the right of abortion.

  (1) As-applied challenge still available: But Kennedy emphasized that the Court was deciding only this broad ***facial*** challenge — which he said could succeed only if the plaintiff showed that the act would be unconstitutional in a "large fraction of relevant cases." If in any case involving a particular plaintiff, the lack of a mother's-health exception meant that the mother's health would be placed in jeopardy, an ***"as-applied"*** challenge could still be brought.

 f. Dissent: Justice Ginsburg wrote a long and passionate dissent, in which she was joined by Stevens, Souter and Breyer.

  i. Lack of mother's-health exception: Ginsburg objected especially to the statute's lack of an exception where the ***mother's health*** was at stake.

  ii. Women deprived of autonomy: Ginsburg also criticized the statute for "depriv[ing] women of the ***right to make an autonomous choice***, even at the expense of their safety." "[T]his way of thinking," she said, "***reflects ancient notions about women's place*** in the family and under the Constitution — ideas that have long since been discredited."

 g. Effect of Ginsburg's replacement by Barrett: Changes in Court personnel since the 2007 *Gonzales* decision (e.g., the replacement of Justice Ginsburg by Justice Barrett) make it near-certain that the present Court would decide *Gonzales* the same way — by upholding the federal statute — if the case arose today.

VI. OTHER SUBSTANTIVE DUE PROCESS ISSUES: CONTRACEPTION, CHILD REARING, THE RIGHT TO MARRY, SEXUAL EXPRESSION, AND THE "RIGHT TO DIE"

 A. Post-*Roe* regulation of contraception (*Carey* case): Only one Supreme Court case after *Roe v. Wade* has dealt with the regulation of ***contraception***. In that case, ***Carey v. Population Services Int'l***, 431 U.S. 678 (1977), the Court struck down a New York statute which: (1) prohibited anyone but a licensed pharmacist from distributing contraceptives to persons over 16;

and (2) entirely prohibited the sale or distribution of contraceptives to minors under the age of 16, except by prescription.

1. **Pharmacists-only rule:** The rule allowing only pharmacists to distribute contraceptives to adults was subjected to *strict scrutiny* (because it bore on the "fundamental" right to decide whether or not to procreate). Since the limitation reduced access to contraceptives, and lessened price competition, that restriction had to be justified by some "compelling" state interest. The interests advanced by the state (e.g., protecting health) were not compelling, so the provision was struck down. Six Justices agreed on this point.

2. **Ban on sale to minors:** As to the complete ban on non-prescription sales of contraceptives to minors, seven Justices agreed that the ban violated the right of privacy, but they were split 4-3 as to the appropriate rationale.

B. **Family relations:** One of the most striking expansions of substantive due process doctrine in recent years has been in the area of *family relations*. In a number of cases, individuals' desires to live together, to marry, or to raise their children in a certain way have come face to face with the state's desire to regulate zoning, marriage, child-rearing or other areas of public concern.

1. **"Fundamental rights" frequently found:** In general, the Supreme Court has in recent years found that a person's decision about how to conduct his family life often rises to the level of a "fundamental right." Consequently, the state may interfere with such a decision only when it shows that the interference is necessary for the fulfillment of a compelling public interest.

2. **Zoning and the "non-nuclear family":** Thus the government may not pass *zoning regulations* which impair the ability of family members to reside together, even if the family is an "extended" rather than "nuclear" one. In *Moore v. East Cleveland*, 431 U.S. 494 (1977), the Court struck down a zoning ordinance which allowed only members of a single "family" to live together.

    a. **"Family" defined:** The ordinance's definition of "family" was a restrictive one, which prevented the plaintiff from living with her two grandsons, who were first cousins. (She would have been permitted to live with two grandsons had they been brothers rather than cousins.)

    b. **Extended family protected:** A four-Justice plurality opinion (authored by Justice Powell) concluded that the right of members of a family, even a non-nuclear one, to live together was a liberty interest, and that state impairment of that interest must be "examine[d] carefully." Although the state interests advanced in support of the ordinance were legitimate ones (e.g., preventing overcrowding, traffic congestion and burdens on the local school system), these interests were only marginally advanced by the ordinance.

    c. **Dissents:** Four Justices dissented in *Moore*. Several of the dissenters contended that the right of members of an extended family to live together was not "fundamental," and that therefore a "mere-rationality" test, rather than heightened scrutiny, should be applied. The dissenters also warned that reference to "traditional values" would lead to widespread and standardless judicial invalidation of state legislative action.

    d. **Stevens' deciding vote:** Only four Justices followed the Powell analysis. The plaintiff won because Justice Stevens concurred on the grounds that the ordinance had no substantial relation to any state interest, and violated the plaintiff's *property* rights.

Thus it is unclear whether a case involving the rights of extended family members to reside together as lessees rather than landowners would yield the same result.

    e. ***Moore* distinguished from *Belle Terre*:** The *Moore* plurality took pains to distinguish that case from *Belle Terre v. Borass*, 416 U.S. 1 (1974), where a majority of the Court upheld a zoning restriction which excluded most groups of **unrelated** people from living together. The *Belle Terre* majority found that unrelated persons had no "fundamental" right to live together. (In particular, no fundamental right of association or privacy was found to be involved.)

        i. **Reconciliation:** Comparing *Moore* and *Belle Terre* illustrates that it is *family relations, not the right of individuals to choose with whom they live*, that the Court has honored with "fundamental rights" status.

3. **Child-rearing:** Parents clearly have a substantive due process right to direct the *upbringing and education of their children.*

    a. **Older holdings:** The Court has long recognized this right. See, e.g., *Pierce v. Society of Sisters (supra*, p. 174), holding that parents' substantive due process right to direct their children's education was violated by a rule requiring all children to **attend public schools** rather than private schools.

    b. **Right to decide who visits the child:** A recent example of a parent's right to direct the upbringing her child came in *Troxel v. Granville*, 530 U.S. 57 (2000), where most members of the Court seemed to agree that a parent has a fundamental due process interest in *determining which people outside the nuclear family will have access to the children.*

        i. **Facts:** In *Troxel*, a state-court judge ordered the mother of two minor girls to give monthly *visitation privileges* to the girls' paternal **grandparents**. The judge did so under a state statute that allowed a court to "order visitation rights for any person when visitation may serve the best interest of the child."

        ii. **Plurality:** There was no majority opinion in *Troxel*. But at least six members of the Court appeared to believe that the compulsory visitation here violated the mother's due process rights. A four-Justice plurality said that "the liberty interest at issue in this case — the interest of parents in the care, custody, and control of their children — is perhaps the **oldest of the fundamental liberty interests recognized by this Court**" (citing *Meyer v. Nebraska* and *Pierce*). The plurality went on to say that the visitation statute as applied in this case "unconstitutionally infringes on that fundamental parental right." The plurality did not suggest that the custodial parent's decision on visitation issues must always be respected by the state. But the opinion did say that where a parent is fit, a court deciding whether to grant visitation rights "must accord at least *some special weight* to the parent's own determination" about whether the proposed visitation would be in the child's best interests.

        iii. **Concurrences:** Two other justices who concurred, Souter and Thomas, agreed with this analysis. In fact, Justice Thomas said that to the extent the Court's precedents recognized a parent's fundamental interest in determining the details of child-rearing, he would apply *strict scrutiny* to infringements of that interest. (The plurality did not say what standard of review it was using.)

iv. Significance: So at least six members of the Court that decided *Troxel* seem to be on record as saying that a parent (at least a fit custodial parent) has a ***fundamental liberty interest*** in controlling the ***care and custody of her child***, and that the state's machinery for ordering visitation rights must attach ***significant weight*** to the ***custodial parent's judgment*** on visitation matters.

4. **Right to marry*:*** The ***right to marry*** is viewed by the Supreme Court as being "fundamental"; substantial interferences with that right will therefore not be sustained merely because they are "rational." This principle now (since 2015) applies to ***both opposite-sex*** and ***same-sex*** marriage.

   a. **Opposite-sex couples (*Zablocki v. Redhail*):** Before 2015, the only significant cases in which the modern Court addressed the issue of whether the right to marriage is fundamental for due process purposes were cases involving the right of ***opposite-sex couples*** to wed. The most important such case was ***Zablocki v. Redhail***, 434 U.S. 374 (1978).

      i. **Facts of *Zablocki*:** In *Zablocki*, the plaintiff attacked a Wisconsin law which required that any parent who was under court order to ***support a minor child*** not in his custody meet two requirements before being permitted to remarry: (1) payment of all court-ordered support; and (2) a demonstration that the child was not currently, and was not likely to become, a public charge (i.e., supported by welfare). Plaintiff attacked the statute on both equal protection and substantive due process grounds.

      ii. **Statute stricken:** The Court voted 8-1 to strike the statute. Five Justices, in an opinion by Marshall, felt that the right to marry was a sufficiently fundamental one that a ***"direct and substantial" interference*** with it should be ***subjected to strict scrutiny.*** (The Marshall opinion was, ultimately, an equal protection opinion, but its discussion of "fundamental rights" and strict scrutiny is highly relevant to substantive due process law.)

         (1) State interest here not compelling: Applying strict scrutiny to the statute at issue, Justice Marshall concluded that the state's interests were "legitimate and substantial," but that the state's method of furthering these interests ***unnecessarily interfered*** with the fundamental right to marry.

      iii. **Indirect interference is not subject to test:** But the Marshall opinion was careful to note that where a regulation merely had some ***incidental effect*** upon the ability to marry, without ***"significantly" interfering*** with that ability, only a ***"mere-rationality"*** test would be used. (But the statute at issue in Zablocki obviously significantly interfered with the ability-to-marry of anyone covered.)

   b. **Same-sex marriage:** Although *Zablocki* established in 1978 that the right of *opposite-sex couples* to marry is "fundamental" for substantive due process purposes, it remained unclear for more than another three decades whether *same-sex* couples have a similar fundamental right. Then, in the seminal case of ***Obergefell v. Hodges***, 135 S.Ct. 2584 (2015), a 5-4 majority of the Court resolved this issue ***affirmatively: same-sex couples have a fundamental liberty interest in being permitted to marry***, and no countervailing governmental interest is sufficiently strong to allow states to forbid same-sex marriages.

i. **Our discussion:** Our principal discussion of *Obergefell* occurs in the chapter on equal protection (*infra*, p. 356), since the case was decided on both equal protection and substantive due process grounds. Here, we'll discuss only the reasoning by which the majority concluded that same-sex couples have a right to marry that is fundamental for substantive due process purposes.

ii. **Kennedy's opinion generally:** The *Obergefell* majority, in an opinion by Justice Kennedy, cited *Zablocki* and other opposite-sex-marriage cases for the proposition that *"the right to marry is fundamental under the Due Process Clause."* Kennedy conceded that all of these cases had "presumed" a relationship involving opposite-sex partners. But, Kennedy said, these cases had identified "essential attributes," based in "history, tradition, and other constitutional liberties," that were "inherent" in the "intimate bond" of marriage.

iii. **Why marriage is fundamental:** Kennedy identified *four "principles and traditions"* that, he said, "demonstrate that the reasons marriage is fundamental under the [Due Process Clause of the] Constitution *apply with equal force to same-sex couples."*

   (1) **"Individual autonomy":** The first principle was that the "right to personal choice regarding marriage" is *"inherent in the concept of individual autonomy."* Decisions about marriage, like choices about contraception, procreation and childrearing (all of which have been held to be fundamental for due process purposes), are, Kennedy said, "among the *most intimate that an individual can make."* He quoted the Court's statement in *Loving v. Virginia* (*infra*, p. 265) that "The freedom to marry, or not marry, a person of another *race* resides with the individual and cannot be infringed by the State." That same principle, Kennedy said, applies to the privacy/autonomy interest of "two men or two women" to make the "profound choice[]" to marry.

   (2) **Support for key two-person union:** Kennedy's second principle making the right to marry fundamental was that that right "supports a two-person union *unlike any other in its importance* to the committed individuals." Marriage, Kennedy said, "responds to the universal fear that a lonely person might call out only to find no one there." And, he said, same-sex couples should have the same right as opposite-sex couples to enjoy this intimate association.

   (3) **Support of children:** The third principle making the right to marry fundamental, Kennedy said, is that the right *"safeguards children and families and thus draws meaning from related rights of childrearing, procreation, and education."* If the children of same-sex couples are denied the *"recognition, stability, and predictability marriage offers,"* Kennedy said, these children will *"suffer the stigma of knowing their families are somehow lesser."* Therefore, laws banning same-sex marriage *"harm and humiliate the children of same-sex couples."*

   (4) **Social benefits accorded to marriage:** Finally, Kennedy said, the fact that there are many *benefits that society chooses to confer only on married couples* contributes to making the right to marry a fundamental right. The states "have throughout our history made marriage the basis for an *expanding list of*

governmental rights, benefits, and responsibilities," relating to matters like taxation, property rights, hospital access, adoption rights, campaign finance restrictions, child custody and support rules, and many others. Furthermore, a valid marriage under state law is a "significant status for over ***a thousand provisions of federal law."*** There ought to be ***"no difference between same- and opposite-sex couples"*** with respect to the benefits that government chooses to confer based on marital status.

iv. **No level of scrutiny specified:** Curiously, Kennedy's opinion never said what *level of scrutiny* is appropriate for judicial review of laws abridging this right that he found to be fundamental for due process purposes.

   (1) **Something more than mere-rationality review:** It's pretty clear by negative implication that the opinion is not applying typical easy-to-satisfy ***"mere-rationality" review***, of the sort applied to regulations that do not substantially interfere with any fundamental right (see *supra*, p.172). But the opinion gives us no clue about ***how much more stringent*** than mere-rationality the standard for review is to be. Is it to be ***"strict scrutiny,"*** so that the regulation will be struck down unless "necessary" to achieve a "compelling" state interest? Or is the review merely ***"mid-level"*** or ***"semi-strict,"*** meaning that the state must merely show that its regulation is "closely linked" to the achievement of an "important" governmental objective?

   (2) **Too soon to predict the standard that will be used:** As of this writing (early November, 2020), it's still unclear whether the Court will apply strict scrutiny to regulations that do not completely forbid same-sex marriage, but indirectly (though intentionally) place some ***significant burdens*** on such marriages, perhaps by withholding some benefits that the state chooses to give to married opposite-sex couples.

   Example: Suppose a state makes it harder for both members of a married same-sex couple to adopt a given child who's not related to either, than it does for married opposite-sex couples. It's likely that the Court would strike down the statute as a violation of due process (or equal protection). But it's not clear whether the Court, acting post-*Obergefell*, would apply strict scrutiny or a less-rigorous (semi-strict) review. See *infra*, p. 361, for a discussion of such an adoption-rights issue under an equal protection analysis.

5. **Right of natural father:** Under the family law of most states, the father of a legitimate child may block that child's adoption. But most states do not give a similar veto right to the natural father of a child born ***out of wedlock***, unless the father has "legitimated" his child (by obtaining a court order). In *Quilloin v. Walcott*, 434 U.S. 246 (1978), a Georgia law following this pattern was challenged by an unwed father who had attempted to block the adoption of his eleven-year-old son (whom he had never legitimated or had custody of) by the child's stepfather. The Supreme Court unanimously *rejected* the challenge.

   a. **Due process conclusion:** The Court held that the statute did not violate the Due Process Clause. The Court reasoned that the state had a legitimate interest in preserving existing family units; since the plaintiff had never lived with the child, or sought custody of him, the statute as applied here preserved existing families and was therefore arguably in the best interests of the child.

    b. Father lives with child: The father in *Quilloin* had never ***lived with*** his child. Where a man has fathered a child out of wedlock but has lived with the child for some substantial period, or has formed a ***significant relationship*** with the child, it is not so clear that a state can deprive the father of a veto power over the child's adoption. In fact, a majority of the present Court seems to believe that an unwed father who has lived with or has developed a substantial relationship with the child has a substantive due process right to maintain that relationship.

        i. ***Michael H* case:** Thus in *Michael H. v. Gerald D.*, 491 U.S. 110 (1989), five justices seemed to agree with the proposition that "Although an unwed father's biological link to his child does not, in and of itself, guarantee him a constitutional stake in his relationship with that child, such a link combined with a substantial parent-child relationship will do so." (The quoted remark was by a four-Justice plurality; a fifth Justice, Stevens, seemed to agree with this statement, though he believed, unlike the plurality, that the state here had done what was required to protect that interest.)

C. Sexuality, including homosexuality: A person's ***sexual conduct*** — apart from any issues of procreation or family life — receives substantive due process protection. The Court so held in an important 2003 decision ***invalidating*** a Texas law ***criminalizing homosexual sodomy***, ***Lawrence v. Texas***, 539 U.S. 558 (2003).

    1. Holding in *Lawrence*: In *Lawrence*, the majority said that "liberty presumes an ***autonomy of self*** that includes freedom of thought, belief, expression, and ***certain intimate conduct***." While the case directly holds only that states may not criminalize private homosexual conduct between consulting adults, the expansive language used by the majority suggests that the Court is willing to recognize a fairly broad autonomy/liberty interest in ***private consensual adult sexual conduct*** generally.

        a. Overruling of *Bowers v. Hardwick*: *Lawrence* is especially significant because it squarely overruled a fairly fresh precedent, the Court's decision in ***Bowers v. Hardwick***, 478 U.S. 186 (1986).

    2. *Bowers v. Hardwick*: Before we can understand the significance of *Lawrence*, we must understand what the Court did in *Bowers*, the decision that *Lawrence* overruled.

        a. Facts of *Bowers*: In *Bowers,* the plaintiff, who was openly gay, challenged a Georgia statute making it a crime to perform or submit to "any sexual act involving the sex organs of one person and the mouth or anus of another[.]" The statute did not on its face distinguish between heterosexual and homosexual behavior. Violations were punishable by a prison sentence of up to 20 years.

        b. Statute upheld: By a 5-4 vote the Court in *Bowers* **upheld** the statute against the plaintiff's substantive due process attack. The majority, in an opinion by Justice White, phrased the issue as being "whether the Federal Constitution ***confers a fundamental right upon homosexuals to engage in sodomy[.]***"

            i. Not a fundamental right: The majority asserted that the Court had regarded and should regard as "fundamental" only those liberties that are either ***"implicit in the concept of ordered liberty"*** or ***"deeply rooted in this Nation's history and tradi-***

tion." Homosexual sodomy was not such a liberty under either of these formulations, the majority found. In view of the fact that, until 1961, all 50 states outlawed sodomy, and 24 still did, any claim that the right to practice sodomy was "implicit in the concept of ordered liberty" or "deeply rooted in this Nation's history and tradition" was "at best, *facetious*."

    c. Blackmun's dissent: A dissent by Justice Blackmun (in which Brennan, Marshall, and Stevens joined) disagreed not only with the result reached by the majority but with the proper framework for analyzing the Georgia statute.

        i. What case is about: The case was not about "a fundamental right to engage in homosexual sodomy" as the majority argued, said the dissenters. Rather, it was about the much broader constitutional *"right to be let alone."* And, the dissenters said, the Georgia statute violated this right as prior decisions had interpreted the right.

3. *Lawrence* overrules *Bowers*: That's where constitutional law on homosexual conduct stood for 17 years until 2003, when *Lawrence* came along to overturn *Bowers*.

4. Facts of *Lawrence*: *Lawrence* came about when the Houston Police entered the apartment of one of the two Ds through an unlocked door. (The police were responding to a reported disturbance involving a weapon. Although the Supreme Court's opinion doesn't say so, the neighbor who made the report was later convicted of filing a false report.) The police discovered the two Ds, both men, having sex.

    a. Texas anti-sodomy statute: The Ds were charged with violating a Texas statute that made it a crime to "engage[] in deviant sexual intercourse with another individual of the same sex." "Deviate sexual intercourse" was defined to include (i) any contact between the genitals of one person and the mouth or anus of another, or (ii) the penetration of the genitals or anus of another by an object. The Ds were not only arrested but held in custody overnight, then tried, convicted, and fined.

5. Majority opinion: Justice Kennedy, joined by four other justices (Stevens, Souter, Ginsburg and Breyer), delivered the opinion for the Court in *Lawrence*. That opinion found that the Texas statute violated the Ds' substantive due process rights, and concluded that *Bowers* had been wrongly decided. (Justice O'Connor supplied a sixth vote for striking down the statute, but on equal protection grounds, as described below.)

    a. Review of older cases: Kennedy's opinion began by reviewing a number of the Court's older substantive-due-process cases that touched on sexual conduct, and that emphasized some form or another of a right to privacy. Kennedy noted that *Griswold* (*supra*, p. 175), in the course of striking down state restrictions on contraception, had described the protected interest as a right to privacy, and had emphasized the *"protected space of the marital bedroom."* Similarly, Kennedy observed, *Roe v. Wade* had recognized that "the protection of liberty under the Due Process Clause has a substantive dimension of fundamental significance in defining the rights of the person."

    b. Review of *Bowers*: Against this backdrop, Kennedy reviewed the *Bowers* decision. He noted that the majority's decision in *Bowers* phrased the issue as "whether the Federal Constitution confers a fundamental right upon homosexuals to engage in sodomy[.]" But, Kennedy now concluded, that very phrasing of the issue "discloses the Court's own failure to appreciate the extent of liberty at stake. To say that the issue in

Bowers was simply the right to engage in certain sexual conduct ***demeans the claim*** the individual put forward, just as it would ***demean a married couple were it to be said marriage is simply about the right to have sexual intercourse.***" Laws like the one in *Bowers* and the one here "have more far-reaching consequences, touching upon the ***most private human conduct, sexual behavior***, and in the ***most private of places, the home***."

    i. **Emerging recognition of liberty interest in sex:** Kennedy argued that American "laws and traditions in the ***past half century***" showed "an ***emerging awareness*** that liberty gives ***substantial protection*** to adult persons in ***deciding how to conduct their private lives in matters pertaining to sex***." Kennedy asserted that this "emerging recognition" "should have been apparent when *Bowers* was decided."

    ii. **Post-*Bowers* developments:** Post-*Bowers* developments, too, had cast doubt on *Bowers*' validity, Kennedy said. For instance, whereas 25 states had laws prohibiting homosexual sodomy at the time of *Bowers*, that number had now been reduced to 13. And even in those states, there was now a "pattern of non enforcement" as to consulting adults acting in private. Continuing *Bowers* as precedent ***"demeans the lives of homosexual persons."***

c. **Conclusion:** Kennedy concluded that ***"Bowers was not correct when it was decided, and it is not correct today.*** It ought not to remain binding precedent." Therefore, it was now overruled. The Ds "are ***entitled to respect for their private lives.*** The state ***cannot demean their existence or control their destiny*** by ***making their private sexual conduct a crime.*** The right to liberty under the Due Process Clause gives them ***the full right to engage in their conduct without intervention of the government.*** ... The Texas statute ***furthers no legitimate state interest*** which can justify its intrusion into the ***personal and private life of the individual***."

    i. **What wasn't covered:** Kennedy also stressed that there were various types of statutes that were ***not covered*** by the *Lawrence* decision: "The present case does not involve ***minors***. It does not involve ***persons who might be injured or coerced*** or who are situated in relationship where ***consent might not be easily refused***. It does not involve ***public conduct*** or ***prostitution***." And, he said, it "does not involve whether the government must give formal recognition to any relationship that homosexual persons seek to enter," an obvious reference to the issue of ***same-sex marriage***.

d. **Rational basis review:** Notice that while Kennedy's opinion is filled with broad-reaching language about the importance of the interest being served (e.g., that the right to liberty under the due process clause protects the "full right to engage in [sexual] conduct without intervention of the government"), the opinion does *not* classify the interest in pursuing homosexual conduct as being a ***fundamental*** interest. Instead, the opinion applies ***rational-basis review***, and strikes down the statute on the grounds that it ***"furthers no legitimate state interest."***

6. **O'Connor's concurrence:** Justice O'Connor concurred that the Texas statute was invalid. However, she reached this conclusion on ***equal protection*** rather than due process grounds. The Texas statute here applied only to sodomy between same-sex partners, not to sodomy between opposite-sex partners. Thus Texas was treating the same conduct differently "based solely on the participants." Texas justified its statute as furthering the "promotion of morality." But, O'Connor concluded, *"moral disapproval"* of a group like homosexuals, like a "bare desire to harm" a group, is "an interest that is *insufficient to satisfy rational basis review* under the Equal Protection Clause."

7. **Scalia's dissent:** Justice Scalia, joined by Chief Justice Rehnquist and Justice Thomas, dissented. He criticized the majority for applying "an *unheard-of form of rational-basis review* that will have far-reaching implications beyond this case."

a. **Rational relation:** Scalia disagreed with the core of the majority's position, that the law here was not rationally related to the promotion of a legitimate state interest. The Texas statute here "seeks to further the belief of its citizens that certain forms of sexual behavior are '*immoral and unacceptable*'." But this was the same interest, he said, that was furthered by "criminal laws against *fornication, bigamy, adultery, adult incest, bestiality,* and *obscenity.*" Therefore, "if, as the Court asserts, the promotion of majoritarian sexual morality is not even a *legitimate* state interest, *none of the above-mentioned laws can survive rational-basis review.*"

i. **Same-sex marriage:** Scalia was especially fearful that the majority's logic would lead inexorably to a constitutionally-recognized right to *homosexual marriage*.

(1) **Good prediction:** Scalia turned out to be a good predictor of future steps by the Court. As we saw above, in the 2015 case of *Obergefell v. Hodges, supra,* p. 199, the Court indeed held, by a 5-4 vote, that same-sex couples have a fundamental liberty interest in being allowed to marry.

Note: For more about the Court's recent treatment of gay rights issues, including same-sex marriage, see our extensive discussion of this topic beginning *infra*, p. 352, in the chapter on equal protection.

D. **The "right to die":** Should a *terminally ill* or *comatose* patient have the right to choose to *"die with dignity"*? The so-called *"right to die"* is really a series of sub-issues, on which the law is just starting to develop. The Supreme Court has issued two major decisions, one on the "right to *decline unwanted medical procedures*" (*Cruzan v. Missouri Dept. of Health, infra,* p. 206) and the other on the "right to *commit suicide*" (*Washington v. Glucksberg, infra,* p. 207).

As the result of these two decisions, there are several major propositions that we can recite at this point:

❑ A competent adult has a Fourteenth Amendment "liberty" interest in *not being forced to undergo unwanted medical procedures*, including artificial life-sustaining measures.

❑ The state has an important countervailing interest in *preserving life.* At the very least, this interest entitles the state to require, before it allows "pulling the plug," *"clear and convincing evidence"* that a now-incompetent patient would have voluntarily declined the life-sustaining measures.

❑ Terminally-ill patients do *not* have a general liberty interest in *"committing suicide."* Nor do they have the right to *recruit a third person* to help them commit suicide (e.g., a physician who would prescribe a fatal does of drugs).

Virtually everything else in this "right to die" area remains unsettled.

1. **The *Cruzan* case:** The Supreme Court's sole "right to decline artificial life-sustaining measures" case so far was the important 1990 case of ***Cruzan v. Missouri Department of Health***, 497 U.S. 261 (1990).

   a. **Facts:** Nancy Cruzan suffered severe brain damage in an automobile accident. Since 1983, she had lain in a "persistent vegetative state," i.e., a coma in which she had no awareness or cognition but continued to breathe without a respirator. All medical authorities agreed that there was virtually no chance that she would ever become conscious again or be aware of her surroundings. She was kept alive by means of a ***feeding and hydration tube*** implanted in her stomach. She was cared for in a Missouri state hospital, and the state was paying for her care.

   b. **The claim:** Nancy's parents asked the hospital to end the artificial nutrition and hydration procedures. Everyone agreed that she would die if these procedures were terminated. But the hospital refused to do this without a court order. Nancy's parents claimed in court that Nancy had a Fourteenth Amendment due process right not to be kept alive by unwanted medical procedures.

      i. **"Living will" statute:** But Missouri had a "living will" statute, which was interpreted by the state supreme court to mean that even if Nancy had such a Fourteenth Amendment right, the statute prevented the right from being exercised except upon "clear and convincing" evidence that Nancy would not have wanted the life-sustaining procedures used here. The court concluded that such clear and convincing evidence was not present, and it thus denied Nancy's parents' claim.

   c. **Supreme Court affirms:** The U.S. Supreme Court, by a 5-4 vote, agreed that Missouri's continuation of the life-sustaining procedures here did ***not violate*** Nancy's Fourteenth Amendment rights. The majority opinion, by Chief Justice Rehnquist, turned largely on procedural issues:

      i. **Right exists:** The majority opinion began by holding that "a competent person has a constitutionally protected ***liberty interest*** in ***refusing unwanted medical treatment*** ... "

      ii. **"Clear and convincing" standard:** But the problem, the majority wrote, was that Nancy was obviously not a competent person who could make a present informed and voluntary choice to discontinue the lifesaving procedures. So the question became, was Missouri entitled to require that such procedures be discontinued only when there is ***"clear and convincing"*** evidence that this is what Nancy would have wanted? The court answered ***"yes"*** to this question — Missouri's interest in safeguarding human life was strong enough that the state was entitled to "guard against potential abuses" by imposing the clear and convincing standard.

         (1) **Standard not satisfied:** The majority then concluded that the Missouri Supreme Court had not committed "constitutional error" when it decided that here there was no clear and convincing evidence that Nancy would have wanted the hydration and the nutritive procedures stopped. The evidence con-

sisted mainly of Nancy's statements to a housemate, about a year before the accident, that she would not want to live as a "vegetable."

d. Dissent: Four members of the Court dissented in *Cruzan*. The principal dissent was by Justice Brennan (joined by Marshall and Blackmun). Brennan contended that Nancy not only had a constitutionally-protected liberty interest in declining unwanted medical procedures, but that this interest far outweighed any general countervailing state interest in preserving life.

e. Significance: So *Cruzan* establishes two major propositions:

[1] a competent adult has a constitutionally-protected Fourteenth Amendment liberty interest in ***declining unwanted medical procedures*** (though we don't know whether this interest may sometimes be outweighed by the countervailing general state interest in preserving life); and

[2] where the patient is ***incompetent***, the state may constitutionally refuse to allow these medical procedures to be terminated except where there is ***"clear and convincing evidence"*** that this is what the patient would have wanted.

2. Right to commit suicide: Suppose that the patient is a competent adult who desires to die. If the adult wishes simply to "pull the plug," i.e., terminate life-preserving medical treatment, *Cruzan* seems to hold or at least strongly suggest that the state may not deny that privilege. A distinct, and tougher, issue is whether the state may forbid a competent adult from taking ***active steps*** to ***commit suicide***.

Thus suppose a patient suffering from terminal cancer desires to commit suicide by taking, say, an overdose of barbiturates. May the state forbid this conduct? And, more interestingly, may the state ***forbid others***, including ***doctors***, from ***assisting*** in this conduct? The answer to both questions is now generally ***"yes,"*** as the result of a landmark pair of 1997 Supreme Court decisions.

a. Supreme Court denies right to commit suicide (*Washington v. Glucksberg*): In these two 1997 decisions, the Supreme Court held that ***neither the Due Process Clause nor the Equal Protection Clause*** was violated by a state's ban on assisting another person (even a terminally-ill one) to commit suicide. We'll focus here on the Court's decision dealing with the Due Process Clause issue, ***Washington v. Glucksberg***, 521 U.S. 702 (1997).

b. Statutory ban: *Glucksberg* involved Washington's ban on "promoting a suicide attempt." The state defined this crime as "knowingly caus[ing] or aid[ing] another person to attempt suicide," and made it a felony.

c. Rehnquist's majority opinion: Justice Rehnquist wrote the Court's opinion in *Glucksberg*. Four other Justices (O'Connor, Scalia, Kennedy and Thomas) joined his opinion. The remaining four Justices agreed with the result (that the Washington statute was not unconstitutional) but not necessarily with Rehnquist's reasoning.

i. Broad level of generality: Rehnquist phrased the issue at a very high level of generality: "whether the 'liberty' specially protected by the Due Process Clause includes a ***right to commit suicide*** which itself includes a right to ***assistance*** in doing so." (Thus Rehnquist rejected the Ninth Circuit's narrower phrasing of the issue: "whether there is a liberty interest in determining the time and manner of one's death.")

ii. **No historical right:** To answer this question, Rehnquist began by canvassing past and present laws on the subject. He noted that "for over 700 years, the Anglo-American common-law tradition has punished or otherwise disapproved of both suicide and assisting suicide." And by the time he was writing his opinion, he noted, in virtually every state — and in almost every western democracy — it was a crime to *assist* in suicide. Although the states had begun to re-examine this prohibition in light of modern medical technology, the prohibition remained on the books practically everywhere, he pointed out.[9]

iii. **Not a fundamental right:** Rehnquist then concluded that any due process liberty interest in *committing suicide* was certainly *not a "fundamental"* interest.

(1) **Rationale:** He noted that the Court had always been reluctant to expand the list of fundamental due process interests "because guideposts for responsible decisionmaking in this uncharted area are scarce and open-ended." Only rights or interests that were *"deeply rooted in this Nation's history and tradition"* could be fundamental. And, in view of the nearly universal past and present prohibition of suicide or assisting suicide, the asserted interest in committing suicide did not come close to meeting this "deeply rooted" test.

(2) *Cruzan* **distinguished:** Rehnquist then distinguished the interest recognized in *Cruzan, supra*, from the one asserted here. *Cruzan* may have recognized a liberty interest in declining unwanted life-sustaining treatment, but that interest "was not simply deduced from abstract concepts of personal autonomy." Rather, the interest recognized in *Cruzan* derived from "the common-law rule that forced medication was a battery, and the long legal tradition protecting the decision to refuse unwanted medical treatment." So the right recognized in *Cruzan* was "entirely consistent with this Nation's history and constitutional traditions." The interest in committing suicide with another's assistance "may be just as personal and profound as the decision to refuse unwanted medical treatment, but it has never enjoyed similar legal protection."

iv. **State's interest in regulation was "rational":** Having decided that the liberty interest in assisted suicide was not "fundamental," Rehnquist then turned to the issue of whether there were any limitations at all on the state's right to ban such suicides. Rehnquist actually ducked the issue of whether there was a *non-fundamental* liberty interest in assisted suicide. Instead, he seemed to say that even if such a non-fundamental interest existed, the state merely had to show that its ban was "rationally related to legitimate government interests." Rehnquist quickly concluded that the state easily satisfied this test.

(1) **Interest in preserving human life:** First, Rehnquist said that the state had an *"unqualified interest in the preservation of human life."*

---

9. As of this writing (July, 2016), five states have some form of legal assisted suicide: California, Montana, Oregon, Vermont and Washington. Cf. www.wikipedia.com, "Assisted Suicide in the United States," retrieved July 21, 2016.

(2) Protecting integrity of medical profession: Also, the state had an interest in protecting the ***integrity of the medical profession:*** physician-assisted suicide could "undermine the trust that is essential to the doctor-patient relationship by blurring the time-honored line between healing and harming."

(3) Protecting the vulnerable: Next, Rehnquist wrote, the state had an interest in ***"protecting vulnerable groups*** — including the poor, the elderly, and disabled persons — from abuse, neglect and mistakes." There was a "real risk of ***subtle coercion*** and ***undue influence*** in end-of-life situations."

(4) Slippery slope: Finally, the state could rationally fear that legalizing physician-assisted suicide would set it down a ***slippery slope*** towards "voluntary and perhaps even involuntary ***euthanasia***."

(5) State interests were rational: These various interests were, Rehnquist wrote, "unquestionably important and legitimate." And Washington's outright ban on assisted suicide was "at least reasonably related" to the promotion of these interests.

v. **The concurrences:** There were several concurrences. Several Justices agreed only with the result reached by Rehnquist, and believed that the issue had been incorrectly phrased by him.

vi. **O'Connor's concurrence:** Justice O'Connor, concurring, supplied the critical fifth vote in support of Rehnquist's opinion. She agreed that there was "no generalized right to 'commit suicide.'" But she seemed to leave open the possibility that a terminally-ill patient suffering great pain might have a ***limited right*** to have a physician prescribe medication to ***alleviate that suffering***, even where this would hasten death. O'Connor thought that there was no need to address that question here, since Washington (and New York, the state whose statute was at issue in the companion case) did not forbid such prescriptions.

d. **Significance:** So where does *Glucksberg* leave us?

i. **No generalized "right to commit suicide":** Clearly, the case establishes that there is no ***generalized*** right to commit suicide, let alone a right to enlist the assistance of others in doing so. And, in fact, it's pretty clear that even the class of "terminally ill patients in severe pain" do not have such a generalized right.

ii. **Right to be free of pain:** But *Glucksberg* was a ***facial*** challenge, essentially a claim that the statute couldn't constitutionally be applied to *any* terminally-ill competent patient. The Court has carefully left the door open to ***"as applied"*** claims. Thus a future plaintiff might well succeed with a claim that a particular state ban on suicide or suicide-assistance has infringed ***that particular patient's*** autonomy-based due process interest. For instance a terminally-ill, competent patient, whose pain can't be reduced by any method that wouldn't bring about death, might well succeed with a constitutional claim if the state prevented him from getting any relief.

iii. **States free to permit:** Lastly, it is of course the case that the states are ***free to permit assisted suicide***, if they want to. See, e.g., the Oregon voter initiative, *supra,* p. 208, permitting assisted suicide in some circumstances.

E. **Other assorted autonomy issues:** The "autonomy" branch of right-to-privacy law has raised a number of other interesting issues, on most of which the Supreme Court has not yet spoken. Some of these are as follows:

1. **Autonomy of mental processes:** The autonomy branch of the right to privacy probably encompasses an individual's right to what might be called *"freedom of thought processes."* That is, the courts have recognized certain limits on what the government may do to *shape the minds* of individuals.

   a. **"Mandatory incantation":** Thus the government does not generally have the right to condition receipt of benefits upon what Tribe (pp. 1315-16) calls *"mandatory incantation."* For instance, a state may not require a flag salute and *recitation of the Pledge of Allegiance* as a condition of receiving public education. *West Virginia State Bd. of Educ. v. Barnette,* 319 U.S. 624 (1943).

   b. **Freedom of inquiry:** Similarly, the government may not generally restrict students' *freedom of inquiry.* See, e.g., *Meyer v. Nebraska (supra,* p. 174) (state may not ban teaching of foreign languages, at least in private schools); see also *Board of Education v. Pico (infra,* p. 592) (First Amendment bars school board from removing books from school library for "narrow[ly] partisan or political [reasons].") However, a state is probably substantially free to limit the subject matter that is studied as part of the *required curriculum* in the public schools, so long as no other constitutional provision is violated (e.g., the separation of church and state, as violated by public-school prayer sessions, discussed *infra,* p. 663).

   c. **Private use of pornography:** Similarly, a person has the constitutional right to possess and use *pornographic* or other objectionable materials in private. See *Stanley v. Georgia,* 394 U.S. 557 (1964) (discussed more fully *infra,* p. 562). This is true even where the material could be completely banned from *sale.*

   d. **Drug statutes distinguished:** But the government does have the right to make possession of specified *drugs* illegal, even though what makes the drug objectionable is its effect upon mental processes (e.g., LSD or marijuana).

2. **Rights of committed mentally retarded:** *Mentally retarded persons* who have been *involuntarily committed* have been recognized by the Court to have the substantive due process right to be kept in a *safe environment,* and not subjected to *undue bodily restraint.* In addition, such persons may have a limited right to *training. Youngberg v. Romeo,* 457 U.S. 307 (1982).

3. **Prohibition of risk-taking:** Attempts by the state to control the *amount of risk* to which an individual may expose himself, may be questioned on autonomy/privacy grounds.

   a. **Motorcycle helmet rules:** The best-known, and most criticized, example of a government attempt to limit risk-taking is the requirement that *motorcyclists wear helmets,* a requirement imposed by statute in many states. Helmet requirements have generally been upheld.

   b. **Seat belts:** Similarly, laws requiring that motorists wear *seat belts* have been challenged on autonomy/privacy grounds. These attacks, too, have generally failed.

4. **The right to travel:** The *"right to travel"* from state to state is sometimes viewed as being part of the constitutionally-protected "right to privacy." For instance, Tribe (pp. 1378-80) includes this right within his chapter called "rights of privacy and personhood."

However, because the right-to-travel cases (especially *Shapiro v. Thompson*) have often involved equal protection considerations, our discussion of the right is postponed until the chapter on equal protection. See *infra*, p. 381.

5. **Right to occupation:** The right to *engage in one's chosen occupation* could be viewed as one of the elements of privacy/autonomy. Recall that since the demise of *Lochner*, the courts have been reluctant to give more than minimal substantive-due-process weight to "economic" rights. Nonetheless, in at least some kinds of situations, state interference with the right to practice one's chosen occupation is being subjected to more than minimal scrutiny.

    a. **Arbitrary deprivation:** The state may not prevent someone from practicing his chosen occupation for *completely arbitrary reasons*. Thus in *Schware v. Board of Bar Examiners of New Mexico*, 353 U.S. 232 (1957), the Court held that state qualifications to practice law "must have a rational connection with the applicant's fitness or capacity," and that plaintiff's prior membership in the Communist Party did not have such a rational connection with his fitness to practice law.

    b. **Equal protection:** Similarly, rules which deprive members of a *narrow* (and perhaps generally disadvantaged) *group* from practicing a profession are subject to attack, on both substantive due process and equal protection grounds. Thus in *Hampton v. Mow Sun Wong*, 426 U.S. 88 (1976), the Court held that the right to work in the federal Civil Service was important enough to be classed as an "interest in liberty." Consequently, Civil Service Commission rules barring aliens from the civil service could be upheld only if they were "justified by reasons which are properly the concern of [the Civil Service Commission]." Under this test, which appeared to be more than a "mere-rationality" standard, the rules could not be sufficiently justified, and were therefore violative of Fifth Amendment due process.

F. **No right to be protected from privately-imposed harm:** Virtually all of the substantive due process claims we have examined so far are ones in which the plaintiff was asserting the right to be free of *governmentally-imposed restrictions* that impair his life, liberty, or property. Suppose, however, that a person's life, liberty, or property are threatened not by the government itself, but by a *private person*; can one have a substantive due process right to be *protected by the government* from this third-party interference?

In a pair of cases, the Supreme Court has essentially answered *"no"* to this question. As the Court said in the first of those cases, *DeShaney v. Winnebago County Department of Social Services*, 489 U.S. 189 (1989), "[T]he Due Process Clauses generally confer *no affirmative right to governmental aid*, even where such aid may be necessary to secure life, liberty, or property interests of which the government itself may not deprive the individual."

1. *DeShaney:* The tragic facts of *DeShaney, supra,* pose the problem with utmost clarity. P was a boy who was repeatedly beaten by his father, to the point of permanent, severe retardation. The Ds were county social-welfare officials who received repeated complaints that P was being beaten, had reason to believe that this was the case, but did nothing to help P. (In fact, at one point the state took custody of P temporarily, then returned him to his father.) P's lawsuit argued that the Ds had deprived P of his liberty without due process of law, by failing to intervene to protect him from his father.

    a. **Claim rejected:** By a 6-3 vote, the Court *rejected* P's claim. The purpose of the Due Process Clause, the majority said, is "to protect the people from the State, not to ensure that the State protect[s] them from each other." Thus the Due Process Clause does not impose any duty upon the state to provide substantive services within its borders, whether these services are safety-protection, medical services, adequate housing, or anything else. The state's obligation under the Due Process Clause is simply to avoid affirmatively injuring a citizen's life, liberty or property without due process.

2. ***Castle Rock***: The later case of *Castle Rock v. Gonzales*, 545 U.S. 748 (2005) posed a related question: may government by its **express pronouncements** in a statute **give a citizen an affirmative right of protection** against third-party harm, such that that right *will* constitute a substantive due process property interest? The Court's answer was that such a result is theoretically possible, but that it will **rarely occur**, and in any event did not occur in the case at hand.

    a. **Facts:** *Castle Rock*, like *DeShaney*, involved tragic facts. P (Mrs. Gonzales) obtained from a Colorado court a **restraining order** compelling her estranged husband to stay away from P and her three daughters. Several weeks after being served with the order, the husband kidnapped the three daughters in violation of the order. Over the next five hours, P repeatedly asked the Town of Castle Rock police to arrest the husband, but the police refused to do so, apparently due to a policy of not normally making arrests for violation of restraining orders. Later that night, the husband came to the police station and was killed in a gunbattle with police; inside his truck, the murdered bodies of his three daughters were found.

    b. **P's claim:** P sued the town on the theory that she had had a due process property interest in having the police enforce the restraining order, and that the police, by their policy of not enforcing restraining orders, had deprived her of this property interest without due process.

        i. **Colorado statute:** In making this claim, P was not relying on the broad assertion (as had been made in *DeShaney, supra*) that government has a generalized duty to protect its citizens by making an arrest where there is probable cause to do so. Instead, P relied on a very specific and recently-passed Colorado statute designed to reduce domestic abuse; the statute provided that a peace officer "shall use every reasonable means to enforce a restraining order," and "shall arrest ... a restrained person when the peace officer has information amounting to probable cause that ... the restrained person has violated or attempted to violate any provision of a restraining order[.]" P asserted that this very specific statutory language demonstrated that Colorado intended to give her a due-process-protected property right.

    c. **Claim rejected:** By a vote of 7-2, the Court concluded that Colorado **had not in fact conferred upon P a due-process-protected property interest** in having the police enforce the restraining order. In an opinion by Justice Scalia, the Court reasoned that P's claim of a property interest failed in three distinct respects:

        i. **Not mandatory:** First, the Colorado statute did not truly make enforcement of restraining orders **mandatory**. "A well established tradition of police **discretion** has long coexisted with apparently mandatory arrest statutes ... [A] true mandate of police action would require some stronger indication [of mandatoryness] from the Colorado Legislature" than was present here.

ii. **No entitlement to enforcement:** Second, even if the statute should be interpreted to make enforcement of restraining orders "mandatory," this would not necessarily mean that Colorado had intended to give a private person in P's position "an entitlement to enforcement of the mandate." Scalia reasoned that "Making the actions of government employees obligatory can serve various legitimate ends other than the conferral of a benefit on a specific class of people."

iii. **Not a property interest:** Finally, even if Colorado had meant to confer a true entitlement on P, it was not necessarily the case that this entitlement would amount to a "property" interest for due-process purposes. Nearly all the cases in which the Court had recognized a government entitlement as constituting "property" (cases like *Roth, supra*) had involved entitlements that constituted *direct* substantive benefits to the plaintiff (e.g., welfare payments, or a job). Here, the benefit sought by P was an *indirect* one — the right to have government take some action (an arrest) vis a vis a third person, not vis a vis the right-holder. Scalia suggested that any entitlement to an indirect benefit from government's taking an action against a third person was not properly viewed as a due-process "property" interest.

iv. **Conclusion:** In summary, Scalia said, *Castle Rock* and *DeShaney* taken together mean that "the benefit that a third party may receive from *having someone else arrested* for a crime generally *does not trigger protections under the Due Process Clause*, neither in its procedural nor in its 'substantive' manifestations." He added that this result "reflects our continuing reluctance to treat the 14th Amendment as a '*font of tort law*.'"

Quiz Yourself on
SUBSTANTIVE DUE PROCESS — PROTECTION OF NON-ECONOMIC RIGHTS

28. The state of Aha has enacted a statute that proscribes what the statute refers to as "unnatural sexual acts." The acts described include oral sex. The statute applies to conduct between married persons as well as to conduct between unmarried persons, but contains an exemption for conduct that takes place in a dwelling that is the residence of one or both parties. Joe and Martha Danzig, a married couple, were vacationing at the Happy Times Motel, when a state police officer burst into the room acting on a tip (reasonable-seeming but erroneous) that the couple was using drugs. The officer happened to see Joe and Martha engaging in oral sex at that moment, and arrested them.

(a) If Joe and Martha want to challenge the charges on constitutional grounds, what is their best argument? _____

(b) Will this argument succeed? _____

29. A number of states have enacted regulations bearing on specific aspects of abortion. Consider the following:

(a) The state of Aloha provides that no abortion may be performed within the state if at the moment of the procedure the fetus is more than three months old.

(b) The state of Brie provides that no abortion may be performed on a married woman unless she signs an affidavit that she has notified her spouse. However, the prohibition does not apply if the married woman instead signs an affidavit that she and her husband are not living together, or that her husband is not the father of the child, or that she has not given notice because she fears that he will abuse her if he finds out that she is planning an abortion. The statute is challenged by P, a woman who is two months pregnant, wants an abortion, and does not want to notify her spouse (with whom P lives, whom she believes to be the father of the child, and who is not likely to abuse her if she tells him she wants an abortion).

(c) The state of Chaucer provides that "No physician shall perform or induce an abortion in this state unless, at the time of the abortion procedure, the physician has patient-admitting privileges at a hospital located within 20 miles of the facility in which the procedure is performed." The preamble to the statute says that it was enacted for the purpose of ensuring that if a woman should encounter medical complications arising out of the abortion procedure, she can be admitted to a hospital for emergency treatment without delay. The statute replaces a previously-in-force provision (the "old statute") that required any physician providing an abortion to have made arrangements in advance with a physician having admitting privileges at a local hospital; the earlier statute was enacted for the same purpose of ensuring prompt hospital treatment in case of complications from an abortion. Prior to enacting the new statute, the legislature did not conduct any hearings or otherwise consider evidence about the number of women who, under the old statute, had suffered abortion-related medical complications requiring hospitalization. The statute is challenged by P, a physician who wishes to perform abortions in Chaucer, and who does not have admitting privileges at any local hospital. At a trial, P produces evidence (not rebutted by the state) that during the prior 10 years when the old statute was in force, no woman was admitted — or sought to be admitted — to a hospital for emergency treatment of post-abortion complications on the day on which she received the abortion. P also shows that most hospitals in Chaucer will not grant admitting privileges to a physician unless the physician demonstrates that he or she will send a regular flow of patients to that hospital, a showing that neither P nor most abortion providers in the state will be able to make precisely because abortions so rarely leads to medical complications that require hospitalization.

State whether each of these provisions is constitutional. (Assume that the suits in (a) and (c) are attacks on the face of the statute, and that the attack in (b) is "as applied.") _____

30. In recent years, in the state of North Rockland, there has been an increase in the number of marginally-funded, educationally-inadequate private schools, as well as a rise in the number of parents who have been teaching their children at home rather than sending them to the public schools. The North Rockland legislature has, therefore, just passed a statute providing that every child between the age of 6 and 16 must be educated in the state's public schools. Parents who do not comply face criminal punishment. The statute does not allow any exceptions for even educationally-sound private schools or educationally-sound home instruction. Paula, the parent of a seven-year-old son, wishes to educate him at home. Paula was until last year a first-grade teacher in a state public school, and all concerned agree that she is well qualified to teach her child at home provided that she does so full time, which she expects to do. Paula has sued to overturn the statute, as applied to her and her son, on substantive due process grounds.

(a) What standard of review should the court use in deciding Paula's suit? _____

(b) Will the statute be found constitutional as applied to Paula and her son? _____

31. The state of Centuria has a criminal statute prohibiting "sodomy," defined to include any instance in which one person's mouth or anus touches another person's genitals. Century Village, a town in Centuria, has a school-board regulation providing that any person who the school board finds to have violated any state statute involving moral turpitude shall be dismissed, and further providing that a violation of the sodomy ban shall be deemed to constitute moral turpitude. Darwin, a non-tenured teacher at Century Village High School, was involved in a sexual relationship with Fred. After Darwin broke up the relation-

ship, Fred sent a video to the Century Village school board, showing Darwin and Fred involved in conduct of the sort proscribed by the Centuria criminal statute. The school board viewed the video, concluded that Darwin had violated the statute, and dismissed Darwin. In recent years, the statute has rarely been enforced, and on those rare occasions has been enforced principally against same-sex sodomy. Darwin has now attacked his firing on the grounds that it violates his substantive due process rights. Assume that issues of procedural due process are ignored.

(a) What standard should the court use for deciding Darwin's challenge? _____

(b) Was Darwin's firing constitutional? _____

32. The town of Tinsel originally did not have any written regulation concerning the beard or hair styles of fire fighters. At the time Jordan was hired onto the fire fighting force, he had a beard and hair that was neatly combed but of shoulder length. After Jordan had been on the force two years, Tinsel enacted a regulation providing that no male firefighter could wear a beard or hair extending below his neck. Jordan has challenged this regulation as violating his substantive due process rights. Tinsel has defended the regulation on the grounds that: (i) uniformity of hairstyle is necessary to generate a feeling of esprit de corps among firefighters; and (ii) facial hair and long hair are more likely to catch fire even if the person dons the usual safety equipment.

(a) What standard should the court use in deciding whether Jordan's substantive due process rights have been violated? _____

(b) Is the regulation constitutional? _____

33. Two years ago, Pedro signed a "living will," in which he directed that in the event he should ever be in a persistent vegetative state, with no real likelihood of improvement, he should not be artificially respirated or hydrated. Pedro was then in a car accident, and lapsed into a deep coma (a persistent vegetative state) from which, all the doctors who have seen him agree, he is very unlikely to emerge. The hospital where he is being kept is willing to disconnect the respirator and hydration unit, but only if Wanda, Pedro's wife, signs a form agreeing with this step and waiving her right to sue. Wanda refuses to sign this document, arguing that although pulling the plug may well be what Pedro wanted (she does not dispute that he signed the living will while competent) she herself is opposed on moral and religious grounds to pulling the plug. Pedro's brother has been appointed Pedro's guardian *ad litem*, and has brought suit for a court order directing the hospital to discontinue life support even without Wanda's consent.

(a) What is the strongest constitutional argument that Pedro's brother can make as to why the plug should be pulled? _____

(b) Should the court order that the plug be pulled? _____

(c) Now, suppose that Pedro, instead of having had a car accident, is in the last stages of terminal cancer, and is in extreme pain. He is competent, and wishes to have his physician, Doctor, prescribe a fatal dose of morphine so that Pedro can commit suicide. The state makes it a crime to help anyone commit suicide, no matter what the circumstances. Doctor goes to court to seek a declaratory judgment that the ban on assisting suicide is unconstitutional as applied to these facts. Should the court grant Doctor's request? _____

———————

Answers

28. (a) That the charges violate the defendants' substantive due process right to "privacy."

(b) Yes, probably. The Supreme Court has held that every individual has a "zone of privacy," and that government action which invades that zone will be found to violate the individual's substantive due process rights unless the government action is necessary to achieve a compelling governmental objective (strict scrutiny). The Supreme Court has never explicitly held that the sexual acts of a married couple, taken in private, fall within the zone of privacy for all purposes. However, the Court has held (in *Griswold v. Connecticut*) that the right to privacy is violated when the state interferes with a couple's attempts to use birth control. Later cases suggest that state interferences with a married couple's sexual intimacy would similarly violate the right to privacy, assuming that the conduct took place in private (even if it took place in a hotel room or other non-residential but non-public setting). See, e.g., *Lawrence v. Texas*, the homosexual-sodomy case, where the majority opinion refers to "an emerging awareness that liberty gives substantial protection to adult persons in deciding how to conduct their private lives in matters pertaining to sex." In summary, since Joe and Martha are married and were performing the activity in private, their conduct probably fell within the protected zone of privacy. (It is a bit less clear that their "right of privacy" argument would prevail if they had been unmarried, or engaged in an adulterous relationship.)

29. **(a) Unconstitutional.** Under *Whole Woman's Health v. Hellerstedt*, the states may not place **"undue burdens"** on the right of abortion. A state regulation will constitute an undue burden if the regulation has the purpose or effect of placing a "substantial obstacle" in the path of a woman seeking an abortion of a **nonviable fetus**. *Id.* Since a four- or five-month-old fetus is certainly not viable even under present medical advances, the blanket prohibition on abortions during this time frame would almost certainly be found to be a "substantial obstacle" and thus an "undue burden." (But a state probably *could* bar all abortions *after* the fetus becomes viable.)

(b) Unconstitutional, probably. *Planned Parenthood v. Casey* struck down a spousal notification provision. The provision here, while it may contain slightly more escape hatches, would likely be found to be a substantial obstacle to the plaintiff (who is not covered by any of the escape hatches). Notice that the attack here is "as applied" rather than "on the face" of the statute. That is, the suit argues that the statute directly violates the rights of the plaintiff, rather than asking the Court to prevent the statute from being enforced against anyone because it violates the rights of persons not before the Court. The present Court would likely find that the statute acts as an undue burden *upon P*, even if that Court wouldn't allow a facial attack on the spousal notification provision. (The pre-*Hellerstedt* opinion in *Gonzales v. Carhart* indicates that the Court will allow facial attacks only if the plaintiffs prove that the statute would be unconstitutional "in a large fraction of relevant cases"; the plaintiffs in a facial attack might not be able to make this "large fraction" showing, given the various escape hatches.)

(c) Unconstitutional. An abortion regulation will be unconstitutional if *either its purpose or effect* is to place a **"substantial obstacle"** in the path of a woman seeking an abortion of a pre-viable fetus. Or, under a slightly different formulation of the standard, the regulation will be unconstitutional if it imposes an **"undue burden"** on pre-viability abortions. *Whole Woman's Health v. Hellerstedt*. Not all burdens on abortion are unconstitutional; only those burdens that are "undue" violate women's substantive due process rights. A reviewing court will classify the burden as "undue" if the burdens imposed by the restriction **outweigh** the benefits it confers. And at least where the benefits claimed by the legislature are **not medically certain**, the reviewing court is not to give "uncritical deference" to the legislature's judgment about medical benefits, but is instead to make its **own factual review** of the existence and size of those benefits.

The statute here, and the factual setting behind it, are almost identical to one of the two Texas provisions struck down by the Supreme Court in *Hellerstedt*. There, the majority concluded that a requirement that abortion physicians have local-hospital admitting privileges conferred no medical benefit at all compared with the prior statute (which merely required the provider to have a working arrangement with *another* physician who did have such admitting privileges). This was so in part because even under the old statute, extremely few if any post-abortion emergency hospital admissions occurred, especially on the actual day of the abortion (which was the only time the provider's ability to arrange an emergency admission would be even theoretically applicable). On the "burden" side, the Court noted that abortion providers can rarely obtain admitting privileges, because the very safety of the abortion process means that a provider usually can't generate the frequent hospital admissions that hospitals typically require as a condition of granting admitting privileges; therefore, requiring providers to obtain unobtainable admitting privileges places a sizable burden on the availability of abortions. When this burden was balanced against what the Court found to be non-existent medical benefits, the former clearly outweighed the latter, making the burden in *Hellerstedt* "undue." Here, there is nothing about the facts of the Chaucer statute that is materially different from the admitting-privileges requirement struck down in *Hellerstedt*, so it is virtually certain that the present Court would strike down the statute here as well.

30. **(a) Strict scrutiny, probably.** That is, the statute will probably be struck down unless shown to be ***necessary*** to achieve a ***compelling*** state interest. The question is really whether the right to make core decisions about how one's children shall be educated is a ***"fundamental"*** right. The Supreme Court has not addressed this issue directly in recent years. However, several cases (discussed further in part (b) below) suggest that the Court would hold that the right to direct the education of one's children is indeed "fundamental," in which case strict scrutiny must be applied to any governmental regulation that substantially impairs that right.

(b) No, probably. In *Pierce v. Society of Sisters* (a 1925 case), the Court struck down a state statute requiring children to attend public schools. The decision seems to have been on substantive-due-process-like grounds, and seems to have applied essentially strict scrutiny. Similarly, in more recent years, the Court has held that parents have a fundamental right to decide who may visit the child; *Troxel v. Granville.*

Assuming that the right to choose how one's children are to be educated is in some sense fundamental, it is very unlikely that the statute here could survive strict scrutiny. Ensuring a good education for children is certainly an important state objective, and probably a "compelling" one. However, it is highly unlikely that foreclosing all options other than public schools is a "necessary" means of attaining that objective. For instance, allowing a program of home instruction by one who is clearly a qualified elementary school teacher certainly seems to be an adequate way to assure a good education. And the state could adopt a monitoring program to make sure that home study programs satisfy a minimum quality standard. So the statute will probably flunk strict scrutiny, if strict scrutiny is applied.

31. **(a) The "rational relation," not "strict scrutiny," standard.** The Supreme Court has held that a state may not criminalize sodomy defined in this way. *Lawrence v. Texas* (2003) (p. 202). But in reaching this conclusion, the Court applied the easier-to-satisfy rational-relation standard. However, the Court found that such a ban on sodomy — generally enforced only against homosexual sodomy — could not satisfy even the rational-relation test, because it pursued only the illegitimate aim of expressing moral disapproval of homosexuality. The Court would presumably use the same rational-relation standard in evaluating whether a public body may fire a person for engaging in such sodomy.

(b) No, probably. Although the Court would (as noted in part (a) above) probably apply the rational-relation standard to the school-board regulation here, it is likely that the regulation would be found invalid even under that relatively easy-to-satisfy standard. The essence of the regulation is that one who violates a state statute forbidding a particular act of turpitude may be fired. Since the underlying state statute is no longer valid in light of *Lawrence*, it is hard to believe that the Court would find that it was rational for the school board to fire someone for violating this no-longer-valid statute. This is especially likely given that the governmental objective that the school district seems to be pursuing here — punishing gay people for "moral turpitude" — is the very one that *Lawrence* found to be illegitimate. The conclusion that the state was pursuing an illegitimate objective would be buttressed by the Court's several cases holding that "a ***bare [governmental] desire to harm a politically unpopular group"*** cannot be a legitimate governmental objective. (See, e.g., *U.S. v. Windsor* (2013), using this rationale while striking down Congress' refusal to recognize state-sanctioned same-sex marriages; the Court found that Congress was motivated solely by anti-gay animus.)

32. (a) The "rational relation" standard, not strict scrutiny. The choice of standard depends on whether the right of a firefighter to wear a beard, etc., is found to be "fundamental." In a case almost completely on point, *Kelley v. Johnson*, the Supreme Court held that a policeman's right to wear his hair as he wished was not "fundamental," and that the hair-length regulation there should be judged on a rational relation standard.

(b) Yes, probably. Assuming that the rational relation standard is used, the regulation here almost certainly passes muster. The town certainly has a legitimate interest in preserving *esprit de corps* and promoting safety. The contribution of short hair to fulfillment of these objectives may be questionable, but it is certainly "rational." (For instance, the town could reasonably have believed that long-haired male firefighters would not fit in as well.) Certainly the comparable hair-length regulation in *Kelley* was found to be rationally related to a legitimate governmental objective, and was thus upheld, so the same result is likely here.

33. (a) That Pedro's substantive due process rights would be violated by forcing him to be kept on artificial life support.

(b) Yes, probably. The Supreme Court has never explicitly faced the issue of whether a person who signs a living will has a substantive due process (or other constitutional) right to have that directive obeyed. But in *Cruzan v. Missouri Dept. of Health*, the Court suggested that a competent adult has a constitutionally-protected liberty interest in declining unwanted medical procedures. The Court might well hold that this interest is a "fundamental" one. If so, the state would have the right to decline to obey the directive only if the refusal was necessary to achieve some compelling governmental interest.

It is highly unlikely that there is any compelling governmental interest here that could only be achieved by keeping Pedro on life support. Certainly Wanda's interest in preserving her own religious or moral objectives would be unlikely to outweigh Pedro's right to control his own destiny. Therefore, the Court will probably order that the plug be pulled even without Wanda's consent (and the Court will probably immunize Hospital from suit by Wanda). (But *Cruzan* does recognize that the states have a significant governmental interest in requiring ***clear evidentiary proof*** about what the patient's wishes really are, so that if Pedro had not signed the living will, the state could probably refuse to accept, say, weak oral testimony from relatives about what Pedro "would have wanted.")

(c) No, probably. The Supreme Court decided in *Washington v. Glucksberg* that state prohibitions on assisted-suicide are not facially invalid, because there is no general right to commit suicide or to enlist another's assistance in doing so. *Glucksberg* seems to apply even where the plaintiff is a competent, terminally-ill person who desires escape from pain. However, it's possible that Pedro or his doctor could convince the Court that his "as applied" challenge (as opposed to the broad "facial" challenge that lost in

Glucksberg) is narrow enough that he should win: he could argue that where a fatal dose of medication is the *only way* he can escape unbearable pain, it's a violation of his personal autonomy to be denied that relief. (See Justice Breyer's concurrence in *Glucksberg*, recognizing a "right to die with dignity," which he said would encompass "personal control over the manner of death, professional medical assistance, and the avoidance of unnecessary and severe physical suffering — combined." It seems pretty clear that Breyer would give Pedro the relief he seeks on these facts.)

VII. PROCEDURAL DUE PROCESS

A. **Introduction:** We turn now to an element of due process that is quite distinct from that with which the previous part of this chapter was concerned. The requirement that the government act with "***procedural*** due process" derives, like the requirement of substantive due process, from the Due Process Clauses of the Fifth Amendment (in the case of the federal government) and the Fourteenth Amendment (in the case of the states). Recall that both clauses prevent the government from depriving any person of "***life, liberty***, or ***property***, without due process of law."

1. **State rules:** In the following discussion, unless otherwise noted, we are talking about the Fourteenth Amendment Due Process Clause, and limits on ***state*** action. However, the same rules generally apply to the federal government via the Fifth Amendment.

2. **No interest in governmental regularity** *per se:* It is crucial to understand that the Due Process Clause ***does not bar the government from procedural irregularities per se. Only when "life," "liberty" or "property" are being taken*** is the government required to act with procedural correctness. If none of these interests is implicated by a particular government act, the government may act ***as arbitrarily or unfairly as it wishes*** (at least insofar as the Due Process Clause is concerned). As one commentator has put it, "Procedural due process … is evidently not a free standing human interest." 62 CORNELL L. REV. 452 (quoted in L,K&C, p. 626).

   Example: Suppose a state government announces that it will hire a new secretary for the head of a state agency. P is superbly qualified. The state interviews P, but awards the job to X, who can't type, but who is the daughter of a prominent local politician. Even if P can prove that the state's action was utterly arbitrary or unfair, P has not established any violation of her procedural due process rights. The reason is that P did not have any "property" or "liberty" interest in the job opening (see *infra*, p. 220), so there was simply no protected interest on which any procedural due process rights could hang.

   a. **Significance:** Thus most of our discussion of procedural due process will focus on the issue of just what types of interests are deemed to be ones in "liberty" or "property," such that they may not be impaired without procedural due process? (Interests in "life" are imperiled by government action only in relatively rare circumstances, principally capital punishment; there, the interest in "life" is so clearly at stake that it is obvious that the government must act with procedural correctness.)

      i. **Distinguished from substantive due process:** The need to focus carefully upon exactly what constitutes "liberty" and "property" in the procedural due process area contrasts sharply with the practice in the substantive due process area. In the latter context, it has rarely been an issue in the Supreme Court's decisions whether "liberty" or "property" was implicated; "liberty" has been assumed to include "just about every interest of significance to an individual." Gunther (12th Ed.), p. 583. (Of course, if the interest involved is not deemed "fundamental," only a very small state justification is necessary to support its impairment; but the interest in "liberty" or "property" is nonetheless assumed to exist in virtually every substantive due process situation.)

    b. **Three-part historical analysis:** The Supreme Court's definition of "liberty" and "property" has undergone marked variation over the years. Our treatment divides the Court's approach to defining these terms into three major stages: pre-1970, early 1970s and post-1972.

    c. **What process is due:** After a comprehensive discussion of the meaning of "liberty" and "property," we turn to a much shorter analysis of a second issue: Once it is determined that a particular government action implicates an interest in "liberty" or "property," **what "process" is due**? That is, must a hearing be given? Must counsel be permitted?, etc.

  3. **Individual adjudications:** One important difference between procedural due process and substantive due process is that a right to the former will only exist where the government action at issue involves an *individualized determination.*

    a. **Illustration of substantive question:** Thus suppose a state establishes broad, mechanical, requirements (e.g., age, education, residence) which must be met before one may be licensed to practice a certain profession. These requirements will be tested solely by use of a substantive due process analysis (i.e., is a fundamental interest at stake; if not, does the rule have some rational relation to a legitimate state objective?)

    b. **Illustration of procedural question:** On the other hand, if a state imposes requirements against which each individual must be carefully, and subjectively, evaluated, the need for procedural due process may also be triggered. Thus if the professional licensing procedure requires an evaluation of "good moral character," the elements of procedural due process (e.g., the right to be heard, the right to an explanation, etc.) must be given. See Tribe, p. 682-83.

    c. **Simultaneously valid and invalid:** Thus a regulation may simultaneously be valid from the viewpoint of substantive due process and invalid from the perspective of procedural due process.

B. **"Liberty" and "property" before 1970:** The Supreme Court has, historically, taken a broad view of what constitutes "liberty" and "property." As the Court said in *Meyer v. Nebraska* (*supra*, p. 174), the interest in "liberty" includes "not merely freedom from bodily restraint but also the right of the individual to *contract*, to engage in any of the common *occupations* of life, to acquire useful knowledge, to marry, establish a home and bring up children [and] to worship God according to the dictates of … conscience." Although the Court has never defined "property" explicitly, this term, too, has always been interpreted liberally.

  1. **Public benefits:** But before 1970, there was one notable area in which the Court was reluctant to find that a "liberty" or "property" interest existed. This was the area of *benefits flowing from the public sector*, including *government employment* and monetary benefits (e.g., *welfare*). The Court traditionally took the view that such items were a *"privilege"* not a "right," and that they could therefore be withdrawn without procedural regularity. This view is sometimes referred to as the "right/privilege dichotomy." See Tribe, pp. 680-81.

   a. Constitutionally impermissible reasons: However, even under this traditional view that public-sector benefits were privileges, not rights, it was apparently the case that these privileges could not be withdrawn for *reasons violative of other constitutional protections*. For instance, it was clear prior to 1970 that the government could not fire a worker for exercising his right to free speech off the job.

      i. Right to hearing: A separate issue is whether a worker's mere *claim* that he has been fired or denied government benefits for such unconstitutional reasons entitles him to a due process hearing. The Supreme Court has still not explicitly decided whether such a mere claim of unconstitutional action, without additional evidence, suffices to trigger the need for procedural due process. Tribe, p. 682 and n. 34.

C. Growth in the '70s of "entitlements": During the early 1970s the Supreme Court held that many types of government benefits previously thought to be mere "privileges" rather than "rights" were *in fact interests in liberty or property*, which could therefore not be taken without procedural due process.

   1. Welfare benefits (*Goldberg v. Kelly*): The first, and perhaps most important, of these decisions was *Goldberg v. Kelly*, 397 U.S. 254 (1970), in which the Court held that a *welfare recipient* must be given an "evidentiary hearing" before his benefits may be terminated. Welfare payments, for a person statutorily entitled to receive them, were not "mere charity," but were a *right* protected by the Constitution against arbitrary withdrawal.

D. Narrowing of "entitlements" theory: But the expansionary process described above posed a real risk: more and more transactions by state and federal governments might be deemed to impair liberty or property interests, until the entire day-to-day activities of those governments were rendered completely subject to constitutional review (and until the judicial system was drowned by due process claims). Consequently, after the early 1970s the Burger Court began to curtail the types of public benefits which would be deemed to create an interest in liberty or property. This scaled-back view of what constitutes liberty or property remains basically in effect today.

E. The tenure cases (*Roth* and *Perry*): The best-known example of the Court's cutting back is *Board of Regents v. Roth*, 408 U.S. 564 (1972), a *university tenure* case. But a companion case, *Perry v. Sindermann*, 408 U.S. 593 (1972), seemed to put an important brake on the retreat in *Roth*.

   1. *Roth*: In *Roth*, plaintiff was given a non-tenured one-year contract to teach at Wisconsin State University. The University declined, without giving reasons, to hire him after the one-year period. Under Wisconsin law, decisions on hiring for non-tenured positions were left totally to the discretion of University officials. The Supreme Court held that plaintiff's interest in being rehired was not an interest in "liberty" or "property," and that he therefore had no right to procedural due process.

      a. Rationale: The Court's opinion emphasized that the "weight" (i.e., the importance) of the plaintiff's interest was irrelevant; it was the "nature" of that interest that counted.

b. Not a "liberty" interest: Plaintiff's interest was not one in "liberty," the Court said, because the state's decision not to rehire plaintiff did not include charges which might damage his reputation (e.g., a charge of dishonesty or immorality), nor was he barred from a broader class of employment (e.g., all other jobs in state universities). Had either of these things occurred, the Court indicated, plaintiff's "liberty" would have been affected, and he would have had the right to procedural due process.

   i. Change in law: However, the Court's suggestion that damage to plaintiff's reputation would have been sufficient to invoke a "liberty" interest is probably no longer good law. In the later case of *Paul v. Davis,* (discussed *infra*, p. 223), the Court held that a person's interest in reputation alone is not a constitutionally-protected liberty interest.

c. Not "property" interest: Nor was plaintiff's interest in being rehired a *"property"* interest. Such an interest did not exist merely because the individual had a "need" for a benefit, or even a "unilateral expectation" of it; rather, he must have had a *"legitimate claim of entitlement"* to it.

   i. Scope defined by state law: Whether or not such a "legitimate claim of entitlement" to the benefit existed was, the Court held, to be determined *by reference to state law*. Since Wisconsin law made it clear that rehiring decisions in non-tenured cases were to be completely discretionary, plaintiff had no such entitlement.

d. Present enjoyment required: The *Roth* Court observed that the Fourteenth Amendment due process protection of property applied to interests "that a person has *already acquired* in specific benefits." This remark seems to mean that *unless a person is already enjoying a benefit, he has no procedural due process rights* (at least arising from the "property" as opposed to "liberty" branch) if the benefit is denied to him.

   i. Initial application: Thus where the state turns down an *initial application* for such benefits as welfare, government employment or parole, it may be the case that no procedural due process rights attach, even though the applicable statute or precedents make the applicant eligible for the benefit. But the Supreme Court has never squarely focused on this issue.

e. Marshall's dissent: Justice Marshall, one of three dissenters in *Roth*, advocated the extraordinary view that "every citizen who applies for a government job is entitled to it unless the government can establish some reason for denying the employment," and that this entitlement constituted a Fourteenth Amendment "property" right.

2. *Perry v. Sindermann's* contrasting view: Despite *Roth's* severe approach, the companion case, *Perry v. Sindermann*, indicates that *informal practices or customs* may be sufficient to create a *legitimate claim of entitlement* to a benefit.

a. Facts: The plaintiff in *Perry*, like the one in *Roth*, was untenured. However, he had taught for ten years, and alleged that the college where he worked had a *"de facto"* tenure program, and that the college administration had created an "understanding" that he had tenure under that program.

b. Holding: The Court held that plaintiff was entitled to a hearing on his *de facto* tenure claim, and that such a claim, if proven, gave plaintiff a property interest. Such an interest will be found to exist if there are "mutually explicit understandings" supporting a claim of entitlement.

F. Breadth of injury is weighed: The ***breadth*** of the public benefit denied is likely to be considered by the Court, especially in public employment cases. For instance, a governmental decision not to hire or rehire a person for one particular government job is much less likely to be held to be violative of a "liberty" or "property" interest than is a decision that the individual may not hold ***any*** government job. See *Board of Regents v. Roth, supra*, p. 221.

G. Freedom from arbitrary procedures: Some commentators have suggested that the courts should recognize, as a ***substantive aspect of liberty***, certain elements of procedural fairness. Professor Van Alstyne, for instance, advocates recognizing ***"freedom from arbitrary adjudicative procedures"*** as an element of "liberty." 62 CORNELL L. REV. 487 (quoted in L,K&C, p. 635). Similarly, Rabin, 44 U. CHI. L. REV. 60 advocates a "right to a ***reasoned explanation*** of government conduct that is contrary to the expectations the government has created by conferring a special status upon an individual." (Quoted in L,K&C, p. 646.)

   1. Significance: These proposals would effectively amount to making procedural due process a "free standing" right which can exist without the presence of any unrelated liberty or property interest. The Supreme Court has never indicated any willingness to do this. See *supra*, p. 219.

H. Narrowing of protected "liberty" interests: In *Bishop*, as noted, the Court appeared to limit constitutionally-protected "property" interests to those which exist under an explicit provision of state law or contract; other sources of substantive property rights (e.g., justifiable expectations, a common-law tradition, etc.) seemed to have been excluded. Very much the same kind of cutting back has also taken place in the definition of ***"liberty,"*** principally as the result of *Paul v. Davis*, 424 U.S. 693 (1976).

   1. Facts of *Paul*: Plaintiff, after being arrested for shoplifting, was listed as an "active shoplifter" in a flyer which the police circulated to hundreds of local merchants. After the shoplifting charges were dismissed, plaintiff sued the police under 42 U.S.C. §1983 (*infra*, p. 452), which allows recovery from public officials for violation of constitutional rights.

   2. Holding: By a 5-3 vote, the Supreme Court held that plaintiff's ***interest in his reputation,*** by itself, was ***not a constitutionally-protected "liberty" or "property" interest.***

   3. Federalism considerations: The majority view in *Paul* seems to have been motivated largely by a desire to ***avoid the federalization of tort law***, and to keep suits alleging wrongdoing by state government officials from deluging the federal court system.

I. Rights of students: The Court has not cut back on the definition of "liberty" and "property" in all contexts. For instance, it has given an expansive reading to these terms in the ***school*** environment. Thus in *Goss v. Lopez*, 419 U.S. 565 (1975), the Court held that a suspension from public school constituted deprivation of a constitutionally-protected property interest. (*Goss'* holding as to the type of procedure required in the suspension situation is discussed *infra*, p. 233.)

J. What process is due: Once a court concludes that a constitutionally-protected "liberty" or "property" interest has been impaired, the issue becomes: ***What process is due?*** While full consideration of this question is generally covered in other courses (particularly *Administrative Law*), a brief outline of the Courts' treatment of the issue is given here.

   1. Traditional adversary model: The early 1970s saw the Supreme Court require an extremely broad set of procedural protections before the government could take away what the Court found to be a "property" interest. For instance, in *Goldberg v. Kelly*, 397

U.S. 254 (1970) (also discussed *supra*, p. 221), the Court held that an ***evidentiary hearing*** was required before welfare benefits could be terminated. In *Goldberg* and cases following it, the Court seemed to be moving towards a view that in order for the government to take administrative action which might affect a person's "property" or "liberty" interest, the full panoply of procedural safeguards typically imposed in court proceedings was required.

a.   **Wide range of procedures:**   This approach, if followed to its logical conclusion, would have guaranteed not only the right to a hearing, but such protections as the right to ***call witnesses***, the right to ***counsel***, the right of ***cross-examination***, the right of ***judicial review***, etc.

2.   **Withdrawal towards a "balancing" test:**   Provision of such a full set of guarantees any time a "property" or "liberty" interest was at issue would obviously have been extremely expensive, time-consuming, and perhaps administratively impossible. Therefore, in the late 1970s, just as the Court cut back on its notion of what constitutes a "property" or "liberty" interest (see *supra*, p. 221), so it cut back on its interpretation of exactly what procedures are required where a liberty or property interest is at issue.

a.   **Balancing test:**   The Court's present view may be summarized as calling for use of a ***"balancing test,"*** in which the costs of requiring a particular set of procedures will be weighed against the benefits from the use of those procedures.

b.   **Illustrated in *Mathews*:**   This balancing test was first formulated in ***Mathews v. Eldridge***, 425 U.S. 319 (1976). In holding that disability benefits could be terminated without a prior evidentiary hearing (a sharp contrast with the holding in *Goldberg v. Kelly*, the welfare benefits case), the Court listed the factors to be balanced.

i.   **One side of equation:**   On one side of the equation are: (1) the strength of the private interest that would be affected by the official action (so that the bigger the individual's stake in the outcome, the more safeguards would be required), and (2) the "risk of an erroneous deprivation of such interest through the procedures used, and the probable value, if any, of additional or substitute procedural safeguards." These two factors are presumably to be multiplied together in some way.

ii.   **Other side of equation:**   On the other side of the equation is "the government's interest, including the function involved and the fiscal and administrative burdens that the additional or substitute procedural requirement would entail."

iii.   **Mathematical form:**   Thus the *Mathews* balancing test might be expressed in the following mathematical terms, where "A" is the additional procedural safeguard to which the individual asserts that he is entitled: procedural safeguard, *A*, will be required if and only if

(amount at stake for individual) x (likelihood that administrative error will be reduced by using *A*) $<$ cost to the government of granting A

c.   **Application in *Mathews*:**   The Court applied this equation in *Mathews* as follows:

i.   **Lower stake:**   First, unlike the welfare payments at issue in *Goldberg*, the disability payments were less likely to be the individual's sole source of income, so his stake was lower than in *Goldberg*.

    ii. Value of safeguard: Second, the value of an evidentiary hearing was less than in *Goldberg*, because the disability issue turned upon a medical assessment of the worker's physical or mental condition, which assessment could probably be evaluated through written documents rather than oral testimony.

    iii. Burden on government: Thirdly, the burden of supplying a full administrative hearing was likely to be substantial, and the cost of it "may in the end come out of the pockets of the deserving since resources available for any particular program of social welfare are not unlimited."

    iv. Conclusion: Therefore, the Court concluded, no evidentiary hearing was required before termination of disability benefits.

  d. Firing of tenured employee: Where the protected interest being terminated is a **public-sector job**, the required procedural safeguards are similarly determined by a balancing test. Thus in *Cleveland Bd. of Ed. v. Loudermill*, 470 U.S. 532 (1985) (also discussed *infra*, p. 233), the Court weighed a tenured employee's interest in retaining his employment against the government's interest in having a quick way to fire unsatisfactory employees; the Court also factored in "the risk of an erroneous termination."

    i. Conclusion: The *Loudermill* Court then concluded that although "some kind of a hearing" was required prior to the discharge of the plaintiff, that hearing was required to include only "oral or written notice of the charges against him, an explanation of the employer's evidence, and an opportunity to present his side of the story." It did *not* include the right to a **full evidentiary hearing** of the sort imposed in the welfare-benefits context in *Goldberg v. Kelly, see supra*, p. 221. Requiring a full adversarial evidentiary hearing would "intrude to an unwarranted extent on the government's interest in **quickly removing an unsatisfactory employee.**"

3. Traditional civil litigation: When a person's property is at stake in a traditional *civil lawsuit*, the range of procedural protections required by the Constitution is broad. Certainly as a matter of practice, and probably as a matter of constitutional due process, the state may not take property as the result of a lawsuit — even if the suit is brought by a private party against another private party — without granting such protections as the right to call witnesses, the right to counsel, the right of cross-examination, and the right of judicial review. A meaningful treatment of what constitutes due process in the civil litigation context is beyond the scope of this outline.

  a. Unlimited discretion: One aspect of the right to due process in the civil litigation context is that a litigant has the right to be free of excessive *discretion* on the part of *juries*. For instance, when a state allows juries to award tort damages against a defendant, the state must give at least some guidance to the jury on when it may allow an award, and in what amount.

  b. Punitive damages: In some circumstances the award of *punitive damages* may violate the defendant's due process rights.

    i. Ratio of actual to punitive: A punitive damages award will violate due process if it is *"grossly excessive." BMW of North America v. Gore*, 517 U.S. 559 (1996).

      (1) Ratio of punitive to compensatory: One of the most important factors in whether an award of punitive damages is grossly excessive is the *ratio* of the *punitive damages* to the *actual damages.* The Court has said that "*few awards* [significantly] exceeding a *single-digit ratio* between punitive and compensatory damages ... will satisfy due process." *State Farm Mut. Automobile Insur. Co. v. Campbell*, 538 U.S. 408 (2003).

Example: In one of the few cases in which the Supreme Court has found that a punitive damages award was so excessive that it violated the defendant's due process right, the court attached a lot of weight to the fact that the punitive award to P was *500 times* the amount of his actual harm as determined by the jury. *BMW of North America, supra.*

ii. **Reprehensibility:** Another of the key factors in the due process analysis is the *reprehensibility* of the defendant's conduct — the more reprehensible the conduct, the higher the amount of punitive damages that may be awarded without violating due process. *State Farm Mut. Automobile Insur. Co. v. Campbell, supra.*

iii. **Conduct vis a vis strangers to the litigation:** Only the defendant's conduct *towards the plaintiff*, not its conduct towards *strangers to the litigation,* may be taken into account by the jury in setting the amount of punitive damages. *Philip Morris USA v. Williams*, 549 U.S. 346 (2007).

Example: P (Jesse Williams), a smoker, sues D (a large tobacco manufacturer) for fraud in having knowingly and falsely led P to believe that smoking was safe. P's attorney tells the jury to "think of how many other Jesse Williams in the last 40 years in the state of Oregon there have been. [Cigarettes] are going to kill ten [of every hundred]." The judge refuses D's request that the jury be instructed that in assessing punitive damages, the jury should not punish D for the impact of its alleged misconduct on other persons, who may bring lawsuits of their own. The jury awards P $821,000 in compensatory damages and $79.5 million in punitive ones.

Held, for D, which is entitled to a new trial. "[T]he Constitution's Due Process Clause forbids a State to use a punitive damages award to punish a defendant for injury that it conflicts upon nonparties [who are] strangers to the litigation." That's so because a defendant threatened with punishment for injury to a non-party has no opportunity to respond (e.g., by showing that the other victim is not entitled to damages because she did not rely on the defendant's statements). Furthermore, permitting punishment for injuring a nonparty victim "would add a near standard-less dimension to the punitive damages equation." *Philip Morris USA, supra.*

c. **Judicial bias:** A litigant also has a procedural due process right to be free of a *large risk of bias on the part of the judge hearing the case.* That right was first recognized by the Supreme Court in an important 5-4 decision, *Caperton v. A.T. Massey Coal Co.*, 129 S.Ct. 2252 (2009). *Caperton* means that in those states (39 at last count) that *elect judges, large judicial campaign contributions* by one party in a pending case can give the other party a procedural due process right to have the judge in question *removed from the case*.

i. **Facts of *Caperton*:** The plaintiffs in *Caperton* were small mining companies and their executives, who claimed that the much larger Massey Coal Company had improperly driven them out of business. The plaintiffs obtained a $50 million damage award from a West Virginia jury. Massey appealed to the West Virginia Supreme Court.

    (1) Campaign contributions: While the appeal was pending, the head of Massey, Don Blankenship, spent a total of $3 million in an effort to have sitting Justice McGraw defeated for reelection and replaced by Brent Benjamin. The $3 million was (the majority found) "more than the total amount spent by all other Benjamin supporters and three times the amount spent by Benjamin's own committee."

    (2) Benjamin wins, votes for Massey's position: Benjamin won the election (by a 53% margin), repeatedly refused to recuse himself from the appeal, and became part of a 3-2 majority that threw out the $50 million verdict against Massey. The plaintiffs who had been stripped of their jury verdict argued that their constitutional due process rights had been violated by Benjamin's refusal to recuse himself for bias.

  ii. Majority finds due process violation: By a 5-4 vote, the Court agreed with the plaintiffs that Benjamin's refusal to recuse himself violated their constitutional due process rights. In an opinion by Justice Kennedy (who joined with the four liberal numbers of the Court), the majority held that due process could be violated not just by proof of "actual bias," but also by a *"serious risk of actual bias ...* based on *objective and reasonable perceptions*[.]" And such a risk of bias occurs "when a person with a personal stake in a particular case had a *significant and disproportionate influence in placing the judge on the case* by *raising funds or directing the judge's election campaign* when the case was pending or imminent."

    (1) "Rare instances": The majority rejected the dissenters' fear of a "flood of recusal motions" and of "unnecessary interference with judicial elections." The facts here were, Kennedy said, "extreme by any measure." Findings of bias that rise to the level of due process violations, Kennedy predicted, would be "confined to rare instances."

  iii. Dissenters fear flood of challenges: The four dissenters feared that the majority's new due process right would create more problems than it solved. In the principal dissent, Chief Justice Roberts said that the majority's "probability of bias" standard "cannot be defined in any limited way," and would inevitably lead to an increase in groundless allegations that judges are biased. The result, he said "will do far more to erode public confidence in judicial impartiality than an isolated failure to recuse in a particular case."

4. Criminal defendants and prisoners: *Criminal defendants* obviously receive extensive procedural due process protections during the course of their trial. If convicted, the defendant will lose her liberty for a substantial period, and perhaps even her life. So the procedural protections that criminal defendants get during trial are at their broadest: right to counsel, right to present witnesses, right to confront opposing witnesses, etc. The procedural protections given to criminal defendants are typically covered in a criminal procedure course, and are beyond the scope of this outline.

a. **Rights of convicted prisoners:** Once a criminal defendant has been **convicted**, the defendant loses many, but not all, procedural due process protections. A large body of case law has arisen concerning both the substantive and procedural due process protections to be given to **prisoners**. Again, full coverage of those cases is beyond the scope of this outline, but here are a few of the key principles:

   i. **Limited rights:** Prisoners "do not shed all constitutional rights at the prison gate." *Sandin v. Conner,* 515 U.S. 572 (1995). However, the needs of prison administration, and society's right to punish crimes, entitle prison authorities to impose restraints on a prisoner's physical freedom even beyond the mere fact of incarceration, and give the authorities a **broad right** to decide on the **particular restraints** without furnishing a full array of procedural protections during the decision-making.

      (1) **The "atypical and significant hardship" test:** Prison officials who give extra punishment to a prisoner or change his terms of confinement won't commit a substantive due process violation, and don't need to observe procedural due process protections during their decision-making process, so long as their action doesn't "impose[] *atypical and significant hardship* on the inmate in relation to the *ordinary incidents of prison life.*" *Sandin, supra.*

         ❏ For instance, a prisoner who is charged with disobeying prison regulations is not entitled by due process to **present witnesses** during the disciplinary hearing, even if the hearing leads to his being put in solitary confinement for 30 days. *Sandin, supra.*

         ❏ Similarly, an inmate does not have a constitutionally-protected liberty interest in **not being transferred** from a medium-security prison to a maximum-security prison, because "'[c]onfinement in any of the State's institutions is within the **normal limits or range of custody** which the conviction has authorized the State to impose." *Meachum v. Fano,* 427 U.S. 215 (1976).

         ❏ Unless a statute gives the right, a prisoner does not have a constitutionally protected interest in being **given parole**. So parole boards may, in the absence of a statute imposing particular procedural requirements on them, act arbitrarily. *Greenholtz v. Inmates,* 442 U.S. 1 (1979).

      (2) **Severe or stigmatizing punishments:** On the other hand, some conditions of imprisonment are either **so severe, or so stigmatizing**, that the prisoner's substantive due process rights *will* be abridged if prison authorities do not have adequate reasons for their actions, and do not follow adequate procedures.

         ❏ Thus a prisoner probably has a substantive due process right not to be **transferred to a mental institution** without cause. Cf. *Vitek v. Jones,* 445 U.S. 480 (1980) (though in *Vitek,* the situation was complicated by the fact that state law allowed the transfer only if the prisoner "suffers from a mental disease or defect" that could not be adequately treated in the prison).

         ❏ Similarly, some prison **conditions** are so incredibly **punitive** that the prisoner has a constitutionally protected liberty interest in avoiding them.

Thus the transfer of a prisoner to a *"Supermax" facility* was found to implicate the prisoner's liberty interest, where the prisoner was kept in *solitary confinement* in a 7 by 14 foot cell for 23 hours a day with a light on at all times, and with just one hour a day outside his cell (to be spent in an indoor recreation cell). *Wilkinson v. Austin*, 545 U.S. 209 (2005). The Court found that this type of confinement imposed an "atypical and significant hardship," the test under *Sandin, supra*, p. 228, for whether a liberty interest is at stake. (However, the Court found that the prison's procedures prior to imposing the punishment — which included notice of reasons and a "fair opportunity for rebuttal" — were constitutionally sufficient, even though inmates were not given the right to call witnesses.)

b. **Right to appeal:** An issue related to prisoner-rights is whether and when a criminal defendant has a due process right to *appeal his conviction*. The Supreme Court has said in dictum that "a review by an appellate court of the final judgment in a criminal case ... is *not* now a necessary element of due process." *McKane v. Durston*, 153 U.S. 684 (1894). The Court might, nonetheless, today find that there is a due process right to have some sort of criminal appeal. In any event, it is clear that once a state chooses (as all states do) to grant some sort of appeal, the appeals process must *obey certain minimum due process requirements*; thus, for instance, a defendant has a due process right to effective assistance of counsel on a first appeal that is granted of right. *Evitts v. Lucey*, 465 U.S. 387 (1985).

i. **Few rules:** But the Supreme Court has largely stayed out of the business of dictating precisely *what* appellate procedures states must supply once they decide to allow criminal appeals at all. Post-conviction remedies given by the state must, in order to satisfy due process, merely "compor[t] with fundamental fairness." *Pennsylvania v. Finley*, 481 U.S. 551 (1987).

ii. **DNA testing:** The Court's reluctance to prescribe specific methods by which the states must allow convicted defendants to try to overturn their convictions is illustrated in a 2009 case involving *DNA testing*. In a 5-4 case in which Chief Justice Roberts wrote the majority opinion, the Court held that a prisoner has *no independent liberty interest in being given access to DNA evidence to prove his innocence*. *District Attorney's Office for the Third Judicial District v. Osborne*, 129 S.Ct. 2308 (2009).

(1) **Facts:** Osborne, the prisoner, had been convicted of kidnapping and sexual assault 16 years earlier by an Alaska state court. There was ample evidence of his guilt, including testimony by a co-defendant. Osborne had later admitted guilt in the course of parole hearings (a condition of parole). He now sought to test, at his own expense, the DNA evidence that had been preserved following the crime. The Alaska courts rejected his attempts.

(2) **Procedures were not inadequate:** Roberts agreed that Osborne had a constitutional liberty interest in having access to *some* sort of state-law procedures to demonstrate his innocence via newly-discovered evidence. But the state here had supplied such procedures (which Osborne apparently did not qualify for because the state viewed the evidence as not "newly discovered"). Those procedures, Roberts said, would be unconstitutional "only if they are fundamen-

tally inadequate to vindicate the substantive rights provided." And the procedures here did not flunk that easy-to-satisfy standard.

(3) **No "freestanding right":** Most importantly, Roberts rejected Osborne's argument that he had (as Roberts put it) a *"freestanding right to DNA evidence* untethered from the [prisoner's] liberty interests[.]" Forty-four states had already given criminal defendants a specific statutory right to DNA testing (though Alaska had not). And overall, the states seemed to be handling the DNA issue satisfactorily. Therefore, the Court should be "reluctant to enlist the Federal Judiciary in creating a new constitutional code of rules for handling DNA," for fear that this "would force [the Court] to act as policymakers" on a host of related issues (e.g., to decide whether there is "a constitutional obligation to *preserve forensic evidence* that might later be tested").

(4) **Dissent:** The four dissenters in *Osborne* believed that Osborne had some sort of constitutionally-protected liberty interest that the state was abridging by not allowing the DNA testing here, though they did not agree among themselves on the exact nature of that interest. Stevens, joined by two other justices, wrote that Osborne had a substantive liberty interest in being given access to DNA evidence to show his innocence, and that the state's refusal to give him that access while providing no good reason for the refusal "constitutes *arbitrary action* that offends basic principles of due process."

5. **Detention of "enemy combatants" who are citizens:**   One context in which the Court has made use of the *Mathews* balancing test (*supra*, p. 224) for determining what process is due is the *detention of "enemy combatants" during war.* In one of the first cases exploring the President's powers in the post-9/11 war on terrorism, the Court held that if a U.S. citizen is to be held as an enemy combatant, he is entitled to due process, including at a minimum the *right to counsel*, and the right to *go before a neutral decisionmaker* to challenge his designation as enemy combatant. *Hamdi v. Rumsfeld*, 542 US. 507 (2004).

a. **Facts:**   The prisoner in *Hamdi* was Yaser Hamdi, an American citizen who was captured in Afghanistan in 2001 by the Northern Alliance, a coalition fighting alongside U.S. troops to oust the Taliban. The Alliance turned Hamdi over to the U.S. military, which labeled him an "enemy combatant" based mostly on the fact that he had been associated with the Taliban and had surrendered his rifle to the Alliance. The military transferred him to a naval brig in South Carolina. The Bush administration asserted that by designating Hamdi as an enemy combatant, the executive branch obtained the power to hold him in confinement indefinitely, without formal charges or proceedings, so long as the war in which he had been seized continued.

b. **Ruling against government:**   Although the Court's rationale was badly splintered, eight members of the Court concluded that the U.S. did not in fact have the power that the government contended it had, i.e., the power to hold Hamdi without counsel, without charges and without opportunity for some sort of trial.

i. **O'Connor's plurality opinion:**   Justice O'Connor, writing for herself and three other justices (Rehnquist, Kennedy and Breyer) wrote a plurality opinion concluding that Hamdi had the right to due process, at least with respect to pursuing his claim that he was not in fact an "enemy combatant."[10] In determining to what procedural protections Hamdi was entitled, O'Connor said, the **balancing test of Mathews v. Eldridge applied.** That is, the government's interest in the nation's security needed to be balanced against Hamdi's interest in not being deprived of liberty without due process.

(1) Government's interest: O'Connor conceded that the government had a strong interest in "ensuring that those who have in fact fought with the enemy during a war do not return to battle against the United States." She also agreed with the Bush administration that the government's interest in being free to wage a war without the distraction of litigation would be impeded by having to follow a system of trial-like procedures — including discovery into the details of military operations and national defense — before someone captured on the battlefield could be declared an enemy combatant.

(2) Citizen's interest: But Hamdi had strong countervailing interests: the "fundamental nature of a citizen's right to be free from involuntary confinement by his own government without due process of law."

(3) Minimum procedures: O'Connor then spelled out some of the procedural protections to which she believed Hamdi was entitled under the *Mathews* balancing test, if he wished to challenge the correctness of his classification as an enemy combatant:

❏ He was entitled to *"notice of the factual basis* for his classification" (as an enemy combatant);

❏ He was entitled to "a *fair opportunity* to *rebut the government's factual assertions* before a *neutral decisionmaker*";

❏ He had the right of *access to counsel* in connection with the proceedings.

(4) Open questions: But O'Connor also tried not to tie the government's hands unduly. The Court was not being confronted with any particular set of procedures that the government was proposing to use — indeed, the government was contending that it did not have to use *any* procedures at all, and could simply detain Hamdi indefinitely on its own say so. However, O'Connor speculated about certain respects in which procedures *less protective* than the ones guaranteed for a standard criminal trial might nonetheless *suffice* in Hamdi's upcoming challenge to his status as enemy combatant, due to the need to "alleviate [the proceedings'] uncommon potential to burden the Executive at a time of ongoing military conflict." Here are some of O'Connor's speculations:

❏ *Hearsay* "may need to be *accepted* as the most reliable available evidence from the Government."

❏ The Constitution "would not be offended by a *presumption in favor of the government's evidence,"* as long as that presumption "remained a *rebuttable* one"

---

10. Hamdi claimed that he never bore arms against the United States, that he arrived in Afghanistan to do relief work less than two months before 9/11, and that he was trapped there when the U.S. military campaign began.

and as long as "fair opportunity for rebuttal were provided."

❏ Whatever procedures are due, they would ***not*** be due at the moment a citizen was initially captured on the battlefield; instead, the procedures would be due only when the government decided to ***continue to hold*** those it had captured.

❏ Finally, O'Connor said, it was ***not*** necessarily the case that a ***federal district court*** would have to be the one to hear Hamdi's challenge to his confinement. Instead, she said, "there remains the ***possibility*** that the standards we have articulated could be met by an appropriately authorized and properly constituted ***military tribunal.***"

ii. **Souter and Ginsburg concur in judgment:** Justices Souter and Ginsburg, concurring only in part, disagreed with the plurality's conclusion that Hamdi's detention was authorized at all. But they agreed that if he *was* to be detained, he would certainly have ***at least those procedural due process rights that the plurality was willing to give him***. In fact, these two justices indicated that they would give Hamdi even *more* procedural protections than the plurality — for instance, they ***disagreed*** that the government could be given the benefit of a ***presumption*** that Hamdi was an enemy combatant, or that litigating the issue before a ***military tribunal*** might constitutionally substitute for Hamdi's right to bring a habeas corpus petition in federal court.

iii. **Scalia and Stevens dissent:** Two additional Justices, Scalia and Stevens, dissented from the Court's basic holding that a citizen could be held in wartime by the executive branch without full recourse to the traditional right to challenge his imprisonment by means of a habeas corpus petition. Therefore, they strongly disagreed with the plurality's suggestion that Hamdi was due something less than the full-dress procedural due process protections given to any other imprisoned citizen. They criticized the plurality's "unheard-of system in which the citizen rather than the Government bears the burden of proof, testimony is by hearsay rather than live witnesses, and the presiding officer may well be a 'neutral' military officer rather than judge and jury."

iv. **Summary:** So eight members of the Court (all but Thomas) believed that the executive branch could not detain a citizen accused of being an enemy combatant unless the citizen was given ***substantial due process protections*** to allow him to challenge the enemy-combatant designation — at a minimum, protections like ***notice of the details*** of the charge, a right to rebut the charge before a n***eutral decisionmaker***, and the ***right to counsel***. Indeed, four members of the court (Souter, Ginsburg, Scalia and Stevens) seemed to believe that the ***full or nearly-full range of protections*** that would be given to any citizen imprisoned while accused of a crime were due to a citizen held on such enemy-combatant charges.

(1) **Wartime not that different:** *Hamdi* also illustrates that, for the present Court, even the fact that the nation is effectively ***at war*** will not allow the executive branch to dispense with basic due process requirements when it imprisons one of its own citizens. This marks a quite dramatic turnaround from the view of the World War II Court in the 1944 Japanese exclusion case (*Korematsu v. U.S.*, discussed *infra*, p. 264), where the Court held that all citizens of Japanese ancestry on the West Coast could effectively be imprisoned

to prevent them from committing espionage and sabotage. As Justice O'Connor put it in her plurality opinion in *Hamdi*, "[A] state of war is *not a blank check for the President* when it comes to the rights of the Nation's citizens."

6. **Legislature's right to limit procedures:** The Court in *Mathews v. Eldridge* (*supra*, p. 224), although it took a limited view of procedural protections, did seem to be applying constitutional criteria in making its decision. But suppose that the *legislature itself*, in creating a statutory entitlement, *attempts to define the procedures* under which the right may be denied or cut off. Do these legislative principles control?

   a. **No right to limit procedures:** The answer is *"no."* Even where the legislature creates the property or liberty interest in question, *it is not free to establish procedures for terminating that right*. *Cleveland Bd. of Ed. v. Loudermill*, 470 U.S. 532 (1985).

7. **Educational cases:** Issues about what process is due have surfaced repeatedly in cases involving public *education*. A brief summary of the Court's major holdings is as follows:

   a. **Disciplinary suspension:** Where a student is *suspended* for disciplinary reasons for more than a trivial period, due process requires that he be given "oral or written notice of the charges against him and, if he denies them, an explanation of the evidence the authorities have and an opportunity to present his side of the story." *Goss v. Lopez*, 419 U.S. 565 (1975). (In *Goss*, a ten-day suspension was held to be clearly more than trivial.)

   b. **Academic dismissal:** By contrast, where a student is dismissed for *academic* (as distinguished from disciplinary) reasons, no hearing is necessary, since this type of decision is more subjective, and less suited to formal judicial or administrative decision making. *Board of Curators v. Horowitz*, 435 U.S. 78 (1978) (involving dismissal of a medical student because of poor clinical performance and personal hygiene).

Quiz Yourself on
PROCEDURAL DUE PROCESS

34. The town of Corinth advertised an opening for a position as secretary to the City Clerk. The ad described the job briefly, and said nothing about the criteria that would be used to fill it. Jane Brown applied for the job. She was given a typing test, and then an interview with George Crako, the City Clerk. Crako chose somebody else for the job. Brown asked for a statement of why she didn't get the job, but the Clerk's office refused to respond.

   Brown later heard from the grapevine that Crako had told someone else in the department that he thought Brown was probably the best at performing the technical tasks, but that he had declined to hire her because he had heard she was gay. Brown, who was not gay, realized that Crako was probably thinking of another member of the community, Jane Browne, who was widely known to be gay. Brown asked for a hearing at which she could present what she called "information which would cause the Clerk to reverse his decision," but town officials again refused. Brown has now sued, arguing that the procedures used to fill the opening deprived her of her Fourteenth Amendment due process rights. Should the court find in Brown's favor? _____

35. Tennant, a single mother who was receiving Welfare, resided in a public housing project owned by the city of Pretoria. She had lived in the building for over 10 years, pursuant to a series of two-year leases. The rules of the housing project, posted on a bulletin board in the complex, stated that "customarily, resi-

dents who are well behaved and current on all of their obligations will be offered the opportunity to renew their leases upon their expiration." There is no statute or other body of state or local law bearing on whether one in Tennant's position is entitled, as a contractual matter, to a renewal. At the end of Tennant's current two-year term, she was not offered the opportunity to renew her lease. Instead, the apartment was given to a woman who turned out to be the niece of Pretoria's Buildings Commissioner, who would not have been given an apartment had the ordinary informal allocation procedures that had previously been followed in the housing project been followed here. Tennant was at no time given an explanation for why she wasn't permitted to renew, or a hearing regarding the decision.

(a) If Tennant wishes to challenge the city's handling of her tenancy on constitutional grounds, what is the strongest argument she can make? _____

(b) Will this argument succeed? _____

36. Netsville High School, a public high school, was known for its strong boys' and girls' tennis teams. The administration caused to be published in the school newspaper an invitation for tryouts. This invitation included the following sentence: "All students in good academic standing have the right to compete for the 7 spots on each team. These spots will be awarded to the best players." Priscilla, a high school freshman, had not been on the team previously. However, she had had some strong results in non-school tournaments the summer before her freshman year. During tryouts, the head coach watched Priscilla play only briefly. He very quickly reached the conclusion that her game was not mature enough to make her a varsity player. After one day of practice, he cut her from the team. He did not give her any statement of reasons, or opportunity to present her view of why she should make the team; he merely stated that she was "not good enough." The coach awarded team spots exclusively to those who had been on the team in prior years, including at least one girl whom Priscilla had soundly beaten in a non-school tournament the summer before. Priscilla has sued the school board, arguing that the procedures by which she was dropped from the team violated her due process rights to be awarded a post if she was one of the "best players."

Assuming that Priscilla can demonstrate that most tennis coaches would have found her to be one of the seven strongest players trying out for the team, should the judge order the coach to reconsider her status? _____

———————————

Answers

34. **No.** The Fourteenth Amendment's Due Process Clause only prevents the government from depriving a person of "*life*, *liberty*, or *property* without due process of law." Unless Brown can show that she had a "liberty" or "property" interest that was impaired, she will not even get to the point of being allowed to show that fair procedures were not followed. In other words, the Due Process Clause does not bar the government from procedural irregularities per se, only procedural irregularities in connection with the taking of life, liberty or property. It is very clear that a person applying for an initial government position has no liberty or property interest in the position, so the government may turn the applicant down for totally arbitrary or irrational reasons (so long as the reasons are not themselves violations of independently-guaranteed constitutional rights, such as refusing to hire a person because she is, say, black). So the fact that the Clerk's decision was completely "wrong," in the sense that he had the wrong person in mind, is completely irrelevant. We never get to the question of what type of process (e.g., right to a statement of reasons, or right to a hearing) would have been due.

35. **(a) That it violated her right not to have her "property" taken without due process, and that this right included the right to a hearing.**

(b) Yes, probably. The core issue is whether Tennant had a *"property" interest* in her apartment. The Court has held that even *informal practices or customs* may be sufficient to create a *legitimate claim of entitlement* to a benefit. See, e.g., *Perry v. Sindermann* (in which a college was found to have created a de facto tenure program that created in P, a college professor, the "understanding" that he would be entitled to tenure). Here, the statement regarding the customary right of renewal was probably enough to create in Tennant such a legitimate claim of entitlement to renew, in view of the lack of any other law bearing on whether Tennant did indeed have such a right. (If there were a statute or body of case law holding that as a matter of state law there is no right to renew despite a seeming indication to the contrary in a housing project's rules and regulations, then this body of state law would be dispositive, and Tennant would not have any "property" interest.)

If Tennant indeed had a legitimate entitlement to being allowed to renew provided that she was in good standing, then she was presumably entitled to at least a hearing before this property interest could be taken away. (The precise procedures that would have to followed are not clear, but for a right as important as the right to continue to live in subsidized housing, it is likely that some sort of hearing and statement of reasons, however informal, would be required.)

36. **No, probably.** The facts are enough to establish that Priscilla indeed probably had a "property" interest (albeit a weak one) in being awarded a spot if she was in fact one of the best seven players. That is, the notice in the newspaper probably was sufficient to constitute a binding offer on the part of the school to award a place to anyone who tried out and proved that she was indeed among the seven best players, and this contract was enough to give rise to a "property" interest. However, the case really turns on exactly what procedures were "due" to Priscilla when it came time to determine whether she was in fact one of the seven best players. The Supreme Court uses a *balancing test* for deciding whether a particular set of procedures should be required once a property interest (or liberty interest) is at stake. On one side is placed the amount at stake for the individual, multiplied by the likelihood that administrative error will be reduced by using the procedure in question; on the other side is the cost to the government of granting that procedure.

Here, the amount at stake for Priscilla is relatively weak, compared with, say, the right to continue receiving welfare benefits or the right to keep one's job. The likelihood that "administrative errors" would be reduced by requiring, say, a statement of reasons before anyone is cut, or a right to present one's case, is relatively small — a coach would still have to be the decision-maker, and that decision would still be based principally on what the coach saw, so that a hearing and statement of reasons are unlikely to reduce error by much. Conversely, there is a substantial cost to the government (here, the school board) in having to set up detailed, judicially-challengeable procedures for awarding every spot on an athletic team. Consequently, the court is very likely to decide that such litigation-like procedures as a statement of reasons and an opportunity to present one's case are not worth their cost.

(On the other hand, probably an applicant who has a property interest in being allowed to compete for a spot on the team at least has the right to marginally "fair" procedures, so that, for instance, an applicant who could show that the coach favored the coach's own child or own private-coaching pupils might be able to show that her procedural rights had been violated.)

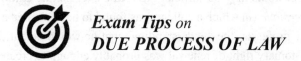

Exam Tips on
DUE PROCESS OF LAW

In virtually any fact pattern where an individual or company is not permitted to do something, you must be alert to the possibility that there is a *due process* violation. A large portion of all essay questions with complex fact patterns will raise at least one due process issue. Here are the most important things to keep in mind:

☞ If your problem involves one of the odd-ball, less-major Bill of Rights guarantees (e.g., the Second Amendment right to keep weapons for *self-defense*, or the Eighth Amendment right not to be required to pay *excessive fines*), check whether your problem involves the applicability of that guarantee to a *state or local government.* If it does, point out that the guarantee has been *"selectively incorporated"* into the meaning of 14th Amendment DP *unless* you're dealing with the Fifth Amendment prohibition on criminal trials without a *grand jury indictment* or the Seventh Amendment's right to *jury trial* in a *civil* case.

☞ Determine whether it is an issue of *substantive* DP or *procedural* DP that you're faced with.

    ☞ In a *substantive* DP problem, the government is completely taking away a whole group's ability to do something, and there is no issue of whether the particular plaintiff falls into the governmentally-defined group or not. (*Example:* The state says, "No woman may have an abortion after the third month of pregnancy." If the facts make it clear that P is a woman who is four months pregnant, we have a substantive DP problem, not a procedural DP problem.)

    ☞ In a *procedural* DP problem, the overall issue is whether P as an individual does or does not fit into the legislatively-defined group, and the sub-issue is what if any individualized, case-specific, procedures must be followed before the government can determine which group P falls into. (*Example:* A city says, "Public school teachers may only be fired for acts of moral turpitude." If there is an issue about whether P did or did not commit such an act, then we're dealing with procedural due process, i.e., the procedures used to determine whether P did or did not commit such an act.)

☞ If you're dealing with a *substantive* DP problem, decide immediately whether the right at issue is *fundamental* or non-fundamental.

    ☞ Remember that the only rights that are fundamental for substantive DP purposes are those that involve the *"right of privacy"* or *"right of autonomy."* The key examples are:

       ☞ The right to *marry*. And keep in mind that since 2015, the fundamental status of the right to marry covers not just opposite-sex couples but also *same-sex couples.* Cite to *Obergefell v. Hodges* on this point.

       ☞ The right to *bear* (or decide *not* to bear) *children*.

       ☞ The right to decide how to *rear* one's children.

☞ Perhaps the right to decline *unwanted medical treatment* (and possibly the right to *commit suicide* if competent and terminally ill).

☞ Possibly, the right to control one's *dress* and *personal appearance*.

☞ If you conclude that the right is "fundamental," state that the court must generally *strictly scrutinize* the regulation. The state *bears the burden* of defending its regulation. The state loses unless *both* the following are true:

☞ The state is pursing a *"compelling"* (not just "legitimate") objective; and

☞ The means chosen by the state are *"necessary"* to achieve that compelling end. (If there are *less restrictive means* that would do the job just as well, or almost as well, then the means chosen aren't "necessary.")

Note: But note that in the special case of the fundamental right to *engage in same-sex marriage,* we don't *know* for sure whether the Supreme Court uses strict scrutiny; we just know from *Obergefell* that bans on same-sex marriage are invalid (but the majority in *Obergefell* might have reached this conclusion even while using some review standard less rigorous than strict scrutiny).

☞ By contrast, if you conclude that the right involved is *non-fundamental*, then state that *"mere-rationality"* review is used. That is, the state just has to be:

☞ Pursuing a *legitimate governmental objective*; and

☞ Doing so with means that are *rationally related* to that objective.

☞ If the government regulation is essentially *economic*, you should almost certainly conclude that the rights involved are non-fundamental, and apply the mere-rationality test. The same is true of most health, safety or other "social welfare" legislation — unless it treads on one of those narrow areas (marriage, child-bearing, child-rearing, "right-to-die"), it's non-fundamental, and you should be using "mere-rationality" review.

☛ Be sure to distinguish between the *Fifth* Amendment's DP Clause and the *Fourteenth* Amendment's DP Clause. If the regulation is imposed by the *federal* government, the relevant clause is the Fifth Amendment. If the regulating is being done by a state or local government, the Fourteenth Amendment is the relevant one.

☛ Here's an overview of some of the most testable issues relating to the substantive due process protection given to *fundamental* rights:

Abortion

☞ A pregnant woman's interest in *abortion*, of course, gets some substantive DP protection. Your professor will expect you to know that this is so, as a general proposition.

☞ What's the *standard* for assessing whether a regulation of abortion is constitutional? *Answer:* Whether the regulation places an *"undue burden"* on (or poses a *"substantial obstacle"* to) women seeking pre-viability abortions. The burden is "undue" if the burdens on abortion access *outweigh the benefits* from the regulation. Reducing the use of abortion on *moral* grounds does *not* count as a permissible "benefit," but *"health benefits" to the pregnant woman do* count. But only *actual* health benefits — not ones claimed by the state but unsupported by medical evidence — can count on the benefits side of the balancing. (Cite to *Whole Woman's Health v. Hellerstedt*.)

☞ The particular abortion sub-issues you're most likely to be tested on are:

☞ Whether the state may require that the woman's **spouse** be given **notice** prior to the abortion (the answer is *"no"*);

☞ Whether a **minor** may be required to have **parental consent** (the answer is generally *"yes,"* but there must be a "judicial bypass" as an alternative);

☞ Whether abortions **after the fetus is "viable"** may be **forbidden** or tightly regulated (the answer is pretty clearly *yes"*);

☞ Whether rules tightly regulating **who may perform** abortions, or in **what types of facilities**, are constitutional. (*Answer:* Unconstitutional if the measures have no real incremental benefits to women's health, or if the burdens that they have the purpose or intent of imposing on abortion-access outweigh whatever health benefits the state is citing. *Examples:* A state may not require abortion doctors to have local-hospital patient-admitting privileges, or require that abortion facilities meet the stringent space, staffing, etc. standards that "ambulatory surgery centers" are required to meet. *Hellerstedt*.)

☞ If the regulation interferes with **sexual** activities, distinguish between interferences with the rights of **married** couples, and virtually all other types of sex.

☞ Thus if your facts involve a government attempt to make certain practices unlawful when practiced between members of a **married** couple in **private**, you should usually be applying strict scrutiny, and you should conclude that the interference violates substantive DP.

☞ Where the activity consists of **homosexual sex** outside of marriage, you should conclude that (1) the activity is **not** "fundamental," and the regulation is therefore not to be strictly scrutinized; but that (2) the **"mere-rationality"** review that's used should have real **"bite,"** and should be used to **strike down** as "irrational" any regulation that seems motivated solely by the majority's **"moral disapproval."**

Example: If government bans "sodomy" in a way that restricts gay sexual activity, say that even under mere-rationality review the measure must be struck down as an irrational substantive due process violation of the right to sexual expression. Cite to *Lawrence v. Texas*.

☞ Here are some other contexts where you might find that fundamental interests are being impaired in violation of substantive DP:

☞ The state has impaired **same-sex couples'** right to **get married** to each other (e.g., by defining marriage as exclusively "between a man and a woman") — cite to *Obergefell v. Hodges* for the proposition that no unit of government may impair this fundamental right.

☞ Relatives are being prevented from ***living together*** (e.g., by restrictive ***zoning*** rules such as the no-cousins rule in *Moore v. East Cleveland*).

☞ Parents are being deprived of freedom to choose how their child is to be ***educated*** (e.g., a state statute banning home-study or private-school education, or unduly restricting these alternatives) or how the child is to be ***raised at home*** (e.g., a state court order compelling a mother to give lengthy visitation rights to the child's paternal grandparents).

☛ Whenever you have government denying a person a job, license, benefit, etc., consider whether the individual was entitled to ***procedural due process***, and if so, whether the requirements of procedural DP were complied with.

☞ First, make sure that there is ***government action*** in the denial. (*Example:* If the facts tell you that a private employer is firing someone, you never get to the issue of procedural due process because there is no state action.)

☞ Next, check to make sure that what is being denied is ***"life," "liberty"*** or ***"property."***

☞ You'll never have to worry about "life" being taken unless your fact pattern deals with the death penalty in criminal cases.

☞ Here are some typical situations where "liberty" is at stake:

☞ P is deprived of the right to ***drive***;

☞ P is denied a ***license*** that she needs in order to practice her profession (e.g., law, medicine, accounting, teaching, or even truck-driving or tour-guiding);

☞ P is deprived of the right to ***raise his family***, because of charges of child abuse or neglect.

☞ Most commonly, though, you'll see fact patterns suggesting that ***"property"*** may have been taken.

☞ Many situations involve government ***benefits***. If you are ***already*** getting the benefit, the government is probably depriving you of a "property" interest if it tries to ***terminate*** the benefit. On the other hand, if you are first ***applying*** for the benefit, then you probably do not yet have a property interest, so the government probably does not have to use procedural DP — it can arbitrarily or irrationally reject your application.

☞ Here are some typical kinds of government benefits that pop up on exam questions:

❏ receipt of ***welfare*** payments;

❏ right to occupy ***public housing***;

❏ right to take certain ***courses*** in public school, or to participate in ***extracurricular activities*** sponsored by the public school.

☞ Remember that a key part of the analysis is whether state law, or perhaps even government custom, gives P a ***"legitimate claim of entitlement"*** to have the benefit continue. (*Example:* If a statute, regulation or even an informal document like a benefit handbook indicates the circumstances under which a particular benefit will be granted or continued, then a person is likely to have a "property" interest in the benefit on the terms provided in the statute, regulation, etc.)

☞ When you're dealing with a state or local government *job*, the same analysis applies: if you've already got the job, you may or may not have a "legitimate claim of entitlement" to it (depending on what state law says about how and when you can be fired). If you do have a legitimate claim of entitlement, then you have a "property" interest that can only be taken away by complying with procedural DP. If you don't have a legitimate claim, then you have no procedural DP rights either.

☞ If you've decided that P has a "property" or "liberty" interest that is being taken away, you know that P is entitled to some sort of procedural DP. Now, you must decide exactly *what procedures* are due to P.

☞ Here, remember to do a *balancing* test: for each procedural safeguard that may or may not be due, weigh the state's interest in making a prompt disposition against the damage to P in being denied the safeguard.

☞ If P has been awarded *punitive damages* against D, consider the possibility that the award is so excessive (or so inappropriately takes account of harm done by D to persons not present in the litigation) that the award violates D's due process rights.

☞ Some of the procedural safeguards that you should consider are (in ascending order of the burden that they typically put on the state):

❏ the right to receive a *statement of reasons* why the benefit is being cut off;

❏ the right to a *hearing* at which P can plead her case;

❏ the right to have *counsel present* at the hearing;

❏ the right to *appeal* the adverse decision to a higher body.

In general, you should conclude that P has the right to counsel and appeal only where the proceedings are criminal or quasi-criminal, but you should be relatively quick to conclude that P has a right to a statement of reasons or a hearing, even in a non-criminal situation such as loss of a job or loss of a financial benefit.

CHAPTER 10

EQUAL PROTECTION

ChapterScope

The Equal Protection Clause is part of the Fourteenth Amendment. It provides that "no state shall make or enforce any law which shall … deny to any person within its jurisdiction equal protection of the laws." Here are the key concepts concerning equal protection:

- **Classifications:** The Clause imposes a *general* restraint on the governmental use of *classifications*, not just classifications based on race but also those based on sex, alienage, illegitimacy, wealth, or any other characteristic.

- **Federal government:** The direct text of the Clause applies only to state governments. But the *federal* government is also bound by the same rules of equal protection — the Fifth Amendment's Due Process Clause is interpreted to bar the federal government from making any classification that would be a violation of the Equal Protection Clause if done by a state.

- **Government action only:** The Equal Protection Clause (and the Fifth Amendment's Due Process Clause) apply *only to government action*, not to action by private citizens. This is the requirement of *"state action."*

- **"As applied" vs. "facial":** There are two different types of attacks a plaintiff may make on a classification:

  - ❏ **Facial:** If P attacks a classification that is clearly written into the statute or regulation, he is saying that the statute or regulation violates equal protection *"on its face."*

  - ❏ **"As applied":** If P's claim is that the statute/regulation does not make a classification on its face, but is being *administered* in a purposefully discriminatory way, then he is claiming that the statute/regulation is a violation of equal protection *"as applied."*

- **What the Clause guarantees:** The Clause in essence guarantees that *people who are similarly situated will be treated similarly*.

- **Three levels of review:** There are three levels of review that are used in judging whether governmental classifications violate the Equal Protection Clause:

  - ❏ **Strict scrutiny:** At one end of the spectrum, the Court gives *"strict scrutiny"* to any statute that is based on a "suspect classification" or that impairs a "fundamental right." Where strict scrutiny is invoked, the classification will be upheld only if it is *necessary* to promote a *compelling* governmental interest. The three suspect classes are *race*, *national origin* and (for some purposes) *alienage*. The rights that are "fundamental" are principally the right to *vote*, the right to have access to the *courts*, and the right to *migrate interstate*.

  - ❏ **Middle-level review:** In a few situations, the Court uses a *middle level* of review, less demanding than "strict scrutiny." This level is used for *"semi-suspect"* classifications, i.e., those based on *gender* and *illegitimacy*. Under mid-level review, the means chosen by the legislature (i.e., the classification) must be *substantially related* to an *important* governmental objective.

❑ **Ordinary "mere-rationality" review:** At the easiest-to-satisfy end of the spectrum, we have the "mere-rationality" standard. This standard applies to all classifications that are not based on a "suspect" or "semi-suspect" classification (i.e., that do not involve race, national origin, alienage, gender or legitimacy) and do not impair a "fundamental right" (i.e., do not impair the right to vote, access the courts or migrate interstate). Under this standard, the classification will be upheld so long as it is conceivable that the classification bears a ***rational relationship*** to a ***legitimate*** governmental objective. Almost every classification survives this easy review.

     ❑ **Economic regulation:** Almost every ***economic*** and ***tax*** classification is reviewed under this easy standard.

■ **Suspect classifications:** When a classification involves a ***suspect class*** (race, national origin and, for some purposes, alienage), here are the key features of how courts do their review:

❑ **Purposeful:** Strict scrutiny will only be applied where the differential treatment of the class is ***intentional*** on the part of the government. If the government enacts a statute or regulation that merely has the unintended incidental ***effect*** of burdening, say, blacks worse than whites, the Court will ***not*** use strict scrutiny.

❑ **Strict equals fatal:** Once the Court decides that a suspect classification is involved and that strict scrutiny must be used, the scrutiny is almost always ***fatal*** to the classification scheme. For instance, only one purposeful racial or ethnic classification has survived strict scrutiny by the Supreme Court since 1944.

❑ **Segregation:** The clearest example of a classification involving a suspect class and thus requiring strict scrutiny is ***segregation***, the maintenance of physical separation between the races. Official, intentional segregation based on race or national origin is a violation of the Equal Protection Clause.

■ **Race-conscious affirmative action:** Government programs that attempt to ***assist*** racial or ethnic ***minorities*** (i.e., ***affirmative action*** programs), and that do so in an explicitly race- or ethnically-conscious way, are strictly scrutinized just the same as those that purposefully ***disadvantage*** minorities.

■ **Gender:** ***Sex-based*** classifications get ***middle-level review***. If government intentionally classifies on the basis of sex, government must show that it is pursuing an ***important*** objective, and that the sex-based classification scheme is ***substantially related*** to that objective.

❑ **Benign as well as invidious:** The same standard of review is used whether the sex-based classification is "invidious" (intended to harm women) or ***"benign"*** (intended to help women, or even intended to redress past discrimination against them).

■ **Illegitimacy:** Classifications disadvantaging ***illegitimate*** children are "semi-suspect" and therefore get middle-level review.

■ **Fundamental rights:** There will be strict scrutiny not only when a "suspect classification" is used, but also when a ***"fundamental right"*** is burdened by the classification selected by the government. Whenever a classification burdens a "fundamental right," the classification will be subjected to strict scrutiny ***even though the people who are burdened are not members of a suspect class***.

❏ **List of rights:** The right to *marry*, to *vote* in state and local elections, to have access to *courts*, and to *travel interstate*, are the rights that have been recognized as fundamental for equal protection purposes.

I. INTRODUCTION

A. Operation of the Clause: Here is a broad summary of the operation of the Equal Protection Clause, as the Supreme Court currently interprets the Clause.

1. **State and federal actions:** The guarantee of equal protection applies to actions by *both* the *state* and *federal* governments. However, the federal guarantee comes from a distinct source.

   a. **State and local governments:** The Equal Protection Clause of the Fourteenth Amendment itself applies only to *state and local governments* ("[n]o state shall deny … "). Local governments are deemed to be subdivisions of the state, and therefore fall within the ban.

   b. **Federal government:** Nothing in the Constitution explicitly requires that the federal government provide equal protection of the laws. But where the federal government makes a classification which, if it were by a state, would violate the Fourteenth Amendment's Equal Protection Clause, the Court has *treated this as a violation of the Fifth Amendment's Due Process Clause* (a clause that is, of course, *directly applicable* to the federal government). See, e.g., *Bolling v. Sharpe*, 347 U.S. 497 (1954). See also N&R, pp. 595-597.

2. **Applies only to making of classes:** The Equal Protection Clause *prevents governments from making improper classifications.* What makes a classification "proper" is, of course, the subject of this chapter. But it should be noted that if a classification scheme is proper, the issue of *which class a particular individual belongs in* is *not* an equal protection matter. Instead, this will be a matter of statutory interpretation and, possibly, the Due Process Clause. The Equal Protection Clause itself applies only to the *making* of the classifications, not to the adjudication of individual situations. N&R, p. 597.

   a. **Caveat:** But a statute which, on its face, does not draw any classifications may nonetheless be *applied* in a way that indicates that classes *are in fact being drawn* in the *administrative process*. In such a situation, the courts will examine the administratively-derived classifications just as they would review ones which were apparent on the face of the statute.

   Example: Suppose that a state passes a statute instituting a literacy test for voters in statewide elections. Even though the statute does not draw any impermissible classifications on its face, if it is applied by local officials in a way that purposefully discriminates against blacks (i.e., treats blacks as one class and whites as another, and penalizes the former), the Equal Protection Clause is violated. But a court review of the determination that a *particular voter* is in fact illiterate would be carried out pursuant to the Due Process Clause, not the Equal Protection Clause.

3. **"As applied" vs. "facial" attacks:** Notice that in the above "Caveat," we referred to how a statute is "applied." This points up the need to make an important distinction between *"as applied"* attacks on statutes and *"facial"* attacks. (The distinction exists for

all sorts of attacks on statutes, but here, we're concentrating on the Equal Protection Clause, so we'll use illustrations involving that Clause.)

If P attacks a classification that is clearly written into the statute or regulation, he is claiming that Equal Protection is violated by the statute or regulation *"on its face,"* without the need to examine how it is applied to P. If P's claim is that the statute does not make a classification on its face, but is being *administered* in a purposefully discriminatory way, then he is claiming that the statute or regulation is a violation of equal protection *"as applied."*

> **Example:** A statute that says "you must be a citizen to vote" creates a classification scheme "on its face" — citizens vs. non-citizens. P might therefore attack this statute on its face, arguing that the classification written into the language of the statute is always invalid, i.e., invalid without reference to how it is applied in any particular concrete situation, such as P's own situation.
>
> By contrast, if P claims that in actual administration, blacks are required to prove citizenship but whites are not, then his equal protection claim would be on the statute "as applied."

  a. **Same standards for both:** Either kind of attack — facial or "as applied" — may be made. Both follow essentially the same principles. For instance, if no suspect classification or fundamental right is involved, the classification scheme will violate the Equal Protection Clause if it's not rationally related to a legitimate state objective, whether the scheme is on the face of the statute or merely in the way the statute is applied.

  b. **Why distinction matters:** However, it is considerably *harder for P to prevail with a facial attack.* When P makes an "as applied" attack, P can win if P can show that the statute cannot constitutionally be applied *against P* — the fact that the statute could be constitutionally applied to some other hypothetical person or situation won't save it from being found invalid in P's suit. By contrast, at least in theory, if P makes a facial attack, P can generally win only if P shows that there are *no circumstances in which the statute is valid.* See *U.S. v. Salerno*, 481 U.S. 739 (1987) ("A facial challenge to a legislative Act is, of course, the most difficult challenge to mount successfully, since the challenger must establish that no set of circumstances exists under which the Act would be valid.") [1]

4. **What the Clause guarantees:** The Equal Protection Clause, at bottom, mainly guarantees (1) that people who are s*imilarly situated* will be *treated similarly.* Occasionally, the Clause is also interpreted to guarantee (2) that people who are *not* similarly situated will *not be treated similarly.* Tribe, p. 1438.

> **Examples:** As an example of a violation of Type (1), consider intentional racial segregation in the public schools — this is a failure to treat people who are similarly situated (blacks and whites, at least with respect to public education, though perhaps not with respect to, say, sickle-cell anemia) similarly to each other. As an example of a violation of Type (2), consider a hypothetical statute (see Tribe p. 1438) requiring vot-

---

1. In reality, the Supreme Court doesn't seem to treat facial challenges quite as strictly as this formulation would suggest — often the Court seems to uphold a facial challenge even though there are at least some applications of the statute that would be constitutional. See 46 Stan. L. Rev. 235, 236 (1994). But there's no doubt that facial challenges are harder to win than as-applied challenges.

ers to come to the polls personally regardless of their physical capacity to do so — a court might conclude that this is a denial of the equal protection right of the handicapped to be treated differently with respect to voting. *Id.*

a. **Most cases are of Type (1):** The vast majority of successful equal protection challenges involve a violation of Type (1), that is, a ***refusal to treat similarly-situated persons similarly.***

b. **Type (2) cases difficult to win:** ***Occasionally***, however, an equal protection claim based on ***Type (2)*** may succeed. That is the plaintiff may win with a claim based on government's refusal to treat differently-situated classes differently. But Type (2) claims are ***difficult to raise successfully*** — in most scenarios, courts ***don't*** interpret the Equal Protection Clause as imposing a meaningful requirement that government treat differently-situated individuals differently.

   i. **Wealth/poverty classifications:** Most claims that ***wealth/poverty classifications*** violate the Equal Protection Clause are claims of this Type (2) variety. See *infra*, p. 383. That is, the plaintiff is claiming that when the government ***demands payment*** for goods or services (e.g., imposes poll taxes) or ***refuses to pay for benefits*** (e.g., refuses to pay for appellate transcripts for indigent defendants), it's a violation of equal protection principles for the government not to ***treat the rich and poor differently.*** In other words, the claimant is asserting that the ***charges must be reduced*** or eliminated, and/or that the benefit in question must be funded by government, if the claimant is poor. However, such wealth-based discrimination claims have usually ***failed*** — the claims have been sustained only where the government scheme impairs one of certain narrowly-defined ***"fundamental rights"*** (e.g., the right to vote or to appeal a criminal conviction). See Tribe, p. 1439, n. 19.

5. **Must look at statute's objectives:** What does it mean to say that two persons are "similarly situated" or "differently situated"? Obviously, two persons may be similarly situated in some respects and differently in others. For instance, a randomly-selected black person and white person might be similarly situated in many respects (e.g., their right to vote or obtain a job) but differently situated in others (e.g., their statistical susceptibility to sickle-cell anemia). In nearly all instances, the "differentness" or "sameness" of people in the context of equal protection analysis is determined by reference to the ***objectives of the statute*** being analyzed.

   Example: The California "statutory rape" law makes men criminally liable for intercourse with a woman under eighteen but does not make women liable for intercourse under any circumstances. Whether this statute violates equal protection (by treating men and women differently for criminal liability purposes) must be determined by looking at the legislature's ***objective*** in enacting, or maintaining, the statute.

   Here, the principal purpose was to discourage illegitimate teenage pregnancies. The legislature could reasonably have concluded that men are differently situated from women, because the woman already has the deterrent of an unwanted pregnancy. The statute therefore roughly "equalizes" the deterrence on the sexes. Thus it is only by looking at the goal of preventing teenage pregnancy that the "sameness" or "differentness" of men and women who engage in the forbidden intercourse may be evaluated.

See *Michael M. v. Superior Court*, 450 U.S. 464 (1981) (discussed in more detail *infra*, p. 276).

a. **Intent and causation:** Common-sense concepts like *"intent"* and *"causation"* may furnish the legislature with a valid basis for treating groups differently. For instance, where two actions produce the same result, the legislature does not violate equal protection where it criminalizes one action and not the other, if one action was taken with intent to produce the result, and the other action was not.

6. **Over- and under-inclusive classifications:** Consider now the usual equal protection claim that persons who are similarly situated have been treated differently (i.e., a type (1) claim, as organized *supra*, p. 244). The way most classifications work is that they *identify a trait* present in some people, and presume a certain connection between that trait and the legislative goal. This goal may be either the prevention of a harm or the furthering of a good; for our discussion here, we will presume that it is a prevention of a harm. (The analysis would be the same for furthering of a good.)

a. **Three main mismatches:** There are three major ways there might be a mismatch in the "fit" between the Trait upon which the legislative has based its classification, and the Harm the legislature is trying to prevent: (1) *"under-inclusiveness"*; (2) *"over-inclusiveness"*; and (3) a *combination* of under- and over-inclusiveness.

Our sample fact pattern: To illustrate these three main mismatches between Trait and Harm, let's consider the statute construed in *Massachusetts Board of Retirement v. Murgia*, discussed *infra*, p. 253. That statute required all uniformed state police to retire at the age of 50. The purpose of the statute was to help keep the police force free of officers whose physical health would not be sound enough for them to perform their duties.

i. **"Under-inclusive:"** It might be the case that all persons who have the Trait contribute to the Harm, but that persons without the Trait *also* contribute to the Harm. Such a classification scheme is called *"under-inclusive."* For instance, if all officers over 50 are in poor health, but some officers under 50 are also in poor health, the scheme is under-inclusive.

ii. **"Over-inclusive":** Conversely, all persons who contribute to the Harm might have the Trait, but some people who have the Trait might not contribute to the Harm. In this situation, the classification is said to be *"over-inclusive."* In the retirement example, the classification is over-inclusive if all officers in poor health are over 50, but some officers over 50 are in good health.

iii. **Over- and under-inclusive:** The final type of mismatch is one that has attributes of both (i) and (ii), i.e., one that is *both over- and under-inclusive*. Although this sounds impossible, it is in fact probably the most common type of classification. The way this occurs is that the classification is over-inclusive as to some groups of people but under-inclusive as to others. In the retirement example, for instance, it is almost certainly the case that some officers over 50 are healthy (so that the statute is over-inclusive as to these healthy older-than-50 people), and at the same time that some officers who are under 50 are unhealthy (so that the statute is under-inclusive as to these sick younger-than-50 officers).

7. **Significance of under- and over-inclusiveness:** Although these categories are useful ways of labeling what a given classification is doing, attaching the correct label says very little about whether the Court will find the classification to be violative of equal protection or not. [2]

   a. **Little review of under-inclusiveness:** The Court *rarely* in practice invalidates an *under-inclusive* law.

      i. **Rationale:** The Court has often justified this reticence by asserting that legislatures are permitted to solve problems *"one step at a time,"* i.e., to regulate certain aspects of a harm without regulating all. Or, as the idea was expressed in *Railway Express Agency v. New York*, 336 U.S. 106 (1949) (discussed *infra*, p. 249), "[i]t is no requirement of equal protection that all evils of the same genus be eradicated or none at all. … "

   b. **Review of over-inclusiveness:** You might think that *over-inclusive* laws would be subjected to greater judicial scrutiny than under-inclusive ones. After all, while the worst that can be said for under-inclusive laws is that they fail to burden some who ought logically to be burdened, an over-inclusive law actually *places a burden on one on whom it should not fall*.

      i. **Little scrutiny:** But in practice, over-inclusive laws *don't* get more scrutiny than under-inclusive ones, assuming that no suspect or semi-suspect classification or fundamental interest is at stake.

8. **Summary of present standards of review:** A key feature of the way the courts interpret the Equal Protection Clause is that the *"standard of review"* varies depending on the type of classification and the type of right involved. There are essentially *three different review standards* that the courts use, and the plaintiff's probably of success varies sharply depending on which standard the court finds to be applicable.

   a. **Ordinary "mere-rationality" review:** The *least probing* standard of review applies to statutes which are *not based upon a "suspect classification,"* and do not involve the *"quasi-suspect"* categories implicitly recognized by the Court (principally gender and illegitimacy). The statutes reviewed under this lowest-level scrutiny are generally ones which involve mainly *economic issues*. Just as the Court has, ever since the decline of the *Lochner* philosophy, declined to give more than minimal *substantive due process review* to economic legislation (see *supra*, p. 171), so the Court has declined to impose very searching review of such legislation under the Equal Protection Clause.

      i. **The test:** Therefore, in this least-scrutiny area, the Court "will ask only whether it is *conceivable* that the classification bears a *rational relationship* to an end of government which is *not prohibited* by the Constitution." N&R, p. 601. This test is sometimes called (and we'll call it here) the *"mere-rationality"* standard.

---

2. Our discussion here of under- and over-inclusiveness assumes that the classification does *not* involve a *"suspect"* or *"semi-suspect"* classification, and does not involve a *"fundamental right."* These terms are discussed beginning at Par. (b) "Strict scrutiny" on p. 248. In other words, we're talking here about the ordinary "mere-rationality" review that's given to the least-problematic tier of economic and social-welfare legislation.

(1) Under- or over-inclusiveness: This easy-to-satisfy mere-rationality standard applies whether the classification is "under-inclusive," "over-inclusive," or simultaneously under- and over-inclusive. (See *supra*, p. 246.)

b. **Strict scrutiny:**   At the other end of the spectrum, the Court will give *"strict scrutiny"* to any statute which either: (1) is based upon a *"suspect classification"* or (2) impairs a *"fundamental right."* (The meaning of these two terms is discussed extensively beginning *infra*, p. 256.) Classifications based on *race* are a classic example of a "suspect" class; the right to *vote* is an important example of a fundamental right.

   i.   **The test:**   Where strict scrutiny is invoked, the classification will be upheld only if it is *necessary* to promote a *compelling* governmental interest. Thus not only must the objective be an extremely important one, but the "fit" between the means and the end must be extremely tight.

c. **Middle-level review:**   In a few situations, the Court has engaged in scrutiny that is more probing than the "mere-rationality" test, but less rigid than classical "strict scrutiny." This is called *"middle-level"* or *"intermediate level"* review. This middle-level standard is used principally in cases involving classifications based on *gender* and *illegitimacy*, and in some cases involving access to the judicial process. N&R, pp. 602-603. Classifications based on *alienage* are also sometimes viewed as being based on this middle-level review, and it's possible that classifications based on *sexual orientation* are now effectively being reviewed under this standard (see *infra*, p. 358).

   i.   **Test:**   Where the middle level of review is applied, the test is usually stated as follows: the *means* chosen by the legislature (i.e., the classification) must serve *important governmental objectives* and must be *substantially related* to achievement of those objectives. In this middle-level situation, therefore, (1) the legislative *objective* must be an *important* one (but not necessarily "compelling") and (2) the *fit* between means and end must be *reasonably tight* (not almost perfect, as in a strict scrutiny situation). See, e.g., *Craig v. Boren*, 429 U.S. 190 (1976), a sex-discrimination case discussed *infra*, p. 321.

II. ECONOMIC AND SOCIAL LAWS — THE "MERE-RATIONALITY" STANDARD

A. **Deferential review:**   As noted, where neither a suspect class nor a fundamental right is implicated, the Court will review a classification with extreme deference, and with a heavy presumption of constitutionality. Most general *"economic"* and *"social welfare"* legislation falls within this limited review category.

1. **Mere-rationality review:**   The standard for lowest-level review is generally phrased as the *"mere-rationality"* test. That is, the statute will not be stricken if it's conceivable that there is some *rational relation* between the means selected by the legislature and a *legitimate* legislative objective.

B. **Broad reading of "legitimate public objective":**   Although the legislature's "purpose" or *"objective"* in enacting a statute must be "legitimate," the courts give *extreme deference* to the legislature's right to define its objectives. Thus of the relatively few cases in which general economic and social policy has been struck down on equal protection grounds in the last fifty years, even fewer have been based upon a finding that the legislature's "objective" was not "legitimate."

1. **Search for objectives:**   The Court often reviews various "conceivable" objectives which *might have* motivated the legislature, if it is not clear from the legislative history what the precise objectives were. (See *infra*, p. 250.) So long as there is at least one conceivable objective which is legitimate and which is rationally related to the means selected, the possibility that another, illegitimate, objective might have motivated the legislature will be ignored by the Court.

2. **Great deference:**   Furthermore, any objective that does not strike the Court as being grossly unfair or totally irrational will be upheld. The fact that the Court thinks that the objective behind the legislation is *unwise* will not be sufficient to make it "illegitimate."

3. **Not all objectives legitimate:**   Yet not every objective that motivates a legislature will be found by the Supreme Court to be "legitimate."

   a. **Discrimination against out-of-state competitors:** For instance, *promoting the success of in-state business over out-of-state competitors* has been held *not* to be legitimate. In *Metropolitan Life Ins. Co. v. Ward*, 470 U.S. 869 (1985), the Court invalidated, on equal protection grounds, an Alabama statute that taxed out-of-state insurance companies at a higher rate than in-state ones. Alabama argued that the statute was a reasonable means of achieving its objective of promoting its domestic insurance industry. But the Court (by a 5-4 vote) concluded that "promotion of domestic business by *discriminating against nonresident competitors* is not a legitimate state purpose."

   b. **Animus towards unpopular groups:**   Similarly, legislation that is motivated solely by *"animus"* or *"hostility"* towards a *politically-unpopular group* (e.g., gay people or "hippies") will be held not to be legitimate. See *infra*, p. 251.

C. **"One step at a time" approach:**   A key feature of "mere-rationality" review is that legislation will not be invalidated merely because the legislature dealt with only one part of a problem. That is, the legislature may deal with a problem *"one step at a time."* This is really another way of saying that a statute which is "under-inclusive" is not necessarily invalid.

   Example: A New York City traffic regulation bans the placing of advertising on vehicles, except that the owner of a vehicle is permitted to advertise his own products. The purpose of the regulation is to reduce traffic hazards. The act is challenged on the theory that a vehicle carrying advertising for the vehicle's owner is no less distracting than a vehicle carrying advertising for others. Also, the challengers point out that other traffic hazards (e.g., "vivid displays on Times Square") have not been banned.

   Held, the regulation is not a violation of equal protection. "It is no requirement of equal protection that all evils of the same genus be eradicated or none at all[.]" *Railway Express Agency v. New York*, 336 U.S. 106 (1949).

D. **Determining a statute's "purpose":**   Before a court can determine whether the purpose of a statute is "legitimate," and that there is a sufficiently close link between means and end, it must somehow determine *what the "purpose" is.* The Supreme Court seems always to have held that so long as *one* of the purposes of the statute is legitimate, and sufficiently closely linked to the means, the statute will be valid under lowest-level review. But the Court has vacillated over the years about *where to look* to find the possible purposes.

1. **"Actual" legislative purpose:**   Obviously, if the statute itself, either within its text, or in its preamble, contains a statement of purpose, that statement will control. Similarly, if the legislative history of the bill discloses a purpose, that will control. In these two situations, the Court is relying on the legislature's *"actual"* purpose.

   a. **Combination of goals:**   The legislature will often have *more than one* objective in mind when it passes a statute. It seems clear that so long as the challenged classification is rationally related to *any one* of these actual objectives, the statute will be sustained, even if it is not rationally related to the others (or the others are not "legitimate" objectives).

2. **"Conceivable basis" standard:**   The quest for the legislature's "actual" purpose may be complicated by either of two possibilities: (1) that neither the statute nor its legislative history discloses *any* clear purpose; or (2) that apart from the stated purpose(s) there may have been *other objectives* which, either solely or in combination with the stated purpose(s), in fact induced the legislature to pass the bill.

   One way in which the Court has dealt with these possibilities is by being willing to consider *any purpose which the statute's defenders* (i.e., the litigant seeking to have the statute upheld) can assert as having been *the,* or even *a,* consideration which *"may"* have motivated the legislature. If the Court agrees that this purpose "may" have motivated the legislature, and that purpose is "legitimate" and rationally related to the means used by the legislature, the statute will be upheld *even if there is no "hard" evidence that that purpose was in fact a motivation* to the legislature.

   a. **Illustration:**   For instance, in *U.S. Railroad Retirement Bd. v. Fritz*, 449 U.S. 166 (1980), six members of the Court held that so long as there was a *"plausible"* reason for Congress to have made the classification scheme it did, lowest-level equal protection review was satisfied; it was *"constitutionally irrelevant whether this reasoning in fact underlay the legislative decision,"* since the Court had "never insisted that a legislative body articulate its reasons for enacting a statute."

   b. **Facts of *Fritz*:**   The facts of *Fritz* show that whether or not one insists on an "actual" legislative purpose may sometimes make a difference in the outcome. In *Fritz*, Congress modified a prior scheme, by which persons who worked long enough for both railroad and non-railroad employers could obtain retirement benefits under both the railroad and social security systems. In order to preserve the solvency of the railroad retirement system, Congress eliminated this double-benefit "windfall."

      i. **Order of employment significant:**   To accomplish this, Congress set up four classes; depending on the class into which he fell, a person got either full windfall, reduced windfall, or no windfall benefits at all. At issue in *Fritz* was that portion of the scheme which, within the class of persons who had worked for railroads more than ten years but less than twenty-five, and who had not yet retired when the act took effect, gave different treatment to those who had worked first for a non-railroad employer than to those who had worked first for a railroad. A person in the former situation received at least a reduced windfall; one in the latter received none. Thus the order of jobs was the sole basis for the statutory distinction.

      ii. **Majority view:**   The majority, as noted, was willing to accept any proffered statutory "purpose," whether actually relied upon by the legislature or not. They reasoned that Congress "may" have been attempting to preserve limited windfall benefits only for "career" railroad employees, and that persons still working in railroading (as a second career) when the act went into force were more likely to be "career" railroad workers than those who had left railroading before the act came into force. Since this was a "plausible reason" for Congress' action, it was sufficient to save the statute.

    iii. Dissent: But the ***dissent***, since it required an ***"actual"*** legislative purpose, reached an opposite result. By looking to the legislative history, the dissent concluded that Congress' actual intent was ***not*** to eliminate any "vested" benefit, and that Congress did not intend to deprive members of plaintiff's class of their windfall (which the dissent called an "earned benefit"). Thus, in the dissent's opinion, the classification was ***not rationally related*** to any actual government purpose; therefore, the classification should not have survived even mere rationality review.

  c. Inconsistent purpose: Since, under the *Fritz* majority's view, any "conceivable" purpose advanced by a statute's defender will, if it rationally relates to the classification, be sufficient to validate the statute, a side effect is probably that the Court may consider even those "conceivable" purposes which, the statute's text and history show, ***could not have been*** the ***"actual"*** purpose of the statute.

3. Court imagines "hypothetical" purpose: On occasion, the Court has gone even further than in *Fritz*, and has simply used ***its own imagination*** to ***"hypothesize"*** a theoretical objective which the legislature "might have" been pursuing when it enacted the statute. Here, too, if this ***hypothetical purpose*** is adequate, the statute has been upheld. When the Court has been inclined to proceed in this manner, it has stated that it will overturn statutory classifications "only if no grounds can be ***conceived*** to justify them." *McDonald v. Board of Election*, 394 U.S. 802 (1969).

E. Legal disabilities motivated by "animus" towards unpopular groups: Occasionally, the Court has examined legislation that it finds to have been motivated by ***"animus"*** or ***"hostility"*** towards a ***politically-unpopular group***. The Court has been willing to ***strike down*** such legislation even though only "mere-rationality review" is supposedly being used. In so doing, the Court has said that the ***desire to harm an unpopular group*** cannot be a ***"legitimate governmental objective."*** These "animus by government" cases may be said to apply mere-rationality review ***"with bite."***

1. Discrimination against hippies: The first case to illustrate this principle that discrimination motivated solely by hostility towards an unpopular group may flunk even mere-rationality was a 1973 case involving what the court found to be congressional animus against "hippies," ***U.S. Dep't of Agric. v. Moreno***, 413 U.S. 528 (1973).

  a. Facts: Congress changed the Food Stamp program to exclude any household that had two or more unrelated members. As the Supreme Court later characterized the change, it "was intended to ***prevent so-called 'hippies' and 'hippie communes' from participating"*** in the program.

  b. Struck down: The Court found that this change did not even satisfy mere-rationality review. "For if the constitutional conception of 'equal protection of the laws' means anything, it must at the very least mean that ***a bare congressional desire to harm a politically unpopular group cannot constitute a legitimate governmental interest."***

Therefore, a congressional desire to discriminate against hippies could not meet the requirement of a legitimate governmental interest.

2. **Ban on protection of gays:** The Court's main use of this "intent to harm unpopular groups" analysis has been in several cases involving the rights of **gays and lesbians.**

   a. ***Romer v. Evans* and denial of discrimination protection:** First, in a 1996 case, the Court struck down an amendment to the Colorado Constitution that would have **prevented the state or any of its cities from giving various protections** (e.g., protection against **"discrimination"**) to gays or lesbians. *Romer v. Evans*, 517 U.S. 620 (1996). The Court found that the amendment's sole purpose was to injure homosexuals. (*Romer* is discussed further in our detailed treatment of classifications directed to sexual orientation, *infra*, p. 354.)

   b. ***Windsor* and the federal definition of marriage:** Then, in another gay-rights case, the Court relied on *Moreno*'s "desire to harm a politically unpopular group" language to hold that **Congress could not define marriage** in such a way as to refuse to recognize, for federal purposes, a same-sex marriage entered into under state law. *U.S. v. Windsor*, 133 S. Ct. 2675 (2013), discussed *infra*, p. 355.

   c. ***Obergefell* and bans on same-sex marriage:** Finally, in the 2015 decision in *Obergefell v. Hodges,* 135 S.Ct. 2584 (2015) (*infra*, p. 356), the majority stuck down bans on **same-sex marriage**. The majority opinion doesn't state what standard it is using, but mentions the **"long history of disapproval** of [same-sex] relationships," and says that bans on same-sex marriage harm gay couples by "serv[ing] to **disrespect and subordinate them."** The majority opinion clearly reflects a standard that is at least as rigorous as "mere-rationality with bite."

3. **The mentally retarded:** Another category that seems to have benefited from a somewhat more rigorous version of mere-rationality review in recent decades is the **developmentally delayed**. In **City of Cleburne v. Cleburne Living Center**, 473 U.S. 432 (1985), the Court struck down a Texas city's denial of a special use permit for the operation of a group home for the **"mentally retarded."**[3]

   a. **Rationale:** The Court refused to treat mental retardation as an explicitly "quasi-suspect" classification like gender or illegitimacy (see *infra*, p. 347). Yet while purporting to apply a "mere-rationality" standard, the Court quite clearly gave the challenged classification a more rigorous review than it has given to purely economic regulations. As in the above cases involving gays and "hippies," the Court seems to have been motivated to use a more-rigorous-than-usual variant of "mere-rationality" review because of the widespread prejudice against the retarded — the Court noted that "there have been and there will continue to be instances of discrimination against the retarded that are in fact invidious[.]"

F. **Highly deferential standard:** But cases like *Moreno, Romer v. Evans, Windsor,* and *City of Cleburne* — in which "mere-rationality" review nonetheless leads to invalidation under the Equal Protection Clause — are the **exception,** not the rule, even in recent decades. Especially where the case does **not** seem to involve a government purpose to discriminate against a politi-

---

3. I recognize that the term "mentally retarded" has been replaced by the less-insulting term "developmentally delayed." But since the Court in *Cleburne* repeatedly used the phrase "mentally retarded," I use it here in my description of the case.

cally-unpopular group (like hippies, gays or the developmentally delayed), the Court continues to give **great deference** to the legislature in cases involving economic and social legislation without the presence of a suspect or semi-suspect class or a fundamental right.

1. **Means-end link need not be empirical:**   One aspect of this deference is in the doctrine that there need not be *in fact* a link between the means selected by the legislature and a legitimate objective. All that is required is that the legislature *"could rationally have believed"* that there was such a link.

   Example: A state statute bans the sale of milk in plastic non-returnable containers, but allows such sale in other types of non-returnable containers, including paperboard cartons. Several justifications are proffered in support of the bill, including: (1) that the elimination of plastic cartons will encourage use of environmentally-superior containers; (2) that banning just plastic containers will cause less economic dislocation within the milk industry than banning both plastic and paperboard simultaneously; and (3) that the law will help to conserve energy. The statute's challengers attempt to show that the statute will not in fact achieve any of these three objectives.

   Held, the statute is not a violation of the Equal Protection Clause. Whether or not the statute will *in fact* achieve any of its objectives is **irrelevant**. The only question is whether the legislature "could rationally have decided" that it would meet these objectives. The burden is on the statute's challengers to show that "the legislative facts on which [a] classification is apparently based could not reasonably be conceived to be true by the governmental decision-maker." Here, whether the classification scheme would meet one or more of these objectives was *at least debatable*. By that fact alone, it cannot be said that the legislature acted irrationally, and the statute must be upheld. *Minnesota v. Clover Leaf Creamery Co.*, 449 U.S. 456 (1981).

2. **Loose means-end fit suffices:**   Since all that is required is that the means-end relationship be close enough that its rationality is *"debatable,"* a *very loose fit between means and ends will be acceptable*.

   a. **Age-discrimination case (*Murgia*):** For instance, in *Massachusetts Bd. of Retirement v. Murgia*, 427 U.S. 307 (1976), a Massachusetts statute required state police officers to retire at age 50. All parties conceded that the objective of the statute was to maintain a physically-fit police force. The statute was upheld, even though some (perhaps many) officers over 50 were not in poor physical health, making the statute over-inclusive. In other words, the fact that the "fit" between the *means chosen* (mandatory retirement over 50) and the *end* being pursued (physically-fit officers) was *very loose did not matter*: it was enough that the means-end fit was *not so attenuated as to be irrational*.

      i. **Availability of tighter fits irrelevant:** Furthermore, the fact that a *tighter-fitting, less-discriminatory means* of measuring physical health was *available* (e.g., annual physical examinations) did not make the less-than-best-fitting means selected by the statute impermissible.

      ii. **Not suspect class:**   The decision in *Murgia* turned largely on the fact that the Court *declined* to treat the classification based on *age* as a *"suspect"* class, on the theory that old age "marks a stage that each of us will reach if we live out our normal span ... " (Justice Marshall, in dissent, argued that the age classification should be subjected to ***middle-level*** scrutiny, because older workers "constitute a class subject to repeated and arbitrary discrimination in employment." In Marshall's view, the statute certainly could not survive such middle-level scrutiny, because of its over-inclusiveness.)

    iii. Still not suspect: By the way, a post-*Murgia* case shows that the Supreme Court still views age as not being a "suspect" class. See *Gregory v. Ashcroft*, 501 U.S. 452 (1991), upholding a scheme by which state judges are required to retire at age 70. The Court held that it was not irrational for the state to distinguish between judges older and younger than 70, nor was it irrational for the state to distinguish between judges and other state employees of the same age, who were not subject to mandatory retirement.

G. Summary of Court's approach: In summary, the Supreme Court takes a generally ***deferential*** equal protection approach to ***economic and social legislation.*** However, this deference is not complete. The principal features of the present Court's review in these areas may be summarized as follows:

    1. Purpose need not be actual: The law will be upheld if the means chosen by the legislature bear a ***rational relation*** to ***any conceivable*** legitimate legislative purpose (at least if proffered by any representative of the state, and perhaps even if thought of only by members of the Court); this will be so even though there is no evidence that this was the ***actual*** purpose motivating the legislature.

    2. Means-end link: It is not necessary that there be an ***actual***, empirical, link between the means selected by the legislature and the (actual or theoretical) legislative objective. All that is necessary is that the legislature could ***"rationally have believed"*** that there was a link between the means and the end. And the legislature will be deemed to have been capable of such a belief so long as it is "debatable" whether such a means-end link exists (even though the Court suspects that it probably does not).

    3. Unpopular trait: Finally, if the classification involves a politically unpopular trait or group, thereby suggesting bias on the part of the majority, the Court is likely to subject the statute to a somewhat more probing review, even where the Court refuses to apply "strict" or "middle level" scrutiny. Examples are statutes that single out "hippies" (*U.S. Dept of Agric. v. Moreno*), ***gays and lesbians*** (*Romer v. Evans* and *Windsor*), and the ***mentally retarded*** (*City of Cleburne*).

Quiz Yourself on
EQUAL PROTECTION — ECONOMIC & SOCIAL LAWS

37. The state of Chartreuse has delegated to the state bar association the job of determining requirements for the practice of law. Until recently, the bar association imposed no continuing legal education requirements. However, there has been a large rise in the number of malpractice actions against lawyers in the state, some of which appear to derive from the fact that lawyers have not kept pace with changing legal principles. Also, there has been a rise in the disdain with which the public in Chartreuse holds lawyers. The bar association, therefore, imposed a mandatory continuing legal education requirement of 12 course-hours per year. The state imposes on doctors a continuing education requirement of only 4 hours per year. There is strong evidence that, in general, changes in medicine happen faster than changes in law. Amos, a lawyer in Chartreuse, has challenged the continuing legal education requirement on the grounds that by imposing a much higher requirement on lawyers than on doctors, the state has violated his equal protection rights. Assume that the state bar association's conduct constitutes state action.

(a) What standard should the court use to test whether the legal education requirement satisfies the demands of equal protection? _____

(b) Will Amos' attack succeed? _____

38. The town of Solon established a regulation that all members of the fire department must retire at the age of 50. The Town Council enacted the regulation after reading a news report that in a neighboring town, a 53 year-old firefighter with a bad back was unable to carry a child out of the fourth floor of a burning building, leading to the child's death. The Town Council members reasoned that on average, those over 50 are less able to perform the highly demanding physical functions of firefighting than those under 50. Prentice is the Chief of the Solon Fire Department. His duties are exclusively desk-bound. He has just turned 50, and has challenged the retirement regulation, as applied to him, on the grounds that it violates his right to equal protection. Will Prentice's attack on the regulation succeed? _____

Answers

37. **(a) The court should ask whether the classification is rationally related to a legitimate state objective.**

(b) No. Unless there is a suspect or semi-suspect class involved, or a fundamental right, the Supreme Court will uphold a state legislative classification against equal protection attack so long as the classification scheme bears a ***rational relation*** to some ***legitimate legislative objective***. The desire to have lawyers be better trained, and to increase public confidence and reduce suits, certainly seem to constitute legitimate governmental objectives. The link between the classification system chosen and the objective being pursued does not have to be a close one. In fact, there does not need to be an actual empirical link between means and end, merely a ***rational belief*** on the part of the legislature that there is a link between means and end. Here, a bar association (acting as a government body) certainly could rationally have believed that lawyers who take mandatory legal education will be more up to date, and thus less likely to make mistakes through outmoded training. The fact that doctors might need refresher courses even more than lawyers will be ignored by the court, because reform may take place ***"one step at a time"*** (i.e., the government does not commit an equal protection violation every time it addresses one aspect of a problem without solving all related aspects).

38. **No.** As in the prior question, the threshold issue is what standard of review the court will give to the challenged classification. Unless a suspect or quasi-suspect class, or a fundament right, is at issue, the court will use the "mere-rationality" standard. The Supreme Court has held repeatedly that age is not a suspect or semi-suspect class. See, e.g., *Mass. Bd. of Retirement v. Murgia* (police officers may be required to retire at age 50). Therefore, the Court applies mere-rationality review to age-based classifications such as the one here. The goal of assuring that each firefighter is fit for the particular duties of the profession is clearly a legitimate one. There is some question about whether the means chosen (outright ban on all over-50 firefighters) is a good way to accomplish that objective, since there are less drastic alternatives (e.g., testing of each applicant, or an exemption for those who perform only desk duties). But all that is required between means and end is a ***rational relation***. Here, the blanket-ban approach was certainly a rational way of assuring physical fitness, even though it was not the best possible approach or even a very well-tailored one. The classification will be upheld unless it is completely irrational, which this one is certainly not.

III. SUSPECT CLASSIFICATIONS, ESPECIALLY RACE

A. Suspect classes generally: We turn now to "suspect" classifications, i.e., statutory classifications which, because they give distinct treatment to a group that has historically been the victim of discrimination, are subjected to *"strict scrutiny."*

    1. Race and national origin: The paradigmatic example of a suspect classification is, of course, *race*. The other principal example is *national origin*.

    2. Alienage: Some Court cases appear to make *alienage* a suspect classification as well, but more recent cases make such large exceptions to the strict scrutiny of alienage classifications that alienage is probably more properly viewed as involving "middle-level" scrutiny; the subject is therefore discussed along with other middle-level scrutiny classes *infra*, p. 340.

    3. Five subject areas: In our treatment of suspect classes, five principal subject areas are addressed: (1) What groups have been so frequently the object of discrimination and prejudice that classifications disfavoring them should be labeled as "suspect"? (2) To what extent must discrimination be shown to be "purposeful" before it is outlawed by the Equal Protection Clause? (3) How rigorous must "strict" scrutiny be? (4) How does one demonstrate that public facilities (especially schools) have been *racially segregated*, and what are the remedies for such segregation? and (5) To what extent may the government make *"benign"* use of suspect classifications (i.e., the problem of "affirmative action")?

B. Groups covered: Classification based on *race* is, of course, the classic example of a "suspect" classification, because of our nation's long history of both public and private racial discrimination. In addition to blacks (the group Congress of course intended most explicitly to assist by means of the Equal Protection Clause), *any other racial group* may, if made the object of a classification intended to disfavor that group, invoke strict scrutiny. See, e.g., *Yick Wo v. Hopkins, infra*, p. 257, treating as suspect administrative discrimination against Asians.

    1. National origin: Apart from blacks, Asians, and other minorities that are clearly racially distinct, a classification based on *national origin* is also suspect. Thus in *Hernandez v. Texas*, 347 U.S. 475 (1954), discrimination against *Mexican-Americans* with regard to jury service was treated in the same way that discrimination against blacks would have been.

    2. Extension in *Croson*: Discrimination against *any* racial group will merit strict scrutiny, even if that group has *never been the subject of widespread discrimination.* A majority of the Supreme Court so concluded in *City of Richmond v. J.A. Croson Co.*, discussed extensively *infra*, p. 301. So if a city discriminates in favor of, say, black contractors at the *expense of white contractors,* this discrimination must be subjected to strict scrutiny (and probably struck down), as happened in *Croson*.

        a. Ethnic groups: Probably the rationale of *Croson* means that any intentional discrimination against a particular *ethnic* group also must be strictly scrutinized, even if the group has not been the victim of widespread prejudice or discrimination. Thus if Whites of Anglo-Saxon Protestant descent were discriminated against in favor of other groups (e.g., Whites of Italian or Mediterranean descent), strict scrutiny would presumably be required even though White Anglo-Saxon Protestants have historically rarely been discriminated against.

3. Other classes: Thus far, the Court has not treated as fully "suspect" classifications based on any grounds other than race and national origin. (But see the discussion of classes treated as "semi-suspect," e.g., sex and illegitimacy, *infra*, pp. 319 and 346.)

a. Wealth: Of special significance has been the Court's refusal to treat classifications based on *wealth* as "suspect." This refusal is discussed *infra*, p. 383.

C. "Purposeful" discrimination: A classification will not be deemed to be "suspect," and therefore subject to strict scrutiny, unless the Court finds that there was a legislative *intent* to discriminate against the disfavored group. That is, the mere fact that a law has a less favorable *impact* on a minority group than it has on the majority is not sufficient to constitute a violation of equal protection. As is discussed in more detail below, a demonstration of disproportionate impact is *a factor* in the equal protection analysis, but it can never by itself suffice; proof of *intentional* discrimination is required.

1. Three ways to show purpose: Purposeful discrimination may appear in any of three ways: (1) the law discriminates *on its face*, i.e., by its explicit terms; (2) the law, although neutral on its face, is *administered* in a discriminatory way; and (3) the law, although it is neutral on its face and is applied in accordance with its terms, was enacted with a purpose of discriminating, as shown by the law's legislative history, statements made by legislators, the law's disparate impact, or other circumstantial evidence of intent.

2. Some examples: Following are some examples of statutes found to have been "purposefully discriminatory," and therefore violative of the Equal Protection Clause:

Example — facially discriminatory: A state statute provides that "all white male persons who are twenty-one years of age who are citizens of this State shall be eligible to serve as jurors." P, a black, is convicted of murder by a jury from which all blacks have been removed pursuant to the statute.

Held, the act on its face discriminates against blacks, and therefore violates the Equal Protection Clause. *Strauder v. West Virginia*, 100 U.S. 303 (1880).

Note: Where a law is found to discriminate "on its face," the Court will *not* require that it be shown to have had an actual discriminatory *impact* in the case at hand. Thus in *Strauder*, P was not required to show that he would not have been convicted by a jury containing blacks, or even to show that some blacks would have been seated on the jury had the statute not been in force. The mere *risk* of discriminatory impact was sufficient, given the facial discrimination.

Example — discrimination in administration: A San Francisco ordinance bars the operation of hand laundries in wooden buildings, except with the consent of the Board of Supervisors. The Board gives permits to all but one of the non-Chinese applicants, but to none of nearly 200 Chinese applicants.

Held, although the ordinance is neutral on its face, there was discrimination in its administration, and this discrimination violates the Equal Protection Clause. *Yick Wo v. Hopkins*, 118 U.S. 356 (1886).

Example — discriminatory purpose shown by circumstantial evidence: Burke County, Georgia elects its five-member Board of Commissioners via an at-large system. Whites are only in a slight majority in the voting-age population, but no black has ever been elected to the Board.

Held, although the at-large system was facially neutral (and although it was not originally adopted, in 1911, for discriminatory purposes), it has been maintained by the state legislature for discriminatory purposes, and has a discriminatory impact on the county's black citizens. In addition to the fact that no black has ever been elected to the Board (which would not by itself be sufficient to show discriminatory purposes), (1) the history of discrimination against blacks with respect to party affairs, primary and general elections; (2) the unresponsiveness of the county's elected officials to the needs of the black community; and (3) the fact that the state legislature's maintenance of the at-large system was basically due to the county's own state representatives (who desired to maintain a system that excluded black participation), all support an **inference** of intentional discrimination. *Rogers v. Lodge*, 458 U.S. 613 (1982).

3. **Proving discriminatory purpose:** If a statute is shown to discriminate on its face, no showing of discriminatory purpose will be necessary. And if those making a discriminatory-administration claim can show that administrators to whom discretion is entrusted have applied the law in a way that is disadvantageous to the suspect class, no additional showing of legislative or administrative motive will be necessary (though the defenders of the law can attempt to rebut the case with an innocent explanation of the disparate administration). In the third situation, however, that of the law which is facially neutral and is applied according to its terms, the difficulties of proving "discriminatory purpose" are much greater.

   a. **No general rule:** There is no general rule that describes exactly how one demonstrates an intent to discriminate on the part of the legislature. Like proof of any other sort of intent, the use of **circumstantial evidence** is required.

   b. **"De jure" vs. "de facto" discrimination:** In any situation where a discriminatory purpose is found to exist, the discrimination is termed **"de jure"** (roughly "by law"). If, on the other hand, a law is found not to result from a discriminatory purpose, then the discrimination will be termed **"de facto"** (even if a discriminatory **effect** has resulted). The most common use of the terms, of course, is to describe the two types of **public school segregation** (with *de jure* segregation being the only judicially redressable one; *infra*, p. 270).

4. **General requirement of purpose (*Washington v. Davis*):** Prior to 1976, it was not completely clear that an intent to discriminate *was* in fact required, if there was a discriminatory **impact** upon a suspect class. But in that year, ***Washington v. Davis***, 426 U.S. 229, set forth an explicit requirement that an intent to discriminate be found before an equal protection racial discrimination claim would be upheld.

   a. **Facts of *Washington v. Davis*:** *Washington v. Davis* involved a suit brought by unsuccessful black applicants for positions as Washington, D.C. policemen. They had failed a written test of verbal ability and reading comprehension, which blacks failed **four times as frequently** as whites. The plaintiffs claimed that this differential impact made the hiring process violative of equal protection even though those who composed or selected the test had no intent to discriminate against blacks. (The plaintiffs also produced evidence suggesting that performance on the test did not necessarily correlate with job performance.)

b. **Holding:** The Supreme Court held that racial discrimination violative of the Equal Protection Clause exists only where it is a product of a ***discriminatory purpose***. While a showing of disproportionate racial impact is *a* factor in ascertaining intent, ***it can never by itself be sufficient to prove discriminatory intent***. Here, other facts, including the D.C. Police Department's affirmative efforts to recruit more black policemen, negated any finding of a discriminatory purpose in the use of the test (which was used throughout the federal Civil Service).

   i. **Comparison to Title VII:** The *Washington* Court conceded that under Title VII of the 1964 Civil Rights Act, a hiring practice which disqualifies a substantially disproportionate number of blacks will be stricken, even without a showing of discriminatory intent. But the Court declined to establish a "no-intent" standard where the source of the discrimination claim was simply the Equal Protection Clause, as distinguished from a specifically-worded congressional statute.

   ii. **Rationale:** The Court was especially concerned that if an intent requirement were not imposed in Equal Protection cases, this might ***invalidate "a whole range of tax, welfare, public service, regulatory, and licensing statutes*** that may be ***more burdensome to the poor and to the average black than to the more affluent white."*** In a footnote, the Court listed numerous statutory schemes that might be open to attack under such a standard, including such items as sales taxes, bridge tolls, minimum wage laws and professional licensing requirements.

5. **Other areas of application:** The principle of *Washington v. Davis* has been extended beyond the public employment context, to include such areas as ***jury selection, zoning*** and ***public housing***, and ***voting rights***. It seems apparent that no matter what the subject area, a statute will not be held to establish an impermissible suspect classification merely because of a disproportionately harsh impact on blacks or other minorities.

6. **Need not be sole motive:** Although a discriminatory purpose is required for invocation of strict scrutiny, such a purpose need not be the ***sole*** purpose of the statute. It is enough that that purpose was a ***"motivating factor"*** in the legislature's decision to enact the statute. *Arlington Heights v. Metropolitan Housing Corp.*, 429 U.S. 252 (1977).

   a. **Two motivations:** Thus if there were ***two purposes*** that motivated the legislature to enact a statute, and only one of these was discriminatory against the suspect class, the presence of the second, non-discriminatory motive, will not immunize the statute from strict scrutiny. So long as the legislature would not have passed the statute had the discriminatory motive not been present, the existence of the other motive makes no difference. Cf. *Hunter v. Underwood*, 471 U.S. 222 (1985) (where voting law was enacted to disenfranchise both blacks and poor whites, the fact that disenfranchisement of blacks was a "but-for" motivation for the law was enough to make it a violation of the Fourteenth Amendment).

   b. **Shifting burden of proof:** In fact, the plaintiff only needs to show that an intent to discriminate was a "motivating" or "substantial" factor in the legislature's enactment decision. Once he does this, the ***burden of proof then shifts to the defendant*** to show that the statute ***would have been passed anyway***, even without that intent. If the defendant succeeds in showing this, the requirement of proof of discriminatory purpose will be deemed not satisfied.

i. "But for cause" standard: To put it another way, the issue is whether a discriminatory motive was a *"but for"* cause of the enactment, but the burden of proof is on the defendant once a *prima facie* showing of "motivating factor" has been made by a plaintiff. Thus in *Hunter v. Underwood, supra,* the requisite discriminatory purpose was shown by the fact that a desire to disenfranchise whites would not have been sufficient to lead to the enactment — the attempt to disenfranchise blacks was the "but for" cause of the enactment.

c. Must be "because of" not "in spite of": It follows from this requirement of "but for" causation that the statute must have been enacted *"because of"* a desire to bring about a discriminatory impact, *not merely "in spite of"* the probability of such an impact. This principle was established in a sex-discrimination case, ***Personnel Administrator of Mass. v. Feeney***, 422 U.S. 256 (1979), but it seems clear that this rule will be applied in racial discrimination cases as well.

i. Facts of *Feeney:* In *Feeney,* P, a woman, challenged a Massachusetts civil service statute which gave an *absolute hiring preference* to any veteran who obtained a passing score on a competitive exam. Since, at the time the suit was brought, over 98% of the veterans in Massachusetts were men, the preference operated overwhelmingly to the benefit of males and to the detriment of females.

ii. Holding: The Supreme Court held that the statute was not intentionally gender-based, either overtly or covertly. A significant number of *men* were also non-veterans. Therefore, "[t]oo many men are affected by [the law] to permit the inference that the statute is *but a pretext* for preferring men over women."

(1) "In spite of" not enough: The Court was willing to accept the plaintiff's contention that the legislature *in fact knew* that the law would be heavily unfavorable to women. But it rejected her further syllogism that, because a person "intends the natural and foreseeable consequences of his voluntary actions," the inevitable disproportionate impact proved an intent to discriminate. "Awareness of consequences" was *not* sufficient to prove "discriminatory purpose"; only if the legislature chose its course *"because of,"* and *not* merely *"in spite of,"* its adverse effects upon women, could there be said to have been intentional discrimination. And the Court found no evidence that the disparate effect upon women was, in the legislature's mind, anything more than a foreseeable but *undesired* and inevitable by-product of the basic decision to favor veterans. Therefore, the preference did not violate the Equal Protection Clause.

7. Passage of time: Suppose that a legislature enacts, for discriminatory motives, a provision that disadvantages a suspect class. It is apparently the case that *no matter how long a time elapses*, that provision continues to be a violation of equal protection so long as it has a discriminatory impact.

a. Extension of principle: Thus in theory even a pre-Civil War statute shown to have been enacted for the purpose of disadvantaging blacks could be struck down today if the law were shown to currently disfavor blacks.

8. Use of statistics: Since disproportionate impact will be considered as *a* factor in measuring discriminatory intent (though it can never be the sole factor), the equal protection claimant will often attempt to use ***statistical analysis*** to show the degree of disproportionate impact. In general, the Court has ***allowed*** such statistical proof.

    a. Heavy weight in subjective discretion cases: Statistical evidence will be especially persuasive where the claim is that an ***individual selection process*** is being discriminatorily performed by administrative officials. See N&R, pp. 622-624. In this situation, it is difficult to gauge the subjective intent of the administrators in any other manner; also, there is less reason for the courts to defer to these officials' subjective decisions than there is to defer to the legislature's own acts.

    Example: When court officials have selected panels of ***prospective jurors*** by using questionnaires, in-person screening or other factors by which the officials become aware of each prospective juror's race, proof of major statistical deviation from the voting population's racial makeup has generally been enough to establish a *prima facie* case of discrimination. But where the selection process does not involve any discretion by the officials (e.g., random selection from tax lists) the occurrence of statistical underrepresentation of minorities has not been enough to make even a *prima facie* case of discrimination. N&R, p. 623.

    b. Prosecutors' peremptory challenges: Statistics are similarly one of the ways to prove discrimination by ***prosecutors*** in their use of ***peremptory challenges***.

        i. Race-based challenges not allowed: Peremptory challenges enable either side to excuse a certain number of potential jurors "without cause." Prosecutors may not use such challenges based solely on the race of the juror. For instance, a prosecutor may not, in the trial of a black defendant, exclude all black jurors on the theory that such jurors are more likely to side with a black defendant than a white juror would be. ***Batson v. Kentucky***, 476 U.S. 79 (1986).

        (1) Statistical proof: Statistical proof — i.e., proof that the prosecution has consistently declined to seat black jurors in trials of black defendants — is one way to show that the prosecution has violated this general principle.

        (2) Other methods: But other ways of showing impermissible racial bias, not involving statistics, also exist. For instance, ***within the defendant's own case***, the prosecutor's questions during voir dire, or even the pattern of his use of challenges, may support an inference of discrimination. Once the inference of discrimination arises, the burden shifts to the prosecution to explain away the racial exclusion. *Batson, supra*.

        (3) Gender-based challenges: By the way, a state may no longer allow litigants to make ***gender-based*** peremptory challenges, either. See *J.E.B. v. Alabama*, discussed further *infra*, p. 331.

    c. Voting rights: Statistical evidence can also be important in establishing a discriminatory purpose in ***voting rights*** cases.

    Example: Black voters attack an "at-large" voting scheme; they argue that use of this arrangement (rather than a series of electoral districts) was intended to dilute the black vote. *Held* (by the Supreme Court), proof of discriminatory purpose, not just effect, is needed. But it's relevant that although blacks compose nearly 54% of the population and 38% of the registered voters in the county, no black has ever been elected to the county Board of Commissioners. Therefore, the trial court's finding that the requisite proof of discriminatory purpose has been made is affirmed — the fact that no black had ever been elected is "important evidence of purposeful exclusion." *Rogers v. Lodge*, 458 U.S. 613 (1982),

D. Other requirements for strict scrutiny: For discrimination to be subject to strict scrutiny, it is not sufficient that it be "purposeful." It must also be of an especially *"invidious,"* or *prejudicial*, sort. In practice, this has meant that the discrimination must be on the grounds of either *race* or *national origin*.

1. ***Carolene Products* footnote:** The basic theory behind strict scrutiny for these types of discrimination remains that expressed by Justice Stone in his *Carolene Products* footnote: "Prejudice against **discrete and insular minorities** may be a special condition, which tends seriously to **curtail the operation of those political processes** ordinarily to be relied upon to protect minorities, and which may call for a **correspondingly more searching judicial inquiry.**" *U.S. v. Carolene Products Co.*, 304 U.S. 144 (1938).

   a. **Tribe's formulation:** Or, as Tribe has put the idea, special judicial protection is given to those groups which, because of "widespread, insistent prejudice against them," occupy the position of *"perennial losers in the political struggle."* Tribe, p. 1454.

2. **Immutability:** It is sometimes suggested that a classification is more likely to be treated as suspect if it is based upon an *immutable* trait, which race and natural origin certainly are. (Immutability also goes some of the way towards explaining the middle-level scrutiny given to classifications based on alienage, illegitimacy and gender, all discussed beginning *infra*, p. 319.)

   a. **Criticism:** However, it is not obvious why the fact of immutability should make a difference. As Professor Ely has pointed out, "[c]lassifications based on physical disability and intelligence are typically accepted as legitimate, even by judges and commentators who assert that immutability is relevant." Ely, p. 150.

3. **Stereotypes:** It is also often suggested that the prevalence of *stereotypes* concerning a group makes it more likely that classifications disadvantaging that group will be found to be "suspect." See, e.g., Justice Blackmun's statement in *Bakke* (*infra*, p. 282) that "[r]acial and ethnic distinctions where they are stereotypes are inherently suspect and call for exacting judicial scrutiny."

   a. **Criticism:** However, the term "stereotype" really means little more than an imperfect generalization. Since almost all legislation involves an imperfect generalization (in the sense that nearly all statutes are under- or over-inclusive or both), it would never do to impose strict scrutiny on any legislation based on a stereotype.

   b. **Incidence of falseness:** Perhaps generalizations whose *incidence of falseness is unduly high* are what should be strictly scrutinized. However, determining what is "too high" is difficult. For instance, as Ely suggests, if a generalization were used to determine who should be subject to capital punishment, virtually *any* occurrence of falsity would be intolerably high; by contrast, if the legislature is trying to identify persons susceptible to heart attacks in order to keep them from piloting commercial aircraft, a high rate of false generalization, perhaps well over 50%, would be appropriate. Ely, p. 156.

    c. Ely's solution: Ely suggests that "[t]he cases where we ought to be suspicious are not those involving a generalization whose incidence of counterexample is 'too high,' but rather those involving a generalization whose incidence of counterexample is *significantly higher than the legislative authority appears to have thought it was*." *Id.* at 157.

    4. Modern Court's view: One Supreme Court case, in discussing why the class of "close relatives" should not be treated as suspect, gave a catalogue of factors the modern Court will view as leading towards strict scrutiny: "As a historical matter, [close relatives] have not been *subjected to discrimination*; they do not exhibit *obvious, immutable,* or *distinguishing characteristics* that define them as a *discrete group*; and they are not a *minority* or *politically powerless*." *Lyng v. Castillo*, 477 U.S. 635 (1986).

E. How strict is "strict scrutiny": Once the decision to apply strict scrutiny has been made, the statute will be upheld only if it is found to be *necessary* (not merely appropriate) to the attainment of some *compelling* (not merely desirable) governmental objective. As Professor Gunther has put it, this scrutiny has generally been "'strict' in theory and 'fatal' in fact." 86 HARV. L. REV. 8.

    1. Rationale for strict scrutiny: Both the requirement of a "compelling" objective and that of "necessary" means to that objective can be seen as aspects of the same judicial goal: to assure that suspect classifications are used only in those very rare situations where the high cost of sanctioning official invidious discrimination is outweighed by the even higher cost of not doing so.

        a. Weightiness of objective: An additional reason for requiring, in strict scrutiny cases, that the state objective be "compelling" is that such a requirement represents *a way of ferreting out discriminatory purposes*. Even if the means-end fit is perfect (i.e., the means is the only way of establishing that particular end), if the end that is advanced as a justification is *insubstantial*, one can legitimately suspect that this end is merely a *pretext*, and that what really motivated the decision was, say, racial prejudice. See Ely, p. 148.

            i. Illustration: For instance, suppose a school principal seats African Americans on one side of the stage at a graduation ceremony, and whites on the other, and justifies the choice by claiming that this arrangement is more esthetically appealing. The objective here is so trivial that one could fairly suspect that it was a pretext to cover racial discrimination. See Brest, *Processes of Constitutional Decision-Making*, p. 489 (1975) (quoted in Ely, p. 148).

        b. "Necessary" means: The requirement that the means selected (the suspect classification) be "necessary" to attainment of the goal expresses the view that *less discriminatory alternatives* must *always* be used if they are available to attain the goal. In fact, less discriminatory alternatives may sometimes be required to be used even if they will *not* achieve the compelling goal *quite as well* as the discriminatory means. That is, some degree of sacrifice of the legislative objective may be required in the name of equality of treatment.

    2. Strict scrutiny nearly always fatal: As an illustration of the strictness with which "strict scrutiny" is applied, consider that only once since 1944 has the Supreme Court **upheld** a governmental classification based on a racial or national-origin classification to which strict scrutiny was applied.

a. **May be changing:** However, as the present Supreme Court has expanded the use of strict scrutiny, it may, paradoxically, have become *easier* for a measure to survive that scrutiny. Thus in *Adarand Constructors* (*infra*, p. 306), a case applying strict scrutiny to race-based federal affirmative action programs, the Court went out of its way to "dispel the notion that strict scrutiny is 'strict in theory, but fatal in fact.' "

   i. **Affirmative action in admissions:** The one post-1944 context in which a race-based governmental classification has actually survived strict scrutiny by the Court illustrates that strict scrutiny may now be less likely to be fatal. That context involves the use of affirmative action in **university admissions.** See, e.g., *Grutter v. Bollinger* (*infra*, p. 283), a 2003 case in which the Court upheld the University of Michigan Law School's right to give an admissions preference to black and Hispanic applicants in order to obtain a "diverse" entering class, as long as this preference was granted as part of an individualized evaluation process that treated race as merely one "plus factor" among others.[4]

3. ***Korematsu:*** Before 2003's *Grutter* decision, the last case in which a racial or ethnic classification **survived** strict scrutiny was ***Korematsu v. U.S.***, 323 U.S. 214 (1944), the infamous ***Japanese Exclusion Case***. (Ironically, *Korematsu* was the first case in which race was explicitly referred to as a "suspect" criterion.)

   a. **Facts:** *Korematsu* involved a post-Pearl Harbor military order excluding all persons of Japanese ancestry from certain areas of the West Coast, and resulting in their effective imprisonment. The order was applied against citizens as well as non-citizens.

   b. **Holding:** The Court upheld the order, despite its suspectness. It did so on the theory that there was a **compelling need** to prevent espionage and sabotage, and that there was no practical and sufficiently rapid way for the military to distinguish the loyal from the disloyal.

   c. **Dissent:** Three Justices dissented in *Korematsu*. The strongest dissent was that of Justice Murphy, who argued that the majority's view relied on the "assumption that all persons of Japanese ancestry may have a dangerous tendency to commit sabotage and espionage. ... " He contended that individualized loyalty hearings, at least for those persons who were American citizens, could have been held. Another dissenter, Justice Jackson, pointed out that no attempt was made anywhere in the United States to exclude German or Italian aliens (thus suggesting that the order was based at least in part on racial prejudice, though Justice Jackson did not explicitly so charge).

   d. **Criticism:** Commentators have almost universally scorned *Korematsu* as one of the worst betrayals of Americans' constitutional rights in the Supreme Court's history. See sources cited in L,K&C, p. 1263, n. c.[5]

___

4. But the post-*Grutter* case of *Parents Involved in Community Schools v. Seattle School District No. 1* (*infra*, p. 294), in which the Court struck down the use of race in public-school pupil assignments, suggests that strict scrutiny in the Roberts Court will generally still be very strict indeed.

5. *Korematsu* was finally officially overruled in 2018, in *Trump v. Hawaii*; see *infra*, p. 686.

    i. **Military necessity:**   Obviously, even the *Korematsu* Court would not have upheld a racial distinction like the one at issue there, if it were not for (what the Court perceived as) extreme emergency. What is most troubling about the decision is not the Court's conclusion that the governmental objective was compelling (since prevention of espionage and sabotage clearly was), but rather, the Court's loose definition of means "necessary" to achieve that objective.

4. **"Separate but equal" treatment:**   Strict scrutiny has traditionally been reserved for those classifications which operate to the *disadvantage* of a racial or ethnic minority. But suppose that a classification *utilizes* race, but does not explicitly disadvantage either blacks or whites. In this situation, claims that there has been "equal application of the law" have usually failed; the school desegregation cases (including the rejection of the *"separate but equal" theory, infra*, p. 267) are the most notable example.

    Example 1: A Virginia statute prohibits marriage between a white and a non-white. The state rebuts an equal protection attack by contending that the statute applies "equally" to whites and blacks, since members of each race are punished to the same degree.

    Held, the statute violates equal protection. The statute contains a racial classification, and the fact that it has "equal application" does not immunize it from strict scrutiny. Since the legislative history shows that the statute was enacted to "preserve the racial integrity" of citizens (i.e., whites), the statute has only an invidious, discriminatory, purpose, and has no "legitimate overriding" one. ***Loving v. Virginia***, 388 U.S. 1 (1967).

    Example 2: Seattle's public-school system, in order to reduce school-by-school racial imbalance, sometimes makes the decision whether to allow a student to transfer into a particular school based solely on whether that student would improve the racial balance in the school.

    Held, this race-based scheme, even though it is not intended to systematically disadvantage any race, must be strictly scrutinized (and will be struck down). *Parents Involved in Community Schools v. Seattle School District No. 1*, infra, p. 294.

    a. **Special traits:**   There may, however, be *special traits* applicable to one race or ethnic group which, if they serve as the basis for a classification, do not necessarily lead to invidious discrimination.

    i. **Alcohol susceptibility:**   For instance, there is respectable evidence that Native American and Eskimos are abnormally susceptible to *alcohol*; a number of states therefore bar the sale of alcohol to these races. While the Supreme Court has never decided the issue, the Court might well hold that such a classification is not invidious, and does not disadvantage the races at which it is directed. If so, such a statute would probably be upheld.

    ii. **Sickle-cell test:**   Similarly, a state might require that all African Americans undergo testing for *sickle-cell anemia*. Again, such a statute would probably be upheld on the theory that it is benign rather than invidious. See L,K&C, p. 1264, n. 2. The same would presumably be true of a requirement that persons of Jewish ancestry undergo testing for Tay Sachs disease.

    iii. Overbreadth: However, these statutes could be subject to attack on an ***overbreadth*** theory, i.e., a theory that the government may not use racial groups as a substitute for an individualized determination. Such an argument seems unlikely to succeed where individualized treatment would be impractical (e.g., testing all racial groups for all genetic defects, even though a particular defect could almost never occur in most of the races). But where individualized judgments *are* feasible, the Court may well insist upon them even though the use of race as an initial screening device makes matters simpler.

    iv. Relation to affirmative action: This issue of "special traits" is related to the much broader issue of "affirmative action," i.e., the extent to which racial classifications may be used to advantage, rather than disadvantage, the minority race. The affirmative action area is discussed more fully *infra*, p. 274.

5. Racial classes and the political process: The Court has not hesitated to strictly scrutinize, and strike down, uses of racial classes as part of the ***political process.***

    a. Identification of candidates: For instance, the Court struck down a law requiring each ***candidate's race*** to appear on the ballot, in *Anderson v. Martin*, 375 U.S. 399 (1964). The *Anderson* Court apparently believed that, in light of private attitudes towards African Americans at that time and place, the statute was designed to help white candidates.

    b. More difficult procedures: Similarly, legislation which, for a racially discriminatory purpose, ***modifies the political process*** to make certain types of political action more difficult, may be subject to strict scrutiny. Thus in ***Hunter v. Erickson***, 393 U.S. 385 (1969), after the Akron City Council adopted a fair housing ordinance, the voters amended the city charter to prohibit any ordinance dealing with racial discrimination in housing, unless it had first been approved by a majority of the voters.

        i. Holding: The Supreme Court held that this charter amendment was violative of equal protection, on the theory that it: (1) was an "explicitly racial classification," and (2) clearly made it more difficult to enact anti-discrimination ordinances than other types of ordinances (which automatically passed into law following enactment by the Council).

6. Other areas: Some other areas in which the state has used racial classifications are as follows:

    a. Security: Prison officials sometimes ***separate prisoners by race*** in order to quell racial tensions or riots. However, *Johnson v. California*, discussed *infra*, p. 317, holds that a prison system's decision to routinely segregate newly-arrived prisoners by race must be ***strictly scrutinized.***

    b. Official records: The state may keep official statistics by race, if, but only if, the statistics serve some useful purpose (e.g., a sociological one). Thus the recording of the race of a husband and wife in every divorce has been upheld (*Tancil v. Woolls*, 379 U.S. 19 (1964)), but the keeping of separate lists of blacks and whites in voting and tax records was held to be without useful purpose, and therefore violative of equal protection, in a companion case (*Virginia Board of Elections v. Hamm*, 379 U.S. 19 (1964)).

    c. Child custody and adoption: Some states take race into account in decisions on ***adoption*** and ***child custody***. The use of racial considerations for these purposes will certainly be subject to strict scrutiny, and few if any such uses will survive that review.

i. **Child custody:** The one case decided by the Supreme Court in this area concerned child custody. In ***Palmore v. Sidoti***, 466 U.S. 429 (1984), two white parents were divorced, and custody of the child was given to the mother. The mother then married an African American, and the Florida courts transferred custody to the father on the grounds that if the daughter remained with her mother and step-father, she would become "vulnerable to peer pressures [and] suffer from the social stigmatization that is sure to come." The Supreme Court unanimously reversed, finding that the Florida court's order could not survive strict scrutiny. The Court conceded that the private biases on which the Florida court relied were probably real ones, but held that the law ***may not, directly or indirectly, give effect to such private prejudices***. (In strict scrutiny terms, the Court apparently held that the state's goal of awarding custody based on the "best interests of the child" was a sufficiently compelling one, but that bowing to private prejudices was not a necessary means of accomplishing that goal.)

ii. **Adoption:** If a state were to impose a rule that in ***adoption*** situations, the adoptive parent and the child must be of the same race, there is little doubt that the rationale of *Palmore* would dictate that the state rule be struck down. It is less clear whether race may be considered as ***one factor among many***. The rationale of *Palmore* would appear to mean that the possibility of prejudice and social rejection may not be considered by adoption authorities even as one factor among many. However, the broader interest in ensuring that the adoptive parents and child are culturally compatible, and that the child will feel a sense of unity with the adoptive parents, might well be recognized as a compelling one.

F. **Segregation and its remedies:** Most of the racial classifications discussed above imposed fairly direct, visible, burdens on racial or ethnic minorities. But some, like the miscegenation statute in *Loving v. Virginia*, purported to treat all races "identically," even though they used a racial classification. The most important example of government action which classifies by race, but which, superficially at least, does not explicitly disadvantage minorities, is ***segregation***, i.e., the maintenance of physical separateness between the races.

1. **Summary of issues:** Since 1954, officially-sanctioned segregation not only in the public schools but in other areas has been treated as a ***clear violation of equal protection***. Therefore, the principal issues related to segregation have been not whether intentional segregation violates the Constitution, but rather: (a) How does one distinguish between "intentional," or *de jure*, segregation (which is unconstitutional) and unintentional, or *de facto*, segregation (which is not)? and (b) What are the ***remedies*** for official segregation? Prior to a discussion of these issues, however, some history is in order.

2. **The "separate but equal" doctrine (*Plessy v. Ferguson*):** Initially, the Supreme Court's view was that ***"separate but equal" treatment did not violate equal protection***. This doctrine was formulated in ***Plessy v. Ferguson***, 163 U.S. 537 (1896), where the Court upheld a Louisiana law calling for separate-but-equal accommodations for white and black railroad passengers.

a. **Rationale:** The majority reasoned that laws such as this one related only to "social" equality, not to political or civil equality. Social equality was not, the Court held, a goal of the Equal Protection Clause, and could be attained only through ***voluntary*** *action* by individuals, not by statutes.

   i.   **Not badge of inferiority:**   Also, the Court reasoned, the law itself did not "stamp … the colored race with a badge of inferiority." If African Americans felt inferior under the law, "it is not by reason of anything found in the act, but solely because the colored race chooses to put that construction upon it."

b. **Dissent:**   The first Justice Harlan, in a classic dissent, argued that the law did indeed violate equal protection. Although it appeared facially neutral, "[e]very one knows that [it] had its origin in the *purpose*, not so much to exclude white persons from railroad cars occupied by blacks, as to *exclude colored people* from coaches occupied by or assigned to white persons." The statute therefore interfered with the personal freedom of African Americans.

   i.   **"Color blindness":**   Harlan then added, in an oft-cited remark, that "*our Constitution is color-blind*." Some have argued that Harlan meant this remark to include "benign" or "reverse" discrimination based on race.

3. ***Brown v. Bd. of Ed.:***   *Plessy v. Ferguson's* validation of "separate but equal" segregation remained the law until 1954. (However, in a series of pre-1954 cases involving graduate school education, the Court found that facilities available to African Americans were not in fact "equal" to those given to whites.) Then, in ***Brown v. Board of Education***, 347 U.S. 483 (1954), the Court explicitly *rejected the "separate but equal" doctrine*, at least insofar as public education was concerned.

a. **Rationale:**   The Court reasoned that even where all-black and all-white schools were equal in terms of "tangible" factors, intangible factors necessarily prevented children who were restricted to all-black schools from receiving equal educational opportunities. In particular, racial segregation "generates [in African American students] a feeling of inferiority as to their status in the community that may affect their hearts and minds in a way unlikely ever to be undone. … Separate educational facilities are *inherently unequal.*"

   i.   **Expert opinion:**   In reaching this conclusion, the Court also relied on the findings of psychologists and educators who had concluded from their research that segregation gave African American pupils a sense of inferiority, which in turn impaired their motivation to learn and their success at learning.

   ii.   **Fourteenth Amendment's history irrelevant:**   One factor upon which the *Brown* Court did *not* particularly rely was the *legislative history* of the Fourteenth Amendment itself. The Court noted that, at the time that Amendment was adopted, blacks in the South were not educated at all, and even in the North there was no compulsory public education system for whites, let alone blacks. Therefore, nothing in the legislative history of the Amendment gave the Court any real clue about what Congress intended with respect to school segregation. Instead, the Court decided to focus on public education as it stood in 1954, not as it stood when the Amendment was adopted in 1868.

4. **Criticism of empirical basis:**   A casual reading of *Brown v. Bd. of Ed.* gives the impression that the Court was relying principally upon *social science* and *empirical evidence*, i.e., factual evidence that segregation indeed harms African American students. But if that is the basis for the Court's decision, it may be criticized. As one commentator has said, "I

would not have the constitutional rights of Negroes — or of other Americans — rest on any such flimsy foundation as some of the scientific demonstrations in these records. [Behavioral science findings] have an uncertain expectancy of life." 30 N.Y.U. L. REV. 157-58.

a. **Possibility of new evidence:** For instance, one could imagine new findings suggesting that, where there are truly equal tangible facilities, African American students do ***better*** in segregated schools than as a minority in a school where they are subject to hostility, and possibly violence, from the white majority. See Wechsler, *Toward Neutral Principles of Constitutional Law*, 73 HARV. L. REV. 33.

b. **Change in African Americans' views:** Furthermore, since such a psychologically-focused theory turns on African Americans' own feelings about segregation, such a theory would presumably no longer be valid if a majority of black students or parents in a given community preferred separation. Constitutional requirements could then theoretically vary from town to town, depending on the views of local African Americans; such a result would not foster the uniformity and predictability usually considered desirable in constitutional (or other) law.

5. **Other public facilities:** Although *Brown* by its terms applied only to schools, the Court extended its rejection of the "separate but equal" doctrine to many ***other public facilities*** during the following ten years.

6. **Implementation of *Brown (Brown II)*:** The Court in *Brown*, by pronouncing official segregation to be a violation of equal protection, did not by that pronouncement alone do much to modify the actual educational patterns of Kansas or any other state. It was only by a long series of "implementation" decisions that a significant reduction in school segregation came about. The first of these implementation decisions was a continuation of *Brown* itself; in *Brown v. Board of Education*, 349 U.S. 294 (1955), the so-called ***Brown II*** decision, the Court did several significant things:

a. **Lower federal courts:** It gave the ***federal district courts*** primary responsibility for supervising desegregation because of their "proximity to local conditions" and the "possible need for further hearings."

b. **Equitable principles:** The Court gave no precise guidelines for carrying out desegregation. Instead, it directed the district courts to use "***general equitable principles.***"

c. **"All deliberate speed":** A plaintiff whose constitutional rights have been violated by state action would normally be entitled to ***immediate*** relief. But, apparently because it feared the chaos and violence that might develop if attempts were made to carry out desegregation instantly, the Court authorized the district courts to take into account the public interest in eliminating desegregation "in a systematic and effective manner." However, the burden of proving any need for delay was placed upon the school boards, and the lower courts were ordered to implement desegregation "with ***all deliberate speed.***"

7. **Aftermath of *Brown*:** For almost a decade after *Brown*, the Supreme Court ***rarely intervened*** in the desegregation process, leaving this to the federal district courts and to local politics. However, in *Cooper v. Aaron*, 358 U.S. 1 (1958), where the governor of Arkansas had used the National Guard to block desegregation of a Little Rock high school, all nine Justices refused to grant to the Little Rock Board of Education a 2 1/2 year delay in deseg-

regation. The Court refused to allow the constitutional rights of African American children to be compromised by actions of the governor and the legislature, even though the school board itself had made good-faith efforts to desegregate.

8. **Specific rules for desegregating:** Then, beginning in a 1963 case, the Court began to lay down much more specific guidelines concerning what means were acceptable for implementing desegregation. Some of the important principles which emerged from this line of cases are as follows.

  a. **Minority-to-majority transfer invalid:** Some school districts rezoned to create schools that would be initially desegregated, but then permitted any student whose race was in a minority in a particular school to transfer to a school where he would be in the majority. These *"minority-to-majority" transfer plans* were invalidated in *Goss v. Board of Education*, 373 U.S. 683 (1963), on the grounds that such schemes "inevitably lead toward segregation of the students by race."

  b. **Closing of public schools:** A county's scheme to *close its public schools* rather than comply with a desegregation order, and then to fund white-only private schools through state and local tax credits and grants, was rejected in *Griffin v. County School Board*, 377 U.S. 218 (1964). The Court indicated that a county could under some circumstances close its public schools, but that it could not do so for an *unconstitutional purpose*, which avoiding desegregation obviously was.

  c. **"Freedom of choice" plans rejected:** Many districts adopted *"freedom of choice"* plans, under which any student could attend the school of his choice. In *Green v. County School Board*, 391 U.S. 430 (1968), a small school district had about a 50% African American population, two schools, and little residential segregation. After the "freedom of choice" plan had been in operation for three years, no white child had chosen to go to the formerly black school, and 85% of the black students remained in that school.

  i. **Holding:** In these circumstances, the Court held, the plan *did not adequately desegregate* the schools. Once a school system had been officially segregated, the Constitution required that it be converted to a "unitary, non-racial system of public education."

  ii. *Green's* **focus on effect, not intent:** *Green* is probably most significant not for the fact that it rejected "freedom of choice" plans, but for the fact that it was the first case in which the Supreme Court attached explicit importance to the *effect* of desegregation measures, and not merely to the *intent* with which those measures were enacted. Once official segregation existed, *good intentions* on the part of the school board *were not sufficient*; whatever affirmative measures were needed to bring about a unitary, non-racial system must be implemented. This doctrine has essentially continued in force to date.

9. *Swann v. Charlotte-Mecklenburg:* Perhaps the most important case giving guidance to the district courts and school boards concerning the techniques of desegregation came in *Swann v. Charlotte-Mecklenburg Board of Education*, 402 U.S. 1 (1971). In *Swann*, the Court made the following rulings:

  a. **Must have *de jure* segregation:** The federal courts may not order a school board to adjust the racial composition of any of its schools (*no matter how great the racial* *imbalance as between schools*) unless there has been a finding that there was *officially-maintained* (i.e., intentional or *de jure*) segregation. Thus a federal court may *not* order *de facto* segregation, no matter how severe, to be cured by adjustment of racial balance. (However, the Court noted, the school board itself could constitutionally exercise *discretion* to adjust racial balances, "in order to prepare students to live in a pluralistic society. … ")

b. Racial quotas: Once official segregation is found, the court may, in determining the appropriate remedy, consider what the *ratio* is of black students to white students for the district as a whole. While the court may *not* require that every school in the district have *precisely that ratio*, the district-wide ratio may be considered as a "useful starting point in shaping a remedy."

c. Single-race schools: The fact that one or more schools that are completely or almost completely *single-race remain* in a district does *not* necessarily mean that desegregation has not yet been accomplished. But such schools must be carefully scrutinized by the court, and it is up to the school board to show that the racial concentration in these schools is not due to official segregation but to other causes (e.g., residential patterns).

d. Rezoning: *Rezoning*, i.e., the redrawing of attendance zones, is a *permissible* technique for remedying segregation. Furthermore, the new zones do *not* necessarily have to be either "compact" or *contiguous*. Thus the Court approved, in *Swann* itself, a system of *"pairing"* and *"clustering"* schools from non-contiguous parts of the city. The effect of this scheme was to combine predominantly African American schools with predominantly white schools, so as to bring racial balance to each school in the pair or cluster.

i. Not usable for *de facto cases*: Again, the Court emphasized that such an order could never be given to remedy *de facto* segregation; it was only because the school authorities presented the lower court with a "loaded gameboard" that this kind of alteration of attendance zones was permissible.

e. Busing: The Court also *approved busing* as a means of bringing about desegregation. "Desegregation plans cannot be limited to the walk-in school." The scheme ordered in *Swann* was valid, because it did not result in excessive amounts of busing, compared with the amount being done voluntarily by the district prior to the desegregation order.

i. Danger to health or education: However, the Court indicated that a busing scheme would not be upheld if "the time or distance of travel is so great as to risk either the health of the children or significantly impinge on the educational process."

f. Later unintentional imbalances allowed: *Swann* and later cases establish that once the effects of official segregation have been even *temporarily remedied*, later imbalances caused by *changing residential patterns* or other non-official conduct *may not be cured by federal court order.* (The school board itself, of course, always remains free to cure such imbalances as a matter of discretion; the board simply cannot be forced by a federal court to do so.)

i. Illustration: A post-*Swann* case illustrates this principle, and demonstrates that court-supervised desegregation will not necessarily ever lead to a desegregated school system. In *Board of Education v. Dowell*, 498 U.S. 237 (1991), the Court held that as long as the school board had complied in good faith with the desegregation decree (which it had apparently done for the six prior years), and as long as the vestiges of past *de jure* discrimination had been eliminated ***"to the extent practicable,"*** the desegregation decree should be lifted and the school district allowed to revert to a system of neighborhood schools. This was true even though, evidence showed, 33 of the 64 elementary schools would then be either more-than-90% black or more-than-90% white. (If the present residential segregation was due to the prior official school segregation, then obviously the Supreme Court's "vestiges of past discrimination removed" standard would not be satisfied. But if the residential segregation was due primarily to ***people's personal choices about where to live***, then, the Supreme Court indicated, the court desegregation order would have to be lifted and the district could revert to neighborhood — and thus *de facto* segregated — schools.) See more about ending federal-court supervision of desegregation, *infra*, p. 274.

10. **Desegregation in the North:** For the first twenty years following *Brown*, virtually all of the Supreme Court's school desegregation cases involved the South, where segregation was generally ***required by law*** at the time *Brown* was decided. These cases thus presented the Court with little need to distinguish between *de jure* and *de facto* segregation, or to prescribe methods for determining whether a school board had intended to segregate — all racial imbalance which the Court evaluated could be linked quite directly to statutorily-required segregation. But then, starting in 1974, the Court began to hear cases involving claimed segregation in the ***North***, where there was virtually no statutorily-authorized segregation at the time of *Brown v. Bd. of Ed.* In a series of Northern cases, the Court attempted to lay down some rules for dealing with a number of new issues, most of them relating to the *de facto/de jure* distinction.

11. ***Keyes* (the Denver case):** The first Northern case was ***Keyes v. School District #1***, 413 U.S. 189 (1973), involving the Denver system. Segregation in Colorado had never been statutorily required. But the district court found that Denver school authorities had used gerrymandered attendance zones, school construction policies, and other devices to purposely keep one part of the city's school system, the Park Hill area, racially segregated. The Supreme Court then made the following rulings for dealing with this and other cases where there was no statutorily-mandated segregation:

    a. ***De jure* requirement maintained:** The Court repeated that only *de jure* segregation, not *de facto* segregation, could be redressed by court action, and emphasized that *de jure* segregation would be found to exist only where there was a ***purpose or intent*** to segregate.

    b. **Segregation of one part of district:** The most important aspect of *Keyes* is in the Court's treatment of the ***effects*** of a finding that there was intentional segregation as to ***one substantial part*** of a ***larger*** metropolitan district. Such a finding could, the Court held, have one or both of the following effects:

        i. **Dual system:** The finding of intentional segregation of a substantial portion of the district would create a ***prima facie case*** that there was a "dual" school system, i.e., that the ***entire district*** was segregated. This *prima facie* demonstration of a dual system could be rebutted only if the school board showed that the segregated part should be viewed as a ***separate, unrelated*** area, and that segregation in that one part had no effect on the others.

   ii. **Probative of segregative intent:** Even if the school board succeeded in showing that the district was divided into unrelated areas, the finding of segregative intent as to one area (the Park Hill area) would create a ***presumption*** that segregated patterns in the other areas were intentional, not coincidental. This presumption, in turn, could only be rebutted if the school board showed either that: (1) segregative intent was not in fact one of the motivating factors in the board's actions as to these other areas (it would not be enough to show that some hypothetical "innocent" motivation "could" have produced those actions by the board); or (2) past segregative acts by the school board did not "create or contribute to the current segregated condition" of the schools. Thus the board would have to prove ***either lack of intent***, or ***lack of a causal connection*** between intent and segregation.

   c. **Summary:** Thus, as a practical matter, a plaintiff who is able to show segregative intent as to one portion of a large school district enjoys an enormous tactical advantage over his adversary: the burden of proof is shifted entirely to the school board to explain away segregated conditions in other portions of the district.

   d. **African Americans and Hispanics aggregated:** The *Keyes* Court defined as segregated any school having a ***combined*** predominance of African Americans ***and Hispanics***. It did so on the theory that these groups had suffered "identical discrimination in treatment," at least in the Southwest. This conclusion had the effect of identifying more segregated schools than if African American enrollment alone were considered.

12. **Interdistrict remedies:** Many of the country's big-city school districts are now predominantly African American. If a city's school system is shown to be *de jure* segregated, may a federal judge order a remedy which ***includes suburban school districts***? In ***Milliken v. Bradley***, 418 U.S. 717 (1974), the Court answered this question, for most purposes, in the ***negative***. The case was decided by a 5-4 split.

   a. **Facts:** The school district for the city of Detroit is predominantly African American. The Detroit suburbs, consisting of numerous towns each having its own school district, are predominantly white. A federal trial judge, after concluding that the city had practiced *de jure* segregation, concluded that a Detroit-only desegregation plan would not be effective, since many schools would remain more than 75% African American. He therefore ordered that 53 surrounding suburban communities participate in the desegregation plan.

   b. **Majority holding:** Justice Burger, writing for a majority of the Court, reversed. He cited the general principle of equity that "[t]he scope of the remedy is determined by the nature and extent of the constitutional violation." Thus there could be a cross-district remedy ***only if there had been a cross-district wrong***, i.e., segregation in Detroit that ***caused an effect in the suburbs***, or vice versa.

      i. **Practical problems:** Burger also pointed to the practical problems that would result from a cross-district desegregation order. Difficult jurisdictional issues would arise regarding the right to levy taxes, the right to establish attendance zones, the authority to locate and construct new schools, etc. And such consolidation would weaken the strong tradition of local control over public education.

      ii. State's role irrelevant: The majority also rejected the dissent's argument (an argument also advanced by the district court), that there had been significant participation by the *state of Michigan* in the Detroit segregation. Even assuming that this was so (which the majority denied), the constitutional right of black students in Detroit was merely "to attend a unitary school system *in that district*."

    c. Dissent: The four dissenters in *Milliken* produced two opinions, the main one by Justice White.

      i. White's dissent: White's dissent stressed that the city of Detroit was a *subdivision of the state*, and that it was the state, not the locality, that must "respond to the command of the Fourteenth Amendment." Justice White simply saw no historical support for a rule that desegregation remedies must stop at the district line.

13. Segregated colleges and universities: So far, we've spoken only about segregation in the context of elementary schools up through high schools. Where government has intentionally segregated in a *college or university*, the same basic rule applies: this *de jure* segregation violates the Equal Protection Clause and must be dismantled. See *U.S. v. Fordice*, 505 U.S. 717 (1992).

14. Ending District-Court supervision: More than 50 years have now passed since *Brown v. Board of Ed.* Some school districts have been under federal-court supervision for desegregation for nearly that entire time. When does that supervision end? It ends when the school district has been "*restored to unitary status*." That is, supervision (and constitutionally-mandated desegregation efforts) must end as soon as the *effects* of the *official* segregation have been eliminated. Supervision will *not* necessarily last until the system is truly integrated.

    a. Neighborhood re-segregation: So the fact that *neighborhoods* have become *re-segregated* (after school desegregation began) based *on private housing decisions*, and that this has led to re-segregated local schools, can't be used to justify extending federal-court supervision.

    b. White flight: Similarly, the fact that busing or other desegregation methods have caused *whites* to *flee* the school district entirely for the surrounding suburbs, leaving the former *de jure* segregated city system heavily minority, can't be used to delay the end of judicial supervision. See *Missouri v. Jenkins*, 515 U.S. 70 (1995).

    c. Use of race for pupil assignments: Once unitary status has been restored, any use of race in making pupil assignments will be strictly scrutinized, as if the official segregation had never occurred. That's what happened in the Louisville portion of *Parents Involved in Community Schools v. Seattle School District No. 1*, *infra*, p. 294 — the fact that *de facto* segregated housing patterns had caused individual schools to become racially isolated once again was not a reason to allow race-conscious pupil assignments to occur, a majority of the Court believed.

IV. AFFIRMATIVE ACTION AND "BENIGN" DISCRIMINATION

    A. "Benign" discrimination generally: We live in a world in which governments, universities, major corporations, etc., are all trying (or at least claim to be trying) to reverse the effects of past discrimination. Yet, past discrimination often cannot be reversed without treating people differently, based upon explicit consideration of the very criterion on which the past discrimination was based (e.g., race or sex).

1. **Problem:** Not surprisingly, such attempts to remedy past discrimination (sometimes called *"benign"* or *"reverse"* discrimination, and more frequently, *"affirmative action"*) present major constitutional questions in their own right. Probably the most important is: What standard should be used to review the "benign" use of a "suspect" classification, such as race? Since classifications which disadvantage a racial minority will be strictly scrutinized, and may be justified only where they are "necessary" to fulfill a "compelling" governmental objective (see *supra*, p. 263), is the same strict scrutiny required of "affirmative action" attempts based on race?

   a. **Strict scrutiny:** The answer is *"yes,"* the same strict scrutiny is required of "affirmative action" attempts based on race as is required of race-based classifications that disadvantage a minority. This is the result of the landmark decision in *City of Richmond v. J.A. Croson Co.*, discussed *infra*, p. 301.

2. **Sex considered before race:** Before we begin our discussion of the benign use of racial classifications, however, we will discuss the benign use of *sexual* classes. Although discrimination against women is not viewed with the same extremely high level of suspicion as is discrimination against African Americans (compare *supra*, p. 256 with *infra*, p. 319), the reverse discrimination precedents in the sexual area laid important groundwork for *Croson* and other racial affirmative action cases.

B. **Benign use of sex classes:** Where a sexual classification *disadvantages* women, it is subjected to "middle-level" scrutiny. That is, the gender-based classification must be "substantially" related to the achievement of "important" governmental objectives. (See *Craig v. Boren, infra*, p. 321.) Perhaps surprisingly, statutes which make sexual classifications which *favor* women, even if enacted solely to remedy past anti-female discrimination, are judged by exactly the same formal standard: the statute will be stricken if the sex-based criterion is not substantially related to an important governmental objective. Thus to put it colloquially, the legislature gets no explicit "brownie points" for attempting to remedy past sexual discrimination.

   1. **"Means" aspect most important:** However, there is a sense in which a statute that favors women in an attempt to remedy past discrimination may implicitly be subject to gentler review. The Supreme Court has generally acknowledged that the aim of remedying a particular type of past sexual discrimination is itself a worthy and "important" governmental objective. Thus most of the pro-women statutes have passed or failed the Court's middle-level scrutiny principally on whether the *means* part of the test was satisfied, i.e., whether there was a "substantial relationship" between the statute and the discrimination which was to be remedied.

      a. **Alimony:** Thus an Alabama statute which allowed *alimony* to be awarded only against men was stricken by the Court because of its weakness in the "means," rather than the "end," part of the test. In *Orr v. Orr*, 440 U.S. 268 (1979), the Court recognized that the statute helped serve an important governmental objective, namely, compensating women for discrimination during marriage. But an outright ban on alimony awards against women was *not substantially related* to the worthy objective.

         i. **Rationale:** The Court observed that the relative financial need of the parties was already required to be considered as part of the divorce process, so that there was no need to use sex as an automatic "proxy for financial dependence." Furthermore, the only women who would be given extra protection by the statute were those who were *not* financially needy; thus the statute's main effect was at odds with its stated purpose.

2. **Difficulty of verifying "benignness":** Observe that it is not always so easy to verify whether discrimination that is claimed to be "benign" really *is*. For instance, a legislature which takes the general view (as Alabama's apparently did, in *Orr, supra*) that women invariably need to be protected may, although claiming that it is helping them by special legislation, in actuality be *reinforcing a negative and untrue stereotype of them.*

3. **Attempt to remedy past discrimination:** Where a gender classification is used in an attempt to remedy *specific, objectively-verifiable* past discrimination against women (rather than to perpetuate stereotypes of women's dependency), the statute is much more likely to be upheld.

    a. **Remedy for job discrimination:** Thus in *Califano v. Webster*, 430 U.S. 313 (1977), the Court unanimously *upheld* a Social Security Act provision which in computing a wage earner's "average monthly wage" (upon which benefits are based) allowed women to exclude three more lower-earning years than a man could.

        i. **Rationale:** The Court found that this provision was not the result of "archaic and overbroad generalizations" about women, but was rather the result of prior objectively-verifiable discrimination which had barred most women from all but the lowest-paying jobs. Thus the measure directly, even though only partially, remedied past discrimination.

4. **Statutory rape:** A necessary (though not sufficient) condition for "benign" sex discrimination to be legal is that men and women be *differently situated*, in a way relevant to the statute's purpose. Of all the possible differences between the sexes, the clearest ones are of course *biological*. For instance, the fact that *only women may become pregnant* led a majority (albeit a bare one) of the Court to declare California's *statutory rape law valid*, even though it applied only to male defendants, in *Michael M. v. Superior Court*, 450 U.S. 464 (1981).

    a. **Nature of statute:** The statute involved in *Michael M.* made it a crime to have sexual intercourse with a female under the age of eighteen. Thus only men could be liable for "statutory rape" (more precisely, "unlawful sexual intercourse").

    b. **Plurality upholds statute:** A four-Justice plurality upheld the statute (with Justice Blackmun, concurring in the judgment, supplying the fifth vote). The plurality acknowledged that, since the statute discriminated based on sex, it could be upheld only if the classification bore a "substantial relationship" to "important governmental objectives" (the "middle-level scrutiny" standard of *Craig v. Boren, infra*, p. 321). This test could only be met if men and women were situated differently, in a way that was relevant to the statutory purpose.

        i. **Statutory purpose:** The plurality found it obvious that the purpose of the statute was to *prevent illegitimate teenage pregnancies*. This purpose was also, the plurality held, an "important governmental objective."

        ii. **Substantial relation:** The fighting issue in the case, however, was whether there was a *substantial relation* between this important objective and the classification chosen. The plurality felt that there was, for two reasons: (1) Since only women can become pregnant, the male had no direct disincentive from having sex with an unmarried minor. The statute therefore served to "roughly 'equalize' the deterrence on the sexes." (2) Enforcement of the statute was more feasible if the girl was exempted from prosecution, since a successful prosecution would normally require her testimony, which she would generally not give if she might be subjected to prosecution.

c. **Dissent:** Four Justices dissented, in opinions written by Justices Brennan and Stevens. The dissenters believed that, even if prevention of illegitimate pregnancy was the statute's goal (something they were not convinced of), the male-only prosecution scheme *did not substantially advance* that objective. They felt that a statute which applied equally to the woman would be a still stronger deterrent (even assuming that *enforcement* might be more difficult). As Justice Stevens put it, "the fact that a class of persons is especially vulnerable to a risk that a statute is designed to avoid is a reason for making the statute applicable to that class."

5. **Draft registration of women:** The federal government's historical refusal to require the *draft registration* or *conscription* of women might be viewed as "benign" sex discrimination. In *Rostker v. Goldberg*, 453 U.S. 57 (1981), the Court *upheld male-only draft registration*. However, the Court did not view the case as involving affirmative action but rather, military necessity.

a. **Facts:** The draft registration process is simply a way of maintaining an inventory of available personnel who may be drafted in the event of a military emergency. An actual draft, in turn, would almost certainly be principally for the purpose of drafting *combat* troops. At least until the Persian Gulf War, the policy of both Congress and the armed services had been that women should not serve in combat. The issue in *Rostker* (at least for the majority) was whether the policy against use of women in combat was sufficient to allow Congress to decline to require registration of women.

b. **Majority upholds exclusion:** Six Justices held that the exclusion of women from registration was *not* a violation of equal protection. The majority did not clearly articulate the test to which it was subjecting the regulation. However, it rejected the government's request that a "mere-rationality" standard be used, and implied that it was applying the "heightened scrutiny" (i.e., middle-level scrutiny) standard of *Craig v. Boren*.

c. **Factors:** In upholding the exclusion of women despite this middle-level scrutiny, the majority relied upon the following factors:

    i. **Deference to Congress in military affairs:** In the area of *military affairs*, Congress' authority is extremely broad, and the courts should show even greater-than-usual deference to congressional decisionmaking.

    ii. **Not unthinking stereotype:** Congress gave careful, and reasoned, consideration whether to register women. In contrast to several other legislative schemes previously reviewed by the Court, the decision not to register women was not the "accidental by-product of a traditional way of thinking about women."

    iii. **Not eligible for combat:** As noted, women were currently not eligible for combat. (The constitutionality of this restriction was not before the Court.) According to the majority, the purpose of registration is to prepare for the possible drafting of combat troops. Since women would not be drafted for combat posts under the present scheme, the government was justified in not registering them. Because of the combat restrictions, this was a case in which men and women "are ***simply not similarly situated*** for purposes of a draft or registration for a draft."

6. **Present "exceedingly persuasive justification" standard:** It's not clear whether gender-based schemes that the Court finds to be truly "benign" or compensatory will have to meet the same tough standard that non-benign gender-based enactments now have to meet. In the 1996 decision in *U.S. v. Virginia, infra,* p. 324, the Court held that gender-based schemes like the one there (maintenance of all-male status for the Virginia Military Institute) could be sustained only if the state showed an ***"exceedingly persuasive justification"*** that the Court would look at with "skeptical scrutiny." But the scheme in that case was clearly *not* a "benign" one, or one that was motivated by a desire to redress past discrimination; it was instead an old scheme that (the Court found) derived from stereotypes about gender roles. It's still not clear whether the post-1996 "exceedingly persuasive justification" standard will be applied to schemes that attempt to reverse prior discrimination against one sex or the other.

C. **Race:** We turn now to the "benign" use of ***racial*** classifications. Just as in the sex-based area, the scrutiny is the same "middle level" one for both "benign" and non-benign discrimination, so race-based classification will receive the same ***strict*** scrutiny whether the classification is supposedly "benign" (i.e., an attempt to help previously disadvantaged racial minorities) or invidious (an attempt by the white majority to hurt African American or other racial minorities). This is the result of *City of Richmond v. J.A. Croson Co.*, discussed *infra*, p. 301.

Croson does not mean that a race-based classification will always be struck down. For instance, a governmental body that had previously discriminated against African-Americans in a very clear way might be able to institute a race-based scheme to eradicate the effects of that discrimination. Similarly, a university that wants to obtain a "diverse" class may give a preference to applicants from underrepresented minorities, as long as this is done as part of an individualized process; see *Grutter v. Bollinger, infra,* p. 283. However, any race-based classification will clearly face a ***presumption of unconstitutionality***, even if it is motivated by affirmative action concerns.

1. **Significance:** Therefore, a race-conscious affirmative action plan, whether it is in the area of employment, college admissions, voting rights or anywhere else, must be adopted for the purpose of furthering some ***"compelling"*** governmental interest, and the racial classification must be ***necessary*** to achieve that compelling governmental interest. The only governmental objectives that have so far been endorsed by the Court as possibly supporting race-conscious affirmative action are (1) the ***redressing of clear past discrimination*** and (2) the pursuit of ***diversity*** in a ***student body.*** The former is the kind of affirmative action on which we will be focusing here.

2. **Past discrimination:** When government institutes an affirmative action plan to accomplish the objective of redressing past racial discrimination, two key questions arise: (1) what kind of ***proof*** must there be that there's really been past discrimination? and (2) ***who is it*** who must have discriminated? So far, the Supreme Court hasn't given much guidance on these issues. A reasonable guess would go like this:

a. **No findings needed:** As to question 1 — what kind of proof of discrimination is needed — there must be *quite strong and specific evidence of past discrimination* against African Americans or other racial minorities whom the plan is helping. It's not enough that the government has a general belief that there's been discrimination. Nor is it enough that African Americans are in some sense *"under-represented"* among the job-holders, students, contractors, or whatever "goody" is in issue.

Example: The Richmond, Virginia City Council notices that less than 1% of the city's construction contracts have been awarded to minority-owned businesses in the past five years. It therefore infers that general contractors have discriminated against minority-owned firms, and requires that henceforth, 30% of the dollar amount of all City-funded construction projects must go to minority-owned firms.

Held, this racially-based classification must be subjected to strict scrutiny, and will only be upheld if necessary to achieve a compelling governmental purpose. If there were clear evidence of past racial discrimination by general contractors, the City would have a compelling interest in having its tax dollars not used to support such discrimination by private firms. But here, the city did not have "hard" evidence of such past discrimination. The fact that black-owned firms got only a tiny share of contracts, and made up only a tiny portion of the local contractors' association, was not enough to prove such past discrimination — there was no evidence that there really were more black-owned firms than this, and "the relevant statistical pool for purposes of demonstrating discriminatory exclusion must be the number of minorities qualified to undertake the particular task." *City of Richmond v. J.A. Croson Co.*, 488 U.S. 469 (1989), discussed extensively *infra*, p. 301.

i. **Formal findings probably not necessary:** On the other hand, it's probably not necessary that there be a formal *"finding"* by a court that this discrimination took place. So for instance, if a particular police force had statistically far fewer African Americans than would be expected based on the number of qualified African Americans in the local labor force, this might be enough to demonstrate that there was discrimination; in that case, the police department might be able to voluntarily put in a plan that gave African Americans some preference in the hiring process. Similarly, the department might be able to settle a discrimination suit by agreeing to put in such a plan. But there does have to be quite clear evidence of past discrimination, not mere supposition.

b. **Discrimination by whom:** Now for Question 2 — *who* must have discriminated? Obviously, a race-conscious affirmative action plan is most likely to be upheld if the past discrimination was by the *particular government entity in question.* But suppose that the past discrimination was not by the particular governmental entity involved in the present case (e.g., the particular governmental employer), but was in the same *general domain* (e.g., the *same industry*). In this "different player but same domain" situation, a race-conscious remedy is probably *also justified.* For instance, in *Croson, supra*, the requirement of a "compelling" government objective would likely have been satisfied by hard evidence that general contractors had discriminated against black-owned contracting firms in the Richmond market, even had Richmond itself not discriminated. On the other hand, *the mere fact that there has been general "societal" discrimination is not enough to justify race-conscious measures.*

3. Quotas: One device that is especially vulnerable to Equal Protection attack is the racially-based *quota*. A racially-based quota is an inflexible number of admissions slots, dollar amounts, or other "goodies" set aside for minorities. (For more about the definition of "quota," see sub-paragraph (a) below.) In the aftermath of the decision in *Richmond v. Croson*, it seems probable that ***virtually all racially-based quotas will be struck down even where the government is trying to eradicate the effects of past discrimination*** — the Court will probably say that a quota is not "necessary" to remedy discrimination, that more flexible "goals" can do the job.

> **Example:** Recall the facts of *Croson* — Richmond tried to remedy what it saw as past discrimination against black-owned contracting firms by giving them 30% of future city contracts. Even if there had been hard evidence that there really was discrimination in the past (evidence that Richmond didn't have), and thus even had Richmond been acting in pursuit of a compelling objective (getting rid of past discrimination), Richmond would probably still have lost, because the 30% requirement was a hard-and-fast one, i.e., a quota. A majority of the Court would probably have said that a flexible goal would have done the job just as well — the City could have required general contractors to show that they "tried" to assign 30% of the contracts to black-owned firms, without automatically penalizing them if they failed. Since a flexible goal would have done as well, the quota wasn't "necessary," and Richmond would (probably) have lost.

> **a. What is a "quota":** What, then, will be considered to be a *"quota"*? Apparently the term will now be quite ***narrowly-construed*** following the affirmative-action-in-admissions decision in *Grutter v. Bollinger*, *infra*, p. 283. The majority opinion there says that "properly understood, a 'quota' is a program in which a certain ***fixed number or proportion of opportunities*** are '***reserved exclusively*** for certain minority groups.' ... Quotas 'impose a fixed number or percentage which ***must be attained***, or which ***cannot be exceeded***'." A program that merely contains aspirational *"goals"* does ***not*** thereby become a quota. Nor does a program become a quota merely because membership in a certain group is made a *"plus factor"* — even a very strong plus factor — as long as the plus factor is administered as part of ***individualized evaluations***.

>> **i. Point system:** On the other hand, a system that automatically assigns a certain fixed number of *"points"* for a certain race or ethnicity ***will*** be treated by the present court as being the equivalent of a quota, even though no particular slots are reserved exclusively for members of the minority group. That's the lesson of one of the Court's other major affirmative-action-in-admissions cases, *Gratz v. Bollinger*, *infra*, p. 285.

4. Court-ordered vs. voluntary: Some affirmative action plans are ***ordered by a court*** to remedy past discrimination; other plans are ***voluntarily adopted*** by a public entity to remedy past discrimination. Does it make any difference to the constitutionality of the plan whether it's court-ordered or voluntary? The answer is not yet clear — court-ordered race-conscious remedies may be spared the strict scrutiny given to voluntary plans put in place by legislatures or executive officials, perhaps on the theory that a court-ordered remedy is less likely to constitute disguised political patronage than, say, a legislature's plan.

5. Some contexts: Let us now turn to some special contexts in which affirmative action has been challenged as being itself a violation of the equal protection rights of the white majority. The contexts which we will examine include: (1) school desegregation; (2) voting rights; (3) preferential admissions; (4) minority set-asides; and (5) employment.

D. Desegregation: The theory that the Constitution requires that all government action be *"color-blind"* was *rejected* quite early in one area, that of *school desegregation*. In *Swann v. Charlotte-Mecklenburg Board of Education*, 402 U.S. 1 (1971) (discussed extensively *supra*, p. 270), the Court explicitly upheld the use of race-conscious pupil assignments in order to remedy past intentional segregation.

1. **Effect of *Croson:*** But even in the school desegregation area, *Richmond v. Croson* (*infra*, p. 301) probably makes race-conscious remedies much harder to justify. The Court will presumably apply strict scrutiny to any race-conscious remedy for discrimination, such as pupil assignments or teacher assignments that explicitly take account of race. The Court will have to be satisfied that the race-conscious measure is "necessary" to eradicate the prior segregation, and this may be a hard burden to satisfy.

   a. ***De facto* segregation:** Now suppose that a school district is trying to remedy *de facto* segregation. Here, it is even more clear that any race-conscious remedy will be strictly scrutinized, and probably invalidated, in light of *Croson*. First, the Supreme Court might not even agree that maintaining racially-balanced schools (where the racial imbalance is *de facto* rather than *de jure*) is a "compelling" objective. Even if this objective were found to be compelling, the court would be likely to hold that there are race-neutral alternatives that would cure the problem with acceptable speed, so that race-conscious methods (such as a race-based pupil assignment scheme like the one described in the above example) are not "necessary" to fulfill that objective.

E. Preferential admissions to universities: Next, let's turn to the use of race in *admissions to colleges and universities.* As the result of four decisions since the turn of the century — two 2003 decisions involving the University of Michigan and two decisions involving the University of Texas (one from 2013 and one from 2016) — we now know that:

[1] Public universities and colleges *may explicitly consider minority racial status* as a factor that increases the odds of admission, so as to promote the compelling goal of *"education diversity."*

[2] These institutions *may not award "points" for minority status*, or otherwise pursue *mechanical quota-like schemes,* and must instead evaluate each candidate as part of a *"holistic" review* that treats race as *merely one factor among others.*

[3] Even when an institution uses a non-quota "holistic" race-conscious method, that method must *survive strict scrutiny*. That is, the method may be used *only* if the institution carries the burden of showing that *no workable race-neutral alternatives* would achieve the educational benefits of diversity *as well or almost as well* as the race-conscious method being used.

[4] Despite the need for strict scrutiny of race-conscious admissions schemes, such schemes can *survive* that scrutiny. Thus there has been one recent example of such a scheme's being upheld: when the University of Texas — after failing to achieve a critical mass of otherwise-under-represented African-American and Hispanic students on campus by use of race-neutral methods — adopted a program of considering race as "one factor among many" in the awarding of 25% of the admissions slots, the Supreme Court found the pro-

gram to be *constitutional* (in the second *"Fisher"* opinion).

The four cases are:

❑ *Grutter v. Bollinger*, 539 U.S. 306 (2003) (upholding by 5-4 the University of Michigan Law School's "race as one factor among many" approach);

❑ *Gratz v. Bollinger*, 539 U.S. 244 (2003) (striking down as a violation of equal protection, by a 6-3 vote, Michigan's undergraduate scheme, by which members of favored racial and ethnic groups got an automatic 20 points of the 100 points needed for admission);

❑ *Fisher v. Univ. of Texas*, 133 S. Ct. 2411 (2013) (*"Fisher I"*) (holding that the University of Texas' race-conscious but non-quota-based system would be valid only if the University showed that no workable race-neutral methods were reasonably available, and remanding the case for a determination on this issue); and

❑ *Fisher v. Univ. of Texas*, 579 U.S. __ (2016) (*"Fisher II"*) (concluding that the University of Texas' plan was constitutional under the rules set in *Fisher I*).

1. *Bakke* **decision:**   Before we analyze these four decisions, we need to review briefly the court's only prior decision on affirmative action in the University context, *Regents of Univ. of California v. Bakke*, 438 U.S. 265 (1978). The case is now significant principally for Justice Powell's opinion, which provided the swing vote even though no other justice joined its reasoning fully, but which was adopted 25 years later by a pro-affirmative-action majority in *Grutter*.

   a. **Opinion by Justice Powell:**   Justice Powell wrote that a university should be permitted to *take into account* an applicant's membership in a racial minority as part of the admissions process. But he believed that a racial *"quota"* system, i.e., the explicit reservation of places which could only be filled by minorities, was *unconstitutional*.

      i. **Powell rationale:**   Justice Powell believed that *any racial or ethnic classification*, regardless of the class against which it is directed or the reason for it, must be subjected to *strict scrutiny*. Powell concluded that (1) the need to obtain "the *educational benefits* that flow from an *ethnically-diverse* student body" was a compelling state interest; but (2) it was *not necessary* (and therefore not permissible) to use a *quota* scheme, where certain seats were reserved *exclusively* for members of particular races; instead, this goal could be pursued by considering an applicant's minority status as merely *one factor* in the admissions process (the so-called "Harvard plan").

         (1) **Individual treatment:**   Powell stressed that a Harvard-type "weigh all factors" scheme, unlike the Davis quota scheme, "treats each applicant *as an individual* in the admissions process." As we'll see, this key distinction by Powell — contrasting individualized assessment of each applicant (constitutionally acceptable) with the reservation of particular "slots" for minorities (unacceptable) — was later adopted by a *majority* of the Court, in *Grutter v. Bollinger, infra*, and continued in the two *Fisher* opinions, also *infra*.

2. *Grutter* **and** *Gratz* **together:**   Twenty-five years after *Bakke*, a majority of the Court, in *Grutter* and *Gratz,* effectively *adopted Powell's approach in Bakke,* by holding that:

   [a] Race-conscious admissions measures will *receive strict scrutiny*, and thus must be

narrowly-tailored to achieve a compelling objective;

[b] The pursuit of *diversity in the student body* can be a *compelling objective*;

[c] A *one-student-at-a-time evaluation* in which the student's race is merely one factor among various ones considered is *sufficiently narrowly-tailored*; but

[d] Mechanical approaches resembling *quotas*, such as automatically awarding an applicant a fixed number of *points* towards admission based on his race, are *not narrowly-tailored* and therefore violate equal protection.

We consider *Grutter* and *Gratz* in sequence, followed by the two *Fisher* opinions.

3. ***Grutter*:** In *Grutter*, the Court **upheld** by a 5-4 vote the University of Michigan Law School's admission process, in which the school pursued the objective of diversity by subjectively adding race into the mix when a student's entire application was considered. Justice O'Connor wrote the Court's opinion, in which she was joined by Justices Stevens, Souter, Ginsburg and Breyer.

   a. Facts: The Law School was (and is) an elite, highly-selective one, which at the time in question received more than 3500 applications each year for a class of around 350 students. The Law School's admissions policy required admissions officials to *read each applicant's entire file.* Admission was based upon undergraduate grades, LSAT scores, and a number of "soft" variables (e.g., enthusiasm of recommenders, quality of the undergraduate institution, difficulty of undergraduate courses taken, etc.). One of the soft variables was the extent to which the applicant's presence would *contribute to "diversity"* at the school. More precisely, the Law School sought to increase "*racial* and *ethnic* diversity with special reference to the inclusion of students from groups which have been *historically discriminated against*, like *African-Americans*, *Hispanics* and *Native Americans*, who without this commitment *might not be represented in our student body in meaningful numbers.*"

   i. "Critical mass": The Law School defended its race-conscious admissions policy principally on the grounds that the school was seeking to enroll a "*'critical mass'* of [underrepresented] minority students." The school's officials testified that "critical mass" meant *"meaningful representation,"* which in turn meant "a number that encourages underrepresented minority students to *participate* in the classroom and *not feel isolated.*"

   ii. Numbers: The school *denied* that there was *any particular number*, percentage or range of numbers or percentages that constituted critical mass. During the years in question, the percentage of students in each class that were members of the three favored groups (black, Hispanic and Native American) varied from 13.5% to 20.1%. The Law School denied that this was a quota, but did acknowledge that consideration of race *significantly increased the numbers of minorities* who were admitted and attended.

   b. Plaintiff's argument: P was a white Michigan resident who unsuccessfully applied to the Law School. Her undergraduate GPA and her LSAT scores were, she claimed, higher than those of many minority applicants who were accepted. Consequently, she alleged, the Law School's use of race as what P termed a "predominant" factor constituted a denial of equal protection to her.

c. O'Connor's majority opinion: Justice O'Connor's opinion *applied strict scrutiny* to the Law School's consideration of race as an admissions factor, but concluded that the school's method was *sufficiently narrowly tailored* to achieve the compelling interest in maintaining diversity.

    i. Adoption of Powell *Bakke* opinion: O'Connor's opinion for Court *"endorse[s]* Justice Powell's view [in *Bakke*] that *student body diversity is a compelling state interest* that can *justify the use of race* in university admissions."

    ii. Narrowly-tailored: O'Connor next turned to the issue of whether the particular race-conscious methods adopted by the Law School were *sufficiently narrowly-tailored* to the achievement of the compellingly-important objective of obtaining diversity in the student body.

        (1) No quotas: O'Connor agreed with Powell's position in *Bakke* that a race-conscious program *cannot use a quota system,* "a program in which a certain *fixed number or proportion of opportunities* are 'reserved exclusively* for certain minority groups'."

        (2) "Holistic" review rather than "quota": The Law School's approach was *not* a forbidden quota, O'Connor said. Rather, the Law School "engages in a *highly individualized, holistic review* of each applicant's file, giving serious consideration to *all the ways* an applicant might contribute to a diverse educational environment." The school did *not* give any *"mechanical, predetermined diversity 'bonuses'* based on race or ethnicity" (as the Court found that the undergraduate admissions scheme at Michigan did, in the companion case of *Gratz, infra*).

        (3) Race-neutral alternatives: Finally, O'Connor considered whether the Law School's approach failed to be narrowly tailored because of the availability of *race-neutral alternatives* for achieving the desired diversity. O'Connor agreed that narrow tailoring "require[s] serious, good faith *consideration* of *workable* race-neutral alternatives that will achieve the diversity the university seeks." But she asserted that "narrow tailoring *does not require exhaustion of every conceivable race-neutral alternative,"* only those alternatives that would *serve the governmental interest "about as well."*

        For instance, O'Connor said, the type of *"percentage plan"* advocated by the George H.W. Bush administration — under which all students above a certain class-rank threshold in every school in the state would be guaranteed admission[6] — would not work for graduate and professional schools, and would probably preclude individualized assessments of each student's contribution to other, non-racial, types of diversity.

    iii. "Sunset" after 25 years: But O'Connor cautioned that race-conscious admissions policies "must be *limited in time*." She noted that it had been 25 years since

---

6. We'll see that this sort of race-blind percentage plan, when used for undergraduate admissions, got the implicit approval of most members of the Court in the later 2013 decision in *Fisher v. Univ. of Texas* (*"Fisher I"*), *infra*, p. 287.

Justice Powell's opinion in *Bakke*, and she wrote that "We expect that *25 years from now*, the use of racial preferences will *no longer be necessary*[.]"

d. **Dissents:** The four dissenters — Chief Justice Rehnquist and Justices Kennedy, Scalia and Thomas — each produced a separate dissent. We'll mention only the Rehnquist and Kennedy dissents here.

    i. **Rehnquist's dissent:** The principal dissent was by Chief Justice Rehnquist, in which the other three dissenters also joined. Rehnquist seemed not to object to the majority's belief that a diverse student body could be a compelling governmental objective. But he very much disputed the majority's conclusion that the Law School's approach was a narrowly-tailored method of achieving that objective. Instead, he believed, the Law School's pursuit of "critical mass" was a *"veil,"* which when stripped revealed "a *naked effort to achieve racial balancing.*"

    ii. **Kennedy's dissent:** Like Chief Justice Rehnquist, Justice Kennedy believed that the majority was not in fact applying strict scrutiny. He accused the majority of giving only a "perfunctory" review of the Law School's policy, which he characterized as using critical mass as a "delusion ... to mask its attempt to *make race an automatic factor* in most instances and to achieve *numerical goals indistinguishable from quotas.*"

4. **Gratz:** The same day as the Court decided *Grutter*, it decided *Gratz*, which involved affirmative-action admissions policies at the University of Michigan's main *undergraduate* College in Ann Arbor.

a. **Facts:** There were several different affirmative-action schemes, used by the College in different years, at issue in *Gratz*. For procedural reasons, most of the Supreme Court's eventual analysis concerned the school's policy after 1998. Under that policy, the school used a "selection index," in which *points were awarded* for various characteristics, up to a maximum of 150 points. A minimum of 100 points was needed for admission. An applicant was entitled to an *automatic 20 points* for membership in an *underrepresented racial or ethnic minority group* (the same three groups — blacks, Hispanics and Native Americans — as in the Law School plan at issue in *Grutter*). The significance of these extra 20 points was great: the University conceded that "the effect of automatically awarding 20 points is that *virtually every qualified underrepresented minority applicant is admitted.*"

b. **Rehnquist's majority opinion:** Chief Justice Rehnquist's majority opinion (joined by O'Connor, Scalia, Kennedy and Thomas) concluded that this *point system* was *unconstitutional*, in that it was *not narrowly tailored* to achieve the school's interest in educational diversity.[7] Because Justice Breyer concurred in the result, the vote was 6-3 to strike the point system.

    i. **Does not conform to Powell's opinion:** Rehnquist believed that the College's point system did *not* meet the requirements of Justice Powell's *Bakke* opinion, under which race could be deemed a "plus," but was not to be "decisive." The College's point system was not at all the kind of system that Powell had in mind, Rehnquist said. For instance, the automatic award of 20 points had the effect of

---

7. The majority also rejected a "standing" argument advanced by the dissenters.

making race decisive "for virtually every minimally qualified underrepresented minority applicant."

c. **O'Connor's concurrence:** Justice O'Connor wrote a concurrence, in which Justices Thomas and Breyer joined. Since O'Connor wrote the majority opinion in *Grutter* upholding the Law School's affirmative action plan, her *Gratz* concurrence is important in that it spells out how and why she thought the College's unacceptable plan differed from the Law School's acceptable one.

　　i. **Predetermined points:** O'Connor principally objected to the fact that *far fewer points* were available for diversity characteristics other than the race-oriented ones, and to the fact that the point values were completely *hard-wired* at the outset. Thus she pointed out that diversity contributions like "leadership," "personal achievement" and geographic diversity were capped at much lower levels than membership in an underrepresented race (e.g., 5 points maximum for leadership, compared with the 20 automatic points for being black or Hispanic). Furthermore, "by setting up *automatic, predetermined point allocations*" for all of the diversity characteristics, the system "ensures that the diversity contributions of applicants *cannot be individually assessed*." This was in "sharp contrast" to the Law School's plan, under which admissions officers were able to "make *nuanced judgments* with respect to the contributions each applicant is likely to make to diversity of the incoming class."

d. **Dissent:** Three justices — Stevens, Souter and Ginsburg — dissented in *Gratz*.

　　i. **Ginsburg:** One of these dissents was by Justice Ginsburg (joined by Souter and in part by Breyer).

　　　　(1) **Legacy of discrimination:** Ginsburg emphasized that "the effects of centuries-old law-sanctioned inequality remain painfully evident in our communities and schools." Consequently, she thought, "government decision makers may properly distinguish between policies of *exclusion* and *inclusion*. ... Actions designed to burden groups long denied full citizenship stature are not sensibly ranked with measures taken to hasten the day when entrenched discrimination and its after effects have been extirpated."

5. **"No workable race-neutral alternatives" (*Fisher I* and *II*):** For 10 years after *Grutter* and *Gratz*, the Supreme Court did not hear any university preferential-admissions cases. Then, over the space of three years it issued two opinions in a single case involving the University of Texas' race-conscious undergraduate admissions scheme, one in 2013 and the other in 2016. We'll call these "*Fisher I*" and "*Fisher II*." Two main principles emerged from the two opinions:

[1] A race-conscious university admissions system must *satisfy strict scrutiny*, including a demonstration that *no workable race-neutral admissions methods are available* to satisfy the university's goal of "educational diversity"; but ....

[2] A well-constructed race-conscious plan can *survive* that strict scrutiny, as shown by the Court's approval of the Texas plan in *Fisher II*.

In Par. 6, we'll review *Fisher I*, and in Par. 7, *Fisher II*.

6. ***Fisher I* requires absence of workable race-neutral alternatives:** In 2013, the Court decided ***Fisher v. Univ. of Texas at Austin (Fisher I)***, 133 U.S. 2411 (2013), a 7-1 decision that surprised many for its near-unanimity. *Fisher I* did not explicitly make new law, but it emphasized that the Court will take seriously the principle that race-conscious admissions are permissible only if ***no workable race-neutral alternatives are available.***

a. **Overall significance of case:** The Court indicated that the ***tightness of the link*** between race-conscious admissions and the goal of greater educational diversity must be ***much more closely scrutinized*** than had previously seemed to be the case. As the Court put it in *Fisher*, a court reviewing a challenged race-conscious admissions scheme "must ultimately be satisfied that ***no workable race-neutral alternatives*** would produce the ***educational benefits of diversity.***" And on this issue of availability of workable race-neutral alternatives, the Court said that ***no deference*** is to be given to the university's own judgment or expertise.

b. **The Texas admissions system:** The University of Texas at Austin used an unusual two-tier method for admitting undergraduates. The system evolved from a series of court decisions and actions by the Texas Legislature, which we won't go into here. But the basic structure worked like this:

[1] **The "Top Ten" component:** Under a ***"Top Ten Percent Plan"*** enacted by the Texas legislature, any student attending a public high school in Texas who finished in the ***top 10% of her high school class*** was ***guaranteed admission*** to any public Texas university (including U. Texas at Austin), assuming that the high school met certain academic standards.[8] About 75% of admitted freshman were admitted under this Top Ten Percent Plan,[9] without any consideration of the student's race (or, indeed, of any other individual attribute of the student). Because of the ***high degree of racial segregation*** from one high school to the next in Texas, use of the Top Ten Percent Plan increased the percentage of black and Hispanic students at Texas/Austin beyond what it had previously been.

[2] **The "holistic" race-conscious method:** Whatever slots remained open after the admission of applicants who qualified under the Top Ten Percent rule were then filled by the best-scoring applicants to emerge from a process of ***"holistic review,"*** in which ***race was expressly considered,*** but was just one factor among many. This "race as one factor" method was designed to comply with *Grutter, supra.* At a point before Ms. Fisher applied, the University added race-consciousness to its pre-existing holistic review method; it did so for the express purpose of increasing still further the percentages of black and Hispanic students — traditionally underrepresented throughout the Texas public university system — beyond what

---

8. Some of the details of this plan are not fully disclosed in the Supreme Court's various opinions in *Fisher*; I've taken some details from the Fifth Circuit opinion that approved the University's plan as the plan was applied to the plaintiff, Ms. Fisher.

9. It's not clear from either the Supreme Court or the Fifth Circuit opinions what percentage of the entering class was filled by Top Ten Percent members in the year in which Ms. Fisher applied. But in the years just before the Supreme Court's decision, by order of the legislature 75% of slots were generally reserved for Top Ten Percent applicants, with the remainder reserved for the next-tier "holistic method" described in the following paragraph.

resulted from use of the Top Ten Percent rule.

    (1) Smaller classes and "critical mass": The University decided to add race consideration to the holistic method in large part because the school's analysis of individual classes showed that *smaller classes* — those containing between *five and 24 students* — rarely contained a *"critical mass"* of black and Hispanic students. (Recall that in *Grutter*, the University of Michigan Law School successfully argued that its race-conscious holistic system helped achieve a "critical mass" of minority students. See *supra*, p. 283.)

c. **P's application and suit:** The plaintiff, Abigail Fisher, who is white, narrowly missed graduating in the top 10% of her high school class, making her ineligible for admission under the Top Ten Percent rule. Her score under the holistic method was also not high enough to give her a seat. She brought a federal suit against the University, claiming that the University's use of race in the holistic method prevented her from gaining admission, and violated her equal protection rights.[10]

d. **Lower courts' decision:** The District Court granted summary judgment in favor of the University, and the Fifth Circuit affirmed. The Fifth Circuit reasoned that *Grutter* required the court to give *substantial deference* to the University, both as to the University's conclusion that educational diversity was a compelling governmental interest, *and* as to the University's determination that the particular admissions plan chosen by the University was narrowly tailored to achieve this interest.

e. **Kennedy's majority opinion, generally:** The Supreme Court *reversed* the Fifth Circuit. Justice Kennedy's opinion was joined by six of the seven other members who heard the case — only Justice Ginsburg dissented. (Justice Kagan recused herself, presumably because she had worked on the case while serving as the Obama administration's solicitor general.)

f. **Diversity as a compelling interest:** Kennedy first dealt with the *"compelling objective"* side of the strict-scrutiny equation. Kennedy quoted, approvingly, *Grutter*'s conclusion that "obtaining the *educational benefits of student body diversity is a compelling state interest* that can *justify the use of race* in university admissions."

g. **Narrowly-tailored means-end fit:** But the heart of Kennedy's opinion — and his rationale for overturning the courts below — dealt with the other half of the strict-scrutiny equation, the *tightness of the fit between the means and the end*. "The University must prove," he said, that *"the means* chosen by [it] to attain diversity are *narrowly tailored to that goal."*

    i. **No deference:** As to whether the University had borne its burden of proving the requisite narrow tailoring, he said, "the *University receives no deference*" from the court. The court, not the University, is to determine whether the particular admissions scheme chosen is *"specifically and narrowly framed"* to achieve the sought-after diversity. True, the court "can take *account of a university's experience and expertise* in adopting or rejecting certain admissions processes." But the

---

10. After being denied admission by Texas, P entered Louisiana State University, from which she had graduated by the time the Supreme Court decided her case.

burden of proof on means-end fit must ***remain at all times on the University***, he said.

ii. **Exhaustion of race-neutral alternatives:** Next, Kennedy described how the court was to make the determination of whether race-consciousness is "necessary" for diversity. He conceded that the required narrow tailoring "does ***not require exhaustion of every conceivable race-neutral alternative***." But, he continued, strict scrutiny "does require a court to ***examine with care***, and ***not defer to***, a university's '***serious, good faith consideration of workable race-neutral alternatives***.'"

h. **Kennedy's summary:** Finally, Kennedy gave a summary of what universities would have to do to successfully defend their race-conscious admissions plans:

> "In order for judicial review to be meaningful, a university must make a showing that its plan is ***narrowly tailored*** to achieve the ***only interest*** that this Court has approved in this context: the benefits of a ***student body diversity*** that 'encompasses a . . . ***broa[d] array of qualifications and characteristics*** of which ***racial or ethnic origin is but a single though important element***' " (citing Powell's *Bakke* opinion).

i. **Ginsburg's dissent:** The only ***dissenter*** in *Fisher I* was Justice Ginsburg. She argued that the lower Texas courts had correctly applied *Grutter*, and had correctly concluded that Texas's holistic race-conscious plan was narrowly tailored to achieve educational diversity, as *Grutter* required.

i. **"Neutral alternatives" are not unconscious:** Ginsburg rejected the contention that supposedly "race neutral" alternatives were available to Texas, and should be used to the exclusion of any race-conscious method. In particular, she said, the Top Ten Percent rule was in reality not ***race neutral at all***; the Texas legislature had adopted this percentage-based plan in explicit reliance on Texas' pattern of "***racially segregated neighborhoods and schools***[.]" She concluded that "[i]t is ***race consciousness***, not blindness to race," that "***drives such plans.***"

ii. **Explicit race-consciousness is better:** Since *Grutter* had allowed explicit consideration of race, she said, an admittedly-race-conscious plan like Texas' holistic method was superior to percentage-type systems: approaches to educational diversity "that ***candidly disclose*** their consideration of race [are] preferable to those that ***conceal it***."

7. **University of Texas' position upheld on remand (*Fisher II*):** As part of *Fisher I*, the Supreme Court ***remanded*** the case to the Fifth Circuit, with instructions that that court reconsider the case in light of the principles set out in *Fisher I*. As we'll see, the Fifth Circuit then ***upheld*** the constitutionality of the University of Texas' affirmative action plan, and the Supreme Court ultimately (in "*Fisher II*") ***affirmed*** that ruling. So as the result of *Fisher I* and *II* taken together, UT's affirmative action plan was decisively found to be ***constitutional***.

a. **Result in Fifth Circuit:** On remand following *Fisher I*, a three-judge panel of the Fifth Circuit concluded that the University's affirmative action plan satisfied the Supreme Court's guidelines for how strict scrutiny should be applied. See *Fisher v. Univ. of Texas at Austin*, 758 F.3d 633 (2014). In a 2-1 decision, a majority of the panel found that Texas' "holistic" plan (the race-conscious part that was engrafted onto the Top Ten Percent Plan) was indeed ***narrowly-tailored*** to achieve the compelling objective of attaining a critical mass of educational diversity.

b.   Affirmed by Supreme Court: By a 4-3 vote,[11] the Supreme Court ***affirmed*** the Fifth Circuit's conclusion that the Texas plan ***survived*** the required strict scrutiny and was therefore not a violation of Ms. Fisher's equal protection rights. See ***Fisher v. Univ. of Texas***, 136 S.Ct. 2198 (2016) (***"Fisher II"***).

The majority opinion was written by Justice Kennedy. Kennedy's conclusion that the UT plan was constitutional represented a major evolution of his views on affirmative action in education — his *Fisher II* opinion marked the ***first time he had ever voted to uphold a race-conscious affirmative action plan*** in any context.

i.   Framing of issue: In *Fisher II* (as in *Fisher I*), the sole issue was whether the race-conscious holistic review part of the UT admissions program (see *supra*, p. 288) was constitutional. In other words, the constitutionality of the ***Top Ten Percent Plan*** (p. 287) — under which by order of the Texas Legislature three-quarters of the admission slots were reserved for applicants who ranked in the top 10% of their high school class — was ***not at issue*** in *Fisher II*.

ii.   Race as "factor of a factor of a factor": Kennedy noted that the only time in which the holistic review procedure considered each applicant's race was ***early in the process***, as part of the calculation of a multi-factor "PAI/AI score" that also included non-racial considerations such as leadership potential, extracurricular activities, socioeconomic status of the applicant and her high school, etc. Therefore, Kennedy said, race was only a "***'factor of a factor of a factor'*** in the holistic-review calculus."

iii.   Arguments by Ms. Fisher rejected: Kennedy then turned to various arguments made by Ms. Fisher in support of her claim that the holistic-review plan failed to satisfy strict scrutiny. He rejected each of these contentions. We consider two of these arguments.

(1)   Argument: "Top Ten Percent Plan" created critical mass: Ms. Fisher argued that if obtaining critical mass was the compelling objective the University was pursuing, the race-conscious holistic-review process ***was not a necessary means of achieving*** that compelling objective, because the University had ***already achieved*** critical mass via its earlier use of the ***Top Ten Percent Plan*** combined with UT's original ***non-race-conscious*** version of holistic review.

As to this argument, Kennedy conceded that a university "bears a ***heavy burden*** in showing that it had not obtained the educational benefits of diversity ***before*** it turned to a race-conscious plan." But, he said, UT had successfully ***borne*** that burden here. Between 1996 and 2003, for instance, the percentage of African-American students enrolled remained flat at 4.1%, a ***"stagnation"*** indicating that UT's pre-race-conscious methods had ***not been adequate*** to

---

11. Justice Scalia died in 2016, shortly before the oral arguments in *Fisher II*, and had not been replaced by the time *Fisher II* was decided. Justice Kagan recused herself because, as U.S. Solicitor General before joining the Court, she had submitted a brief in *Fisher I* in support of UT.

enroll an adequate number of "students who can offer underrepresented perspectives."

(2) Other race-neutral methods available: Then, Fisher made perhaps her most promising argument: that race-conscious methods were not a *"necessary"* means of achieving the University's compelling interest in educational diversity because there were *"numerous other available race-neutral means"* of achieving that same interest. Most specifically, she suggested that the University could have selected a *larger percentage* — perhaps even *all* — of its student body through the *Top Ten Percent Plan.*

Kennedy took seriously this argument that expansion of the Top Ten Percent Plan was an available alternative. But he agreed with the contention made by Justice Ginsburg in her dissent in *Fisher I*, that plans like the Top Ten Percent Plan may be *facially* neutral but are adopted for the purpose of boosting minority enrollment, work only because they rely on *"racially segregated neighborhoods and schools,"* and are *driven by "race consciousness, not blindness to race*[.]"

Furthermore, he said, "privileging one characteristic above all others" (in this case, class rank) *"does not lead to a diverse student body."* And such a policy would create *"perverse incentives for applicants"*; for instance, as Justice Ginsburg had argued back in her 2003 dissent in *Gratz* (see *supra*, p. 286), such plans "encourage parents to *keep their children in low-performing segregated schools*, and discourage students from *taking challenging classes* that might lower their grade point averages." Therefore, Kennedy said, "an effective admissions policy cannot prescribe, realistically, the exclusive use of a percentage plan."

iv. **Deference to universities:** In a final passage, Kennedy seemed to say that when universities are deciding what types of diversity they wish to encourage, the schools are *entitled to greater deference* than might have been expected from the tone of *Fisher I*. Here in *Fisher II*, Kennedy wrote that "[a] university is in large part *defined by those intangible 'qualities which are incapable of objective measurement* but which make for greatness.'" Therefore, he continued, *"Considerable deference is owed* to a university in *defining those intangible characteristics, like student body diversity,* that are *central to its identity and educational mission."*

(1) Caution: But in that same final passage, Kennedy warned that universities like UT *would not get a free pass* from the courts in deciding how and when to use race-conscious methods to pursue educational diversity. A university like UT, he said, which "now has at its disposal *valuable data* about the manner in which different approaches to admissions may foster diversity or instead dilute it," must "continue to *use this data to scrutinize the fairness* of its admissions program."

v. **Dissent:** The main *dissent* in *Fisher II* was by Justice Alito (in which Roberts and Thomas joined). That dissent, at 51 pages, was more than twice as long as the majority opinion.

(1) "Turns affirmative action on its head": Alito was especially critical of UT's argument that race-conscious methods were needed because the ***Top Ten Percent Plan*** (which Alito viewed as race-neutral) was ***not an adequate method*** of achieving the university's goal of educational diversity. He pointed out that in *Fisher I*, UT had argued in a brief that a race-conscious component of its admissions plan was needed in order to admit "the African-American or Hispanic child of ***successful professionals*** in Dallas." Alito described UT's refusal to rely on the Top Ten Percent Plan exclusively as an ***attempt to favor affluent minorities*** over "students from poor families who attend schools in which the student body is predominantly African-American or Hispanic."[12] And, he said, that refusal ***"turns affirmative action on its head,"*** because "[a]ffirmative-action programs were ***created to help disadvantaged students."***

(2) Undue deference to University: Alito also criticized the *Fisher II* majority's "uncritical deference to UT's self-serving claims" that the university had narrowly tailored its race-conscious methods to its goals. That deference "blatantly contradicts" the Court's statement in *Fisher I* that ***"it is for the courts, not for university administrators***, to ensure that an admissions process is ***narrowly tailored."*** Here UT had formulated its goals in various "vague" ways — most generally as "the educational benefits of diversity," and more specifically as "demographic parity, classroom diversity, intraracial diversity, and avoiding racial isolation." But these vaguely-articulated goals were ***"so broad and imprecise"*** that it would be impossible for a court to ***determine whether the race-conscious means being used were narrowly-tailored to achieve them.***

vi. **Effect of changes in Court's membership:** The Court has undergone major change since *Fisher II* was decided. Two years after supplying the winning vote for, and writing, the majority opinion in *Fisher II*, Justice Kennedy retired and was succeeded by the more-conservative Justice Kavanaugh. Then, Justice Barrett, a Trump appointee, replaced Justice Ginsburg following the latter's death. Given the resulting probable rightward-shift on the Court, it seems likely that going forward a majority will look much less favorably on the constitutionality of race-based affirmative action programs like the UT program approved in *Fisher II*.

8. **Present status of race-conscious university-admissions policies:** So what, then, do the four university affirmative-action cases, *Grutter, Gratz, Fisher I* and *Fisher II,* establish?

a. **Strict scrutiny theoretically always applicable:** If any part of the admissions process takes conscious consideration of any applicant's race, it remains the case that a reviewing court ***must apply strict scrutiny*** to the process. That is, the university will bear the burden of showing affirmatively ***both*** that:

[1] the university is seeking to achieve a ***"compelling"*** (not just "important") objective; and

---

12. Alito pointed out that UT later abandoned this "child of professionals" argument: the University asserted in *Fisher II* that Ms. Fisher's claim that UT wanted to favor "affluent minorities" was "a fabrication." But, Alito said, UT really *had* made the argument before renouncing it, and the Fifth Circuit panel had "bought a version of that claim."

[2] the race-conscious methods that the university has chosen are ***narrowly-tailored*** to achieve that objective. That is, the selected means must be ***"necessary"*** to achieve the objective, in the sense that no non-race-conscious methods will achieve the objective as well or even almost as well.

See *Fisher II.*

b. **"Educational diversity" is the only compelling objective:** In the university admissions context, the ***only*** governmental objective that has ever been recognized by the Supreme Court as "compelling" (and thus as sufficient to survive strict scrutiny) is the interest in ***"educational diversity."***

   i. **Not compelling to match state demography:** For instance, an interest in having the racial or ethnic breakdown of the student body ***resemble the demography*** of, say, the state in which the university is located, is ***not*** by itself a compelling objective.[13]

   ii. **Educational benefits that flow from diversity:** When the Court says it accepts as compelling the objective of "educational diversity," that phrase is shorthand to mean ***"the educational benefits that flow from student body diversity."*** *Fisher II.* More specifically, the Court has recognized that student body diversity leads to various specific educational benefits: it ***"promotes cross-racial understanding***, helps to ***break down racial stereotypes***, and enables students to ***better understand persons of different races.*** " (*Fisher II*, quoting *Grutter.*)

   (1) "Critical mass": The Court has never defined how much, or what type of, student body diversity is required to deliver these educational benefits from diversity. But the Court *has* agreed that achievement of a ***"critical mass"*** of students from each of various university-designated otherwise-under-represented minorities ***is*** part of what is needed for these educational benefits to accrue. (*Fisher II.*)

c. **Core principle of affirmative action preserved:** Even though race-conscious admissions procedures will be strictly scrutinized, that strict scrutiny will ***not*** necessarily prove ***fatal***. The core idea behind affirmative action in higher education — to take account of applicants' race in an effort to ensure educational diversity — has ***survived*** the quartet of cases ending in *Fisher II*. Synthesizing these four cases, a race-conscious scheme is ***likely to be upheld*** as long as the university can make two main showings:

[1] Critical mass: that the university is pursuing the educational benefits of student body diversity (and student body diversity can be defined to include the achievement of a ***"critical mass"*** of students from each of multiple racial minorities at the individual course-by-course level); and

[2] No acceptable alternatives: that there exist ***no "workable" non-race-conscious methods*** capable of achieving these educational benefits of diversity ***as well (or almost as well)*** as race-conscious methods. And in measuring whether non-race-

---

13. See, e.g., *Fisher II*: "[T]he compelling interest that justifies consideration of race in college admissions is ***not an interest in enrolling a certain number of minority students.***"

conscious methods will achieve the same benefits from diversity as-well-or-almost-as-well, the university's interest in having an ***academically-excellent*** student body counts significantly (so that a race-neutral method that produces educational diversity, but only by means of a significant lowering of academic excellence, is not achieving the diversity benefits "almost as well").

Note: But see *supra*, p. 292, for the possible effects of the post-*Fisher-II* changes to the composition of the Court.

    d. **Acceptable methods:** When the Court is deciding whether the particular race-conscious methods adopted by a university are sufficiently narrowly tailored to the achievement of the educational benefits from diversity, ***"quota"*** systems are ***bad***, and ***"holistic"*** methods (i.e., ones that involve ***"individualized" consideration of each student***) are good.

        i. **Can't use points or quotas:** Thus any system in which a certain ***pre-defined number of "points"*** is ***automatically given*** to any student who belongs to a particular minority racial or ethnic group, in a way that gives the recipients a large admissions advantage, will likely be struck down as a ***forbidden quota system***. Such a mechanical quota system was struck down in *Gratz*, and nothing post-*Gratz* changes the anti-quota principle.

        ii. **Individualized consideration of multiple factors:** By contrast, the Court is far more likely to find the requisite narrow tailoring if the race-conscious aspect of admissions is part of a ***"holistic" system*** in which each applicant is given ***individual consideration*** as to ***various*** intangible traits, ***not just race or ethnicity.***

    e. **Deference to university's fact-finding and judgment:** A key issue is the ***degree of deference*** that the reviewing court may or must give to the fact-finding and judgments the university made in the course of formulating its race-conscious plan. The two *Fisher* cases suggest that the university is entitled to ***much greater deference*** when it is (1) deciding ***what types of educational diversity*** it wishes to pursue (and why) than when it is (2) selecting particular race-conscious ***methods*** (where the issue is whether the selected methods are narrowly tailored to achieving the identified diversity).

F. **Admissions to public secondary schools by race-conscious pupil-assignments (the *Parents Involved* case):** To what extent may a ***public school system*** make ***race-conscious pupil-assignment decisions*** in order to combat racial imbalances in the district's schools? As a result of a 2007 decision that was the Roberts Court's first consideration of affirmative action, ***no individual student's race may be considered in making that student's school assignment.*** The case, ***Parents Involved in Community Schools v. Seattle School District No. 1***, 552 U.S. 701 (2007), was a bitter 5-4 split, with Justice Kennedy siding with the four conservative members of the Court in striking down the race-conscious school-assignment plans from Seattle and Louisville, Kentucky at issue there. The case marks an important extension of the Court's recent tendency to strictly scrutinize, and usually invalidate, race-conscious affirmative action decisions by governments.

    1. **The assignment plans:** Both Seattle's and Louisville's race-conscious pupil-assignment plans were essentially ***voluntary*** as opposed to court-ordered. Seattle had never been under court order to desegregate its schools. Louisville had once been under such a court order, but prior to the use of the plan at issue court supervision had ceased because the district had been found to have eradicated the vestiges of official segregation. Both districts enacted plans that *occasionally took account of race,* in an effort to prevent individual schools from becoming *racially isolated*.

a. **Seattle plan:** Under the Seattle plan, *race served as a "tiebreaker"* for the assignment of incoming ninth graders to certain of the city's high schools. Ninth graders were asked to state their preferences; if a school was "oversubscribed" (more students listed it as their first choice than there were slots), a series of tiebreakers was used. The first tiebreaker gave a preference to students with a sibling already enrolled at the school.

The next tiebreaker was what the litigation was about. In the district as a whole, 41% of students were white, and 59% "nonwhite" (a designation that apparently included Asian Americans, African Americans and Latinos). But due to housing patterns, the north end of the city was predominantly white and the south end predominantly non-white. If the school in question was not within 10 points of the district-wide white/nonwhite ratio, the tiebreaker went in favor of *an applicant whose race would bring the school into better balance.* So, for instance, if a school was more than 51% white (i.e., more than 10 percentage points above the 41% district-wide percentage of whites), the tiebreaker would go in favor of a black applicant over a white applicant. Out of a total of about 20,000 high school students in a typical year, about 300 were affected by the race-based tiebreaker (see the dissent of Justice Breyer). The plaintiff was a nonprofit corporation consisting of parents of students who had been or might be denied admission to their first-choice high school on account of the student's race.

b. **The Louisville plan:** In Louisville, a federal court dissolved a prior desegregation order in 2000, finding that the system had been desegregated to the extent feasible. The following year, the school district continued to use the pupil-assignment rules at issue (which had been put into effect during the desegregation-order years), in an attempt to prevent individual schools from becoming racially isolated due to housing patterns. About 34% of the district students were black; most of the remaining 66% were white. The plan allowed students to transfer from their initially-assigned school to another, but a transfer was not allowed if the transferee school had a black enrollment of less than 15% or more than 50% and the *transfer would worsen the imbalance.* The plaintiff was an individual, Crystal Meredith, who sought to transfer her kindergärtner son Joshua from an assigned school 10 miles from his house to a school that was only 1 mile from his house; he was denied the transfer on the grounds that the transferee school he selected was outside the 15-50% racial guidelines, and his presence would worsen the imbalance.

2. **Both plans ruled invalid:** The court ruled that both the Seattle plan and the Louisville plan *violated the equal protection clause by considering race.* Four members of the Court, led by Chief Justice Roberts, concluded that *any* use of race in the context of school assignments would be unconstitutional. (I refer to this bloc as the *"plurality."*) Another four-member bloc, led by Justice Breyer's dissent, asserted that both plans were constitutional. The case therefore turned on *Justice Kennedy's concurrence*; he concluded that the taking into account of racial considerations would *not always* be unconstitutional in the school-assignment context, but that the particular plans here — which involved *categorizing each student by race* and then making some students' assignments depend on that race — was an unconstitutional use of race.

3. The Roberts plurality opinion: Chief Justice Roberts' plurality opinion was joined in full by Justices Scalia, Thomas and Alito. He concluded that both the Seattle and Louisville plans failed the requisite strict scrutiny on two grounds: first, the districts were ***not pursuing a compelling governmental interest***, and second, the race-conscious ***means*** chosen by the districts were ***not narrowly tailored to meet*** whatever governmental interests they were designed to pursue.

a. Strict scrutiny required: Roberts began by summarizing the standard that the Court's emerging conservative majority had imposed for race-conscious affirmative action plans in cases like *Gratz* (*supra*, p. 285) and *Adarand* (*infra*, p. 306): "When the government distributes burdens or benefits on the basis of ***individual racial classifications***, that action is ***reviewed under strict scrutiny***. ... In order to satisfy this searching standard of review, the school districts must demonstrate that the use of individual racial classifications in the assignment plans here under review is 'narrowly tailored' to achieve a 'compelling' government interest."

b. No compelling interest being pursued: Roberts began by examining the issue of what governmental interests being pursued by the two cities could be considered "compelling."   There were only two governmental interests, Roberts said, that the Court had recognized in prior school cases as being "compelling": ***"remedying the effects of past intentional discrimination"*** and "the interest in ***diversity in higher education"*** recognized in *Grutter* (*supra*. p. 283).

i. Past intentional discrimination: Roberts rapidly dismissed the first of these objectives from the present cases: the Seattle school system had never been shown to be segregated by law and had never been under a court-ordered desegregation decree; and the Louisville system had been found to have eradicated all vestiges of official segregation prior to the use of the race conscious plan under analysis here. So neither city could justify its plan based on combating the effects of past intentional discrimination.

ii. Educational diversity: Roberts spent far more time explaining why he believed that neither plan could be found to have been enacted in support of the second objective, the interest in ***diversity***. The objective upheld in *Grutter* was ***not "focused on race alone,"*** he said, but was rather the interest in "***all factors*** that may contribute to student body diversity," including such factors as a student's having lived or traveled abroad, fluency in several languages, overcoming of personal adversity, community service, and the like. Here, by contrast, "When race comes into play, it is decisive by itself. It is ***not simply one factor*** weighed with others in reaching a decision, as in *Grutter*; it is the factor."

(1) White / nonwhite distinction: Even worse, Roberts said, both plans manifested only a ***"limited notion of diversity,"*** viewing race exclusively in white/nonwhite terms (Seattle) or black/other terms (Louisville). For instance, under the Seattle plan, a school with 50% Asian-American students and 50% white would be considered "balanced" but one that was 30% Asian-American, 25% African-American, 25% Latino and 20% white would not. Roberts could not see how this classification scheme could be said to be in pursuit of an enrollment that was "broadly diverse," the objective upheld in *Grutter*.

iii. **Directed to "racial balance":** Roberts also rejected the school districts' argument that the race conscious plans here pursued a compelling interest in a *racially integrated learning environment*, in which students would learn more and become better socialized. Roberts declined to decide whether pursuit of educational benefits flowing from racial diversity might ever be a compelling interest because, he said, the plans here pursued *"only ... racial balance, pure and simple,*" an objective this Court has repeatedly condemned as *illegitimate.*" Accepting racial balancing as a compelling state interest, he said, "would justify the *imposition of racial proportionality throughout American society,"* a tactic that would have *"no logical stopping point."*

c. **Lack of tight means-end fit:** Even if the interests being pursued by the school districts were compelling, Roberts went on to say, the particular race-conscious *means* selected by the districts were not *necessary for achieving those interests.* In both cities, the use of the racial guidelines resulted in the *shifting of only a few students*, suggesting to Roberts that "other means would be effective." Furthermore, he said, cases like *Grutter* had interpreted the requirement of narrow tailoring to require "serious, good faith consideration of workable and race-neutral *alternatives*"; the districts here had flunked that requirement, by failing to show that they had even considered race-neutral methods.

d. **Mantle of *Brown*:** Roberts then argued that the plurality's position, not the dissent's, was true to the legacy of *Brown v. Board of Education.* "It was not the inequality of the facilities but the fact of *legally separating children on the basis of race* on which the Court relied to find a constitutional violation" in *Brown.* Even the plaintiffs in *Brown*, he said, had argued (and he quoted from their 1953 brief) that "the Fourteenth Amendment prevents states from according differential treatment to American children on the basis of their color or race." In sum, he wrote, *"The way to stop discrimination on the basis of race is to stop discriminating on the basis of race."*

4. **The Kennedy concurrence:** Justice Kennedy, in a concurring opinion, supplied the key fifth vote to strike down the Seattle and Louisville plans. But he *disagreed* sharply with the plurality's view that a school system may *never take race into account* as part of a voluntary system of pupil assignments.

a. **Diversity as a compelling educational goal:** Kennedy agreed with the plurality that since both plans "classify individuals by race and allocate benefits and burdens on that basis," the plans were to be subjected to strict scrutiny. But Kennedy rejected the plurality's conclusion that the districts had not identified any compelling interest that they were pursuing. For Kennedy, *"diversity*, depending on its meaning and definition, *is a compelling educational goal* a school district may pursue." (At the end of his opinion, Kennedy was even more specific about what interests should be deemed compelling: a school district had a compelling interest in both *"avoiding racial isolation"* and in "achiev[ing] a *diverse student population."* As to the latter, "race may be one component of that diversity, but other *demographic* factors, plus *special talents and needs*, should also be considered.")

b. **Not narrowly tailored:** But Kennedy voted to strike the plans because, even if they were enacted in pursuit of a compelling objective, they did not manifest the *tightness of means-end fit* required under strict scrutiny. In the case of Seattle, for instance, even accepting as appropriate goals Seattle's desire to reduce racial isolation and promote the educational benefits of diversity, Kennedy could not see how Seattle's use of the ***white / non-white distinction as the sole racial classification*** furthered those goals. Less than half of Seattle's student body was white, yet the district had used "the ***crude racial categories of 'white' and non-white' ''*** as the basis for its assignment decisions.

Kennedy cited with approval the plurality's criticism that under the Seattle plan, a school with 50% Asian-American students and 50% white students, and with no black, Native-American or Latino students, would qualify as balanced, whereas a school with 30% Asian-American, 25% African-American, 25% Latino and 20% white students would not. "Far from being narrowly tailored to its purposes, this system threatens to defeat its own ends[.]" "Individual racial classifications" like the ones used here, he said later in his opinion, were permissible "only if they are a ***last resort*** to achieve a compelling interest," and neither district had satisfied this last-resort standard.

c. **Plurality criticized:** But Kennedy also believed that the ***plurality*** had ***gone much too far in its insistence on complete color-blindness.*** He criticized Roberts' ***"all-too-unyielding insistence that race cannot be a factor*** in instances when, in my view, it ***may be taken into account.''*** The plurality opinion, he said, was "too dismissive of the ***legitimate interest*** government has in ensuring all people have ***equal opportunity*** regardless of their race."

Kennedy was especially unwilling to accept the plurality's apparent belief that "the Constitution requires school districts to ***ignore the problem of de facto resegregation*** in schooling." If the plurality was suggesting that the Constitution required that state and local authorities "must ***accept the status quo of racial isolation*** in the schools," the plurality was ***"profoundly mistaken.''***

i. **Right to consider race:** Kennedy believed that school authorities were entitled to use "race-conscious measures" to address the goal of offering "an ***equal educational opportunity*** to all of their students." But authorities had to "***address the problem in a general way*** and ***without treating each student in different fashion solely on the basis of a systematic, individual typing by race.***"

(1) **Allowable methods:** Kennedy pointed to several ***race-conscious methods*** that a school district ***might use*** without running afoul of his "no individual typing by race" rule:

❑ "strategic ***site selection*** of new schools" based on consciousness of neigborhood demographics;

❑ "drawing ***attendance zones*** with a general recognition of the demographics of neighborhoods";

❑ "allocating ***resources for special programs***";

❑ "***recruiting students and faculty*** in a targeted fashion" and

❑ "tracking enrollments, performance, and other statistics by race."

(2) Rationale: Kennedy believed that these methods, although they were race conscious, did not need to be strictly scrutinized because they "do not lead to different treatment based on a *classification that tells each student he or she is to be defined by race*[.]"

d. **Summary:** In sum, Kennedy was willing to allow some use of race in the student assignment process, but not the broad use of race, including *student-by-student classification*, that the dissent would allow. The dissent's approach, he said, had "no principled limit and would result in the *broad acceptance of governmental racial classifications in areas far afield from schooling*." Kennedy stressed "the dangers presented by individual [racial] classifications," dangers that he said "are not as pressing when the same ends are achieved by *more indirect means*."

5. **The dissent:** The principal dissent was by Justice *Breyer*, who was joined by Stevens, Souter and Ginsburg.[14] Breyer disagreed with virtually every step of the plurality's analysis, saying that the plurality's views "threaten a *surge of race-based litigation*," violated long-established precedent, and were likely to jeopardize *Brown*'s promise of progress towards racial equality.

a. *De jure / de facto* **distinction rejected:** At the outset, Breyer rejected the importance the plurality gave to the distinction between *de jure* and *de facto* segregation. Both Seattle and Louisville had had racially segregated schools, and had long struggled to reduce that racial isolation. For Breyer, the fact that Seattle had never been under a formal court finding of official segregation, and that Louisville's official segregation had been declared eradicated, should not have deprived either district of the power to make voluntary use of race-conscious factors in pupil assignments.

b. **Gentler form of strict scrutiny:** Breyer also believed that the plurality was misinterpreting the legal standard set by then-recent cases on raced-based affirmative action, like *Adarand* and *Grutter*. He conceded that those cases seemed to require that strict scrutiny be applied to all race-based classifications. But he thought that in practice, these cases applied a far more forgiving form of strict scrutiny to "racial classifications that seek to *include*" than to "racial classifications that harmfully *exclude*." And he believed that the plans here were entitled to the more forgiving version of scrutiny, because what was at issue here was "not a context that involves the use of race to decide *who will receive goods or services* that are normally distributed on the basis of merit and which are in short supply" but instead, a context of "racial limits that seek, not to keep the races apart, but to *bring them together*." Therefore, Breyer said, he thought that the plan should be given merely a *"careful review,"* not a review that was " 'strict' in the traditional sense of that word[.]"

c. **Meets even true strict review:** But even if full-fledged strict scrutiny were applied, Breyer said, the plans here passed muster: they were *narrowly tailored* to the achievement of a *compelling objective*.

---

14. Justice Stevens wrote his own, briefer, dissent. He found Roberts' reliance on *Brown* to be a "cruel irony," and noted that "history books do not tell stories of white children struggling to attend black schools." For Stevens, the racial classifications here should be viewed differently than the ones struck down in *Brown*, because the ones here "do not impose burdens on one race alone and do not stigmatize or exclude." Stevens closed by lamenting that "It is my firm conviction that no Member of the Court that I joined in 1975 would have agreed with today's decision."

i. **Compelling objective:** Breyer characterized the interest being pursued by the school boards as the interest in *"promoting or preserving greater racial 'integration' of public schools."* He thought that this interest was in turn motivated by several sub-interests: (1) a *historical* interest in "setting right the consequences of prior conditions of segregation"; (2) an *educational* interest in "overcoming the adverse educational effects produced by and associated with *highly segregated schools*" and (3) a *democratic* interest in "helping our children learn to *work and play together* with children of different racial backgrounds." He then asked rhetorically, "If an educational interest that combines these three elements is not 'compelling', what is?"

ii. **Narrow tailoring:** Kennedy next turned to whether the race conscious means chosen by the school boards here were *"narrowly tailored"* towards achievement of this compelling objective in preserving integration. He thought that the answer was yes, even under "the strictest 'tailoring' test." He listed several factors in support of this conclusion:

(1) First, the use of race-conscious criteria here was only a small part of the decision-making process in school assignments, a process that depended mainly on other, non-racial, elements.

(2) Second, he thought that the use of race here was more narrowly tailored than the use of race approved in *Grutter*: here, "race becomes a factor only in a *fraction* of students' *non-merit-based* assignments," whereas in *Grutter*, race affected "*large numbers* of students' *merit-based* applications."

(3) Finally, the history behind each plan showed that it was the product of the district's long efforts to "enhance student choice, while diminishing the need for mandatory busing"; each plan thus made *less use of race* than the plans it replaced, demonstrating how hard the districts had tried to use race in the most narrowly-tailored way that would still accomplish the objective of integration.

6. **Significance:** So what is the significance of the *Parents Involved v. Seattle* case?

a. **Direct impact:** The direct impact on the operation of the nation' public schools seems *not* to be very *large*.

i. **Use of non-racial grounds:** Most importantly, nothing in the *Parents Involved* decision seems to prevent school districts from promoting school-by-school diversity so long as only *non-racial grounds* are used for measuring diversity. Most promising is the use of *socioeconomic status* ("SES"), a factor already used by many districts. For instance, the fact that a student qualifies for the free or reduced-cost federally-financed *school lunch program* gives districts a way to promote socio-economic integration: assignment and transfer policies can be implemented so as to place the same ratio of school-lunch and non-school-lunch (i.e., poor and non-poor) students in each of a district's schools. Because minority students tend to be on average from poorer families, such an SES-based program will also tend to reduce school-by-school racial isolation while being beyond reproach from an equal protection standpoint.

Note: Notice that the use of race-neutral *socioeconomic status* as an allowable proxy for race in the K-12 context is quite analogous to the use of race-neutral *class-rank-percentage systems* like those lauded by the Court in the university-admissions context (see *Fisher, supra*, p. 287).

b. **Indirect impact:** But the case is more significant for what it shows about the rightward drift of the Court from the Rehnquist era to the Roberts era. *Parents Involved* was the Court's first affirmative action decision since Justice O'Connor was replaced by Alito, and that seems to have made a key difference — Justice O'Connor voted with the majority to allow consideration of race in law school admissions in *Grutter*, whereas Justice Alito voted with the plurality in *Parents Involved* (and would almost certainly have voted with the dissent in *Grutter*).

G. **Minority set-asides by states and cities:** Congress and many states and cities have enacted so-called minority *"set-aside"* programs, by which some fixed percentage of publicly-funded *construction projects* must be set aside for minority-owned businesses. Where such a program is enacted by a city or state (as opposed to the federal government), such set-aside programs will be subjected to **strict scrutiny**, and will often be found unconstitutional. This is exactly what happened in the landmark case of ***Richmond v. J.A. Croson Co.***, 488 U.S. 469 (1989), the first case in which a majority of the Court finally agreed on what level of review should be applied to race-conscious affirmative action programs. Because of the significance of *Croson*, it is worth going into the facts and holding in some detail.

1. **Facts:** The city of Richmond, Virginia, enacted a Minority Business Utilization Plan. The plan required prime contractors on construction contracts funded by the city to subcontract at least 30% of the dollar amount of the contract to one or more Minority Business Enterprises, or MBEs. To be an MBE, a business had to be at least 51% owned by minority group members. "Minority group members" were defined to include African Americans, Hispanics, Asians, Indians, Eskimos and Aleuts. An MBE need not be based in the Richmond area: it could be anywhere in America, and still qualify under the set-aside program.

   a. **Rationale:** The City Council declared that its plan was designed to overcome the effects of past discrimination against African Americans in the Richmond-area construction industry, and was thus "remedial" in nature. The Council said it wanted to "promot[e] wider participation by minority business enterprises in the construction of public projects."

   b. **Waiver:** A prime contractor could obtain a waiver from the MBE requirement, but only if he showed that there were no qualified MBEs available and willing to participate in the contract.

2. **Evidence before the Council:** The Council had before it some evidence that there had been extensive racial discrimination in the construction industry:

   a. **None by city:** There was no evidence that the *city itself* had ever discriminated with respect to construction.

   b. **No contracts:** However, there was evidence before the Council that even though Richmond was 50% black, less than 1% of the city's prime construction contracts had been awarded to minority businesses in the prior five years.

   c. **Associations:** Also, most of the contractors' associations active in the area had virtually no minority businesses within their membership.

d. Congressional plan: Lastly, the Council had before it reports issued by Congress, at the time Congress enacted a similar minority set-aside program for federal public works projects. Those congressional findings contained strong evidence that there had been extensive discrimination against African American construction concerns nationwide.

3. **Nature of the claim:** The plaintiff in *Croson* was a white-owned prime contractor seeking a contract to install toilets in the city jail. P claimed that he was unable to find an MBE who could supply 30% of the work at acceptable cost. P sued the city, claiming that the set-aside violated its right to equal protection of the law.

4. **Holding:** The opinion for the Court was written by Justice O'Connor. On some points, she spoke for only a plurality. But on the key point, she spoke for a majority: ***any governmental action that is explicitly race-based must be "necessary" to achieve a "compelling" governmental interest***. In other words, the majority held, race-based affirmative action plans must be subjected to the same ***strict scrutiny*** as are governmental actions that intentionally discriminate ***against*** racial minorities.

   a. Rationale: Justice O'Connor seemed to assert three distinct reasons why race-conscious affirmative action plans must be subjected to strict scrutiny:

   i. No way to tell: First of all, there is ***no easy way to tell*** which racial classifications are ***truly "benign" or "remedial"*** and which ones are ostensibly benign, but in reality motivated by ***"illegitimate notions of racial inferiority or simple racial politics."*** (For instance, since the measure here was enacted by a City Council that had a black majority, it might well have been merely a successful political attempt to get more of the economic pie.) Use of strict scrutiny, Justice O'Connor said, would help "smoke out" the illegitimate use of race by insisting on a compelling governmental objective and a very tight fit between the means chosen and that objective. (See *supra*, p. 263, for a discussion of how strict scrutiny helps to "smoke out" illegitimate objectives.)

   ii. Stigmatic harm: Second, O'Connor asserted, classifications based on race "carry a danger of ***stigmatic harm***." That is, the group "benefited" by an affirmative action program (e.g., African American contractors in Richmond) might in the long run be harmed, because society will ***believe*** that the favored group is ***less competent*** and cannot succeed without special protection.

   iii. Can't get beyond race: Finally, she argued, unless race-conscious affirmative action plans are strictly scrutinized, as a society we will never achieve our goal of becoming truly ***race-neutral***. Justice O'Connor accused Justice Marshall's dissent (discussed below) of advocating a "watered-down version of equal protection review [that] effectively assures that race will always be relevant in American life[.]"

   b. As applied to Richmond plan: Strict scrutiny clearly required that the Richmond plan be struck down, Justice O'Connor thought.

   i. Objective: Although Richmond claimed to be pursuing the objective of overcoming past racial discrimination in construction, there was not nearly adequate proof that this discrimination had in fact occurred. For instance, there was no direct evidence of discrimination by *anyone* in the Richmond construction industry, merely "an amorphous claim that there has been past discrimination."

ii. **Inadequacy of evidence:** The evidence pointed to by the city and by the dissenters was inadequate to make the requisite showing of clear past discrimination, O'Connor thought. For instance: (1) the fact that less than 1% of publicly-funded prime construction contracts in prior years had been given to African American contractors was irrelevant, because there was no showing that *qualified MBEs* represented more than this tiny fraction of overall qualified construction firms in the Richmond area; and (2) the fact that Congress had previously made legislative findings that there was a lot of discrimination against African Americans in the construction industry *nationwide* was almost irrelevant, since the degree of discrimination would vary from market to market, and what was relevant was how much discrimination there was in the *Richmond market*.

iii. **Conclusion:** In conclusion, Richmond, like any other public entity that wants to use race-conscious affirmative action measures, "must *identify* [the] discrimination, public or private, with *some specificity* before [it] may use race-conscious relief."

c. **Tailoring:** Not only did Richmond not show that it had a compelling need to redress past discrimination, it also was unable to show that its plan was *narrowly tailored* to this remedial objective. For instance, there was no showing that *race-neutral* means (e.g., city financing for small firms without regard to the race of their owners) would not increase minority participation adequately.

d. **Sometimes might survive:** Justice O'Connor did not believe that *all* race-conscious remedial plans would necessarily fail this strict scrutiny test. If there was clear evidence of discrimination either by the government or perhaps even by private parties, eradication of this discrimination might be a sufficiently compelling objective. For instance, had there been clear evidence of discrimination by specific general contractors in the Richmond area, eliminating the effects of this discrimination might have been a "compelling" objective, and some sort of race-conscious plan might have been a sufficiently-narrowly-tailored means of correcting that discrimination.

5. **Array of judges:** Five members of the Court in *Croson* agreed with the key proposition that all race-conscious measures, even supposedly "remedial" ones, must be subjected to strict scrutiny. Three justices (Rehnquist, White, and Kennedy) joined O'Connor's opinion on this point; a fifth, Scalia, said in a concurrence that he agreed with this proposition (though he would go even further than O'Connor, and would not allow race-conscious measures *ever* as a means of remedying past discrimination committed by anyone other than the government itself).

6. **Stevens' concurrence:** Justice Stevens, in a concurrence, seemed to agree with the basic holding that where the government institutes a race-conscious measure for remedial purposes, that measure must be subjected to strict scrutiny. But he saw the majority opinion as having an underlying premise that "a governmental decision that rests on a racial classification is *never* permissible except as a remedy for a past wrong," and he disagreed with that premise. That is, he thought that there might be some legitimate public purposes, other than relief of past discrimination, that might be served by race-conscious measures (e.g., "In a city with a recent history of racial unrest, the superintendent of police might

reasonably conclude that an integrated police force could develop a better relationship with the community and thereby do a more effective job of maintaining law and order than a force composed only of white officers").

7. **Dissent:** Three justices dissented. The principal dissent was by Justice Marshall, joined by Justices Brennan and Blackmun.

    a. **Standard:** The dissenters sharply disagreed with the majority's assertion that strict scrutiny was the appropriate standard for measuring race-conscious remedial plans. They believed that ***intermediate level*** scrutiny was the appropriate one: "[R]ace-conscious classifications designed to further remedial goals 'must serve important governmental objectives and must be substantially related to achievement of those objectives. ... ' "

    b. **Rationale:** Marshall asserted that "[a] profound difference separates governmental actions that themselves are ***racist***, and governmental actions that ***seek to remedy the effects of prior racism*** or to prevent neutral governmental activity from perpetuating the effects of such racism." By adopting the strict scrutiny standard, the majority "signals that it regards racial discrimination as largely a phenomenon of the past." Marshall, by contrast, did not believe that the country was "anywhere close to eradicating racial discrimination or its vestiges."

    c. **Important objective:** Under Marshall's proposed ***intermediate-level*** standard of review, the Richmond plan was clearly constitutional. Unlike the majority, he thought that the fact that less than 1% of public construction contracts had gone to minority-owned prime contractors strongly suggested (though it didn't directly prove) discrimination. And he would have given great weight to the congressional findings of past ***nationwide*** discrimination in the construction industry. The evidence taken as a whole, he said, constituted a strong showing that past discrimination had caused the present lack of minority participation in the Richmond construction industry, and therefore made the goal of ***promoting minority participation*** in that industry an ***"important"*** one.

    d. **"Substantially related":** Also, Marshall thought, the particular 30% set-aside was ***"substantially related"*** to achieving this objective. The set-aside applied only to public contracting dollars, and amounted to merely 3% of overall Richmond-area contracting. Also, the Richmond plan did not interfere with any vested right of a contractor to a particular contract; instead, it operated almost entirely prospectively, and was therefore less damaging than a plan which took away a contract already awarded to a white contractor. Finally, while the 30% set-aside was in a sense a quota, it was merely a "half-way" measure — it set a percentage about half-way between the present percentage of Richmond-based minority contractors (nearly zero) and the percentage of minorities in Richmond (50%).

8. **Significance:** What does *Croson* signify about the constitutionality of the many hundreds of minority set-aside programs enacted by states and cities across the country? The Richmond plan was unusually vulnerable, because of the relative weakness of the findings of past discrimination, the relatively high (30%) set-aside, and the relatively narrow procedures for obtaining a waiver. But the case undoubtedly makes it dramatically harder for other set-aside programs to pass constitutional muster as well.

a. **Findings:** Governmental bodies that want to pursue set-asides (or other race-conscious remedial plans) will have to make ***very precise*** legislative findings that there has been past discrimination.

   i. **Discrimination by governmental body:** If there are specific findings that the ***governmental body itself*** has practiced intentional racial discrimination, eradication of the effects of this discrimination will presumably constitute a "compelling" governmental objective. However, governmental bodies will rarely voluntarily make such findings about their own conduct, because of the public relations and legal liability problems this would entail.

   ii. **Discrimination by others:** If the government entity comes up with clear evidence that ***others*** (even private parties) have practiced discrimination in the past, and shows a danger that non-remedial government activity would compound the effects of that discrimination, apparently avoiding this compounding effect will also suffice as a "compelling" governmental objective.

   iii. **Societal discrimination:** Clearly, it is not enough for the governmental body to come up with findings of past ***societal discrimination***. For instance, no matter how clear the evidence was that there had been widespread racial discrimination by society as a whole in the Richmond area, this would have been irrelevant — what counted was discrimination ***in the construction industry***.

   iv. **Inference:** It will also be possible to prove past discrimination by ***inference***. Generally, this can be done by statistics. But the statistics will have to be much more carefully worked out than they were in the Richmond case. For instance, it will not be enough to show that only a tiny percentage of, say, construction contracts go to African American firms. Instead, the government will apparently have to show fairly precisely how many ***qualified*** minority firms there are, and will have to demonstrate that these firms are getting a much smaller percentage of the work than their numbers would indicate.

b. **Other objectives:** The curing of past intentional discrimination is one of ***only two objectives*** every found by the Supreme Court to be "compelling" and to thus justify a race-conscious set-aside plan. For instance, a governmental body's desire to improve the general economic status of its poorer citizens will virtually never justify a race-conscious plan.

   i. **Pursuit of educational diversity:** The only other objective that the Court has ever found to be a "compelling" one that may justify race-conscious measures is the pursuit of ***diversity*** in an ***educational setting***. Recall, for instance, that in *Grutter v. Bollinger, supra,* p. 283, the Court found that a public law school had a compelling interest in seeking broad diversity — including but not limited to racial and ethnic diversity — in its entering class.

c. **Narrowly tailored:** The requirement that the means chosen be very ***"narrowly tailored"*** to meet the compelling governmental objective also makes it very hard for minority set-asides to pass muster.

   i. **Quota:** Probably a rigid ***quota*** will almost always be invalid. Thus even had Richmond set aside only 10% of its contracts for minorities (the figure used by Congress, as opposed to the 30% figure actually used by Richmond), it is hard to imagine that the case would have turned out differently. The Court would almost always conclude that a less rigid plan would have been adequate.

ii. Race-neutral plans: Probably the requirement of narrow tailoring means that the government must first either try out, or at least consciously eliminate, *race-neutral* means before using race-conscious means. Thus the Richmond City Council would presumably have to have either tried race-neutral methods (like giving a preference for small or new construction firms, regardless of the race of their owners), or at least come up with specific findings as to why such race-neutral means would not succeed, before it could be allowed to use race-conscious methods.

iii. Goals: Probably set-asides will at least have to be replaced by less rigid, *"soft"* racial preferences, if racial preferences are to be allowed at all. For instance, Richmond would have had a better chance if it had expressed a *"goal"* or *"preference"* for minorities that would remain in force until 30% of contracts were awarded to minority-owned firms, instead of the hard and fast "quota" which it used. Similarly, a city might fare better if it allowed consideration of race as *one factor* among many to be considered when the city decides who should get a contract. But even a "goal" or "one factor among many" plan will probably be struck down if there is no clear evidence of past discrimination, and no showing that race-neutral means would be inadequate. [15]

H. Set-asides by Congress: The rules are the same for minority set-asides imposed by *Congress*, though this has been true only since mid-1995. In *Adarand Constructors, Inc. v. Pena*, 515 U.S. 200 (1995), the Court overturned prior law and announced that *strict scrutiny must be applied to race-based affirmative action schemes imposed by Congress*, just as it is applied to those imposed by state and local governments.

1. Pre-*Adarand* law (*Metro Broadcasting*): *Adarand* overruled a prior case, *Metro Broadcasting, Inc. v. FCC,* 497 U.S. 547 (1990), which had applied intermediate level review, not strict scrutiny, in judging whether "benign" race-conscious action by Congress violated the equal protection rights of non-minorities.

2. Facts of *Adarand*: The minority preference at issue in *Adarand* was subtle but nonetheless real. Plaintiff (Adarand) was a white-owned construction firm that had bid for a sub-contract to supply guardrails to a federal highway project in Colorado. P's bid was the lowest. But the general contractor took a bid from a minority-owned firm that qualified under federal regulations as a Disadvantaged Business Enterprise (DBE). The prime contractor was not *required* to award the sub-contract to a minority-owned DBE, but it received a financial incentive (10% of the amount of the sub-contract, or 1.5% of the amount of the prime contract, whichever was less) for doing so.

a. Whites can be DBE's: Small white-owned firms could also be DBE's. But a firm owned by an African American, Hispanic or certain other ethnic minority (as well as a firm owned by a woman) was automatically, though rebuttably, *"presumed"* to be dis-

---

15. Again, *university admissions* present a slight exception. The use of goals for minority enrollment to achieve diversity in the student body (rather than to remedy past discrimination) was officially endorsed by the court in *Grutter, supra,* p. 283. But *Grutter* also demonstrates that, as the main text suggests, soft "goals," as opposed to rigid quotas, are far more likely to be found to be an acceptably narrowly-tailored means of achieving whatever compelling interest justifies the use of race-conscious decision making.

advantaged. A firm owned by a white male, by contrast, had to prove disadvantage by "clear and convincing evidence." In any event, P in *Adarand* could not or did not gain DBE status, and the winning bidder for the sub-contract did.

3. **Strict scrutiny applied:** The Court in *Adarand* overruled *Metro Broadcasting*, and held that ***congressionally-authorized race-conscious affirmative action programs must be subject to strict scrutiny***. In other words, the rule of *Richmond v. Croson, supra* — that race-conscious "reverse discrimination" may be upheld only if "necessary" to achieve a "compelling" governmental interest — ***applies to congressional statutes*** the same as it applies to the actions of state and local governments. On this issue, the vote was 5-4; the Court's opinion was by Justice O'Connor (joined by Rehnquist, Kennedy, Thomas and Scalia).

   a. **Rationale:** O'Connor believed that *Metro Broadcasting* should be overruled because it departed from what she said was one of the core principles of the Court's pre-*Metro* cases on affirmative action: the principle of "***congruence***," that "equal protection analysis in the Fifth Amendment area [applicable to the federal government] is the same as that under the Fourteenth Amendment [applicable to state and local government]." No matter what level of government is involved, "[W]henever the government treats any person unequally because of his or her race, that person has suffered an injury that falls squarely within the language and spirit of the Constitution's guarantee of equal protection."

   b. **Strict scrutiny not necessarily fatal:** But O'Connor went out of her way to assure that the use of strict scrutiny did ***not*** necessary mean that the governmental action being reviewed would be struck down: "we wish to ***dispel*** the notion that strict scrutiny is '***strict in theory, but fatal in fact***.' " She suggested that if government is responding to "the ***lingering effects of racial discrimination*** against minority groups," and does so in a ***"narrowly tailored way,"*** even race-conscious methods may survive.

   c. **Particular regulation not addressed:** The Court's opinion did not decide whether the particular set-aside regulations at issue could survive strict scrutiny. Instead, the Court remanded the issue to the lower courts. O'Connor suggested that on remand, the lower courts should consider whether the governmental interest being served was ***"compelling,"*** whether ***race-neutral*** means might have been effective to achieve that interest, and whether the remedy was appropriately ***short-lived*** so as not to "last longer than the discriminatory effects it is designed to eliminate."

4. **Concurrences:** Two members of the majority would have gone even further than O'Connor. Both Scalia and Thomas indicated in concurrences that they would have ruled that race-conscious affirmative action can ***never*** be justified. As Thomas put it, "government-sponsored racial discrimination based on benign prejudice is just as noxious as discrimination inspired by malicious prejudice. In each instance, it is racial discrimination, plain and simple."

5. **Dissents:** The four Justices in the minority wrote three dissents. Perhaps the most interesting dissent was the one by Justice Stevens, since he had voted with the majority in *Croson* to apply strict scrutiny to state and local affirmative action programs.

   a. **Good motives less suspect:** Stevens rejected the majority's "consistency" principle: "There is no moral or constitutional equivalence between a policy that is designed to perpetuate a caste system and one that seeks to eradicate racial subordination. ... The consistency that the Court espouses would ***disregard the difference between a 'No Trespassing' sign and a welcome mat.*** It would treat a Dixiecrat Senator's decision to vote against Thurgood Marshall's confirmation in order to keep African Americans off the Supreme Court as on a par with President Johnson's evaluation of his nominee's race as a positive factor."

   b. **"Congruence" derided:** Stevens also believed that there were at least two strong reasons for rejecting the majority's "congruence" principle, and for giving ***more deference*** to race-based affirmative action efforts by Congress than to state and local programs.

      i. **Special enforcement powers:** First, Congress' powers concerning matters of race were "***explicitly enhanced***" by §5 of the 14th Amendment (which gives Congress the power to "enforce, by appropriate legislation, the provisions of the 14th Amendment"). By contrast, the states' use of race-conscious measures was what the Amendment was specifically directed *against*.

      ii. **Entire nation's representatives:** Second, "federal affirmative-action programs represent the will of our ***entire Nation's elected representatives***, whereas a state or local program may have an impact on ***nonresident entities*** who played no part in the decision to enact it." Just as Congress may burden interstate commerce even though the individual states may not (see *supra*, p. 74), so Congress should have greater leeway to use race to combat the effects of past discrimination, Stevens argued.

  6. **Significance of *Adarand*:** The most important aspect of Adarand is that it ***"federalizes"*** *Croson*: the federal government must satisfy the same "strict scrutiny" standard for race-based affirmative actions as must state and local governments. That is, government may use race only in a way that is "narrowly tailored" to achieve some "compelling" governmental objective.

   a. **Applies to non-set-aside contexts:** *Adarand* does not just apply to minority set-asides or to contracting. It applies equally to ***educational admissions***, ***employment***, and any other domain. For instance, a congressionally-funded scholarship fund that gave a preference to African American and Hispanic students would presumably be subjected to strict scrutiny.

I. **Hiring, lay-offs, and promotions:** Are race-conscious affirmative action programs constitutional when they relate to ***hiring***, ***lay-offs***, ***promotions***, and other ***job-related*** decisions? Voluntary arrangements by a private company do not raise any constitutional issue, since no state action is present. Constitutional issues do, however, arise when a race-conscious employment policy is either:

   ❏ voluntarily entered into by a ***public employer***; or

   ❏ ***imposed*** upon either a public or private employer ***by a court*** as a remedy for a judicial finding of prior discrimination.

No case raising these issues has been decided by the Supreme Court since *Croson* required strict scrutiny for all race-conscious affirmative action measures. Here is what can be said at present about affirmative action plans in the employment area:

1. **Standard:** A race-conscious plan in the employment area, like a race-conscious plan adopted by government in any context, must be ***strictly scrutinized,*** as the result of *Croson*. That is, the government objective must be a "compelling" one, and the means chosen must be very "narrowly tailored" to that objective — "narrowly tailored" seems to mean that there must be no feasible less-restrictive alternative. Thus the employer must either have tried race-neutral methods, or at least come up with a convincing argument as to why such race-neutral methods would not suffice.

2. **Governmental objective:** The Court has now either adjudicated or alluded in dictum to five possible governmental objectives in the employment area, only some of which are sufficiently important to survive scrutiny:

   a. **Redress of past discrimination:** The redress of ***past discrimination*** by the ***particular employer*** enacting the affirmative action program is sufficiently compelling to pass muster with all or nearly all members of the Court.

      i. **Broader discrimination:** Furthermore, it will sometimes suffice that there is evidence of past discrimination in a particular ***industry***, rather than on the part of a particular employer.

   b. **"Societal" discrimination:** On the other hand, the remedying of "***societal***" discrimination, i.e., discrimination by society as a whole, does ***not*** constitute an objective that is important enough to justify use of race-conscious measures.

   c. **Encouragement of "diversity":** It is possible that the goal of promoting "***racial diversity***" in a workforce may sometimes be a sufficiently weighty goal.

      i. **Admissions context as precedent:** We now know, of course, of that the goal of promoting racial diversity in a ***university student body*** can be a compelling governmental interest; that's the core holding of *Grutter v. Bollinger, supra*, p. 283. We will have to see whether promoting racial diversity in a ***workforce*** as opposed to student body can sometimes similarly be compelling. Perhaps where the ***constituency served*** by a workforce is highly ***integrated***, attaining racial diversity among the workforce itself will be deemed especially weighty, as in the case of an inner-city police force or a corrections staff serving a highly integrated prison population. Similarly, where a public workforce itself is highly integrated, having an integrated ***leadership*** at the top of that workforce may be deemed to be compelling, as in the case of the officer corps of our nation's very-integrated armed forces.

   d. **Balanced workforce:** The goal of assuring a "***balanced workforce***," by itself, clearly will ***not*** justify use of race-conscious employment policies. Thus even where, say, a public employer has a smaller percentage of minorities in its workforce than are present in the relevant local labor force, the goal of bringing minority participation up to the labor-pool average will not suffice, in the absence of evidence of discrimination by that particular employer, or at least discrimination by the industry or union covering the labor market in question.

   e. **Furnishing of "role models":** The goal of supplying "role models" to minority students is probably ***not*** a goal adequate to support race-conscious measures. That is, although it may be appropriate to seek some degree of diversity on a high school faculty, it is almost certainly not permissible to give preferences to minorities for the purpose of increasing minority representation on the faculty to match the percentage of minority students.

3. **Narrowly tailored means:** On the "means" side of the equation, employment cases have focused on three broad classes of methods for achieving the various objectives discussed above: (1) goals and "quotas" in hiring; (2) protections against lay-offs; and (3) preferences in promotions.

a. **Hiring goals:** Explicitly race-conscious "*hiring goals*" are generally permissible when they are an attempt to redress *clear past discrimination* by the employer who is using them.

Example: Employer, who has been found by a court to have discriminated against African Americans in the past, is ordered by the court to make best efforts to ensure that 18% of all new employees it hires are African American. African Americans make up 18% of the local labor force for the type of worker commonly employed by Employer. This type of "hiring goal" will probably be found to be constitutional.

i. **Non-victims as beneficiaries:** It does not matter that *non-victims* benefit from the hiring goals. Thus on the facts of the above example, even if it were shown that few or none of the African Americans who obtained jobs from Employer had ever been discriminated against on racial grounds (either by Employer or by other companies), the scheme would remain valid.

ii. **Quotas:** However, "hiring goals" are not the same thing as "*quotas*." Quotas are probably *not constitutional* even where used by an employer who has discriminated in the past. While the difference between a "hiring goal" and a "quota" is fuzzy, the difference mainly relates to *flexibility*. A hiring goal is flexible in the sense that the employer does not adopt a hard-and-fast rule that a particular percentage of new hires *must* belong to the minority, no matter what their relative qualifications. Similarly, if the program is under the supervision of a court, in order to avoid a presumptively unconstitutional quota the court must grant a temporary waiver to the employer if there is a plausible reason why the employer was not able to meet the goals.

iii. **Absolute bar to majority advancement:** The goals cannot act as an *absolute bar to majority advancement*. Thus a goal calling, even briefly, for 100% of new hires to belong to the minority would presumably be unconstitutional, no matter how egregiously the employer had discriminated in the past, and no matter how far the percentage of minorities in the employer's workforce fell below the percentage in the overall local workforce.

iv. **Temporary:** The goals must be *temporary*. That is, they must expire as soon as the percentage of minorities in the employer's workforce equals the percentage in the relevant labor force, since at that point the result of past discrimination has presumably been eliminated.

v. **Percentage of places reserved:** It may be unconstitutional for the goals to call for reservation, even temporarily, of a *higher* percentage of places in the employer's workforce than minorities occupy in the local labor force. This is an issue on which the Court has not yet taken an explicit position.

vi. **Tested against race-neutral means:** Race-conscious hiring goals will probably always be tested against possible *race-neutral* methods. Thus if the employer cannot show that it has considered and rejected for good reason race-neutral means, the race-conscious hiring goal will probably be struck down. For instance, the employer will normally have to show that it has considered *more aggressive recruiting* of minority workers, special training programs for new workers regardless of race, or other methods apart from race-based selection procedures, before the employer may use race-conscious hiring goals.

b. **Lay-offs:** Preferential protections against *lay-offs* are far harder to justify, as a constitutional matter, than are hiring preferences. Since lay-offs affect a worker's present job, rather than merely one of several possibilities for future employment, the harm suffered by "innocent" members of the majority is far greater than in the hiring-preference case. See, e.g., *Wygant v. Jackson Bd. of Educ.*, 476 U.S. 267 (1986) (plurality opinion). Therefore, it seems unlikely that there is any scheme for giving minorities preferential protection against lay-offs that would be supported by a majority of the Court.

c. **Promotion preferences:** Preferences in *promotions* of existing employees fall somewhere between hiring preferences and lay-off preferences in terms of the disruption to the lives of existing employees. Therefore, they are somewhat harder to justify than hiring goals but easier than lay-off preferences. A preferential promotions plan is most likely to survive constitutional scrutiny where it is a closely calibrated attempt to *restore* minority workers to the senior positions they *would have had* in the employer's workforce had the past discrimination never occurred.

4. **Significance of context:** The *context* in which the employment preference occurs is also significant:

a. **Judicial finding:** Where the employer, whether public or private, is found by a court to have discriminated in the past, and the preference scheme is one ordered by the court, the above analysis controls. That analysis would probably also control if the employer settled a serious discrimination suit by agreeing to the preference scheme, but this has not been definitively established.

b. **Voluntary arrangement by private party:** Where the preference scheme is a *voluntary* one enacted by a *private* employer which has *discriminated* in the past, there is no constitutional problem at all because there is no state action.

c. **No past discrimination:** Where the scheme is enacted by a private employer for some purpose other than the remedying of past discrimination by that employer (e.g., to maintain a balanced workforce, or to remedy "societal" discrimination), there is similarly no constitutional problem. (However, there may be problems with Title VII, the main federal anti-discrimination *statute*.)

d. **Voluntary arrangement by public employer:** Where a *public* employer *voluntarily* enacts preferences without evidence that it has discriminated in the past, the Court will presumably *strictly scrutinize* the preference. While this strict scrutiny will make it hard for the voluntary plan to survive, it has a respectable chance of surviving if: (1) there is strong statistical evidence of an imbalance that could not have happened by chance; (2) there is some evidence of discrimination by the industry or unions in the relevant market (even if not evidence of discrimination by the particular employer); and (3) race or sex is merely made "one factor" in the hiring or promotion decision.

J. Drawing of election districts on race-conscious grounds: The process by which the boundaries of *election districts* are drawn has often led *groups of voters* to claim unconstitutional reverse racial discrimination. When election districts are drawn by state legislatures or other government bodies, those drawing the lines almost always take race into account, just as they take account of party affiliation, ethnic breakdown, and other demographics. In light of *Richmond v. Croson, supra,* p. 301, you might think that once the plaintiff could show that she had been disfavored by any significant consideration of race in the drawing of election district boundaries, the Court would automatically give strict scrutiny to the districting scheme. But that is generally *not* the case, as we'll see immediately below.

1. **"Racial gerrymanders" can violate Equal Protection:** Plaintiffs may use the Equal Protection Clause to attack the racially-focused drawing of electoral district boundaries. But the plaintiffs need to show that race was not just *a* factor in the drawing, but rather *the "predominant factor,"* in order to trigger strict scrutiny. Such *"racial-gerrymander" cases* have often proved to be *winnable by the plaintiffs.*

   a. **The "facially irrational" theory (*Shaw v. Reno*):** The first racial-gerrymandering decision by the Court was *Shaw v. Reno,* 509 U.S. 630 (1993). By a 5-4 vote, the Court held that if the plaintiffs could show that the districting scheme was "so *irrational* on its face that it can only be understood as an effort to segregate voters into separate voting districts because of their race," strict scrutiny would be triggered, and the districting struck down unless it was shown to be "narrowly tailored to further a compelling governmental interest."

      i. **Bizarre shape:** The majority in *Shaw* seemed to concentrate on the *shape* of the district. The district at issue in *Shaw* was in fact strangely-shaped and non-compact. Because North Carolina's African American population is relatively dispersed, a long, narrow, irregularly-shaped district was the only way to create two districts that would be majority-black in the state, a goal the state legislature was willing to achieve and the Voting Rights Act may have required. The district as drawn was 160 miles long, and in some places was only as wide as the interstate highway.

         (1) **Remanded:** The Court remanded for a determination of whether this district was so bizarre as to violate the Court's new standard. Later, in *Shaw v. Hunt,* 517 U.S. 899 (1996) (also discussed *infra,* p. 314), the Court held that the district *did* violate the standard.

      ii. **Significance of shape unclear:** The *Shaw* decision left it unclear whether a bizarre shape was a requirement for showing an illegal "racial gerrymander," or whether instead *any* racially-motivated districting scheme would be strictly scrutinized, with bizarre shape merely being one possible indicator of racial motive.

      iii. **Rationale:** In any event, the majority in *Shaw* made it clear that 5 members of the Court thought that "racial gerrymanders" were bad, and constitutionally suspect, policy. There were two reasons. First, the drawing of district lines based mainly on race would have a *socially-divisive impact* on *voters,* resembling *"political apartheid"* and *"balkaniz[ing]"* us into competing racial factions." Second, racially-motivated districting sends a bad message to the *officials* elected from the gerrymandered districts, that their primary obligation is to ***represent only the members of the racially-dominant group*** rather than the whole constituency.

b. **"Predominant factor" test (*Miller v. Johnson*):** The next racial-gerrymandering case, ***Miller v. Johnson***, 515 U.S. 900 (1995), then made it clear that a bizarre shape is ***not*** a requirement for such a claim, and that all the plaintiffs must prove is that race was a "***predominant factor***" in the drawing of the district lines. Once the plaintiffs make this showing, the Court will use strict scrutiny. *Miller*, like *Shaw*, was a 5-4 vote.

> **i.** **Kennedy's opinion:** The majority opinion in *Miller*, by Justice Kennedy, spoke in broad terms: "Just as the state may not, absent extraordinary justification, segregate citizens on the basis of race in its public parks, buses, golf courses, beaches, and schools," so it may not "separate its citizens into different voting districts on the basis of race."
>
> **ii.** **Facts:** The facts in *Miller* illustrate at least one scenario in which an illegal racial gerrymander will be found. Because Georgia had previously been found to have discriminated against African Americans in voting, it was subject to the "pre-clearance" provisions of the federal Voting Rights Act. Under these provisions, any redistricting plan had to be pre-approved by the Justice Department. The Justice Department (the majority found) took the position that any redistricting plan must create at least three majority-black districts. After initially resisting, the Georgia legislature eventually came up with a plan that included three such districts, including the district at issue here (the 11th). In the litigation, the state essentially conceded that the drawing of the lines for the 11th was done mostly for racial reasons, because of the need to produce three majority-black districts to satisfy the Justice Department. The fact that the district was relatively ***compact***, and no more "irregular" or "bizarre" in its shape than many districts, was not enough to save it, given the race-conscious motives with which it was drawn.
>
> **iii.** **Flunks strict scrutiny:** Because the districting had been done primarily for racial reasons, the Court applied strict scrutiny. The majority found that the lines for the 11th district flunked because the state was not pursuing any "compelling" interest. If the drawing of three majority-black districts had really been necessary to redress past discrimination, the Court suggested, the requisite compelling interest might have been found. But here, the only interest the majority found was the interest in satisfying the Justice Department's rules. And these rules, the majority concluded, were not necessary for eliminating past anti-black discrimination in the state.
>
> **iv.** **O'Connor's concurrence:** Justice O'Connor, who in a concurrence supplied the vital fifth vote to strike the districting plan, suggested that she might make it harder than the other four members of the majority would for plaintiffs to win such challenges. She characterized the standard for those challenging race-conscious districts as being a "demanding one" — plaintiffs must show that the State has "relied on race in ***substantial disregard of customary and traditional districting practices***." Only "***extreme instances*** of gerrymandering" would be subjected to strict scrutiny, she said.
>
> **v.** **Dissent:** As in *Shaw*, four Justices dissented. The principal dissent, by Justice Ginsburg, argued that the majority was unduly expanding *Shaw*. Ginsburg objected to the use of strict scrutiny whenever race was a "predominant factor" —

she believed that this would open the door to federal litigation over the legitimacy of any districting plan that even took account of race.

c. **Additional districts struck down:** A pair of 1996 cases shows that majority-minority districts will in fact frequently be struck down under *Shaw* and *Miller*. See *Bush v. Vera*, 517 U.S. 952 (1996) and *Shaw v. Hunt*, 517 U.S. 899 (1996). In this pair of cases, the Court struck down *all four* of the districts whose constitutionality it considered, on the grounds that in each, race was the predominant factor.

d. **Significance:** So what do *Shaw* and *Miller*, taken together, say about analyzing claims that racially-conscious redistricting schemes violate the Equal Protection clause? Here are some thoughts:

  i. **Race-consciousness still allowed:** States are not prevented from being *"race conscious"* when they draw lines, as long as race does not become the *"predominant factor."* Plaintiffs must show (using Justice O'Connor's words in *Miller*) that the state "relied on race in substantial disregard of customary and traditional districting practices." So if race is heavily considered, but so are such (traditional) objectives as protecting incumbents, keeping "communities of interest" (e.g., large urban neighborhoods) together, using county and precinct lines, and not diluting the voting strength of other ethnic groups (e.g., Irish Americans), the plan probably survives.

   (1) **Race as predominant factor:** But the fact that the people drawing the district lines consider other factors in addition to race certainly *won't immunize* the districting scheme from being invalidated for making race the "predominant factor." The Supreme Court will take a very detailed look at exactly *how* the line-drawers went about their business, and won't hesitate to find that race was the most important factor. For instance, in *Bush v. Vera, supra*, p. 314, a plurality of the Court attached great weight to the fact that the legislature used maps and computer programs that *provided racial data at the block-by-block level*, but other data (e.g., incumbency and political affiliation) only on a broader basis; this fact helped convince these Justices that race was more important to the line-drawers than all other factors taken together, including incumbency.

  ii. **Minority districts vulnerable:** *"Majority-minority"* districts are clearly *vulnerable,* in light of *Shaw* and *Miller*. Any plan that seems to have been motivated principally by a desire to create the maximum possible number of such districts will be open to attack.

   (1) **Compliance with Voting Rights Act:** But *compliance with the Voting Rights Act can* apparently supply the requisite "compelling" state objective to support intentional creation of majority-minority districts. This is demonstrated by a post-*Shaw/Miller* 2006 case, *League of United Latin American Citizens v. Perry*, 548 U.S. 399 (2006), in which six members of the Court agreed that compliance with the VRA can be a compelling state objective that justifies drawing race-conscious district lines. So if the creation of one or more majority-minority districts was in fact necessary to comply with the VRA's requirement that the political processes be *"equally open to minorities,"* a

solid six-justice majority of the Roberts Court would apparently uphold the districts even though race was in some sense the predominant factor.

    iii. Dispersed racial majority: Districting authorities will find it toughest to avoid a violation where African Americans or other racial minorities are *widely dispersed*. For instance, the plan struck down in *Miller* was weakened by the fact that it reached from the outskirts of Atlanta in the middle of the state to Savannah, on the coast 260 miles away. By contrast, districts that are relatively *compact*, and that consist completely of neighborhoods within a single large city, are more likely to survive.

2. Use of redistricting commissions: As we've just seen, redistricting schemes carried out by the state legislature have often been successfully attacked as being intentional racial gerrymanders. Also, litigants have often attacked a different sort of gerrymander, so-called *"partisan gerrymanders,"* by which the party that dominates the state legislature draws district lines (including lines for congressional districts) in a way that effectively dilutes the votes of the other party.[16] To avoid legal and other troubles relating to gerrymandering, a number of states have taken some or total responsibility for redrawing district lines away from the state legislature and given that responsibility to a *nonpartisan or bipartisan commission.*

    a. Successful in Arizona case: This transfer of redistricting power to a commission seems to be *valid*, at least from a constitutional point of view: as the result of the Court's 5-4 vote in *Arizona State Legislature v. Arizona Independent Redistricting Commission*, 135 S.Ct. 2652 (2015), states whose lawmaking procedures allow voters to make law by the *initiative process* will *not violate* the U.S. Constitution if the voters pass an initiative that *takes the redistricting function away from the state legislature* and turns it over to a nonpartisan or bipartisan commission.

        i. Facts: In *Arizona State Legislature*, voters used the initiative process to pass "Proposition 6," which modified the state constitution so as to take redistricting away from the Legislature and give it to an independent commission. The Legislature then filed a federal suit challenging the federal constitutionality of Proposition 106's stripping from it all role in drawing congressional districts. The suit claimed that the Proposition violated the U.S. Constitution's *"Elections Clause,"* Art. I, § 4, cl. 1, which says that "The Times, Places and Manner of holding Elections for Senators and Representatives, shall be *prescribed in each State by the Legislature thereof*; but the Congress may at any time by Law make or alter such Regulations[.]"

        ii. Majority allows: By a 5-4 vote, the Court, in an opinion by Justice Ginsburg, concluded that the Elections Clause *did not mean* — as the Arizona Legislature asserted it did — that *only laws passed by the Legislature itself* could establish the rules governing elections. The main purpose of the Clause, Ginsburg said, was to *"empower Congress to override state election rules,"* not to *"restrict the way States enact legislation."* The Clause therefore did not change the "characteristic

---

16. Suits challenging non-racially-inspired partisan gerrymanders were ruled *non-justiciable* by the Supreme Court, in an important 2019 decision. See *Rucho v. Common Cause*, *infra*, p. 758.

of our federal system" that "States retain autonomy to ***establish their own governmental processes.***"

K. Harm to members of minority: Thus far, we have implicitly assumed that race-conscious affirmative action programs disadvantage only the majority, if they disadvantage anyone. But suppose that such a program, while it perhaps benefits ***most*** members of the previously-disadvantaged minority, ***harms certain members of the minority class.*** Does the existence of this harm render the plan a violation of equal protection? So far, the Supreme Court has not had to face this issue.

   1. Housing: One area in which the question may arise involves attempts to prevent ***"tipping"*** in residential areas. Such attempts have generally taken one of two forms: (1) the expenditure of public funds to create a program of ***"benign steering"*** in which prospective purchasers are shown homes solely in areas where they will contribute to integration rather than segregation (e.g., African Americans would not be shown homes in areas already containing more than, say, 40% blacks); (2) actual racial ***quotas*** in ***public housing projects.***

      a. No clear rule for "benign steering": With respect to the ***"benign steering"*** programs, there have been very few decisions. But it seems probable that such plans would be ***upheld***, since the plans do not prevent members of the minority from living wherever they wish — the plans simply use public funds in a way that encourages integration.

      b. Absolute quotas: Absolute racial quotas for public housing projects, on the other hand, seem more difficult to justify, since such quotas will lead to a person's being absolutely deprived of a particular good (an apartment in a particular project) solely on the ground of his race. Probably the majority's opinion in *Richmond v. Croson* (see *supra*, p. 301), casting doubt on whether a racial preference is ever truly "benign," means that an absolute racial quota for public housing projects will be strictly scrutinized and in fact struck down.

   2. Racial balance in schools: Similarly, suppose that a school board, in an attempt to maintain integration in an area that seems to be suffering from "white flight," decrees that only a limited percentage of African Americans living in a particular school district may attend the neighborhood school, but that all whites may.

      a. Effect of *Croson*: Recall that *Richmond v. Croson* (*supra*, p. 301) apparently requires strict scrutiny of *any* race-conscious government decision. Although preventing "white flight" might be found to be a compelling governmental objective, it is doubtful that a majority of the Court would conclude that an explicitly race-conscious plan that permits all white students in a neighborhood to attend their local school, but deprives African Americans of this right, is a "necessary" means of solving the white flight problem. (Instead, a majority of the Court would probably conclude that magnet schools, anti-racist public relations programs, and other race-neutral means could and must be used to deal with the problem.)

      b. Voluntary one-race schools: As a twist on the usual integration problems, suppose that African American (or Hispanic or other minority) students decide that ***they*** wish to have a segregated school, dormitory or facility limited to their own race. May the majority accede?

  i. **Possible justification:** Such voluntary segregation could be justified on the grounds that it promotes racial pride and cohesiveness on the part of groups which have been the victims of long discrimination and consequent poor self-image.

  ii. **Criticism:** Yet making a school or dormitory off-limits to whites certainly deprives them of a good solely on the grounds of race. *Richmond v. Croson* (*supra*, p. 301) certainly seems to require that such single-race facilities must be subjected to **strict scrutiny**. If strict scrutiny were applied, it seems unlikely that the Court would find that one-race facilities were a **necessary** means of promoting racial pride or cohesiveness among minorities. Special courses in black culture, a representative proportion of minority instructors, etc., certainly seem like adequate and less-intrusive ways of achieving the same result.

L. Law enforcement, prison administration and military operations: Governments sometimes make race-conscious decisions not in order to redress past discrimination, but in order to further **operational** needs, especially in the **law-enforcement, prison administration** and **military** contexts. The Supreme Court's only modern-era decision in these areas — which applied strict scrutiny to a state's policy of racial segregation in the **cell assignments of recently-arrived prisoners** — suggests that race-conscious policies will be **strictly scrutinized** despite governments' operational needs in these contexts. That ruling came in *Johnson v. California*, 543 U.S. 499 (2005).

1. **Facts of *Johnson*:** *Johnson* involved California's unwritten policy under which, when prisoners entered a new correctional facility, they were racially segregated in double cells for up to 60 days. (After the initial up-to-60-day period, prisoners were allowed to choose their own cellmates.) The state defended this segregative practice as being "necessary to prevent violence caused by racial gangs."

2. **Subjected to strict scrutiny:** Of the eight members of the Court who expressed an opinion (Chief Justice Rehnquist did not participate), six agreed that the state's policy **must be strictly scrutinized.** In an opinion by Justice O'Connor, the Court remanded the case to the lower courts for a determination whether the segregative policy could survive the strict scrutiny standard.

    a. **Applies to all classifications:** O'Connor noted that the Court had held that " '*all* racial classifications [imposed by government] ... must be analyzed by a reviewing court under strict scrutiny' " (quoting *Adarand*, supra).

    b. **"Benign" use irrelevant:** California defended its segregation policy on the grounds that it was a "neutral" one that "neither benefits nor burdens one group or individual more than any other group or individual." But O'Connor quickly dismissed this rationale: the Court had "rejected the notion that separate can ever be equal – or 'neutral' – 50 years ago in *Brown v. Board of Education*," and there was no reason to resurrect that notion now.

    c. **Might increase racial hostility:** Indeed, O'Connor said, the use of racial classifications in prison housing assignments might well **"breed further hostility** among prisoners and reinforce racial and ethnic divisions. By perpetuating the notion that race matters most, racial segregation of inmates 'may exacerbate the very patterns of [violence that it is] said to counteract.' " She noted that virtually all other states and the federal government "manage their prison systems without reliance on racial segregation." And she rejected the argument that the operational needs of prison administration dictated a different result: "[C]ompliance with the 14th Amendment's ban on racial discrimination is not only consistent with proper prison administration, but also bolsters the legitimacy of the entire criminal justice system."

    i. Might still survive: O'Connor emphasized that the Court was not deciding whether California's policy here could *survive* the required strict scrutiny — that would be left to the courts below. But she noted that "prisons are dangerous places, and the special circumstances they present may justify racial classifications in some contexts."

3. Dissent: Justice Thomas, joined by Justice Scalia, dissented in *Johnson*. Thomas thought that "The Constitution has always demanded less within the prison walls," and believed that the Court should adopt a *"deferential standard* for reviewing prisoners' constitutional claims."

4. Other contexts: *Johnson* suggests that the present Court will *apply strict scrutiny* to any race-conscious government policy, even in the demanding operational areas of law enforcement, prison administration and the military. However, it is probably the case that in these areas, race-conscious schemes have a better chance of surviving the requisite strict scrutiny than in many other areas. Here are some domains in which the issue might arise:

    a. Police: *Police departments* have sometimes preferred black applicants to white ones not in order to remedy past discrimination, but in order to have more African American policemen available for duty in predominantly-black neighborhoods, where it is felt that African American officers will have better rapport. Such a plan might even survive the strict scrutiny presumably required by *Croson* and *Johnson*.

    b. Prison guards: Similarly, there have been attempts to hire more minorities as *prison guards*, in order to match more closely the racial composition of the prison population. Such a plan might well be sustained, on the grounds that the state's interest in reducing racial strife in the prison system is a compelling state interest.

    c. Officer corps in military: The U.S. armed forces, too, have adopted explicitly-race-conscious means to develop more minority officers (e.g., by relaxing admissions criteria for the military academies). Given the heavily integrated rank-and-file in the military (e.g., 32% of rank-and-file were black or hispanic in 2002), and the much lower percentage of minority officers, it seems likely that the present Court would approve limited race-conscious methods. See Justice O'Connor's opinion for the court in *Grutter, supra,* p. 283, commenting favorably (albeit in dictum) on the armed services' use of affirmative action to ensure an integrated officer corps.

M. Popular votes to repeal affirmative action: Given that race-conscious affirmative action is sometimes constitutional,[17] what happens if some unit of government *voluntarily adopts* a presumably-constitutional affirmative action approach to some problem, and the electorate responds by *voting to overturn the plan* and to make it much *harder to institute* this sort of affirmative action in the future? Assuming that a state's law and constitution allow such a binding popular vote, does the electorate's use of its voting power to abolish previously-insti-

---

17. For instance, recall in the area of university admissions, a public university may constitutionally treat race as a "plus" factor if there is no other way to fulfill the compelling objective of maintaining educational diversity. See *Grutter v. Bollinger, supra,* p. 283 and *Fisher v. Univ. of Texas (Fisher I), supra,* p. 287.

tuted affirmative action *itself constitute the denial of equal protection* to members of minority groups that would in theory have benefited from the affirmative action?

As the result of a 2014 case, *Schuette v. Coalition to Defend Affirmative Action (BAMN)*, 134 S.Ct. 1623 (2014), the answer will generally be *"no."*

1. **Result of *Schuette*:** *Schuette* means that voters are generally[18] *free to repeal an affirmative action plan*, and to *change the political process* in a way that intentionally makes it harder for affirmative action to be instituted in the future. For instance, voters may choose to ban affirmative action by *amending the state constitution* in a way that can only be undone by another constitutional amendment. And voters may do this even though their vote to ban race-conscious affirmative action has both the *purpose and the effect* of making it harder for future voters to restore race-based affirmative action than for future voters to undo all other kinds of governmental actions the electorate disapproves of.

2. **Application in *Schuette*:** The facts of *Schuette* illustrate how voters may now successfully change the rules in such a way. In *Schuette*, the effect of the Court's decision was to allow the voters of Michigan to change the state constitution so as to *prohibit officials in the state's public universities from employing affirmative action in admissions*, even though the Court had previously upheld one of the very affirmative action plans that the voters were now abolishing.

V. CLASSIFICATIONS BASED ON SEX

A. **Introduction:** When examining a racially-conscious statute, it is generally not too difficult to ascertain whether the statute was intended as "benign" affirmative-action legislation designed to benefit a disadvantaged minority, or was, rather, garden-variety discrimination *against* a racial minority. But when one examines a statute which classifies by *gender*, it will usually be much more difficult to decide whether the statute is "benign" (i.e., beneficial to women) or not.

1. **Prior cases:** Many of the cases arguably involving benign sex-based classifications were discussed *supra*, p. 275, in conjunction with the general discussion of affirmative action. We turn now to the remainder of the sex-classification cases. The statutes in many of these cases may seem neither more nor less "benign" than those considered previously, so that the prior materials should be reviewed together with the ones which follow.

2. **Rarely outright hostility:** The reason for the difficulty of determining "benignness" is that legislatures have almost never acted out of *hostility* or *ill-will* towards women. Nearly all gender-based legislative classifications have evolved out of some kind of desire to *"protect"* women.

   a. **Early laws:** Early statutes typically did so on the theory that a woman's place was *at home raising children*, and that women therefore needed to be protected from a whole list of dangers lurking in the male-dominated world outside the home: alcohol, physical labor, jury duty, etc.

---

18. I say "generally" because *Schuette* does not cover the special situation in which the prior affirmative action plan was enacted in order to *undo state-sponsored or state-encouraged racial discrimination.* In this situation, there are pre-*Schuette* cases suggesting that voters are *not* necessarily free to repeal affirmative action measures that some unit of government enacted to redress the discrimination.

b. Later laws: A second group of laws, generally enacted after 1960, were protective in another way: they attempted to **undo the effects** of past paternalistic attitudes which had curtailed opportunities for women.

c. Intermediate standard throughout: Perhaps surprisingly, the Court today ostensibly applies a **single** standard to all gender-based classifications, whether these are found to be truly compensatory or merely paternalistic and stereotypical: **any gender-based classification must be "substantially related" to "important" governmental objectives**. This is, of course, the **intermediate level** of scrutiny, also applicable to illegitimacy and, perhaps, alienage. (See *supra*, p. 248.)

   i. "Exceedingly persuasive justification": The Court, as the result of a 1996 case, applies intermediate scrutiny in a quite **rigorous** way, which makes it **closer to strict scrutiny** than to "mere-rationality" review. As the result of *U.S. v. Virginia, infra*, p. 324, the defenders of a gender-based scheme must show an **"exceedingly persuasive justification"** for the scheme, and the Court will apply **"skeptical scrutiny."** The Court still officially applies the intermediate-level test ("substantially related to an important governmental objective"), but the government won't often pass this test.

   ii. Stereotypical thinking vs. attempt to reverse discrimination: A gender-based scheme is especially likely to be invalidated where it is an older one that arguably stems from a **traditional, stereotypical** way of thinking about gender roles, rather than a newer one that is intended to **combat past discrimination** against women. See *U.S. v. Virginia, infra*, p. 324 (all-male status of Virginia Military Institute struck down, based in part on the state's stereotypical views of the skills and interests of men vs. women).

B. Traditional deference by Court: Until 1971, the Supreme Court treated classifications based on gender as not meriting any special scrutiny, so that the highly deferential "mere-rationality" test was applicable. Thus a statute was upheld if the Court could find it to be **rationally related** to some **legitimate state objective**, usually the preservation of women's "proper role."

> **Example:** A Michigan law provides that no woman may obtain a license to tend bar unless she is the wife or daughter of the male owner of a licensed tavern. The state argues that bar-tending by women may cause "moral and social problems" but that oversight of the barmaid by her husband or father will minimize these problems.
>
> *Held*, statute upheld. The state could forbid *all* women from working in bars. This is so despite the possibility that public attitudes have changed, since "[the] Constitution does not require legislatures to reflect sociological insight, or shifting social standards. ... " Furthermore, it was not irrational for the legislature to conclude that the social and moral problems posed by having women tend bar would be less grave where the barmaid's husband or father was available to supervise. Therefore, the statute is not invalid. *Goesaert v. Cleary*, 335 U.S. 464 (1948). (*Goesaert* was later explicitly disapproved by the Supreme Court, in *Craig v. Boren, infra*, p. 321.)

C. Stricter review: But in the early 1970's, the Court began to give more than trivial review to gender-based classifications.

1. ***Reed:*** This occurred first in *Reed v. Reed*, 404 U.S. 71 (1971), where a statute preferring men over women as administrators of estates was struck down. The Court purported to apply the traditional "mere-rationality" standard. But in rejecting the state's contention that the preference reduced the workload of probate courts by eliminating hearings on the merits, the Court was clearly putting more bite into the traditional standard than it had done previously.

2. **Explicit strict scrutiny:** The "mere-rationality" standard for gender-based classifications was then explicitly ***rejected*** by the Court in *Frontiero v. Richardson*, 411 U.S. 677 (1973). In fact, that case went virtually to the other extreme, with a plurality holding that classifications based on sex, "like classifications based upon race, alienage, or national origin," are "inherently suspect and must therefore be subjected to strict judicial scrutiny."

3. **Retreat to "intermediate scrutiny":** The Court then settled (permanently, it now appears) on an ***"intermediate"*** level of scrutiny for ***gender-based classifications, whether "benign" or not.*** This standard was formulated in ***Craig v. Boren***, 429 U.S. 190 (1976).

   a. **Facts of *Craig*:** *Craig v. Boren* was a successful challenge to an Oklahoma statute which forbade the sale of "3.2% beer" (supposedly non-intoxicating) to males under the age of 21, and to females under the age of 18. A bartender who lost income from not being allowed to sell to men 18 to 20 brought suit against the state, asserting that the statute denied equal protection to this group of men.[19]

   b. **Standard articulated:** The Court articulated the applicable standard as being that "classifications by gender must serve ***important*** governmental objectives and must be ***substantially*** related to achievement of those objectives."

      i. **New standard not explicit:** The majority did not explicitly announce that it was applying a new standard different from either the traditional "mere-rationality" test or the "strict scrutiny" reserved for suspect classifications and fundamental rights. In fact, the Court purported merely to be applying standards established in previous cases, including *Reed* and *Frontiero*. But the concurring and dissenting opinions clearly viewed the majority as having formulated a third, ***middle***, level of scrutiny.

   c. **Defense of statute:** Oklahoma defended the statute on the grounds that it promoted traffic safety, since, statistically, 18- to 20-year-old males were arrested for drunken driving much more frequently than females in the same age group. (2% of males and .18% of females in that age group were arrested for drunk driving.)

   d. **Insufficient correlation:** The majority found this statistically-based defense ***insufficient.***

      i. **Maleness not "proxy":** First, since such a small portion even of *males* in the relevant age group were convicted of drunken driving, maleness could not serve as a "proxy" for drinking and driving.

---

19. Note that the plaintiff bartender was not claiming that *his own* constitutional rights were violated — he was asserting the constitutional rights of his 18-to-20-year-old potential male customers, who were not parties. By allowing the plaintiff's suit to proceed, the Court was recognizing an exception to the usual rule that a litigant may not assert the constitutional rights of persons not before the court. See the discussion of this third-party-standing aspect *infra*, pp. 741-742, Par. [2].

    ii. Non-intoxicating beverage: Secondly, even if 18- to 20-year-old males did drive while drunk with a sufficiently greater frequency than similarly-aged females, this did not establish that the state's regulation of *3.2%* beer was reasonable, since that beverage was supposedly non-intoxicating.

    iii. Only sale prohibited: Lastly, the statute only prohibited the *selling* of the beer to males, not their *drinking* it once they acquired it (perhaps via a purchase by an 18- to 20-year-old female companion).

    iv. Poor overall fit: Thus, overall, the *"fit"* between the *means* of regulation selected (ban on sale of 3.2% beer to 18- to 20-year-olds) and the *end* sought to be achieved (promotion of traffic safety) was simply *too tenuous* to constitute the required *"substantial relation"* between means and end.

  e. Dissent: Justice Rehnquist, dissenting, argued that the case should be judged according to a "mere-rationality" standard. He apparently would not have objected to intermediate-level scrutiny for discrimination *against women*, but saw no reason why discrimination against *males* should be given any greater scrutiny than that given to the great majority of other statutes attacked on equal protection grounds.

    i. Means-end "fit": Rehnquist also objected to the majority's conclusion that the statute was invalid because the *fit* between being an 18- to 20-year-old male and driving while drunk was unduly tenuous. In his opinion, what counted was not the relative size of the percentage of young males who drank, but *whether this percentage was higher than for females*. Since there was evidence that, however few young males were arrested for drunken driving, it was far more proportionately than the number of females, he found the connection between regulation of 3.2% beer and promotion of traffic safety "rational," meriting upholding of the statute.

  f. "Exceedingly persuasive justification": But the "intermediate" level of review is today *quite difficult to meet*. A 1996 case holds that the state must show an *"exceedingly persuasive justification"* for a gender-based scheme, and that the courts must give "skeptical scrutiny" to such a scheme. See *U.S. v. Virginia, infra,* p. 324. So even though intermediate-review remains the official standard, it's a standard that's closer to strict scrutiny than to mere-rationality.

D. Middle-level review not always fatal: However, the intermediate-level scrutiny now given to gender-based classifications, although substantially more probing that the traditional "mere-rationality" standard, has by no means proven to be universally fatal to the statutes examined.

  1. Most interests "important": Almost every governmental interest urged in support of a gender-based statute has been found *"important"* and therefore sufficient to meet the first prong of the test. The sole exceptions have been: (1) *"administrative convenience"* (see, e.g., *Frontiero v. Richardson,* 411 U.S. 677 (1973) (*supra,* p. 321); and (2) providing women, but not men, with "a choice of educational environments" (rejected as a rationale for a single-sex admissions policy in *Mississippi University for Women v. Hogan, infra,* p. 328).

    a. Must be "actual" objective: But to qualify as an important governmental objective, the objective must be one that *"actually"* motivated the legislature, as opposed to one that is articulated after the gender-based scheme was adopted. See *U.S. v. Virginia* (the

VMI case), *infra*, p. 324 ("a tenable justification must describe actual state purposes, not rationalizations for actions in fact differently grounded").

2. **"Substantially related":** The requirement that the means chosen be ***"substantially related"*** to the end has had considerably more bite. But it, too, has frequently been satisfied.

> **Example 1:** In *Michael M. v. Superior Court*, 450 U.S. 464 (1981) (discussed more fully *supra*, p. 276), the Court held that California could constitutionally make men but not women liable for sexual intercourse with a partner under the age of 18. The state's asserted purpose of protecting against teenage pregnancy was deemed important, and punishing the man but not the woman was held to be "substantially" related to achievement of that end — only women could become pregnant, so that a criminal sanction against men "equalized" the deterrence on the sexes. Also, women would be less likely to report statutory violations if they themselves could be punished, so that a gender-neutral statute might be unenforceable.

> **Example 2:** Congress was permitted to require that only men register for the draft, in *Rostker v. Goldberg*, 453 U.S. 57 (1981) (discussed more extensively *supra*, p. 277). Since the purpose of draft registration was to facilitate eventual drafting of combat troops, and since only men were eligible for combat, the male-only registration scheme was "closely related" to the purpose of the statute.

> **Note:** One can disagree about whether the means chosen in *Michael M.* and *Rostker* are indeed substantially related to the ends sought to be achieved by those two statutes. But if one accepts the majority's characterization of the aims of those two statutes, it does seem that ***neither*** was enacted as "the accidental by-product of a ***traditional way of thinking about females***" (*Califano v. Webster, supra*, p. 276). It is the latter sort of statute, typically enacted more than 60 years ago, that is the sort most likely to fail to withstand intermediate-level scrutiny. See, e.g., *U.S. v. Virginia*, discussed immediately below.

a. **Some imprecision allowed:** Even if the fit between the means chosen by the legislature and the governmental objective is ***far from perfect***, the Court may nonetheless conclude that there *is* the required "substantial relation" between means and end. A good illustration of the imprecision that the Court will tolerate came in ***Nguyen v. INS***, 533 U.S. 53 (2001), where the Court held that Congress could make it easier for the out-of-wedlock child of an American mother to achieve citizenship than for such a child of an American father.

 i. **The statutory scheme:** Congress has set up some detailed rules for determining the citizenship of a child who is born abroad, and out of wedlock, to parents one of whom is an American citizen and the other of whom is not. These rules make it easier for the child to become an American citizen if the American parent is the mother. When the American parent is the mother, the child is ***automatically*** deemed an American citizen at birth. But when the American parent is the father, the child will become a citizen only if, before the child turns 18, the father's paternity is legally established by one of several specified means (e.g., the father acknowledges paternity in writing under oath, or a court finds paternity).

ii. Holding: By a 5-4 vote, the Court ***upheld*** this scheme against an equal protection claim by the son of an American father who never took any of the legitimating steps before the son turned 18. The majority reasoned that by imposing the requirement of one of three legitimizing steps before the child was 18, Congress was promoting parent-child bonding by requiring "that an ***opportunity for a parent-child relationship occur*** during the ***formative years*** of the child's minority." And the fact that none of the legitimizing steps would *necessarily* indicate that a parent-child bond had developed did not mean that the requisite substantial relation between means and end was absent, for "***none*** of our gender-based classification equal protection cases have required that the statute under consideration must be ***capable of achieving its ultimate objective in every instance.***"

iii. Dissent: Justice O'Connor, dissenting in *Nguyen*, argued that there was not even close to a substantial relation between the means chosen by Congress and Congress' supposed objectives. For instance, with respect to the supposed congressional interest in making sure that there was an "opportunity" for father-child bonds, she contended that the way to promote that objective would have been to require that there actually *be* a real father-child relationship, not to require that *proof* of that relationship be obtained by the time the child was 18. Instead, O'Connor believed, Congress' scheme was based on an "overbroad sex-based generalization," and reflected "a ***stereotype*** … 'that mothers are significantly more likely than fathers … to develop caring relationships with their children.'"

Note: But a slightly different part of the same citizenship statute at issue in *Nguyen* has been struck down as an equal protection violation. See *Sessions v. Morales-Santana, infra*, p. 326, where the Court held that it violated equal protection for Congress to give unwed citizen-mothers living abroad the benefit of a shorter pre-birth U.S.-residency requirement in order to pass their citizenship on to their children than the residency rule that applied to similarly-situated citizen-fathers.

E. Stereotypical thinking rejected: The Court is especially likely to strike down a gender-based classification system that seems to be based on ***faulty generalizations*** or ***stereotypes*** about the ***differing abilities and interests of the two sexes***.

1. ***U.S. v. Virginia* (VMI case):** The most dramatic example of a law that the Supreme Court has struck down on account of the legislature's use of stereotypical gender-based assumptions is ***U.S. v. Virginia***, 518 U.S. 515 (1996), where the Court held that Virginia's ***publicly-operated men-only military academy***, Virginia Military Institute (VMI), ***violated equal protection***.

   a. **Facts:** Virginia had operated VMI as a men-only institution since its founding in 1839; the school's purpose was and is to develop "citizen-soldiers." VMI was the only single-sex school among Virginia's 15 public universities. Virginia's principal defense of its single-sex policy was that three aspects of VMI's approach — its extremely rigorous physical training, its technique of depriving students of privacy, and its "adversative" approach (under which entering students are extensively hazed, in a manner comparable to Marine Corps boot camp) — would have to be materially changed if the school were made co-ed. Instead, the state sought to create a less rigorous program for women — but still one in theory devoted to developing citizen-soldiers — at a pre-existing all-women private liberal arts college, Mary Baldwin College.

b. **Holding:** By a surprisingly broad 7-1 majority, the Court held that: (1) Virginia's policy of excluding women from VMI was a violation of women's equal protection rights; and (2) the program at Mary Baldwin College was not sufficiently comparable to the VMI program to redress the injury. The majority opinion by Justice Ginsburg was a sweeping one:

  i. **No "overbroad generalizations":** Ginsburg began by noting that gender-based classifications "must not rely on *overbroad generalizations* about the different talents, capacities or preferences of males and females. . . . [Gender-based] classifications may not be used, as they once were . . . to create or perpetuate the legal, social, and economic inferiority of women."

   (1) **Suitable for some women:** Ginsburg rejected Virginia's claim that the VMI program would have to be materially changed if women were admitted. It may be true that, as Virginia asserted, *most* women wouldn't like the rigorous, adversative martial VMI program, and would prefer a more cooperative program. But the experience of women in the U.S. military academies, and in the U.S. military, suggested that these fears were overblown. In any event, there were clearly *some* women for whom the existing VMI program was an attractive and suitable program, and Virginia could not deprive these unusual women of the opportunity to attend VMI. "*[G]eneralizations about 'the way women are,'* estimates of what is appropriate for *most women*, no longer justify denying opportunity to women whose talent and capacity place them *outside the average description*."

   (2) **Diversity policy:** Virginia had also defended its men-only rule as being in furtherance of a state policy of "diversity in educational approaches." But the majority rejected this objective as well, concluding that this was not an "*actual* state purpose," given that Virginia had no women-only public universities, and that the no-women policy at VMI dated from a time when Virginia did not offer any sort of public higher education for women.

  ii. **Mary Baldwin program insufficient:** The majority then concluded that the proposed women-only program at Mary Baldwin would *not constitute an adequate remedy* for the equal protection violation caused by VMI's men-only status. To remedy an equal protection violation, the solution would have to "place [victims] in the *position they would have occupied in the absence of discrimination*," and "to eliminate [so far as possible] the discriminatory effects of the past." The Mary Baldwin program would not be in any way the equivalent of VMI: it would be a *"pale shadow"* of VMI.

  iii. **"Exceedingly persuasive justification" needed:** The majority opinion was also notable for the *stricter tone* with which it applied mid-level scrutiny. Sex-based classifications have to undergo *"skeptical scrutiny,"* and will be upheld only if the state demonstrated an *"exceedingly persuasive justification"* for any gender-based governmental action.

   (1) **Objective must be one that really motivated state:** Perhaps the most important aspect of this "skeptical scrutiny" is that when the government articulates a justification for the gender-based classification, this justification

"must describe *actual state purposes*, not rationalizations for actions in fact differently grounded." Thus when Virginia asserted that its policy fulfilled the objective of diversity-in-education, the Court's response was not that this wasn't an important objective (or that the men-only program wasn't closely related to achieving that objective), but that this wasn't the state's *real* objective, merely a pretext.

iv. **Dissent:** The lone dissenter was Justice Scalia.

    (1) **Objection to majority's standard:** Scalia objected first to the majority's choice of standard. He claimed that while the majority admitted to having changed the traditional intermediate level of review, it was in fact substituting a new and improper "exceedingly persuasive justification" standard that contradicted the reasoning of the Court's prior gender cases. In Scalia's view, this standard was an "*unacknowledged adoption* of what amounts to (at least) *strict scrutiny*."

    (2) **Satisfies mid-level review:** Scalia believed that operation of VMI as an all-male school *satisfied mid-level review* when that standard was properly applied. The state had an important interest in achieving the educational diversity provided by single-sex colleges. And when Virginia elected to have an all-male school that used the adversative model (VMI) and an all-female school that used the cooperative model (the new Mary Baldwin program), it had selected a strategy that was "substantially related" to the achievement of that interest in diversity.

2. **Child-rearing by unmarried parent living abroad (*Morales-Santana*):** Just as the VMI case, *supra*, applied a quite rigorous form of mid-level review to strike down the "overbroad generalization" about gender differences at issue there, so a 2017 case on *immigration and citizenship* demonstrates that the Court continues to apply rigorous review to laws that reflect *outdated stereotypes about gender roles* in *child-rearing*. In that case, *Sessions v. Morales-Santana*, 137 S.Ct. 1678 (2017), the Court voted by 6-2 to strike down on equal protection grounds a federal law that made it easier for unwed *female U.S. citizens living abroad to pass on their citizenship to their foreign-born children* than for similarly-situated male citizens to do so.

a. **The statutory scheme:** *Morales-Santana* involved several related rules embodied in the Immigration and Nationality Act (INA), all dealing with the U.S. citizenship of a child born abroad, when one parent is a U.S. citizen at the time of birth and the other parent is not. (We'll call the child whose citizenship is at issue "C".) Here are the rules as they stood at the moment (in 1962) when P, the litigant who was arguing he received citizenship at birth, was born:

    [1] **Married couple:** If C's parents were *married* and living abroad at the moment of C's birth, the rule was that the U.S.-citizen parent must have *resided in the U.S.* for at least *ten years* prior to the birth (of which five had to be after the age of 14). (§ 1401.) So in this "married" scenario, it didn't matter whether the U.S. citizen was the mother or the father.

    [2] **Unmarried citizen-father:** Where C's parents were *unmarried* and living abroad at the moment C was born, if the U.S. citizen-parent was the *father*, the same rule

as in [1] applied: the father must have resided in the U.S. for at least ten years prior to the birth, of which five had to be after the age of 14. (§ 1409(a), incorporating the general rule of § 1401.) In other words, Congress made the general rule of [1] applicable to the children of an unmarried citizen-father, so that children of an unmarried citizen father were treated the same as the children of a citizen married to a non-citizen (whether the citizen in the married couple was the mother or the father).

[3] **Unmarried citizen-mother:** But where C's parents were unmarried and living abroad at the moment C was born, and the citizen was the ***mother***, Congress established a special rule to ***benefit the mother and her children:*** the mother could transfer her U.S. citizenship to her foreign-born child C if the mother had had ***just one year*** of continuous residence in the U.S. prior to the chid's birth. (§ 1409(c).)

b. Supreme Court agrees with P on equal protection claim: The Supreme Court, by a 6-2 vote, held that the statutory scheme ***violated the equal protection rights*** of unmarried fathers who were U.S. citizens. The majority opinion was by Justice Ginsburg; of the eight justices who participated,[20] six agreed that the statute violated equal protection principles. (The other two did not disagree, but said in a concurrence that it was unnecessary for the court to decide the constitutional question.)

i. Mid-level review: Ginsburg began her analysis by pointing out that under the Court's modern-era decisions, laws that grant or deny ***benefits*** "on the basis of the sex of the qualifying parent" are subject to the ***"heightened scrutiny"*** that the court gives to all gender-based classifications. Under this heightened standard of review, the defenders of the challenged statute would have to show an ***"exceedingly persuasive justification"*** (citing *U.S. v. Virginia*, the VMI case, *supra*) for the gender-based classification.

ii. Conclusion: Ginsburg concluded that the government had ***failed*** to establish the required "exceedingly persuasive justification" for preferring unmarried citizen-mothers over unmarried citizen-fathers.

iii. Defense of the statute: The U.S., in defense of the distinction the statute made between unmarried citizen-fathers and unmarried citizen-mothers, argued mainly that Congress had been trying to ensure a ***"connection between the child* to become a citizen and the *United States."***

(1) Rationale for favoring mother: Why then, did Congress distinguish between an unwed citizen-father and an unwed citizen-mother? Congress seemed to be applying the "familiar stereotype" (Ginsburg's phrase) according to which "unwed citizen ***fathers* ... would *care little about, and have scant contact with,* their *nonmarital children.***" But in the case of an unwed citizen ***mother***, Ginsburg said, Congress believed that "there was no need for a prolonged residency prophylactic: The alien father, who might transmit foreign ways, was ***presumptively out of the picture.***"

---

20. Justice Gorsuch joined the Court after oral argument in the case.

    (2) Based on stereotypes: For Ginsburg, this "connection to the U.S." rationale did not come close to surviving mid-level review. For one thing,[21] the distinction between mothers and fathers did not meet the "important governmental interest" prong of heightened scrutiny. The Court had previously held, she said, that "no important governmental interest is served by laws grounded [as § 1409(a) was] in the *obsolescing view* that 'unwed fathers [are] invariably *less qualified and entitled* than mothers' to take responsibility for nonmarital children."

F. **Remedial statutes:** If the Court finds that a gender-conscious statute represents an attempt to *remedy past discrimination* against women, both prongs of the intermediate-level test will almost certainly be found to be satisfied.

  1. **Redress for lower earnings:** For instance, in *Califano v. Webster*, 430 U.S. 313 (1977) (*supra*, p. 276), the Court upheld a Social Security provision by which a female worker's "average monthly wage" (against which social security benefits are calculated) could exclude three more lower-earning years than a male worker's. The Court found this provision to be a strictly remedial one, whose purpose was one of "redressing our society's longstanding disparate treatment of women," not one of "role-typing" women by casually assuming that they are "the weaker sex" or are "more likely to be child-rearers or dependents."

  2. **Remedy must be specific:** But it is not enough that the statute is intended to improve the position of women. It must also be the case that this improvement comes *in a particular narrowly-defined sphere*, in which women have *previously been disadvantaged*. An especially vivid illustration of this rule came in *Mississippi University for Women v. Hogan*, 458 U.S. 718 (1982), in which the Court struck down Mississippi's policy of barring men from the University's School of Nursing.

    a. **Facts of *MUW v. Hogan*:** The Mississippi University for Women (MUW) is a state university that has enrolled only women since its establishment in 1884. The School of Nursing was not established until 1971. The nursing school, like the other university departments, allowed men to audit courses but not to take them for credit. The plaintiff, Hogan, was denied admission to the degree program at the nursing school, which was located in the town where he lived and worked. There were co-ed degree programs at other Mississippi-supported nursing schools, but he would have had to commute a substantial distance to attend any of them.

    b. **Holding:** A five-Justice majority (in one of the first opinions authored by Justice O'Connor) *struck down* the women-only policy of the nursing school. The majority opinion applied the intermediate level of scrutiny prescribed by *Craig v. Boren*; Justice O'Connor then added her own gloss on that standard, arguing that an "exceedingly persuasive justification" must be shown for any sex-based classification. The statute was unable to survive this scrutiny.

    c. **Not affirmative action:** Most significantly, Justice O'Connor rejected the state's assertion that the single-sex admissions policy *compensated for discrimination*

---

21. A second problem for Ginsburg was that even if the "connection to the U.S." rationale *had* been a sufficiently important objective, the means-end fit between the gender-based means that Congress chose, and this objective, was not nearly close enough to meets the requirements of mid-level review.

against women and was therefore "educational affirmative action." Such a "compensatory purpose" justification would be valid, the Justice stated, only if members of the sex benefitted by the classification "actually suffer a *disadvantage related to the classification*." In the present case, this would have required a showing that women were disadvantaged *in the field of nursing*, not merely in the general sphere of education or employment.

    i. Nursing as woman's field: The state made no such showing regarding nursing. In fact, Justice O'Connor noted, the evidence was just the contrary: nursing in Mississippi (as well as in the rest of the country) was widely viewed as exclusively a woman's job. Thus the single-sex policy of the nursing school in fact merely *perpetuated a stereotype about proper roles for women*, and had nothing to do with compensation for past discrimination.

G. Discriminatory purpose required: In the sex-discrimination cases which we have examined so far, there was usually little dispute about whether the statute was intended to classify on the basis of sex. Most of the statutes explicitly mentioned sex, and the main issue was whether the classification was justifiable. But it is important to remember that, in sex-discrimination cases as in race-discrimination ones, the plaintiff is nonetheless required to show a *discriminatory purpose*, not merely a discriminatory *effect*.

1. *Feeney:* One illustration of this requirement is *Personnel Administrator of Massachusetts v. Feeney*, 442 U.S. 256 (1979) (discussed more fully *supra*, p. 260). In *Feeney*, the Court held that Massachusetts' absolute veterans' preference for civil service jobs did not violate equal protection, even though over 98% of the veterans in Massachusetts were men. Only "purposeful discrimination" against women could give rise to an equal protection violation — "[T]he Fourteenth Amendment guarantees equal laws, not equal results." (The fact that Massachusetts legislators may have *foreseen* that the statute would operate to women's extreme detriment was not enough; an equal protection claim could be valid only upon proof that the legislature acted in part "because of," not merely "in spite of" adverse effects on women.)

2. Use of biological factors: A legislature's use of *biological factors* may similarly cause a disparate effect upon the two sexes. Again, only if there is proof that the disparate effect was *intended* by the lawmakers will the statute be struck down on equal protection grounds. *Geduldig v. Aiello*, 417 U.S. 484 (1974), purports to be an illustration of this principle.

    a. Facts: *Geduldig* involved a provision of California's disability insurance system which excluded coverage for "disability that accompanies normal pregnancy and childbirth."

    b. Holding: The Court held that the statute did not violate the Equal Protection Clause, because it did not use an intentionally *sex-based classification*. There was no evidence that the distinction based on pregnancy was a pretext designed to effect invidious discrimination against women. "The program divides potential recipients into two groups: pregnant women and nonpregnant persons. While the first group is exclusively female, the second includes members of both sexes. The fiscal and actuarial benefits of the program thus accrue to members of both sexes."[22]

        i. Mere-rationality standard: Therefore, the legislature's choice of conditions to be covered or not covered, being "gender neutral," needed simply to satisfy the "mere-rationality" test. The state's legitimate interests in keeping the insurance system solvent and in making benefits adequate for those conditions covered, were rationally related to the means chosen (exclusion of pregnancy-related conditions).

3. **Explicit differentiation by sex:**   But where the statute itself *explicitly differentiates* based on sex, the Court will give heightened scrutiny to a justification based on biological considerations.

   a. **Parents of illegitimate children:**   For instance, a New York statute giving the mother of an illegitimate child, but not the father, the right to *veto the child's adoption*, was invalidated by the Court (5-4) in *Caban v. Mohammed*, 441 U.S. 380 (1979). The father, mother and child in *Caban* had lived together for several years as a family. The majority concluded that New York could not deny the father the right to block an adoption by withholding consent, if it gave this right automatically to the mother; there was no "universal difference," at every stage of a child's development, between the closeness of the father-child relationship and that of the mother-child one.

      i. **Other adoptions:**   But the majority emphasized that the state was free to differentiate between mothers and fathers as to adoptions taking place while the child was *still an infant*, or where the child was past infancy but the father had *not participated* in its rearing.

   b. **Wrongful death action:**   But not all schemes which treat the father of an illegitimate child less favorably than the mother will be struck down. For instance, in *Nguyen v. INS* (*supra*, p. 323), a 2001 case, the Court upheld a federal statute that allowed a mother who is a U.S. citizen to automatically confer U.S. citizenship on her illegitimate child, while a father who is a citizen must take one of several affirmative steps before the child turns 18 in order to confer citizenship. The majority relied heavily on the theory that the mother automatically establishes ties to the child merely by giving birth and being present at the birth, whereas the father does not have such automatic ties.

4. **Co-ed bathrooms and lockerrooms:**   Public bathrooms, lockerrooms, sleeping quarters and other facilities related to *intimate bodily functions* of course generally remain sex-segregated. The Court has not explicitly dealt with this sort of segregation, but there is little reason to believe that such facilities-separation would be struck down as violative of equal protection.

   a. **Privacy argument:**   Perhaps the best argument against a finding of an equal protection violation in this context is that sex-segregated facilities such as these are not expressions of invidious discrimination, but rather, expressions of the recognized desire for *sexual privacy*. Recall that the Court has recognized a substantive, constitutionally-protected, "right of privacy" (*supra*, p. 175), which seems to be applicable in this situation.

---

22. But four members of the Court in 2012 called for *Geduldig* to be overruled. In a dissent in *Coleman v. Court of Appeals of Maryland*, 132 S.Ct. 1327 (2012), Justice Ginsburg (joined by Justices Breyer, Sotomayor and Kagan), said that "it is simply false that a classification based on pregnancy is gender-neutral. ... Rather, discriminating on the basis of pregnancy [b]y definition . . . discriminates on account of sex; for it is the capacity to become pregnant which primarily differentiates the female from the male."

H. "As applied" challenges: So far, nearly all of the challenges to gender-based classifications we have considered have been "facial" ones, i.e., ones directed to gender-based classifications that are present in the text of the statute or regulation itself. But remember that the Equal Protection Clause also allows for ***"as applied"*** challenges — if the plaintiff can show that government has ***enforced*** a neutral-sounding provision in a way that discriminates against one or the other gender, this discrimination, too, will have to satisfy mid-level review.

    1. Peremptory challenges: Consider, for instance, statutes that allow for civil or criminal litigants to use ***peremptory challenges***, by which potential jurors may be dismissed without any showing of cause. The Court has held that the use of peremptory challenges to ***exclude all women*** from a jury cannot survive mid-level review, and thus violates equal protection. *J.E.B. v. Alabama*, 511 U.S. 127 (1994).

       a. Rationale: The Court phrased the issue as being "whether discrimination on the basis of gender in jury selection substantially furthers the State's legitimate interest in achieving a fair and impartial trial." It then answered "no," concluding that the assumption that women jurors will have certain types of attitudes in certain cases (such as the paternity case that was at issue in *J.E.B.*) reinforced stereotypical assumptions about women. So, just as a state may not permit litigants to strike jurors peremptorily on the grounds of race (see *Batson v. Kentucky*, discussed *supra*, p. 261), so the state may not allow gender-based strikes.

Quiz Yourself on

EQUAL PROTECTION — SUSPECT CLASSES, AFFIRMATIVE ACTION AND CLASSIFICATIONS BASED ON SEX

39. The state of Minnetonka has enacted an adoption statute that specifies the criteria to be used when public agencies make adoption placements. (No private adoptions are permitted in the state.) According to the statute, the "racial compatibility" between the child and the adoptive parents is the most important factor to be considered, though many other factors are also to be considered. Peter and Jill, a white couple in their 40's, wished to adopt a child. They learned that a large number of African American children were being raised in state-sponsored orphanages, because no homes could be found for them. The couple applied to a state adoption agency, requesting to adopt any African American child under the age of four, who was currently living in an orphanage. The adoption agency replied, "Because applicable statutes require us to give racial matching heaviest weight in making adoption placements, and because you are seeking a relatively young child who may well be placeable with a racially-compatible, i.e., African American family in the future, we cannot grant your request." Peter and Jill have sued in federal court for a ruling that the statute providing for race-matching violates their equal protection rights. They have presented evidence that African American children are staying longer in orphanages than white children who are otherwise similar, and that this lengthier stay is due in part to the heavy statutory weight placed on race-matching.

    (a) By what standard should the court test the constitutionality of the race-matching statute as it applies to Peter and Jill? _____

    (b) Should the court agree with Peter and Jill's contention that their equal protection rights have been violated? _____

40. Carolene High School, a public high school, has for years maintained special remedial reading classes. Students can take these classes in lieu of the regular English class, if they are shown to have learning disabilities or otherwise shown to be behind on their reading skills. Students of African American ancestry make up 12% of the student body of the high school. Forty-five percent of the students in the remedial reading program are African American. Because of reduced federal aid to education and a local recession, the school board has reluctantly concluded that it must reduce expenditures. Therefore, it has cancelled the remedial reading program, which is about 15% more expensive per student than the regular English program. The school board has not cut funding for the honors English program, which similarly costs about 15% more per student than regular English. About 9% of the students in the honors English program are African American. All of the evidence is that the school board made the decision it did on the honest belief that the honors program accomplishes more per dollar and strengthens the school system more, than does the remedial reading program. Carl, an African American student enrolled in the remedial reading program, has now challenged the termination on the grounds that it violates his right to equal protection.

   (a) What standard should the court use in deciding Carl's challenge? _____

   (b) Will Carl's challenge succeed? _____

41. Smithville is a small town located near the Canadian border. A significant minority of the children attending Smithville High School are American citizens of French-Canadian descent. The school board has just canceled the honors French program. The decision was made by the school principal, an American of Anglo-Saxon descent, who told school board members, "If we keep running an extensive French program, we'll just attract more Americans of French-Canadian ancestry to the town, and soon they'll be a majority." Since the school board was completely dominated by Anglo-Saxon Americans, they concurred with the decision. Jacques, an American student at the school of French-Canadian descent, has sued the school district, arguing that the cancellation has violated his constitutional rights.

   (a) What standard of review should the court use to judge the school district's cancellation decision?
   _____

   (b) Will Jacques' challenge succeed? _____

42. Same facts as prior question. Now, however, assume that the town of Smithville, and its school board, both contain a majority of Americans of French-Canadian descent. The board has now voted to dramatically expand the French program, and to cancel the honors English program. Strong evidence suggests that the board was motivated by a desire to attract more French-Canadian Americans into town, and to solidify this group's majority over Anglo-Americans. Does either of your answers to question 41 change here, and if so, how? _____

43. The city of Monroe enacted an ordinance providing that 10% of all procurements of office supplies in the city for the coming year must be purchased from office supply companies majority-owned by either African Americans or Hispanics, the two largest ethnic groups in the city. African Americans and Hispanics together make up a substantial minority (approximately 40%) of the city's population. The City Council did not conduct legislative hearings or investigations prior to enacting the bill. However, minutes of the Council's deliberations show that Council members enacted the bill primarily because they felt that minority business people, especially in the office supply industry, had had less general economic opportunity than white-owned firms, and that the 10% set-aside was the best way to increase the opportunities for minority owned companies. At the moment the bill was enacted, firms owned by African Americans or Hispanics amounted to approximately 10% of the total office supply companies in the city, but these companies did only about 4% of the total office supply business in the city, since the average minority-owned firm was much smaller than the average white-owned firm.

Anglo Office Supply, a white-owned office supply firm, has challenged the Monroe set-aside on equal protection grounds.

(a) What standard should the court use in evaluating the constitutional sufficiency of the set-aside?

_____

(b) Will Anglo's attack succeed? _____

44. A statute in the state of Ames confers upon the board of education of any city in the state the right to exercise control of assignments of students to public schools in the city. Bigtown, Ames' largest city, exhibits a large degree of racial segregation in housing. Years ago, a federal court found that this racially-segregated housing pattern came about solely through private housing choices, and was not significantly encouraged by any intentional governmental action. Last year, the popularly-elected Board of Education of Bigtown instituted a system under which elementary school students were assigned to (and bused to) schools that were not necessarily near the student's home, for the express purpose of reducing racial imbalances in the city's elementary schools. (Assume for purposes of this question that the assignment and busing plan did not violate any student's constitutional rights.) In response to the widely-publicized Bigtown plan, anti-busing forces in Ames convinced the state's voters to approve a voter initiative that amended the state Constitution so as to forbid any city Board of Education in the state from enacting a mandatory busing plan. (Assume that this initiative was a valid means of amending the state constitution.)

Some minority children in Bigtown have sued the state, contending that the initiative is an intentional race-based classification, one that modifies the state's political processes so that local governments' use of busing to overcome racial isolation are made much more difficult to enact than government plans to use busing for all non-racially-oriented purposes. Therefore, the plaintiffs say, the initiative must be strictly scrutinized, and struck down as a violation of their right to equal protection, unless shown to be necessary to achieve a compelling governmental purpose. Are the plaintiffs correct about the level of review to be given to the initiative? _____

45. The Oneanta state legislature mandated that any employer with five or more employees grant a paid six-month maternity leave to any woman who gave birth while on the company's payroll. The legislature imposed no requirements regarding paid or unpaid family leave for men who had just had a child. In deciding to enact the measure, the legislators relied principally on evidence that various rising social problems, such as drugs and crime, were caused in part by the rise in working women and a consequent failure of mothers to bond with their infants. Frank, the father of a newborn infant who wished to have a paid paternity leave, has challenged the statute on the grounds that it violates his equal protection rights.

(a) What standard should the court apply in evaluating Frank's challenge to the maternity-leave statute? _____

(b) Will Frank's attack succeed? _____

46. Congress was dismayed by statistics indicating that although African Americans and Hispanics now compose approximately 15% of America's university-age population, these two groups comprise only 7% of enrollees at colleges and universities nationally. Most members of Congress believed that the shortfall was due to the residual effects of past official discrimination by state and local governments, including public university systems. Therefore, Congress enacted a statute providing that any college or university receiving federal funds was required to treat an applicant's African American or Hispanic status into

account as a "positive factor," and to "make best efforts" to enroll as high a percentage of African American and Hispanic students as are present in the school-age population for the geographical area being served by that college or university. The statute further provided that statistics regarding actual enrollments would be treated as follows: a university would be rebuttably presumed to have failed to comply with the statute if the number of African American and Hispanic students actually enrolled was less than 80% of what would be predicted from the pool of recent high school graduates in the region from which the university draws the bulk of its enrollees. The statute's preamble recited Congress' belief that enrollment disparities stemmed in major part from past governmental discrimination, but neither the statutory text nor the statute's legislative history either (1) described the particulars of this discrimination (e.g., whether it was national, whether it was by universities or other governmental actors, etc.) or (2) considered whether race-neutral methods might suffice to cure the lingering effects of the discrimination. Penny, a white female with good grades and test scores, was denied admission to Statesville University, a large and prestigious public university. She sued the University, pointing out that her grades and test scores were above the average for those accepted at the University, and arguing (correctly, as a factual matter) that but for the federally-required racial preference, she would probably have been admitted. She therefore contends that the federal statute violates her equal protection rights.

(a) What standard should the court use in deciding whether the federal statute violates Penny's equal protection rights? _____

(b) Will Penny's attack succeed? _____

47. In the state of Delta, 12% of recent high school graduates are African-American. The state's premier public university, Delta State, has historically made its decisions about whom to admit on a "holistic basis." Under the holistic system, admissions officials look at the student's entire academic and extracurricular profile, without ever explicitly treating (or even knowing) the student's race as a factor. Two years ago, the university's administration observed that its entering freshman class during the prior four years had been, on average, 6% black. A survey done by the university administration then determined that 75% of seminar classes at the university — "seminar" meaning classes having between 5 and 16 students — contained either zero or one African-American student. In a survey of currently-enrolled African-American students, many reported feelings of loneliness and racial isolation. The administration decided that it would be vital to admit — and hopefully enroll — a substantially greater number of African-American students, so as to increase the critical mass of such students in seminar classes sufficiently to reduce the percentage of seminar classes without at least two black students from 75% to about 45%, and thereby to increase the overall educational diversity of the student body. To that end, the admissions department considered two different plans, Plan A and Plan B. (The administration reasonably concluded, after extensive research, that apart from these two plans, there were no other apparently-workable admissions schemes that offered an opportunity for raising the number of African-American students to the desired level without compromising other major attributes of the entering class.) Under Plan A, half the entering class's seats would no longer be allocated on the holistic method, and would instead be subjected to a "Top Seven Percent" arrangement, under which any applicant who had been in the top 7% of his in-state public high school graduating class would automatically be offered admission. A statistician consulted by the university predicted that because of the highly segregated nature of Delta's public high schools, the adoption of Plan A would result in many more offers to (and acceptances by) black students, so that the percentage of seminar classes without at least two black students would likely drop from 75% to about 45%. Under Plan B, the university would amend its existing holistic plan so that race could be explicitly considered as one factor among many; under this plan, all seats would be allocated under the newly-revised

race-conscious holistic plan. Admissions officials determined, after some modeling, that Plan B would result in an increase in black students (and a decrease in seminars with fewer than two black students) comparable to that anticipated from Plan A.

Admission officials decided to use Plan B instead of A. They made this choice mainly because they reasonably concluded that Plan B would result in the admission of a significantly more-highly-credentialed group of black students than Plan A, since Plan B would enable the school to attract a significant number of black students graduating in the top 15% (but not top 7%) of their class at relatively affluent and high-achieving majority-white public high schools in the state. Paula, a white non-Hispanic student who graduated 5th in her class of 100 at a high-achieving in-state suburban high school, was denied admission to Delta State. She has sued the university in federal district court, alleging that its use of Plan B violated her federal equal protection rights by discriminating against her because she was white. The university has defended on the grounds that its use of Plan B, although admittedly race-conscious, conforms with applicable Supreme Court precedents. Assume that had Plan A been in force instead of Plan B, Paula would have automatically been offered admission.

(a) Which party, Paula or Delta State, bears the burden of proof on the issue of whether Paula's equal protection rights have been violated by Delta State's use of Plan B? _____

(b) What standard of review should the trial court use in deciding whether the party who bears the burden of proof (as identified in your answer in (a)) has carried that burden? _____

(c) When the court applies the review standard you specified in (b), which party is likely to win? _____

Answers

39. (a) The court should apply strict scrutiny, and ask whether the statute is necessary to achieve a compelling governmental objective.

(b) Yes, probably. The Supreme Court has generally given strict scrutiny to any race-based classification scheme, even if it does not appear to be enacted for the purpose of disadvantaging African Americans. In a somewhat analogous situation involving child custody, the Court held that child custody decisions could not be made by taking into account race-matching or social prejudices; see *Palmore v. Sidoti*. So unless the mandatory consideration of race here is shown to be a necessary method of achieving a compelling state objective, it will be struck down. The state undoubtedly has a compelling interest in guaranteeing that a child be raised by a family that will be compatible. All other factors being equal, a racial match probably will make it easier for the child to develop a strong sense of identity. However, it is hard to see where the mandatory first-preference for a racial match is a "necessary" means of achieving state objectives, especially in light of evidence that it may keep children in institutional care longer. Therefore, the odds are that the court will find that the "necessary means" part of the equation has not been satisfied, and will strike down the mandatory first preference. (But a scheme merely requiring that race be considered as one factor among many, without making it the most important factor, probably would survive even strict scrutiny.)

40. (a) The court should use the mere-rationality standard, not the strict scrutiny standard.

(b) No, probably. Race is a "suspect category," and classifications based on race are therefore ordinarily subject to strict scrutiny. However, strict scrutiny will only be applied where the court finds that there was a governmental *intent* to discriminate against the disfavored group. The mere fact that a law has a less favorable *effect* on a racial minority than it has on the majority is *not* sufficient to trigger strict scrutiny. Disparate effect can be used as circumstantial evidence of an intent to discriminate, but such evidence is not dispositive. Here, the facts tell us that an intent to disfavor African American students was not present on the part of the school board. Therefore, strict scrutiny will not be applied, and instead the "rational relation" standard will be used. Under this standard, the classification will be upheld so long as it is rationally related to the achievement of a legitimate state objective. Here, cutting an expensive program is certainly rationally related to saving money for the school system, and saving money is certainly a legitimate state of objective in a time of economic hardship.

41. **(a) Strict scrutiny.** Classifications based on *national origin* are suspect. Similarly, classifications based on ethnic ancestry are suspect. So whether the French-Canadians are being discriminated against because they or their ancestors came from another country, or because they are part of a different ethnic group that speaks a different language, they are clearly a suspect class. Since all the evidence indicates that the decision was made for the purpose of disadvantaging members of this group (i.e., the disadvantage was not merely an inadvertent effect of action taken for some other reason), the requisites for strict scrutiny have been satisfied.

(b) Yes. Once strict scrutiny is applied, the challenged classification will only be upheld if it is necessary to achieve a compelling governmental objective. Preventing a particular group of citizens from becoming a majority in a town or school system is certainly not a compelling state objective (and probably not even a "legitimate" objective). Therefore, even if the challenged classification is a "necessary" means of achieving that objective, the classification must fall.

42. **No.** Discrimination against *any* racial, ethnic or national-origin group will be strictly scrutinized, even if that group has traditionally not been the victim of widespread prejudice or discrimination. Thus even discrimination against whites of Anglo-Saxon Protestant descent will be strictly scrutinized. This is the result of *City of Richmond v. J.A. Croson Co.*, striking down a minority set-aside program that disadvantaged whites. So the analysis, and outcome, should be exactly the same as in the prior question.

43. **(a) Strict scrutiny.**

(b) Yes. The facts here are fairly similar to those of *Richmond v. Croson*. That case makes it clear that any race-based affirmative action scheme will be strictly scrutinized, and will thus be struck down unless it is necessary to achieve a compelling governmental objective. Here, the scheme has at least two shortcomings, each of which is probably separately fatal. First, the city is not trying to remedy past official discrimination, or even explicitly trying to remedy past unofficial discrimination — the facts tell us merely that there has been an inequality of "economic opportunity," which is not the same as racial discrimination. In the absence of a legislative finding of discrimination in the office supply industry in the city of Monroe itself, any attempt to give a racial preference would probably be struck down regardless of how that preference was carried out. Secondly, the plan here is essentially a *quota* — it allocates a particular fixed percentage of city contracts for minority-owned firms. Rarely if ever will quotas be found to be a "necessary" means of redressing even clear past discrimination — certainly a city needs to consider, and probably try, less restrictive measures first, such as voluntary goals, an outreach program to solicit more bids from minority-owned firms, or some other means that is less hard-and-fast than an absolute set-aside.

44. **No.** The 2014 decision in *Schuette v. BAMN* establishes that voters are generally *free to repeal a race-conscious affirmative action plan*, and to change the *political process* in a way that intentionally makes it harder for a comparable race-conscious affirmative action plan to be instituted in the future. *Schuette* itself upheld a voter initiative to change a state's constitution so as to forbid a particular type of race-con-

scious affirmative action (in that case, a preference for admission to state universities), even though the initiative had the purpose and effect of making race-conscious government action much harder to institute than other sorts of comparable government action. (For instance, *Schuette* allowed the state to say, in effect, that residents lobbying for a race-conscious admissions preference must get the state constitution amended, whereas residents lobbying for a non-race-conscious admissions preference in favor of, say, alumni, merely have to persuade the university officials to grant it.) *Schuette* will control the outcome here: since the facts tell us that the problem in question (racial isolation in schools) came about through private housing decisions rather than by any government action, the voters are free to roll back government's attempt to use race-conscious means to deal with the problem, even though those race-conscious means (pupil assignments and busing) would not themselves have violated anyone's constitutional rights.

45. **(a) Mid-level scrutiny, i.e., whether the statute is "substantially related" to the achievement of an "important" governmental objective.** (*U.S. v. Virginia* says that gender-based classifications will now need an "exceedingly persuasive justification," and will be "skeptically scrutinized," but the case seems not to officially reject mid-level scrutiny, merely to indicate that mid-level scrutiny will now be applied in a rigorous way.)

(b) Yes, probably. Government classifications involving suspect or semi-suspect claims are evaluated by the same standard regardless of whether the purpose is to discriminate against the traditionally disfavored class or to redress past discrimination. In other words, there is no easier standard for "affirmative action." Thus the Supreme Court applies the same mid-level review to all gender-based classes, whether the classification is old-fashioned discrimination against women or affirmative action designed to improve the lot of women. In both cases, the gender-based classification will be upheld only if it is substantially related to the achievement of important governmental objectives.

Here, encouragement of bonding between parent and newborn child is probably an "important" governmental objective. However, a court would probably conclude that there is no "substantial relation" between a mother-only parental-leave program and achievement of this objective. It is highly likely that whatever social problems are caused by not having either parent at home during a child's infancy, those problems can be redressed as well or almost as well by having the father be at home. Therefore, a scheme that entitled either parent, but not both parents, to take a paid maternity leave would accomplish the legislative purposes as well or almost as well as the mother-only scheme. Consequently, the court will probably, thought not certainly, strike down the statute.

In general, courts are likely to strike down any statute that reflects *stereotypes* about the "proper place of women." See, e.g., *U.S. v. Virginia*, finding Virginia's belief that VMI's intense military training program is unsuitable for women to be an unconstitutional generalization about "the way women are." The scheme here — which implies that a mother's place, but not a father's place, is to be home with the newborn infant — reflects similar stereotypical thinking.

46. **(a) Strict scrutiny — the statute must be necessary to achieve a compelling governmental objective.**

(b) Yes, probably. There are three key issues here: (1) whether the fact that the preference was enacted by *Congress* rather than by a state or local government should change the standard for judicial review; (2) whether Congress' attempt to *wipe out past discrimination* renders the measure constitutionally acceptable; and (3) whether the Court's decision in *Grutter v. Bollinger*, allowing race-conscious university admissions, affects the answer.

As to the first issue — whether the fact that the preference was enacted by *Congress* rather than by a state or local government should change the standard for judicial review — the answer is *"no."* Because of the decision in *Adarand Constructors v. Pena*, strict scrutiny will be given to race-conscious congressionally-enacted affirmative action plans. Since the statute clearly classifies on the basis of race, it falls within this rule.

As to the second issue — whether Congress' desire to wipe out past governmental discrimination renders the measure acceptable — the answer is again *"no."* The eradication of past governmental discrimination is indeed probably a "compelling" goal. However, the preference probably would ***not*** be found to be ***"necessary"*** for the rooting out of the effects of past governmental discrimination. Congress did not make detailed ***findings*** about which geographical regions this discrimination exists in, or about which governmental units (e.g., universities versus other governmental actors) caused it. Also, there is no indication that Congress considered ***race-neutral means*** (e.g., use of "socio-economic" criteria rather than racial ones) as a possible way to solve the problem. As the Court said in another race-conscious university-admissions case, *Fisher v. Univ. of Texas* (2013), strict scrutiny "require[s] a court to examine with care, and not defer to, a university's '*serious, good faith consideration of workable race-neutral alternatives.*'" If there was a *"workable race-neutral alternative available"* to the university, then the race-conscious means can't be deemed to have been "necessary." *Id*. There's no evidence here that Congress ever gave "serious, good faith consideration" of race-neutral alternatives to see whether they might be workable.

The "rebuttable presumption" used here is better than an outright quota, but *Adarand, supra*, which involved a similar presumption-based scheme, suggests that racially-based presumptions will nonetheless be hard to justify (though the *Adarand* Court didn't actually decide whether the preference there survived strict scrutiny). Also, the Court might give slightly greater deference to Congress than it would to a state or local body. Nonetheless, the best guess is that the statute here would be struck down.

As to the final issue — whether the Court's decision in *Grutter v. Bollinger*, allowing race-conscious university admissions, changes the outcome — the answer once again is *"no."* Race-conscious affirmative action was allowed in *Grutter* because the majority was satisfied that the University there was pursuing the compelling goal of achieving diversity in the student body, and doing so in a narrowly-tailored way by use of individualized evaluations of each applicant. Here, there is no indication that Congress was seeking true diversity in each student body — Congress seems to have been nakedly pursuing *"racial balancing"* (i.e., making the portion of minority students at each university mirror the local student-age population), and the *Grutter* majority opinion makes it clear that this is not a legitimate objective. The numerically-based presumption of illegality just makes things worse, since such a presumption is more like the point system struck down by the Court in *Gratz v. Bollinger* than it is like the individualized evaluations upheld by the Court in *Grutter*. The Court's post-*Gratz* decision in *Parents Involved in Community Schools v. Seattle School District*, where a majority struck down pupil-assignment plans that gave a preference to students whose presence would lessen the racial imbalance in the target public school, further buttresses the conclusion that the racial preference here would be found to be in essence an illegitimate quota or "racial balancing" plan. The same is true of the even-more-recent decision in *Fisher, supra*, repeating *Grutter*'s holding that strict scrutiny will be applied to any race-conscious admissions method, and quoting approvingly *Parents Involved*'s statement that "Racial balancing is not transformed from 'patently unconstitutional' to a compelling state interest simply by relabeling it 'racial diversity.'"

47. **(a) Delta State.** Plan B, by amending the holistic method to explicitly take account of a student's race, makes use of a suspect classification (race). When government uses a suspect classification and is challenged on equal protection grounds, the burden of proof as to whether the classification is constitutional is

imposed on the government. So it will be up to Delta State to show, by a preponderance of the evidence, that its use of a race-conscious admissions method was constitutional.

(b) Strict scrutiny. That is, Delta State will have to show that Plan B was a *"necessary" means* of accomplishing a *compelling governmental interest.* So a reviewing court would (1) first decide whether the achievement of greater "educational diversity," as Delta State has defined such diversity here (attainment of a critical mass of African-American students on campus), represented a "compelling" governmental interest; and (2) if the answer to (1) was "yes," then decide whether the particular race-conscious admissions plan now being used, Plan B, was "necessary" to achieve that compelling interest. Under the Court's case law, the issue of whether the race-conscious means are "necessary" translates to the question of "whether [the] university could achieve sufficient diversity without using racial classifications." *Fisher v. Univ. of Texas* (2013) ("*Fisher I*"). If there was a "workable race-neutral alternative available" to the university, then the race-conscious means won't be deemed to have been "necessary." *Id.*

(c) Delta State, probably. As noted in part (b) above, Delta State will win only if Plan B survives strict scrutiny, an outcome that will require the university to show that Plan B was "necessary" to achieve a "compelling" governmental interest. So first, the trial court will have to determine whether the university's pursuit of greater educational diversity — defined here as having sufficient African-American students on campus that 55% of seminar classes will have two or more such students — is a "compelling" interest. The answer to this question is almost certainly "yes" — the Court has held that "the *educational benefits* that flow from *student body diversity*" constitute a compelling interest. *Fisher v. Univ. of Texas* (2016) ("*Fisher II*"). (The requisite diversity is not defined as, say, mechanically matching the racial or ethnic composition of the overall statewide population; rather, to be compelling the diversity must deliver "educational benefits" like "promoting cross-racial understanding" and helping to "break down racial stereotypes." *Id.*) The University of Texas (UT) argued in *Fisher II* that reducing the number of courses containing zero or one black student was a concrete measure of the desired student-body diversity (in part since it would have the benefit of reducing black students' feelings of racial isolation), and the *Fisher II* majority agreed that this goal was "compelling." So here, it's pretty clear that the trial court will accept as a compelling interest Delta State's desire to obtain enough African-American students that no more than 45% of seminar classes will have zero or one such student (i.e., will accept the university's categorization of this figure as reasonably defining a "critical mass" of such students).

The trial court will then consider whether Plan B is a "necessary" means of achieving this compelling interest in obtaining the educational benefits of increased student-body diversity. This issue translates to the question of whether there is a *"workable race-neutral alternative* available" that would achieve essentially the same diversity benefits, without unacceptable "side effects." On this "means-end fit" prong of strict scrutiny, the university will likely prevail. In *Fisher II*, a majority of the Court found that a similar race-conscious plan adopted by UT was a necessary means of achieving diversity, because there was no apparent workable race-neutral alternative available to UT. *Fisher II* includes several rulings that are relevant to the means-end-fit aspect of our current problem: (1) the Court gave UT credit for having evaluated the need for race-conscious methods "with care," and for having made a "reasonable determination" that such methods would be needed to achieve critical mass; (2) the Court found that UT behaved reasonably in concluding that using a Top Ten Percent Plan (in which the supposedly-race-neutral criterion of having a class rank in the top 10% of one's high school class was the sole method of choosing the entire incoming class) would not lead to a truly diverse student body, and would create "perverse incentives" like encouraging parents to "keep their children in low-performing segregated [high] schools." Applying these rulings to our facts here: (1) a court would almost certainly give Delta State credit for having carefully and reasonably determined that there were no plausible race-neutral means of achieving critical mass beyond Plan A and Plan B; and (2) the court would also likely conclude that insofar as using Plan A ("fill half the seats through a class-rank-only-based plan") would lead to a significantly academically-weaker student body than Plan B, Delta State reasonably determined that Plan A was not "workable" in terms of the university's overall aspirations (including the achievement of academic excellence).

There is, however, one respect in which Delta State's plan is more troubling than the UT plan approved in *Fisher II*: in *Fisher II*, the portion of the class that was filled by race-conscious means (as approved by the Court) was just 25%, whereas here, Delta State is proposing to use a "race as one factor among many" for *all* the incoming slots; so the plan here uses race as a bigger part of the entire admissions structure than was approved in *Fisher II*. But a fair reading of the majority's language in *Fisher II* — especially its general criticisms of class-rank-based admission systems — suggests that a lower court trying to apply *Fisher II* on our facts would conclude that Delta State's rejection of use of the class-rank-based Plan A for even half the class as not "workable" would not be second-guessed by the court. So it seems likely, though not certain, that Delta's use of Plan B would pass muster as to both the "compelling interest" and "narrow tailoring of means to end" prongs of strict scrutiny.

VI. CLASSIFICATIONS BASED ON ALIENAGE

A. **Alienage generally:** Recall that in deciding whether or not to treat a particular type of classification as "suspect," the Court has given substantial weight to whether the class which is disadvantaged is a "discrete and insular minority," i.e., a minority which is politically powerless and which has historically been discriminated against. (See *supra*, p. 262.) We have already seen that race, and its close relative national origin, have been treated by the Court as suspect classifications (*supra*, p. 256). In general, the Court has also purported to apply strict scrutiny to classifications disadvantaging **aliens**. However, the status of alienage classifications is much less clear than those of race and national origin.

   1. **Definition:** "Alienage," as the term is used by the Court, means "***not having U.S. citizenship***." Thus the term is not co-extensive with "national origin," since (1) discrimination against a person because he is of a particular national origin might occur even if he is a citizen (e.g., discrimination against a Mexican-American); and (2) discrimination against aliens often takes the form of discrimination against *all* aliens, without regard to their country of origin.

   2. **Powerless and discriminated against:** Aliens as a class do seem to bear the two principal traits which make a minority "discrete and insular." It seems clear that aliens as a class are "***politically powerless***," since they are not permitted to vote. And it is at least arguable that there has been traditional discrimination against aliens (though much of this is probably more easily explained as either discrimination against persons of particular national origins, or discrimination against undocumented, i.e., "illegal," aliens).

      a. **Not "immutable":** But one factor often relied upon by the Court in establishing that a given classification is "suspect" is lacking in the case of aliens: "***immutability.***" Thus in the case of race and national origin (and also in the cases of sex and illegitimacy, both subject to intermediate-level scrutiny), the trait is **beyond the power of the individual to change it.** But in the case of an alien, at least one who is legally in this country, there will normally come a time when he becomes **eligible for citizenship**; at that moment, of course, his alienage is no longer immutable.

     i. Significance: The "mutability" of the alienage trait may explain, at least in part, the wavering quality of the Court's commitment to strict-scrutiny treatment for the trait. This seems, for instance, to have been a sub-theme in the majority's handling of *Ambach v. Norwick, infra*, p. 342, involving two aliens who were already entitled to citizenship but who declined to claim it.

   3. Federal preemption: Unlike nearly all the other classifications typically reviewed under equal protection analysis, those based on alienage raise significant questions of *federal supremacy* and *preemption*. This is because the Constitution vests in the federal government full authority to deal with issues of immigration.

     a. Consequence: Therefore, when a state classifies in a way that disadvantages aliens, a relevant question is: Is this disadvantaging consistent with the fact that the federal government has permitted the aliens in question to reside in this country (or, in the case of "illegal" aliens, with the fact that the federal government has *not* so permitted them).

     b. Increasing importance: While issues of federal supremacy have not usually been dispositive in cases involving state treatment of aliens, the supremacy aspect seems to be becoming increasingly important. For instance, both the majority and the minority in *Plyler v. Doe* (a case deciding that illegal aliens may not be barred from free state education) relied in part on their views about whether such a ban comported with congressional immigration policy. See *infra*, p. 343.

B. General rule of "strict scrutiny": In the early 1970's, the Court began to treat discrimination against aliens as calling for *strict scrutiny*. There were three main cases in which such scrutiny was applied, and the statute under review invalidated:

   1. Welfare benefits: First, the Court held that states *cannot deny welfare benefits* to aliens. *Graham v. Richardson*, 403 U.S. 365 (1971). The opinion deemed aliens to be a "discrete and insular minority," and held that the state's fiscal interest in preserving limited resources for its citizens was not a sufficiently strong countervailing governmental interest.

     a. Rationale: The opinion noted that *aliens pay taxes* (from which the funds to pay welfare benefits come), just as citizens do.

   2. Bar admissions: Then, the Court held that states may not prevent resident aliens from *practicing law*. *In re Griffiths*, 413 U.S. 717 (1973). None of the state interests supposedly served by the ban (e.g., maintaining "high professional standards" and having lawyers serve as "officers of the court") was sufficiently closely linked to exclusion of aliens to overcome strict scrutiny.

   3. Civil service: Lastly, the Court held that a state may not bar aliens from holding positions in the state *civil service. Sugarman v. Dougall*, 413 U.S. 634 (1973).

C. *Sugarman* exception: But in what was to become an extremely important dictum, the Court in *Sugarman* stated that a state *could* prevent aliens from holding state *elective* executive, legislative and judicial positions, and even important *nonelective* positions in any of the branches of state government.

   1. Rationale: The Court reasoned that such persons "perform *functions that go to the heart of representative government*." Therefore, just as a state could exclude aliens from voting, it could exclude them from "participation in its democratic political institutions."

2. **Consequence:** This "exception" to the principal doctrine of *Sugarman* has ***virtually swallowed the rule***. See, e.g., *Cabell v. Chavez-Salido, infra,* p. 342, placing "Spanish-speaking Deputy Probation Officers" within the *Sugarman* exception. See generally Sullivan & Gunther, pp. 812-13.

3. ***Sugarman* exception interpreted broadly:** The trend towards interpreting the *Sugarman* exception extremely broadly, so as to bar aliens from a wide range of state employment, began with *Foley v. Connelie,* 435 U.S. 291 (1978), where the Court held that New York could prevent aliens from becoming ***state troopers***. Since state troopers were engaged in "execution of broad public policy," and since they held a large degree of ***discretion*** in doing so, they fell within the *Sugarman* exception.

4. **Public school teachers:** The *Sugarman* exception was broadened again, when the Court permitted New York to bar aliens from becoming ***public school teachers. Ambach v. Norwick***, 441 U.S. 68 (1979), a 5-4 decision.

   a. **Facts:** The bar in *Ambach* applied to all aliens except those who had "manifested an intention to apply for citizenship." Plaintiffs refused to apply for citizenship even though they were eligible for it.

   b. **Standard:** The majority in *Ambach* expressed the test as being whether the employment was a ***"governmental function,"*** i.e., a function which was ***"bound up with the operation of the state as a governmental entity. ... " Public school teaching, in the majority's opinion, qualified under this standard.***

   c. **Application of test:** Since public school teaching fell within the exception rather than the rule of *Sugarman*, only a mere-rationality review was appropriate, and the classification passed muster under that review.

5. **Probation officers:** ***Deputy probation officers*** were added to the list of jobs from which aliens may be barred, in *Cabell v. Chavez-Salido,* 454 U.S. 432 (1982) (another 5-4 decision).

6. **Notaries public:** In the only post-*Sugarman* case in which the Court found *Sugarman* not applicable, the Court held that ***notaries public*** do ***not*** perform "functions that go to the heart of representative government." *Bernal v. Fainter,* 467 U.S. 216 (1984). Since the duties of a notary public are "essentially ***clerical*** and ***ministerial***," aliens may be barred only if the state can establish a justification that survives strict scrutiny (which the state was not able to do in *Bernal*).

7. **Summary of present position:** It seems clear, then, that the present majority of the Court will allow states to ban aliens from any post involving a ***"political"*** rather than "economic" function, and that any post ***related to education or law enforcement*** is likely to be found "political." In fact, it is not even at all clear that *Griffiths* (the attorney case) would be decided the same way under the present Court, though *Bernal* (the notary case) may indicate that it would.

D. **The federal government:** Suppose a classification disadvantaging aliens is made by the ***federal government***, rather than by a state. As noted, the Equal Protection Clause would not directly apply to the government's action; instead, the Fifth Amendment Due Process Clause would be interpreted to impose requirements similar to those which the Equal Protection Clause places upon the states. But because of the federal government's ***exclusive responsibility for supervising immigration***, a given instance of discrimination against aliens, if made by the federal government, will be reviewed with ***greater deference*** than would the same type of discrimination when carried out by a state.

1. **Balancing test:** Roughly speaking, the Court has ***"balanced"*** the federal government's interest in controlling the terms of immigration against the alien's right to fair treatment.

2. **Administrative agency action:** The Court has granted this greater deference more readily to actions taken directly by Congress and the President than to action taken by ***administrative agencies***. See, e.g., *Hampton v. Mow Sun Wong*, 426 U.S. 88 (1976) (regulation issued by the Civil Service Commission barring resident aliens from jobs in the federal Civil Service is struck down, though ban would not necessarily have been invalid if promulgated directly by the President or Congress).

3. **Medical benefits:** In the Court's only case where ***Congress itself*** discriminated against certain aliens, the Court ***upheld*** congressional power to do so. In ***Matthews v. Diaz***, 426 U.S. 67 (1976), the Court held that Congress could impose the double requirement that aliens be both admitted for permanent residence and have resided continuously in the U.S. for five years, in order to receive Medicare. The Court (a unanimous one) stressed Congress' ***full power over immigration***, a power which justified some discriminations against aliens which might not be permitted to the states.

E. **Education of illegal aliens:** In all the cases considered in this section thus far, the aliens who claimed to be discriminated against were ***legally present*** in this country. But what are the rights of aliens who have not been legally admitted, i.e., so-called ***"illegal"*** or ***"undocumented"*** aliens? The Supreme Court has not yet dealt with the rights of ***adult*** illegal aliens. But it has established that illegal aliens of ***school age*** may ***not***, consistent with the Equal Protection Clause, be charged a ***fee for public school education. Plyler v. Doe***, 457 U.S. 202 (1982).

1. **Facts of *Plyler:*** *Plyler* involved a Texas statute which: (1) denied local school districts funds for education of illegal-alien children; and (2) allowed school districts to deny free public education to such children.

2. **Majority strikes statute:** By a 5-4 vote, the Court ***struck down*** the statute as violative of equal protection. The majority opinion required several steps to reach this result:

    a. **Protected by Fourteenth Amendment:** First, the Court rejected Texas' argument that the Equal Protection Clause applies only to state action against "any person within [the state's] jurisdiction," and that illegal aliens are not "within Texas' jurisdiction" at all. The Court concluded, as a matter of legislative history, that the Clause was intended to cover ***any person physically within a state's borders***, regardless of the ***legality*** of his presence.

    b. **Intermediate scrutiny applied:** The Court then devoted much of its opinion to determining the proper level of scrutiny. It concluded that ***intermediate-level scrutiny*** was appropriate here, since both the powerless nature of the group and the importance of education were factors.

        i. **"Not suspect class":** The Court explicitly ***rejected*** the suggestion that illegal aliens should be treated as a ***"suspect class."*** Entry into the class was a ***voluntary*** act (since entry into the nation was voluntary), in contrast to the involuntary nature of membership in other suspect classes. Also, illegal immigrant status was clearly not a constitutional irrelevancy, since Congress possessed, and had exercised, the power to exclude certain aliens, and the states could "follow the federal direction."

    ii. Not mere "rational relation": But "mere-rationality" review was not sufficient, either. Although the action by adult aliens in illegally entering this country was voluntary, the action of their *children* was *not*. Also, public education, while not a "right" guaranteed by the Constitution, was certainly more important than other social welfare "benefits." Denying these children an education would render them illiterate, and would thus prevent them from advancing based on their individual merit and from becoming useful members of society.

c. Congressional policy: Texas argued that Congress' failure to admit these children, and indeed its "apparent disapproval" of their presence, gave the state authority to treat them less favorably than citizens and resident aliens. The majority agreed that if Texas' denial of public education to these children was indeed in accord with an "identifiable congressional policy," Texas' action might well be valid. But, the majority believed, this denial *was not in accord with any identifiable congressional policy*. For instance, there was no evidence that Congress had ever even considered conservation of state educational resources as a reason for restricting immigration.

d. State interest supporting action: Texas also asserted three interests of its own which, it believed, justified the denial of free public education. But the Court did not find any of these interests sufficiently weighty to overcome the intermediate-level scrutiny.

    i. Prevent influx: First, the state contended that its statute might help *stem the flood* of illegal immigrants. But the Court found this a "ludicrously ineffectual" way of stemming this tide, especially in view of an alternative measure: prohibiting the *employment* of illegal aliens.

    ii. Preserving high quality of education: Texas also contended that illegal alien children imposed an especially heavy burden on the state's ability to provide *high quality public education*. But, the majority responded, even if excluding the children would improve the overall quality of education (an assertion as to which the Court found no evidence), Texas still bore the burden of showing why *this particular group of aliens*, as distinguished from documented aliens, was the appropriate one to exclude. Texas was unable to discharge this burden, since documented and undocumented alien children were "basically indistinguishable" in terms of their educational needs.

    iii. Less likely to remain resident: Finally, Texas claimed that illegal alien children were less likely than other children to remain within the state and therefore less likely to put their education to use there. The Court also rejected this claim, essentially because it found nothing in the record to suggest that this was true as a factual matter.

e. General "conservation of resources" argument: The majority also rejected Texas' more general claim, that it had an interest in *preserving the state's limited educational resources* so that it could spend these on the education of its lawful residents. The majority found it easy to dismiss this argument, by resort to precedent. Preservation of scarce resources was simply *never a sufficient reason* for denying those resources to one particular group; this had already been established in the case of welfare benefits (*Graham v. Richardson, supra*, p. 341).

    i. **Comparison:** The Court's response to this "scarce resources" argument is similar to its rejection of "administrative convenience" as a grounds for discrimination against a particular group (e.g., married servicemen in *Frontiero v. Richardson, supra*, p. 321). In the most general sense, the fact that the state saves money, time, effort, etc. is *never by itself enough to justify the selection of a particular group to bear the brunt of the state's conservation efforts* (at least where the group is one which receives the benefit of intermediate-level or strict scrutiny).

3. **Dissent:** Justice Burger dissented in *Plyler*, joined by three other members of the Court (White, Rehnquist and O'Connor).

    a. **Unduly result-oriented:** First, Burger objected to the general way in which the majority arrived at the decision to use intermediate-level scrutiny. Since the majority was not treating illegal aliens as a suspect class nor education as a fundamental right, the Court was "[p]atching together bits and pieces of what might be termed quasi-suspect-class and quasi-fundamental-rights analysis [making the Court] guilty of an unabashedly result-oriented approach. ... " In the dissent's view the majority's theory had so little generality that it established "little more than that the level of scrutiny employed ... applies only when illegal alien children are deprived of a public education."

    b. **Voluntariness irrelevant:** Burger also objected to the fact that the majority took into account the "involuntariness" of the children's presence in this country. For Burger, it was simply irrelevant that the trait upon which the discrimination was based (illegal presence) was involuntary. For instance, the state could distinguish between mentally-ill persons and mentally-healthy ones, even though the condition of the former might be beyond their control. Nor was it relevant that the Court had previously given intermediate-level scrutiny to classifications based on illegitimacy; here, the discrimination was not based merely on "status of birth" but on a congressionally-unsanctioned illegal presence.

    c. **Education:** Burger also objected to the extra weight that the majority gave to the interest in education, as distinguished from other governmental benefits. He contended that *Rodriguez (infra*, p. 365) had definitively established that education was not a "fundamental right," and that therefore, the fact that it was education which was being denied (as opposed to, say, welfare, medical care or housing) could not make any difference to the level of scrutiny applied.

    d. **Rational relations:** Since neither the plaintiff's illegal alien status nor the nature of education should, in Burger's opinion, trigger any special scrutiny, he believed that the *"mere-rationality" test was the appropriate one.*

        i. **Application of test:** Not surprisingly, Burger found that denial of free public education to these children was rationally related to legitimate interests held by Texas. The state had an interest in preserving its fiscal resources, and could reasonably conclude that it had no obligation to spend those resources on education for persons illegally in the country. Also, the state had a legitimate interest in attempting to curb the influx of illegal immigrants; denial of public education might not be the most effective way of accomplishing this end, but that means was not completely irrational.

    ii. Congressional policy: The dissent also argued that the *federal* government's exclusion of illegal aliens from various social welfare programs (e.g., the food stamp and AFDC programs) supported the rationality of a state's excluding such aliens from state programs.

4. Scope of case unknown: Because the majority, in deciding to apply intermediate-level scrutiny in *Plyler*, relied upon the *combination* of a disadvantaged group (illegal aliens) and an unusually important interest (education), the Court avoided the need for deciding whether *either* of these factors *by itself* might justify intermediate scrutiny.

    a. Intermediate review for illegal aliens: Thus it remains a possibility that *other types of discrimination against illegal aliens* (even if not involving something as basic as the complete denial of education) *might nonetheless trigger intermediate-level scrutiny.*

    b. Complete denial of education: Similarly, it is possible that the *complete denial of education* to any group (even one without the special powerlessness that marks illegal aliens) might be given intermediate-level or even strict scrutiny, despite the fact that lesser variations in the furnishing of education are subjected only to "mere-rationality" review (under *Rodriguez, infra*, p. 365).

VII. ILLEGITIMACY

A. Discrimination against illegitimates: Many states have statutes which disadvantage illegitimate children. The discrimination may take the form of ineligibility to take by intestate succession, inability to sue for the parent's wrongful death, disentitlement to claim a presumption of dependency (relevant for receipt of certain government benefits, such as social security survivors' benefits), etc.

B. Present state of the law: The Supreme Court has vacillated considerably over the years on how classifications based on legitimacy should be treated. Here is a summary of the present state of the law:

1. Mid-level review: *Mid-level review* is used. That is, the classification disadvantaging illegitimates must be substantially related to an important governmental objective. *Clark v. Jeter*, 486 U.S. 456 (1988).

2. Claims can't be flatly barred: Consequently, the state cannot simply bar unacknowledged illegitimate children from bringing wrongful death actions, from having any chance to inherit, etc. Such children must be given at least *some reasonable opportunity* (typically, via a proceeding brought by their mother) to obtain a *judicial declaration of paternity.* Once they obtain such a declaration, they must be *treated equivalently to children born legitimate.*

    a. No short statutes of limitation: Furthermore, the statute of limitations on paternity claims must be no longer than is reasonably needed to fulfill the state's interest in, say, weeding out stale or fraudulent claims.

Example: Pennsylvania passes a statute of limitations saying that no action for child support may be brought on behalf of an out-of-wedlock child unless the action is brought before the child turns 6. *Held*, the statute violates the child's equal protection rights. Since the classification is based on out-of-wedlock status, it will be upheld only if it is substantially related to an important governmental objective. Concededly, Pennsylvania has an interest in avoiding the litigation of stale or fraudulent claims. But the 6-year statute of limitations is not "substantially related" to the achievement of that interest. *Clark v. Jeter, supra.*

VIII. MENTAL RETARDATION AND MENTAL ILLNESS

A. Mental retardation: The Supreme Court has refused to treat *mental retardation* as a quasi-suspect classification. *City of Cleburne v. Cleburne Living Center*, 473 U.S. 432 (1985).

1. **Rationale:** The Court in *Cleburne* advanced four reasons why it would not be appropriate to accord heightened scrutiny to classifications based on mental retardation:

    a. **Judicial second-guessing undesirable:** First, the states have a legitimate interest in giving special treatment to the mentally retarded, because of their "reduced ability to cope with and function in the everyday world." The treatment to be given to the mentally retarded is "a difficult and often a technical matter, very much a task for legislators guided by qualified professionals and not by the perhaps ill-informed opinions of the judiciary." If heightened scrutiny were given to classifications based on mental retardation, the judiciary would be more likely to be required to make "substantive judgments" about the legislative handling of the retarded, judgments which it is ill-equipped to make.

    b. **No antipathy by lawmakers:** Secondly, the array of national and state legislative responses to the plight of the mentally retarded (responses which, in general, *benefit* the retarded) show that there is no "continuing antipathy or prejudice" on the part of lawmakers.

    c. **Not politically powerless:** Thirdly, the very fact that these legislative responses have occurred "negates any claim that the mentally retarded are politically powerless in the sense that they have no ability to attract the attention of the lawmakers."

    d. **Other groups:** Finally, if quasi-suspect status were given to the "large and amorphous class" of the mentally retarded, there would be no "principled way" to deny quasi-suspect status to a number of other groups, including the aging, the disabled, the mentally ill, and the infirm. And this kind of expansion is something the courts should be "reluctant" to embark upon (though the Court did not say why).

2. **D flunks mere-rationality review:** As it happened, the fact the retarded were not given quasi-suspect status in *Cleburne* did *not* mean that the retarded plaintiffs lost the case. Although the Court purported to apply only the "mere-rationality" standard (by which the classification would be upheld so long as it was rationally related to some legitimate governmental objective), the particular governmental classification at issue in *Cleburne* was *struck down*. The defendant municipality's refusal to grant a "special use permit," required by the municipal zoning ordinance before a group home for the mentally retarded could be operated, was found not to be even rationally related to any legitimate state pur-

pose. Rather, the denial of the permit seemed to "rest on an ***irrational prejudice*** against the mentally retarded."

    a. Rigorous application of test: The Court appeared to be applying the "mere-rationality" test with considerably ***more rigor — and less deference to the government —*** than it has done in most recent cases involving that test (as to which, see *supra*, p. 252). So the standard might fairly be called mere-rationality review ***"with bite."***

3. Dissent: Three members of the Court (Marshall, Brennan, and Blackmun) disagreed with the Court's refusal to give the mentally retarded quasi-suspect status. They contended that the mentally retarded have been subject to a " 'lengthy and tragic history' … of segregation and discrimination that can only be called grotesque." They argued that at least where what is at issue is the right of the retarded to establish a group home (the right to "establish a home" being clearly a "fundamental liberty"), heightened scrutiny should be given to any regulation that burdens their right to do so.

    a. Majority's rationale rejected: The three Justices dissenting on this point also contended that the majority's reasoning was illogical:

        i. Legislation irrelevant: For instance, the fact that extensive legislation had recently been enacted to protect the retarded did not mean that there was no ongoing discrimination against the retarded, or that this group was necessarily less needful of the benefits of heightened scrutiny. The dissenters pointed out that "race-based classifications [did not become] any less suspect once extensive legislation had been enacted on the subject."

        ii. Relevance of trait: The dissenters also could not see why the fact that retardation was relevant to *some* types of regulation should mean that it was relevant to the kind of regulation here. "That a characteristic may be relevant under some or even many circumstances does not suggest any reason to presume it relevant under other circumstances where there is reason to suspect it is not. A sign that says 'men only' looks very different on a bathroom door than a courthouse door." For the dissenters, the fact that retardation is irrelevant in some circumstances, when coupled with a history of discrimination against the retarded, was enough to require heightened scrutiny.

4. Significance: Beyond establishing that mental retardation will not be treated as a quasi-suspect classification, *Cleburne* appears significant for at least two other reasons:

    a. Hostility to heightened scrutiny: The case probably indicates that a majority of the present Court is ***reluctant*** to establish ***additional "quasi-suspect" classes.*** The majority went out of its way to indicate that it thought quasi-suspect status should not be given to certain other classifications that arguably merit it, such as "the aging, the disabled, the mentally ill, and the infirm." Therefore, few if any new entries into the catalogue of quasi-suspect classes can be expected from the present Court.

    b. Burdens vs. benefits: The case also seems to confirm the Burger/Rehnquist Court's reluctance to treat a classification as more suspicious when it is used to ***burden*** the historically-disadvantaged group than where it is used to ***benefit*** that group. Recall that in the case of gender-based classifications, the Court gives the same level of review (intermediate scrutiny) to such classifications whether they purport to benefit women or not. Similarly, in the case of mental retardation, the Court will apparently apply the same level (rigorous "mere-rationality" review, but not intermediate-level scrutiny) to the classification, regardless of whether the particular classification in question appears to have been motivated by a desire to benefit or to burden the retarded.

B. Mental illness: The Court has never explicitly decided whether classifications based on *mental illness* should be treated as quasi-suspect.

    1. Unlikely to be quasi-suspect class: However, in light of *Cleburne*, it seems very unlikely that the Court would give the mentally-ill quasi-suspect status.

    2. "Mere-rationality with bite": However, the mentally ill, like the mentally retarded, have often been discriminated against, and do bear some of the traits of a "discreet and insular minority." (See *U.S. v. Carolene Products Co., supra,* p. 262.) Therefore, although the Court would probably give to classifications based on mental illness only low-level "mere-rationality" review, it may apply that level of review in the same fairly stringent way (mere-rationality *"with bite"*) that it did to the mental-retardation classification in *Cleburne*.

IX. GENERAL PRINCIPLES OF MIDDLE-LEVEL SCRUTINY

A. General principles: Once a court decides that traditional deferential, "mere-rationality" review is appropriate, it is almost a foregone conclusion that the statute will be upheld. Conversely, if the court decides to apply strict scrutiny, the statute will almost invariably be struck down. Thus in these two situations, it is not usually important to focus on exactly how the review takes place; the important thing is how the choice of standards gets made. By contrast, the decision to apply "middle-level" or "intermediate" review does not by any means dispose of the matter; the precise way in which the court applies the middle-ground scrutiny thus becomes extremely important. This section reviews briefly some of the principles that seem to be guiding the courts in applying intermediate-level review.

B. Importance of objective: The *objective* sought to be achieved by the statute must be *"important,"* even if it need not be "compelling" (as required in strict scrutiny situations).

    1. Little "bite": However, this requirement has not proven to have a lot of bite, since most asserted state objectives have been found to be "important." However, there are some exceptions, such as "administrative convenience" and "conservation of scarce resources" (see *supra*, p. 344).

C. Close means-end fit: The *means* chosen by the state must be *"substantially related"* to achieving the important objective. That is, the *means-end fit* must be a *reasonably tight one*.

    1. Less-restrictive alternatives: Looking at this requirement another way, the demands of intermediate scrutiny are more likely to be satisfied if there are *no available alternatives* that would carry out the asserted objectives as well or better, without causing needless disadvantage to anyone.

    2. Smoking out bad motivation: One reason for requiring a close means-end fit is that it furnishes a way of *"flushing out" unconstitutional motivation*. See Ely, p. 146 (regarding strict scrutiny); see also *supra*, pp. 263-263. That is, if the state claims that a particular objective was the motivation behind the statute, yet the means is not closely related to the ends, the court will be justified in suspecting that the asserted motivation was not the real one (which may have been an unconstitutional one).

D. **Refusal to hypothesize state purpose:** Recall that in the area of general social and economic welfare legislation, where "mere-rationality" review is all that is applied, the Court seems to be willing to consider possible objectives to which the means chosen by the legislature are rationally related, even though there is no evidence that this objective *in fact* motivated the legislature. (*Supra*, p. 250.) In the intermediate-review area, however, the Court *will not hypothesize a state objective*; only those objectives which are shown (by the terms of the statute, legislative history, or otherwise) to have *actually motivated the legislature* will be considered. If none of these actual objectives is sufficiently "important," or sufficiently tightly related to the means chosen, the statute will be struck down.

> **Example:** In *Trimble v. Gordon*, 430 U.S. 762 (1977), the state argued that one purpose of its ban on intestate succession by illegitimates was to enforce the "presumed intention" of intestate decedents. The Court rejected this asserted objective, stating "[we] do not think [the law] was enacted for this purpose [and] we will not hypothesize an additional state purpose. … "

Quiz Yourself on
EQUAL PROTECTION — ALIENAGE AND ILLEGITIMACY

48. The state of Pacifica enacted a statute providing that no person who is not a U.S. citizen could hold title to beach-front land located in the state. Pacifica's west coast consists entirely of ocean-front property. The statute was enacted in part because state residents were annoyed that Japanese nationals and citizens of other Pacific rim countries were paying high prices for Pacifica beach-front property, making it harder for U.S. citizens living in Pacifica to compete for ownership of that property. Yukio, a Japanese citizen who resides permanently in the United States, and who wishes to buy ocean-front property in Pacifica, has sued to have the statute overturned on the grounds that it violates her equal protection rights.

    (a) What standard of review should the court give to the Pacifica statute? _____

    (b) Will Yukio's attack succeed? _____

49. The city of Xenon was concerned that many applicants for posts as public school teachers in the town, and some hires, were foreigners who spoke with a hard-to-understand accent. Therefore, the Xenon school board enacted a regulation that henceforth, all new hires for the post of school teacher in the local school system must at the time of their application be United States citizens. Ted, an Englishman married to an American citizen, was a permanent resident of the U.S. but had no desire to become a U.S. citizen (even though his marital status entitled him to become one). Ted sued Xenon to have its citizens-only rule overturned, on the grounds that it violated his equal protection rights.

    (a) What standard should the court use in reviewing the Xenon citizens-only provision? _____

    (b) Will Ted's attack on the provision succeed? _____

50. The village of Tesla had a fine school system, generally believed to be better than that of surrounding towns. Tesla is located less than 100 miles from the border with Mexico, and has a large number of both Mexican Americans as well as undocumented aliens from Mexico. In order to discourage enrollment by students who in fact reside in other towns, the village enacted a set of strict regulations providing that

only students who satisfied two conditions could attend the village's schools: (1) they had a bona fide residence within the village limits; and (2) they were either U.S. citizens or resident aliens. One effect of this regulation, as intended by the town elders, was to make undocumented aliens unable to attend the village schools even if they resided in the village. The principal motive for the no-illegal-aliens rule was to conserve tax dollars, because undocumented aliens on average pay lower property taxes, and education in the state is financed principally through property taxes. The village allowed an exception to its enrollment restrictions for anyone willing to pay a tuition fee of $4,000 per year.

Pedro, a resident of Tesla who was undocumented, sued the village, arguing that as applied to him the enrollment restrictions violated the Equal Protection Clause.

(a) When the court reviews Pedro's challenge to the enrollment restrictions, what standard of review should it use? _____

(b) Will Pedro's attack succeed? _____

51. The state of Rigor provides that no illegitimate child may receive any part of his or her father's estate if the father dies intestate. This statutory exclusion applies even if there has been a judicial finding of paternity prior to the father's death. When Stuart was 11, he was found (in a proceeding brought on his behalf by his mother) to be the illegitimate son of David. Two years after this finding, David died intestate. Stuart has sued for a declaratory judgment that the state's exclusion of him from an intestate share of David's estate violates his, Stuart's, equal protection rights.

(a) What standard of review should the court use in examining the exclusion of illegitimate children from the intestacy scheme? _____

(b) Will Stuart's attack succeed? _____

_____

Answers

48. (a) Strict scrutiny.

(b) Yes, probably. Discrimination against aliens (at least aliens who are legally in this country) is to be strictly scrutinized, because aliens as a class are politically powerless and frequently discriminated against. Therefore, any statute that discriminates against aliens on its face, or whose purpose is to disadvantage aliens, will be struck down unless it is necessary to achieve a compelling governmental interest. Here, the state's interest in keeping land prices low for American citizens is almost certainly not "compelling." In any event, discrimination against aliens is not a "necessary" way to achieve that objective, since there are other less-discriminatory options available (e.g., price controls that apply to everybody).

49. (a) The mere-rationality standard.

(b) No. As noted in the answer to the prior question, discrimination against aliens is generally subjected to strict scrutiny. However, under the so-called "*Sugarman* exception," this strict scrutiny does not apply to discrimination against aliens who apply for jobs that ***"go to the heart of representative government."*** The Court has held that the post of public school teacher falls within this "heart of representative government" exception, because of a teacher's opportunity to "influence the attitudes of students towards government, the political process, and a citizen's social responsibilities." *Ambach v. Norwick.* Therefore, only a mere-rationality review is used, and the regulation will be upheld if it is rationally related to the achievement of a legitimate state objective. Here, the regulation almost certainly satisfies this standard. Hiring teachers who can be easily understood is surely a legitimate state objective, and there is at least a rational relation between citizenship and ease of understanding (since non-citizens on average probably have harder-to-understand accents than citizens).

50. **(a) Intermediate-level review, under which the measure will be invalidated unless it is "substantially related" to the achievement of an "important" governmental objective.**

(b) Yes, probably. The Court held in *Plyler v. Doe* that intermediate-level review should be given to any state law denying free public-school education to illegal aliens of school age. In *Plyler*, the Court held that the various state interests advanced there (e.g., preventing an influx of illegal immigrants, conserving tax dollars, etc.) were not sufficiently weighty to overcome this mid-level review. The enrollment restriction here is essentially identical to that struck down in *Plyler*. The fact that non-residents of the village are also excluded is irrelevant — the key fact is that among residents of the village, those who are illegal aliens are excluded, whereas those who are citizens or resident aliens are allowed. Even if the village shows that it has to spend tax dollars on educating these additional students, and even if it is able to show that it does not get state aid to compensate it for these incremental burdens, the interest in conservation of resources is likely to be found insufficient to overcome the mid-level review (and similar fiscal interests were found insufficient in *Plyler* itself).

51. **(a) Mid-level review.**

(b) Yes, probably. After waffling a lot about what the appropriate level of review is for classifications that disadvantage illegitimates, the Supreme Court has finally held that intermediate scrutiny should be used. That is, the statutory classification that disadvantages illegitimates must be "***substantially*** related to an ***important*** governmental objective." Here, the state's total exclusion of illegitimates from intestate succession, even those who have been found by a reliable court proceeding to be the decedent's child, is very unlikely to be found to be substantially related to the achievement of an important state objective. (For instance, while the state may have an important objective of repelling false claims of paternity, this objective is not advanced at all by excluding one who has, during the decedent's lifetime, been found to be truly his child.) See *Trimble v. Gordon*, 430 U.S. 762 (1977), roughly matching the facts of this case, and striking down the total exclusion.

X. UNEQUAL TREATMENT OF GAYS, AND THE BANNING OF SAME-SEX MARRIAGE

A. Issues generally: A critical and controversial issue in equal protection over the last two decades has been the status of ***gays and lesbians***: to what extent may government ***classify people on the basis of their sexual orientation***, or otherwise intentionally disfavor homosexuals?

The Supreme Court has issued four major gay-rights opinions since 1996, all of which have been decided ***in favor of the gay party***. Here's a summary of where this quartet of cases has left the law of equal protection:

❑ **Right to same-sex marriage:** Same-sex couples have a ***fundamental right to be married.*** Therefore, states must ***issue marriage licenses*** to gay couples, and states (and the federal government) must ***recognize*** same-sex marriages entered into in other jurisdictions.

❑ **No "semi-suspect" status:** The Court has ***not*** so far ***treated*** classifications based on sexual orientation as having official ***"semi-suspect"*** or ***"suspect"*** status. So when the Court hears a challenge to a classification based on sexual orientation and not involving a fundamental right, the Court seems to use some form of easy-to-satisfy *"mere-rationality"* review, not mid-level review (which is given to semi-suspect classifications, like gender) or strict scrutiny (given to suspect classifications, like race and ethnicity).

❏ **Mere-rationality "with bite":** However, in cases not involving a fundamental right,[23] although the Court appears to apply mere-rationality review, it has in fact given *much less deference* to the legislature's sexual-orientation-based classification system than is typically applied in mere-rationality cases. The level of review used can fairly be described as "mere rationality *with bite.*"

❏ **Animus towards unpopular minority:** A persistent theme in these decisions has been the majority's conclusion that legislative classifications based on sexual orientation have historically been *based solely on animus towards a disfavored minority*, and that such animus *cannot be a "legitimate governmental interest."* Therefore, the Court concludes, the classification system fails mere-rationality review because of the lack of a legitimate interest. (See *supra*, p. 251, for a more general discussion of the Court's decisions turning on a finding of legislative animus towards disfavored minorities.)

1. **Four major cases:** The majority opinion in each of these four major gay-rights cases was written by Justice Kennedy. The cases, listed in the order in which they were decided, are:

   ❏ *Romer v. Evans*, a 1996 case in which the Court struck down a state constitutional amendment that would have prohibited any local government from *giving various anti-discrimination protections* to gays and lesbians.

   ❏ *Lawrence v. Texas*, a 2003 decision in which the Court struck down a *state's criminalizing of same-sex "sodomy"* between consenting adults. The case was decided based on substantive due process rather than equal protection grounds, which is why we discuss it in the chapter on due process (see *supra*, p. 202). But because the Court used a quite stringent form of mere-rationality review, *Lawrence*, like the three cases decided mostly on equal protection grounds that we're considering here, exemplifies the modern Court's trend of giving unusually close review to laws that single out gays.

   ❏ *U.S. v. Windsor*, a 2013 decision in which the Court struck down a key definition in the federal Defense of Marriage Act (DOMA), under which only opposite-sex couples could be deemed married for federal purposes. The effect of the decision was that *if a same-sex couple was married under the law of a state*, the federal government *could not treat the couple any differently* than it would treat a *heterosexual couple* married under that same state's law.

   ❏ *Obergefell v. Hodges*, a 2015 decision in which the Court expanded on *Windsor* by holding that *all states must allow same-sex couples to marry*, and must recognize same-sex marriages entered into in other jurisdictions.

We discuss *Romer*, *Windsor* and *Obergefell* here, since these three cases were decided mainly on equal protection grounds.

---

23. As noted, the *right to marriage* is now deemed fundamental, so the text of this paragraph does not apply to the claim that states violate the Constitution when they refuse to allow same-sex marriage.

B. Singling out of gays because of animus (*Romer v. Evans*): The first case in the quartet described above was *Romer v. Evans*, 517 U.S. 620 (1996). There, the Court **struck down** a Colorado constitutional amendment that would have **prevented the state or any of its cities from giving certain protections to gays or lesbians**. The Court found that the measure flunked "mere-rationality" review on two separate grounds: there was no legitimate state interest in fact being served, and the means chosen by the state were not rationally related to the (possibly legitimate) interest that the state asserted.

1. **Facts:** The Colorado provision, known as "Amendment 2," modified the Colorado constitution to provide that neither the state nor any subdivision (including state agency, city or school district) shall "enact, adopt or enforce any statute, regulation, ordinance or policy whereby **homosexual, lesbian or bisexual orientation**, **conduct**, practices or relationships shall constitute or otherwise be the basis of or entitle any person or class of persons to have or claim any **minority status**, quota preferences, **protected status** or **claim of discrimination**."

    a. **Bans anti-discrimination laws:** The main practical impact of Amendment 2 was that it prevented both the state legislature and any city from passing statutes or ordinances that would **protect gays and lesbians from discrimination**. For instance, the cities of Aspen, Boulder and Denver had all passed (prior to the enactment of Amendment 2) ordinances barring discrimination against gays in housing, employment, education, public accommodations, and the like; each of these ordinances would apparently have been wiped out by Amendment 2. Only by re-amending the state constitution — something requiring a state-wide referendum — could gays obtain any protection against discrimination on the basis of sexual orientation.

2. **Holding:** By a 6-3 vote, the Court struck down Amendment 2, even though the majority used only "mere-rationality" review. The opinion by Justice Kennedy relied on several grounds:

    a. **Gays not put in "same position" as others:** Colorado defended the amendment on the grounds that it merely (in Kennedy's words) "puts gays and lesbians in the **same position** as all other persons" and "does no more than deny homosexuals **special rights**." But Kennedy found this interpretation "implausible." The amendment in fact singled gays out for **worse** treatment than other groups: "Homosexuals, by state decree, are **put in a solitary class** with respect to transactions and relations in both the private and governmental spheres. The amendment **withdraws from homosexuals, but no others, specific legal protection** from the injuries caused by discrimination[.]"

    b. **Desire to harm is not a legitimate interest:** Kennedy then asserted that Amendment 2 "seems inexplicable by anything but **animus toward the class that it affects**." He quoted approvingly the statement in *U.S. Dep't of Agric. v. Moreno*, 413 U.S. 528 (1973) (discussed *supra*, p. 251), that "If the constitutional conception of 'equal protection of the laws' means anything, it must at the very least mean that a **bare . . . desire to harm a politically unpopular group cannot constitute a legitimate governmental interest**."

    c. **"Protection of liberties of landlords or employers" rationale rejected:** Colorado argued that Amendment 2 was rationally related to the protection of **other citizens' freedom of association**, in particular the freedom of landlords or employers who have personal or religious objections to homosexuality. Kennedy did not reject this as a legitimate state interest. But he found the ***means-end fit*** to be so loose that it was not credible that this free-association interest was even part of what had motivated the state: "The breadth of the Amendment is so far removed from these particular justifications that we find it impossible to credit them."

    d. Conclusion: Kennedy concluded by saying that "Amendment 2 classifies homosexuals not to further a proper legislative end but to make them ***unequal to everyone else***. This Colorado cannot do. A State ***cannot so deem a class of persons a stranger to its laws***."

3. Dissent: The dissent, by Justice Scalia (joined by Rehnquist and Thomas) was unusually vitriolic. Scalia accused the majority of ***"tak[ing] sides in the culture wars,"*** and said that its striking down of the Amendment was "an act, not of judicial judgment, but of political will."

    a. No singling out: Scalia rejected the majority's view that Amendment 2 singled out homosexuals for unfavorable treatment. All the Amendment did was to say to gays that "they may not obtain preferential treatment without amending the state constitution."

    b. Rationally related: Scalia believed that the Amendment was in fact reasonably related to a legitimate governmental interest. That interest was the prevention of "***piecemeal deterioration of the sexual morality*** favored by a majority of Coloradans." And a measure that merely denied homosexuals "preferential treatment" was surely an appropriate means of achieving that end.

C. The federal Defense of Marriage Act struck down (*Windsor*): In ***U.S. v. Windsor***, 133 S. Ct. 2675 (2013), the Court decided that ***when a same-sex couple has been married under the law of a state***, the federal government ***may not treat the couple any differently***, for federal-law purposes, than it would treat a ***heterosexual couple*** married under that same state's law.

The *Windsor* decision invalidated, on essentially equal protection grounds, a major part of a 1996 federal statute called the ***Defense of Marriage Act***. The effect of *Windsor* was that any same-sex couple who had been married under the law of a state that permitted same-sex marriage was then entitled to the ***same federal benefits*** as any opposite-sex married couple.

1. The 1996 Defense of Marriage Act (DOMA): In the mid-1990s, a majority of Congress wanted to make sure that even if some states decided to recognize same-sex marriages, unwilling states or the federal government would not have to follow suit. Congress tried to accomplish this by passing, in 1996, the ***Defense of Marriage Act (DOMA),*** 1 U.S.C. § 7 and 28 U.S.C. §1738C.

    a. Federal recognition of state's same-sex marriage: DOMA, as enacted by Congress, had two independent provisions. The provision that was at issue in *Windsor* (***"§3"***) said that the ***federal*** government ***didn't have to recognize a same-sex couple as being married*** — even if they were married under state law — for purposes of any *federal* benefits or federal regulations.

    b. States allow same-sex marriage: By the time of the Supreme Court's 2013 decision in *Windsor*, 12 states and the District of Columbia had granted same-sex couples the right to marry.

        i. DOMA's consequence: Section 3 of DOMA meant that no federal statute or regulation — dealing with ***income tax, estate tax, immigration, health insurance***, etc. — was *permitted* to treat a same-sex couple that had been legally married in any of these states as being married for federal purposes.

2. **Kennedy's opinion strikes down DOMA:** By a 5-4 vote, the Court held that section 3 of DOMA was an *unconstitutional infringement* of the *rights of same-sex couples whom state law regarded as properly married.* The majority opinion was by Justice Kennedy. He was joined by the four members of the Court's liberal wing, Justices Ginsburg, Breyer, Sotomayor and Kagan.

  a. **Basis for Kennedy's opinion:** It's not so easy to state which constitutional provision(s) Kennedy found DOMA to have violated, or what standard of review he used.

  b. **Equal protection as basis:** Kennedy's opinion seemed to rely *mainly on equal protection*, and secondarily on *substantive due process*. He asserted that DOMA should be subjected to *more than casual review*, to determine whether it was a constitutionally "obnoxious" discrimination; he then decided that DOMA could not survive this review.

    i. **Summary:** In summary, Kennedy said, *"no legitimate purpose* overcomes [DOMA's] purpose and effect to *disparage* and to *injure* those whom the State, by its marriage laws, sought to *protect in personhood and dignity."* By treating married same-sex couples as "living in marriages *less respected* than others," Congress had violated the Fifth Amendment's guarantees of equal protection and due process.

3. **Dissents:** The Court's four most conservative members — Roberts, Scalia, Alito and Thomas — *dissented*.

  a. **Scalia's dissent:** The most extensive dissent was by Justice Scalia, who delivered a stinging criticism of the majority's handling of the merits.

    i. **"Mere-rationality:"** Scalia gave his own answer to the standard-of-review issue that Kennedy had avoided: that DOMA's classification between same-sex and opposite-sex state-consecrated marriages should be reviewed *"only for its rationality."* Judged by this mere-rationality standard, for Scalia this was an easy case, because §3 of DOMA was rationally related to the achievement of several legitimate objectives (e.g., having a *"uniform federal definition of marriage,"* to deal with issues such as a same-sex couple that marries in a state where same-sex marriage is legal and then moves to one where it is not).

D. **States must allow same-sex marriage (*Obergefell*):** The same majority that decided *Windsor* then, two years later, announced a broader proposition: that there is a *constitutionally-guaranteed right to same-sex marriage.* In *Obergefell v. Hodges*, 135 S.Ct. 2584 (2015), the Court held by a 5-4 vote that *all states* must: (1) *issue marriage licenses to same-sex couples*; and (2) *recognize all same-sex marriages entered into in other states.*

1. **Based on both equal protection and due process:** The decision in *Obergefell* was based on *both* the *Equal Protection* and the *Substantive Due Process* Clauses — state laws banning same-sex marriages were found to violate both the equal protection and the substantive due process rights of gay and lesbian couples who wished to marry. We'll conduct our detailed discussion of *Obergefell,* here in the context of equal protection.[24]

---

24. For how *Obergefell* fits into the Court's substantive due process case law, see *supra*, pp. 199-201.

2. **Setting of case:** Between the Court's 2013 decision in *Windsor* and its 2015 decision in *Obergefell*, there was a strong movement across the U.S. towards recognizing a right to same-sex marriage. Four of the five federal circuits to confront the issue between *Windsor* and *Obergefell* found that the states could not constitutionally ban same-sex marriages. The sole exception was the Sixth Circuit, which combined for review four district-court decisions (involving same-sex-marriage bans in Ohio, Tennessee, Michigan and Kentucky), and concluded that the Constitution did not require the states to allow same-sex marriage. This Sixth Circuit case was the decision on appeal to the Supreme Court in *Obergefell*.

   a. **State courts and legislatures:** Apart from decisions by the federal courts of appeal, various state-court opinions and legislative changes had already, prior to *Obergefell*, eliminated many bans on same-sex marriage. Consequently, by the day in June 2015 when the Supreme Court handed down *Obergefell*, same-sex marriage was already legal in 37 states and the District of Columbia, leaving only 13 states (including the four states covered by the Sixth Circuit's *Obergefell* decision) with bans in place. Thus *Obergefell* directly changed the laws of only these 13 states.

3. **The various plaintiffs:** In the various cases consolidated in *Obergefell*, the plaintiffs were 14 same-sex couples, as well as two men whose same-sex partners had died. All of the plaintiffs contended that state officials, by obeying state laws that either forbade the issuance of marriage licenses to same-sex couples and/or refused to recognize out-of-state same-sex marriages, violated the plaintiffs' constitutional rights.

4. **Kennedy's majority opinion:** Justice Kennedy wrote the Court's opinion, as he had written each of the Court's three major prior opinions that had gradually enhanced the constitutional rights of gays and lesbians.

   a. **Importance of marriage:** Kennedy began by describing, in the lofty tone he often used, the importance of marriage. He referred to the "transcendent importance of marriage," which in its customary man-and-woman configuration "always has ***promised nobility and dignity to all persons***, without regard to their station in life." The institution has "existed for millennia and across civilizations," and is "essential to our most profound hopes and aspirations."

   b. **Marriage as a "fundamental right" for due process:** Kennedy then turned from this abstract discussion of marriage to the first substantive question presented by the case: is the right of a same-sex couple to be married under state law a ***"fundamental right"*** for purposes of the Fourteenth Amendment's guarantee that a person's "liberty" may not be infringed upon in a way that violates the person's right to **substantive due process**? After a long discussion of cases in which the Court had found *opposite*-sex marriage to be a "fundamental" right for substantive due process purposes, Kennedy concluded that the factors making marriage fundamental for due process ***apply equally to the same-sex marriage context.*** (We discuss the due process aspects of the decision at greater length *supra*, pp. 199-201, as part of our discussion of the substantive due process rights of gays and lesbians.)

   c. **Marriage as fundamental for equal protection analysis:** Next, Kennedy asserted that marriage should be considered a fundamental right ***for equal protection purposes,*** just as for substantive due process purposes.

i. **Application to same-sex marriage:**   In the same-sex-marriage context, Kennedy said, use of both equal protection and due process analysis was appropriate. Not only did the bans on same-sex marriage "burden the liberty of same-sex couples" (giving rise to the due process violation), but the bans also *"abridge central precepts of equality."* These laws *"are in essence unequal: same-sex couples are denied all the benefits afforded to opposite-sex couples* and are barred from exercising a fundamental right."

(1) **History of disapproval:** Kennedy also indirectly referred to a factor that has often been central in cases in which the Court has chosen to review a given classification with more-than-usual rigor: the fact that the classification *disadvantages certain isolated minorities.* He mentioned the *"long history of disapproval* of [same-sex] relationships," and suggested that this history added to the "grave and continuing harm" marriage bans impose on gay couples, by "serv[ing] to *disrespect and subordinate them."*

ii. **No review standard mentioned:** Curiously, nowhere in his opinion did Kennedy say *what standard of review* he was applying in his equal protection analysis. So we are left to parse the opinion for clues as to the standard.

(1) **More than "mere rationality":** It's pretty clear from the result in *Obergefell* that the standard Kennedy applied was *not* the typical easy-to-satisfy *"mere-rationality"* standard, used in reviewing run-of-the-mill economic and social-welfare legislation. (See *supra*, p. 248.) But did Kennedy use the *"strict scrutiny" standard* (like that used concerning classifications based on race or ethnicity)? Or was it *"intermediate review"* (like the standard used for classifications based on gender)? Or, as a final alternative, was it what might be called *"mere-rationality with bite,"* which seems to be the standard the Court has used in some other recent cases involving classifications based on sexual orientation (see *supra*, p. 252)? As of this writing (early October, 2020), the answer remains unclear.

(2) **Significance of fundamental right:**   But one thing *does* seem clear: the relatively-demanding equal-protection review that Kennedy applied (whatever its precise dimensions) stemmed not *just* from the fact that the classification disfavored gays, a historically marginalized and discriminated-against category. Rather, the *fundamental importance* of *marriage as an institution* seems to have been an essential part of Kennedy's decision to impose relatively rigorous review of the fact that the marriage laws in question treated gays less favorably than opposite-sex couples.

d. **Rebuttal to the "await legislative action" argument:**   Kennedy also addressed the main argument made by the dissent: that whatever the social merits of same-sex marriage, respect for the democratic process demanded that any change in the definition of marriage be made by the people's *elected representatives, not by unelected judges.*

i. **Kennedy's answer:** Kennedy's answer stressed that *protection of individual rights against the will of the majority* was precisely what the individual-liberty provisions of the Constitution were designed to ensure. "The dynamic of our constitutional system is that *individuals need not await legislative action before* *asserting a fundamental right."* He continued, "An individual can invoke a right to constitutional protection when he or she is harmed, *even if the broader public disagrees and even if the legislature refuses to act."* He quoted *West Virginia Bd. of Ed. v. Barnette* (see *infra*, p. 592): "*Fundamental rights may not be submitted to a vote; they depend on the outcome of no elections."*

5. **Dissents:** Each of the four Justices in the minority — Roberts, Scalia, Alito and Thomas — wrote a separate dissent. The dissents all sounded one major theme: that the decision on whether to allow same-sex marriages should be *left to the elected legislatures of each state*, not to nine unelected members of the Supreme Court. We'll focus on the dissents of Roberts and Scalia.

   a. **Roberts' dissent:** Chief Justice Roberts signaled the depth of his disagreement with the majority by reading his dissent from the bench, the first time he had done so in his 10 terms on the Court.

      i. **Should be left to legislature:** Roberts believed that it was not the Supreme Court's place to decide what the rules of marriage should be. *"[T]his court is not a legislature,"* he said. "Whether same-sex marriage is a *good idea should be of no concern to us."*

      ii. **Not a "fundamental right":** Roberts rejected the idea that the liberty interest guaranteed by the Fourth Amendment included a fundamental right to same-sex marriage. He seemed to concede implicitly that in some contexts (perhaps he had in mind opposite-sex adult couples), the right to marriage might indeed be "fundamental." But, he said, "The fundamental right to marry *does not include a right to make a State change its definition of marriage"* to extend beyond the traditional one-man-one-woman formulation.

      iii. **Not an irrational restriction:** Roberts then dismissed in passing a question that the majority had not addressed: were states' bans on same-sex marriages so *"irrational"* that they should be struck down under even the easy-to-satisfy mere-rationality test for cases where no fundamental right or suspect class is at issue?[25] Roberts' quick answer was in the negative: "a State's decision to maintain the meaning of marriage that has persisted in every culture throughout human history *can hardly be called irrational."*

      iv. **Judicial overreach:** Roberts harshly criticized the majority for overstepping its constitutional role, calling the majority's decision *"an act of will, not legal judgment."* The majority, he said, "omits even a pretense of humility, openly relying on its desire to *remake society according to its own 'new insight' into the 'nature of injustice.' "*

         (1) **"Basis of human society for millennia":** At this point, in a passage that many observers identified as the most memorable of his dissent, Roberts summed up the consequences of the majority's overreaching: "[T]he Court invalidates the marriage laws of more than half the States and orders the *trans-*

---

25. The majority didn't *need* to address this issue, because it found that even in the case of same-sex couples, the right to marriage is fundamental; therefore, restrictions on that right were to be reviewed by a standard that (although unspecified by the majority) was clearly at least somewhat more rigorous than the usual "mere-rationality" review used in situations not involving fundamental rights or strict and semi-strict classifications.

formation of a social institution that has formed the basis of human society for millennia, for the Kalahari Bushmen and the Han Chinese, the Carthaginians and the Aztecs. Just who do we think we are?"

b. **Scalia's dissent:** The most notable of the other three dissents was by Scalia, a dissent that was unusually cutting even for him. Scalia said he agreed with all of the detailed points made by Roberts' dissent, which he joined. But he wrote separately to call attention to what he said was the majority's *"threat to American democracy."*

     i. **Robs people of "freedom to govern themselves":** The majority's holding, Scalia said, was the "furthest extension one can even imagine" of a development he had long criticized: "the Court's *claimed power* to *create "liberties"* that the Constitution and its Amendments *neglect to mention."* By claiming that power to create new liberties, he said, the majority was "rob[bing] the People of [their] *most important liberty*: ... the *freedom to govern themselves."*

     ii. **Nine unelected lawyers:** He called the majority's approach *"a naked judicial claim to legislative — indeed, super-legislative — power."* The majority was imposing a "system of government that makes the People *subordinate to a committee of nine unelected lawyers,"* a system that "does not deserve to be called a democracy." The majority was now "engaging in a *judicial Putsch."*

6. **Significance of case:** Here are the most significant principles that *Obergefell* establishes:

a. **Fundamental right under substantive due process clause:** The right to marriage, including the right of two people of the same sex to marry, is a *"fundamental" aspect of "liberty,"* for purposes of interpreting the Fourteenth Amendment's guarantee that liberty will not be infringed without due process. Therefore, *substantial interferences* with that right will be subjected to at least somewhat closer-than-normal judicial review.

b. **Fundamental right for equal protection purposes:** Similarly, government distinctions treating same-sex couples less favorably with respect to access to marriage than opposite-sex couples will be deemed interferences with the fundamental right of marriage *under the Equal Protection Clause.* This fundamental-rights treatment seems to mean that government regulations that intentionally make it harder for same-sex couples to marry than for opposite-sex couples (or give them lesser benefits from marrying) will be more rigorously reviewed by the courts. (However, as I discuss below, we don't know how *much* tougher the level of review will be.)

c. **Federal, state and local governments:** The fundamental status of the right to same-sex marriage is binding on *all levels of government,* federal, state and local.

d. **Right to a marriage license:** *Obergefell,* taken together with its new grant of "fundamental right" status to same-sex marriage, means that any unit of government that confers upon *opposite-sex couples* the right to marry must confer the *same right to same-sex marriage.* Most obviously, this means that since all states authorize marriages to take place between opposite-sex couples that meet certain requirements (e.g., age and residency), all states must similarly *authorize marriages between same-sex couples meeting those same requirements.*

e. **Right to same consequences once married:** It also seems clear that no level of government may intentionally give same-sex married couples *less favorable benefits* or other treatment as the result of being married than that government gives to opposite-sex couples.

    i. **Birth certificates:** One vivid application of the *Obergefell* principle requiring "no less favorable treatment for same-sex married couples" has already been supplied by the Supreme Court. Two years after *Obergefell*, the Court summarily decided[26] in *Pavan v. Smith*, 137 S.Ct. 2075 (2017), that it *violates Obergefell* for a state to deny same-sex *female married couples* the right to *have both women listed* on the *birth certificate* of a child conceived by *anonymous sperm donation*, given that the state lists the husband from an opposite-sex couple in that same anonymous-sperm-donation situation.

    ii. **Divorce, adoption, taxation, etc:** *Obergefell* and *Pavan* make it clear that a state may not treat same-sex married couples less favorably than opposite-sex couples with respect to *divorce*, *child custody*, *adoption*, *state income and estate taxation*, or any other aspect of law that derives from a couple's status of being married.

    Example: Consider one of the same-sex couples who were plaintiffs in *Obergefell*, April DeBoer and Jayne Rowse. The two wanted to be able to *both* adopt each child whom they decided to bring into the family. But Michigan limited the class of people who could adopt any given child to (1) opposite-sex married couples and (2) one single individual. This meant that DeBoer and Rowse could not, pre-*Obergefell*, both adopt the same child. (Then, if the adopting parent died the other would have no legal rights regarding the child.)

    The decision in *Obergefell* makes it clear that not only must Michigan permit DeBoer and Rowse to marry, but it must then permit the two of them to adopt the same child if it would permit both members of an opposite-sex couple to adopt a given child.[27]

7. **Open questions:** Here are a couple of the important issues left open by *Obergefell*:

    a. **Strict scrutiny for interference with fundamental right to marriage?** Recall that Justice Kennedy's opinion for the court in *Obergefell* never actually stated *what standard of review* the Court was using. The opinion concludes that the "right to marriage" is "fundamental" for both equal protection and substantive due process purposes, and that this is true whether the couple that wishes to marry is same-sex or opposite sex. And normally in cases involving significant interferences with what the Court finds to be a fundamental right, the court specifies that *strict scrutiny* (or perhaps *semi-strict scrutiny*) is to be used. But Kennedy's opinion in *Obergefell* *never specifies what standard of review he is using* to find the statute unconstitutional.

    i. **Less-than-outright ban:** This lack of specificity on the standard of review is likely to matter not so much on whether states may make it harder for same-sex couples to *get* married than opposite-sex ones (it's clear from *Obergefell* that the

---

26. "Summarily" means that the Court acted without a briefing on the merits by either party, and without oral argument. That is, the Court went from granting *certiorari* directly to deciding the case on the merits.

27. But whether the principle behind *Obergefell* means that *unmarried* same-sex couples must be treated identically to unmarried opposite-sex couples with respect to adoption, or with respect to any other incident of state law, is not yet clear; see *infra*, p. 362.

answer to this is "no"), but on whether states may write or interpret their laws in a way that gives **lesser benefits** to gay couples on account of their marriage than it gives to opposite-sex couples.

Example: Suppose a state, when it employs people, offers an employee's opposite-sex spouse fully-subsidized health insurance, but only offers *half*-subsidized health insurance to an employee's same-sex spouse. Suppose further that the state defends this distinction on the grounds that its financial resources are limited, and it cannot immediately afford to cover the full cost of benefits for this new, unanticipated class of spouses.

Intuitively, it seems likely that the "fundamental right to marriage" theory of *Obergefell* will be interpreted to mean that the state will lose if a same-sex couple brings an equal protection challenge. But is the court to reach this result by using strict scrutiny? Mid-level review? Or perhaps just "mere-rationality with bite" (see *supra*, p. 251)? We won't know until the Supreme Court gives us further guidance.

b. **Suspect status of anti-gay laws outside of the marriage context:** Another category of questions left open by *Obergefell* concerns government's right to treat gays and lesbians less favorably than straight people **outside of the right-to-marry context.**

i. **Lack of textual support in *Obergefell*:** Claims by gay individuals, or by unmarried gay couples, that government is unconstitutionally discriminating against them on the basis of their sexual orientation don't seem to get much support from any actual language in *Obergefell*. Nowhere in the majority opinion does Kennedy even hint at **what level of review** is to be applied to those classifications that are drawn based on sexual orientation, but that do not involve the right to marry.

(1) **Not necessarily a suspect or semi-suspect class:** In particular, the majority gives no hint — as many gay activists had hoped it would — that homosexual orientation outside of the marriage context is to be treated as constituting a **"suspect class" or "semi-suspect class,"** the way the Court treats classifications based on race (a suspect class; see *supra*, p. 256) or **gender** (a semi-suspect class; see *supra* p. 322).

(2) **Disfavoring of gays may be allowable outside of marriage context:** If the Court eventually concludes that same-sex orientation outside of marriage **does not constitute a suspect or semi-suspect class,** then as we've seen earlier, two important consequences will follow:

[1] Equal protection review would merely have to satisfy the easy-to-meet **"mere-rationality"** standard i.e., (the law just has to be rationally related to the achievement of a legitimate state objective); and

[2] The **burden of proof** would be on the person **challenging** the classification, not on the government.

So if it turns out that unfavorable classifications based on sexual orientation outside of the marriage context are not deemed suspect or semi-suspect (and assuming no fundamental right is at issue), gays will get only the **relatively minimal protection conferred by mere-rationality review**, which rarely leads to striking down the classification.

ii. **Discrimination vs gays or the transgendered as "sex discrimination":** As we just noted in passing in (b)(i)(1) above, the Court gives intermediate-level review, rather than mere-rationality review, to classifications based on "***gender***," i.e., "***sex***." Members of the L.G.B.T. community have argued for years that intentional discrimination based on a person's ***same-sex orientation*** or ***gender identity*** (e.g., ***transgender*** status) should be considered to be discrimination based on "sex," for both statutory and constitutional-equal-protection purposes. If this argument were accepted, intentional government discrimination against ***gay or transgender individuals would be subjected to close equal protection scrutiny, and likely invalidated.***

(1) **Opinion on statute (*Bostock*):** We have at least a hint that the Court would accept this argument for purposes of the Equal Protection Clause. In a 2020 opinion interpreting the main federal employment-discrimination ***statute***, "Title VII," a majority of the Supreme Court ***agreed with this pro-LGBT argument***. In *Bostock v. Clayton County*, 140 S.Ct. 1731 (2020), the Court held that the statute's prohibition of employment discrimination ***"because of"*** a person's ***"sex" includes discrimination on account of the person's being gay or transgender.*** The opinion does not discuss any constitutional issues; but the Court's reasoning can plausibly be extended to the equal protection context if the employer is found to be a "state actor" (see *infra*, p. 431).

c. **Free speech and free exercise rights of opponents to same-sex marriage:** A last major issue involving *Obergefell* arises when a private ***business operator*** resists a ***state anti-discrimination law*** by claiming a First Amendment ***free-speech*** or ***free-exercise-of religion*** right to ***refuse to supply services in connection with a same-sex wedding.***

i. **Expressive component of good or service:** The business operator's First Amendment claim is likely to be especially powerful when the same-sex couple requests goods or services that are to be ***customized*** by the supplier to meet the specific needs of the same-sex wedding ceremony.

Example: Suppose the state of Equality enacts a statute, Proposition 100, prohibiting any person operating a place of public accommodation from discriminating on grounds of "sexual orientation." Ted and Bob (the Ps), two gay men who are about to marry, see an online advertisement for a flower shop operated by D, which reads, "Let me use my artistry to create a one-of-a-kind floral arrangement for your special occasion." They visit the shop, and disclose to D that they want a custom arrangement for their wedding, with the phrase "Ted and Bob, married under God, now and forever" to be written in the middle. D declines, saying "My religious beliefs prohibit me from creating custom arrangements that celebrate same-sex weddings." At the Ps' request, the state charges D with violating Proposition 100. D defends on the grounds that both her free-speech and free-exercise-of-religion rights would be violated by compelling her to deliver this message, with which she disagrees. The case goes to the U.S. Supreme Court.

It seems more likely than not that the present Court would find for D, especially on Free Exercise Clause grounds. Cases like *Tandon v. Newsom* (*infra*, p.

707) demonstrate that since Justices Kavanaugh and Barrett have joined the Court, it has become even more solicitous of free-exercise claims. So there would probably be five or more votes to hold that D's free-exercise rights require the state to exempt her from having to perform this highly-expressive task.

XI. FUNDAMENTAL RIGHTS

A. Introduction: In most of the equal protection cases that we've discussed so far, the decision to apply more than extremely deferential "mere-rationality" review was made because of the peculiar nature of the *group* burdened by the statutory classification. But there is another way in which more-than-deferential equal protection review may be triggered: If the classification burdens a *"fundamental right"* or "fundamental interest," the classification will be subjected to strict scrutiny, *regardless of the characteristics of the people who are burdened*.

1. **Meaning of "fundamental":** There are two general classes of rights which are deemed "fundamental," so that any interference with them will give rise to strict equal protection scrutiny. The first consists of rights which are *independently and explicitly guaranteed by some other constitutional provision* (distinct from the Equal Protection Clause). The second consists of rights which are not independently and explicitly given by other constitutional provisions, but which are felt to be both important and implicitly granted by the Constitution, so that large deviations in equality as to them are viewed as suspect.

   a. **Example of first class:** A primary example of the first type of "fundamental right," one independently guaranteed by constitutional provisions apart from the Equal Protection Clause, is the right of *interstate migration* (see *infra*, p. 381). While there is some dispute as to exactly which part of the Constitution guarantees this right, it is clear that the right exists apart from the Equal Protection Clause. Nonetheless, the Equal Protection Clause will be used to strictly scrutinize a classification which restricts the migration rights of some but not all citizens. See *Shapiro v. Thompson, infra*, p. 381.

   b. **Example of second class:** As an example of the second type of fundamental right, one which does not exist outside the Equal Protection Clause and therefore relies entirely on that clause for its vindication, consider substantial interferences with the *right to vote* in state elections (see *infra*, p. 369). Thus a law imposing a $1.50 poll tax on anyone who wished to vote was strictly scrutinized and invalidated under the Equal Protection Clause, in *Harper v. Virginia Board of Elections, infra*, p. 369.

2. **Developed by Warren Court:** Strict scrutiny of classifications impairing fundamental rights began in the Warren Court. The three principal areas in which that Court found fundamental rights to be at stake were: (1) the *right to vote* (and the related right to participate as a candidate); (2) the right to *use the courts*; and (3) the right of *interstate migration*. (Each of these is considered in its own section below).

   a. **Proposals for extensions:** Proponents of a broad reading of the fundamental rights doctrine argued that that doctrine should also be applied in a number of other contexts; most interestingly, they contended that this treatment should be used to strictly scrutinize legislation impairing equal access to *"necessities"* (e.g., welfare, housing, and education). The Warren Court never dealt with the fundamental rights doctrine's applicability to such necessities.

3. **The post-Warren Court:** The post-Warren Court has for the most part *declined to expand the list* of fundamental rights beyond the broad areas recognized by the Warren Court. For instance, *"necessities"* like *welfare* and *education*, despite their conceded societal importance, have been held *not to be fundamental*.

   a. **Right to marry:** On the other hand, in various post-Warren-era cases the Court has held that the *right to marry is* fundamental, for equal protection (as well as substantive due process) purposes. Thus the Court has found that *same-sex couples* have a fundamental right to marry. See *Obergefell v. Hodges*, 135 S.Ct. 2584 (2015), discussed extensively *supra*, p. 199 and p. 356.

B. **Education:** The prime example of the Court's refusal in the post-Warren era to treat "necessities" as fundamental rights is the Court's refusal to give fundamental-rights status to *education*. In *San Antonio Ind. School Dist. v. Rodriguez*, 411 U.S. 1 (1973), the Court held (by a 5-4 vote) that there is *no fundamental right* to equality in *public-school education*.

   1. **Facts:** In *Rodriguez*, the plaintiffs claimed that Texas' system of financing public education violated equal protection, because it relied principally on local property taxes. This meant that districts with a high property tax base per pupil consistently spent more on education than those with a low base were able to do.

   2. **Majority's holding:** The majority rejected the plaintiffs' two main arguments: (1) that residents of property-base-poor districts formed a "suspect class," especially since (the plaintiffs contended) poorer families tended to live in districts with smaller property tax bases; and (2) that education was a fundamental right, inequalities in the distribution of which must be strictly scrutinized.

   3. **Not suspect class:** The majority rejected the *"suspect class"* theory in large part because the majority simply disagreed that the poorest families lived in the districts with the smallest tax bases. The Court conceded the validity of the plaintiff's contention that districts with smaller property tax bases spent less money per pupil on education; but this fact did not make residents of those districts a suspect class.

      a. **Rationale:** These residents had "none of the *traditional indicia of suspectness.*" The class was *"large, diverse, and amorphous* … unified only by the common factor of residence in districts that happen to have less taxable wealth. … " Members of the class had not been subjected to a history of *"purposeful unequal treatment,"* nor relegated to a position of *political powerlessness* so as to require "extraordinary protection from the majoritarian political process."

      b. **Wealth:** The Court implied, though it did not state, that even a class composed entirely of poor people would not by that fact alone be "suspect." See *infra*, p. 384, for additional discussion of the Court's refusal to treat wealth as a suspect classification.

   4. **Not fundamental interest:** Most of the majority's opinion was devoted to explaining why the deviations in per pupil expenditures did not constitute interference with a *fundamental right*. Most critically, the majority stated that the *"importance"* of a service performed by a state does not determine whether it is "fundamental" for equal protection purposes. " '*Relative societal significance*' of an interest is *irrelevant*. Rather, the issue is whether *the right is 'explicitly or implicitly guaranteed by the Constitution.' "*

      a. **Education not guaranteed:** By this standard, education was not "fundamental." It was certainly not explicitly guaranteed by the Constitution. The plaintiffs argued that a right to education was implicitly guaranteed by the Constitution, because education was essential to effective exercise of First Amendment freedoms and the right to vote. The majority responded that **absolute equality** in education was certainly not guaranteed, even implicitly, by the Constitution.

5. **Absolute deprivation issue not addressed:**   But the Court in *Rodriguez* seemed to acknowledge the possibility that an **absolute deprivation** of education, if imposed on some group, might nonetheless be found to be an impairment of a fundamental right: "Even if it were conceded that some identifiable quantum of education is a constitutionally protected prerequisite to the meaningful exercise of either [the First Amendment or the right to vote], we have no indication that the present [Texas] system fails to provide each child with an opportunity to acquire the **basic minimal skills** necessary." Only the less-than-absolute **differences** among districts were at issue in *Rodriguez*.

6. **Rational relation test:**   Since neither a suspect class nor a fundamental right was at issue, the majority held in *Rodriguez*, the traditional "mere-rationality" test applied. The Texas system **passed** this test. The scheme had been enacted (the majority appeared to find) for the purpose of giving each **local district** a large **measure of control** over the education given to its residents, a goal which the majority found legitimate.

    a. **Imperfect means-end fit not fatal:**   The Court conceded that some districts (the ones with a lower property tax base) had less control over spending than others. But this was merely a slight imperfection in the means-end fit, an imperfection which did not negate the existence of a "rational relationship" between the means chosen (use of local property taxes) and the ends sought (local control). It was not mandatory that the "least restrictive alternative" be selected.

7. **Dissents:**   Four Justices dissented; we'll focus on the one by Marshall.

    a. **Marshall's dissent:**   Marshall disagreed with the majority's view that only those rights that are "explicitly or implicitly guaranteed by the Constitution" should be treated as "fundamental" for equal protection analysis.

        i. **Marshall's proposed test:**   Marshall proposed his own test for "fundamentality." The issue should be "the extent to which constitutionally guaranteed rights are **dependent on interests not mentioned in the Constitution**. As the nexus between the specific constitutional guarantee and the non-constitutional interest draws closer, the non-constitutional interest becomes more fundamental[.]" For instance, the right to appeal from a criminal conviction is "fundamental," he said, because of its close interrelationship with the Fourteenth Amendment's specific guarantee of due process of law.

            (1) **Education as "fundamental":**   By this test, education was a fundamental right, since it "directly affects the ability of a child to exercise his First Amendment interests. ... " Similarly, educated persons exercise the right to vote more frequently than those who are not educated.

            (2) **Sliding scale:**   Throughout his dissent, Justice Marshall was apparently not suggesting that full-fledged "strict scrutiny" should be given to the Texas statute. Rather, he seemed to be arguing in favor of a **"sliding scale"** of review, whereby the degree of scrutiny in equal protection cases, instead of being a

rigid two-pole scheme, would vary along a ***continuum*** depending on the importance of the interest and the suspectness of the classification.

8. **Significance of *Rodriguez:*** We will discuss *Rodriguez* again in the treatment of wealth classifications *infra*, p. 384. For now, several significant principles may be deduced from the case: (1) whether a right or interest is "fundamental" is determined by whether it is ***expressly or impliedly guaranteed by the Constitution, not*** by its ***"societal importance"***; (2) by this standard, the right to public education (or, at least, the right to ***equality in the expenditures made for one's public education***) is ***not fundamental***; and (3) for a classification related to wealth to be "suspect," it must probably both be against a discrete, insular, historically-discriminated-against and powerless class, and involve an almost total deprivation of the good in question, not mere inequality in the amount of that good given.

C. **Marriage as fundamental right:** The Court has recognized ***marriage*** as a fundamental right for equal protection (as well as substantive due process) purposes.

1. **Marriage by parent who is in default on child support:** For example, the Court has held that the right to marry is sufficiently fundamental that it is a violation of equal protection for a state to deny a marriage license to a parent who is in default ***on making court-ordered child-support payments***. See *Zablocki v. Redhail*, 434 U.S. 374 (1978), which we discuss extensively in the context of substantive due process (*supra*, p. 199), but which is essentially an equal protection decision.

2. **Same-sex marriage:** Similarly, the Court has decided that the right to marry is sufficiently fundamental that states may not deny marriage licenses to ***same-sex couples.*** See *Obergefell v. Hodges*, 135 S.Ct. 2584 (2015), discussed extensively *supra*, p. 356. The *Obergefell* majority concluded that the right of all couples — both same-sex and opposite-sex — to marry is fundamental for both equal protection and substantive due process purposes.[28]

D. **Adult sexual relations:** An interesting question is whether the Court will come to recognize certain forms of ***adult sexual relations*** as being fundamental rights for equal protection purposes. The Court has not yet done so. Indeed, in the now-overruled case of *Bowers v. Hardwick* (*supra*, p. 202), the Court held that there was ***no*** "fundamental right [of] ***homosexuals*** to engage in sodomy" (a due-process decision that seemed to have implications for equal protection analysis as well). Even when *Bowers* was overruled by *Lawrence v. Texas* (*supra*, p. 202), the Court still did not recognize the interest in adult ***same-sex sexual relations*** as being "fundamental."

1. **Unusually-rigorous review:** But *Lawrence*'s use of ***unusually-rigorous*** rational-relation review, and that case's striking down of statutes ***criminalizing gay sodomy***, suggest that a majority of the present Court may well view adult sexual expression — whether same-sex or different-sex — as effectively being of more-than-usual importance (perhaps ***"quasi-fundamental"***) for both substantive-due process and equal-protection purposes.

---

28. However, the majority opinion in *Obergefell* did not expressly say that because marriage is a fundamental right, regulations that significantly impair that right must be strictly scrutinized, which is the usual standard of review that the Court applies to significant burdens on a fundamental right. But the fact that the majority proceeded directly from labeling the marriage right fundamental to striking down all bans on same-sex marriage suggests that the Court was ***applying some form of heightened review***, if not actual strict scrutiny. See *supra*, p. 358.

2. Same-sex intimacy: Also, language in the majority opinion in the same-sex-marriage case of *Obergefell v. Hodges* suggests that **sexual intimacy** is part of the package of values that makes **marriage** a fundamental right for both same-sex and opposite-sex couples. See, e.g., the majority's statement that "The nature of marriage is that, through its enduring bond, two persons together can find other freedoms, such as expression, **intimacy**, and spirituality." If the freedom to pursue intimacy is part of what makes marriage a fundamental right, perhaps the right to pursue adult sexual intimacy even outside of marriage will ultimately be classified as fundamental too.

E. Voting rights: For some purposes, the Court seems to treat the **right to vote** in state and federal elections as being fundamental. But the case law on how extensively the states may regulate this right, without abridging any fundamental aspect of the right, is extremely confusing.

1. No limits on states' power to regulate state and local elections: To begin with, the Constitution does not place any explicit limits on the power of states to control state and local elections. Relying in part on this constitutional silence, the Court has held over the years that the states may exercise substantial control over the right to vote.

    a. State right to regulate voter qualifications: For instance, the states have the right to determine **voter qualifications** for state elections, so long as they do not exercise that right in a way which violates any specific constitutional prohibitions (or any statute which Congress has enacted pursuant to a constitutional provision). Thus states may require that voters be of **reasonable age**, and that they be **citizens and residents** of the state.

        i. State regulation of federal voter qualifications: By the way, the Constitution indirectly gives the **states** the right to set voter qualifications not just for state elections but for **federal** ones. Article I, §2 provides that voters in House of Representatives elections shall have the same qualifications as such voters need for voting in elections for the state legislature, and the Seventeenth Amendment, §1, provides the same for election of U.S. Senators. (Article I, §4 gives Congress the right to **override** these state-created voter qualifications for federal elections. But Congress has no such right of override of qualifications for state elections, so that state power there is exclusive.)

2. Voting as fundamental right: Yet voting is integrally related to the First Amendment right to free speech, including political expression. Furthermore, maintenance of other constitutionally-guaranteed civil rights and liberties depends on public officials' accountability to the electorate. Therefore, the Court has sometimes labeled the **right to vote** in state and local (as well as federal) elections as **"fundamental."**

    a. Strict scrutiny: Because the right to vote is "fundamental," the Supreme Court has — but only in some circumstances — subjected laws that impair some group's right to vote to **strict scrutiny**. The Court's cases are quite jumbled in this area, and it's hard to articulate a single standard for when the Court will use strict scrutiny. It's also hard to predict whether a particular measure will **survive** that strict scrutiny, an outcome that happens more often in voting-rights cases than in other areas.

    b. The "unrelated to voter qualifications" test: In deciding whether to use strict scrutiny, the Court seems to place great weight on whether the voting regulation is reasonably **"related to voter qualifications."**

i. **Not reasonably related (strict scrutiny):** If the Court decides that the regulation is *not* "reasonably related to voter qualifications," then the Court **uses strict scrutiny**, and will probably strike down the regulation. As we'll see below, poll taxes, property-ownership requirements and duration-of-residence requirements fall into this strictly-scrutinized-and-generally-struck-down category.

ii. **Reasonably related (intermediate review):** If, on the other hand, the Court decides that the regulation *is* reasonably related to voter qualifications, then the Court generally does **not** use strict scrutiny. Instead, it uses some less stringent review method (typically, an intermediate-level **balancing test**), and is likely to **uphold** the measure. Basic residency requirements, voter ID requirements, and regulations disenfranchising felons all fall into this category; see *infra*, p. 371.

3. **Not reasonably related to voter qualifications:** Let's first look at various types of regulations that the Court has found to be **not reasonably related to voter qualifications**, and as to which it has therefore **applied strict scrutiny.**

a. **Poll tax:** The seminal area in which regulations have been found not to be reasonably related to voter qualifications is the imposition of a **poll taxes.** A poll tax, no matter how minor, creates an inequality in the right to vote that must be strictly scrutinized, and struck down as an Equal Protection violation. Thus in **Harper v. Virginia Board of Elections**, 383 U.S. 663 (1966), the Court struck down an annual poll tax of only $1.50, imposed as a prerequisite for voting.

   i. **Rationale:** The Court began by holding that the right to vote was fundamental, because it was "preservative of all rights." Therefore, inequality in its distribution was to be "closely scrutinized" (i.e., strictly scrutinized).

      (1) **Application of strict review:** The tax in *Harper* could not survive such scrutiny, even though the state clearly had a right to charge standardized fees for the exercise of other types of rights (e.g., a fee for a driver's license). The means-end link there did not have the requisite tightness, because "wealth, like race, creed, or color, is not germane to one's ability to participate intelligently in the electoral process."

   ii. **Dissent:** Three dissenters in *Harper* contended that a "mere-rationality" rather than "strict scrutiny" standard should be applied. If this were done, they argued, the statute should be upheld, since it was rationally related to several legitimate state objectives, including promotion of civic responsibility (on the theory that "people with some property have a deeper stake in community affairs ... ").

b. **Ballot restricted to "interested voters":** Another type of inequality which has often (but not always) been strictly scrutinized and invalidated is the requirement that voters **own property** or otherwise have some **"special interest"** entitling them to vote. Such requirements tend to exist not in general elections, but in elections on **special issues** (e.g., bond issues) or for **special boards** (e.g., water districts).

   i. **Summary:** The law in this area is somewhat confused. In general, the Court has been suspicious of state claims that only a certain group is "interested" in the results of an election. If, however, the state proves that only members of that group do indeed have a major objective interest or "stake" in the issue (as opposed to a subjective curiosity about it), the limitation may be upheld. But if the state doesn't succeed in making that proof, then the Court will strictly scrutinize, and probably invalidate, the limitation.

ii. School board elections: Thus in *Kramer v. Union Free School District No. 15*, 395 U.S. 621 (1969), the Court **struck down** a New York statute which limited **school district** elections to persons who either: (1) owned or leased property within the district; or (2) were parents of children in the district's public schools. The Court said that any requirement which had the effect of giving the franchise to some residents but not others (apart from reasonable requirements of age and citizenship) must be *"carefully scrutinized"* to determine whether the scheme was *"necessary* to *promote* a compelling state interest."

(1) Means not sufficiently tailored: By this standard, the statute here was inadequate. The state's asserted interest in limiting elections to persons "primarily interested" in, or "primarily affected" by, the elections might be a legitimate objective (the Court did not decide). However, the **means chosen** (property ownership or rental) was an inadequate way of reaching that goal, since some people who had a substantial interest in the outcome of the elections were excluded (e.g., plaintiff, who was a 31-year-old bachelor stockbroker living with his parents), while other people without a real interest could vote (e.g., "an uninterested unemployed young man who pays no state or federal taxes, but who rents an apartment in the district[.]"). The means was "not sufficiently tailored" to the goal of limiting the vote to people "primarily interested" in school affairs.

(2) Dissent: The three dissenters in *Kramer* argued that some linedrawing was essential to lawmaking, and that discrepancies like the one here were the inevitable results of such linedrawing.

iii. Exception for "special purpose" body: However, if the Court finds that the governmental unit for which elections are being held has a **limited purpose** which **disproportionately affects** only one group, the franchise may be limited to that group. Thus *"special purpose bodies"* may restrict the vote to persons who are directly affected by the body's activities.

(1) Water district: For instance, votes for a special-purpose *"water storage district"* can be **limited to landowners**, and can be on a "one acre, one vote" basis. See, e.g., *Ball v. James*, 451 U.S. 355 (1981) (even though water district finances its operations by selling electricity to hundreds of thousands of residents, the vote can be limited to landowners because the district can't enact laws, and doesn't perform "normal functions of government").

c. Duration-of-residence requirements: Requirements that voters have **resided within the state** for **more than a certain time** prior to Election Day are strictly scrutinized.

i. *Dunn v. Blumstein*: Thus in **Dunn v. Blumstein**, 405 U.S. 330 (1972), Tennessee's duration-of-residency requirements (one year in the state and three months in the county) were struck down, both on the ground that they interfered with the fundamental right to vote and on the ground that they impaired the right to travel. (The "right to travel" aspects of the case are discussed briefly *infra*, p. 383.)

(1) Fifty-day statutes: But *shorter* residency requirements have been *upheld*, on the theory that these are merely methods of ensuring that the person *really is a resident.* Thus the Court has twice *upheld fifty-day* residency requirements, on the grounds that such a period is needed to allow the state to maintain accurate voting lists. See, e.g., *Marston v. Lewis*, 410 U.S. 679 (1973).

4. **Reasonably related to voter qualifications:** Let's look now at some types of regulations that the Court has found to be *reasonably related to voter qualifications*, and thus to be reviewed by a *less-than-strict-scrutiny* standard. Typically, the standard the Court uses is some form of *intermediate-level* review. As the Court said in the leading case in this area, "When a state election law provision imposes only *'reasonable, nondiscriminatory restrictions'* upon the First and Fourteenth Amendment rights of voters, the state's important regulatory interests are generally sufficient to justify" the restrictions. *Burdick v. Takushi*, 504 U.S. 428 (1992).

   a. **Voter identification requirements:** For example, a state requirement that every voter *present a photo ID* was *upheld* under this non-strict-scrutiny standard, in *Crawford v. Marion County Election Board*, 128 S.Ct. 1610 (2008).

      i. **Facts:** In *Crawford*, Indiana required any voter casting a physical (as opposed to absentee) ballot to *present a government-issued photo ID at that time.* The state offered a free qualifying photo ID to anyone who could prove residence and identity.

      ii. **Challenge:** The plaintiffs brought a "facial" Equal Protection challenge to the statute. That is, they argued that the statute should be struck down for *all* voters, not just for particular voters to whom they posed especially great burdens. The plaintiffs argued that the photo ID requirement was analogous to a poll tax, and should thus be subjected to strict scrutiny and invalidated as the poll tax was in *Harper v. Virginia Bd. of Elections* (*supra*, p. 369).

      iii. **Challenge rejected:** A 6-member majority *rejected* the facial challenge, and the argument that the statute should be strictly scrutinized. There was no majority opinion, because the six Justices split on the proper rationale. But all six Justices who voted to uphold the statute agreed that *strict scrutiny was not appropriate.*

         (1) Plurality: An opinion signed by three of these six Justices (Stevens, joined by Roberts and Kennedy) asserted that prior cases had held that *"evenhanded restrictions that protect the integrity and reliability of the electoral process itself"* are not "invidious" and therefore should not be strictly scrutinized. Instead, these three said, a *"balancing approach"* should be used, under which the interests being pursued by the state in making the regulation must be balanced against the burdens imposed. (We'll call this the plurality opinion.) At least for this facial attack, the plaintiffs had not carried their burden of showing that *enough voters were significantly burdened* by the photo-ID requirement, or that the burdens on those voters were sufficiently great and unfair, as to outweigh the state's interest in combatting in-person voter fraud. (But the plurality seemed to leave open the possibility that in a later *"as applied"* suit, particular voters without photo IDs might show that *as to them,* the ID requirement *did* constitute an unconstitutionally great burden.)

(2) Concurrences: In a separate concurrence in the judgment, three more justices (Scalia, joined by Thomas and Alito) agreed with the plurality opinion that strict scrutiny should not be given to any voter regulation that imposes what the concurrence called "nonsevere, nondiscriminatory restrictions." And, the concurrence said, a regulation that places "ordinary and widespread burdens, such as those requiring 'nominal effort' of everyone, are not severe" (and therefore should not trigger strict scrutiny). The photo ID requirement here was the sort of "non-severe" widespread burden that should be judged even more deferentially than the plurality opinion would have judged it. The state's burden of justification should be *"minimal,"* Scalia said, so that the state's interests *merely needed to be "reasonable,"* a standard which Scalia thought was easily met here.

iv. **Dissent:** There were three dissenters (Souter, joined by Ginsburg, in one dissent, and Breyer in another).

(1) Souter: Souter contended that even if the plurality opinion's balancing test was used, the photo ID requirement here should be struck down, because a significant number of voters lacked the requisite photo ID and would therefore be seriously burdened. By contrast, the state's main interest — its need to combat in-person voter fraud — had not been demonstrated to be a significant one. (Souter pointed out that Indiana had *"not come across a single instance* of in-person voter impersonation fraud in all of [the state's] history.")

(2) Breyer: Breyer's dissent asserted that the photo ID requirement had the effect of imposing on a significant number of voters — those without a driver's license or other valid form of photo ID, a group largely made up of the poor, elderly or disabled — a disproportionate burden, perhaps more severe than the $1.50 poll tax struck down in *Harper*. And, he believed, a statute that placed a "disproportionate burden" on a class of voters (here, the class without photo IDs) should be struck down.

v. **Summary:** So as the result of *Crawford*, at least six members of the Roberts court are on record as believing that as long as a restriction on voting rights is an "*even-handed* [one] that *protect[s] the integrity and reliability* of the electoral process itself," *strict scrutiny should not be used.* And these six further agree that the requirement of a photo ID for all persons casting physical ballots is an evenhanded restriction that should not be strictly scrutinized. But these six are evenly split about whether the standard of review that should be used is (1) a moderately-severe balancing test (the plurality's view) or (2) a very deferential standard under which, when the impact of the restriction is "not severe," the state's burden of justification should be "*minimal*" so that the state's interests merely need to be "*reasonable*" (the Scalia concurrence's view).

b. **Denial of vote to felons:** Many states deny the vote to *felons*, even ones who have served their sentence and finished any parole. It's clear that such measures won't receive strict scrutiny, and will at least as a general matter be upheld. Such disenfranchisement was *upheld* by the Court in *Richardson v. Ramirez*, 418 U.S. 24 (1974). The Court relied on the rarely-invoked §2 of the Fourteenth Amendment, which calls for reduced representation for states which deny the vote to residents, but which makes this sanction inapplicable in cases of "participation in rebellion, or **other crime**." The majority in *Richardson* felt that §2 demonstrated Congress' intent to permit disenfranchisement as a sanction for crime.

c. **Burden on right to vote by limiting voter's choices:** The restrictions we have examined so far typically had the effect, where they applied at all, of **preventing the voter from voting at all**. But suppose the state regulation of voting merely has the effect of **"burdening"** the right to vote, by **limiting the voter's choices**. Here, as in the voter-ID and disenfranchisement-of-felons scenarios just discussed, the Court does **not** use strict scrutiny; instead, the Court balances the degree of burden against the magnitude of the state's interest, and the Court is slow to strike down the regulation. It was in such a case involving a voter-choice-limiting regulation that the Court first articulated the rule relied on by the plurality in *Crawford*, supra, that "When a state election law provision imposes only **'reasonable, nondiscriminatory restrictions'** upon the First and Fourteenth Amendment rights of voters, the state's important regulatory interests are **generally sufficient** to justify" the restrictions. *Burdick v. Takushi*, 504 U.S. 428 (1992).

  i. **Ban on write-in votes:** For example, in *Burdick*, the Court held that Hawaii could **completely ban** all **write-in votes**. So long as the state gave candidates reasonable access to the ballot (thus preserving each voter's interest in having a reasonable choice of candidates), the state was not required to protect each voter's interest in being able to vote for **any** candidate of his choosing.

5. **Inequality in ballet-counting procedures:** As the result of the Court's decision that effectively handed the 2000 presidential election to George W. Bush over Al Gore, voters now seem to have some sort of equal protection right to have their votes **counted according to uniform standards**. **Bush v. Gore**, 531 U.S. 98 (2000).

a. **Facts:** The election came down to the vote in Florida. The Florida Supreme Court ordered that a statewide recount of all "undervotes" be conducted. ("Undervotes" are ballots on which, according to the machine tabulation, no candidate was selected.) The U.S. Supreme Court issued a stay blocking the continuation of this recount, then decided that no constitutionally-acceptable recount could be completed within the time available.

  i. **Chads:** Most Florida counties had a punch-card system which required a voter to perforate the ballet by a stylus. The ballots in dispute were mainly ones in which the voter did not completely perforate the ballot, making the vote uncountable by machine. Many of these ballots left a piece of the card hanging by one, two, or three corners (a "hanging chad") or contained mere indentations indicating perhaps that the voter had tried but failed to punch the card (an "indented chad").

  ii. **No uniform standards:** The Florida Supreme Court ordered a hasty manual statewide recount of all of these undervotes, without specifying uniform standards for determining when a vote should count. For example, it was left to each county's election commissioners to decide whether an indented chad should count.

  iii. **Partial counts accepted:** The Florida Supreme Court also ordered that in those instances where counties had reported partial counts from recounts that had not been finished by the prior state-law deadline, those partial recount totals be accepted as legal votes.

b. Holding: By a 5-4 vote, the U.S. Supreme Court ruled that the entire recount procedure violated voters' equal protection rights. The Court's conservative bloc (Rehnquist, Scalia, Thomas, O'Connor and Kennedy) voted together to form a majority, and the liberal bloc (Stevens, Souter, Breyer and Ginsburg) dissented.

    i. Rationale: The unsigned per curiam opinion for the Court said that "The right to vote is protected in more than the initial allocation of the franchise ... Having once granted the right to vote on equal terms, the state may not, by later arbitrary and disparate treatment, value one person's vote over that of another." To the majority, the recount mechanisms "do not satisfy the ***minimum requirement*** for ***non-arbitrary treatment of voters*** necessary to secure the fundamental right [to vote]. ... The formulation of uniform rules to determine intent ... is practicable and, we conclude, necessary." The majority pointed out that "the standards for accepting or rejecting contested ballots might vary not only from county to county but indeed within a single county from one recount team to other."

    ii. Not enough time: Normally, the equal protection problem would have been taking care of by ordering the Florida Supreme Court to issue uniform standards for the recount. But the high court was ruling on Dec. 12th, and the 12th was already the last day on which the state could certify its vote and still be certain that that vote would not be challenged in Congress. That is, Dec. 12 was the last day to use the "safe harbor" built into the federal system. The five members of the majority believed that holding a fresh constitutionally-adequate recount, and requiring Florida to miss the safe harbor, would have violated Florida's own election code, made binding upon the presidential election by the Constitution. Therefore, there could be no recount, and the original Florida certification of Bush as the winner stood.

c. Dissent: Of the four dissenters in *Bush v. Gore*, two (Souter and Breyer) believed that the lack of uniform standards indeed raised serious equal protection problems. But those two believed that the way to handle the problem was to remand to the Florida Supreme Court with instructions that the state could try to get the recount done, with uniform standards, by the Dec. 18 final deadline. The other two dissenters (Stevens and Ginsburg) believed that the equal protection problem was not substantial.

d. Significance: *Bush v. Gore* probably does not have much significance for future elections. The majority took pains to observe that "[o]ur consideration is ***limited to the present circumstances***, for the problem of equal protection in election processes generally presents many complexities." However, the case probably does stand for at least the vague proposition that there are some equal-protection limits to how much variation is tolerable in the standards for determining whether a ballot is a legal vote.

6. Dilution of votes: The Court has also recognized a voter's ***fundamental right*** not to have his vote ***diluted*** by use of electoral districts that are not constructed strictly on the basis of ***population***. The "reapportionment" cases (especially *Reynolds v. Sims*, the case establishing "one man, one vote" as a constitutional principle) are discussed as part of the treatment of political questions, *infra*, p. 754.

7. Fifteenth Amendment: When you analyze a governmental action that arguably restricts of the right to vote, do not overlook the ***Fifteenth Amendment***, which in §1 says that "The right of citizens of the United States to *vote* shall not be denied or abridged by the United States or by any State on account of *race, color, or previous condition of servitude*." (§2, a provision analogous to §5 of the Fourteenth Amendment, see *infra*, p. 453, gives Congress the power to "enforce this article by appropriate legislation.") As we have already seen, most restrictions on the right to vote are given Fourteenth Amendment due process/ fundamental rights analysis. But occasionally, a direct limit on the right to vote on racial grounds will be found to violate the Fifteenth Amendment.

> **Example:** The Hawaiian Constitution provides that the trustees of the Office of Hawaiian Affairs (OHA) may be elected solely by persons who are descendants of the original Native Hawaiians who inhabited the island prior to Captain Cook's arrival in 1778. *Held*, this provision constitutes racial discrimination in voting, and therefore violates the Fifteenth Amendment. *Rice v. Cayetano*, 528 U.S. 495 (2000).

F. Access to the ballot: Related to the "right to vote" is the right of a person to *be a candidate*, and of members of a *political party* to *place their candidate on the ballot*.

1. **State interest in regulating elections:** Before we look at whether these "rights" to ballot access really exist in a constitutional sense, consider the state's interest in *limiting* the presence of candidates and parties on a given ballot. There are two main interests which a state may be pursuing when it attempts to control the number of candidates or parties listed: (1) the interest in *reducing voter confusion*; and (2) the interest in maximizing the probability that the winning candidate will have received a *majority* of the *popular vote*. See N&R, p. 877. If these goals are not met, there is a danger that the result will be "only the cacophony of an atomized body politic, not the orchestrated voice of an electorate." Tribe, p. 1097.

2. **Interest of candidates, parties and voters:** However, there are a number of countervailing interests in easy ballot access, on the part of: (1) individuals who wish to be candidates; (2) members of minor or newly-formed parties; and (3) the voters themselves. These interests may be summarized as follows:

   a. **Interest in being a candidate:** Individuals clearly have an *interest in being a candidate*. While the Supreme Court has never recognized this interest as being a "fundamental right" (and has probably implicitly decided that it is not), the interest clearly has some constitutional weight. It is related to the First Amendment right of free speech, and to the general right to participate in the political process.

   b. **Party's right of association:** A group of individuals has a strong interest in being able to *band together to form a political party*. In fact, *freedom of association*, guaranteed by the First Amendment (see *infra*, p. 605) clearly requires that they be permitted to do so. It is less clear, however, that freedom of association requires that they be permitted to be an *effective* party, in the sense of being able to place their candidates on the ballot. In general, the Supreme Court has held that this right of association does mean that parties with *significant popular support* must be given *reasonable opportunities to appear on the ballot*.

   c. **Voters' interest in suitable candidate:** The *voters* have an interest in being offered a variety of candidates representing a *range of political views*. While there is certainly no constitutional requirement that every voter be offered a candidate matching the voter's own views, a system which consistently prevented participation by candidates representing particular controversial views (at least if shared by a significant part of the electorate) would probably be constitutionally suspect. See Tribe, p. 1100, n. 13.

3. **Candidate eligibility rules:** Some requirements concern the *eligibility* of the *individual candidate*. Since there is no general "right to be a candidate" which the Supreme Court has been willing to recognize as fundamental, these restrictions are generally reviewed under the highly deferential "mere-rationality" standard. Thus *minimum age* requirements, and requirements that the candidate have *resided for a certain period of time* in the state or district where he is seeking office, have generally been *upheld*, on the grounds that they are rationally related to a legitimate state interest (e.g., the interest in having elected officials who have reasonable experience and maturity, and who have an interest in matters concerning their constituency). See Tribe, pp. 1100-01.

   a. **Violation of other constitutional right:** Candidate eligibility requirements may not, of course, violate any other *independent* constitutional right. For instance, if a state imposed an unusually long *state residency* requirement for candidacy (e.g., four years), a strong argument could be made that such a requirement violates the individual's *right to interstate migration* (*infra*, p. 381), or at least that the requirement should be given scrutiny. See Tribe, p. 1101.

4. **Party organization and popular support:** Many states require candidates to be *affiliated with a political party* in order to obtain a place on the ballot. (Special rules, usually fairly burdensome, govern independent candidacies.) Yet only those parties that have demonstrated a certain amount of *popular support* are generally entitled to place their candidates on the ballot. In some states, the popular support requirements (perhaps coupled with requirements of an elaborate party structure, and use of nominating conventions) are quite burdensome; in such states, candidates from the two major parties have an even greater than usual advantage.

   a. **Overall Supreme Court view:** The Supreme Court has decided several major cases concerning the extent to which such popular-support and organizational requirements may be placed upon newly-formed or minor parties. These cases do not yield an easily-stated unified principle. However, the cases taken together do seem to hold that: (1) states may, in order to keep ballots from becoming confusingly large, require parties (or independent candidacies) to show a *significant amount of community support*; but (2) the restrictions may not be so great that minority parties or independent candidates have *no realistic chance* of getting on the ballot. See Tribe, p. 1110-01.

   b. *Williams* **case:** The first of the cases, *Williams v. Rhodes*, 393 U.S. 23 (1968), was quite easy to decide, since the ballot access restrictions there were so severe that even a party with significant popular support stood almost no chance of getting on the ballot.

      i. **Facts:** The Ohio law struck down in *Williams* required a minor party (defined as one which had not received 10% of the votes in the previous gubernatorial election) to meet, as a condition to getting on the presidential ballot, three stringent requirements: (1) the filing, earlier in the election year, of petitions signed by *15%* of the number of votes cast in the prior gubernatorial election; (2) the creation of an *elaborate party structure*; and (3) the conducting of *primaries*. The statute also *forbade independent* and *write-in* candidacies. The law was challenged by the

American Independent Party, whose candidate, George Wallace, was blocked from the 1968 presidential ballot.

c. Statute struck down: A majority of the Court found that the scheme violated the equal protection rights of minority parties, since it made it *"virtually impossible"* for a new party, even one with hundreds of thousands of members, to get a place on the ballot, and therefore gave a large advantage to the two existing major parties.

   i. Interests implicated: The majority found that two specific constitutional interests were impaired by the statute: (1) the right of individuals to *associate* for advancement of their political beliefs; and (2) the right of *voters* to *"cast their votes effectively."* These interests were sufficiently important that *strict scrutiny* should be applied to the state law.

   ii. State interests inadequate: None of the state's asserted interests was sufficiently compelling, when measured under this strict test. For instance, the state's desire to promote the two-party system might be legitimate (the Court did not decide), but giving a permanent monopoly to two *particular* parties, Republicans and Democrats, was clearly not.

d. *Jenness:* The next case, *Jenness v. Fortson*, 403 U.S. 431 (1971), marks the other end of the spectrum, i.e., a set of restrictions so lenient that they were clearly constitutional.

   i. Facts: *Jenness* was a challenge to a Georgia rule which permitted independent candidates (i.e., ones with no party affiliation) to appear on the ballot, but only if they filed petitions with the signatures of at least 5% of the number of votes in the previous election. Petitions could be filed later in the election year than they could in *Williams*.

   ii. Holding: The Court found this situation vastly different from that in *Williams*, and quickly upheld the scheme. A key distinction was that Georgia, unlike Ohio, "in no way freezes the status quo, but implicitly recognizes the potential fluidity of American political life."

e. Middle-ground cases: If *Williams* and *Jenness* represent two ends of the spectrum of ballot-access restrictions, later cases discuss restrictions that are somewhere in the middle. In these later cases, the Court has seemed to apply a kind of mid-level review: The Court upholds the ballot-access measure as long as it is a *"reasonable and non-discriminatory"* way of achieving an *"important"* state interest, such as the maintenance of "ballot integrity" or "political stability."

   i. Organization requirement: For instance, a Texas requirement that minor parties hold precinct, county and state *nominating conventions* was *upheld*, in *American Party of Texas v. White*, 415 U.S. 767 (1974). The key factor was the lack of discrimination against minor parties; since *major* parties in Texas were required to hold these three types of conventions in order to promulgate party platforms, the minority parties were not placed at a relative disadvantage. (But in a state where the major parties do *not* hold such conventions, presumably the requirement that minority parties do so would be a violation of their right to equal protection.)

   ii. Ban on fusion candidates: Similarly, the Court has held that a state may prohibit a party from putting a *"fusion"* candidate on the ballot, i.e., a candidate who has *already been nominated by another party.* Timmons v. Twin Cities Area New Party, 520 U.S. 351 (1997). The minor party in *Timmons* argued that the rule against fusion candidates abridged its freedom of association (mostly by giving popular candidates a large disincentive to accept the minor party's early nomination). But the Court upheld the rule, on the grounds that it was a "reasonable [and] nondiscriminatory" way of achieving the state's "important regulatory interests" in "ballot integrity" and "political stability."

   f. Empirical test: In gauging the effect of signature requirements, organizational requirements, etc., the Court generally takes into account the ***actual historical success or failure*** that minor parties have had in getting on the ballot. Obviously, the more often minor parties or independent candidates have in fact succeeded in getting on the ballot, the less likely the Court will be to find a violation of equal protection. See Tribe, p. 1111.

5. Filing fees: *Filing fee* requirements imposed on candidates will be struck by the Court, if they prevent ***indigent*** candidates from appearing on the ballot. In *Lubin v. Panish*, 415 U.S. 709 (1974), the Court unanimously invalidated a California filing fee set at a percentage of the salary for the position being sought (a $700 fee in plaintiff's situation). The Court reasoned that a state may not charge a candidate filing fees which he is incapable of paying, unless it gives him alternative means of getting on the ballot (e.g., by filing a petition demonstrating popular support).

6. Right to be a candidate: *Lubin* spoke in terms of the right of an indigent candidate to get on the ballot, not the right of ***voters*** to choose an indigent candidate. This seems to be the closest the Court has come to suggesting that there may be ***an independent constitutional right to be a candidate***. See Tribe, p. 1111. However, the existence of such a right is not at all clear, in light of the Court's failure to find such a right in other cases.

G. Access to courts: Existence of a classification based on ***wealth*** has never, by itself, been enough to trigger strict scrutiny. But where the state ***imposes fees*** which have the effect of preventing the poor from gaining access to a significant constitutionally-protected right, the Court has sometimes been willing to apply strict scrutiny. This was the case, for instance, with respect to the poll tax and with respect to candidate filing fees (*supra*, pp. 369 and 378). The Court has at times made the ***litigation process*** another such area; state-imposed fees or other economic barriers which prevent the poor from ***gaining access to the courts*** may be subjected to strict scrutiny, if the particular type of judicial access being sought is found to be sufficiently important.

1. No general principle: The Court's course in the area of judicial access has been confused and changing, so that it is difficult to state a general principle. Generally, the Court has shown a greater likelihood of striking down barriers to the pursuit of judicial remedies in ***criminal cases*** than it has in most ***civil*** contexts.

2. Equal protection vs. due process: Nor is it clear whether equal protection or due process is the relevant doctrine in these cases. Sometimes, the Court has seemed to hold that ***due process*** is what matters: if fundamental procedural fairness requires that all persons, rich or poor, be given a particular type of judicial access, the Court will order this to be done, without focusing on the distinction between rich and poor. In other cases, however, the issue has been one of equal protection: if the type of access sought is judged to be highly important, the Court has decided that what the rich are permitted to pay for, the poor must be given, in order to avoid what the Court sees as the unfairness which would inhere in making the access in question available only to those who can pay for it.

    a. Equal protection dominant: The **equal protection** aspect appears to have **dominated** the Burger/Rehnquist Court's decisions. However, the due process aspect crops up from time to time (e.g., in *Little v. Streater, infra,* p. 380, involving an indigent paternity defendant's right to blood-grouping tests).

3. Not "fundamental" rights: The Court has generally **not** labeled the rights at issue in these judicial-access cases as *"fundamental"* ones. But it has conceded that the rights at issue are highly important, and that they merit at least some extra measure of constitutional protection. Unlike the right-to-vote cases, where the right itself was "fundamental," and therefore was sufficient to trigger strict scrutiny, the judicial-access cases have generally involved strict scrutiny only where there was a **combination** of a *"quasi-suspect" wealth classification* (usually in the form of a state-imposed *fee*) *and* an **important interest.**

4. Cutting back by Burger/Rehnquist Court: The most important cases giving special protection to judicial access by the poor came during the Warren era. In both the criminal and civil areas (probably more so in the latter), post-Warren Courts have curtailed, though not completely overturned, the Warren-era results.

5. Transcripts: The first Warren-era case involved the right of indigents to a *trial transcript* in *criminal appeals.* In *Griffin v. Illinois,* 351 U.S. 12 (1956), the Court held that the state *must provide indigent criminal defendants with a trial transcript,* if such a transcript is *necessary for effective appellate review.*

    a. Rationale: *Griffin* was decided on both equal protection and due process grounds. In ringing rhetoric (which was never taken to its logical conclusion in subsequent, harder cases), the Court observed that "[t]here can be no equal justice where the kind of trial a man gets depends on the amount of money he has."

    b. Harlan dissent: But Justice Harlan, in dissent, made a point which has had continued relevance in cases involving wealth criteria. He observed that in the usual equal protection case, the state *makes a classification,* and places disabilities upon persons falling on one side of the classifying line. Here, by contrast, by charging a fee for transcripts the Court was *not making any classification at all*; it was simply failing to "alleviate the consequences of differences in economic circumstances that exist wholly apart from any state action."

        i. Consequence: Consequently, Harlan argued, the majority was imposing on states "an affirmative duty to lift the handicaps flowing from differences in economic circumstances" and was interpreting equal protection to require that "Illinois must give to some what it requires others to pay for." This was not the meaning of the Equal Protection Clause, Harlan contended.

    c. No "right" to an appeal: Even the majority agreed with Harlan that there was **no "right" to an appeal**; the state could, for instance, provide that a criminal trial was simply the final judicial event. But what the states could not do, in the majority's view, was to grant an appeal to some (those who could pay for a transcript) and not to others.

6. Counsel during appeal: Then, the Warren Court held that indigent criminal defendants had the right to the *assistance of counsel* on appeal, at least if: (1) this was the first appeal taken in the case; and (2) the appeal was granted as a matter of right (not judicial discretion) to all persons. *Douglas v. California*, 372 U.S. 353 (1963). The decision was, like *Griffin*, based on both equal protection and due process grounds.

7. **Discretionary appeals:** *Douglas* did not deal with the right to appointed counsel in *discretionary* appeals. But in the later case of *Ross v. Moffitt*, 147 U.S. 600 (1974), the Court explicitly **refused** to find such a right in discretionary appeals.

   a. **Rationale:** Most of the majority's opinion was addressed to the equal protection argument. The majority distinguished *Douglas*, on the grounds that the interest in equal access to appellate review was "one of degrees," and that denial of counsel's assistance in discretionary appeals (e.g., appeals to the highest state court or petitions for *certiorari* to the U.S. Supreme Court) was only a "relative handicap," much less severe than lack of counsel during the initial appeal of right.

   b. **Dissent:** Three dissenters, Douglas, Brennan and Marshall, contended that the *Douglas* rationale should be applied even with respect to discretionary appeals.

8. **Civil litigation:** Indigents have also argued that filing fees and other payments to the state should be waived for them in *civil litigation*. But such arguments have generally been *unsuccessful*; in only one category of action, loosely *"family law,"* has the Court agreed that indigents are entitled to access to the civil courts.

   a. *Boddie:* The main family-law decision involved *divorce.* That case was **Boddie v. Connecticut**, 401 U.S. 371 (1971). The parties seeking divorce were welfare recipients who could not pay the $60 filing fee. The Supreme Court agreed that *denial of access to divorce was a violation of the plaintiffs' due process rights.*

      i. **State monopolization as factor:** Two factors were found by the Court to be basic to this due process conclusion: (1) marriage occupies a *fundamental place* in our society's scheme of values; and (2) the *state* has a *monopoly* on the means for dissolving this relationship. Thus access to divorce is quite different from use of the civil courts for the *resolution of private disputes*; in the latter situation, other, nonjudicial, means of resolution are generally available.

   b. **Not applicable to bankruptcy:** Post-Warren Courts have taken an extremely narrow view of what other situations, apart from family law, entitle indigents to civil court access. For instance, indigents do *not* have a right to a waiver of the $50 filing fee for *bankruptcy*, the Court held in **U.S. v. Kras**, 409 U.S. 434 (1973).

   c. **Review of welfare terminations:** Similarly, the Court has held that indigents could be forced to pay a $25 filing fee in order to gain judicial review of *welfare-benefit terminations. Ortwein v. Schwab*, 410 U.S. 656 (1973). By the same 5-4 majority as in *Kras*, the Court held that welfare payments were in the area of "economics and social welfare," and thus had "far less constitutional significance" than the interest in divorce.

   d. **Other family-law contexts:** But the Court *has* granted fee relief to indigents in two contexts that are theoretically civil, but that have a *family-law* dimension:

      i. **Paternity suits:** First, in *Little v. Streater*, 452 U.S. 1 (1981), the defendant was an indigent against whom a *paternity action* had been brought. The Court held that he was entitled to *state-subsidized blood grouping tests* to determine whether he could have been the child's father.

ii. **Termination of parental rights:** Then, the Rehnquist Court held that where a child's father successfully sued to have the child's mother's ***parental rights terminated*** so that the child could be adopted by the father's wife, the state had to pay for a ***trial transcript*** to be used by the mother on ***appeal***. *M.L.B. v. S.L.J.*, 519 U.S. 102 (1996). In that case, the decision seemed to turn more on the "quasi-criminal" nature of the proceeding than on the fact that it involved family-law matters. But the Court characterized "the interest of parents in their relationship with their children" as being "fundamental."

e. **Summary:** So where the proceeding is nominally ***"civil,"*** an indigent has ***no general right to fee relief.*** Thus actions for ***bankruptcy*** and for review of ***welfare terminations*** fall into this general "no equal protection right to fee relief" category. But an indigent *does* have an equal protection right to fee relief in three situations falling within the family-law area: actions for ***divorce***, for ***determinations of paternity***, and for ***termination of parental rights***.

H. **The right to travel:** We live in a federal system, one of the basic principles of which is that ***any American is free to travel from state to state***, and to ***change his state of residence*** or employment whenever he desires. This ***"right to travel"*** (or, a better way of putting what is usually being litigated, this ***"freedom of interstate migration"***) is not explicitly given by any one constitutional provision. But the Court has nonetheless treated the right as ***"fundamental."*** Consequently, when a state treats ***newly-arrived residents*** significantly ***less favorably*** than those who have lived in the state longer, strict equal protection scrutiny may be triggered.

1. ***Shapiro v. Thompson:*** The classic case applying strict equal protection scrutiny to classifications penalizing the "right to travel" (or to migrate interstate) is ***Shapiro v. Thompson***, 394 U.S. 618 (1969). In that case, the Court invalidated the denial by two states and the District of Columbia of ***welfare benefits*** to residents who had ***not resided in the jurisdiction for at least a year.***

a. **"Right to travel" rationale:** By requiring the one-year waiting period, the states were impairing the "fundamental right of interstate movement," the Court held. The Court declined to locate this right in any particular constitutional clause. Rather, the right derived from the fact that "the nature of our federal union and our constitutional concept of personal liberty unite to require that all citizens be free to travel throughout the length and breadth of our land. … "

b. **Severe impact:** Furthermore, what was being denied to newly-arrived residents was something of ***extreme importance*** — welfare aid "upon which may depend the ability of the families to obtain the ***very means to subsist*** — food, shelter, and other ***necessities of life.***"

c. **Strict scrutiny:** Because of this major interference with freedom to travel, the Court applied ***strict scrutiny***, requiring that the one-year waiting period be ***necessary*** to achievement of a ***compelling governmental interest***. None of the interests asserted by the state was sufficient.

i. **Unconstitutional objectives:** In fact, several of the asserted state interests were flatly unconstitutional. For instance, the state's argument that it wished to preserve the financial integrity of the state welfare program by preventing an influx of indigent newcomers was itself flatly inconsistent with the newcomers' right to travel interstate.

ii. Other interests: Other interests asserted (e.g., providing an "objective test of residency," discouraging fraudulent collection of payments from more than one state, etc.) were legitimate. But these interests were not "compelling," and could in any event have been served by less drastic means.

d. Dissent: There were three dissenters in *Shapiro*. The most important of the dissents was by Justice Harlan, who was especially concerned about the importance the majority attached to the fact that the newcomers might be deprived of "food, shelter, and other necessities of life" — Harlan feared that the Court might ultimately apply strict scrutiny to any classification bearing on the availability of such "necessities," an exception which he said would "swallow the standard equal protection rule" and make the Court a "super-legislature."

   i. Fifth Amendment: Harlan also thought that the right of interstate movement, which he conceded was an independently-valid constitutional right, could be and should be protected by resort to the ***Fifth Amendment's Due Process Clause*** rather than by the Equal Protection Clause.

e. Aftermath of *Shapiro*: Justice Harlan's fear that the Court would find a generalized fundamental right to the ***"necessities of life,"*** triggering strict equal protection scrutiny whenever the state failed to guarantee those necessities to all citizens, never materialized. The Court's subsequent treatment of "necessities" is discussed in the section on wealth classifications, *infra*, pp. 383-385. But the Court's recognition in *Shapiro* of a fundamental right to interstate travel, and its application of strict equal protection scrutiny of any classification impairing that right, have remained good law.

2. Deterrent or penalty: The *Shapiro* Court did not make clear exactly what sort of effect on the right to interstate travel must occur before that right would be impaired sufficiently so as to trigger strict scrutiny. The Court might have meant that the right was impaired only where the residency requirement was so obviously burdensome that it had a ***deterrent effect*** on interstate migration. But later cases have construed *Shapiro* to mean that the right to travel is impaired wherever it is ***"penalized,"*** even if there is no actual deterrence. Thus since the one-year residency requirement for welfare payments caused substantial hardship to those who moved to the state (as the *Shapiro* Court found), this would be sufficient to trigger strict scrutiny, ***even if there was no showing that anyone actually declined to migrate*** because of the requirement.

   a. Medical benefits: The principle that merely a "penalty," not an actual deterrent effect, is required to trigger strict scrutiny, was illustrated in the post-*Shapiro* case of ***Memorial Hospital v. Maricopa County***, 415 U.S. 250 (1974). That case struck down an Arizona requirement of one year's residence as a condition for indigents to receive free non-emergency ***medical care***. The ability to receive such care was clearly not a significant deterrent to interstate migration, since it was unlikely that people would change or decline to change their state of residence to receive such care. Nonetheless, denial of the medical care was a "penalty" on the right to migrate, the Court held. As such, it was to be subjected to strict scrutiny, which it did not survive.

   i. Definition of "penalty": But, the Court in *Memorial Hospital* held, not all differences in treatment between residents and non-residents are "penalties"; only inequalities in distribution of ***"vital government benefits and privileges"*** are sufficiently severe to be considered penalties. The right to medical care was as much a "basic necessity of life" as were the welfare payments in *Shapiro*, so inequality in their distribution was a penalty.

    b. Divorce: Other government-supplied benefits have been found to be less important, so that their denial to newcomers does ***not*** trigger strict scrutiny. For instance, Iowa's requirement that a person reside in that state for one year before suing a non-resident there for ***divorce***, was ***upheld***, in *Sosna v. Iowa*, 419 U.S. 393 (1975).

        i. Rationale: The majority did not speak in terms of "penalties." But it held that a requirement that a person wait one year for a divorce was a ***less severe hardship*** than waiting one year for medical benefits or welfare assistance — in the latter situation, some part of what was being sought would never be obtained (benefits applicable to the one year wait). In the divorce situation, by contrast, the plaintiff would ultimately end up with the very thing sought, i.e., an adjudication of divorce.

        ii. Stronger state interest: Furthermore, the countervailing state interest was much stronger in the divorce situation. In the welfare benefits and medical care cases, the state's interests were largely those of budget concerns and administrative convenience. Here, by contrast, the state had a strong interest in ***not becoming a "divorce mill"*** whose divorce decrees might be susceptible to collateral attack.

3. *Bona fide* residence requirements: Nothing in the Constitution, however, prevents the state from requiring that persons show that they are ***bona fide residents*** before receiving public services or benefits.

4. Voting rights: Some cases previously discussed in the ***voting rights*** area involve a right-to-travel component. For instance, in *Dunn v. Blumstein*, 405 U.S. 330 (1972) (*supra*, p. 370) Tennessee's duration-of-residency requirements for voting were strictly scrutinized not only because they burdened the fundamental interest in voting, but also because they impaired the interest in interstate travel.

5. Privileges or Immunities Clause as alternate rationale: Recall that there has been some confusion about just where in the Constitution the "right to travel" is granted. For instance, *Shapiro v. Thompson* (*supra*, p. 381) failed to specify where in the document the right was provided. But a 1999 case suggests that the "right to travel" should be founded upon the ***Fourteenth Amendment's Privileges or Immunities Clause,*** which prohibits any state from abridging "the privileges or immunities of citizens of the United States." That case, *Saenz v. Roe*, 526 U.S. 489 (1999), is discussed *infra*, p. 399.

I. Wealth classifications: During the Warren Court, there were some indications that a broad range of government programs which arguably failed to take account of the special needs of the ***poor*** might be subjected to strict scrutiny.

1. Possibility of suspect class: Some observers expected this to happen by the placing of "wealth" on the list of ***suspect classifications***.

2. Possible "fundamental interest" in "necessities": Alternatively, there were hints that the Warren Court might find a fundamental right or interest in the ***"necessities of life,"*** like food, shelter or clothing.

3. Post-Warren Court declines to expand view: But the Warren Court never explicitly held either that wealth without more was a suspect classification or that statutes impairing the right to "necessities" of life, without more, impaired a fundamental interest. The post-Warren Court has explicitly *refused to support either of these propositions*.

4. **Not suspect classification:** For instance, in *James v. Valtierra*, 402 U.S. 137 (1971), the majority held that *wealth classifications*, unlike, say, racial ones, *simply do not trigger any heightened scrutiny.* The Court therefore upheld a California constitutional amendment providing that no low-income housing projects could be built in any community without achieving majority support in a popular referendum. The non-suspect nature of wealth classifications seems to have been reiterated (though this is not completely clear) in the school financing case, *San Antonio Ind. School Dist. v. Rodriguez, supra*, p. 365.

5. **No fundamental interest in "necessities":** Similarly, in a series of cases the Court also rejected claims that various *"necessities of life"* were fundamental interests whose impairment should trigger strict scrutiny.

   a. **Welfare benefits:** The first such area was that of *welfare benefits*. In *Dandridge v. Williams*, 397 U.S. 471 (1970), the Court upheld a Maryland welfare scheme which set a maximum monthly payment of $250, regardless of family size or need.

      i. **Rationale:** The majority reasoned that the statute, like all welfare schemes, lay in the area of "economics and social welfare" and therefore called only for "mere-rationality" review. The scheme satisfied this deferential standard, since it bore a rational relation to several legitimate state objectives (e.g., encouraging employment by prohibiting payments that might compare favorably with what a job would provide).

      ii. **Marshall's "sliding scale" dissent:** Justice Marshall dissented in *Dandridge*. He conceded that strict scrutiny was not appropriate. But he also disagreed with the majority's finding that the traditional, deferential, "mere-rationality" test was the correct one. Instead, he gave the first major exposition of his *"sliding scale"* theory: Rather than a rigid "two-tier" standard, by which all statutes are given either extreme deference or strict scrutiny, the degree of review should be adjusted along a *spectrum*, depending on: (1) the type of classification; (2) the *"relative importance* to individuals in the class discriminated against of the governmental benefits that they do not receive;" and (3) the strength of the interests *asserted by the state* in support of the classification. When this analysis was applied to the facts of *Dandridge*, Marshall concluded that a significant degree of scrutiny should be given, since the welfare recipients' interest in the benefits was large, and (Marshall believed) the state's asserted interest in its scheme relatively weak. The scheme was not sufficient to withstand this significant scrutiny, he contended.

   b. **Housing:** Similarly, the right to *housing* is *not* a constitutionally fundamental one. See *Lindsey v. Normet*, 405 U.S. 56 (1972), where the Court applied deferential "mere-rationality" review to a state statute making it relatively easy for landlords to evict tenants if the landlord claimed that the rent had not been paid.

   c. **Difficulties with contrary approach:** A contrary approach, holding that there *is* a fundamental interest in necessities, would pose large problems.

      i. **Extension of state's role:** It is true that the Court has required states to pay for certain goods rather than charging indigents for them (e.g., trial transcripts in *Griffin* and appellate counsel in *Douglas*). But the goods there, as well as in the "right to vote" cases, were used in ***areas in which the state is already dominant***. An extension of the fundamental rights doctrine to include necessities like food and shelter would expand the state's obligations into huge new areas, which until now have been left ***principally to the private sector***.

    ii. Other difficulties: Furthermore, there would be major difficulties in having courts determine issues like: (1) What level of food, shelter, clothing, etc. is so essential that one has a fundamental right to it? and (2) Does the claimant already have the resources to be able to purchase these goods? (and if he has part of the resources needed, what part?) Nor would it be appropriate for the court to be deferential to the legislature's statutes or regulations governing these matters, since the very idea of a fundamental right is that it is one as to which claims of impairment must be strictly scrutinized by the judiciary.

6. Procedural safeguards: Keep in mind that in the welfare context and in cases involving other governmental benefits, ***procedural safeguards*** may accomplish part of the protection of the poor that the post-Warren Court has been unwilling to impose in the name of equal protection. See, e.g., *Goldberg v. Kelly*, 397 U.S. 254 (1970) (*supra*, p. 221), holding that a person's welfare benefits may not be terminated without an administrative hearing at which certain procedural standards are adhered to.

Quiz Yourself on

EQUAL PROTECTION — UNEQUAL TREATMENT OF GAYS; FUNDAMENTAL RIGHTS

52. The state of Concord regulates the procedures by which publicly-run adoption agencies are to decide which would-be adopting parents are to be matched with children who are available for adoption. The regulations say that if the agency has received applications from more than one "qualified" person or couple, the agency is to give a higher preference to "a married husband and wife living together" than to "an adult couple living together not consisting of a husband and wife." (The latter category still gets higher preference than "an unmarried adult living with no other adults in the household.") Judicial interpretations have made it clear that the phrase "married husband and wife" does not include married same-sex couples, even though same-sex marriage is fully recognized in Concord. Bill and Ed, two men who are married to each other and who live together in Concord, wish to adopt a healthy white infant (they don't care which particular one, as long as he or she fits these basic requirements). No public adoption agency has been willing to place any such infant with Bill and Ed, because all these agencies have at least one "qualified" married opposite-sex couple for each infant. Bill and Ed have therefore sued the state in federal court, arguing that the preference scheme violates their constitutional rights. At trial, the state presents testimony by a professor of psychology that adoptees turn out to be, on average, "slightly better-adjusted" as young adults when raised by married opposite-sex couples than when raised by married same-sex couples. Bill and Ed do not offer rebuttal evidence on this point — they simply claim that a level of judicial review more demanding than ordinary "mere-rationality" review must be applied to this regulation, and that under *any* tougher-than-conventional-mere-rationality-review, the regulation here cannot survive.

    (a) What standard of review should the federal court use in deciding the merits of the plaintiffs' claim?

_____

    (b) Which party will prevail on the merits, if the standard of review you specified in (a) is applied?

_____

53. The state of Booth has enacted a statute governing the issuance of absentee ballots in state elections. Under the statute, any male under the age of 65 will be issued an absentee ballot only upon written proof that the applicant will be unable to be present at the voting place on the scheduled day for the election. If the applicant is a female, however, no written proof is required, and the applicant's statement that she cannot be present at the polling place is accepted at face value. The motivation for the statute was the legislature's belief that many women voters are the mothers of infants, who cannot easily get to the polling place to vote. Marvin, a male resident of Booth, has attacked the requirement of written proof on the grounds that it violates his Fourteenth Amendment equal protection rights.

    (a) What standard should the court use in reviewing the requirement of written proof? _____

    (b) Will Marvin's attack succeed? _____

54. The county of Gardenia has established a Forest Conservation District. The purpose of this district is to levy a special tax on owners of forested property, and to use these funds to buy certain parcels of forested property in the county from willing sellers so that the property can remain forested. The ultimate purpose of the District is to ensure that there is enough forested land that erosion will not get a foothold locally, something that would happen if many forested parcels become denuded by logging. The district is to be administered by a Board of Directors having five members. The five members are to be elected annually. Only owners of forested property in the county are permitted to vote in the election for directors. Bruce, the owner of non-forested real estate, has sued for a declaration that the "one person, one vote" principle has been violated by this arrangement.

    (a) What standard of review should the court use in deciding Bruce's challenge? _____

    (b) Will Bruce's attack succeed? _____

55. The state of Illowa provided that in order for a "minor" party to have its presidential candidate appear on the ballot, the party must file petitions containing the signatures of 15% of all eligible voters in the state. (A party was defined as "minor" if it had not received at least 10% of the votes cast in the state in the previous presidential election.) The petition had to be filed nine months before the general election. Also, a minor party did not qualify for the ballot unless it conducted a primary election. Other Illowa electoral provisions prevented anyone from running for President as an independent, and did not allow for write-in candidacies for President. The Anti Washington Party, a newly-formed party dedicated to "throwing the rascals out of Washington," wished to have its candidate appear on the Illowa presidential-election ballot. The AWP sued on the grounds that these restrictions violated the equal protection rights of minority parties, as well as the freedom-of-association rights of party members.

    (a) What standard should the court use in hearing this challenge? _____

    (b) Will the AWP's attack on the restrictions succeed? _____

56. The state of Amazonia has a program called MedAmaz, which provides emergency medical assistance for indigent citizens. Under the rules for the program, a person who has moved to Amazonia is not eligible to receive emergency medical care until he or she has resided in the state for at least one year. Penelope, who moved to Amazonia three months ago from Ohio, needed an emergency appendectomy. The hospital refused to perform it because she did not meet the residency requirement, and Penelope almost died. Now, she has sued the state for damages, arguing that the residency requirement violated her right to equal protection of the laws.

    (a) What standard of review should the court use? _____

(b) Will Penelope's attack succeed?   _____

57. The state of New Canada has set its maximum welfare payment at $1,250 per month. For families of one child through three children, extra sums are paid for each additional child (with the $1,250 figure being paid for a family with three children). The net effect of the scheme is that a family does not receive any extra money for children after the first three. A further effect is that for a family of five children, the maximum paid by the state is 25% less than the federal poverty level. Hilda, a single mother of five children, whose only income comes from New Canada welfare payments, has sued the state, arguing that her family's equal protection rights have been violated, in that the state has discriminated against large families such as hers.

(a) What standard of review should the court use in evaluating the statute?   _____

(b) Will Hilda's attack succeed?   _____

Answers

52. **(a) Unclear, but at least "mere-rationality with bite."** The case most on point is *Obergefell v. Hodges* (2015), where the Court by 5-4 struck down all state bans on same-sex marriage, after holding that such bans violate the "fundamental right" of marriage, under both the substantive Due Process Clause and the Equal Protection Clause. The majority opinion in *Obergefell* didn't specify **what standard of review** the Court was using. But we know that the opinion ended up striking down all state bans on same-sex marriage, and that it did so without even conducting a discussion of either the objectives being pursued by the defendant states or of the tightness of the fit between these objectives and the "means" chosen (a total ban on same-sex marriages). This result seems to show that some standard **more rigorous than ordinary mere-rationality review** (which is a review standard that's so easy to satisfy that the court will uphold a regulation so long as the state has used a means that's merely "rationally related" to the achievement of some "legitimate" state objective) was implicitly being used by the majority. But as of this writing, there is no way to know whether the standard to be used is "strict scrutiny," "mid-level review," or even "mere-rationality with bite."

But *Obergefell* involved a **complete ban** on same-sex marriage, so it was relatively easy for the majority to decide that if the right to marriage is "fundamental" (which the majority decided it was), the ban substantially interfered with that fundamental right. But here, the state *isn't* denying same-sex couples the right to marry — the state is merely treating same-sex married couples less well with respect to **one feature or benefit** stemming from married status, the degree of preference in adoptions. (And note that under the regulation, same-sex married couples still get preference over single adults.) So we have to ask, does the regulation here "substantially impair" the fundamental right of marriage? If it doesn't, it's not clear that anything more rigorous than easy-to-satisfy ordinary mere-rationality review is called for.

Obergefell's emphasis on **child-rearing as one of the key factors** that *makes* the right to marriage fundamental suggests that the *Obergefell* majority *would* view the adoption-restriction here as substantially impairing the fundamental right of marriage, especially from the standpoint of equal protection. Recall that *Obergefell* says that same-sex marriage bans "breach central precepts of equality," in that "same-sex couples are **denied all the benefits** afforded to opposite-sex couples." Here, it's true that the state is not denying gay couples *all* benefits that it gives to opposite-sex couples, but it is clearly treating same-sex couples less favorably with respect to a major benefit that the state has chosen to confer on opposite-sax married couples. So it seems probable that the Court (at least the *Obergefell* majority) would view the adoption regulation here as denying gays equality as to a key benefit of marriage, and thus as substantially impairing their right of marriage. And if the court *did* decide that a fundamental right was being significantly infringed by the adoption regulation here, the court would almost certainly apply a review standard at least as severe as "mere-rationality with bite" (though whether this would lead to striking the regulation is discussed in the next part of this answer).

(b) Unclear, but probably the plaintiffs, Bill and Ed. Since we don't know what the standard of review will be, beyond the strong likelihood that it will be at least as tough as "mere rationality with bite," we can't predict the outcome with great confidence. But even in cases that seem to apply just this relatively-forgiving "mere-rationality with bite" standard — like *U.S. v. Windsor* (*supra*, p. 356), striking down the federal Definition of Marriage Act — the Court seems to have viewed regulations singling out gay couples (particularly married gay couples) for less-favorable treatment than opposite-sex couples as not being supported by even a *legitimate* (let alone "important" or "compelling") state interest. So if the court believes that the regulation here was adopted out of visceral dislike for same-sex couples, the regulation would be unlikely to survive even mere-rationality with bite. However, here the state has articulated a plausible and significant interest not present in the case of total bans on same-sex marriage: an interest in maximizing the adjustment of adoptees. Therefore, the ultimate result would likely turn not only on what standard of review the court chooses to apply, but also on whether the court believes that the state has shown a *reasonably close fit* between the *means* chosen (a denial to same-sex married couples of the highest preference in adoption, but not a complete ban on such adoptions) and this important state objective.

The state's social science evidence about adjustment, given that it was unrebutted by the plaintiffs, might be found to be strong enough to establish a reasonably close means-end fit. But notice that the state's expert witness testified only to a "slightly" better average adjustment when adoptees are raised by an opposite-sex couple. Yet the adoption preference here acts in a very *outcome-determinative way*: because there are always enough married opposite-sex couples, benefiting from the highest priority, available to adopt every healthy white infant, the preference operates as *almost an absolute ban* on the type of adoption the plaintiffs are seeking. The near-absolute nature of the preference, when coupled with the slight advantage the state is pursuing, makes it likely that the court would hold that the state has *not* established that its preference system is sufficiently *closely related* to the admittedly-important state goal of maximizing adoptees' well-being so as to satisfy even mere-rationality with bite.

53. **(a) Strict scrutiny — the differential treatment must be necessary to achieve a compelling governmental interest.**

(b) Yes. Normally, a statutory scheme that distinguishes on the basis of gender must undergo merely mid-level review, i.e., it must be "substantially related" to the achievement of an "important" governmental interest. However, because the right to vote is *"fundamental,"* classifications disadvantaging this right are subjected to strict scrutiny. Therefore, unless the state can show that distinguishing between men and women in issuance of absentee ballots is necessary to achieve a compelling governmental interest, the restriction must fall. Here, even if the state is pursuing some kind of compelling interest (perhaps the need to avoid the fraudulent use of absentee ballots), it is highly unlikely that the gender-based discrimination chosen here is a "necessary" means to achieve that interest. For example, a provision that *each* person who wants to use an absentee ballot must furnish a written excuse would appear to be a satisfactory way to handle the fraud problem.

54. **(a) "Mere-rationality" review.**

(b) No, probably. Normally, any deviation from the "one person, one vote" principle, will be strictly scrutinized, and will probably be found to violate the Equal Protection Clause. But the Supreme Court has made a limited exception for *"special purpose"* bodies, that is, governmental units having a strictly limited purpose which disproportionately affects only one group. In that situation, the right to vote may be limited to the disproportionately-affected group. Here, since all funds disbursed by the district come from taxes on the owners of forested lands, and only such owners can receive the disbursed funds, this standard is probably satisfied. If so, the court will only give mere-rationality review to the arrangement. Since limiting votes for a body to those who have some interest in the body's actions is a rational way to achieve the body's purposes, the mere-rationality standard is probably satisfied. See *Ball v. James.*

55. (a) Strict scrutiny.

(b) Yes, probably. States are certainly entitled to impose ballot restrictions to ensure that only parties with a certain degree of popular support appear on the ballot. However, where ballot restrictions are so severe that they prevent virtually any but the two established parties from getting candidates on the ballot, these restrictions will be strictly scrutinized and probably struck down. The restrictions here seem to be so severe that they would be almost impossible to meet, so the court will probably invalidate the restrictions. See *Williams v. Rhodes*, one of the few ballot-access cases containing a restriction so severe that the statute was struck down; the restrictions here are virtually identical to those in *Williams.*

56. (a) Strict scrutiny.

(b) Yes, probably. Normally, when the state furnishes free goods or services, and does not discriminate against a suspect class, only a "mere-rationality" level of review is used. But when the state is dispensing a *"vital government benefit or privilege," and* the state treats *newly-arrived residents* significantly less favorably than those who have lived in the state longer, strict scrutiny is used. The Supreme Court has held that even non-emergency medical care is a "vital government benefit or privilege" (*Memorial Hospital v. Maricopa County*), so emergency care certainly would be. The one-year residency requirement has the effect of treating recently-arrived people less favorably, so the conditions for strict scrutiny are met. It is doubtful that there is any state interest here that is "compelling" (the state's fiscal interest probably is not), and even more doubtful that a flat ban on any assistance to those who have not yet lived in the state for a year is a "necessary" method of achieving the state's objectives.

57. (a) The "mere-rationality" standard.

(b) No. First, large families (or any particular family size) have has never been found to constitute a "suspect" or "semi-suspect" class. Nor are poor people members of such a class. Hilda's only hope would be to establish that one has a "fundamental interest" in the "necessities of life." However, the Supreme Court has explicitly held that welfare benefits and other "economic necessities" are *not* fundamental interests. See, e.g., *Dandridge v. Williams* (no fundamental interest in welfare benefits). Therefore, any classification system used by the state in allocating such economic necessities is judged by the easy-to-satisfy "mere-rationality" standard. Here, the state's scheme bears a rational relation to several legitimate state objectives (e.g., encouraging employment by prohibiting payments that might compare favorably with what a job would provide).

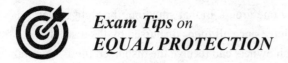

Exam Tips *on*
EQUAL PROTECTION

Equal protection issues, like due process ones, are often hidden, and are likely to be part of almost any complex fact pattern. It is not uncommon for 20-25% of a total Con. Law exam to consist of equal protection issues, scattered throughout multiple fact patterns. Here's what to look for:

☞ Above all else, anytime you see a legislative *classification* — a placement of people or businesses into *two or more groups* — think about the possibility that the classification might violate equal protection.

   ☞ For there to be an equal protection problem, the issue must be whether the government has behaved reasonably in *setting up* the classes in the first place. If the issue is whether the government has correctly placed an *individual* into the "right" group or class, you have a problem of procedural due process, not equal protection. (*Example:* If the government says, "All firefighters must retire at age 55," there is an EP problem because the issue is whether the government can set up the classes in this way. But if the government says, "Any firefighter too weak to do the work will be discharged," and the government then says, "Norman, you are too weak," the issue of whether Norman has been treated fairly is a procedural DP issue, not an EP issue, because the issue is whether the government has given Norman procedural regularity in deciding which class he falls into.)

   ☞ For there to be an EP problem, there must be *"discrimination"* against members of one of the classes, i.e., one class must be treated intentionally less favorably than the other. Use the adjective *"invidious"* to describe the required discrimination.

☞ If you state that P can make an EP attack on the classification at issue, state whether the attack would be "on the statute's *face*" or "*as applied*." Remember that a "facial" attack is used where the statute itself in its text discriminates against a class; an "as applied" attack is used where discrimination against one class stems from how the statute or regulation is *carried out*. (*Examples:* If government imposes a literacy test, or allows public prosecutors to use peremptory challenges, you're likely to be dealing with an "as applied" test.)

☞ Examine whether the discrimination is being practiced by a *state/local* government, or by the *federal* government. If it's the state or local government, then you're using the Fourteenth Amendment's EP Clause. If it's the federal government, you're using the Fifth Amendment's Due Process Clause, which by the process of "reverse incorporation" includes the principle of equal protection. (Especially in multiple choice tests, Profs like to give you an instance of federal discrimination and then try to tempt you to make a choice that involves "the Fourteenth Amendment's Due Process Clause," which is the wrong answer for the reason just stated.)

☞ Once you have identified an EP problem, devote extreme efforts to choosing the correct *level of review*. Remember that there are three levels used in evaluating EP situations:

☞ **Strict scrutiny** is used where either a classification is based upon a **suspect class** (race, national origin or alienage) or where the classification impairs the exercise of a **fundamental right** (e.g., the right to vote or the right to change your state of residence).

☞ **Mid-level** review is used for two "semi-suspect" classifications, those based on **gender** and **illegitimacy**.

☞ The **"mere-rationality"** standard is used for all other types of classifications.

Suggestion: After you identify the issue, immediately state what the likely standard of review is, including details of that test. (*Example:* "Since the classification here is on the basis of gender, the Court will use a mid-level standard of review. That is, the Court will strike down the statute unless it is shown to be important to the achievement of a substantial governmental objective.")

☛ Here are the main things to remember about the **"mere-rationality"** standard, and the places where it is used:

☞ If the classification relates to **economic** regulation, you will almost certainly be using the "mere-rationality" standard. (*Examples:* The state says no one can put a sign on a rooftop, but gives an exception for a sign advertising goods produced by the owner of the building. Or, the state taxes one group more heavily than another (e.g., there's a sales tax on "refined petroleum," but not on "unrefined petroleum").)

☞ Most types of **"social welfare"** classifications will also be judged by the "mere-rationality" standard. (*Examples:* Discrimination based on **age**; discrimination against **aliens** where the function relates to the heart of representative government (see further discussion of aliens below); discrimination in the issuance of **licenses** or **permits**; discrimination against **out-of-staters**; discrimination against the **poor** (in the sense that government fails to pay for things the poor need that the rich can pay for themselves).)

☞ If there's no suspect or semi-suspect class or fundamental right, and the government is trying to **combat an evil**, you'll probably note that the government has only attacked **part** of that evil. The question becomes whether the government has violated EP by not attacking the other evil. Here, you should say something like: "The regulation is valid, because the government is entitled to combat evils **one step at a time**." You might then want to cite to *Williamson v. Lee Optical Co.* (*Example:* The government requires lawyers, but not doctors, to take mandatory continuing education — this is OK, because the government may combat the evil of non-up-to-date professionals one step at a time.)

☞ If the government is trying to **single out an unpopular group** (but one that doesn't get suspect or semi-suspect status) for unfavorable treatment, indicate that although only "mere-rationality" review is used, that review will be applied "with bite," and the scheme may well be struck down. For instance, unequal treatment of **gays** and the **mentally retarded** may fall into this category.

☛ If the classification has to do with **race**, here are the key things to remember:

☞ Race is a **"suspect class."** Therefore, any intentional discrimination based on race —

either in the face of the statute/regulation, or in the way it is applied — must be ***strictly scrutinized***. That is, the classification must be struck down unless it is ***necessary*** to achieve a ***compelling governmental interest***. You should almost always conclude that this standard is ***not*** satisfied. Typically, your reason will be because there is some alternative non-race-conscious method of handling the problem, so the race-conscious means are not "necessary."

☞   Remember that race as a suspect classification will not be deemed to be involved unless government is acting with the ***purpose***, ***not just the effect***, of classifying based on race. (*Example:* If government takes an action which happens to disadvantage more blacks than whites, there's no suspect class, and thus no strict scrutiny, unless there's evidence that government acted with the purpose of disadvantaging blacks.) ***This is the single most commonly tested aspect of strict scrutiny***.

　　☞   Your fact pattern will usually ***not*** contain a racial classification "on its face." Yet, the facts will indicate to you that some racial group is affected more than other groups. This should be your tip-off that you have an " 'effect' vs. 'purpose' " problem.

　　☞   Keep in mind, however, that ***circumstantial evidence*** can always be used to show that government has the ***intent*** to discriminate against the unfavored group, and that the effect is not merely an unintended by-product. (*Example:* If government chooses grand jurors from the rolls of registered voters, the fact that this produces far fewer black grand jurors than other methods would is admissible as circumstantial evidence that the government really intended to discriminate against black grand jurors.)

☞   Remember that the discrimination must be ***"invidious."*** That is, there must be an attempt to treat some racial group in a ***less favorable***, stigmatizing, way. You will want to examine whether this element of "invidiousness" is present whenever the governmental scheme tends to merely ***record*** racial differences, or to impose some kind of racial ***"matching."*** (*Examples:* If the government publishes the race of each political candidate, or the government requires that the race of an adoptive parent match the child's race, or the government imposes a sickle-cell test applicable only to African Americans, you'll want to examine whether there is a "stigmatizing" or "invidious" discrimination. Often, but not always, you will conclude that the answer is "yes.")

☞   Be on the lookout for ***segregation*** — any government program that intentionally ***separates*** the races, or intentionally encourages the races to separate themselves, is likely to be invidious and thus needs to be strictly scrutinized. (*Example:* If a state university allows dormitories to classify themselves, by vote of the existing residents, as "primarily black" or "primarily white," this probably represents intentional governmental support of segregation, and probably requires strict scrutiny.)

☛ Special rules apply to race-conscious ***affirmative action***:

☞   ***Strict scrutiny*** is applied to the affirmative action situation just as much as to the "invidious" situation. Cite to *Richmond v. Croson* when you have a race-conscious affirmative action program.

☞ Typically, the only governmental objectives that are strong enough to overcome strict scrutiny in the affirmative action context are: (1) the eradication of **past discrimination** by government (and only if the discrimination is shown by **clear evidence**) and (2) the pursuit of **diversity** in a **student body**.

☞ The fact that it's **Congress**, rather than state or local government, that's doing the affirmative action now makes **no** formal difference — strict scrutiny is still applied. (Cite to *Adarand* if a congressional act is at issue.) However, you may want to allude to the possibility that even though the Court applies strict scrutiny, it may end up giving **slightly greater deference** to Congress' conclusion that race-conscious measures are needed, than it would to a similar conclusion by a state or local body.

☞ Be on the lookout for race-conscious affirmative action in **university admissions**. Here, say that this is OK (because obtaining the "educational benefits" of student-body diversity can be a compelling objective) *if* the school (1) evaluates each applicant as an **individual**; (2) treats minority-race as merely **one "plus factor" among others**; (3) **doesn't use mechanical means** (like **quotas** or a fixed number of "points") to obtain the desired number of minority-group admittees; and (4) proves that there were no **"workable race-neutral alternatives"** available to achieve the desired "educational diversity."

☞ Cite to the four cases of *Grutter v. Bollinger* (race as an individualized "plus factor" ~~is~~ *Gratz v. Bollinger* (mechanical point systems are not OK); *Fisher v. Univ. of Texas I* ("*Fisher I*") (workable race-neutral methods for achieving student-body diversity must be shown to be unavailable); and *Fisher v. Univ. of Texas II* ("*Fisher II*") (a race-neutral admissions scheme based solely on high-school-class-rank is probably not a "workable" means of achieving student-body diversity, so the availability of such a plan doesn't prevent the university from instead using a race-conscious plan that better promotes diversity).

☞ Also, be on the lookout for race-conscious **pupil-assignment plans** for **public elementary or high schools.** Here, any plan that classifies each student's race, and makes any pupil assignment based on whether the student's presence would improve or worsen the target school's racial imbalance, will almost certainly flunk the requisite strict scrutiny. Cite to *Parents Involved v. Seattle School District* on this point.

☞ It's generally OK for voters to **abolish a race-conscious affirmative action plan** previously instituted by government, as long as the plan being abolished wasn't adopted to remedy government's own previous racial discrimination. And that's true even though the voters intentionally make race-conscious plans harder for government to adopt than other sorts of government programs. (*Example:* Voters may amend a state's constitution to abolish the existing practice by public universities of giving racial minorities preferences in admissions. That's true even though the voters leave the universities free to use other admissions preferences, such as for athletes. Cite to *Schuette v. BAMN.*)

☞ Here are some contexts in which race-conscious affirmative action programs may pop up on exams:

☞ preferential **admissions** to universities and public schools (see above);

☞ minority set-asides in the award of public **construction** and other **contracts**;

☞ allocation of public-sector **jobs** (including layoffs and promotions as well as original hiring);

☞ the drawing of **election districts**.

☛ The drawing of classifications based on **national origin** is also to be strictly scrutinized. However, exams rarely pose a national-origin problem.

☛ Here's what to look for when there is a classification based on **gender**:

☞ Remember that **mid-level** review is used for gender-based classifications. That is, the governmental objective must be **"important,"** and the means must be **"substantially related"** to that objective. (But note that this mid-level review is a pretty tough standard, with the court requiring an "exceedingly persuasive justification," and giving "skeptical scrutiny." Cite to *U.S. v. Virginia*, the VMI case, as the source for these descriptions of how the mid-level review is to be conducted.)

☞ Remember that the same review standard is in theory used whether the sex-based classification is **"invidious"** (intended to harm women) or **"benign"** (intended to help women). Any classification that derives in part from "stereotypical" views about women (e.g., that women's place is in the home, or that women are physically weak) is especially likely to be struck down.

☞ Where the classification disadvantages **men**, the same rules apply: mid-level review is used.

☞ As with race-conscious discrimination, only governmental action whose **purpose**, not mere effect, is to discriminate against one gender, will be considered. (*Example:* A strength requirement for paramedics would not be subjected to mid-level review, if the requirement's purpose was not to discriminate against women, and it was merely an unintended effect that fewer women than men could qualify.)

☞ Here are some areas where gender-based classifications have popped up on exams:

☞ (1) The government provides that pregnant women in the workforce are to be treated differently than all others, e.g., with respect to exposure to toxic substances. (This is not necessarily true gender discrimination, since women who are not pregnant are not impacted, so probably you don't apply mid-level review, just "mere-rationality" review.)

☞ (2) Women are given different school activities than men. (*Example:* Women are not allowed to play football. Probably it's appropriate to use mid-level review, but the classification system will probably survive that review in light of the different average size and strength of women.)

☛ Classifications based on **illegitimacy** are also "semi-suspect" and thus get mid-level review. Most commonly, you would be tested on a state statute that discriminates against illegitimates with respect to the right to **inherit**.

☞ Discrimination against *aliens* is very frequently tested.

  ☞ As a *general* rule, remember that discrimination against aliens is subjected to **strict scrutiny**. (*Examples:* A state's refusal of welfare benefits to aliens, or its refusal to let an alien practice a profession, will be strictly scrutinized.)

    ☞ Note that discrimination against "aliens" typically refers to discrimination against **legal** aliens. Probably strict scrutiny is **not** used for discrimination against **illegal** or "undocumented" aliens.

  ☞ Remember that there is a key **exception** to the general rule of strict scrutiny: where the alien has applied for a **job** that goes to the **"heart of representative government,"** only mere-rationality review is used. Most government jobs that have a **policy**, **law enforcement** or **education** component fall within this "representative government" exception. (*Examples:* Jobs as a public school teacher, police officer, or probation officer are all within the exception, so the state merely has to be rational in its decision to close these positions off from foreigners.)

    ☞ But there are some jobs that are sufficiently ministerial that they do not fall within the "representative government" exception. (*Examples:* Secretary in a governmental agency; meter reader for a publicly owned electric utility.)

☞ Classifications impairing a **"fundamental right"** are tested less frequently than those involving a suspect or semi-suspect class. Nonetheless, these classifications sometimes pop up on exams.

  ☞ The **right to marriage** is a fundamental right, and that right now includes the right to **same sex marriage.** (Cite to *Obergefell v. Hodges* on this point.) So if government treats *married same-sex couples less favorably* than married opposite-sex couples in ~~mention~~ the strong possibility that the classification will be subjected to ~~close~~ scrutiny.

  Example 1: When a married couple have a child conceived by anonymous sperm donation, state law says that if the couple is opposite-sex, the "husband's" name must be put on the child's birth certificate, even though the husband by definition couldn't be the child's biological father. But when the married couple consists of two women one of whom has conceived by use of anonymous sperm donation, the state refuses to list the non-birth-mother's name on the certificate. Note that this disfavoring of same-sex married couples violates the *Obergefell* principle; cite to *Pavan v. Smith* for this result.

  Example 2: Suppose state adoption regulations make it harder for a same-sex married couple to both adopt the same child than for an opposite-sex married couple. You should say that the court will probably give fairly tough scrutiny (though not necessarily strict scrutiny) to the classification, on the grounds that it significantly impairs the fundamental right to same-sex marriage.

  ☞ Any impairment of the right to **vote** is an impairment of a fundamental right, and thus strictly scrutinized, if it is **not reasonably related to determining the voter's qualifications.**

Examples: (1) Poll taxes; (2) a requirement that the voter have resided in the jurisdiction for one year before the election; and (3) a requirement that the voter be a landowner or tenant, are generally not reasonably related to determining the voter's qualifications. Therefore, they'll be strictly scrutinized and struck down.

☞ But if the measure *is* reasonably related to determining the voter's qualifications, then it will be subjected only to **mid-level review**, and probably upheld.

Examples: (1) A requirement that a voter present a government-issued photo ID; and (2) A requirement that a voter prove that he's a bona fide resident (e.g., by having lived in the jurisdiction for 50 days) won't be strictly scrutinized, and will probably be upheld.

☞ A person's right to be a **candidate** seems to be "semi-fundamental," and thus gets more-than-mere-rationality review. (*Example:* A high candidate filing fee that is imposed even on indigent candidates violates EP.) Similarly, restrictions that unfairly keep **new, not-yet-established, political parties** off the ballot get this semi-fundamental review.

☞ Access to the **courts** is sometimes a "fundamental interest." Look for situations where the state imposes a **fee** that it refuses to waive for indigents. The two contexts that count are **criminal** cases (so that the state may not charge an indigent for a trial transcript or for counsel) and **family law** cases (so that the state may not charge a filing fee to indigents who want a **divorce**). But other types of civil access (e.g., small claims court or bankruptcy court) are not deemed "fundamental," so the state's refusal to subsidize indigents gets only mere-rationality review.

☞ The **"right to travel"** (really the right to **change** one's state of **residence** or **employment**) is "fundamental."

☞ Therefore, look for patterns where the state imposes a substantial **waiting period** on newly-arrived residents: if they have to do this wait before they get some **vital governmental benefit** (e.g., **welfare**), a fundamental right has been impaired. But non-vital benefits are not "fundamental" (so that there's only mere-rationality review where the state makes newcomers wait for, say, low in-state university tuition rates).

☞ The right to **"necessities"** is **not** fundamental. So if your fact pattern involves the state's refusal to equalize the right of indigents to such items as **public school education, food, shelter or medical care**, you probably need to apply only "mere-rationality" review, not strict scrutiny fundamental interest review.

CHAPTER 11

MISCELLANEOUS CLAUSES: 14TH AM. PRIVILEGES OR IMMUNITIES; TAKING; CONTRACT; RIGHT TO BEAR ARMS; EX POST FACTO; BILLS OF ATTAINDER

ChapterScope

This Chapter considers several clauses that have little in common except that they protect individuals against specific types of government conduct. The most important concepts in this Chapter are:

■ **Privileges or Immunities:** The 14th Amendment has a "Privileges or Immunities" Clause. But this clause is very narrowly interpreted: it only protects the individual from state interference with his rights of *"national"* citizenship (principally the right to *travel from state to state* and the right to *vote in national elections*).

■ **"Taking" Clause:** The Fifth Amendment's "Taking" Clause provides, essentially, that the government may take private property under its power of "eminent domain," but if it does take private property, it *must pay a fair price*.

❑ **Land-use regulations:** What the government calls mere "regulation" may occasionally amount to a "taking" for which compensation must be paid. This happens mostly in cases of *land-use regulation*. For a land-use regulation to avoid being a taking, it must satisfy two requirements: (1) it must *"substantially advance legitimate state interests"*; and (2) it must *not "deny an owner economically viable use of his land."*

■ **"Contract" Clause:** The "Contract" Clause provides that "no state shall... pass any... law impairing the obligation of contracts." The meaning of this Clause depends on whether the government is impairing its own contracts or contracts between private parties:

❑ **Public contracts:** If the state is trying to escape from its *own financial obligations*, then the Court will *closely scrutinize* this attempt: the state's attempt to "weasel" will be struck down unless the modification is *"reasonable* and *necessary* to support an *important* public purpose."

❑ **Private contracts:** But when the state is re-writing contracts made by *private parties*, the state merely has to be acting *"reasonably,"* a much easier-to-satisfy standard. (And if the state's action is a *generally applicable* rule that has only the incidental effect of impairing contracts, the Contract Clause does not apply at all.)

■ **Right to Bear Arms:** The Second Amendment has been held to guarantee private individuals the right to keep firearms at home for purposes of self-defense.

■ **Ex Post Facto Laws:** Both the state and federal governments are prohibited from passing any "ex post facto" law. An ex post facto law is a law which has a *retroactive punitive effect*. So government may not impose a punishment for conduct which, at the time it occurred, was *not punishable*. Nor may government *increase* the punishment for an offense over what was on the books at the time of the act.

▪ **Bills of Attainder:** Both state and federal governments are prohibited from passing any "bill of attainder." A bill of attainder is a legislative act which "applies either to *named individuals* or to *easily ascertainable* members of a group in such a way as to *punish* them without a *judicial trial*."

I.   THE 14TH AMENDMENT'S PRIVILEGES OR IMMUNITIES CLAUSE

A. **"Privileges or Immunities" Clause:** The *"Privileges or Immunities"* Clause of the Fourteenth Amendment comes at the beginning of the second sentence of Section I: "No State shall make or enforce any law which shall *abridge* the privileges or immunities of citizens of the United States. ... " At least some of the members of Congress who participated in the drafting of the Fourteenth Amendment expected and hoped that this Clause would constitute a substantial restraint on state government action against individuals. See Tribe, p. 550.

   1. *Slaughterhouse* **Cases:** But the Supreme Court did not take this view. In the *Slaughterhouse Cases*, 83 U.S. (16 Wall.) 36 (1873), the Court held (5-4) that the Fourteenth Amendment's Privileges or Immunities Clause merely forbade state infringement of the rights of *national* citizenship, *not the rights of state citizenship.*

      a. **Facts of *Slaughterhouse* Cases:** The *Slaughterhouse Cases* arose when Louisiana passed a law giving a monopoly on New Orleans-area slaughterhouses to a particular company. Butchers not included in the monopoly claimed that the statute deprived them of the opportunity to practice their trade, and thereby violated the Thirteenth and Fourteenth Amendments. The plaintiffs' most serious argument was that the statute was a denial of the privileges or immunities of Louisiana citizenship, including the *right to practice one's calling.*

      b. **Argument rejected:** But the Supreme Court *rejected* all of the plaintiffs' contentions, including the privileges or immunities argument. *"Fundamental" civil rights,* including the right to *practice one's calling,* were the *domain of the states,* not the federal government, the Court said. Therefore, the plaintiffs should look to Louisiana law for protection; if there was no protection under Louisiana law (as apparently there was not), the plaintiffs were out of luck, since the Privileges or Immunities Clause added nothing to their rights in this area.

      c. **Minority view:** The four *dissenters* in the *Slaughterhouse Cases* flatly rejected the majority's limited reading of the Fourteenth Amendment Privileges or Immunities Clause. The correct reading, the dissent contended, was that the Clause guaranteed to every U.S. citizen that his "fundamental rights," rights which "belong to the citizens of all free governments," would not be infringed by any state. These fundamental rights included the right to "pursue a lawful employment in a lawful manner."

   2. **View of clause until 1999:** Until 1999, the *Slaughterhouse* majority's view of the Fourteenth Amendment Privileges or Immunities Clause prevailed. For 125 years after that decision, *only one state law was ever invalidated* under the Clause, and that decision was

soon overruled. Only a few rights of "national" (as opposed to "state") citizenship were deemed protected, such as the right to ***travel physically from state to state***, to petition Congress for redress of grievances, to ***vote in national elections***, to enter federally-owned lands, and to be protected while in the custody of U.S. marshal (see *Twining v. New Jersey*, 211 U.S. 78 (1908)), and these were rarely even claimed to be abridged by state laws.

3. **View expanded in *Saenz*:** But then, a surprising 7-2 decision in 1999 dramatically breathed some narrow but real new life into the Fourteenth Amendment Privileges or Immunities Clause. In ***Saenz v. Roe***, 526 U.S. 489 (1999), the Court held that the clause protects a particular and important aspect of the so-called "right to travel," namely the right of a person who has ***recently become a citizen*** of a state to the same privileges enjoyed by ***longer-standing citizens*** of that state. *Saenz* became only the second case in 125 years to strike down a state law on Fourteenth Amendment P-or-I grounds.

    a. **Welfare rights:** *Saenz* involved the right of a newly-arrived resident in California to receive the same state ***welfare benefits*** as a person who had been in the state longer. California, acting under express congressional authority, said that anyone who had resided in the state for less than one year would receive welfare benefits no greater than the level of benefits the person had received in her prior state of residence. (45 of the 49 other states had lower benefit levels than California.) Although California denied that the purpose of its provision was to deter the migration of poor people into California, the lower federal courts in *Saenz* found that this was indeed the statute's purpose.

    b. **Struck down:** The Court found that California's rule setting welfare benefits based on the recipient's state of prior residence violated the Fourteenth Amendment P-or-I Clause: ***"[T]he Clause does not tolerate a hierarchy of 45 subclasses of similarly situated citizens based on the location of their prior residence."*** Even if California was acting for the purpose of reducing expenditures (rather than in order to deter in-migration of poor people), using a means predicated on length of state citizenship was not acceptable, since a family's financial needs were not dependent on how long it had been in the state or where it had previously resided.

        i. **Strict scrutiny:** The Court in *Saenz* seems to have applied ***strict scrutiny*** to California's rule disfavoring recent newcomers: the Court said that "[n]either mere rationality nor some intermediate standard of review should be used to judge the constitutionality of a state rule that discriminates against some of its citizens because they have been domiciled in the State for less than a year." California's fiscal justification did not come even close to satisfying this strict standard of review.

    c. **Significance:** So *Saenz* probably means that the Fourteenth Amendment Privileges or Immunities Clause requires the states to ***satisfy strict scrutiny*** before they may ***treat newly-arrived residents less favorably than those of longer standing.***

        i. **Bona fide residence requirements:** One last note: *Saenz* probably does not change the rule that a state is entitled to impose a ***requirement of bona fide residency as a pre-condition to receiving state benefits***.

4. **Distinguished from Article IV Clause:**   It is important to distinguish the Fourteenth Amendment Privileges or Immunities Clause from the Privileges and Immunities Clause of *Article IV, §2* (described *supra*, p. 104). To summarize the distinction: The Fourteenth Amendment Clause bars a state from abridging any U.S. citizen's rights of "national" citizenship (of which the most important now seems to be the right to travel, and relocate, from one state to another). The Article IV Clause protects rights of "state" citizenship, but only when a non-resident of the state is not treated the same as a resident with respect to an important state right, essentially a right involving commerce.

II. THE "TAKING" CLAUSE

A. **The Taking Clause generally:**   Governments, both state and federal, have the right to *take private property for public use, provided that "just compensation" is paid.* This power is known as the right of *"eminent domain."* Nothing in the Constitution explicitly confers this eminent domain power upon either the federal or state governments. But the Fifth Amendment, originally intended to apply solely to the federal government, provides that "private property *[shall not] be taken for public use, without just compensation."* This so-called Taking Clause is at least a "tacit recognition that the power to take private property exists." N&R, pp. 438-440.

1. **Two major issues:**   A full discussion of the eminent domain power, and the accompanying obligation to pay just compensation, is beyond the scope of this outline. (The subject is treated more extensively in *Emanuel* on *Property.*) For present purposes, we are interested in the general aspects of two issues: (1) what is the borderline between a *"taking"* (for which compensation must be paid) and a mere *"regulation"* (for which no compensation is due)? and (2) when is a taking made for *"private"* rather than "public" use, so that there is no right of eminent domain, even if compensation is paid? The first of these issues is the more important.

2. **States subject to rules:**   The federal government, as noted, is explicitly bound by the Fifth Amendment's ban on the taking of private property for public use without just compensation. But the Supreme Court has repeatedly held that *state governments* are similarly prohibited, by the Fourteenth Amendment's Due Process Clause, from taking private property without paying for it. However, since the Fourteenth Amendment Due Process Clause does not refer explicitly either to takings or to compensation, the theory by which the just compensation requirement is imposed on the states is not clear.

   a. **Competing views:**   In any event, the Supreme Court has held that essentially the same standards for determining when there has been a taking, and what constitutes just compensation, should be applied to the states as to the federal government.

B. **The taking/regulation distinction, generally:**   If the court finds that private property has been "taken" by the government, compensation must be paid. But if the state merely *regulates* property use in a manner consistent with the state's "police power," then *no compensation needs to be paid,* even though the owner's use of his property, or even its value, has been substantially diminished. It thus becomes crucial to distinguish between a compensable "taking" and a non-compensable "regulation." Most of the cases requiring a distinction between taking and regulation have involved *land-use regulations*; these include zoning regulations, environmental-protection rules, landmark preservation schemes, and other schemes by which the government does not attempt to take title to a landowner's property but does regulate his use of that property.

Here are some of the principles governing when a land-use regulation will be so extensive that it should be viewed as a taking for which compensation must be paid.

1. **Physical occupation:** If the government makes or authorizes a ***permanent physical occupation*** of the property, this will ***automatically*** be found to constitute a taking, no matter how minor the interference with the owner's use and no matter how important the countervailing governmental interests. In ***Loretto v. Teleprompter Manhattan CATV Corp.***, 458 U.S. 419 (1982), the Court formulated this *"per se"* rule, and applied it to invalidate a statute which required landlords to permit cable television companies to ***install their cable facilities on the landlord's rental property.*** (The scheme permitted landlords to charge the cable companies what was in most instances a maximum one-time fee of $1.) The case is discussed in more detail *infra*, p. 405.

2. **Diminution in value:** The more drastic the ***reduction in value*** of the owner's property, the more likely a taking is to be found. For instance, in ***Pennsylvania Coal Co. v. Mahon***, 260 U.S. 393 (1922), a landowner had bought the surface rights to land, and the house on it, under a chain of title which reserved to a coal company the right to mine coal from under the property. Thereafter, Pennsylvania enacted a statute preventing subsurface mining where a house might be caused to sink. The effect of the statute was to bar the coal company completely from mining under the owner's land.

    a. **Holding:** The Supreme Court held in *Mahon* that the regulation so utterly impaired the right to mine coal that it was nearly the equivalent of an appropriation or destruction of the coal. Therefore, the regulation was a taking, which could not be carried out without compensation to the coal company. The Court, in a majority opinion by Justice Holmes, noted that "while property may be regulated to a certain extent, if regulation goes too far it will be recognized as a taking."

    b. **Dissent:** But a dissent, by Justice Brandeis, argued that the regulation was merely "the prohibition of a noxious use," and therefore did not require compensation. (The "noxious use" factor is discussed immediately below.)

    c. **Result may no longer be valid:** The result in *Pennsylvania Coal* may no longer be valid. In *Keystone Bituminous Coal Ass'n v. DeBenedictis*, 480 U.S. 470 (1987), the Court by a 5-4 vote upheld a modern (1966) Pennsylvania version of the statute struck down in *Pennsylvania Coal*. The 1966 statute required that 50% of the coal beneath existing public buildings and dwellings be left in place to provide surface support. The majority made some efforts to distinguish *Pennsylvania Coal*, but there is so little difference between the two statutes that it seems likely that *Pennsylvania Coal* would turn out the other way if decided today.

        i. **Principle still applies:** However, the general ***principle*** for which the case is cited — that ***the more drastic the reduction in value of the owner's property, the more likely a taking is to be found*** — remains ***valid***. (*Keystone* also illustrates that where the state is acting to prevent ***harm to the public***, the courts will be very reluctant to invalidate the regulation as a "taking." See the discussion of the "prevention of harm" rationale, *infra*.)

C. Denial of all economically viable use of land: Since as we've just seen the more drastic the reduction in value of the owner's property, the more likely a taking is to be found, it's not surprising that the Court has imposed a *flat rule* that a taking automatically occurs where an owner has been deprived of *all economically viable use* of his land. See *Agins v. Tiburon*, 447 U.S. 255 (1980).

1. **Particular use eliminated:** Cases in which such an extreme taking by deprivation of economically viable use is found are rare. The fact that the *particular* use made by the plaintiff has been completely foreclosed *will not be enough.*

   Example: For instance, suppose a parcel contains an aluminum smelter worth $100 million, and the city where the smelter is located then bans all smelting. The fact that P's particular land use — operation of the smelter — has been totally foreclosed will not be enough to make the regulation a "taking," because P is still free to convert the smelter to some other use, or even to raze it and put up some other structure (or sell it to someone who will).

2. **Total ban:** On the other hand, a *total and permanent ban* on the *building* of *any structure* on property *is* likely to be enough to deny the owner "all economically viable use" of his land, and thus to constitute a taking automatically.

   Example: South Carolina, in order to protect its coastline from continued erosion, enacts the Beachfront Management Act, which defines certain "critical areas" of erosion danger, and bars any owner of a lot in a critical area from building any permanent habitable structure on the parcel. P is the owner of two parcels which, at the time he bought them for nearly $1 million, were allowed to have houses built upon them; passage of the Act has the effect of *preventing P from building any permanent structure on either lot.* P contends that this "regulation" deprives him of all economic use of his property, and thus constitutes a taking.

   Held (by the U.S. Supreme Court), if P has truly been deprived of all economically viable use of his property, a "taking" has occurred. It is up to the South Carolina courts to decide whether P has really been deprived of all economically viable use. If he has been, a taking exists even though the state is trying to protect the health and safety of residents (unless the state already had, under the "background principles of the state's law of property and nuisance" the right to prevent the particular use by P, an issue to be decided by the state courts on remand; this aspect of the case is described *infra*, p. 404, Par. 2). *Lucas v. South Carolina Coastal Council*, 505 U.S. 1003 (1992).

3. **Temporary moratorium on development:** In *Lucas*, the ban on all economically viable use of P's property purported to be permanent. What happens if the government merely imposes a *temporary* delay on all economically viable use of property, as where a planning board institutes a *"moratorium"* on development of certain property — is the government automatically required to pay just compensation for this delay? As a result of a post-*Lucas* case decided in 2002, the answer is *"not necessarily"* — the court will instead consider *all the surrounding circumstances* to determine whether the delay of all economically viable

use was so severe as to require that compensation be paid. ***Tahoe-Sierra Preservation Council, Inc. v. Tahoe Regional Planning Agency***, 535 U.S. 302 (2002).

  a. **Categorical ruling rejected:** The Supreme Court, by a 6-3 vote, ***refused*** to find a categorical right to compensation for such a temporary delay in the right to make any economically-viable use of one's property. In an opinion by Justice Stevens, the court said that "the answer to the abstract question whether a temporary [development] moratorium effects a taking is neither 'yes, always' nor 'no, never'; the answer depends upon the ***particular circumstances*** of the case."

    i. **Distinction:** The Court distinguished sharply between ***physical*** takings and ***regulatory*** takings. Even a temporary physical occupation of P's property entitles him to compensation. But a similar rule for temporary regulatory takings would wreak havoc: "Land-use regulations are ubiquitous. ... Treating them all as *per se* takings would transform government regulation into a ***luxury few governments could afford.*** By contrast, physical appropriations are relatively rare, easily identified, and usually represent a greater affront to individual property rights."

    ii. ***Lucas*** **marginalized:** So as the result of *Tahoe-Sierra*, the *Lucas* decision is ***marginalized***. As Justice Stevens put it in *Tahoe-Sierra*, "the categorical rule in *Lucas* was carved out for the 'extraordinary case' in which a regulation ***permanently*** deprives property of all value; the ***default rule*** remains that, in the regulatory taking context, we require a more ***fact specific*** inquiry."

  b. **Significance:** *Tahoe-Sierra* does *not* mean that a ban on all economically-viable use of one's property need not be compensated merely because it turns out to be temporary. The case merely means that there is no ***automatic*** right to compensation — instead, the surrounding circumstances must be considered in deciding whether there has been a taking. For example, if the property actually ***increased in value*** during the moratorium, that would probably strongly cut against a finding that there had been a taking.

D. **"Prevention of harm" or "noxious use" rationale:** A regulation rather than a taking is likely to be found where the property use being prevented is one that is ***harmful*** or "***noxious***" to others. For instance, a zoning ordinance may properly prevent the operation of a steel mill in the middle of a residential neighborhood; in general, anything which the common law would recognize as a public or private ***nuisance*** may be barred by regulation, without the need for compensation.

  1. **Favoring one private interest over another:** Occasionally, a zoning or other public decision that a land use is "noxious" will be the product of a clear decision to ***favor one private interest over another***. Nonetheless, the fact that a private interest, rather than the "public interest" as a whole, is being benefited, will not render the regulation a compensable taking.

  Example: Many red cedar trees in the state of Virginia are infected with cedar rust, a disease that is highly dangerous to apple orchards. Virginia passes a law requiring the destruction, as a public nuisance, of all red cedar trees within a prescribed distance from an apple orchard. Cedar owners are paid only the cost of removing their trees, not the value of the trees.

Held, the ordinance, and the consequent uncompensated destruction of the cedars, were not a compensable taking. The state had the right to conclude that apple orchards were more important to the state economy than cedars, and its decision to sacrifice the latter to save the former did not violate due process. *Miller v. Schoene*, 276 U.S. 272 (1928).

   a. **Bar must fall within common-law nuisance principles:**   However, the mere fact that the legislature has labeled a certain use as being "harmful" or "noxious" is *not enough* to ensure that the land-use restriction will be found to be a regulation rather than a taking. If a land-use regulation is so severe that it deprives the owner of "all economically beneficial use of his land," then the restrictions must "do no more than duplicate the result that could have been achieved in the courts — by adjacent land owners … under the State's law of *private nuisance*, or by the State under its complementary power to abate nuisances that affect the public generally[,]" In other words, the legislature cannot suddenly decide that a particular use is so harmful that it should be immediately banned, if the ban will deprive an owner of all economically viable use of his land, and if the common law principles of nuisance would not allow the state to get the use forbidden by a court.

E. **Zoning, environmental and landmark-preservation rationales:** Many cases involve a land owner's claim that *zoning, environmental,* or *landmark-preservation regulations* constituted a regulatory taking. In these cases, the owner is rarely able to show that the regulation deprived her of "all economically viable use" of her property. Therefore, owners rarely prevail with their regulatory-taking claim.

   1. **Zoning regulation:**   In cases where *zoning regulations* impair an owner's use of his property, the Court has been especially reluctant to find a compensable taking. A zoning ordinance will not be stricken as violative of due process unless it is *"clearly arbitrary and unreasonable*, having no substantial relation to the public health, safety, morals or general welfare." *Moore v. East Cleveland*, 431 U.S. 494 (1977).

      a. *Moore:*   *Moore* itself was an extremely rare invalidation of a zoning ordinance. The ordinance there allowed only members of a "family" to live together, and defined "family" so narrowly that a grandmother was barred from living with her two grandchildren, one by each of two different children.

   2. **Environmental regulation:**   Regulations designed to protect the *environment* are usually similarly subjected to only mild review, even if the property owner's ability to use his land is substantially circumscribed.

      a. **Caveat:**   But again, remember that if the regulation *completely deprives* an owner of *economically viable use of his land,* and that regulation cannot be justified under common-law nuisance principles, a "taking" will occur even if the government's objective is to protect the environment. See *Lucas v. South Carolina Coastal Council, supra*, p. 402.

   3. **Landmark preservation:**   *Landmark preservation* schemes, like zoning and environmental regulations, will *seldom* constitute a taking. In *Penn Central Transportation Co. v. New York City*, 438 U.S. 104 (1978), the Court found that the New York City Landmarks Preservation Law did not effect a taking of plaintiff's property.

a. **Facts:** Plaintiff was the owner of Grand Central Terminal, which was designated as a "landmark" under the Law. As a consequence, the building's exterior was required to be kept "in good repair," and administrative approval was necessary for any alteration. Plaintiff sought such approval to construct a 55-story office building above the Terminal, but this request was denied on the grounds that the new structure would clash with the Terminal's beaux arts facade.

b. **Holding and rationale:** A six-Justice majority held that so long as landmark preservation is carried out as part of a **comprehensive** preservation scheme, development of individual landmarks may be curtailed without effecting a taking. The New York City statute met the requirement of comprehensiveness. The opinion found landmark preservation schemes to be akin to zoning laws (although the Court conceded that the effect of a preservation scheme typically falls heavily upon a few, in contrast to the widespread impact of a zoning scheme).

   i. **Use of "transferable development rights":** In determining that there was no taking, the Court took into account the fact that New York City gave the owners of landmark buildings so-called "transferable development rights" (TDRs), which could be used to increase the permissible size of other, non-landmark, buildings owned by the same owner. Because, in the Court's opinion, these TDRs had value, the economic impact on the owner of a landmark building fell short of what would be required before a taking could be found.

c. **Dissent:** Justice Rehnquist, joined by two other members of the Court, dissented from the *Penn Central* holding. The regulation here was a taking, the dissent contended, because it was a serious destruction of property, and was not justified either under the "nuisance" rationale (see *supra*, p. 403) or the rationale of zoning-type laws.

F. **Physical occupation:** We saw earlier (*supra*, p. 401) that where government makes a **physical occupation** of private property, that occupation is treated as an automatic "*per se*" taking, for which the government must pay compensation **no matter how minor** the occupation's **economic impact** on the landowner.

1. **Where occupation is permanent and continuous:** This rule that a physical occupation amounts to a *per se* compensable taking has long been clear in those situations in which the occupation is essentially a **permanent and continuous** one.

    Example: A New York statute (1) says that any landlord must permit a cable television company to install its cable facilities on the landlord's property, and (2) limits the landlord to a one-time $1 fee as compensation.

    Held, no matter how small the economic impact from the installation is on the value of the landlord's property, the installation is a "taking" for which compensation must be paid. When government action brings about a "permanent physical occupation of property," a Fifth Amendment taking occurs "without regard to whether the action achieves an important public benefit or has only minimal economic impact on the owner." *Loretto v. Teleprompter Manhattan CATV Corp.*, 458 U.S. 419 (1982) (also discussed *supra*, p. 401).

2. **Temporary occupation:** But as the result of a 2021 decision, this same principle — that a physical occupation commanded by government *automatically* amounts to a compensable taking — now normally applies even where the occupation is a **temporary and/or intermittent one**. In that case, **Cedar Point Nursery v. Hassid**, 141 S.Ct. 2063 (June 23, 2021), the Court held that a state law allowing union organizers to come onto crop growers' property from time to time to recruit workers was a *per se* taking of the growers' property.

   a. **Facts:** A California labor regulation required agricultural employers to allow *labor unions to come onto the work site* and *meet with workers* there for up to 120 days per year. On each of those days, the access could be for an hour before work, an hour after work, and an hour during the lunch break.

   b. **Majority finds a taking:** By a 6-3 vote, the conservative majority held that this compelled "physical appropriation" *was a per se taking,* with *no need for the courts to consider the size of the economic harm* the appropriation caused to the value of the land. Furthermore, Chief Justice Roberts' majority opinion said, such physical appropriations constitute *per se* takings even if the appropriation is **intermittent** rather than permanent: "The fact that a right to take access is exercised *only from time to time* does not make it any less a physical taking."

      i. **Not a mere "regulation":** Roberts agreed with the dissent that if the scheme here had merely functioned to *"regulate"* the growers' use of their property, the *"per se"* rule governing physical appropriations would *not* have been triggered, and there would have been no taking unless the economic harm to the owner was significant. But Roberts *disagreed* with the dissenters' conclusion that California here was *merely regulating land-use.*

      True, the government action here "comes garbed as a regulation[.]" But California was not merely restricting a property owner's ability to use his own property. Rather, the state was *appropriating the owners' "right to exclude others,"* which Roberts called "one of the most treasured rights of property ownership." The state was then temporarily transferring that right of exclusion to a third party (the union). The state was therefore *making a "physical appropriation" of property* — triggering an automatic Takings Clause obligation to compensate the owner — not merely "regulating" how the owner could use his land.

   c. **Dissent:** The Court's three liberal justices, in an opinion by Breyer (joined by Sotomayor and Kagan), *dissented.* Breyer believed that the access provision here was a classic form of land-use *regulation*, *not a physical appropriation* that might constitute a *"per se"* taking.

      i. **Shopping center case as precedent:** Breyer believed that the scheme here could and should be found to be a non-taking regulation based on the Court's earlier decision in a case involving access to a *privately-owned shopping center.* In *Prune Yard Shopping Center v. Robins*, 447 US. 74 (1980), a state constitution required that any privately-owned shopping center permit individuals to enter the property to exercise their rights to free speech. The Court in *Prune Yard* held that the access right did *not* constitute a Fifth Amendment taking: although the provision allowed the individuals to "physically invade" the property, the temporary nature of the access, and the lack of any evidence that the access would unreasonably impair the property's value, made the provision a regulation rather than a *per se* taking. Breyer thought that the *Prune Yard* holding ***"fits this case almost perfectly,"*** especially since the regulation here "grants a far smaller group of people the right to enter landowners' property for far more limited times in order to speak about a specific subject."

  ii. Widespread impact: Breyer worried that the majority's rationale would treat as *per se* takings "large numbers of ***ordinary regulations*** in a host of different fields that, for a variety of purposes, permit temporary entry onto (or an 'invasion of') a property owner's land." These regulations, he said, included "activities ranging from ***examination of food products*** to ***inspections for compliance*** with ***preschool licensing requirements.***"

   (1) Roberts' rebuttal: Roberts' majority opinion rejected this concern. Roberts said that government could rely on several exceptions to avoid having "government health and safety inspection regimes" constitute *per se* takings. For instance, he wrote, government could "***condition the grant of a benefit such as a permit, license, or registration*** on ***allowing access for reasonable health and safety inspections***"; the use of such conditions would turn the access into a valid regulation rather than a *per se* taking.

G. Subsequent owner who takes with notice of restriction: Suppose the case is one of those relatively uncommon ones in which the land-use restriction is so great that a taking will be deemed to have occurred. What happens if the person who owns the property at the time the regulation is put into effect does not sue, but a ***subsequent buyer*** — who buys the property ***with knowledge*** of the restriction — then sues on a takings theory?

1. New buyer may sue: The Supreme Court has held that the subsequent buyer ***may proceed*** with the suit just as the original owner could have. A contrary rule, the Court held, would enable the state in effect "to put an expiration date on the Takings Clause." This ought not to be the rule, the Court continued, because "[f]uture generations, too, have a right to challenge unreasonable limitations on the use and value of land." *Palazzolo v. Rhode Island*, 533 U.S. 606 (2001)

H. Dedications, and the requirement of a tight means-end fit: The Supreme Court has for the last several decades required, in at least some kinds of cases, a ***very close fit*** between the ***means*** chosen by the state (i.e., the particular land-use regulation selected) and the governmental ***objective*** being pursued. In this category of cases, even a compelling state interest will be to no avail if the means chosen by the government are not quite closely tailored to advance that interest.

1. Applies only to "dedications": This approach requiring a tighter means-end fit applies, so far, only in the special case in which the government attempts to require property owners to ***"dedicate"*** (i.e., ***give away***) to the public some piece of land, cash or other property in return for approval of a land-use permit.

2. Summary of rule: As the Court has summarize this approach to dedications, "a unit of government ***may not condition the approval of a land-use permit*** on the owner's ***relin-***

quishment of a portion of his property unless there is a ***'nexus'*** and ***'rough proportionality'*** between the government's demand and the effects of the proposed land use." *Koontz v. St. Johns River Water Mgmt. Dist.*, 133 S. Ct. 2586 (2013).

a. **Contrast with other areas of regulation:** This requirement of a tight means-end fit in land-use cases involving dedications contrasts quite sharply with the Court's easy-to-satisfy standard in other economic regulation contexts, where all that is required is that the relation between the means chosen and the end being pursued be ***"merely rational"*** (see *supra*, pp. 171 and 248).

We'll look at the three main cases in which the Court has imposed its tough approach to dedications. In these cases, the Court in sequence decided that:

[1] When government makes a permit conditional on a dedication, the means chosen by government (the particular dedication required) must ***"substantially advance"*** the land-use objective that the government is pursuing. (See *Nollan*, immediately below);

[2] There must be a ***"rough proportionality"*** between the ***burdens*** that issuance of the land-use permit would cause to the public, and the ***benefits*** that would accrue to the public from the dedication. (See *Dolan*, *infra*, p. 409.)

[3] The above two requirements apply not only where the government ***grants*** the permit ***on condition*** that a dedication be made, but also where the government ***denies the permit outright***, while ***"suggesting"*** that the outcome would be different — i.e., that the permit would be issued — if the landowner voluntarily makes the dedication. (See *Koontz*, *infra*, p. 410.)

3. **The "substantially advance" requirement:** The first case announcing tougher standard for dedications was ***Nollan v. California Coastal Commission***, 483 U.S. 825 (1987). There, the Court required that the ***means chosen*** by the government (the dedication required as a condition to the permit) ***"substantially advance"*** the governmental ***objective*** being pursued. Or, as the Court also put it, there must be an ***"essential nexus"*** between the dedication exacted as a condition to issuance of the permit, and the "legitimate state interest" being pursued by government in demanding the dedication.

a. **Facts:** The land-use regulation at issue in *Nollan* said that the Ps could rebuild their house on their beach front property only on condition that they first ***gave the public an easement*** across a sandy strip of the property adjacent to the ocean. The government body that issued the regulation was mainly concerned that the Ps would replace their small bungalow with a much bigger house, thus blocking the public's view of the beach.

b. **Holding:** By a 5-4 vote, the Court held that the Commission's conditioning the issuance of the building permit upon transfer of the easement ***amounted to a taking***, for which compensation must be paid. In arriving at this conclusion, the majority opinion (written by Justice Scalia), reasoned as follows:

[1] If the government had simply ***required the Ps to give the public an easement*** over their property, this would clearly have been a taking, since it would be a "permanent physical occupation" (even though no particular individual would

be permitted to station himself permanently on the property);

[2] On the other hand, an outright *refusal* by the government to grant the permit would *not* constitute a taking, so long as the refusal "substantially advanced a legitimate state interest" and did not "deny an owner economically viable use of his land"; and

[3] The granting of the permit *subject to conditions* must be evaluated by the same standard as an outright refusal would have been. Therefore, *only if the conditions* attached to the grant of the permit *"substantially advance"* — or have an *"essential nexus"* with — *the legitimate state interests being pursued* will the conditions be valid.

c. **Loose means-end fit:** Requirement (3) was *not satisfied* on the facts of *Nollan*, in the majority's view, because the *harms feared* by the government would *not be cured or even materially lessened* by the means chosen (the easement). For instance, there was no reason to believe that the easement would reduce obstacles to viewing the beach created by the new house, since the easement would only help people already on public beaches north or south of the Ps' property. In the majority's view, the building restriction was "not a valid regulation of land use but 'an out-and-out *plan of extortion.*'"

4. **The "rough proportionality" requirement:** After *Nollan*, in an even more striking use of rigorous review, the Court held that when a city conditions a building permit on some *"give back"* ("dedication") by the owner, there must be a *"rough proportionality"* between the *burdens on the public* that the permitted development would bring about, and the *benefit* to the public from the give back on which the permit was conditioned. This "rough proportionality" standard was announced in *Dolan v. City of Tigard*, 512 U.S. 374 (1994).

a. **Facts:** In *Dolan*, P was a property owner who wanted to enlarge the plumbing and electric supply store she ran on the property. D, the city of Tigard, issued her a permit to do this, but conditioned the permit on P's willingness to (among other things) convey a 15-foot strip of land on her property to the city, to be used as a bicycle pathway. (She would have been required to convey approximately 10% of the property.) The city, at the time it asked for the trade-off, asserted two reasons for it: (1) P would be paving over a larger part of her property, thus expanding the "impervious surface" and *worsening the danger of flooding* from a nearby creek; the unpaved pathway would help soak up some of the flood waters; and (2) P's bigger store would *increase automobile traffic* to her site; the bike path, by increasing the attractiveness of biking, might result in a *countervailing decrease in car traffic.*

b. **P's attack:** P attacked the requirement that she convey the 15-foot strip as an unconstitutional taking of her property without compensation.

c. **Court agrees:** The Court, by a 5-4 vote, *agreed* with P that the trade-off requirement was an unconstitutional taking of P's property. The Court first repeated *Nollan*'s statement that there had to be an "essential nexus" between the permit condition exacted by the city, and the "legitimate state interest" being pursued.

> **i. Satisfied:** The Court found this requirement *satisfied* here. There was a nexus between preventing flooding from the creek and limiting development on P's property. Similarly, there was a nexus between reducing traffic congestion and providing for an alternative means of transport, biking.

d. "Rough proportionality": But the novel part of the Court's holding came in the imposition of a *second* requirement that any permit condition must now meet: there must be a *"rough proportionality"* between the size of the give-back demanded by the city and the burden to the public caused by P's proposed development (for which the give-back was supposed to compensate).

> **i. Not satisfied:** The Court found that the city here had *not* satisfied this "rough proportionality" requirement. For example, although the city had calculated somewhat precisely the number of additional car trips per day that would be caused by P's expansion, the city had not tried to show how much of this traffic *would be reduced by the proposed bikeway* — it was not enough for the city to conclude, as it had, that the proposed bikeway *"could"* offset some of the traffic demand (though a finding that the bikeway "would" or "was likely to" offset some of the demand would apparently have sufficed).

5. Denial of permit plus suggestions for a cure: *Nollan* and *Dolan* were both cases in which the government *granted* a permit, but *conditioned the grant* on the owner's compliance with what the Court later found to be inappropriate conditions (the exaction). Suppose, instead, that government *denies* the permit outright, but then *suggests* that if the land owner were to make some specified dedication, or pay some specified sum of money to be used on another parcel, the permit denial might be reversed. Does government's use of this structure — *"denial with suggestions for a cure"* — change the analysis? The court answered this question in the *negative* in *Koontz v. St. Johns River Water Mgmt. Dist.*, 133 S. Ct. 2586 (2013).

a. Facts: P, the owner of wetlands property, was required to get a permit for a state-run Water Management District in order to that develop the property. Under state law, the District could issue the needed permit only if it was satisfied that P was mitigating the environmental damage the development would cause. P proposed particular mitigation measures to the District, but the District rejected them as insufficient, and indicated it would not issue the permit. However, the District indicated that if P was willing to pay for certain improvements to wetlands property owned by the District, the District would issue the permit. P refused this suggestion, the District refused to issue the permit, and P sued the District on a *Nollan/Dolan* taking theory.

b. Issue: The issue was whether *Nollan* and *Dolan* applied to situations like this, in which the government never issues a conditional permit, but instead denies the permit outright while indicating that the owner could change the results by making a particular dedication or paying for some improvement on other land.

c. State loses: The Court answered, by a 5-4 vote, that *Nollan* and *Dolan* **apply even to this "suggestion" scenario.** The majority opinion, by Justice Alito, said that the principles behind *Nollan* and *Dolan* "do not change depending on whether the government *approves a permit on the condition* that the applicant turn over property or *denies a permit because the applicant refuses* to do so."

    i. **Rationale:** Alito reasoned that a contrary rule would enable governments to *evade Nollan* and *Dolan*. "[A] government order stating that a permit is *'approved if'* the owner turns over property would be subject to *Nollan* and *Dolan*, but an identical order that uses the words *'denied until'* would not." The form of words used should not make a constitutional difference, he said.

6. **Significance:** *Nollan, Dolan* and *Koontz* demonstrate a much harsher review by the Court of land-use regulations. We now have a scheme whereby, when government conditions some land-use permission on the owner's "give-back" of a significant property right — or even suggests that permission won't be granted until the owner makes such a give-back — two conditions must be met:

❑ the means chosen by the local government unit must *"substantially advance"* a legitimate aim; and

❑ the benefit to the public from the give-back must be *"roughly proportional"* to the harm caused by the new land use.

I. **Requirement of "public" use:** Recall that the Taking Clause says that private property shall not be taken *"for public use"* unless just compensation is paid. This language has been interpreted by the Supreme Court as prohibiting the taking of private property for *private use, even if just compensation is made*. Thus the federal government (and, under an analogous interpretation of the Fourteenth Amendment, a state government) cannot simply take private property from one person, and give it to another, without any public purpose.

1. **"Public use" construed broadly:** However, the Supreme Court has construed the requirement of a "public use" quite *broadly*. Here are two principles illustrating just how broadly the Court stretches the phrase:

❑ So long as the state's use of its eminent domain power is *"rationally related* to a *conceivable public purpose,"* the public use requirement is satisfied. *Hawaii Housing Authority v. Midkiff*, 467 U.S. 229 (1984).

❑ The property *need not be open to the general public after the taking.* As the first rule above suggests, all that "public use" means is that the property be used for a "public purpose." *Kelo v. New London*, 545 U.S. 469 (2005). Therefore, the fact that the property is *turned over to some private user* does not prevent the use from being a public one as long as the public can be expected to derive some benefit (e.g., economic development) from the use. *Midkiff, supra.*

2. **Transfer to private owner:** The principle that there can be a public use even though the property is *turned over to a private user* is illustrated by *Hawaii Housing Authority v. Midkiff, supra*. There, the Court upheld a scheme whereby Hawaii used its eminent domain power to acquire lots owned by large landowners, and transferred them to the tenants living on them, or to other non-landowners. Since there was tremendous inequality in land ownership (on Oahu, the most urbanized island, 22 landowners owned 75.5% of the privately-owned land), and since thousands of homeowners had been forced to lease rather than to buy the land under their homes, the state's scheme was a rational attempt to remedy a social and economic evil. As with any other state conduct sought to be justified as an exercise of the police power, all that was required was that the legislature *"rationally could have believed"* that the act would *promote a legitimate objective;* the scheme here easily passed this test.

3. **Urban renewal and economic development:**   Similarly, the public use requirement can be met even though the government is pursuing the diffuse goal of *"economic development,"* and even if it is doing so by condemning parcels in *non-blighted* areas. This was the controversial result in a 5-4 decision in the 2005 case of *Kelo v. New London, supra.*

   a. **Facts:**   In *Kelo*, the long-struggling city of New London, Connecticut wanted to revitalize itself economically by carrying out a redevelopment plan that included building a $300 million research facility for the Pfizer pharmaceutical company, plus an adjacent conference hotel, residences and pedestrian "riverwalk" along the Thames River. The city believed that the development plan would create jobs, generate tax revenue, and revitalize the downtown. The plaintiffs were the owners of about 15 properties condemned by the city. These properties were mostly owner-occupied houses; none was in poor condition, but all were in the development area.

   b. **Ps' claim:**   The plaintiffs claimed that a city's decision to take non-blighted property for the purpose of economic development was not a "public use."

   c. **Majority upholds taking:**   By a 5-4 vote, the Supreme Court disagreed with the plaintiffs and *upheld the condemnation.* Justice Stevens wrote for the majority.

      i. **Only a "public purpose" is required:**   Stevens began by saying that the requirement of public use did *not mean that the property had to be made open to, or used by, the public at large.* All that was required was that there be a *"public purpose"* behind the taking. Furthermore, the concept of "public purpose" was to be broadly defined, reflecting the court's "longstanding policy of *deference to legislative judgments* in this field."

      ii. **Application:**   Stevens then quickly concluded that New London's plan here met the requirement of public purpose. The city's economic development plan was "carefully formulated," and "comprehensive in character." The city believed that the plan would create new jobs and increased tax revenue. Therefore, Stevens concluded, it easily met the requirement that it serve a public purpose.

   d. **Dissent:**   Justice O'Connor *dissented*, joined by Chief Justice Rehnquist and Justices Scalia and Thomas. She would have held that takings for the *purpose of economic development* are *simply not constitutional,* because they are not for public use. "Under the banner of economic development, all private property is now vulnerable to being taken and transferred to another private owner, so long as it might be upgraded — i.e., given to an owner who will use it in a way that the legislature deems more beneficial to the public[.]"   Indeed, O'Connor could not see *any logical limit* on government's power under the majority's approach: *"The specter of condemnation hangs over all property.* Nothing is to prevent the State from replacing any Motel 6 with a Ritz-Carlton, any home with a shopping mall, or any farm with a factory."

e. **Raw transfer to the politically favored:** After *Kelo*, does the "public use" requirement have any bite at all? The answer seems to be "very little." One sliver of continuing significance is hinted at by a concurrence by Justice Kennedy, in supplying the fifth vote to uphold New London's plan. Kennedy asserted that if a taking were clearly shown to have been *"intended to favor a particular private party*, with only *incidental or pretextural public benefits,"* it would be invalid. (That obviously hadn't happened in *Kelo*, since New London's plan was a comprehensive one, and since the identity of most of the private beneficiaries was unknown at the time the plan was formulated.)

III. THE "CONTRACT" CLAUSE

A. **The "Contract" Clause generally:** One of the few protections against state action given to individuals in the body of the Constitution (as distinguished from the Bill of Rights or other amendments) comes in Article I, §10: "No State shall … pass any … Law i*mpairing the Obligation of Contracts.* … " This so-called Contract Clause by its terms applies only to the states. But a similar or identical rule has been held applicable to the federal government, by virtue of the Fifth Amendment's Due Process Clause. See *Lynch v. U.S.*, 292 U.S. 571 (1934); see also Tribe, p. 613.

1. **Purpose:** The Contract Clause was enacted principally for the purpose of protecting creditors against *debtor relief laws*, by which the obligations of debtors were often postponed or even completely lifted. Such protection of creditors' rights was thought to be necessary for the economic development of the country. See N&R, p. 406.

2. **Extension to public grants:** But the Clause was quickly extended to include the prevention of the impairment of "public" contracts, i.e., contracts between the government and private parties.

3. **Two-part discussion:** Our discussion below is divided into two aspects: (1) the use of the Contract Clause to protect *public* agreements, i.e., those to which government is a party; and (2) the use of the Clause to protect agreements between private parties. There is reason to believe that the Supreme Court today favors stricter review of cases falling within (1) than of those coming within (2).

B. **Protection of public agreements:** Until 1977, it appeared that the Supreme Court had virtually abandoned the Contract Clause as a limitation on states' rights to modify "public" contracts.

1. **Some elements remain (*U.S. Trust* case):** But the Clause has turned out to have some real bite left in it, due in large part to *U.S. Trust Co. v. New Jersey*, 431 U.S. 1 (1977). That case marked the first time in almost four decades that the Supreme Court invalidated a state law on Contract Clause grounds. The case indicates that the Court will scrutinize somewhat closely a state's attempt to *escape* from its *financial obligations*, and will only permit such an escape where a *significant public need* exists that cannot be reasonably handled in any other way.

a. **Facts of *U.S. Trust:*** In a 1962 bond issue, the Port Authority of New York and New Jersey promised bondholders that certain revenues pledged as security for the bonds would not be used to finance unprofitable passenger railroad systems in the future. In

1974, New York and New Jersey retroactively repealed this covenant, so that the pledged revenues (including bridge and tunnel tolls) could be used to improve rail service. U.S. Trust Co., one of the bondholders, sued on the grounds that the repeal violated the Contract Clause.

b. Contract Clause found violated: The Supreme Court found, by a 4-3 majority, that the repeal violated the Contract Clause. The majority opinion, by Justice Blackmun, stated this test: an impairment of contractual obligations will be constitutional only if it is "*reasonable* and *necessary* to support an *important public purpose*."

   i. "Necessity" defined: A contractual impairment was "necessary" only when the state's public interest objectives could not be met by *less drastic* modification of the contract. Here, alternative means existed for improving mass transit (and also of discouraging automobile use, a second major state goal).

   ii. "Reasonable" defined: An impairment was "reasonable," as the Court used the term, only if the modification was induced by *unforeseen developments* occurring after the original contract was made. Here, the public need for mass transit improvements was *quite foreseeable* at the time the covenant to bondholders was made in 1962. Since the impairment wasn't necessitated by developments unforeseen at the time of the original contract, the impairment violated the Contract Clause.

C. Protection of private contracts: The principal purpose of the Contract Clause was to curtail populist *debtor-relief* laws. The Framers' fears of such laws seem to have been justified; most of the *private-agreement cases* under the Contract Clause have indeed involved debtor relief. The development of Contract Clause doctrine in private-agreement cases has been roughly similar to that in the public-agreement situations discussed above: originally a fairly broad use of the Clause to strike down legislation, a near abandonment of the Clause during the 20th century, and a slight resuscitation by the Court beginning in the Burger era.

1. Debtor relief laws: The Court has steadily cut back on the use of the Contract Clause as a limitation on debtor relief laws. It remains the case that a state legislature may not completely absolve debtors of obligations incurred prior to the legislature's action. But whereas the Contract Clause was once a barrier to any impairment of creditors' rights, the impact of the Clause has been curtailed in a number of ways.

2. Prospective only: Insolvency laws may relieve debtors from obligations contracted *after* the law is enacted. That is, only *retroactive* laws are barred by the Contract Clause. *Ogden v. Saunders*, 25 U.S. (12 Wheat.) 213 (1827).

3. Remedies: Although a creditor's basic rights may not be impaired, his "*remedies*," i.e., the means by which he enforces those rights, may be modified. For instance, extensions of time can be given. This distinction between rights and remedies is an obscure and difficult one; but the basic idea is that the underlying obligation may not be impaired, although the creditor's right to strict compliance with all aspects of the contract may be modified.

4. Protection of public interest: An even broader exception to the Contract Clause is that debtors' obligations may be modified where a *vital public interest*, especially an economic emergency, so demands.

a. *Blaisdell* case: One of the best known modern Contract Clause cases, ***Home Building & Loan Ass'n v. Blaisdell***, 290 U.S. 398 (1934), involved such an emergency modification of debtors' obligations. That case involved a Minnesota statute, enacted at the height of the Depression, which allowed local courts to ***give relief from mortgage foreclosure sales.*** The courts were permitted to give extensions from such sales, provided that the mortgagor paid "all or a reasonable part" of the property's fair income or rental value. The measure was intended to apply to mortgages issued prior to the date of the law; i.e., the statute was retroactive.

   i. Right to protect public interest: The Supreme Court ***upheld*** the statute, on the theory that the state had at least the right to temporarily delay enforcement of a mortgage's literal terms, where "vital public interests" would otherwise suffer. In view of the enormous economic emergency which gave rise to the statute, the modification was a limited and reasonable one. The Court stressed that principal remained due, interest continued to run, the right of foreclosure would ultimately be restored, and the statute would (the Court assumed) be rescinded once the economic emergency was over.

5. Renaissance of the Clause (The *Allied Structural Steel* case): The Contract Clause has been saved from extinction in private-agreement cases, just as *U.S. Trust Case* (*supra*, p. 413) did this in public-contract cases. In ***Allied Structural Steel Co. v. Spannaus***, 438 U.S. 234 (1978), the Supreme Court ***invalidated*** an attempt by Minnesota to ***expand the pension obligations of certain Minnesota employers who closed a plant*** in the state. Perhaps even more than the *U.S. Trust* decision, the *Allied Structural* holding seems to indicate that the Contract Clause may now be used as a significant weapon against state police power regulations which affect contracts.

   a. Facts: The Minnesota statute provided that when certain Minnesota employers closed down their operations in the state, or terminated a pension plan, any employee who had worked for the firm for more than ten years became "vested" in (i.e., ***entitled to benefits under)*** any pension plan the company might have. Allied's pension plan did not provide, in most cases, for vesting until long after ten years of employment; the plan also provided that it could be terminated at any time, with no obligation to those employees who had not yet vested. Shortly after the statute was enacted, Allied closed its plant (which it had planned to do even before enactment). The statute thus required the company to pay pensions to workers, an obligation that the company would not have had absent the statute.

   b. Holding: By a 5-3 majority, the Supreme Court found that the Minnesota statute ***violated the Contract Clause.*** The majority opinion, by Justice Stewart, conceded that the police power allowed the states to make minor, and in a few circumstances substantial, modifications to contracts.

   i. Strict requirements: But the Court held that the modification here was a ***substantial*** one, and that it could therefore be sustained only if a series of factors like those existing in *Blaisdell* (*supra*, p. 415) also existed. The Court read these to include: (1) that there be an ***emergency***; (2) that the measure be enacted to protect a "***basic societal interest, not a favored group***"; (3) that the relief be "appropriately ***tailored***" to the emergency; (4) that the modifications be "***reasonable***" in scope; and (5) that the statute be ***limited to the duration of the emergency.*** The Court found that factors (1) and (2) were not present, since the legislative history did not disclose any major emergency to which the statute was a response, and since, in the Court's view, only a very limited number of employers and employees would be affected. The Court also implied that the effect on a company like Allied was also so drastic and permanent that conditions (3), (4) and (5) were not met either.

   ii. **Violation of reasonable expectations:** The majority also objected to the fact that the statute imposed a "sudden, totally unanticipated, and substantial ***retroactive*** obligation." This, coupled with the fact that Minnesota had never regulated the area of pensions previously, seemed to the majority to violate Allied's ***reasonable expectations*** about what it was getting into when it started a pension plan.

   c. **Dissent:** Justice Brennan dissented (joined by Justices White and Marshall). Brennan argued that the Minnesota statute simply created an "additional, supplemental duty of the employer," and that the Contract Clause, in its prohibition on the "impairment" of contractual duties, did not prohibit the creation of new duties.

D. **More deferential standard:** The *U.S. Trust* and *Allied Steel* cases represented significant revitalizations of the Contract Clause, in the case of public and private agreements, respectively. However, developments following these two decisions suggest that the Court will not invalidate much state legislation on Contract Clause grounds. In 1983, the Court articulated a new standard of review for Contract Clause challenges, a standard which is apparently applicable to both public and private agreements. Although the Court claimed to be relying principally on *U.S. Trust* and *Allied Steel*, this newly-formulated standard of review seems to be ***significantly more deferential*** to state legislative judgments. ***Energy Reserves Group, Inc. v. Kansas Power and Light Co.***, 459 U.S. 400 (1983).

   1. **Three-part test:** In *Energy Reserves*, the Court articulated the following three-step test for evaluating Contract Clause challenges:

      a. **Threshold inquiry:** First, the court must make a "threshold inquiry" as to "whether the state law has, in fact, operated as a ***substantial impairment*** of a contractual relationship."

      b. **Legitimate public purpose:** If this threshold inquiry yields an affirmative result (i.e., the court finds that there has been a "substantial impairment"), the state must demonstrate that it has a ***"significant and legitimate public purpose"*** which the regulation is intended to serve.

      c. **"Reasonable and appropriate":** If the state does show such a "legitimate public purpose," the court must then take the final step of determining "whether the adjustment of 'the rights and responsibilities of contracting parties [is based] upon ***reasonable conditions*** and [is] of a character ***appropriate to the public purpose***'" asserted in support of the regulation.

   2. **Distinction between public and private contracts:** The three-part *Energy Reserves* test applies both to contracts in which the state is a party and to purely private contracts. However, the Court seems likely to apply that test with ***significantly greater strictness*** where

the state is attempting to make *its own contractual obligations less burdensome*. In a footnote, the *Energy Reserves* Court cited approvingly the statement in *U.S. Trust* that *when the state is a party to the contract*, "complete *deference* to a legislative assessment of reasonableness and necessity is *not appropriate* because the State's *self-interest* is at stake."

IV. THE SECOND AMENDMENT "RIGHT TO BEAR ARMS"

A. Text of the Amendment: The Second Amendment provides: "A well regulated Militia, being necessary to the security of a free State, the right of the people to *keep and bear Arms*, shall *not be infringed*."

B. Applicable to private individuals (the *Heller* case): Until recently, the Amendment had never been recognized by the Supreme Court as giving *private citizens* the right to keep firearms. But in a stunning 2008 case, decided by a 5-4 vote, *District of Columbia v. Heller*, 128 S.Ct. 2783 (2008), the Court struck down the District of Columbia's strict gun-control laws on Second Amendment grounds. The majority asserted that "the inherent right of self-defense has been central to the Second Amendment right," and concluded that the *Amendment confers on private individuals a right to keep basic firearms, including handguns, at home for self-defense.*

1. **Significance of *Heller*:** The only significant prior Supreme Court decision on the meaning of the Second Amendment, a 1939 case, had been widely interpreted as saying that the Second Amendment gave no rights to private individuals, and merely protected the right of "well regulated militias" (now known as state National Guard units) to keep their members armed while on duty. But *Heller* concluded that this was not the correct reading of the 1939 case, and that the Amendment confers on private citizens, not just militias, the right to keep at least some kinds of weapons for self-defense and recreational purposes.

2. **D.C. statute:** The D.C. gun-control statute at issue in *Heller* was among the two or three strictest such statutes in America. The statute contained two distinct prohibitions that were challenged:

   ❏ First, the statute effectively *banned the possession of handguns in the home* — only registered firearms could be kept, and handguns could not be registered.

   ❏ Second, the statute required that firearms other than handguns (e.g., *rifles* and shotguns) could only be kept in the home if they were kept *unloaded* and either *disassembled or disabled* by a trigger lock.

3. **Challenge by P:** The plaintiff, Dick Heller, was a police officer who wanted to keep a handgun in his house. He asserted that each of the above two prohibitions violated his Second Amendment right to bear arms.

4. **Majority upholds:** By a 5-4 Vote, the court *agreed* that *both provisions* of the D.C. statute violated P's Second Amendment rights. The majority opinion was by Justice Scalia, and may well be his most important majority opinion since he joined the Court in 1986. Four members of the majority were those generally considered the conservative bloc of the court — in addition to Scalia they included Chief Justice Roberts and Justices Thomas and Alito. The critical fifth vote was supplied by Justice Kennedy, as has so often been the

case in the Rehnquist and Roberts courts.

a. **Language and history:** Scalia's opinion began by considering the history and language of the Second Amendment. He separately analyzed the "prefatory" clause ("A well regulated Militia, being necessary to the security of a free State...") and the "operative" clause ("the right of the people to keep and bear Arms shall not be infringed").

    i. **Operative clause:** As to the meaning of the *operative* clause, Scalia pointed to several elements that he said demonstrated that the clause was intended to give rights to *individuals*, not just to members of state militias. For instance, the operative clause codified a ***"right of the people,"*** and the use of this phrase by other constitutional provisions (e.g., the First Amendment's assembly-and-petition clause) demonstrated that the phrase customarily referred to individual rights, not collective ones, he said.

    ii. **Prefatory clause:** Next, Scalia analyzed the ***prefatory*** clause, that is, the reference to "a well regulated militia, being necessary to the security of a free State..." As to the meaning of a "well regulated militia," Scalia rejected the dissent's reading of this term as being limited to officially-organized state-militias. For Scalia, the term "the militia" referred to ***"all males physically capable of acting in concert for the common defense,"*** and the adjective "well-regulated" implied merely "the imposition of proper discipline and training." So the prefatory clause was not inconsistent with Scalia's "individual rights" interpretation, he argued.

    iii. **Historical purpose:** Scalia then analyzed the ***historical purpose*** of the Amendment. The history behind the enactment of the Second Amendment, he said, was that English tyrants had eliminated the ability of "the militia" (i.e., able-bodied men) to resist tyranny "not by banning the militia but simply by taking away the people's arms," enabling a standing army supporting the tyrant to "suppress political opponents." Consequently, Scalia asserted, "[t]he threat that the new Federal Government would destroy the citizens' militia by taking away their arms was the reason that right ... was codified in a written constitution."

    iv. **Summary of history and language:** In sum, the history leading to the enactment of the Second Amendment, and the common 18th-century meaning of the phrases used in it, convinced Scalia that the framers intended to grant individual citizens the right to bear arms for self-defense, not merely to confer such a right upon official state militias.

b. **Later interpretations:** Scalia then argued that ***post-enactment interpretations*** of the Second Amendment had reached this same conclusion, that the Amendment conferred an individual right to bear arms for self-defense.

    i. **Distinguishing *Miller*:** Scalia paid special attention to *U.S. v. Miller*, 307 U.S. 174 (1939), the Supreme Court's principal prior case on the meaning of the Second Amendment. *Miller* involved criminal charges of transporting an unregistered short-barreled shotgun; the Court rejected the defendants' argument that their conduct was protected by the Second Amendment.

(1) Dissent's view rejected: The dissent in *Heller* contended that in *Miller*, the Court had held that *only military uses of guns were protected by the Amendment.* But Scalia disagreed about what *Miller* said: *Miller* said "only that the Second Amendment does not protect those weapons not typically possessed by law-abiding citizens for lawful purposes, such as short-barreled shotguns." So for Scalia, *Miller* was not inconsistent with the *Heller* majority's conclusion that the Amendment protects the rights of law-abiding citizens to possess guns for self-defense.

c. **What the amendment protects:** Having concluded that the Amendment protects at least some rights of non-military individuals to bear arms, Scalia now turned to the *scope* of the right. On this score, he conceded that the right was *not absolute or unlimited.* The majority was not, he said, "cast[ing] doubt on long-standing prohibitions on the possession of firearms by *felons* and the *mentally ill*, or laws forbidding the carrying of firearms in *sensitive places such as schools and government buildings*, or laws imposing *conditions and qualifications* on the *commercial sale* of arms."

   i. **"Dangerous and unusual weapons":** Furthermore, Scalia said, the Amendment protects only the carrying of weapons that were *"in common use at the time"* the Amendment was enacted, so that *"dangerous and unusual weapons"* (quoting an 18th century commentator) would *not* be protected. Scalia seemed to be saying that what he called "weapons that are most useful in military service — M-16 rifles and the like," may be banned because they were not in common use at the time the Amendment was enacted.

d. **Application to D.C. statute:** Scalia then applied his reading of the Second Amendment to the D.C. statute before the Court. He addressed both of the District's bans: the complete ban on handgun possession, and the requirement that any non-handguns kept at home be kept in unloaded and inoperable form.

   i. **Ban on handguns:** As to the absolute handgun ban, Scalia asserted that "the *inherent right of self-defense* has been *central* to the Second Amendment right." And, he said, D.C.'s complete ban on handgun possession in homes "amounts to a prohibition of an *entire class of 'arms'* that is *overwhelmingly chosen by American society* for that lawful purpose." Since handguns were the favored method of self defense in the home, a complete ban on them violated the Amendment.

   ii. **Requirement that guns be unloaded and trigger-protected:** Scalia then turned to the requirement that any gun the possession of which is not completely forbidden (e.g., rifles and shotguns) be kept *unloaded and inoperable* in the home. This requirement, he said, "makes it impossible for its citizens to use [such guns] for the core lawful purpose of self-defense and is hence unconstitutional." Therefore, this requirement, too, violated the Second Amendment.

e. **Rejects "interest-balancing" approach:** Scalia did not specify exactly *what standard of review* should be used in evaluating government actions that impact Second Amendment rights. But Scalia did reject the standard proposed by Justice Breyer in his dissent (see *infra*, p. 420). Breyer proposed an *"interest-balancing inquiry"*; for any regulation that significantly implicated competing constitutionally-protected interests,

Breyer would ask merely whether the statute burdens a protected interest in a way or to an extent that is *"out of proportion"* to the statute's beneficial effects on some other protected interest. But Scalia dismissed this approach, saying that "a constitutional guarantee subject to future judges' assessments of its usefulness is no constitutional guarantee at all." In any event, he said, the Second Amendment "surely elevates above all other interests the *right of law-abiding, responsible citizens to use arms in defense of hearth and home.*"

f. Application to Heller: Scalia then wrapped things up by saying that so long as the plaintiff (Heller) was not "disqualified from the exercise of Second Amendment rights,"[1] the District of Columbia *must permit him to register his handgun* and must *issue him a license* to *carry it in the home.*"

5. Dissents: Four Justices *dissented,* in two separate opinions.

a. Stevens' dissent: The principal dissent was by Justice Stevens (joined by Justices Souter, Ginsburg and Breyer). Stevens reached a completely opposite conclusion from Scalia's as to the purpose and intent of the Second Amendment. The Amendment, he said, "was adopted to protect the right of the people of each of the several States to *maintain a well-regulated militia.* It was a response to concerns ... that the power of Congress to disarm the state militias and create a national standing army posed an intolerable *threat to the sovereignty of the several states."* The framers had not evidenced "the slightest interest in limiting any legislature's authority to regulate *private civilian uses* of firearms."

b. Breyer's dissent: Justice Breyer wrote a separate dissent, in which Stevens, Ginsburg and Souter joined. Breyer fully agreed with Stevens' argument that the Second Amendment only protects militia-related, not self-defense-related, interests. But, he said, even if the Amendment *were* read to protect self-defense-related interests, the D.C. statute should be found not to violate the Amendment.

  i. Interest-balancing: Whenever a governmental regulation "significantly implicates *competing constitutionally protected interests* in complex ways," Breyer said, the Court does and should use an explicit *"interest-balancing inquiry."* That is, the Court should ask "whether the statute burdens a protected interest in a way or to an extent that is *out of proportion to the statute's salutary effects upon other important governmental interests."*[2]

   (1) Deference to legislature's empirical judgment: A key feature of the interest-balancing approach advocated by Breyer is, he said, that the Court *"defers to a legislature's empirical judgment* in matters where a legislature is likely to have *greater expertise and greater institutional fact-finding capacity."* Thus here, the legislature (of D.C.) concluded that a handgun ban would meaningfully reduce crime, and did so after a careful consideration by the relevant committee of extensive evidence about the link between handguns and urban

---

1. Scalia seemed to be referring to classes of people whose right to possess arms may be nullified, such as felons and the mentally ill.

2. This is essentially a form of intermediate scrutiny, as Breyer correctly characterizes it.

violence. The only role of the courts should be to "assure that, in formulating its judgments, the legislature has ***drawn reasonable inferences based on substantial evidence.***" And D.C. had easily met this standard here, Breyer said.

6. **Applies to states and cities:** *Heller* applied only to the federal government, since the District of Colombia is part of that government. But in a post-*Heller* case, ***McDonald v. City of Chicago***, 561 U.S. 742 (2010), a 5-4 majority of the Court decided that the Second Amendment ***applies the same way to state and local governments as it applies to the federal government.***

   a. **Facts of *McDonald*:** *McDonald* involved the very strict gun-control laws of two cities, Chicago and Oak Park, Ill. The ordinances effectively banned possession of handguns by almost all private citizens residing there. As in *Heller*, the plaintiffs were private citizens who wanted to keep guns in their homes for self-defense.

   b. **Majority says incorporation applies:** Five members of the Court agreed that the Second Amendment applies to state and local governments, not just to the federal government. However, no majority agreed with on *why* this should be. Justice Alito wrote for a four-justice plurality, and Justice Thomas, in a concurrence, added the fifth vote but on a different theory.

      i. **Alito's plurality opinion:** Justice Alito (joined by Roberts, Kennedy and Scalia), said that the Second Amendment was ***incorporated*** into the 14th Amendment's ***Due Process Clause***, and thereby made applicable to the states.

      ii. **Thomas and the P-or-I Clause:** Justice Thomas supplied the needed fifth vote, but he disagreed on the appropriate rationale. Thomas believed that the appropriate means to make the Second Amendment applicable to state and local governments was by use of the 14th Amendment ***"Privileges or Immunities" Clause*** (*supra*, p. 398), not by incorporation into the 14th Amendment's Due Process Clause.

      iii. **Remanded:** The Court did not decide whether the two city ordinances violated the Second Amendment; instead, it remanded the cases to the lower courts to decide this question.

   c. **Dissent:** Justices Stevens, Ginsburg, Breyer and Sotomayor ***dissented***, in separate opinions by Stevens and Breyer. The dissenters believed that *Heller* had been incorrectly decided. But even if it had been correct, the dissenters would not have applied it to state and local governments, because they believed that the right to keep arms in the home for self-defense was ***not "intrinsic to ordered liberty,"*** as rights must be in order to be selectively incorporated into the Fourteenth Amendment Due Process Clause.

      i. **Stevens:** Stevens, for instance, argued that there was no evidence that the right to keep a gun for self-defense was "critical to leading a life of ***autonomy, dignity, or political equality.***" He said that the fact that ***other advanced democracies***, including those sharing our British heritage, generally ***regulate firearms extensively*** "tends to weaken [the argument] that the right to possess a gun of one's choosing is fundamental to a life of liberty."

7. Standard to be used: It is unclear what *standard* the court will use for reviewing governmental restrictions that impair Second Amendment rights. Justice Scalia avoided answering this question in *Heller*, saying merely that "under any of the standards of scrutiny that we have applied to enumerated Constitutional rights," the District's complete ban on handguns in the home would "fail constitutional muster." And the Court didn't address this issue of standard-of-review in *McDonald*, either.

    a. Intermediate-level review: The most likely outcome is that the Court will end up judging gun-control regulations by use of some variant of *mid-level review.*

        i. Substantial-relation-to-important-interest: The traditional form of mid-level review requires that the means chosen by government be *"substantially related"* to the achievement of an *"important"* governmental interest. (This is the formulation used in several free-speech areas such as regulation of commercial speech; see *infra*, p. 572.) There is a good chance that this version of mid-level review will prove to be the ultimate standard.

    b. Effect on gun laws: Even though we now know from *McDonald* that the Second Amendment applies to state and local gun laws, it's not clear that governments will lose very much of their practical power to regulate gun use.

        i. Handgun bans: *Heller* and *McDonald* together pretty clearly mean that a *total ban on handgun possession* in the home would be unconstitutional, as would a requirement that non-handguns be stored in an inoperable and unloaded manner. So, for instance, Chicago's virtually complete ban on handguns — at issue in *McDonald*, but as to which the Supreme Court remanded to the lower courts — is vulnerable. But few cities, and no states, regulate handguns nearly as extensively as D.C. and Chicago do, so these other governments' restrictions may well survive.

        ii. Licensing: It seems likely that *licensing requirements* will *not* be found to violate the Second Amendment as long as the procedures for obtaining a license are *not unreasonably burdensome*, and are directed towards keeping guns out of the hands of people who do not have a Second Amendment right to possess them. So, for instance, since *Heller* makes it clear that government may ban *felons* and the *mentally ill* from possessing guns, a licensing requirement that would deny permits to such people — and that would give government a reasonable amount of time to check whether the applicant fell into these categories — would presumably be *valid* even if some form of strict scrutiny were used.

        iii. Concealed-carry permits: Similarly, it seems likely that the Amendment will be found not to prohibit governments from banning the *carrying of concealed weapons in public places.* The majority opinion in *Heller* commented, seemingly approvingly, that "the majority of the 19th century courts to consider the question held that prohibitions on carrying concealed weapons were lawful under the Second Amendment or state analogues."

        iv. Barring certain types of weapons: One last open question is the *types of weapons* the possession of which is guaranteed by the Second Amendment. Scalia's opinion in *Heller* seems to agree that the 1939 *Miller* opinion was correct in holding that only those weapons that were *"in common use at the time"* the Amendment was adopted are protected, and that (in the words of an 18th Century commentator) *"dangerous and unusual weapons" may be prohibited*. So presumably governments may ban the possession of modern weapons that are much more advanced and dangerous than those existing in 1791, such as *machine guns, assault rifles* and the *sawed-off shotguns* at issue in *Miller*.

    v. Summary: So although the Second Amendment now recognizes some sort of individual right to bear arms, that right is likely to be found to be subject to *heavy governmental regulation.* At the end of the day, it may well be the case that of gun regulations actually adopted by states or cities somewhere, only the very most extreme measures — like the virtually-total ban on handguns, and the requirement of trigger-locking of guns stored at home, both of which were invalidated in *Heller* — will be struck down.

V. *EX POST FACTO* LAWS

A. Constitutional prohibition of *ex post facto laws*: The Constitution prevents both the federal and state governments from enacting *ex post facto* laws. See Article I, §§ 9 and 10, respectively. An *ex post facto* law is one which has a *retroactive punitive effect*. This can happen in any of four ways:

    1. Definition altered: The law retroactively *alters the definition* of a crime, so that an act that wasn't a crime at all at the time it was committed is now defined as a crime; or

    2. Aggravation: The law retroactively *aggravates a crime*, re-defining it so as to make it a greater offense than it was when it was committed (e.g., by transforming what would have been manslaughter into murder);

    3. Increased punishment: The law *increases the punishment* for an act that was a crime when it was committed; or

    4. Rules of evidence: The law *alters the rules of evidence*, by allowing a conviction based on lesser evidence than was required at the time the act was committed.

Calder v. Bull, 3 U.S. 386 (1798) .

B. Criminal conduct only: The ban on *ex post facto* laws applies only to measures which are *criminal* or *penal.*

    1. Ambiguity: However, the dividing line between criminal and civil penalties is not always clear. The following are major illustrations of what measures have and have not been considered criminal (and therefore barred or not barred by the *ex post facto* clause when applied to conduct occurring before enactment of the measure).

        a. Criminal: The following have been found to be criminal measures:

        i. Imprisonment: Any measure calling for *imprisonment;*

        ii. Criminal fine: Any other punitive measure which the government identifies as being part of its system of criminal punishment. For instance, if the statute defining a particular crime states that violators will be ***fined*** upon conviction, the fine will be treated as a criminal measure falling within the *ex post facto* clause.

b. Not criminal: Conversely, other types of measures, even though they may be "punitive" in the broad sense, are deemed civil rather than criminal, and therefore ***not*** subject to the ban on *ex post facto* laws.

i. Professional disqualification: Thus laws disqualifying convicted felons from certain ***professions*** (e.g., the practice of medicine) are not deemed penal, usually on the theory that such measures are a reasonable way of ensuring that the professions are practiced only by those who are fit for them.

ii. Deportation: Similarly, laws providing for the ***deportation*** of persons based on certain acts committed before the enactment of the deportation measure are not penal, and therefore not subject to the *ex post facto* ban.

C. Increase in punishment: Any ***increase*** in the ***severity*** of a criminal punishment, compared with that authorized at the time the act was committed, violates the *ex post facto* clause. (But a retroactive ***reduction*** of a penalty does not.)

1. "Prior offense" measures: But ***"prior offense"*** measures (i.e., measures providing for ***more severe criminal penalties*** for a given crime if the offender has been previously convicted of ***other offenses***) are ***not*** subject to *ex post facto* laws merely because the prior convictions occurred before the measure was enacted.

> **Example:** D is convicted of burglary in 2000, and again in 2001. In 2005, the legislature enacts a statute providing that robbery shall carry a prison term of one to five years, but that where the defendant has been previously convicted of two other felonies, the term shall be one to fifteen years. D is convicted of robbery in 2007 for a robbery he committed in 2006. He may be sentenced to fifteen years, even though the only grounds for the harsher-than-ordinarily-permitted sentence is criminal activity (the first two burglaries) committed before the increased-penalty statute was enacted. Cf. Tribe, p. 637.

D. Rationale for ban: The usual rationale for the *ex post facto* ban relates to the concept of ***"fair notice"*** — it is felt to be unfair to punish a person for an act which, at the time he committed it, he could not have known was subject to such a penalty.

1. Knowledge of who will be affected: But another possible rationale is that the legislature should not be permitted to act "with knowledge of whom [the new measures] would adversely affect and how." Tribe, p. 640, n. 26. This rationale is similar to that behind the ban on bills of attainder, discussed immediately *infra*.

VI. BILLS OF ATTAINDER

A. Constitutional provision: The Constitution prohibits both the federal government and the states from passing any ***"bill of attainder."*** Article I, §§ 9 and 10, respectively. The term "bill of attainder" has been interpreted to include not only the English bill by that name (which condemned named individuals to death and prohibited inheritance of their property) but also the English "bill of pains and penalties," which included lesser penalties. See Tribe, pp. 641-42.

1. **Coverage:** Thus the prohibition covers any legislative act which "appl[ies] either to *named individuals* or to *easily ascertainable members of a group* in such a way as to *inflict punishment* on them without a judicial trial ... " *U.S. v. Lovett*, 328 U.S. 303 (1946).

> **Example:** In response to charges made by the House Un-American Activities Committee, Congress passes a measure which prohibits the payment of salaries to three named federal agency employees, on the grounds that they are engaged in "subversive activities."
>
> *Held*, the act is invalid as a bill of attainder, since it applies to named or easily-identified individuals, and punishes them without a judicial trial. *U.S. v. Lovett, supra.*

B. **Rationale for clause:** The rationale for the ban on bills of attainder rests in the concept of *separation of powers*. The process of deciding which individuals should be subject to punishment is inherently a judicial process, and must be performed by the judicial branch, not by the legislature. Because of the political non-independence of the legislature, and its extreme responsiveness to popular will, it must act by rules of *general applicability*, not ones directed at specific individuals (at least where matters of punishment are concerned).

C. **Definition of "punishment":** The Bill of Attainder Clause applies only to legislative *"punishment"* of specific individuals or narrowly-defined groups. But recent cases have defined "punishment" somewhat broadly, to include measures having not only a "retributive" function, but also measures whose purpose is "rehabilitative," "deterrent" or "preventative." Thus a ban on union participation by Communist Party members was deemed "punishment" (and was thus a bill of attainder) even though the ban's purpose was to prevent strikes. See *U.S. v. Brown*, 381 U.S. 437 (1965).

1. **Pure regulation not covered:** However, measures which are taken solely for the purpose of *regulation*, and which have no substantial stigmatizing element, are not prohibited by the Bill of Attainder Clause, even though they may contain aspects that are unfavorable to certain individuals. For instance, in *Hawker v. New York*, 170 U.S. 189 (1898), a ban on the practice of medicine by convicted felons was justified on the grounds that it was solely a regulatory measure.

Quiz Yourself on

MISCELLANEOUS CLAUSES *(ENTIRE CHAPTER)*

58. The state of Okansas has a state-paid health plan, whereby the state pays the medical bills of indigent families after a $1,000-per-family annual deductible. Because of the generosity of this plan, the state has become concerned that some impoverished residents of other states offering less-generous (or no) medical coverage have been moving to Okansas to take advantage of the plan. Therefore, the Okansas legislature has provided that a family moving to Okansas from another state shall, for its first year of genuine residence in Okansas, be entitled only to those medical-bill payments that the family would have received in the state in which it previously resided.

    (a) You represent a poor family that has just moved to Okansas from Nebraska, which has no indigent medical coverage at all. What is the best constitutional argument you can make that Okansas' provision violates your client's rights? _____

(b) Will the claim you make in (a) succeed? _____

59. Mill Co. has operated a steel mill in the Township of Fuschia for many years. Mill Co. owns both the factory and the land on which it is located. The mill has always obeyed all state and federal pollution control requirements. However, operation of a steel mill is inevitably a somewhat messy enterprise, with a fair amount of noise, smoke, etc. As the township has become more affluent and residential in character, the inhabitants have become increasingly unhappy with having a steel mill in their midst. Now, the township has amended its zoning ordinance so as to provide that no "heavy industry" (defined in a way that includes Mill Co.'s steel mill and a variety of other manufacturing operations) shall be permitted to operate anywhere in the town after four years from the ordinance's adoption. The effect of the ordinance is that Mill Co. or the next owner of its property may build houses, stores or warehouses on the site, but not operate a heavy manufacturing plant. Although the end of the four-year period is still two years away, Mill Co. wishes to challenge the ordinance.

(a) Assuming that the ordinance was enacted in a procedurally satisfactory manner, what is the strongest argument that Mill Co. can make attacking the constitutionality of the ordinance as applied to it?

_____

(b) Will this argument succeed? _____

60. The village of Green Valley wished to incinerate its trash and garbage in an ecologically sound way, rather than using up scarce landfill. It also wished to raise revenue as part of the process. Therefore, it entered into an arrangement with Waste Co., a trash management company. The arrangement provided for Waste Co. to build an incinerator in Green Valley, and for Waste Co. to pay Green Valley a 50¢ per ton "franchise fee" for every ton of trash or garbage processed by the plant over a 15-year period. (Waste Co. would make money by charging the public a fee for each load processed.) In return, Green Valley agreed to require by law, for the 15 years, that all trash and garbage produced in the town be sent to the Waste Co. facility. The arrangement operated as expected for the first five years, during which time Waste Co.'s fees to the town averaged about $2 million per year.

Then, New Co., another waste company that competed with Waste Co., proposed a new deal to Green Valley. New Co. asked Green Valley to require that trash (i.e., dry refuse) but not garbage (wet refuse, such as food remains) be sent to *its* facility. In return, New Co. would pay Green Valley a minimum of $1.5 million per year. Green Valley agreed, and changed its laws so that now, the Waste Co. plant would only get garbage, and the New Co. plant would get the trash. The net effect was that Green Valley's receipts went from $2 million a year to $3 million per year. (Green Valley, like most municipalities, could certainly benefit from the extra $1 million per year, but the town is not faced with extreme financial hardship.) The effect on Waste Co. was to reduce its profits by $500,000 per year.

(a) If Waste Co. wishes to challenge Green Valley's conduct on constitutional grounds, what is its best argument? _____

(b) Will this attack succeed? _____

61. Last year, Byer purchased a small shopping center in the town of Happy Farms. There were several other similar shopping centers in town, as well as various other types of retail stores. At the time of the purchase, Happy Farms allowed retail stores to operate seven days a week, 24 hours a day, if they wished. At the time of the purchase, the shopping center had so called "percentage leases" with its tenants, whereby the rent paid was a percentage of the retail sales generated by the stores. Each percentage lease required the store owner to maintain hours on Sunday from noon to 6:00 p.m. Byer computed the amount that it was appropriate for him to pay for the center based on this flow of percentage rent. Six months after Byer made the purchase, Happy Farms changed its zoning ordinance to prohibit any retail store from opening on Sunday. This action (taken at the request of certain small store owners who wanted to be able to take Sundays off without losing sales to their competitors), caused Byer's tenants to suffer a 10% drop in revenues, which translated into a substantial loss of rent for Byer.

Byer now asserts that the Sunday closing law constitutes an impairment of his contractual rights, in violation of the Obligation of Contracts Clause. Is Byer's assertion correct? State your reasons.

_____

62. In 2008, Dennis had sex with a 14-year-old girl, who purported to give consent. However, the state's criminal statutes regarded sex with a female under the age of 15 as statutory rape, regardless of ostensible consent. The penalty for rape was a prison sentence of up to five years. In 2009, the state legislature changed the penalty for statutory rape from a maximum of five years to a maximum of 10 years. Dennis was tried and convicted in 2010, and was sentenced to a prison term of seven years.

(a) If Dennis wishes to attack his conviction and/or sentence on constitutional grounds, what is his strongest argument? _____

(b) Will this argument succeed? State your reasons. _____

63. The Phrenic Brotherhood is a small, dedicated group of religious fundamentalists, located throughout the United States, whose stated mission is to dissuade the U.S. from opposing the rise of the religion of Phrenology throughout the world. Certain acts of terrorism have been traced to the Brotherhood, though it is not known who in particular committed these acts. The state of New Righteous, in response to a recent act of terrorism in the state thought to be associated with the Brotherhood, passed the following statute: "No member of the group known as the Phrenic Brotherhood shall be hired or retained on the payroll of any branch of the government of this state." Oren, who was employed as a file clerk at the New Righteous Department of Social Security, was known to his superior to be a member of the Brotherhood. The superior, citing the newly enacted statute, fired Oren.

(a) If Oren wishes to attack the statute on constitutional grounds, what argument (putting aside any argument based directly upon the First Amendment) has the best chance of success for him?

_____

(b) Will this attack succeed? _____

———————————————

Answers

58. (a) That it violates the "right to travel," a right protected by the 14th Amendment's Privileges or Immunities Clause.

(b) Yes, probably. The Court held in *Saenz v. Roe* that a state may not provide that when a family moves into the state, for one year after arrival the family's welfare payments shall be limited to the amount that the family would have received in their prior state of residence. The Court reasoned that this violates the "right to travel" — one of the rights of "national citizenship" guaranteed by the 14th Amendment's P-or-I clause — because the state's action was irrational except as an attempt to carry out the forbidden objective of discouraging poor people from moving into the state. There is no reason why the same principle shouldn't apply here, since we're told the state's action is based upon this same unlawful motive.

59. (a) That the ordinance constitutes a "taking" in violation of the Fifth Amendment.

(b) No, probably. The Fifth Amendment provides that "nor shall private property be taken for public use, without just compensation." This clause, though by its terms applies only to the federal government, also applies to states and municipalities via the Fourteenth Amendment's Due Process Clause. An enactment that is labelled a "land-use regulation" will generally not constitute a "taking," unless it "den[ies] an owner economically viable use of his land." Here Mill Co. is not being deprived of **all** economically viable use of its land — it is free to build houses, stores or warehouses on the site. The fact that the **particular** use being made of the property at this moment is now being foreclosed is not enough to meet this "no economically viable use" standard. See, e.g., *Goldblatt v. Hempstead* (town does not commit a "taking" where it bans the continued operation of a sand and gravel pit). If the ordinance had **immediately** taken effect, without any "amortization" period (here, four years), this might have tipped the balance in favor of a finding that a taking had occurred. But the amortization period, together with the fact that the mill owners had already had many years to derive value from the plant, remove this difficulty.

60. (a) That it violated the Obligation of Contracts Clause.

(b) Yes, probably. Art. I, Section 10, provides that "no State shall … pass any … Law impairing the Obligation of Contracts. … " This provision applies both to states and to municipalities. The Clause has been interpreted by the Supreme Court to mean that a state's attempt to **escape from its financial obligations** will be sustained only where a **significant public need** exists that cannot be **reasonably handled** in any other way. Here, Green Valley has in effect modified the terms of its agreement with Waste Co., by changing the law so that Waste Co. no longer gets the town's trash. The fact that Green Valley is somewhat better off financially as a result of this decision, and even the fact that the gain to Green Valley is greater than the loss to Waste Co., will not be enough to meet the requirement that there be a significant public need that cannot be reasonably handled in any other way. Court decisions show that an impairment will be "reasonable" only if it was induced by **unforeseen developments** occurring after the original contract was made; here, it was certainly foreseeable that some other waste management company might come along with a more financially attractive deal. Also, the Court has refused to merely balance the benefit to the public against the damage to the other party to the contract. See *U.S. Trust Co. v. New Jersey*. If Green Valley had been on the verge of insolvency, with this modification able to make the difference, then the impairment might stand; however, the facts do not indicate this level of hardship. Therefore, the Court would probably find that the Obligations of Contracts Clause was violated.

61. No. The Obligation of Contracts Clause applies only where the state takes an action that is **specifically directed** at contractual obligations. If the state applies a **"generally applicable rule of conduct"** which has the **incidental by-product** of impairing contractual obligations, the Contract Clause does not apply at all. See *Exxon Corp. v. Eagerton*. Here, Happy Farms has enacted a generally applicable rule, one requiring Sunday closings. The fact that certain contractual obligations (the store owners' contractual duty to remain open on Sundays) happen to be impaired is irrelevant. Therefore, we never get to the point of even determining whether the impairment here was justified by pressing needs of public policy (as we would have to do in a situation where the state specifically directed its new law at contractual obligations).

62. (a) That it is an *ex post facto* law.

(b) Yes. The Constitution prevents a state government from enacting an *ex post facto* law; see Art. I, Section 10. An *ex post facto* law is one which has a retroactive punitive effect. Some *ex post facto* laws are ones which outlaw conduct that was not criminal at the time it was committed. But there is a second kind of *ex post facto* law: one which **increases** the **severity** of a criminal punishment, compared with that authorized at the time the act was committed. Here, Dennis could not have been sentenced to more than five years in prison at the moment he committed the offense, so his sentence now constitutes a violation of the *ex post facto* ban.

63. (a) That the statute violates the prohibition on bills of attainder.

(b) Yes, probably. The Constitution prohibits both the federal government and the states from passing any "bill of attainder." (See Art. I, Section 10, for the provision as it applies to states.) The term covers any legislative act which "applies either to *named individuals* or to *easily ascertainable members of a group* in such a way as to *inflict punishment* on them without a judicial trial. ... " Here, since the Phrenic Brotherhood is a relatively small group, and its members are fairly easily ascertained, the requirements seem met. Assuming that dismissal from the state payroll is found to be "punishment," the law seems to be a bill of attainder. Measures taken solely for the purpose of *regulation*, and which have no substantial stigmatizing element, are not prohibited by the Bill of Attainder Clause. Here, however, since the law applies to all state government jobs, and applies without respect to whether the individual has a specific intent to espouse the terrorist beliefs of some Brotherhood leaders, the law seems more like punishment than regulation. Especially since there is a risk that freedom of association values will be infringed, the Court will probably conclude that the law is a bill of attainder. See, e.g., *U.S. v. Brown* (law making it a crime for a Communist Party member to serve as an officer of a labor union is struck down as a bill of attainder).

Exam Tips on
MISCELLANEOUS CLAUSES

The Clauses covered in this Chapter are easy to miss on an exam, because each applies to fairly specialized facts and is likely to be buried within a much larger fact pattern. Most of your work will therefore consist of spotting the issue; once you do so, analyzing it correctly shouldn't be too hard. Here are some things to look for:

☛ If your fact pattern happens to involve a person who is prevented from *travelling* from state to state, or blocked from *voting* in a national election, consider whether the *14th Amendment's Privileges or Immunities Clause* has been violated. Also, if the state is discriminating against people who recently moved into the state, the clause is probably violated. (But if your fact pattern involves a target state that discriminates against out-of-staters who have not moved into the target state, probably it's the *Article IV* P&I Clause, *not* the 14th Amendment P&I Clause, that's been violated.)

☛ If you have a fact pattern that involves *land-use regulation* by the state or federal government, be alert to a *Takings* Clause issue.

    ☞ The main kinds of regulations that should put you on notice to look for a Takings problem are: (1) *zoning* regs; (2) *environmental-protection* regs; and (3) *landmark-protection* regs. In general, if government is telling the owner, "You can't do such-and-such with your property" or "If you want to do such-and-such with your property, you'll have to submit to the following conditions ... ," there is likely to be a Takings issue.

    ☞ Remember that for a land-use regulation to avoid being a taking it must *not deprive an owner of all economically viable use* of his land.

☞ The typical zoning regulation, which is generally-applicable and leaves the owner with at least some reasonable alternative uses of the property, will **not** normally be a "taking."

☞ But a **permanent ban** on constructing any building on a lot **would** be a "taking," if there was no economically attractive use of the property (e.g., recreational) that did not involve construction.

☛ If your fact pattern has the government **"rewriting the rules"** in a way that seems to **change previously-executed contracts**, consider whether the **"Contract"** Clause has been violated.

☞ Where government is trying to escape from **its own "bad deals,"** you should be quick to find a Contract Clause violation. Remember that the Court scrutinizes this type of government action closely, and will allow it only if a **"significant public need"** exists that cannot be reasonably handled in any other way.

☞ Where government is re-writing contracts made by **private parties**, remember that the judicial review is not so tough. So long as the government is dealing with an emergency, and protecting broad social interests (rather than a narrow, favored group), the Court will uphold any contract-rewriting that is **"reasonable"** in the circumstances.

☞ If the state applies a **"generally applicable** rule of conduct" that merely has the **incidental by-product** of impairing contractual obligations, the Contract Clause **doesn't come into effect at all**. This element is perhaps the most frequently tested aspect of the Contract Clause.

☛ **Ex post facto** laws are fairly easy to spot — whenever you see government **making something a crime** that wasn't a crime when it was done, or **increasing the penalty** for something beyond what was on the books when it was done, you may have an *ex post facto* violation.

☞ Remember that only **"criminal"** penalties, not "civil" or "regulatory" ones, are covered. Often this distinction is what's being tested.

☛ **Bill of attainder** issues are rare. Only when you see the legislature trying to punish a group that is so **narrowly-defined** that it's possible to name all the affected people in advance, should you even think about bill of attainder. Typical example: The legislature holds that members of a particular named **organization** may not hold a certain post or receive a certain benefit.

CHAPTER 12

STATE ACTION

ChapterScope

Nearly all of the rights guaranteed by the Constitution to individuals are protected only against interference **by government**. This is sometimes called the requirement of *"state action."* However, sometimes even a private individual's actions are found to be "state action," and thus subject to the Constitution. Here are the main concepts in this Chapter:

■ **"Public function" doctrine:** Under the *"public function"* doctrine, if a private individual or group is entrusted by the state to perform functions that are traditionally viewed as ***governmental in nature***, the private individual becomes an agent of the state, and he constitute "state action." Therefore, his acts must obey the Constitution.

■ **"State involvement" doctrine:** Alternatively, a private individual's conduct may be transformed into "state action" if the state is ***heavily involved*** in those activities. This is the *"state involvement"* branch of state-action doctrine. Examples are where:

❏ the state *"commands"* or *"requires"* the private person's action;

❏ the state *"encourages"* the private party's actions;

❏ the state and the private actor have a *"symbiotic"* or *"mutually beneficial"* relationship;

❏ the state is *"entangled"* with the private actor (e.g., they act together to carry out the action being challenged).

I. INTRODUCTION

A. Only state conduct covered: Nearly all of the rights and liberties which the Constitution guarantees to individuals are protected only against interference **by governmental entities**. For instance, the guarantees of due process and equal protection, given by §1 of the Fourteenth Amendment, are introduced by the words "No State shall. ... "

   1. Self-executing rights: In fact, of the constitutional rights which are "self-executing" (i.e., capable of enforcement by courts even without specific congressional legislation enacted to enforce the right), *only* the Thirteenth Amendment's prohibition on slavery (discussed *infra*, p. 456) includes private as well as governmental conduct. See Tribe, p. 1688, n. 1.

   2. Need for "state action" doctrine: Therefore, in virtually every litigation in which an individual argues that his ***constitutional rights have been violated,*** the court can grant relief ***only if it finds that there has been state action***, i.e., some sort of ***participation by a governmental entity*** sufficient to make the particular constitutional provision applicable. This chapter examines the various ways in which the Supreme Court has gone about determining whether state action exists.

   3. Sometimes apparent: In many instances, the existence of state action will be so apparent that this will not be a real issue. For instance, whenever the constitutional claim is that a *statute or regulation itself* violates the Constitution (e.g., by being racially discriminatory), the existence of state action is apparent. Similarly, the existence of state action is clear in the case of a claim that a state official, while engaged in performance of his duties, has violated the plaintiff's constitutional rights. The issue arises only where the specific action alleged to interfere with a constitutional right is taken by a *private individual*, i.e., one not acting on behalf of the government.

   a. Two sides: In this situation, the defendant typically argues that there cannot have been a constitutional violation because there has been no state action. The plaintiff, in contrast, typically contends that the state has in some way encouraged, benefitted from, or at least acquiesced in the private individual's conduct, thereby furnishing the requisite state involvement.

4. Governmental units: Putting aside the *degree* of governmental action required, the term "government" is broadly defined for purposes of determining the existence of "state action." Not only actions taken by the state, but those taken by any of its *subdivisions*, will count as state action. Thus actions by a *city, county, municipally-owned utility*, etc., will all qualify. Furthermore, in the case of those constitutional rights which are protected against interference at the hands of the federal government, *any federal instrumentality* (e.g., any federal agency or commission) will be included.

   a. Government-run corporation: In fact, even a *corporation* will be treated as a governmental entity, if it's set up by the government, remains under governmental control, and furthers governmental objectives. Thus *Amtrak* was found to be part of the federal government, for First Amendment purposes, because it was created by the U.S., the President appoints a majority of its board of directors, and it carries out the federal mission of avoiding the extinction of private passenger-train service. *Lebron v. National Railroad Passenger Corp.*, 513 U.S. 374 (1995).

5. Confusing doctrines: The Supreme Court has been largely unable to formulate rules about when the degree of state involvement is sufficiently great to convert a private person's conduct into "state action." Instead, the Court has said, in essence, that each case must be judged on its own facts. The result is a series of cases that are difficult or impossible to reconcile, and a consequent inability of observers to predict how the next case will be decided.

B. Early interpretations of "state action": The greatest importance of the state-action requirement is in connection with the Fourteenth Amendment's equal protection and due process guarantees.

1. *The Civil Rights Cases:* The first significant articulation by the Supreme Court that these Fourteenth Amendment rights are applicable only where state action is present was in the *Civil Rights Cases*, 109 U.S. 3 (1883).

   a. Facts: The *Civil Rights Cases* involved the Civil Rights Act of 1875, in which Congress prohibited all persons from denying, on the basis of race, any individual's equal access to inns, public transportation, theaters and other places of public accommodation. The statute was clearly applicable to private conduct. The question before the Court was whether Congress had the *power* to enact such a statute.

   b. Holding: In deciding the case, the Court made three main holdings, which have varying degrees of acceptance today.

c. **Applicable solely to state action:**   First, the Court held that the guarantees of equal protection and due process, given by §1 of the Fourteenth Amendment, apply by their own terms *solely to state action*. This holding remains valid today, at least in the sense that, in the *absence* of congressional legislation, the courts *will not find conduct that is exclusively private to be violative of these Fourteenth Amendment guarantees.*

d. **Congress without power:**   Secondly, the Court held that the grant to Congress in §5 of the Fourteenth Amendment of the power to enforce these guarantees did *not authorize Congress to regulate solely private conduct*. §5 "does not authorize Congress to create a code of municipal law for the regulation of private rights. ... " The only lawmaking power given to Congress under §5 of the Amendment, the Court held, was the ability to pass laws to prevent the *states, by their own action*, from interfering with these rights.

   i. **Probably no longer the law:**   It is not clear whether this aspect of the *Civil Rights Cases* remains good law, but it probably does not. There is no case in which a majority of the Court has held, in a single opinion, that §5 of the Fourteenth Amendment allows Congress to reach purely private conduct. But six Justices in *U.S. v. Guest*, 383 U.S. 745 (1966), in two separate opinions, argued that Congress has such power. See the fuller discussion of this issue *infra*, p. 454.

e. **Thirteenth Amendment inapplicable:**   Lastly, the Court held that the statute could not be justified as an exercise of the *Thirteenth* Amendment. The Court conceded that that Amendment is *applicable to private as well as state conduct*, since it prevents private individuals from holding others in slavery. But the Amendment by its terms bars only "slavery [and] involuntary servitude," and the Court took a narrow view of this phrase. Refusal to allow blacks to use public accommodations was simply not a "badge of slavery."

   i. **Overruled:**   This narrow view of what constitutes a "badge of slavery" prohibited under the Thirteenth Amendment has clearly been overruled, at least with respect to Congress' power to enact *legislation* to enforce that Amendment (an enforcement power given in §2 of the Amendment.) See, e.g., *Jones v. Alfred H. Mayer Co.*, 392 U.S. 409 (1968), discussed *infra*, p. 456. But the Court has continued to take a narrow view of the definition of slavery when analyzing state or private conduct directly, where there is no relevant congressional statute. Only conduct involving *actual peonage* (e.g., state laws imprisoning workers who violate labor contracts) has so far been held directly violative of the Amendment itself. See Tribe, p. 1688, n. 1.

f. **Statute invalidated:**   Since there was, in the majority's view, no satisfactory constitutional basis for the 1875 Civil Rights Act, the Act was *invalidated.*

g. **Dissent:**   Justice Harlan, in dissent, objected to the majority's view of both the Thirteenth and the Fourteenth Amendments.

   i. **Broad view of Thirteenth:**   As to the Thirteenth, he believed that freedom from slavery necessarily entailed not only the liberation from physical bondage, but also the eradication of all *"burdens and disabilities"* suffered by black people because of their race. Therefore, he believed that Congress could prevent black people from being denied, on grounds of race, those *"civil rights"* which white people have. In his opinion, these civil rights included the right to use inns, public transport, and other public facilities.

    ii. Harlan's Fourteenth Amendment view: With respect to the Fourteenth Amendment, Harlan pointed to a part of §1 that the majority ignored, the provision that "[a]ll persons born or naturalized in the United States and subject to the jurisdiction thereof, are citizens of the United States and of the State wherein they reside." He believed that this section gave blacks *state citizenship*, and that this grant of state citizenship in turn entitled them to "exemption from race discrimination in respect of *any civil right belonging to citizens of the white race* in the same State." As in the case of the Thirteenth Amendment, he believed that these civil rights included access to public accommodations. (Apart from this argument, Harlan also contended that railroad companies, innkeepers, etc., since they serve the public and are subject to state regulation, should be viewed as *agents of the state*, so that their conduct constitutes state action for equal protection and due process purposes.)

  2. Consequence of case: The *Civil Rights Cases*, and other cases decided shortly thereafter that took an equally narrow view of congressional power, had a devastating effect on Congress' ability to prevent the emergence of virtual apartheid in the South. It was not until the 1940s that some meaningful limits on unofficial racial discrimination were imposed; this happened principally through a broadening of the concept of "state action," a process described below.

C. Modern approach to state action: The narrow view of what constitutes "state action," implicit in the *Civil Rights Cases*, remained in force until the 1940s. Then, the Court began to broaden the concept of state action, with the result that various acts that were carried out by private persons, not state officials, were nonetheless attributed to the state. The Court has used a number of theories (or, perhaps "descriptions" is a better term) to explain why particular private conduct is so closely linked to official conduct that it should be considered state action. The cases generally seem to fall into two main groups: (1) those in which the private activity is attributable to the government because the private actor is fulfilling a *"public function"*; and (2) those in which the various connections (the *"nexus"*) between the state and the private actor are sufficiently great that the state can be said to be *involved in*, or even to have *"encouraged,"* the private activity which is being complained of. We will consider each of these lines of cases in turn.

  1. Limitations by post-Warren Court: In both of these areas, the broadening of the state action concept culminated during the Warren era. The Burger/Rehnquist/Roberts Court has clearly stopped the state action concept from further expansion, and in numerous respects appears to have in fact narrowed it.

  2. Relation between two doctrines: The relation between the "public function" doctrine and the "nexus" doctrine remains somewhat obscure. Apparently, the party who is attempting to show that his adversary's conduct constitutes state action will prevail if he can show *either* that that adversary performed a "public function" *or* that there was a sufficient "nexus" of contacts between the state and the adversary to justify subjecting the latter to constitutional prohibitions.

II. THE "PUBLIC FUNCTION" APPROACH

A. The "public function" approach generally: The *"public function"* doctrine holds that when a private individual (or group) is entrusted by the state with the performance of functions that are *governmental in nature*, he becomes an agent of the state and his acts constitute state action. This public function analysis at one time appeared to be potentially extremely broad-sweeping. But the Burger/Rehnquist Court has cut back the doctrine substantially, principally by insisting that the function be one that is normally "exclusively" reserved to the state. See *infra*, p. 437.

B. The *White Primary Cases*: The "public function" analysis seems to have had its start in the so-called *White Primary Cases*. In a series of decisions, the Court held that despite state attempts to delegate more and more of the nominating process to private political parties, the *entire electoral process is a public function* and the political parties are acting as agents of the state. Therefore, they may not practice racial discrimination.

1. Discrimination by political parties: For instance, where a state convention of Democrats established a rule that only whites could vote in the Texas Democratic Primary, the racial restriction was held to be violative of the Fifteenth Amendment, in *Smith v. Allwright*, 321 U.S. 649 (1944).

2. Extended to pre-primary: This rationale was carried even further in *Terry v. Adams*, 345 U.S. 461 (1953), where state action was found even in the racially-restrictive *"pre-primary"* elections held by the Jaybird Democratic Association, a group whose candidate almost always won the ensuing Democratic Primary (usually unopposed).

   a. Rationale: There was no majority opinion, but the prevailing rationale appeared to be that the state, by inaction, had permitted this unofficial pre-election to *usurp the role of the official primary* (which, under *Smith*, was itself an integral part of the election process). Several of the Justices seemed to rely on the fact that the state's tolerance of private discrimination reflected a *purposeful* decision to maintain a racially discriminatory system of elections. See Tribe, p. 1708.

3. Scope of rationale: It is not clear how broadly applicable the rationale of the *White Primary Cases* is. It does not seem likely that all or most other conduct by political parties will be deemed to be state action; for instance, the selection of party chairmen would probably not be held to be the performance of a public function. Nor is it clear that discrimination based on grounds other than race, even in the primary process, would necessarily be held to be state action; the *White Primary Cases* were founded on the Fifteenth Amendment, which applies only to racial discrimination. Thus a party which limited its membership solely to men, or solely to Protestants, might well be found not to be engaged in state action. See Tribe, p. 1119, n. 11.

C. Company towns and shopping centers: A second major area in which "public function" analysis developed concerned actions taken by the owners of *company towns* and *shopping centers.*

1. Issue: The issue in these cases was whether the owner of the property had the right to use *state trespass laws* to keep out people who wished to *speak* or *distribute literature* on the property. Where operation of the property was held to be a public function, First Amendment guarantees became applicable, barring the use of state trespass laws. By contrast, where there was no public function, there were no First Amendment rights and the owner therefore had the ability to keep the outsiders off his property.

2. **Company town:**   The first of this line of cases involved a company town. In *Marsh v. Alabama*, 326 U.S. 501 (1946), a Jehovah's Witness was charged with criminal trespass for distributing religious literature in the town of Chickasaw, Alabama, a town **wholly owned** by the Gulf Shipbuilding Corporation. The Court held that, since the town was just like any other town (except for the fact that title to the real estate was vested in a private company), **operation of the town was a public function**. Prior cases had held that ordinary non-private towns could not bar distribution of religious literature, under First Amendment principles; these principles were therefore applicable to Chickasaw as well.

   a. **Public access:**   The *Marsh* Court attached some importance to the fact that the town was not limited to housing, but also included a downtown shopping district, which was accessible to and freely used by outsiders. The Court's stress on this fact may mean that privately-owned communities that are **purely residential**, as well as **camps for migrant workers**, are **not** fulfilling public functions, since these are typically not used by outsiders. Later cases, discussed *infra*, holding that shopping centers are not by themselves engaged in public functions, seem to buttress this more limited view of what types of property will be found to be used for public functions.

   b. **Balancing:**   Strict logic would indicate that, since Chickasaw fulfilled a "public function," **any activity** taken in connection with its administration would be subjected to constitutional scrutiny. For instance, by this analysis, any person hired as a **sanitation worker** under a contract would presumably have the right to procedural due process before being discharged. Yet the *Marsh* Court's analysis leaves open the possibility that the operation of a town may be a public function only for **some, but not all**, purposes. The opinion seems to call for a **balancing test**, whereby "the constitutional rights of owners of property" are balanced against the right of the people to "enjoy freedom of the press and religion."

      i. **Application:**   Under such a balancing test, the right of a town worker not to be discharged without a fair hearing might be found to weigh less heavily on the scale than did the right to distribute literature, and might lead to a decision that such firings are not part of the town's public function. A similar holding might be made in response to charges that the town refused to hire, say, women for sanitation positions.

3. **Shopping centers:**   For a while, it appeared that **shopping centers** would also be treated as engaged in a public function, so that First Amendment guarantees, at least, would be applicable to activities there. But cases so indicating were overruled in 1976 by **Hudgens v. NLRB**, 424 U.S. 507 (1976).

   a. **Facts and holding:**   In *Hudgens*, union members who were engaged in a labor dispute with one of the stores in a shopping mall attempted to picket in the open area and the parking lot of the mall. A majority of the Court held that, prior cases to the contrary notwithstanding, a large self-contained **shopping center** was **simply not the equivalent of the company town** in *Marsh*, and that **no First Amendment guarantees were applicable to activities in it.**

   b. **State of company-town cases:**   *Marsh* itself presumably remains good law. But the effect of *Hudgens* is to limit *Marsh* to its own facts; thus operation of a company-owned town will be deemed a public function, but operation of property that supplies less than a full range of municipal services will not be.

D. Parks and recreation: Operation of a ***park*** has been considered the exercise of a "public function."

1. ***Evans case:*** Thus in *Evans v. Newton*, 382 U.S. 296 (1966), a park in Macon, Georgia had been left in trust by Senator Bacon, with the proviso that it be used only for whites. At first, the City of Macon acted as trustee and enforced the proviso; then, it was replaced by private trustees who did the same.

   a. **Holding:** The Supreme Court held that operation of the park in a racially discriminatory manner violated the Fourteenth Amendment. One reason for this conclusion was that the services rendered even by a private park were "***municipal in nature***"; like fire and police departments, a park "***traditionally serves the community.***"

   b. **Aftermath of case:** The Supreme Court was subsequently required to decide whether the reverter in Senator Bacon's will, which was to be triggered if the park was no longer racially restricted, could constitutionally be enforced by the state. It concluded that it could, in *Evans v. Abney*, discussed *infra*, p. 440.

2. **Present status:** It is unlikely that the "public function" analysis of *Evans v. Newton* will be extended to include other types of recreational facilities, such as ***country clubs*** or ***amusement parks.*** The post-Warren Court has held that only those functions which are traditionally "***exclusively***" performed by the state will be deemed public functions. A footnote to Justice Rehnquist's majority opinion in *Flagg Bros., infra*, p. 437, suggests that "parks for recreational purposes" do not fit into this category, and that the real explanation for *Evans* lay in the city's day-to-day involvement in the park's maintenance. Thus if the issue were to arise again, purely private operation of even an ordinary park might no longer be held to be a public function.

E. The requirement of state "exclusivity": In the post-Warren years, the Court has dramatically narrowed the situations in which "public function" analysis will apply, by requiring that the function be one which has traditionally been ***exclusively*** the domain of the government. The Court has used this exclusivity requirement on a number of occasions to reject the application of the public function doctrine.

1. **Utilities:** Operation of a ***privately-owned utility*** licensed and regulated by the state was held ***not*** to be performance of a public function, in ***Jackson v. Metropolitan Edison Co.***, 419 U.S. 345 (1974).

   a. **Rationale:** Public function analysis is applicable, the Court said, only where the function has ***been "traditionally and exclusively performed"*** by the government. This exclusivity requirement was not met by operation of the utility in *Jackson*, the Court concluded; this was demonstrated by the fact that state law did not ***obligate*** the state to furnish power.

      i. **"Public interest" rationale rejected:** The *Jackson* Court explicitly rejected the argument that all heavily regulated businesses "***affected with a public interest***" should be treated as exercising public functions.

2. **Warehouseman's lien:** The impact of the exclusivity requirement was still more evident in a case in which the Court held that sale by a ***warehouseman*** of goods stored with him in

which he had a ***warehouseman's lien*** for unpaid storage charges was ***not a public function***. *Flagg Bros., Inc. v. Brooks*, 436 U.S. 149 (1978).

    a. Rationale: The majority, in an opinion by Justice Rehnquist, rejected the contention that resolution of private disputes was traditionally an exclusive government function. Here, for instance, Rehnquist argued, the dispute need not have been settled by the warehouseman's sale: the owner of the goods could have brought a replevin action, or could have sued for damages based on her claim that she had not authorized the storage.

3. Nursing homes: Operation of ***nursing homes***, including the making of decisions about patient care, was found ***not*** to be a public function, in *Blum v. Yaretsky*, 457 U.S. 991 (1982). The majority seemed to be imposing still another requirement for application of the public function doctrine: that the activity be one which the state is ***required*** to provide by statute or by the state constitution. Since the state was not required to supply nursing home, or other medical, care, no public function was involved. (Other aspects of the case are discussed *infra*, p. 441.)

4. Private school: The Court has held that operation of a ***private school***, even one whose income comes primarily from public grants, is ***not*** a public function. *Rendell-Baker v. Kohn*, 457 U.S. 830 (1981). Provision of education is not the "exclusive" prerogative of the state, even though it's a function normally provided by the state out of public funds.

5. Community-access cable TV channel: The operation of a ***public access TV channel on a cable system*** is ***not*** a public function if the channel is operated by a private company. Therefore, the operator of the channel is not a state actor, and ***can engage in viewpoint discrimination*** of the sort that would trigger First Amendment Free Speech strict scrutiny if done by government. See *Manhattan Community Access Corp. v. Halleck*, 139 S.Ct. 1921 (2019).

    a. Narrow decision: All members of the Court agreed in *Halleck* that *Jackson, supra*, holding that the public-function doctrine ***requires that the function have been "traditionally and exclusively performed"*** by the government, ***represents current law*** that does not need to be changed. And all agreed that without more, operation of a cable TV system is not a traditional public function, because such operation, even though *often* performed by government, is not "***exclusively***" performed by it.

F. Future of "public function" doctrine: In summary, the "public function" doctrine has been ***substantially narrowed*** by the post-Warren Court. The doctrine now seems to apply where two quite stringent conditions are met: (1) the function is one which has traditionally been performed ***exclusively*** (not just mostly) by the state; and (2) some statute or state constitutional provision ***in fact requires the state*** to perform the function.

1. Where satisfied: The present Court seems to regard only two groups of prior cases as meeting these requirements: the maintenance of ***streets*** (in *Marsh v. Alabama*, the company-town case) and the maintenance of an ***electoral system*** (in the *White Primary Cases*).

III. "NEXUS" — THE SIGNIFICANCE OF STATE INVOLVEMENT

A. The "nexus" theory generally: The second broad branch of the state action doctrine relates not to the type of activity carried out by the private actor, but to the ***conduct of the govern-***

ment. If the government is sufficiently ***"involved"*** in the private actor's conduct or ***"encourages"*** that conduct, or ***benefits from*** it, the private party's acts will be deemed state action, and subjected to constitutional review. A common catch-all way of referring to this branch of state-action analysis is to call it the ***"nexus"*** approach; that is, the issue is the nexus, or ***points of contact***, between the state and the private actor.

B. **"Commandment":** One way in which the state can become responsible for a private party's conduct is by ***commanding*** that conduct. Some examples of commandment are so obvious that no one would dispute the presence of state action; for instance, if the state ordered private restaurant owners to serve only white customers, both the order, and the private owners' execution of it, would be state action.

1. **Facially neutral law:** Much more interesting are those situations where the state, by ***applying facially neutral laws, enforces private agreements*** with the result that one person is judicially ordered to discriminate against another. Even the application of such neutral laws may be construed as a commandment to discriminate, and therefore state action.

2. ***Shelley v. Kraemer:*** The classic illustration of this principle is ***Shelley v. Kraemer***, 334 U.S. 1 (1948).

   a. **Facts of *Shelley*:** *Shelley* involved the enforceability of ***racially restrictive covenants***. Most homeowners in an area had entered into a covenant that their property would not be owned by anyone but Caucasians for 50 years. When blacks bought homes from willing white owners despite the covenants, other whites, who were owners of properties also subject to the covenants, sued to block the blacks from taking possession. The issue before the Supreme Court was whether the state courts could award the white plaintiffs the relief they sought, without violating the Fourteenth Amendment.

   b. **Holding:** The Supreme Court held that ***judicial enforcement*** of the restrictive covenant ***would constitute state action***, and would therefore violate the Fourteenth Amendment. "[B]ut for the active intervention of the state courts, supported by the full panoply of state power, [defendants] would have been free to occupy the properties in question. ... " Nor was it relevant that enforcement by the state occurred because of a longstanding ***common-law***, rather than ***statutory***, policy of granting such enforcement.

      i. **Not inaction:** The Court also noted that this was not a case in which the state was simply remaining ***inactive***, while one private person discriminated against another. The *Shelley* Court stressed that the case involved ***willing sellers*** as well as buyers, so that it was only the state's coercive judicial machinery which would cause the discrimination to occur.

3. **Damage actions:** Suppose the white plaintiffs in *Shelley* had sought not an injunction against the black purchasers, but ***money damages*** against the ***white sellers***. Granting this relief, too, would be state action and a violation of the Fourteenth Amendment, the Court held in ***Barrows v. Jackson***, 346 U.S. 249 (1953).

   a. **Rationale:** The Court's rationale was that awarding such relief would impede an agreement between an otherwise willing seller and buyer just as the injunction sought in *Shelley* would have, since the seller would be either completely dissuaded from selling to a black by the possibility of a damage action, or at least motivated to charge black buyers a higher price to cover a possible damage award.

4. Scope of *Shelley* uncertain: The scope of *Shelley* (and *Barrows*) is highly unclear.

  a. Broad reading: A broad reading of *Shelley* would be that anytime a person's decision to discriminate, or an agreement between two or more people to discriminate, is enforced or left undisturbed by the state's legal system (even pursuant to a facially neutral legal rule), state action exists.

  i. Refusal to sell: By this reading, if a white homeowner who had signed a racially restrictive covenant like the one in *Shelley* simply ***refused to sell*** to a black in reliance on the covenant, the judiciary's refusal to ***prevent*** the white from relying on the agreement would be state action and thus unconstitutional.

  ii. Refusal to serve: Similarly, by this reading of *Shelley*, a restaurant owner's decision not to allow black civil rights workers to conduct a sit-in on his premises could not constitutionally be backed up by use of the state's trespass laws, even though this law was a facially neutral provision that entitled any property owner to decide who may come on his property.

  b. Narrower reading: But a strong case can be made that the proper reading of *Shelley* is much ***narrower***. For instance, there is reason to believe that the rationale of *Shelley* was meant to apply ***only*** to those situations where there are a ***willing seller and buyer***, and the state is asked to use its power affirmatively to prevent them from consummating their sale. (This reading is suggested by the *Shelley* Court's statement that this was not a case "in which the states have merely abstained from action, leaving private individuals free to impose such discriminations as they see fit.")

  i. Narrower view probably accurate: Subsequent Supreme Court cases certainly have not disproved the narrower view of *Shelley*. For instance, the great lengths to which the Court has gone to develop other theories for finding state action (such as the "symbiosis" rationale of *Burton v. Wilmington Parking Authority, infra*, p. 442) suggest that mere invocation of neutral state laws to preserve individuals' "right" to discriminate probably does not constitute state action. The Court's refusal to rely on the broader reading of *Shelley* in sit-in cases decided in the 1960s also lends some support to this narrower view of *Shelley*.

5. Reverter in deed: In any event, if a private agreement calls for discrimination, it is not unconstitutional state action for a court to enforce a provision in the agreement dealing with the contingency that the discrimination is held unenforceable. This was demonstrated by ***Evans v. Abney***, 396 U.S. 435 (1970), a further development in the litigation of which *Evans v. Newton (supra*, p. 437) was a part.

  a. Facts: After *Evans v. Newton* established that Baconsfield Park could not be operated in a racially discriminatory way, the state trial court determined that, since fulfillment of Senator Bacon's intent was no longer possible, the trust should ***terminate*** (presumably causing the property to close as a park), and the property should revert to the Senator's heirs. This reversion was called for by operation of Georgia law in the event of a trust's termination.

  b. Ruling upheld: The Supreme Court held that this state ruling did ***not violate*** the Fourteenth Amendment. The only discrimination was by Senator Bacon, not by the state's laws calling for reversion. This situation was distinguishable from *Shelley*, the majority held, because in *Shelley*, the state court was called upon to ***enforce*** a private scheme of discrimination; here, the state ruling, rather than enforcing discrimination, in fact nullified discrimination by preventing the park from being used by either blacks or whites.

6. **Delegation:** The Court since the '80s has taken a quite narrow view of the circumstances in which the state will be deemed to have "***commanded***" particular actions by private persons. If any real degree of ***discretion*** is delegated to the private party, this will probably be enough to relieve the state of responsibility for those private actions, even though they take place within a fairly rigid framework of state-created rules. For instance, in *Blum v. Yaretsky*, 457 U.S. 991 (1982), a class of Medicaid patients in private nursing homes unsuccessfully claimed that decisions by the homes to discharge them or send them to facilities giving less extensive (and less costly) service constituted state action.

   a. **Facts:** The patients contended that the decisions on level-of-care, although made in individual cases by the nursing home's staff, were tightly circumscribed by the state rules, and that the state therefore bore responsibility for these decisions.

   b. **Claim rejected:** But a majority of the Court, in an opinion by Justice Rehnquist, disagreed. The actual discharge or transfer decisions were based on "medical judgments," which were made by independent nursing home professionals who were not controlled by the state. Therefore, these decisions were not state action.

C. **"Encouragement" by the state:** If *Shelley v. Kraemer* may be seen as a case where the state "commanded" the discrimination (by attempting to enjoin the willing white sellers from selling to the black purchasers), other cases have found that the state has "***encouraged***" discrimination. Such encouragement, too, will constitute state action, and may thus trigger a constitutional violation.

1. **Repeal of civil rights laws as "encouragement":** Such an "encouragement" theory was used in ***Reitman v. Mulkey***, 387 U.S. 369 (1967). In *Reitman*, the Court found state action where California voters amended their constitution to prohibit the government from interfering with any private individual's right to discriminate in the sale or lease of residential real estate. An immediate effect (and purpose) of the constitutional amendment was to overturn two statutes which barred some sorts of private residential housing discrimination. The California Supreme Court, in striking the constitutional amendment, found that its purpose and effect would inevitably be to encourage private discrimination. The U.S. Supreme Court, in affirming, agreed that this was ***encouragement*** by the state, ***not even-handedness***.

   a. **Deference to state court finding:** The U.S. Supreme Court, in agreeing that the constitutional amendment would have the effect of encouraging private discrimination, gave deference to the California court's finding that, "in the California environment," the amendment would have this effect.

   b. **Scope of *Reitman*:** Even giving *Reitman* a broad reading, it seems extremely ***unlikely*** that the ***mere failure by a state to forbid private discrimination constitutes state action***. Thus had California simply never enacted any legislation or regulation dealing with private housing discrimination, its inaction would almost certainly not be deemed state conduct. Even had it enacted legislation, the ***mere repeal*** of the statute(s) by the legislature would probably not have been state action, since a strong argument could be made that such a repeal merely restored the status quo. It was probably only the fact that the change was made to the state's ***constitution***, and thus acted as a bar to enactment of fair housing legislation in the future, that state "encouragement" was found.

D. "Symbiosis" between state and private actor: Another way in which the state can become so involved with private discrimination that the latter will be subjected to constitutional scrutiny is if there is a "symbiotic," i.e., ***mutually beneficial***, relation between the state and the private discriminator. That is, if there are ***extensive contacts*** between the state and the private party, in such a way that each benefits from the other's conduct, the requisite state involvement may be found.

1. **The *Burton* case:**   The classic example of such a symbiotic relationship is ***Burton v. Wilmington Parking Authority***, 365 U.S. 715 (1961).

    a. **Facts:**   *Burton* involved the relationship between a parking building owned and run by the Wilmington Parking Authority (a state agency) and a restaurant run by a private company within the building, under a 20-year lease between the Authority and the company. The restaurant refused to serve blacks. (No provision in Delaware or federal law at the time required private companies to do so.) A black who was refused service contended that the Authority's involvement with the restaurant was sufficiently great as to make the private discrimination "state action" violative of the Fourteenth Amendment.

    b. **State action found:**   The Supreme Court agreed that ***state action was present***. The Court relied heavily on various indications that the restaurant was essential to successful operation of the overtly public facility (the parking portion). For instance, the project could not have been financed without rents from commercial tenants like the restaurant. Furthermore, since the restaurant claimed that its business would be hurt if it were forced to serve blacks, the "profits earned by discrimination" were indispensable elements in the project's financial success.

    c. **No relevant lease provision:**   Unlike the constitutional amendment in *Reitman*, nothing the state did in *Burton* expressly conferred on the restaurant the right to discriminate. The lease was completely silent on the issue of discrimination. But the Supreme Court held that, in view of the symbiotic relation between the parties, the state had an ***affirmative obligation*** to insert a non-discrimination requirement in the lease (which, under state law regarding leases of public property, it had the power to do). This obligation could not be avoided even upon a showing by the state of perfect good faith, and of a complete absence of desire to encourage discrimination.

    d. **Scope of *Burton*:**   As with many of the other state action decisions, it is difficult to gauge the scope of *Burton*. The case probably does ***not*** stand for the proposition that any time the state has the power to prevent discriminatory use of public property, it must exercise that power. For instance, if the Authority had ***sold*** the entire building as surplus, it seems unlikely that an anti-discrimination clause in the deed would be constitutionally required. A key aspect of *Burton* is undoubtedly that the state ***benefited*** heavily from the lease, and may in fact have benefited from the discrimination itself (since the absence of an anti-discrimination clause probably made the restaurant willing to pay higher rents). In fact, *Burton* may be seen as a case in which there was ***circumstantial evidence*** that the ***government itself had racially discriminatory motives*** in failing to prohibit the private discrimination. See Tribe, p. 1701, n. 13.

E. Involvement or "entanglement" by state: There are some situations in which the state is so heavily *involved* in or "entangled with" private action that, even though the state does not *benefit* from or encourage the private conduct (thus ruling out the "symbiosis" approach, *supra*, p. 442) the court will nonetheless attribute to the state the private conduct.

1. **Licensing by the state:**   Where the state *licenses* a private entity to perform a particular function, it is often claimed that the act of licensing is sufficient state involvement to make the private conduct state action. But in general, the Supreme Court has *rejected* such claims.

    a. **Liquor license:**   The best-known case on state action through licensing is ***Moose Lodge No. 107 v. Irvis***, 407 U.S. 163 (1972), involving a liquor license.

        i.   **Facts:**   In *Moose Lodge*, the Lodge, a private club, refused service to the black guest of a member. The guest contended that, since the state had given the club one of a limited number of liquor licenses, this act of licensing was sufficient to render the club's discrimination state action.

        ii. **Claim rejected:**   The Supreme Court disagreed, holding that the mere fact that a state grants a license to an entity does not transform the latter's conduct into state action, *even where the number of licenses is limited*. (But the majority hinted that the result might have been different if the licenses were limited in such a way that clubs holding them had a "*monopoly*" in the dispensing of liquor.")

        iii. **"Significant involvement" standard:**   The majority phrased the issue as being whether the state was *"significantly involved"* with invidious discrimination. The mere fact of licensing did not constitute such significant involvement. The Court distinguished this situation from that in *Burton*, where there was a "symbiotic relationship" between a public restaurant and a public building; here, by contrast, there was a *private* club in a private building.

        iv. **Dissent:**   Three Justices dissented. One of the dissents, written by Justice Douglas, conceded that as a general rule, the activities of a private club were beyond the reach of the Constitution, even if the club operated pursuant to some sort of license. But this case was different, he contended, because there was a "state-enforced *scarcity of licenses*" that restricted the ability of blacks to obtain liquor. If individuals wanted to form a club that would serve blacks, they would have to buy an existing club license, and would have to pay a *monopoly price*; the creation of this monopoly scheme was directly attributable to the state. Therefore, Douglas contended, the Lodge's discrimination was state action.

2. **Grant of monopoly:**   Related to the problem of licensed businesses is that of "natural monopolies," i.e., areas of commerce where, usually because of high capital requirements, only one business can profitably exist. Such natural monopolies are usually *highly regulated*, since there is no competition to keep their charges reasonable. Yet despite this intense regulation, actions by these monopolies will *not* generally be deemed state action. The classic example is conduct of a public *utility*.

    a. ***Jackson v. Metropolitan Edison:***   The Court refused to find that the conduct of an electric utility, which had a monopoly in its area, constituted state action, in ***Jackson v. Metropolitan Edison Co.***, 419 U.S. 345 (1974). Consequently, plaintiff's claim that her electric service should not have been turned off for nonpayment without notice and fair hearing was unsuccessful. The Court was not convinced that the state had really "granted" the utility a monopoly (since the monopoly was a "natural" one). But even if it had, this was not sufficient to transform the utility's activities into state action, because there was an "insufficient relationship between the challenged actions of the [utility] and [its] monopoly status."

b. **Dissent:** Three Justices dissented in separate opinions. Two of them believed that the state *had* conferred a monopoly on the utility, and appeared to believe that this fact justified subjecting the utility's actions to constitutional review. One of the dissenters, Justice Marshall, pointed out that an important part of the state's regulatory program was its decision not to have the state itself *compete* with private utilities, and to regulate the latter "in a multitude of ways to ensure that the [utilities'] service will be the functional equivalent of service provided by the State." (See the discussion of the majority and dissent's viewpoints on this "public function" issue *supra*, p. 437.)

3. **State funding:** The fact that a private entity *receives substantial state funding* will not by itself convert its activities into state action. Thus in *Rendell-Baker v. Kohn*, 457 U.S. 830 (1982), the Court held that a *private school*, whose income came primarily from public funding, and which was regulated by public authorities, was not committing state action when it fired employees.

4. **"Joint participation":** The necessary state involvement with a private party *will* be found where the private party and a state official have *jointly participated* in the activity being challenged. This "joint participation" theory was used to find state action in *Lugar v. Edmondson Oil Co.*, 457 U.S. 922 (1982).

a. **Facts:** *Lugar*, like *Flagg Bros. (supra*, p. 437), involved a creditor's right to summarily seize or dispose of his debtor's property. In *Lugar*, the creditor (Edmondson) sued to collect a debt, and obtained a pre-judgment attachment against the property of the debtor, Lugar, which had the the effect of preventing Lugar from being able to sell it (though he remained in possession). To obtain the attachment, Edmondson was required only to file an *ex parte* petition stating a belief that Lugar might dispose of the property in order to defeat his creditors; a clerk of the court then issued a writ of attachment, which was executed by the sheriff.

b. **Holding:** The Court held that because the clerk and sheriff acted *together with* Edmondson, Edmondson's conduct in obtaining the attachment was state action. Therefore, Edmondson could be held liable for violating Lugar's constitutional rights if (as Lugar alleged) the attachment statute failed to comply with the requirements of due process.

c. **Limited scope:** But only Lugar's allegation that the *statutory procedure itself* was unconstitutional, *not* Edmonson's alleged *misuse* of the statute, was held to involve state action. Misuse of a properly-drafted statute was not "conduct that can be attributed to the state," because such misuse did not give rise to a "[constitutional] deprivation ... caused by the exercise of some right or privilege created by the state or by a rule of conduct imposed by the state. ... "

d. **Peremptory challenges as joint participation:** For another illustration of the principle that joint participation between the state and a private party can be enough to transform the private party's action into state action, consider the use of *peremptory juror challenges* in trials. The Court has held that when a *private litigant* — either a civil litigant or a defendant in a criminal case — uses peremptory challenges to exclude jurors on racial grounds, this conduct constitutes state action and therefore violates the Equal Protection Clause. See *Edmonson v. Leesville Concrete Co.*, 500 U.S. 614 (1991) (in a civil case, private litigants cannot exercise their peremptory challenges in a racially discriminatory manner); *Georgia v. McCollum*, 505 U.S. 42 (1992) (same rule for criminal defendants).

     e. Regulation of interscholastic athletics: For yet one more illustration of how joint participation between the state and a private party can constitute state action, consider the regulation of ***interscholastic athletics*** within a state. In a 2001 decision, the Court held that although high school interscholastic athletics within a state were regulated by a nominally private association, the association was a state actor due to the extensive participation of state entities in the association's affairs. The fact that 84% of the association's members were public high schools, and the fact that educators from those public schools were fulfilling their own job responsibilities when they worked with the association, contributed to the Court's conclusion that the association was a state actor. See *Brentwood Academy v. Tenn. Secondary School Athletic Assoc.*, 531 U.S. 288 (2001), discussed more extensively *infra*, both immediately below and on p. 446.

5. "Entwinement": A 2001 decision suggests that where the links between a state entity and a private group are so extensive that the two can fairly be said to be ***"entwined,"*** this entwinement will itself be strong evidence that the private group should be deemed to be a state actor. In *Brentwood Academy v. Tenn. Secondary School Athletic Assoc.*, 531 U.S. 288 (2001) (also discussed immediately *supra*, and *infra* at p. 446), the majority said that "Entwinement will support a conclusion that an ostensibly private organization ought to be charged with a public character and judged by constitutional standards; entwinement to the degree shown here requires it."

     a. Facts: *Brentwood* involved the question whether an Association regulating secondary-school athletics within a state should be treated as a state actor. The Court found two types of public-private entwinement in *Brentwood*. First, the State Board of Education was intertwined with the Association in numerous ways (e.g., the Board appointed non-voting members to the Association's committees). Second, most of the public secondary schools within the state not only belonged to the Association but performed some of their official functions (e.g., the running of interscholastic sports programs) in close conjunction with the Association. These two forms of entwinement justified the conclusion that the Association's conduct constituted state action.

6. Acquiescence by the state not enough: Mere ***acquiescence*** by the state in the private individual's conduct is not enough to make the latter "state action." The government must ***actively encourage*** or ***facilitate*** the private conduct, not merely ***tolerate*** it. This is true even where the state has the clear power to ***prevent*** the challenged private conduct, but chooses not to exercise that power.

     Example 1: A utility files with the State Public Utilities Commission a tariff, which among its terms states a right to terminate a customer's service for nonpayment. The Commission does not object to this provision.

     Held, the utility's practice of terminating service for nonpayment, without giving notice or an opportunity for a hearing, is not transformed into state action merely because the Commission (a state agency) allowed it. (A prior case in which a utility's conduct was carefully scrutinized by a utilities commission, and in which the commission ultimately praised the practice as improving service, was distinguishable, since there, the state placed its "imprimatur" on the practice). *Jackson v. Metropolitan Edison Co.*, 419 U.S. 345 (1974), also discussed *supra*, p. 437.

Example 2: The state, by enacting the Uniform Commercial Code, grants a warehouseman a lien for unpaid storage charges against goods deposited with him, and permits him to sell these goods to satisfy the lien. Plaintiff, whose goods are about to be sold in this manner, argues that the sale constitutes state action, and that its terms must therefore satisfy procedural due process.

Held, the carrying out of the sale does ***not*** constitute state action. The state has merely ***permitted, not encouraged***, such sales by warehousemen. Plaintiff's claim is merely that the state has refused to act (i.e., that it has refused to bar the sale), and mere inaction by the state cannot transform private acts into state acts. *Flagg Bros., Inc. v. Brooks*, 436 U.S. 149 (1978) (also discussed *supra*, p. 437).

Note: A dissent by Justice Stevens in *Flagg Bros.* argued that the majority's distinction between "permission" and "compulsion" cannot be the determining factor in state-action analysis. Under the majority's rationale, the state could also pass a statute providing that "any person with sufficient physical power [may] acquire and sell the property of his weaker neighbor"; such sales would then not be state action. Justice Stevens instead believed that state action was present, because the state had delegated to a private party what was essentially a state function, the non-consensual transfer of property to satisfy debts.

7. **Recognition by state:** If a state ***formally recognizes*** the role played by a private association in a particular type of state-organized activity, that recognition will itself make it more likely that the association will be deemed to be a state actor. Thus in a 2001 case in which the Court found that a state association regulating interscholastic secondary-school athletics was a state actor, the Court relied heavily on the state's recognition of the association's special role as regulator of the athletic activities of public junior-high and high schools. *Brentwood Academy v. Tenn. Secondary School Athletic Assoc.*, 531 U.S. 288 (2001).

Quiz Yourself on
STATE ACTION *(ENTIRE CHAPTER)*

64. Pablo, an American of Hispanic origin, attempted to receive treatment at Green Valley Hospital. He believes that he was denied admission solely because he was Hispanic. Green Valley Hospital is owned by the Little Sisters of Green Valley, a private religious order. Pablo has brought suit against the Little Sisters, arguing that they have violated his right to equal protection under the Fourteenth Amendment. Assuming that the facts are as asserted by Pablo, will his suit succeed? _____

65. A statute enacted by the state of Albatross makes it a felony for any individual to "interfere with any right guaranteed by the Equal Protection Clause of the Fourteenth Amendment of the U.S. Constitution." Delbert was the manager of a housing project funded and operated by a federal housing agency. Delbert refused to rent to a family solely because they were black. If Delbert is charged with violating the Albatross statute, should he be convicted? _____

66. Ninety percent of the kindergarten-through-twelfth-grade students who attend school in the state of Mongoose attend public schools. The other 10% attend private schools, some of which are parochial and some of which are not. Beaver Academy is a non-sectarian private school, 40% of whose operating funds are supplied by the state as part of an innovative program to encourage excellence in education. The state does not prescribe any aspect of the Beaver curriculum, beyond checking to make sure that students achieve a minimum level of competency in core subjects like reading. Pamela, a sixth-grade student, has brought suit against Beaver Academy, asserting that she was denied admission to Beaver solely on the grounds that she is black. Because Mongoose has extremely limited civil rights statutes, Pamela's suit consists solely of the assertion that the school's failure to admit her violated her Fourteenth Amendment equal protection rights. Assume that Pamela's factual assertions are true.

(a) When Pamela attempts to prove the presence of state action, what doctrine offers her the best chance of success? _____

(b) Will Pamela's suit succeed? _____

67. State U is a large public university located in the fairly small town of Arborville. Students at the university represent a substantial share of the local demand for housing. Much of the housing stock in Arborville consists of two-family homes, in one part of which the owner lives and the other part of which is rented to students. State U's housing department maintains a list of local homeowners who have such housing to offer to students. State U allows a homeowner to indicate his or her racial or ethnic preferences on the listing; thus one who prefers whites may request that a "W" designation be affixed, one who prefers blacks that a "B" be affixed, etc. The university does not charge for these listings. Because State U does not have enough dormitory space to house all students, the availability of private housing like that contained in the list is an important resource for the university. There is evidence that some homeowners who have participated in the list would not do so if they were not able to indicate their racial preferences and thus reduce the possibility of an embarrassing face-to-face refusal to rent to minorities.

Bernard, a black student at State U, has been unable to find what he considers suitable housing. He believes that there are substantially fewer housing units available to black students than to white students, and that on average the ones that are available to blacks are either more costly or less attractive. Assume that no federal or state statute bars discrimination by an owner/occupier of a two-family house in the selection of a tenant. Bernard has sued State U for an injunction against continued use of the racially-coded housing list, on the grounds that the U's maintenance of that list violates his equal protection rights.

(a) What is the best argument Bernard can make as to why maintenance of the list violates his equal protection rights? _____

(b) Assuming that many private landowners on the list are in fact discriminating against black students, and that black students on average have to pay more for less attractive accommodations than whites when they rent from the list, should Bernard's request for an injunction be granted? _____

Answers

64. No. The Fourteenth Amendment, like all aspects of the Constitution (except the Thirteenth Amendment) only restricts ***government*** action. Here, the facts tell us that Green Valley Hospital is operated by a private religious order. Since there is no government involvement, there cannot be an equal protection violation.

65. No. This is essentially a "trick question." The Fourteenth Amendment applies only to conduct by ***state*** and ***local*** governments. Therefore, any conduct by or on behalf of the housing agency here could not have violated the Equal Protection Clause, because it was conduct of the federal government, not the state government. Delbert therefore did not cause any interference with equal protection rights. (Equal protection *principles* are binding on the federal government via the Fifth Amendment's Due Process Clause, and these equal protection principles are interpreted the same way as are the Fourteenth Amendment's equal protection principles. But the question here has been carefully worded to refer only to conduct that violates the Fourteenth, not the Fifth, Amendment.)

66. **(a) The "public function" doctrine.**

(b) No. The "public function" doctrine holds that when a private actor (or group) is entrusted by the state with the performance of functions that are governmental in nature, that actor or group becomes an *agent of the state* and his/their acts constitute state action. However, for the "public function" doctrine to apply, the function must be one which has traditionally been *exclusively* the domain of the government. The Court has held that the providing of education is *not* the exclusive prerogative of the state, even though it is a function normally provided by the state out of public funds. Therefore, the "public function" doctrine will not apply to Beaver. See *Rendell-Baker v. Kohn*, refusing to treat a private school as involving a public function, even where the school's income came primarily from public grants. (It is also conceivable that the state might be found to have been so heavily "involved" or "entangled" in the private school here that state action should be found, but the Court has held that mere government funding of a private actor's operations does not convert those private operations into state action, so this argument, too, would almost certainly fail.)

67. **(a) That there is a symbiotic relationship between State U and the private landowners, sufficient to turn the private acts of discrimination into state action.**

(b) Yes, probably. If the state is deeply involved with private discrimination, that private discrimination can sometimes be viewed as itself being state action. One of the ways this can happen is if there is a *"symbiotic,"* i.e., mutually beneficial, relation between the state and the private discriminator. Here, a strong argument can be made that the university is benefitting greatly from private acts (the rental of housing to State U students), and that the private discriminators are receiving important benefits from the state (free listings and a free flow of potential tenants).

To the extent that the pool of homeowners willing to list their properties has been increased by the coding option, it can be argued that State U has actually achieved a benefit not just from the overall listing program, but from the very acts of discrimination being complained of; if so, this makes it even more likely that state action would be found. All in all, there is a better than even chance that State U would be found to be so heavily involved with the private acts of discrimination that state action should be found in the maintenance of the list. The symbiosis here is reminiscent of that in *Burton v. Wilmington Parking Authority* (where restaurant paid rent for space in publicly-owned building, discrimination by restaurant was state action).

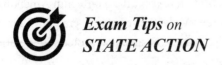

Exam Tips on STATE ACTION

You need to be on the lookout for State Action problems in any question that involves the rights of individuals (i.e., due process, equal protection, freedom of expression, freedom of religion, etc.). Remember that these constitutional guarantees only come into play when government is acting. Here are some specific things to watch for:

☞ Before you start to write about how the due process, equal protection, or other guarantee has been violated, make sure that there is "state action," i.e., that the challenged action is really **action by the government**, or at least that the challenged action can somehow be **ascribed** to the government.

☞ If a private individual is doing something that would clearly pose constitutional problems were it done by government, that's a tip off to a state action problem. Examples:

> A private apartment owner refuses to rent to a black;
>
> A private employer refuses to hire a person because of her gender;
>
> A private shopping center refuses to allow P to distribute political campaign literature.

☞ In all of these situations, there will be no state action (and thus no constitutional violation), unless additional facts are presented that somehow tie the state in to the private actor's conduct.

☞ Be alert to situations where the only action is by a private individual, but the activity in question is one that is a **"public function,"** i.e., a function **"traditionally" done by the states.** Thus you may have at least an issue of whether a "public function" is being performed if your facts involve any of the following:

> a private (but partly state-funded) **school**;
>
> a privately-operated **park**;
>
> a **political party** conducting a primary or other party business;
>
> a **"company town;"**
>
> a person taking some action typically done by the **judicial system** (e.g., a seller or lender foreclosing on collateral).

☞ Remember that today, the "public function" doctrine applies only where the function has traditionally been done **"exclusively"** by the states. This requirement knocks out a large percentage of the cases (including at least the private-school situation above).

☞ Also, be on the lookout for situations where the state is somehow heavily **"involved"** in the private actor's actions. The common scenarios for this are:

☞ The state has **"commanded"** or **"required"** the private action. (*Example: Shelley v. Kraemer*, where the state, by enforcing restrictive covenants, in effect commanded private individuals not to sell their homes to blacks.)

> ☞ *Testable issue:* May the state enforce some **neutral state law** where this has the effect of facilitating private discrimination? (*Example:* Where a private store owner refuses to serve blacks and wants them evicted, does the state's use of its trespass laws turn the property owner's action into "state action?" The answer is probably "no," as long as the state is evenhanded in how it uses the trespass law.)

☞ The state has **"encouraged"** the private action.

☞ The state has a *"symbiotic relationship"* with the private action, i.e., the state and the private actor **benefit from each other's conduct**. Classic illustration: *Burton v. Wilmington Parking Authority* — the state builds a state-operated building, and rents space in it to a restaurateur who discriminates; because the state is getting major benefits from the restaurateur's operations, his conduct is transformed into "state action."

☞ The state is heavily *"involved," "entangled"* or *"entwined"* in the activity.

   ☞ Where the state merely *licenses* the private activity, that's not enough involvement or entanglement to produce state action. (*Example:* Where government gives a liquor license to a private club, that's not enough to turn the club's discriminatory actions into state action. *Moose Lodge v. Irvis.*)

   ☞ But where state entities *participate* heavily in the private activity, and the state *recognizes* that activity as being closely related to important state concerns, this will probably be enough entanglement to make the activity state action.

   Example: A state statute provides that a private association of high schools, all of which are located within a single state, has the role of regulating interscholastic sports in the state. Most association members are public high schools, and nearly all public high schools are members. The association's activities will probably found to be so entwined with state concerns as to make the association a state actor. (*Brentwood Academy*)

CHAPTER 13

CONGRESSIONAL ENFORCEMENT OF CIVIL RIGHTS

ChapterScope

This Chapter involves several aspects of Congress' power to enforce the Amendments enacted immediately after the Civil War. The main concepts are:

■ Congress has special powers to enforce the Civil War Amendments, i.e., the 13th, 14th, and 15th Amendments.

■ Congress probably can't prohibit *purely private discrimination* under the 14th and 15th Amendments.

❏ But Congress *can* prohibit purely private discrimination under the *13th* Amendment, if it finds that the discrimination is a *"badge or incident of slavery."*

■ Congress does not have power to *define the scope* of the Civil War Amendments. Only the federal courts may do this.

❏ So Congress may not *"expand"* the meaning of these Amendments, i.e., define them in a way that causes more government action to run afoul of these Amendments.

❏ Nor may Congress *"reduce"* the scope of these Amendments. Thus once the Supreme Court says for instance, that the Equal Protection Clause prohibits a certain kind of government action, Congress can't use its enforcement powers to say, in effect, "The conduct shall no longer be deemed to be a violation of the Equal Protection Clause."

I. INTRODUCTION

A. Issues presented: This chapter examines Congress' power to *enforce* the Amendments enacted immediately after the Civil War, i.e., the Thirteenth, Fourteenth and Fifteenth Amendments. There are two main issues regarding this power:

1. **Reaching private actors:** To what extent may Congress enact legislation pursuant to these Amendments so as to reach *purely private conduct*, given that these Amendments (at least the Fourteenth and Fifteenth) only refer to conduct *by the states?*

2. **Interpreting the Amendments:** What power does Congress have to *interpret* these Amendments *differently from the Supreme Court*, with respect to: (i) *remedies* to impose for what the Court and Congress both would agree constitutes violations of these Amendments; and (ii) the *substantive content* of these rights?

B. Applicable statutes: Our focus will be upon the constitutional boundaries of Congress' power to enforce the amendments, not upon the precise interpretation of the statutes which Congress has in fact enacted. Nonetheless, a brief overview of the existing statutory framework is helpful. Our summary of this framework is done from the perspective of statutes now on the books.

1. **Civil provisions:** A number of statutes *grant civil rights* as distinguished from those imposing criminal penalties:

    a. **General equal rights:** The most general grant of civil rights is made under what is today 42 U.S.C. §1981. That section gives all persons within the United States the same right "as is enjoyed by white citizens" to *make and enforce contracts*, to sue, and to be subject to identical punishments, taxes, and other treatment by the government. This statute was originally enacted as part of the Civil Rights Act of 1866, which was premised on the Thirteenth Amendment (since the Fourteenth did not yet exist).

    b. **Property rights:** What is now 42 U.S.C. §1982 gives all United States citizens the *same property rights* as whites have, including rights of inheritance, purchase and sale and lease. This provision, too, was part of the 1866 Civil Rights Act, and was given a broad reading by the Court in *Jones v. Alfred H. Mayer Co., infra,* p. 456.

    c. **Deprivations "under color of law":** 42 U.S.C. §1983 allows a private suit for damages to be brought against any person who, *"under color of any statute"* or other law, deprives the plaintiff of *"any rights, privileges or immunities secured by the Constitution and laws."* §1983, one of the best-known of all federal statutory provisions, has often been used to bring suit against *state and local government officials who violate individuals' civil rights.* It derives from the 1871 Civil Rights Act, and relies on at least the Fourteenth Amendment, and perhaps the Thirteenth, for constitutional authority.

    d. **Private conspiracies:** Two or more persons who *conspire* to deprive anyone of *equal protection* or *equal privileges and immunities under the law*, may be subjected to civil suit under 48 U.S.C. §1985(c). This provision, which derives from the 1871 Civil Rights Act, appears to be applicable *even where there is no state action*, so long as access to a federally-guaranteed right is infringed or sought to be infringed. The constitutionality of this statute's application to conduct involving only private persons is suggested, but not made explicit, in *U.S. v. Guest, infra,* p. 454.

2. **Criminal statutes:** Two statutory provisions, deriving (like the ones above) from the post-Civil War period, provide *criminal penalties* for roughly the same types of conduct for which private civil actions are permitted by those provisions summarized in (c) and (d), respectively, above.

    a. **Color of law:** Thus the criminal analog to §1983's civil "color of law" provision is 18 U.S.C. §242, which imposes a fine or imprisonment upon any person who *"under color of any law*, statute, ordinance, regulation or custom," willfully deprives another of any rights protected by the Constitution or federal statutes, on account of *color, race or alienage*. If death results from the deprivation, life imprisonment is authorized.

    b. **Private conspiracies:** The criminal analog to §1985(c)'s civil conspiracies provision is 18 U.S.C. §241, setting criminal penalties for *conspiring* to "injure, oppress, threaten, or intimidate any citizen in the free exercise or enjoyment of any right or privilege secured to him by the Constitution or the laws of the United States."

3. **Modern statutory additions:** Major civil rights laws enacted in the 1960's have added some important new provisions. Among these are the following:

a. **Public accommodations:** Discrimination in the furnishing of ***public accommodations*** is banned, and made subject to private and governmental civil suits in the Public Accommodations Title of the Civil Rights Act of 1964, 42 U.S.C. §2000a *et seq.* This title was based on Congress' power to regulate interstate commerce, not its power to enforce the Civil War Amendments. See *supra*, p. 29.

b. **Voting:** Various provisions to ensure ***the right to vote*** were contained in the 1965 Voting Rights Act, 42 U.S.C. §1973, including measures to restrict the discriminatory use of literacy tests and other voter registration requirements. The Act is discussed in the treatment of *South Carolina v. Katzenbach, infra*, p. 464.

c. **Fair housing:** Important restrictions on the ability of private entities and individuals to discriminate in the sale or rental of ***housing*** were contained in Title VIII of the 1968 Civil Rights Act, the Fair Housing Title.

d. **Violence:** ***Violent interference*** with a person's enjoyment of his civil rights, even if it is not part of a conspiracy (as is required for application of 18 U.S.C. §241) and even if it involves no state action (as is required for 18 U.S.C. §242) is prohibited by 18 U.S.C. §245, part of the 1968 Civil Rights Act.

II. CONGRESS' POWER TO REACH PRIVATE CONDUCT

A. **Purely private conduct:** The Fourteenth and Fifteenth Amendment, by their terms, apply only to *state* interferences. As we saw in the previous chapter, the Court has (especially in recent years) read this state action requirement to impose substantial "bite." But §5 of the Fourteenth Amendment, and §2 of the Fifteenth Amendment, explicitly grant Congress the power to *enforce* each of those amendments *"by appropriate legislation."* Thus the issue arises, to what extent may Congress "appropriately" enforce the Fourteenth and Fifteenth Amendments by ***proscribing conduct which the Court would not construe to be "state action?"***

1. **Some latitude:** While the precise answer to this question has never been decided, it seems clear that Congress has at least some latitude, and that certain types of private conduct unaccompanied by state involvement may nonetheless be prohibited.

   a. **Link to state conduct:** For instance, private conduct which ***prevents state officials*** from giving equal protection or due process to others may clearly be prohibited by Congress. Similarly, private conduct which intentionally interferes with rights guaranteed to an individual by federal constitutional provisions *other than* the Fourteenth Amendment (e.g., the ***right to travel interstate***) may be barred by Congress.

   b. **Gray area:** The principal gray area is the extent to which Congress may prevent ***purely private discrimination*** by one individual against another, where no state facilities, programs or rights are directly involved. For instance, may Congress prohibit discrimination by small private social clubs that hold no state licenses?

B. **Early decision:** The first time Congress' power to regulate private discrimination was considered, that power received an extremely narrow reading by the Court. Recall that in the *Civil Rights Cases*, 109 U.S. 3 (1883), discussed *supra*, p. 432, a majority of the Court held that, since only state action could violate the Fourteenth Amendment, Congress' enforcement power ***only permitted it to restrict state action***, and not private conduct.

1. **Consequence:** Under the logic of the *Civil Rights Cases* (though this was not made explicit in the opinion), Congress did not even have the power to prevent one private individual from forcibly blocking another's exercise of the right to vote in state elections, the right to attend public schools, or other exercises of state rights. Such private conduct would presumably be in violation of state law, but it would not itself be a violation of "equal protection of the [state] laws;" only action *by* the state could be that. And Congress' enforcement power was limited to enactment of those statutes which were needed to *prevent the state* from abdicating its equal-protection obligations.

C. **The *Guest* case:** This extremely narrow view of congressional power under the Fourteenth Amendment was not re-examined until the 1960's. Then, in *U.S. v. Guest*, 383 U.S. 745 (1966), six members of the Court stated that Congress could, under §5 of the Fourteenth Amendment, reach a substantial range of *private racially discriminatory conduct*. But since three Judges did so in one concurring opinion and the other three in another, *Guest* did not produce a single majority articulation of the scope of Congress' right to reach private conduct.

1. **Facts of *Guest*:** *Guest* concerned a prosecution for criminal conspiracy under 18 U.S.C. §241 (see *supra*, p. 452). The defendants were private individuals. The first count of the indictment charged them with conspiring to interfere violently with the rights of several blacks to use state-owned facilities.

2. **Court's opinion:** The opinion for the Court, written by Justice Stewart, avoided deciding whether §241 could constitutionally be applied to racially discriminatory, but entirely private, interference with the use of public facilities, as charged in the first count. It did so by pointing to the possibility that the indictment might be claiming, although ambiguously, that *state officials participated* in the interference.

3. **Concurrences:** Six Justices, in two concurrences, were willing to go further. They thought that the first count of the indictment was constitutional even if it charged only purely-private conduct, with no participation by state officials.

   a. **Clark's concurrence:** One concurrence, by Justice Clark, reasoned that "[t]he specific language of §5 [of the Fourteenth Amendment] empowers the Congress to enact laws punishing all conspiracies — *with or without state action* — that interfere with Fourteenth Amendment rights." But he gave no explanation of *why* §5 should be read so as to dispense with any requirement of state action.

   b. **Brennan's concurrence:** Justice Brennan's separate concurrence, however, *did* deal with the question Justice Clark ducked. Brennan believed that §5 gave Congress the power to make any law which it concluded was *"reasonably necessary* to protect a right created by and arising under" the Fourteenth Amendment. Thus he would apply the same standard as applied by Chief Justice Marshall in *McCulloch v. Maryland*, in interpreting "the Necessary and Proper" Clause.

      i. **Application of test:** In Brennan's view, Congress could reasonably have concluded that prevention of *private* interference with access to state-owned facilities was a reasonably necessary means toward preventing *governmental* interference with that access. In fact, he believed that Congress could punish *all* conspiracies that interfered with Fourteenth Amendment rights, even if no state officers were involved.

D. *Morrison* wipes out the expansive interpretation of *Guest*: For 34 years after *Guest*, no one knew whether the views of the six concurring justices in *Guest* — that Congress could use its §5 remedial powers to reach purely private conduct that interfered with Fourteenth Amendment rights — represented good law. But in a case decided in 2000, ***U.S. v. Morrison***, 529 U.S. 598 (2000) (also discussed *supra,* p. 34), the Court decided by a 5-4 vote that the concurrences in *Guest* did *not* represent a holding of the Court, and should be disregarded. Consequently, it is now clear that ***it is not within Congress' §5 powers to reach purely private conduct,*** even if that conduct interferes with rights protected by the Fourteenth Amendment.

   1. **Context:** *Morrison* involved a federal statute, the Violence Against Women Act, which allowed women who had been the victims of gender-motivated violent crimes to sue the perpetrator in federal court. When the defendant attacked the statute as beyond Congress' powers, the plaintiff argued (among other things) that even if the statute reached purely private conduct, that private conduct consisted of attempts to violate women's equal protection rights, and was therefore reachable on the theory of the six concurring justices in *Guest*.

   2. **Claim rejected:** But the five-justice majority in *Morrison* squarely **rejected** this argument. The Court conceded that the three-Justice concurrence authored by Justice Brennan in *Guest* represented a real view on the merits that Congress could use its §5 powers to reach purely private conduct that interfered with Fourteenth Amendment rights. But the *Morrison* majority pointed out that the other three concurring justices in *Guest*, led by Justice Clark, had given no explanation at all for their similar views. Consequently, Clark's statement that Congress could reach purely private conduct was ***"naked dicta"*** that could not be added to the opinions of the Brennan group for pruposes of deriving a constitutional holding.

      a. **Conclusion:** Therefore, the *Morrison* majority concluded, *Guest* said nothing authoritative about whether Congress could reach purely private conduct, and the *Civil Rights Cases* still represented prevailing law. Under the *Civil Rights Cases*, purely private action that interferes with rights protected by the Fourteenth Amendment is simply beyond Congress' §5 remedial powers.

E. Current state of the law: So here's what the present law seems to be regarded Congress' use of its Fourteenth Amendment §5 powers to reach conduct by private individuals:

   1. **Conduct not relating to public officials:** Where Congress tries to reach purely private conduct that has ***nothing to do with state officials***, it's now clear as the result of *Morrison* that Congress cannot do this under its §5 enforcement powers.

      Example: In *Morrison* itself, we saw that Congress could not use its §5 remedial powers to give private citizen *A* a federal cause of action against private citizen *B* merely because *B* practiced gender discrimination against *A* of a sort that would have been a Fourteenth Amendment violation had *B* been acting under color of state law. The same would clearly be true if *B* was a private individual who practiced *racial* discrimination against *A* (e.g., *B* refused to rent an apartment to *A* on racial grounds, and Congress tried to use its §5 powers to give *A* a federal cause of action against *B*).[1]

   2. **Interference with state officials:** On the other hand, suppose that Congress merely prohibits private individuals from ***interfering with state officials' attempts*** to furnish equal protection or due process. Here, it seems clear that Congress' action *does* fall within its §5 remedial powers, notwithstanding *Morrison*.

Example: Suppose that Congress makes it a federal crime for a private individual to prevent or attempt to prevent a public School Board official from complying with a federal court's school-desegregation order. Since the private action being regulated is closely tied to state action (the school board desegregation efforts), it seems clear that Congress has acted validly under its Fourteenth Amendment §5 remedial powers.

3. **Private-state interaction:** Finally, where a private party acts in *conjunction with a state official*, it is quite clear that Congress may punish the private conduct. In fact, 18 U.S.C. § 242 (the statute preventing discriminatory action committed "under color of law") is applicable even to the private actors in this situation.

   a. *Price* **case:** For instance, in *U.S. v. Price*, 383 U.S. 787 (1966), the Court held that private individuals who acted together with local law enforcement officials in the infamous 1964 murder of three civil rights workers near Philadelphia, Mississippi, acted "under color of law" (and could therefore be charged under § 242) even though they themselves were not law enforcement officers.

F. **The Thirteenth Amendment and private conduct:**   §1 of the *Thirteenth* Amendment provides that "[n]either slavery nor involuntary servitude, except as a punishment for crime ... shall exist within the United States. ... " §2 gives Congress the power to "enforce this [amendment] by appropriate legislation." Because the Thirteenth Amendment, unlike the Fourteenth and Fifteenth, is *not explicitly limited to governmental action*, the Amendment has proved to be a useful source of congressional power to reach certain private conduct.

   1. **Originally narrowly construed:**   The Court has always conceded that Congress could reach purely private conduct under the Thirteenth Amendment; this was one of the holdings of the *Civil Rights Cases*, discussed *supra*, p. 432. However, the Court, beginning with those cases, took a very narrow view of the *type* of conduct which the Thirteenth Amendment forbade. The Amendment, and any congressional statutes enforcing it, could only deal with slavery and its *"badges and incidents"*; private *discrimination*, even in the furnishing of transportation, hotels and other accommodations, did not constitute a badge of slavery prohibited by the Thirteenth Amendment.

   2. **Broadened in *Jones v. Mayer*:**   This narrow view of the Thirteenth Amendment's scope was dramatically broadened in a startling case, *Jones v. Alfred H. Mayer Co.*, 392 U.S. 409 (1968). That case held that Congress had the power, under the Thirteenth Amendment, *"rationally to determine what are the badges and incidents of slavery."* Furthermore, it held, Congress' definition of those badges and incidents could rationally be a very *broad* one, broad enough to encompass private racial discrimination in *real estate transactions*.

      a. **Facts:**   In *Jones*, plaintiffs complained that defendant (a private developer) refused to sell them a house solely because they were black. Plaintiffs claimed that this was a violation of 42 U.S.C. §1982, which provides that "[a]ll citizens of the United States

---

1. Remember, we're talking here only about whether Congress' *Fourteenth Amendment* enforcement powers can be used. In the rental situation, other congressional powers, such as the Commerce power and the *Thirteenth* Amendment's enforcement power (see *infra*, p. 456), could clearly be used. That's why, for instance, 42 U.S.C. §1982's grant of equal rights to "inherit, purchase, lease, sell, hold, and convey real and personal property" without racial discrimination is clearly still valid notwithstanding *Morrison* — it's almost certainly valid under the Commerce power, and certainly valid under the 13th Amendment (see *Jones v. Alfred H. Mayer Co.*, *infra*, p. 456).

shall have the same right, in every State and Territory, as is enjoyed by white citizens thereof to inherit, purchase, lease, sell, hold, and convey real and personal property." §1982 derives from the 1866 Civil Rights Act, which was enacted solely in reliance on the Thirteenth Amendment, since the Fourteenth had not yet been enacted. Defendant argued that even if §1982 was not intended to apply to private conduct (which Defendant claimed it was not), such conduct could not constitutionally be reached under the Thirteenth Amendment.

b. Holding: The Supreme Court disagreed, finding that the statute was *within Congress' power under the Thirteenth Amendment*. §2 of the Amendment, giving Congress enforcement powers, allowed Congress to pass "all laws necessary and proper for abolishing all badges and incidents of slavery in the United States" (quoting the *Civil Rights Cases*). And this section gave Congress the right rationally to determine *what the badges and incidents of slavery are*. This "rationality" test was satisfied here, since it was not irrational of Congress to conclude that barriers to enjoyment of real property were badges of slavery; "when racial discrimination herds men into ghettos and makes their ability to buy property turn on the color of their skin, then it too is a relic of slavery."

c. Potentially broad impact: *Jones* seems to acknowledge Congress' power to define the "badges and incidents of slavery" in almost any way it wishes, so long as the definition is rational.

d. Possible limitations: However, this view of *Jones* seems unduly broad. For instance, while Congress' power to define "slavery and its incidents" may indeed be broad, it is not clear whether Congress may treat anything other than *racially motivated* (or *ethnically* motivated) discrimination as coming within the Amendment.

i. Protection of whites: It does seem clear that Congress may use its Thirteenth Amendment enforcement powers to protect *groups other than blacks* against racial discrimination.

ii. Non-racial discrimination: Apart from discrimination based on race, Congress may probably use the Thirteenth Amendment to prohibit private discrimination on grounds of *ancestry*, or *ethnic characteristics*. However, the Court has never squarely addressed the issue of whether the Thirteenth Amendment can support legislation banning these types of discrimination.

iii. Other types of discrimination: The Court has never explicitly indicated that Congress may use the Thirteenth Amendment to prohibit invidious discrimination on *grounds other than race, ancestry, or ethnic background*. So, for instance, it is highly questionable whether Congress could, say, ban purely private discrimination against *gays*, lawyers, or other unpopular groups under authority of the Thirteenth Amendment.

iv. Purposeful discrimination: In any event, whatever discrimination is banned under authority of the Thirteenth Amendment must probably be *purposeful* and *invidious*.

3. Self-executing scope of amendment: Keep in mind that this broad view of the "badges and incidents of slavery" applies only where Congress has enacted a *statute* under its powers to enforce the Thirteenth Amendment. Where the *direct*, self-executing meaning of the

Amendment itself, absent any statute, is concerned, the Court gives a very narrow reading to "badges and incidents of slavery" — perhaps only peonage is included.

> **Example 1:** Suppose that a state passes a law stating that "any owner of residential real estate may discriminate on the basis of race in the sale or lease of that property." Assume that Congress has not passed any statute which would conflict with this state statute. A court probably could ***not*** strike down the state statute on the grounds that it violated the Thirteenth Amendment — that Amendment has practically no self-executing scope.

> **Example 2:** Suppose that a state passed a statute providing that where one person owes a debt to another and cannot pay, the former may be required to work at minimum wage for the latter until the debt is paid off, and that a person who refuses to do such mandatory labor shall be sent to prison. Even in the absence of a federal statute prohibiting this kind of compulsory work, a court probably would hold that the state statute violates the Thirteenth Amendment — the self-executing scope of the Thirteenth Amendment, while very narrow, probably does cover true "peonage," and this state statute would probably be held to involve peonage.

G. Violation of other constitutional rights: So far, we have considered only private conduct which may be barred by congressional statutes relying on the Civil War Amendments. But there are also some rights which are secured by ***other constitutional provisions*** (that is, apart from the Thirteenth, Fourteenth and Fifteenth Amendments) which are applicable against private, not just state, interference.

1. **Right to travel:** Perhaps the most important of these is the ***right to travel from state to state***. See, e.g., *U.S. v. Guest*, 383 U.S. 745 (1966) (other aspects of which are discussed *supra*, pp. 396-98), in which the Court held that Congress was authorized to punish purely private conspiracies to interfere with the exercise of this right (although the Court did not point to any specific constitutional provision as being the source of this right).

2. **Other examples:** Other constitutional rights that are applicable against private interference include: the right to ***vote*** in ***federal primary*** and ***general elections***, the right to ***inform federal officials of violations of federal law***, and the right to ***assemble to petition Congress*** for a redress of grievances. See Justice Harlan's concurrence in *U.S. v. Guest*, 383 U.S. 745 (1966), for his catalogue of such rights.

   a. **Tie-in with civil rights statutes:** These rights are ***not*** necessarily ***self-executing***. That is, it is not clear that one private citizen may recover damages against another, or obtain an injunction against him, for violation of any of these rights, unless a congressional statute so provides. But the post-Civil War civil rights statutes, especially the criminal and civil conspiracy provisions, 18 U.S.C. §§241 and 1985(c) respectively, authorize the federal courts to give civil and criminal relief for certain types of violations of ***any*** constitutional provision, not merely the provisions of the Thirteenth, Fourteenth and Fifteenth Amendments.

III. CONGRESS' POWER TO REMEDY VIOLATIONS OF THE CIVIL WAR AMENDMENTS

A. General problem: We turn now to several questions about the extent of Congress' powers under the Civil War amendments extends:

[1] What kinds of explicitly "remedial" actions may Congress take? (We consider this question generally in Paragraph (B) below, and specifically in the case of voting rights in Paragraph (C), *infra*, p. 460.)

[2] If Congress disagrees with the Supreme Court about the ***proper scope*** of the rights guaranteed by the Thirteenth, Fourteenth or Fifteenth Amendment, may Congress use its remedial powers to ***change the meaning and scope*** of these guarantees? (We discuss this in its own section, section IV, *infra*, p. 464.)

[3] Under what circumstances may Congress ***abrogate*** the states' ***Eleventh Amendment immunity***, so as to let ***private citizens recover money damages*** from a state that violates a federal statute enacted under authority of the Civil War Amendments? (On this question, see section V, *infra*, p. 467).

As to (1), the brief answer is, "a very broad, but not unlimited, range of measures." As to (2), the brief answer is "no." As to (3), the brief answer is, "only if Congress' response is proportional to the state's threatened constitutional violations."

B. Congress' broad "remedial" powers: It is clear that congressional power to adopt ***"remedial"*** legislation concerning the Thirteenth, Fourteenth and Fifteenth Amendments is ***extremely broad,*** though not unlimited.

1. **Reference to "Necessary and Proper" clause:** Congress' power to enforce these Amendments is to be judged generally by reference to the ***"Necessary and Proper"*** clause (*supra*, p. 18). That is, as long as the ***means*** chosen by Congress are ***"rationally related"*** to achieving an objective that one of these Amendments is designed to fulfill, Congress has not exceeded its enforcement authority.[2]

2. **Can act based on state law's effect rather than purpose:** For instance, if Congress reasonably fears that the ***effect*** of a state law will be interferences with a right guaranteed by one of these three Amendments, Congress can prohibit the state law from being enforced. That's true even if it's clear that the members of the state legislature did not, when they enacted the law, have a ***purpose*** of promoting violations of any of the Amendments.

> **Example:** Congress enacts the Voting Rights Act (discussed extensively below) pursuant to its powers to enforce the Fifteenth Amendment, which prohibits racial discrimination in voting. One section of the V.R.A. says that certain states and local governments with a history of intentional discrimination in voting must get federal pre-approval before making any change to the state's voting regulations, if the "effect" of the change may be to abridge voting rights on the basis of race. Rome, Georgia, a city that is required to get pre-approval for various voting-related changes, argues that since §1 of the Fifteenth Amendment prohibits only intentional discrimination, Congress has exceeded its §2 enforcement powers by prohibiting practices based solely on the practices' possible discriminatory effect.
>
> *Held*, Rome loses. The Court will assume, without deciding, that the city is correct in its contention that §1 of the Fifteenth Amendment itself bars only state action that is

---

2. As we'll see below, there is one important limitation on this principle, the "congruent and proportional" standard for judging Congress's exercise of its Fourteenth Amendment enforcement powers; see *City of Boerne v. Flores*, *infra*, p. 464.

intended to discriminate in voting based on race. But even if that's true, Congress has **broad discretion** in choosing what enforcement methods to use, at least where the defendant has previously violated one of the Civil War Amendments — Congress must merely act rationally in making that choice. Here, "Congress could rationally have concluded that, because electoral changes by jurisdictions with a demonstrable history of intentional racial discrimination in voting create the risk of purposeful discrimination, it was proper to prohibit changes that have a discriminatory impact." *City of Rome v. U.S.*, 446 U.S. 156 (1980).

C. **The Voting Rights Act:** Most cases about how far Congress' "remedial" powers extend under the Civil War amendments have concerned the constitutionality of *voting-rights* measures adopted by Congress beginning in the 1960's. The most important such measure is the *Voting Rights Act*, the first version of which was enacted by Congress in 1965.

1. **Historical background of the V.R.A.:** Reconstruction-era efforts by Congress to eradicate racial discrimination in voting in the South were only marginally successful, and most of the federal statutory provisions were repealed in 1894. Meanwhile, many of the southern states enacted *literacy tests* and other tests that were often used to deny blacks the franchise. The Fifteenth Amendment was of course theoretically available for relief in these situations, but litigation under it was generally time-consuming and difficult. Even when states or counties *were* ordered by the courts to eliminate one discriminatory practice or another, they were often able to devise some new scheme by which to perpetuate racial discrimination in voting. Initial statutory efforts by Congress in 1957, 1960, and 1964 proved largely ineffective.

2. **Voting Rights Act of 1965:** Therefore, Congress enacted the *Voting Rights Act of 1965* (the *V.R.A.*), designed to eradicate racial discrimination in voting in part by *preventing it from occurring*, as opposed to detecting and punishing it after the fact.

   a. **Suspension of any "test or device":** The most important aspect of the Act, from the perspective of Congress' power to enforce the Fifteenth Amendment, was its treatment of *literacy tests* and other *voter eligibility standards*. The Act *suspended*, for an initial period of five years, literacy and similar voter-eligibility tests in any state or political subdivision, if the U.S. Justice Department made an administrative finding that the jurisdiction *had used such tests* as of the last election, and had had an unusually *low voter turnout* in that election.

      i. **No intent required:** Thus the V.R.A. applied special anti-discrimination administrative rules to certain states and local governments, regardless of whether the jurisdiction had ever been found to have had an *intent* to discriminate on racial grounds.

3. **Upheld in *South Carolina v. Katzenbach*:** The V.R.A.'s scheme of suspending all literacy and other voting tests in pre-identified states was *upheld* by the Supreme Court in *South Carolina v. Katzenbach*, 383 U.S. 301 (1966).

   a. **"Rationality" standard:** The Court in *Katzenbach* construed Congress' power to enforce the Fifteenth Amendment *broadly*. It held Congress could use *"any rational means"* to enforce that Amendment's ban on racial discrimination in voting.

   b. **Ban on tests rational:** The particular congressional scheme at issue in *Katzenbach* — banning tests or devices in any jurisdiction where they coincided with less-than-

50% registration — *satisfied the rationality standard.* This was so because there was evidence presented to Congress that all of the areas known to have practiced racial discrimination in voting shared these two characteristics. Also, the use of tests or devices clearly furnished a means of carrying out racial discrimination, and low registration figures were an obvious symptom of such discrimination.

c. **Court's own view of literacy tests:** *South Carolina v. Katzenbach* demonstrates that Congress' remedial powers under §2 of the Fifteenth Amendment permit Congress to **outlaw practices which the Court would not on its own find to violate §1 of that Amendment,** as long as these practices are **reasonably closely related** to practices that *would* violate §1. (But, as we'll see from the 2013 *Shelby County* case, if Congress wants to outlaw practices that don't necessarily manifest a discriminatory intent, Congress must be acting based on "current conditions.")

d. **Discriminatory effect:** A post-*Katzenbach* case on the Voting Rights Act confirms that Congress's §2 remedial powers give it the power to ban even practices that are discriminatory **only in their effect,** not their purpose. See *Rome v. U.S.*, 446 U.S. 156 (1980), discussed *supra*, p. 460. In other words, if Congress reasonably fears that a state will commit intentional discrimination, Congress can "remedy" that discrimination **in advance,** by banning a given practice that would have the **effect** of hurting minority voters, whether or not there's proof that the jurisdiction proposing to use that practice did so for discriminatory **purposes.**

4. **Obligation to rely on current data (*Shelby County v. Holder*):** Nearly everyone would agree that the massive, purposeful racial discrimination by the southern states that gave rise to the original 1965 version of the V.R.A. has dramatically **decreased** in recent years. Does the passage of long periods — and the consequent large **reduction in purposeful discrimination** — mean that a specific remedy that once fell within Congress's Fifteenth Amendment enforcement powers might now **exceed those powers**?

A major 2013 decision shows that the answer in some instances is *"yes."* That is, if in the present era Congress wants to use its Fifteenth Amendment enforcement powers to prevent future violations of the Amendment — rather than punish past violations — Congress must **adjust the measures it uses** to reflect **current rather than historical voting circumstances.** The decision is **Shelby County v. Holder**, 133 S.Ct. 2612 (2013), a 5-4 decision, which because of its overruling of a major and long-standing part of the V.R.A. is worthy of detailed discussion.

a. **Summary of holding:** The Court held in *Shelby County* that because Congress relied only on **40-year-old data** when it identified certain state and local governments and required them to get federal "preclearance" for many voting-related changes, Congress exceeded the scope of its Fifteenth Amendment enforcement powers. So these preclearance requirements of the V.R.A. — which in many ways are the heart of the V.R.A. — are as of this writing **unenforceable**, and will remain so unless and until Congress passes a new law using much more up-to-date voter information as the basis for identifying covered jurisdictions.

b. **The preclearance procedures:** You can't understand *Shelby County* without a fairly detailed understanding of the V.R.A.'s *"preclearance"* scheme. Under that scheme, mainly specified in §5 of the Act, any state or subdivision of a state that has been determined to have a certain *history* of voter discrimination based on race or color cannot make any change to its registration or other electoral processes without getting advance approval (i.e., "preclearance") from the U.S. Justice Department.

i.   **"Coverage formula":** An integral part of the preclearance scheme is the idea of a ***"coverage formula,"*** which the V.R.A. uses to determine *which jurisdictions* are to be required to preclear their voting-related changes. When the V.R.A. was first passed in 1965, §4 of the Act specified a formula to be applied by the U.S. Justice Department for *identifying* those states or subdivisions of states likely to have previously practiced large-scale racial discrimination.

ii. **Consequence of being on list:**   Under the original V.R.A. (as well as its subsequent versions), if a state or local government appeared on the Justice Department's coverage list, the government ***could not change any of its voting procedures*** — ranging from minor changes like moving a polling place or changing the hours for voting, all the way to major changes like redistricting — without getting ***preclearance*** either from the Justice Department or from a federal court in Washington DC.

iii. **Initial list:**   The initial coverage list compiled by the Justice Department soon after the V.R.A.'s 1965 passage included six entire states, all in the deep South — ***Alabama, Georgia, Louisiana, Mississippi, South Carolina and Virginia*** — as well as several counties in other states. (Although the coverage list changed slightly in the ensuing decades, all of these six states remained covered as of the 2013 *Shelby County* decision, and a couple of new ones, such as Texas, were added.)

iv. **Original "sunset" provision:**   In the initial 1965 V.R.A., these preclearance procedures were set to ***expire automatically after five years***, on the theory that the voting discrimination to which they were addressed would likely have been remedied by then.

   (1) **Reauthorized:**   But in the ensuing decades, Congress repeatedly ***reauthorized*** the preclearance and coverage-formula provisions.

   (2) **Coverage formula unchanged:**   In what became the critical aspect of the *Shelby County* litigation, Congress in the 2006 reauthorization ***maintained the coverage formula as it had stood in 1975***. This meant that the sole factors used to determine what jurisdictions would be subject to preclearance were whether the jurisdiction had ***used a voting test in 1972*** and whether the jurisdiction had had less than 50% voter registration or turnout in ***that year***. So no post-1972 developments could count at all, either to include or exclude a jurisdiction.

c.   **Shelby County's suit:**   Now, on to the *Shelby County* case. Shelby County, in Alabama, brought a challenge to the constitutionality of both §4's coverage formula (which included all local governments in Alabama) and §5's preclearance procedures. The county claimed that each of these sections went beyond Congress' powers. The lower federal courts rejected the challenge, concluding that both of the sections were proper exercises of Congress' Fifteenth Amendment enforcement powers.

d.   **Majority strikes down §4:** The Supreme Court, by a 5-4 vote, ***struck down*** §4's ***coverage formula.*** The majority opinion was by Chief Justice Roberts. He was joined by the three other conservatives (Scalia, Thomas and Alito), and got the decisive fifth vote from the frequent swing justice, Kennedy.

   i. **Nature of decision:** Roberts did not decide whether the basic §5 *preclearance* procedure was constitutional. But he held that the *particular coverage formula* used in §4 was beyond Congress' Fifteenth Amendment enforcement powers, because that formula was *based on 40-year-old data* and thus *did not adequately reflect current conditions.*

   ii. **Originally a valid approach:** Roberts agreed that when the original coverage-formula approach to preclearance was enacted in 1965, it was a *proper exercise* of Congress' powers: requiring certain states to obtain federal permission before enacting any change to their voting laws was *"strong medicine,"* but Congress had properly determined that this step was needed to combat *"entrenched racial discrimination"* in voting. And the coverage formula — "the means of linking the exercise of the unprecedented authority with the problem that warranted it" — *"made sense."*

   iii. **"Our country has changed":** But, Roberts said, *"our country has changed"* since 1965.

   (1) Change in voter turnout patterns: He pointed out that Census Bureau data from the most recent (2012) elections showed that African-American voter turnout *exceeded* white voter turnout in five of the six states originally (and still) covered by the preclearance requirement, and was only one half of one percent behind the white turnout in the sixth state.

   iv. **Current data not used:** Then came the nub of Roberts' analysis: Congress, in the recent 2006 reauthorization of the V.R.A., *had not taken into account "current conditions"* when it reenacted the previously-used coverage formula. It was true that Congress had conducted extensive *hearings* prior to the reauthorization. But Congress had not *used this record* to design a new formula based on current conditions. Instead, Congress had "reenacted *a formula based on 40-year-old facts having no logical relation to the present day."*[3] The "extraordinary and unprecedented features" of the V.R.A. had been reauthorized *"as if nothing had changed."*

   (1) Conclusion: This failure by Congress to use data reflecting current conditions made the coverage formula unconstitutional, he said.

   e. **Ginsburg's dissent:** Justice Ginsburg *dissented*, in an opinion joined by the Court's three other liberals, Breyer, Sotomayor and Kagan. Ginsburg's two major themes were that (1) the majority had failed to give the *requisite deference* to Congress's judgment about what means were required to combat discrimination in voting; and (2) the V.R.A. as reauthorized was far better calibrated to current conditions than the majority gave it credit for being.

   i. **Summary:** In summary, Ginsburg said, Congress' own judgment about what means fell within its power to enforce the Civil War amendments "by appropriate

---

3. This statement is factually correct: no event occurring after the 1972 elections had any effect on what jurisdictions would be covered by the formula. See *supra*, p. 462.

legislation" merited the Court's "***utmost respect.***" The Court "errs egregiously" by overriding Congress' decision.

f. **Significance:** *Shelby County* means that unless and until Congress is able to ***agree on a new coverage formula***, the preclearance regime of §5 might as well not exist, since ***no jurisdiction can be subject to it.***

   i. **Conduct of elections:** Most observers think that it's very unlikely that Congress will be able to ***agree on a new coverage formula*** anytime soon. (That's the reason, politically speaking, why the existing formula was left unchanged in the 2006 reauthorization, even though huge majorities in both houses voted for reauthorization.)

   (1) **Tougher Voter ID rules:** The unenforceability of pre-clearance means that all states and subdivisions are now free to ***make whatever changes they wish to their election procedures*** without seeking advanced federal approval. In the aftermath of *Shelby County*, the most dramatic impact of the decision has been that several states that had previously been subject to preclearance have enacted or announced more rigorous ***voter identification*** requirements. These include measures such as requiring a ***government-issued photo ID*** as a prerequisite for registration and prohibiting same-day voter registration. Some of these states have also moved to ***limit early voting.*** See generally, *NY Times*, August 13, 2013 (p. A11) and August 8, 2013 (p. A1).

IV. CONGRESS' POWER TO REDEFINE THE MEANING AND SCOPE OF CONSTITUTIONAL GUARANTEES

A. **Substantive modifications:** Most of the time, when Congress claims to be using its power to enforce the Civil War amendments, Congress is clearly acting for ***"remedial"*** purposes — that is, the statute is designed to combat what, by the Court's own opinions, constitute past or prospective violations of these Amendments. Even in *Shelby County*, although the Court found that Congress went beyond its powers, there was no doubt that Congress was seeking mainly to prevent what the Court agreed would have been violations of the Fifteenth Amendment.

But other legislation enacted by Congress from time to time under its Civil War Amendment enforcement powers is harder to justify on a "remedial" theory. This latter type of legislation seems to constitute an attempt by Congress to ***redefine the meaning and scope of constitutional guarantees themselves.*** Can Congress do this?

1. **Congress may not redefine scope of guarantees:** After decades of uncertainty, the Court in 1997 finally decided that Congress may ***not*** do this — ***it's up to the Court alone, not Congress, to define the scope of constitutional rights,*** even rights (such as those given by the Fourteenth Amendment) as to which Congress has an explicit remedial power.

2. ***Boerne v. Flores:*** The landmark case in which the Court found that Congress has ***no right to specify the substantive contours of constitutional rights*** was ***City of Boerne v. Flores***, 521 U.S. 507 (1997). In that case, the Court held that Congress could not use its Fourteenth Amendment remedial powers to prevent local governments from unintentionally burdening individuals' religious freedom in certain ways. The decision's effect was to pre-

vent Congress from effectively overruling a prior Supreme Court decision about the meaning of the Free Exercise clause.

a. Statutory and caselaw background: Before we can understand *Boerne*, we have to understand a bit about that prior Court decision, and Congress' response to it.

   i. Prior Court decision: In 1990, the Supreme Court decided *Employment Division v. Smith* (*infra*, p. 700), a case about the meaning of the First Amendment's guarantee of the free exercise of religion. The Court reversed its prior doctrine, and held that where a state enacts a criminal ban that is generally applicable, the state may automatically enforce that ban — without any balancing of the government's interest against the individual's interest — even where the ban has the effect of substantially interfering with an individual's exercise of his religion. (The ban at issue in *Smith* prevented Native Americans from making their traditional religious use of the drug peyote.)

   ii. Congress' response: The *Smith* decision was very unpopular. Congress responded in 1993 by overwhelmingly passing the "Religious Freedom Restoration Act" (RFRA). The RFRA forced federal, state and local governments to apply pre-*Smith* law, by which no government action that had the effect of "substantially burdening" a person's exercise of religion could be taken unless that action was the least restrictive means of accomplishing a "compelling governmental interest." (In other words, Congress was effectively saying that any governmental action that substantially burdened the exercise of religion had to survive strict scrutiny.)

   iii. Based on Congress' Fourteenth Amendment remedial power: In applying its new rule to state and local governments, Congress relied on its Fourteenth Amendment remedial powers: since the First Amendment (including the guarantee of free exercise of religion) is made applicable to the states through the Fourteenth Amendment's guarantee of due process (see *supra*, p. 164), Congress reasoned that it could tell the states how to enforce that free-exercise guarantee as a means of "enforcing" due process.

b. Result: In *Boerne v. Flores*, the Supreme Court held that the RFRA was ***unconstitutional***. Writing for a 6-3 majority, Justice Kennedy said that "[Congress] has been given the power 'to enforce,' ***not the power to determine what constitutes a constitutional violation.***" (In fact, even the three dissenters agreed that Congress did not have the power to define substantive aspects of the Fourteenth Amendment.)

   i. Rejection of *Katzenbach v. Morgan*: Justice Kennedy admitted that there was language in a prior Court opinion, *Katzenbach v. Morgan*, 384 U.S. 641 (1966), which he said "could be interpreted as acknowledging a power in Congress to enact legislation that expands the rights contained in §1 of the Fourteenth Amendment." But he said that this was not the best interpretation of what *Katzenbach* was saying.

   ii. Effects would be unbounded: Kennedy then argued that allowing Congress to expand or contract the scope of constitutional guarantees would produce an unstable, easily-changed Constitution: "If Congress could define its own powers by altering the Fourteenth Amendment's meaning, no longer would the Constitution be 'superior paramount law, unchangeable by ordinary means.' It would be 'on a level with ordinary legislative acts, and, like other acts, . . . alterable when the legislature shall please to alter it' [citing *Marbury v. Madison*]. Under this approach, it is difficult to conceive of a principle that would limit congressional power. . . . Shifting legislative majorities could change the Constitution and effectively circumvent the difficult and detailed amendment process contained in Article V."

iii. RFRA struck down: Justice Kennedy then concluded that the RFRA in fact modified the scope of the free exercise clause, rather than merely enforcing that clause.

(1) Congress can sometimes prohibit state statutes: Kennedy acknowledged that Congress could sometimes prevent states from enacting certain types of statutes that were not facially unconstitutional, as a method of preventing likely constitutional violations. For instance, in the Voting Rights Act provision upheld in *Katzenbach v. Morgan*, Congress could, and did, prohibit states with a history of voting-rights violations from applying literacy tests.

(2) The "congruence and proportionality" test: Kennedy then set forth a new test for when Congress has gone beyond its Fourteenth Amendment §5 remedial powers: He conceded that Congress must have "wide latitude" in determining where the line is between an appropriate remedial provision and an improper substantive re-definition of a Fourteenth Amendment right. But, he said, "there must be a *congruence and proportionality* between the injury to be prevented or remedied and the means adopted to that end."

(3) RFRA out of proportion: But the RFRA, Kennedy said, flunked this "congruence and proportionality" test. It was "so *out of proportion* to [any] supposed remedial or preventive object that it cannot be understood as responsive to, or designed to prevent, unconstitutional behavior. It appears, instead, to attempt a substantive change in constitutional protections." Therefore, it was invalid.

iv. Dissent: Three Justices dissented in *Boerne*. But even the three dissenters agreed that Congress can't expand or contract the scope of constitutional guarantees, even the scope of the Fourteenth Amendment guarantees as to which Congress has an explicit remedial power. (These Justices dissented only because they disagreed with the *Smith* decision, and therefore didn't believe that Congress was in fact modifying the scope of the Free-Exercise clause from what these dissenters believed that scope should be.)

c. Significance: The main significance of *Boerne*, taken together with Eleventh Amendment cases decided in its aftermath (like *Kimel v. Florida Bd. of Regents, infra*, p. 468), is to establish two related propositions, both captured in the above-noted phrase that Congress' use of its enforcement powers under § 5 of the 14th Amendment must be *"congruent and proportional"* to the harm that's being remedied:

[1] Congress has power under § 5 of the 14th Amendment to allow private plaintiffs to sue the state *only if Congress properly found widespread unconstitutional state conduct in the area in question,* and ...

[2] Even if Congress properly found such widespread unconstitutional conduct by the state, Congress must choose *narrowly-tailored methods* for combating the state conduct.

V. CONGRESS' POWER TO ABROGATE THE ELEVENTH AMENDMENT, AND THUS AUTHORIZE PRIVATE DAMAGE SUITS AGAINST THE STATES FOR DISCRIMINATION

A. **Private money-damage suits against states for discrimination:** Congress often prohibits a certain type of *discrimination*, and then attempts to make *state and local governments*, not just private individuals, obey the prohibition. Sometimes, Congress goes even further, and attempts to *give private individuals the right to bring private actions* for *money damages* against a *state or local government* that commits the prohibited discrimination.

  1. **Significance of Eleventh Amendment:** But because of the existence of the *Eleventh Amendment* (described below), it will often turn out that Congress *has overstepped its boundaries* by such an attempt to let private individuals sue state and local governments for discrimination.

  2. **Must use Civil War Amendment remedial powers:** As we'll see in a minute, if Congress wants to subject the states to private money-damage suits for violating federal anti-discrimination laws, Congress *must act under its Civil War Amendment enforcement powers*, not under its other powers such as the Commerce Clause. That means that a special restriction the Court has placed on Congress' powers to enforce the Civil War amendments significantly limits Congress' ability to let private citizens sue state governments for discrimination.

B. **The Eleventh Amendment:** The Eleventh Amendment says, in brief, that the *states are immune* from being sued for *money damages by private citizens in federal court*. We discuss the Amendment in much greater detail later in this outline (see p. 746).

  1. **Congress' power to abrogate the immunity:** It's always been clear, however, that Congress has in some circumstances the power to *abrogate* the states' Eleventh Amendment immunity from private suits. But the Supreme Court's view of how and when Congress can do so has changed over the years.

    a. **Cannot use Commerce powers:** Originally, nearly everyone thought that Congress could use its extremely broad *Commerce Clause* powers to abrogate the states' Eleventh Amendment immunity. That is, it was thought that Congress could ban a particular type of discrimination by use of its Commerce powers, and under those same powers (i) require the states to comply with the ban, and (ii) strip their Eleventh Amendment immunity so that private citizens could sue the state for violation of the federal ban. But in the 1996 case of *Seminole Tribe v. Florida* (discussed further *infra*, p. 748), the Court surprised the world by holding that the Commerce powers *cannot* serve as the basis for a congressional abrogation of the Eleventh Amendment.

    b. **Can use Civil War Amendment powers:** On the other hand, it's always been clear that Congress *may* rely on its *Civil War Amendment remedial powers* as the source of authority for a general anti-discrimination statute. And under those powers (unlike the Commerce power), Congress can not only ban discrimination that would violate the Civil War amendments, but can subject state governments to the ban, and *abrogate the states' Eleventh Amendment immunity*, so as to let private victims sue a discriminating state for damages.

2. **"Congruent and proportional" rule:** But when Congress wants to regulate the states and subject them to private damage suits, there's an important rub. Remember that when Congress purports to use its Civil War Amendment enforcement powers (at least its Fourteenth Amendment powers), there must be a *"congruence and proportionality"* between the constitutional injury that Congress is trying to prevent or redress, and the means that Congress has chosen. (That's the key holding of *Boerne v. Flores*, *supra*, p. 464.)

   a. **Consequence:** This "congruence and proportionality" rule can easily get in Congress' way. Suppose Congress prohibits a certain form of discrimination (e.g., age discrimination in employment), includes state governments within the ban, and then purports to strip the states of their Eleventh Amendment immunity so that state employees can sue the state for damages if the state discriminates against them. If the Supreme Court then decides that Congress used a remedy so broad that it was not "congruent and proportional to" the problem, then Congress's attempt to abrogate the Eleventh Amendment immunity will be *invalid*, and employees won't in fact be able to sue the states for damages even though that was Congress' intent.

C. **Age and disability discrimination:** This scenario — Congress fails in its attempt to make the states liable in private money-damage suits alleging discrimination — has in fact unfolded on several occasions. For instance, in a pair of decisions the Court held that when Congress tried to make the states (acting as employers) liable in federal court for *age and disability discrimination*, Congress *exceeded* its Fourteenth Amendment §5 remedial powers. *Kimel v. Florida Bd. of Regents*, 528 U.S. 62 (2000) and *Bd. of Trustees of Univ. of Alabama v. Garrett*, 531 U.S. 356 (2001). We'll discuss *Kimel* first.

   1. **The ADEA statute (*Kimel*):** Back in the 1960s, Congress passed the Age Discrimination In Employment Act (ADEA), which prohibits various forms of age discrimination in employment. Congress expressly subjected the states to the ADEA's requirements when they act as employers. And for quite awhile, state employees often successfully sued the states in federal court for damages for age discrimination based on ADEA violations.

      a. **State arguments after *Seminole Tribe* and *Boerne*:** But after the 1996 decision in *Seminole Tribe* and the 1997 decision in *Boerne v. Flores*, states started defending these private ADEA suits with the following pair of arguments:

         [1] the states can be liable for ADEA violations only if Congress was acting properly under its power to enforce the equal protection clause of the Fourteenth Amendment (since that's the only clause of the Thirteenth, Fourteenth and Fifteenth Amendments that even arguably has anything to do with age discrimination); and

         [2] Congress didn't find that the states were *significant violators of equal protection* when they discriminated on the basis of age, so making the states obey the ADEA as a means of combating equal protection violations was not a "congruent and proportional" response to an equal protection problem, as required by *Boerne v. Flores*.

      b. **States win:** In *Kimel*, the state of Florida *prevailed* with this 2-pronged argument. The only real question was whether argument [2] would convince the Court. Five members of the Court concluded that the argument had merit.

i. **Lack of discriminatory history by state:** The majority noted that prior to passage of the ADEA, older persons were ***not commonly the victims of equal protection violations at the hands of state or local governments.*** Older workers had not been subjected to a "history of purposeful unequal treatment," and were not a "discrete and insular minority." Therefore, as the Court had previously decided in *Mass. Ret. Bd. v. Murgia* (*supra*, p. 253), state discrimination on the basis of age need only survive mere-rationality review, not some form of a ban scrutiny.

ii. **No congruence or proportionality:** Consequently, any attempt by Congress to subject the states to extensive age-discrimination rules ***could not possibly have been a "congruent and proportional" response*** to equal protection violations, as required by *Boerne*. This meant that individual employees could not constitutionally be permitted to recover damages for ADEA violations against state or local employers.

2. **Same result for disability discrimination under ADA (*Garrett*):** Then, a year after *Kimel*, the Court reached a similar conclusion about Title I of the ***Americans with Disabilities Act (ADA).*** Just as *Kimel* found that Congress did not have §5 remedial power to subject the states as employers to ***age***-discrimination rules, the Court held in a 5-4 ruling in *Bd. of Trustees of Univ. of Alabama v. Garrett*, 531 U.S. 356 (2001) that Congress did not have §5 power to bar the states from discriminating against ***employees with disabilities***, as it tried to do in Title I.

   a. **Lack of adequate proof:** The ADA was a more modern statute than the ADEA (at issue in *Kimel*), and Congress tried hard to document, through extensive hearings, that the states as employers often discriminated unconstitutionally against the disabled. But this showing, too, failed to satisfy a majority of the Court. The majority conceded that the states may often have discriminated against disabled employees. But since the disabled were not a suspect or semi-suspect class, the only discrimination against them that would be a violation of the Fourteenth Amendment was ***"irrational"*** discrimination. And, the majority found, Congress despite its efforts failed to identify "***a pattern of irrational state discrimination in employment*** against the disabled."

   b. **Lack of congruence:** Furthermore, the majority concluded in *Garrett*, the ***remedy*** chosen by Congress in the ADA ***lacked "congruence and proportionality"*** to any equal protection violations that the states may have been guilty of, just as had been the case in *Kimel*. For the ADA required states to spend hard dollars to modify existing facilities to make them readily accessible to disabled employees; that duty of accommodation went far beyond what could possibly have been required to address whenever small equal protection violations the states may have been guilty of.

   c. **Significance:** So the Eleventh Amendment means that a state, when it acts as an employer, is not liable for money damages if it discriminates against a disabled employee or applicant in a way that would violate the ADA.

D. **Significance of standard of review:** The cases we've examined so far involving the "congruence and proportionality" requirement — that is, the cases discussing when Congress may abrogate the Eleventh Amendment and make the states defend private damage suits in federal court — have involved Congress' efforts to legislate in areas where the states' actions, if challenged on constitutional grounds, would receive ***only mere-rationality review.*** For instance, when a state is alleged to have discriminated in employment on the basis of age or disability

— the types of discrimination at issue in *Kimel* and *Garrett* — equal protection review of the states' conduct would involve just the easy-to-satisfy mere-rationality level of review, since neither age nor disability has ever been found to be a suspect or semi-suspect category, and employment is not a fundamental right.

1. **Class or right triggering heightened scrutiny:**   But now, suppose that Congress is trying to combat state discrimination either based on a ***suspect or semi-suspect category***, or involving a ***right that is "fundamental"*** for due process or equal protection purposes. Does the fact that a ***heightened level of review*** gets used in these contexts[4] entitle Congress to act ***more aggressively*** when it tries to include states in a private-damages remedy for the discrimination in question?

   The answer seems to be ***"yes."*** That is, if the discrimination involves a suspect or semi-suspect category (or a fundamental interest), the courts will apparently be ***quicker to conclude*** that when Congress gave individuals a right to sue the states in federal court for this type of discrimination, Congress acted in a way that *was* "congruent and proportional," and thus proper under §5, than where the area requires only mere-rationality review.

2. **Court access for disabled:** For instance, in *Tennessee v. Lane*, 541 U.S. 509 (2004), a 5-Justice majority concluded that Congress had power to permit federal court suits against the states for money damages under Title II of the Americans with Disabilities Act (ADA), at least for activities relating to ***access to courts***.

   a. **Court access:**   Title II provides that no disabled person can be excluded from participating or getting the benefits of any "***services**, programs or activities of a **public entity**,*" or be discriminated against by such an entity. The plaintiffs in *Lane* were paraplegics who sought damages because they did not have adequate access to court services. One plaintiff, for instance, was required to crawl up stairs to answer criminal charges, because the county courthouse had no elevator.

   b. **Compared with Title I of ADA:**   Recall that in *Garrett* (*supra*, p. 469), a narrow majority of the court held that Congress could not authorize damage suits against states for violations of Title I of the ADA, which covers employment discrimination. But Justice O'Connor changed sides from *Garrett* to *Lane*, forming a majority for the proposition that Congress had power to allow damages for Title II violations, at least in the court-access area.

      i. **Rationale:** The majority reasoned that the ***right of access to courts*** is subject to ***"more searching judicial review"*** than the rational-relation review used in disability-discrimination-in-employment cases like *Garrett*. Furthermore, there was much clearer evidence before Congress that the states had failed to ensure equal treatment for the disabled in the provision of state services (Title II) than there was that the states as employers had discriminated against disabled employees (Title I).

E. **Right to allow damages for actual constitutional violations:** Congress is always free to give private individuals a right to sue the states in federal court for damages for ***actually vio-***

---

4. Remember that for suspect categories like race and alienage, the Court uses strict scrutiny (see *supra*, p. 256), and for a semi-suspect category like gender the Court uses mid-level review (*supra*, p. 321). Similarly, when an equal protection or due process violation is alleged regarding a right that the court deems to be "fundamental," the Court uses strict scrutiny here as well. See, e.g., equal protection challenges involving voting rights (*supra*, p.368) or access to courts (*supra*, p. 378).

lating the individual's constitutional rights, and when Congress does so it doesn't have to worry about the "congruent and proportional" rule. It's only when Congress acts "*prophylactically*" — when it forbids the states from taking some action that wouldn't necessarily violate anyone's constitutional rights, but which action is somehow *related* to possible constitutional violations that Congress is trying to prevent — that Congress' response must be "congruent and proportional" to the constitutional violations that Congress is trying to avoid.

> **Example:** The federal ADA statute requires states (as well as private citizens) to accommodate disabled persons' access to certain public facilities. The statute lets state prisoners sue the state for violating these rights. P, a disabled prisoner, sues the state for actual damages caused to him when his disability is not accommodated (his cell isn't big enough for him to turn his wheelchair around in it).
>
> *Held*, it was within Congress' power to let P sue the state on these facts. Because P's suit is premised on an actual violation of his 14th Amendment liberty interest (not merely based on a federal statute enacted out of a general fear that states or private citizens would discriminate), the Court will not consider whether this ADA disabilities-access provision is "congruent and proportional" to the constitutional violations feared by Congress. *U.S. v. Georgia*, 126 S.Ct. 877 (2006)

F. 3-step analysis: So to summarize this welter of cases regarding Congress' power under § 5 of the Fourteenth Amendment to authorize federal-court damage suits against states, you should follow a three-level analysis:

❑ First, ask whether the state conduct that the plaintiff is complaining of was an *actual violation* by the state of the plaintiff's *constitutional rights.* If the answer is yes, then Congress can clearly grant the plaintiff the right to recover damages against the state in federal court, without worrying about whether its response is congruent-or-proportional to the violation. Cf. *U.S. v. Georgia, supra.*

❑ Now, assuming that the state conduct complained of by the plaintiff was not an actual constitutional violation, ask whether the federal statute that creates the private right of action (i.e., the right of the plaintiff to sue for damages) deals with an area that involves *either a suspect or semi-suspect class or a fundamental right.* If the answer is yes, then, since the Court applies some form of *heightened scrutiny* to this area, the Court will be quite likely to find that Congress' decision to allow a damages suit *meets the "congruent and proportional" requirement* and is thus constitutional. (See *Tennessee v. Lane supra*, p. 470.)

❑ Finally, assume that the answer to both of the above questions is "no." Now, Congress has power under §5 of the Fourteenth Amendment to allow the plaintiff to sue the state *only if Congress found widespread unconstitutional state conduct in the area in question.* And even if such widespread conduct was found, Congress must choose *narrowly-tailored methods* for combating the state conduct. This is all captured in the slogan that Congress' response must be *"congruent and proportional"* to the pattern of unconstitutional state actions relied on by Congress. (See *Bd. of Trustees of Univ. of Alabama v. Garrett, supra*, p. 469).

Quiz Yourself on

CONGRESSIONAL ENFORCEMENT OF CIVIL RIGHTS *(ENTIRE CHAPTER)*

68. The U.S. Congress has decided that it would now be desirable to extend the reach of federal anti-discrimination laws to the rental of units in 1-4 family homes, which have previously been exempt from such laws. Therefore, Congress proposes to make it a crime for any homeowner, regardless of the size of his dwelling or the number of units in it, and regardless of whether the owner resides in it, to decline to rent to another person on the grounds of the latter's race, ethnic group or national origin. Do Congress' remedial powers under the Fourteenth Amendment furnish adequate constitutional support for this statute? _____

69. Same facts as prior question. Now, however, assume that you are asked to find a constitutional basis for the proposed statute other than the Fourteenth Amendment and other than the Commerce Clause. What provision would you point to? _____

70. After a sharp right-ward shift in the politics of the nation, Republicans and conservative Democrats gained a majority in both houses of Congress. They passed, and the President signed into law, a statute providing as follows: "It shall be a federal felony for any person to perform an abortion on a woman who is more than three months pregnant, unless the pregnancy was caused by rape or incest or the abortion is necessary to save the woman's life." Assume for purposes of this question that if a state passed a comparable statute, Supreme Court precedents already on the books would compel the conclusion that the state statute was an unconstitutional violation of women's right of privacy. A woman and her doctor have challenged the federal statute on the grounds that it is a violation of the right to privacy, as embodied in the Fifth Amendment's Due Process Clause. Will this attack on the statute succeed? _____

Answers

68. No, probably. The Fourteenth Amendment is generally triggered only where there is "state action." Thus the clause dealing with equal protection provides that "[n]o State shall make or enforce any law which shall … deny to any person within its jurisdiction the equal protection of the laws." On the other hand, §5 of the Fourteenth Amendment grants Congress the power to enforce that amendment "by appropriate legislation." The issue is whether Congress may "appropriately" enforce the Equal Protection Clause by proscribing private, as opposed to governmental, conduct.

Certainly some types of private conduct may be reached under Congress' remedial powers. For instance, Congress may prevent a private person from interfering with a state official's attempts to furnish equal protection (e.g., Congress may punish private individuals to who prevent local school board officials from carrying out desegregation). But where the conduct being proscribed is *purely* private, involving the interaction of one private individual with another, it is clear that Congress' power to enforce the Equal Protection Clause does not extend that far; see *U.S. v. Morrison.*

69. The Thirteenth Amendment. The Thirteenth Amendment provides that "[n]either slavery nor involuntary servitude, except as a punishment for crime … shall exist within the United States. … " The Thirteenth Amendment, unlike the Fourteenth and Fifteenth, is thus not explicitly limited to governmental action. Section 2 of the Thirteenth Amendment gives Congress the power to "enforce this [amendment] by appropriate legislation." This §2 remedial power has been construed to mean that Congress has the right to decide what the ***"badges and incidents of slavery"*** are. If Congress makes a finding that one of the badges and incidents of slavery is the refusal of private homeowners to rent to others on the basis of race, the Court would uphold the proposed statute here as a valid exercise of this remedial power. All that is required is that Congress act "rationally" in determining that a particular aspect of private conduct is indeed a badge or incident of slavery, and Congress' conclusion here would certainly be found to be "rational." See *Jones v. Alfred H. Mayer Co.* (Thirteenth Amendment is broad enough to let Congress conclude that private racial discrimination in real estate transactions is a badge or incident of slavery).

70. **Yes, probably.** The question boils down to, "May Congress reduce the substantive content of individuals' constitutional rights?" The answer to this question is "no." The Court held in *Boerne v. Flores* that Congress' power to enforce the Civil War Amendments does not include the power to redefine the substantive boundaries of the rights given by those Amendments. Here, Congress has tried to reduce the substantive contours of a woman's substantive due process right to abortion, and under *Boerne* (and other Court cases), Congress may not do this.

Exam Tips on
CONGRESSIONAL ENFORCEMENT OF CIVIL RIGHTS

Exam questions on the subjects covered in this Chapter are relatively rare. Here are the few things to keep in mind:

☛ Probably most important, the 14th and 15th Amendments cannot be used to reach ***purely private conduct***, i.e., conduct not involving the state in any way. (This is another way of stating that "state action" is required.) But where government action and private action ***combine***, then Congress can reach this activity. (*Example:* Congress can make it a crime for a private citizen to interfere with government desegregation efforts.)

☛ Sometimes tested: The ***13th*** Amendment is the only Amendment that can reach ***purely private conduct***. That is, Congress gets to say what is a "badge or incident of slavery," and to then forbid it. *Example:* Congress can ban purely private discrimination in housing, under authority of the 13th Amendment. *Jones v. Alfred H. Mayer Co.*

   ☞ This means that the 13th Amendment can be the basis for federal anti-discrimination legislation that would otherwise have to be based on the Commerce Clause.

   ☞ The 13th Amendment can be used to ban racial discrimination against ***non-blacks*** (e.g., whites, Asians, etc.).

   ☞ Testable issue: Can Congress ban, under the 13th Amendment, discrimination on ***other than racial grounds***? Probably Congress can attack discrimination based on ***national origin*** and ***ethnicity***, but not on other characteristics (e.g., gender or sexual orientation). Also, probably only ***purposeful*** discrimination can be reached.

☛ Where Congress is trying to combat a clear problem of ***discrimination by a state***, its ***remedial*** powers are ***relatively broad***. So as long as Congress is behaving rationally in combatting discrimination, you should conclude that it is acting constitutionally under its power to enforce the 13th, 14th and 15th Amendments.

   ☞ But where Congress wants to use its remedial power to ***prevent*** state discrimination that has not yet occurred, Congress must act on ***reasonably up-to-date information*** about where discrimination is likely to be occurring.

Example: Congress uses its 15th Amendment remedial powers to single out certain states, and to require only those states to get federal preapproval of any changes to state voting laws. Congress can't rely solely on 40-year-old voter data as the basis for picking which states must get the federal preapproval. (*Shelby County v. Holder.*)

☞   Also, even where Congress is using its 14th Amendment powers to combat state discrimination, Congress' response must be ***"congruent and proportional"*** to the discrimination — Congress can't choose methods that are much ***broader*** than the discrimination being cured. (*Boerne v. Flores.*) So Congress can't ban certain state discriminatory conduct, and then make the states liable in damages to private plaintiffs for that conduct, unless Congress had evidence that the states frequently violated people's constitutional rights in that area.

Example: Suppose Congress rationally concludes that states, acting as employers, occasionally (but not frequently) violate the 14th Amendment equal protection rights of disabled employees. Congress still can't give state employees the right to sue the state for damages for violating the statute — the states have 11th Amendment immunity from private damage suits, and that immunity can be overcome only by proof that Congress' response was congruent and proportional to widespread state discrimination of the type being addressed, something not present here. (*Bd. of Trustees of Ala. v. Garrett.*)

☞   But where the area of discrimination that Congress is trying to prevent is one that gets ***heightened scrutiny*** (i.e., involves a ***suspect or semi-suspect class***, or a ***fundamental right***), then Congress can allow private damages based on a ***lesser showing*** that the states have discriminated.

Example: Congress orders state and private employers to give employees various rights to take unpaid leave to care for sick family members. In doing so, Congress is acting to combat gender discrimination. Even if the states have practiced only occasional leave-related gender discrimination against their employees, Congress can still let state employees sue for violations of the state, because gender-discrimination gets heightened (mid-level) review. (*Nevada Dept. of Hum. Res. v. Hibbs*)

☞ Occasionally, you'll notice buried in a fact pattern that Congress is arguably ***expanding*** or ***contracting*** the ***scope*** of a right guaranteed under one of the Civil War Amendments. Say that under *Boerne v. Flores*, Congress may ***neither*** expand nor contract the boundaries of any constitutional right, even under Congress' power to "enforce" the Civil War Amendments.

CHAPTER 14

FREEDOM OF EXPRESSION

ChapterScope

The First Amendment provides, in part, that "Congress shall make no law … abridging the freedom of speech, or of the press. … " These rights (plus the accompanying "freedom of association") are often grouped together as "freedom of expression." Here are the key concepts relating to freedom of expression:

- **Content-based vs. content-neutral:** Courts distinguish between *"content-based"* and *"content-neutral"* regulations on expression.

  - ❏ **Content-based:** If the government action is *"content-based,"* the action will be generally subjected to *strict scrutiny*, and the action will usually be struck down.

  - ❏ **Content-neutral:** On the other hand, if the government action is *"content-neutral,"* the government's action is subjected to a much easier-to-satisfy test, and will usually be upheld.

  - ❏ **Classifying:** A governmental action that burdens expression is "content-based" if the government is *aiming* at the *"communicative impact"* of the expression. By contrast, if the government is aiming at something other than the communicative impact, the action is "content-neutral," even if it has the *effect* of burdening expression.

- **Analysis of content-based government action:** Where a government action impairing expression is "content-based," here's how courts analyze it:

  - ❏ **Unprotected category:** If the speech falls into certain pre-defined *unprotected* categories, then the government can more or less completely ban the expression.

    - ❏ **Listing:** The main "unprotected" categories are: (1) obscenity; (2) fraudulent misrepresentation; (3) defamation; (4) advocacy of imminent lawless behavior; and (5) "fighting words."

  - ❏ **Protected category:** All expression not falling into one of these five categories is *protected*. If expression falls within the protected category, then any government ban or restriction on it based on its content is *presumed to be unconstitutional*. The Court subjects any such regulation to *strict scrutiny* — the regulation will be sustained *only* if it (1) serves a *compelling governmental objective*; and (2) is *"necessary,"* i.e., drawn as *narrowly as possible* to achieve that objective. Very few content-based restrictions on protected-category expression can survive that scrutiny.

- **Analysis of content-neutral regulations:** If the government restriction is *content-neutral*, here is how the Court analyzes it:

  - ❏ **Three-part test:** The government must satisfy a *three-part test* before the regulation will be sustained, if the regulation substantially impairs expression:

    - ❏ **Significant governmental interest:** First, the regulation must serve a *significant governmental interest*;

❏ **Narrowly tailored:** Second, the regulation must be *narrowly tailored* to serve that governmental interest; and

❏ **Alternative channels:** Finally, the state must *"leave open alternative channels"* for communicating the information.

■ **The public forum:** Speech that takes place in a *"public forum"* is often harder for government to regulate.

❏ **Content-based:** If a regulation is *content-based*, it makes no difference whether the expression is in a public forum: strict scrutiny will be given in any event.

❏ **Neutral "time, place and manner":** But if a regulation is *content-neutral,* then the fact that the speech does or does not take place in a public forum makes a difference. Usually, we're talking about *"time, place and manner"* restrictions here.

❏ **Non-public forum:** When expression takes place in a *non-public forum*, the regulation merely has to be *rationally related* to some *legitimate* governmental objective, as long as equally effective alternative channels are available.

❏ **Public forum:** But where the expression takes place in a *public forum*, the regulation has to be *narrowly drawn* to achieve a *significant* governmental interest (roughly *intermediate-level* review). It is still necessary (but not sufficient) that the government leaves alternative channels available.

❏ **What are public forums:** "True" public forums are: (1) streets; (2) sidewalks; and (3) parks. Also, places in which a public government *meeting* takes place are probably true public forums.

❏ **Designated-public:** There are also *"designated-public"* forums. These are locations where the government has decided to open the place to particular open-expression purposes. The rules are essentially those for true public forums, except that government may at any time decide to close the forum.

❏ **Non-public forums:** Other public places are "non-public forums." Here, government regulation merely has to be rationally related to some legitimate governmental objective, as long as alternative channels are left open. (*Examples:* Airport terminals, jails, military bases, courthouses, schools used after hours, and governmental office buildings.)

■ **Defamation:** The First Amendment places limits on the extent to which a plaintiff may recover tort damages for *defamation*.

❏ **Plaintiff as public official or public figure:** Where P is a *public official* or *public figure*, he may only win a defamation suit against D for a statement relating to P's official conduct if P can prove that D's statement was made with either *"knowledge* that it was false" or *"reckless disregard"* of whether it was true or false.

■ **Obscenity:** Expression that is *"obscene"* is simply *unprotected* by the First Amendment. (But the mere *private possession* of obscene material by an adult may *not* be made criminal.)

■ **Commercial speech:** Speech that is *"commercial"* gets First Amendment protection. But this protection is more limited than protection given to non-commercial speech:

❑ **Truthful speech:** Content-based restrictions on truthful commercial speech get only mid-level review: the government must be: (1) *directly advancing* (2) a *substantial* governmental interest (3) in a way that is *reasonably tailored* to achieve the government's objective. (This compares with strict scrutiny of content-based restrictions on non-commercial speech.)

❑ **False, deceptive or illegal:** False or deceptive commercial speech, or speech proposing an *illegal transaction*, may be forbidden by the government.

▪ **Freedom of association:** First Amendment case law recognizes the concept of *"freedom of association."* If an individual has a First Amendment right to engage in a particular expressive activity, then a *group* has a "freedom of association" right to engage in that same activity as a group.

I. GENERAL THEMES

A. Text of First Amendment: The First Amendment provides that "Congress shall make no law … abridging the *freedom of speech*, or of *the press*; or the right of the people peaceably to assemble, and to petition the Government for a redress of grievances."

1. **Related rights:** There are thus several distinct rights which may be grouped under the category "freedom of expression": freedom of *speech*, of the *press*, of *assembly*, and of *petition*. Additionally, there is a well-recognized "freedom of association" which, although it is not specifically mentioned, is derived from individuals' rights of speech and assembly.

B. Two broad classes: When government "abridges" freedom of speech, its reasons for doing so can be placed into two broad classes. The first is that the government is restricting the speech *because of its content*, that is, because of the *ideas or information contained in it*, or because of its general subject matter. The second reason for abridgment has nothing to do with the content of the speech; rather, the government seeks to avoid *some evil unconnected with the speech's content*, but the government's regulation has the *incidental by-product* of interfering with particular communications.

1. **Two tracks:** The Supreme Court has implicitly recognized that the dangers posed by governmental action taken for the first reason are different (and generally more severe) than those posed by regulation carried out for the second reason. Therefore, the Supreme Court's rules for determining whether the government has violated the First Amendment differ depending on whether the governmental control falls within the first class or the second.

a. **Track one (communicative impact):** Where the government's conduct falls within the first class, which Tribe summarizes as governmental actions "aimed at *communicative impact*," he has labeled the appropriate analysis *"track one"* analysis. (Tribe, p. 791).

b. **Track two (noncommunicative impact):** Where the government's conduct falls within the second class (which Tribe describes as government actions "aimed at *noncommunicative impact* but nonetheless having *adverse effects on communicative opportunity"*), he calls the relevant analysis *"track two."* Tribe, p. 792.

  c. We adopt terms: For ease of labeling, we will follow the same "track one" and "track two" terminology.

2. Some examples: Following are some examples of governmental actions punishing or restricting speech, and the track into which each falls:

    Example 1 (track one): The state forbids pharmacists to advertise the prices of prescription drugs, because it is afraid that the public will buy drugs at the lowest available price and will therefore receive low-quality goods and service. This case falls within "track *one*," since the speech is being regulated because of the government's fears about consumers' reaction to the speech's *content*. See *Virginia Pharmacy Board v. Virginia Consumer Council*, 425 U.S. 748 (1976) (invalidating the restriction, as discussed *infra*, p. 565).

    Example 2 (track one): The state forbids "maliciously and willfully disturb[ing] the peace or quiet of any neighborhood or person [by] offensive conduct." D is convicted under the statute for wearing a jacket bearing the words "Fuck The Draft" in a corridor of the county courthouse. The case should be analyzed under "track *one*," since the asserted offensiveness caused by D results *solely from the content* of his communication. (To see this, observe that bystanders who *could not read English* would *not* have been offended.) See *Cohen v. California*, 403 U.S. 15 (1971) (reversing D's conviction, as discussed *infra*, p. 519).

    Example 3 (track one): Under Maryland tort law, if a speaker (D) intentionally makes outrageous statements attacking another person (P), P may be able to recover against D for intentional infliction of emotional distress (IIED). In a federal-court diversity case based on Maryland tort law, a jury grants P (the father of a Marine killed in Iraq) a civil judgment for IIED against the Ds, who are members of a church that thinks God punishes the U.S. military for tolerating homosexuality. The IIED consists of the Ds having carried, during and nearby the Marine's funeral, picket signs attributing the Marine's death to God's desire to punish the military for not rooting out homosexuality.

    Maryland's constitutional authority to allow such a recovery under its substantive tort law, notwithstanding the Ds' First Amendment right to speak out on matters of public interest, is to be analyzed under "track *one*." That's because the "outrageousness" of the Ds' messages on the picket signs results solely from the content of those messages. (If the Ds' statements on the picket signs addressed to P constituted pleasant rather than nasty messages, the statements wouldn't be "outrageous" — so giving the jury power to impose liability for IIED is a content-based rather than content-neutral regulation.) See *Snyder v. Phelps*, 131 S.Ct. 1207 (2011), *infra*, p. 520 (reversing the verdict against the picketers as a violation of their First Amendmen right not to have their statements on public affairs be regulated on content-based grounds).

    Example 4 (track two): A city prohibits the use of sound trucks which emit "loud and raucous noises" while operating on the streets. The ordinance should be analyzed under "track *two*," since the harm which the government seeks to prevent is *independent of the content* of the messages being amplified — even a listener who *could not understand English* would be a victim of the harm. See *Kovacs v. Cooper*, 336 U.S. 77 (1949) (upholding such a ban, as discussed *infra*, p. 512).

Example 5 (track two): A city forbids distribution of leaflets, because it wishes to prevent littering. The case should be analyzed under "track *two*," since the harm sought to be avoided exists regardless of what information is contained on the leaflets. (In fact, even *blank* leaflets could end up being litter.) See *Schneider v. State*, 308 U.S. 147 (1939), striking the ban (on the grounds that the First Amendment requires a less restrictive alternative, such as only punishing actual littering; the case is discussed *infra*, p. 506).

C. Analysis of "track one" cases ("content-based" regulation): If a case falls within "track *one*" — that is, the government is trying to restrict expression based on its *communicative impact* — courts generally *"strictly scrutinize"* the regulation. Here's a more specific catalog of the rules that apply to such "content based" restrictions:

1. **Unprotected vs. protected categories:** There are certain categories of expression (e.g., defamation) that the Supreme Court has long identified as being essentially *"unprotected"* for First Amendment purposes. (See p. 486 for a list of these categories.) But most expression does *not* fall within these special unprotected categories. Since the rules for when and how government may restrict expression on account of its content vary based on this distinction, it's important to keep track of the two types of categories; therefore, we'll use the phrases *"unprotected categories"* and *"protected category"* to refer to the two types.

2. **Speech in the main "protected category":** For speech in the broad *"protected category,"* such as everyday speech on *core political issues,* it is simply *not open to the government to argue that the speech is harmful* because of its content, and that it should be suppressed or punished.

   a. **Strict scrutiny required:** So when government tries to regulate such protected-category speech on account of the speech's contents, the Supreme Court will *strictly scrutinize* the regulation: the government bears the burden of showing "that its regulation is necessary to *serve a compelling state interest* and that it is *narrowly drawn* to achieve that end." *Widmar v. Vincent*, 454 U.S. 263 (1981).

   b. **Comparable to strict scrutiny elsewhere:** The techniques of strict scrutiny in this area are therefore comparable to those used in the due process (*supra*, p. 173) and equal protection (*supra*, p. 263) contexts.

   c. **Marketplace of ideas:** The rule requiring strict scrutiny of content-based restrictions on speech falling within the ordinary "protected category" reflects the view, implicit in the First Amendment, that *it is not the government's place to suppress ideas because they are "wrong."* Rather, as Justice Holmes put it in his dissent in *Abrams v. U.S.*, 250 U.S. 616 (1919) (discussed more extensively *infra*, p. 491), there is to be *"free trade in ideas,"* and truth will become accepted through "the *competition of the market."*

Example: Consider Example 1, *supra*, p. 478, in which the state prohibited pharmacists from advertising their prices for prescription drugs. The state contended that barring this information would be in the public interest, since a contrary policy would lead people to be interested only in price, and therefore to receive low-quality goods or services.

The Court conceded the plausibility of the state's claim. But it held that the weighing of the state's interest in protecting its citizens versus the value of free-flowing information was *not the Court's or the Virginia legislature's to make.* "It is precisely this kind of choice between the dangers of suppressing information, and the dangers of its misuse if it is freely available, *that the First Amendment makes for us." Virginia Pharmacy Board v. Virginia Consumer Council*, 425 U.S. 748 (1976) (discussed more extensively *infra*, p. 565).

  d. **Consequences if regulation is of "protected category" speech:** Here are some of the consequences that flow from the fact that the Court uses strict scrutiny to review content-based restrictions of *"protected category"* speech:

    i. **Effect of more speech:** Any time *more speech* could eliminate the evil feared by the state, the Court will conclude that the regulation is *not "necessary"* to prevent that evil (no matter how serious the evil is). This is simply an application of the general principle, previously noted, that whenever possible, "harmful" speech must be fought by more expression, not by government-imposed silence.

    ii. **Other speakers' opportunities irrelevant:** The government may not claim that the content of the expression has been adequately articulated by *other speakers*, and that proponents of *different viewpoints* on the issue should be given a chance to speak instead.

    iii. **Other times and places irrelevant:** The government may not claim that the speaker can make his point just as well in *some other place*, at *some other time*, or in *some other manner*. Once the government is seen to be objecting to a message based on its content, *not even a "trifling" or "minor" interference with expression will be tolerated by the courts*.

  e. **"Viewpoint based" restrictions, generally:** The most obvious type of scenario in which a restriction will be found to be "content-based" (and thus subjected to strict scrutiny) is one in which government has singled out a certain *"message"* or *"viewpoint,"* and imposes *restrictions on that message or viewpoint on account of its communicative content.* We'll refer to such restrictions as being *"viewpoint based."*

    i. **Time, place and manner restrictions that are viewpoint based:** Government rarely attempts to prohibit specific messages *entirely*; rather, when government imposes "viewpoint based" restrictions, it typically does so by *limiting the time, place or manner* in which the message can be delivered. But even modest time, place and manner restrictions will *trigger strict scrutiny* if the restriction is "viewpoint based," i.e., if it applies only to certain messages or viewpoints.[1]

    ii. **Illustration:** A good example of a classic "viewpoint based" time, place and manner restriction came in *Boos v. Barry*, 485 U.S. 312 (1988). There, a Washington D.C. statute that prohibited the display of certain messages on *signs near foreign embassies* was strictly scrutinized (and struck down), even though people

---

1. As we'll see at greater length *infra*, p. 507, time, place and manner restrictions will be subject instead to the less-rigorous "mid-level" standard of review if the court is satisfied that the restriction is *truly content-neutral* rather than content-based. But where a time, place and manner restriction is found to single out particular viewpoints for greater restrictions (i.e., the regulatory scheme is found to be content- or viewpoint-based), strict scrutiny applies even if people who want to express the discriminated-against message are left with many alternative places, times or methods for delivering it.

who wanted to deliver that sort of message were left with lots of alternative venues in which to do so.

(1) Facts of *Boos*: The statute in *Boos* prohibited the display of any *sign within 500 feet of a foreign embassy* if that sign tended to bring that foreign government into *"public odium"* or *"public disrepute."* The statute was obviously "viewpoint based" — that is, only certain messages (those bringing the foreign government into "public odium" or "public disrepute") were prohibited from being delivered near embassies.

(2) Strict scrutiny applied: Since the statute was viewpoint based, the Court subjected it to *strict scrutiny:* the statute could survive only if the restriction was found "necessary" to serve a "compelling" state interest. And if a less speech-restrictive statute would have achieved the compelling interest as well or even almost as well, the statute wasn't "necessary" to achieve the goal.

(3) Result: The Court concluded that the D.C. statute *failed* this nearly-impossible-to-satisfy standard. Even if the District's interest in preserving the dignity of foreign diplomats was "compelling" — something the Court did not decide — more *narrowly-drawn measures* (e.g., a ban on *harassing foreign officials*) would have furthered that interest adequately.

f. Bans on discussing "either side" of issues are "viewpoint based": Most of the "track one" statutes we've looked at so far have singled out *particular messages* for disfavor, based on the content of the message. For instance, Example 1 on p. 478 singled out a particular type of message-content for restrictive treatment — pharmacists' advertisements of the prices of prescription drugs.

But for purposes of applying the principle that "viewpoint based" restrictions must be strictly scrutinized, a statute will *also* be held to be viewpoint based even if the statute singles out a *whole category* of speech, *not just a particular "point of view,"* for negative treatment based on the speech's message content. Thus a regulation that restricts people from making arguments about a contested issue, regardless of which *side* of the issue the speaker supports, will nonetheless be held to be viewpoint based (and therefore content based) — the fact that the restriction is *"even handed"* won't be enough to insulate it from strict scrutiny.

i. Restriction on "hate speech" or "offensive" speech (*Matal v. Tam*): So for instance, suppose that government limits messages for the theoretically-admirable purpose of *protecting whole groups of people* from being emotionally damaged by *"hate speech"* or *"offensive speech."* Even though the restriction applies to protect *all* groups equally, that fact won't prevent the courts from treating the restriction as "viewpoint based" and thus *triggering strict scrutiny.*

A 2017 case involving the federal government's unsuccessful attempt to ban *derogatory terms* from being used as *registered trademarks* furnishes a vivid illustration of this principle. See *Matal v. Tam*, 137 S.Ct. 1744 (2017).

(1) The statute in *Matal*: *Matal* involved a federal statute that denied federal trademark registration for any trademark "which may *disparage ... persons*, living or dead, *institutions*, *beliefs*, or national symbols, or bring them into *contempt, or disrepute.*" (This is the so-called "disparagement clause.")

(2) The rock group named "The Slants": The Ps were a rock group called "The Slants," who sought trademark registration for that name. "Slants" is (the Supreme Court found) a "derogatory term for persons of Asian descent." The members of the band were Asian-Americans who believed that by taking this slur as the name of their group they could help "reclaim" the term and "drain its denigrating force." The U.S. Patent and Trademark Office (PTO) denied the registration application on account of the disparagement clause. The Ps claimed that the PTO's denial of registration for this reason violated their free speech rights.

(3) Supreme Court agrees with the Ps: The Supreme Court *agreed* with the Ps that the denial infringed their right of free speech. All eight justices who participated[2] agreed that the disparagement clause constituted **unconstitutional "viewpoint discrimination."**

(4) The plurality: Writing for a four-justice plurality, Justice Alito concluded that even though the disparagement clause *"evenhandedly* prohibits disparagement of *all* groups" (e.g., trademarks that "damn Democrats and Republicans, capitalists and socialists, and those arrayed on both sides of every possible issue"), the clause was "viewpoint discrimination," because *"[g]iving offense is a viewpoint."*

(5) The concurrence: Justice Kennedy, writing for himself and three other justices who did not sign the plurality opinion, agreed with the plurality that the disparagement clause **constituted viewpoint discrimination.** The disparagement clause "reflects the government's **disapproval of ... messages it finds offensive,"** making the clause *"the essence of viewpoint discrimination."*

ii. **Restriction on "scandalous" or "immoral" trademark:** Similarly, if government restricts speech on the grounds that it is *"scandalous"* or *"immoral,"* that restriction, too, will be viewed as a *viewpoint-based regulation* that must be strictly scrutinized.

A 2019 case illustrates this principle. That case, ***Iancu v. Brunetti***, 139 S.Ct. 2294 (2019), was similar to *Matal v. Tam, supra*, in that both cases invalidated the federal trademark statute's ban on the registration of a category of trademarks.

(1) The statute in *Iancu*: *Iancu* involved a federal statutory provision denying trademark registration for any trademark that comprises *"immoral[] or scandalous matter."*

(2) The mark P sought to register, "FUCT": P sought a registration for the trademark "FUCT," which he had been using on his clothing line. The Patent and Trademark Office (PTO) refused the registration, on the grounds that the mark was "extremely offensive" and thus "immoral or scandalous." P asserted that the ban on registration of immoral-or-scandalous trademarks constituted viewpoint-based regulation, which P said triggered – and could not survive – strict scrutiny.

---

2. Justice Gorsuch did not participate, because he joined the Court after oral argument.

(3) Court agrees with P: The Court *agreed with P*, and *struck down* the "immoral or scandalous" provision. The majority opinion by Justice Kagan consulted the dictionary definitions of "immoral" and "scandalous," and found that both terms had *meanings tied to concepts of morality.* Therefore, Kagan said, the statute "distinguishes between two *opposed sets of ideas*: those *aligned with conventional moral standards* and those *hostile* to them."

The statute's use of "immoral and scandalous" therefore constituted, on its face, viewpoint bias, triggering strict scrutiny. And the provision could not survive that scrutiny.

3. **Distinctions based on viewpoint versus ones based on "topic":** Probably the greatest danger of content-based restrictions on speech is that government will *favor certain messages over others,* and will thereby *censor private expression.* That's why the Supreme Court has long interpreted the First Amendment as requiring strict scrutiny of such restrictions. All of the examples we've considered so far of content-based restrictions are ones in which it's clear that the government was singling out speech *based on the particular viewpoint or message it contained.* But there's *another* type of content-based regulation, one that does not single out particular viewpoints. This consists of restrictions based on what can loosely be called the speech's *"topic"* or *"subject matter."* And this type of regulation, too, will be subjected to *strict scrutiny*, and probably struck down as a a First Amendment violation.

   a. **Combined rules on modes and topics:** Such "topic-specific" restrictions virtually never occur in the form of a government ban on *all* discussion of a topic. Instead, they usually occur as a more limited restriction, on only the use of a particular *medium or mode of expression* to discuss a *particular topic.*

   b. **Signage regulation, generally:** A common way government might try to regulate a combination of a particular mode of expression and a particular topic — without any apparent intent to favor particular messages — is by a local government's regulation of *signage.* Most cities tightly regulate how and when *signs may be posted by private citizens* — these regulations typically require private signs to be no more than some stated *maximum size*, be posted for no more than a *certain duration*, be limited to a certain *number* or to certain *places*, etc.

      i. **Regulation applies similarly to all signs:** If a regulation applies the same way to *all* signs — regardless of the "type" of sign or the sign's "subject matter" — the regulation will be presumed to be content-neutral (i.e., to fall within "track two"), and will *not* be subject to strict scrutiny.

      ii. **Regulations apply differently depending on subject matter:** But frequently, even where a city doesn't intend to disfavor any particular message, the city divides signs into *multiple categories*, and treats certain categories as meriting fewer restrictions than others, perhaps for reasons as innocuous as preventing "visual litter." As we'll see in the discussion of *Reed v. Gilbert* immediately below, such category-based regulation schemes will be *strictly scrutinized*, and likely to be *struck down* as violations of the First Amendment.

   c. **Signage regulation struck down in *Reed v. Gilbert*:** A unanimous 2015 decision, ***Reed v. Town of Gilbert,*** 135 S.Ct. 2218 (2015), shows that as soon as government tries to impose any sort of differential regulation of *signage* based on even the broadest categorizing of the signs' subject matter, the regulation will be found to be content-based, will be *strictly scrutinized*, and will in all probability be *struck down*.

i.   Ordinance in *Reed*: *Reed* involved the signage ordinance of the Town of Gilbert, Arizona. The Town required a permit before the posting of any sign that was not classified as "exempt" under the ordinance. Of the various categories of exempt signs, the two most relevant to the case were:

[1] *"Ideological Signs,"* a catch-all category of signs used for noncommercial purposes that did not fall into any other, more specific, category. Apparently this category included *political speech* that was *not* related to any current *election campaign.* Ideological Signs were treated quite *favorably*, in that they could be up to 20 square feet in area, could be placed in all zoning districts, and were not subject to limits on how long they could remain posted.

[2] *"Temporary Directional Signs,"* which included, most relevantly, signs giving the particulars of *events to be held by non-profit groups*, such as the time and place for church services. These signs were treated much less favorably than Ideological Signs — they could be no larger than 6 square feet; could number no more than four on a single property at once; and had to be put up no more than 12 hours before the event and taken down within an hour afterwards.

ii. The conflict: The plaintiffs were the Good News Community Church and its pastor. Because the Church was cash-strapped, it wanted to publicize its services cheaply; posting signs around town was the main way it chose. The Church and the pastor sued the Town, arguing that the ordinance violated their rights of free speech by allowing them to keep their signs up for a far shorter time each week than if the sign had been an "Ideological" one.

iii. Court strikes the statute in opinion by Thomas: All nine Justices agreed with the plaintiffs that the statute *violated the plaintiffs' First Amendment rights.* For our present discussion of content-neutrality, what's most significant is that all nine Justices agreed that the ordinance was *content-based,* even though it did *not* appear to be motivated by a desire to *suppress any particular message.* Therefore, all Justices agreed, it had to be *strictly scrutinized*, and invalidated. We'll focus on Justice Thomas' opinion, in which he announced the result and gave a rationale that five other Justices supported.

(1) Strict scrutiny is triggered: The ordinance was clearly content-based, due to its *on-its-face classification based on subject matter and purpose.* Therefore, Thomas said, the Court was required to *subject it to strict scrutiny.* Thus the Town bore the burden of demonstrating that the Code's differentiation between Temporary Directional Signs and other types of signs, such as Ideological Signs, *"furthers a compelling interest and is narrowly tailored to that end."*

(2) Easy to strike down: In Thomas' view (which on this point was shared by all Justices), the Town had *not* come even remotely close to satisfying this very difficult burden. The Town had cited only two governmental interests in support of the distinction: preserving the town's *aesthetic appeal*, and *main-*

taining traffic safety. Even if these were compelling interests (which Thomas assumed but did not decide), the distinctions used in the code were "hopelessly *underinclusive.*"

For instance, the Town "cannot claim that placing strict limits on temporary directional signs is *necessary to beautify* the Town while at the same time *allowing unlimited numbers of other types of signs that create the same problem.*"

   iv. **Concurrence only in result:** But three members of the Court disagreed with parts of Thomas' reasoning, and therefore concurred only in the result. Justice Kagan (joined by Ginsburg and Breyer) agreed with Thomas that the Court does, and should continue to, apply strict scrutiny to facially content-based regulations of speech "when there is any *'realistic possibility that official suppression of ideas is afoot.'* " And she agreed that, because there is such a possibility of suppression when the regulation on its face differentiates "on the *basis of viewpoint,*" or restricts "discussion of an *entire topic*" in public debate, strict scrutiny is needed in *those* instances. But, she said, in cases where hidden official suppression of ideas *is "not realistically possible,"* the Court should perhaps *"relax our guard* so that *'entirely reasonable' laws* imperiled by strict scrutiny can *survive.*"

     (1) **Examples:** Kagan agreed that the present statute was not one of those cases where hidden official suppression was "not realistically possible"; that's why she concurred in the result. But Kagan gave several examples of categories of signs that, under the majority's standard, could not be given any preference without being struck down, but that she thought might be constitutionally permissible. For instance, according to the majority's analysis a town could not give preference for signs informing passersby *"where George Washington slept,"* unless the town could show a compelling interest in doing so. Kagan predicted that courts across the U.S. would now have to invalidate the "entirely reasonable" sign restrictions of *thousands of towns.* "

  d. **Rule on distinctions between various "topics" or "subjects":** So to summarize, cases like *Reed v. Gilbert*, *supra*, mean that the requirement of content-neutrality effectively bars the government not only from (1) showing favoritism as between differing *points of view* (or "messages") on a particular subject, but also from (2) placing a *particular topic or subject-matter* off-limits (or subjecting it to time-place-and-manner restrictions) while not so limiting discussion of other issues or subjects. The case in the following example demonstrates restriction (2) in a context *not* involving signage.

Example: The New York Public Service Commission, using its power to regulate utilities, orders the utilities not to discuss, as part of their monthly billing materials, the *desirability of nuclear power.*

Held, this order violates the utilities' right of free speech. "The First Amendment's hostility to content-based regulation extends not only to restrictions on particular viewpoints, but also to prohibition of public discussion of an *entire topic*." *Consolidated Edison v. Public Serv. Commission*, 447 U.S. 530 (1980).

4. **Content-based regulation of speech falling into an unprotected category:** The cases we've just reviewed in Pars. 2 and 3 above — e.g., *Boos, Matal,* and *Reed v. Gilbert* — are ones in which the speech that was subjected to content-based restrictions did *not* fall within any category recognized by the Supreme Court as a predefined *"unprotected category."* Now, let's look at *what the unprotected categories are,* as well as the rules for evaluating content-based restrictions on speech that *does* fall within one of these categories.

a. **List of categories:** Here is a list of these unprotected categories, as the Supreme Court has recognized them:

[1] *"Incitement."* This category includes advocacy of *imminent lawless behavior* (p. 495), as well as the utterance of *"fighting words,"* i.e., words that are likely to precipitate an immediate physical conflict (p. 516);

[2] *Obscenity* (p. 559);

[3] *Misleading or deceptive speech (i.e., fraud)* (p. 571);

[4] Speech *integral to criminal conduct* (p. 571), such as speech that is part of a *conspiracy* to commit a crime or speech *proposing an illegal transaction*; and

[5] *Defamation* (p. 552).

i. **Few if any new additions:** The unprotected status of the five above categories has existed for decades, though the precise contours of some of the categories have varied a bit. But over the last few decades, the Supreme Court *has refused to add any new entries* to this unprotected-categories list.

(1) **Animal-crush videos:** For example, the Court has refused to add to the list of unprotected-categories the class of *"depictions of animal cruelty."* See *U.S. v. Stevens,* 130 S.Ct. 1577 (2010).

(2) **No "false statements" category:** Similarly, the Court has declined to establish an unprotected category consisting of *"factually-false statements."* See *U.S. v. Alvarez,* 132 S.Ct. 2537 (2012), *infra,* p. 558.

b. **Court's change of approach in 1992:** What are the rules for when government may engage in content-based regulation of speech that falls within one of these unprotected categories? Until about 1992, such speech could be regulated in a content-based way as long as the regulation satisfied the very lenient *"mere rationality"* review standard, not strict scrutiny. But since a 1992 decision, a majority of the Court seems to have *abandoned* this distinction between the protected-categories situation and the unprotected-categories situation: in *either* case, *viewpoint based restrictions will now be strictly scrutinized.* See *R.A.V. v. St. Paul,* 505 U.S. 377 (1992) (discussed further *infra,* p. 523).

i. **Significance of categories:** Since viewpoint based restrictions are now strictly scrutinized even where the restricted speech falls within an unprotected category, what significance remains to the fact that particular speech does or does not fall within an unprotected category? The main consequences of the unprotected/protected distinction now are probably that:

[1] Government may *completely proscribe* materials falling in an unprotected cat-

egory (so long as government acts in a content-neutral manner within the category); by contrast, government obviously may not enact such a total ban on materials not falling within an unprotected category; and

[2] ***Time/place/manner*** restrictions on speech in public forums will be ***presumptively valid*** when applied to unprotected categories, but will be subjected to careful "mid-level" review (see *infra*, p. 507) in the case of protected categories.

5. **Blurry line between content-based and content-neutral:** The dividing line between content-based and content-neutral regulation can sometimes be ***blurry***, with the Court deeply split about which side of the line a particular regulation falls.

     a. **Speech outside of abortion clinics (*McCullen* case):** A recurring scenario in which the justices have differed about whether the regulation is content-neutral is that of attempts to regulate conduct on public property ***outside of abortion clinics.*** Suppose a state creates a ***buffer zone*** on the street and sidewalk near a clinic entrance, from which all persons without clinic-related business are excluded ***without reference to what message***, if any, they want to deliver. Assume further that when the state enacts the buffer zone, the legislature has only one goal in mind: preventing violence and intimidation by ***anti-abortion protesters*** against women visiting the clinic. Does the fact that the zone on its face excludes *everyone, regardless of message,* who has no business at the clinic, prevent the regulation from being content-based? In a 2014 case, ***McCullen v. Coakley***, 134 S.Ct. 2518 (2014) (also discussed *infra*, p. 515), the Supreme Court split 5-4 on this issue, with the bare majority concluding that the state had ***succeeded in acting in a content-neutral way.***

         i. **Statute in *McCullen*:** *McCullen* involved a Massachusetts law that excluded all persons from standing on streets and sidewalks in an area 35 feet around the entrance to any abortion clinic, except those with clinic-related business.

         ii. **Held not to be content-based:** The plaintiffs who challenged the statute contented that it was in fact a ***content-based restriction of speech***, because, as they (correctly) pointed out, "virtually all speech affected by the [statute] is speech concerning abortion." But Chief Justice Roberts, writing on this point for a majority of the Court, ***disagreed*** with the plaintiffs' conclusion.

         (1) Reasoning: Roberts conceded that the statute, by creating buffer zones only around abortion clinics, had the ***"inevitable effect"*** of restricting abortion-related speech more than speech on other subjects. But this fact wasn't enough to make the act content-based: ***"A facially neutral law does not become content based simply because it may disproportionately affect speech on certain topics."***

         iii. **Dissent:** But four members of the Court ***disagreed*** with Robert's conclusion that the statute was content-neutral. A concurrence by Justice Scalia (joined by Kennedy and Thomas) argued that the statute was obviously content-based: "[It] blinks reality to say [that] a blanket prohibition on the use of streets and sidewalks where ***speech on only one politically controversial topic is likely to occur*** — and where that speech can ***most effectively be communicated*** — is not content-based." Scalia went on, "Would the Court exempt from strict scrutiny a law banning access to the streets and sidewalks surrounding the site of the Republican National Convention? Or those used annually to commemorate the 1965 Selma-to-Montgomery civil rights marches? ... Surely not."

D. Analysis of "track two" cases ("non-content-based" regulation): Let us turn now to the analysis of a case which belongs on "track *two*," that is, one in which the government's interest in regulation *does not relate to the communicative impact of the expression*. Regulations of the *"time, place and manner"* of speech (assuming that they do not mask discrimination based on the communicative content of the speech) fall within "track two." The abortion-protest case discussed on p. 487 above, *McCullen*, is an example (according to a majority of the Court) of such a content-neutral regulation.

1. General principles: Analysis on "track two" depends on whether or not the expression takes place in a *"public forum."* (This term includes traditional public places like streets and parks, and is further defined *infra*, p. 532.)

   a. Public forum: Where the expression takes place in a public forum, the regulation must not only be *content-neutral* (which it must be no matter what the forum, unless the expression falls within an "unprotected category" as discussed above), but it must also *not close adequate alternative channels* for communications, and it must be *narrowly-tailored* to serve a *significant governmental interest*. This is effectively a "middle level of review," halfway between mere-rationality and strict scrutiny.

   i. "Convenience" not enough: An important aspect of this mid-level review is that regulations that impair the use for expressive purposes of such public forums may *not* be justified merely by the government's *convenience* (e.g., a ban on handbills to prevent littering).

   b. Private places: Where the expression takes place in a location that is *not* a public forum, it's much easier for the government to regulate the expression:

   i. Insubstantial restraint: If the impairment of expression caused by the regulation is *not substantial*, the state must merely show that its regulation is *rational* (assuming, as always, that the restraint is content-neutral).

   ii. Substantial: If the impairment of expression *is* "substantial," the state must show that its own interest is even more substantial. But in contrast to the public-forum situation, the state can prove that a restraint on expression in a non-public-forum is not substantial by showing that there are *alternate channels* by which the speaker can reach the same audience with the same message. Tribe, p. 982.

E. Regulation of "pure conduct": So far, we have assumed that "expression" is somehow being regulated by the government. But how do we decide whether what is being regulated *is in fact "expression"*? The fact that what is being regulated is "conduct" rather than "pure speech" is not dispositive — a long line of Supreme Court cases holds that "expressive conduct" receives First Amendment protection just as "pure speech" does. (For instance, marching down the street in a protest is in a sense "conduct," but it is also clearly "expression." See the discussion of this conduct/speech distinction *infra*, p. 509.) But some conduct may contain such a *small* component of expression that it is found to be *not protected by the First Amendment at all*.

1. Supreme Court's test: The Supreme Court has articulated a two-part test for determining whether conduct possesses sufficient *"communicative elements"* to trigger the First

Amendment protection: it must be the case that **both**: (1) an "intent to convey a **particularized message** was present"; and (2) "the likelihood was great that the message would be **understood** by those who viewed it." *Spence v. Washington*, 418 U.S. 405 (1974).

> **Example:** A court might hold that panhandling on the street has so little expressive content that it gets no First Amendment protection at all. The court might reason that the express or implied statement "Please give me money" (or even "Please give me money because I'm poor") does not really convey any communicative element that would be so understood by the people to whom it is addressed. (The Supreme Court has never decided whether panhandling gets any First Amendment protection.)

II. ADVOCACY OF ILLEGAL CONDUCT

A. Introduction: If any kind of speech can lay claim to special constitutional protection, it is probably speech of a *political* nature. Our entire system of representative government operates on the assumption that political and social change will come about peacefully, through public discussion, rather than through violence.

1. **Dangerous speech:** Yet, certain types of political speech may seem to most of us to pose a threat to the very system of representative democracy which freedom of speech is supposed to ensure. For instance, speech calling for immediate assassination of the President, or the institution of a military coup, seems dangerous to tolerate. However, once the government is permitted to prevent or punish some types of political speech, there arises the threat that those in power may also **stifle legitimate dissent.**

2. **Advocacy of illegal conduct:** Since early 20th century, when the Supreme Court first began its serious grappling with the limits of valid political speech, the Court has generally tried to distinguish between, on the one hand, general **political dissent** and advocacy of **abstract theories** (which may not be punished), and on the other hand, **incitement** of **particular illegal acts** (which constitutes an "unprotected category," and may therefore be punished). But the Court has vacillated dramatically during this period in drawing the line between these two types of speech. Most commentators agree that the current standard, articulated in 1969 in *Brandenburg v. Ohio*, 395 U.S. 444 (1969) (discussed *infra*, p. 495) gives substantially greater protection to political speech than the various tests in force before it.

B. The "clear and present danger" test: For most of the 20th century prior to *Brandenburg*, the dividing line between legal advocacy and illegal incitement of criminal acts was drawn by use of the *"clear and present danger"* test. Under this test, speech could be punished as an attempt to commit an illegal act if the speech created a "clear and present danger" that the illegal act *would come about* (even if it never in fact occurred).

1. *Schenck:* The test was first articulated by Justice Holmes (speaking for a unanimous Court) in **Schenck v. U.S.,** 249 U.S. 47 (1919). The case arose in a wartime context, and involved the degree to which citizens had a constitutional right to oppose the First World War.

   a. **Facts:** In the 1917 Espionage Act, Congress made it a crime, *inter alia*, to "willfully cause or attempt to cause insubordination, disloyalty, mutiny, or refusal of duty, in the military or naval forces of the United States," or to "willfully obstruct the recruiting or enlistment service" of the U.S. The defendants were not charged with violating the

Act, but rather, with *conspiring* to violate it. The defendants had sent two draftees a document opposing the draft, calling it "despotism," and urging the draftees, "[d]o not submit to intimidation." But the document *did not explicitly advocate illegal resistance* to the draft; it merely advocated *peaceful measures,* such as petitioning for repeal of the Conscription Act.

b. **Holding:**   Nonetheless, the Court unanimously found that the defendants *could constitutionally be convicted* of conspiracy to violate the statute. Whether or not a given utterance is protected by the First Amendment depends, Holmes wrote, on the circumstances; the defendants' document might have been constitutionally protected, for instance, in time of peace. The issue was "whether the words used are used in such circumstances and are of such a nature as to create a *clear and present danger* that they will *bring about the substantive evils* that Congress has a right to prevent." Whether the defendants' conduct in fact posed a "clear and present danger" was a factual issue, the jury's disposition of which the Court refused to disturb.

c. **Crying "fire" in theater:**   In his *Schenck* opinion, Holmes illustrated his assertion that not all speech was constitutionally privileged by posing the now-famous example of *falsely crying "fire!" in a crowded theater.*

   i. **Criticism:**   However, the nature of crying "fire!" in a crowded theater seems dramatically different from the speech in *Schenck*; for one thing, the false cry of "fire" is clearly understood by its listeners to be a statement of *fact,* not an exhortation or expression of opinion as the *Schenck* document obviously was. Also, if one believes that the best way to combat false speech is by combatting it in the "marketplace of ideas" (a view espoused by Holmes himself in *Abrams v. U.S., infra,* p. 491), the two situations are clearly different: there is not time to argue with the cry of "fire!", but probably ample time to argue about the merits of conscription.

2. *Frohwerk* **and** *Debs:*   Very shortly after *Schenck,* Justice Holmes wrote two more opinions, for a unanimous Court, upholding Espionage Act convictions against First Amendment arguments.

   a. *Frohwerk:*   One of these, *Frohwerk v. U.S.,* 249 U.S. 204 (1919), involved writers of editorials criticizing the draft in a German-language newspaper. Holmes' opinion seemed to *shift the burden of proof to the defendants* — because of the lack of clarity of the record on appeal, it was "impossible to say that it might not have been found" that the publication might have been enough to "kindle a flame" of draft resistance.

   b. *Debs:*   The other case, *Debs v. U.S.,* 249 U.S. 211 (1919) is perhaps even more disturbing to those who believe that general opposition to government policies, unaccompanied by explicit advocacy of illegal acts, ought to be protected by the First Amendment. The defendant in *Debs* was the well-known socialist and presidential candidate Eugene V. Debs, who made a speech opposing the First World War. Debs' conviction of obstructing military recruitment was upheld by the Court.

   i. **Weak standard:**   Although Holmes purported to be applying the "clear and present danger" standard, he phrased it as merely requiring that the words have as their *"natural tendency and reasonably probable effect"* the obstruction of recruitment. As in *Schenck,* the Court refused to reject the jury's finding that Debs' speech met this test.

ii. **Criticism of *Debs*:** The "clear and present danger" standard which the *Debs* opinion purported to apply gave very little protection to Debs. There was, for instance, no evidence that any obstruction of recruitment actually occurred as a result of the speech. Holmes did not acknowledge that there was a difference between mailing anti-draft leaflets *directly* to draftees (as in *Schenck*) and addressing a general audience. Debs' conviction was "somewhat as though George McGovern had been sent to prison for his criticism of the war [in Vietnam]." 40 U. CHI. L. REV. 237 (quoted in L,K&C, p. 653, n.a.).

3. **Holmes' dissent in *Abrams*:** It was not until *Abrams v. U.S.,* 250 U.S. 616 (1919) that application of the "clear and present danger" standard was sufficient to produce even so much as a dissent against a conviction for anti-war speech. In that case, Justice Holmes' dissent (joined by Justice Brandeis) finally placed some First Amendment "bite" into the standard; *Abrams* is one of his best-known dissents.

a. **Facts:** The defendants in *Abrams*, American socialists of Russian-Jewish birth, were convicted of violating a newly-added section of the Espionage Act, which prohibited the urging of any curtailment of war production with intent to hinder the United States' prosecution of the War. The defendants had published two pro-Bolshevik leaflets, which attacked the United States' production and supplying of arms that might be used against Russia (against whom the U.S. had not declared war); neither leaflet was pro-German, and in fact one was violently against German militarism. The leaflets urged workers not to make bullets which would be used not only against Germans but Russians as well.

b. **Majority view:** The key factual issue in the case was whether the defendants had the requisite intent to interfere with the war effort *against Germany*. The majority conceded that the defendants' *primary* purpose may have been only to aid the Russian Revolution. But "[m]en must be held to have intended … the effects which their acts were *likely to produce*." Curtailment of production to protect Russians could not have been accomplished except by also impairing the war effort against Germany, the majority believed, so that the intent requirement was satisfied. (The majority also went out of its way to emphasize, repeatedly, that the defendants were self-proclaimed "anarchists.")

c. **Holmes' dissent:** Much of Holmes' dissent was on the fairly pedestrian issue of intent. Unlike the majority, he believed that an actor does not "intend" a consequence "unless that consequence is the aim of the deed." By this standard, the defendants simply had no intent to interfere with the war effort against Germany, however likely that possible outcome may have seemed to them.

i. **Value of free speech:** But Holmes' dissent is best known for its more general words about the value of free speech. He articulated what could be called the "marketplace of ideas" theory: he urged *"free trade in ideas,"* and argued that "[t]he best test of truth is the power of the thought to get itself accepted in the competition of the market. … " The importance of allowing ideas to compete with each other, he argued, was so great that even opinions which we "loathe and believe to be fraught with death" should not be suppressed, "unless they so imminently threaten immediate interference with the lawful and pressing purposes of the law that an immediate check is required to save the country."

4. Criticism of "clear and present danger" doctrine: Holmes' "clear and present danger" doctrine has been criticized on a number of grounds.

    a. Not very protective: First, at least as it was applied in early cases, the doctrine obviously did not give very much protection to freedom of speech, since the defendants in *Schenck, Frohwerk, Debs*, and *Abrams* were all convicted, without a showing that the words of any of them actually brought about a substantive evil.

    b. Opinion about threat: Second, the test, since it relies upon the fact-finder's opinion about the immediacy of a specific threat (e.g., obstruction of military recruitment), makes political speech particularly vulnerable to the mass hysteria which tends to strike in times of national crisis. For instance, the test gave the least protection to speech during the First World War and during the McCarthy anti-Communist scare, as discussed below.

    c. Ineffectiveness rewarded: Finally, the test seems to say that any kind of speech is permissible *as long as it is ineffective*, making the test a very peculiar way of carrying out the First Amendment notion of political change through peaceful speech rather than through violent action.

C. The Learned Hand test: Because of these weaknesses in the "clear and present danger" test, Judge Learned Hand, one of the greatest federal district and appeals court judges in our history, articulated a different test, one focusing *solely on the words spoken, not on the surrounding circumstances*. Hand's test was put forth in *Masses Publishing Co. v. Patten*, 244 F. 535 (S.D.N.Y. 1917), a pre-*Schenck* decision.

1. Terms of test: Hand believed that words could be punished if they "counsel or advise others to *violate* the law as it stands," but not if they are merely *critical* of the law.

    a. Application: The speech at issue in *Masses* consisted of anti-war cartoons and text which criticized the War and the draft, and which expressed great sympathy for draft resisters. Yet for Hand, this was still only *abstract advocacy* of the anti-war position, not a direct call to violate the law. Consequently, he found the materials beyond Congress' power to prohibit or punish.

2. Significance: The main significance of Hand's test is that it makes the *likely effects* of the speech *completely irrelevant*. Even if it were shown that the materials in fact caused many readers to resist the draft illegally, the publication would still be beyond Congress' reach. By the same token, if the publication *did* constitute a *direct call* to violate the law, it would be punishable *even if it was utterly ineffectual*.

3. Fate of Hand test: Hand's test was immediately rejected; not even the federal court of appeals in *Masses* itself was willing to affirm it. Instead, the "clear and present danger" test prevailed for the next 50 years. But the Hand approach has ultimately had its day; *Brandenburg v. Ohio (infra*, p. 495) incorporates the main aspects of that test, though it adds aspects of "clear and present danger" as well.

D. Statutes directly proscribing speech: In the cases considered thus far, the legislature proscribed *acts*, not speech; speech became relevant only because the prosecution claimed that the speech constituted an attempt, or conspiracy, to bring about the forbidden act. Later, however, legislatures began enacting statutes which *directly forbade* certain types of speech. A major debate erupted on the Court about whether the "clear and present danger" test applies to prosecutions under such statutes as well.

1. **Test not applied:** The argument was won, at least temporarily, by those who claimed that the "clear and present danger" test had *no application* in this instance, and that the legislature's *own conclusion* that certain types of speech were *intrinsically dangerous* was to be respected.

2. ***Gitlow:*** Thus in ***Gitlow v. New York***, 268 U.S. 652 (1925), the Court construed the New York "criminal anarchy" statute, which banned advocating (orally or in writing) the overthrow of a government by assassination or other violent means. The defendant, a socialist, was involved in the publication of a "Left-wing Manifesto," which advocated establishment of a dictatorship of the proletariat through mass strikes and other "revolutionary mass action."

   a. **Majority view:** There was no showing at trial that the publication had posed any present danger of governmental overthrow or other substantive evil. Nonetheless, the majority *upheld* the defendant's conviction.

      i. **Rationale:** The "clear and present danger" test of *Schenck* was only to be applied "in those cases where the statute merely prohibits certain *acts* involving the danger of substantive evil, *without any reference to language* itself. ... " Here, by contrast, the legislature had *already* determined that *certain types of language* (advocacy of violent overthrow of the government) posed a risk that substantive evils would result. It was not open to the Court to dispute the legislature's judgment and to conclude that, in a particular case, utterances coming within the statute were not dangerous.

      ii. **No immediacy requirement:** Furthermore, there was no requirement that the legislature proscribe only speech advocating *definite* or *immediate* action. Thus the defense that the Manifesto called only for action at some indefinite time in the future was unavailing.

   b. **Dissent:** A dissent by Justice Holmes (joined by Justice Brandeis) argued that the "clear and present danger" test *should* be applied on these facts. Under this test, he argued there should be no conviction because the Manifesto "had *no chance* of starting a *present conflagration*." But Holmes did not respond directly to the majority's argument that the test should not be applied where the legislature has directly forbidden certain types of speech.

3. ***Whitney:*** The legislature's right to ban a certain type of speech, regardless of the substantive dangers posed by it, was presented again in ***Whitney v. California***, 274 U.S. 357 (1927).

   a. **Facts:** The California Criminal Syndicalism Act forbade the knowing membership in any organization advocating the use of force or violence to effect political change. Miss Whitney, who did not deny being a member of the Communist Labor Party, was convicted even though she did not agree with the Party's advocacy of violent means of change, and had in fact voted for a more temperate plank.

   b. **Holding:** But a majority of the Court upheld the conviction, believing that the legislature's conclusion that mere knowing membership in an organization advocating criminal syndicalism was substantively dangerous, "must be given great weight."

   c. **Brandeis' dissent:** Justice Brandeis' concurrence in *Whitney* (joined by Holmes) is one of his most eloquent on free speech.

i. **The value of free speech:** Brandeis' concurrence is most remembered for its general discussion of the value of free speech. An orderly society *cannot be maintained merely through fear and enforced silence*, for "fear breeds repression … repression breeds hate … [and] hate menaces stable government." On the contrary, "the path of safety lies in the opportunity to discuss freely supposed grievances and proposed remedies. … *[T]he fitting remedy for evil counsels is good ones.*" This might be thought of as the *"safety valve"* theory of free speech (in contrast to the view that human expression is an end in itself, not merely a means to maintenance of order).

ii. **Emergency:** For Brandeis, it followed that anytime bad ideas could be combatted by good ones, this combat, rather than suppression of the bad ideas, must be allowed to take place. Only where "the incidence of the evil apprehended is so *imminent* that it may befall *before there is opportunity for full discussion*" may speech be prohibited or punished. Furthermore, even if the danger is imminent, it may not be suppressed unless it is *"relatively serious"*; for instance, advocacy of the right of pedestrians to cross unfenced vacant lands could not be prohibited, even if there were imminent danger that such advocacy would lead to trespass.

iii. **Concurrence:** However, Brandeis' opinion was cast as a concurrence, not a dissent, because in Brandeis' opinion the defendant had not raised the appropriate constitutional claims at the trial level.

d. **Overruled:** *Whitney* was explicitly overruled in *Brandenburg v. Ohio*, 395 U.S. 444 (1969), discussed extensively *infra*, p. 495.

E. **Threat of communism and the Smith Act:** During and immediately following the Second World War, fears of an international communist threat became even more pronounced. One response was the passage by Congress in 1940 of the Smith Act, which was similar to the New York Criminal Anarchy Statute upheld in *Gitlow (supra*, p. 493).

1. **The *Dennis* case:** The most important Smith Act case was *Dennis v. U.S.*, 341 U.S. 494 (1951), in which the Court purported to apply the "clear and present danger" standard, but did so in a manner that gave dramatically *less First Amendment protection* to political speech than Holmes or Brandeis would presumably have wanted.

a. **Facts:** The defendants were convicted under the Smith Act of conspiring to advocate the overthrow of the United States Government, and of conspiring to reorganize the U.S. Communist Party, which the prosecution claimed was a group that advocated such overthrow.

b. **Majority upholds:** A majority of the Court *upheld* the conviction. The opinion, by Justice Vinson, purported to be applying the "clear and present danger" test. However, the majority refused to interpret the test as requiring that there have been a clear and present danger of an *actual attempt* to overthrow the government; the Holmes test "cannot mean that before the Government may act, it must wait until the putsch is about to be executed, the plans have been laid and the signal is awaited."

i. **Adoption of Hand balancing test:** Instead, the majority applied a test which had been formulated by Learned Hand, writing for the appeals court below: the test was "whether the *gravity* of the 'evil', *discounted by its improbability,* justifies such invasion of free speech as is necessary to avoid the danger." (Hand thus abandoned his *Masses* test, and instead tried to reshape the Holmes test.) Here, the evil (violent overthrow of the government) was so great that even a ***small, non-imminent***, chance of success justified curtailing the speech.

    c. Significance of *Dennis*: *Dennis* represents "the temporary eclipse of the Holmes-Brandeis formulation of the clear and present danger test." Tribe, p. 846. Once the evil's ***seriousness*** became a ***substitute*** for its ***immediacy,*** speech could be restricted ***no matter how remote its anticipated consequences***.

F. The modern standard: Today, the Supreme Court generally gives ***greater protection to free speech***, at least in the political area, than it has given in previous eras.

    1. *Brandenburg*: The present status of freedom of political speech is best expressed in ***Brandenburg v. Ohio***, 395 U.S. 444 (1969), a case in which the Court combined the most speech-protective aspects of ***both*** the ***"clear and present danger"*** test and the ***"advocacy/incitement"*** distinction.

        a. Facts: Defendant was a leader of an Ohio Ku Klux Klan group. He was charged with violating Ohio's Criminal Syndicalism Statute, which (like that of California, sustained in *Whitney v. California, supra*, p. 493) forbade the advocacy of crime or violence as a means of accomplishing industrial or political reform.

        b. Holding: The Court (in a unanimous *per curiam* opinion) ***struck down*** the Ohio statute, without considering whether the defendant's actual speech could have been properly proscribed.

            i. New test: In so doing, the Court articulated new requirements which a statute proscribing speech must meet. Speech advocating the use of force or crime can be proscribed only where two conditions are satisfied:

            [1] the advocacy is ***"directed to inciting or producing imminent lawless action"***; ***and***

            [2] the advocacy is also ***"likely to incite or produce such action."***

    2. Significance of new test: The two-part *Brandenburg* standard is usually viewed as combining aspects of both the Holmes and Hand tests, in a way that gives "double protection" to speech.

        a. Holmes aspect: The Holmes "clear and present danger" legacy is reflected in the requirement that the speech be "***likely*** to incite or produce" ***imminent*** unlawful action. Thus the concern with immediate, likely, consequences remains.

        b. Hand aspect: But *Brandenburg* also reflects Hand's insistence that what should be restricted is only direct advocacy of ***action***, not mere advocacy of ***abstract doctrine***. This distinction is imposed by the requirement that the speech be ***"directed"*** (i.e., ***intended***) to ***"inciting*** or ***producing"*** an unlawful response.

        c. Consequence: Apparently, therefore, no speech that would have been protected by ***either*** the Holmes or Hand tests may be prohibited under *Brandenburg*.

        d. Application to Ohio statute: The significance of the *Brandenburg* test is illustrated by the way the Court applied it to the Ohio statute at issue there. The Ohio act punished all advocacy of the "duty, necessity or propriety of crime [or] violence ... as a means of accomplishing industrial or political reform. ... " This language was sufficiently broad that it forbade advocacy of the ***abstract doctrine*** of violent political change, as well as incitement to imminent unlawful action. Therefore, it was held unconstitutional, even though some applications of it might have been constitutional (an illustration of the "overbreadth" doctrine, discussed below).

3. **Severity of harm:** The *Brandenburg* test does not explicitly take into account the ***severity*** of the harm which is threatened. Reading *Brandenburg* literally, a speaker who advocated use of nuclear weapons for terrorist purposes, but only after a one-year moratorium, could not be punished (since the harm would not be "imminent"). Conversely, one who incited his listeners to jaywalk immediately could be punished. Tribe (p. 849, n. 59) advocates taking into account seriousness, at least on the less-serious side of the spectrum.

4. ***Whitney* overruled:** *Brandenburg* explicitly overruled *Whitney v. California, see supra*, p. 493, which had upheld a Criminal Syndicalism statute nearly identical to that struck down in *Brandenburg*.

5. **Other modern cases:** Other cases decided in the late 60's or later present additional illustrations of the twin modern requirements of: (1) ***incitement*** (as distinguished from abstract advocacy); and (2) harm that is ***imminent*** (as distinguished from remote).

   a. ***Bond:*** The Court held that the Georgia House of Representatives' exclusion of Julian Bond from membership violated his First Amendment rights, in *Bond v. Floyd*, 385 U.S. 116 (1966). Bond, an opponent of the war in Vietnam, had joined a statement of "sympathy with, and support [of] the men in this country who are unwilling to respond to a military draft." The Georgia House reasoned that Bond could not truthfully swear to "support the Constitution of this State and of the United States." But the Court held that Bond could not be penalized for his statement, since it did not constitute a call for unlawful draft resistance, but was merely a ***general, abstract***, declaration of opposition to the war.

   b. ***Watts:*** A black anti-war activist, in a speech, said "[i]f they ever make me carry a rifle, the first man I want to get in my sights is L.B.J. They are not going to make me kill my black brothers." He was convicted under a law making it a crime intentionally to threaten to kill the President. In *Watts v. U.S.*, 394 U.S. 705 (1969), the Court reversed the conviction, on the grounds that the circumstances showed that the speaker did not intend to make a ***"true threat"*** but rather, to state his ***political opposition*** to the President (albeit in a "very crude, offensive" way). The Court relied especially on the fact that the "threat" was conditional, and that the audience responded by laughter.

   c. ***Hess:*** *Bond, Watts* and *Brandenburg* were all decided during the Warren era. But the post-Warren Court has also applied the *Brandenburg* standard. One instance is *Hess v. Indiana*, 414 U.S. 105 (1973), growing out of a campus anti-war demonstration in which demonstrators blocked a street until they were moved off it by the police. Defendant then said "We'll take the fucking street later [or again]." (The record was ambiguous as to the precise word used.) The Court found this to be protected speech, rather than an unprotected incitement to illegal action. Construed least favorably to the defendant, the statement was "nothing more than advocacy of illegal action at ***some indefinite future time***"; only words intended to produce (and also likely to produce) ***imminent*** disorder could be punished.

6. **Mere membership not enough (*Scales*):** Are there some organizations that are so subversive that ***mere knowing membership*** in them can be forbidden? The answer so far has

been *"no"* — membership in a group can be punished only if the member is an *active* (not passive) member who *specifically intends to further the organization's illegal ends.* *Scales v. U.S.*, 367 U.S. 203 (1961).

a. **"Active support" is enough:** On the other hand, a post-9/11 decision shows that although government may not be entitled to make "mere membership" in an organization illegal, the state *can* constitutionally prohibit virtually any kind of *active support* of an illegal organization, even support that is intended to further the organization's *legal* aims. See *Holder v. Humanitarian Law Project*, 130 S.Ct. 2705 (2010), in which the Court upheld a federal statute making it a crime to provide *"material support"* to a designated foreign terrorist organization, and defining "material support" in an exceptionally broad way.

i. **What the statute forbids:** The statute in question in *Holder* let the U.S. Secretary of State designate an entity as a *"foreign terrorist organization."* Once an organization had been designated in that way, it was then a federal crime to give the organization "material support or resources." "Material support" was defined to include not just financial support, but also a number of intangible services such as *"training"* and the giving of *"expert advice or assistance."*

ii. **The plaintiffs:** Two of the organizations put on the terrorist list were the Kurdistan Workers' Party (which had the aim of establishing an independent Kurdish state in southeast Turkey) and the Liberation Tigers of Tamil Eelam (which aimed to created an independent Tamil state in Sri Lanka). The plaintiffs were various American citizens and organizations that wanted to train members of these groups in how to use international law to resolve their disputes peacefully, and also wanted to engage in political advocacy on their behalf. The plaintiffs claimed that the statute was inconsistent with *Scales* — they argued that it effectively made mere membership in the organization illegal, even if the member wanted to pursue only the organization's lawful aims.

iii. **Statute upheld:** By a 6-3 vote, the Court *upheld* the statute against First Amendment attack. In an opinion by Chief Justice Roberts, the Court said that *Scales* was irrelevant, because that case did not deal with the issue of whether the giving of material support to an organization could constitutionally be forbidden. The statute here did not criminalize "mere membership" (as the one in *Scales* had done), but instead criminalized the giving of "material support" to the organization. There was no constitutional difficulty, Roberts said, with prohibiting material support of an illegal organization (at least a foreign one), even if the supporter did not have a specific intent to further the organization's illegal aims.

(1) **Freeing up of resources:** Roberts argued that even support of a terrorist organization's *legitimate* aims could be *harmful*. For instance, such support *"frees up other resources within the organization* that may be put to violent ends." And that support "helps *lend legitimacy* to foreign terrorist groups — legitimacy that makes it easier for those groups to persist, to recruit members, and to raise funds — all of which facilitate more terrorist attacks."

(2) **Statute is limited:** But, Roberts asserted, the statute applied only to material support that was *"coordinated with or under the direction of"* the designated terrorist organization, not *"independent* advocacy that might be viewed as

promoting the group's legitimacy." So *Holder* does not answer the question of whether Congress could make it a crime to engage in truly independent advocacy on behalf of a terrorist organization.

    iv. Dissent: Three justices (Breyer, joined by Ginsburg and Sotomayor) dissented in *Holder*. They argued that the statute should be strictly scrutinized, because it authorized the criminal prosecution of those who engage in the communication and advocacy of political ideas. The dissenters were especially troubled by the majority's argument that the forbidden support "helps lend legitimacy" to terrorist groups; the dissenters believed that there was "no natural stopping place" once this argument was accepted — "speech, association and related activities on behalf of a group will often, perhaps always, help to legitimate that group."

  b. "Incitement" law today: *Holder* suggests that today, as we are actively waging the war on terror, the Supreme Court will be **quicker to uphold government restrictions on subversive or terrorist organizations** than it was in the relatively liberal 1960s era in which *Brandenburg* and *Scales* were decided. True, *Brandenburg* and *Scales* technically remain the law: mere advocacy of even violent political change cannot be forbidden unless the speaker is calling for imminent lawless action, and mere membership in even the most dangerous organization cannot be flatly prohibited. But *Holder* means that any support beyond pure advocacy or membership — even **"training"** of an organization's personnel, or **"advocacy"** that is coordinated with the organization — **may be criminalized**, and that's true even if the support is intended to further only the organization's *legal* objectives.

    i. Less free-speech protective: That's a less free-speech-protective approach than pre-9/11 cases seemed to allow. See Bollinger (quoted at SST&K, p. 1066, n. 5), presciently saying in 2002 that "the fact that the last 30 years since *Brandenburg* have been remarkably peaceful and prosperous means that the understandings we now have about the meaning of free speech have not really been tested ... [J]ust about every time the country has felt **seriously threatened** the First Amendment has **retreated**."

III. OVERBREADTH AND VAGUENESS

  A. Overbreadth: Because of the especially great importance of freedom of expression in our constitutional scheme, the Supreme Court has developed several techniques of statutory analysis to make sure that that freedom gets the extra protection it requires. One of these techniques is the use of the doctrine of **"overbreadth."**

    1. Definition: A statute is overbroad if, in addition to proscribing activities which may constitutionally be forbidden, it **also** sweeps within its coverage speech or conduct which is **protected by the guarantees of free speech or free association**. See *Thornhill v. Alabama*, 310 U.S. 88 (1940).

    2. Significance: There are two respects in which the doctrine of statutory overbreadth changes the usual rules of constitutional litigation:

      a. Standing: First, a litigant who is attempting to have a statute ruled unconstitutional must normally show that it is unconstitutional **in its application to him.** For instance, in a First Amendment case that does not involve overbreadth, the challenger to a statute must show that his own speech or conduct was protected by the First Amendment. But the overbreadth doctrine permits the challenger to prevail if he can show that the statute, applied according to its terms, would violate the First Amendment rights of persons not now before the Court. Thus overbreadth can be viewed as an *exception to the usual requirements of "standing"* (see *infra*, p. 731), by which a person is not normally permitted to assert the constitutional rights of others, only his own. Or to put it in terms of the usually-employed set of labels, most constitutional attacks are required to be *"as applied"* attacks (the plaintiff is saying that the statute is unconstitutional "as applied" to her, i.e., the statute violates *her own rights*), whereas an overbreadth attack is a *"facial"* attack, i.e., an attack *"on the face"* of the statute, saying that it's invalid *no matter to whom it's applied*.

    i. **Statute's application to challenger:** In fact, where overbreadth analysis is applied, the Court simply *assumes* that a more narrowly-drawn statute *could* constitutionally proscribe the challenger's own conduct. Ordinarily, the Court never even decides this question explicitly; by deciding to apply overbreadth analysis, it is able to decide instead the usually *easier* question of whether the statute by its terms covers hypothetical constitutionally-protected conduct by third parties.

  b. **Statute found void on its face:** Secondly, in the usual situation, where a court finds a statute to be unconstitutional it will simply *excise* the statute's unconstitutional applications, *leaving the statute in force* as to those situations where its application would be constitutional. But where overbreadth is applied, the statute is *completely struck down*. That is, the statute is found to be *void "on its face."* Until a different statute is enacted (a more limited one, applying only where it may constitutionally do so), or until another court with authority construes the statute more narrowly (in a way that forbids only constitutionally-proscribable speech or conduct), the statute is simply unenforceable against *anyone*.

3. **Rationales:** There are two main rationales for using the overbreadth doctrine in First Amendment cases:

  a. **"Chilling effect" on speech:** First, the mere existence of an overly broad statute (that is, a statute which by its terms forbids some protected speech) is likely to have a *"chilling effect"* on free speech. Some people whose speech the statute could *not* constitutionally reach (and who thus would presumably prevail in court if they spoke and then litigated the statute's application to them) might simply be *intimidated* into *not exercising their right to speak*.

    i. **Explanation:** As Justice Marshall put it in a dissent to *Arnett v. Kennedy*, 416 U.S. 134 (1974), an overbroad statute "hangs over [people's] heads like a Sword of Damocles. … That this Court will ultimately vindicate [a person] if his speech is constitutionally protected is of little consequence — for the value of a sword of Damocles is that it hangs — not that it drops." He added that the focus of the overbreadth doctrine "is not on the individual actor before the court but on others who may forgo protected activity rather than run afoul of the statute's proscriptions."

  b. **Selective enforcement:** Secondly, an overly-broad statute is highly vulnerable to *selective enforcement* by the authorities, i.e., enforcement that discriminates against certain classes of people or certain points of view. The problem of selective enforcement exists in any statute. But the risk is greater in the case of an overbroad one, since the statute gives officials, by hypothesis, not only the opportunity to treat people differently (a problem with any statute, since it is always possible to prosecute only one of two people who may constitutionally be prosecuted), but also the chance to *violate the constitutional rights* of one person without violating those of another.

Example: Assume that a town ordinance proscribes "all demonstrations, involving 100 or more persons, held in public streets." This ordinance by its terms applies both to activity which may constitutionally be proscribed (e.g., demonstrations that include violence or a substantial breach of the peace) as well as to those which may *not* be constitutionally prohibited (peaceful demonstrations, conducted at an appropriate time, without causing major interference with traffic).

Within the class of activities to which the statute may *not* constitutionally be applied, there is an open invitation to the police to allow their own views about acceptable content to color their decision. For instance, they may "look charitably at a post game victory celebration in the streets of a college town [but] not feel the same way about an antiwar demonstration." See 43 CHI. L. REV. 38 (quoted in L,K&C, p. 733). Therefore, the statute will be found to be overbroad, and thus void "on its face"; that is, it may not be applied even to activity which *could* constitutionally be proscribed by a more narrowly-drawn statute (e.g., demonstrations that include violence to bystanders).

4. **Doctrine cut back — "substantial" overbreadth now required:** However, the modern Court has significantly *curtailed* the use of overbreadth analysis in First Amendment cases. It has done so principally by requiring that the overbreadth be *"substantial,"* compared with the legitimate applications of the statute. This requirement was first set forth in *Broadrick v. Oklahoma*, 413 U.S. 601 (1973), a case which remains the best statement of the modern Court's view on overbreadth.

   a. **Facts:** §818 of Oklahoma's Merit System Act prohibited civil servants from engaging in certain political activities, including taking part in the management or affairs of any political party or campaign, and soliciting for campaign contributions. Broadrick, who had campaigned for a superior and had solicited money for him, challenged §818 on overbreadth (as well as vagueness) grounds. He pointed out that §818 had been construed as applying to such political expression as the wearing of political buttons and the displaying of bumper stickers, which (he asserted) were constitutionally-protected free speech activities. Therefore, he contended, the section must be struck down, regardless of whether his own activity could have been constitutionally proscribed by a more narrowly-drawn statute.

   b. **Holding:** By a 5-4 vote, the Court *rejected* Broadrick's claims, spending most of its time on the overbreadth one.

   c. **Speech vs. conduct:** The opinion distinguished between statutes primarily regulating conduct and those directly governing speech. In situations involving the latter, the Court did not modify the overbreadth rule. But in the case of statutes *governing conduct*, where the conduct happens to have an expressive content, the "strong medicine" of complete invalidation of the statute should not invariably be applied. Instead, the majority believed, for facial invalidation to be appropriate, "the overbreadth of a statute must not only be real, but *substantial* as well, judged in relation to the statute's plainly legitimate sweep." Where the overbreadth is not substantial, unconstitutional applications should be rooted out one at a time, by analysis of the particular fact situations in which successive litigants find themselves.

d. Application: The Oklahoma statue, under this analysis, ***did not call for overbreadth treatment***. The statute was primarily directed at ***conduct*** (taking part in a political campaign), not at pure speech. The statute was ***not "substantially overbroad,"*** since in the majority's judgment, it applied to a "substantial spectrum of conduct" that could constitutionally be subjected to state regulation.

    i. Some protected applications: The Court conceded that the statute by its terms could be applied to the wearing of political buttons or the use of bumper stickers, and that these might be constitutionally-protected expressions. But such potential unconstitutional applications of the statute were ***not numerous enough compared with the body of permissible applications***, so there was no "substantial overbreadth."

    ii. Applied to litigant: Since Broadrick's own conduct was clearly regulable rather than protected, the statute was upheld as applied to him.

e. Makes hard cases easy: The overbreadth doctrine, even with its requirement of "substantial" overbreadth, often has the effect of ***making "hard" cases into "easy" ones***. That is, a case that would be a difficult one if it had to be decided on its own facts often becomes easy once the statute can be taken literally and applied to a substantial number of other hypothetical situations, as to which it would clearly be unconstitutional. See Sullivan & Gunther, p. 1346.

B. Vagueness: The doctrine of ***"vagueness"*** is similar, but not identical, to that of overbreadth. A statute will be held void for vagueness if the conduct forbidden by it is so ***unclearly defined*** that persons "of common intelligence must necessarily ***guess at its meaning*** and differ as to its application." *Connally v. General Construction Co.*, 269 U.S. 385 (1926).

1. Constitutional basis: Theoretically, the proscription against vagueness stems from the Due Process Clause's requirement that people be given ***fair notice*** of what conduct is prohibited. But many void-for-vagueness holdings stem more from violations of other constitutional provisions, particularly the First Amendment. In the First Amendment area, an unduly vague statute has the same ***"chilling"*** effect on speech or association as does an overbroad one: a person does not know whether or not his conduct will ultimately be held to be constitutionally protected, so he declines to exercise his right of speech or association.

2. Curbing discretion: The other main function of the vagueness doctrine is to ***curb the discretion*** afforded to law enforcement officers or administrative officials. Observe that this danger, too, is also a danger posed by an overbroad statute (*supra*, p. 499).

3. Distinguished from overbreadth: Yet vagueness and overbreadth are quite distinguishable doctrines. Their differences can be illustrated by the following example:

Example: Statute I prohibits anyone from "publicly display[ing] a red flag [as] a sign, symbol or emblem of opposition to organized government." Statute II prohibits anyone from "publicly displaying a red flag for any purpose whatsoever."

Statute I is unconstitutionally ***vague***, because there is no way to tell whether it is meant to apply to peaceful displays of opposition to the political party currently in office, or to other constitutionally-protected expressions of political opposition. (See *Stromberg v. California*, 238 U.S. 359 (1931), so holding.)

Statute II is unconstitutionally overbroad. It is obviously not "vague," since its meaning is perfectly clear. But since by its terms it appears to apply to constitutionally-protected conduct, and since there is no "bright line" rule to separate out the constitutional from unconstitutional applications, neither a member of the public nor a court has an easy way to articulate what the statute may constitutionally cover.

Note: These two statutes show that vagueness and overbreadth are both, in part, attempts to deal with the same problem. Both statutes leave the user uncertain about which applications of the statute may **constitutionally** be imposed. The main difference is that in the overbreadth situation, the vagueness is "latent"; for this reason, overbreadth has been called "really a special case of the problem of vagueness." See Freund, *The Supreme Court of the United States* (quoted in L,K&C, p. 732).

Quiz Yourself on

FREEDOM OF EXPRESSION — GENERAL THEMES; ADVOCACY OF ILLEGAL CONDUCT; OVERBREADTH AND VAGUENESS

71. Darwin and 10 others were all members of the basketball team of State U, a public university. The Chancellor of State U had recently suspended Xavier, one of the members of the team, from both the team and the school for alleged cheating in an exam. At 10:00 a.m. on a Tuesday morning, Darwin and his 10 teammates stood in front of the University administration building, which contained the Chancellor's office. They carried signs saying, "Reinstate Xavier"; they also chanted and sang. The Chancellor happened to be away from the office that day (unbeknownst to Darwin and his friends), and nobody in the building was considering Xavier's case at the time.

A statute of the state in which State U is located provides as follows:

"No group of 10 or more persons shall demonstrate on the sidewalk or other public way in front of a state or local government office building during business hours, unless the demonstration is related to matters currently under consideration by government officials working in the building. Violation of this provision shall be punishable as a misdemeanor."

Darwin has been charged with violating this section. He wishes to defend on the grounds that the section violates his First Amendment freedom of expression.

(a) What is the best argument he can make as to why his First Amendment rights would be violated by a conviction? _____

(b) May Darwin constitutionally be convicted of violating the provision? _____

72. The city of Munford has enacted the following ordinance: "No person shall attempt to give to passersby on any sidewalk or public thoroughfare any handbill during a Restricted Time Period. 'Restricted Time Period' shall mean the hours between 8:00 and 9:30 a.m. and the hours between 4:30 and 6:00 p.m., Monday through Friday. 'Handbill' is defined to include any piece of printed literature, four pages or less, dealing with a single topic." The purpose of the definition is to cover advertising circulars and brochures, but not to cover newspapers and magazines. The ordinance was enacted in response to two fears: (1) that during the busy rush hour, people were handing out so many handbills that the flow of pedestrian traffic was frequently impaired; and (2) that an extraordinary amount of litter was being generated when people who had handbills thrust into their hands dropped them on the sidewalk. Kermit, a political candidate who was giving out brochures in support of his own candidacy, was charged with violating the statute. Kermit now argues that a conviction would violate his First Amendment rights. Should the Court agree?

———————————

73. Picketers picket on the public street adjacent to the house of CEO, the head of a company that makes drones used in an unpopular foreign war. The signs they carry contain intentionally hurtful messages (e.g., "CEO is a cowardly murderer"). The state common law of intentional infliction of emotional distress (IIED) allows recovery for any "outrageous and intentionally offensive" language carried on a picket sign near the plaintiff's house. In a suit brought by CEO against the picketers, a jury imposes a $100,000 civil judgment in favor of CEO. May the judgment be constitutionally imposed? ———————————

74. Leonard, a resident of a state that bordered Mexico, believed that the federal government should vastly increase the physical barriers to illegal immigration from Mexico. One day he went to a park that was frequented by people on both sides of the immigration issue. Before a moderately interested audience of about 20 people, all of whom had come to the park for other purposes, Leonard began to make a speech. He said, "If the federal government doesn't start doing a whole lot more to keep out illegal immigrants, we'll have to make 'em do it. Let's start by building up an arsenal of automatics and machine guns. Eventually, we'll have guerilla cells throughout the Southwest to make the federal government's life such a hell they'll build the kind of huge border fence we need." A few of the listeners applauded, one asked a question, but no one took any other action in apparent response to Leonard's speech. Immediately after his speech, Leonard was arrested by the police for violating §123 of a state statute. That statute provided that it is a felony to "advocate insurrection against the state or federal government or any local subdivision thereof." Leonard now defends on the grounds that a conviction would violate his First Amendment rights. May Leonard constitutionally be convicted of violating the statute? ———————————

75. Robert was a tenured teacher in a public high school, in the state of Cartesia. He was also a member of NAMBLA, the National Association of Man Boy Love Affairs. NAMBLA's charter says that it is dedicated to the furtherance of social and sexual interaction between men and boys. Cartesia makes it a crime for an adult male to have sexual relations with a boy under the age of 17. Robert knows the aims of NAMBLA, and supports those aims; in fact, he himself has in the recent past had sexual relations with a boy. School officials, worried about recent publicity concerning teachers who belong to NAMBLA, asked Robert and all other teachers at the school to sign an affidavit stating that "I am not now nor have I ever been a member of NAMBLA." (The affidavit said nothing else.) School officials announced that if a teacher did not sign the affidavit, they would consider that refusal to sign presumptive evidence of unfitness to be a teacher. Robert has so far refused to sign the affidavit. He wishes to challenge the constitutionality of the school's insistence that he sign.

(a) What is the strongest argument Robert can make as to why the affidavit requirement is unconstitutional? ———————————

(b) Will Robert's attack on the requirement's constitutionality succeed? ———————————

76. Becky, a young woman, walked topless on the boardwalk of Straitsville. She was arrested for violating a town ordinance that banned "lewd or lascivious public conduct." The statute contains no other relevant language, and there is no legislative history. For purposes of this question, assume that it would be possible to draft a statute in such a way that it could constitutionally proscribe appearing topless in public. Instead, concern yourself only with whether Becky may be convicted for violating *this* statute.

(a) What is Becky's strongest argument as to why she cannot constitutionally be convicted of violating the statute? _____

(b) Will Becky's argument succeed? _____

Answers

71. **(a) That the section is a content-based regulation on speech, and is thus invalid unless necessary to achieve a compelling state interest.**

    (b) No. Government may impose reasonable regulations on the "time, place and manner" of speech that takes place on public forums. However, government's right to do this is contingent on its behaving in a *content-neutral* way. If government chooses to allow some messages and not allow others based on the content of the speech, then the restriction will be strictly scrutinized, and will be struck down unless it is: (1) necessary to achieve a compelling objective; and (2) narrowly drawn to achieve that objective. See, e.g., *Widmar v. Vincent.*

    Here, government allows messages that pertain to matters under discussion inside the office building, but not messages pertaining to other matters. The government might defend on the grounds that it has not objected to the content of the messages, but has merely allowed some whole "categories" of speech while not allowing other whole categories. However, even distinctions among topics or categories is typically found to be content-based. See, e.g., *Consolidated Edison v. Public Serv. Comm.* (state may not prevent utilities from discussing the issue of nuclear power's desirability, because "[t]he First Amendment's hostility to content-based regulation extends not only to restrictions on particular viewpoints, but also to prohibition of public discussion of an entire topic.") In any event, the speech here is taking place in a public forum, so the court will be especially reluctant to allow such a broad interference with it.

72. **Yes.** First, we need to analyze whether the restriction is *content-based.* A regulation can be found to be content-based even though it does *not* appear to *favor any point of view* over another. Thus in addition to regulations that favor certain messages or points of view, content-based regulations are defined so as to also include regulations that (a) *place a particular topic or subject matter off-limits*, or (b) *require discussions of some topics or subject-categories* to meet *more stringent time-place-and-manner restrictions* than other topics or subject categories. [*Reed v. Town of Gilbert* (2015)] [483-485] A court would almost certainly say that the restriction here falls within category (b), since publications are treated differently depending on whether they discuss only a single subject or multiple subjects. Therefore, the court will almost surely classify the restriction here as content-based.

    When government engages in content-based regulation of expression, the restriction will be *strictly scrutinized*, and will be struck down unless it is: (1) necessary to achieve a compelling objective; and (2) narrowly drawn to achieve that objective. It's very unlikely that the regulation here can survive that strict scrutiny. Even if the two objectives cited by the town (avoiding impairment of traffic flow during rush hour, and avoiding litter) are "compelling," the *means* chosen by the town (a *complete ban* on the distribution of short single-topic hand-bills during rush hour) is deeply *"underinclusive."* That is, the town has chosen *not* to restrict the distribution of free magazines and newspapers in the same places and time slots, even though that distribution poses essentially the same dangers. A dramatically underinclusive regulation will rarely be found to satisfy the very tight "means-end fit" requirement imposed by strict scrutiny. See, e.g., *Reed v. Gilbert, supra*, striking down a town's tighter regulation of some types of signs than others, after the Court found that the regulation showed a fatal under-inclusiveness similar to the one here.

73. **No.** It would be a violation of the picketers' First Amendment rights for them to be held liable under this

statute, because such liability would effectively allow for content-based regulation of the picketers' speech, and cannot survive strict scrutiny. The case is comparable to *Snyder v. Phelps*, where picketers located on a public street who carried signs that intentionally offended the family of a soldier killed in Iraq were found to be shielded on First Amendment grounds from state-court liability for IIED.

74. No. The government may forbid a person from advocating illegal conduct, such as insurrection or over-throw of the government. However, under *Brandenburg v. Ohio*, speech advocating such illegality may only be proscribed if two conditions are satisfied: (1) the advocacy is directed to inciting or producing *imminent* lawless action; and (2) the advocacy is *likely* to incite or produce such action. Here, neither of these requirements seems to be met. Leonard is not calling for *imminent* illegality — he says "let's start … ," but he does not indicate that action should take place immediately. Furthermore, although his statement about having guerilla cells could probably be interpreted as a call for illegality, his statement about "building up an arsenal" is not necessarily a call for illegality, since there are many legal ways to buy guns, even automatics and machine guns. Even if the court decides that Leonard was attempting to incite imminent lawless action, it is pretty clear that there was very little risk that his speech was *likely* to produce that effect, since he had only a small crowd in front of him, they were in the park for other reasons, and they did not in fact respond with immediate illegal actions.

75. (a) That it is overbroad. A statute or regulation is overbroad if, in addition to proscribing activities which may constitutionally be forbidden, it also sweeps within its coverage future conduct which is protected by the guarantees of free speech or free association.

(b) Yes, probably. The government is clearly entitled to insist that Robert not commit crimes, and that he not advocate that others imminently commit crimes. However, the government may *not* make mere membership in an organization, without more, a crime, and it may not deprive a person of a government job or benefit for being merely a member or for refusing to say that he is not a member. Here, the affidavit merely requires Robert to say that he has not been a member; since Robert would be entitled to be a mere member of NAMBLA, so long as he did not agree with its aim of advocating imminent commission of the crime of man-boy love, the affidavit requirement would punish some membership that is constitutional. Robert's own membership here is *not* constitutionally protected, since he in fact knows of NAMBLA's stated aims and supports those (illegal) aims. But under the overbreadth doctrine, Robert is permitted to say, in effect, "The affidavit requirement would be unconstitutional if applied to (hypothetical) other people who merely belong to NAMBLA without supporting its criminal aims, so it should be struck down as facially invalid."

Under the requirement of *"substantial* overbreadth," the overbreadth doctrine would not be applied unless the invalid applications of the requirement are substantial compared to the legitimate applications. Here, however, this requirement of substantial overbreadth is probably satisfied, since quite a number of people are likely to belong to NAMBLA just to get information about the law and politics surrounding this question rather than to advocate or practice illegal man-boy sex. Therefore, Robert's overbreadth attack will probably succeed.

76. (a) That the statute is unconstitutionally vague.

(b) Yes, probably. A statute will be held void for vagueness if the conduct forbidden by it is so unclearly defined that a person of ordinary intelligence would not know what is forbidden.

Here, the statute uses the words "lewd or lascivious," but furnishes no further information about what type of conduct is being forbidden. A reasonable observer would probably be in doubt as to whether it is necessarily lewd for a woman to appear topless. Because of the ordinance's lack of specificity, undue discretion is given to local law enforcement officials, who depending on how they felt about Becky or top-lessness generally could decide to look the other way rather than making an arrest. Therefore, while the city might be entitled to ban women from appearing topless in public if the ordinance specifically applied to toplessness, the formulation here is probably unconstitutionally vague.

IV. REGULATION OF CONTEXT — "TIME, PLACE AND MANNER"

A. Context regulations generally: Recall that the state is somewhat more free to regulate expression when it does so for reasons independent of the speech's communicative content (a "track two" situation) than where the regulation is motivated by the expression's content (the "track one" case). Or, to put it another way, the state is substantially freer when it acts in a *content-neutral* manner. This section discusses various factual settings in which the state has claimed (not always successfully) that it is merely regulating the *"time, place and manner"* of speech and is therefore entitled to "track two" analysis.

   1. **Rules for "track two" cases:**   In general, the Court has applied a *balancing test* to determine whether the government's interest in content-neutral regulation of speech-related conduct outweighs the speaker's (or his listeners') interest in a particular form of communicative activity. But in performing this balancing test, the Court in effect places a "thumb on the scale" on the side of free expression, to reflect the exceptional importance of such expression.

   2. **Disproportionate impact:**   In performing the balancing test, the court will take into account the extent to which the regulation "falls *unevenly upon various groups* in … society." Tribe, p. 980. For instance, the poor cannot generally afford television spots or full-page newspaper announcements; they must use cheaper means such as demonstrations, leafletting and door-to-door canvassing. Therefore, regulations which inhibit these economical forms of expression will be especially closely scrutinized because of their unequal impact.

   3. **Public forum:**   Speech in a *"public forum"* (defined *infra*, p. 532) may not be restricted, even in a content-neutral way, unless the restriction is a *narrow one* which is *necessary* to serve a *significant governmental interest*. Tribe, p. 982. Thus citizens have in essence a *"guaranteed access"* to streets, parks and other public forums. See *Hague v. CIO*, 307 U.S. 496 (1939): "The privilege [to] use the streets and parks for communication of views on national questions may be regulated in the interest of all; [but] it must not, in the guise of regulation, be abridged or denied."

      a. **Mere inconvenience:**   This "guaranteed access" to public forums is implemented by several rules not applicable to non-public-forum situations. In a public forum context, *mere inconvenience* to the government will *not suffice* to outweigh the interest in public expression. Also, the government must use the *least restrictive means* of achieving its legitimate content-neutral objectives.

      Example: Ordinances in several cities completely forbid distribution of leaflets. The cities claim that the bans are necessary to prevent littering.

      Held, the flat bans violate the First Amendment. The objective of keeping the streets clean is insufficiently substantial to justify preventing a person with a right to be on a public street from giving literature to one who wants to receive it. Also, the state's objective can be met by means which place less of a burden on the freedom of expression (e.g., punishing only those who actually litter). *Schneider v. State*, 308 U.S. 147 (1939).

    b. Alternative places or times: Similarly, where a public forum is involved, the fact that the same message may be expressed by the speaker at a ***different place*** or time, or in a different manner, will not by itself suffice to validate a content-neutral restriction on the expression.

4. Non-public forum: By contrast, where the expression does ***not*** take place in a "public forum," the analysis depends on whether the regulation constitutes a ***substantial interference*** with communication. Here, the existence of alternatives is relevant — the availability of a different time, place, or manner for expressing the same message is likely to mean that the regulation's interference with speech is not substantial. If there is no substantial interference with expression, the state must merely show a ***rational justification*** for the regulation (assuming that it is content-neutral). Tribe, p. 982.

5. General rule for "time, place and manner" rules: Where a regulation is claimed to be a valid ***"time, place and manner"*** regulation, the Court now applies the following ***three-part test,*** which is essentially a ***"mid-level" of review.*** The regulation will not be valid unless it satisfies ***all*** of these these three requirements:

   ❏ It must be "justified without reference to the content of the regulated speech"; that is, it must be ***content-neutral*** (thus avoiding "track one" analysis);

   ❏ It must be ***"narrowly tailored"*** to serve a *"**significant** governmental interest."* (The requirement that the regulation be "narrowly tailored" to serve the interest means that it must be the case that the interest cannot be equally well-served by a means that is substantively less intrusive of First Amendment interests. See *Clark v. Community For Creative Non-Violence*, 468 U.S. 288 (1984));

   ❏ It must "***leave open alternative channels*** for communication of the information." *Metromedia, Inc. v. San Diego*, 453 U.S. 490 (1981).

Note: The above test does not explicitly distinguish between speech which takes place in public forums and that which does not. However, the ***second*** and ***third*** of the above requirements are ***interpreted more stringently in the public forum situation.*** As noted, "mere governmental convenience" (e.g., prevention of littering) is not treated as a "significant governmental interest" where a public forum is involved, and the availability of other public forums or other times for using the one at issue is not deemed to constitute "alternative channels."

    a. Mid-level standard: As noted, this 3-part standard for time, place and manner regulations essentially amounts to a ***middle level of review:*** it will ***not*** almost-inevitably lead to an ***invalidation*** of the regulation (as ***strict scrutiny*** does), but at the same time it's a ***meaningful obstacle*** for the regulation (unlike "mere-rationality" review, used for things like reviewing most social-welfare and economic regulation). The mid-level standard also ***shifts the burden of proof to the government*** to defend the regulation, instead of placing it on the speaker to show why the regulation violates the speaker's First Amendment rights.

B. Requirement that means be "narrowly tailored" to the objective: As we noted above (*supra*, p. 544), any regulation of "time, place and manner" must not only serve a significant government interest, but must be *"narrowly tailored"* to achieving that interest. In fact, the issue of whether the regulation is sufficiently narrowly tailored tends to be the main battlefield on which litigants fight over the validity of time, place and manner regulations.[3]

1. **Meaning of "narrowly tailored":** What does it *mean* for a law regulating expression to be "narrowly tailored" to the achievement of a state interest? The answer is that the law *must not "burden substantially more speech than is necessary* to further the government's legitimate interests." *McCullen v. Coakley*, 573 U.S. __ (2014) (discussed in more detail *infra*, p. 515). So it's not fatal that the law forbids *a bit more speech* than would be strictly necessary to achieve the state's interest, but it can't be the case that the law blocks *"substantially"* more speech than is necessary.

2. **Restriction often fails:** Time, place and manner restrictions are often found to *fail* this "narrowly tailored" prong of mid-level review. That's because government, while acting to combat a clearly-significant evil by content-neutral means, often through imprecise drafting ends up *silencing substantially more speech* than is really needed.

3. **Use of social-networking sites by registered sex offenders:**   A good example of a time, place and manner law that the Court has struck down as being substantially more speech-restrictive than needed was the statute struck down in *Packingham v. North Carolina*, 582 U.S. __ (2017). There, all eight justices who participated[4] agreed that a North Carolina law making it a felony for a *registered sex offender* to use a *"commercial social networking Web site"* was *not narrowly tailored* to the admittedly-important state interest in *preventing sexual abuse of minors.*

   a. **The statute:** The statute defined the concept of a "commercial social networking Web site" quite broadly. The Supreme Court found that such highly popular sites as *Facebook, LinkedIn* and *Twitter* would all fit within this definition, and would thus be off-limits to any registered sex offender.

      i. **P's conviction:** P, as a 21-year-old college student, had sex with a 13-year-old girl and was convicted of statutory rape. Eight years later, he logged into Facebook and posted a single message celebrating getting a traffic ticket dismissed. By virtue of this post alone, P was convicted of felony violation of the statute. He argued that the statute violated his freedom of expression, because it was not sufficiently narrowly-tailored to meet the state's goal of preventing sexual abuse of minors.

   b. **U.S. Supreme Court strikes the statute:**   The Supreme Court agreed with P: the statute was not sufficiently narrowly tailored to pass mid-level review. The majority opinion was by Justice Kennedy, who was joined by four other justices.

      i. **Mid-level scrutiny applied:** Kennedy assumed, without deciding, that the statute was content-neutral and thus subject to intermediate scrutiny. Therefore, he noted, the law could survive only if it was *"narrowly tailored* to serve a *significant* gov-

---

3. That's because there are many governmental interests that qualify as "significant," so the majority of interests asserted by government in support of any given time, place and manner regulation will satisfy the "significant interest" prong of middle-level review.

4. Justice Gorsuch did not participate, since he joined the Court after the case was argued.

ernment interest." And it would be found narrowly tailored only if it *did not "burden substantially more speech than is necessary to further the government's legitimate interests"* (quoting *McCullen v. Coakley*, discussed *infra*, p. 515).

ii. **Speech greatly burdened:** The bulk of Kennedy's opinion was devoted to estimating *how extensively the statute burdened the speech* of registered sex offenders like P. Kennedy found the burdens to be *extreme:* "the statute here enacts a prohibition *unprecedented in the scope* of *First Amendment speech it burdens*."

   (1) **Nature of Internet:** Kennedy commented on the *First Amendment significance of the Internet generally.* "Cyberspace," he said, today encompasses *"the most important places (in a spacial sense) for the exchange of views[.]"*

   (2) **Reach of social-media sites:** Furthermore, Kennedy said, users of what he called *"Internet social networking services"* — the type of services covered by the statute, like Facebook, LinkedIn or Twitter — "employ these websites to *engage in a wide array* of protected First Amendment activity on *topics 'as diverse as human thought.' "*

   (3) **Broad impact on expression:** Therefore, Kennedy said, the statute had a *devastating impact on sex offenders:* "North Carolina with one broad stroke *bars access* to what for many are the *principal sources* for *knowing current events, checking ads for employment, speaking and listening in the modern public square,* and otherwise *exploring the vast realms of human thought and knowledge."*

iii. **Broader than necessary to achieve the desired benefit:** Kennedy then turned to the *"benefit" side* of the narrow-tailoring analysis. North Carolina asserted that its law fulfilled a "preventative purpose of *keeping convicted sex offenders away from vulnerable victims."* Kennedy concluded that the state had *not met* its "burden to show that *this sweeping law is necessary or legitimate to serve that purpose."*

   (1) **Narrower laws might survive:** But Kennedy indicated that a *more narrowly-drawn prohibition,* covering just *some* types of Internet access by registered sex offenders, might be narrowly-tailored enough to *survive* intermediate-level review. For instance, he said, the First Amendment probably permits a state to "prohibit a sex offender from engaging in conduct that *often presages a sexual crime,* like *contacting a minor* or *using a website to gather information about a minor*."

4. **State need not pick least-restrictive alternative:** Although a content-neutral regulation of "time, place and manner" must be *"narrowly tailored"* to serve an important governmental interest, the requirement of narrow tailoring does *not* mean that the state must choose the *least-restrictive* or least-intrusive means of achieving its objective. Instead, the state must merely avoid choosing means that are *"substantially broader* than necessary to achieve the government's interest." *Ward v. Rock Against Racism*, 491 U.S. 781 (1989). In other words, the fact that an alternative method would have interfered somewhat less with expression while still fulfilling the government's objectives, is irrelevant — all that is required is that the means-end fit be *fairly close*, not perfect.

Example: To cut down on complaints by citizens that rock concerts in the city's parks are too loud, New York City imposes a requirement that rock performers use only city-provided sound equipment and sound technicians.

Held, this requirement is a valid "time, place and manner" restriction. It's true that the city might have found a less-restrictive means of solving the loudness problem (e.g., by monitoring the performances and punishing performers who exceeded pre-defined sound limits). But the availability of less-restrictive means of regulating volume is irrelevant: since the means chosen by the city were not "*substantially* broader than necessary" to keep sound low, the requirement that the means be "narrowly tailored" to serve the government's interest is satisfied. *Ward v. Rock Against Racism, supra.*

C. **"Leave open alternative channels" requirement:**   The third and final requirement for a "time, place and manner" regulation is that it "*leave open alternative channels* for communication of the information." See *supra*, p. 507. Usually, a regulation that satisfies the other requirements (content-neutral, and narrowly tailored to serve a significant governmental interest) will also satisfy this final requirement. But occasionally, the requirement does turn out to make a difference. It is especially likely to do so where the government tries to foreclose an *entire medium* or *method* of communication, and the method is so easy-to-use or inexpensive that other channels simply are not substitutes.

1. **Use by individuals:** In general, the more a particular method is likely to be used by *individuals* who are trying to disseminate core political messages without spending a lot of money, the more likely the method is to be found so vital that its prohibition fails to leave open "alternative channels." Thus complete bans on *handbills* (see *supra*, p. 506) or on the display of *homemade signs* are likely to be struck down as not leaving open alternative channels.

    Example: The City of Ladue, Missouri generally prohibits "signs," and defines that term broadly. All residential signs are prohibited except for "identification signs" and "for sale" signs. P places an 8.5 x 11 inch sign in the second story window of her home, stating "For Peace in the Gulf." The city asserts that P's sign must come down, and defends its ordinance on the grounds that it is merely a "time, place and manner" regulation whose purpose is to minimize the visual clutter associated with signs.

    Held, for P. By forbidding residents from displaying virtually any "sign" on their property, the city "has almost completely foreclosed a venerable means of communication that is both unique and important." The city has not "[left] open ample alternative channels for communication. … Residential signs are an unusually cheap and convenient form of communication. Especially for persons of modest means or limited mobility, a yard or window sign may have no practical substitute." Therefore, even though the city's ordinance may be content-neutral, and even assuming that the ordinance is narrowly tailored to serve a significant governmental interest, it unconstitutionally infringes P's free speech. *City of Ladue v. Gilleo*, 512 U.S. 43 (1994).

D. **Licensing:**   One way in which governments often attempt to regulate speech or expressive conduct is through *licensing* or *permit* requirements, by which official permission is required *in advance* of a public address, march, solicitation campaign, or other expressive activity.

1. **Multiple techniques:** The Court has used a number of techniques to ensure that such requirements will not stifle the freedom of expression:

   a. **Content-neutrality:** The government must apply the permit requirement in a ***content-neutral*** manner. If, for instance, a permit is required before any parade, the officials charged with granting or denying permit requests ***may not take into account the ideas or politics being espoused*** by the paraders. (Only if the content of the expression places it within an "unprotected category," such as "advocacy of imminent illegal activity," may this content be taken into account.)

      i. **Consequence:** Thus if the government wishes to have its advance-permit requirement sustained in a particular fact situation, it will almost certainly have to show either that the case belongs on "track two" rather than "track one," or that the speech's content falls into an unprotected category.

      ii. **Fee based on content of speech:** For example, the government almost certainly cannot charge a ***different fee*** for the license or permit, based on the content of the speech. In fact, the government may not vary the fee according to the ***costs of security*** that the government will bear in connection with the expression, because such costs will inevitably depend on the content of the speaker's message, and the hostility generated by that message. Cf. *Forsyth County v. The Nationalist Movement*, 505 U.S. 123 (1992).

   b. **Excessive administrative discretion:** The grounds upon which a permit may be denied must be set forth ***specifically***, and ***narrowly***, in the ordinance. If the official charged with granting or denying permit applications is given ***too much discretion***, the ordinance will be voided for overbreadth, vagueness, or both (see *supra*, p. 498).

      Example: A municipal ordinance forbids the distribution anywhere within the town of "literature of any kind," unless a permit has first been obtained from the City Manager. D is convicted of violating the ordinance for distributing religious literature published by the Jehovah's Witnesses.

      Held, the ordinance is an unconstitutional violation of freedom of speech. It gives a censor's power to the City Manager, since his right to deny a permit is not tied to the avoidance of littering or disorderly conduct, or to regulation of time and place. Because the ordinance is void on its face (for what would today be called overbreadth), D was not required to seek the permit and then challenge its denial in court; she was free to disregard the permit requirement and to challenge the ordinance after her arrest. *Lovell v. Griffin*, 303 U.S. 444 (1938).

2. **Prior restraint:** One of the reasons the courts look with particular disfavor on permit requirements is that these amount to ***prior restraint*** on the freedom of speech. That is, in contrast to statutes which merely ***punish*** certain types of expressive conduct ***after*** they have occurred, the permit requirement, if enforced, prevents the expression from ever taking place at all.

   a. **Restraint of press:** The Court's hostility to prior restraints on free expression is even more noteworthy in the case of the ***press***. See, e.g., *Near v. Minnesota*, discussed *infra*, p. 628.

3. **General right of regulation:** However, if the statute or ordinance *does* adequately constrain administrative discretion, does require content-neutrality, and does have an adequate

means-end fit, it will be upheld if it is a ***reasonable means of ensuring that public order is maintained.***

> **Example:** The Ds (Jehovah's Witnesses) are charged with holding a parade on public streets, in violation of a state statute that requires a permit before any "parade or procession" is held on a public street. The statute sets forth elaborate procedural requirements for the hearing of such permit requests. The Ds claim that the advance-permit requirement abridged their First Amendment rights.
>
> *Held*, ordinance sustained (and the Ds' conviction affirmed), because: (1) the statute required ***content-neutrality*** in the issuance of permits; and (2) the Ds would, if they had applied for a permit, have had an unqualified right to a permit so long as their proposed parade was to be at a time and place where it would not unduly disturb public use of the streets. The government's interest in not having overlapping parades, and in having advance notice so as to be able to ensure proper policing, furnished adequate justification for the permit requirement. *Cox v. New Hampshire*, 312 U.S. 569 (1941).

E. Intrusive speakers vs. right to be left alone: One way in which the state has sometimes justified content-neutral regulations on expressive activity is by claiming that the would-be audience has an interest in ***not being forced to listen*** to the speaker's message. The Court has not been completely unsympathetic to this "right to be left alone." But it has generally held that it is ***up to the unwilling listener*** (or viewer) to ***avoid the undesired expression***, and that the state may not issue a blanket proclamation shielding both the willing and unwilling from the expression.

1. Loudspeakers: Thus the Court has carefully scrutinized restrictions on ***loudspeakers*** and ***soundtrucks***. Where such restrictions give ***uncontrolled discretion*** to local officials, they will be struck down (just like other types of overbroad or vague permit schemes, discussed above).

    a. "Loud and raucous noises" prohibitable: But if administrative discretion is sufficiently restricted, and the statute is not overbroad or vague, regulation of amplification devices will be permitted, as a valid regulation of the "time, place and manner" of expression.

        i. Loudspeakers: For instance, in *Kovacs v. Cooper*, 336 U.S. 77 (1949), the Court ***upheld*** a ban on all amplification devices operated in public places which emit ***"loud and raucous noises."*** The municipality's interest in avoiding distractions to traffic, and in protecting the "quiet and tranquility" of its inhabitants, was sufficient to justify the regulation, despite the "preferred position of freedom of speech." (It is not clear whether the logic of the majority opinion in *Kovacs* would allow a city to ban ***all*** public amplification devices, since it is not clear whether all such devices make "loud and raucous noises.")

        ii. Regulating sound equipment: Similarly, the Court held that New York City could require that any musician performing in a public forum (the bandshell in Central Park) use city-provided sound-amplification equipment and sound technicians. The city had a significant governmental interest in protecting citizens from unduly loud sounds, and the regulation was not substantially broader than necessary to achieve that interest. *Ward v. Rock Against Racism* (other aspects of which are discussed *supra*, p. 509).

2. **The captive audience:** Whenever speech is directed towards a ***captive audience***, that is, one which ***cannot easily avoid exposure*** to the speech, this is a factor which the Court will weigh in favor of ***allowing restriction*** on that form of expression. A number of cases show how the presence of a captive audience is a factor making the Court more willing than usual to allow restrictions on expression:

    a. **Print advertising on city buses:** For instance, in *Lehman v. Shaker Heights*, 418 U.S. 298 (1974), the Court upheld restrictions on some but not all types of print advertising on city-owned buses. The Court held that the fact that commercial advertising was accepted did not give political candidates a right to have *their* advertising accepted; the majority relied in part upon the city's interest in limiting access so as to reduce "the risk of imposing upon the captive audience."

    b. **Picketing in front of residence:** Similarly, the Court has held that a municipality may ban all ***picketing*** in front of a ***particular residence***, in order to protect the inhabitants of that house from hearing or seeing unwanted messages. *Frisby v. Schultz*, 487 U.S. 474 (1988), also discussed *infra*, p. 534.

    c. **Women visiting abortion clinics:** Finally, ***women*** who are ***visiting abortion clinics*** or other health-care offices can get some protection from unwanted expression. See, e.g., *Hill v. Colorado*, 530 U.S. 703 (2000) (*held*, a state may create a 100-foot ***"buffer zone"*** around the entrance to any health-care facility, in which no one may make an unwanted approach to within eight feet of another person in order to counsel that person, pass out a leaflet, or picket).

    d. **No general rule:** But don't think that the Court has adopted a broad rule that the public has an absolute ***"right to be left alone,"*** even in special contexts like the entrances to abortion clinics. For instance, the Court has struck down, post-*Hill*, a statute that completely prohibited unauthorized persons from being present in a 35-foot buffer zone around abortion-clinic entrances. See *McCullen v. Coakley*, *infra*, p. 515. So even in the abortion context, it is clear that citizens in public places must tolerate some unwanted messages — government may prevent ***"harassment,"*** but it ***may not forbid or restrict the delivery of all or some messages in advance*** even if government correctly believes that most of the recipients would find the messages unwelcome.

F. **Canvassing and soliciting:** The interest in being left alone also plays a role in the case law on ***canvassers and solicitors***. Here, too, however, this interest has been merely one factor in the balancing of society's interest in regulating the form of expression against the speaker's interest in unrestrained communication.

1. **Significance of place:** The *place* in which the canvassing or solicitation occurs is important; the Court has granted greater weight to the rights of canvassers and solicitors in ***public places*** than at ***private residences*** (though even as to the latter, access may not be completely cut off by a blanket ban).

2. **Mailboxes:** The Court's concern with the sanctity of the home has led it to be sympathetic to legislative acts which restrict access to ***home mailboxes***.

    a. **Homeowner's right to block receipt:** Thus a congressional provision allowing a homeowner who has received what he (in his sole judgment) believes to be "erotically arousing or sexually provocative" material to obtain a post office order requiring the mailer to remove the homeowner's name from its mailing lists, was upheld in *Rowan* *v. Post Office Dept.*, 397 U.S. 728 (1970). The Court found that "[t]he right of every person 'to be let alone' must be placed in the scales with the right of others to communicate." Whatever rules might apply outside the home, "[a] mailer's right to communicate *must stop at the mailbox* of an unreceptive addressee."

    b. Not public forum: The mailer's "right of access" to home mailboxes was further undermined when the Court upheld a federal statute which prohibited depositing *unstamped materials in home mailboxes,* in *U.S. Postal Service v. Greenburgh Civic Assns.*, 453 U.S. 114 (1981). There, several civic groups argued that they had a constitutional right to deliver messages to local residents by placing unstamped pamphlets and notices in such mailboxes. But the Court held that *home mailboxes do not constitute a "public forum,"* even though they are in effect controlled by the government; therefore, any reasonable, content-neutral, regulation of their use was permissible.

3. Personal visits at home: Those who wish to solicit or canvass by making *personal visits* to homes have received substantial First Amendment protection from the Court, notwithstanding the homeowner's interest in being left alone. In general, the Court has taken the view that *it is up to homeowner himself to indicate his desire to be left alone* (in which event the state may enforce that desire); the state may not simply *assume* that all homeowners wish to be undisturbed.

    Example: An ordinance prohibits anyone from distributing handbills to residents by either ringing their doorbell or otherwise calling them to the door. (Nor is there any way to get a permit that would allow this.) The town defends this prohibition on privacy grounds. *Held*, this flat ban on canvassing is unconstitutional, because less restrictive alternatives are available (e.g., letting a homeowner post a no-soliciting sign, and then making it an offense for anyone to ring the bell of such a person). *Martin v. Struthers*, 319 U.S. 141 (1943).

4. Heightened scrutiny: Even where an ordinance regulating canvassing is written in a way that does not give officials undue discretion, it will not pass constitutional muster if it: (1) directly and substantially impairs protected First Amendment expression; and (2) is not substantially related to achievement of a *"strong, subordinating interest."* This two-part test was applied to invalidate an ordinance barring door-to-door or in-the-street solicitation by charitable organizations that do not use at least 75% of their receipts for "charitable purposes" (defined to exclude overhead and solicitation expenses). *Schaumburg v. Citizens For Better Environment*, 444 U.S. 620 (1980).

5. Solicitation in public places: Where canvassing or solicitation occurs in *public places*, essentially the same constitutional standards apply as in the door-to-door situation. That is, the regulation must be content-neutral, and authorities may not be given excessive discretion in determining who may solicit, or in what manner. Reasonable "time, place and manner" regulations which satisfy both of these requirements will be upheld, so long as they serve a *significant governmental interest* and *leave open ample alternative channels* for communicating the same information.

    a. Less judicial tolerance: But since the "governmental interest" and "alternative channel" factors inevitably involve a kind of balancing, the Court has been *less tolerant* of regulations on solicitation done in public forums than in the door-to-door situation (where the governmental interest in having citizens be left alone is stronger).

G. Protest and persuasion on public property outside of abortion clinics: The interest in being left alone frequently arises in the context of *abortion clinics*. Opponents of legalized abortion frequently seek to *picket* on public streets and sidewalks around the entrance to such clinics, and from there attempt to *persuade* women approaching the clinic entrance that they should reconsider getting abortions. In general, the Supreme Court has been quite *protective of the free-speech rights of abortion protesters* in this public-forum scenario, in the face of government regulations that claim to protect the interest of clinic patrons to be free of unwanted communications.

   1. Summary: The Court has not denied government *all* tools to prevent harassment and unwanted communications outside abortion clinics. For instance, the Court has held that government may ensure that the entrance is *not physically blocked*, and that no patron is *harassed*. But the Court has *struck down* government attempts to establish sizable *"buffer zones"* around clinic entrances, within which no sort of speech is permitted. And the Court has done this even where it is convinced that government is attempting to act in a content-neutral way (by proscribing *all* speech, regardless of the viewpoint expressed, in the buffer zone).

   2. *McCullen* case: The most important case illustrating the Court's protection of the expressive rights of abortion opponents on public property is a 2014 decision, ***McCullen v. Coakley***, 134 S.Ct. 2518 (2014), involving a Massachusetts attempt to create a buffer zone around abortion clinics.

      a. Facts: A 2007 Massachusetts statute made it a crime for any person knowingly to *stand* on a "public or sidewalk" *within 35 feet* of an entrance or doorway to any place (other than a hospital) at which abortions are performed. The Ps in *McCullen* were abortion opponents who wished to "approach and talk to women outside such facilities," in the hopes of dissuading them from having abortions. The statute meant that the Ps could not make such an approach to any woman within 35 feet of a clinic entrance, even if the woman being approached gave no indication that she would find the approach unwelcome.

         i. Broader than prior law: Massachusetts enacted the 2007 statute after a more narrowly-drafted 2000 statute (imposing an 18-foot buffer) had failed to curtail what the state characterized as a history of harassment and violence outside abortion clinics in the state.

      b. Unanimously struck down: The Supreme Court *unanimously struck down* the newer statute as a violation of the abortion opponents' free-speech rights. In an opinion by Chief Justice Roberts, the Court found that *even though the statute was content-neutral,*[5] the statute *forbade more speech than necessary,* and therefore violated the Court's rules on content-neutral time-place-and-manner regulation.

         i. Statement of level of review: Roberts began by stating the familiar rule that *mid-level review* is to be given to content-neutral time-place-and-manner regulations substantially affecting traditional public fora like streets and sidewalks, which have a "special position" in terms of First Amendment protection. He continued, "[G]overnment's ability to restrict speech in such locations is *'very limited.'* "

---

5. As was discussed *supra*, p. 487, four members of the Court disagreed with Roberts' finding of content-neutrality.

Even if the government regulation is content-neutral, it must be *"narrowly tailored to serve a significant governmental interest."* And for a time-place-or-manner regulation to qualify as narrowly tailored, it must *not "burden substantially more speech than is necessary to further the government's legitimate interests."*

  ii. **Buffer zones aren't narrowly tailored:** It was clear to Roberts (and indeed, to *every* member of the Court) that the Massachusetts statute *wasn't sufficiently narrowly tailored* — that it burdened substantially more speech than necessary to achieve the various interests cited by the state. These interests included "ensuring *public safety* outside abortion clinics, preventing *harassment and intimidation* of patients and clinic staff, and combating deliberate *obstruction* of clinic entrances." But, Roberts said, the state had numerous *other means available to it* to accomplish these objectives.

    (1) **Other methods available:** For instance, the statute itself already had a provision making it a separate offense to *block another person from entering or exiting* an abortion clinic. And if more protection was needed, the legislature was free to follow federal law and make it a crime to intimidate or interfere with anyone to prevent them from obtaining "reproductive health services."

H. **The hostile audience and "fighting words":** One of the "unprotected categories" of speech consists of so-called *"fighting words,"* that is, words which are likely to make the person to whom they are addressed *commit an act of violence* (probably against the speaker). "Fighting words" receive no First Amendment protection, because, like other unprotected categories (e.g., defamation, obscenity, etc.) they are not normally part of any "dialogue" or "exposition of ideas." But the Supreme Court today keeps this exclusion within tightly circumscribed bounds.

  1. *Chaplinsky:* The "fighting words" doctrine originated in *Chaplinsky v. New Hampshire*, 315 U.S. 568 (1942).

    a. **Facts:** The defendant in *Chaplinsky* was a Jehovah's Witness who called the city marshall a "goddamned racketeer" and "a damned fascist," and then got into a fight with him on the sidewalk. He was convicted under a broadly-worded statute, which provided that "no person shall address any offensive, derisive or annoying word to any other person who is lawfully in any street or other public place … " But the New Hampshire Supreme Court had interpreted the statute to bar only "words *likely to cause an average addressee to fight."*

    b. **Conviction upheld:** The conviction was *upheld*. The Supreme Court believed that the defendant's words were indeed ones which would *likely provoke the average person to retaliate*. It then held that among the classes of speech which are not protected by the First Amendment are "fighting words," which the Court defined as "those which by their very utterance *inflict injury* or *tend to incite an immediate breach of the peace."* Such words are *"no essential part of any exposition of ideas*, and are of such *slight social value as a step to truth* that any benefit that may be derived from them is clearly outweighed by the social interest in order and morality."

    c. **Two branches:** Observe that this *Chaplinsky* formulation defines "fighting words" quite broadly — in addition to words which are likely to incite an immediate fight, words are also included which "inflict injury." Here, we are concerned only with words likely to provoke a fight or other breach of the peace.

2. **Limitations on doctrine:** The Court realized, soon after *Chaplinsky*, that giving a broad scope to the "fighting words" doctrine would lead to the swallowing up of important First Amendment protections. Therefore, the Court has *limited* the "fighting words" doctrine in a number of ways.

    a. **"Stirring to anger" not enough:** To constitute "fighting words," it is not enough that the speaker's words *make the listeners angry; incitement to violence* (whether or not the violence actually ensues) is required. For instance, in *Terminiello v. Chicago*, 337 U.S. 1 (1949), D made a race-baiting speech, which attracted an angry crowd; the speaker then denounced the crowd as "snakes" and "slimy scum." The Supreme Court reversed D's conviction under a breach-of-the-peace statute which the trial court had interpreted to include speech which "stirs the public to *anger* [or] *invites dispute*," as well as speech which creates a disturbance.

        i. **Rationale:** The Supreme Court reasoned that speech which "stirs the audience to anger" or "invites dispute" is *protected* under the First Amendment and that, in fact, *the most valuable expression may well be that which, because it is provocative and challenging, produces these emotions*. Therefore, the statute (as interpreted by the trial judge) was *overbroad* on its face; D's conviction had to be reversed, regardless of whether *his actual words* could have been made criminal under a more narrowly-drawn statute covering only words likely to incite violence.

    b. **Crowd-control required:** Wherever the police have the physical ability to *control the angry crowd* as a means of preventing threatened violence, they *must do so* in preference to arresting the speaker for using "fighting words." For instance, in *Cox v. Louisiana*, 379 U.S. 536 (1965), 2,000 civil rights demonstrators picketed a courthouse; about 75 policemen separated the demonstrators from 100-300 whites gathered on the other side of the street. The Court, in reversing the breach of peace conviction of the demonstration's leader, rejected the state's claim that the conviction was justified because "violence was about to erupt" — the Court relied in part on the fact that the police could have "handled the crowd."

        i. **"Heckler's veto":** Observe that a contrary rule, allowing the police to silence a speaker whenever the audience threatens violence, would legitimate what has been called the *"heckler's veto."* That is, members of the audience would gain the right to silence any speaker with whose ideas they did not agree.

    c. **Mere dislike of speaker's identity not sufficient:** If it is the *mere identity* or lawful acts of the speaker or demonstrator, *not his threatening words or actions*, which lead the police to believe that violence is imminent, the "fighting words" doctrine may *not* be applied.

        i. **Civil rights sit-ins:** For instance, in several breach-of-peace cases involving civil rights sit-ins of segregated facilities, the state was able to justify its fear of imminent violence only by asserting that the *mere fact that blacks were using segregated facilities* made whites likely to attack them. Even if this anticipation of whites' response was accurate, it was constitutionally irrelevant, since the blacks' use of these facilities was not evidence of any crime. See *Garner v. Louisiana*, 368 U.S. 157 (1961). See also Tribe, p. 854.

3. **Doctrine sometimes applicable:** But these *are* occasional situations in which none of these exceptions or limitations applies, and the "fighting words" doctrine is applicable. These will be those situations in which "imminent spectator violence cannot be satisfactorily prevented or curbed by means of crowd control techniques, and … the speech itself is the apparent cause of the impending disorder." Tribe p. 855.

   a. *Feiner:* The last true "fighting words" conviction sustained by the Court was in ***Feiner v. New York***, 340 U.S. 315 (1951).

      i. **Facts:** D, a left-wing college student, made a street-corner speech in which he called President Truman a "bum" and the American Legion a "Nazi Gestapo," and said that blacks should "rise up in arms and fight for [legal rights]." One member of the racially-mixed crowd said that if the police did not get that "son of a bitch" off the stand he would do it himself. D refused to heed requests from the police to stop speaking, and was then arrested for disorderly conduct.

      ii. **Conviction upheld:** A majority of the Court believed that D's conduct constituted *incitement to riot*, and that his arrest was motivated by the police's legitimate desire to prevent a fight, not by disagreement with the content of D's message. The Court conceded that "the ordinary murmurings and objections of a hostile audience cannot be allowed to silence a speaker," but implied that the crowd response here went beyond that. Therefore, the Court *upheld* D's conviction.

      iii. **Black's dissent:** But Justice Black dissented, disagreeing with the majority's view of both the facts and the law. As a factual matter, he did not agree that violence was imminent; he believed that D had in reality been arrested and convicted for the unpopularity of his views, not the tendency of his speech to induce violence. He also believed, as a legal principle, that the police must, before interfering with a lawful speaker, make "*all reasonable efforts to protect him … even to the extent of arresting the man who threatened to interfere.*" (Black believed that the majority's opinion implied that there was no such requirement.)

      iv. *Feiner* **to be read narrowly:** However, the present Court would probably construe *Feiner* quite *narrowly*, and it is not at all clear that the case would be decided the same way if it arose today. In particular, the Court is probably less inclined to accept the police's self-justifying rationales for their action ("We didn't think we could control the crowd.") See Tribe, p. 855.

4. **Relation to "clear and present danger":** The problem of "fighting words" is similar to, and in some ways a subset of, the problem of advocacy of illegal conduct (*supra*, p. 489). Just as under *Brandenburg, supra*, p. 495, only speech which is intended to advocate *imminent* lawless action, and which is in fact *likely* to result in such action, may be punished, so only those words which are likely to result in violence that cannot be prevented in any other way (e.g., by controlling the crowd) will be preventable or punishable under the "fighting words" doctrine.

   a. **Perhaps no longer valid:** This requirement of imminent unpreventable violence is so strict that many commentators doubt that the fighting words doctrine has much real practical value today. For instance, it is probably the case that there are no words which by themselves are "automatically" fighting words — each utterance has to be evaluated *in context* to determine whether there were actual listeners who were likely to resort to violence. This, coupled with the fact that no regulation has been upheld under the fighting words exception since *Feiner* in 1951, may render the doctrine largely irrelevant.

I. **Offensive words and the sensitive audience:** A related issue is whether the government may prevent or punish words which listeners will find *offensive*, even though these words are not likely to lead to actual violence. In general, the Court has *not* allowed government to suppress speech or expressive conduct on the grounds that others would find it "offensive," at least where matters of *public interest* rather than purely private interests are at stake.

1. **Foul language:** Most of the cases involving "offensive language" have focused upon *profanity*. Generally, the Court has held that statements *may not be punished merely because they are profane* and are therefore offensive to their listeners. These cases, even though they involve "four-letter-words" with a sexual connotation, must be sharply distinguished from speech that is "obscene"; here, we deal with statements whose tone is *not erotic*, so that the law of obscenity is irrelevant.

    a. ***Cohen v. California:*** The most important case involving the state's right to ban offensive language of the profane sort is ***Cohen v. California***, 403 U.S. 15 (1971). The case stands basically for the proposition that *profane, offensive language is nonetheless First Amendment speech*, and may not be suppressed under the guise of regulating the "manner" of speech.

       i. **Facts:** Cohen wore a jacket bearing the legend "Fuck the Draft" in a corridor of the Los Angeles County Courthouse, where women and children were present. He was convicted of violating a statute prohibiting the intentional "disturb[ing] the peace or quiet of any … person [by] offensive conduct."

       ii. **Conviction reversed:** The Court, in a classic opinion by Justice Harlan, *reversed the conviction* on First Amendment grounds. In so doing, Harlan rejected a number of arguments advanced by the state.

       iii. **Not obscene:** Harlan found that the legend on the jacket was *not obscene*. An expression is obscene only if it is "in some significant way, erotic." No erotic "psychic stimulation" could reasonably have been expected to result when anybody read the jacket.

       iv. **Not "captive audience":** The state claimed that *Cohen's* message had been "thrust upon unwilling or unsuspecting viewers," and that the state had the power to protect such *"captive audiences"* from offensive language. But Harlan's opinion took a narrow view of what constitutes a true "captive audience." Those in the courthouse could have "avoid[ed] further bombardment of their senses simply by *averting their eyes*."

       v. **Right to purge offensive language:** Lastly, Harlan rejected the state's most general claim, that it had the right to ban certain expletives in order to "maintain what [officials] regard as a *suitable level of discourse* within the body politic." He stressed that the First Amendment's general function is to *"remove governmental restraints for the arena of public discussion."* Only where speech falls within relatively narrow pre-established categories may government regulate its form or content; none of these exceptions was applicable here. But Harlan also found more specific reasons for finding that the state could not ban expressions like Cohen's from public discourse:

(1) No stopping point: First, there was no principled way to distinguish "fuck" from other words. Yet the state clearly did not have the right to "cleanse public debate to the point where it is grammatically palatable to the most squeamish among us." The preferable constitutional result was simply to *leave matters of "taste and style" to the individual*, especially since "[o]ne man's vulgarity is another's lyric."

(2) Emotional content: Secondly, this was not simply a situation in which Cohen chose vulgar words to express an idea that could have been equally well expressed by more polite language. The language chosen by Cohen, like much expression, conveyed not only an intellectual idea, but also *"otherwise inexpressible emotions."* The Constitution protects this *"emotive function"* of speech just as much as the cognitive content of expression.

(3) Smokescreen for censorship: Finally, governments might often ban particular words as a *smokescreen* for banning the *expression of unpopular views*. "One [cannot] forbid particular words without also running a substantial risk of suppressing ideas in the process."

2. **Emotionally hurtful speech:** A second important category of speech that is entitled to full First Amendment protection even though offensive is speech that is *emotionally hurtful* to the listener. No matter how much psychic pain the speech inflicts — indeed, is *intended* to inflict — on the listener, the speech gets *full First Amendment protection*, as long as

[1] The speech is on a matter of *public* (not purely private) *interest*; and

[2] The pain comes from the *content* of the message (i.e., the attempted state regulation is "content-based" as discussed *supra*, p. 477).

A 2011 case striking down a state's right to allow recovery for speech that under state law constituted *intentional infliction of emotional distress* (IIED) is the leading illustration of this principle. That case, which upheld the First Amendment right of picketers to use hateful speech to attack the character of a dead soldier at his funeral, is *Snyder v. Phelps*, 131 S.Ct. 1207 (2011).

a. **Facts:** The speakers in *Snyder* were members of a small church, the Westboro Baptist Church of Topeka, Kansas, founded in 1955 by Fred Phelps and still run by him and his family in the 2000s, when the events in the suit took place. The church members' core belief was that God hates homosexuality and hates (and punishes) the U.S. military for tolerating homosexuality.

i. **Protest strategy:** The church members' main First Amendment activity has long been to picket military funerals. *Snyder* grew out of one such picketing session, in which the church members carried hateful signs on public land adjacent to the Maryland funeral of a Marine Lance Colonel killed in Iraq, Matthew Snyder. Matthew's father, Albert Snyder, saw the signs on a TV broadcast after the funeral and became severely distressed at their content. He brought a federal-court diversity action based on substantive Maryland law for the tort of IIED. He ultimately obtained a civil judgment for $4 million in combined compensatory and punitive damages against the church members. The issue was whether that — or indeed any — civil judgment could be enforced without violating the church members' First Amendment rights. (The Supreme Court's answer turned out to be a very clear "no," as we'll see.)

(1) Hateful signs: The picketers at the Snyder funeral carried signs with messages like "God Hates the USA/Thank God for 9/11," "God hates fags," and "Thank God for Dead Soldiers." The picketers' message was apparently that Matthew and other soldiers had been killed in combat because God wanted to punish the United States for tolerating homosexuality. Some viewers seem to have assumed that the picketers were saying that Matthew was himself gay; in any event, Matthew was not in fact gay.

(2) On public property: A key aspect of the case was that the protest took place entirely on a small plot of *public land adjacent* to a public street. Picketing took place 1,000 feet from the church where the funeral was held; none of the church members ever entered the church or the cemetary, or in any way interfered with the funeral.

b. **The Ds win:** In an opinion by Chief Justice Roberts that seven members of the Court (all but Alito) joined, the Court held that allowing Matthew's father Albert to recover any damages at all would be a *violation* of the Ds' First Amendment right to *speak freely on a matter of public interest.*

i. **The test:** Roberts began by saying that whether the First Amendment prohibited holding the church members liable for their speech "turns largely on whether the speech is of *public* or *private* concern." Speech on matters of "*public* concern" is "at the *heart* of the First Amendment's protection" and "occupies the *highest rung* of the hierarchy of First Amendment values [making it] entitled to special protection." By contrast, if the speech involved solely a "*purely private* matter," it would "*not implicate the same constitutional concerns*" because there would be "no potential *interference with a meaningful dialogue of ideas.*"

ii. **Public concern:** Roberts then quickly concluded that the speech here was indeed on a matter of *public* concern. Speech involves a matter of public concern when it either (1) "can be fairly considered as relating to *any matter of political, social, or other concerns to the community,*" or (2) "is a subject of *legitimate news interest.*" The fact that the statement is "inappropriate or controversial" is *irrelevant* to the question of whether it involves a matter of public concern. The messages on the picket signs here "may fall short of refined social or political commentary" but those messages were clearly designed to *speak on a broad public issue*, and indeed, to reach as broad a public audience as possible.

iii. **Content-based rather than content-neutral:** Roberts was also in no doubt about whether the governmental regulation here (namely, the availability of a *tort recovery* under state law) was of the forbidden *content-based* variety rather than an easier-to-justify *content-neutral* "time, place and manner" regulation. Maryland *could* indeed have imposed some content-neutral time, place and manner regulation, such as prohibiting picketing within a specified short distance of a funeral service or procession.

(1) Content-based jury deliberations: But that isn't what happened here: the substantive tort law of Maryland gave the jury the right to allow recovery for *"outrageousness,"* a concept that has an *"inherent subjectiveness about it"* that would make the jury *"unlikely to be neutral with respect to the content of the speech."*

c. **Alito dissent:** The sole member of the Court to believe that the First Amendment did not bar Albert Snyder from recovering was Justice Alito, who dissented. He believed that notwithstanding the First Amendment, any speaker *may not "intentionally inflict[] severe emotional injury on private persons* at a time of intense emotional sensitivity by launching *vicious verbal attacks* that make no contribution to public debate."

d. **Nazi-Skokie dispute:** Before *Snyder*, the leading case showing that speech may not be banned merely because it is emotionally hurtful was a federal Court of Appeals case involving plans by an American Nazi group to demonstrate in front of the Skokie, Illinois Village Hall. Skokie is a predominantly-Jewish community, and about 5,000 of its residents were survivors of the concentration camps. When the village learned of the Nazis' demonstration plans, it passed an ordinance to ban the demonstration.

    i. **March could not be banned:** But the Seventh Circuit explicitly *rejected* the argument that the village had the right to prevent a substantive evil, the "infliction of psychic trauma on resident Holocaust survivors." *Collins v. Smith*, 578 F.2d 1197 (7th Cir. 1978).

        (1) Rationale: The court in *Collins* agreed that the demonstration might be shocking to the village's residents. But any shock effect would be due to the *content of the ideas expressed*, and "public expression of ideas may not be prohibited merely because the ideas are themselves offensive to some of their hearers."

3. **Strict scrutiny to be used:** If the state *does* want to regulate speech on the grounds of its offensive content, the courts will use *strict scrutiny* to review the regulation, and the regulation will *virtually never survive that strict scrutiny.*

a. *Snyder v. Phelps*: *Snyder v. Phelps, supra*, illustrates this — once the Supreme Court determined there that allowing a recovery for intentional infliction of emotional distress constituted a form of content-based regulation of speech related to a public issue, the reversal was virtually automatic.

b. **Offensive trademarks (*Matal*):** A 2017 case involving *federal trademarks* similarly illustrates that government attempts to silence offensive speech will be *strictly scrutinized,* and almost always struck down. In *Matal v. Tam,* 137 S.Ct. 1744 (2017) (also discussed *supra*, p. 481 and *infra*, p. 569), the federal trademark registration statute contained a "disparagement clause," under which the Patent and Trademark Office (PTO) was told to disallow the registration of any trademark that "may *disparage ... or bring ... into contempt*" any "persons, living or dead, institutions, beliefs, or national symbols[.]" Under PTO regulations, a mark would be denied registration if the PTO examiner found that it was "disparaging to a substantial composite of the referenced group."

    i. **Rationale:** All eight Justices who participated in *Matal* agreed that denying registration to any trademark that would be "offensive to a substantial percentage of the members of any group" **constituted viewpoint discrimination.** And all agreed that the viewpoint discrimination here violated the Ps' freedom of expression.

J. Regulation of "hate speech": As we just saw, government may generally not prevent or punish words on the grounds that listeners will find them hurtful or otherwise offensive. Groups interested in eliminating discrimination against *minorities* have argued that an exception should be made for *"hate speech"* directed against racial minorities, women, homosexuals, and other traditionally disfavored groups. State legislatures have generally agreed — all but four states have some form of "hate crime" law criminalizing bias-motivated speech or acts.

However, if government *singles out bias-motivated speech*, criminalizing it while not criminalizing other types of angry speech, the government can properly be accused of acting in a forbidden *content-based* rather than content-neutral way. In a series of three cases since 1992, the Supreme Court has tried to lay out some rules for when government may single out hate speech and punish it specially. Two of the three cases have involved *cross burning*, a particular form of hate speech that has a long history of expressing racial hatred (and, often, of preceding racial violence).

1. **Three rules:** These three cases stand for the following main propositions, which represent a general rule about what the state may not ban, and three exceptions to that major rule:

   ❑ **General ban:** A ban on speech or conduct intended or likely to incite anger or violence based solely on *particular listed topics or motives* — such as race, color, religion or gender hatred — is *impermissibly content-based.* That's true even if all the speech/conduct banned falls within an *"unprotected"* category such as, here, *"fighting words."* (See *R.A.V., infra.*)

   ❑ **Worst examples:** However, a state *may* impose a content-based ban on *particular instances* of unprotected speech if the ban forbids *only the very worst examples* illustrating *the very reason the particular class of speech is unprotected.* (Thus the state may choose to criminalize just the very most dangerous "fighting words," the very most obscene obscene images, etc.) (*R.A.V.*)

   ❑ **Penalty-enhancement statutes:** Also, a state may identify particular generally-applicable criminal proscriptions, and may then choose to punish *more severely* those criminal acts that happen to be motivated by hate than those not motivated by hate. This is called the *"penalty enhancement"* approach. For instance, from within the overall class of acts that constitute criminal vandalism or arson, the state may punish vandalism or arson more seriously if it's motivated by bias against particular groups. (*Wisconsin v. Mitchell, infra,* p. 526.)

   ❑ **All intimidating acts:** Finally, a state may select a particular type of expressive act (e.g., cross-burning), and punish *all instances* where that act is done with a purpose of *intimidating or threatening* someone, even though the state doesn't punish other types of intimidating or threatening acts. (*Virginia v. Black, infra,* p. 526.)

2. **The general principle of *R.A.V. v. St. Paul*:** The first of this trio of Supreme Court cases on hate-speech was *R.A.V. v. City of St. Paul*, 505 U.S. 377 (1992). The case involved a *cross-burning*, but seems applicable to anti-hate-speech laws in general.

a. Facts: In *R.A.V.*, D and several other teenagers allegedly burned a homemade cross inside the fenced yard of a black family that lived across the street from D; the incident took place in the middle of the night. D was prosecuted under the St. Paul "Bias-Motivated Crime Ordinance," which provided that "whoever places on public or private property a symbol, object, appellation, characterization or graffiti, including, but not limited to, a burning cross or Nazi swastika, which one knows or has reasonable grounds to know arouses anger, alarm or resentment in others on the basis of *race, color, creed, religion or gender* commits disorderly conduct and shall be guilty of a misdemeanor." D contended that the ordinance violated the First Amendment in two respects: (1) it was substantially overbroad; and (2) it was impermissibly content-based.

b. Court agrees: The Court unanimously agreed that the ordinance, on its face, violated the First Amendment. However, the Court was bitterly split, 5-4, on the proper rationale.

c. Opinion of the Court: Justice Scalia, joined by four other Justices (Rehnquist, Kennedy, Souter and Thomas), wrote the opinion for the Court. Scalia concluded that the law was ***impermissibly content-based***, because "it prohibits otherwise permitted speech solely on the basis of the subjects the speech addresses."

i. Only applicable to "fighting words":   The Minnesota Supreme Court, in construing the ordinance, had concluded that it was intended to apply only to *"fighting words"* (see *supra*, p. 516), not to bias speech that would not threaten an immediate breach of the peace. Scalia believed that he had no choice but to accept the Minnesota court's construction of the statute.

ii. No content-based regulation of unprotected categories: The Supreme Court had previously held, as noted (see *supra*, p. 516) that fighting words are an "unprotected category" under the First Amendment. But Scalia's opinion asserted that ***even when government is regulating a supposedly "unprotected" category, it may not do so in a content-based manner***.

(1) Examples: Scalia gave two examples of what he considered to be impermissibly content-based regulations of "unprotected" categories: The government may proscribe libel, but it may not make the further content discrimination of proscribing *only* libel critical of the government. Similarly, a city council may not enact an ordinance prohibiting only those legally obscene works that contain criticism of the city government.

iii. Ordinance unconstitutional: By Scalia's standard, the St. Paul ordinance was clearly ***unconstitutional***, even though applicable only to generally-unprotected "fighting words." The ordinance was certainly content-based, because it applied only to fighting words that insult or provoke violence "on the basis of *race, color, creed, religion or gender*" — abusive language, no matter how vicious or severe, was permitted under the ordinance unless it was addressed to one of the *"specified disfavored topics"*; fighting words used to express hostility based on political affiliation, union membership or homosexuality, for instance, were not covered by the ordinance.

(1) Viewpoint based: In fact, Scalia said, the ordinance was not only content-based but "*viewpoint* based." That is, where two opposing sides had a confrontation concerning a matter of race or religion, one side could use fighting words while the other could not. "One could hold up a sign saying, for example, that all 'anti-catholic bigots' are misbegotten; but not that all 'papists' are, for that would insult and provoke violence 'on the basis of religion.'" St. Paul has no authority, Scalia asserted, "to license one side of a debate to fight free-style, while requiring the other to follow Marquis of Queensbury Rules."

iv. Remedy: Proponents of the ordinance argued that even if it was content-based, it could survive the strict scrutiny given to content-based regulations because it was necessary to serve a compelling state interest. Scalia conceded that the state had a compelling interest in safeguarding the rights of traditionally-disfavored groups, including their right to live in peace where they wish. But he argued that the ordinance was not "*necessary*" to achieve this state interest, because there were "*adequate content-neutral alternatives.*" In particular, St. Paul could enact an ordinance prohibiting *all* fighting words, not merely fighting words motivated by racial, religious or other specifically-enumerated biases. To Scalia, burning a cross in someone's front yard is "reprehensible," but St. Paul had "sufficient means at its disposal to prevent such behaviour without adding the First Amendment to the fire."

d. Concurrence: The main concurrence in *R.A.V.* (by Justice White, joined by Blackmun, O'Connor and, in most respects, Stevens) read more like a dissent.

i. Unprotected categories: Justice White believed that where a category is "unprotected," the states are *not* prevented from regulating it on the basis of content. "It is inconsistent to hold that the government may proscribe an *entire category* of speech because the content of that speech is evil … but that the government may not treat a *subset of that category differently* without violating the First Amendment; the content of the subset is by definition worthless and undeserving of constitutional protection."

(1) Overbreadth: But White nonetheless agreed with the result in the case. White believed that the case should instead have been decided on *overbreadth* grounds. He interpreted the Minnesota court to have ruled that the ordinance prohibited expression that "by its very utterance" causes "anger, alarm or resentment." By this interpretation, the ordinance reached not only words tending to incite an immediate breach of the peace (words which may constitutionally be proscribed), but also words and expressive conduct that cause *only* hurt feelings, offense, or resentment (words and conduct which may not be constitutionally proscribed). Since the ordinance reached both protected and unprotected speech, it was *overbroad*, and thus invalid.

3. Enhancement-of-penalty statutes: The Court's approach in *R.A.V.* invalidates many anti-hate crime statutes that, like St. Paul's, define certain activities as a *new, separate, crime*.

a. Enhancement-of-penalty statutes may be valid: But *R.A.V.* does *not invalidate* statutes that approach the hate-speech problem in a quite different way: these statutes punish *existing crimes* like vandalism and arson *more seriously* if the prosecution shows that the crime was motivated in part by one of the listed types of bias. The Court found such a *"penalty enhancement"* statute to be *valid*, in *Wisconsin v. Mitchell*, 508 U.S. 476 (1993). This unanimous decision seems to validate all of the dozens of state and local hate-crime laws of the "penalty enhancement" variety throughout the country.

b. **Facts:** In *Wisconsin v. Mitchell*, D, a black teenager, was convicted of aggravated battery, a crime that in Wisconsin ordinarily carries a maximum sentence of two years in prison. However, there was strong evidence that D had selected his victim, V, based on race; for instance, he pointed to V, told his friends, "There goes a white boy; go get him," then led them in a severe beating of V. Under Wisconsin's statute, the *maximum sentence* for aggravated battery was *increased* to seven years because of D's race-based selection of a victim.

c. **Statute upheld:** The Court unanimously held that this penalty-enhancement scheme did not violate D's First Amendment rights, and thus *upheld* the statute.

  i. **Defendant's argument:** D argued in *Mitchell* that since the only reason for the enhanced sentence was his discriminatory motive for selecting his victim, the statute punished his beliefs. Therefore, he argued, the penalty-enhancement statute was no more constitutionally acceptable than the ban on certain "fighting words" struck down in *R.A.V.*

  ii. **Speech/ conduct distinction:** But the Court rejected this argument. In doing so, the Court relied heavily on the distinction between speech and conduct. The ordinance struck down in *R.A.V.* was explicitly directed at expression, whereas the penalty-enhancement statute here was aimed at *conduct*, and this conduct was completely unprotected by the First Amendment. (That is, there is no constitutional protection for the act of battery, whatever the actor's motive.)

  iii. **Analogy to anti-discrimination laws:** The Court also observed that many other statutes punish a defendant based on his motive for acting. For instance, federal Title VII makes it unlawful for an employer to discriminate against an employee "because of such individual's race, color, religion, sex, … ," yet that statute has always been found to conform with the First Amendment.

4. **Ban on all acts intended to intimidate:** Finally, in the most recent cutting back on the general rule of *R.A.V.*, the Court has held that *all instances* of a certain type of expressive act — such as cross-burning — may be prohibited if done for the purpose of *intimidation or threat*, even if other intimidating acts with expressive content are not prohibited. *Virginia v. Black*, 538 U.S. 343 (2003).

a. **Statute:** The statute at issue in *Black* made a crime to burn a cross in a public place or on the property of another, if done "with the intent of *intimidating any person or group of persons.*" The statute also added a clause (we'll refer to it here as the "prima facie" clause) saying that "Any such burning of a cross shall be *prima facie evidence* of an intent to intimidate[.]"

b. **Main provision upheld:** The Court's opinion in *Black* was fragmented — there was no opinion that spoke for a majority on all points. But there were separate majorities for two propositions: (1) that government may *single out cross burning* as a particularly virulent form of intimidation, and may thus *ban all cross burnings done with* *intent to intimidate* even while not banning other expressive acts intended to intimidate; and (2) that the statute here was **unconstitutional** (though no majority agreed about why).

    i. **Government may single out cross-burning:** As to proposition (1), a majority of the Court in *Black* agreed that "[i]nstead of prohibiting all intimidating messages, Virginia may choose to **regulate this subset of intimidating messages** in light of cross burning's long and pernicious history as a **signal of impending violence.**"

    c. **Significance:** *Black* is significant mainly for the proposition that a properly-constructed statute may **ban a particular type of intimidating expression** — such as cross burning — while **declining to ban other types of intimidating expressions**.

K. **All speech not necessarily created equal (the disfavoring of indecent speech):** Implicit in *Cohen v. California, supra,* p. 519, is the principle that all constitutionally-protected expression is **created equal** in the eyes of the First Amendment, so that the government **may not prefer certain ideas or subject matter to others.** But a number of cases suggest that certain types of expression, while not directly suppressible on the grounds of their content, are viewed as inherently **less valuable** and may therefore be **regulated more extensively** than speech closer to the "core" of First Amendment values, such as political speech. This less-favored of speech seems to include mainly speech that is "*indecent*."[6] This is sometimes referred to as the "*two-tier*" theory of First Amendment protection.[7]

    Example: New York criminalizes the distribution of non-obscene materials showing **children engaged in sexual conduct.** The ban covers such sexually-explicit materials even if they are not obscene (e.g., materials that have serious literary value, a factor that automatically prevents them from meeting the formal definition of "obscene"; see *infra,* p. 561).

    Held, the ban does not violate the First Amendment. Materials showing children engaged in sexual conduct, even if the materials are not "obscene," have an "exceedingly modest, if not *de minimis,*" First Amendment value. The state has a countervailing, compellingly strong interest in stopping sexual exploitation of child actors. Therefore, the First Amendment does not demand that the state allow distribution of such materials. *New York v. Ferber,* 458 U.S. 747 (1982) (discussed further *infra,* p. 563.)

    1. **Consequences of being "lesser-valued" speech:** So in what way may lesser-valued speech such as indecent speech be more extensively regulated than high-value speech? Sometimes, the low-value speech may be completely banned; more commonly, its "secondary effects" can be regulated.

    2. **Complete ban:** Occasionally, as in the indecent-speech-involving-minors area at issue in *Ferber, supra,* the Court has allowed government to **completely ban** the speech despite its

---

6. *Commercial* speech also seems to be somewhat less-favored. See *infra,* p. 565.

7. Don't confuse this "two-tier" theory with the "two track" analysis on p. 477 *supra.* "Two-tier" refers to the Court's distinction based on the "value" of the speech. "Two track" refers to two ways of analyzing restrictions on speech, one track for content-based regulations and the other for content-neutral "time, place and manner" regulations.

slight First Amendment value.

3. **The "secondary effects" doctrine:** But a more important practical difference between high-value and low-valued speech is that the *"secondary effects"* doctrine seems to apply to this lesser-valued speech.

    a. **Nature of doctrine:** Under the secondary effects doctrine, if the court is satisfied that the government was merely trying to eliminate the undesirable *non-content-related consequences* of an expressive activity — things like increased crime or declining property values — the regulation will be found to be *content-neutral* and will be given only relatively un-strict "track two" review.

        i. **Regulation passes review:** Furthermore, in cases qualifying for the secondary effects doctrine, the Court seems very willing to find that the measure *passes* that track two review. That is, the Court typically accepts that the government is indeed pursuing an important interest, and that the regulatory means being chosen appropriately further that interest while leaving open adequate alternative channels for communication.

    b. ***Erie v. Pap's* expands the doctrine to allow a complete ban:** For instance, a 2000 case holds that the secondary effects of lower-valued speech may entitle government to *completely ban* the disfavored expressive conduct (not merely limit the speech to a certain geographical area). The case is *Erie v. Pap's A.M.*, 529 U.S. 277 (2000).

        i. **Facts:** *Pap's* was a *"nude dancing"* case. The city of Erie, Pa. passed an ordinance that required live dancers to wear at least "pasties" and a "G-string." (Neither the city nor anyone else claimed that nude dancing was obscene and therefore constitutionally unprotected.) The city said that it was attacking not the expressive content of nude live entertainment, but rather its secondary effects, such as violence, sexual harassment, public intoxication, prostitution, and the spread of sexually transmitted diseases. The ban applied throughout the city, not just in a delimited area (as a prior Supreme Court case had approved). A nightclub that presented live nude dancers attacked the ordinance.

        ii. **Plurality:** The Court *upheld* the ordinance. However, there was no majority opinion on the underlying constitutional issues. A four-Justice plurality (opinion by O'Connor, joined by Rehnquist, Kennedy and Breyer) found that the secondary effects doctrine applied, so that the ordinance should be judged by the more-forgiving track two analysis for *content-neutral* time, place and manner regulations.

            (1) **Bad motivation irrelevant:** In fact, to the plurality it didn't even matter that the city may have been *motivated in part* by a desire to *suppress particular expression*. According to the plurality, as long as *one* of the purposes of the regulation was to combat secondary effects, it didn't matter that government also had the motive of suppressing speech.

            (2) **Passes track two analysis:** The plurality then found it easy to conclude that the ordinance satisfied the track two "time, place and manner" standard.

        iii. **Additional votes:** Justices Scalia and Thomas concurred. They believed that because the ordinance was a "general law regulating conduct and not specifically directed at expression," the ordinance was *not subject to First Amendment scru-*

tiny at all. Therefore, they agreed that the ordinance easily passed constitutional muster.

    iv. 6 votes for using secondary effects analysis: So *Erie v. Pap's* demonstrated that there were at least six votes on the Court for holding that even an ***absolute government ban*** on a particular form of expressive conduct motivated by a desire to combat the conduct's ***secondary effects*** is to be viewed as ***content-neutral***, and may be upheld if the ban is a reasonably effective means of combating those effects.

    v. Limited to indecency or other less-favored speech: So far, the secondary effects doctrine has not been applied outside of the ***indecency*** context. Thus as far as we know, government can't attack what it says are the bad secondary effects of protected speech other than indecency (e.g., ***core political speech***) except by surviving strict scrutiny.

L. Regulation of indecency in media: A number of cases have dealt with ***indecency in the media***. A brief summary of the Court's holdings is that the government has substantial latitude in regulating indecent expression on the ***public airwaves,*** but much less latitude when it tries to carry out such regulation in media that are more one-on-one, such as ***phone systems,*** modern individually-addressable ***cable TV systems,*** and ***computer networks*** such as the ***Internet.***

1. Public airwaves: The government has the power to regulate non-obscene "indecent" material broadcast over the ***public airwaves*** (standard broadcast ***radio and TV***).

2. Regulation of indecency on phone, cable and computer systems: But when government tries to limit indecency in ***other media*** that are not as intrusive and widely-disseminated, the limits will be ***strictly scrutinized.*** These cases have involved ***phone networks*** ("dial-a-porn"), ***cable TV*** systems, and the ***Internet.***

    a. Cable programming: For instance, if government tries to perform content-based regulation of indecent speech on ***cable TV systems***, the court will use ***strict scrutiny***.

        i. Less restriction permissible: Therefore, much less regulation of indecency will be tolerated in the cable TV area than in the over-the-air broadcast area, because of cable's technological ability to ***block access on a household-by-household basis.*** Since content-based restrictions will be strictly scrutinized, any reasonably-effective less-restrictive alternative must be used. Therefore, government, instead of curtailing transmission of indecent material to *all* households, must instead give cable operators the right to offer blocking to ***just those households that want it.***

    b. Indecency on the Internet: What about ***"cyberspace,"*** and in particular the ***Internet***? Is the Internet more like over-the-air broadcasting (as to which the Court has traditionally allowed substantial government regulation), or is it more like books and newspapers (which receive the greatest First Amendment freedom)? The Supreme Court has answered this question by saying that the Internet ***more closely resembles books and newspapers,*** and is therefore deserving of the ***utmost freedom from content regulation***. The Court did so in two major opinions concerning Congress' efforts to restrict the access of ***minors*** to ***indecent content*** over the Internet.

        i. *Reno v. ACLU*: The first of the two cases was ***Reno v. American Civil Liberties Union***, 521 U.S. 844 (1997). The plaintiffs attacked two provisions of the federal Communications Decency Act (CDA). The first provision made it a crime to use a "telecommunications device" to transmit any communication which is "obscene or ***indecent***," while "***knowing that the recipient*** of the communication is under 18 years of age." The second made it a crime to "use any interactive computer service" to "display in a manner ***available to a person under 18***," any communication that uses ***"patently offensive"*** language or images. (For easy reference, we'll call the first provision the "knowing transmission" provision and the second the "make available" provision.) Both provisions were directed mainly at the Internet.

(1) Unanimously struck down: All nine Justices agreed that at least parts of the CDA were ***unconstitutional***. The Court's opinion was by Justice Stevens, who found the CDA to be both overly vague and overbroad.

(2) Less risk of intrusion: Stevens concluded that the burden on government to justify content regulation of the Internet was much greater than for such regulation of over-the-air broadcasting. Over-the-air broadcasting merited regulation in part because there was no way to adequately ***protect the listener from unexpected messages.*** By contrast, the risk that a computer user would ***stumble upon*** indecent material by accident was ***"remote,"*** because "a series of affirmative steps is required to access specific material." So cases allowing tight regulation of indecency in the over-the-air context (like *FCC v. Pacifica*, *infra*, p. 640) furnished no support for a finding that the CDA was constitutional.

(3) Statute found overbroad: Stevens concluded that the statute was ***overbroad***, because it restricted the free-speech rights of *adults*. "In order to deny minors access to potentially harmful speech, the CDA effectively suppresses a large amount of speech that ***adults have a constitutional right to receive*** and to address to one another." For instance, if one member of a 100-person chat group was a minor, the entire group would be foreclosed from discussing an "indecent" topic, even though the 99 adults clearly had a right to discuss that topic.

(4) Fails strict scrutiny: This suppression of protected adult speech had to survive ***strict scrutiny***, Stevens said. Therefore, the government had to show that there was ***no less restrictive alternative*** that would accomplish the same ends. The government had failed to carry this burden, he concluded. For instance, the government might have just imposed the less-restrictive alternative that indecent material be "tagged" so that user-installed filters could block it.

ii. **Replacement statute is also found invalid:** After *Reno*, Congress tried to fix the CDA's constitutional problems by enacting a replacement statute, the ***Child Online Protection Act (COPA)***. But in ***Ashcroft v. American Civil Liberties Union***, 542 U.S. 656 (2004), the Court found that COPA, too, was very likely a violation of the First Amendment. (Because of the preliminary-injunction posture of the case, the Court did not definitively decide the statute's constitutionality.)

(1) Terms of statute: COPA made it a crime to put on to the Web content that was "harmful to minors." Material was deemed "harmful to minors" if it was either obscene or was designed to appeal to minors' prurient interests in a "patently offensive" way that lacked serious literary or other value to such minors. (Minors were defined as persons under 17.) Web operators were given an affirmative defense if they screened minors from access by some ***age-verification mechanism***, such as by requiring a credit card or by "any other reasonable measures that are feasible under available technology." So basically, COPA said that anyone who wanted to operate a commercial Web site containing material that might be harmful to minors had to impose a mechanism for checking that only adults used the site.

(2) Lower court issues injunction: A federal district court issued a preliminary injunction against COPA, on the grounds that it, like the CDA before it, violated the First Amendment rights of adults.

(3) Supreme Court agrees with injunction: By a 5-4 vote, the Supreme Court held that the lower-court had ***not abused its discretion in entering the injunction.*** Justice Kennedy's opinion for the majority began by repeating *Reno*'s holding that if a statute suppresses a large amount of speech that adults have a constitutional right to receive, the government must bear the burden of showing that there are ***no less-restrictive alternatives*** that would be at least as effective.

(4) Filtering not shown to be less effective: Kennedy concluded that the government had not borne this burden of proof here. In particular, he focused on ***"blocking and filtering software"*** that could voluntarily be installed by users on their own computers. Such filtering software would clearly be less restrictive than the age-verification scheme required by COPA; for instance, an adult with children could simply turn off the filter when the adult wanted to use the computer. Therefore, the injunction should be permitted to stand while the case was tried on the merits, and the statute would be found valid only if the government could show (as seemed very unlikely) that the statute was in fact the ***least-restrictive available means of effectively blocking minors*** from accessing indecent Internet material.

(5) Dissent: The four dissenters, led by Justice Breyer, believed that COPA did indeed satisfy the least-restrictive-alternative requirement. They believed that COPA blocked very little content that was not in fact obscene (and thus forbiddable even to adults).

iii. **Significance:** Here are some of the things that *Reno v. ACLU* and *Ashcroft v. ACLU* seem to establish:

(1) Broad protection for Internet: The Internet, and publicly-available computer networks in general, deserve the same ***very broad First Amendment protection as books and newspapers,*** not the lesser protection given to scarce over-the-air broadcast media. (*Reno*.) This means that any "time, place and manner" restriction on the Internet will have to be very closely linked to the achievement of an important governmental interest.

(2) Protection of rights of adults: When government tries to protect minors from non-obscene material, government must make great efforts to see to it that the ***rights of adults*** to access material that they have a constitutional right to access are not inadvertently hampered. *Reno*. (So a ban on putting non-obscene "indecent" material in any place where minors might see it infringes the rights of adults, since adults have a right to see the material and the ban will dissuade people from making the material broadly available.)

(3) **No-restrictive available alternatives:** Indeed, if government *is* going to make it harder for adults to access material that they have a First Amendment right to see — even if "harder" means imposing a hurdle as relatively small as requiring the user to prove that she is in fact an adult — government must bear the burden of proving that there are *no less-restrictive available alternatives.* For example, if Congress wants to impose an age-verification requirement, Congress would have to prove that this device is less restrictive, or more effective, than filtering software voluntarily installed by private (adult) users, clearly a hard-to-make showing. (*Ashcroft.*)

M. **The public forum:** We turn now to a detailed discussion of the *public forum* as a factor in determining whether governmental regulation that purports to be merely of the "time, place and manner" of expression nonetheless violates the First Amendment.

1. **Recap of rules:** To recapitulate briefly how the status of a place as a public or non-public forum fits into the constitutional analysis, here is a summary of the relevant rules:

    a. **Content-based regulation:** If the regulation occurs because the government objects to the *communicative impact* of the expression (i.e., the government is not being content-neutral), it *does not make a difference* whether the expression takes place in a public forum or not; in either event, the governmental regulation is presumptively invalid, unless the expression falls in a pre-defined "unprotected category" (or, apparently now, if it falls within a class of speech that has "lesser social value," such as the "offensive" or "indecent" speech in *American Mini Theatres* and *Pacifica* or the child pornography in *Ferber).*

    b. **Content-neutral regulation in a public forum:** But assuming the regulation is *content-neutral,* then if the speech occurs in a *public forum*, it (and conduct related to it) can only be regulated in *narrow ways* which the government shows to be *necessary* to serve *significant governmental interests*. Tribe, p. 982. The availability of *alternative channels* for the communication will *not* by itself be enough to make the regulation valid.

        i. **Designated public forum:** Some government-owned property is viewed as a *"designated public forum."* This happens where government makes the decision to open non-public-forum property to broad expressive uses. (*Example:* Government decides to let any student group use its classrooms for any expressive activity.) The same rules (given in (b) above) apply to designated public forums as to true public forums, but government can at any time *change its mind* and remove the designation, making the site or use a non-public forum. (For more about designed public forums, including how they are defined, see p. 535 *infra*.)

    c. **Content-neutral regulation in a non-public forum:** Where the speech does *not* occur in a public (or designated public) forum, the state's right to regulate it in a content-neutral manner depends on whether the regulation's interference with expression is *"substantial"* or not.

i. **Substantial interference:** If the interference *is* substantial, the same rule applies as in the public-forum situation: the regulation must be narrowly drawn, and necessary to serve some significant government interest.

ii. **Insubstantial interference:** But if the interference is ***not substantial***, the government must only show a ***rational justification*** for its regulatory scheme. Tribe, p. 982. The government's scheme may allow access to some speakers and some subject matters while excluding others, "so long as the distinctions drawn are reasonable in light of the purpose served by the forum and are ***viewpoint neutral***." *Cornelius v. NAACP Legal Defense and Educational Fund*, 473 U.S. 788 (1985).

iii. **Alternative channels:** One significant difference between expression occurring in a public (including designated public) forum and that occurring in a non-public forum is that in the latter situation, the ***availability of equally effective alternative channels*** is ***sufficient to make the interference "insubstantial"*** (so that the "rational relation" test is all that has to be met). Tribe, p. 982.

2. **Necessary for significant state interest:** In applying the rule that content-neutral regulations of speech in public forums must be narrow ones that are necessary to serve significant governmental interests, the Court has held that ***mere administrative convenience does not suffice*** as a governmental interest. Recall, for instance, that a city's interest in keeping its streets clean was held not to constitute a sufficient justification for a ban on distribution of handbills, in *Schneider v. State*, 308 U.S. 147 (1939) (*supra*, p. 506).

a. **Safety:** But a need to ***control crowds*** to prevent ***physical danger*** from say, demonstrators or their audience, *will* suffice, provided that the Court is convinced that the crowd-control justification is not really a smokescreen for censorship (non-content-neutrality), and provided that there is no problem of vagueness or overbreadth (so that administrative discretion is held within acceptable limits).

b. **No right to make communication-free zones:** On the other hand, government's interest in preventing people from being ***bothered*** by hearing possibly-unwelcome messages will generally ***not*** justify government in ***putting certain public forums completely off-limits to expression.*** Government may forbid *harassment*, and may forbid one person from continuing a discussion with another if the latter indicates that she does not want the conversation to continue. But government generally may not act ***prophylactically***, by ***forbidding in advance all communication in a certain public place*** merely because government fears that much of the communication will be unwelcomed by the intended recipient.

i. **Conversations outside abortion clinics:** The issue of government's right to put certain public fora off-limits for communication arises most often in the case of ***abortion clinics***. Opponents of abortion frequently attempt to station themselves on public property near the entrances to clinics, so that the opponents can from there either engage in protest (e.g., by holding signs opposing abortion), or attempt to persuade prospective clients of the clinic that they should reconsider their plans.

(1) **First Amendment right upheld:** In general, the Supreme Court has ***protected*** the rights of abortion opponents to protest and communicate on public property near the entrance to abortion clinics. For more about regulation of speech near abortion clinics, see the discussion of *McCullen v. Coakley*, 134 S.Ct. 2518 (2014) *supra*, p. 515.

c. Access to public and private places: The need to allow *access* to *public and private buildings* will clearly justify some regulation of demonstrators. For instance, at least where less-intrusive measures have not worked, a judge may enjoin protesters or picketers from *blocking access* to the place that they are picketing.

d. Traffic flow: Even the need to keep streets *free for ordinary traffic* may justify *limited* regulation of marchers or demonstrators (e.g., a requirement that they use a street that is not a main thoroughfare).

3. Private places: Even where expression takes place in a *private* place, content-neutral regulations may be found to so impair the freedom of expression that the First Amendment has been violated. This will be true where the channel of communication being impaired *has no adequate substitutes.*

> **Example:** The City of San Diego bans all billboards containing non-commercial messages, apart from a few narrowly-defined exceptions. The City raises the defense (among others) that the ordinance is a reasonable "time, place and manner" restriction.
>
> *Held*, the ban is not a valid "time, place and manner" restriction; such restrictions, to be valid, must not only be content-neutral, but must also serve a significant governmental interest and *"leave open ample alternative channels for communication of the information."* Here, the parties stipulated that many advertisers rely on outdoor advertising because other forms of advertising are "insufficient, inappropriate and prohibitively expensive." Thus these other forms of advertising do not represent adequate alternative channels. *Metromedia, Inc. v. San Diego*, 453 U.S. 490 (1981).

a. Other locations: In private-forum situations, there is no general rule to predict when alternative channels will be found to be "adequate." One rule of thumb that seems to have emerged, however, is that a different *location* (as distinguished from a different medium) is much more likely to be an adequate substitute when it is in the *same city* as the location which has been placed under restriction, than where this alternative location is in a neighboring city.

4. "True" or "traditional" public forums: Let us now consider in more detail the various types of forums. First, and easiest to analyze are *"true" public forums,* sometimes referred to as *"traditional"* public forums. These are forums that by custom, rather than by any explicit government decision or designation, are completely public.

The clearest examples of a completely public forum, recognized as such since the 1930's, are *streets, sidewalks and parks.* See *Hague v. C.I.O.*, 307 U.S. 496 (1939) ("Use of the streets in public places [for assembly and debate of public questions] has, from ancient times, been a part of the privileges, immunities, rights and liberties of citizens.") Even a *quiet street* in a *residential neighborhood* is a true public forum. See *Frisby v. Schultz, supra*, p. 534, so holding (but concluding that the state nonetheless was entitled to ban all picketing on a residential street in front of a particular house).

a. Rules: Remember the *rules* applicable to true public forums:

❑ any *content-based* regulation will be *strictly scrutinized* (regulation must be necessary to achieve a compelling governmental interest) and rarely sustained; and

❑ any *content-neutral* "time, place and manner" regulation must be *narrowly drawn* to serve *significant governmental interests*, while leaving open adequate *alterna-*

tive channels for the communication.

5. Designated public forums: An additional class consists of what are called *"designated public forums."* These are public facilities as to which the government *has made the decision to open the place up to a broad range of expressive activities.* (As we explain below, these are treated essentially the *same way as true public forums*.)

  a. Municipal theater: For instance, a *municipal theater* that is held open as a place where *any group* may put on productions becomes a designated public forum, and certain groups or productions may not be excluded merely because a different theater is available. See *Southeastern Promotions, Ltd. v. Conrad*, 420 U.S. 546 (1975) (city theater may not exclude production of "Hair," even though some other, privately-owned theater in the city was available).

  b. School classrooms: The same would be likely to be true of *school classrooms*, if the school district has decided to let practically *any* community group or school group use the premises *after hours.* Such a decision makes the classrooms (at least after hours) a designated public forum, at which point the government can't allow or disallow particular groups to use the rooms based on agreement/disagreement with the group's message.

  c. Social-media Internet websites: It now seems that *major portions of the Internet* will be treated by the Supreme Court as constituting a designated public forum (or maybe even a "true" public forum). In *Packingham v. North Carolina* (discussed more extensively *supra*, p. 508), the Court held that mid-level scrutiny must be given to content-neutral restrictions on *"commercial social networking Web sites,"* such as the North Carolina statute at issue there.

   i. Status of "cyberspace": In support of that conclusion, Justice Kennedy's majority opinion said that *"a street or a park is a quintessential forum* for the exercise of First Amendment rights"; he then observed that "While in the past there may have been difficulty in identifying the *most important places* (in a spatial sense) for the exchange of views, today the answer is clear. It is *cyberspace* — the *'vast democratic forums of the Internet'* in general."

   ii. "Internet social networking services": Kennedy then focused his analysis on "Internet social networking services" — the types of sites covered by the statute at issue. Kennedy found that this category included sites like Facebook, LinkedIn and Twitter, and said that "social media users employ these websites to engage in a *wide array of protected First Amendment activity* on topics *'as diverse as human thought.'* " Therefore, he said, the state's decision to place these social media websites off-limits to certain users (registered sex offenders) had to undergo mid-level review, which it could not survive.

   iii. Significance: So it sounds as though a majority of the Court that decided *Packingham* believes that social media websites on the Internet — and perhaps other types of websites as well — are now such important avenues for First Amendment expression that even content-neutral time, place and manner restrictions on a person's access to such sites are to be analyzed by the same mid-level-review standard as are restrictions on expression occurring in true public forums like public streets and parks or in designated public forums (see Par. (d) below).

iv. **Internet websites as private property:** Observe that the major Internet social-media websites like Facebook are *privately-owned*, not government-owned. And until recently, virtually all of the Court's public-forum decisions involved publicly-owned property, like streets and parks. But *Packingham* seems to mean that the fact that a particular place for expression is privately owned does *not* prevent that place from being *treated as a designated public forum* when the source of the restriction on expression is the government rather than the private owner.

(1) **Restriction by owner of site:** Assuming that social-media websites are now to be analyzed similarly to public streets and parks, what happens if restrictions on expression there are *imposed by the website's private owners* — should such restrictions be limited by the First Amendment? The answer seems to be *"no,"* though the Supreme Court has never squarely faced the issue.

Example: Suppose that according to Facebook's own (i.e., not government-mandated) "terms of service," no person who is registered as a sex offender under the law of his state of residence may post on Facebook. Suppose further that Facebook learns that P is such an offender, and cancels his user ID under the terms of service. Can P argue that First Amendment principles (or perhaps common-law "public policy" principles inspired by the First Amendment) prevent Facebook from imposing this restriction on him given that government wouldn't be allowed to do so?

It seems clear that P will *lose* with this argument. The fact that the restriction comes from a private person (the site owner) who is not acting at any government's request will itself suffice to deprive P of a First Amendment claim. And it's unlikely that the courts will recognize any sort of federal or state "common-law right to free expression" "inspired" by First Amendment concerns.[8]

d. **Rules:** Once a place becomes a designated public forum, the *same rules apply as apply to true public forums:* (1) content-based regulation will be strictly scrutinized; and (2) content-neutral "time, place and manner" regulation must be narrowly drawn to serve significant governmental interests, while leaving open adequate alternative channels for the communication.

i. **Government may change its mind:** The only difference between a true public forum and a designated public forum is that with a designated forum, government may at any time *change its mind*, and *remove the designation* — at that point the forum becomes a non-public forum (see immediately below), which may be subjected to much greater "time, place and manner" regulation.

6. **Non-public forums:** A final category consists of those public facilities which are used for purposes *not particularly linked to expression*. Such a facility is usually referred to as a *"non-public forum"* (or sometimes, a *"limited public forum"*). Of the three categories

---

8. For an analogous situation, consider speech restrictions imposed by the private owners of *shopping centers*, discussed *infra*, p. 541. The Court now holds that such shopping centers are *not* the equivalent of public forums; therefore, the private owner of such a center may restrict speech there without thereby violating the speaker's First Amendment rights.

of public areas, this group offers the *least* constitutionally-protected access for First Amendment expression. The government regulation of expression in a non-public forum must merely be:

[1] *reasonable* in light of the *purpose served* by the forum; and

[2] *viewpoint neutral*.

See, e.g., *Int'l Soc. for Krishna Consciousness, Inc. v. Lee*, 505 U.S. 672 (1992).

a. **Reasonableness:** The requirement of *"reasonableness"* has relatively little bite here, as in the due process and equal protection areas. Government may limit speech in the non-public forum even if *less restrictive alternatives are readily available*, and even if the restriction chosen is not the *"most reasonable."*

Example: The public authority that operates the three major New York City airports bans all repetitive solicitation of money within the terminals, and all distribution of literature.

Held, because airport terminals are not public forums, the regulation of expression within them must merely be reasonable. The ban on face-to-face solicitation of money is reasonable, because "passengers who wish to avoid the solicitor may have to alter their path, slowing both themselves and those around them [with the result that] the normal flow of traffic is impeded." Also, face-to-face solicitation presents risks of duress and fraud. (But, a different majority of the Court holds, the sale and distribution of literature may *not* be banned; at least one member of the Court believes that such regulation is not even "reasonable.") *Int'l Soc. for Krishna Consciousness, Inc. v. Lee, supra*.

b. **Viewpoint neutrality:** But the requirement of *viewpoint neutrality* has a real impact in these non-public-forum cases. The government can restrict speech across the board in these forums, but it can't restrict speech by *preferring some messages or perspectives over others.*

   i. **Can't bar religious viewpoint, even if it involves worship:** The most dramatic example of the requirement of viewpoint-neutrality for non-public forums is that when a government allows use of *public facilities* by various (even though not all) community groups, *religious groups* must be given *equal access.*

      (1) **Funding of student activities:** For instance, where a public university funds a broad range of *student publications*, it may not exclude publications on the grounds that they are religiously-oriented. See *Rosenberger v. Univ. of Virginia*, discussed *infra*, p. 538.

   ii. **Candidate forums on government-owned TV:** Similarly, government must be viewpoint-neutral when it organizes a debate or forum for *competing political candidates*. See *Arkansas Educational Television Comm'n v. Forbes*, 523 S. Ct. 666 (1998), holding that a state-owned TV station which held a candidates' forum was not entitled to choose which candidates to invite based upon the candidate's political views (but also holding that the station did not violate this principle).

   iii. **Even spending must be viewpoint-neutral:** The requirement of viewpoint-neutrality is so strict that it applies even to activities that are *funded by the govern-*

ment. Thus government may *not* choose to *fund some third-party activities and not others, based on the viewpoints expressed*.

Example: The University of Virginia (a public university) funds certain student publications, by paying for their printing costs. The University disqualifies from this funding any publication that "primarily promotes or manifests a particular belie[f] in or about a deity or an ultimate reality." P is the publisher of *Wide Awake*, a student newspaper that gives a "Christian perspective" on the University. P argues that the University's refusal to fund *Wide Awake* violates his free-speech rights. The University concedes that its policy puts a whole subject — religion discussed from a proselytizing perspective — off limits, but claims that its policy is viewpoint-neutral. (For instance, the university points out that those opposing the practice of religion are equally excluded.)

Held, for P (by a 5-4 vote). The regulation here was *not* viewpoint-neutral. "The University does not exclude religion as a subject matter but selects for disfavored treatment those student journalistic efforts with religious editorial viewpoints." Nor does the fact that the University is spending money make any difference: If the University were disseminating only its own messages, it would not have to fund opposing viewpoints. But once it chooses to fund some *third-party viewpoints* (i.e., some student-run publications), it may not choose which ones to fund based on the viewpoint of the speaker. (Also, requiring the University to fund publications like P's does not violate the Establishment Clause. See *infra*, p. 663.) *Rosenberger v. University of Virginia*, 515 U.S. 819 (1995).

(1) Can ban discrimination by others: But when government gives a subsidy to certain organizations, it *may* require as a condition of the subsidy that the organizations themselves *not discriminate against certain viewpoints.* When government pursues such an *"all-comers"* policy, the Court has held, government is not engaging in forbidden viewpoint based discrimination. See *Christian Legal Society Chapter v. Martinez*, 130 S.Ct. 2971 (2010), a 5-4 decision set out in the following Example.

Example: The University of California's Hastings College of Law gives official recognition and some funding only to those organizations ("Registered Student Organizations," or RSOs) that comply with the school's nondiscrimination rules (the "all-comers" policy). The all-comers policy requires any RSO to accept all students who apply, and also forbids RSOs from discriminating on the basis of various specified criteria, one of which is sexual orientation. P (the Christian Legal Society) refuses to accept any student who engages in "unrepentant homosexual conduct," or who holds religious convictions different from those contained in a "Statement of Faith" the Society has adopted. Hastings refuses to grant P the RSO status because of these limits on who may join. P claims that the all-comers policy violates the First Amendment requirement that when government restricts access to limited public forums (i.e., nonpublic forums) the restriction must be both reasonable and viewpoint neutral.

Held, for Hastings: the all-comers policy is constitutional. The policy is viewpoint neutral: "[It is] hard to imagine a more viewpoint-neutral policy than one requiring all student groups to accept all comers." The requirement that student groups accept all applicants is " 'justified without reference to the content [or viewpoint] of the regulated speech.'" (Also, the all-comers requirement is *reasonable* for several reasons, including that Hastings could reasonably conclude that (1) an equal-access policy promotes the educational experience, and (2) in light of the fact that RSOs get school funding, no Hastings student should be forced to fund a group that would reject her as a member.)

(The four dissenters argue that the policy is not in fact viewpoint neutral because it "single[s] out one category of expressive associations for disfavored treatment: groups formed to express a religious message. Only religious groups [are] required to admit students who [do] not share their views.") *Christian Legal Society Chapter v. Martinez, supra.*

c. **"Subject neutrality" not required:**   The requirement of neutrality in non-public forum cases is merely one of *"viewpoint* neutrality," *not "subject neutrality."* Thus "[a] speaker may be excluded from a non-public forum if he wishes to address a *topic* not encompassed within the purpose of the forum ... or if he is not a member of the class of speakers for whose special benefit the forum was created. ... [But] the government violates the First Amendment when it denies access to a speaker solely to suppress the *point of view* he espouses on an otherwise includable subject." *Cornelius v. NAACP Legal Defense and Educational Fund, Inc.*, 473 U.S. 788 (1985).

Example: The federal government says that non-profits may solicit from federal employees in the workforce by using a particular fundraising mechanism administered by the federal government. However, no agency that seeks to influence the outcome of elections or the determination of public policy through politics, lobbying or litigation, may participate. *Held*, the government may exclude litigation and advocacy organizations, assuming that it is acting in a viewpoint-neutral way. *Cornelius, supra.*

d. **Particular types of places that are non-public forums:**   The Court is increasingly quick to find that particular publicly-owned places are *non-public forums*. The test is whether the government has intended to create *"general access for a class of speakers"* (in which case the forum is true public or designated public) or, instead, *"selected access for individual speakers"* (in which case the forum is probably non-public). *Arkansas Educational Television Comm'n v. Forbes*, 523 U.S. 666 (1998). In most cases where the issue has been discussed by the Court, a non-public forum has been found.

i. **Airport terminals:**   An *airport terminal* is a non-public forum. *Int'l Soc. for Krishna Consciousness v. Lee*, 505 U.S. 672 (1992).

(1) **Rationale:**   Six members of the Court in *Krishna* believed that an airport terminal was a non-public forum. The majority opinion, by Chief Justice Rehnquist, asserted that public forums have two principal characteristics: they have *traditionally* been used for purposes of assembly and expression, and they have as a *"principal purpose ... the free exchange of ideas."* Airports do not satisfy either of these tests: only recently have they been made available for speech activity, and their principal purpose is to facilitate travel and make a regulated profit, not to facilitate free expression.

ii. Other transportation hubs: What about *subways, bus stations, railroad stations,* and other publicly-owned and operated parts of transportation systems? The rationale of the majority's opinion in the *Krishna* case suggests that these, too, will be found to be non-public forums — they have not traditionally been used for purposes of free expression (with the possible exception of big-city subways), and their principal purpose is transportation, not expression.

iii. Jails: Another good example of a non-public forum is the *jailhouse*. Jailhouses serve the limited function of housing prisoners, and nearly any type of expressive conduct, whether by prisoners or members of the public, is likely to be seen as incompatible with this basic purpose.

iv. Military bases: Similarly, *military bases* may be placed off-limits to political speakers. In *Greer v. Spock*, 424 U.S. 828 (1976), a majority of the Court so held, reasoning that the purpose of a military base is to "train soldiers, not to provide a public forum." The policy against political campaign appearances was also justified by the "American constitutional tradition of a politically neutral military under civilian control."

v. Use of school facilities by student groups: Where facilities and funding are made available by a public school system to *student groups* (not to all members of the public generally), this usage will be classified as falling within the non-public-forum category. See *Christian Legal Society Chapter v. Martinez*, 130 S.Ct. 2971 (2010), *supra*, p. 538 (Court uses the phrase "limited public forum," but it's clear the Court means the same thing as "non-public forum.")

vi. School mail system: A *school system's* internal *mail* system, including teachers' mailboxes, has been held to fall into this non-public-forum category. *Perry Education Ass'n v. Perry Local Educators' Ass'n*, 460 U.S. 37 (1983). The fact that the official teachers' union, as well as a number of other outside organizations (e.g., YMCA and Cub Scouts) were permitted to use the mail system was not enough to convert the system into a public forum. Therefore, the school district's rule that no "school employee organization" except the official union could use the system was valid.

vii. Governmental workplace: A *governmental workplace* will apparently be treated as a non-public forum. In *Cornelius v. NAACP Legal Defense and Educational Fund*, *supra*, p. 539, the Court held that a charitable campaign held at federal workplaces fell into the non-public forum category.

viii. Candidates' debates or fora: When government organizes a *forum or debate for political candidates,* this will often be a non-public forum. For instance, in a case in which a state-owned TV station organized a televised debate to which the two leading candidates for a congressional seat were invited, the court found that the forum was a nonpublic one, because the debate "did not have an open-microphone format," i.e., the station did not make its debate "generally available to candidates" for that seat. Therefore, the station was within its rights not to invite plaintiff, a minor candidate (so long as the station made its decision based upon an objective determination of the plaintiff's lack of strength rather than upon lack of enthusiasm for his views). *Arkansas Educational Television Comm'n v. Forbes*, 523 U.S. 666 (1998).

ix. **Internet connections in libraries:** *Internet connections at public libraries* appear not to constitute public forums. Therefore, the government may require libraries receiving federal funding to install anti-pornography filters on any computer connected to the Internet. See *U.S. v. Amer. Library Ass'n.*, 539 U.S. 194 (2003) (4-justice plurality holds that "a public library does not acquire Internet terminals in order to create a public forum for Web publishers to express themselves, any more than it collects books in order to provide a public forum for the authors of books to speak." A fifth Justice, Breyer, in concurring, says he agrees with this determination.)

x. **Buses:** *Buses* that are part of a municipally-owned transit system also appear to fall within the category of non-public-forum facilities. See *Lehman v. Shaker Heights*, 418 U.S. 298 (1974), where a plurality reached this conclusion.

xi. **Utility poles:** *Utility poles* owned by the government are not a public forum, so that a city may prevent the posting of signs on them, in order to reduce "visual blight." See *Los Angeles v. Taxpayers For Vincent*, 466 U.S. 789 (1984).

N. **Right of access to private places:** In most of the First Amendment cases which we have examined so far, the speaker sought to use *public property* to deliver his message. In a few of the other cases above, he sought to use his own property, or that of a willing owner (e.g., billboard advertisers in *Metromedia v. San Diego, supra*, p. 534). We turn now to the rights of a speaker to use *private property, against the owner's will*, for expressive purposes. In this group of cases, speakers have in effect argued that there should be recognized certain *"private forums,"* to which the government should guarantee speakers access, just as it guarantees access to public forums like streets and parks.

1. **Rationale:** The main argument in support of recognizing a guaranteed right of access to certain private forums is that a contrary view would *close off many important channels of communication*. The mere fact that government itself has not closed down these channels is of small consolation, "[f]or if no one will rent an unpopular speaker a hall or print the speaker's views, it may be of little use that the government has not gone out of its way to muzzle the speech." Tribe, p. 998.

2. **Shopping centers:** The main type of "private forums" to which speakers have asserted a guaranteed right of access is *shopping centers*.

   a. **Initial success by claimants:** Speakers asserting a right to access to privately-owned shopping centers were, initially, partly *successful* — the Court held that a center's owner could not constitutionally be permitted to use state trespass law to bar peaceful union picketing of a store in the center.

   b. **Change of law:** But the Court eventually changed its mind, and concluded that the First Amendment does *not* guarantee any speaker a right of access to a privately-owned shopping center, even if the speech relates to the center's (or its tenants') operations. *Hudgens v. NLRB*, 424 U.S. 507 (1976).

   c. **Present rule:** So neither labor picketers, anti-war activists *nor any other citizens have a First Amendment right to express themselves in shopping centers over the property owner's objection*.

   d. **Access guaranteed by state constitution:** Although there is no right of access to a shopping center under the First Amendment to the federal constitution, at least one state, California, has interpreted ***its own constitution*** as guaranteeing such a right. In *Prune Yard Shopping Center v. Robins*, 447 U.S. 74 (1980), the Court held that this interpretation of the California State Constitution did not violate a shopping center owner's federal right of free speech, nor his right not to have his property taken without just compensation.

V. SYMBOLIC EXPRESSION

A. Problem generally: Just as expression may consist of speech accompanied by conduct (e.g., a protest march), so expression may sometimes consist solely of ***non-verbal actions***. The Supreme Court has for a long time been willing to recognize that certain non-verbal conduct is protected by the First Amendment (e.g., *Stromberg v. California*, 283 U.S. 359 (1931), striking a statute prohibiting display of a red flag as a symbol of opposition to organized government). Yet the Court has been wary of giving generalized First Amendment protection to any act which is an attempt to convey a message; this reluctance stems principally from the fear that granting such protection would legitimatize actions like political assassinations, Patty Hearst-type bank robberies, pouring blood on draft records, and other violent actions. See Tribe, p. 601.

1. Two-track analysis: The Court's recent cases on symbolic expression seem to have implicitly followed the "two-track" method of analysis (*supra*, p. 477). That is, where the Court believes that certain symbolic expression is prohibited because the government objects to the ***communicative content*** of the expression (what we're calling "track one"), the Court applies ***strict scrutiny***. Conversely, where the Court believes that the government's interest in regulating the conduct has nothing to do with the conduct's expressive content ("track two"), a more-easily-satisfied balancing test is applied, in which the interest being pursued by the state may well be found to outweigh the individual's interest in using that particular mode of expression.

2. Draft card burning: The Court's choice of "track two" rather than "track one" analysis seems to have been dispositive in the well-known case involving a conviction for ***draft card burning, U.S. v. O'Brien***, 391 U.S. 367 (1968).

   a. Facts: O'Brien and several others burned their draft cards in public, as part of a protest against the war in Vietnam. They were convicted of violating an amendment to the draft laws making it a crime to "knowingly destroy [or] mutilate" a draft card.

   b. Court finds right to regulate: O'Brien contended that the burning was "symbolic speech" protected by the First Amendment. But the Court held that even if this were true, conduct combining "speech" and "non-speech" elements could be regulated if four requirements were met:

   [1] the regulation was within the constitutional power of the government;

   [2] it furthered an ***"important or substantial governmental interest"***;

   [3] that interest was ***"unrelated to the suppression*** of free expression"; and

   [4] the ***"incidental restriction"*** on First Amendment freedoms was ***"no greater than is essential*** to the furtherance" of the governmental interest.

   The *O'Brien* Court found that all of these requirements were satisfied.

Note: This four-part test continues to be the one used by the Court for analyzing "time, place and manner" regulations. Therefore, it's worth memorizing.

    i. **"Track two" analysis:** The four-part test turns out to be indistinguishable from what we've been calling "track two" analysis (see *supra*, p. 488). The requirement that the governmental interest be "unrelated to the suppression of free expression" is a somewhat clumsy and conclusory way of saying that the harm which the regulation seeks to avoid must not stem from the ***communicative content*** of the conduct; this is the key finding of "content neutrality" that places a case on "track two" rather than "track one." Requirement (4) is equivalent to the "track two" requirement that content-neutral regulations of conduct in public forums must not close alternative channels for communication.

c. Content-neutrality: The Court in *O'Brien* identified several governmental interests served by the prohibition on draft-card destruction, interests the Court said were all ***"limited to the non-communicative aspect*** of O'Brien's conduct." For instance, the government had an interest in making sure that all draft-age males had in their possession a document indicating their availability for induction in an emergency. This and the other governmental interests were "important and substantial," and could not have been achieved with any less impact on O'Brien's freedom of expression. Therefore, his conviction did not violate the First Amendment, the Court concluded.

d. Relevance of motive: O'Brien argued that Congress' ***"purpose"*** or ***"motive"*** in enacting the statute was the improper one of suppressing dissent. But the Court rejected this argument, concluding that ***congressional "purpose" was simply irrelevant to a statute's constitutionality, so long as there was a legitimate governmental interest which could support the statute*** (whether or not Congress actually relied on it).

    i. **Still a rule:** It apparently remains the case that in First Amendment cases, the existence of a legitimate non-content-based government interest can save a statute that burdens expressive conduct, even if one of the government's motives is to suppress or oppose the message being communicated.[9]

3. Protest in schools: The Court's initial judgment about whether or not the government's regulation of symbolic expression is targeted at the expression's communicative impact will usually be dispositive. This was true in *Cohen*, and also true in another Vietnam-War-protest case, ***Tinker v. Des Moines School District***, 393 U.S. 503 (1969). In *Tinker*, several high school and junior high school students were suspended for wearing black armbands as a symbol of opposition to the War; a rule forbidding the wearing of such armbands had been adopted by school officials two days before, in anticipation of the protest.

a. Free expression right upheld: The Court held that the prohibition on armbands ***violated*** the students' First Amendment rights. What was being suppressed was not "actu-

---

9. Notice, though, that the same "motive irrelevant" rule doesn't apply to at least some constitutional rules *outside* the First Amendment area. For instance, the legislature's motivation is often relevant in *equal protection* cases; see, e.g., *Washington v. Davis*, 426 U.S. 229 (1976), *supra*, p. 258, holding that the absence or presence of government intent to commit racial discrimination is relevant in equal protection cases.

ally or potentially disruptive conduct," but rather, something that was nearly "pure speech."

i.   **Wish to avoid controversy:**   The authorities seem to have acted out of a wish to *avoid controversy* which might stem from the students' silent expression of opinion about the War. But this fear was not a valid reason for banning the expression: "Undifferentiated fear or apprehension of disturbance is not enough to overcome the right to freedom of expression."

ii. **Other symbols not barred:**   The lack of content-neutrality in the school officials' conduct was also shown by the fact that they did not prohibit the wearing of *all* political or other controversial symbols; buttons for national political campaigns, and even the Nazi iron cross symbol, were permitted.

b.   **"Track one" analysis:**   Thus the *Tinker* Court seems to have applied conventional "track one" analysis, under which any regulation of expression which is done because of the communicative impact of the expression will be strictly scrutinized, and allowed only if necessary to serve a compelling governmental interest.

i.   **Possibility of "track two":**   But, the Court indicated, had the students' act "materially and substantially interfere[d] with the requirements of *appropriate discipline* in the operation of the school," the officials would have been justified in preventing it. If the officials had been able to show that they acted for this reason, this presumably would have been the equivalent of showing that they were content-neutral, and would thus have entitled them to the less stringent review of "track two."

c.   **Regulation of hair and clothing:**   The Court in *Tinker* explicitly declined to deal with the constitutionality of school regulations dealing with *hair length, clothing type*, and other aspects of *personal appearance* which arguably have an expressive content. Nor has the Court ever been willing to confront this issue after *Tinker.*

i.   **Lower courts:**   Most lower courts have held that such aspects of personal appearance are not sufficiently communicative as to be entitled to full First Amendment protection. However, particular regulations have sometimes been struck down on the grounds that they infringe the personal liberty protected by the *Fourteenth* Amendment. See Tribe, p. 1386. .

4.   **Sleeping in park:**   The low level of scrutiny given to content-neutral regulations that affect symbolic expression was again demonstrated in *Clark v. Community For Creative Non-Violence*, 468 U.S. 288 (1984). There, the Court held that a National Parks Service *ban on sleeping in public parks* did *not* violate the First Amendment rights of demonstrators who wished to sleep in tents in two Washington D.C. national parks in order to dramatize the plight of the homeless. (The Court assumed, without deciding, that sleeping in connection with the demonstration constituted symbolic expression.)

a.   **Application of test:**   The Court found that the regulation was valid under the four tests of *U.S. v. O'Brien, supra*, p. 542. Most significantly, the Court found a substantial governmental interest in "maintaining the parks in the heart of our capital in an attractive and intact condition," and concluded that the ban on sleeping furthered this interest by limiting the extent and duration of demonstrations like the one involved here.

B. Flag desecration: One context in which the right of symbolic speech is important is the area of *flag desecration*: nearly all states (as well as the federal government) make it a crime to mutilate or otherwise desecrate an American flag. Most such statutes seem to have been enacted for the purpose of preserving the flag as a symbol of *national unity*, or some similar rationale. If such a statute, either on its face or as applied, applies to some flag-related conduct but not others based on the actor's *message*, the Court will presumably apply strict scrutiny, and will therefore probably strike the statute.

1. ***Texas v. Johnson:*** This is what happened in ***Texas v. Johnson***, 491 U.S. 397 (1989), the first of the Court's two highly controversial decisions on flag burning.

   a. **Statute:** The Texas statute at issue in *Johnson* made it a crime to "intentionally or knowingly desecrate … a state or national flag." "Desecrate" was defined to mean "deface, damage, or otherwise physically mistreat in a way that the actor knows will *seriously offend* one or more persons *likely to observe* or discover his action."

   b. **Facts:** Johnson, the defendant, participated in a political demonstration outside the 1984 Republican National Convention in Dallas. At the end of the demonstration, he unfurled an American flag, doused it with kerosene, and set it on fire. While the flag burned, the protestors chanted, "America, the red, white, and blue, we spit on you." Johnson was charged with violating the desecration statute; at his trial, several witnesses testified that they had been seriously offended by the flag burning, and he was convicted.

   c. **Holding:** By a 5-4 vote, the Court held that the Texas statute violated the First Amendment as applied to Johnson's acts. The majority opinion was written by Justice Brennan.

      i. **"Track one" analysis:** The key to the result reached by the majority was that the Court applied what we have called "track one" analysis. That is, the majority determined that the prosecution of Johnson was *"directly related to expression."* In reaching this conclusion, the Court reviewed the two objectives that Texas asserted it was pursuing: (1) preventing breaches of the peace; and (2) preserving the flag as a symbol of nationhood and national unity. As to objective (1), the majority simply disbelieved that preventing breaches of the peace was what had motivated Texas on these facts (since no disturbance of the peace either actually occurred or was threatened by this particular flag burning). As to objective (2), the need to protect the flag as a symbol of national unity would only be implicated if the defendant's conduct had a contrary message associated with it, so this objective was "directly related to expression" and thus called for track one scrutiny. The content-based nature of the statute was illustrated by the fact that particular conduct was covered only if an observer's likely reaction would be to be "seriously offended" — the offense could only flow from the message accompanying the act. (For instance, if D had burned the flag as a means of respectfully disposing of it because it was dirty or torn, he would not have offended anyone, and he would not have been convicted under the statute.)

      ii. **Strict scrutiny applied:** Since Johnson was prosecuted only because of the content of the particular message he was conveying, the Court applied strict scrutiny to the statute. "If there is a bedrock principle underlying the First Amendment, it is that the Government may not prohibit the expression of an idea simply because society finds the idea itself offensive or disagreeable." Here, Texas's objective — preserving the flag as a symbol of national unity — may have been worthy, even "compelling." But the means chosen by Texas to serve that objective were not necessary ones. First, the majority didn't believe that the nation's belief in the cherished significance of the flag would be undermined by acts of mutilation; indeed, these acts might produce the opposite result. Second, the government could combat such acts by acts of its own, such as giving the remains of the flag a respectful burial (as one witness to Johnson's burning did).

     d. Dissent: Four members of the Court bitterly dissented. The principal dissent was by Justice Rehnquist (joined by White and O'Connor). The dissenters thought that a state could prohibit the burning of a flag without violating the First Amendment prohibition on suppression of ideas. "The flag is not simply another 'idea' or 'point of view' competing for recognition in the market place of ideas." Also, the dissenters thought that flag burning is so inherently inflammatory that it inevitably threatens a breach of the peace, and thus could be analogized to "fighting words" and deprived of First Amendment protection entirely. In a separate dissent, Justice Stevens thought that the flag, even though it is in a sense an intangible asset, could be protected from desecration just as, say, the Lincoln Memorial could be protected from having a political message spray-painted upon it.

   2. The federal statute: The problem with the Texas statute in *Texas v. Johnson* seemed to be the statute's proscription of flag burning that would "seriously offend" observers — this reference to "offensiveness" made it clear that only flag burning intended to convey a particular message (disrespect) was proscribed by the statute. Therefore, immediately after the *Johnson* decision, the U.S. Congress tried to enact a *federal* flag burning statute that would ban all or most flag burning without being content-based and thus unconstitutional. This federal statute, the Flag Protection Act of 1989, punished anyone who "knowingly mutilates, defaces, physically defiles, burns, maintains on the floor or ground, or tramples upon any flag of the United States. ... " However, even though the statute avoided any reference to conduct that would "offend" an observer, the Supreme Court, by a 5-4 vote, found that this statute, too, was a violation of the First Amendment. *U.S. v. Eichman*, 496 U.S. 310 (1990).

     a. Rationale: The five-justice majority in *Eichman* found that despite the more careful wording, this statute, like the one in *Johnson*, was content-based. "Although the [Act] contains no explicit content-based limitation on the scope of prohibited conduct, it is nevertheless clear that the government's asserted *interest* is 'related to the suppression of free expression' ... and concerned with the content of such expression." The majority noted that the government was asserting its interest in preserving the flag as a *symbol for certain national ideals*; this goal was intimately related to the content of the burner's message (so that, for instance, a person's secret burning of the flag in his basement would not threaten this symbolic meaning of the flag). Since Congress was attempting to "suppress ... expression out of concern for its likely communicative impact," the statute had to be strictly scrutinized. It failed that scrutiny. (Interestingly, Justice Scalia was part of the five-member majority voting to strike down the statute, a surprise given his generally conservative views.)

   3. Significance: As a result of *Johnson* and *Eichman*, there is probably no way for government (whether state or federal) to "wipe out flag burning." Even if the statute uses the most content-neutral language (e.g., "No one may burn a flag under any circumstances"), the statute will presumably be struck down so long as the Court believes that it was *motivated* by a desire to preserve the symbolic value of the flag. Therefore, a constitutional amendment is probably the only way to prevent such acts.

Quiz Yourself on

"TIME, PLACE AND MANNER" RESTRICTIONS; SYMBOLIC EXPRESSION

77. Centerville is a small town. Its two biggest streets are Broadway and Main. After several recent parades and demonstrations that badly snarled traffic, Centerville's City Council enacted an ordinance that forbade all parades from taking place on either Broadway or Main. The ordinance did not forbid parades on the other, smaller streets in town. There is no evidence that the ordinance was motivated by hostility to particular types of parades, and the ban has been enforced even-handedly as to all parades. Citizens Against Corruption, a group wishing to protest what it believed was corruption in the mayor's office, paraded in an organized way down Broadway, and its leaders were arrested. The city has asserted that its ban on parades is a valid "time, place and manner" regulation.

    (a) What standard should the court use in evaluating the ordinance as applied here? _____

    (b) Should the court uphold the ordinance, and convict the marchers, under the test you specified in (a)? _____

78. An ordinance in the town of Harmony provides that "no demonstration or parade involving more than 20 persons shall take place on the town's streets, parks or other city-owned property without the prior issuance of a permit." The permit is free, and is to be granted by the mayor's office, "if the mayor concludes, acting in a reasonable manner, that the proposed activity would not be detrimental to the overall community, taking into account the "time, place and manner" of the activity." Firebrand, the head of a local group of anarchists, wished to conduct a demonstration in the park, at which he planned to urge his followers to immediately attempt a "sit in" of the mayor's office. The mayor, without knowing the precise purpose of the demonstration and knowing only that it was to be a demonstration against the local government, refused to issue the permit. In announcing the refusal, the mayor stated that "there has been too much demonstration, and not enough cooperation, around here recently." Firebrand then brought suit for an injunction against continued application of the permit requirement, and for a declaratory judgment that the permit requirement as drafted was unconstitutional. Should the court find the ordinance unconstitutional on its face? _____

79. Same facts as prior question. Now, however, assume that Firebrand ignored the ordinance, did not ask for a permit, and held a demonstration involving 30 people in a city park. He was arrested and charged with violating the ordinance. He now wishes to defend on the grounds that the ordinance is overbroad and thus facially invalid. Assuming that the ordinance is indeed overbroad, should the court acquit Firebrand? _____

80. The town of Lawton had a very carefully worded permit requirement. For any demonstration or parade involving more than 30 people, a permit was required, application for which must be made at least one hour prior to the close of business on the day before the proposed activity. Under the terms of the ordinance, the police commissioner was required to issue the permit, subject only to the rule that if in the commissioner's reasonable judgment, a breach of peace would be likely to occur which could not be controlled with the manpower available to the Lawton Police Department, the permit could be denied until such later date as proper police protection could be arranged (by borrowing from other police departments, if necessary).

Rouser, a radical, applied late on Friday afternoon to make a speech on Saturday. Because past speeches by Rouser had led to skirmishes, and because the commissioner believed that under weekend police schedules only three officers would be available (a number which the Commissioner believed would not be sufficient if problems should occur), the Commissioner turned down the request for a permit, and suggested that Rouser wait until the following Saturday. A local Justice of the Peace Court was open Friday night, and the Justice would have had jurisdiction to issue an injunction against the permit requirement. However, Rouser did not seek an injunction. Instead, Rouser gave his speech anyway, and no violence occurred. Rouser was charged with violating the permit requirement. He is now defending on the grounds that he was wrongfully denied the permit, because there was not in fact a serious threat of a breach of the peace, and that even if there was one, the presence of three officers would have been sufficient.

Assuming that the court agrees with Rouser's factual contentions about the danger of breach of the peace, should Rouser be acquitted? _____

81. The city of Blue Bell has enacted an ordinance providing as follows: no "canvasser or solicitor" may ring the doorbell of a private home, or knock on the door of a private home, where her purpose is to distribute handbills or to solicit an order for goods, services or charitable contributions. The ban does not prevent a person from simply sticking advertising material under the door or into the mail slot, so long as there is no bell-ringing or door-knocking. The purpose of the ordinance is to avoid disturbing residents (including those who work nights and sleep days), and also to prevent crime (e.g., people who want to see into the residence to "case the joint" for a later burglary).

Delrina, a Jehovah's Witness, was charged with violating the statute in that she rang doorbells so that she could personally hand inhabitants the literature requesting donations to the Jehovah's Witness organization. She has defended on the grounds that the ordinance represents an unconstitutional infringement of her right to free expression. May Delrina be convicted? _____

82. The city of Crooklyn had two substantial ethnic populations that were frequently at odds with each other, Middle-eastern Moslems and Orthodox Jews. After complying with a city requirement calling for a permit before the making of a public address, Mohammed, a self-proclaimed Islamic Fundamentalist, gave a speech in a park in Crooklyn. There were approximately 100 Islamic followers in the audience, as well as a group of about 30 Orthodox Jews. The Jews carried signs opposing Mohammed. Mohammed then made various anti-Semetic inflammatory statements, such as "Jews are corrupt" and "Jews control the U.S. government." He also addressed the Jews in the audience, saying, "You Jews in the audience today, you're not fit to kiss the dung-stained shoes of my poorest follower." At no time did Mohammed urge his audience to attack any of the Jewish onlookers or to otherwise commit immediate illegal acts.

Some of the Jews in the audience began to shake their fists and yell back at Mohammed; five of them then began to move towards the podium with upraised fists. There were 15 police officers at the scene to prevent disturbances, most of them ringed around the podium. They immediately arrested Mohammed and charged him with violating an ordinance prohibiting anyone from inciting a riot or causing a breach of the peace. Mohammed has defended on the grounds that his arrest violated his freedom of expression.

(a) What doctrine can the prosecution point to as justifying the arrest? _____

(b) Do First Amendment principles prevent Mohammed's conviction? _____

83. The Women's Health Alliance is a clinic that principally performs abortions. Abortion protesters decided to demonstrate outside the clinic. The protesters waved signs containing messages such as "Abortion Equals Murder." Whenever the protesters saw a woman leaving the clinic, they shouted, "Baby Killer," at her. The protesters remained at least 20 feet away from the front door of the clinic, and they did not block anyone's access to or from the clinic. All protesting took place on public property. A local ordinance forbids "the making of any public statement or the showing of any sign where the speaker knows the statement or sign is likely to be offensive to the person to whom it is addressed." May a protester who has waved the sign and shouted the epithet described above be convicted of violating the statute?

_____

84. State U, a public university, recently added the following provision to its Student Code: "No student or faculty member shall address to any other student or faculty member any verbal slur, invective, insult or epithet based on the addressee's race, ethnicity, gender, handicap or sexual orientation." The penalty for a first offense is suspension, and for the second offense is expulsion. Desmond, a white student at the university, addressed the following remark to Vera, a black student, "You nigger, go back to Africa where you belong." State U has commenced disciplinary proceedings against Desmond. You are the university's general counsel. The president has asked you the following question: "May the university constitutionally suspend Desmond for making this remark?" If your answer is "no," please describe the types of changes that might be made in the Code to alleviate the problem. _____

85. The state of Morality makes it a crime to post any "indecent" photo on a computer system located in the state, if the computer is connected by means of a physical wire or a telephone line to any other computer. "Indecent" is defined to include "any photo of a naked man or woman that would be offensive when measured by local community standards." The legislature means for its prohibition to apply even to pictures that would not be "obscene," including photos having significant artistic value. The legislature's purpose is to prevent minors from seeing indecent material. *Playpen* magazine puts a photo of a naked woman (which is not obscene under U.S. Supreme Court rulings) on its dial-in computer, located in Morality. Peter, a 16-year-old, dials in and retrieves the photo. A local prosecutor in Morality prosecutes the owner of *Playpen*, Hugh, and shows that Hugh had ordered that the photo be placed on the system. May Hugh constitutionally be convicted? _____

86. The Grand Union Station is a large train station owned and run by a public agency, the Tri-State Transit Authority. The Authority has enacted a "policy statement," prominently posted on the walls of the Station, which says, in part, that "no person or organization shall solicit for funds within this Station." Hussan, a member of the Hari Krishna religious sect, approached numerous passengers in the Station one day, asking each one, "Would you like to contribute to my religious organization?" Authority police stopped him and politely but forcibly removed him from the station for violating the no-solicitation policy. The police appear to enforce the no-solicitation rule uniformly, i.e., they stop everyone from soliciting, regardless of whether the solicitation is religiously-oriented, regardless of whether it appears to be "begging" or on behalf of an organized charity, etc.

    (a) Is the Station a "public forum" for purposes of First Amendment analysis? _____

    (b) Was the police's treatment of Hussan constitutional? _____

_____

Answers

  77. (a) The ban must be: (1) content-neutral; (2) narrowly tailored to serve a significant governmental interest; and (3) leave open alternative channels for communication of the information.

(b) No, probably. The facts indicate to us that the ban is content-neutral both in terms of the purposes for which it was enacted and the way in which it is applied. However, it seems not to be "***narrowly tailored*** to serve a ***significant*** governmental interest." Since the proposed speech would take place in the most traditional of all public forums — the streets — mere convenience, such as avoiding traffic obstructions, probably does not qualify as a "significant governmental interest." Also, there are more narrowly-tailored restrictions that could be used, such as an advance permit requirement which would give the police time to detour traffic and thereby reduce disruption. Finally, the requirement that alternative channels be left open is strictly construed in a public-forum context; the fact that there may be other public places (e.g., smaller streets) where the same expression is allowed will not generally be enough to qualify as an adequate alternative channel.

78. Yes. An advance permit requirement will be upheld if it is content-neutral, adequately constrains administrative discretion, and is a reasonable means of insuring that public order is maintained. However, in order to avoid giving the official charged with granting or denying permit applications too much ***discretion***, the grounds upon which a permit may be denied must be set forth ***specifically*** and ***narrowly*** in the ordinance. Here, the standard given for granting or denying a permit — that the proposed activities "not be detrimental to the overall community" — gives the mayor virtually uncontrolled discretion, and acts as an invitation to him to behave in a content-based way. This excessive discretion makes the statute overbroad and vague. Therefore, even though Firebrand's own proposed conduct might be capable of being prohibited by an appropriately-drawn ordinance, the ordinance here must be struck down as invalid on its face.

79. Yes. If a permit that is required prior to the exercise of First Amendment rights is unconstitutional ***on its face***, the speaker is ***not required*** to apply for a permit. He may decline to apply, then speak, and avoid conviction on the grounds of the permit requirement's unconstitutionality. See, e.g., *Lovell v. Griffin*. Because a statute that is overbroad is facially invalid, this rule applies to overbreadth claims. Therefore, Firebrand may assert overbreadth even though he failed to ever apply for a permit.

80. No. Where a permit requirement is not facially invalid (e.g., not unduly vague or overbroad), and the speaker's claim is merely that he has been wrongfully denied a permit, the speaker ***must seek judicial relief*** before speaking. That is, for an "as applied" as opposed to "facial" challenge to a permit requirement, one who ignores the denial of the permit loses the right to object to the permit scheme's unconstitutionality. There is an exception where the applicant shows that he could not have obtained prompt judicial review of the administrative denial of the permit; however, the facts here tell us that Rouser could have obtained judicial review prior to the time for the speech, if he had wanted to do so.

81. No. As with any "time, place and manner" restriction, the ordinance will be valid only if it is content-neutral, is narrowly tailored to serve a significant governmental interest, and leaves open alternative channels for communicating the information. Here, probably the requirement of content-neutrality is satisfied (unless there is evidence that, say, Jehovah's Witnesses were a special target of the ordinance). The government probably has a significant government interest in preventing homeowners from being disturbed at home when they do not want to be. However, it is doubtful that the ordinance is "narrowly tailored," since there are less restrictive alternatives (e.g., permitting a homeowner to indicate on his door that he does not wish to be disturbed by solicitors) — when the city makes a blanket assumption that ***no*** homeowner wishes to receive a solicitor, this is probably not a sufficiently narrowly tailored approach. Furthermore, it is doubtful whether alternative channels have been left open, since for many types of organizations, door-to-door and face-to-face is the only affordable means, given the large expense associated with, say, newspaper and TV advertising. Upon facts similar to these, the Court struck down a blanket ban. See *Watchtower Bible and Tract Soc. v. Stratton* (ban on solicitation without prior permit is unconstitutional).

82. (a) The "fighting words" doctrine.

(b) Yes, probably. Among the classes of speech which are not protected by the First Amendment are "fighting words," which the Court has defined as "those which by their very utterance … tend to incite an immediate breach of the peace." *Chaplinsky v. New Hampshire*. However, there are several exceptions and clarifications to the "fighting words" doctrine, which make it seldom applicable. One of those exceptions is that if the police have the physical ability to **control the angry crowd** as a means of preventing threatened violence, they **must do so** in preference to arresting the speaker for using "fighting words." *Cox v. Louisiana*. Here, it seems probable that the 15 police officers could have either arrested or at least restrained those Jews who were moving forward towards the podium, and probably any other hostile Jew in the audience. At the very least, the police needed to make some effort to do this, rather than immediately arrest the speaker.

83. No. In general, government may not forbid speech merely because it would be *"offensive"* to the listener. For example, language cannot be forbidden merely because it is profane. *Cohen v. California* (D cannot be punished for wearing a jacket bearing the legend "Fuck the Draft"). Here, the statute is phrased specifically to reach only "offensive" conduct, so it runs afoul of this principle. Furthermore, the statute is probably unconstitutionally vague, since a reasonable reader of it would not know exactly what types of language would be forbidden.

84. No. The problem is that the ban here is *content-based*. That is, it proscribes only certain types of speech, based on the content or message of that speech. Thus insults based on race, ethnicity and three other attributes are banned, but insults based on other attributes are not (e.g., the addressee's politics, intelligence, short or tall stature, etc.). Even if the university interprets the ban so as to bar only "fighting words," this will not be enough to save the statute, because *R.A.V. v. City of St. Paul* (striking down an anti-cross-burning statute) establishes that government may not ban some fighting words but not others, based on the words' precise message. The best way for State U to solve the problem is to amend its code so as to ban "all slurs, invectives, insults or epithets that would have the likely effect of either inducing the listener to respond with violence, or which would be likely to create in the listener an apprehension of imminent physical harm." Such a formulation would essentially ban all fighting words, plus all words that would constitute an assault; these two categories may clearly be constitutionally proscribed, as long as the proscription occurs in a content-neutral way. (Of course, this re-write would fail to prohibit a lot of hate speech, so it would not be a perfect solution, but at least it would be content-neutral.)

85. No. The Supreme Court has held that computer networks are more like newspapers than like broadcast TV, and that content-based restrictions on what is placed on such networks must therefore be strictly scrutinized. See *Reno v. ACLU*. Applying strict scrutiny, the measure is clearly unconstitutional, since it's content-based (only materials with an "indecent" message are proscribed), and it's not narrowly tailored towards the (admittedly "compelling") objective of keeping indecent materials away from minors — for instance, the state could give parents free filtering software that would block access to these materials by minors. See *Ashcroft v. ACLU*. Furthermore, the statute is overbroad: it applies to viewing by adults (who have a right to see the photo), as well as to viewing by minors (who probably don't have a First Amendment right to see such a photo, though this is not completely clear). Since the rights of adults are being curtailed in a content-based way, the statute will surely fail strict scrutiny. *Reno v. ACLU*.

86. (a) No. The Supreme Court has held that airport terminals are not "public forums," even though they are public places. *Int'l Soc. for Krishna Consciousness, Inc. v. Lee*. Assuming that train stations are analyzed the same way as are airport terminals — which seems virtually certain — the terminal here falls into the category of "non-public forum." Non-public forums are public facilities that are used for purposes that are not especially linked to expression; thus the terminal here is primarily linked to transportation, and has never historically been viewed as a center for expression.

(b) Yes. A non-public forum offers the ***least*** constitutionally-protected access for First Amendment expression. Government regulation of expression in a non-public forum must merely be: (1) ***reasonable*** in light of the ***purpose*** served by the forum; and (2) ***viewpoint neutral***. See *Krishna v. Lee, supra*. The Court in *Krishna* held that these tests were met by a ban on funds solicitation in airport terminals; presumably the same analysis would apply to the fund solicitation in the train station here. The ban on face-to-face solicitation of money was found to be reasonable in *Krishna* because such solicitation might slow pedestrian traffic within the terminal, interfering with its transportation-related function. (But a ***total ban*** on ***literature distribution*** was found not to be even "reasonable" in *Krishna*.)

VI. DEFAMATION, INTENTIONAL INFLICTION OF EMOTIONAL DISTRESS, AND THE BANNING OF "FALSE SPEECH"

A. **Regulation of defamatory and other false speech:** Recall that there are certain pre-defined categories of speech that receive no, or virtually no, First Amendment protection. (See *supra*, p. 489). These include such categories as obscenity, "fighting words," and commercial fraud. We concentrate here on one of those unprotected categories, ***"defamation,"*** i.e., the making of ***false statements*** that are ***damaging to reputation***. We also consider ***intentional infliction of emotional distress*** (*infra*, p. 556) as well as the more general problem of whether government may forbid speech on the grounds that it is ***factually false*** (see *infra*, p. 557).

B. **Initially no protection:** Initially, the Supreme Court took the view that any language treated as ***defamatory*** under state law was not entitled to First Amendment protection. For instance, in *Chaplinsky (supra*, p. 516), the Court included libelous statements in the list of categories which are "no essential part of any exposition of ideas," and as to which there is therefore no First Amendment protection.

C. *New York Times v. Sullivan:* But the Court eventually concluded that the First Amendment protections for speech and the press place at least ***some limits on the rules states may establish for defamation actions***. This limiting process occurred initially in ***New York Times Co. v. Sullivan***, 376 U.S. 254 (1964), where the Court concluded that the First Amendment requires that a defense for ***"honest error"*** be allowed in the case of false statements made about ***public officials*** relating to their ***official conduct***.

   1. **Facts:** Plaintiff in *New York Times* was a public official one of whose duties was supervising the Montgomery, Alabama Police Department. He alleged that the *Times* had libeled him by printing an advertisement that stated that the Montgomery police had attempted to terrorize Martin Luther King and his followers. (Plaintiff was not even named in the advertisement; but under Alabama libel law, criticism of the department of which he was in charge was deemed to reflect on his reputation.)

      a. **Truth as affirmative defense:** The libel law of Alabama, like that of most states at the time, provided for ***strict liability***. That is, a publisher could not avoid liability by showing that he reasonably believed his statement to be true, if it was in fact false.

Furthermore, although "truth" was an available defense under Alabama law, it was an **affirmative defense** as to which the defendant bore the burden of proof. Therefore, although the factual errors in the *Times* ad were minor (e.g., that Dr. King had been arrested seven times, rather than the actual four times), and even though there was no showing that the *Times* ought to have known that the ad prepared by others contained falsehoods, the paper was nonetheless subjected to a $500,000 libel judgment. The net result was that familiar rules of libel gave Alabama's "white establishment" a formidable weapon with which to punish the *Times*, and any other proponents of civil rights. See Tribe, p. 863.

2. **Libel judgment reversed:** A unanimous Supreme Court *reversed* the damage award. In so doing, the Court for the first time established that *state defamation rules are limited by First Amendment principles.*

   a. **Robust debate:** The Court viewed this case as one involving *criticism of government policy*, not merely factual statements about an individual. Debate on public issues must be "uninhibited, robust, and wide open," and may often include "vehement, caustic, and sometimes unpleasantly sharp attacks on government and public officials." Requiring critics of official conduct to guarantee the truth of all their factual assertions would lead to *self-censorship*, rather than free debate.

      i. **Sedition Act:** The Court found that the effect of Alabama's libel rules was similar to that of the original federal Sedition Act of 1798. The Sedition Act made it a crime to publish any "false scandalous and malicious writings" against the federal government with intent to bring it into "contempt or disrepute." Although the Act expired before the Supreme Court determined its constitutionality, the view that the Act violated the First Amendment had "carried the day in the court of history," according to the *New York Times* Court. So, here, criticism of government public officials could not be curtailed, without violating the First Amendment.

3. **Formal rule:** The Court was not content merely to strike the libel judgment as a disguised ban on criticizing the government. Instead, it articulated a formal rule, so that future speakers would not have to worry about liability for libel in similar circumstances: the First Amendment prohibits a *public official* from recovering damages for a defamatory falsehood *relating to his official conduct* unless he proves that the statement was made with *"actual malice"* — that is, *"with knowledge that it was false* or with *reckless disregard of whether it was false or not."* The case thus establishes a *"constitutional privilege for good faith critics of government officials."* Tribe, pp. 864-65.

   a. **Knowing or reckless falsity:** *New York Times* requires the public official to prove that the defendant *knew* his statement was false, or *recklessly disregarded* whether it was true or not. It is *not* enough for the official to show that a *"reasonably prudent man"* would not have published the statement, or would have investigated further before publishing. Rather, there must be evidence to permit the conclusion that "the defendant *in fact entertained serious doubts* as to the truth of his publication." *St. Amant v. Thompson,* 390 U.S. 727 (1968). Thus at least with respect to statements published about public officials relating to their duties (and also statements about "public figures," see *infra*), *"ignorance is bliss."* Tribe, pp. 870-71.

D. **Extension to "public figures":** The *New York Times* "actual knowledge or reckless disregard of the truth" test was extended to include *"public figures"* in *Curtis Pub. Co. v. Butts* and

Associated Press v. Walker, both reported at 388 U.S. 130 (1967). In these cases both the University of Georgia football coach and a prominent retired Army General were held to be public figures.

1. **"Public figure" narrowly defined:**   However, the Court has read the "public figure" category **narrowly** in cases since *Butts* and *Walker*. The Court has recognized three classes of public figures: (1) those who have **"general fame** and notoriety in the community," who are public figures for **all** purposes; (2) those who have "voluntarily **injected themselves** into a **public controversy** in order to influence the resolution of the issues involved," who are public figures **only** with respect to **that controversy**; and (3) **"involuntary** public figures," who are directly **affected** by the actions of public officials, such as a **defendant in a criminal case** (who would be an involuntary public figure with respect to news items concerning that case). See *Gertz v. Robert Welch, Inc.,* 418 U.S. 323 (1974) (discussed extensively *infra*).

2. **Meaning of "voluntarily injected":**   The Court will not be quick to conclude that a person has "voluntarily injected" himself into a controversy (required for category (2) above). For instance, in *Time, Inc. v. Firestone*, 424 U.S. 448 (1976), *Time* incorrectly reported that one of the grounds for Ms. Firestone's divorce was adultery. The Court found that she was not a "public figure," even though she had held some press conferences during the divorce trial, and even though the trial itself had been widely reported in the Miami newspapers. (Nor did Ms. Firestone's extensive activities before the trial as a prominent member of Palm Beach society make her a public figure.)

3. **"Involuntary" class narrow:**   Similarly, category (3), that of "involuntary public figures," has also been narrowly construed by the Court; such involuntary figures will be relatively rare.

E. **Private figures:** The *New York Times* standard does **not** apply to suits by **private figures**. That is, where the plaintiff is neither a public official nor a public figure, there is **no constitutional requirement** that he prove that the defendant **knew his statement to be false or recklessly disregarded the truth. Gertz v. Robert Welch, Inc.,** 418 U.S. 323 (1974).

1. **Facts:**   The plaintiff, Gertz, was a locally well-known lawyer who represented the family of a youth who was killed by a policeman. Defendant, publisher of a John Birch Society magazine, falsely attacked Gertz as having helped "frame" the policeman and as being a communist.

2. **Negligence standard permitted:**   The Supreme Court held, 5-4, that in libel actions brought by **private figures**, the First Amendment **does not forbid use of a simple negligence standard**. The states are free to decide whether they wish to establish negligence, recklessness or knowing falsity as the standard (but they **may not impose strict liability).**

   a. **Reasoning:**   The majority reasoned that private individuals are both more vulnerable, as well as more deserving of recovery for defamation, than public figures. They are more **vulnerable** because public figures generally have "significantly greater access" to the media, and can use that access to counteract false statements. They are **deserving** of extensive protection against defamation, because public figures have generally "voluntarily exposed themselves to increased risk of injury from defamatory falsehoods," unlike private persons.

3. **Punitive damages not allowed:** The majority also held that, if a private figure shows only negligence on the part of the defendant, rather than recklessness or knowing falsity, he *may not recover presumed or punitive damages*. ("Presumed" damages are ones awarded where there is no proof of actual harm, but the jury believes that damage would ordinarily result from a defamatory communication like the one in issue.) The Court imposed this limitation because the state's interest in giving broader protection to private figures only justified awarding "compensation for *actual* injury."

4. **Who is private figure:** In holding that Gertz himself was a private figure, the Court implicitly took a narrow view of the term "public figure." Gertz was a well-known lawyer locally, and had agreed to take a case which he knew would attract substantial publicity. Nonetheless, Gertz had not achieved "general fame or notoriety in the community" (so that he was not public figure for all purposes); similarly, he was not a public figure for the limited purposes of this case, because he had played only a "minimal role" in it.

5. **Dissents:** The four dissenters differed significantly among themselves in reasoning. For instance, Justice Brennan continued to believe (as he had in *Rosenbloom v. Metromedia, Inc.*, 403 U.S. 29) that the *New York Times* standard should be applied to private-person libel actions arising out of events of "public or general interest." But Justice White argued the quite opposite position that the *Gertz* majority should not even have stripped the states of their right to apply *strict liability* in suits brought by private persons.

6. **Proof of falsity:** As noted, one aspect of *Gertz* is that the states may not impose strict liability, even in cases brought by private figures. This aspect of *Gertz* was broadened in the later case of *Philadelphia Newspapers, Inc. v. Hepps*, 475 U.S. 767 (1986), where the Court held that the private figure suing a media defendant must bear the burden of proving not only "fault," but also the *falsity* of the defendant's statement. That is, *Gertz* has been held to replace the common-law rule *presuming* falsity. (This holding applies only where the suit involves a matter of "public interest"; the presumption of falsity is probably constitutional where there is no matter of public concern, in light of *Dun & Bradstreet, Inc. v. Greenmoss Builders, Inc., infra*, p. 556.)

F. **Non-media defendants:** Both *New York Times* and *Gertz* involved *media* defendants, and in those cases the Court relied heavily on freedom-of-the-press considerations, especially the need to prevent media self-censorship. It is not clear whether the public-figure standard of *New York Times* and the private-figure standard of *Gertz* also apply where the *defendant* is a *private person* or other *non-media defendant*.

1. **Possibility of different standard:** Thus it is possible that such defendants might be liable *without* a showing of reckless disregard or knowledge of falsity when they defame a public official or public figure. Similarly, they might even be *strictly liable* where they defame a *private* figure.

   a. **Unlikely:** However, no Supreme Court case after *Gertz* has made a constitutional distinction between media and non-media defendants, and it's *unlikely* the Court will do so in the future. That's especially true now that the rise of the Internet has dramatically blurred the distinction between media and non-media speakers. (For instance, if the Court were to hold non-media defendants to a stricter standard in defamation cases, should an amateur blogger who blogs once a week be deemed a "media" speaker or a "non-media" one?)

G. Statements of no "public interest":   If the communication does *not involve any matter of "public interest,"* special constitutional rules apply. These were laid down in *Dun & Bradstreet, Inc. v. Greenmoss Builders, Inc.,* 472 U.S. 749 (1985).

    1. Facts: D was a credit reporting agency which falsely reported to several subscribers that P, a small corporation, was insolvent. The issue in the case was whether presumed and punitive damages could be awarded without a showing of reckless disregard for the truth or actual knowledge of falsity.

    2. Result: Although no opinion commanded a majority of the Court, the divided Court affirmed an award of both types of damages. Three Justices thought that presumed and punitive damages could be awarded even without a showing of reckless disregard for the truth or knowledge of falsity if the statements did not involve any issue of "public interest"; two more Justices thought that *Gertz* was entirely wrongly decided (and thus that presumed and punitive damages should be allowed to all private plaintiffs, regardless of whether an issue of public interest was involved).

    3. Consequences: Thus *Dun & Bradstreet* seems to put a majority of the Court behind two constitutional principles:

        a. Presumed and punitive damages: First, where a private plaintiff sues concerning statements that involve no issue of public interest, he can recover *presumed and punitive damages without* a showing that the defendant recklessly disregarded the truth or knew of the falsity of his statement. This is the actual result of *Dun & Bradstreet.*

        b. Strict liability: Secondly, *Dun & Bradstreet* probably means that where a private figure sues on a statement relating only to matters of private concern, *he is not constitutionally required to show even ordinary negligence* in order to recover. (At least one member of the Court that decided *Dun & Bradstreet,* Justice White, concurring, stated that he believed this result to follow from *Dun & Bradstreet.*)

H. Statements of opinion: The Supreme Court has refused to give special First Amendment protection for statements of *"opinion."* So some statements, even though they express opinions, may be the subject of defamation actions. But only when a statement contains or implies a statement of *provably false fact* may the suit proceed. *Milkovich v. Lorain Journal Co.,* 497 U.S. 1 (1990).

    1. Holding: In *Milkovich,* the Supreme Court held that statements of opinion *get no special First Amendment protection.* However, the majority opinion in *Milkovich* makes it clear that the Court's prior First Amendment rulings will ensure that statements of *pure* opinion are not found to be defamatory. The Court observed that these prior cases require any libel plaintiff to prove: (1) that the statement is *"false"*; and (2) that the statement can be reasonably interpreted as stating *"actual facts"* about an individual. A pure statement of opinion (e.g., "In my opinion Mayor Jones shows his abysmal ignorance by accepting the teachings of Marx and Lenin.") would not be actionable, because it: (1) is not provably false; and (2) cannot reasonably be interpreted as stating actual facts about the plaintiff.

I. Intentional infliction of emotional distress: The *New York Times* standard also applies to actions for *intentional infliction of emotional distress (IIED).* That is, a public figure or public official may recover against the publisher who causes such distress only if he can prove that the publication contained a false statement of fact published either with knowledge that the statement was false or with reckless disregard as to whether it was true or not. The Supreme Court so held in *Hustler Magazine v. Falwell*, 485 U.S. 46 (1988).

1. **Facts:** The facts of *Hustler* vividly illustrate this extension of *New York Times* to suits for emotional distress. Hustler Magazine published a parody of an advertisement for Campari Liqueur, which portrayed P (the Reverend Jerry Falwell) as a drunken hypocrite who had sex with his mother. The ad contained a legend at the bottom, "Ad parody, not to be taken seriously." A jury found that the parody could not reasonably be understood as describing actual facts about Falwell; the jury therefore rejected his libel claim, but gave him an award for intentional infliction of emotional distress.

2. **Holding:** All eight members of the Court who heard the case agreed that Falwell could *not* receive such an award consistent with the First Amendment. The Court observed that "even when a speaker or writer is motivated by hatred or ill-will, his expression [is] protected by the First Amendment." The Court noted that political parody and satire is an important element of political speech, and believed that there is no way to distinguish such "core" political speech from the kind of satire involved here. The "outrageousness" of the speech here did not furnish an acceptable distinction, because that term is inevitably highly subjective.

3. **Remains good law:** *Hustler* remains good law in a general sense, as we know from a 2011 case: actions for IIED can violate the First Amendment if they make it too easy for the plaintiff to establish liability. *Snyder v. Phelps*, 131 S.Ct. 1207 (2011), *supra*, p. 520, involved a suit against a private-figure defendant, but on a matter of public interest. So it raised a somewhat different issue than *Hustler* (where the defendant was a public figure, requiring the plaintiff to show actual malice). But *Snyder*, like *Hustler* before it, establishes that as a general principle suits for IIED will violate a civil defendant's First Amendment right to content-neutrality unless the plaintiff can show that the state law of IIED, when it allows the content of the defendant's message to trigger liability, can survive strict scrutiny (a standard that a state's common law of IIED will rarely meet).

J. **False statements of fact outside the defamation context:** Successful actions for defamation necessarily involve a factually-false statement. And as we've just seen, despite cases like *New York Times v. Sullivan*, the First Amendment does not generally prevent governments from forbidding defamatory (and thus factually false) speech. The treatment of defamation raises a more general question: can government *categorically forbid factually-false statements*, even ones that are *not* defamatory? Could a state, for instance, *make it a crime to "tell a lie"?*

1. **Content-based regulation:** Keep in mind that a ban on making false statements would be a form of *content-based regulation*: if there are two statements made in exactly the same context, punishing the "false" one and not the "true" one would require government to regulate based on the message being delivered.

2. **Can't generally forbid false statements:** Given the extreme scrutiny given to content-based regulation of speech, it's not surprising that the brief answer to the question, "Can government generally forbid lying?" is *"no."* Except for a few narrow *pre-defined sub-categories* (defamation, fraud, and perjury, for instance), as to which there is a long-standing consensus that the type of false speech in question is especially likely to cause severe harm, government *may not forbid statements merely on the grounds that they are factually false.*

3. **Can't criminalize lying about military medals (*U.S. v. Alvarez*):** The principle that government may not ban factually-false speech not falling into the few pre-defined specially-harmful categories was demonstrated in *U.S. v. Alvarez,* 132 S.Ct. 2537 (2012). The Court held by a 6-3 vote that Congress' decision to make it a crime for a person to falsely state that he had won certain *military medals* violated the First Amendment.

    a. **The Stolen Valor Act:** In the federal *"Stolen Valor Act"* of 2005, Congress made it a crime for any person to falsely state, even orally, that he had been "awarded any decoration or medal authorized by Congress for the Armed Forces of the United States." Alvarez falsely claimed, in a public meeting, that he had been awarded the Congressional Medal of Honor 20 years before.

    b. **6 votes against the Act:** Six members of the Court *agreed with Alvarez* that the Act violated the First Amendment. No opinion commanded a majority, because the six justices were not in agreement about how stringent a test should be used to evaluate the law.

    c. **Plurality:** A four-Justice plurality opinion (written by Justice Kennedy, and joined by Roberts, Ginsburg and Sotomayor) applied "exacting scrutiny" — essentially, *strict scrutiny* — to the statute, and concluded that the statute could not survive that scrutiny.

       i. **"No First Amendment value" argument rejected:** The government argued that false statements "have *no First Amendment value* in themselves," and are therefore not entitled to constitutional protection. But the plurality *rejected* this "categorical" assertion. True, certain categories of false statement could be restricted — categories like defamatory statements, perjury, and fraudulent statements intended to extract some material benefit from another (e.g., fraudulent commercial speech). But outside of these few pre-defined categories where there was inevitably some special harm caused by the falsehood, the Court had *never held that false statements are without constitutional protection*, and the plurality wasn't willing to do so now.

       ii. **Strict scrutiny applied:** In fact, the plurality held, even though the Act barred only false statements, the Act needed to be subjected to "the *most exacting scrutiny.*" The plurality conceded that the government's interest in ensuring that the public's general perception of military awards not be diluted by false claims was a compelling interest. But no matter how compelling the government's interest, the statute could survive only if the particular restriction imposed was *"actually necessary"* to achieve that interest.

          (1) **Alternatives available:** The plurality concluded that the government had not made this showing of "actual necessity." In particular, the government had not shown why *"counterspeech"* would not suffice. For instance, in the case of false claims concerning the Congressional Medal of Honor (the most-heavily-punished type of violation under the Act, and the one with which Alvarez had been charged), the government could combat the lying problem by creating an *online database* that would list Medal of Honor winners, making it "easy to verify and expose false claims."

d. **Two additional votes:** Justice Breyer (joined by Kagan) agreed with the plurality that the Act was unconstitutional, making 6 votes for that proposition. But Breyer applied *"intermediate scrutiny"* rather than the plurality's strict scrutiny. Even under this easier-to-satisfy standard, however, the statute could not survive, because the government had not shown that a "more finely tailored statute" could not adequately address the harms. For instance, the statute might be rewritten to require that the false statement "caused specific harm" or was "material."

e. **Dissent:** Three Justices dissented, contending that the statute was constitutional. Justice Alito (joined by Scalia and Thomas) pointed out that the statute was narrowly drafted, and reached only "knowingly false statements about *hard facts directly within a speaker's personal knowledge."* Also, he said, the statute was "strictly *viewpoint neutral*" — it reached *all* false statements about medals, whether the statements disparaged or commended the military or the system of military honors.

   i. **Harmful:** On the other hand, Alito said, the lies forbidden by the statute "inflict substantial harm," because they *"debase the distinctive honor"* of military awards, by making them *seem more common* than they really are. This debasement harms military morale.

   ii. **No First Amendment protection:** The dissent asserted that "false statements of fact *merit no First Amendment protection in their own right."* Alito conceded that in many areas (e.g., defamation suits brought by public figures), government needs to "extend a measure of strategic protection" even to false statements, in order to ensure sufficient *"breathing space"* for protected speech, so that protected (and truthful) speech is not *"chilled."*

      (1) **Act is narrow:** But, Alito said, the Stolen Valor Act was not one of those situations requiring that some false statements be tolerated in order to avoid a chilling of protected speech. The Act presented *"no risk at all that valuable speech will be suppressed,"* leading Alito to conclude that the Act was fully constitutional.

VII. OBSCENITY

A. **Generally unprotected:** Obscenity, like defamation and "fighting words," was listed in *Chaplinsky* (*supra*, p. 516) as being a type of speech *unprotected by the First Amendment*. But again, as with defamation, the states are no longer completely free to define obscenity however they wish, and to then punish the distribution or sale of the material so defined.

1. **Attempt to define:** Instead, the Supreme Court has attempted to lay down specific guidelines for what materials may, compatibly with the First Amendment, be punished as "obscene." However, none of these attempts to define "obscenity" has turned out to be specific enough to give legislatures and lower courts reliable guidance about what materials are covered. Therefore, the Supreme Court has remained very much in the business of deciding, case by case, whether given materials meet the Court's definition.

2. *Roth:* The first case which required the Court to face directly the issue of whether obscene materials are protected by the First Amendment was *Roth v. U.S.*, 354 U.S. 476 (1957). In *Roth* (in an opinion by Justice Brennan), the Court confirmed what its dictum in

Chaplinsky had suggested — that "obscenity is not within the area of constitutionally protected speech or press." But the Court also held that First Amendment concerns *limit the acceptable definition of "obscenity."*

   a. **Definition of "obscene":**   The Court formulated its own definition of "obscenity": *"whether to the average person, applying contemporary community standards, the dominant theme of the material taken as a whole appeals to prurient interest."* The Court purported to be repeating the definition of obscenity laid down in certain prior lower-court cases. However, the definition seems to have been intended as a *minimal constitutional standard*; that is, the state could not, consistent with the First Amendment, ban a given item as obscene unless it satisfied this *Roth* definition.

   b. **Meaning of "prurient":**   The Court defined "prurient" as "material having a tendency to excite lustful thoughts." (But in a much later case, the Court interpreted this definition of "prurient" to *exclude* materials which, although they "excite lustful thoughts," provoke "only normal, healthy sexual desires." *Brockett v. Spokane Arcades, Inc.*, 472 U.S. 491 (1985). However, the *Brockett* Court did not define its phrase "normal, healthy sexual desires.")

   c. **Redeeming social value:**   Of primary importance to the *Roth* Court was distinguishing between obscenity and "the portrayal of sex ... in *art, literature and scientific works*." The latter must be given full constitutional protection. It is not clear from the Court's opinion whether, apart from the definition cited above, there is an *additional* requirement for obscenity that the work not constitute art, literature, or other category having social value. But the Court did say that "all ideas having even the *slightest redeeming social importance*" are to be protected (and, implicitly, are to be judged not obscene).

   i. **Ambiguity:**   If a work had some serious social value (e.g., of a literary nature), but its dominant theme was nonetheless one which "excites lustful thoughts" and is therefore "prurient," it is simply not clear whether the material could be obscene under *Roth*. (In any event, the presence of a small amount of "redeeming social importance" is *no longer sufficient* to prevent a work from being obscene, under *Miller v. California*, the presently-applicable test, discussed *infra*, p. 561.)

3. **Post-*Roth* cases:**   In a long string of post-*Roth* cases, the Court was forced to decide whether particular materials were obscene under the *Roth* definition. In many instances, no majority of the Court could agree on a single rationale, though of course there was always either a majority of the Court believing that the materials were obscene or a majority believing that they were not. From *Roth* until 1973, in fact, no majority of the Court ever agreed on a definition of obscenity.

   a. **Stewart's remark:**   Perhaps the most candid, and certainly the most famous, comment made during the post-*Roth* period on the difficulties of defining "obscenity," was that of Justice Stewart. Concurring in *Jacobellis v. Ohio*, 378 U.S. 184 (1964), he conceded that he might never be able intelligibly to describe "hard core pornography," which he believed to be the only type of material bannable under *Roth*. However, he observed, *"I know it when I see it*, and the motion picture involved in this case is not that."

B. *Miller:* Finally, in **Miller v. California**, 413 U.S. 15 (1973), five Justices agreed on a **new definition** of "obscenity," one which was built upon the *Roth* definition but which also resolved some additional issues.

1. *Miller's* **definition:** *Miller* laid out the following three-part test (all parts of which must be met) for identifying material which may be banned as obscene:

   a. the *"average person*, applying **contemporary community standards"** would find that "the work, *taken as a whole*, appeals to the *prurient* interest" (citing *Roth*);

   b. the work "depicts or describes, in a **patently offensive way, sexual** conduct specifically defined by the applicable state law" and

   c. the work, taken as a whole, *lacks "serious literary, artistic, political, or scientific value."*

2. **Changes:** This definition changes or clarifies prior law in two major respects:

   a. **"Community" standards:** The *Miller* majority explicitly **rejected** the argument that what appeals to the "prurient interest" or is "patently offensive" should be determined by reference to a **national standard**. What counts are the standards of the **local community** where the prosecution is taking place. Thus "the people of Maine or Mississippi [need not] accept the public depiction of conduct found tolerable in Las Vegas, or in New York City."

   b. **Limited to "hard core" sex:** *Miller* also establishes that the states may ban as obscene only depictions or descriptions of *"hard core"* sexual conduct. Since the states must *be specific* about what sexual conduct is being banned (in order to satisfy the First Amendment need for "fair notice" of what is forbidden, and in order to avoid a chilling effect on expression), the Court provided several examples of materials which could be banned:

      i. **Ultimate sexual acts:** "Patently offensive representations or descriptions of *ultimate sex acts*, normal or perverted, actual or *simulated"*;

      ii. **Other:** "Patently offensive representations or descriptions of *masturbation, excretory functions*, and *lewd exhibition* of the *genitals*."

      Note: Later Court cases show that mere *nudity*, by itself, is *not obscene*, and indeed gets some First Amendment protection. See, e.g., *Erie v. Pap's A.M., supra*, p 528.[10]

3. **Dissents:** Four Justices dissented in *Miller*. The reasoning of three of them was more fully expressed in their dissent to a companion case decided the same day, *Paris Adult Theatre I v. Slaton*, discussed *infra*.

4. **Some limits on right to define terms:** Notwithstanding *Miller's* "community standards" approach, the Court will impose some limits on the right of the local community to apply its own interpretation of the meaning of terms like "patently offensive" or "prurient interest." For instance, the Court has made it clear that the definition of "prurient interest" (part of the definition of obscenity in *Miller*, and in *Roth, supra*, p. 559) *may not include* a concept of lust that encompasses "only normal, healthy sexual desires." *Brockett v. Spo-*

---

10. However, 7 members of the Court held in *Pap's* that totally nude dancing, though not obscene, could nonetheless be prohibited as part of a content-neutral attempt to combat nude dancing's "secondary effects." See *supra*, p. 528.

kane Arcades, Inc., 472 U.S. 491 (1985). That is, the community is not free to say, in effect, that material that excites "normal, healthy sexual desires," and that does not incite sexual responses above and beyond these normal ones, is "prurient" or "offensive."

C. Private possession by adults: The mere ***private possession*** of obscene material by an adult ***may not be made criminal. Stanley v. Georgia***, 394 U.S. 557 (1969).

   1. Rationale: In reaching this conclusion, the Supreme Court relied both on the weakness of the state's interest in controlling private possession of obscenity, and on the strength of the individual's interest in not being forbidden such private usage. The state's interest was only the weak one of "protect[ing] the individual's mind from the effects of obscenity." The individual's interest was directly contrary, and much stronger: that of ***not having his thoughts controlled***. "If the First Amendment means anything, it means that a State has ***no business telling a man, sitting alone in his own house, what books he may read or what films he may watch.***"

      a. Two interests: Thus the *Stanley* rule relied on two distinct interests held by individuals: the First Amendment interest in having free access to ideas, and a distinct ***privacy*** interest in not having what one does in one's own home made the subject of government scrutiny.

   2. Possession of child pornography: There is one important exception to *Stanley's* rule that private possession of obscene material by an adult may not be made criminal: the states may criminalize even private possession of ***child pornography***. See *Osborne v. Ohio*, discussed *infra*, p. 563.

   3. No right to supply consenting adults: Since *Stanley* recognized a right held by consenting adults to possess and use obscenity in their homes, it would not have been illogical for the Court also to conclude that there was a right to ***supply*** obscene materials to such adults. But the Court has refused to extend the rationale of *Stanley* in this manner.

      a. Mailing of obscene material: For instance, government may make it a crime to ***mail*** obscene materials to consenting adults. *U.S. v. Reidel*, 402 U.S. 351 (1971). *Reidel* concluded that the focus on *Stanley* had been on "freedom of mind and thought and on the privacy of one's home" (the privacy strand of *Stanley*), and that *Stanley* did not recognize any First Amendment right to acquire obscene materials from commercial suppliers.

      b. Adult movie theaters: Similarly, the holding of *Paris Adult Theatre I v. Slaton,* 413 U.S. 49 (1973), that there is no right to ***show obscene movies to consenting adults***, represents an unwillingness to carry the rationale of *Stanley* beyond its immediate facts.

D. Protection of children: The Court has developed special doctrines to give the states additional authority to protect ***children*** from pornography. Two sorts of dangers are involved: (1) that children may ***read, view or listen*** to pornography; and (2) that children may be induced to ***take part in sexual conduct*** in order to be ***filmed*** for pornographic pictures and movies.

   1. Protection of children as audience: A state may prohibit the distribution of sexually explicit materials to children, even though those materials would not be obscene if distributed to an adult.

      a. Can't impair access of adults: But if the state wants to keep materials that are sexually explicit (but not obscene) out of the hands of minors, it must do so in a way that does ***not substantially impair*** the access of ***adults*** to those materials. That is, the state must ***narrowly tailor*** its regulations so that the materials are forbidden ***only*** to minors.

2. **Children as photographic subjects:** A state may also ban the distribution of materials ***showing children engaged in sexual conduct, even though the material is not legally obscene***. In reaching this conclusion, the Court in ***New York v. Ferber***, 458 U.S. 747 (1982) relied on the state's "compelling," surpassingly important, interest in ***preventing the sexual exploitation and abuse of children*** who are photographed for production of such materials.

   a. **Private possession may also be banned:** The state's interest in preventing the sexual exploitation and abuse of children is so strong that even the ***private possession*** of sexually explicit nude pictures of children may be prohibited. In the post-*Ferber* case of *Osborne v. Ohio*, 495 U.S. 103 (1990), the Court upheld a statute criminalizing most private possession of nude pictures of children. Even though *Stanley v. Georgia* (*supra*, p. 562) had held that adults have a First Amendment right to privately possess pornography, the *Osborne* Court held that materials showing children are different: the state's interest in preventing the pornographic exploitation of children is much stronger than the interest in protecting the minds of adults, so any First Amendment interest in possessing nude pictures of children is outweighed by this anti-child-exploitation interest. And this is true even if the materials are ***not "obscene,"*** merely ***"indecent."***

3. **Virtual child pornography:** On the other hand, government may ***not*** ban non-obscene ***"virtual child pornography,"*** by forbidding either ***computer-generated images*** that appear to be of children having sex, or explicit images of ***young-looking adults posing as minors***. In *Ashcroft v. Free Speech Coalition*, 535 U.S. 564 (2002), the Court rejected the federal government's argument that barring such virtual images was necessary to restrain the market for actual child pornography, and therefore necessary to protect children.

4. **Protection against non-obscene violence:** Government's extensive power to protect children by banning them from access to non-obscene materials applies only where the materials involve ***sexual content***, not where the materials involve ***violent conduct*** without any direct sexual connection.

   a. **Violent video games:** Thus in a 2011 case, *Brown v. Entertainment Merchants Ass'n*, 131 S.Ct. 2729 (2011), the Court struck down a California law that prohibited the sale or rental of ***"violent video games"*** to minors. The Court reasoned that ***"video games qualify for First Amendment protection,"*** in the same way as ***books, plays and movies*** do, and the obscenity exception to the First Amendment does not apply to violent games any more than it does to violent books, if there is no direct depiction of sexual conduct.

E. **Protection of animals, and the "animal crush video" issue:** Just as the state has an interest in avoiding the harm to children that inevitably occurs during the filming of child pornography (as in *N.Y. v. Ferber*, *supra*, p. 563), animal-rights activists have claimed that government ought to be able to prevent the harm to ***animals*** that inevitably occurs during the making of videos depicting animal cruelty. But a 2010 case, *U.S. v. Stevens*, 130 S.Ct. 1577 (2010), demonstrates that any attempt by government to prevent such harm will have to be ***narrowly constructed*** to avoid First Amendment problems.

1. **Facts of *Stevens*:** *Stevens* involved a federal statute that made it a crime to create, sell or possess any depiction of "animal cruelty," if done for "commercial gain" and in violation

of any federal or state law existing in the place where the video was created, sold or possessed. The statute gave an exemption for a depiction that has "serious religious, political, scientific, educational, journalistic, historical or artistic value." The legislative history of the statute showed that it was designed to eliminate the market for ***"crush videos,"*** videos depicting the intentional torture and killing of small animals, often by showing women slowly crushing the animals to death with their bare feet or high-heeled shoes.

    a.　The defendant: But in *Stevens*, D was convicted not for selling a crush video, but for selling videos of ***dogfights*** involving pitbulls. D argued that the statute was an unconstitutional infringement of his First Amendment rights.

2.　D wins: By an 8-1 vote, the Supreme Court ***agreed*** with D, on overbreadth grounds. There might well be portrayals of animal cruelty that government *could* constitutionally ban in order to avoid harm to animals. But the statute here criminalized a far ***greater range of content*** than could be prohibited consistently with the First Amendment. For instance, the statute covered depictions in which a living animal was "wounded or killed," even if no cruelty was involved. It was true that the statute applied only where the conduct depicted was against the law of the state where the video was made, possessed, or sold. But the statute by its terms would apply to, say, the depiction of hunting done by a particular method that was legal in the place where it happened, but illegal in the place where the resulting video was possessed or sold. Therefore, ***a substantial number of the possible applications of the statute*** were unconstitutional. That made the statute ***void on its face*** under the doctrine of ***substantial overbreadth*** (*supra*, pp. 500-501).

F.　Other issues: Here are a few other substantive rules regarding obscenity laws:

1.　Book without pictures: A book without pictures, in which sexual acts are ***verbally described***, may nonetheless be obscene under the *Miller* test.

2.　Community standards: In *Miller*, the Court held that the "community standards" by reference to which terms like "patently offensive" should be defined did not have to be national. In *Jenkins v. Georgia*, and its companion case, *Hamling v. United States*, both reported at 418 U.S. 87 (1974), the Court ***rejected*** the argument that the standards should have to be at least ***statewide***. Thus an obscenity case can be tried in a small, conservative rural town, and the ***standards of that town*** may be made the relevant ones (though the judge is not ***precluded*** from allowing evidence of standards in other communities).

    a.　Venue for federal suits: Permitting local community standards to control becomes especially significant in view of state and federal prosecutors' ability to pick as the venue for trial ***any town through which the allegedly obscene materials have passed***. The federal statute prohibiting the mailing of obscene matter, for instance, has been held to allow venue ***anywhere along the route that the mailed material travels***, not just the point of mailing or receipt.

        i.　Consequence: Thus a publisher or distributor who wishes to sell his materials nationally must face the possibility that any small town anywhere in the country through which a mail train or truck carrying one copy of the materials passes may be selected by federal prosecutors as the venue for a criminal trial. That place's local standards for determining what is "patently offensive," "prurient," etc. will then control.

3. **Scienter:** The seller of an obscene work may not be convicted unless the prosecution proves *scienter*, that is, knowledge by the defendant of the **contents** of the materials. *Smith v. California*, 361 U.S. 147 (1959). (But there is no requirement that the prosecution prove that the defendant knew, as a conclusion of law, that the materials were obscene. Thus "ignorance of the law is no excuse" in obscenity prosecutions, any more than it is in most other contexts. See *Hamling v. U.S.*, 418 U.S. 87 (1974).)

VIII. COMMERCIAL SPEECH

A. **Overview:** Like libel, obscenity and a few other types of speech, most kinds of *"commercial speech"* were traditionally viewed as being an "unprotected category" totally outside the scope of the First Amendment. But just as the Court in recent decades has held that the states do not have an unlimited right to ban or regulate speech merely by labeling it "libelous" or "obscene," so the Court has now given substantial First Amendment protection to speech which can be described as "commercial."

1. **Extensive change:** In fact, in some senses this change towards more extensive First Amendment protection has been even greater in the commercial-speech area than in the areas of defamation and obscenity: in the latter two areas, the Court has simply limited governments' ability to define these areas as broadly as they wish. Once speech falls within the allowable definition of "libel" or "obscenity," it is completely without First Amendment protection. But most types of commercial speech, by contrast (all types except those that are misleading or that propose illegal transactions), are now *entitled to some First Amendment protection*. However, this protection is generally not as extensive as that reserved for speech nearer the "core" of First Amendment values, especially "political" speech.

B. **The *Virginia Pharmacy* revolution:** Since a 1976 case, the Court has held that *even "purely commercial" speech is entitled to First Amendment protection. Virginia Pharmacy Bd. v. Virginia Consumer Council*, 425 U.S. 748 (1976).

1. **Facts:** *Virginia Pharmacy* involved a state statute making it "unprofessional conduct" for a pharmacist to *advertise prescription drug prices.*

2. **Statute stricken:** This ban was held by the Court to violate the First Amendment. The Court conceded that this case involved speech that was *purely* commercial, and that the only "idea" expressed was "I will sell you the *X* prescription drug at the *Y* price." Nonetheless, the Court held, such wholly commercial speech was protected by the First Amendment.

   a. **Informational value:** In reaching this conclusion, the Court relied on society's strong interest in "the *free flow of commercial information*." Here, for instance, consumers, especially poor ones, had a compelling interest in who was charging how much for what drug.

   b. **Weak state interest:** The countervailing state interest in suppressing price advertising was that of maintaining "a high degree of professionalism on the part of licensed pharmacists," an interest implicated by the possibility that advertising might lead to aggressive price competition, which might in turn lead to shoddy services. But this interest amounted to saying that consumers would be best protected *if kept in igno-*

rance. And, the Court concluded, the First Amendment ***flatly forbids the state from deciding that ignorance is preferable to the free flow of truthful information***.

3. **Exceptions:** However, the Court hinted that although purely commercial speech is entitled to First Amendment protection, that protection might be ***less extensive*** than for other types of speech. ***False or misleading*** advertising could clearly be prohibited (whereas such statements when made about public figures cannot be, unless there is actual malice — see *New York Times v. Sullivan, supra*, p. 552). Similarly, ***broader regulation of "time, place and manner"*** might be justified, and the strong ***presumption against prior restraints*** might not apply.

4. **Audience's right to information:** Apart from the fact that it recognizes purely commercial speech as being entitled to First Amendment protection, *Virginia Pharmacy* is of interest because it demonstrates the Court's recognition of a First Amendment right to ***receive*** information. Prior First Amendment cases had almost all involved the right to ***express*** oneself, that is, to be a ***disseminator*** rather than a recipient of information.

   a. **Third-party rights:** By contrast, the successful plaintiffs in *Virginia Pharmacy* were in fact consumers (the recipients of the information), not pharmacists (the disseminators of the information). It is not yet completely clear whether disseminators of information may assert the third-party rights of their audiences in First Amendment cases, though it seems probable that they may. This would be an exception to the usual rules of standing (discussed *infra*, p. 731), which normally permit a litigant to assert only that his ***own*** rights have been violated.

5. **No right to ban "For Sale" signs:** The rationale of *Virginia Pharmacy*, especially the principle that dissemination of even purely commercial information may not be barred because that information would be "harmful," was later applied in *Linmark Associates, Inc., v. Willingboro*, 431 U.S. 85 (1977). There, the Court unanimously held that a racially-integrated town's prohibition on ***real estate "For Sale" and "Sold" signs*** violated the First Amendment, despite the town's interest in stemming "white flight."

   a. **Suppression of truthful information:** The fatal flaw of the *Linmark* ordinance was that it, like the ban in *Virginia Pharmacy*, was an attempt to protect the public (residents of the town) by ***keeping them in ignorance***. The town's claim that the information about sales might cause residents to act "irrationally" would, if accepted, permit "every locality in the country [to] suppress any facts that reflect poorly on the locality."

6. **"Track one":** *Virginia Pharmacy* and *Linmark* can be viewed as classic "track one" cases (see *supra*, p. 477). That is, in those cases the government tried to suppress information based on the chance that the ***communicative impact*** of the message might cause harm. Such "track one" abridgements will be allowed only where they either fall into pre-defined "unprotected categories" or survive strict scrutiny; the point of *Virginia Pharmacy*, of course, is that "commercial speech" is no longer such an unprotected category.

   a. **Later case:** But the later case of *Central Hudson Gas, infra*, p. 568, indicates that such content-based restrictions may be upheld if they are a ***narrow and direct means*** of pursuing ***substantial governmental interests***, essentially a type of "***intermediate***" scrutiny.

C. Regulation of lawyers: First Amendment protection for commercial speech has also been conferred by the Court in several cases involving regulation of the way in which *lawyers* acquire clients.

1. Newspaper advertising in general: The first of these cases established that states *may not ban all newspaper advertising of legal services*. In *Bates v. State Bar of Arizona*, 433 U.S. 350 (1977), the Court upheld by a 5-4 vote the right of a "legal clinic" to offer in newspaper advertisements certain routine services at "very reasonable fees."

2. In-person solicitation: The majority in *Bates* explicitly excluded considerations of whether lawyers could be barred from *in-person solicitation* of clients. But in a pair of 1978 cases, the Court held that some (though not all) types of in-person solicitation of clients may be banned. The two cases were at absolute opposite ends of the spectrum in terms of the acceptability of the lawyer's conduct. Therefore, it is hard to know where the line will be drawn between solicitation that may constitutionally be prohibited and that which may not.

   a. Pecuniary gain: *Ohralik v. Ohio State Bar Ass'n*, 436 U.S. 447 (1978) represented the most prohibitable kind of solicitation, classic *"ambulance chasing."* There, the Court held that a state may forbid *in-person solicitation* for *pecuniary gain*. So a state may forbid the kind of conduct at issue in *Ohralik*, in which the lawyer solicited accident victims in person, to induce them to let him represent them for a contingent fee.

   b. Right of association: The other case, *In re Primus*, 436 U.S. 412 (1978), represented the kind of solicitation that is least objectionable and most worthy of protection.

      i. Facts: Primus, a South Carolina lawyer who did occasional work without pay for the ACLU, wrote a letter to a woman who had allegedly been illegally sterilized as a condition to her further receipt of Medicaid benefits; the letter offered the ACLU's free services in filing a lawsuit on her behalf. Primus, like Ohralik, was disciplined for violating anti-solicitation rules.

      ii. Punishment reversed: But the Supreme Court held that Primus *could not constitutionally be punished* for what she did. Her letter, and the ACLU litigation itself, were attempts to further her *political and ideological goals*. Therefore, her conduct implicated her interest in *free "political expression"* as well as *freedom of association*, both core First Amendment values. (This was the same sort of associational activity that the Court had earlier protected in *NAACP v. Button*, *infra*, p. 600.) These First Amendment interests were sufficiently strong that the state could *not* use *prophylactic measures* because of the mere potential for overreaching, fraud or other abuse; instead, Primus could only be disciplined if there was a showing that her solicitation had *in fact* led to one of these harms.

   c. Some in-person solicitation allowed: A much more recent case suggests that some types of *in-person solicitation* by professionals will be *allowed*, and that it was the unusually *vulnerable and susceptible condition* of the prospective clients in *Ohralik* that made the difference there. See *Edenfield v. Fane*, 507 U.S. 761 (1993), striking down Florida's ban on direct, in-person uninvited solicitation of business owners by Certified Public Accountants.

D. Commercial speech doctrine curtailed (*Central Hudson Gas*): *Virginia Pharmacy* seemed to hold that the states may not suppress even "purely commercial" speech, so long as the speech was not false or misleading and did not propose an illegal transaction. But later cases show that *Virginia Pharmacy* cannot be read this broadly: while purely commercial speech is entitled to *some* First Amendment protection, it *does not receive the full range* of that Amendment's protection. See ***Central Hudson Gas v. Public Service Commission***, 447 U.S. 557 (1980).

1. **The *Central Hudson* case:** In *Central Hudson*, the Court laid down a formal *four-part test* to determine whether a given regulation of commercial speech violates the First Amendment. This test indicates that, even apart from the states' right to prevent misleading speech or speech that proposes illegal transactions, the government has *significantly more power to regulate commercial speech* than might have been supposed from a simple reading of *Virginia Pharmacy*.

   a. **Facts:** In *Central Hudson Gas*, the New York State Public Service Commission (PSC) banned all "promotional advertising" by electric utilities. The stated purpose of the ban was to conserve energy; "promotional advertising" was defined as advertising intended to stimulate the purchase of utility services (so that all other types of advertising by utilities, including "institutional" ads, were permitted).

   b. **Four-part test:** Before analyzing the ban, the Court reviewed prior commercial speech cases, and derived for the first time a *four-part test* for determining whether a given regulation abridges the First Amendment.

      [1] **Protected speech:** First, courts must determine whether the commercial speech is protected *at all* by the First Amendment. All commercial speech receives at least partial protection except for: (1) speech that is *misleading* or *fraudulent*; and (2) speech that *concerns unlawful activity*. (The contours of these two exceptions are discussed further, *infra*, p. 571.) Speech that falls into one of these exceptions raises no First Amendment issues at all, and may thus be fully regulated by the government.

      [2] **Substantial government interest:** Second, the court must ask whether the *governmental interest* asserted in support of the regulation is *"substantial."* If not, the regulation will be struck down without further inquiry. If the interest is substantial, the government must still meet the final two parts of the test.

      [3] **Interest "directly advanced":** Third, the court will decide whether the regulation *"directly advances"* the governmental interest evaluated in part (ii) of the test. If it does not, the regulation will be struck down. If it does, it will still have to meet the fourth part of the test.

      [4] **Means-end fit:** Finally, the court will ask whether the regulation is *"not more extensive than is necessary"* to serve the government interest. If it *is* more extensive than necessary, the regulation will be struck down. (But a post-*Central Hudson Gas* case has watered down this "not more extensive than is necessary" test. Today, all that is required of the fit between the means and the end is that the means be *"reasonably tailored"* to serve the governmental objective, so that some looseness in the means-end fit will be tolerated where what is regulated is commercial speech. See *Edenfield v. Fane*, discussed further, *infra*, p. 572.)

c. **Application to facts:** The Court in *Central Hudson* then applied its test to the facts there.

    i. **Protected speech:** Utilities' promotional advertising was clearly speech ***protected*** by the First Amendment, satisfying part (i). The Court rejected the argument that advertising by a monopolist has no value; for one thing, even a monopolistic electric utility faces competition from alternative energy sources.

    ii. **State interests:** The state asserted two interests in support of its ban: conservation of energy and maintenance of a fair and efficient rate structure (which, the state contended, would have been impaired by an increase in usage, because of the peculiarities of the rate structure). The Court agreed that each of these interests was ***substantial***.

    iii. **Direct link:** The Court found that there was a ***direct link*** between the ban and one (but not the other) of the asserted state interests, that of energy conservation. (The link between promotional advertising and inequitable rates was, by contrast, too speculative to satisfy the "direct link" requirement.)

    iv. **Least-restrictive alternative:** With respect to the ban as a way of promoting energy conservation, part (iv) was ***not satisfied***; the ban was ***more extensive than needed*** to further that interest. For instance, it prevented a utility from promoting the use of electricity even for those applications where it was a more efficient power source than that currently being used.

d. **Rehnquist dissent:** Justice Rehnquist was the sole dissenter in *Central Hudson*. He thought that the majority's four-part test did not give the government enough power to regulate commercial speech, and that the test gave commercial speech falling within the First Amendment protection that was "virtually indistinguishable" from that given to non-commercial speech. Rehnquist believed that the regulation here was more an economic regulation than a restraint on "free speech." Therefore, he would have given it "virtually complete deference," in contrast to what he viewed as the majority's resurrection of the discredited doctrine of *Lochner v. New York* (see *supra*, p. 167).

2. **Viewpoint discrimination under the *Central Hudson* test:** In *Central Hudson* itself, the Court did not expressly address whether the regulation there — banning promotional advertising by electric utilities — was "viewpoint based." So *Central Hudson* doesn't say squarely whether that case's more-forgiving *"mid-level"* standard of review applies even when government is ***selecting one particular viewpoint to restrict especially thoroughly*** (as opposed to the strict-and-usually-fatal review applied to viewpoint based restrictions on *non*-commercial speech, as discussed *supra*, p. 479).

a. **No definitive answer:** No Supreme Court case decided post-*Central-Hudson* (i.e., post-1980) has ever squarely addressed this issue. But probably the answer will turn out to be that in the case of a viewpoint-based restriction, strict scrutiny, not just mid-level review, is the appropriate standard even though the case involves "just" commercial speech.

    i. **Hard for government to win:** But even if it should turn out that for a majority, mere mid-level review of viewpoint-based regulation of commercial speech *is* the applicable standard, government will usually find it quite ***difficult*** to convince the court that government's choice to discriminate based on viewpoint is *sufficiently narrowly tailored* to the achievement of a substantial government interest.

E. **Advertising of lawful but harmful products:** Advertising of unlawful products may clearly be prohibited under *Central Hudson Gas*. But what about the advertising of products or services that are *lawful*, but believed by the legislature to be *harmful*? Examples include *cigarettes*, *liquor*, and *gambling*.

1. **Regular commercial-speech rules apply:** The Court's relatively pro-free-speech approach towards regulation of commercial speech generally — applying fairly-tough *mid-level review* to such regulations (see *supra*, p. 572) — seems to *apply the same way to "vice" products* as to products or services not generally considered harmful. This tough attitude towards speech regulation in this area is shown by the Court's *rejection* of several arguments commonly made in favor of regulation of arguably harmful products:

    a. **Right to ban product irrelevant:** The fact that the state could have *banned the sale of the product completely* probably does *not* confer on the state the right to ban or tightly regulate *commercial speech about the product.* That's so because the Court seems to agree that banning speech about certain conduct may often be *more intrusive* than banning the conduct itself.

        i. **Rationale:** Thus in *44 Liquormart v. Rhode Island*, 517 U.S. 484 (1996) (also discussed immediately *infra*), the Court unanimously held that a state statute forbidding the *advertising of liquor prices* violated the First Amendment, even though the state would have had the freedom to *ban all liquor sales.* Justice Stevens, speaking for a plurality in *44 Liquormart*, said, "We think it quite clear that *banning speech* may sometimes prove *far more intrusive* than banning conduct. ... [A] local ordinance banning bicycle lessons may curtail freedom far more than one that prohibits bicycle riding within city limits. ... The text of the First Amendment ... presumes that *attempts to regulate speech* are *more dangerous than attempts to regulate conduct*." Based on recent cases, it's likely that a majority of the present Court would agree that a legislature's right to ban the sale of a product does not confer a right to issue content-based regulations seeking to sell the product.

    b. **"Consume less" objective will fail:** If the government's sole justification for limiting advertising of the legal-but-assertedly-harmful product is that the limitation will cause people to *consume less* of the item, it will be extremely *difficult* for the limitation to pass muster. First, the government will have to show that the limit "*significantly*" reduces consumption, and this will generally be quite hard to do. Second, the government will have to show that no means are available that are significantly *less intrusive*; since the government will almost always be free to *increase taxes* on the item, or to *regulate how and where it can be sold*, or to conduct an educational campaign showing its dangers, it's again unlikely that the government will succeed in making the required showing that materially less restrictive alternatives don't exist.

        Example: Rhode Island prohibits all advertising of liquor prices, except for price tags displayed with the merchandise and not visible from the street. The state defends the prohibition on the grounds that price advertising will lead to lower prices, and lower prices will lead to increased consumption, a result at odds with the state's interest in "temperance."

Held, the prohibition violates the First Amendment. First, the three-part test of *Central Hudson Gas supra*, p. 572) requires that any regulation of commercial speech ***"directly advance"*** the state's interest. This "directly advance" requirement means that the regulation must "significantly," not just slightly, advance the state's goal. Here, there is no evidence that prohibiting price advertising ***significantly*** curtails alcohol consumption. Second, *Central Hudson Gas* also requires that a regulation of commercial speech be ***"no more extensive than necessary."*** The ban fails this requirement, too, since the state could have limited alcohol consumption by less restrictive means, such as increased taxation, limits on per capita purchases, or educational campaigns.[11] *44 Liquormart v. Rhode Island*, 517 U.S. 484 (1996).

   c. Protect minors: Finally, if the government's principal justification is to prevent ***minors*** from gaining access to, or being enticed by, the "vice" product, government will have to ***tailor its methods very tightly*** so that there is no undue interference with the rights of ***adults*** to obtain or learn about the product.

   i. Tobacco regulation: As the Court said in a case striking down Massachusetts' restrictions on the advertising of smokeless tobacco and cigars, "no matter how laudable the state's interest in preventing minors' access to tobacco products, the state may not regulate advertising in a way that interferes materially with the legitimate rights of the tobacco industry, and its ***adult customers***, to exchange truthful information." *Lorillard Tobacco Co. v. Reilly*, 533 U.S. 525 (2001).

F. Current status: The ***current status*** of the protection given to "commercial speech" may be ***summarized*** as follows:

1. Misleading or deceptive statements: Commercial speech that is ***misleading*** or ***deceptive***, or that ***proposes an illegal transaction***, is ***not*** entitled to ***any*** First Amendment protection at all. That is, misleading or deceptive speech is deemed to fall within an "unprotected category" of speech (see *supra*, p. 486), and commercial speech falling within an unprotected category gets no First Amendment protection at all.

   a. Potential to mislead: Even speech which merely has a ***potential*** to mislead may be regulated. But if information may be presented in ***either*** a misleading or a non-misleading way, the state must attempt to prohibit ***only*** the misleading method (i.e., it must use the ***least-restrictive alternative***). *In re R.M.J.*, 455 U.S. 191 (1982).

   b. Integral to criminal conduct: Speech that is ***integral to criminal conduct*** is not protected.

   i. Proposing an illegal transaction: So, for instance, speech that ***proposes an illegal transaction*** doesn't receive any First Amendment protection. See, e.g., *Pittsburgh Press Co. v. Human Relations Commission*, 413 U.S. 376 (1973), upholding an order forbidding newspapers from publishing sex-designated help-wanted col-

---

11. The two arguments discussed here — that the measure failed because there was no evidence that it significantly diminished alcoholic consumption, and because less restrictive means would have sufficed — were joined only by a plurality of the Court. But all 9 members of the Court agreed with the result, that Rhode Island's ban violated the First Amendment.

umns. The Court reasoned that such columns act as an aid to illegal sex discrimination in employment.

    ii. Conspiracy: Similarly, speech that is part of a ***conspiracy*** to commit a crime ("We hereby agree to rob the First National Bank") may be punished, because such speech is unprotected.

2. **Three-part test:** If the commercial speech *is* covered by the First Amendment (i.e., the speech does not fall within an "unprotected category"), then — even if the regulation is ***content neutral*** — the restriction will be upheld only if the state shows that it:

[1] ***directly advances*** ...

[2] a ***substantial governmental interest*** ...

[3] in a way that is ***reasonably tailored*** to achieve that objective.

(These are essentially the last three prongs of *Central Hudson Gas*.) This is basically ***"mid-level"*** (or ***"intermediate-level"***) review.

    a. **Content based:** And if the regulation is *not* content neutral, the regulation must survive strict scrutiny, even though what's being regulation is commercial speech.

3. **"Reasonably tailored means":** Part (3) of the *Central Hudson Gas* test requires that the content-neutral regulation of commercial speech be "no more restrictive than necessary" to achieve the government's objective. But several post-*Central Hudson Gas* cases show that the Court is ***not*** taking the phrase "no more restrictive than necessary" ***literally***, as if it meant "least restrictive possible alternative." Instead, all that is required of the means-end fit is that the means be ***"tailored in a reasonable manner"*** to serve the government objective, i.e., that the means advance the objective in a ***"direct and material way."*** *Edenfield v. Fane*, 507 U.S. 761 (1993).

    a. **Looseness of means-end fit:** The fact that there may be ***some other means*** that would serve the government interest as well, while restricting the commercial speech less, will ***not be fatal***. In other words, some degree of ***looseness in the means-end fit*** will be ***tolerated*** when what is being regulated is commercial speech. See *Board of Trustees of SUNY v. Fox*, 492 U.S. 469 (1989).

    b. **Can still have "bite":** But the not-so-demanding means-end test still has considerable ***"bite"***: If the Court is convinced that there is some alternative method of achieving the same end as well or almost as well, with ***significantly less interference*** with protected speech, the Court will not hesitate to ***strike down*** the restriction. Indeed, the Court will generally place upon the government the burden of ***showing*** that ***proposed less-restrictive alternatives would not adequately fulfill*** the governmental objective being sought. See *Thompson v. Western States Medical Center*, 535 U.S. 357 (2002).

    c. **Internal consistency required:** An important factor in whether the means will be found not to be unecessarily restrictive is whether the means selected by the government are ***internally consistent*** — where the means are not self-consistent, the Court is likely to find that the scheme is too irrational to advance the stated objective sufficiently.

    Example: A federal statute prohibits beer manufacturers from listing their beverage's alcohol content on the label. The federal government defends the ban on the grounds that it's needed to prevent brewers from engaging in "strength wars," in which each maker increases its beer's alcohol content and then tries to lure drinkers by advertising the high content.

Held, the statute violates the brewers' free speech rights. The federal government does not prohibit alcohol strength listings in advertising, only on labels. Similarly, the government doesn't ban such listings for the labels of wines and spirits, only beer. These inconsistencies make the scheme so irrational that it does not "directly and materially advance" the objective of preventing strength wars. *Rubin v. Coors Brewing Co.*, 514 U.S. 476 (1995).

d. **Some chance of success:** A second factor in determining whether the means are reasonably tailored to the government objective is whether the means have a ***reasonable probability of achieving the objective*** at least some of the time. The means-end fit will be too loose if it "provides only ***ineffective or remote support*** for the government's purpose" (*Edenfield, supra*), or if there is ***"little chance"*** that the restriction will advance the state's goal (*Greater New Orleans Broadcasting Assoc.*, 527 U.S. 173 (1999).

Example: Massachusetts regulates indoor advertising for smokeless tobacco and cigars in a number of ways. One restriction is that advertising for such products cannot be placed lower than five feet above the floor of any retail establishment located within 1,000 feet of any school or playground. The purpose of the regulation is to make tobacco products less appealing to minors, by limiting minors' exposure to advertising about the products.

Held, the restriction is unconstitutional. The five-foot rule "does not seem to advance" the state's goal. "Not all children are less than five feet tall, and those who are certainly have the ability to look up and take in their surroundings." Therefore, the height restriction "does not constitute a reasonable fit" with the state's goal. *Lorillard Tobacco Co. v. Reilly*, 533 U.S. 525 (2001) (also discussed *infra*, p. 571).

e. **Fear of bad public decisions not sufficient:** Government's fear that if the commercial information is divulged to the public, the public will make ***"bad decisions"*** is not a legitimate state objective. "Fear that people would make bad decisions if given truthful information cannot justify content-based burdens on speech." *Sorrell v. IMS Health Inc.*, 131 S.Ct. 2653 (2011).

G. **Constitutionally-protected products:** The use of some products is so tightly tied in with the ***exercise of constitutional rights*** that sale of the product could ***not*** constitutionally be banned; therefore, advertising of these products may also not be banned or heavily regulated. For instance, since there is a constitutional right to use ***contraceptives***, a ban on the advertising of contraceptives would not be any more constitutional than would a ban on the sale of them. Indeed, the Court held this to be the case, in *Bolger v. Youngs Drug Products Corp.*, 463 U.S. 60 (1983).

Quiz Yourself on

DEFAMATION, OBSCENITY AND COMMERCIAL SPEECH

87. Joe was the owner of "Joe's Jewelry," a jewelry store that was the only such store in the town of Liberty. Since Liberty was a small town, most people knew who Joe was, but they didn't know much about his

personal life, and he had never been involved in politics. One day, the local newspaper, the *Liberty Post*, reported that Joe had shot Tim, a shopper in the store, based on Joe's mistaken belief that Tim was attempting to rob the store. In fact, Tim was shot in Joe's store, but by Pete, Joe's employee, who Joe then immediately fired. (Tim was not in fact trying to shoplift, and Pete simply made a bad mistake.) Joe has brought a libel action against the *Post*. The state's policy is to allow a libel recovery whenever such a recovery would be allowed at common law and would not be forbidden by the U.S. Constitution. At the end of the case, the judge charged the jury that Joe could recover against the *Post* if the jury found that the *Post* had been negligent, but not if it found that the *Post* had made a non-negligent error as to the underlying facts. Does this charge correctly reflect the relevant constitutional principles? _____

88. After Emilio failed to pay numerous traffic tickets, the police came to his house to arrest him on a bench warrant. While they were standing inside the foyer of his house making the arrest, they saw copies of two unusual publications. One was *Kiddie World*, which contained pictures of nude adolescents; the adolescents were suggestively posed, but were not engaged in real or simulated sexual activities. The second publication was *Barnyard Illustrated*, which consisted exclusively of pictures of men and women having real or simulated sex with a variety of barnyard animals, including sheep and goats. A state ordinance forbids the sale or possession of "any pictorial material containing sexually explicit photographs that are obscene under prevailing constitutional standards." Assume that Emilio can be shown to have known the contents of both of these magazines.

(a) Can Emilio be convicted for violating the ordinance as to *Kiddie World*? _____

(b) Can Emilio be convicted for violating the ordinance as to *Barnyard Illustrated*? _____

89. Congress has concluded that the nicotine used in cigarettes is "highly addictive." Congress has also concluded that cigarette advertising causes many minors (who under federal and state laws can't legally buy the product) to take up smoking. Therefore, Congress has now banned all print advertising for cigarettes. Together with a prior ban on broadcast advertising for cigarettes, this means that billboards and handbills are now the only allowable means of advertising cigarettes. The cigarette industry asserts that this near total ban violates its right of free expression.

(a) What is the test that the Court will use in evaluating the constitutionality of the ban? _____

(b) Is the statute constitutional? _____

Answers

87. Yes, probably. The first question is whether Joe is a ***"public figure."*** If he is a public figure, he may not be permitted to recover unless he shows "actual malice" on the part of the *Post*, i.e., that either the *Post* had knowledge that its statement about who did the shooting was false, or that the *Post* acted with "reckless disregard" of whether the statement was false or not. So if Joe is a public figure, then the judge's instruction is wrong. Joe might be held to be an "involuntary public figure" because of his involvement in this matter of obvious public interest; however, since he is not a criminal defendant, and since the Court has construed the "involuntary public figure" category narrowly, probably Joe does not fall into this category. Joe is certainly not a generally famous person (even locally), nor one who has voluntarily injected himself into a public controversy, so he probably doesn't fit into either of the other public figure categories recognized by the Court.

If Joe is in fact a "private figure," then the judge's charge is correct. Under *Gertz v. Robert Welch,* where P is neither a public official nor a public figure, there is no constitutional requirement that he prove that the defendant knew his statement to be false or recklessly disregarded the truth. (On the other hand, the state would not be permitted to grant Joe a recovery based on strict liability; the First Amendment requires that the *Post* be proven to be at least negligent, even in a suit brought by a private figure.)

88. **(a) Yes.** On these facts, Kiddie World is probably not, strictly speaking, "obscene" under Supreme Court definitions. The reason is that mere nudity, without any attempt to portray sexual activity, is not considered "obscene." However, the state's interest in preventing the sexual exploitation and abuse of children is so strong that states may prohibit the sale, and even the private possession, of sexually explicit nude pictures of children, even though these are not strictly speaking "obscene." *Osborne v. Ohio.*

(b) No. The material here is almost certainly "obscene." Under *Miller v. California,* material is obscene if it depicts "patently offensive representations or descriptions of ultimate sex acts, normal or perverted. … " It must be the case that the average person, applying contemporary community standards, would find that the work taken as a whole appeals to the prurient interest, and that the work taken as a whole lacks serious literary, artistic, political or scientific value. These tests all seem to be satisfied by the material here. However, the mere ***private possession*** of obscene material by an adult may not be made criminal. *Stanley v. Georgia.* Therefore, even though the state might be able to punish the person who sold the magazine to Emilio, it may not punish Emilio for knowingly possessing the material in his house. (As noted in part (a), possession of material showing sexually explicit photos of children does not come within the purview of *Stanley.*)

89. **(a) In theory, the four-part test of *Central Hudson Gas v. Public Service Comm.*,** as modified by later cases. First, the Court will determine whether the commercial speech is protected at all by the First Amendment; commercial speech receives at least partial protection so long as it is not "misleading" and does not propose unlawful activity. Next, the Court asks whether the governmental interest in support of the regulation is ***"substantial."*** Third, the Court decides whether the regulation ***"directly advances"*** the governmental interest being sought. Finally, the Court asks whether the restriction is ***"not more extensive than is necessary"*** to serve the governmental objective. (But some post-*Central Hudson* cases suggest that when a ban on advertising is premised on the idea that less advertising of a harmful product will lead to less consumption, the Court may apply **strict scrutiny**, not the mid-level standard of *Central Hudson Gas.* So the *Central Hudson Gas* test might not be applied here.)

(b) Unclear, but the statute would probably be struck down. Even if the not-so-hard-to-satisfy *Central Hudson Gas* test were applied, the restriction would probably not survive. General cigarette advertising is not "misleading" and does not propose unlawful activity (since Congress has not outlawed the sale of cigarettes), so the speech gets some First Amendment protection. It's true that the government's interest in preventing additional people (especially minors) from becoming "addicted" certainly seems to be "substantial." It's also true that a ban on all print advertising certainly seems to "directly advance" the objective of preventing the creation of new smokers, given the power of advertising. However, *44 Liquormart* says that the anti-consumption impact of the regulation must be "significant," and it's not clear that the impact here would qualify. Furthermore, it's not clear whether the ban is "not more extensive than is necessary" to serve this interest, since there are some less-restrictive methods (e.g., a broader anti-smoking campaign, or higher taxes) that haven't been tried yet.

It may be that the fact that the users that Congress is principally targeting are ***minors***, who under state and federal law can't be legal purchasers of the product, may lead the Court to give more deference to the restriction here than it did to the no-liquor-price-ads restriction struck down in *44 Liquormart.* But in

Lorillard Tobacco Co. v. Reilly, the Court struck down several state regulations against smokeless tobacco advertising where the regulations were designed to protect minors (e.g., a ban on outdoor advertising, and a rule that advertising within a retail store had to be at least five feet above the floor). In *Lorillard,* the Court said that regardless of the importance of protecting minors, "the state may not regulate advertising in a way that interferes materially with the legitimate rights of the tobacco industry, and its ***adult customers***, to exchange truthful information." So protection of minors probably won't be enough to save the statute here from being found to flunk the *Central Hudson Gas* requirements that the government regulation (1) *significantly* reduce the use of the harmful substance; and (2) be "*not more extensive than necessary*" to serve the state interest.

IX. REGULATION IN THE CONTEXT OF POLITICAL CAMPAIGNS

A. **Money in political campaigns, generally:** In the modern political campaign, speech and the expenditure of money seem inevitably to go hand in hand. Whether money is spent by a private citizen who is contributing to a candidate, by a political action committee which runs advertisements backing or opposing certain candidates, or by a candidate himself, campaign spending has a strong expression component. Yet if corruption and the appearance of corruption are to be curbed, and if the cynical view that the richest candidate generally wins is to be proved wrong, some sorts of limits on campaign spending are probably necessary.

1. **General principles:** In a series of cases beginning in 1976, the Supreme Court has attempted to work out a line dividing those types of election spending which the states or the federal government may prohibit from those which are constitutionally-protected. While this line is a somewhat blurry one, several basic principles have emerged:

   ❑ ***Contributions*** made by individuals or groups to individual candidates, to Political Action Committees (***PAC***'s) or to political parties, may be ***limited in dollar amount***, so long as the limits are not so low as to substantially interfere with candidates' and parties' ability to ***run a competitive election campaign.***

   ❑ On the other hand, ***independent expenditures by individuals***, as well as by ***corporations and unions,*** may ***not*** be limited at all.

   ❑ Similarly, expenditures by ***candidates from their own funds*** may ***not*** be limited at all.

   ❑ Congress may not treat ***corporations*** and unions ***less favorably than individuals*** (e.g., by preventing corporations from paying for independent election-time ads out of their own treasuries).

B. ***Buckley v. Valeo:*** The seminal case on the First Amendment implications of campaign-finance regulation is ***Buckley v. Valeo***, 424 U.S. 1 (1976), in which the Supreme Court upheld some but not all provisions of the Federal Election Campaign Act of 1971 (FECA), as amended in 1974 (shortly after Watergate).

1. **Statutory provisions:** Of the several provisions of the Act whose constitutionality the Court reviewed in *Buckley*, two are of concern to us here: (1) the Act's limitation on ***individual political contributions*** to $1,000 to any single candidate per election (with a corollary $25,000 limit on ***aggregate*** contributions by any one individual in any year); and (2) its limitations on ***expenditures***, including a $1,000-per-year limit on ***independent*** expen-

ditures by individuals and groups on behalf of a "clearly identified" candidate, various limits on expenditures *by a candidate* from personal or family funds, and various limits on *total* campaign spending.

2. **Result:**   In brief, the Court's *per curiam* decision **sustained** the contribution limits, but found **unconstitutional** the limits on independent expenditures by individuals, on expenditures by a candidate from personal or family funds, and on aggregate campaign spending.

3. **Contribution limits upheld:**   The Court applied what it called its "closest scrutiny" to the *contribution* limits. But despite the close scrutiny, the Court **upheld** the limits, on the following analysis:

    a. **Marginal restriction:**   Although these limits placed some quantity restriction on political expression, the restriction was only *"marginal."* Since a dollar contribution does not communicate the "underlying basis" for the contributor's support of the candidate, the amount of "communication" being done by the contributor *does not increase* as the size of the contribution increases — whatever expression takes place when a contribution is made derives from the "undifferentiated, symbolic act of contributing," whose symbolism is largely independent of dollar amount.

    b. **Strong governmental interest:**   On the other side of the scale, the governmental interest supporting the limits was a powerful one, that of limiting the *actuality and appearance of corruption* resulting from large individual contributions, which are sometimes made to secure a political *quid pro quo* from the candidate. *No less restrictive alternative* would have been adequate; for instance, anti-bribery and disclosure laws could not deal fully with the need to root out all apparent as well as actual opportunity for corruption.

    c. **Aggregate limits struck down:** The contribution limits at issue in *Buckley* included not only a limit of $1000 to any single candidate per election, but also a $25,000 limit on *aggregate contributions* by an individual to *all* federal candidates in any one year. The Court in *Buckley* **sustained this aggregate limit**, just as it sustained the limit on contributions to a single candidate. But whereas the *per-candidate* limit on individual expenditures remains constitutional as of this writing (late 2014), the *aggregate limit was struck down* in 2014 as a violation of the free-speech rights of individual contributors. That holding, in *McCutcheon v. FEC*, 134 S.Ct. 1434 (2014), is discussed *infra*, p. 580.

4. **Expenditures by individuals:**   In contrast to its ruling upholding contribution limits, the Court in *Buckley* **struck down** the limitations on *expenditures* by *individuals acting independently* from candidates. The Court concluded these independent-expenditure limits imposed *"direct and substantial restraints* on the quantity of political speech," and unconstitutionally limited political expression "at the core … of First Amendment freedoms." For instance, the restrictions would have made it impossible for an individual or association legally to take out a single quarter-page advertisement backing a particular candidate in a big-city newspaper.

    a. **State interest insufficient:**   When viewed with the requisite "exacting scrutiny," the governmental interest in combating corruption, asserted in support of the limits on expenditures by individuals, was *inadequate*.

i. **Wouldn't eliminate *quid pro quos*:** First, not all apparent or actual *quid pro quo* deals would be eliminated, since the limits applied only to expenditures "advocating the election or defeat" of a "clearly identified candidate," so that ads could still be run supporting the candidate's *views* (as part of a *quid pro quo*), without expressly advocating his election.

ii. **Complete independence reduces danger:** Secondly, the expenditure limits only applied where the expenditures were made *totally independently* of the candidate and his campaign; spending which was controlled by or coordinated with the campaign was treated as a contribution. Where such complete independence existed, a carefully-orchestrated *quid pro quo* was less likely, the Court concluded, making the need for the contribution limits less pressing.

5. **Spending of candidate's own money:** The Court in *Buckley* also struck down limits on the amount that a *candidate* could spend from his *own personal or family funds*. The interest in preventing actual or apparent corruption did not apply to this situation, since obviously a candidate would not bribe himself. And the interest in *equalizing the resources* of competing candidates was not well served by the spending limit, since a candidate who spent less of his own money than his opponent could nonetheless outspend the latter by raising more money from outside sources. Therefore, no state interest was sufficient to outweigh the candidate's own "First Amendment right to engage in the discussion of public issues and vigorously and tirelessly advocate his own election. ...."

   a. **Still valid:** This principle that the amount a candidate may spend from his own resources may not be capped remains intact — and indeed has been expanded — in the Roberts court. See the discussion on p. 586 of *Citizens United*, where the Court held that even *corporations and unions*, not just individuals, must be permitted to *spend uncapped amounts* of their own funds to buy advertising for or against a candidate, as long as the corporation or union acts independently of the candidate.

6. **Limits on total campaign spending:** Finally, the Court struck down limits on what a candidate could *spend from all sources combined*. Candidates have a First Amendment right to spend as much as they wish to promote their own political views, and the governmental interest in curbing the skyrocketing costs of political campaigns is not sufficient to outweigh that right, the Court held. (But Congress may create a scheme for *publicly funding* elections, in which case the candidate *may* be required to choose between respecting an aggregate spending limit and losing the public subsidy.)

7. **Other opinions:** Only three Justices joined the Court's *Buckley* opinion in its entirety. Five others concurred only in part, and one did not participate.

   a. **Burger's concurrence:** Justice Burger dissented from the plurality's upholding of the contribution limits. In his view, contributions, no less than expenditures, were ways of communicating. Contributions were simply a way of "pooling" money, and were thus associational activities comparable to, say, volunteer work; therefore, freedom of *association* as well as freedom of speech required that these not be restricted unless there was no less-restrictive satisfactory alternative. In Burger's view, anti-bribery laws and disclosure requirements could solve the corruption problems inherent in large contributions just as they could in the expenditure context.

   b. **White's concurrence:** Justice White, like Justice Burger, saw no principled distinction between expenditures and contributions. But in sharp contrast to Justice Burger's view, White believed that **both** the contribution and expenditure limits were **valid**. He disagreed with the plurality's equation of money with speech. Also, he would have deferred much more completely to Congress' superior knowledge of what motivates politicians, and to its conclusion that expenditure limits on both private citizens and candidates are needed to accomplish the goals of preventing bribery and corruption and equalizing "access to the political area."

8. **Buckley remains valid (*Randall v. Sorrell*):** A 2006 decision involving Vermont's campaign-finance reform statute shows that **Buckley's general approach remains valid** in the Roberts Court. That case, *Randall v. Sorrell*, 548 U.S. 230 (2006), held that:

   ❏ limits on **candidate expenditures** remain flatly **unconstitutional**, as *Buckley* had held them to be; and

   ❏ limits on **contributions** will often be constitutional (as the ones in *Buckley* had been held to be), but the particular Vermont limitations at issue were so low (e.g., $400 per election cycle for gubernatorial candidates) that they **interfered with candidates' ability run a competitive election**, and thus **violated** the First Amendment.

   Note: Although as *Randall* illustrates limits on the amount that one individual may contribute to a *single* candidate remain constitutional (provided the limit is not so low that it interferes with candidates' ability to run competitive campaigns), limits on the **aggregate** amount that an individual can contribute to **all candidates collectively** are **no longer valid**. That is, the aggregate-contribution limits approved in *Buckley*, and then tacitly re-approved in *Randall*, were later overturned, in the 2014 case of *McCutcheon v. FEC*, discussed *infra*, p. 580.

9. **Attempts to level the candidate playing field:** In the decades after *Buckley*'s ruling that limits on a candidate's expenditure of her own personal funds violated her First Amendment rights, both Congress and many states have sought to find other ways to **reduce the advantages held by wealthy candidates willing to spend their own funds**. Essentially, legislatures have devised arrangements under which, if a wealthy candidate spends a large amount of his own or well-heeled contributors' funds, the opposing non-wealthy candidate gets to **"level the playing field"** by either **qualifying for public financing**, or being able to **receive larger private donations** than would otherwise be allowed.

   But in a pair of decisions, one from 2008 and the other from 2011, the Court by a 5-4 vote has **struck down two of these "level the playing field" structures,** one created by Congress and the other by Arizona. In both cases, the majority's theory was that the **wealthy candidate's** right to **spend on her campaign** was being **substantially and unconstitutionally burdened** by having that spending trigger extra campaign money for the non-wealthy opponent.

   a. **Millionaire's Amendment:** The first of the cases involved a federal statute, the so-called **"Millionaire's Amendment,"** passed by Congress in 2002. This amendment said that when a candidate for the House of Representatives spent more than $350,000 of his own funds, the candidate's **adversary** could receive individual contributions at **three times the usual rate** (i.e., subject to a per-donor limit of $6,900 rather than the usual $2,300). The idea was to "even the playing field," so that the millionaire candidate wouldn't have an unfair advantage from his ability to self-fund without limit. But in ***Davis v. F.E.C.***, 128 S.Ct. 2759 (2008), the Court by a 5-4 vote found that the Millionaire's Amendment ***violated the First Amendment rights of wealthy candidates.***

    i.   **Burden on speech:** The majority agreed with the plaintiff (a wealthy candidate) that the amendment required candidates to "choose between the First Amendment right to engage in unfettered political speech and subjection to discriminatory fund-raising limitations." Therefore, the amendment imposed a ***"substantial burden"*** on the exercise of the First Amendment right to use personal funds for campaign speech, triggering strict scrutiny. And the amendment could not withstand that strict scrutiny.

  b. **Right to public funding:**   The second case involved an Arizona statute that created a ***voluntary public financing system*** to fund the primary and general campaigns of candidates for state office. Candidates could agree to limit their own spending to $500, and thereby receive public funds. The key innovation was that during the course of the campaign, if a candidate who did not take the public option then spent more than a certain amount of her own money (or raised more than a certain amount from contributors), the publicly-funded candidate would ***get additional equalizing or matching funds.*** In *Arizona Free Enterprise Club's Freedom Club PAC v. Bennett*, 131 S.Ct. 2806 (2011), a five-Justice majority found that this violated the First Amendment rights of the privately financed candidate, because it ***"substantially burdens protected political speech without serving a compelling state interest."***

    i.   **Rationale:** The majority relied on the rationale of the decision in the "Millionaire's Amendment" case (*Davis v. FEC, supra*). Since "each personal dollar spent by the privately financed candidate results in an award of almost one additional dollar to his opponent," the structure "forces the privately financed candidate to ***'shoulder a special and potentially significant burden'*** when choosing to exercise his First Amendment right to spend funds on behalf of his candidacy."

    ii. **Dissent:** The four dissenters, in an opinion by Justice Kagan, believed that the matching-funds mechanism here was perfectly proper. Far from substantially burdening speech, the program ***"creates more speech* and thereby *broadens public debate."***

C. **Limits on aggregate contributions by an individual (*McCutcheon*):** You'll recall that in *Buckley v. Valeo*, the Supreme Court upheld not only limits on the amount that an individual can contribute to a single candidate, but also limits on the ***aggregate*** amount that an individual can contribute to ***all*** candidates during an election cycle. Thus a federal law providing that no individual could contribute more than $25,000 in any year to all candidates for federal office was found in *Buckley* to be constitutional on the same basis as the limit on per-candidate contributions: that such limits are needed to ***combat the actuality and appearance of corruption***, including the reality or appearance that the candidate is implicitly promising favorable action in return for a large contribution (a "*quid pro quo*").

But although the limit on the amount an individual may contribute to a *single* candidate has so far *survived* the Roberts Court's hostility to campaign-finance laws, ***the aggregate-contribution limit has not survived.*** In ***McCutcheon v. FEC***, 134 S.Ct. 1434 (2014), the Court held by a 5-4 vote that limits on the amounts that an individual may contribute in a year to ***all federal candidates***, and, separately, to ***all political committees***, ***violate the free-speech rights of individual***s who want to make bigger aggregate contributions.

1. **Regulations at issue in *McCutcheon*:** *McCutcheon* involved the contribution limits for the 2013-14 federal election cycle. During this cycle, federal campaign restrictions prohibited an individual from contributing more than $48,600 to all federal candidates, and from giving more than $74,600 to all non-candidate-controlled political committees. These *"aggregate"* restrictions were on top of "base" restrictions limiting how much an individual could contribute to any *one* candidate ($5,200, counting both the primary and general elections) or to any one political committee ($5,000).

2. **Plaintiffs:** The two plaintiffs — a donor and a political party — challenged these aggregate limits as a violation of their First Amendment rights.

3. **Struck down by 5-4 vote:** The Supreme Court, in a 5-4 victory for the conservative bloc of the Court, ***struck down the aggregate limits as violations on the free speech rights of contributors.*** The main opinion was a plurality opinion by Chief Justice Roberts (joined by Justices Scalia, Kennedy and Alito); the fifth vote came from Justice Thomas, who concurred in the result.

   a. **Relation between base and aggregate limits:** Roberts conceded that the Court had long held that the *base* limits — the maximum contribution by one donor to one candidate — serve the permissible objective of combating corruption and the appearance of it. (The plaintiffs in *McCutcheon* did not challenge the base limits.) The question was whether the *aggregate* limits, too, could be found to serve the anti-corruption objective. The federal government, defending the aggregate limits, argued that the answer was yes; for one thing, the government said, the aggregate limits would make it harder for donors and political parties to ***circumvent the base limits.***

   b. **Only corruption-prevention an allowable objective:** But Roberts rejected this "circumvention" defense of the aggregate limits. He noted that over the past 40 years since *Buckley*, the Court had recognized only *one* legitimate governmental interest supporting restrictions on campaign finances: *"**preventing corruption** or the **appearance of corruption.**"*

      i. **Narrow view of corruption:** Furthermore, Roberts said, the Court had decided that there was only *one* type of activity that would qualify as "corruption" of the sort that could be fought by finance regulation: *"**'quid pro quo' corruption or its appearance.** That Latin phrase captures the notion of a **direct exchange of an official act for money.**"*

   c. **No impact on *quid-pro-quo* problem:** Under this narrow view by which only measures that target *quid pro quo* corruption could survive, the aggregate limits were ***fatally flawed,*** Roberts said. The government had argued that the aggregate limits helped in the fight against corruption by making it harder for contributors to evade the base limits. But Roberts concluded that the aggregate limits "do ***little, if anything, to address [the circumvention] concern***, while ***seriously restricting participation*** in the democratic process." That was enough to make the limits invalid under the First Amendment.

   d. **Thomas adds fifth vote:** The fifth vote to uphold the aggregate limits came from Justice Thomas, who concurred in the judgment. Thomas would have gone even further than the plurality — he would have ***overruled*** *Buckley*'s core distinction between limits on *contributions* (which *Buckley* decided did not need to be strictly scrutinized) and limits on *expenditures* (which *Buckley* and later cases have strictly scrutinized).

Thomas believed that limits on both contributions and expenditures should be strictly scrutinized. He left little doubt that if the base limits upheld by *Buckley* (and never overturned since) were subjected to such scrutiny, they too, like the aggregate limits, should and would be struck down.

4. **Dissent:** Justice Breyer dissented in *McCutcheon*, in an opinion joined by Justices Ginsburg, Sotomayor and Kagan.

    a. **Evisceration:** Breyer believed that the outcome in *McCutcheon*, when taken together with that in *Citizens United* (see *infra*, p. 586) striking down limits on corporations' independent expenditures, *"eviscerates our Nation's campaign finance laws*, leaving a remnant incapable of dealing with the *grave problems of democratic legitimacy* that those laws were intended to resolve."

5. **Significance:** So as the result of *McCutcheon*, a donor may now donate the maximum per-candidate amount (currently $5,200 per election cycle) directly to *as many federal candidates as the donor wishes.* And the same is true of political committees: the donor may give the $5,000 (current) limit to as many political committees as he or she desires. Thus, even apart from the unlimited "independent expenditures" that a wealthy donor might make to urge the election of particular candidates, the donor could give, for instance, an aggregate of nearly $2.8 million to all Republican House and Senate candidates ($5,200 x 535 candidates) in a single election cycle, as well as an even larger amount to a collection of political committees not under the control of any individual candidate.

D. **"Soft money" and pre-election "issue ads" (*McConnell, Wisconsin Right to Life* and *Citizens United*):** The federal campaign finance reform measures approved by the Court in *Buckley* turned out not to be tremendously effective over the several decades that followed. Sophisticated and wealthy donors and advocacy organizations — and the national political parties — bypassed these measures by various devices, most notably the institutions of *"soft money"* and *"issue ads."* Finally, Congress responded by enacting the Bipartisan Campaign Reform Act of 2002 ("BCRA"), popularly known as the *McCain-Feingold Act* after its chief Senate sponsors. In an important trio of decisions, the Court first approved the key measures of the BCRA, but then (after a switch in Court personnel) reversed itself by striking one of the two key measures.

The three cases are: *McConnell v. Federal Election Comm.*, 540 U.S. 93 (2003) (approving both key measures, mostly by a 5-4 vote); *Federal Election Commission v. Wisconsin Right to Life*, 127 S.ct. 449 (2007) (dramatically narrowing the scope of the ban on election-time issue ads, also by a 5-4 vote); and *Citizens United v. Federal Election Commission*, 130 S.Ct. 876 (2010) (stripping nearly all the rest of the BCRA's regulation of such issue ads, by holding, again by a 5-4 vote, that *corporations and unions can't be treated worse than individuals*). *Citizens United*, in particular, is the most important campaign-finance decisions by the Court since *Buckley*.

1. **Twin targets of the BCRA:** The BCRA addressed the two practices that Congress believed were the most egregious ways in which wealthy donors and special-interest groups were corrupting and distorting the federal election process:

    a. **Soft money:** First was the giving of *"soft money"* donations. Political contributions whose amounts were regulated by the FECA (the act upheld in *Buckley*) were and are known as *"hard money"* donations. But the FECA as interpreted by the Federal Election Commission treated certain donations and expenditures as not falling within this regulated, hard-money classification; these unregulated sums are what is known as soft money. For instance, donors could contribute ***unlimited soft-money sums to the Democratic and Republican national parties*** (or special committees run by those parties), and the parties could then ***re-spend the money*** however they wanted as long as the funds were not used to expressly advocate the election or defeat of a particular candidate. Such large soft-money donations could be given by wealthy individuals, corporations, labor unions, and anyone else, as long as the funds were used in this no-advocacy-of-election-or-defeat-of-a-specific-candidate manner.

  i. **Get-out-the-vote and other uses of soft money:** So, for instance, the national political parties could raise large sums from wealthy donors, then spend those sums on activities like ***get-out-the-vote drives*** (directed at voters expected to vote for the party putting on the drive), and ***generic party advertising*** (e.g., "Vote for the Democratic ticket this November 2nd.")

b. **Issue ads:** The second practice that was upsetting Congress was the use of ***special-issue broadcast ads*** by groups like ***corporations*** and ***labor unions***. If a corporation or union wanted to buy an ad expressly advocating the election or defeat of a particular candidate, that ad had to be paid for with hard (and thus tightly-regulated) dollars, and lots of information about the sponsor of the ad had to be disclosed. But if the sponsor avoided the "magic words" — i.e., words expressly advocating a particular candidate's election or defeat — then the ad could be funded by ***unlimited sums furnished by the corporation or union***, and with no disclosure of the sponsors' identity. These ads are generically known as ***"issue ads"*** (and ones attacking rather than supporting a particular candidate are known as ***"attack ads"***).Thus a Republican-leaning advocacy group might purchase ads attacking Democratic Congressman Joe Smith's voting record on Social Security, and then conclude, "Call Joe Smith and tell him to stop weakening Social Security." These attack ads were in fact often ***more effective*** than direct "vote for [or against] Jane Doe" ads.

2. **Congress attacks the twin evils:** So by enacting the BCRA, Congress tried to curb the abuses associated with both unregulated soft money and with issue ads purchased by that unregulated money. In doing so, Congress believed that it was acting to reduce not only corruption but the ***appearance*** of corruption, stemming from wealthy donors' apparent attempt to purchase access to office holders. The heart of the BCRA consisted of Titles I and II.

a. **Title I on soft money:** Title I of the BCRA was Congress' attempt to plug the soft-money loophole. The main provision in Title I ***prohibited the national political parties and their committees from soliciting, receiving or spending any soft money.*** As the *McConnell* majority later summarized this provision, Title I "takes national parties out of the soft-money business."

b. **Title II on issue ads:** Title II mainly ***prohibited corporations*** and ***labor unions*** from using their general funds for ***broadcast advertisements naming specific candidates for federal office near election time.***

  i. **Electioneering Communications:** Title II defined a new category called ***"Electioneering Communications,"*** which consisted of ***TV and radio ads***, broadcast within 60 days before a general election or 30 days before a primary, and referring to an ***identified candidate*** for federal office.

    ii. **Ban on ads:** Title II then said that ***corporations and labor unions may not use their general funds to pay for Electioneering Communications,*** and must instead pay for these with money from their Political Action Committees (see *supra*, p. 576).

    iii. **Significance:** Since PAC's are ***subject to contribution limits*** and other types of regulation (e.g., the requirement that the names of individual donors be ***publicly disclosed***), Title II significantly restricted the ways in which ***corporations*** (including ***non-profit advocacy corporations*** like the ACLU and the NRA) could pay for and carry out their own election-time broadcast advertising.

3. **The twin evils meet different fates:** Both Title I on soft money and Title II on issue ads were promptly attacked in multiple litigations. As we'll see below, as of mid-2010, Title I's ***soft-money*** restrictions have ***survived*** constitutional scrutiny, but Title II's restrictions on ***corporations' and unions' right to pay for issue ads*** have been completely ***overruled*** as First Amendment violations. We consider the attacks on each title independently, first Title I (in Paragraph 4) and then Title II (in Paragraph 5).

4. **Title I (soft-money ban) survives:** The ban on ***soft-money donations*** imposed by Title I of the BCRA has, at least for now, survived First Amendment attack. That happened in *McConnell, supra*, the 2003 case that was the first, and least successful, of the trio of First Amendment attacks on the BCRA.

    a. **Attacked by odd grouping:** In *McConnell*, a consortium of non-profit groups attacked the constitutionality of the BCRA, including such unlikely allies as the American Civil Liberties Union and the National Rifle Association. (They attacked both Title I and Title II; here, we cover the Title I attack, with the Title II attack postponed to p. 585 below).

    b. **Court upholds Title I in *McConnell*:** The *McConnell* Court ***upheld the constitutionality of Title I***, as part of a decision ***upholding nearly all of the BCRA***.[12] The majority opinion on Title I was jointly authored by Justices Stevens and O'Connor (joined by Souter, Ginsburg and Breyer). Most of the case was decided on a 5-4 vote.

        i. **Rationale:** The majority wrote that soft money had enabled candidates and parties to ***circumvent*** FECA's limits. The majority agreed with the congressional drafters of Title I that there was ample evidence to support the conclusion that large soft-money contributions to the national political parties had had a ***corrupting influence***, or at the very least had given rise to the ***appearance*** of corruption. There was "no meaningful distinction between the national party committees and the public officials who control them." There was evidence that "candidates and donors alike [have] exploited the soft-money loophole, the former to increase their prospects of election and the latter to ***create debt on the part of officeholders***, with the national parties serving as ***willing intermediaries***[.]" Therefore, it was not a violation of donors' First Amendment rights for Congress to regulate donations so as to curb the reality or appearance of that corruption.

---

12. The one part of the Act that was struck down was a ban on contributions by ***minors*** — Congress was worried that rich parents would funnel, through their minor children, contributions in excess of the hard-money limits. But the Court said that there was no evidence that such evasions were occurring.

c. Dissents in *McConnell*: Four justices — Kennedy, Scalia, Thomas and Rehnquist — ***dissented*** from the majority's wholesale upholding of Title I in *McConnell*.

   i. Scalia's dissent: Justice Scalia's dissent said that the majority had "smiled with favor upon a law that cuts to the heart of what the First Amendment is meant to protect: the right to ***criticize the government***." In particular, he thought the law improperly allowed Congress to ***insulate its own incumbent members against criticism*** by political parties and corporations. The BCRA might be "evenhanded" in the sense that it similarly prohibited criticism of those running *against* incumbents. But "this is an area in which ***evenhandedness is not fairness***. [If] incumbents and challengers are limited to the same quantity of electioneering, ***incumbents are favored.***"

d. Present status: Title I's ban on soft-money donations ***remains in force***. Nothing in the revolutionary case of *Citizens United* (*infra*, pp. 586-587), giving corporations and unions the same independent-campaign-spending rights as individuals, directly invalidates the soft-money ban upheld in *McConnell*.

   i. Vulnerable: However, notice that Title I treats the ***national political parties less favorably*** than all other non-candidate election players, since outside groups (e.g., Political Action Committees) may receive unlimited donations to use for electioneering, whereas the national political parties may not. The same logic that led the Court in *Citizens United* to say that Congress couldn't radically disfavor one type of player (corporations) as to issue ads, arguably applies the same way to prevent Congress from disfavoring one type of player (national political parties) as to political fund-raising. Therefore, Title I may not survive in a post-*Citizens United* world.

5. Title II (issue-ad ban) struck down: Recall (p. 583 *supra*) that Title II of the BCRA banned ***issue ads***, i.e., pre-election ads mentioning a candidate, paid for by corporations or unions. That ban, unlike Title I's ban on soft-money, has ***not survived*** in the Supreme Court.

a. Title II initially upheld: In *McConnell*, *supra*, a majority of the Court thought that Title II, like Title I, was ***constitutional***. Those attacking Title II argued that under *Buckley*, speakers had an absolute First Amendment right to engage in "issue advocacy" (as opposed to express advocacy of the election or defeat of a particular candidate). But the majority disagreed: corporate-paid broadcast ads near the time of an election, mentioning specific candidates, were just as clearly intended to influence the election as were the type of express-advocacy ads regulated under *Buckley*. Therefore, it did not violate the First Amendment for these issue ads to be regulated in the same way.

b. Reversal of Court's view on Title II: But beginning four years after *McConnell*, and following a change in the Court's membership, the Court ***reversed itself*** as to Title II's ban on issue ads near election time. In a pair of cases, *FEC v. Wisconsin Right to Life* (2007) and *Citizens United v. FEC* (2010), Justice O'Connor's replacement by Justice Alito produced a ***switch*** to 5-4 the other way, with the ultimate result that ***even corporations and labor unions may run whatever issue ads they want during political campaigns***, as long as they ***operate independently*** of the candidate.

c. Narrowed in *Wisconsin Right to Life*: First, in *FEC v. Wisconsin Right to Life*, 551 U.S. 449 (2007), the Court dramatically narrowed the scope of the ban on issue ads.

d. Ban overturned (*Citizens United*): Then, in the much more important ***Citizens United v. FEC***, 130 S.Ct. 876 (2010), by the same 5-4 alignment as in *Wisconsin Right to Life*, the Court explicitly ***overruled*** the part of *McConnell* that had upheld Title II. *Citizens United* establishes that ***corporations have a full measure of First Amendment protection in the area of politics***, and that Congress may not prohibit them from using their ***general funds to run campaign advertising***, as long as the corporation ***acts independently*** of the candidate.

  i. Facts: Citizens United, a non-profit organization that was the plaintiff, made a documentary presenting an unflattering portrait of then-presidential candidate Hillary Clinton. Citizens United wanted to pay for a cable TV video-on-demand presentation of the movie shortly before the 2008 Democratic presidential primary. Regulations of the Federal Election Commission prohibited Citizens from paying for this broadcast with its unrestricted funds, on the theory that this would be a forbidden corporate-paid "electioneering communication." Citizen United sued the FEC for a ruling that its free speech rights had been violated.

  ii. Plaintiff wins: By a 5-4 vote, Citizens United ***prevailed***. In a very broad opinion by Justice Kennedy, the majority held that Title II's ban on corporate issue ads violated corporations' free speech rights.

   (1) *Austin* and *McConnell* overruled: In reaching this conclusion, Kennedy's opinion squarely overruled the Title II holding of *McConnell* (*supra*, p. 585). The opinion rejected the rationale that corporate campaign speech could be limited because of its distorting effects. To Kennedy, this rationale would ***reach too far***: "If the ***anti-distortion rationale*** were to be accepted ... it would permit government to ***ban political speech*** simply because the speaker is an association that has taken on the corporate form." Nor did Kennedy believe that independent corporate campaign expenditures could be banned in order to ***prevent corruption*** or the appearance of corruption; an anti-corruption rationale justified limits on contributions to *candidates*, he said, but there was no evidence that independent corporate expenditures that were ***not coordinated*** with a candidate fostered corruption or the appearance of corruption.

   (2) Censorship: Kennedy concluded that banning corporations from making independent expenditures to broadcast political messages ***amounted to censorship***: "When government seeks to use its full power, including the criminal law, to ***command where a person may get his or her information*** or ***what trusted source he or she may not hear***, it ***uses censorship to control thought.*** ... The Government ***may not suppress political speech*** on the basis of the ***speaker's corporate identity.***"

  iii. Dissent: Justice Stevens (joined by Justices Ginsburg, Breyer and Sotomayor) ***dissented*** from the key holding in *Citizens United*, that Title II's ban on corporate-funded issue ads violated corporations' free speech rights.

   (1) Rationale: Stevens believed that Congress was entitled to ***distinguish between corporate and human speakers.*** Lawmakers have a "compelling constitutional basis" to guard against the ***potentially-damaging effects of corporate spending*** in local and national elections, he said, a basis reflected in the the special limitations that Congress had imposed on corporate campaign spending ever since a 1907 law. The majority's rule "threatens to ***undermine the integrity of elected institutions*** across the Nation."

(2) Antidistortion and anticorruption: Stevens argued that regulation of corporate electioneering expenditures was a necessary means of avoiding corporations' ***unfair influence in the electoral process***. Unregulated corporate expenditures would be likely to ***drown out non-corporate voices***, and to "generate the impression that corporations dominate our democracy." The majority's approach was premised on the idea that "there is no such thing as too much speech." This might be true "if individuals ... had ***infinite free time*** to listen to and contemplate every last bit of speech uttered by anyone, anywhere[.]" But, he continued, "[i]n the real world, we have seen, corporate domination of the airwaves prior to an election may ***decrease the average listener's exposure to relevant viewpoints***[.]"

iv. **Unions:** *Citizens United* dealt directly only with speech by corporations, not by other types of entities such as ***labor unions*** (who were also forbidden by Title II to run issue ads). But the rationale of the case is broad — the majority says that for First Amendment purposes, the particular form of legal organization doesn't matter. Therefore, *Citizens United* strongly implies that independent campaign spending by labor unions ***cannot be barred or heavily regulated — or treated much differently*** — than such spending by individuals.

v. **Significance:** *Citizens United* essentially ***removes all dollar limits on corporations' and labor unions' direct campaign spending.*** As long as the corporation or union acts "***independently***" of the candidate that it is supporting, and discloses to the world that that is what it is doing, is ***no limit to how much the entity can spend*** to advocate the election or defeat of a particular candidate, right up until election day.

6. **Prognosis:** So here is where federal regulation of ***soft money*** and ***issue ads*** seems to stand after *McConnell* and *Citizens United*:

❏ Title I's ban on ***soft money contributions to the national political parties*** remains ***constitutional.*** There is no indication that a majority of today's post-*Citizens-Unitied* Court disagrees with *McConnell*'s conclusion that Congress can constitutionally fight the appearance of corruption by tightly regulating the making of ***cash contributions to candidates or parties.***

❏ Title II's ban on "***electioneering communications***" is ***defunct*** — all types of speakers, including ***corporations and unions***, can spend ***apparently-limitless sums*** from their general treasuries to advocate for or against particular candidates, as long as the spending is "***independent***," i.e., not coordinated with the candidate.

❏ Consequently, corporations, unions and ***non-party special-interest groups*** (e.g., party-independent Political Action Committees, or "***PAC's***") all have the opportunity to exert ***more influence*** on elections than before these two decision, because of their ability to spend limitless sums on political ads. Conversely, the ***national political parties*** have probably ***lost influence*** relative to these other kinds of groups, since the political parties' fundraising abilities are restricted and the independent entities' fundraising and fund-spending abilities are not.

❏ The core distinction dating back to *Buckley* — between ***contributions*** to candidates, and ***independent spending*** to help elect a candidate — ***remains in effect***. Contributions can be heavily regulated (because they give the appearance of corruption), whereas independent expenditures cannot (because they're less likely to feed corruption or the appearance of it). This distinction continues to be much criticized, but there's no sign the present Court is ready to abandon it.

E. Campaign spending by political parties: Campaign spending by ***political parties*** on behalf of congressional candidates ***may not be limited***, as long as the party is working *"independently"* of the candidate rather than in "coordination" with her. This was the result of the pre-*McConnell* case of *Colorado Republican Federal Campaign Committee v. Federal Election Commission*, 518 U.S. 604 (1996) (*"Colorado Republican I"*).

   1. Limited by BCRA: But the BCRA (*supra*, p. 582) means that such spending by political parties is limited, because the parties are now restricted to ***raising only tightly-regulated hard-money donations*** from which to make even such candidate-independent expenditures.

   2. Limits on coordinated spending are constitutional: Furthermore, it is ***constitutional*** for Congress to limit campaign spending by parties that *is **coordinated*** with the candidate. The court so concluded in *Federal Election Commission v. Colorado Republican Federal Campaign Committee*, 533 U.S. 431 (2001) (*"Colorado Republican II"*).

F. How low can limits be set: We know from *Buckley* that government can set a dollar limit on campaign contributions, and we also know from that case that a $1,000 limit (in 1976 dollars) per-contributor/per-candidate is valid. But may the limits constitutionally be ***set even lower***? As the result of a 2000 case, *Nixon v. Shrink Missouri Government PAC*, 523 U.S. 666 (2000), we know that the answer is ***yes***: as long as the limitation is not so radical as to ***"render contributions pointless,"*** it will be ***sustained*** even though it buys far less campaign speech than $1,000 did in 1976. (So, for instance, a limit of $1,075 in donations for statewide offices was upheld in *Shrink Missouri*.)

   1. Applies to states: *Shrink Missouri* means that the ***states*** may limit campaign contributions for state elections, just as *Buckley* and *McConnell* said that Congress may do for federal elections.

   2. Some limits are too low: In only one case has the Court concluded that contribution limits were ***unconstitutionally low***. In *Randall v. Sorrell, supra,* p. 579, the Court concluded that Vermont's limits — for instance, a $400 limit on what an individual or party could contribute to a candidate for governor during a two-year election cycle — were so low as to "disproportionately burden" the First Amendment rights of candidates, parties and volunteers. Only in a truly extraordinary case — where the limits are so low that they prevent challengers from making an effective campaign against incumbents, for instance — will the Court find that the limits are unconstitutionally low. (No majority of the Roberts Court has been able to agree on a standard for determining when contribution limits are "too low.")

G. Corporate and judicial expression during campaigns: We turn now to two special issues involving regulation of campaign speech:

[1] to what extent may political expression be regulated on account of the fact that the speaker is a *business* or *corporation*?; and

[2] in places where *judges* must run for electoral office, what restrictions may be placed upon the candidates' *campaign speech* and their efforts to *raise campaign funds*?

The Supreme Court has issued one decision on the first issue, and two on the second. The decision in the corporate case went in favor of the corporate speaker. In the two judicial-election cases, the earlier decision was in favor of the judicial speech claim, while the later one upheld a much narrower regulation on judges' campaign-finance efforts.

1. **Corporate political expression:** On the issue of campaign-related speech by *businesses* and *corporations*, the Court has held that political expression may not be denied First Amendment protection merely because its source is a *corporation* rather than an individual. In *First National Bank of Boston v. Bellotti*, 435 U.S. 765 (1978) the Court, by a 5-4 vote, struck down a Massachusetts ban on *corporate political advocacy*. The decision relied on the *public's right to know*, rather than on the corporation's right to speak.

    a. **Reaffirmed in *Citizens United*:** *Citizens United* (*supra*, p. 586) makes it clear that *Bellotti* is still good law. The majority in *Citizens* cited *Bellotti* for the proposition that "First Amendment protection extends to corporations." After *Citizens United*, it is clear that independent political expression by a *business or corporation* cannot be *treated any less favorably* than such expression by an *individual*.

2. **Campaign speech in judicial elections:** In 39 states, at least some judges are *popularly elected* rather than appointed. In these states, there is a risk that candidates for judgeships will, in order to get elected, say things or do things that may conflict with a judge's ethical obligations once elected.

    For instance, the candidate may *announce how she would rule* on a controversial issue likely to come before her court, in which case the due process rights of the litigants might be impaired. Or, in order to defray the costs of running a campaign, the candidate may *solicit funds* in a way that creates a risk that contributors (who may include potential litigants as well as lawyers) will *expect and perhaps receive favorable treatment* if the candidate wins office, raising an obvious appearance of *corruption*.

    a. **Split decisions:** The Supreme Court's two decisions on regulations limiting the campaign speech and financial activities of judicial candidates are, as noted, *split*. A 2002 case struck down a state law that barred judicial candidates from expressing their opinions about legal issues that may come before the court, but a 2015 case upheld a much narrower regulation that blocked judicial candidates from personally soliciting campaign contributions. We'll look at each decision in turn.

    b. **Ban on discussion of "legal or political issues" (*White* case):** In the earlier case, the Court gave broad First Amendment protection to speech by judicial candidates, comparable to protection long given to candidates for legislative or executive office. The case was *Republican Party of Minn. v. White*, 536 U.S. 765 (2002). There, the Court struck down a Minnesota rule that a candidate for judicial office shall not *"announce his or her views on disputed legal or political issues."*

i. **Purpose of the rule:** Drafters of the rule reasoned that when a candidate publicly makes known her views on issues that may come before her court, the *due process rights* of later litigants are likely to be abridged.

ii. **Struck down:** By a 5-4 vote, the Court struck down Minnesota's rule, on the theory that it violated the *First Amendment rights of judicial candidates.* The opinion, by Justice Scalia, conceded that opposition to judicial elections "may be well taken." But, he said, "the First Amendment does not permit [opponents of judicial elections] to achieve [their] goal by leaving the principle of elections in place while *preventing candidates from discussing what the elections are about."*

iii. **Dissent:** The four dissenters contended that the Minnesota rule was a reasonable way for Minnesota to pursue its legitimate goal of maintaining judicial impartiality.

c. **Ban on direct solicitation of contributions (*Williams-Yulee* case):** In the more recent case, again by a 5-4 vote, the Court *upheld* a Florida rule that prohibited judicial candidates from *personally soliciting campaign contributions.* See *Williams-Yulee v. Florida Bar*, 135 S.Ct. 1656 (2015).

   i. **Canon of Ethics:** Florida adopted a whole set of Canons of Judicial Conduct. One of them, Canon 7C(1), was based on a similar provision from the American Bar Association's Model Dode of Judicial Conduct. 7C(1) provided that a candidate running for an elective judgeship:

   > *shall not personally solicit campaign funds*, or solicit attorneys for publicly stated support, but *may establish committees* of responsible persons to secure and manage the expenditure of funds for the candidate's campaign and to obtain public statements of support for his or her candidacy. *Such committees are not prohibited from soliciting campaign contributions* and public support from any person or corporation authorized by law.

   So under the Canon, the candidate herself could not "personally solicit" campaign contributions, but a campaign committee run by others *could* solicit campaign contributions on behalf of the candidate.

   ii. **Canon is attacked:** P (Ms. Yulee, a lawyer) wrote, signed and mailed a letter to local voters in which she announced her candidacy for a county court judgeship, and asked for small contributions (from $25 to $500) to be made payable to her campaign. The Florida bar then filed a complaint against her for violating Canon 7C(1)'s ban on personal solicitation of campaign funds. She defended by asserting that she had a First Amendment right to solicit campaign funds.

   iii. **Majority upholds the Canon:** Five members of the Court, in an opinion by Justice Roberts, held that this relatively narrow restriction on candidates' speech did *not* violate their First Amendment rights.

      (1) **Strict scrutiny applied:** Roberts first decided that because the solicitation-of-contributions ban restricted P's speech based on its content, the restriction would have to *survive strict scrutiny.* That is, it would pass constitutional muster "only if the restriction is *narrowly tailored to serve a compelling interest.*"[13]

(2) A compelling interest: But Roberts wrote that this was one of the *"rare cases* in which a speech restriction *withstands* strict scrutiny." First, the state's interest in "protecting the *integrity* of the judiciary" and "maintaining the public's *confidence in an impartial judiciary,"* taken together, constituted "a state interest of the highest order," and thus a "compelling" interest. In fact, he said, the state's interest in maintaining public confidence in the integrity is even more important in the case of *judicial* elections than in the context of *legislative* and *executive* elections: "Politicians are expected to be appropriately *responsive to the preferences of their supporters,"* whereas "In deciding cases, a judge is *not to follow the preferences of his supporters*, or *provide any special consideration to his campaign donors."*

(3) "Raises a red flag": Roberts then turned to the issue of whether the ban here was sufficiently *narrowly tailored* to achieve this compelling objective regarding integrity. P argued that the ban was fatally underinclusive, in that Canon 7C(1) "allows a judge's *campaign committee* to solicit money, which arguably reduces public confidence in the integrity of the judiciary just as much as a judge's personal solicitation." And Roberts conceded that a law's underinclusivity *"raises a red flag"* in First Amendment strict scrutiny cases (in part by "rais[ing] 'doubts about whether the government is in fact pursuing the interest it invokes, rather than disfavoring a particular speaker or viewpoint'.")

(4) Narrowly tailored: But, Roberts said, "the First Amendment *imposes no freestanding 'underinclusiveness limitation'."* A state "need not *address all aspects of a problem in one fell swoop,"* and the ban here "aims squarely at the conduct *most likely to undermine public confidence* in the integrity of the judiciary: *personal requests for money by judges and judicial candidates."* So the ban was indeed narrowly tailored to achieve the compelling state interest in judicial integrity, thereby surviving strict scrutiny.

X. SOME SPECIAL CONTEXTS

A. Scope: We now examine several particular contexts in which special First Amendment problems have arisen. Generally, these special problems arise because the First Amendment comes into conflict with unusually strong "public policy" interests, for instance, the interest in running an effective public-school system, or in the smooth administration of justice.

---

13. Only two of the four Justices who agreed with the result reached by Roberts — that the Canon was constitutional — agreed with him that strict scrutiny was the appropriate standard. The other two (Ginsburg and Breyer, both concurring only in the result) would have applied a less rigorous standard (though they didn't say what it was), making five Justices to hold the ban constitutional. But the four dissenters (Scalia, Kennedy, Alito and Thomas) all believed that strict scrutiny was required, and that the ban could *not* survive that strict scrutiny. So one majority of the Court — Roberts plus the four dissenters — believed that strict scrutiny was the appropriate standard, but a different majority (Roberts, plus two others who joined his reasoning, and another two who concurred only in result) believed that the ban could survive whatever scrutiny that particular Justice thought was the right standard. (But only one Justice, Roberts, simultaneously thought *both* that the standard to use was strict scrutiny and that the statute could survive.)

B. Schools: The conflict between First Amendment values and society's substantial interest in pursuing other important values can be seen clearly in the ***public school*** context. On the one hand, the public school system is the community's principal means for transmitting knowledge and values from one generation to the next; this process unavoidably involves teaching students how, and sometimes what, to think. See 96 HARV. L. REV. 151. Yet students and teachers have First Amendment rights, which they do not completely surrender when they enter the school.

1. **Reluctance to intervene:**   The Supreme Court has generally been reluctant to intervene in school authorities' handling of school operations. The Court will not intervene in those operations unless "basic constitutional values" are "directly and sharply implicate[d]." *Epperson v. Arkansas*, 393 U.S. 97 (1968).

2. **Illustrations of interference:**   But the Court has, nonetheless, occasionally held that school authorities have violated the First Amendment or other constitutional rights of students or teachers. For instance, the Court has held that the state ***may not forbid*** the ***teaching of foreign languages***; see *Meyer v. Nebraska*, 262 U.S. 390 (1923) (decided on substantive due process grounds; see *supra*, p. 174). Similarly, the Court has held that school children ***cannot be required to salute the flag; West Virginia Bd. of Ed. v. Barnette***, 319 U.S. 624 (1943). And recall that a student's right to wear an armband and to protest symbolically against the Vietnam War was not permitted to be suppressed by school authorities, at least where this was done to suppress a particular point of view; *Tinker v. Des Moines School District*, 393 U.S. 503 (1969) (*supra*, p. 543).

    a. **Permissible purposes:**   However, school authorities may act to preserve ***discipline***, the ***rights of other students***, and the ***educational function of the school***. For instance, the Court in *Tinker* indicated that the armband display could have been prohibited if there had been a showing that it did or would substantially interfere with school work or discipline.

3. **Choice of materials to be taught:**   Perhaps the most difficult First Amendment issue in the school context is the extent to which that Amendment restricts educators' choices of ***curriculum*** and ***teaching materials***. Educators must of course be given the right to determine what is to be taught in the public schools. Yet there is a potential conflict between this right and the First Amendment principle that "no official, high or petty, can prescribe what shall be orthodox in politics, nationalism, religion, or other matters of opinion. ... " *West Virginia Bd. of Ed. v. Barnette, supra.*

    a. **School libraries:**   The only Supreme Court case to deal directly with this conflict did so in a limited context, the right of school authorities to ***remove books from a school library***. In ***Board of Education v. Pico***, 457 U.S. 853 (1982), a plurality of the Court held that such a removal must not be carried out in a ***"narrowly partisan or political manner,"*** or for the purpose of denying students access to ***ideas with which the authorities disagree.***

        i.   **Facts:**   The school board in *Pico* ordered nine books to be removed from its high school and junior high school libraries, including Richard Wright's *Black Boy* and Eldridge Cleaver's *Soul on Ice*. The books were all on a list published by a conservative parents' group and were labelled by the board as "anti-American, anti-Christian, anti-Semitic, and just plain filthy."

ii. **Holding:** Because of the procedural posture, the Supreme Court did not directly decide whether the school board had violated the Constitution in ordering the removal of the books. The plurality did, however, articulate what it saw as the appropriate constitutional standard: a school board has wide authority in determining what books to remove from a library, but it may not remove books for the purpose of ***denying access to ideas for political or partisan reasons***. As an extreme example, the plurality noted that a Democratic school board could not, motivated by party affiliation, order the removal of all books written by Republicans.

b. **Curriculum and textbooks:** It is hard to know what standard the Court will apply to the issue of school authorities' discretion to select the ***curriculum*** and ***required textbooks***. Although, as noted, the Court will probably recognize greater discretion here than in the library-book-removal situation of *Pico*, it is not clear that this discretion will be much broader. Something like *Pico*'s ban on "narrow partisan or political motives" will probably be applied in this situation as well. For instance, it is doubtful that a majority of the Court would uphold a school board's rule that no teacher may express in class the opinion that the war in Vietnam was morally and legally wrong.

   i. **Teacher's own expression of views:** At the same time, ***individual teachers*** may probably take actions which a school board would not be permitted to take on a system-wide basis. For instance, a teacher may certainly constitutionally express to his students a view about the morality or legality of the Vietnam War, whether or not the school system may formulate an "official" view on the same subject; this distinction is appropriate because an individual teacher's views do not represent an "official" or "orthodox" position in the same way that a system-wide position does.

4. **Speech by students:** What about ***speech by students?*** Students do not "shed their constitutional rights to freedom of speech or expression at the schoolhouse gate." *Tinker v. Des Moines School District*, 393 U.S. 503 (1969), discussed more extensively, *supra*, p. 543. Thus in *Tinker*, the Court held that the First Amendment rights of several high school and junior high school students were abridged when they were suspended for wearing black armbands in school as a symbol of opposition to the Vietnam War.

   However, the Supreme Court has recognized some important ***limits*** on *Tinker*. Two of the more important are that school authorities are free to limit student speech when:

   [1] the limit is needed to ***maintain school discipline*** and fulfill the school's ***educational mission***; or

   [2] the speech ***advocates illegality***, at least in the special case of ***drug use***.

   We'll examine each of these exceptions in more detail, in Pars. (a) and (b) below. Then, in Par. (c), we'll discuss speech that occurs off-campus.

   a. **Maintenance of discipline and the school's mission:** Notwithstanding *Tinker*, school authorities have a strong and valid interest in ***maintaining school discipline and in carrying out their educational mission.*** Pursuit of these goals will sometimes entitle the authorities to regulate speech in a way that would not be permissible outside the school context. The cases of *Bethel School District No. 403 v. Fraser* and *Hazelwood School District v. Kuhlmeier* illustrate this principle.

i. **Speech at a school assembly (*Bethel*):** In *Bethel School District No. 403 v. Fraser,* 478 U.S. 675 (1986), a high school student addressing a high school assembly gave a speech that school authorities found to be lewd. The speech, made in support of a candidate for a student government office, contained an elaborate sexual metaphor (e.g., "Jeff Kuhlman is a man who takes his point and pounds it in. ... He doesn't attack things in spurts — he drives hard, pushing and pushing until finally — he succeeds."). School authorities suspended the speaker and removed him from the list of candidates for commencement speaker.

   (1) **Disciplinary action upheld:** The Court ***upheld*** the disciplinary actions over the student's claim that they violated his freedom of expression. "The undoubted freedom to advocate unpopular and controversial issues in schools and classrooms must be balanced against society's countervailing interest in ***teaching students the boundaries of socially appropriate behavior.*** " When balanced in this way, the school's interest in prohibiting "vulgar and lewd speech" outweighed whatever First Amendment interests the student might have had, especially since the penalties were ***"unrelated to any political viewpoint," i.e., they were content-neutral.***

ii. **Student newspaper (*Hazelwood*):** Similarly, school officials may exercise editorial control over the contents of ***student newspapers*** if they do so in a way that is ***reasonably related to legitimate pedagogical concerns. Hazelwood School District v. Kuhlmeier***, 484 U.S. 260 (1988).

   (1) **Facts:** Thus in *Hazelwood*, the Court upheld a school principal's decision to remove two articles from the student newspaper: (1) a story describing three students' experience with pregnancy; and (2) a story discussing the impact of divorce on students at the school. The principal believed that the first story might indirectly identify the students (even though their names weren't used), and that its references to sexual activity and birth control were inappropriate for some of the younger students at the school. He believed that the second article, which in the draft the principal saw identified a student who blamed her father for her parents' divorce, unfairly denied the father the chance to respond.

   (2) **Holding:** A majority of the Court held that where a school a ***sponsors an activity***, in such a way that students and others may reasonably perceive the activity as ***bearing the school's imprimatur***, the school's right to restrict student speech is much greater than in the *Tinker* situation (*supra*, p. 543). In *Tinker*, the students who wore armbands were not in any school-sponsored activity; they merely happened to be on school property, but did not forfeit their right of free speech. But expression that occurs during the course of a school-sponsored publication, theatrical production, or other school-sponsored activity may be subject to school authorities' control "so long as [the authorities'] actions are ***reasonably related to legitimate pedagogical concerns.***"

   (3) **Application:** Applying this "reasonable relation" test, a majority found that the school principal acted reasonably: based on the facts as the principal then knew them, suppression of the articles was reasonably related to the school

objectives of protecting privacy, shielding younger students from inappropriate subject matter, and teaching journalistic fairness.

b. **Advocacy of illegal drug use:** Both of the above cases (*Bethel* and *Hazelwood*) were ones in which either school discipline or the school's pedagogic mission was at stake, so it seemed relatively painless for the Supreme Court to carve out an exception from *Tinker* to justify the regulation of student speech. Where the student speech does *not* place discipline or the school's pedagogic mission in danger, the Court has been less likely to approve regulation. Thus in the core scenario typified by *Tinker* — student engages in political or social expression in a way that cannot plausibly be thought to pose discipline or pedagogic problems – *Tinker* remains the law, and restraints on student expression will be strictly scrutinized. But the Court has carved out one special *exception* to this general rule: speech ***advocating the use of illegal drugs*** may be restricted. That was the holding of ***Morse v. Frederick***, 551 U.S. 393 (2007).

   i. **Facts:** In *Morse*, students at a public high school were permitted to leave school to observe the carrying of the Olympic Torch; the excursion was treated as a school trip. One of the students, Frederick, while watching the Torch procession, unfurled a banner that said "BONG HiTS 4 JESUS." (No one seems confident of what the banner was supposed to mean, though it seemed to express the owner's view that marijuana use was a good thing.) The principal demanded that Frederick take down the banner, because she thought it encouraged illegal drug use in violation of school policy; she also suspended him from school.

   ii. **Action upheld:** The Court held that the confiscation of the banner and suspension of Frederick ***did not violate*** his First Amendment rights. The Court concluded that "a principal may, consistent with the First Amendment, restrict student speech at a school event, when that speech is reasonably viewed ***as promoting illegal drug use.***" That was true even though the speech here could not reasonably be viewed as a threat to the school's discipline or mission. The Court reasoned that schools have "an important, perhaps compelling" interest in deterring drug use by schoolchildren.

c. **Off-campus speech:** So far, all the student-speech cases we've discussed involved speech that occurred either ***on campus*** (e.g., *Tinker* itself, where the students wore the anti-war armband at the school) or during the course of a ***school-sponsored off-campus activity*** (e.g., *Morse v. Frederick*, where the student displaying the "Bong Hits" banner did so during a school trip). But how much speech-regulation may the school impose when the speech in question ***takes place off-campus,*** and the student is ***not speaking as part of a school-sponsored event?*** As a result of an important 2021 case, ***Mahanoy Area School District v. B.L.***, 141 S.Ct. 2038 (2021), we can make several general statements about a school's power to regulate such off-campus speech:

   [1] The fact that the speech occurs off-campus and not as part of a school event ***does not completely prevent*** the school from ***regulating*** the content or manner of the speech; but ...

   [2] The school's authority to regulate is ***generally much weaker*** than it is where the speech occurs on-campus or as part of a school-sponsored off-campus activity; and ...

   [3] Unless the speech falls within a few special categories (e.g., harassment, fighting

words, obscenity, or significant disruption of school activities), the speech receives ***at least as much constitutional protection*** as if it had occurred ***on-campus*** or during the course of a school-sponsored off-campus activity.

i. **Facts of *Mahanoy*:** *Mahanoy* concerned speech by B.L.,[14] a student at Mahanoy Area High School, a public school in a small town in Pennsylvania. B.L. tried out for the varsity cheerleading squad at the end of her freshman year, but was rejected and instead offered a spot on the junior varsity. When she got this news, she and a friend went to a local convenience store on a Saturday, from which B.L. used her smartphone to post two photos on Snapchat, a social media application. Snapchat allowed her to send these photos so that they could be viewed by her Snapchat "friends" (of which she had about 250), but would vanish after 24 hours.

   (1) **Content of the photos:** One of the photos showed B.L. and her friend with their middle fingers raised. The caption read: "Fuck school fuck softball fuck cheer fuck everything."

   (2) **The images spread:** Before the Snapshot photos vanished, one of B.L.'s "friends," a member of the cheerleading squad, took screenshots of them, and showed them to her mother, who was a cheerleading coach. The images spread, and several cheerleaders, appearing "visibly upset" about the photos, asked the cheerleading coaches about them; one discussion occurred during an algebra class taught by one of the coaches.

   (3) **School's response:** The cheerleading coaches, together with the principal, decided that because the posts used profanity in connection with a school extracurricular activity, the posts violated team and school rules. B.L. apologized, but the coaches nonetheless ***suspended her from the junior varsity cheerleading squad*** for the upcoming year.

ii. **The suit and the lower-courts' rulings:** B.L. and her parents sued the school district in federal court, claiming that the suspension violated B.L.'s First Amendment right of free speech. Both the district court and a 3-judge panel of the Third Circuit on appeal ***held in B.L.'s favor***, reasoning that the posts were protected under *Tinker* (*supra*, p. 543).

iii. **Supreme Court finds for B.L.:** The Supreme Court, by an 8-1 vote, agreed that the suspension ***violated B.L.'s right of free speech.*** The Court's opinion was written by Justice Breyer.

   (1) **Cites the *Tinker* decision:** Breyer began by repeating what *Tinker v. Des Moines* (*supra*, p. 543) said about the First Amendment rights of students: students ***"do not 'shed their constitutional rights to freedom of speech or expression,'*** even 'at the school house gate.' " But, he noted, *Tinker* recognized that schools have a ***special interest*** in regulating speech that ***"materially disrupts classwork*** or involves ***substantial disorder or invasion of the rights*** of others."

---

14. Because B.L. was a minor when the case began, the Supreme Court's opinion refers to her only by her initials.

(2) Rejects lower court's "off campus" rationale: Breyer then turned to the question of whether public schools had the same *"special interest"* in regulating student speech if the speech took place *off-campus*. For Breyer, the answer was a *qualified "yes"*: "[W]e do *not believe* the special characteristics that give schools additional license to regulate student speech *always disappear* when a school regulates speech that takes place off campus."

(3) List of scenarios: Breyer gave examples of scenarios in which the school's "regulatory interests" would *remain significant* even though the speech took place off-campus. These included situations involving:

❏ "serious or severe *bullying or harassment* targeting *particular individuals"*;

❏ *"threats* aimed at *teachers or other students"*;

❏ the *"failure to follow rules* concerning *lessons*, the *writing of papers*, the *use of computers*, or participation in other *online school activities"*;

❏ "breaches of *school security devices*, including *material maintained within school computers."*

(4) No "broad, highly general" rule: When the Court granted *certiorari* in *Mahanoy*, observers hoped that it would articulate a *general* rule about whether and how schools could regulate off-campus speech. But Breyer's opinion *declined* to do that.

(5) Features of off-campus speech: However, Breyer *was* willing to mention *three features of off-campus speech* that, he said, *"diminish the strength* of the unique educational characteristics that might call for [giving the school] special First Amendment leeway." Here were the three features:

❏ First, in relation to off-campus speech, "a school . . . *will rarely stand in loco parentis,"* because "off-campus speech will normally *fall within the zone of parental,* rather than school-related, *responsibility."*

❏ Second, "from the student speaker's perspective, regulations of off-campus speech, when coupled with regulations of on-campus speech, *include all the speech a student utters during the full 24-hour day."* Consequently, "courts must be *more skeptical* of a school's efforts to regulate off-campus speech, for doing so *may mean the student cannot engage in that kind of speech at all."* He continued, "When it comes to *political or religious speech* that occurs outside school or a school program or activity, the school will have a *heavy burden to justify intervention."*

❏ Finally, Breyer said, "the school itself has an interest in *protecting a student's unpopular expression,* especially when the expression takes place off campus." He continued, "America's public schools are the *nurseries of democracy,"* and must *"protect[] unpopular ideas*, for popular ideas have less need for protection."

Breyer said that the Court would "leave for future cases" the job of deciding "where, when, and how these features mean the speaker's off-campus location will make the critical difference[.]" But the present case provided one example of how the features would be applied.

(6) "Pure speech" protected by First Amendment: Before applying the three factors making the off-campus location of B.L.'s speech significant, Breyer described how her speech fit within broad freedom-of-expression principles. Her speech consisted of *"criticism of the rules of a community* of which B.L. forms a part." The post was therefore "the kind of *pure speech* to which, were she an adult, the First Amendment would *provide strong protection."*

(7) Application of law to facts — factors helping B.L.: It was then time for Breyer to apply the three factors to the particular facts of the case; the issue was whether the school's interest in regulating student speech was strong enough to overcome the fact that the speech here occurred off-campus. Breyer began by listing the ways in which B.L.'s off-campus location — together with the factors that limited the impact of the speech — cut *in favor of B.L.*:

❏ The speech occurred *"outside of school hours."* (It took place on a Saturday.)

❏ The speech came from a *"location outside the school"* (the convenience store).

❏ The speech *did not identify the school.*

❏ The speech *did not "target any member of the school community* with *vulgar or abusive language."*

❏ The speech was *transmitted "through a personal cell phone"* (i.e., *not* through a device *owned by the school*).

❏ The speech was directed "to an audience consisting of [B.L.'s] *private circle of Snapchat friends."*

In sum, Breyer said, although B.L.'s speech "risk[ed] transmission to the school itself," the above attributes of that speech *"diminish[ed]"* the school's *interest* in punishing B.L., according to the three broad features Breyer had previously articulated (summarized in Sub-par. (5) above).

(8) Application of law to facts – factors helping the school: Breyer then listed the factors that *cut in favor of the school district's interest* in regulating (and in this case, punishing) B.L. for her speech. Breyer broke the district's interests into three broad categories, and concluded that as to each category, the district's interest was *weaker* than the district claimed. Here were the categories:

[1] **"Teaching good manners":** First, the district claimed an interest "in *teaching good manners* and consequently in *punishing the use of vulgar language* aimed at part of the school community." But this interest was

"weakened considerably" by the fact that B.L. spoke *"outside the school on her own time,"* which meant that the school was not "stand[ing] in *loco parentis*."

Apart from the district's lack-of-*in-loco-parentis* status, the district's interest in "teaching good manners" was also weakened by the fact that the school presented *"no evidence of any general effort* to *prevent students from using vulgarity outside the classroom."*

[2] **"Preventing disruption":** Next, the school argued that it was "trying to *prevent disruption* ... within the bounds of a school-sponsored *extracurricular activity*." But Breyer concluded that the school had not produced any evidence of a *"substantial disruption"* of a school activity. The school had merely shown that discussion of B.L.'s post had taken "at most 5 to 10 minutes of an Algebra class for 'just a couple of days'," and that some members of the cheerleading team were "upset." But under *Tinker*, the school must show that "its action was caused by *something more than a mere desire to avoid the discomfort and unpleasantness* that always accompany an unpopular viewpoint"; the disturbance here did not meet this "demanding standard."

[3] **"Team morale":** Finally, the school claimed that it acted out of a *"concern for team morale."* But Breyer said that there was no evidence of any *"serious decline"* in team morale.

(9) Summary: In sum, Breyer concluded, B.L.'s post presented a situation in which the various interests that the school was pursuing when it punished that speech were *so weak* — especially in light of the off-campus nature of the post — that the school's action *violated* B.L.'s First Amendment rights. The school may have viewed B.L.'s post as "unworthy of ... robust First Amendment protections[.]" But, Breyer concluded, *"sometimes it is necessary to protect the superfluous in order to preserve the necessary."*

iv. **Dissent:** Only Justice Thomas refused to join Breyer's opinion. In a dissent, Thomas argued that at the time the First Amendment was made applicable to the states via the Fourteenth Amendment, it was "well settled" that schools could *"discipline students for off-campus speech or conduct that had a proximate tendency to harm the school environment."* The majority had failed to supply any "good constitutional reason" to depart from this "historical rule," he said.

C. **Furnishing of legal services by lay groups:** As part of their interest in regulating the *legal profession*, states have a strong interest in preventing any conduct which interferes with the relationship between a client and his attorney. One concern which many states have had is that people or organizations might *stir up litigation* in which they have no direct pecuniary interest, and might then exercise control over the handling of the law suit, control which should normally be solely in the hands of the lawyer and client. Most states would, for instance, prohibit the creation of a for-profit corporation whose purpose is to advertise to personal-injury victims the availability of contingent-fee representation, and to receive a commission, or "forwarding fee" from the lawyer to whom the corporation assigns a case; even under the modern

Court's relaxed view of lawyer advertising, such prohibitions would almost certainly be upheld.

1. **Rights and political expression:** However, these valid state interests may sometimes conflict with the interests of an organization in *furthering political goals* or obtaining economic benefits for its members, by notifying individuals of their legal rights, referring them to lawyers, or paying their legal bills. In general, where a *lay organization* (i.e., one not composed solely of lawyers) is able to make a respectable claim that it is engaged in *associational activities* when it gives such advice, referrals or funding, these freedom-of-association rights will *prevail* over the state interest in regulating the attorney-client relationship.

2. *NAACP v. Button:* The classic case demonstrating the strength of such associational interests is *NAACP v. Button*, 371 U.S. 415 (1963), in which the Supreme Court upheld the NAACP's right to refer to lawyers individuals who were willing to become plaintiffs in public school desegregation cases, and to pay these plaintiffs' litigation expenses.

    a. **Facts:** In *Button*, Virginia made it a crime for any organization to employ or compensate any attorney "in connection with any judicial proceeding in which [the organization] has no pecuniary right or liability." The state also forbade any organization to "control" or "exploit" the lawyer-client relationship, or to "intervene between client and lawyer." The Virginia NAACP brought about school desegregation cases by encouraging parents to become plaintiffs, by referring them to non-NAACP-staff lawyers, and by paying all litigation expenses. The Virginia courts held that these activities violated both the anti-control and anti-compensation rules.

    b. **Activities held protected:** But the Supreme Court held that the NAACP's activities were "modes of *expression* and *association* protected by the First and Fourteenth Amendments," and *could not be prohibited* under the state's power to regulate the legal profession. The Court reasoned that the litigation promoted by the NAACP was not a "technique of resolving private differences," but was rather a means for achieving equal treatment for blacks, and was thus a *"form of political expression."*

3. *Primus:* *Button* has been extended, to allow an *individual lawyer* to solicit clients as part of her *pro bono* work on behalf of the ACLU. See *In re Primus*, 436 U.S. 412 (1978) (discussed more extensively *supra*, p. 567).

D. **Government as speaker or as funder of speech:** So far, nearly everything we have said in this chapter concerns the role of government as the regulator of speech by non-government actors. But sometimes, *government itself wishes to speak*. And sometimes, government wishes to give *financial support* to certain speech by others. In these two contexts — government as speaker, and government as funder of speech — government seems to have at least somewhat greater ability to prefer one viewpoint over another than it does when it merely regulates. However, the law governing these two special contexts is far from settled.

1. **Government as speaker:** When government wishes to *be a speaker itself*, it is pretty clear that government may *say essentially what it wants*, and is not subject to any real rule of viewpoint neutrality. As the Court noted in *Pleasant Grove City v. Summum*, 555 U.S. 460 (2009) (discussed more fully *infra*, p. 603), "The Free Speech Clause restricts government regulation of private speech; *it does not regulate government speech.*"

a. No obligation to fund opposing viewpoints: Furthermore, when government — acting as a speaker — uses its own funds to deliver a particular message, government is *not thereby obligated to also fund other points of view* on the same topic.

Example: "When Congress established a National Endowment for Democracy to encourage other countries to adopt democratic principles, it was not constitutionally required to fund a program to *encourage competing lines of political philosophy* such as communism and fascism." *Rust v. Sullivan*, 500 U.S. 173 (1991) (also discussed *infra*, pp. 625-625).

2. **Government as funder of third-party speech:** But a much tougher question arises when government *funds speech by third parties*, who are essentially expressing their own beliefs rather than the government's. Here, may government be non-viewpoint-neutral, by funding only those viewpoints of which it approves? The answer is heavily dependent on the details of the government funding.

a. **Use of agents to deliver government's message:** Government *may* use content-based criteria when government is selecting third parties who will serve as the *government's agents* in *spreading the government's own message*. As the Court said in *Rosenberger v. University of Virginia*, 515 U.S. 819 (1995), "we have permitted the government to *regulate the content of what is or is not expressed* when it is the speaker or when it *enlists private entities to convey its own message.*"

Example: The federal government funds certain family-planning "projects" (essentially, clinics) that are operated by private parties. The program's regulations say that while a person (e.g., a doctor) is working in such a clinic, that person may not discuss the possibility of an abortion with a pregnant clinic patient.

Held, this limitation of private speech does not violate the First Amendment. *Rust v. Sullivan*, 500 U.S. 173 (1991). As the Court later summarized this aspect of *Rust* (in *Rosenburger, supra*), "the government did not create a program to encourage private speech but instead *used private speakers* to *transmit specific information pertaining to its own program*. We recognized that when the government appropriates public funds to *promote a particular policy* of its own it is *entitled to say what it wishes.*"

b. **No forbidding of some topics or messages for disfavor:** On the other hand, if government decides to *fund* (or allow on public property) *some expressions of private citizens' own views,* government must generally *behave not only in a content-neutral but also a subject-neutral way.* That is, government cannot (1) decide that it's going to subsidize or facilitate private messages on various topics, but then (2) decline to fund (or exclude from the discussion) a few *disfavored topics or messages*.[15]

i. **Religion:** For example, government cannot decide to fund a broad range of expressive activities and then exclude expressive activities that are *mainly religious.*

---

15. Note that here, we're not talking about the situation in which government selects agents to disseminate what the public will realize is government's *own* message (a topic we discussed *supra*); we're talking about the situation in which government gives funding to private speakers (or gives them access to public property, even non-public-forum public property, see Par. 6(b) *supra*, p. 537), and in effect decrees, "Say whatever you want, but you can't use this funding to deliver Message X or to speak on Subject X."

Example: Recall the facts of *Rosenberger* (*supra,* p. 538): The University of Virginia (a public university) funds certain student publications, by paying for their printing costs. The University disqualifies from this funding any primarily-religious publication.

Held, this exclusion violates the free speech rights of student religious organizations. If the University were disseminating only its own messages, it would not have to fund opposing viewpoints. But once it chooses to fund some ***third-party viewpoints*** (i.e., some student-run publications), it may not choose which ones to fund based on the viewpoint of the speaker. *Rosenberger v. University of Virginia*, 515 U.S. 819 (1995).

c. **Unconstitutional conditions:** Similarly, if government decides to award public funding for a privately-run program, the doctrine of ***"unconstitutional conditions"*** may prevent government from conditioning the funding on the recipient's agreement to give up its right to speak on certain topics, or requiring the recipient to deliver certain messages. The doctrine of unconstitutional conditions, especially as applied to free speech, is a quite confused area of the law, which we discuss in its own section *infra*, p. 623.

d. **Government as patron of excellence:** Suppose that government acts a ***"patron"*** by giving subsidies to a ***select number*** of speakers. In this context, it appears that the Court will ***not*** require government to remain rigidly viewpoint-neutral. In this type of "reward for excellence" situation, the government cannot be expected to fund every speaker, so it is entitled to some degree of discretion in what speakers, and messages, it wishes to fund.

Example: The National Endowment for the Arts gives various grants to artists of unusual merit. Congress requires the NEA, in deciding which artists should receive grants, to "tak[e] into consideration general standards of decency and respect for the diverse beliefs and values of the American public." The Ps (various artists) bring a facial challenge to this requirement that the standards be taken into account, arguing that it's inconsistent with *Rosenberger*'s holding that when a public university funds student publications, it cannot exclude those with religious content.

Held, the artists lose. *Rosenberger* is ***inapplicable***, and that NEA statute is ***constitutional*** on its face: "[Any] content-based considerations that may be taken into account in the grant-making process are a consequence of the ***nature of arts funding***. ... The 'very assumption' of the NEA is that grants will be awarded according to the 'artistic worth of competing applications,' and ***absolute neutrality is simply 'inconceivable.'***" (But the "decency" requirement here is very general, and the Ps aren't claiming that it's being used to discriminate against the Ps' particular viewpoints. "If the NEA were to leverage its power to award subsidies on the basis of subjective criteria into a penalty on disfavored viewpoints, then we would confront a different case.") *National Endowment for the Arts v. Finley*, 524 U.S. 569 (1998).

3. **The boundary between government-as-speaker and government-as-facilitator-or-funder-of-private-speech:** As we've just seen, government can behave in a non-content-neutral way when it is the ***speaker***, but generally ***not*** when it is the ***funder or facilitator of private citizens' speech***. But the boundary line between government speech and government-facilitated private speech can sometimes be blurry.

a. **Monuments and plaques (*Pleasant Grove v. Summum*):** One scenario in which it may be unclear whether the speech is by the government occurs when a message is *inscribed* on a piece of tangible property — a *monument or a plaque*, for example — by a private citizen who then *donates* the property to government and asks that it be permanently *displayed*. If government accepts and permanently displays the item, is government a speaker (making it free to reject other messages) or a facilitator of private-party speech (making it obliged to accept similar property expressing other views)?

As the result of a 2009 case, where government accepts and permanently displays the monument or plaque, government is likely to be found to be *acting as a speaker*, and thus is free to *reject other similar donations* of tangible items bearing messages that government does not agree with. See *Pleasant Grove City v. Summum*, 555 U.S. 460 (2009).

   i. **Facts:** Prior to the litigation, Pleasant Grove, Utah, had permanently placed in a local park 11 displays and monuments donated by private groups. One of these was a Ten Commandments monument donated in 1971. Members of the Summum religion then asked the city to accept and display in the same park a monument showing the "Seven Aphorisms," which Summum adherents believe were brought down from Mt. Sinai by Moses before he brought down the Ten Commandments. The proposed Summum monument was similar in size and nature to the Ten Commandments one.

   ii. **The Ps' argument:** The Summum members argued that when Pleasant Grove accepted and displayed the Ten Commandments and other monuments, the effect was to turn the park into a public forum, thereby requiring the city to accept other kinds of monuments and displays on a content-neutral basis.

   iii. **Held to be government speech:** But the Supreme Court held unanimously that the monument display was *government speech*, which therefore did not have to be content-neutral. Justice Alito's opinion said, "Although a park is a traditional public forum for *speeches and other transitory expressive acts*, display of a *permanent monument in a public park* is not a form of expression to which forum analysis applies. Instead, the placement of a permanent monument in a public park is best viewed as a *form of government speech* and is therefore *not subject to scrutiny under the Free Speech Clause*." So the city was permitted to reject the monument from the Summum congregants.

b. **Specialty license plates:** Another context in which reasonable people can differ about whether government is the speaker involves *state-issued specialty license plates*, which allow vehicle owners to pay the state extra to display certain pre-approved *slogans or images*. In the one Supreme Court case on the subject so far, the Court held by a 5-4 vote that the message on the plate was a *form of government speech*, thereby entitling the state to *reject messages it found offensive*. See *Walker v. Tex. Div., Sons of Confederate Veterans, Inc.*, 135 S.Ct. 2239 (2015).

   i. **Facts:** The Texas Department of Motor Vehicles Board gave organizations and individuals the chance to design a particular "specialty" license plate, by proposing a plate design containing a slogan, image or (most commonly) both. If the

Board accepted a proposed design, vehicle owners could pay extra to use the specialty plate.

(1) Proposed plate: The Texas Division of the Sons of Confederate Veterans ("SCV") proposed a specialty design displaying the *Confederate battle flag.*

(2) Rejected by Board: The Board *rejected* the proposed design, saying that public comments had shown that "many members of the general public find the design offensive ... [and] associate the confederate flag with organizations *advocating expressions of hate* directed toward people or groups [in a way] that is demeaning to those people or groups."

(3) Positions of the parties: SCV sued the Board, arguing that its rejection of the proposed plate *constituted viewpoint based regulation* in violation of SCV's First Amendment rights. The Board defended on the theory that the plate and its contents constituted *speech by the government,* a conclusion that if accepted would give the government wide latitude to reject messages it found offensive.

ii. **State wins by 5-4:** By a 5-4 vote, the Court found *in favor of the Board* — the specialty plates *constituted government speech*, entitling the government to reject messages it found offensive. The majority opinion, by Justice Breyer, reasoned that the factors relied on by the Court in *Pleasant Grove City v. Summum, supra,* showed that the plates here should be viewed as government speech just as the monuments displayed by government in *Summum* had been found to be government speech.

(1) Rationale: Breyer's opinion pointed to several factors — taken from the analysis in *Summum* — that he said caused the plates here to constitute government speech:

❏ First, the *"history of license plates"* shows that when the plates contain more than state names and vehicle identification numbers, the plates *"long have communicated messages from the States."*

❏ Second, Texas license plates are "often *closely identified in the public mind with the state."*

❏ Finally, Texas *"maintains direct control"* over the messages on its specialty plates, and carefully *reserves the right to approve each specialty plate design*, thereby allowing the state "to *choose how to present itself* and its constituency."

Taken together, these factors convinced the majority that the specialty plates here "are similar enough to the monuments in *Summum* to call for the same result" (that the plates, like the monuments, *were government speech*).

iii. **Dissenters:** Four justices dissented, in an opinion by Alito (joined by Roberts, Scalia and Kennedy).[16] Alito concluded that (1) the license plates were not government speech; and (2) SCV's core contention was correct: in enacting the specialty plate program, the state had *created a limited public forum*, and once it did so, it *could not discriminate based on viewpoint.*

(1) Alito's thought experiment: As to conclusion (1), Alito proposed a thought experiment: "Suppose you sat by the side of a Texas highway and studied the license plates on the vehicles passing by. You would see ... an impressive array of specialty plates [with] more than 350 varieties. ... You might see plates bearing the name of a high school, a fraternity or sorority, the Masons, the Knights of Columbus ... a favorite soft drink, a favorite burger restaurant, and a favorite NASCAR driver." He then asked, rhetorically, "As you sat there watching these plates speed by, **would you really think** that the sentiments reflected in these specialty plates are the **views of the State of Texas** and not those of the owners of the cars?"

(2) "Pure viewpoint discrimination": As to conclusion (2), Alito noted that the Board had rejected the plate design "because it concluded that many Texans would find the flag simply **offensive**." This was, he said, **"pure viewpoint discrimination."** And the Court's precedents, he said, made it clear that the government cannot practice viewpoint discrimination when it furnishes a limited public forum.

XI. THE FREEDOM OF ASSOCIATION, THE RIGHT NOT TO SPEAK OR ASSOCIATE, AND THE DENIAL OF PUBLIC JOBS OR BENEFITS

A. Freedom of association generally: The First Amendment does not explicitly mention the freedom of **association**. But in numerous cases, the Supreme Court has held that that freedom derives by **implication** from the explicitly-stated right of speech, press, assembly and petition.

1. **Limited scope:** However, the freedom of association has not been broadly construed by the Court. For instance, the Court has never held that any activity which an individual may lawfully do by himself, he is constitutionally entitled to do in concert with others. Rather, all that has been recognized is "a right to join with others to pursue goals **independently protected** by the First Amendment." Tribe, p. 1013. These goals include **political advocacy**, the pursuit of **unionization in the workplace, literary expression** and **religious worship**, among others.

   a. **No general right of "social association":** Since there is a special freedom of association only where the goals being pursued are independently protected by the First Amendment, there is no special freedom to engage in **"social association."** That is, a group of people do not have any specially-protected First Amendment right to gather together for social purposes such as dancing, partying, watching a sporting event, etc. These events are not primarily expressive events, so there is no special First Amendment right to **gather** for purposes of engaging in these events.

2. **Strict scrutiny:** Government is not absolutely forbidden to impair the freedom of association, just as it is not absolutely forbidden to interfere with freedom of speech. However, before the government may significantly interfere with protected associational activity,

---

16. Notice that Thomas, who customarily votes with the conservative bloc on the Court, joined the four-member liberal bloc on this case. Since he did not write a concurrence, it's not clear why he parted company with the conservatives this time.

two showings must be made: (1) that the governmental interest being pursued is a ***compelling*** one; and (2) that that interest cannot be achieved by means ***less restrictive*** of the freedom of association. In other words, ***strict scrutiny*** is normally applied. See *NAACP v. Alabama*, 357 U.S. 449 (1958) (discussed further *infra*, p. 616), holding that "[s]tate action which may have the effect of curtailing the freedom to associate is subject to the closest scrutiny."

    a. Anti-discrimination measures: One governmental interest that is often found to be compelling — as well as not achievable without restrictions on First Amendment freedoms — is the interest in ***preventing discrimination*** based on race, sex, or other suspect criterion. For instance, the Supreme Court has held that Minnesota could constitutionally require the Jaycees to admit women members, even though there might be some impairment of existing members' freedom of association or freedom of speech. ***Roberts v. United States Jaycees***, 468 U.S. 609 (1984).

        i. Rationale: Minnesota's desire to eliminate discrimination in "places of ***public accommodation***" (found as a factual matter to include quasi-commercial organizations like the Jaycees) was a compelling interest which the state was achieving through the least restrictive available means.

        ii. California Rotary case: Similarly, the Court has held that California was constitutionally empowered to force Rotary Clubs in that state to admit women, because "the relationship between Rotary Club members is not the kind of intimate or private relation that warrants constitutional protection." *Board of Directors of Rotary International v. Rotary Club of Duarte*, 481 U.S. 537 (1987).

B. Right not to associate, generally: The Court has also recognized, in effect, a right ***not*** to associate. That is, an individual has a general First Amendment right ***not to be compelled by the government to associate with, or support, the speech or expressive activities of persons or groups of which the individual does not approve.***

    1. Contexts where the right applies: There are several major contexts in which this "right not to associate" comes into play. Here's a preview of most of the ones we'll be examining:

        a. Right not to give financial support: A person has a free-association right not to be ***compelled to give financial support*** to an organization whose message the person disagrees with. Most significantly, this means that government may not require a ***public employee*** to join, or even ***pay dues to, a union that represents the employee*** in collective bargaining. See Paragraph (C) below, p. 607.

        b. Veto on unwanted participants and unwanted members: A group has a free-association right not be ***forced to accept a participant in an event*** if that person's participation would interfere with the group's expressive activities. See Paragraph (D) below, p. 609. Similarly, a group has a free-association right not to be forced to allow ***unwanted members*** into the group. See Paragraph (E) below, p. 610.

        c. Right not to have membership in group be illegal: A person has a free-association right not to have the government ***criminalize membership in the group.*** See Paragraph (F) below, p. 611.

d. Right to public jobs and benefits: A person may have a free-association right not to have a ***public-sector job,*** or a ***license or benefit issued by the government,*** be denied because of the person's associational activities. See Paragraph (G) below, p. 611.

e. Right to refuse to disclose organizational affiliation: A person may have a free-dom-of-association right not to be required to ***disclose her associational activities*** as a condition to receiving a government job or benefit. See Paragraph (H) below, p. 615.

C. Right to avoid compulsory financial support: An important aspect of the "right not to associate" is a person's right not to be compelled to ***give financial support to organizations or activities*** where the money will be used to ***disseminate messages with which the person disagrees.*** This right has played out most significantly in the context of laws ***forcing public employees to pay dues to a union*** that represents them. The Supreme Court has interpreted the right very broadly: as the result of the 5-4 decision in ***Janus v. AFSCME***, 138 S.Ct. 2448 (2018), government employees who choose not to join the union that represents them have a ***First Amendment right to refuse to contribute even one dollar towards the costs of collective bargaining.***

1. Payments toward cost of bargaining (*Janus*):   Pre-*Janus* law had held that it was not a violation of non-union-members' free-association rights to force them to contribute towards the costs of the collective bargaining function. But *Janus* changed this, by holding that where a government worker exercises her (First Amendment) right to decline to join the union that represents her, she also has a First Amendment right ***not to be required to pay any fee at all, even a fee that would be used solely to help cover the costs of collective bargaining.***

a. How issue arose: *Janus* involved an Illinois ***"agency shop" provision,*** which as we'll see allowed public-employee unions to charge non-union members for the costs of collective bargaining.

i. Pre-*Janus* agency-fee statutes: Prior to *Janus*, states were free to require, or not require, non-union-member government employees to pay their share of the cost of the union's bargaining-related activities. Twenty-two states, including Illinois, enacted such statutes, making them "agency shop" states. The rest passed "right to work" statutes, which prohibited deduction of agency fees from non-members without their consent. That was the state of play when the Court decided *Janus*.

ii. Janus' attack on the statute: Janus, the plaintiff in the case, worked for the Illinois Department of Healthcare and Family Services as a child support specialist; he had declined to join the union that represented most Illinois public employees (the American Federation of State, County, and Municipal Employees, "AFSCME"). Under the Illinois agency-shop statute, the union was allowed to charge Janus an "agency fee" (by having the fee withheld from his wages) covering the union's direct costs of fulfilling its collective-bargaining obligation; the union set these at about 78% of full union dues. Janus asserted in the litigation that in view of Illinois' "fiscal crisis," he opposed certain positions the union had been taking in collective bargaining. Therefore, he said, the non-member agency fees charged to him were ***"coerced political speech"*** in violation of his First Amendment rights. This was exactly the argument that had been foreclosed by the decision in *Abood*.

b.   **Majority agrees with plaintiff's argument:**   By a 5-4 vote, the Court *agreed with plaintiff Janus' argument.* Justice Alito, joined by the other conservative-leaning Justices (Roberts, Kennedy, Thomas and Gorsuch), said that even though the agency fees in theory related only to the union's collective-bargaining activities, the compulsory-fee arrangement *"violates the free speech rights of nonmembers* by *compelling them to subsidize private speech* on matters of substantial public concern[.]"* Therefore, the union could no longer have the agency fee deducted from a non-member's wages; only if the non-member affirmatively consented to pay would the union receive the fee.

    i.   **"Exacting scrutiny" test is chosen:**   To reach this result, Alito had to select a *standard* to be used in determining whether the agency-fee statute violated the First Amendment rights of non-union-members. He selected a standard the Court had used in other compulsory-speech contexts, one using *"exacting scrutiny."* [17] Under "exacting" scrutiny, he said, the compelled subsidy must "serve a *compelling state interest* that cannot be achieved through *means significantly less restrictive of associational freedoms."*

    ii.   **Test is flunked:**   Alito then quickly determined that for several reasons, the Illinois statute could not satisfy the exacting-scrutiny standard. For example, he said, even if the statute promoted the state's interest in combating "free riding," combating free riding was *not a "compelling"* state interest.[18]

c.   **Dissent:**   The four liberal members of the court dissented in *Janus.* The principal dissent, by Justice Kagan (joined by Breyer, Ginsburg and Sotomayor) said that the majority "overthrows a decision entrenched in this nation's law — and in its economic life — for over 40 years." The Court's opinion, she said, "prevents the American people, acting through their state and local officials, from making important choices about workplace governance. And it does so by *weaponizing the First Amendment,* in a way that unleashes judges, now and in the future, to intervene in economic and regulatory policy."

d.   **Significance:**   So as the result of *Janus,* even when a government-employee workplace is represented by a union, each non-union-member's right to avoid subsidizing other persons' speech means that *the union may not charge the non-member for any part of the cost of the union's bargaining activities.*

    i.   **Impact on unions:**   The decision is a big financial blow to the activities of public-employee unions. In fact, it's a big blow to union power in the U.S. generally, since a much higher percentage of public-sector employees are represented by unions than is the case in the private sector.

---

17. More precisely, Alito *applied* "exacting scrutiny" without deciding whether even this standard was sufficiently demanding. He cited a prior holding that, he said, "questioned whether [the exacting scrutiny] test *provides sufficient protection* for free speech rights"; he implied that *true "strict scrutiny"* might be required. But, he said, since the Illinois statute "cannot survive even under the more permissive [exacting scrutiny] standard," there was no need to "decide the issue of strict scrutiny."

18. Alito also suggested, without deciding, that the agency-dues provision here did not in fact combat free riding, at least when the provision was applied to Janus. He quoted, sympathetically, Janus' argument that "he is not a free rider on a bus headed for a destination that he wishes to reach but is more like a person *shanghaied for an unwanted voyage."*

D. Veto on unwanted participants: The "right not to associate" extends well beyond the right not to have to give financial support to groups or causes of which one disapproves. Another important aspect of the right is that a group has a First Amendment right *not to be forced to accept participants whose presence would interfere with the group's expressive activities.*

1. **Parade:** For instance, private parties who conduct a *parade* may exclude unwanted members — or at least unwanted messages — from the parade. Thus in *Hurley v. Irish-American Gay, Lesbian, and Bisexual Group of Boston*, 515 U.S. 557 (1995), the Court held unanimously that Massachusetts could not require a private group that conducts a St. Patrick's Day parade in Boston to include gay and lesbian marchers marching under their own banner.

   a. **Expressive conduct:** The "right not to associate" is closely related to the *"right not to speak,"* which the Court has also long recognized.[19] Thus in *Hurley*, the parade organizers were in fact willing to have gays and lesbians in the parade — the fight was about whether the gays should be allowed to march in their own unit *under their own banner*. The Court found that a parade inevitably has expressive content, and that gays marching under a banner would be sending a message (presumably a message supporting gay rights and gay lifestyles) that the parade organizers had a right to refuse to endorse. "It boils down to the choice of a speaker not to propound a particular point of view, and that choice is presumed to lie beyond the government's power to control," the Court said in *Hurley*.

2. **Must be perceived as group's own speech:** But the right of a group not to be forced to accept co-participants of whose message the group disapproves applies *only* where the *group's own "message" will be affected by the unwanted participation.* This principle is demonstrated by *Rumsfeld v. FAIR*, 547 U.S. 47 (2006), where the Court upheld the constitutionality of the "Solomon Amendment," under which Congress said that any university could receive certain federal funding only if all parts of the university, including its law school, gave the same on-campus access to military recruiters as to recruiters from other employers.

   a. **The claim:** A group of law schools argued in *FAIR* that since the military discriminates against gays, the Amendment unconstitutionally forced the schools to *support a message they abhorred*; the plaintiffs contended that by forcing the schools to serve as host for on-campus military recruiting, the Solomon Amendment infringed the schools' freedom not to associate with the military just as directly as the forced participation of gays in *Hurley* infringed the rights of the St. Patrick's Day parade organizers.

   b. **Argument rejected:** But the Court in *FAIR* *disagreed* with the plaintiffs' assertion that the two cases were the same. The compelled-speech cases like *Hurley* turned on the fact that "the *complaining speaker's own message was affected* by the speech it was forced to accommodate." Thus in *Hurley* itself, the parade was expressive, and a law forcing the inclusion of an unwanted group altered the expressive content of the parade. In *FAIR*, by contrast, "[A]ccommodating the military's message *does not affect the law schools' speech,* because *the schools are not speaking when they host interviews and recruiting receptions.* Unlike a parade organizer's choice of parade

---

19. For more about the "right not to speak," see *infra*, p. 621.

contingents, a law school's decision to allow recruiters on campus *is not inherently expressive* ... Nothing about recruiting suggests that law schools agree with any speech by recruiters, and nothing in the Solomon Amendment restricts what the law schools may say about the military's policies."

E. Right to exclude from membership in group: Just as the "right not to associate" means that a group may veto the participation of unwanted outsiders in the group's activities (see, e.g., *Hurley, supra*, p. 609), this right also means that an association has a First Amendment interest in *not being forced to accept unwanted members*.

> **Examples:** For instance, the rights of a Democratic club would probably be impaired if the government forced the club to admit registered Republicans as members. And the rights of NAACP members would be impaired if the organization were forced to admit, say, Nazi supremacists or Ku Klux Klanners.

1. Gays in the Boy Scouts: The most dramatic example of this "right to exclude from membership" branch of the right not to associate came in ***Boy Scouts of America v. Dale***, 530 U.S. 640 (2000), where the Court held that because opposition to homosexuality was part of the Scouts' "expressive message," the Scouts' freedom of association was violated by a state anti-discrimination law that barred the group from excluding gays as adult members.

a. Ouster upheld: By a 5-4 vote, the Court found for the Scouts. The majority, in an opinion by Justice Rehnquist, concluded that the Scouts had an "official position" that avowed homosexuals should not be Scout leaders, and that homosexual conduct was in the Scouts' view incompatible with the requirement that a Scout be "morally straight." Given this viewpoint, Rehnquist wrote, requiring that the Scouts keep Dale as an adult member would "at the very least, force the organization to ***send a message***, both to the youth members and the world, that the Boy Scouts ***accept homosexual conduct*** as a legitimate form of behavior." It didn't matter that the Scouts were not formed "for the purpose" of opposing homosexuality — as long as being forced to admit a practicing homosexual would ***impair the organization's message***, this was enough to trigger a strong First Amendment interest, one which the state's anti-discrimination interest could not overcome.

i. Strict scrutiny: Chief Justice Rehnquist didn't expressly say that he was using strict scrutiny. But he rejected the *O'Brien* content-neutral standard, which he characterized as an "intermediate standard of review," and he appears to have in fact used a variant of strict scrutiny.

b. Dissent: The four dissenters did not disagree with the general proposition that an organization cannot be forced to accept members whose presence would materially impair the group's message. But they disagreed about the application of this test here. As Justice Stevens' principal dissent put it, the Scouts had never — at least outside of various litigations — made a ***"clear, unequivocal statement"*** of opposition to homosexuality. And such a clear statement, in his view, was necessary before an organization could claim an infringement of its associational rights. All the Scouts had done was to "adopt[] an exclusionary membership policy" without any "shared goal of disapproving of homosexuality."

2. Compulsory membership won't necessarily interfere with expression: As *Boy Scouts* implies, the more ***central and unequivocal*** the organization's views on a particular matter, the ***greater the interference*** with associational rights will be if the organization is forced to accept a member with opposing views. Therefore, if a particular point of view is *not clearly articulated by the organization*, or *not especially central* to the organization's mission, compulsory membership by one with opposing views or conduct may *cause so little harm* that a countervailing governmental objective may outweigh the associational interest. And where that governmental interest is the possibly-compelling interest of reducing discrimination, the government is especially likely to prevail.

   a. **Illustration:** This is what happened, for instance, in *Roberts v. United States Jaycees*, *supra*, p. 606: the originally all-male membership of the Jaycees had a First Amendment interest in not being required to accept women as members, but the organization's no-women stance was (the Court found) *not very central* to the organization's purposes. Consequently, this relatively weak interest was outweighed by the state's compelling interest in banning discrimination in places of public accommodation, an interest which could not be fully achieved by narrower measures.

F. Illegal membership: Government may not make it *illegal* to *merely be* a *member of an association or group*. Membership in a group may only serve as an *element* of a criminal offense if the following *additional requirements* are satisfied:

   [1] the group is *actively engaged in unlawful activity*, or *incites* others to *imminent lawless action* (in such a way that the incitement is punishable as a "clear and present danger" under the modern *Brandenburg* test, *supra*, p. 495); and

   [2] the individual member *knows* of the group's illegal activities, and has the *specific intent* of furthering the group's illegal goals.

This series of requirements evolved through the case law on subversive advocacy and the "clear and present danger" text, a subject treated in detail *supra*, p. 489.

G. Denial of public job or benefit: The freedom of association may be unconstitutionally abridged if a *job in the public sector*, or a license or benefit issued by the government, is denied because of the applicant's associational activities. This possibility arises most commonly where a job or license is denied on the grounds of the applicant's membership in the *Communist Party* or other subversive group.

   1. No ban based solely on membership: A public job or other public benefit *may not be denied merely on the basis of the applicant's constitutionally-protected membership in a group or organization*.

   2. Subversive group: Therefore, unless an individual's group activities could be made *illegal*, those group activities cannot be grounds for denying him a job, license to practice law, or other public benefit.

   a. Same test as for outright ban: Thus the test applied in the public-job-or-benefits context is the same as the two-part test used connection with the *outright outlawing* of subversive group activity (see *supra*, Par. (D)).

   Example: A state statute provides for the discharge of any public employee who knowingly becomes a member of the Communist Party or of any party whose purposes include overthrow of the state government, if the employee has knowledge of this unlawful purpose. *Held*, the statute violates the First Amendment, because it does not also require that the employee have the "specific intent" to further the organization's illegal aims. *Elfbrandt v. Russell*, 384 U.S. 11 (1966).

3. **Patronage hirings and dismissals:**   The use of *political patronage* presents special free association problems: when a person or party who controls public-sector jobs gives those jobs out as a means of rewarding faithful party workers, applicants without political connections can plausibly claim that they have been discriminated against based on their political affiliation (or lack of one).

   a. **Rule for ordinary jobs:** In general, the Supreme Court has *agreed* with such claims, at least in the usual case where effective performance of the job does not depend on political affiliation. The rule is that in making *hiring, promotion and dismissal* decisions concerning such ordinary jobs, party affiliation may *not* be a factor. *Rutan v. Republican Party of Illinois*, 497 U.S. 62 (1990).

      i. **Massive patronage rejected:**   The facts of *Rutan, supra*, show the kind of patronage scheme that will *not* be allowed. Plaintiffs alleged that the Republican governor of Illinois prohibited any hiring, firing or promotions for any state office except on his "express permission," and that only those who had voted for or supported the Republican party in past years were favored. The Court held that these employment practices, if proven, violated the First Amendment free association rights of those not given special treatment.

   b. **Inherently political posts:**   On the other hand, some government posts are by their nature so bound up with party affiliation — so *inherently "political"* — that the "wrong" party affiliation can get in the way of effective job performance. In that scenario, party affiliation *may* be considered in hiring and firing. For instance, "Democrats have no right to consideration on equal terms with Republicans when the newly elected Republican government of a state is choosing a speech writer or a high-level special assistant." Tribe, p. 1018.

      i. **"Effective performance" test:** The test is "whether the hiring authority can demonstrate that party affiliation is an *appropriate requirement* for the *effective performance* of the public office involved." *Branti v. Finkel*, 445 U.S. 507 (1980).

         (1) **Assistant public defender:**   The one Supreme Court case deciding whether party affiliation was appropriately required for effective job performance is *Branti, supra*. There, the Court held that two Republican *assistant public defenders* could *not* be discharged on party-affiliation grounds when a Democrat was named to head the public defender's office. The majority reasoned that a rank-and-file public defender's *effectiveness* depends on how he handles his client's needs, not on any partisan political interests.

4. **Loyalty oaths:**   Normally, denial of a job or license based on associational activities does not occur as the result of extensive investigation by the government. Rather, such denials have generally occurred where the applicant or employee is required to take an *oath* that he has not belonged to certain types of organizations, or engaged in other activities, and he is unwilling or unable to take such an oath.

   a. **Rule:**   In general, the rule regarding such *"loyalty oaths"* is that one may not be required to state that one has not performed a certain act, or that one will not perform it in the future, unless actual *performance* of that act would be grounds for discharge. That is, the permissible scope of such oaths is co-extensive with the scope of grounds for *non-hiring or discharge.* See *Cole v. Richardson*, 405 U.S. 676 (1972).

i.   **Illustration:**   For instance, recall that a person may not be discharged for membership in an organization advocating overthrow of the government, unless she had *knowledge* of the organization's purpose and *specific intent* to further that purpose. Consequently, a person may also not be required to swear a blanket oath that she has never been a member of an organization advocating such overthrow — language referring to the affiant's knowledge of the illegal purposes, and to her specific intent to further them, must be inserted into the oath itself.

5.   **Speech critical of superiors:**   Thus far, we have examined the denial of public jobs and benefits for *associational* activities. Similar issues arise when the government attempts to deny a public job or benefit because of a person's *speech*-related activities. For instance, under what circumstances may a government employee be fired for *criticizing his superiors?*

a.   **"Public concern" as key factor:**   The key issue is whether the speech involves a matter of *"public concern."* Governmental attempts to fire or otherwise penalize its employees for speech on matters of "public concern" will be *strictly scrutinized*, but speech on matters that are *not* within this category will receive substantially less protection. ***Connick v. Myers***, 461 U.S. 138 (1983).

i.   **Public concern:**   Where speech involves a matter of *"public concern,"* the Court held in *Connick*, the judiciary must carefully examine the justification given by the state for penalizing the speech, and must strike a *balance* between the free speech rights of the employee and the "interest of the State, as an employer, in promoting the efficiency of the public services it performs[.]"[20]

ii.   **Matters not of "public concern":**   By contrast, where the matters discussed by the employee are *not* ones of public concern, the court should give "a wide degree of *deference* to the *employer's judgment.*" The employer's interest in, for instance, avoiding "the *disruption of the office* and the *destruction of working relationships*" should be *weighed heavily*.

> **Example:** P is an assistant D.A. After learning that she has received an unwanted transfer to a new post within the D.A.'s office, she gives her coworkers a questionnaire soliciting their views on a number of matters concerning the office, including whether they have "confidence in" particular superiors, and whether they ever "feel pressured to work in political campaigns on behalf of office supported candidates." The D.A., upon learning of the questionnaire, views it as an act of insubordination, and fires P for both the questionnaire and for refusing to accept the transfer.
>
> *Held* (5-4), P's firing is sustained. The D.A. reasonably believed that P's actions would "disrupt the office, undermine his authority and destroy close working relationships." Since the questionnaire as a whole touched only slightly on matters of "public concern," the D.A.'s judgment is entitled to great deference. (But if matters of public interest been been more plainly implicated in the questionnaire, less deference would be due the D.A.'s judg-

---

20. But there's a major exception to this rule of *Connick*: under *Garcetti v. Ceballos*, discussed *infra*, p. 614, if the speech occurs "pursuant to the employee's *official duties*," it *doesn't* get this significant protection, even if it involves a matter of public concern.

ment, and a much stronger showing of danger to the efficiency of the office would be required to sustain the firing.) *Connick, supra.*

    iii. **Expansive reading to "public concern":** The Court has sometimes given a surprisingly broad reading to the definition of "public concern," the key definition used by *Connick* for determining whether a public employer can fire an employee for speech-related reasons.

> **Example:** P is a 19-year-old black clerical employee in the office of D (the County Constable). When P hears of John Hinckley's attempted assassination of President Reagan, P says (in the office) to a co-worker who happens to be her boyfriend, "If they go for him again, I hope they get him." The remark is overheard by another co-worker, who informs D about it; D fires P.
>
> *Held* (by 5-4 vote), P's dismissal violated her First Amendment rights. P's comment was on a matter of "public concern," thus satisfying the first prong of the *Connick* test. Taken in the context in which it was made, the remark was essentially a commentary on the President's policies and the attempted assassination, both of which were matters of public concern. Since the statement touched on a matter of public concern, the dismissal could only be upheld if the State bore the burden of justifying the discharge on legitimate grounds. Any justification had to take into account the context in which the statement was made, including "time, place and manner." Here, P had no policy-making or law-enforcement responsibilities and her statement had no discernible impact on the functioning of the Constable's office, so the State failed to justify the dismissal. *Rankin v. McPherson,* 483 U.S. 378 (1987).

  b. **Need not have "property" interest:** Observe that in the "speech critical of superiors" cases (*Connick,* for instance), the employee has a qualified right not to be fired for First Amendment activity even if she has no *"property"* interest in the job. This is very different from the rule in cases brought under the Due Process Clause (see *supra,* p. 222), under which the employee has no right to due process before being fired unless she is found to have had a property interest in the job.

  c. **Speech must not occur as part of job responsibilities:** There's a very important exception to the *Connick* rule. In order for speech on matters of public concern to get the protection of *Connick,* the speech *must not be made "pursuant to the employee's official duties."* So speech on matters of public concern made in furtherance of the public employee's *job functions* receives *less First Amendment protection* than speech the employee makes as a "citizen" acting outside of his job. The Court announced this principle in *Garcetti v. Ceballos,* 547 U.S. 410 (2006).

    i. **Facts:** The plaintiff in *Garcetti* was a supervising lawyer in the L.A. County District Attorney's Office. P was called on to investigate whether an affidavit prepared by a deputy sheriff to obtain a search warrant was properly done. After his investigation, P wrote a memo to his supervisor concluding that the affidavit had been improperly done, and recommending dismissal of the criminal case premised upon it. This memo precipitated a chain of events at the end of which P claimed, his superior retaliated against him for writing the memo. The D.A.'s office retorted that P's act of writing the memo was not entitled to First Amendment protection because the memo was created as part of P's job responsibilities.

ii. **Court agrees:** By a 5-4 vote, the Court agreed with the D.A.'s position: "[W]hen public employees make statements *pursuant to their official duties,* the employees are *not speaking as citizens* for First Amendment purposes, and *the Constitution does not insulate their communications from employer discipline."* Here, because P's investigation and the ensuing memorandum were part of his job responsibilities, the employer had the right to regulate the content and manner of P's speech.

(1) Rationale: The majority reasoned that "employers have heightened interests in *controlling speech made by an employee in his or her professional capacity* ... Supervisors must ensure that their employees' official communications are accurate, demonstrate sound judgment, and *promote the employer's mission."*

iii. **Dissent:** The four dissenters conceded that the majority was correct to recognize a government employer's important interest in ensuring that employees who speak for it while doing their work have competence, honesty and good judgment. But the dissenters, led by Justice Souter, would nonetheless apply a *Connick*-style *balancing* when on-the-job speech implicates matters of public concern — they thought that the government's interest in job performance could sometimes be *outweighed* by the employee's interest in speaking (and the public's interest in hearing the speech) on matters of public concern. For Souter, such a balancing was appropriate, for instance, "when a public auditor speaks on his discovery of embezzlement of public funds, when a building inspector makes an obligatory report of an attempt to bribe him, or when a law enforcement officer expressly balks at his superior's order to violate constitutional rights he is sworn to protect."

6. **Imposition of burdens:** So far, we have talked about the award by the government of *benefits* (e.g., public-sector jobs). But a similar rule applies where the government metes out *burdens*. That is, the government may not use as a basis for selecting which individuals are to be burdened the individuals' exercise of constitutionally-protected rights (or any other constitutionally-illicit criterion, e.g., race). This is true even if the government would otherwise have the right to place that burden upon the individuals in question. For instance, "there are First Amendment problems if only Democrats, or only critics of government, or only Socialists, are selected for *income tax audit*." Gunther, 1985 Supp., p. 66. The same is true of any other government prosecution or penalty.

H. **Compulsory disclosure (*Americans for Prosperity v. Bonta*):** Sometimes, interference with associational freedoms will be alleged where the government requires a group, such as a charity or a political party, to *disclose who its members or contributors are*. The group might be required to make the disclosure *to the government* (with or without government's promising to keep the contents *secret*); or, the group might be required to make a *public filing* of the information. In either scenario, a 2021 case establishes that such a government-mandated disclosure requirement will be subjected to *"exacting scrutiny,"* essentially a form of *intermediate-level review*.[21] This exacting-scrutiny standard requires that the type of disclosure being compelled must be at least *"narrowly tailored* to the government's asserted interest," though

---

21. See *supra*, pp. 320 and 572 for examples of intermediate-level review in other contexts.

not necessarily the "*least restrictive means* of achieving that end." ***Americans for Prosperity Foundation v. Bonta***, 141 S.Ct. 2373 (July 1, 2021).

1. **Earlier case of *NAACP v. Alabama*:**   Before we get to the *Americans for Prosperity* case, we need to review an earlier case, the first modern-era case in which the Supreme Court recognized that when government compels a group to disclose its members, this mandatory disclosure might violate the members' First Amendment freedom of association. That case was ***NAACP v. Alabama ex rel. Patterson***, 357 U.S. 449 (1958), a case arising from the Civil Rights struggle in the south.

   a. **Facts of *NAACP*:** Here's a brief summary of the facts of the *NAACP* case, as recounted in the majority's later opinion in *Americans for Prosperity*. The NAACP opened an Alabama office that supported desegregation in higher education and public transportation. NAACP members were then threatened with economic reprisals and violence. As part of the state's efforts to drive the organization out of the state, the Alabama Attorney General demanded that the group ***turn over its membership lists.***

   b. **Holding:** The Supreme Court held that such compulsory disclosure ***violated*** the group's members' freedom of association. As the *Americans for Prosperity* opinion summarized the holding in *NAACP*, "[b]ecause NAACP members faced a risk of reprisals if their affiliation with the organization became known — and because Alabama had demonstrated no offsetting interest 'sufficient to justify the deterrent effect' of disclosure, . . . the State's demand violated the First Amendment."

      i. **No standard of review announced:** The *NAACP* opinion did not specify ***what standard of review*** should be used for determining whether Alabama's disclosure scheme violated the plaintiff's' First Amendment rights. (At the time, in 1958, the Supreme Court had not yet even articulated either "strict scrutiny" or "intermediate review" as possible standards for reviewing First Amendment or other constitutional challenges.)

2. **Facts of *Americans for Prosperity*:** Returning now to the *Americans for Prosperity* case, California required any tax-exempt charity that solicited contributions in that state to file copies of the charity's "Form 990" with the state's Attorney General. The Form 990 is a form every charity is required to file annually with the federal Internal Revenue Service (IRS); the form requires the charity to list the names and addresses of any donor who contributed more than $5,000 in the relevant year. California was thus requiring every charity soliciting contributions in the state to tell the state the ***names and addresses of every major donor.*** The state promised to keep the information ***confidential***; however, prior to the suit, the Attorney General office had inadvertently posted at least 2,000 Form 990s to the Department's website, thus making their contents public.

   a. **The state's interest:** In California, one of the jobs of the Attorney General's office is to ***supervise charitable fundraising.*** The Attorney General defended the Form 990 disclosure requirement as a means of furthering the state's interest in ***preventing "charitable fraud and self-dealing."***

      i. **Efficiency argument:** Even had there been no automatic "up-front" disclosure scheme, the Attorney General would have been free to subpoena the Form 990 from any particular charity the A.G. wanted to investigate. But, the state said, collecting all Form 990s up-front ***improved the efficiency*** of the Office's regulatory efforts.

b. Two plaintiffs bring suit: The disclosure requirement was attacked in separate suits brought by two charities (the "Ps") associated with conservative causes. The Ps argued that by requiring them to file their Form 990s, the state was violating each charity's (and the charity's donors') First Amendment freedom of association. In part because of the inadvertent leaks of Form 990s mentioned above, the Ps argued, the disclosure scheme and related leakage risks made it ***harder for them to fund-raise***, by subjecting their donors to the risk of reprisals and harassment from the public.

    i. Facial attack: An important aspect of the Ps' suit was the Ps' claim that the disclosure requirement was not only a violation of freedom-of-association "as applied" to each P and its donors, but was also ***invalid "on its face,"*** i.e., that it could not constitutionally be applied to *any* charity.[22]

3. The holding: By a 6-3 vote, the ***Ps prevailed*** in the Supreme Court. The Court (a) subjected the California disclosure scheme to ***"exacting scrutiny,"*** then (b) concluded that the scheme ***could not survive that scrutiny***, and (c) determined that the scheme was in fact ***invalid on its face.*** The Court's opinion was by Chief Justice Roberts.

    a. Relevance of *NAACP*: Roberts began by explaining the importance of a group's interest in maintaining the ***privacy of its members' identities.*** He quoted from the *NAACP* opinion, *supra*: ***"privacy in group association*** may ... be indispensable to preservation of freedom of association, particularly where a group ***espouses dissident beliefs."***

    b. "Exacting scrutiny" as the standard: Roberts then noted that after *NAACP*, the Court had concluded that the appropriate standard of review for compulsory-disclosure schemes is the *"exacting scrutiny" standard.*

        i. More about the "exacting scrutiny" standard: Under the exacting scrutiny standard, Roberts said, there must be "a ***substantial relation*** between the disclosure requirement and a ***sufficiently important governmental interest***." And, he continued, "To withstand this scrutiny, the strength of the governmental interest must ***reflect the seriousness of the actual burden*** on First Amendment rights."

        ii. The means-end fit: Roberts then discussed ***how tight the means-end fit*** — the fit between the disclosures required by the government and the important governmental interest(s) being pursued — must be in order to satisfy the exacting-scrutiny standard. The government, he said, does ***not*** need to choose the ***"least restrictive means"*** of achieving the relevant interest. But, he continued, the means must be ***"narrowly tailored"*** to the achievement that asserted interest.

    c. Applying the "important interest" requirement: Roberts then turned to ***applying*** the exacting-scrutiny standard to the actual California disclosure regime at issue. As to the "sufficiently important governmental interest" prong — i.e. the "end" being sought by government — Roberts quickly conceded that California's interest in "preventing wrongdoing by charitable organizations" was indeed *"sufficiently important."*

    d. Applying the "narrowly-tailored" requirement: Roberts then applied the other prong of exacting scrutiny — that the means chosen must be *"narrowly tailored"* to

---

22. For the distinction between "as applied" challenges to the constitutionality of a government action and "facial" challenges, see *supra*, p. 499.

the governmental interest which that means promotes. As in most constitutional challenges triggering either intermediate-review or strict scrutiny, the *"tightness of fit"* between the end and the means was where the problem lay. Here, Roberts said, there was a *"dramatic mismatch"* between the A.G.'s interest in combating fraud and the broad disclosure regime he implemented.

i.   **No instances:** For starters, the A.G. had not been able to point to even a *"single, concrete instance"* in which the collection of a Form 990 had done anything to "advance the Attorney General's investigative, regulatory or enforcement efforts."

ii. **Need for universal production:** Furthermore, Roberts said, even if the A.G. *had* actually relied on up-front collection in some cases, that modest reliance would fall "far short" of the means-end fit required by the exacting-scrutiny standard. This prong required the state to show that "universal production" was needed *"in light of any less intrusive alternatives."*

(1) **Subpoenas as an alternative:** The A.G. had argued that alternative means of obtaining the Form 990s — such as *subpoenas* or *letters announcing an audit* — were less efficient than up-front collection. But, Roberts said, the record showed that the A.G. had never even *"considered"* these alternatives to universal up-front collection, weakening the A.G.'s claim that this was not a viable less-intrusive alternative.

(2) **"Administrative efficient not a sufficient goal:** Roberts concluded that the main interest that California was pursuing by its universal up-front disclosure regime was not investigating fraud but rather, achieving *"ease of administration."* However, he said, the highly burdensome up-front disclosure system was *not narrowly-tailored* towards achieving this relatively weak state interest in "mere administrative convenience."

e. **Scheme is "facially invalid":** Roberts then turned to the issue that may well prove to be the most far-reaching aspect of the decision: whether the disclosure regime was *"invalid on its face."* So far, we've seen how his majority opinion decided that the disclosure scheme here violated the freedom-of-association rights of the two particular plaintiff charities who brought the suit (making this at least a successful "as applied" challenge). But should the majority conclude that the scheme also violated the free-association rights of most or all charities *not presently before the court?* If so, the Court could find that the scheme was "facially invalid," i.e., that it could not constitutionally be enforced against *any* charity.

i. **The test:** Roberts noted that it's easier for the plaintiff to succeed with a "facial challenge" in First Amendment cases than in cases involving other parts of the Constitution. Outside of the First Amendment area, a plaintiff bringing a facial challenge has to show either that (a) "no set of circumstances exists under which the [law] would be valid"; or (b) the law lacks a "plainly legitimate sweep."[23] But where a challenge is based on the First Amendment, there is a separate, easier-to-satisfy standard for establishing that a law is facially invalid: "a law may be inval-

---

23. For more about facial challenges, see *supra*, p. 244.

idated as *overbroad*[24] if a *substantial number* of its applications are unconstitutional, judged in relation to the statute's *plainly legitimate sweep.* "

    ii. Statute flunks the test: Roberts said he had "no trouble" concluding that by this test, California's disclosure scheme *was overbroad*: "The *lack of tailoring* to the State's *investigative goals* is categorical — *present in every case* — as is the *weakness* of the State's interest in *administrative convenience.*" It *didn't matter* that the plaintiffs had not shown that a substantial number of charities would be *subjected to harassment and reprisals* — if the statute had *satisfied exacting scrutiny* (by being narrowly tailored to the achievement of an important governmental interest), then it *would* have been appropriate for the Court to grant only as-applied treatment, rather than facial-invalidation.

    But where, as here, a disclosure scheme does *not* survive exacting scrutiny, then *even the theoretical risk of a chilling effect is enough* to make the scheme facially invalid. "When it comes to the freedom of association, the protections of the First Amendment are *triggered not only by actual restrictions* on an individual's ability to join with others. ... The *risk of a chilling effect on association is enough* [for facial invalidity], '[b]ecause First Amendment freedoms *need breathing space to survive.*' "

4. The dissent: Justice Sotomayor — joined by Breyer and Kagan — *dissented* in *Americans for Prosperity*.

    a. Actual burden must be shown by Ps: Sotomayor agreed with Roberts that publicizing individuals' associations with a particular group might chill the group's and its members' freedom of association by exposing them to harassment and reprisals. But in the Court's prior decisions, what had always mattered were the risks that *"actually result[ed] from disclosure"*; only after the plaintiffs showed an *actual burden* had the Court then required means-end tailoring, and the level of that tailoring was proportional to that particular burden. But now, she said, the Court had abandoned that established approach, by "holding that narrow tailoring applies to disclosure requirements *across the board,* even if there is *no evidence that they burden anyone at all."*

    i. No need for exacting scrutiny: Sotomayor sharply disagreed with this approach. The plaintiffs here had not produced *any* "evidence of tangible burdens" at all. Therefore, there was no need for the Court to perform any exacting scrutiny.

    b. Tailor the level of scrutiny to the degree of burden: Similarly, Sotomayor contended, in heightened-scrutiny cases the Court had always *adjusted* the required tightness of means-end fit in order to match the *magnitude of the burden* the government was placing on the group's freedom of association. Now, the majority was unwisely shifting from this "nuanced approach" to a *"one size fits all"* test — no matter whether the burdens the government was placing on associational rights were slight, heavy, or nonexistent, the Court was requiring that the disclosure regime *always be narrowly tailored.* This created a significant risk that disclosure requirements that should be constitutional would be struck down, Sotomayor said.

---

24. When a law attacked on First Amendment grounds is found to be "overbroad," that overbreadth is a form of facial invalidity; consequently, the overbroad law may not be enforced against *anyone*, even persons who were not part of the plaintiff group when the suit against the statute was brought. See *supra*, p. 498.

    c. Overbreadth: Finally, Sotomayor was especially critical of the majority's conclusion that the disclosure scheme was *"facially invalid"* — and thus could not be enforced against *any* charity — rather than merely invalid "as applied" to the two charities who had brought the suit. She conceded that facial attacks are (and should be) easier to win in the First Amendment area than in other contexts, because of the risk that imprecisely-drawn regulations will have a broad chilling effect on speech or association.

    But even in the First Amendment area, she said, the Court had never allowed a facial attack to succeed unless the regulation was shown to be unconstitutional in a *"substantial number of … applications* … judged *in relation to* the statute's *plainly legitimate sweep."* Here, given the desire of many charitable donors to have their donations publicized, the plaintiffs had "fail[ed] to show that a substantial proportion of those affected would prefer anonymity, much less that they are objectively burdened by the loss of it."

    d. "Marked with a bull's-eye": In sum, Sotomayor said, the Court had *"mark[ed] reporting and disclosure requirements with a bull's-eye."*

5. **Possible extensions to other disclosure regimes:** The logic of *Americans for Prosperity* seems to render unconstitutional a *wide variety of state and federal disclosure requirements,* not just in the area of charitable donations but also in the domain of *campaign finance.*

    a. IRS charitable disclosure requirements: For instance, recall that the requirement struck down in *Americans for Prosperity* was that each non-profit file with the state the non-profit's IRS Form 990, listing each significant donor's identity and the amount they contributed. The Court's logic almost certainly *applies equally* to the *filings required by the IRS itself*: the long-established requirement that non-profits file the Form 990 with the IRS seems now to be facially invalid (and thus unconstitutional) as to *all nonprofits and their donors,* even where there is no evidence that any donor's willingness to contribute to any charity has been *actually chilled* by that filing requirement. See Chemerinsky, *"Supreme Court Opens Door for Dark Money…,"* Sacramento Bee, Aug. 4, 2021.

    b. Campaign-finance disclosure laws: Beyond the charitable-donation area, *Americans for Prosperity* also seems to cast into serious doubt every state and federal law requiring *campaign-finance disclosure.* As one observer writes, "Any *candidate or political party* can claim that having to reveal its donors will chill association," and the case makes it "clear that no proof of actual harm is required." Chemerinsky, *op. cit.* Therefore, unless the state or federal government can carry the hard-to-satisfy burden of showing that its disclosure requirement is "narrowly tailored" to the government's interest in, say, combating the buying of elections, the disclosure scheme will apparently be struck down as to *all candidates and all donors.*

I. **The bar membership cases:** Cases on qualifications for *admission to the bar* are a kind of hybrid, raising problems both as to the grounds for denial of publicly-conferred benefits (the license to practice) as well as issues of the scope of required disclosure. Most of the bar cases have involved state qualification procedures designed to deal with *subversive* activities. Here's what seems to be the present state of affairs about bar-admission inquiries:

1. **No disqualification:** The state cannot ask the candidate a question whose *sole function* is to determine whether the candidate has been a knowing member of an organization which advocates forcible overthrow of the government. Thus *knowing membership* in such an organization, without more, *can't be the basis* for denying admission. *Baird v. State Bar of Arizona*, 401 U.S. 1 (1971).

2. **Screening device:** However, the state *can* use a *two-part question*, where the first part acts merely as a *screening device.* Thus the state can ask the initial question, "Have you ever been a member of an organization which advocates forcible overthrow of the government, while knowing that that was the organization's aim?" Then, if the answer is "yes," the state can ask the follow-up question, "Do you *support* this aim?" An affirmative answer to this second question (or a refusal to answer it) can apparently then be grounds for denying bar admission. *Law Students Research Council v. Wadmond*, 401 U.S. 154 (1971).

J. **The "right not to speak":** In discussing the *Hurley* case, *supra*, p. 609, I noted that the "right not to associate" is closely related to the *"right not to speak."* Let's talk now in more detail about this right not to speak. The Court has long held that part of a person's freedom of expression is the *right not to be forced* by the government to *express a message* that the person does not wish to express.

1. **Pledge of allegiance:** In an early case, the Court held that a state law requiring all public school students to *salute and pledge allegiance to the U.S. flag* violates their freedom of expression. *West Virginia State Board of Educ. v. Barnette*, 319 U.S. 624 (1943). In *Barnette*, the Court noted that the pledge and salute "require[] *affirmation of a belief and an attitude of mind*[.]" Were the Court to uphold the compulsory pledge and salute, "we [would be] required to say that a Bill of Rights which guards the individual's right to speak his own mind [leaves] it open to public authorities to *compel him* to *utter what is not in his mind,*" something the Court refused to do.

2. **"Live free or die" on license:** Similarly, the Court held that New Hampshire could not criminally punish vehicle owners who covered up the *state motto "Live Free or Die"* on their state-issued *license plates,* if the motto was at odds with the owner's moral or religious beliefs. See *Wooley v. Maynard*, 430 U.S. 705 (1977): "[W]here the State's interest is to *disseminate an ideology,* ... such interest cannot outweigh an individual's First Amendment right to *avoid becoming the courier* for such message."

3. **Required notices in "crisis pregnancy centers":** A business operator's "right not to speak" has even been extended to include the right not to be required to *post government-drafted notices* that deliver a disclosure message with whose content the operator disagrees. In a 2018 case, the Court held that California violated the free-speech rights of *"crisis pregnancy centers"* when the state passed a law requiring that such centers post a notice informing patients of the availability of public family-planning services *including abortions*. The case was *National Institute of Family and Life Advocates v. Becerra*, 138 S.Ct. 2316 (2018).

   a. **The statute:** California enacted the California Reproductive Freedom, Accountability, Comprehensive Care, and Transparency Act ("FACT" Act), which required clinics that primarily serve pregnant women to provide certain *state-specified notices.* Of greatest interest to us on the compelled-speech issue is the Act's requirement that licensed clinics post a notice (1) telling women that *the state provides free or low-cost* *family-planning services, including abortions,* and (2) supplying a phone number to call.

b. **Attack on the statute:** A group of "crisis pregnancy centers" — pro-life organizations that offer services to pregnant women, and that the state said "aim to discourage and prevent women from seeking abortions" — claimed that the notice requirement violated their free-speech rights by requiring them to deliver a state-sponsored message with which they disagreed. The plaintiffs sought a preliminary injunction against the notice requirement, which the lower courts denied.

c. **Court agrees with plaintiffs:** By a *5-4 vote,* the Supreme Court *agreed* that the *plaintiffs were likely to succeed* on the merits of their free-speech claim, and therefore granted them an injunction against the notice requirement pending further proceedings in the lower court. The Court divided under familiar ideological lines, with the conservatives (including Justice Kennedy as the deciding fifth vote) upholding the free-speech claim, and the four liberals dissenting. The majority opinion was by Justice Thomas.

  i. **No special rule for "professional speech":** The lower courts had held that the clinics were engaged in *"professional speech,"* and that the standard for reviewing government regulation of such speech should therefore be *less stringent* than for ordinary speech. But Thomas rejected this view: except in a few special circumstances not at issue here, the standards for reviewing government restrictions on speech, he said, are *the same where the speech is "professional" as when it is not.*

  ii. **Strict scrutiny:** Thomas wrote that the notice the licensed clinics were required to post was a *"content-based regulation of speech."* The state was requiring clinics to "provide a *government-drafted script* about the availability of state-sponsored services[.]" "By compelling individuals to *speak a particular message,"* Thomas said, the state *"alter[s] the content of [their] speech[.]"* Thomas suggested, though he did not explicitly hold, that in view of his finding that professional speech should not be any easier for government to regulate in a content-based way than other speech, the appropriate standard of review should be strict scrutiny.

  iii. **Can't survive even intermediate-level review:** But Thomas saw no need to apply strict scrutiny here because, he said, the notice requirement "cannot survive *even intermediate scrutiny."* He didn't expressly recite what intermediate scrutiny would involve in this context, but he seemed to be saying that this level of view requires a showing that the means chosen by the state was *closely drawn to achieve a substantial state interest.*

  iv. **Application of standard:** The only interest the state had asserted here, Thomas said, was the interest in "providing low-income women with *information about state-sponsored services[.]"* And even if that was a substantial interest, the notice required here was *"not sufficiently drawn* to achieve" that interest, because the notice requirement was "wildly *underinclusive,"* in that it *exempted many similar types of clinics* from a similar requirement.

  v. **Remanded:** The majority in *National Institute* did not conclusively find that the notice requirement was unconstitutional — the Court merely found that the plaintiffs would likely win on the merits, and therefore granted an injunction against enforcement of the notice while the case was fully litigated below.

d. Dissent: Justice Breyer (joined by Ginsburg, Sotomayor and Kagan) *dissented*. He noted that the majority's rule applied heightened scrutiny to any government rule that compels an individual to "speak a particular message." But, he said, this rule would cast into doubt the constitutional validity of *"virtually every disclosure law,"* since nearly all disclosure laws require individuals 'to speak a particular message.'" The majority's view, if taken literally, "could radically change prior law, perhaps placing much *securities law or consumer protection law at constitutional risk[.]"*

i. Bad consequences for regulation of professionals: Breyer noted that the majority opinion said it was willing to recognize an exception for laws that "require professionals to disclose factual, noncontroversial information in their 'commercial speech,'" but only in the narrow situation where the disclosure *"relates to the services that [the regulated professionals] provide."* But the majority's narrow exception meant that *numerous disclosure requirements* routinely imposed on the medical or legal professions — but not relating to the professionals' own services — would now have to be subjected to heightened scrutiny. For instance, statutes requiring hospitals to tell parents about *child seat belts*, or to tell parents of newborns about diseases for which a *vaccine is available*, would have to be closely scrutinized (and probably struck down) as content-based restrictions on the hospitals' right to reject compelled speech. Breyer believed that such disclosure laws should be upheld as falling within the Court's modern-era, post-*Lochner*[25] practice of treating "ordinary economic and social legislation" as "rais[ing] little constitutional concern."

XII. UNCONSTITUTIONAL CONDITIONS

A. Unconstitutional conditions generally: Government actions sometimes raise the problem of *"unconstitutional conditions."* The problem arises "when government attaches *constitutionally troublesome 'strings'* to *government benefits*, such as housing, employment money, or licenses." S,S,S,T&K pp. 1608-09. Most often — but not always — the "string" is that the recipient of the government benefit must, in order to get the benefit, agree to *waive her freedom of expression*.

1. Statement of doctrine: To deal with this problem, the Court sometimes invokes the doctrine of unconstitutional conditions in order to strike down the condition. When the doctrine applies, it holds that "government *may not grant a benefit on the condition that the beneficiary surrender a constitutional right*, even if the government may *withhold that benefit altogether*." 102 HARV. L. REV. 1415. The idea behind the doctrine is that what the government may not do *directly*, it may not do *indirectly* either. *Id.*

Example: Suppose that the Republican-controlled legislature of a state passes a statute saying that no one may get or keep a job working for the state — no matter how low-level the position or what the requirements of the position are — unless the per-

---

25. See *supra*, p. 170, for a discussion of how the Court eventually rejected *Lochner v. N.Y.*'s close scrutiny of garden-variety social and economic legislature.

son signs a pledge not to criticize any elected Republican official during the employment.

The Supreme Court would undoubtedly invoke the doctrine of unconstitutional conditions to strike down this statute as a violation of state employees' freedom of expression. Every citizen has the right to criticize politicians, and letting the state condition all state employment on the waiver of this right amounts to letting the state do indirectly what it could not to directly.[26]

2. **Guiding principles:** The Court seems to apply the doctrine somewhat inconsistently. But following are three principles that seem to explain the outcome in most of the Court's unconstitutional-condition cases. (See S,S,S,T&K p. 1615.) We have already covered most of these principles in earlier parts of this chapter, especially in the discussion of government's rights as funder of speech, *supra*, p. 601.

[1] **Government uses agents to deliver government's own speech:** Government is *permitted* to say pretty much whatever it wants *when the government is itself the speaker.* (See *supra*, p. 601.) Furthermore, government is permitted to *select agents* to deliver the government's own message. (*Supra*, p. 601.) Therefore, government is free to *pay agents* to deliver the government's message, and to *condition that payment* on the agent's willingness to *waive his otherwise-protected right* to engage in speech that would contradict or garble the government message the agent is being paid to deliver.

Example: Congress provides funding for a public-education campaign called "Smoking Kills." The funding pays for lecturers to travel the country giving anti-smoking speeches. It's clear that Congress may insert into its contract with any lecturer a provision saying, "In any public lecture you are giving as part of the 'Smoking Kills' program, you shall make no statement inconsistent with the view that smoking is inherently hazardous."

By doing so, Congress has not attached an unconstitutional condition to its lecture contract; the nature and advertising of the program make it clear that any lecturer who is speaking under the auspices of the program is delivering the government's own message, so it is not unconstitutional for the government to insist on speakers who will faithfully deliver the message that the government has selected.

[2] **Limits on use of government's payments:** Government is also free to set up *"subsidy programs,"* under which government funds private groups to help them carry out some function. And when government does this, it is free to *refuse* to allow *the subsidy dollars to be used for particular activities opposed by government*, including otherwise-constitutionally-protected activities like *speaking* on certain topics, *performing abortions*, or lobbying legislators. (But this exception applies only when the restriction limits just the use of the actual *dollars paid by the government*, not when the program restricts the grantee's freedom to engage in other activities being pri-

---

26. Notice that I've designed this hypothetical statute so that it applies even where the state has no legitimate interest in curbing the criticism. If such a law instead only applied, say, to high-ranking policy-making employees to prevent them from publicly criticizing their own superiors while performing the functions of the job, the unconstitutional-conditions doctrine wouldn't apply. In this situation, the Court would almost certainly hold that the government has an overriding interest in assuring that high-level employees don't impair their own performance or that of their superiors by on-the-job criticisms of superiors. See *Garcetti v. Ceballos, supra*, p. 614.

vately funded. As to this latter situation, see [3] below.)

Example: Recall the facts of *Rust v. Sullivan* (*supra*, p. 194): Congress has long provided federal grants to help private citizens operate family-planning clinics. Any program using these grants is known as a "Title X project." The Secretary of Health and Human Services then makes a new interpretation of the grant program, under which every Title X project is prohibited from "counselling [patients] concerning the use of abortion" or from "encourag[ing] or promot[ing] abortion." Grantees who have been receiving funds argue that this new condition violates their and their patients' freedom of speech, by stripping the grantees of the right to counsel a patient that she has a constitutionally-protected right to have an abortion in certain circumstances.

Held, the new interpretation is not an unconstitutional condition, and does not violate the First Amendment. "[T]he Government is not denying a benefit to anyone, but is instead simply insisting that *public funds be spent* for the purposes for which they were authorized." A critical distinction is between the "project" (the particular activity paid for by the grant funds, namely operating a family-planning clinic), and the "grantee" (the individuals or group that are running the project). The way the statute and interpretation are written, a Title X *grantee* can continue to engage in abortion advocacy or counselling; the grantee simply is required to conduct those activities "through programs that are *separate and independent from the project* that receives Title X funds."[27] *Rust v. Sullivan*, 500 U.S. 173 (1991).

[3] **No "leveraging" by government:** But although government may (as described in [2] above) put conditions on how the government funds will be used inside a government-subsidized privately-run program, government may not impose conditions that "seek to *leverage funding* to *regulate speech outside the contours* of the [government] *program itself*."

Example 1: Congress gives funding to noncommercial TV and radio stations, but only on condition that they do not do any editorializing, even with private funds.

Held, the no-editorializing rule is an unconstitutional condition. Congress had the power to limit how subsidy dollars are spent. But here, Congress went beyond that power, by preventing all editorializing by even stations that didn't use federal funding for this purpose. For the no-editorializing condition to have been constiututional, Congress would have had to give a station a way to use private funds for editorializing as long as the station made sure not to use the federal grants for these editorializing purposes. *FCC v. League of Women Voters*, 468 U.S. 364 (1983).

Example 2: Congress gives large money grants to various nongovernmental organizations that are fighting HIV and AIDS. Congress says that no funds may be given to any group "that does not have a *policy explicitly opposing prostitution[.]*" (This is the "Policy Requirement.") The Ps are various non-profits that fear that if they obey the Policy Requirement and adopt an explicitly anti-prostitution message, their mission

---

27. Indeed, that's the way Planned Parenthood and other recipients of Title X funding operated after *Rust* — they set up federally-funded clinics to do non-abortion-related family planning such as distribution of contraceptives, and separately set up non-federally-funded abortion clinics.

will be adversely affected (e.g., they may find it harder to persuade prostitutes to promote condom usage).

   Held (6-2),[28] for the Ps; the Policy Requirement is an unconstitutional condition. The Court's cases on unconstitutional conditions have distinguished between "conditions that define the limits of the government spending program, [i.e., that] specify the activities Congress wants to subsidize" (which are constitutional) and "conditions that seek to leverage funding to regulate speech outside the contours of the program itself" (which are unconstitutional). It may sometimes be hard to tell on which side of the line a particular condition falls. But here, the Policy Requirement falls on the unconstitutional side of the line. "By demanding that funding recipients adopt — as their own — the Government's view on an issue of public concern, the condition by its very nature affects 'protected conduct outside the scope of the federally funded program.'" *Agency for Int'l Dev. v. Alliance for Open Soc'y Int'l, Inc.*, 133 S. Ct. 2321 (2013).

XIII. SPECIAL PROBLEMS CONCERNING THE MEDIA

   A. Summary of issues: Certain First Amendment problems arise only where the First Amendment right is being asserted by a member of the *media*, i.e., professional *publishers* and *broadcasters*. The four issues which we address that pertain specially to the media are:

   1. Does the press have a special role to play under the First Amendment, so that it has *rights* which an *ordinary member of the public would not?*

   2. Under what circumstances, if any, may the media be *restrained* from publishing or broadcasting material (as distinguished from being punished after such dissemination has already occurred)?

   3. Does a journalist have any greater rights to *resist governmental demands for information* known to the journalist, than does an ordinary member of the public? and

   4. Do the media have any First Amendment *right of access* to information *within the government's possession* or control?

   B. Special role for the press: The First Amendment explicitly prohibits abridgment of the freedom "of the press," in addition to protecting the freedom "of speech." On its face, this language suggests that the organized press is entitled to somewhat greater First Amendment protection than are ordinary members of the public; otherwise, the explicit reference to the press would seem to be redundant.

   1. **Not yet recognized:** However, in no case has a majority of the Court ever recognized the Press Clause of the First Amendment as having independent constitutional significance. Yet, neither has the Court ever squarely held that the Clause is redundant.

   2. **Laws of general applicability:** The Court has heard a number of cases in which the press argued that it should receive an *exemption* from rules of general applicability. The Court has virtually always *denied* any special exemption for the press. For instance, if a state's generally applicable procedural rules allow a person to be forced to give *testimony* to a grand jury or petit jury, then the press must obey those rules like anyone else. See

---

28. Justice Kagan recused herself.

Branzburg v. Hayes, infra, p. 634. Similarly, the same rules apply to the issuance of **search warrants** to search a publisher's premises as apply to searches of a non-publisher. *Zurcher v. Stanford Daily, infra,* p. 636. And newspapers may be made to pay damages for violating contractual promises of **confidentiality**, the same as any private citizen may be. See *Cohen v. Cowles Media Co., infra,* p. 638.

a. Access right: There is one situation in which the press may have rights superior to those of the public at large. The press may have a right of **access** to newsworthy information within the government's control — such a right of access for the press, based on general free-expression principles, may have been recognized by the Court in the *Richmond Newspapers* case, *infra,* p. 638.

3. Government can't single out press: Regardless of whether the press has special rights, what is clear is that government may not **single out** the press for **unfavorable** treatment.

a. Taxation: This has been clearest in cases involving **taxation**. The government may not impose a tax that applies to newspapers (or all media) but that is not generally applicable. Thus in **Minneapolis Star & Tribune Co. v. Minnesota Comm'r of Revenue**, 460 U.S. 525 (1983), the Court held that a special Minnesota "use tax" applicable only to the cost of **paper and ink** consumed in the production of **publications**, violated the First Amendment.

i. Rationale: The Court did not find any evidence that the Minnesota legislature had tried to censor or chill the press. But the tax was a special one, not part of the state's generally-applicable use tax. Therefore, the Court concluded, the state had "singled out the press for special treatment." Consequently, the tax had to be strictly scrutinized — it would be invalid unless "necessary to achieve an overriding governmental interest."

ii. "Chilling" effect: There was evidence that the particular tax here was not especially burdensome to the press (since it was at the same percentage rate as the general state sales and use taxes, and applied only to paper and ink, not to the total price of the newspaper). Nonetheless, because the state had singled out the press, the "**political constraints** that prevent a legislature from passing crippling taxes of general applicability are weakened, and the threat of burdensome taxes becomes acute." The **mere threat** of crippling taxes might well have a censorial effect, the Court argued.

iii. Strict scrutiny test failed: The statute was not able to withstand the strict scrutiny to which the Court subjected it. The state's interest in raising revenue might be a compelling one (the Court did not say); but the singling out of the press for a special tax was **not a necessary means** of achieving that objective. The state could, for instance, simply have made newspaper sales part of the **general state sales tax** already in force.

iv. Dissent: Justice Rehnquist, in dissent, argued that not all "differential treatment," but only that differential treatment which **burdens** the press, should be strictly scrutinized. Here, he calculated, the use tax was **more favorable** to the press than, say, a sales tax set at the same percentage, but applicable to the newspaper's gross revenues. Therefore, there was a "benefit" to the press, not a "burden."

b. Taxation based on content: Where a tax operates differently upon different members of the press depending on the **content** of a publication, it is even more likely to be found invalid. In the post-*Minneapolis Star* case of *Arkansas Writer's Project, Inc. v. Ragland*, 481 U.S. 221 (1987), an Arkansas statute that taxed general interest magazines, but exempted newspapers and other special-interest publications, was invalidated by the Court. The fact that the tax did not discriminate among particular *views*, merely among subject areas, was not sufficient to save the statute.

   i. Exemption that is denied to large category: On the other hand, where a generally-applicable tax is applied to most media as well as to non-media, and an exemption is given to a certain media segment, denial of the exemption to the rest of the media seems **not** to be unconstitutional. Thus if a state has a generally-applicable sales tax on goods and services, it may decide to cover cable TV services while continuing to exempt newspapers, magazines, and satellite broadcast services. *Leathers v. Medlock*, 499 U.S. 439 (1991). The idea seems to be that as long as it is not the case that a small segment of the media is singled out for negative treatment, the fact that some segment of the media *is* given an exemption is irrelevant.

C. Prior restraints: A key aim of the drafters of the First Amendment was to forbid any system of **prior restraints**, similar to the English licensing scheme, by which nothing could be published without government or church approval. This aim remains a vital part of modern First Amendment doctrine, so that any governmental action which prevents expression from occurring (as distinguished from punishing it once it has occurred) is **presumed to be constitutionally invalid**. This is all the more true where the prior restraint is directed against the organized press. See Tribe, p. 1041.

   1. Procedural obstacles: The dangers of prior restraints also stem from the fact that procedural rules applied in American courts make such restraints more likely to **"chill"** the exercise of First Amendment rights than would a subsequent punishment. Where a person is sought to be punished *after* his speech-related conduct, he is completely free to raise the claim that the statute at issue is unconstitutional, either on its face or as applied to him. But where a person is enjoined *prior* to his expressive act, and yet goes ahead and does that act anyway, he will not be permitted to argue that either the underlying statute or the injunction was unconstitutional as applied to him (though he may argue that the statute was void on its face). See, e.g., *Walker v. City of Birmingham*, 388 U.S. 307 (1967). Thus an unconstitutionally-imposed prior restraint is likely to cow the defendant into forgoing his First Amendment rights, at least during the length of time it takes to conduct an appeal. See Tribe, pp. 1042-45.

   2. Examples of prior restraints: There are two basic types of pre-publication restraints. One consists of governmental orders and court injunctions telling a particular person that he cannot engage in a certain type of communication. The other consists of a scheme requiring a **license or permit** before a particular type of expression may be engaged in. Movie-censorship schemes are illustrations of the latter category. All of the cases involving the organized press, with which we are concerned here, are of the governmental-order or court-injunction type.

   3. *Near v. Minnesota:* The classic case articulating the heavy presumption against prior restraints is **Near v. Minnesota**, 283 U.S. 697 (1931).

a. **Facts:** In *Near*, a state procedure for closing down as a public nuisance any "malicious, scandalous and defamatory newspaper" was used to permanently enjoin the publication of a newspaper which criticized local officials.

b. **Holding:** In striking the injunction as an unconstitutional infringement of free speech, the Court held that the primary aim of the First Amendment was to prevent pre-publication restraints. The proper remedy for false accusations against public officials was by a post-publication libel action, not by a pre-publication procedure which the Court found to be tantamount to censorship.

   i. **Exceptional cases:** The prohibition on prior restraints, in the *Near* Court's view, was almost, but not quite, complete. There could be a few "exceptional cases" in which prior restraint would be permissible; the Court gave as illustrations actual obstruction of recruitment for the armed forces, and publication of "the sailing dates of transports or the number and location of troops."

   ii. **Burden of proof:** One aspect of the Minnesota statute to which the Court took particular exception was that the *burden of proof* was placed *upon the publisher* to show his truthfulness or good faith, rather than on the party seeking the injunction to show falsity or malice. However, nothing in the *Near* opinion (or in subsequent case law) suggests that placing the burden of proof in these issues on the party seeking the injunction would validate such a generalized prior restraint scheme.

4. **Pentagon Papers case:** The only other case to reach the Court on the issue of prior restraint of political speech is the famous *Pentagon Papers* case, *New York Times Co. v. U.S.*, 403 U.S. 713 (1971). This case establishes that the press has *almost absolute immunity* from pre-publication restraints. See Tribe, p. 1039.

   a. **Facts:** *The New York Times* and *The Washington Post* began publishing portions of a secret Defense Department study (popularly known as the "Pentagon Papers") of U.S. policy in Vietnam. The government sought an injunction against the two papers to prevent further publication. The government conceded that the Papers discussed only historical events which transpired prior to 1968, but argued that publication would prolong the War by giving the enemy information useful to it and would embarrass our diplomatic efforts.

   b. ***Per curiam* opinion:** The opinion of the Court was a brief *per curiam* one, which recited prior case law that there is a heavy presumption against the constitutionality of prior restraints, but which contained no other reasoning. By a 6-3 vote, the Court determined that the government was *not entitled* to the injunctions.

   c. **Nine separate opinions:** *Every member* of the Court wrote a separate opinion, and no majority of the Court agreed on a precise rationale for the decision. The opinions fell into three broad categories: Justices Black and Douglas argued that there could *never* be a prior restraint on the press; Justices Brennan, White, Stewart and Marshall contended that there could be prior restraint in extraordinary circumstances, but that the present case did not qualify; and Justices Burger, Harlan, and Blackmun believed that prior restraint was appropriate here.

d. Absolutist view: Justices Black and Douglas appeared to be saying that *ever* to permit the publication of news to be enjoined would "make a shambles of the First Amendment."

    i. Criticism: But as Professor Cox has pointed out, in 94 HARV. L. REV. 6, "Surely [Black and Douglas] would not have ruled during World War II that a newspaper had a constitutional right to publish for Nazi eyes the knowledge that, because of … cryptographic work … British authorities were reading the orders of the Nazi High Command."

e. Possible restraints: The four other Justices in the six-man majority believed that prior restraint of news publication could sometimes occur, but not in this case. This group, consisting of Brennan, Stewart, White and Marshall, argued that there must be a *virtual certainty* that grave damage to the country would result if publication were not enjoined; as Justice Stewart, joined by White, expressed the test, there must be a showing that disclosure "will *surely result* in *direct, immediate, and irreparable damage* to our Nation or its people."

    i. Danger not substantially certain: Most or all of these Justices seemed to believe that publication would *probably* damage the nation. It was only because there was not a *substantial certainty* of such damage that they voted to strike the injunction.

    ii. Absence of statutory authorization: To all of these four Justices except Brennan, an important weakness of the government's position was that *no statute* provided for an injunction against news publication in circumstances like these. Separation of powers principles made it impermissible for the Court to issue an injunction where Congress had declined to act. (But Justices Stewart and White seemed to say that even in the *absence* of statutory authorization, a certainty of direct, immediate and irreparable damage to the country might permit issuance of an injunction. This view would probably command a majority of the Court today. See 94 HARV. L. REV. 7.)

f. Dissent: Three Justices, Harlan, Burger and Blackmun, dissented. They criticized the haste with which the Court heard and decided the case. (Less than one week elapsed between filing of the case and announcement of the decision.) Only one Justice, Harlan, formulated a test for evaluating the constitutionality of such injunctions.

    i. Harlan's test: In Harlan's view, the Court's role should be limited to determining: (1) whether the subject matter of the dispute lies within the *proper scope* of the *President's foreign relations power*; and if the answer is "yes," (2) whether the determination that disclosure would irreparably impair the national security was personally made by the head of the relevant executive department, here, the Secretary of State or Secretary of Defense. If the answer to this question, too, was "yes," the injunction should be upheld.

    ii. Rationale: Harlan argued that it was a violation of separation of powers principles for the judiciary to go beyond these two inquiries and to "redetermine for itself the probable impact of disclosure on the national security."

g. Receipt of stolen goods: As is well known, the newspapers' source for the Pentagon Papers was Daniel Ellsberg, who was given them in confidence while he did work for the government. Had the government been able to show that the newspapers were *receivers of stolen goods*, by showing that the newspapers were aware that Ellsberg's making and distributing copies was a violation of his obligation of confidentiality, it is possible that the Court might have found this to be grounds for an injunction. No subsequent case to reach the Court has faced this question squarely.

    i. Difficulty: One difficulty with allowing an injunction based on such a receivership-of-stolen-goods theory is that "requiring a newspaper to decide at its peril whether information that it has received about an official proceeding is confidential would have a chilling effect upon the publication of legitimate news." 94 HARV. L. REV. 12.

5. The *Progressive* H-bomb case: At least one court has interpreted the *Pentagon Papers* case to *permit* an injunction against publication of newsworthy information if a statute so authorizes, and if the danger is sufficiently compelling. In *U.S. v. The Progressive, Inc.*, 467 F. Supp. 990 (W.D. Wis. 1979), the district court enjoined a magazine from publishing an article containing *technical information about the H-bomb*. At least some of the materials had previously been declassified. But the U.S. convinced the court that these materials, taken together with other classified information (also sought to be released by the magazine), could pose a direct threat to national security by possibly "allow[ing] a medium size nation to move faster in developing a hydrogen weapon."

    a. Rationale: The judge reasoned that two main considerations made this case distinguishable from the *Pentagon Papers* case: (1) here, a statute, the Atomic Energy Act, authorized an injunction against publication of certain information relating to the use or manufacture of nuclear weapons (including some of the information in the proposed article); and (2) publication might well lead to nuclear proliferation, which in turn might lead to "thermonuclear annihilation for us all."

    b. Balancing test: The court then balanced the dangers to the paper's First Amendment rights against the danger to the nation. As to the former, although the injunction might interfere with the magazine's broadly-defined First Amendment rights, it would not interfere with its "laudable crusade to stimulate public knowledge of nuclear armament and bring about enlightened debate on national policy questions." The balance was struck in favor of the injunction; the "disparity of risk" between the danger to the nation and the damage to the paper's First Amendment rights justified what the court conceded was "the first instance of prior restraint against a publication in this fashion in the history of this country."

    c. Outcome: Before the paper's appeal could be heard, the government's attempt to get a permanent injunction against it was dropped, because the information was published elsewhere.

6. "Gag orders" and preservation of fair trials: The media's exercise of its First Amendment rights may sometimes come into conflict with a *criminal defendant's right to a fair trial*. Extensive pre-trial publicity, including disclosure of confessions (possibly inadmissible) by the defendant, may make it much more difficult to find jurors who can be impartial. Nonetheless, the United States has never gone even a single step towards the English rule, which makes illegal the pre-trial publication of information that might cause prejudice.

a.   **Standard for biased jury:**   If the defendant can show that the jury was biased against him, he is entitled to a *reversal* of his conviction. But it is *not* sufficient for him to show that the jurors had *knowledge before they were sworn in about the facts and issues involved in the case* — requiring complete ignorance would be virtually impossible in important trials, given today's mass communications. Rather, the defendant must show that the jury was *prejudiced* against him as the result of pre-trial publicity.

b.   **Publicity during trial:**   Similarly, publicity *during* the trial may be so great that, if the jury is exposed to it, the defendant's right to a fair trial will be found to have been violated. See, e.g., *Sheppard v. Maxwell*, 384 U.S. 333 (1966), the famous Sam Sheppard murder case, where massive prejudicial publicity during the trial, to which the jury was exposed, was held to be grounds for reversal; the Court observed that the problem could have been avoided by *sequestering* the jury for the length of the trial.

c.   **Gag orders:**   Because of these dangers of publicity, especially before the trial begins, trial judges have sought ways of assuring that they will be able to find an unbiased jury. One appealing method that some seized upon is the *"gag order,"* a pre-trial order *prohibiting the press from publishing certain types of information* about the case. But as the result of the one case involving a gag order to reach the Court, such orders will *almost never be constitutionally permissible*. That case is *Nebraska Press Ass'n v. Stuart*, 427 U.S. 539 (1976).

   i.   **Facts of *Nebraska Press:***   In *Nebraska Press*, a man was about to be tried for a heinous mass murder, which had attracted widespread media attention. The trial judge, in order to assure his ability to select an unprejudiced jury, issued an order prohibiting the press from reporting any confessions or admissions by the defendant, or any other fact "strongly implicative" of him, until after impaneling of the jury.

   ii.   **Holding:**   The Supreme Court held unanimously that the gag order *violated* the press' First Amendment rights.

   iii.   **Majority opinion:**   The majority opinion was written by Chief Justice Burger, with whom four other Justices joined. Burger declined to hold that a ban on pre-trial publicity could *never* be constitutional. Instead, he applied a test long ago advocated by Learned Hand for subversive-advocacy cases: the restraint should be allowed only if the "gravity of the 'evil,' discounted by its improbability" is greater than the damage from impairment of First Amendment rights.

   (1)   **Standard not met:** Here, Burger said, this test was not satisfied. The trial judge's conclusion that pretrial publicity would impair the defendant's rights "was of necessity *speculative*," rather than certain. Furthermore, the trial judge should have considered *other alternatives* for reducing the harmful effect of such publicity (e.g., change of venue, postponement of trial, careful *voir dire*, restricting statements by the lawyers, police and witnesses, etc.). Finally, the trial judge should have considered whether his gag order would even be effective, in view of the rumors which usually circulate in a sensational case. On balance, then, it was not sufficiently established that the benefits of the gag order outweighed its First Amendment dangers.

d. Significance: *Nebraska Press* probably presents about the strongest case imaginable for a gag order furthering the right of fair trial. Therefore, the result of that decision is that such orders will virtually never be constitutional, at least as long as the press acquires its information without violating the law.

e. Distinguished from subsequent punishment: What made the order in *Nebraska Press* a "prior restraint" was not simply that it forbade publishing a certain type of material; it was that the restriction took the form of an order applicable to one particular, specifically-identified factual setting (this particular trial). Had the *legislature* made it a *crime* to publish prejudicial information in advance of *any* criminal trial, such a statute could *not properly be termed a prior restraint*, and would *not* necessarily be unconstitutional.

   i. Analysis: General First Amendment principles might be interpreted to make such a statute violative of freedom of expression, but the heavy presumption against prior restraints would have nothing to do with the decision.

f. Silencing the lawyer: The "gag order" in *Nebraska Press* was directed at the media; the case establishes that such press-directed orders will rarely be constitutional. But courts have a far greater ability to issue a constitutional gag order against the *lawyers* in the case, as the result of a post-*Nebraska Press* case decision. In *Gentile v. State Bar of Nevada*, 501 U.S. 1030 (1991), the Court held that states may prevent a lawyer from making any statement that would have a *"substantial likelihood of materially prejudicing"* an adjudicative proceeding. The Court upheld a Nevada rule patterned on the American Bar Association's Model Rule (prohibiting statements posing a substantial likelihood of material prejudice) over the lawyer's claim that a "clear and present danger" standard should be used.

g. Closure orders: Since trial judges will almost never be permitted to use a pre-trial gag order directed at the press, an obvious alternative is for them simply to *close pre-trial proceedings to the public (and press)*. The use of such closure orders, at least where they are limited to pretrial proceedings and are not opposed by either the prosecution or the defense, was upheld by the Supreme Court, in *Gannett Co. v. DePasquale*, discussed *infra*, p. 638.

D. Governmental demands for information held by press: First Amendment issues may arise when the government seeks *disclosure* of information *obtained by the press* during its news-gathering activities, but not yet published. Typically, the government seeks such disclosure as part of its *law enforcement* efforts. The two Supreme Court cases on point, one involving a grand jury investigation and the other the use of an *ex parte* search warrant, indicate that the press is *not entitled to any special First Amendment protection* against what would otherwise be proper compulsory disclosure of information obtained during news-gathering.

1. Indirect impact on First Amendment rights: Observe that the nature of the interference with First Amendment expression is quite different in this compulsory-disclosure setting than in the prior restraint area. In the latter setting, restraint is almost always sought *because of the communicative impact* which publication would have; thus prior restraints almost always call for "track one" analysis (to use Tribe's term), and strict scrutiny is obviously appropriate. But in the compulsory disclosure area, any interference with First Amendment expression (e.g., the drying up of information from informants, because they are afraid their confidentiality will not be preserved) is *incidental to,* not the purpose of, the disclosure. Therefore, these cases call for "track two" analysis, which as noted (*supra*, p. 488) is handled by a much less stringent balancing of harms and benefits. Therefore, it is not surprising that the Supreme Court has been much less quick to accept the press' arguments in the compulsory-disclosure area than in the context of prior restraints. See 94 HARV. L. REV. 55.

2. ***Branzburg* and grand jury investigations:**   In ***Branzburg v. Hayes***, 408 U.S. 665 (1972), the Court held by a 5-4 vote that requiring newsmen to testify before **grand juries** concerning **information obtained from confidential sources** during news-gathering does **not** violate the First Amendment. In so deciding, the Court **rejected** journalists' requests for at least a **qualified privilege** to refuse to disclose the **identities of confidential sources** or the **information** received from them.

   a. **Journalists' argument:**   The argument raised by Branzburg and two other journalists was that news-gathering often requires confidential sources, who agree to supply the journalist with otherwise unavailable information only if non-disclosure of the informant's name and/or some of the information is promised. If a grand jury could compel disclosure, the journalists argued, not only the source of the particular information sought, but other confidential sources in the future, would be dissuaded from talking to journalists.

   b. **Holding:**   In rejecting the claim for a privilege, the Court held that such a privilege had never been found to exist, and that journalists had always been viewed as having the **same duty as any other citizen** to disclose to grand juries information about crime. The majority was not convinced that a significant portion of information supplied by confidential sources would dry up, especially since such information was widely available to newsmen even though no privilege had ever been recognized.

      i. **Balancing:**   Even if significant impairment of confidential sources did occur, the majority saw no reason why "[t]he public interest in possible future news about crime from undisclosed, unverified sources" should take precedence over the governmental interest in prosecuting crimes about which journalists possess evidence.

      ii. **Definitional problem:**   Also, the majority saw a **definitional** problem: recognition of a privilege would require the courts either to decide that only the "organized press" should be protected (and to define that term), or to make the privilege dangerously broad by protecting "lectures, political pollsters, novelists, academic researchers, dramatists" and anyone else claiming to be informing the public and to be relying on confidential sources.

   c. **Qualified privilege rejected:**   The majority also rejected even a **qualified** privilege, by which disclosure of confidential information could not be compelled unless the state showed that a crime had been committed and that the journalist possessed relevant information not available from other sources.

   d. **Protection against harassment:**   But the majority preserved the right of a journalist to obtain relief against **harassment**, e.g., a subpoena issued not to pursue law enforcement ends but for the purpose of disrupting the reporter's relationship with his news sources (perhaps because of official displeasure with the newsman's work). However, so long as the questions were relevant and material, and were part of a good faith grand jury investigation, the newsman could not decline to answer.

e. Powell's concurrence: The crucial fifth vote was supplied by Justice Powell, who although he joined the Court's opinion submitted a separate concurrence as well; this concurrence made the result of the case somewhat ambiguous. Whereas the other four members of the majority rejected a qualified privilege, and left room only for a defense of harassment, Justice Powell's concurrence stated that claims of privilege should be decided on a *case-by-case basis*, by balancing freedom of the press against the obligation of all citizens to give relevant testimony. Powell suggested, for instance, that a newsman may obtain relief if he can show that he has been asked for information bearing "only a remote and tenuous relationship to the subject of the investigation," or that his confidential sources would be compromised "without a legitimate need of law enforcement."

f. Dissent: Three of the four dissenters in *Branzburg* did not argue for an absolute privilege against grand jury disclosure of confidential sources. But they did support a type of *strict scrutiny* of such compulsory disclosure, by which the government would have to make three showings before a reporter could be required to reveal confidences: (1) that there is "probable cause to believe that the newsman has information which is *clearly relevant* to a *specific probable violation of law*;" (2) that the information cannot be obtained by "*alternative means* less destructive of First Amendment rights"; and (3) that the government has a "compelling and overriding interest" in the information.

    i. Relation to Powell's view: As the dissenters pointed out, this type of qualified privilege may not be so different from the position taken by Justice Powell. The absolute position taken by the other four members of the majority, by contrast, would "annex the journalistic profession as an investigative arm of government," the dissenters argued.

3. Limited scope of ruling: In addition to grand jury proceedings, the rationale of *Branzburg* obviously applies to *criminal trials* as well. But it is not clear that the theory of *Branzburg* also deprives newsmen of a constitutional privilege regarding testimony in *civil suits*. Some lower courts have granted a *qualified privilege* in this situation, which may be overcome only by a showing that the confidentially-obtained information is not available from other sources. See N&R, p. 1051.

4. Shield laws: The majority in *Branzburg* noted that Congress and state legislatures are free to enact *statutes* granting to newsmen a privilege against disclosure of confidential sources or information in grand jury or other proceedings. More than half of the states have, either before or after *Branzburg*, conferred such a privilege by means of so-called *"shield laws."*

a. No Court decisions: The Supreme Court has not yet had occasion to determine whether some applications of such a shield law unconstitutionally interfere with other constitutional rights, most notably a criminal defendant's Sixth Amendment *right to a fair trial.*

b. *Farber* case: One well-known state court case, involving a trial judge's order to a reporter to produce interview notes in connection with a murder case, concluded that such a shield law *must yield to the defendant's Sixth Amendment rights. In re Farber*, 394 A.2d 330 (N.J. 1978).

5. ***Ex parte* search warrants:** Another press claim for special protection against compelled disclosure for law enforcement purposes failed in *Zurcher v. Stanford Daily*, 436 U.S. 547 (1978). There, the Court upheld an ***ex parte warrant*** for the search of a student newspaper's offices, based on probable cause to believe that photographs of a riotous demonstration might be found there.

   a. **Usual rules applied:** The majority opinion spent most of its time talking about the Fourth Amendment, not the First, and saw no reason to depart from usual principles allowing the issuance on probable cause of *ex parte* warrants (that is, warrants issued without notice to the person whose property is to be searched).

   b. **Qualified privilege rejected:** As in *Branzburg*, the Court ***rejected*** the press' request for at least a ***qualified*** privilege, under which an *ex parte* warrant would be issued only where there was reason to believe that a ***subpoena*** might lead to the destruction of the evidence.

E. **Disclosure of confidential or illegally-obtained information:** To what extent may government prohibit the media from ***disclosing information*** that government believes ought to be ***secret***? The interests that government may be trying to protect can include the ***privacy of individuals***, the ***rehabilitation of juvenile offenders***, or the maintenance of ***national security***, among others. A good summary of the Court's decisions in this area is that "[i]f a newspaper *lawfully obtains truthful information* about a matter of ***public significance*** then [government] officials may not constitutionally punish publication of the information, absent a ***need ... of the highest order***." *Smith v. Daily Mail Publishing Co.*, 443 U.S. 97 (1979).

1. **Information about legal proceedings:** A number of the Court's decisions concerning publication of "secret" material have involved information about ***legal proceedings*** or ***law enforcement***. Here, government has almost always been ***unsuccessful*** in ***making it a crime to publish*** legally-obtained truthful information. Here are some examples:

   ❏ A broadcaster may not be held civilly liable for ***publishing the name of a rape victim***, if the name is learned from the reading of a publicly-filed indictment. *Cox Broadcasting Corp. v. Cohn*, 420 U.S. 469 (1975).

   ❏ A state may not make it a crime for a newspaper to report (accurately) that a state judicial commission is contemplating an ***investigation of a particular sitting judge***. *Landmark Communications, Inc. v. Virginia*, 435 U.S. 829 (1978).

   ❏ A newspaper cannot be punished for publishing the ***name and photo of a juvenile offender***, where the newspaper obtained the name from witnesses to the crime and from law-enforcement officers who investigated it. *Smith v. Daily Mail Publishing Co.*, 443 U.S. 97 (1979).

2. **Information obtained by means of a crime:** An important sub-question is whether this rule — that publication of newsworthy confidential information may not be criminalized absent an extremely strong state interest — applies even to ***illegally-obtained*** information.

   a. **Where publisher has acted illegally:** If the ***publisher itself*** has ***acted illegally*** in obtaining the information, then it is quite clear that government ***may make it a crime*** to punish the information, no matter how newsworthy it is.

      Example: Suppose that, in 1974, a reporter for the *Washington Post* broke into the White House and found a tape that recorded White House officials conspiring to burglarize the Democratic National Committee's offices. If the *Post* published a transcript of that tape, it's quite clear that a state could constitutionally punish the paper for the publication (apart from the break-in), because the newspaper obtained the information as a result of a crime by its own employee.

b. **Where private party has acted illegally but publisher has not:** On the other hand, the fact that the secret information was originally obtained illegally by a person *acting independently* of the eventual publisher is *not* enough to allow publication to be made criminal, at least where the material has significant newsworthiness.

i. **Illegal interception of cellphone calls:** A vivid illustration of this principle occurred in a 2001 case in which a radio station played a tape of a cellphone conversation that had been intercepted in violation of a federal wiretapping law. Because the interception occurred without the participation of the station, and because the conversation involved important public events, the station could not be prosecuted for the broadcast. *Bartnicki v. Vopper*, 532 U.S. 514 (2001).

(1) **Facts:** In *Bartnicki*, the conversation was a cellphone conversation between two officials of a teachers union, who were discussing a bitter contract negotiation that they were having with the local school board. During the conversation, one of the officials said that if the board remained intransigent, it might be necessary for the union to go to board members' homes and "blow off their front porches." An unknown person intercepted the conversation in violation of federal law and sent it anonymously to a radio station, which broadcast it. The two officials sued the station for damages, as allowed by federal and state wiretap statutes prohibiting the disclosure of intercepted telephone conversations.

(2) **Holding:** By a 6-3 vote, the Court held that the station could not constitutionally be held liable for damages — the extreme newsworthiness of the conversation outweighed the strong governmental interest in protecting the privacy of electronic communications. The majority conceded that the government had a strong interest in deterring illegal interceptions, but believed that barring publication by a third person who did not participate in the interception would not significantly deter the illegal conduct.

(3) **Newsworthiness:** It seems clear that the extremely strong *newsworthiness* of the conversation in *Bartnicki* — which contained not only news about the bitter negotiation but a possible threat to people's physical safety — played a key role in the Court's decision.

(4) **Significance:** So what we know from *Bartnicki* is merely that where a publisher innocently comes into possession of illegally-intercepted conversations, and those conversations involve matters of unusually great public interest, the publisher may not be punished for disseminating them. There is a good chance that where the conversation involves matters that are *not* of major public interest (e.g., trade secrets or personal gossip), publication *can* be criminalized. And, of course, the person who does the illegal intercepting may be punished for publishing, no matter how great the public interest in the intercepted conversation.

3. **Enforcement of confidentiality promises:** Now consider one last aspect of government's power to enforce the confidentiality of information: if a journalist promises confidentiality to a source and then breaches that promise by publishing the confidential information, may the state allow the source to recover damages? The brief answer is "yes" — the Supreme Court has held that the states may ***enforce such confidentiality promises*** as they would any other contract, without thereby running afoul of the First Amendment. *Cohen v. Cowles Media Co.*, 501 U.S. 663 (1991).

F. **Right of access to government-held information:**   Much newsworthy information is ***within the government's possession*** or control. Until recently, nothing in any Supreme Court decision supported any First Amendment right on the part of the press to have ***access*** to this newsworthy information. Thus although the press has long been recognized to have a broad First Amendment right to publish information which it obtains, the press has ***not*** been constitutionally entitled to ***assistance in obtaining information.*** Such a right of access has still not been explicitly recognized by the Court, but the decision in *Richmond Newspapers, Inc. v. Virginia*, discussed *infra*, p. 638, upholding a right of access to criminal trials, may presage some form of right of access to government-controlled newsworthy material.

1. **Access to jails:**   Several cases have established that the press has little or no special right of access to information about ***prison conditions***.

   a. ***Pell*** **and** ***Saxbe:***   In the companion cases of *Pell v. Procunier*, 417 U.S. 817 (1974) and *Saxbe v. Washington Post Co.*, 417 U.S. 843 (1974), the Court ***upheld*** state and federal regulations ***prohibiting press interviews*** with any specific prisoner. The Court rejected First Amendment claims raised by both the media and by prisoners. The majority opinion in both cases, by Justice Stewart, relied mainly on the fact that the regulations ***treated the press no worse than they did members of the general public.*** While the First Amendment prevents the government from interfering with the media's attempt to gather news, it does ***not*** "require government to accord the press special access to information not shared by members of the public generally."

2. **Access to pretrial proceedings:**   Trial judges are ***not*** permitted to issue pretrial ***"gag orders"*** in order to preserve the defendant's right to an unbiased jury, except where the danger to the defendant's right to a fair trial is unusually great. See *Nebraska Press Ass'n v. Stuart,* 427 U.S. 539 (1976). Therefore, some courts have instead ***closed pretrial proceedings to the public****.* In *Gannett Co. v. DePasquale*, 443 U.S. 368 (1979), the Court held that such pretrial closure orders are at least ***sometimes constitutional***; the Court's opinion may even mean that the press and public ***never*** have a First Amendment right to attend such pretrial proceedings.

3. **Closure of criminal trials:**   One key question left unresolved by *Gannett* was whether a criminal defendant's interest in a fair trial could be preserved by ***closing the entire trial*** to the public. In ***Richmond Newspapers, Inc. v. Virginia***, 448 U.S. 555 (1980), the Court answered this question largely in the ***negative***, holding that "absent an ***overriding interest*** articulated in findings," the First Amendment requires that "[t]he ***trial of a criminal case must be open to the public***." Although the vote was 7-1, there was no majority opinion, and the precise scope of the decision remains unclear.

   a. **Significance of case:**   At a minimum, *Richmond Newspapers* establishes that the public and press have a First Amendment right to attend criminal trials, and that entire trials can be closed only if that right is outweighed by ***overriding*** interests which ***can-***

not be satisfied by less restrictive means. Whether the decision means more than that is not clear.

    i. Civil trials: It seems probable that the decision is also applicable to *civil trials*, since such trials, like criminal ones, have traditionally been open to the public, and since there is a strong public interest in observing the administration of civil justice. Several of the Justices in *Richmond Newspapers* specifically stated that they believed the decision to be applicable to such civil proceedings.

    ii. Pretrial context: The First Amendment right of access to criminal trials recognized in *Richmond Newspapers* has been extended to certain **pretrial proceedings**. For instance, the public has a right to attend the *voir dire* of the jury; see *Press Enterprise Co. v. Superior Court*, 467 U.S. 501 (1984).

    iii. Closure of portions of trial: Trial judges presumably retain their traditional power to close **certain portions** of a criminal trial in order to protect the integrity of the proceedings. For instance, testimony of a particular witness might be held outside of the presence of the public, in order to prevent other witnesses from hearing his testimony and adjusting their own to match it (though sequestration of subsequent witnesses is a preferable technique for solving this problem). Also, any trial proceedings **not held in the presence of the jury** (e.g., discussions of the admissibility of evidence) probably may be closed to the public.

    iv. Limited seats: Also, the right of access to public trials does not mean that *every* person who desires to see a particular trial has a right to do so. Obviously, courtrooms have limited seating, and a trial judge may use a reasonable scheme of allocating seats. However, the First Amendment right recognized by *Richmond Newspapers* probably does require that **at least some seats be given to media representatives**.

  4. Less-restrictive alternative required: Although *Richmond Newspapers* established that there is a First Amendment right to access to criminal trials, *no* Justice suggested that that right is an *absolute* one. The test for determining when that right is outweighed by other countervailing interests has been developed in later cases.

    a. *Globe Newspapers*: In *Globe Newspapers v. Superior Court*, 457 U.S. 596 (1982), the Court applied what amounted to a traditional *strict scrutiny* standard: access to criminal trials may be denied only if the denial is "necessitated by a **compelling governmental interest**, and is **narrowly tailored to serve that interest**." Under this test, a Massachusetts statute was unconstitutional in *requiring* the exclusion of the press and public from the courtroom during the testimony of any minor who is allegedly the victim of a sex offense.

G. Regulation of broadcast media: The Supreme Court has always recognized that the **broadcast** media may be subject to *closer regulation* than newspapers and other non-broadcasters. The closer regulation of broadcasters derives from the fact that broadcast frequencies are a **naturally scarce** commodity — whereas there can in theory be an unlimited number of newspapers serving any particular market, the technology of broadcasting is such that there could only be a strictly limited number of television and radio stations serving any particular market. (This distinction is, in practical terms, much less convincing in today's world of UHF and cable television, massive FM as well as AM radio, Internet video, etc., than it was when broadcasting was largely limited to VHF television and AM radio. But the Court has not fundamentally altered its willingness to tolerate closer regulation of the broadcast media.)

1. **Means of regulation:** This regulation has generally been carried on through the Federal Communications Commission (FCC). The Court has several times sustained the FCC's power to ensure various types of *public access* to the broadcast media. See, e.g., *Red Lion Broadcasting Co. v. FCC,* 395 U.S. 367 (1969), in which the Court upheld the FCC's "fairness" doctrine, by which broadcasters are compelled to grant individuals the right to reply on the air to political editorials or personal attacks. Similarly, the Court is probably more willing to tolerate closer regulation of *context* where the source of speech is a broadcaster; see, e.g., *FCC v. Pacifica Foundation,* 438 U.S. 726 (1978), in which the Court permitted the FCC to ban language that was "indecent" (but not "obscene") from the airwaves during afternoon hours when children were likely to be in the audience.

2. **"Mere-rationality" review for content-neutral regulations:** Where regulations against broadcasters are *content-neutral*, these regulations are judged very deferentially, essentially according to the "mere-rationality" standard. For instance, *Red Lion, supra,* seems to have applied "mere-rationality" review to the FCC's fairness doctrine, on the theory that that doctrine is essentially content-neutral.

3. **Middle-level scrutiny for content-based restrictions:** However, where the regulation against broadcasters is *content-based*, the Court seems to apply a *middle-level scrutiny*, more stringent than "mere-rationality" review. But even here the standard of review reflects the Court's view that broadcasters should be subjected to tighter regulation because of their access to scarce airwaves: the mid-level review given to content-based broadcasting regulations is clearly less stringent than the "strict" (and almost always fatal) review given to content-based regulations against newspapers and other non-broadcasters. (See *supra,* p. 479.) This middle-level scrutiny was demonstrated in *FCC v. League of Women Voters,* 468 U.S. 364 (1984), a 5-4 decision.

   a. **Ban on editorializing struck down:** In *League of Women Voters,* the Court struck down (by a 5-4 vote), a congressional prohibition on *editorializing* by public broadcasters who receive federal funding. The majority viewed the ban as being non-content-neutral. The test set forth by the Court was that such restrictions impinging on broadcasters' First Amendment rights will be upheld only if they are *"narrowly tailored* to further a *substantial governmental interest,* such as ensuring adequate and balanced coverage of public issues. … "

   b. **Test not satisfied:** The Court concluded that the ban on editorializing could not survive this middle-level review. For instance, Congress may have had a substantial governmental interest in making sure that public broadcasters did not become "vehicles for governmental propagandizing" as the result of federal funding, but there were other, more narrowly-tailored, ways of making sure that government did not interfere with the broadcasting judgment of station officials.

4. **Cable gets greater free speech:** The Court has held that *cable* television is, in effect, *somewhere between broadcast TV and newspapers* in terms of the amount of government regulation of speech that operators must tolerate.

   a. **Content-neutral regulation:** Thus where the regulation of cable TV is *content-neutral, mid-level review* is to be used. In *Turner Broadcasting System, Inc. v. FCC,* 512 U.S. 622 (1994) (*"Turner I"*), the Court held that where cable TV operators are subjected to content-neutral regulations, mid-level review, not the easy-to-satisfy "mere-rationality" standard used in the over-the-air broadcast cases, should be used.

i. **Regulations upheld:** But content-neutral governmental regulation of cable TV certainly can sometimes *pass* constitutional muster, even though mid-level rather than rational-relation review is used. For instance, Congress has enacted "must carry" provisions, which require cable TV systems to devote some of their channels, free of charge, to the retransmission of local broadcast TV stations. In a successor to *Turner I, supra,* the Court upheld these must-carry rules after mid-level review. The Court gave special deference to Congress' legislative findings on the need for must-carry, because Congress was better equipped than the judiciary to "amass and evaluate the *vast amounts of data*" bearing on legislative questions, especially ones concerning "regulatory schemes of the *inherent complexity*" and "assessments about the likely interaction of *industries undergoing rapid economic and technological change.*" *Turner Broadcasting System Inc. v. FCC,* 520 U.S. 180 (1997) (*"Turner II"*).

b. **Content-based regulation:** Where cable TV operators and programmers are regulated in a *content-based* way, *strict scrutiny* must be used. See *U.S. v. Playboy Entertainment Group, Inc.,* 529 U.S. 803 (2000).

Quiz Yourself on

REGULATION IN POLITICAL CAMPAIGNS; SPECIAL CONTEXTS; FREEDOM OF ASSOCIATION; DENIAL OF PUBLIC JOBS OR BENEFITS; SPECIAL PROBLEMS OF THE MEDIA

90. The legislature of the state of Langdell decided that there was too much money being spent on political campaigns in the state. Therefore, the legislature passed a statute providing for several limits on how much money could be spent in any year in connection with any person's campaign to be elected to a statewide office. These limits included the following:

[1] No donor could contribute more than $5,000 per year to any one candidate.

[2] No candidate could spend more than $250,000 of his or her own funds on advertising or promoting that candidate's election.

[3] No donor could give a total of more than $50,000 to all statewide candidates together.

[4] No individual could expend more than $10,000 in trying to bring about the election or defeat of a candidate other than himself, even if the individual's spending was done entirely independently of any candidate.

Which of these restrictions violates the free speech rights of the person whose spending is being limited?

---

91. The State of Unionville enacted a statute providing that any union representing government employees in the state may withhold from the paycheck of each non-union-member an amount in lieu of dues (a "mandatory agency fee") equal to the union's cost of representing that member in collective bargaining. The Unionville State Teachers Union therefore charges each teacher in the state's public schools who chooses not to join the union a mandatory agency fee equal to 75% of the amount each union member pays in dues. Pete, a teacher who has not joined the Union, sues it, claiming that the mandatory agency fee violates his freedom of expression, by forcing him to subsidize union speech that he disagrees with. (He claims that the Union's pursuit of higher teacher salaries is worsening Unionville's budget deficit.)

(a) What standard should the court use in reviewing the mandatory agency fee statute? _____

(b) Applying that standard, should the court agree with Pete that the agency fee violates his First Amendment rights? _____

92. Patti was the starting point guard for the girls' varsity basketball team at Prep, a public high school in Prep township. Coach, the team's head coach, after repeatedly telling Patti that she had been shooting too much and passing too little, benched Patti for most of the next three games. On the Sunday following the last benching, Patti, from her home, posted a TikToc video showing her shooting a basketball, with a text superimposed over it reading, "Fuck Girls Basketball. I'm sooo tired of being benched for 'excess shooting,' even though I'm the best shooter on the team." The post was seen by two of Patti's teammates. Three hours after posting the video, Patti removed it, but by then one of the two teammates who saw it, Angela, had emailed a screenshot of it to Coach, together with a message from Angela saying, "I'm really upset about this – Patti's complaining is bad for team morale." The next school day, Coach criticized Patti for the post, and Patti immediately apologized. Nonetheless, Coach suspended Patti from the team for the rest of the season, with the explanation that "Your vulgar language, and your public criticism of my coaching decisions, are conduct detrimental to the team's welfare, for which a season-ending suspension is an appropriate punishment."

Patti has now brought a federal-court civil suit against the Prep Board of Education (the "Board of Ed"), arguing that the suspension has infringed her freedom of expression. At a bench trial, the parties together have proved the above facts. The Board of Ed defends by arguing that the suspension was an appropriate punishment given that Patti's post violated both (1) the school's written policy against "vulgar or lewd language in connection with a school-sponsored extra-curricular activity"; and (2) a second written policy of the school, barring "language or conduct that substantially disrupts an extra-curricular activity." No evidence has been presented concerning any team member's knowledge of, or reaction to, Patti's post prior to the suspension, except for Angela's message to Coach. Nor has any evidence been presented about whether the Board of Ed has ever attempted to prevent or punish other episodes in which a student has made (in person or on social media) off-campus remarks containing vulgar or lewd language in connection with a school activity.

Should the judge find that the Board of Ed (acting through its employee, Coach) has violated Patti's freedom of expression, and why? _____

93. There have been several bombings of government office buildings on the island of Puerto Rico recently. After each bombing, an anonymous caller has told the local newspaper that the bomb was planted by "People for a Free Puerto Rico" (PFPR), an organization dedicated to using any means necessary to end Puerto Rico's status as a United States territory and establishing it as a sovereign nation. There is evidence that the PFPR was able to plant the bombs so successfully inside the buildings because its members or sympathizers have jobs in government agencies located in those buildings, who could furnish information and access for placement of the bombs. To deal with the threat, the territorial government of Puerto Rico has now imposed a requirement that any new applicant for any government position must before being hired sign a loyalty oath stating, among other things, that "I am not a member of the People for a Free Puerto Rico or of any group advocating the use of force to alter the territorial status of Puerto Rico." Ramona, an applicant for a position as a clerical worker in the Puerto Rican government, has declined to

sign the oath, without specifying her reasons. Can the government constitutionally decline to hire her on the grounds that she has refused to sign? _____

94. Sheryl was a low-level clerk in her state's Department of Motor Vehicles. News reports were published stating that Horace, the Commissioner of the Department of Motor Vehicles (and thus, ultimately, Sheryl's boss) may have taken payments from Computer Systems Inc. in return for helping Computer Systems get a contract to install a large new computer system at the Department. Horace protested his innocence, and the District Attorney eventually decided that no charges should be brought. Shortly thereafter, Sheryl said to a co-worker, while on the job, "I still think Horace took the money, and I think he's a crook." Another employee who overheard the remark reported it to Horace, who immediately fired Sheryl for insubordination and fomenting discord in the Department. Under the relevant Civil Service rules, Sheryl was an at-will employee who had no reason to expect continued employment. Sheryl now seeks a court order restoring her position, on the grounds that she was fired in violation of her First Amendment rights. Should the court grant reinstatement to Sheryl? _____

95. The state of West Carolina has assigned to the state's Attorney General's office the responsibility for ensuring that charities that solicit in the state do not commit fraud. Years ago, the A.G. promulgated a rule ("Rule 100") requiring any charity that solicits more than $10,000 in total donations in any year from West Carolina residents to report to the A.G. the names and addresses of any donor (whether residing in West Carolina or not) who has contributed more than $5,000 in that year. Rule 100 includes a promise by the A.G.'s office that it will keep any reported information secret from the public. (However, several years ago, due to a clerical error in the office, the Rule 100 donor reports from several charities were made publicly available on the office's website.) The administrative history of Rule 100 shows that it was enacted so that if the A.G.'s office ever had reason to suspect that a given charity was committing fraud in soliciting, that charity's up-to-date donor information would already be present in the A.G.'s files, eliminating any need for the office to subpoena records from the charity at the start of an investigation.

Toys for Kids, a Nevada-based charity that raises about $100,000 per year from West Carolina residents, has sued the A.G.'s office in federal court, claiming that Rule 100 violates Toys' (and its donors') First Amendment freedom of association. The charity argues that given the risk that the identities of its donors might be leaked by mistake (as happened previously), Rule 100 cannot survive the relevant standard of review — whatever that standard is — because any interest the A.G.'s office may have in combating fraudulent solicitations can be adequately served by the less-intrusive alternative of issuing document subpoenas to a particular charity when and if the office has reason to suspect the charity of fraud.

(a) What standard should the court use in determining whether Rule 100, as applied to Toys, violates Toys' and its donors First Amendment freedom of association? _____

(b) Using the standard you supplied in part (a), should the court find that Rule 100 is unconstitutional as applied to Toys? _____

(c) For this part only, assume (whether the assumption is correct or not) that the court finds that Rule 100 unconstitutionally violates Toys' freedom of association. Should the court also hold that the Rule is invalid "on its face," i.e., that it cannot constitutionally be applied to *any* charity, including those not presently before the court? _____

96. P.J. Summers, a former football player turned sports announcer, was charged with the brutal murder of his wife. While in police custody, Summers gave a confession. In pretrial hearings, the trial judge determined that the *Miranda* rules had not been complied with, and decided that the confession would not be admissible at the trial. The press learned of the confession through pretrial proceedings in open court, and did not

act improperly in obtaining this information. Prosecutors decided to try Summers as a principal in the murder, and also decided to charge B.C. Scowling, a long-time friend of Summers, as an accomplice. Both trials were to be held simultaneously (but in front of separate juries) in proceedings conducted by Judge Jones.

Judge Jones was very worried that disclosures about the confession might make it difficult or impossible to impanel a jury that would be fair to Summers. Therefore, several days before jury selection was to start, Jones issued two orders from the bench: (1) he ordered that no newspaper, magazine or broadcaster report the existence or details of the inadmissible confession until after the jury had been picked (once the jury was picked, it could be sequestered, so that prejudicial disclosures would not matter anymore); (2) he also ordered that no lawyer on the case, including the lawyer for Scowling, disclose to the press or to anyone else the existence of Summers' confession. (There was reason to believe that Scowlings' lawyer planned to say in a public press conference, "My client is innocent; P.J. confessed, and in his confession he said that he acted alone").

    (a) Is the judge's order in part (1) constitutional? _____

    (b) Is the judge's order in part (2) constitutional? _____

97. Roger is a reporter for the Hillsdale Star, a local newspaper. In the most celebrated crime to hit Hillsdale in many years, Joshua, an eight-year-old boy, was found strangled in front of his house. The police have not found any suspects. One week after the killing, Roger published an article saying, "A source that I cannot identify saw the crime from a distance, and believes that the perpetrator was a young white male about 22 years old, six feet tall, weighing about 175 pounds." In the ensuing months, the police have never been able to find this or any other witness to the crime. The prosecutor called Roger in front of a grand jury, and demanded that he identify the witness who served as his source. Roger stated under oath that the witness was fearful that the killer would kill her to silence her. Roger further stated that he had signed a written pledge to the witness that he would never reveal her name; only in response to this pledge did the witness agree to speak to him. Roger did say, however, that the witness lived in the neighborhood and that in his opinion, she could be identified by good police work. The judge then ordered Roger to disclose the witness' identity, or be found in contempt of court. Roger refused. There is no state law relevant to the issue. Can Roger constitutionally be found in contempt and imprisoned until he divulges the name of the witness? _____

Answers

90. All but [1], and even the continuing validity of [1] is not certain. In a series of campaign-finance decisions beginning with the 1976 decision in *Buckley v. Valeo*, the Supreme Court has steadily broadened the types of limits that it has found to be unconstitutional restrictions on free speech. (The Court has consistently held that campaign spending is a form of speech, and is thus protected by the First Amendment, so that significant restrictions on such spending must survive strict scrutiny.)

As to [1], *Buckley* held that the interest in preventing corruption and the appearance of corruption (the *only* interest the Court has ever found to justify limits on campaign financing) justifies some limitations on donations by a single donor to a single candidate. The $5,000 limit here nearly matches the $5,200 per year federal-election donation limit in existence in 2014, the year when the Court made its decision in *McCutcheon v. FEC* on the related issue of "aggregate" donation limits. Since the Court has not so far struck down the federal limits, the $5,000 limit presumably remains a valid means of achieving the compelling governmental interest in combating corruption and its appearance. (But the Court's tendency to strike an ever-broadening array of campaign-finance limits suggests that even this right to limit single donor-donee contributions may not remain in force indefinitely.)

[2] is clearly unconstitutional, under *Buckley* itself — the Court there held that limits on the amount that a candidate may spend from his own personal funds in order to get elected cannot be justified on the grounds that they serve the interest in avoiding corruption (since a candidate would not bribe himself). And the government's asserted interest in "leveling the playing field" (equalizing the resources of competing candidates) has been expressly rejected by the Court as an interest that can justify limits on campaign spending.

[3] is also clearly unconstitutional, under the 2014 decision in *McCutcheon v. FEC*. That decision rejected federal "aggregate" donation limits, which prevented any donor from giving more than $48,600 to all federal candidates collectively (as well as from giving more than $74,600 to all non-candidate political committees collectively). The *McCutcheon* Court found that any limits on aggregate donations are not necessary to serve the anti-corruption interest (repeatedly held by the Court to be the only interest which may support campaign-finance limits); therefore, the comparable state limit in [3] would undoubtedly also be struck down by the Court.

[4] is, too, clearly unconstitutional, and would have been so ever since the 1976 *Buckley* decision. The Court held in *Buckley* that where a person makes campaign-related expenditures ***independently*** of the candidate, there is no serious danger of a "quid pro quo," so that the government's interest in avoiding even the appearance of corruption is not significantly implicated. Therefore, a person (as well as a corporation — see *Citizens United v. FEC* (2010)) may spend unlimited funds urging the election or defeat of any candidate in any election, as long as the spender acts completely independently of any candidate.

91. **(a) An "exacting scrutiny" standard, by which the agency fee scheme will be struck down unless it "serves a compelling state interest that cannot be achieved through means significantly less restrictive of associational freedoms."** That's the standard the Supreme Court articulated for exactly this type of mandatory agency fee statute, in *Janus v. AFSCME* (2018).

(b) Yes. In *Janus*, the Supreme Court held that an Illinois mandatory agency fee statute virtually identical to the one here violated non-union-members' free speech rights, by "compelling them to ***subsidize private speech*** on matters of substantial public concern." The Court in *Janus* reasoned that the only interest advanced by Illinois in support of its statute — preventing "free riding" by non-union-member employees who get the benefit of the union's collective bargaining efforts without having to pay for those efforts — was not a "compelling" interest. The same would be true of the statute here. Therefore, the court must conclude that the Unionville statute violates the free expression rights of Pete and all other public employees who choose not to join the union.

92. **Yes, because the Board of Ed's interest in regulating Patti's off-campus speech was weaker than had the speech taken place either on campus or during a team event, and that interest was outweighed by Patti's First Amendment right to criticize the way in which a school activity is conducted.** The facts here are quite similar to those in *Mahanoy Area School District v. B.L.* (2021), where the Court found that the one-year-long suspension of a student (P) from the school's cheerleading squad for making a similar social-media post while off-campus violated P's freedom of expression. *Mahanoy* establishes that a school has a legitimate interest in regulating off-campus student speech that concerns school activities, but that this interest is ***relatively weak*** in an off-campus-speech scenario like this one, because (1) the school is not acting "*in loco parentis*" (as it would if the speech occurred either on-campus or during an off-campus school activity itself); (2) if the school were allowed to tightly regulate such off-

campus speech in addition to on-campus speech, every student's right to speak would be impaired for all 24 hours of the day; and (3) a school must "protect unpopular ideas," because public schools are the "nurseries of democracy."

Here, the two interests that the Board of Ed claims to have been pursuing are relatively weak (as they were in *Mahanoy*). As to the interest in avoiding "vulgar or lewd language" in connection with a school activity, the facts stipulate that the school district did not present any evidence that it has *generally* attempted to police the politeness of off-campus speech about school activities; this matters, because a similar lack of evidence caused the *Mahanoy* Court to view the school's interest in civility there as relatively weak. As to the school's interest in avoiding disruption of school activities, the fact that the only evidence of disruption in *Mahanoy* consisted of a few minutes in which a couple of P's teammates told teachers that they were "upset" by P's posts led the Court to view any disruption that occurred as minor; the same conclusion is appropriate here, where the only evidence of disruption was an email from one student (Angela), saying without elaboration that she was upset. Therefore, given that the judge is required to follow *Mahonoy* (the Court's only modern decision on when schools may regulate off-campus speech relating to school activities), the judge should find that any interest in regulation held by the Board of Ed was outweighed by Patti's First Amendment right to comment freely and publicly on school activities.

93. **No.** One may not be required to state in a loyalty oath that one has not performed a certain act (or that one will not perform it in the future) unless ***actual performance*** of that act would be grounds for discharge. One may not be discharged for membership in an organization advocating overthrow of the government or other illegality, unless one has ***knowledge*** of the organization's purpose and ***specific intent*** to further that purpose. Consequently, one may not be required to swear a blanket oath that one has not been a member of such an organization — language referring to the swearer's knowledge of the illegal purposes, and to her specific intent to further them, must be inserted into the oath. Since the oath here does not refer to Ramona's specific intent to use force to alter the Puerto Rican government, she cannot be penalized for refusing to sign it. See *Cole v. Richardson*.

94. **Yes, probably.** When government attempts to deny a public job or benefit because of a person's speech-related activities, the level of judicial review depends on whether the speech related to matters of ***"public concern."*** If the speech did relate to matters of "public concern," then the Court gives something like strict scrutiny to the situation, striking a balance between the free speech rights of the employee and the state's interest as an employer in conducting its activities efficiently. *Connick v. Myers*. Here, the speech is clearly relating to a matter of public concern, i.e., whether the head of the department took a bribe. Since Sheryl was engaging in core political speech, her interest in being allowed to do so was a strong one. On the other side of the equation, Sheryl was a low-level clerk, not a policy-making official; therefore, her speech was unlikely to have created a severe additional threat to the department's efficiency, especially since other people inside and outside the department were undoubtedly discussing the same much-publicized issue anyway. *Rankin v. McPherson*. Consequently, a court would probably conclude that Sheryl's free speech interest outweighed the department's interest in maintaining smooth operations; if so, the court should order Sheryl reinstated.

By the way, it makes a difference that here, Sheryl's statement was ***not required as part of her job duties.*** *Garcetti v. Ceballos* establishes that where an employee speaks as part of her official duties, what she says ***gets no First Amendment protection at all.*** So if, say, Sheryl's official duties had included the obligation to make a report about any conflicts-of-interest she observed on the job, her statement, "Horace took money from Computer Systems in violation of our Department's conflict-of-interest rules," made in her officially-required report, would not get First Amendment protection, and Sheryl would now not be entitled to reinstatement. So it's only because Sheryl was speaking "as a citizen" (not as an employee) to her co-worker that she gets protection under *Connick v. Myers.*

Lastly, observe that because Sheryl was an at-will employee, she could be fired at any time for "no reason"; even so, under *Connick* she had a First Amendment right not to be fired for the ***particular*** reason that she was exercising her free speech rights.

95. **(a) The "exacting scrutiny" standard, by which the disclosure requirement must be "narrowly tailored" to the achievement of a "sufficiently important governmental interest."** The Supreme Court articulated this standard in a case involving a California disclosure requirement very similar to the one here; see *Americans for Prosperity Foundation v Bonta* (2021).

(b) Yes, the court should find that Rule 100 unconstitutionally violates the free association rights of Toys and its donors. The *Americans for Prosperity* case, *supra,* involved a California requirement that charities raising more than a certain total annual amount from California residents file with the state A.G.'s office a copy of the charity's federal IRS filing ("Form 990") listing the identity of significant donors. The California rule was obviously similar to Rule 100 here. The Court in *Americans for Prosperity* concluded that (1) there was a significant risk that the public would learn the identity of donors appearing on the Form 990 (as the A.G.'s office had inadvertently allowed to happen in the past); (2) members of the public might therefore harass the charity and its donors based on the leaked information; and (3) the disclosure requirement was not "narrowly tailored" to achieving the state's concededly-important goal of reducing fraudulent solicitations, because the A.G.'s office could have used the ***less-burdensome alternative*** of waiting until it had reason to suspect a particular charity of fraud, and then subpoenaing the Form 990 from the charity. That same reasoning applies here, since West Carolina (like California in *Americans for Prosperity*) could have achieved its anti-fraud objective by using the less-burdensome method of waiting until it had suspicions about a particular charity and then subpoenaing the donor records from the charity.

(c) Yes, the court should find Rule 100 unconstitutional "on its face." This is exactly what the Supreme Court did as to the California disclosure requirement struck down in *Americans for Prosperity, supra.* In the First Amendment area, the ***"overbreadth"*** doctrine makes it especially easy for a court to find a law to be invalid on its face: the law will be struck down as overly broad "if a ***substantial number*** of its ***applications*** are unconstitutional, judged in ***relation to the statute's plainly legitimate sweep.***" *Id.* The Court in *Americans for Prosperity* decided that in First Amendment cases in which the law (such as the disclosure requirement there) fails the relevant "exacting scrutiny" test, then even the mere ***"theoretical risk"*** that the law will have a ***"chilling effect"*** on the freedom of association will compel the court to rule that the law is overbroad and thus invalid on its face. The same conclusion is required on our facts, since (as described in Part (b)) Rule 100 fails "exacting scrutiny," and will thus be deemed to have a chilling effect on the freedom of association of donors to any charity covered by the Rule, including charities not before the court.

96. **(a) No.** "Gag orders" — that is, pretrial orders prohibiting the press from publishing certain types of information about the case — are virtually never constitutionally permissible. See *Nebraska Press Ass'n v. Stuart.* A gag order is a species of prior restraint, so it can be allowed only if its benefits substantially outweigh its First Amendment dangers, something that will virtually never happen. Here, there are other methods available to the judge to help assure a fair trial (e.g., careful *voir dire* to make sure that each juror has either not heard about the confession or understands that it is to be absolutely disregarded). (A gag order might be allowed if the press had ***illegally*** gotten the information, e.g., by bribing a member of the police department to release sealed information; but where the press comes by the information legally, a

gag order preventing it from disseminating the material will almost never be upheld.)

(b) Yes, probably. States may prevent a lawyer from making any statement that would have a *"substantial likelihood of materially prejudicing"* an adjudicative proceeding. *Gentile v. State Bar of Nevada.* The state must give guidelines that are reasonably specific about what kinds of disclosures are and are not allowed. The ban here, which refers specifically to the facts of the confession, seems to have adequate specificity. While some sorts of gag orders might unconstitutionally restrict a defense lawyer's right to defend his client in the public eye (e.g., the states probably can't prevent a lawyer from asserting that his client is innocent, or from generally describing the client's proposed defense), references to a co-defendant's inadmissible confession are probably the sort of unduly prejudicial remarks that a lawyer falling within the court's jurisdiction may be barred from making.

97. **Yes.** The First Amendment is not violated when a reporter is required to testify before a grand jury concerning information obtained from confidential sources during newsgathering. In fact, reporters are not even entitled to a *qualified privilege* to refuse to identify their sources or information received from those sources — thus a reporter, like any other citizen, may be required to divulge information that could be obtained by police or prosecutors from other sources. *Branzburg v. Hayes.* (Over half of the states have enacted *statutes* that grant reporters a privilege against disclosure of confidential sources or information. If such a "shield law" existed here, it would prevent Roger from being held in contempt on these facts.)

 Exam Tips on
FREEDOM OF EXPRESSION

Freedom of expression typically makes up a larger portion of a full-year Con. Law exam than does any other single topic. Almost any regulation of an individual's conduct may pose a free expression issue, so think very broadly. Here are some particular things to keep in mind:

☛ Remember that free expression issues are posed not just where government is regulating "speech" but also where government is regulating *"conduct"* that includes an *expressive component.* So for each activity that's being restricted, first deal with the issue: "Is there an expressive component to the activity?" If you answer "yes," you've got a free expression issue. (*Example:* Panhandling on the subway has been held to be expressive — and thus protected — conduct.)

☛ Always keep in mind the five *"unprotected categories,"* the categories thought to be of *so little value* that they get *no First Amendment protection at all* (as long as government is not singling out particular disfavored *viewpoints,* something that will trigger strict scrutiny even for an unprotected category). If your facts fall into an unprotected category, you don't have to worry about whether the government is unreasonably restraining expression, as long as government is being content-neutral.

    ☞ Here is a list of the five unprotected categories:

        [1] *"Incitement."* This category includes advocacy of *imminent lawless behavior,* as well as the utterance of *"fighting words,"* i.e., words that are likely to precipitate an immediate physical conflict.

[2] *Obscenity*.

[3] *Misleading or deceptive speech (i.e., fraud)*.

[4] Speech *integral to criminal conduct*, such as speech that is part of a *conspiracy* to commit a crime or speech *proposing an illegal transaction*.

[5] *Defamation*.

Example: A state can flatly *forbid all obscenity,* without even trying to make its ban narrowly tailored to achieve a significant governmental interest (something government would have to do for a content-neutral regulation outside an unprotected category).

☛ Once you've identified a situation where government is "substantially impairing" protected speech or expressive conduct, decide whether the regulation is *"content-neutral"* or not.

   ☞ A tip to help you decide: Ask whether the harm the government is trying to prevent would exist to the same degree if the listener/reader didn't understand English. If the answer is "no," the government's action is probably content-based.

   ☞ Always consider the government's *motive* in regulating the speech — the issue is what the government wished to do: did it want to suppress/control ideas, or did it really want to regulate "secondary" concerns not related to the expressive content?

☛ If you decide that the regulation is "content-based," apply *strict scrutiny*. That is, write that the regulation must be struck down unless the government shows that the restriction is *necessary* to achieve a *compelling* governmental purpose. You should almost always then conclude that the government restriction can't survive. (Usually, the key reason will be that there is some less restrictive way to deal with the problem, even if that less restrictive way is not an absolutely perfect way of handling the problem.)

   ☞ One commonly-tested scenario: A public school district allows community groups to use the school for their own purposes after hours. A particular group is denied access because of the type of activity, or because of the group's controversial views. (Typically, you should conclude that the restriction here is content-based, and therefore apply strict scrutiny.)

   ☞ Keep in mind that strict scrutiny for content-based regulations limits a state's right to *impose civil liability for hurtful speech.* So, for instance, be ready to say that there is a First Amendment violation if the state lets a person against whom *intentionally-offensive speech is directed* recover under state law for *intentional infliction of emotional distress (IIED).* (Cite to *Snyder v. Phelps*, where funeral picketers were shielded from IIED liability.)

   ☞ For a regulation to be "content-neutral," the regulation must be more than just *"viewpoint"* neutral. "Content neutral" means "without reference to the content." And that, in turn, means that restrictions that put *whole topics* off limits — or *circumscribe discussion* of certain topics — are not content-neutral.

Example: Assume the federal government refuses to allow people to register *trademarks* for *"offensive"* terms, like "Nigger" or "Kike." Say that this prohibition is content-based (not content-neutral), so that it must be strictly scrutinized (which the restriction here won't survive). Cite to *Matal v. Tam* (federal government can't use a "no offensive trademarks rule" to refuse registration for "Slants," because the rule can't survive strict scrutiny).

☛ If you conclude that the regulation is truly "content-neutral," use a three-part test. For instance, any regulation of the ***"time, place and manner"*** of demonstrations or other expressive conduct will be analyzed by this test if you find that it is content-neutral. Here are the three parts (***all*** of which must be satisfied):

☞ The regulation must serve a "***significant*** governmental interest";

☞ The regulation must be ***narrowly tailored*** to achieve that objective; and

☞ The regulation must leave open adequate ***alternative channels*** for communication.

☞ Look most closely at the ***second*** of the above parts most closely: whether the regulation is ***narrowly-tailored*** to achieving the governmental interest. When content-neutral restrictions are subjected to mid-level review and the government loses, the narrow-tailoring requirement is usually the reason. Remember, if the restriction burdens ***"substantially more speech than is necessary"*** to achieve the objective, that will mean that the restriction wasn't narrowly-tailored, thus flunking mid-level review.

Example: A state passes a statute making it a felony for any person convicted of sexual assault of a minor to post any message on any social-media website, including Facebook. P, who has such a conviction, makes a one-sentence post on Facebook having nothing to do with sex or minors, and the state prosecutes him. The statute is a violation of P's First Amendment freedom — even though the state has a more-than-significant interest in preventing convicted sex-offenders' use of the Internet to locate new underaged victims, the statute restricts much more expression than would be reasonably necessary to achieve that objection. (However, a statute that just prohibited P from posting on, say, a website designed for minors would probably *not* fail to be narrowly-tailored to meet the state's stop-sexual-assault-of-minors objective.) (Cite to *Packingham v. North Carolina.)*

Note: In assessing any "time, place and manner" restriction, consider whether a ***public forum*** is involved. The "narrowly tailored" and "alternative channels left open" requirements are ***more strictly construed when a public forum is involved.*** (The public forum is discussed further below.)

☛ Always consider whether either of two key First Amendment doctrines applies:

☞ First, ***overbreadth***. Remember that most litigants in Con. Law are not permitted to assert the rights of others. But under First Amendment overbreadth, P is allowed to assert that the government regulation violates the rights of a person who is not now before the court. (*Example:* A city bans the sale of "sexually explicit" materials. P is charged with violating the statute. The materials sold by him are clearly obscene. Yet, he can defeat the prosecution by showing that the ban also applies to non-obscene sexually explicit materials, which cannot be constitutionally prohibited.)

☞ Second, ***vagueness***. Remember, a statute or regulation is unconstitutionally vague if a person of normal intelligence wouldn't know whether the action in question was forbidden or not. (*Examples:* Statutes forbidding conduct that is "demeaning," "offensive," or "disruptive to public order" might all be found to be unconstitutionally vague, because it is not clear where the line is between what they do and do not proscribe.)

☛ Many exam questions involve a speaker who tries to rouse the crowd to take *subversive* or *illegal action*. Be on the lookout for persons charged with "inciting to riot," "urging the overthrow of the government," "advocating illegal conduct," or the like. When you have such a fact pattern, check for three things:

☞ Was the riot or illegality *imminent*, as opposed to something that would take place at a later date? Only speech urging imminent illegality may be punished. (*Example:* If the speaker says, "Start thinking about forming guerrilla units ... ," the required imminence is not present.)

☞ Was the advocacy *intended* to produce illegality? (If illegality was the *unintended by-product* of the speaker's speech, he can't be punished for it.)

☞ Was the advocacy *likely* to produce the illegality? Ineffectual efforts don't count. (*Example:* If people are in a park for other purposes, happen to listen to the speaker, and then go about their business, the "likely to produce illegality" requirement probably is not met.)

☛ When government attempts to require a *license* or *permit* before expressive activity (typically a speech or demonstration) may occur, here are the things to check for:

☞ Make sure that the license/permit requirement is truly *content-neutral*, both as written (i.e., "on the face" of the statute) and as applied (i.e., as the permits are actually handed out by officials). A permit/license requirement cannot be used as a smoke-screen for suppressing unpopular views or unpopular topics.

☞ Make sure that the scheme does not give *excessive discretion* to the official charged with issuing the permit. (*Example:* If the fact pattern tells you that the permit is to be issued "based on the Police Commissioner's overall assessment of the good of the community," that's excessive discretion.) This is a commonly tested aspect.

☞ Profs frequently test on whether a speaker has a right to *ignore* a permit requirement.

   ☞ If the permit requirement is unconstitutional *on its face* (e.g., it's content-based, in that it requires a permit for certain topics but not others), the speaker is *not* required to apply for a permit. He may decline to apply, speak, and then defend on the grounds of the permit requirement's unconstitutionality.

   ☞ But if the permit is not facially invalid, only unconstitutional *as applied* to the speaker, then the speaker generally does *not* have the right to ignore the requirement. He must apply for the permit, then seek prompt judicial review rather than just going ahead and speaking. (But an exception exists where the applicant shows that *sufficiently prompt judicial review* of the denial was not available.)

   ☞ When the speaker is judicially *enjoined* from speaking, marching, etc., he generally may *not* ignore the injunction and then raise the constitution as a defense in a subsequent contempt proceeding. Instead, he must seek prior judicial review.

☞ If the above requirements are satisfied, then the permit requirement is valid. (*Example:* A permit will not be invalid merely because it is issued upon conditions that the marchers or demonstrators not block the public's access to a particular place, e.g., an abortion clinic or government building.)

☛ Be on the lookout for expression that may constitute ***"fighting words."*** These are words that are likely to induce the addressee to ***commit an act of violence***, typically against the speaker. Government may forbid fighting words, or punish them after they are spoken.

☞ But be skeptical of claims by the government that the speech in question really constituted "fighting words." Most importantly, remember that the police must ***control the crowd*** if they have the ability to do so — they can't stand back, then punish the speaker for rousing the crowd to violence.

☞ Also, distinguish fighting words from mere ***"offensive speech."*** Speech may not be forbidden merely because the listeners are likely to find it offensive. (*Examples:* Nazis demonstrating in front of Holocaust survivors, or black students calling white students "honkey" at a public university, are probably not using "fighting words," merely "offensive speech" — unless the circumstances made violence very likely, the speech cannot be forbidden.)

☞ Look out for attempts to restrict ***"hate speech."*** A ***broad ban*** on ***all fighting words*** is OK. So is a broad ban on all words or acts intended to ***harass*** or ***intimidate*** others. Government can even single outs certain intimidating acts and forbid them (e.g., ***cross burnings***, when done as a threat or intimidation), while declining to forbid other intimidating acts (e.g., burnings in effigy). But government ***can't forbid just those fighting words or threats that are motivated by particular kinds of hatred*** (e.g., racial or gender hatred). (Cite to *R.A.V. v. St. Paul* on this point.)

Example: University, a public university, passes a speech code that says "All students are forbidden to harass or threaten other students on the basis of race, gender, or sexual orientation. Violations are punishable by suspension." Since the code bans just certain types of harassment or threats (those based on race, gender and sexual orientation) and not others (e.g., those based on political affiliation), the code is a content-based regulation, and must be strictly scrutinized. It will probably fail that scrutiny, since there are content-neutral alternatives that are less restrictive of speech and will do the job almost as well (e.g., a code banning *all* harassments and threats, regardless of the speaker's motive).

☞ Speech cannot be banned on the mere grounds that it is ***profane***. This merely makes it "offensive," not "obscene" or "fighting words." (*Example:* D can wear a jacket saying, "Fuck the Draft." Cite to *Cohen v. California*.)

☞ Whenever you're dealing with a ban on "offensive" conduct or "harassment," consider the possibility that there may be a ***vagueness*** problem with the regulation.

☛ Whenever your fact pattern involves a restriction on speech that takes place in a ***public forum***, note this fact, and try to explain what difference it makes.

☞ The fact that the expressive conduct is taking place in a public forum only makes a difference if the regulation is content-neutral. Assuming that it is content-neutral, the principal difference is that we use ***mid-level review*** (the restriction must be ***narrowly drawn to serve a significant governmental interest***, while leaving open adequate alternative channels for the communication) as opposed to "mere-rationality" review for non-public-forum speech.

☞ The classic *"traditional"* public forums are: ***streets***, ***sidewalks***, ***parks***. There are also ***"designated"*** public forums, where government has decided to open the place to a broad range of expressive activity (e.g., an open City Council meeting or a school whose classrooms are made available after hours to any community group); the same rules apply to designated forums as to true forums, except that government can change its mind and make the place a non-public forum.

☞ The mere fact that something is public property does not mean it is a public or designated-public forum. There are public spaces that are ***"non-public forums,"*** as to which "mere-rationality" review is all that is used. (*Examples:* Airport terminals, jails, military bases, courthouses, government office buildings.)

☞ But even in a non-public forum, regulation must still be ***rational*** and ***viewpoint-neutral***. Be especially alert for a violation of viewpoint-neutrality when government ***excludes religious groups*** from benefits that it gives to a wide range of non-religious groups.

Example: A school district allows a variety of local community groups to use elementary school classrooms after hours to run programs promoting the "general welfare." However, the district excludes from this program any activity or group that is "primarily of a religious nature." This will be unconstitutional viewpoint based discrimination, even though school classrooms used this way are probably a non-public forum.

☞ Even if a private group is somehow involved in speech, check to see whether ***government*** is the ***real speaker.*** If the real speaker is government, ***don't use public-forum analysis.*** Instead, say that government-as-speaker can behave in a content-based way, delivering just the message it wants.

Example: A private group donates a message-bearing monument that a city government decides to take and display in a park. Government will be deemed to be the speaker by virtue of its decision to accept and display the monument. Therefore, the city can discriminate based on the message: the city doesn't have to accept other donated monuments with messages that the city doesn't approve of. [Cite to *Pleasant Grove v. Summum.*]

☞ If you apply ***mid-level review*** to a content-neutral time-place-and-manner restriction on speech in a public forum, be sure to stress that the required ***"narrow tailoring"*** means that there must be a ***quite tight fit between the means and the end*** — the law will not survive if there's ***some less-speech-restrictive way*** to achieve the state's objective as well (or even ***"almost as well"***).

Example: A state bans all demonstrations within a 35 foot "buffer zone" around the entrance to any abortion clinic, to avoid harassment and blocking of the clinic entrance. Even if the court believes this is content-neutral, the fact that the state has other means to achieve these important objectives [e.g., a specific ban on harassment, or a ban on blocking the entrance] means that the buffer zone ban is not narrowly-tailored to the state's objectives, and is a violation of protesters' free speech rights. [Cite to *McCullen v. Coakley*]

☛ Fact patterns often involve speech that takes place on *private property*. Here are the two aspects that are most frequently tested:

☞ The *public* has no First Amendment right of access to private property. (*Example:* A person does not have a First Amendment right to distribute literature in a privately-owned shopping center.)

☞ Government may limit an owner's right to use, or to rent his property to others, for expressive purposes. Here, use standard "time, place and manner" analysis, except that no public forum is involved. Therefore, the regulation will usually be upheld if it is content-neutral and other avenues are left for the message. (*Example:* Government may prevent owners from putting signage on their property advertising their wares, as long as the ban applies to all types of signage, and there are other advertising channels available.)

☛ The same rules apply to regulation of *"symbolic expression"* as apply to speech and speech-mixed-with-conduct. "Symbolic expression" refers to *non-verbal acts*.

☞ For instance, if government wants to ban destruction of the flag, it must do so in a content-neutral way (e.g., it cannot ban flag burning that is intended as a means of political dissent while allowing flag burning that is intended as a means of destroying worn-out flags).

☛ Remember that when the government regulates *defamation*, there are First Amendment limitations:

☞ Most important, under *New York Times v. Sullivan*, if P is a *public official* or *public figure*, he may only win a defamation suit against D for a statement relating to P's official conduct if P can prove that D's statement was made either "with *knowledge* that it was false" or "with *reckless disregard*" of whether it was true or false. Use the phrase "actual malice" to describe this requirement.

☞ Be sure to examine whether the plaintiff is truly a public or, rather, private figure. If P is a private figure, he merely has to prove negligence rather than "actual malice."

☞ Remember that in an action for "intentional infliction of emotional distress," P must, similarly, follow *New York Times v. Sullivan* and prove "actual malice," if P is a public figure.

☛ Remember that government *can't generally make it a crime to "tell a lie."* Government can forbid making factually-false statements within certain long-established *pre-defined categories* (e.g., defamation, perjury, fraud). But outside those categories, government can't pass a law making it a crime to lie, even if the lie would be likely to cause harm.

Example: Congress can't make it a crime to falsely state that the speaker has received the Congressional Medal of Honor. Cite to *U.S. v. Alvarez* on this point.

☛ *Obscenity* is frequently tested. Here are some of the most commonly-tested sub-issues:

☞ The relevant standard is the *"community"* standard — if the relevant sale and trial take place in a small town in Kansas, what counts is whether the average member of that town would find that the work as a whole appeals to the "prurient" interest.

☞ The fact that the work shows *nakedness* is not enough — there must be real or simulated sex that is described or portrayed.

☞ Remember that no matter how obscene the work is, its *private possession* by an adult in the privacy of his own home cannot be punished. (But the *seller* can still be punished.)

☞ Be sure to distinguish between material that is truly "obscene," and material that's merely *"indecent."* Mere nakedness, for instance, doesn't make something obscene (e.g., because of the possibility that the material may have artistic or social value, or because the material may not be "patently offensive.")

☞ So if government tries to regulate "indecency," indicate that the material gets First Amendment protection and that government has to satisfy strict scrutiny.

Example: Congress prohibits the furnishing of "indecent" material on the Internet, hoping to keep this stuff away from minors. You should apply strict scrutiny, and strike down the restriction, because the total ban is overbroad — the ban covers material that could be proscribed because it's obscene, but also material that's not obscene and thus protected as to adults. Cite to *Reno v. ACLU.*

Same analysis if Congress, trying to avoid having minors access indecent material, says that a Web site can show such material only if the user is required to provide proof that he is an adult; this will flunk strict scrutiny if a less-restrictive and equally-effective alternative — say, user-installed filtering — is available. Cite to *Ashcroft v. ACLU.*

☞ But government has a relatively free hand to regulate the *"secondary effects"* of indecent speech. (*Example:* A town can ban live nude dancing if it reasonably believes that nude dancing establishments contribute to increased drug use, prostitution, etc.)

☛ Ascertain whether the regulated speech is *"commercial"* (as opposed to core political) speech. Commercial speech is speech proposing a sale or other commercial transaction. Here are the things to remember about regulation of commercial speech:

☞ If the commercial speech is truthful and proposes a *legal* transaction, the Court uses *mid-level review.* The restriction survives only if it: (1) *directly advances* (2) a *substantial* governmental interest (3) in a way that is *"not more extensive than is necessary"* to achieve the government's objective. This is true even if the regulation is *content-based.* (So it's somewhat easier for government to do content-based regulation of commercial speech than of non-commercial speech, as to which strict scrutiny has to be used.)

☞ If the speech is *false*, *deceptive* or proposes an *illegal transaction*, government can *flatly ban* it.

☞ Profs frequently test on whether the government may prohibit or regulate truthful advertising about products that are *harmful* but *lawful*. Generally, this regulation gets mid-level review, which it will often *flunk* because *substantially less-restrictive means are available*. (*Examples:* If government tries to prohibit or tightly regulate truthful advertising for *cigarettes*, *liquor* or *gambling*, the Court is likely to say that less-restrictive means like educational campaigns, or higher taxes, must first be tried. Cite to *Lorillard*, the Mass. case that banned outdoor tobacco advertising, on this point.)

☞ Restrictions on *lawyer advertising* are often tested. Except for some *in-person solicitation* by profit-motivated lawyers seeking clients, states generally can't block truthful advertising. (*Example:* States can't block a public interest lawyer or advocacy group from soliciting clients, even through direct mail or in-person contacts.)

☛ Be on the lookout for the First Amendment implications of *restrictions on campaign financing*. The government *may* place monetary limits on *direct contributions* by one donor to one candidate. But most other campaign-finance limits are likely to be found to be a *violation of citizens' free speech rights*.

> *Example:* Government may not place *any limit at all* on how much a person (or corporation) may spend to advocate the election of a particular candidate, as long as the spender/advocate is *acting independently* of the candidate's own efforts. Cite to *Buckley v. Valeo* and *Citizens United*.

☛ If the regulation is of *public school students*, state that the courts apply a "balancing" test: the student has a limited right of free speech, to be balanced against the administration's right to *carry out its educational mission* and to *maintain discipline*. (So officials may not suppress students' speech merely because they disagree with it on ideological or political grounds, but they may ban profanity, or ban school-newspaper stories that would disturb the school's educational mission, such as stories about sex.)

☞ Where the student speech takes place *off-campus*, and is *not part of a school-sponsored extra-curricular activity*, say that the school may nonetheless be entitled to regulate the content or manner of the speech. But mention also that the school's interest in regulation is considerably *weaker* than in the case of in-school speech. Cite to *Mahanoy*.

Example: P tries out for shortstop on the varsity baseball team at Public High, but the coaches choose X instead, and put P on the junior varsity. From his home that evening, P tweets, "Fuck Public High Baseball. The coaches chose X instead of me for shortstop because X's dad lobbied them relentlessly." No other team member complains about the tweet, but the school suspends P for the year from the junior varsity under a school rule prohibiting "disruptive conduct in connection with a school activity."

You should say the P's free expression has been violated: since the speech took place off-campus (and not directly as a part of a school-sponsored activity), the school's interest in regulating that speech was relatively weak, especially since the team members' lack of reaction suggests that the tweet was not very disruptive. P's interest in commenting about a matter of public concern (his allegation that the coaches are unfairly responding to parental lobbying) outweighs the school's weak interest in regulation.

☛ If you have a fact pattern that involves *group activity* of an expressive nature, refer to the protected *"freedom of association."* (*Example:* If a group gets together and pursues class action litigation, their right to do so is protected by the associational freedom.)

    ☞ Remember that there's also a "right *not* to associate"; for instance, a group can't be required to take unwanted members whose presence will detract from the group's expressive activities. (*Example:* The NAACP can't be forced to accept white supremacists as members.)

☛ Be alert for situations in which government may be forcing a person or group to deliver a *government-drafted message* that the person or group *disagrees* with. The modern Court *strictly scrutinizes* these "you must deliver the following message" attempts by government, and typically strikes them down as violations of free expression.

    Example 1: A state says to pro-life "pregnancy crisis centers," "You must post a poster in your waiting room that tells women that the state provides low-cost abortions." This is an unconstitutional impairment of each center's free-expression right not to be required to deliver a message of which the center disapproves. [Cite to *Nat'l Institute v. Becerra*]

    Example 2: A state statute allows any public-employee union to charge non-members for the union's pro-rata costs of representing the non-member in collective bargaining. The statute violates each non-member's free-speech right to refuse to give financial support to a message (in this case, a collective bargaining position) that the non-member disagrees with. [Cite to *Janus v. AFSCME*]

☛ Many fact patterns involve the denial of *public jobs or benefits* to persons based upon their expressive conduct. This is a very commonly tested area. Here are some key aspects to keep in mind:

    ☞ In general, the standard for whether government may refuse to hire, or may fire, based on expressive conduct is the same as for when government may *prosecute*. (*Example:* Since a person may not be prosecuted for belonging to an organization unless there is a showing that he had the specific intent to further the organization's illegal aims, so a person may not be fired for belonging to the organization without such a showing of specific intent.)

    ☞ A person may be required to sign a *loyalty oath* as a condition for getting or keeping a public job, but he may not be forced to promise to refrain from doing anything that he would be constitutionally permitted to do. (*Example:* You may be forced to sign a loyalty oath that you have not belonged to the Communist Party while specifically intending to further the overthrow of the government, but you may not be required to sign a loyalty oath stating simply that you do not belong to the Communist Party — since you can't be prosecuted for mere membership without specific intent to further illegal aims, you can't be forced to sign a loyalty oath that you won't be a mere member.)

    ☞ There is an *exception* to these limits: you can be deprived of expressive freedom where the expression would truly interfere with your *job performance*. (*Example:* Civil servants can be forced to choose between their jobs and engaging in partisan political activities, since there's a strong governmental interest in making sure that civil servants don't get coerced into campaigning for their elected bosses.)

☞ Where a public *benefit* as opposed to a job is at stake, there is no "performance" exception, and it's hard for government to restrict free speech. (*Example:* A person's right to continue as a tenant in public housing, or to receive welfare payments, generally can't be made contingent upon their forfeiting their freedom of expression, because they generally don't have a "performance" obligation that would be impaired by pursuit of expressive conduct or speech.)

☛ Look out for *"unconstitutional conditions,"* where government *unfairly conditions* the award of funding or other benefits on the recipient's *waiver of constitutional rights.*

☞ Government *can* sometimes require as a condition to giving you a financial benefit (e.g., a subsidy) that you waive your right to free expression. But that condition can generally apply only to *how you use the particular government-supplied funds*, not how you spend *non-subsidy dollars*. Cite to *Agency for Int'l Dev. v. Alliance for Open Soc'y Int'l, Inc.*

☛ If your question involves restrictions placed on the *media* (publishers or broadcasters), there are some special considerations:

☞ If the governmental action consists of a *prior restraint*, you should almost certainly conclude that the restraint is not valid. For instance, if the government is trying to get an injunction against a newspaper that will publish a story, it's almost impossible for the government to succeed.

☞ The media must obey a *subpoena* (e.g., to give information to a grand jury) pretty much the same as a private citizen must.

☞ The press does not get any special *right of access* to government-held information, beyond what the public as a whole has.

☞ Some issues turn on the *type of media*:

☞ *Over-the-air broadcast radio and tv* may be subjected to somewhat greater *"time, place and manner" regulation* than print media, because these are scarce resources, and they are potentially intrusive (someone may stumble upon unwanted content while dial-turning).

☞ *Print publications*, and the *Internet*, by contrast, are neither scarce nor intrusive. So these media get *very great freedom* from "time, place and manner" regulation.

CHAPTER 15

FREEDOM OF RELIGION

ChapterScope

Here are the key concepts involving "freedom of religion":

- **Two clauses:** There are two distinct clauses in the First Amendment pertaining to religion:

  - ❏ **Establishment Clause:** First, there is the ***Establishment Clause***. That clause prohibits any law "respecting an establishment of religion." The main purpose of the Establishment Clause is to prevent government from ***endorsing*** or ***supporting*** religion.

  - ❏ **Free Exercise Clause:** The second clause is the ***Free Exercise*** Clause. That clause bars any law "prohibiting the free exercise of religion." The main purpose of the Free Exercise Clause is to prevent government from ***outlawing*** or seriously ***burdening*** a person's pursuit of whatever religion (and whatever religious practices) she chooses.

- **Applicable to states:** Both religious clauses, by their terms, apply only to action taken by ***Congress***. However, both clauses are interpreted to apply also to the ***states***, by means of the Fourteenth Amendment's Due Process Clause.

- **Establishment Clause:** The purpose of the Establishment Clause is to put a ***wall between church and state***. Mainly, this means that government must stay out of the business of religion. (*Example:* Government can't intentionally prefer one religion over another religion.)

  - ❏ **Three-part test:** Government action that has some relationship to religion will violate the Establishment Clause unless it satisfies ***all three parts*** of the following test:

    - ❏ **Purpose:** First, the government action must have a ***secular legislative purpose***.

    - ❏ **Effect:** Second, the government action's principal or ***primary effect*** must ***not be to advance*** religion. (But ***incidental effects*** helpful to religion do not violate this prong.)

    - ❏ **Entanglement:** Finally, the governmental action must not foster an ***excessive government entanglement*** with religion.

- **The Free Exercise Clause generally:** Under the Free Exercise Clause, the government is barred from making any law "prohibiting the free exercise" of religion. The Free Exercise Clause prevents the government from getting in the way of people's ability to practice their religions.

  - ❏ **Includes conduct:** The Free Exercise Clause prevents the government from unduly burdening both a person's abstract "beliefs" as well as a person's religiously-oriented ***conduct***. Most real-world problems relate to regulation affecting conduct.

    - ❏ **Non-religious objectives:** Free exercise problems most typically arise when government, acting in pursuit of ***non-religious objectives***, either: (1) forbids or burdens conduct which happens to be ***required*** by someone's religious beliefs; or (2) conversely, compels or encourages conduct which happens to be ***forbidden*** by someone's religious beliefs.

    - ❏ **Intentional vs. unintentional burdens:** The Free Exercise Clause prevents the government from unduly interfering with religion whether the government does so ***intentionally*** or ***unintentionally***.

❏ **Intent:** If the interference is ***intentional*** on government's part, then the interference is subjected to the ***most strict scrutiny***, and will virtually never survive.

❏ **Unintentional burden:** If the government ***unintentionally burdens*** religion, the Free Exercise Clause is still applied. Here, however, the Court uses a somewhat less stringent form of strict scrutiny. (In fact, if the government makes certain conduct a ***crime***, and this unintentionally burdens the exercise of religion, the Court does not use strict scrutiny at all, and instead uses "mere-rationality" review.)

❏ **Coercion required:** The Free Exercise Clause only gets triggered where government in some sense ***"coerces"*** an individual to do something (or not to do something) against the dictates of his religion. If the government takes an action that unintentionally happens to make it harder for a person to practice his religion — but without coercing him into taking or not taking some action as an individual — the Free Exercise Clause does not apply.

I.   INTRODUCTION

A. **Two clauses:**   The First Amendment contains two distinct clauses designed to protect religious freedom. One is the ***Establishment*** Clause, which prohibits any law "respecting an establishment of religion." The other is the ***Free Exercise*** Clause, which bans laws "prohibiting the free exercise" of religion.

B. **General function of clauses:**   These two clauses are designed to protect the same basic value, the freedom of every individual to worship (or not worship) as he wishes, without governmental interference. The two clauses have been summarized as requiring "that government neither engage in nor compel religious practices, that it effect no favoritism among sects or between religion and nonreligion, and that it work deterrence of no religious belief." *Abington School District v. Schempp*, 374 U.S. 203 (1963) (Goldberg, J. concurring).

C. **Conflict between clauses:**   However, in some contexts the two clauses ***conflict.***

   1. **Illustration:**   Consider, for instance, state financial assistance to private schools, including parochial schools. If such aid is given, a strong argument can be made that the Establishment Clause is violated, since government is assisting parochial schools in an activity that has a strong religious component. Yet if such aid is not given, while public schools are given large amounts of assistance, a claim can be made that students' free exercise of religion is infringed, because economic burdens force them to abandon parochial schools for public ones.

   2. **No solution:**   The Supreme Court has not yet found a precise way of harmonizing the two clauses. The Court has asserted that government rules must be ***"neutral"*** towards religion. But the Court has used the concept of neutrality in such a vague way that the term does not aid in the solution of any of the difficult cases of conflict between the clauses.

D. **Application of clauses to states:**   Although the First Amendment by its terms only restricts legislative action by ***Congress***, the two religion clauses, like most of the other guarantees of the Bill of Rights, have been incorporated into the Fourteenth Amendment's due process guarantee, and thereby made ***applicable to the states***. See, e.g., *Everson v. Board of Education*, 330 U.S. 1 (1947) (application of Establishment Clause to states).

II. THE ESTABLISHMENT CLAUSE

A. Background: The basic purpose of the Establishment Clause is, in the words of Thomas Jefferson, to erect "a ***wall of separation*** between church and state." However, the image of a "wall" does not help very much in determining what types of state actions violate the Clause.

1. Specific prohibitions: There are some types of governmental actions which clearly violate the Establishment Clause. The majority cataloged some of these in *Everson v. Board of Education, supra:*

    a. No official church: Neither a state nor the federal government may ***set up an official church.***

    b. No coercion: Government may not "***force*** [or] ***influence*** a person ***to go to*** or to ***remain away*** from church against his will or force him to ***profess a belief*** or ***disbelief*** in any religion."

    c. Punishment for beliefs: No one may be "***punished*** for entertaining or professing ***religious beliefs or disbeliefs***, for church ***attendance*** or ***non-attendance.***"

    d. No preference: Government may not ***prefer*** one religion over another. Also, government may not prefer religion to non-religion.

    e. Participation: Government may not ***participate in the affairs*** of religious organizations, and such organizations may not ***participate*** in the affairs of government.

    Note: Some of these prohibitions (e.g., the right not to be punished for one's religious beliefs) are also protected by the Free Exercise Clause, perhaps even more directly than by the Establishment Clause. Nonetheless, the *Everson* Court purported to be listing solely those prohibitions stemming from the Establishment Clause.

2. Three-part *Lemon* test: Officially, the modern Court applies a ***three-fold test*** to determine whether governmental action violates the Establishment Clause. See ***Lemon v. Kurtzman***, 403 U.S. 602 (1970). Under that test, only if the action satisfies ***each*** of the following conditions will it be ***valid:***

    [1] Secular purpose: The government action must have a ***secular purpose***;

    [2] Effect: Its principal or ***primary effect*** must neither ***advance*** nor ***inhibit*** religion; and

    [3] Entanglement: It must not foster an ***excessive government entanglement*** with religion.

    a. Present Court's discontent with *Lemon*: But there are some strong clues that a majority of the present Court is so ***unhappy*** with the *Lemon* three-part test that the Court may soon ***abandon*** it, or at least ***curtail the situations*** in which it is used.

        i. Abandoned for religious-symbol displays on public land: For instance, as the result of a 2019 case, the Court now seems to have ***abandoned*** the use of *Lemon* for cases involving the ***display of religious symbols on public property***. See *American Legion v. American Humanist Assoc., infra*, p. 674.

ii. **Test not overruled, but ignored:** In other cases, the Court has simply *ignored* *Lemon* as a precedent, without overruling it or explicitly finding it inapplicable to the particular category of Establishment Clause cases in question. That's what happened in a 1994 case, *Board of Education of Kiryas Joel v. Grumet*, discussed *infra*, p. 681. The majority found that the challenged practice there (the establishment of a school district consisting solely of members of a particular Jewish sect) violated the Establishment Clause, but the majority opinion referred only briefly to *Lemon* and did not purport to apply the *Lemon* test.

B. **Religion and the public schools:** The extent to which the government may accommodate religion in operating the *public schools* has provoked much controversy and several important cases. The primary areas of concern are the extent to which the state may: (1) accommodate students' desire to *receive religious instruction* during school hours, or on school property; (2) allow the *reading* of state-composed *prayers* or the Bible, as part of a daily ritual; and (3) *modify the curriculum* in order to accommodate the religious views of some. In general, the Court has permitted the public schools *very little leeway* in pursuing these objectives.

1. **Religious instruction:** One issue is whether public schools may accommodate religion by *releasing students* for *optional religious instruction.*

   a. **Release for classes held elsewhere:** Thus Court has upheld a program in which students who elected to participate were released to receive religious instruction *away from the public school's physical facility.* *Zorach v. Clauson*, 343 U.S. 306 (1952).

   b. **Use of school facilities by student groups:** Similarly, a state-supported school's policy of allowing religious groups to *use its physical facilities* does not violate the Establishment Clause if the policy is *truly neutral* as between religious and non-religious groups. Thus in *Widmar v. Vincent*, 454 U.S. 263 (1981), a state university banned the use of its facilities for purposes of worship by student-run religious groups, but allowed all non-religious student groups to use them. In holding that this policy was unconstitutional on free speech grounds, the Court rejected the university's claim that an equal-access policy would have violated the Establishment Clause.

      i. **Significance of neutrality:** It was precisely the fact that the facilities were also available to *non-religious* groups that prevented the university's policy from being a violation of the Establishment Clause. The Court said in *Widmar* that equal access would not "confer any imprimatur of state approval on religious sects or practices," and the advancement of religion would not be the "primary effect" of such a policy.

      ii. **Religious groups in elementary schools:** Even if it is a public *elementary* school that allows religious groups to meet on the same after-school basis as non-religious groups, there is no Establishment Clause problem, the Court has held. *Good News Club v. Milford Central School*, 533 U.S. 98 (2001). And this is true even if the attendees will be *elementary school students*.

      iii. **Rights for non-religious groups:** But now, suppose that a school allows religious groups to conduct voluntary meetings outside of school hours, but *does not grant this right to non-religious groups*. This policy probably *would* constitute an Establishment Clause violation, on the theory that this type of conduct had the purpose and effect of primarily aiding religion; such a policy would also arguably offend the free speech rights of the non-religious groups. (Paradoxically, the surest way for a school system to stay clear of both Establishment Clause and free speech problems, as well as problems under the Equal Access Act, may be to ban *all* extracurricular activities!)

    c. Funding of student activities: The "equal access" principle of *Widmar* — that a school must treat religious and non-religious activities equally — applies even where what the school is supplying is *funding* for activities, rather than merely access to pre-existing facilities. In *Rosenberger v. University of Virginia*, 515 U.S. 819 (1995), the Court held by a 5-4 vote that it would not be an Establishment Clause violation for the University of Virginia to fund an evangelical Christian student publication on the same basis it funded other student publications, so long as the funds were paid to third parties (e.g., the printer) rather than to the students running the publication. (The Court also said that the University's failure to treat the Christian publication equally was a *free speech* violation; see *supra*, p. 538.)

2. Prayer reading: The official *reading of prayers* in the public schools has several times been held by the Court to *violate* the Establishment Clause.

    a. State-composed prayer: First, the in-classroom reading of a *state-composed* "non-denominational" prayer was held to violate the Establishment Clause, in *Engel v. Vitale*, 370 U.S. 421 (1962). The Court reached this determination even though *no child was compelled to recite the prayer*. Neither this non-compulsory aspect, nor the non-denominationality, saved the scheme, because it was clearly part of a "religious program carried on by government."

    b. Reading from Bible: Similarly, a daily classroom ritual of *reading from the Bible* was struck down in *Abington School Dist. v. Schempp*, 374 U.S. 203 (1963). As in *Engel*, it made no difference that no child was compelled to participate.

    c. Voluntary silent prayer: Furthermore, a state statute that explicitly authorizes *"voluntary" silent prayer* in the public schools will not be saved from constitutional problems merely because the prayer is silent and non-compulsory. Any such statute is to be analyzed according to the three-prong *Lemon* test (*supra*, p. 661) — if the provision has no secular purpose, or has the primary effect of aiding religion, or results in excessive government entanglement with religion, it will be struck down even though each student is given the freedom not to participate in the prayer. Thus the Supreme Court has struck down an Alabama statute which authorized a *one-minute silent period* at the start of each school day which was to be used "for meditation or voluntary prayer." *Wallace v. Jaffree*, 472 U.S. 38 (1985). The vote was 6-3.

        i. Rationale of majority: The *Wallace* majority concluded from various pieces of legislative history that the legislature's *sole purpose* in enacting the statute was to endorse religion, a violation of the first prong of *Lemon*. Since the first prong of *Lemon* was not satisfied, the Court did not need to reach the issue of the statute's conformance with the second and third *Lemon* prongs (primary effect and state entanglement).

    d. Academic study: The school prayer decisions do not prohibit the *study* of the Bible in public schools, as long as this study takes place in a purely *academic manner*. The issue is whether the school, by including Bible study in the curriculum, intends to (or does in fact materially) advance religious beliefs.

e. **Ceremonies:** So far, we have considered only prayers that take place in *classrooms*. Suppose that a school conducts an official *ceremony* or ritual outside the classroom, and prayer is part of that ceremony. At least where school officials can fairly be said to be *sponsoring* the religious message, a prayer will be found to be a *violation* of the Establishment Clause. The Court so held in *Lee v. Weisman*, 505 U.S. 577 (1992). *Lee* also establishes that even a completely *non-denominational* school prayer will violate the Establishment Clause if it is state-sponsored.

   i. **Facts:** *Lee* involved prayers at public middle-school and high-school *graduation ceremonies*. In one instance, a middle-school principal invited a rabbi to deliver a prayer, told him the prayer should be non-sectarian, and gave him a pamphlet (prepared by the National Conference of Christians and Jews) detailing the kinds of prayers that would be appropriate at a public civic occasion. The prayers delivered by the rabbi were indeed non-denominational, and consisted mainly of thanks to God (e.g., "Oh, God, we are grateful to You for having endowed us with the capacity for learning which we have celebrated on this joyous commencement. … Send Your blessings upon the teachers and administrators who helped prepare [the students]"). P was a graduating student who argued that she shouldn't be required to listen to a prayer as part of her graduation ceremony.

   ii. **Practice struck down:** By a 5-4 vote, the Court ruled that the delivery of the prayer in this context violated the Establishment Clause. The five-Justice majority, in an opinion by Justice Kennedy, held that the state here effectively *coerced* students into participating in, or at least supporting, the prayers.

   iii. **Dissent:** Four Justices (Scalia, joined by Rehnquist, White and Thomas) dissented. The dissenters principally argued that there was *no official compulsion* here — P was not required to attend the graduation ceremony at all (thus distinguishing the case from the in-classroom prayer cases), and certainly was not required to join in the prayers in any way, merely to accommodate others who wished to pray.

   iv. **Incidental references to religion:** Suppose that an official ceremony or ritual contains mere *occasional* references to God, which are *incidental* to the ceremony. In this situation, it seems likely that the majority of the Court would *allow* the reference, despite its religious content. For instance, a majority of the Court has indicated in dictum that the use in public schools of the *Pledge of Allegiance*, with its reference to God, does not violate the Establishment Clause, because this is merely a "reference to our religious heritage," rather than an endorsement of religion. *Lynch v. Donnelly*, 465 U.S. 668 (1984). (But see our further discussion of the Pledge issue *infra*, p. 672.)

f. **"Student-sponsored" speeches:** A key aspect of the Establishment Clause problem in *Lee v. Weisman* was that the school clearly endorsed the prayer — the principal invited a rabbi to give the prayer, and gave him instructions about what type of prior to use, making the prayer effectively school-sponsored. In part to get around *Lee*, a number of school districts after *Lee* put in place procedures whereby a *student* can be *elected by the student body* to be a speaker at a school-sponsored event. If the speaker then chooses on her own to give a prayer, the school can plausibly claim that the speech is private speech — posing no Establishment Clause problem — rather than school-sponsored speech. But a post-*Lee* case, in which the Court struck down a pre-football-game prayer delivered by an elected student speaker, suggests that this technique will **rarely be successful**. *Santa Fe Independent School Dist. v. Doe*, 530 U.S. 290 (2000).

   i. Facts: The Sante Fe, Texas, school district handled the problem of whether there should be a pre-football-game prayer by conducting two elections:

   First, the class would vote by secret ballot whether a "statement or invocation" should be delivered before each game, to "solemnize the event." Then, if the vote was yes, a second election would be held to choose the spokesperson to deliver the invocation/statement.

   (1) Prayers delivered: The student body in fact voted to have the invocations, and those invocations turned out to be, the lower court later found, prayers that appealed to "distinctively Christian beliefs."

   ii. Struck down: By a 6-3-vote, the Court found that the school policy **violated** the Establishment Clause.

   (1) Not private speech: The majority rejected the school district's claim that the pre-game invocations should be regarded as **"private speech."** The school policy itself encouraged religious messages (e.g., by providing that the purpose of the message must be to "solemnize the event"). And the fact that the invocation was delivered at a school-sponsored event, over a school-owned public address system, added to the impression that this was school-sponsored, not private, prayer.

   iii. Dissent: The three dissenters in *Santa Fe*, led by Chief Justice Rehnquist, agreed with the district's argument that the prayers should be viewed as private speech, because it was up to the elected students to decide what to say in the pre-game speech.

3. **Modification of curriculum:** The state may not design or modify the **curriculum** of its schools in order to further religion at the expense of non-religion, or one set of religious beliefs over others.

   a. **Anti-evolution laws:** This principle is most vividly demonstrated by the Court's invalidation of an Arkansas **"anti-evolution" statute**, which forbade public school teachers from teaching "the theory or doctrine that mankind ascended or descended from a lower order of animals." *Epperson v. Arkansas*, 393 U.S. 97 (1968). (This statute was an offshoot of a comparable Tennessee statute, which was the subject of the famous 1927 Scopes trial.)

   i. **Rationale:** The *Epperson* Court concluded that the statute violated the Establishment Clause because its **sole purpose** was a religious one: to bar the teaching of a theory that was at odds with the "fundamentalist sectarian conviction" that man was created in the manner described in the Bible. Even if the statute was intended only to prohibit teaching Darwinian theory as "true" (rather than barring even any *explanation* of what the theory says), the law's solely religious motivation was sufficient to make it unconstitutional.

b. Requirement that Bible be taught: May the state require that the biblical theory of creation be taught *in addition to* the theory of evolution? Such a requirement could, of course, be defended on the grounds that it preserves neutrality as between religion and non-religion, and presents all viewpoints. However, if such a requirement were imposed solely or primarily for the same religious *purpose* as the *Epperson* statute, it would violate the Establishment Clause. Thus in one case, the Supreme Court held that a Louisiana statute, the "Balanced Treatment for Creation-Science and Evolution-Science in Public School Instruction" Act, was *motivated solely by religious purposes,* and therefore violated the Establishment Clause. *Edwards v. Aguillard,* 482 U.S. 578 (1987).

    i. Facts: The Louisiana Act forbade the teaching of evolution in public schools unless that teaching was *accompanied by instruction in "creation science."* No school was required to teach evolution or creation science, but if either was taught the other must also be taught.

    ii. Statute stricken: The outcome of the case essentially turned on the extent to which one believed that the Louisiana legislature could have had a valid secular purpose in enacting the statute. Seven members of the Court, represented in a majority opinion by Justice Brennan, concluded that there *could not have been such a secular purpose*.

        (1) Legislative history: Brennan relied heavily upon the *legislative history* of the statute, including statements made by the bill's sponsor and testimony at the legislative hearings by the leading expert on creation science; both of these sources indicated that the theory of creation science includes a belief in the existence of a "supernatural creator," and is thus a religious doctrine.

    iii. Dissent: Justice Scalia, joined by Chief Justice Rehnquist, issued a forceful dissent that challenged the majority's analysis on both factual and legal grounds. Factually, Scalia disagreed that the record was adequate to allow the Court to conclude that the principal or sole motivation for the statute was to advance religious beliefs. Scalia noted that the act recited a secular purpose ("protecting academic freedom") and that the act was endorsed by a vast majority of legislators, only a small minority of whom were members of fundamentalist religious denominations. Furthermore, he stressed, the issue was not whether the statute would actually achieve the purpose of enhancing academic freedom, but merely whether the legislators were *sincere* in believing that it would have this outcome.

    iv. Significance: Observe that the majority approach in *Edwards* — that a religious motivation will invalidate the statute — can mean that when two states adopt an identically-worded statute, the statute may be *valid in one state and invalid in the other*, since the two legislatures may have been differently motivated.

c. No secular purpose: *Epperson* and *Edwards* are two of the few cases in which the religious *purpose* of a law was dispositive. The "purpose" prong of the three-prong Establishment Clause test is that there must be *a* "secular purpose," not that there may not be a religious purpose. Thus if there is *both a religious and secular purpose*, the prong is *not violated*. The statutes in *Epperson* and *Edwards* are two of the few legislative enactments as to which members of the Court could find no conceivable secular purpose. (For another such statute, see the Alabama "voluntary prayer" statute struck down in *Wallace v. Jaffree, supra*, p. 663.)

C. Sunday closing laws: Laws requiring merchants to be *closed on Sunday* do *not* violate the Establishment Clause. *McGowan v. Maryland*, 366 U.S. 420 (1961).

1. **Rationale:** The Court reasoned in *McGowan* that, as these statutes are administered today, they have a *secular purpose and effect:* providing a *uniform day of rest for all citizens*. (The Court believed it irrelevant that the laws were originally enacted for purely religious reasons.)

2. **Overlapping of secular and religious purposes:** Of course, the fact remains that the day chosen for this uniform day of rest is Sunday, the day of religious observance for most Americans. The case therefore illustrates the rule that a statute does not violate the Establishment Clause if it has *both a religious and secular purpose*. See Tribe, p. 1205-06.

   a. **Effect:** Similarly, the fact that the law had both a secular and religious *effect* did not cause a violation of the Establishment Clause, since the religious effect was not the primary, or even major, one. The Court seems correct in viewing the Sunday closing laws as having merely an *incidental* unofficial effect of advancing religion.

3. **Employees' right not to work on Sabbath:** But if a statute relating to Sabbath observance *does* have the primary effect of advancing religion, it will be found to violate the Establishment Clause. For instance, a Connecticut statute requiring all employers (including private employers) to give any employee the day off on that employee's Sabbath, was struck down as violative of the Establishment Clause, in *Thornton v. Caldor, Inc.*, 472 U.S. 703 (1985).

   a. **Rationale:** The statute in *Thornton* went beyond the government's right to "accommodate" the needs of religious observers. There, the preference given to Sabbath observers was an *absolute* one. For instance, suppose that an employer is faced with having to choose which of two employees should have Sunday off: one employee points to Sunday as his Sabbath; the other, who has more seniority, has a pressing and legitimate, but non-religious need for Sundays off (e.g., to have the same day off as his working spouse and school-aged children). The Connecticut statute mandated an absolute preference for the former. The statute thus had the primary effect of "impermissibly advanc[ing] a particular religious practice" (namely, Sabbath observance).

   b. **Non-absolute preference:** But a statute that merely required an employer to make "reasonable attempts" to accommodate the religious interest of workers probably would *not* violate the Establishment Clause.

D. Property-tax exemptions for churches: The granting of *property tax exemptions* to churches generally does *not* violate the Establishment Clause. *Walz v. Tax Commission*, 397 U.S. 664 (1970).

1. **Sales tax exemption violates clause:** On the other hand, some kinds of tax exemptions given to religious groups *will* be held to violate the Establishment Clause. For instance, Texas exempted from *sales tax* all (and only) periodicals "published or distributed by a religious faith and [consisting] wholly of writings promulgating the teaching of the faith and books that consist wholly of writings sacred to a religious faith." This exemption was struck down by the Court in *Texas Monthly, Inc. v. Bullock*, 489 U.S. 1 (1989).

2. **Distinction:** How was the property tax exemption in *Walz* different from the sales tax exemption in *Texas Monthly*? The main difference seems to be that the exemption in *Walz* was part of a **broader scheme** that did not prefer religion over non-religion — property owned by most types of non-profit organizations (including hospitals, libraries, patriotic groups, etc.) was also exempted. In *Texas Monthly*, by contrast, **only** religious writings published by religious groups were exempted, so the exemption's sole purpose (and apparently its principal effect) was to advance religion.

E. **Military and prison chaplains:** Recall that government has some ability to *accommodate* the religious needs of citizens, so long as government is not "sponsoring" official religious practices. The right of public schools to release their students so that they can receive religious instruction outside of the school is one illustration of this principle. The "accommodation" principle is also applicable when government supplies *military chaplains* or *prison chaplains* to soldiers or prisoners who wish to use them, or otherwise accommodates the religious needs of solders or prisoners.

1. **Religious accommodation to prisoners:** For instance, the Court has upheld the Religious Land Use and Institutionalized Persons Act (RLUIPA), which essentially requires all prison systems to accommodate the religious needs of prisoners unless refusing to do so would further a compelling governmental interest by the least restrictive means. See *Cutter v. Wilkinson*, 544 U.S. 709 (2005), discussed *infra*, p. 682. Even though RLUIPA clearly prefers religion over non-religion (e.g., by effectively requiring that prisoners be given the right to attend organized group prayer meetings and the right to wear religiously-dictated non-standard apparel while prisoners who wish to engage in these activities for non-religious reasons are not given the right to do so), the Court found no Establishment Clause violation.

F. **Helping religious groups spread their message:** Recall that one of the prongs of the *Lemon v. Kurtzman* test (*supra*, p. 661) is that the governmental action's principal effect must not be to **advance** religion. Thus government actions whose primary effect is to help religious organizations **spread a religious message** or **obtain converts** would presumably fail this prong and thus violate the Establishment Clause.

> **Example:** Suppose that Congress passed a law providing grants to religious (and *only* religious) organizations, for the express purpose of giving them the financial resources to run expanded membership drives and to explain their beliefs to the general population. This statute would almost certainly violate the "primary effect" prong of *Lemon*.

1. **Incidental effect:** But if grants are made to a wide variety of institutions, only some of which are religiously-affiliated, the fact that some of the recipients happen to be religious organizations who use the funds to spread the organization's religious message will *not* lead to a striking down of the entire statute (though it may cause grants to the particular organizations who use the funds in this way to be struck down). Only if a *significant portion* of the government funding flows to institutions that are *"pervasively sectarian"* will the entire funding scheme be a violation of the Establishment Clause. See *Bowen v. Kendrick*, 483 U.S. 1304 (1988) (where grants are made to public and non-profit private organizations for counseling adolescents about sex and pregnancy, inclusion of religiously-affiliated organizations among the grant recipients doesn't cause an Establishment Clause violation).

G. The "excessive entanglement prong": Recall that the third prong of the test for Establishment Clause violations is that the governmental action must not give rise to *excessive entanglement* on the part of government in the affairs of religion, or vice versa.

1. The "ministerial exception" from government regulation: One consequence of the "no excessive entanglement" rule is that governmental regulation that has the effect of interfering with a religious group's determination of *who is qualified to convey the group's message* and/or *carry out its mission* is likely to violate the Establishment Clause. Religious groups are entitled to a *"ministerial exception,"* under which the group's choice of *who may be a minister or religious leader* will be *immune from regulation*, at least regulation that takes the form of *anti-discrimination* laws.

2. Two cases: The Court has discussed this "ministerial exception" in two cases, *Hosanna-Tabor Evangelical Lutheran Church and School v. EEOC*, 132 S.Ct. 694 (2012) and *Our Lady of Guadalupe School v. Morrissey-Berru*, 140 S.Ct. 2049 (2020). Here is a summary of what the two cases, taken together, say about the scope of the ministerial exception from government regulation.

a. Broad principle: The "ministerial exemption" means that religious organizations must be permitted (1) to decide *who* within the organization *is a minister* ; and (2) to employ *only ministers for particular posts. (Hosanna-Tabor)*

    i. Rationale: Here's the Court's rationale for deciding that the ministerial exception is required by the Establishment Clause: "According the state the power to determine which individuals will minister to the faithful ... violates the Establishment Clause, which *prohibits government involvement in such ecclesiastical decisions." (Hosanna-Tabor)*

b. Anti-discrimination statutes: The main practical consequence of Par. (a) is that where a religious group has determined that a particular position must be filled by a "minister" (as designated by the group), the group is automatically entitled to an *exemption* from *state and federal anti-discrimination laws* regarding that minister. (We'll see how this exemption operates in the Example on p. 669 below.)

c. Discretion in defining "minister": The religious group must be given *extremely wide discretion* in *determining who is a "minister"* for the group. Indeed, it's not really accurate to refer to the exception as one for "ministers" – it's more accurate to say that the exception applies to any employee whom the institution regards as *"educating students in the [institution's] faith." (Our Lady of Guadalupe)*

Example of Pars. (a)-(c): The Ps are two fifth-grade teachers at Catholic elementary schools (each of which is a defendant, i.e., "D"). Each of the Ps sues her school for violating generally-applicable employment laws; one P asserts an age-discrimination claim, and the other a disability-discrimination claim. The Ds defend by arguing that (1) each D has the right to determine whether a particular employee is a "minister"; (2) the two Ds have correctly determined that the Ps are ministers, even though neither of the Ps is an ordained minister, and both teach primarily secular subjects; (3) since each P is a minister, the Ds are entitled (under both the Free Exercise and the Establishment Clause) to an exemption from the otherwise-applicable anti-discrimination laws.

Held (by a 7-2 vote), with the Court's opinion by Justice Alito: *for the Ds.* Both Ps were correctly classified as "ministers," and are therefore not protected by anti-discrimination-in-employment laws. It doesn't matter that neither school gave the employee *the title "minister,"* since many religious traditions do not use that title. Nor does it necessarily matter that the employee did not have *formal religious training*, especially in the case of elementary school teaching, which "does not demand the same formal religious education as teaching theology to divinity students." Instead, "what matters … is *what an employee does*[.]" A religious school is entitled to apply the ministerial exception to a teacher if at the core of the teacher's mission is *"educating young people in their faith,* inculcating [the faith's] teachings, and *training them to live their faith[.]"*

Both of the Ps easily *met this standard.* Each teacher "performed vital religious duties," including "educating and informing students in the Catholic faith[.]" Both teachers *"prayed with their students, attended Mass* with the students, and prepared the children for their participation in other religious activities." Furthermore, each school's own *"explanation of the role* of such employees in the life of the religion in question" was *entitled to considerable weight.* (*Our Lady of Guadalupe*)

i. **Dissent:** Two justices *dissented* in *Our Lady of Guadalupe*, in an opinion by Justice Sotomayor. She pointed out that the two Ps *"taught primarily secular subjects, lacked substantial religious titles and training,* and *were not even required to be Catholic."* Yet because they "taught short religious modules at Catholic elementary schools," the majority was treating them "as 'ministers' of the Catholic faith." This allowed them to be *"fired for any reason, whether religious or nonreligious,* benign or bigoted, without legal recourse." Neither the Establishment Clause nor the Free Exercise Clause required this result, she said.

ii. **Significance:** *Our Lady of Guadalupe* seems to *expand*, in a pretty dramatic way, the group of *employees of religious institutions* that can be treated as "ministers," and thus exempted from employment discrimination laws. The case seems to say that so long as the employer determines that the employee's duties are "vital" to "carrying out the mission of the church," the exemption should apply. As the dissent warned, many *other categories of employees* may turn out to be included in the exemption, including *"coaches, camp counselors,* nurses, social-service workers, *in-house lawyers,* media-relations personnel, and many others who work for religious institutions."

3. **Truth vs. sincerity:** The anti-entanglement prong of the Establishment Clause causes courts to *avoid adjudicating the "truth"* of religious beliefs. But courts are sometimes willing to consider the *sincerity* of professed beliefs.

a. *Ballard:* The truth/sincerity distinction was made in *U.S. v. Ballard,* 322 U.S. 78 (1944), where the defendants, self-professed *faith healers,* were charged with fraudulently soliciting donations. The Court held that the Free Exercise Clause barred the submission to the jury of the truth or falsity of the defendants' faith healing claims: "Men may believe what they cannot prove. They may not be put to the proof of their religious doctrines or beliefs." However, the Court held, a jury could be required to decide whether the defendants were *sincere* in their claims, that is, whether they genuinely (whether or not reasonably) believed these claims.

H. Entanglement by church involvement in government affairs: The anti-entanglement principle will also be violated by the converse problem, that of excessive involvement *by the church in affairs of government.*

1. *Larkin:* For instance, in *Larkin v. Grendel's Den, Inc.*, 459 U.S. 116 (1982), the Court struck down a Massachusetts statute prohibiting issuance of a liquor license to any premises located within 500 feet of a church or school if the church or school makes a written objection to the issuance of the license.

   a. **Rationale:** Giving such a veto provision to churches "enmeshes churches in the exercise of substantial governmental powers," the *Larkin* Court held, and therefore runs afoul of the anti-entanglement principle of the Establishment Clause.

I. Ceremonies, displays and monuments — generally: When the government conducts a *ceremony,* puts on a *display,* or erects a *monument*, and the ceremony / display / monument refers to a religious subject, Establishment Clause problems will often result. In the following two sections, we consider these problems, dividing our discussion into *ceremonies* referring to religious themes (section J) and *displays or monuments* involving religious themes or symbols (section K).

J. Ceremonies: First, consider government-led *ceremonies* referring to God or other religious themes. The fact that God is *occasionally referred to* in a ceremony put on by the government will usually *not* cause the ceremony to violate the Establishment Clause.

1. **Chaplain at sessions of legislature:** For instance, the practice of opening each daily session of a state *legislature* with a *prayer* by a state-paid chaplain does *not violate* the Establishment Clause, the Court held in *Marsh v. Chambers*, 463 U.S. 783 (1983).

   a. **Rationale:** The Court relied principally on the theory that such practices have deep *historic roots*, going back to the First Congress; this fact demonstrated that the congressmen who approved the First Amendment must have believed that use of a chaplain did not violate principles of church-state separation.

   b. **Dissent:** But Justice Stevens, one of three dissenters, argued that the Nebraska legislature's choice of a Presbyterian to hold the position of chaplain for sixteen years, probably in order to reflect the state's primary sect, constituted an illegal "preference of one faith over another."

2. **Chaplain at meetings of town board:** Now, suppose that a prayer is offered not before the opening of the state legislative session but, instead, before the opening of a *town board's meeting*. Further, suppose that, unlike the state-legislature scenario in *Marsh* (which involved a prayer *directed solely to the legislators),* at the town board meeting *members of the public are participants*, and the prayer is directed mainly to them. Does the greater involvement of the public make the town's decision to offer a prayer before each meeting more constitutionally suspect?

   a. **No violation:** The Supreme Court essentially answered *no* to this question by a 5-4 vote in a 2014 case — as long as the practice of having a member of the clergy offer a meeting-opening prayer does not disparage other religions or coerce members of the public into praying, the practice does not violate the First Amendment, the Court held. *Town of Greece v. Galloway*, 134 S. Ct. 1811 (2014).

      i. **Practice upheld:** Five members of the Court — essentially the four-justice conservative bloc at the time plus Justice Kennedy — held that the prayer practice did *not* violate the Establishment Clause. Speaking for all five on most issues, Justice Kennedy wrote that the town's prayer practices were sufficiently like the legislative prayer approved in *Marsh* that the town had behaved lawfully.

b.   Significance: So following *Galloway*, the right of governments at all levels to offer *prayers before public sessions* now seems to be considerably quite firmly entrenched. For instance, it's not a problem for a majority of the Roberts Court that virtually all of the chaplains invited to give prayers are members of a single sect, or that the prayers use extensive sectarian (e.g., references to Christ) rather than non-sectarian language.

   i.   Limits: Only if the prayers *explicitly denigrate other religions, or non-believers, or seek to proselytize* to the public, is there likely to be a Establishment Clause problem in the eyes of the majority.

3.   Pledge of Allegiance: What about the *Pledge of Allegiance*? The Pledge contains the phrase, "One nation, under God, indivisible, with liberty and justice for all." Probably this brief reference to God will not be held to be a violation of the Establishment Clause. The Pledge would probably be viewed as a whole, and when so viewed would probably not be found to have the sole purpose of, or the primary effect of, advancing religion.

a.   Tradition: Also, the Court seems more inclined to allow references to religious themes when the reference is part of a *long-standing tradition* or *historical practice*. The Pledge certainly seems to qualify on this ground.

K. Displays and monuments with religious themes: Great controversy can arise when the government either erects, or makes its property available for private groups to erect, some sort of *display*, *monument* or *presentation* that involves religious themes.

   Examples posing the issue: For instance, suppose the government displays, or allows a private religious group to display, on public property a copy of the *Ten Commandments*, a *nativity scene*, a *Hanukkah menorah*, a *Christian cross*, or some other symbol that has great religious significance. Does the fact that the government is making its property available for such a display violate the Establishment Clause?

1.   The endorsement test: The Court has struggled to come up with a single test for dealing with this class of issues posed by government's facilitating (by funding or by making public property available) a private group's presentation of a religious-themed display or monument. Much of the time (though not always), the Court's test in recent years seems to have been: Would a *reasonable observer* seeing the display or monument conclude that the government was either *endorsing religion in general*, or *endorsing* a *particular religion*? If the answer to either part of the question is "*yes*," the display or monument violates the Establishment Clause. If the answer is "*no*," it does not.

a.   Context: This means that the constitutionality of a given Ten Commandments display, nativity scene, monument featuring a cross, etc., will be a *question of fact*. The most important single factor seems to be the *context* in which the religious symbol is displayed.

   i.   Presented by itself: If the religious symbol is presented *by itself* in what is clearly a space reserved by the government for its own property and its own messages, the Court is likely to conclude that a "reasonable observer" would believe that the government *was* endorsing the religious message.

ii. **Presented near other, non-religious, symbols:** Conversely, the presence of *other non-religious symbols nearby*, or the existence of a *sign* indicating that the display was furnished by private parties without governmental approval, or evidence that the religious material was provided for its historical rather than religious value — any of these factors may well be enough to lead a reasonable observer to the conclusion that government was *not* endorsing religion.

b. **Intent:** Government's *intent or motive* in establishing (or making its property available for) the display or monument is also of vital importance. If the court believes that the government's principal purpose in establishing the display or monument was to *promote or endorse religion* (or some particular religion), this fact by itself will probably lead to a finding of unconstitutionality. *McCreary County v. ACLU,* a Kentucky Ten Commandments case which we'll be reviewing in detail *infra*, p. 674, illustrates how a governmental purpose to advance religion will be fatal.

c. **Passage of time coupled with additional significance:** Lastly, even if, at the time the display or monument was created, a court would have found that government endorsed the religious message (leading to a conclusion that the Establish Clause was violated), the sheer *passage of time* — during which the item acquires *additional non-religious*, purely cultural, significance — may well lead a court considering the matter now to find that a violation of the Clause no longer exists. See, e.g., the *American Legion* case (*infra*, p. 674), in which this passage-of-time component seems to have played a decisive role in the Court's conclusion that a long-standing war memorial displaying a large cross did not now violate the Establishment Clause.

d. **Two categories:** There have been various cases in which the Court has considered whether religiously-oriented displays or monuments in public spaces violated the Establisment Clause. We'll examine the two most important categories covered in these cases: displays of *the Ten Commandments* and displays of *Christian crosses.* We consider each category separately (the Ten Commandments cases in Paragragh L. immediately below, and the leading cross case in Paragraph M. on p. 674).

L. **The Ten Commandments cases:** The Court decided two 2005 companion cases involving public displays of the text of the *Ten Commandments* in public spaces. The cases went in opposite directions, with one finding a display at the Texas State Capitol to be constitutional, and the other finding a display in two Kentucky courthouses to be unconstitutional. The Texas case was *Van Orden v. Perry*, 545 U.S. 677 (2005) and the Kentucky one was *McCreary County v. ACLU of Kentucky*, 545 U.S. 844 (2005).

1. **Two 5-4 decisions:** In each case, the decision was 5- 4. Four members of the court (Rehnquist, Scalia, Thomas and Kennedy) believed both displays were constitutional; four other members (Souter, Stevens, O'Connor and Ginsburg) believed both displays were unconstitutional. The swing vote was Justice Breyer, who therefore made a majority for upholding the Texas display and a different majority for striking down the Kentucky one.

2. **The Texas case (*Van Orden*):** In the Texas case (*Van Orden*), the display was a six-foot high monument containing the text of the King James version of the Ten Commandments. The monument was one of 17 monuments and 21 historical markers installed in 22 acres on the grounds of the Texas Capitol.

a. **Rehnquist's opinion upholds the display:** Chief Justice Rehnquist, in a plurality opinion joined by Scalia, Kennedy and Thomas, concluded that the monument *did not* *violate* the Establishment Clause. With Justice Breyer's vote concurring in the result, this provided the five votes needed to uphold the display. Rehnquist believed that although the Ten Commandments "are religious," they also "have an undeniable *historical meaning,*" since "Moses was a lawgiver as well as a religious leader."

    b. **Breyer supplies the fifth vote:** Justice Breyer concurred in the result and thus supplied the needed fifth vote for upholding the Texas display's constitutionality. For Breyer, this was "a borderline case." The Commandments' text had an undeniable religious message. But the display of which they were part conveyed a *secular message as well,* a message about the historical relation between this religious text and the development of law.

   3. **The Kentucky case (*McCreary County*):**   In the Kentucky case (*McCreary County v. ACLU of Kentucky*), Justice Breyer joined the four dissenters from *Van Orden* to **strike down** two counties' posting of the Ten Commandments. The *history* of that posting — a history that convinced a majority of the Court that government's primary purpose was to endorse religion — was dispositive.

    a. **Facts:** The two counties, McCreary and Pulaski, initially ordered large framed copies of the King James version of the Ten Commandments posted on a stand-alone basis in their courthouses. After the ACLU brought an initially-successful Establishment Clause challenge, the Counties tried to cure the problem by installing a second display, and then a third display.

      i. **The third display:** The third display (which was the subject of the case as it got to Supreme Court) consisted once again of framed copies of the Ten Commandments; however, this time these were accompanied by various other historical, *secular*, documents (e.g., the Magna Carta, the Declaration of Independence and the Bill of Rights), each with a statement about its historical and legal significance.

    b. **Majority strikes down:** Justice Souter, writing for himself and for Stevens, O'Connor, Ginsburg and Breyer, concluded that the third display *violated the Establishment Clause.* Souter relied on the *"purpose"* prong of *Lemon v. Kurtzman* (p. 661) — the display was invalid because it was *not supported by any genuine "secular legislative purpose."*

      i. **Rationale:**   In ascertaining purpose, Souter looked at the history of the three displays. Souter thought that as to the first display, any "reasonable observer could only think that the Counties *meant to emphasize and celebrate the Commandments' religious message."* Then, as to the third display — the one directly at issue — he concluded that the same religious purpose that had motivated the Counties in making the prior displays had continued.

M. **The Christian cross case (*Amer. Legion*):** Our second and final category of "displays and monuments" cases consists of displays of *Christian crosses.* The main such case is a 2019 decision, *American Legion v. American Humanist Assoc.*, 139 S.Ct. 2067 (2019). There, the Court *upheld* the display *by government* of a Christian cross on *public land.* The case represents the Court's most recent Establishment Clause decision, and its first decision about that Clause since Justices Gorsuch and Kavanaugh joined the Court.

   1. **Cross in memory of WWI veterans:**   In *American Legion*, a fractured Court held that it did not violate the Establishment Clause for government to allow a *32-foot-tall Christian* *cross* erected as a *World War I memorial* to remain on public land, or to be maintained by public funds. The case turned in large part on the majority's belief that during the nearly 90 years after the cross's erection, whatever Christian connotation it originally had, had since been blended with *"added secular meaning"* as a tribute to the area's WWI dead.

2. **Facts:** In 1918, a committee of residents of Prince George's County, Maryland, began to erect a 32-foot-high plain white cross (the "Bladensburg Cross" or "the Cross") as a memorial to the county's soldiers who had died in WWI. The committee decided to use such a cross for the memorial because, as the Supreme Court later put it, "the image of row after row of *plain white crosses marking the overseas graves of soldiers* was *emblazoned on the minds of Americans at home*." The American Legion, a private charity, completed the project in 1925. A Maryland state commission (the "Commission") eventually acquired the monument in 1961, and public funds were thereafter used to maintain it. By the time the challenge was filed in 2014, the monument sat on public land (owned by the Commission), where it was now at the center of a busy intersection.

   a. **Suit by Humanist organization:** The monument seems not to have engendered serious church-state controversy until many decades had passed following its 1925 completion. Then, in 2014, the Ps (the American Humanist Association) filed suit, alleging that the Cross's presence on public land, taken together with the (government) Commission's maintenance of the structure, violated the Establishment Clause.

3. **Vote is 7-2 to uphold the Cross:** By a vote of 7-2, the Supreme Court held that the Cross as presently maintained *did not violate* the Establishment Clause, and thus did not need to be moved or removed from the public site. But the Court was badly *fractured* about how the case should be analyzed. There were seven opinions altogether, six of which were contributed by the seven justices who agreed that there was no Establishment Clause violation.

   a. **Two dissenters:** The only members of the Court who thought the Establishment Clause *was* violated by the Cross's current publicly-funded presence on public land were Justices Ginsburg and Sotomayor. (Their dissent is discussed *infra*, p. 676.)

   b. **Alito's opinion:** Justice Alito wrote the main opinion, which spoke for a majority on many but not all points. (On some issues regarding the rationale for upholding the Cross, there *was* no majority.)

4. **Four factors:** Speaking for seven justices, Alito said that there were *four factors* that, taken together, meant that the publicly-funded maintenance on public land of this longstanding religiously-themed monument should *not* be found to violate the Establishment Clause:

   [1] **Hard to determine original purpose:** First, he said, when the case concerns "monuments, symbols, or practices that were *first established long ago,*" identifying their *"original purpose or purposes"* may be *"especially difficult."* Here, the long passage of time between the first planning of the Cross (1918) and the present challenge (2014) meant that it was no longer possible to *"uncover [the] motivations"* for the use of a cross in this or any such WW-I-era memorial.

   [2] **Changes in surrounding area:** Second, Alito said, "as time goes by, the *purposes associated* with an established monument, symbol, or practice often *multiply[.]"* That is, even if a monument's "original purpose" was "infused with religion," the

passage of time may have "*altered the area* surrounding [the] monument in ways that *change its meaning* and provide *new [non-religious] reasons for its preservation.*" This, too, was the situation here, since the Cross "now sits at a busy traffic intersection, and numerous additional monuments [not necessarily religious ones] are located nearby."

[3] **Message may evolve:** Third, Alito wrote, "the *message"* of a monument, symbol, or practice "may *change over time."* With enough time, "religiously expressive monuments … can become *embedded features* of a community's *landscape and identity*," so that the community "come[s] to *value them without necessarily embracing their religious roots."* This had happened here.

[4] **Removal as a non-neutral, hostile, act:** Finally, Alito said, removing long-standing religiously-expressive monuments would *pose its own problems.* "A government that *roams the land, tearing down monuments* with religious symbolism and scrubbing away any reference to the divine will strike many as *aggressively hostile to religion.*" Instead, in the case of a long-established monument like the Cross, the passage of time should "give[] rise to a *strong presumption of constitutionality."*

a. **Breyer's concurrence:** Justice Breyer (joined by Kagan) *concurred*, saying that Alito had "eloquently explain[ed]" why the Cross should be allowed to stay. (That made seven votes for that result.)

b. **Ginsburg's dissent:** Justice Ginsburg – joined by Justice Sotomayor – *dissented*.

   i. **"Symbol of Christian faith":** Ginsburg wrote that "[t]he Latin cross is the *foremost symbol of the Christian faith*[.]" And using the cross as a war memorial *"does not transform it into a secular symbol[.]"* She made this comparison: "Just as a *Star of David* is not suitable to honor Christians who died serving their country, so a *cross* is *not suitable to honor those of other faiths* who died defending their nation." (The county's soldiers who died in WWI were not all Christians.)

   ii. **Endorsement of religious content:** Therefore, she said, by maintaining the Cross on a public highway, the Commission *"elevates Christianity over other faiths,* and *religion over nonreligion.*" She agreed with the majority that "[m]emorializing the service of American soldiers is an … 'unquestionably secular' objective." But, she argued, this objective was *not served* by "displaying a symbol that bears 'a *starkly sectarian message.*'"

      (1) **"Endorsement" effect:** As Ginsburg saw it, when government displays a cross on public property, the government "may be *presumed to endorse [the cross's] religious content."* And government endorsement of the religious content of a monument located on public land, she said, constituted an Establishment Clause violation.

c. **Significance of case:** Here are a couple of the ways in which the majority's opinion in *American Legion* is significant:

   i. **Long-standing practices versus recent ones:** Whether what's at issue is a "monument," a "symbol," or a "practice,"[1] the thing or practice is *less likely* to pose an

Establishment Clause issue if it is a *long-standing* one than if it's a *recently-established* one.

    ii. Rejection of *Lemon* 3-factor test: The case marks the first time a majority of the modern Court has decisively ***rejected the use of the three-part Lemon v. Kurtzman test*** (*supra*, p. 661) in a particular context. *Lemon* will no longer be used in cases of an Establishment Clause challenge to the ***maintenance of religious symbols on government property.***[2]

        (1) Not rejected for all purposes: But neither *American Legion* nor any other case so far has **overruled** *Lemon*, or even explicitly rejected the *Lemon* standard from use in other Establishment Clause contexts.[3] Before *American Legion*, individual members of the Court frequently grumbled about *Lemon*'s inadequacies; but they then usually joined opinions deciding the case before them without either relying on or rejecting *Lemon*.

N. Financial aid to religious schools: Probably the most important and sensitive issue in the whole Establishment Clause area is whether, and to what extent, the government may give ***financial assistance*** to religious schools, or to students at these schools.

    1. Three-prong test: The Court applies the three-prong *Lemon* test in these financial-assistance cases, and in fact it was in such a case that the test was originally formulated. Thus such a program must satisfy each of the following requirements in order to avoid violating the Establishment Clause: (1) it must have a ***secular legislative purpose*** (though it may also have a religious purpose, as long as at least one secular purpose exists); (2) its "principal or primary ***effect***" must neither advance nor inhibit religion; and (3) it must not foster "an excessive government ***entanglement*** with religion." Also, as either an additional requirement or as a sub-requirement of (3), the Court has disallowed programs which are likely to be ***"politically divisive."***

    2. Broad themes: Before we turn to consideration of particular assistance programs, it is worthwhile to summarize some of the broad themes that have characterized the Court's handling of attacks on financial aid schemes.

        a. Lower vs. higher education: The Court has been much less likely to sustain programs which aid ***elementary and secondary*** parochial schools, than it has been to uphold those aiding sectarian ***colleges and universities.*** This distinction stems from the belief that in the elementary and secondary setting, religious instruction ***permeates every aspect*** of the educational process, whereas in the higher education context, it is possible to identify and support those aspects of the institution which are devoted to purely secular objectives. Most of the discussion which follows relates to elementary

---

1. The part of Alito's opinion that attracted the votes of seven members of the Court applied to all three of these categories.

2. See Chemerinsky Csbk (6e), p. 1730: "Justice Alito's majority opinion rejected use of the *Lemon* test in evaluating ***religious symbols on government property.***"

3. See Chemerinsky Csbk (6e), p. 1730, saying that outside the area of religious symbols on government property, *American Legion* "did not overrule *Lemon* or use of the test with regard to other Establishment Clause issues."

and secondary contexts; separate consideration is given to the higher education area beginning *infra*, p. 688.

    b. **Direct vs. indirect aid:** Assistance programs are more likely to be upheld if the aid is given to **students and their parents**, rather than directly to the school, and each parent or student gets to decide at which school to use the benefit. (See, e.g., *Zelman v. Simmons-Harris*, the tuition-voucher case, *infra*, p. 679, making this distinction.) This distinction is based on the theory that it is easier to ensure that the aid is used to fulfill secular objectives if the parents and students, rather than the school, are given control of the money or items being furnished.

    c. **All students:** A program which by its terms assists **all students**, both in public and private schools, is much more likely to be sustained than one which is addressed **solely to religious-school students**.

    d. **Secular effect:** All three of the broad principles just described can be seen as deriving from the basic requirement that the financial assistance have a **primary effect** that is **secular**.

3. **Particular programs:** We turn now to consideration of **particular types** of programs aiding parochial schools or their students.

4. **Transportation:** A program by which parents were reimbursed for the money they spent to **transport** their children to school on **public buses** was upheld, in *Everson v. Board of Education*, 330 U.S. 1 (1947).

    a. **Public school students included:** A key feature of the plan approved in *Everson* was that parents of **public school students** were **included** in the reimbursement scheme. It is highly unlikely that a transportation-reimbursement scheme applicable *only* to religious-school students would be approved by the Court today. The key difference is that the *Everson* scheme can justly be viewed as supplying the secular benefit of "transportation to one's school," and as supplying that benefit in a way that is completely **neutral as between religious and secular institutions**.

5. **Textbooks and other materials:** *Textbooks* may be *loaned* to parochial school students, as long as: (1) a similar policy is followed with respect to public-school and private-non-parochial students; and (2) the textbooks are themselves secular rather than religiously-oriented. See *Board of Education v. Allen*, 392 U.S. 236 (1968).

    a. **Computers and other non-textbook materials:** Similarly, non-textbook materials and equipment, such as **computers**, **audio-visual equipment,** and the like, may be given or lent to religious schools as long as: (1) the materials are themselves non-religious in nature; (2) the materials are **not diverted** for religious purposes (e.g., computers are not used to run religiously-oriented programs); and (3) **all schools** — religious or not — are eligible for the aid on the **same terms**. *Mitchell v. Helms*, 530 U.S. 793 (2000).

6. **Salary supplements:** The state may not subsidize parochial education by reimbursing parochial schools for a portion of **teachers' salaries**, even where this reimbursement is theoretically for the teaching of secular subjects. See, e.g., *Lemon v. Kurtzman*, 403 U.S. 602 (1971). Again, the problem is that there is no way to make sure that these funds are not used for religious purposes, at least not without such surveillance of the teachers' actual conduct that the monitoring itself would constitute excessive entanglement between church and state. *Id.*

7. **Furnishing of teachers:** Suppose the state takes *public-school teachers* (i.e., teachers who are on the public payroll and who do most of their teaching in the public schools) and *sends them into parochial schools* to teach special subjects. Such a program *does not violate* the Establishment Clause, so long as the public-school teachers *teach in a secular manner* and *without curricular interference* by the parochial school. See *Agostini v. Felton*, 521 U.S. 203 (1997), a 5-4 decision.

   a. **Rationale:** Justice O'Connor, writing for 5-member majority, said that there were *"three primary criteria* we currently use to evaluate whether government aid has the *effect of advancing religion,"* and that the program here *did not run afoul* of any of the three: "[I]t does not result in *government indoctrination*; define its recipient by *reference to religion*; or *create an excessive entanglement"* between government and religion.

8. **Services:** Publicly-funded *services* (e.g., testing and counseling) may be supplied to parochial school students. Apparently the only present limitations on such services are that: (1) they must be *offered to all schools* in a way that does not intentionally favor parochial schools; and (2) they must have an *exclusively secular content.* So if, for instance, the state offers testing, counseling, remedial education or other specialized services to all non-public schools, with the quantity of services keyed to the size of the school's enrollment, and with the services having no direct religious content, there is apparently no Establishment Clause problem. That seems to be true even if the principal *effect* of the services is to aid religion.

9. **Tuition vouchers:** *Tuition vouchers* may be given to parents to enable them to pay religious-school tuition, as long as the vouchers may also be used in non-religious private schools. In *Zelman v. Simmons-Harris*, 536 U.S. 639 (2002), a controversial and important case, the Court held by a 5-4 vote that such a tuition voucher plan *did not violate the Clause.* The majority reasoned that any "advancement of a religious message" that the plan facilitated was an *"incidental"* one that resulted from *"the deliberate choices of numerous individual recipients,"* not from the government.

   a. **General approach in *Zelman*:** The Court in *Zelman* seems to have announced a rule for cases involving government funding that finds its way to religious institutions: so long as *private citizens make individual choices* about how to use the funding, the fact that the great majority of the funding *ends up being used in religious institutions,* and for pursuit of religious ends, *does not matter.*

   b. **Facts:** In *Zelman*, the state of Ohio set up a program under which any Cleveland student in kindergarten through 8th grade could receive a voucher of up to $2,250 to attend private school. In the most recent year, 3,700 of the 75,000 students in the Cleveland school district took advantage of the program. Although the program let both religious and non-religious private schools participate, *96% of participating students enrolled in religious schools.* The principal purpose of the program seems to have been to enable students in a failing public school system to afford a private alternative.

   c. **Majority upholds:** Chief Justice Rehnquist was joined by Justices O'Connor, Scalia, Kennedy and Thomas in upholding the constitutionality of the program.

      i. **Reliance on precedent:** The Chief Justice reviewed earlier cases that, he said, had distinguished between "government programs that provide aid *directly* to religious schools" and "programs of *true private choice*, in which government aid reaches religious schools only as a result of the genuine and independent *choices of private individuals*." Programs falling into this latter category — ones that implement private choices — had been consistently upheld, he said. The voucher program here was constitutional because it was a "program of *true private choice*," one that was *"neutral in all respects toward religion."*

    d. Dissents: The four dissenters (Stevens, Souter, Ginsburg and Breyer) wrote three dissents. All viewed the majority's opinion as a major and regrettable change to the Court's prior Establishment Clause doctrines, and all warned that this new approach would likely *trigger major social conflicts.*

    e. Significance: *Zelman* (which remains good law) demonstrates that a majority of the Court will conduct a *quite easy-to-satisfy review* of government programs whose benefits flow to religious organizations. So long as the funding program is *facially neutral* as between religious and non-religious organizations, and so long as the program relies upon *individual citizens to make their own decisions* about which organization shall receive the funding, the fact that the vast majority of the total funding directly advances organizations' religious objectives *does not matter.*

      i. **Possible Free Exercise violation:** In fact, a 2020 case demonstrates that a tuition voucher plan like the one in *Zelman* not only doesn't violate the *Establishment* Clause by including parochial-school students, it *does* violate the *Free Exercise* Clause if such students are *excluded*. See *Espinoza v. Montana Dep't. of Revenue*, discussed extensively *infra*, p. 695.

10. Scholarships for religious study: A generalized program of awarding *scholarship money* or other grants to students will not run afoul of the Establishment Clause, even if some students use the funds to *attend religious institutions that would prepare them for a religious calling.* Thus in *Witters v. Washington Dept. of Services for the Blind*, 474 U.S. 481 (1986), the Court unanimously held that the Establishment Clause was not violated by a state's grant of funds under a vocational rehabilitation assistance program to a blind student who would use the funds to attend a private Christian school, where he would *train to be a "pastor,* missionary, or youth director."

    a. Rationale in *Witters*: As in *Zelman*, *supra*, in *Witters* the key fact preventing the program from having the primary effect of advancing religion was that the payments were made *"directly to the student,* who transmits it to the educational institution of his or her choice[.]" Therefore, "any aid ... that ultimately flows to religious institutions does so only as a result of the *genuinely independent and private choices* of aid recipients."

11. Aid to higher education: Public financial assistance to sectarian *colleges* raises *fewer Establishment Clause problems* than does aid to elementary and secondary schools. Although the Court has applied the usual three-prong test in the aid-to-colleges context, it has found that test to be much more readily met.

O. No intentional preference for one sect over others: Just as the Establishment Clause is violated when government prefers religion over non-religion, so is it violated when the government intentionally *favors a particular sect over other sects*, or over non-religious interests.

As the Court put it in *Larson v. Valente*, 456 U.S. 228 (1982), "The clearest command of the Establishment Clause is that *one religious denomination cannot be officially preferred over another."*

1. **Strict scrutiny:** In fact, if the Court is convinced that government is intentionally preferring some sect(s) over others (rather than aiding religion generally), the Court will *apply strict scrutiny:* the preference will be struck down unless it is "justified by a *compelling governmental interest* and ... *closely fitted to further that interest." Larson, supra.*

   Example: The state of Minnesota originally exempts all religious organizations from complying with various reporting and registration requirements that other charities must obey. The state then cuts back the exemption so that it applies only to the benefit of those religious organizations that receive more than half of their total contributions from members; this is the "50% Rule." (The state says that the Rule is designed to guard against groups that conduct abusive in-person solicitation of non-members.) The "Moonies," a Christian sect that widely solicits funds in public places, claim that the Rule violates the group's rights under the Establishment Clause. The Supreme Court determines that the 50% Rule indeed prefers, on its face, some religious groups (those principally supported by members) over other groups (those, like the Moonies, that are principally supported by non-members).

   Held, for the Moonies. Given that the 50% Rule on its face prefers some religious groups over others, the Court will automatically strictly scrutinize the Rule, and uphold it only if it is "justified by a compelling governmental interest and ... closely fitted to further that interest." Here, even if the state's asserted interest in combating solicitation abuse is compelling (unclear), the 50% Rule is not "closely fitted" to furthering that interest, since nothing in the record suggests that the likelihood of solicitation abuse is closely related to the ratio of member contributions to total contributions. *Larson, supra.*

2. **Accommodation vs. favoritism:** Cases in which government singles out some religious group(s), in a facially-obvious way, by giving it (or denying it) a financial benefit that other religious groups are denied (or are given), are relatively rare. (*Larson, supra*, is one such rare instance.) A much more common way that government runs the risk of being found to unconstitutionally favor one particular religious group over others is where government tries to *"accommodate"* a group's *special needs* by *exempting* the group from a *generally-applicable legal requirement.*

   a. **Conflict:** In these situations of government attempts to "accommodate," there can be a conflict between the Establishment Clause's "no inter-denominational preferences" principle and the fact that sometimes, the *Free Exercise Clause* requires (or at least allows) government to grant a special accommodation. (See *infra*, p. 698, for the Free Exercise side of the accommodation problem.)

   b. **"Accommodation" becomes forbidden favoritism:** Occasionally, the Court has in fact held that government's attempt to accommodate a sect's special needs has crossed the line from permissible accommodation to forbidden favoritism. This happened, for instance, in *Board of Education of Kiryas Joel Village v. Grumet,* 512 U.S. 687 (1994). The case also illustrates that where a state *delegates governmental power* directly to a religious group, a violation of the Establishment Clause is almost certain to be found.

i. **Facts:**   The *Kiryas Joel* case had its origins when a group of Satmar Hasidim, fundamentalist Jews, moved from Brooklyn to the Town of Monroe in upstate New York. In 1977, taking advantage of a New York State law that allows groups of residents within a town to form a smaller village, the Satmars formed the Village of Kiryas Joel. The village was drawn to include just the 328 acres owned and inhabited by Satmars. By the time of suit, the village had a population of about 8,500.

   (1) Isolated: The 8,500 Satmars are vigorously religious and deeply insular. They speak Yiddish as their primary language, segregate the sexes outside the home, forbid TV and radio, and dress distinctly. Except for the handicapped children who were the focus of the suit, all children in the village attend private Jewish schools.

   (2) Handicapped children: Under state and federal laws, all **handicapped** children are entitled to special publicly-funded education services. The Satmars wanted to receive these services without having to send their handicapped children to a neighboring district's public schools (where there were almost no Satmar students).

   (3) Special district: The New York Legislature tried to give the Satmars what they wanted, by passing a special statute that provided that "the territory of the Village of Kiryas Joel ... shall be ... a **separate school district.**" The effect of the statute was to allow a locally-elected board of education to open schools, hire teachers, and impose property taxes to fund the operation. The resulting Kiryas Joel Village School District in fact used its powers very narrowly; the only school or program it ever ran was a special-education program for handicapped children, mostly paid for by state funds. At the time the suit was heard by the Court, the new district served only 40 full-time students, of whom two-thirds were Hasidic children who commuted from outside the village.

ii. **Holding:**   By a 6-3 vote, the Court held that the establishment of the Kiryas Joel Village School District *violated* the Establishment Clause. The majority opinion, by Justice Souter, seemed to say that there were two distinct problems with the way the district was created: (1) **religious criteria** were used to **draw the boundary lines** of the district; and (2) the creation of the district was a **special favor** for a particular religious sect, with no assurances that other similarly-situated groups would receive the same benefits.

c. **Another illustration:**   *Kiryas Joel* is not the only case in which the Court has found a **forbidden preference for one sect over another.** For another such case, see **Larson v. Valente**, 456 U.S. 228 (1982), the "Moonies" case discussed *supra*, pp. 681-681, where a "50% Rule" for determining which religious groups would be tax-exempt discriminated on its face against religious groups that mostly solicited funds in public and in favor of those that solicited mainly from members.

3. **Accommodation found not to be a violation:**   In *Kiryas Joel* and *Larson v. Valente*, one religion or sect was accommodated in preference to another, and the accommodation was found to be an Establishment Clause violation. However, where what is being accommodated is not a particular religion or sect, but rather, the **practice of religion generally**, the Court is much **less likely** to find an Establishment Clause violation.

a. **RLUIPA:** For example, Congress has enacted the Religious Land Use and Institution-alized Persons Act of 2000 (RLUIPA), which requires that the ***religious practices of prisoners*** be given greater accommodation than needs to be given to the non-religious practices of prisoners. The Court has held that this provision does not on its face vio-late the Establishment Clause. See *Cutter v. Wilkinson*, 544 U.S. 709 (2005).

4. **National security, and the entry of foreigners into the U.S. (*Trump v. Hawaii*):** The rule that governmental actions that are motivated by a desire to prefer one sect over another will be strictly scrutinized is subject to an important ***exception***: when the prefer-ence occurs in the context of the federal government's authority to determine ***which non-U.S. nationals may enter the country,*** the courts will use only ***mere-rationality review,*** not strict scrutiny. The Court announced this result in the 2018 "travel ban" case, ***Trump v. Hawaii***, 128 S.Ct. 2392 (2018).

a. **Travel ban:** The ban was contained in a presidential proclamation issued by Presi-dent Trump (the "Proclamation"), which greatly ***restricted entry into the U.S.*** by nationals of eight countries, most of which had majority-Muslim populations. Here is a brief chronology of some of President Trump's comments — both before and after assuming office — on the subject of Muslims' entry to the U.S. and his proposed travel ban, as well as an overview of the various drafts the proposal went through:[4]

❑ In December 2015, then-candidate Trump issued a formal statement in which he said that he was "calling for a total and complete ***shutdown of Muslims entering the United States*** until our country's representatives can figure out what is going on," given the "great hatred towards Americans by large segments of the Muslim population."

❑ In March 2016, Mr. Trump said, ***"Islam hates us.*** . . . [W]e can't allow people coming into this country who have this hatred of the United States . . . [a]nd of people that are not Muslim."

❑ In December, 2016, as President-elect, Mr. Trump was asked whether he would "rethink" his previous "plans to create a Muslim registry or ban Muslim immigra-tion"; he replied: "You know my plans. All along, I've proven to be right."

❑ In January, 2017, one week after taking office, Mr. Trump signed an Executive Order (***"EO-1"***), his first travel ban, entitled "Protecting the Nation From Foreign Terrorist Entry Into the United States." EO-1 did two things: (1) it directed the Secretary of Homeland Security to conduct a ***worldwide review*** of whether foreign governments were supplying adequate ***security-vetting information*** about their nationals seeking to enter the U.S.; and (2) pending that review, it suspended for 90 days the entry of foreign nationals from ***seven majority-Muslim countries*** — Iran, Iraq, Libya, Somalia, Sudan, Syria, and Yemen — that had been previously identified by Congress or prior administrations as posing heightened terrorism

---

4. Most of these details are as recounted in Justice Sotomayor's dissent in the case. Given that the dissent attached great importance to the details of Mr. Trump's many remarks about why he issued the Proclamation and its predecessors, I cover those remarks in some detail. As we'll see, unlike the dissent, the majority concluded that given the facial neutrality-towards-religion of the Proclamation, and the existence of a legitimate security rationale for it, these statements were essentially irrelevant.

risks.

❑ The day after Mr. Trump signed EO-1, one of his advisers described how EO-1 had come about: after Mr. Trump first announced a proposed "Muslim ban," the advisor said, Mr. Trump called the advisor and told him, " 'Put a commission together. Show me the *right way to do it legally'*."

❑ A lower court soon issued a temporary restraining order blocking the entry restrictions in EO-1. As a result, Mr. Trump revoked EO-1 and replaced it with *EO-2*, which again directed a worldwide review and temporarily suspended entry of foreign nationals from certain countries. But this time, the list consisted only of six countries (all of the seven covered by EO-1 except Iraq). An adviser to the President described EO-2 in advance as having "the same basic policy outcome" as EO-1, and said that any changes would address "very technical issues that were brought up by the court" in the EO-1 litigation.

❑ Two Courts of Appeal soon enjoined the entry restrictions of EO-2 from going into effect. In June 2017, the Supreme Court entered a partial stay of these injunctions. That same month, the President used Twitter to describe EO-2 (the version of the ban that was then in litigation before the Supreme Court), as a *"watered down, politically correct version"* of the "original Travel Ban."

❑ In August 2017, Mr. Trump tweeted a reference to an apocryphal story about how U.S. General Pershing in the early 1900's used bullets dipped in pigs' blood to massacre a large group of Muslim insurgents in the Philippines; his tweet then said, approvingly, that after the massacre, "There was no more Radical Islamic Terror for 35 years!"

❑ In September 2017, after the worldwide review had been completed, Mr. Trump issued the Proclamation.

❑ In November 2017, Mr. Trump retweeted three anti-Muslim videos, entitled "Muslim Destroys a Statue of Virgin Mary!", "Islamist mob pushes teenage boy off roof and beats him to death!", and "Muslim migrant beats up Dutch boy on crutches!"

i. Details of the Proclamation: The Proclamation restricted entry into the U.S. by nationals of *eight countries* whose systems for managing and sharing information about their nationals the Department of Homeland Security had found to be inadequate during the review. These were Chad, Iran, Iraq, Libya, North Korea, Syria, Venezuela, and Yemen. Six of these — all but North Korea and Venezuela — were majority-Muslim; those two were added between EO-2 and the Proclamation.[5]

b. "Religious gerrymander" claim: The state of Hawaii and individuals associated with it claimed that the Proclamation violated both (1) the anti-discrimination provisions of a federal statute governing the issuance of visas and (2) the Establishment Clause's ban on preferring some denominations over others. The plaintiffs called the

---

5. Sotomayor's dissent charged that "[T]he inclusion of North Korea and Venezuela ... simply reflect[s] subtle efforts to start 'talking territory instead of Muslim,' precisely so the Executive Branch could evade criticism or legal consequences for the Proclamation's otherwise clear targeting of Muslims."

Proclamation a *"religious gerrymander,"* asserting that it was intentionally devised to apply mainly to countries with majority-Muslim populations, and reflected the President's animus towards Muslims.

    i.   **Injunction by lower courts:**   The lower federal courts, including the Ninth Circuit, found for the plaintiffs. These courts enjoined the entry restrictions on statutory grounds; they did not reach the Establishment Clause issue.

c.   **Ban is upheld:**   But by a 5-4 vote, the Supreme Court reversed. The majority **upheld** the Proclamation, at least as a preliminary matter: the Court dissolved the lower-court injunction against the travel ban, concluding that the plaintiffs had not demonstrated a "likelihood of success" on the merits of either their statutory or their Establishment Clause claims. The majority opinion was written by Chief Justice Roberts.

    i.   **President's remarks didn't matter:**   Roberts didn't review the President's remarks about Muslims in any detail. But he showed some discomfort with the tenor of those remarks. He noted that the plaintiffs had argued that Mr. Trump's words "strike at fundamental standards of respect and tolerance, in violation of our constitutional tradition." Roberts didn't dispute this characterization. But he said, in effect, that the words, however biased or offensive, **didn't much matter** to the outcome of the case: the issue before the Court was "not whether to denounce the statements. It is instead the significance of those statements in reviewing a Presidential directive, neutral on its face, addressing a matter within the core of executive responsibility."

    ii.   **"Fundamental sovereign attribute":**   Roberts then relied heavily on prior case law holding that the power to make decisions about which foreign nationals should be allowed to enter the U.S. — and more generally, decisions about national security matters — constitutes a *"fundamental sovereign attribute."* Under the Constitution's structure, he said, that "sovereign attribute" is to be exercised by Congress and the Executive Branch, *"largely immune from judicial control."* (This portion of Roberts' opinion is discussed more extensively *supra*, p. 125.)

    iii.   **Uses "rational basis review":**   Roberts then turned to a core issue: what **standard of review should be used** in evaluating whether the Proclamation violated the Establishment Clause? Roberts **rejected** the dissent's proposed *"reasonable observer"* standard.[6] Instead, Roberts selected a standard of review that would be nearly impossible for the challengers to satisfy: *"rational-basis review,"* under which the Court would decide "whether the [Proclamation] is **plausibly related to the Government's stated objective** to protect the country and improve [pre-entry] vetting processes."

    iv.   **Application of rational-basis review:**   Once Roberts decided to use rational-basis review, it was a foregone conclusion that he would **uphold** the Proclamation's constitutionality.

---

6. See p. 686 *infra* for how the dissent thought such a standard would work.

(1) Legitimate objective: Roberts found that the interest that the federal government claimed it was advancing — the interest in restricting foreigners who might espouse terrorism — was a "legitimate" one.[7]

(2) Rationally related to this objective: Roberts then took up the second part of the rational-basis test: whether the governmental action was ***rationally related*** to the achievement of this legitimate national-security interest.[8] Here, too, he found that the standard was easily satisfied, for several reasons. For instance:

❏ **"Results of a worldwide review process":** The particular details of the entry ban in the Proclamation reflected "the results of a ***worldwide review process*** undertaken by multiple Cabinet officials and their agencies."

❏ **Other rational aspects:** Also, the details of the Proclamation arguably served the asserted federal interest in national security. For instance, the Proclamation's restrictions were merely ***"conditional"*** ones that would remain in force ***only so long as they were necessary*** to address the inadequate security vetting by the eight countries.

In sum, Roberts said, the federal government had "set forth a sufficient national security justification to ***survive rational basis review."***

v. *Korematsu:* Roberts also, in passing, officially declared the ***overruling*** of *Korematsu v. U.S.* (*supra*, p. 264), the Court's infamous 1944 decision upholding the constitutionality of a war-time Executive Branch order putting most U.S. citizens of Japanese ancestry who lived on the West Coast into internment camps. Roberts said that *Korematsu* "was gravely wrong the day it was decided, has been overruled in the court of history, and — to be clear — 'has no place in law under the Constitution.'"

(1) "Nothing to do with this case": But, Roberts said, despite the dissent's contention otherwise, *Korematsu **"has nothing to do with this case."*** It was "wholly inapt," he said, to "liken that morally repugnant order to [the Proclamation's] facially neutral policy denying certain foreign nationals the privilege of admission."

d. Dissent: The four liberal Justices ***dissented***, in two separate opinions each joined by two members of the Court. The longer and angrier of the dissents was by Justice Sotomayor, who was joined by Justice Ginsburg. Here are the main points that Sotomayor made:

i. "Reasonable observer" test: Sotomayor disagreed vigorously with the majority's choice of the "rational basis" as the standard for review. She believed that the

---

7. For more on how Roberts saw the issue of what objectives are legitimate, see *supra*, p. 125.

8. Roberts' opinion didn't explicitly transition between considering (1) whether the asserted interest was legitimate, and (2) whether the means chosen rationally related to that interest. Instead, he phrased the issues as whether the entry rules here were "expressly premised" on the legitimate interest, and whether those rules "support" the government's claim that it was acting in pursuit of this legitimate interest. But it seems clear from context that Roberts was evaluating whether the required rational-relation-between-means-and-end existed.

correct standard was the ***"reasonable observer" test*** given in the Ten-Commandments-monument case, *McCreary County v. ACLU* (*supra*, p. 674). Applied here, she said, this test would ask "whether a reasonable observer, presented with all 'openly available data,' the text and 'historical context' of the Proclamation, and the ***'specific sequence of events'*** leading to it, would conclude that the ***primary purpose***[9] of the Proclamation is to disfavor Islam and its adherents by excluding them from the country."

(1) Allows consideration of Trump's statement: A key feature of the *McCreary* reasonable-observer standard is that, since it takes into consideration the enactment's "historical context" and the "specific sequence of events" leading to it, the standard allows the Court to ***consider statements of motive and intent*** by the government ***officials*** who sponsored it. (By contrast, the majority's rational-basis standard, since it considers *any* plausible and legitimate governmental interest, whether or not it was the one that actually motivated the enactment, implicitly disregards officials' statements of motive.)

(2) President's motives: Sotomayor summarized the President's motives in issuing the Proclamation this way: "What began as a policy explicitly 'calling for a total and complete shutdown of Muslims entering the United States' has since morphed into a 'Proclamation' putatively based on national-security concerns." But, she said, "this new window dressing cannot conceal an unassailable fact: the words of the President and his advisers create the strong perception that the Proclamation is ***contaminated by impermissible discriminatory animus*** against Islam and its followers."

(3) "Unquestionably" motivated by religious animus: Since the Proclamation's purpose was to disfavor Muslims by excluding them from the U.S., Sotomayor said, that fact alone was enough, under *McCreary*, to make the measure an Establishment Clause violation.

ii. **Comparison to *Korematsu*:** Sotomayor thought there were "stark parallels" between the majority's reasoning here and that of *Korematsu v. U.S.*, the Japanese internment case (*supra*, p. 264). In both cases, she said, the Court "gave a pass [to] an ***odious***, gravely injurious racial classification ***authorized by an executive order***," after the government "invoked an ***ill-defined national-security threat*** to justify an exclusionary policy of sweeping proportion." And in both cases, "the exclusion order was rooted in dangerous stereotypes about ... a particular group's ***supposed inability to assimilate*** and ***desire to harm*** the United States."

e. **Significance of case:** *Trump v. Hawaii* seems to mean that where the Executive Branch takes action in the areas of national security and/or immigration, the Court ***will not give any sort of heightened scrutiny*** to that action, even if there is extensive evidence that the action ***was in fact motivated by bias towards religion or towards a par-***

---

9. Recall that most of the Court's Establishment Clause cases, and certainly *McCreary* itself, have applied the three-part test of *Lemon v. Kurtzman*, *supra*, p. 683. Under that test, the government action will be found to violate the Establishment Clause unless it satisfies ***all three parts*** of the test, one of which is that the enactment ***have a primary purpose that is "secular."***

ticular religious group. In contrast to the strict scrutiny with which the Court reviews *domestic* actions by government that appear to be motivated by anti-religious sentiment, in this foreign-affairs context the Court will use easy-to-satisfy *rational-basis review.*

    i.　Rational-basis review: Under this rational-basis review, the Court will uphold the government action long as the action is rationally related to the achievement of a *plausible and legitimate national-security interest;* any evidence that government *in fact* acted based on an anti-religious motive will essentially be *ignored.*

III.　THE FREE EXERCISE CLAUSE

A.　Introduction: The First Amendment bars government from making any law *"prohibiting the free exercise"* of religion. The Free Exercise Clause, like the Establishment Clause, applies not only to the federal government but also to the states, via the Fourteenth Amendment.

    1.　No forbidding of belief: The Free Exercise Clause flatly forbids the outlawing of any religious *belief.*

    2.　Conduct: The difficult issues arise not in connection with pure beliefs, but in connection with *conduct* that is related to beliefs. Normally, free exercise problems arise when the government: (1) forbids or burdens conduct which happens to be dictated by someone's religious belief; (2) compels or encourages conduct which is forbidden by someone's religious belief; or (3) runs generally-available government-benefit programs that intentionally exclude certain recipients based on the recipient's religious identity.

    3.　General principles: However, not all government actions that fall within one of the above three categories are necessarily violative of the Free Exercise Clause. The Free Exercise analysis depends heavily on the distinction between government action taken with *intent* to burden a religious practice, and government action that merely has an *unintended burdensome effect* on a religious practice:

        a.　Intent: Whenever the *purpose* of a governmental action is to negatively affect a particular type of conduct *because* the conduct is dictated by religion, that action will almost automatically be found to violate the Free Exercise Clause. Such purposeful interference with religion will be *strictly scrutinized*, and almost never upheld.

        b.　Burdensome effect: Where the government action is not motivated by an intent to interfere with religiously-related conduct, but the action nonetheless has that *effect*, as long as the statute is a rule of *"general applicability"* (as opposed to a rule that focuses on religion), an individual's free exercise rights *don't entitle him to an exemption* from the statute. As the Court put it in the key 1990 case on the subject, "the right of free exercise does not relieve an individual of the obligation to *comply* with a *'valid and neutral law* of *general applicability* on the ground that the law *proscribes (or prescribes) conduct* that his religion prescribes (or proscribes).'" *Employment Division v. Smith*, 494 U.S. 872 (1990) (discussed further *infra*, p. 700).

B.　Intent to disfavor religious practice: Where government takes an action whose *purpose* is to forbid or interfere with particular conduct *because* the conduct is tied into the exercise of a religious belief, that governmental action will generally be strictly scrutinized, and almost always struck down, as a violation of the Free Exercise Clause. We'll refer to this type of government action as falling within the *"purposeful discrimination"* branch of the Free Exercise Clause (as opposed to the "incidental burdensome effect" branch, discussed *infra*, p. 698).

1. **Three categories:** Within this "purposeful discrimination" branch of Free Exercise case law, it's reasonable to divide government actions relating to religion into *three different categories*, with the modern Supreme Court's treatment varying depending on which category the government action falls into. Here are the categories:

   [1] **Prohibition or punishment:** Cases in which government actively *prohibits or punishes* a private person's religiously-motivated actions, under circumstances in which the government seems to be acting based on a *desire to discriminate* against a particular religion or against religion generally. In this category, *strict scrutiny* will certainly be applied.

   Example: A city council enacts an ordinance making it illegal to carry out animal sacrifices. The council is shown to have been motivated by prejudice against a particular locally-unpopular religious sect that had been engaging in such sacrifices. The court will surely give the ordinance strict scrutiny, and will strike it down. (Cf. *Church of the Lukumi Babalu Aye, infra*, p. 690, where the Supreme Court strictly scrutinized, and *struck down*, such a prohibition.)

   [2] **Pool of discretionary benefits denied for "essentially religious" uses:** Cases in which government does both of the following: (a) uses its discretion to furnish a financial benefit to a *limited group* of individual recipients, and (b) tells recipients that they may not use the benefit towards any *"essentially religious endeavor,"* like *training for the ministry*. In this situation, the Court will apparently *not* apply strict scrutiny, and will conclude that the carve-out for "essentially religious" uses does not violate the recipient's Free Exercise rights.

   Example: A state scholarship program provides that the scholarships may be used by recipients at any in-state college, even one operated by a religious institution, but may not be used to pursue a degree in the "essentially religious endeavor" of "devotional theology" (e.g., training to be a minister). In *Locke v. Davey, infra*, p. 694, the Court *upheld* such a program against Free Exercise attack.

   [3] **Denial of generally-available benefit:** Cases in which government makes a benefit generally available, but categorically *denies* that benefit for use by or in connection with *any religious organization or any religious activity*. Here, as in Category [1] above, the court will *apply strict scrutiny*, even if the reason for the government's denial is a *desire to separate church and state*, rather than hostility toward religion.

   Example: Montana's state constitution has a "no aid" provision, which forbids public funds to be used to aid any private religious school. The state legislature grants a tax credit of up to $150 to reimburse a family for tuition they spend at a private school, whether the school is a religious school or not. The state Supreme Court invalidates the tax credit on the grounds that it violates the "no aid" state-constitutional provision. *Held* (by the U.S. Supreme Court): (1) the no-aid provision "discriminates based on religious status," so it must therefore be *strictly scrutinized*; and (2) the provision cannot survive that strict scrutiny. See *Espinoza v. Montana Dept. of Revenue*, 140 S.Ct. 2246 (2020), discussed at length *infra*, p. 695.

We consider each of the three categories in more detail below, in Pars. 2-4.

2. **Prohibition or punishment based on government's hostility to religion:** *Category [1]* consists of cases in which government actively *prohibits or punishes* a private person's religiously-motivated actions, under circumstances in which the court concludes that government acted out of *hostility* towards *religion generally,* or towards *a particular religious group.* In this scenario, the courts must *strictly scrutinize* the governmental action, and will almost always end up *striking down that action* as a violation of the Free Exercise Clause.

   a. **Cases are rare:** Cases falling into this "intentional and invidious discrimination" category are relatively *rare*.

   b. **Animal sacrifice case (*Church of the Lukumi Babalu Aye*):** One of the few modern Supreme Court case in which government was shown to have had such an illicit intent to disfavor a particular religion is *Church of the Lukumi Babalu Aye, Inc. v. Hialeah*, 508 U.S. 520 (1993), involving *ritual animal sacrifice* by practitioners of the Santeria religion.

      i. **The Santeria religion:** The plaintiffs in *Lukumi* were members of a church following the Santeria religion. Santeria, practiced most often in Cuba, is a religion whose members perform ritual sacrifices of chickens, pigeons and other animals as part of rites for birth, marriage and death, for cure of the sick, and at other times. The animal is killed by the cutting of its carotid arteries, and is usually (but not in all instances) cooked and eaten.

      ii. **Government's response:** The city of Hialeah, Florida, where the Ps' church was located, enacted a series of ordinances that, taken together, outlawed religious animal sacrifice. The ordinances were written so that their sole effect would be to ban sacrifices by Santeria practitioners; for instance, Kosher slaughter was carefully exempted by defining "sacrifice" so as to exclude slaughter that is "for the primary purpose of food consumption."

         (1) **Motive:** The history behind the ordinances' enactment — such as the supporting statements by Council members, and the public debate concerning the issue — made it clear that the community as a whole disliked the practice of Santeria, and wanted to abolish sacrificial rituals by Santeria practitioners.

      iii. **Ordinance struck down:** *All members* of the Court agreed that the Hialeah ordinances must be *struck down* as a violation of the Free Exercise Clause. Seven Justices believed that the intent of the City Council in enacting the ordinances was to suppress the ritual portion of the Santeria religion, and agreed that governmental action that is intended to disfavor a particular religious practice will almost always violate the Free Exercise Clause.

      iv. **Rationale:** Writing for the Court on most points, Justice Kennedy explained that government action that affects religion will be subjected to the *"most rigorous of scrutiny"* (which it will rarely survive) unless the government act is both: (1) *"neutral"*; and (2) of *"general applicability."*

(1) Not "neutral": Here, Kennedy found, the ordinances were clearly not "neutral," since they were transparently enacted for the ***purpose of disfavoring*** a particular religious practice.

(2) Not "generally applicable": Nor was the ordinance one of ***"general applicability."*** Kennedy seemed to say that the more ***"underinclusive"*** (see *supra*, p. 246) a governmental action is, the less likely it is to manifest the required "general applicability." Here, the ordinances were very underinclusive. For instance, the city claimed that the ordinance was necessary to protect the public health, since sacrificed animals were frequently not properly disposed of; yet the city did not regulate the disposal of animals that had been killed by hunters, or the disposal of leftover food by restaurants.

v. **Net result:** *Lukumi* makes it clear that in what we're calling "Category [1]" cases — those very rare instances where government is shown to have acted for the ***purpose*** of ***burdening or punishing*** a particular type of religiously-motivated act, with government acting out of hostility to the religion or the religious practice — the governmental act will be subjected to strict (and almost certainly fatal) scrutiny.

c. **Hostility during adjudications (*Masterpiece Cakeshop*):** Category [1] also encompasses scenarios in which government behaves with hostility to religion generally (or to a particular religious group) during the course of ***adjudicating*** whether a person is ***entitled to an accommodation*** on religious grounds. This became clear in a 2018 case that raised the issue of whether a business operator may, in violation of a general anti-discrimination statute, ***refuse to sell a good or service*** because obeying the statute would violate his religious beliefs. That case, ***Masterpiece Cakeshop, Ltd. v. Colorado Civ. Rights Comm'n***, 137 S.Ct. 2290 (2018), did not answer the underlying question about when the business person is entitled to a religion-based exemption from the anti-discrimination law; but it did establish that the person is entitled to have his request for an accommodation ***treated by government in a way that does not reflect hostility to religion.***

i. **Availability of exemptions, generally:** Shortly below (p. 698), we'll be examining in detail the extent to which a person is entitled, on free exercise grounds, to an ***exemption*** (or "accommodation") from a generally-applicable rule that happens to burden religious conduct. In brief, the modern rule, as laid down in *Employment Division v. Smith*, 494 U.S. 872 (1990), is that such exemptions will ***rarely*** be available. The *Masterpiece Cakeshop* case involved such a request for exemption, though the Supreme Court there avoided deciding on the merits whether the business operator seeking the exemption was entitled to it.

ii. **Facts of *Masterpiece*:** In *Masterpiece*, Jack Phillips operated a Colorado bakery called Masterpiece Cakeshop. A same-sex couple, Craig and Mullins, visited Phillips' shop in 2012 and said they wanted to order a cake "for our wedding."[10] Phillips told the couple that he does not "create" wedding cakes for same-sex

---

10. At the time, Colorado did not recognize same-sex marriage; therefore, the couple planned to wed legally in Massachusetts and afterwards host a reception back in Colorado. It was for the reception that the couple wanted the cake.

weddings; he said, "I'll make your birthday cakes, shower cakes, sell you cookies and brownies, I just don't make cakes for same sex weddings." The couple left the shop without further discussion. When Craig's mother (who had been with the couple on the visit to the shop) called Phillips the next day to ask why he declined to serve the couple, Phillips said that he does not create wedding cakes for same-sex weddings because of his religious opposition to same-sex marriage (and also because, at the time, such marriages were not legal in Colorado).

(1) Couple files a complaint: The couple soon filed a discrimination complaint against Phillips under the Colorado Anti-Discrimination Act (CADA). At the time, CADA prohibited anyone from denying goods or services in a "place of public accommodation" if the denial was for any reason on a list that included "sexual orientation." The complaint was heard by an Administrative Law Judge (ALJ) working for the state Civil Rights Commission (the "Commission").

(2) Defense by Phillips: In the ALJ hearing, Phillips raised two constitutional defenses. He contended that when the state applied the CADA in a way that required him to create a cake for a same-sex wedding, this compulsion violated (1) his First Amendment right to *free speech* by *compelling him to express a message* with which he disagreed and; (2) his First Amendment right to the *free exercise of religion.*

iii. **Ruling by ALJ and Commission against Phillips:** The ALJ rejected both of these constitutional claims. As to the free-speech claim, the ALJ rejected Phillips' assertion that preparing a wedding cake is a form of protected speech. As to the free-exercise claim, the ALJ concluded that CADA is a "valid and neutral law of general applicability" which, according to *Employment Div. v. Smith* (*infra*, p. 700), a person must obey even if the law requires the person to act in a way that is inconsistent with the person's religious beliefs. The ALJ then concluded that Phillips' refusal to supply the cake violated CADA. The 7-member Commission then upheld the ALJ's finding.[11]

(1) Anti-religion comments: In what later became the central factor in the Supreme Court's decision, during the Commission's deliberation on whether to uphold the ALJ's finding, two members of the Commission made *remarks evincing hostility to religion* during the course of deciding Phillips' case. One of them (let's call him "Commissioner *A*") said that a businessman can believe "what he wants to believe," but he can't *act* on those religious beliefs "if he decides to do business in the state." Commissioner *A* also said, "[I]f a businessman wants to do business in the state and he's got an issue with the — the law's impacting his personal belief system, he needs to look at being able to compromise." The other (Commissioner *B*) said, "Freedom of religion and religion has been used to justify all kinds of discrimination throughout history, whether it be slavery, whether it be the holocaust ... We can list hundreds of situations where freedom of religion has been used to justify discrimination.

---

11. An intermediate Colorado court affirmed the Commission's decision. The Colorado Supreme Court refused to hear Phillips' next appeal, and the case then went to the U.S. Supreme Court.

And to me it is one of the most despicable pieces of rhetoric that people can use to — to use their religion to hurt others."

iv. **Court finds violation of free exercise:** By a vote of 7-2, the Supreme Court held that the Commission had *violated Phillips' free exercise rights* by deciding the case in a way that was *infected by hostility to religion*. The majority opinion, by Justice Kennedy, was notably *narrow*.

(1) **Impermissible hostility to religion:** Kennedy wrote that Phillips was "entitled to the *neutral and respectful consideration of his claims* in all the circumstances of the case." But, Kennedy said, the Commission had not fulfilled that obligation of neutrality towards religion. The Commission's treatment of the case, he wrote, had "some elements of a *clear and impermissible hostility* toward the *sincere religious beliefs* that motivated [Phillips'] objection."

(2) **Two Commissioners' comments:** Kennedy characterized the comments (quoted above) from both Commissioners *A* and *B* as being hostile to Phillips' religious beliefs. Kennedy said that Commissioner *A*'s remarks, although ambiguous, were best interpreted as "inappropriate and dismissive comments showing lack of due consideration for Phillips' free exercise rights and the dilemma he faced." And as to Commissioner *B*, Kennedy was even more critical: "To describe a man's faith as 'one of the most despicable pieces of rhetoric that people can use' is to disparage his religion in at least two distinct ways: by describing it as despicable, and also by characterizing it as merely rhetorical — something insubstantial and even insincere."

(3) **Inconsistent treatment:** Kennedy also concluded that, independently of the remarks of Commissioners *A* and *B*, the Commission as a whole had shown hostility to religion by virtue of treating Phillips' case in a way that was *inconsistent* with how it handled several cases involving what was arguably the opposite issue, requests for wedding cakes bearing religiously-inspired anti-gay decorations. In three other cases, the Commission had held that it was not a violation of CADA for a baker to refuse to create cakes where the customer wanted a decoration, asserted to be motivated by his religious beliefs, that *"demeaned gay persons or gay marriages."* The lower Colorado court concluded that the two situations were distinguishable, because the anti-gay messages were *"offensive"* whereas Phillips had not been asked to convey an offensive message.

But Kennedy *rejected* this distinction, saying that "it is not ... the role of the State or its officials to *prescribe what shall be offensive."* In short, he said, the Commission's rejection of Phillips' religious objection "did not accord" with its acceptance of the conduct of the bakers who refused to make the cakes decorated with religiously-inspired anti-gay messages.

(4) **State can protect gay rights:** But Kennedy emphasized that, although Colorado had not properly found against Phillips on the facts here, the state *retained the general power to protect gay people against discrimination.* He wrote that "Colorado law can protect gay persons, just as it can protect other classes of individuals, in acquiring whatever products and services they

choose on the ***same terms and conditions as are offered to other members*** of the public."

v. Two dissenters: Two justices dissented from the Court's central conclusion that the verdict against Phillips must be overturned. Justice Ginsburg (joined by Sotomayor) believed that Craig and Mullins should win the case, in part because the "comments by ***one or two members*** of one of the ***four decision-making entities*** considering this case"[12] did not justify overturning the entire result of the litigation.

vi. Significance: *Masterpiece Cakeshop* will probably not turn out to be deeply significant. True, it establishes the general proposition that when government adjudicates a person's request for a faith-based exemption from a generally-applicable law, government must behave in a way that does not telegraph hostility to the applicant's religion or to religion generally, as the two members of the Colorado Commission did in such a clumsy way.

(1) Can still deny exemption: But assuming the government seems to behave with the requisite neutrality towards religion, nothing in *Masterpiece Cakeshop* undermines the core holding of *Employment Div. v. Smith* (*infra*, p. 700) that with few if any exceptions, the right of free exercise does not relieve a person of the obligation to comply with a ***valid and religiously-neutral law of general applicability***, even if that law proscribes or requires conduct at odds with his religion.

3. Benefit given to a class, while "essentially-religious" uses are excluded: Turning back now to our three categories, ***Category [2]*** consists of cases in which government: (a) uses its discretion to furnish a benefit to a class of individuals, and (b) excludes any use of the benefit directly in support of ***"an essentially religious endeavor."*** In this situation, the Court will apparently ***not*** apply strict scrutiny, and will typically conclude that the Free Exercise Clause ***has not been violated.***

Example: A state makes a fixed pool of college scholarship money available to a limited group of lower-income students. The scholarship may be used at any in-state college, even one operated by a religious institution. However, the scholarship may not be used to pursue a "degree in devotional theology," i.e., ***training to be a member of the clergy.*** P, who wants to use the scholarship for such training, sues the state.

Held (by the Supreme Court), this exclusion ***does not violate*** P's Free Exercise rights. The state has "merely chosen not to fund a distinct category of instruction." There are "few areas in which a State's anti-establishment interests come more into play" than the area here, where what is at stake is the use of "taxpayer funds to ***support church leaders*** ... one of the hallmarks of an 'established' religion." ***Locke v. Davey***, 540 U.S. 712 (2004).

4. Denial of generally-available benefit: Finally, ***Category [3]*** consists of cases in which government makes a benefit ***generally available to citizens***, except that government inten-

---

12. These four entities were: (1) the ALJ who tried the case; (2) the Commission who affirmed the ALJ's decision; (3) the intermediate appeals court; and (4) the Colorado Supreme Court (which declined to hear Phillips' subsequent appeal).

tionally makes the benefit *unavailable* to those who want to use it *in connection with activities run by a religious institution even though those activities are not themselves religiously-oriented.* As in Category [1] cases, the Supreme Court will *apply strict scrutin*y to the governmental action, and will almost certainly *strike down* the action as a violation of the Free Exercise Clause.

a. **State aid to private schools (*Espinoza*):** This principle was vividly illustrated by a 2020 decision in which the Supreme Court held that if a state *offers scholarships* towards tuition at *private schools*, the state *may not exclude religious schools* from the program. The case was *Espinoza v. Montana Dep't. of Revenue*, 140 S.Ct. 2246 (2020).

b. **Facts of *Espinoza*:** The Montana Legislature set up a program in which donors who funded scholarships for use at private schools were given dollar-for-dollar tax credits for their donations. The program allowed the scholarships to be used at any "qualifying" private school in the state, a term that encompassed virtually any private school, religious or not. After the program was enacted, 94% of the scholarship dollars were used at private schools operated by religious groups.

   i. **The state constitutional provision:** However, the Montana State Constitution contained a provision prohibiting any use of public funds to aid any school *controlled by any "church, sect, or denomination"* (the *"no-aid"* provision). In order to prevent the scholarship program from violating the no-aid provision, the state Department of Revenue enacted an administrative rule ("Rule 1") barring the use of the scholarships at any private school operated by a religious group.

   ii. **The suit:** After Rule 1 was enacted, the Ps — three mothers who wanted to use the scholarships at a church-run school — sued, claiming that the religious-school carveout violated their and their children's Free Exercise rights.

c. **Result in the Montana Supreme Court:** The Montana Supreme Court held that the program as originally enacted by the legislature — i.e., allowing the scholarships to be used at religious as well as non-religious private schools — violated the state constitution's no-aid provision, and thus could not stand as enacted. That court also held that the Department of Revenue had no authority to enact Rule 1. Consequently, the court ruled, *the entire program could no longer operate* — scholarships could not be awarded for use at *either* religious or non-religious private schools. The Ps appealed to the U.S. Supreme Court.

d. **Supreme Court agrees with the Ps:** The U.S. Supreme Court, by a 5-4 vote, held that the state-constitutional no-aid provision, as applied to invalidate the scholarship program, *violated the plaintiffs' Free Exercise rights.* The majority opinion was by Chief Justice Roberts, who was joined by the other four conservative justices.

   i. **Rationale:** Drawing on prior case law,[13] Roberts wrote that "disqualifying *otherwise eligible recipients from a public benefit* 'solely *because of their religious character*' imposes 'a *penalty on the free exercise of religion.*'" That was the sit-

---

13. The main precedent Roberts relied on was *Trinity Lutheran Church v. Comer,* 582 U.S. ___ (2017), a narrow ruling that when a state gave limited financial grants to help schools install rubber playground surfaces made from recycled tires, the Free Exercise Clause prohibited the state from excluding private religious schools from the grants.

uation here, since the no-aid provision barred religious schools — and parents who wished to send their children to such schools — from public benefits "solely because of the religious character of the school."

ii. **Strict scrutiny required:** Therefore, Roberts said, the no-aid provision as applied by the Montana Supreme Court *constituted "status-based discrimination,"* thereby triggering *"the strictest scrutiny."* The state court's use of the provision to exclude religious schools could survive this scrutiny only if the state could show that the provision "advance[s] *'interests of the highest order'"* and was *"narrowly tailored* in pursuit of those interests."

iii. **Fails strict scrutiny:** Roberts concluded that the no-aid provision, as applied to the scholarship program here, *flunked both prongs of strict scrutiny.*

(1) **"Compelling" interest prong:** As to the first prong — whether the state interest being pursued was "of the highest order," also known as a *"compelling" interest* — Montana argued that the no-aid provision served the state's interest in *separating church and state* even "more fiercely" than the U.S. Constitution's Establishment Clause does, and that this interest was a "compelling" one. But Roberts rejected the argument: an interest "cannot qualify as compelling," he said, if it brings about *"the infringement of free exercise"* as the no-aid provision here did.

(2) **Narrow tailoring:** As to the second prong – whether the means chosen by the state were *"narrowly tailored* in pursuit of [the compelling] interests" – Roberts found this prong, too, unsatisfied. The state contended that the no-aid provision, by separating church and state, furthered the state's ultimate interest in *"promot[ing] religious freedom"* by ensuring taxpayers that "their *taxes are not directed to religious organizations"* and by *"keeping the government out* of [religious organizations'] *operations*." But Roberts did not agree that the no-aid provision promoted this interest in religious freedom. For Roberts, a key aspect of religious freedom was the "right[] of parents to *direct 'the religious upbringing'* of their children." And parents often exercise that right by sending their children to religious schools. The no-aid provision, Roberts said, *"penalizes that decision* by *cutting families off from otherwise available benefits* if they choose a religious private school[.]"

iv. **Doesn't advance the interest in "promoting public education":** There was a second compelling objective asserted by Montana, that of *advancing public education* by ensuring that government support was *not "diverted to private schools."* Roberts seemed willing to assume that this was a compelling state interest. But, he said, here too the no-aid provision lacked the required "narrow tailoring" between means and end. The no-aid rule was *"fatally underinclusive,"* because it barred aid only to private *religious* schools, while allowing plenty of diversion of government support to private *non-religious* ones.

v. *Locke v Davey* **distinguished:** Roberts then turned to the meaning of an important earlier precedent that Montana contended justified its no-aid provision. The state argued that its provision was constitutional under *Locke v. Davey, supra,* p. 694. You'll recall that in *Locke,* the Court found that it was not a Free Exercise violation for a state to bar the use of public scholarship funds for the ***training of ministers***. But Roberts concluded that *Espinoza* was ***distinguishable*** from the *Locke* situation.

(1) "Use" versus "status": In *Locke*, the state had merely chosen to fund ***one "distinct category" of instruction,"*** the ***"essentially religious endeavor"*** of ***training a minister to lead a congregation.*** By contrast, in *Espinoza*, Montana's no-aid constitutional provision "bars ***all*** aid to a religious school 'simply because of what it *is*[.]" In other words, *Locke* was distinguishable because it merely denied state funding for a particular "*use*," whereas *Espinoza* denied such funding based on the school's "*status*," a much broader interference with free exercise.

vi. Summary of holding: Roberts summarized the effect of the Court's opinion this way: A state ***may choose not to "subsidize private education."*** But once a state chooses to grant such a subsidy, ***"it cannot disqualify some private schools solely because they are religious."***

e. The dissents: Four justices – the four liberal members – ***dissented*** in *Espinoza*. They did so in three separate opinions, by Justices Ginsburg, Breyer and Sotomayor.

i. *Locke* should control the case: Most of the dissenters believed that the decision in *Locke v. Davey* (*supra*, p. 694) should ***control***. As Breyer (joined on this point by Kagan) argued, Montana here, like Washington in *Locke*, had ***"chosen not to fund … 'an essentially religious endeavor'*** – [namely] an ***education designed to 'induce religious faith'."*** For Breyer, both cases therefore involved "a State's ***decision not to fund the inculcation of religious truths."*** Consequently, *Espinoza* should have been decided the same way as *Locke*, based on the ***long-standing principle*** that a state may constitutionally ***elect not to "forc[e] taxpayers to pay the salaries of those who teach their faith from the pulpit … [or] who teach it in the classroom."***

f. Significance of the decision: *Espinoza* completely ***nullifies any state attempt to exclude religious institutions from receiving otherwise-available public funding.*** So the 37 states that, like Montana, have on their books state-constitutional prohibitions barring religious schools or organizations from receiving otherwise-available funding may no longer single out these entities for less favorable treatment. So if a state ***makes scholarship aid available to private schools (or the schools' students) generally***, it must ***apply exactly the same rules to schools (and their students) affiliated with religious organizations.***

i. Funding an "essentially religious endeavor": However, *Espinoza* does not seem to affect the narrow category we've called Category [2] (*supra*, p. 694), exemplified by *Locke v. Davey*. That is, a state may still apparently refuse to make otherwise-available public funding available for use ***directly in support of an "essentially religious endeavor."*** So a state may still prohibit the use of a generally-available publicly-funded scholarship to pay the tuition for a person's ***training to be a minister*** (the situation in *Locke*), and may apparently still forbid the use of public funds to pay the salary of a ***teacher*** at a religious school if the person teaches ***only purely religious-doctrinal subjects*** (say, the salary of a teacher whose only subjects at a Catholic high school consist of ***Catechism*** classes).

C. Incidental burdensome effect, and required accommodations: Now, let's leave our discussion of government actions that consciously treat religion differently from non-religion, and turn a different type of Free Exercise case, that in which governmental action has the ***unintended effect*** of burdening religiously-motivated conduct. In these cases, a person's religion prohibits an act required by the government, or requires/encourages an act that is forbidden by the government. The issue in such cases is, when do free exercise principles require government to grant an ***exemption or accommodation*** from the act that is ordinarily required or forbidden by the government?

1.   **1990 shift:** Beginning with a 1990 case, *Employment Div. v. Smith* (*infra*, p. 700), the Court's analysis of these exemption cases underwent a profound shift, making it much harder for the free exercise claim to prevail. But then, as we'll see (*infra*, p. 713), the pendulum swung back in 2020-21, restoring to free exercise claimants an easier path to success.

2.   **Pre-1990 law:**   Prior to 1990, the Court seemed to take a relatively pro-free-exercise approach to this problem of unintended burdens on religion. In general, when a government law had the unintended effect of burdening religious exercise, the Court held (or at least claimed to be holding) that the law could be upheld only if it was the ***least restrictive means*** of accomplishing a ***compelling*** state objective. In other words, the Court purported to give ***"strict scrutiny"*** to the government's insistence on applying its statute even to those whose religious exercise would be burdened by enforcement of the statute. Under the strict scrutiny standard, if the state's objective could be served as well, or almost as well, by granting an ***exemption*** to those whose religious beliefs were burdened by the regulation, ***such an exemption had to be given.***

   a.   **Accommodation for Sabbath:**   The most important case demonstrating this pre-1990 "give an exemption where feasible" approach was ***Sherbert v. Verner***, 374 U.S. 398 (1963). Sherbert, a Seventh Day Adventist, was fired for being unwilling to work on Saturdays, her religion's day of rest. All other available jobs required willingness to work on Saturdays. The state refused to give her unemployment compensation benefits, on the grounds that she had declined to accept "suitable work when offered."

      i.   **Holding:** The Supreme Court held that the state's refusal to give Mrs. Sherbert an exemption from the "must be willing to work on Saturdays" rule violated her right to the free exercise of her religion.

         (1) Rationale: The Court reasoned that South Carolina's policy unduly burdened Sherbert's free exercise of her religion, since it forced her to choose between receiving benefits and following her religion. This choice placed "the same kind of burden upon the free exercise of religion as would a fine imposed against [her] for her Saturday worship." Furthermore, there was a ***discriminatory*** component to the state's action, since Sunday worshippers were not put to this choice.

         (2) Strict scrutiny: But the fact that Sherbert's free exercise rights were burdened was not by itself enough to gain her a victory. Rather, the issue became whether there was a ***compelling state interest*** justifying the governmental policy, which could ***not be satisfied by means placing less of a burden*** upon the exercise of religion. In other words, the refusal to give an exemption was to be ***"strictly scrutinized."*** Here, no showing was made by the state that an ***exemp-***

tion for Sabbatarians would prevent the state from achieving its objective (assuring that payments go only to those who were involuntarily unemployed).

ii. **Modern Court's view:** Despite the Court's major change of approach in 1990, the ruling and rationale of *Sherbert* — at least when applied to the same *narrow context of unemployment benefits* — probably remains good law.

b. **Compulsory schooling:** Another major pre-1990 illustration of the principle that exemptions must be given where feasible came in a case involving a state *compulsory-schooling* requirement. In *Wisconsin v. Yoder*, 406 U.S. 205 (1972), the Court invalidated Wisconsin's refusal to exempt 14- and 15-year-old Amish students from the requirement of attending school until the age of 16.

i. **Applying strict scrutiny:** Applying strict scrutiny, the Court said that the state must grant an exemption unless it could show (1) an interest "of the highest order," and (2) that the interest could not be served by means other than denial of an exemption.

ii. **Compelling interest:** The Court found that the state's interest in having its citizens be reasonably well-educated, so that those citizens could participate intelligently in political affairs and become economically self-sufficient, was a compelling one.

iii. **Means-end fit:** But the plaintiffs demonstrated that it was an essential element of their Amish religion that members be informally taught to earn their living through farming and other rural activities, and that compulsory high school education was at odds with that belief. The plaintiffs also proved that nearly all Amish children continue to live in the Amish community throughout their lives. That was enough to convince the Court that the state's interest in education could be adequately served by the less-restrictive means of allowing home-schooling of this particular group of children.

c. **Strict scrutiny not applied:** But in some other pre-1990 cases, the Court did *not apply strict scrutiny* to the government's refusal to give an exemption.

i. **Deference to military judgments:** Sometimes this happened because the Court decided that the case involved a *special context* in which *greater deference* to government was required. For instance, in a case (set forth in the following Example) in which the regulation was imposed by the *military* on its employees, the Court gave *great deference to the military's judgment* about whether granting an exemption would be damaging to the military's interests.

> **Example:** An Orthodox Jewish Air Force captain asserts a Free Exercise right to wear a yarmulke while on duty, in contravention of an Air Force regulation requiring uniform dress. (A yarmulke is a head-covering that Orthodox Jewish men are required by their religion to wear at all times.)
>
> *Held*, for the Air Force: Although a person in military service is not completely without First Amendment rights, "when evaluating whether military needs justify a particular restriction on religiously motivated conduct, courts must give *great deference* to the professional judgment of military authorities concerning the relative importance of a particular military interest." In sum, "the First Amendment does not require the military to accommodate [religious

dress] practices in the face of its view that they would detract from the uniformity sought by the dress regulation." *Goldman v. Weinberger*, 475 U.S. 503 (1986).

ii. **Coercion required:**   Also, the pre-1990 Court limited the scope for strict scrutiny by holding that the Free Exercise Clause only gets triggered where government in some sense *"coerces"* an individual to do something (or not to do something) against the dictates of his religion. Where the government merely takes an action that *unintentionally happens to make it harder for a person to practice her religion* — but without coercing her into taking or not taking some action as an individual — the Court said that the Free Exercise Clause *did not apply.*

Example: The federal government, without intending to affect any religious practice, wants to build a road. The effect will be to destroy Native American ritual grounds.

Held, there has been no impairment of the Native American plaintiffs' free exercise rights, because the plaintiffs are not being coerced into doing or not doing anything — external reality is simply being changed in a way that makes it harder for them to practice their religion. *Lyng v. Northwest Indian Cemetery Protective Ass'n*, 485 U.S. 439 (1988).

D. **The 1990 "generally-applicable rule" case (*Employment Div. v. Smith*):**   As we've seen, before 1990 individuals sometimes successfully argued that they were entitled to an exemption from a government rule on free exercise grounds, but often failed. Then, in 1990, the Court made it even *harder* for individuals to use free exercise grounds to win exemptions from *generally-applicable* government rules that *unintentionally burden* religious conduct. The Court did this in *Employment Division v. Smith*, 494 U.S. 872 (1990).

1. **The *Smith* case itself:**   In *Smith*, the Court, by a 5-4 vote, held that a generally-applicable religiously-neutral law is automatically *enforceable*, regardless of the degree of burden it causes on an individual's religious beliefs. The majority wrote that "the right of free exercise does not relieve an individual of the obligation to comply with a *valid and neutral law* of *general applicability* on the ground that the law proscribes (or prescribes) conduct that his religion prescribes (or proscribes)."

   a. **Facts:**   In *Smith*, the issue was whether Oregon could *criminalize the possession of the drug peyote*, and refuse to give an exemption to American Indians whose use of the drug is a central part of their religious rites.

   b. **Holding:**   Justice Scalia's opinion for the Court said not only that Oregon could refuse an exemption, but also that *no balancing* of the state's interest in its prohibition against the burden on the individual's religious beliefs need even be carried out — so long as the ban on peyote was *generally applicable*, and not motivated by a governmental desire to *affect religion*, the law was *fully enforceable despite the burden on the plaintiffs.* [14]

   c. **Dissents and concurrences:**   The other four members of the Court in *Smith* disagreed with Scalia's "generally applicable" test. In a concurrence by Justice O'Connor, and a dissent by Justice Blackmun (joined by Brennan and Marshall), these four argued that *strict scrutiny* should be applied wherever a generally-applicable law burdened the free exercise of religion. As Justice Blackmun put it, "A state statute that burdens the free exercise of religion … may stand only if the law in general, and the state's refusal to allow a religious exemption in particular, are justified by a compelling interest that cannot be served by less restrictive means."

2. **Significance of *Smith*:** *Smith* means that *any **generally-applicable** regulation, **whether criminal or civil**,* and whether it requires conduct or forbids conduct, will be *fully enforceable and upheld despite an unintentional burden on individuals' religious practices.* So the pre-*Smith* traditional strict scrutiny supposedly given to government's refusal to grant an exemption has been ***abolished***.

3. **Not applicable to intentional discrimination against religion:** Keep in mind that *Smith*, though it makes it dramatically tougher for the plaintiff to win a free exercise challenge to government action, ***only*** applies where the government action has the ***unintentional effect*** of burdening religion. In those rare instances where government acts for the ***purpose*** of disfavoring a particular religious practice, the most rigorous strict scrutiny will still be applied, and the government action will almost always be struck down. See, e.g., *Church of the Lukumi Babalu Aye*, *supra*, p. 690, where the Court found that an ordinance forbidding animal sacrifice was exactly such a government action intended to disfavor religion, and thus struck it down.

E. **Post-*Smith* law generally:** *Employment Division v. Smith **remains the law*** as of this writing (late 2021). But there are strong signs that a majority of the present Court would like to ***overrule*** *Smith* when an appropriate case arises. We discuss these signs *infra*, p. 713. For now, however, let's discuss details of how *Smith* has been ***interpreted*** in the decades since it was decided. Our discussion is divided into four parts:

   [1] When should a law be deemed to be *"generally applicable"*? (See Par. F below.)

   [2] What ***level of scrutiny*** does *Smith* require if the law is found ***not*** to be generally applicable? (See Par. G below.)

   [3] Does *Smith* apply when ***anti-discrimination laws conflict*** with a religious group's right to *"pick its ministers"*? (See Par. H below.)

   [4] Might *Smith* be overruled? (See Par. I below.)

F. **The meaning of "generally applicable":** Recall (see *supra*, p. 700) that in order for a government regulation that allegedly burdens the free exercise of religion to nonetheless be enforceable under *Smith*, the regulation must be a *"law of general applicability."* What kind of laws will be found to ***flunk*** this generally-applicable requirement? There seem to be ***two main categories*** that will cause a law to be found not to be generally-applicable:

   [1] **Individualized exemptions:** First, where government has allowed *"individualized exemptions"* to the law's requirements, i.e., exemptions based on the circumstances of the particular person seeking the exemption; and

---

14. But Scalia's opinion noted, in passing, an exception to the rule it was announcing, an exception that would later prove important. He wrote that the Court's pre-*Smith* decisions "in the unemployment cases" — that is, cases deciding that state could not deny unemployment benefits to an applicant whose unemployment was due to his unwillingness to work on what his religion classified as a sabbath — stood for the proposition that "where the State has in place a system of *individual exemptions*, it may not refuse to extend that system to cases of 'religious hardship' without compelling reason."

[2] **Comparable secular activity:** Second, where government has ***exempted an entire category of secular activities*** from the law's application, if that category is found to be *"comparable"* to the religious activity that has not been granted an exemption.

Let's consider each of these categories. Category [1] is discussed in Par. 1 immediately below; category [2] is discussed in Par. 2 starting on p. 707 *infra*.

1. **Individualized exemptions (*Fulton v. Philadelphia*):** *Smith* says that a law that has the unintended effect of burdening religious expression will be deemed *not* to be "generally applicable" — and thus not eligible for the pro-government status conferred by *Smith* — if the law ***contains a mechanism for recognizing "individualized exemptions"*** to the law. (See the footnote on p. 701 *supra*.) This aspect of *Smith* has become increasingly important as the result of a 2021 decision, ***Fulton v. City of Philadelphia***, 141 S.Ct. 1868 (June 17, 2021). In *Fulton*, the fact that the law in question authorized government to make individualized exemptions from the law's requirements ***caused*** *Smith* ***not to apply;*** consequently, the Court ***strictly scrutinized*** the law as a burden on religious expression, and unanimously struck it down.

   a. **Facts of *Fulton*:** The City of Philadelphia used a roster of private social-services agencies to help the City place children into ***foster homes.*** Each participating agency maintained a list of potential foster homes, which it sent to the City's Department of Human Services. When the Department determined that a child could not remain with her family, the Department would then pick from these lists whatever family it regarded as the most suitable, and would contract for support services from the agency that had listed that family.

      i. **CSS's role:** One of the agencies on Philadelphia's roster was Catholic Social Services, affiliated with the Catholic Church's Archdiocese of Philadelphia, which had long contracted with the Department for CSS to perform foster-care services.

      ii. **The City's requirement:** Standard contracts between the Department and each of the private agencies on its roster, including CSS, required the agency to agree that it would ***not reject a family*** as a prospective foster family based on, among other reasons, the family's *"**sexual orientation.**"* At some point CSS told the Department that the CSS had a policy of ***not certifying same-sex married couples*** as suitable placements for foster children. The Department then said that it would no longer enter into foster-care contracts with CSS unless CSS promised to abandon this refusal to certify same-sex couples.

      iii. **The suit:** CSS sued the Department, claiming that the Department's insistence that CSS be willing to certify same-sex couples in order to receive foster-care contracts violated CSS' free exercise of religion. The Department defended by saying that its no-discrimination rule was a "generally-applicable" rule under *Smith*.

      iv. **The "individualized exemptions" provision:** But CSS had a good response to this defense. It turned out that the standard foster-care contract between the Department and each private agency contained a provision, "Section 3.21," that gave the Commissioner of the Department the power to grant, in the Commissioner's *"**sole discretion,**"* an *"**individual exemption**"* to the standard agreement's non-discrimination rules as to any given placement. CSS argued that the mere availability of this system of discretionary individualized exemptions was enough to prevent the non-discrimination rule from being a "generally-applicable" law of the sort that *Smith* protected against free exercise claims.

b. **CSS scores unanimous win:** The Supreme Court *agreed* with this argument by CSS. In fact, *all nine justices* agreed that the mere existence of the Commissioner's discretionary power to issue individualized exemptions from the anti-same-sex-couples-discrimination policy prevented *Smith* from applying, making the policy a violation of CSS' Free Exercise rights. The opinion was by Chief Justice Roberts.

Roberts' analysis had a number of steps, not all of which were spelled out. Here's how he reached his conclusion that the Department's non-discrimination rule violated CSS' free-exercise rights:

[1] **The "Rule" was a "law":** When the Department decided to enact a rule making it a condition of a given private agency's eligibility to provide the Department with placement services that the agency promise to avoid various types of discrimination (we'll call this the "Rule"), the Rule *constituted a "law"* that, depending on its details, might or might not unacceptably burden the agency's free exercise of religion.

[2] **Law must be "generally applicable":** No matter how great was the Rule's unintended burden on an agency's free exercise of religion, *Employment Div. v. Smith* would completely *insulate* the Department from an agency's claim that the Rule violated the agency's free exercise of religion *only* if the Rule was a "neutral" and — most importantly, for present purposes — a *"generally applicable" law.*

[3] **No "individualized exemptions":** However, in order for a law to be found to be generally applicable (thus qualifying it for the highly pro-government treatment given by *Smith*), the *law must not contain any "mechanism for individualized exemptions."*

[4] **Section 3.21:** Section 3.21 of the Rule — by providing that as to any individual placement by an agency, the Commissioner had the *untrammeled discretion to waive* any otherwise-applicable non-discrimination requirement — was exactly the sort of *"mechanism for individualized exemptions"* whose existence *automatically prevented the Rule from being generally-applicable.*

[5] ***Smith* doesn't apply:** The fact that the Rule was not generally-applicable meant, in turn, that *Smith v. Employment Div.* had *no application* in the case.

[6] **Strict scrutiny:** In the case of a law to which *Smith* doesn't apply, if the law imposes (even *unintentionally*) a *significant burden on religious exercise*, the law must be *subjected to strict scrutiny.* In this context, strict scrutiny means that unless the government can carry the burden of showing that *granting an exemption* from the law to the person whose exercise of religion would be significantly burdened without an exemption would *significantly impair the government's achievement of a compelling objective*, the government *must grant the exemption.*

[7] **Application of strict scrutiny:** It then came time for the Court to *apply strict scrutiny* to the particular facts of *Fulton*. Here's how the Court did so:

❏   Before the litigation began, CSS asked the Department for what amounted to a ***partial exemption*** from the requirement that CSS promise not to discriminate against same-sex couples: if CSS happened to encounter a prospective foster family consisting of a same-sex married couple, CSS proposed that it would behave as it had always previously done, by simply ***referring that same-sex couple to another private agency*** (one that had a similar contractual relationship with the Department, but that was willing to work with such couples). The Department refused to grant that exemption, claiming that such an exemption would impair the Department's ability to achieve its compelling objectives (mainly the goal of attaining ***equality for same-sex couples in the foster-placement process***).[15]

❏   So the question for Roberts became: If the Department had ***granted*** CSS' request that it be allowed to avoid the problem by referring same-sex couples to another agency, would that approach really have ***"significantly impaired"*** the Department's ability to achieve its admittedly-compelling objective of ensuring equality for same-sex couples in the foster-placement process? As we'll see in more detail below, the Court's answer was ***"no"*** — the Department had failed to carry its burden of showing that granting CSS' request would have significantly impaired the Department's ability to achieve that objective.

c.   **Several aspects of the majority opinion:** Let's take a closer look at several noteworthy aspects of Chief Roberts' opinion in *Fulton*:

i.   **Failure to actually grant exemptions is irrelevant:**   The City claimed that the availability of individualized exemptions was irrelevant, because the ***Commissioner had never granted one.*** But Roberts disagreed: "The creation of a ***formal mechanism for granting exceptions*** renders a policy not generally applicable, ***regardless whether any exceptions have been given[.]***"

ii.   **Strict (and fatal) scrutiny:**   Once the Roberts opinion determined that the Rule was ***not generally-applicable,*** the opinion followed existing law by ***applying strict scrutiny*** to the City's refusal to give CSS an exemption from the no-sexual-orientation-discrimination requirement.

(1)   **The test:**   Roberts recited a standard version of what strict scrutiny requires: "a government policy can survive strict scrutiny ***only if it advances "interests of the highest order"*** and is ***narrowly tailored to achieve those interests."*** He then added: "Put another way, so long as the government ***can*** achieve its interests in a manner that does not burden religion, it ***must*** do so."

(2)   **The City's interests:**   What were the interests the government was pursuing? The City asserted that its non-discrimination policy served three interests, each of which the City claimed was compelling:

[1] maximizing the ***number of foster parents***;

[2] ***protecting the City from liability***; and

---

15. For more about the Department's objectives, see Sub-par. (2) on p. 704 *infra*.

[3] *ensuring equal treatment* of prospective foster parents and foster children.

(3) **Appropriate level of generality:** But Roberts pointed out that the City was stating these interests at a *"high level of generality."* Too high, he said: "[t]he First Amendment demands a *more precise analysis,"* one that *doesn't rely on "broadly formulated interests."*

(4) **Interest in denying an exemption:** So then, what were the City's interests, assuming that those interests had to be stated precisely enough to avoid being too "broadly formulated"? Here was Roberts' answer: as to each of the City's broadly-stated objectives, the City would have to show that that objective gave the City a *compelling interest in denying an exemption* to the non-discrimination policy. That is, for each of the three goals, the *burden was on the City* to show that there was not any *more-narrowly-drawn exemption* available — one defined *just broadly enough to avoid substantially burdening the religious practice in question* — that would still let the City achieve its broadly-defined goal of avoiding the evils that would flow from discrimination.

(5) **Exemptions were available:** For Roberts, *none of the City's three broadly-defined goals* — maximizing the number of foster parents, protecting against liability, and ensuring non-discrimination against gay parents or children — *satisfied* this hard-to-meet standard.

Example: For instance, Roberts said, the City's broadly-defined goal of *treating all prospective foster parents and foster children equally* was certainly a compelling one. But the narrow-tailoring issue was whether the City had a compelling interest in *denying CSS an exception* (an exemption under which the agency would be excused from having to supervise the placement of a child in a foster home headed by a same-sex married couple). The mere fact that the Rule adopted by the City allowed the Commissioner to make exceptions in her sole discretion *"undermines the City's contention* that its non-discrimination policies *can brook no departures."* The City had offered "no compelling reason why it has a particular interest in *denying an exception to CSS while making [exceptions] available to others."*

Note: This aspect of the majority opinion — strictly scrutinizing any government refusal to grant a rule-exemption to protect religious practices, if the government grants an exemption for secular activities — seems to demonstrate the Roberts Court's tendency to *grant greater protections to claimants under the Free Exercise and Establishment Clauses* than the Court gives to litigants asserting other constitutional claims, such as claims that government's use of suspect categories violates the Equal Protection Clause. As one law professor has put it, *"Fulton* showed us that the court is disposed to a kind of *tiering of constitutional rights* where some rights are *higher-ranked over others. ... Religious liberty sits at the top tier.* And *equality*, whether it's race-based, sex-based or LGBT equality, enjoys now a kind of *second-class status."* Katherine Franke, quoted in The Wall Street Journal, *"Supreme Court Signals Expansion of Religious Exemptions From Laws,"* June 20, 2021.

iii. Alito's concurrence in the judgment: Justice *Alito* filed an opinion that *concurred* in the judgment in *Fulton*, but not in the majority's reasoning. His concurrence was a lengthy one (five times the length of Roberts' opinion for the Court), and was joined by two of the other most-conservative members of the Court, Thomas and Gorsuch. Most of the concurrence was devoted to explaining why the Court should *overrule Employment Division v. Smith*, and should instead revert to the pre-*Smith* regime of strictly scrutinizing any law — whether generally-applicable or not — that substantially burdens the exercise of religion.

(1) *Fulton* **holding easily evaded:** Alito was harshly critical of the majority's reliance in *Fulton* on the "generally-applicable" requirement of *Smith*. He thought the majority's opinion was ridiculously narrow and easy to evade — the decision *"might as well be written on the dissolving paper sold in magic shops."* He continued, "if the City wants to get around today's decision, it can simply *eliminate the never-used exemption power.* If it does that, then, voilà, today's decision will vanish — and the parties will be back where they started."

(2) Free Exercise as more than a non-discrimination rule: Beyond the easily-evaded holding in *Fulton* that allowing individualized exceptions violates the "generally-applicable" requirement of *Smith*, Alito objected to the core rationale of *Smith* itself. *Smith*, he said, interprets the Free Exercise Clause as "essentially an *anti-discrimination provision:* it means that the Federal Government and the States cannot restrict conduct that constitutes a religious practice for some people unless it *imposes the same restriction on everyone else who engages in the same conduct."*

But, Alito said, the Free Exercise Clause had, before *Smith*, always been interpreted to *do much more* than just forbid discrimination. The Clause "gives a specific group of people (those who wish to *engage in the 'exercise of religion')* the *right to do so without hindrance."* He continued, "the language of the Clause *does not tie this right to the treatment of persons not in this group,"*

(3) Strict scrutiny should be used: Alito therefore concluded that *Smith* was *"wrongly decided[.]"* He called on the Court to overrule the case, and to replace it with pre-*Smith* doctrine, under which, as he summarized it, "A law that imposes a substantial burden on religious exercise can be *sustained only if it is narrowly tailored to serve a compelling government interest."*

iv. Barrett's concurrence: Justice *Barrett* wrote a brief separate concurrence, in which Justices Kavanaugh and Breyer joined.[16] Unlike Alito, Barrett agreed with Roberts that the case could and should be resolved by concluding that the theoretical availability of individualized exemptions was enough to prevent the anti-discrimination law from being "generally applicable," thereby preventing the City's no-discrimination rule from qualifying for protection under *Smith*. But Barrett's

---

16. Kavanaugh joined the entire concurrence, and Breyer joined all but the first paragraph; it's not exactly clear which statement(s) in that paragraph Breyer was unwilling to join.

concurrence briefly discussed whether *Smith* should remain good law. We discuss this part of her concurrence *infra*, p. 714.

d. **City can eliminate the exception-granting structure:** Notice that for a government body that is trying to show that its law is generally-applicable, there is an *easy remedy* to the problem that caused Philadelphia to lose the *Fulton* case: the government can simply *remove the mechanism that allows for individualized exemptions.* So in the Fulton situation, all Philadelphia would have to do going forward would be to repeal Section 3.21 of the Rule, the provision giving the Commissioner the discretion to waive any otherwise-applicable non-discrimination requirement.

2. **Categorical exemptions for secular activities (*Tandon v. Newsom*):** As we've just seen in the *Fulton* case (see Par. 1, beginning on p. 702 *supra*), one way that the availability of exemptions will prevent a law from qualifying for protection under *Smith* is if the availability of an exemption in a particular situation is left to the *discretion* of government officials. But even where the law *does not give officials discretion* to carve out an exemption to cover an individual situation, a different principle announced by the Court in a 2021 opinion, applicable to *"categorical"* exemptions, may similarly prevent the law from qualifying for *Smith*'s pro-government treatment. The 2021 opinion was *Tandon v. Newsom*, 141 S.Ct. 1294 (April 9, 2021).

a. ***Tandon*'s holding in brief:** *Tandon* says that even the existence of a *single "categorical" exemption* — an exemption that is not discretionary, and that *automatically covers all situations* within a particular category — will prevent the law from meeting the generally-applicable requirement of *Smith* if the exemption is for a *secular activity* that the Court finds to be *"comparable"* to the non-exempt religious activity in question.

i. **"Most favored nation" principle:** Many commentators (and I) call this new approach taken by the Court in *Tandon* the ***"most favored nation"*** (or *"MFN"*) approach. The MFN approach has two main effects:

[1] First, the MFN approach dramatically *narrows the reach* of *Smith*, by saying that the mere existence of a categorical exemption to a law to cover a "comparable" secular activity automatically makes the law not "generally applicable"; and

[2] Second (and as a direct consequence of [1]), the MFN approach dramatically *expands the circumstances* in which governments will be *required to grant to religious activities an exemption* from laws that *unintentionally burden* those activities.

b. **A 5-4 *per curiam* decision:** *Tandon* was the most significant in a string of decisions by the Court evaluating state governments' efforts to *reduce the spread of COVID-19* by *temporarily banning certain types of activities.* The decision took the form of a brief *"per curiam"* order.[17] The case was decided by a 5-4 vote, with five of the

---

17. A *per curiam* decision is one in which the opinion for the court is *not signed* by any identified Justice. The majority's choice to issue a *per curiam* opinion was likely due in part to the fact that the suit was a time-pressured request for a temporary injunction, not a full trial "on the merits"; for that same reason, the Court did not receive full briefs from the parties, and did not hear a full set of oral arguments.

Court's six conservative justices (Thomas, Alito, Gorsuch, Kavanaugh and Barrett) voting to issue the unsigned order. The three liberals (Breyer, Sotomayor and Kagan) dissented; Chief Justice Roberts joined them in disagreeing with the order, but did not sign the dissent.

c. **The California regulation:** Like many state executive and legislative branches, California attempted to reduce the spread of COVID-19 by restricting various activities that were thought to amplify the contagion. The particular restriction at issue in *Tandon* ***banned all in-home gatherings of more than three households,*** whether the gathering was for ***religious or for secular purposes,*** and whether it took place ***indoors or outdoors*** (e.g., in a backyard), so long as it was in a home. But the state did ***not*** impose a "no more than three households" restriction on certain activities occurring inside ***commercial premises.*** For instance, ***hair salons*** and ***retail stores*** were among the types of commercial premises that were permitted to host more than three households at a time.[18]

d. **The Ps' claim:** The main plaintiffs in *Tandon* were a pastor (Jeremy Wong) and a lay person (Karen Busch). Each argued that the California restriction prevented them from hosting Bible studies and communal worship services in their homes, if they wanted to host more than two other families. The Ps argued that because California permitted various indoor commercial "personal care" businesses (e.g., hair salons) to operate without a maximum-number-of-households limitation, the restriction was ***not a "generally applicable" one*** as required for protection under *Smith*. Therefore, they said, the regulation had to be strictly scrutinized, and must be struck down.

   i. **The Ps lose in district court:** The Ps lost in the district court (which held that the restriction was a generally-applicable one), and sought an injunction against the restriction while they appealed. After the district court denied the injunction, the Ps appealed that denial, too, to the Ninth Circuit.[19]

   ii. **The Ninth Circuit:** A three-judge panel of the Ninth Circuit, by a 2-1 vote, ***denied*** the emergency injunction, agreeing with the District Court that the restriction was a generally-applicable one, and concluding that no injunction was appropriate because the plaintiffs were not likely to prevail on the merits.

e. **The Supreme Court's ruling:** The plaintiffs then appealed the Ninth Circuit's denial of an injunction pending appeal to the Supreme Court. Because of the emergency nature of the case — the Ps wanted to conduct in-home services immediately — the Court decided the case without oral arguments.

   By a 5-4 vote, the Court ***reversed*** the Ninth Circuit. In a *per curiam* ruling, the five justices in the majority held that because the California restriction ***allowed some comparable secular activities to be held in homes without reference to the number of households present***, the restriction's number-of-household limits on religious activities caused the restriction to ***fail to be "generally applicable."*** Therefore, the restriction did not qualify for the protection of *Smith*, and had to be strictly scrutinized, a review that the majority found the restriction could not survive.

---

18. For the full list of such commercial premises cited by the Court, see Sub-par. ii[1] on p. 709 *infra*.

19. This statement of the facts, and any discussion below of the rulings by the lower courts, comes from the Ninth Circuit opinion, *Tandon v. Newsom*, 992 F.3d 916 (9th Cir. 2021).

i.   **Three principles:**   The short opinion for the Court consisted mostly of three legal principles that, the opinion said, had been made clear by the Court's prior cases:

[1] **"Comparable secular activities":** First, "government regulations are *not neutral and generally applicable,* and therefore *trigger strict scrutiny* under the Free Exercise Clause, whenever they treat *any comparable secular activity* more *favorably than religious exercise.*"[20]

[2] **Meaning of "comparable" activity:** Second, "whether two activities *are comparable* for purposes of the Free Exercise Clause must be judged against the *asserted government interest that justifies* the regulation at issue. . . . Comparability is concerned with the *risks various activities pose, not the reasons why people gather.*"

[3] **Strict scrutiny:** Third, "the *government has the burden* to establish that the challenged law *satisfies strict scrutiny.*" Strict scrutiny includes *narrow tailoring* between means and end. Here, narrow tailoring "requires the government to show that *measures less restrictive of the First Amendment activity could not address* its interest in reducing the spread of ." The Court continued, "Where the government *permits other activities to proceed with precautions*, it must show that the *religious exercise at issue is more dangerous* than those activities *even when the same precautions are applied.* Otherwise, *precautions that suffice for other activities suffice for religious exercise too.*"

ii. **Application of law to facts:**   Given these three principles, the *per curiam* opinion found it easy to conclude that (1) the three-household-maximum restriction was *not "generally applicable"* because the state had not subjected some *"comparable"* secular activities to the same restrictions; (2) the restriction therefore had to be subjected to *strict scrutiny*; and (3) the restriction *could not survive* that scrutiny, because the state failed to carry its burden of showing that *narrower precautions* (like those applied to the comparable secular activities), if used in the Ps' religious activities, would not have been *adequate to reduce* the COVID-spreading risk.

Here's how the majority applied the three principles listed immediately above to the facts of *Tandon*:

[1] **What activities were "comparables":** The majority enumerated *various secular activities* that it said were *"comparable"* to the "at-home religious exercise" in question: *"hair salons*, *retail stores*, personal care services, *movie theaters*, private suites at sporting events and concerts, and *indoor restaurant*s[.]"

[2] **Rationale for determining "comparables":** The majority then explained how a court should determine whether these secular activities were in fact "comparable" to the at-home worship at issue. The Ninth Circuit had said that these secular activities were *not "comparable"* to in-house worship because the secular ones took place in *"public buildings"* and the worship activities

---

20. The italicization of the word "any" is by the Court.

took place in *"private buildings*." But the majority said that this distinction between public and private buildings was *irrelevant* in determining comparability, because *"[c]omparability is concerned with the risks various activities pose, not the reasons why people gather."* (see principle [2] on p. 709.) Since the state had not carried its burden of proving that the risk of COVID transmission would be greater during in-home worship than during the secular activities taking place in public buildings (assuming similar safeguards), that failure of proof was enough to *make the secular activities "comparable"* to the worship activities.

[3] **Strict scrutiny:** Since California was treating the in-home worship activities less favorably than the "comparable" secular activities, the state's restrictions were *not a neutral and generally-applicable law.* Consequently the restrictions needed to be *strictly scrutinized.* (See principle [1] on p. 709.)

[4] **"Same precautions" analysis:** Finally, the majority ruled that the restrictions *failed to satisfy the "narrow tailoring"* that strict scrutiny requires. This conclusion derived from applying principle [3] (*supra*, p. 709), under which the narrow tailoring required by strict scrutiny means that "[w]here the government *permits other [secular] activities* to *proceed with precautions*, [the government] must show that the religious exercise at issue *is more dangerous than those activities even when the same precautions are applied.* Otherwise, *precautions that suffice for other activities suffice for religious exercise too.*"

California had permitted the secular activities to go forward when done with particular precautions (e.g., social distancing). And the state had failed to show that in-house worship would pose a greater danger of COVID transmission than the secular activities would, assuming those same precautions were taken during the two activities. Therefore, the state's refusal to let the in-house worship go forward with the precautions in place constituted a failure to narrowly tailor the restrictions to the state's admittedly-compelling interest in preventing the spread of COVID.

iii. **Injunction granted:** Keep in mind that when the Court issued its *per curiam* opinion under the time pressures of a motion for injunction pending appeal, the Court was *not deciding the underlying merits* of the plaintiffs' claim that their free exercise rights had been violated by the California restriction. The only issue the Court resolved in *Tandon* was, were the plaintiffs *"likely to succeed on the merits* of their free exercise claim" (answer: yes). But because the California restriction ended soon after the Court granted the injunction, this particular set of facts will never receive a *full treatment on the merits* by the Court.

f. **The dissent:** As noted, the *per curiam* opinion in *Tandon* received only five votes. Justice Kagan wrote a *dissent*, which was joined by Justices Breyer and Sotomayor. Chief Justice Roberts did not sign either the *per curiam* or the dissent, but said he would deny the injunction, thus aligning himself with the dissenters in terms of the outcome. (Roberts did not state his reasons.)

Kagan's dissent disagreed with the majority both (1) as to the appropriate *test* for determining whether the restriction was *generally-applicable*, and (2) as to the proper *outcome* even if the majority's test were used.

i.   **Dissent's view of the proper test:** Kagan agreed with the majority that (as she put it), "The First Amendment requires that a State *treat religious conduct as well as the State treats comparable secular conduct."* [21] But she sharply disagreed with the majority's approach to identifying the *correct "comparable" secular activities*, whose treatment by the government must not be more favorable than the government's treatment of the religious activity in question. The majority had classified as "comparable" various types of activities that *took place in business premises* (e.g., "retail stores"). But Kagan believed that the relevant secular activities should be ones that *take place in the home, not in business premises.*

ii. **Application to the facts of the case:** Once the comparable secular activities were defined to consist solely of "in-home" activities, it was easy for Kagan to conclude that California had *met* the most-favored-nation standard. Since California was saying that religious gatherings in homes could not include more than three households, the test was *whether there were any secular activities in homes as to which California allowed more than three households.* And her answer was that there were not: California "has adopted a blanket restriction on *at-home gatherings of all kinds, religious and secular alike."*

(1) **Explanation:** Kagan continued, "California *need not,* as the [majority] insists, *treat at-home religious gatherings the same as hardware stores and hair salons —* and thus *unlike at-home secular gatherings, the obvious comparator here.*" In sum, she said, "the law does *not* require that the State *equally treat apples and watermelons."*

iii. **Result if majority's test accepted:** Furthermore, Kagan said, even if the majority's selection of comparable activities (those taking place in business premises) *was* used, the record showed numerous respects in which these comparables *posed lesser risks of COVID transmission* when the precautions were used than would the in-home religious gatherings accompanied by similar precautions.

(1) **Distinctions:** For instance, when people gather in social settings, "their interactions are likely to be *longer* than they would be in a commercial setting," and the participants are "more likely to be *involved in prolonged conversations*[.]" Similarly, *"private houses are typically smaller and less ventilated"* than commercial establishments. Finally, *"social distancing and mask-wearing* are *less likely* in private settings," and *"enforcement* [of anti-transmission policies] is *more difficult"* than when the activity is in a commercial setting.

---

21. Although she did not expressly say so, Kagan appeared to agree with the Court's adoption of the "most favored nation" standard for determining whether a law is "generally applicable" so as to qualify for protection under *Smith*. For more about the most-favored-nation standard, see *infra*, p. 712.

G. Strict scrutiny under *Smith*, and the "most favored nation" rule: As we saw, a majority of the Court in *Tandon, supra,* adopted what's sometimes called the ***"most-favored-nation" ("MFN") rule*** for analyzing laws that place an unintended burden on religious exercise. The MFN rule has only been an official doctrine since the April 2021 *per curiam* opinion in *Tandon*, so we don't yet know very much about how it will be applied. But here's an early attempt to describe how the MFN approach apparently works:

[1] If government *fails to grant an exemption* from a law for a *category of religious activities* (e.g., "at-home religious services with more than 3 households"), while...

[2] *granting an exemption* from the law for even a *single type* of what a court finds to be a *"comparable" secular activity*, then ...

[3] the law automatically *fails* to be *"generally-applicable"* (so *Smith* does not apply). In that event ...

[4] the government's refusal to grant the exemption to the religious activity *must be strictly scrutinized*, and will be struck down if *not "narrowly-tailored"* to the achievement of the government's compelling objective.

[5] This requirement of "narrow tailoring" means that unless government can carry the *burden of proving* that it can't achieve its objective by a less-intrusive alternative — i.e., by *granting to the religious activity* an *exemption* similar to the one given to the *"comparable"* secular activity — the law *flunks strict scrutiny*, and the refusal to grant an exemption will be *struck down* as unconstitutional.

1. "Same precautions" standard: A key step in the MFN approach is that the court must apply *"narrow tailoring."* That is, the court must decide what kind of exemption(s) must be granted to the religious activity in order to make the scheme not meaningfully more restrictive than the exemption(s) given to the comparable secular activity. As the majority said in *Tandon*, "[w]here the government permits other [i.e. *secular*] activities to *proceed with precautions*, it must show that the *religious exercise* at issue is *more dangerous* than those [secular] activities *even when the same precautions are applied."*

Example: Let's try to imagine how the MFN rule would dictate the narrow tailoring required on the facts of *Tandon*, if the issue were fully tried at the trial-court level.[22] Let's assume that the California COVID restrictions are again attacked by a plaintiff ("P") who wishes to conduct religious services in her home, with *10* couples present. Presumably, P could look at the roster of all secular activities that the state has exempted from its "no more than three households" rule.[23] P could then pick, say, any one or more of these activities as the basis for its narrow-tailoring challenge. Let's suppose that P selects "retail stores" as one category it wants to focus on. P can then

---

22. Remember, the MFN approach, and its requirement of narrow-tailoring, didn't enter the case in Tandon until the case got to the Supreme Court on an application for an injunction pending appeal; therefore, no court made a detailed factual determination about how much risk of COVID transmission would result if in-home services were subject to restrictions similar to the less intrusive restrictions applied to the "comparable" on-commercial-premises activities.

23. Recall that in the *Tandon* opinion, the Court listed "hair salons, retail stores, personal care services, movie theaters, private suites at sporting events and concerts, and indoor restaurants" as among the commercial activities during which California permitted more than three households at a time to gather.

place on California the burden of: (1) identifying *each "precaution"* that is being used by retail stores to reduce the spread of COVID; and (2) showing how and why, if P were to *take substantially similar precautions* for in-home services with 10 households, the risk of COVID spreading *would not be reduced* to about the same level as in the retail stores.

Continuing the analysis, let's imagine that California recommends that indoor retail stores (i) request that staff and customers *wear masks*, (ii) require staff and customers to *show proof of vaccination*, and (iii) *enforce social distancing.* Under *Tandon*, the burden will apparently be on California to show that even if P were to adopt all three of these types of precautions, the risk of the spread of COVID would still be *higher* than in the case of a retail store that imposed the same precautions. Unless California can satisfy this burden, application of *Tandon*'s MFN rule will require the state to *exempt P from the "no more than three households" restriction.*

a. **Vaccine mandates:** One domain in which the most-favored-nation rule is already being litigated is the area of government-imposed *vaccine mandates*. Many state and local governments have recently been requiring that certain groups — medical workers, say, or government employees dealing face-to-face with the public — be *vaccinated against COVID-19*. Some people subjected to these mandates have demanded an exemption on free-exercise grounds; for instance, some have asserted that all available COVID vaccines were originally developed by researchers who used tissues from *aborted fetuses,* causing inoculation to be inconsistent with the claimant's religious beliefs.

   i. **New York statute found vulnerable:** For instance, as of this writing (November 2021), there has already been at least one successful free-exercise challenge to a COVID vaccine mandate. A federal district court has ruled that New York State violated the plaintiff workers' free exercise rights when the state simultaneously (1) refused to even consider granting the workers a religious exemption from the state's mandate that certain healthcare workers be vaccinated against COVID-19, while (2) granting an exemption to a comparable secular category (healthcare workers with a *medical condition*). See *A. v. Hochul*, 2021 U.S. Dist. LEXIS 199419 (N.D.N.Y. Oct. 12, 2021).

H. Anti-discrimination laws, and a group's right to pick its "ministers": There's one other important limitation on *Smith* that has emerged. *Smith* does *not* apply when the government regulation, even though neutral and generally-applicable on its face, would have the effect of *interfering with the internal decision-making of a religious group* regarding the group's *core faith and mission*.

1. **Employment discrimination:** So, for instance, a church will be exempt from a generally-applicable and neutral rule forbidding certain types of *employment discrimination*, if the rule would interfere with the church's right to *select the "ministers"* who will carry out the church's core religious mission. See *Our Lady of Guadalupe School v. Morrissey-Berru*, 140 S.Ct. 2049 (2020) (also discussed *supra*, pp. 669-670).

I. Possible overruling of *Smith*: Many commentators, as well as more than a few past and present members of the Supreme Court, have *criticized Employment Division v. Smith* since it was decided in 1990. There are good reasons to think that *Smith* may well be *overruled* if and when a suitable case comes before the Court.

1. **Most common criticism:** The most common criticism of *Smith* is that it reduces the Free Exercise Clause to ***nothing more than an anti-discrimination principle***, rather than an ***independent source of protection*** against laws that place an ***unintended but substantial burden on religious practices.*** As Justice Barrett said in her concurrence to *Fulton v. Philadelphia*, "as a matter of text and structure, it is difficult to see why the Free Exercise Clause — lone among the First Amendment freedoms — ***offers nothing more than protection from discrimination."***

2. **Five potential votes to overrule *Smith*:** *Smith* remains the law as of this writing (late 2021). But ***five members*** of the present Court are now on record as either calling for the overruling of *Smith*, or as at least being seriously open to that possibility. This lineup is clear from two of the opinions in *Fulton* (*supra*, p. 702):

   [1] **Alito:** Justice Alito, concurring in the judgment in *Fulton*, was joined by Justices Thomas and Gorsuch when he wrote that "*Smith* was ***wrongly decided,"*** and that "the Court's error in *Smith* should now be corrected."

   [2] **Barrett:** Justice Barrett, concurring in full in Chief Justice Roberts' majority opinion, was joined by Justice Kavanaugh when she wrote that there were ***"serious arguments*** that *Smith* ought to be overruled[.]" Then, as we saw in Par. 1 just above, she cast doubt on *Smith* by suggesting that the Clause might well be interpreted to offer something beyond mere "protection from discrimination." These remarks certainly suggest that Barrett and Kavanaugh would seriously consider overruling *Smith* in an appropriate case.

3. **What test should replace *Smith*:** If *Smith* is eventually overruled, the question will of course become, ***what should replace it?*** That is, when a generally-applicable law unintentionally but substantially burdens a person's religious exercise, ***what standard of review*** should courts use to determine whether the Free Exercise Clause requires government to give an exemption to that person? Presumably the standard is *not* one of extreme deference (essentially amounting to no review at all), since that's what happens under *Smith*, and by hypothesis we're assuming that *Smith* is being overruled. But should the "new" standard be ***strict scrutiny?*** Or, should the review be some type of ***"intermediate" scrutiny?*** [24] The five justices who seem eager or at least potentially willing to overrule *Smith* seem to disagree among themselves about what standard of review should replace *Smith*.

   a. **Alito says "strict scrutiny":** For the three most-conservative justices, the answer is, ***"strict scrutiny."*** Thus in Justice ***Alito's*** concurrence in *Fulton* (in which he was joined by Thomas and Gorsuch), he said that the standard should be the "standard that *Smith* replaced," namely, that "[a] law that imposes a substantial burden on religious exercise can be sustained only if it is ***narrowly tailored*** to serve a ***compelling government interest."***

   b. **Barrett suggests something "much more nuanced":** But Justice *Barrett* seems not to agree with Alito. In her *Fulton* concurrence (joined by Kavanaugh), she said that if *Smith* is to be replaced, "the prevailing assumption seems to be that strict scrutiny would apply[.]" But she said she was ***"skeptical*** about swapping *Smith*'s categorical

---

24. This is the standard used to review, for example, content-neutral time, place and manner regulations that burden free expression (*supra*, p. 507): the regulation will be struck down unless it's "substantially related" to the achievement of an "important" governmental interest.

anti-discrimination approach for an *equally categorical strict scrutiny regime*," especially given that the Court's "resolution of conflicts between generally applicable laws and other First Amendment rights — like speech and assembly" had been *"much more nuanced."*

    i. Intermediate review: Barrett didn't say what the "more nuanced" standard was that she would use instead of strict scrutiny. But she cited an opinion (*Gillette v. U.S.*, 401 U.S. 437 (1971)), in which the Court applied a standard requiring the government's interest to be "substantial," a feature of what is usually called *"intermediate review."*

J. Public health regulations: Let's now leave *Employment Div. v. Smith* and its aftermath, and turn to a couple of other Free Exercise topics. One category of regulation sometimes attacked on Free Exercise grounds is that of *public health* rules. The individual raising the Free Exercise claim has generally lost when the health or welfare of others was at issue, but has usually won where *only his own health* or well-being would be jeopardized by an exemption.

    1. Vaccinations: Thus the Court has held that an individual may be required to *receive a vaccination* against disease, even if his religion prohibits such procedures. *Jacobsen v. Massachusetts*, 197 U.S. 11 (1905). This is probably still good law after *Employment Div. v. Smith, supra,* p. 700, since vaccination laws are generally written in a way that makes them neutral, generally-applicable laws, ones that must be obeyed even when they interfere with a person's religious practices.

        a. COVID-19 vaccine mandates: But government mandates that certain people be *vaccinated against COVID-19* have brought to the forefront once again the issue of when government must grant a religious exemption. As the lower-court case discussed on p. 713 *supra* illustrates, if government gives some sort of exemption from the vaccination mandate to one group with a secular reason for needing the exemption (e.g., those with a medical condition that would make it unsafe for them to be vaccinated), then *government must apparently give that same exemption* to a *comparable group* making a free-exercise claim.

    2. Life-saving medical treatment: Where an adult refuses on religious grounds to receive a *blood transfusion* or other *life-saving medical care*, the issues are complex. If the adult is competent, and there is no issue of contagion, it's not clear whether, even post-*Smith*, he can be forced to submit to such care notwithstanding his free exercise rights — a court might well decide that the absence of potential harm to anyone else, combined with considerations of personal autonomy, dictate respecting the adult's right to decline care. The Supreme Court has never decided such a case.

        a. Child or parent of minor: But where the patient is a *child* whose parents object on religious grounds, or the patient is a *parent with minor children*, most courts have *compelled* the treatment, on the theory that the state's interest in safeguarding minors outweighs whatever rights of religious liberty are at stake.

K. What constitutes a "religious belief": A Free Exercise claim, to be valid, must of course involve a "religious belief." Thus the courts are forced to consider not only whether a belief is genuinely held, but whether it is "religious." The Supreme Court has never articulated a formal definition of "religious belief" or of "religion." However, several things are clear about how the Court determines the religiosity of a belief:

1. **Not necessarily theistic:**   The belief, and the system of beliefs of which it is a part, ***need not necessarily recognize a Supreme Being***. That is, non-theistic as well as theistic religions may receive Free Exercise protection. See, e.g., *Torcaso v. Watkins*, 367 U.S. 488 (1961), striking down a state requirement that all holders of public office declare their belief in the existence of God.

2. **Organized vs. unorganized religion:**   The Court will try hard to avoid preferring ***"organized"*** religions (i.e., ones that are well-established, with large numbers of adherents and conventional practices) over ones that are new, unconventional or sparsely-followed.

    a. **Religion practiced by a single person:**   In fact, a person's religious beliefs are entitled to the protection of the Free Exercise Clause even if those beliefs are held by a ***single person*** rather than being part of the teachings of any kind of group or sect. See *Frazee v. Illinois Dept. of Employment Security*, 489 U.S. 829 (1989).

3. **Sincerity:**   Obviously, a court should not sustain a Free Exercise claim unless it is convinced that the belief is ***genuine***. However, in making this determination the court will strive mightily to avoid considering the "truth" or "reasonableness" of that belief. See *U.S. v. Ballard, supra*, p. 670.

4. **Centrality:**   A belief which is claimed to be in conflict with a particular governmental rule must also be ***central*** to the individual's religion; the government should not be required to grant an exemption from a regulation which merely ***inconveniences*** a believer. However, as in the case of gauging whether a belief is "sincerely" held, this decision should be based in part on subjective criteria: if an individual genuinely feels that the conflict is with a belief central ***for him***, his claim should be upheld even though most members of the same sect would consider the belief to be peripheral. Tribe, p. 1249. See, e.g., *Thomas v. Review Bd. Ind. Empl. Sect. Div.*, 450 U.S. 707 (1981), where a Jehovah's Witness' refusal to work in a munitions factory was held to require an exemption from unemployment compensation rules under the Free Exercise Clause, even though there was evidence that another Jehovah's Witness *was* willing to work in the same factory.

Quiz Yourself on
FREEDOM OF RELIGION *(ENTIRE CHAPTER)*

98. The town of Amity has a religiously diverse population. In October, the mayor announced that he and the City Council believed it would be nice to have some sort of public display celebrating the upcoming holiday season. Therefore, he said, a small area would be set aside in Amity's biggest and most centrally-located park, in which a display could be assembled. He established a "Committee for a Happy Holiday," to which he appointed several eminent local citizens. Anyone else who wished to join the committee was permitted to do so. The purpose of the committee was to design and assemble a display. The committee put together a display consisting of: (1) a crèche or nativity scene, portraying the birth of Christ in the manger; (2) a Christmas tree; (3) a Menorah; (4) a Santa Claus riding reindeer; and (5) a banner reading, "Have a Happy Holiday." There was no instance in which a citizen (whether a member of the committee or not) proposed a figure or item that was rejected.

   (a) You are volunteer counsel to the local branch of the ACLU. Your members wish you to bring suit attacking the constitutionality of this display. What constitutional provision should you base your suit on?

   _____

   (b) Will your attack succeed?   _____

99. The state of Carginia requires every religious organization operating in the state to register with the state Attorney General, and to submit financial statements, if the institution wishes to be exempt from state property taxes and state income taxes. (An institution is always free to forgo these tax advantages, in which case it need not register or submit financial statements.) After numerous small community churches, synagogues and mosques claimed that the paperwork involved was terribly burdensome to them, the registration and financial-statement provisions were amended to grant an exemption for any institution "50% or more of whose financial support derives from donations by persons who consider themselves members of the institution."

The state legislature considered eliminating the registration/financial-statement requirement altogether, but did not do so because of a fear that groups that solicit donation from non-members are likely to practice fraud, harassment, and other abuses. There is evidence that the legislature was especially concerned about groups that did their fund-raising by ringing doorbells at private homes, such as "Moonies" and Jehovah's Witnesses. A local group of Jehovah's Witnesses gets most of its financial support by selling Bibles door-to-door to non-members. This group has sued to overturn the statutory scheme as a violation of its Establishment Clause rights. Should the court find in favor of the plaintiff? _____

100. Shortly after being elected, the President announces that he will soon be proposing an Executive Order whose purpose is to (in his words) "drastically reduce Chain Migration from China, by shutting down the China portion of the family-unification visa program." Under that program, Chinese nationals have long been permitted to immigrate to the U.S. when sponsored by a close family member who previously emigrated from China and became a U.S. citizen. In public appearances prior to issuing the Order, the President says that the Order is needed because "Most folks born in China hate us, they don't assimilate into American life when they come here, and they don't share our Judeo-Christian culture — we should be welcoming more immigrants who are Northern-European Christians, and way fewer non-Christian Chinese." The Order, when eventually issued by the President, instructs the State Department to reduce by 95% the number of family-unification visas issued annually to Chinese nationals. The Order states that its sole purpose is to "combat widespread espionage against our military secrets committed by Chinese nationals working for the Chinese government."

Several U.S. citizens of Chinese origin who now want to sponsor their relatives for visas sue the President, seeking an injunction against the Order. The plaintiffs claim that the Order violates their First Amendment Establishment Clause right to be free of religious bias by government in the visa-issuance process. In a federal bench trial, the President's lawyers show (accurately) that in four separate recent espionage cases, Chinese nationals who held family-reunification visas were convicted of stealing military secrets and passing them to the Chinese government. These defense lawyers also present evidence that the various federal agencies charged with protecting national security believe (and believed at the time they helped draft the Order) that dramatically reducing the number of visas issued to Chinese nationals would at least somewhat lower the threat of Chinese-government-sponsored espionage. Based on these facts:

(a) What standard should the court use in evaluating the Order's constitutionality? _____

(b) After applying that standard, should the court grant the injunction? _____

101. The legislature of the state of Largesse was concerned that students in the state's biggest and most financially-troubled city, Bigtown, were not getting a good public-school education. To increase school competition, and to give parents of Bigtown students a choice of schooling options, the Largesse legislature enacted the "Tuition Voucher Plan of 2021" (the "Voucher Plan"). Under the Voucher Plan, the parents of any elementary- or middle-school student living in Bigtown could attend any licensed private non-parochial school in or near Bigtown, and receive a state voucher worth $2,000 to be used towards the private school's annual tuition. A provision in the Largesse state constitution, enacted long ago to further the principle of church/state separation, provides that "No public funds shall be paid to a church or other institution whose primary function is for religious observance." Because the Largesse legislature wanted to avoid violating this provision, the Voucher Plan prohibited the use of the vouchers at any parochial school. Parents of a parochial school student have sued the state, claiming that the exclusion of parochial-school parents from the Plan violates their and their child's Free Exercise rights. Should the court find in favor of the parent-plaintiffs? _____

102. The religion of Weejun is practiced primarily on a small island in the South Pacific Ocean. A number of adherents have made their homes in the West Coast town of Pacifica. The Weejuns speak their own language, and practice their own rituals in a church located in the town. As part of their rituals, the Weejuns drink a beverage called nectaria, made from fermented nectarines. The beverage is smelly and of quite high alcoholic content. Practitioners sometimes get drunk from using it in their rituals. The Weejuns are, in general, relatively uneducated, of lower income status, and seem quite strange to most non-Weejun residents of Pacifica. For some time, non-Weejun Pacificans had been complaining at Town Council meetings that the Weejuns and their nectaria-based rituals were leading to public drunkenness, and a consequent burdening of the police and lowering of Pacifica's "image." The Town Council then enacted an ordinance whose sole provision was to ban the sale or public use of nectaria. "Public use" was defined to include the use in any gathering of more than three people who were not related to each other and who were not meeting in a private home. Since the Weejun church was a free-standing building, the sole effect of the ordinance was to ban the use of nectaria as part of the Weejun church rituals.

   (a) If the members of the Weejun congregation wish to attack the constitutionality of the Pacifica ordinance, what constitutional provision should they rely upon? _____

   (b) What test or standard of review should the court apply in evaluating the challenge you referred to in (a)? _____

   (c) Is the ordinance constitutional, when judged by that standard of review? _____

103. Practitioners of the religion of Parentism believe that it is up to the parents of the child to carry out that child's education, and that the teaching of the child by strangers (i.e., non-parents) is against God's will. Consequently, each child born to parents who practice Parentism is schooled at home, and no private religious schools following the Parentism religion exist. The state of Gomorra has been worried that students who are taught at home by their parents fail to receive necessary socialization, and frequently don't learn needed skills like cooperation, as well as knowledge of more advanced subjects like trigonometry. Therefore, the state has recently enacted a ban on any kind of home education (though parents are free to send their children to any private or religious school they wish, so long as children from more than one family attend). There is no evidence that the Gomorra regulation was motivated by any particular dislike, or even awareness, of Parentism; in fact, the practitioners of Parentism are so few that state education officials are barely aware that they exist. Priscilla, an adherent of Parentism who has been teaching her child Pamela at home, has applied to the state for an exemption from the no-home-schooling requirement, on the grounds that the ordinance would otherwise violate Priscilla's and Pamela's free exercise rights. Must the state grant an exemption so that Pamela may be schooled at home? _____

104. A central element of the Sharkist religion is to possess and pray to a piece of a fin from a Great White Shark. Because the Great White Shark is a nearly extinct species, and because it has been relentlessly

hunted as a source of shark fin soup and other delicacies, the U.S. (acting together with other western nations) has recently enacted a ban on the possession or importing of any fin or other body part from Great White Sharks. When Congress enacted this ban, few if any members of Congress were aware of the existence of the Sharkist religion, which has very few adherents. The federal legislation makes it a felony, punishable by up to five years in prison, to knowingly possess a Great White Shark's fin. Samark, a practitioner of Sharkism, has petitioned the U.S. for an exemption from the ban, contending that the ban violates his free exercise rights. Religious experts estimate that there are fewer than 100 Sharkists in the United States, and that granting them an exemption would have no material effect on the rate at which Great White Sharks are hunted. Must the U.S. grant the exemption? _____

105. After a major 2-month-long recurrence of COVID-19 struck the state of Ames in 2021, the state's Governor issued an Emergency Order. The Order classified as "Red Zones" those census tracts within the state where COVID had been spreading especially fast, and specified that certain activities within Red Zones were forbidden until the rate of new cases declined to a specified "safe" level. One of the provisions of the Order prohibited any "church or synagogue" within a Red Zone from holding a service attended by more than 25 people, even if all congregants wore masks and practiced social distancing, and regardless of the size of the hall in which the service was held. The Order included a similar ban on the presence of more than 25 people within any "place of business" within a Red Zone. However, the Order exempted from this place-of-business closure any "essential business," defined in the Order to include banks, grocery stores, parking garages and chemical manufacturing plants.

First Church, a large church with the capacity to seat over 1,000 congregants, has now sued Ames in federal court seeking an injunction blocking the 25-person limit in the Order from being enforced against it; the church asserts that the limit violates the church's and its members' rights under the First Amendment's Free Exercise Clause. At a hearing on the injunction request, the Church has produced evidence (not challenged by the state) that (i) in the two months prior to the lawsuit, the Church required all congregants to wear masks and socially distance themselves from others (with six feet of space between any two persons not members of the same household, resulting in a limit of 200 congregants per service); and (ii) no cases of COVID occurred among the congregants during the two months.

(a) By what standard of review should the court evaluate the constitutionality of the limit, and why is that the correct standard? _____

(b) Using the review standard you specified in Part (a), should the court grant the injunction, and why or why not? _____

106. The Reverend John Butcher was a self-proclaimed "faith healer." Through programs paid for by his ministry on radio and television, he gave notice to the world that if a person was physically or mentally ill, Butcher would lay hands upon that person and, in most cases, could cure them. Butcher charged a "donation" for each attempt at faith healing, which he said should normally be about equal to one month's wages, payable in advance. Butcher performed dozens of attempted acts of faith healing. Of the first 30 such attempts, 29 ended with the patient/worshipper believing that he or she had not been helped at all; the other one believed that there had been some slight improvement. Butcher's 31st patient, Jones, had cancer; she relied on Butcher's laying on of hands and did not seek medical treatment, which could have cured her. She died of the cancer.

Butcher was prosecuted for the manslaughter of Jones, as well as for financial fraud in her case. The essence of the prosecution was that Butcher did not in fact believe that he had faith healing powers, and purported to have them only as a means to make money. At the trial, the prosecution was permitted to show that 29 of the first 30 patients believed that they had not been helped by Butcher. The judge then charged the jury, "The issue is not whether Butcher's treatments worked, but whether Butcher sincerely believed that they might work. In making this determination of sincerity, you may consider evidence that they did not in fact work, as bearing circumstantially on whether Butcher believed that they might work." Butcher has objected to this charge on the grounds that it infringes upon his free exercise of religion. Is Butcher's argument correct? _____

Answers

98. **(a) The Establishment Clause.** The Establishment Clause of the First Amendment prohibits any law "respecting an establishment of religion." In a general sense, its purpose is to erect a wall between church and state.

(b) No, probably. The Establishment Clause prevents government from ***sponsoring*** or ***endorsing*** one religion over another, or religion over non-religion. A display of religiously-oriented materials at holiday time might indeed be found to constitute an implicit endorsement or sponsorship by the government of religion or of a religious message. In evaluating whether a particular display or ceremony violates the Establishment Clause, the Court generally uses a three-part test (derived from *Lemon v. Kurtzman*). Only if the action satisfies ***each*** of the following conditions will it be valid: (1) it must have a ***secular legislative purpose***; (2) its principal or ***primary effect*** must neither advance nor inhibit religion; and (3) it must not foster an ***excessive governmental entanglement*** with religion.

On facts very similar to these, the Court held by a 5-4 vote that the display did ***not*** violate any of these three tests. *Lynch v. Donnelly*. Here, a court would probably find a secular purpose (to celebrate the holiday, which is a secular government-observed holiday in addition to being one with religious significance). The primary effect of the display would probably not be found to benefit religion in general or Christianity specifically (since the non-religious "holiday spirit" was also being benefitted, and any advancement of religion was somewhat indirect). And there would probably not be found to be undue entanglement between government and religious institutions, since government basically left the space available and allowed citizens to do what they wished without further government intervention. The most important factor would probably be ***context***: here, there were at least some non-religiously-oriented items in the display (e.g., the banner, and the reindeer), so that a reasonable observer would probably not conclude that the display was, overall, a government endorsement of religion. (Observe, however, that *Lynch* was a 5-4 decision, and even a small variation in the items displayed, or in how they came to be displayed, might have resulted in a shift of one vote and thus a change in result.)

99. **Yes.** The facts are similar to those in *Larson v. Valente*. The Court held that this type of scheme benefited one religion or group of religions over another. Therefore, the Court applied ***strict scrutiny***, not the *Lemon* three-prong test. Such a preference of one religious group over others could be sustained only if it was "justified by a compelling governmental interest and … closely fitted to further that interest." Although the state may have an interest in guarding against "abusive solicitation practices," the means selected here are not "closely fitted" to furthering that interest, since there is no reason to believe that the likelihood of solicitation abuse is closely related to the ratio of member contributions to total contributions.

The conclusion that the legislature has "played favorites" here is buttressed by the evidence that the legislature knew it was disfavoring Jehovah's Witnesses and other residential-doorbell-ringers. If there were evidence that the disfavoring of Jehovah's Witnesses was entirely ***incidental***, perhaps strict scrutiny would not be called for.

100. (a) Whether the Order is "plausibly related" to the government's stated (and legitimate) objective of improving the nation's military security. The facts here correspond pretty closely to those of *Trump v. Hawaii* (2018), where the Court upheld President Trump's "travel ban" severely restricting entry into the U.S by nationals of various majority-Muslim countries. There, as here, the President said he was acting to combat a threat to national security. In that case, the Court said that the power to make such national-security decisions is a "fundamental sovereign attribute" of the Executive and Legislative Branches that is "largely immune from judicial control." And, the Court said there, the maintenance of the government's stated objective of preserving national security was a legitimate governmental interest. Consequently, the Court said in the *Hawaii* case, the appropriate standard for reviewing the President's order was ***"rational-basis review,"*** under which the order would be upheld as long as it was "plausibly related" to achieving the stated national-security interest. Presumably, therefore, the same easy-to-satisfy rational-basis review standard will apply here.

(b) No, because, given the multiple espionage arrests cited by the Order, the visa reductions are plausibly related to achieving the stated national-security goal. Under the rational-basis standard of *Trump v. Hawaii*, the court will first determine what governmental interest is being cited in support of the order; the answer is, clearly, the interest in "safeguarding the nation's security" by reducing espionage, an interest analogous to the anti-terrorism interest asserted by the U.S. in the *Hawaii* case. Next, the court will determine whether the means employed in the Order are "plausibly related" to achieving this asserted national-security interest. The *Hawaii* case shows that for a majority of the Supreme Court, it doesn't take much to meet the plausibly-related standard; there, the fact that various federal agencies decided that the travel ban would contribute to combating terrorism, when coupled with the ban's use of various time-limits, exemptions and waivers, was enough to constitute the required "plausible" link between the ban and the objective. So, here, it seems highly likely that the four documented cases of espionage by persons of Chinese origin who received the same type of family-reunification visas as covered by the Order, when taken in combination with the relevant federal agencies' stated belief that reducing the issuance of such visas would reduce espionage, would be enough of a means-end link to satisfy the plausibly-related standard.

What's especially worthy of note is that under *Trump v. Hawaii*, ***countervailing evidence*** that the President's ***actual motive*** in issuing the Order here was really ***religion-based bias*** against non-Christian immigrants from China will essentially be ***disregarded*** if the government claims to be acting to protect national security. So the evidence of the President's public statements about the purpose of the soon-to-be-announced Order — including the strong indications of bias against a particular religious group — will play little if any role in how the court should apply the plausibly-related standard.

101. Yes. In a 2020 decision, the Court held that if a state offers scholarships towards tuition at private schools, the Free Exercise Clause is violated if the state excludes private religious schools from the program. *Espinoza v. Montana Dep't. of Revenue*. The fact pattern here is nearly identical to the one in *Espinoza*, since there, as in our problem, the state's scholarship provision honored a state-constitutional provision prohibiting the use of public funds to aid any church-controlled school. Just as the Court in *Espinoza* held that Montana's scholarship provision needed to undergo strict scrutiny under the Free Exercise Clause, the same scrutiny would be triggered here. The *Espinoza* Court concluded that Montana's exclusion of private religious schools from the generally-available scholarship program failed *both* the ***"compelling objective"*** prong of strict scrutiny and the prong requiring the means chosen to be ***"narrowly tailored"*** to the achievement of the compelling objective. There, the state's asserted objective of furthering "religious freedom" by maintaining strict separation of church and state was found not to be a compelling one, because an interest "cannot qualify as compelling" if it "brings about 'the infringement of free exercise'." And the means chosen by the state – the exclusion of religious schools from the scholarship – was found not to be closely tailored to promoting that interest in religious freedom, because the state was "penalizing," not advancing, religious freedom by "cutting families off from otherwise available benefits if they choose a religious private school[.]"

Here, the court should similarly hold that the state's decision to exclude religious schools from participating in its scholarship program flunks both prongs of strict Free Exercise scrutiny, for the same reasons as in *Espinoza*.

102. (a) The Free Exercise Clause. The First Amendment bars government from making any law "prohibiting the free exercise" of religion. The clause can apply to regulations that are directed at religious beliefs or, more commonly, directed at religiously-oriented **conduct**. Here, we have a regulation that is directed at conduct (the consumption of a particular beverage).

(b) Strict scrutiny. Where government takes an action whose **purpose** is to forbid or interfere with particular conduct **because** the conduct is dictated by a religious belief, the government action is strictly scrutinized and almost always struck down. Here, all the evidence is that the Pacifica Town Council was motivated principally by members' dislike of the Weejun religion and its practitioners, not by a generally-applicable dislike of drunkenness. The facts are roughly analogous to those of *Church of the Lukumi Babalu Aye, Inc. v. Hialeah*, where the Court struck down a ban on ritual animal sacrifice on the theory that the ban was motivated by hostility to practitioners of the Santeria religion. When the Court is deciding whether governmental regulation is designed for the purpose of interfering with a particular religious practice, the extent to which the ordinance is of "general applicability" will be considered; here, the ordinance speaks solely of nectaria, not other beverages of equal alcohol content, and the ordinance affects nobody but practitioners of Weejun. Therefore, a court would almost certainly conclude that there was an intent to interfere with the religious practice, not merely an unintended effect upon religion. Consequently, strict scrutiny must be used.

(c) No. Strict scrutiny in the free exercise context, as in other constitutional contexts, means that the regulation will be struck down unless it is **necessary** to achieve a **compelling** governmental interest. The government's interest here in cutting down on public drunkenness might be "compelling," but the means selected are certainly not "necessary" to achieving that end. For instance, the town could simply have banned public drunkenness, or banned all substances of sufficiently high alcohol content that were very likely to produce drunkenness. The ordinance here is extremely underinclusive (it deals with only one source of drunkenness), demonstrating that it is not "drawn in narrow terms" to accomplish the objective.

103. Yes, probably. The general rule today is as set forth in *Employment Div. v. Smith*: "the right of free exercise does not relieve an individual of the obligation to comply with a **valid and neutral law** of **general applicability** on the ground that the law proscribes (or prescribes) conduct that his religion prescribes (or proscribes)." Applying this principle would mean that Priscilla is not constitutionally entitled to an exemption. But a pre-*Smith* case that is somewhat on point has never been explicitly overruled post-*Smith*, and would probably be re-affirmed today. That case is *Wisconsin v. Yoder*, where the Court held that a state must exempt Amish teenage students from the requirement of attending school until the age of 16. If the case arose today, the Supreme Court would likely preserve *Yoder* by carving out a narrow exception to *Smith* to allow a free exercise claim by parents who want to home-school their children for religious reasons.

104. No. Where government enacts a generally-applicable *criminal prohibition* on a certain type of activity, and government does not intend to burden religious beliefs, government does not have to grant an exemption to those whose religious beliefs or practices are burdened by the prohibition. The facts are analogous to those of *Employment Division v. Smith*, where a state was allowed to refuse to grant American Indians an exemption from the ban on peyote, even though use of the drug was a central part of their religious rites. *Smith* establishes that government does not have to engage in any *balancing* of its interests in its prohibition against the burden on the individual's religious beliefs — so long as the ban is generally applicable, and not motivated by a governmental desire to affect religion, the law is fully enforceable no matter how large the burden on the plaintiff or how small the benefit to the state. Therefore, even though an exemption would not meaningfully interfere with the goal of safeguarding Great White Sharks, no exemption needs to be given.

105. (a) Strict scrutiny, because the limit is not a "generally applicable law," and the rational-relation test used to review generally-applicable laws that potentially impair religious practices therefore does not apply.

Under *Employment Division v. Smith*, when government enacts a "neutral" and *"generally applicable"* law that has the unintentional effect of burdening a person's religious practice, the standard by which the law's constitutionality under the Free Exercise Clause will be reviewed is the easy-to-satisfy *"rational relation" standard,* by which the law will be upheld so long as the means chosen by government are *"rationally related"* to the achievement of a *"legitimate"* governmental objective. But if the court determines that the law in question is *not* "generally-applicable" (or that the law is not "neutral" as to religion), then *Smith does not apply.* In that event, the court is required to apply *"strict scrutiny,"* by which government bears the burden of showing that the means it chose is *"narrowly tailored"* to achieve a *"compelling"* governmental objective. As a general rule, the means chosen *won't* be deemed to be "narrowly tailored" if the governmental objective could have been achieved by means that *interfered less* with the plaintiff's religious practice.

(b) Yes, the court should grant the injunction. The fact that "essential businesses" were exempted from the Order, coupled with the fact that the state didn't show that the risk of COVID's spreading during church services (assuming that the masking and social-distancing measures were in place) would be greater than that risk of spread in these essential businesses if subjected to the same safety measures, prevents the Order from being a "generally-applicable" law. Since the Order is not a generally-applicable law, the court is required to strictly scrutinize it.

Here's a closer look at the case law behind the analysis stated in the prior paragraph: according to the 2021 decision in *Tandon v. Newsom*, if government enacts a law that substantially impairs the ability of a person ("P") to practice their religion because government fears some risk posed by that practice, but government *grants an exemption* from the law for a *category of secular activity* that poses a risk that's *"comparable"* to the risk posed by P's religious practice, then the law *automatically* fails to be a "generally applicable" one. That's the case here: the state has exempted certain categories of business — let's focus on grocery stores — from the 25-person limit, and has not shown that if the same mask and social-distancing measures were enforced as to both grocery stores and church services (but without the 25-person limit in either case), COVID would spread more rapidly in the church services than in the grocery stores. Therefore, the 25-person limit is not a "generally applicable" law, a fact that prevents *Employment Div. v. Smith* from applying. When *Smith* doesn't apply, *Tandon* says that pre-*Smith* law applies, under which the state's decision to deny an exemption from the occupancy limit for church services while granting one for grocery stores must be *strictly scrutinized*.

Under strict scrutiny in this context, the state's decision to deny an occupancy-limit exemption for church services will be struck down unless the state proves that the denial of an exemption for the services (while granting one for grocery shopping) was ***"narrowly tailored"*** to the achievement of a ***"compelling governmental objective."*** Preventing the rapid spread of COVID is undoubtedly a compelling objective. But the court will have to find that the means chosen by government — here, the 25-person occupancy limit on church services, coupled with the absence of such a limit on grocery stores — was *not* "narrowly tailored" to achieve the anti-COVID objective, unless government carries the burden of showing that there were ***no "less restrictive alternatives"*** that would adequately achieve that same objective. Here, the state has not carried this burden; indeed, the fact that other anti-COVID measures adopted by the church (mask-wearing and social-distancing) eliminated all COVID cases for the last two months strongly suggests that these less-restrictive alternatives *do* adequately achieve the anti-COVID objective. Therefore, the reasoning in *Tandon* compels the court to grant the injunction here. (By the way, the facts here are very similar to those of a 2020, i.e., pre-*Tandon*, case, *Roman Cath. Diocese of Brooklyn v. Cuomo*, 141 S.Ct. 63 (2020), where the Court voted 5-4 to enjoin New York state's occupancy limits pending appeal; the case would surely have come out the same way had it been decided after *Tandon*.)

106. **Unclear.** The facts are analogous to those of *U.S. v. Ballard*, where the defendants were faith healers charged with fraudulently soliciting donations. The Court held that the Free Exercise Clause barred the submission to the jury of the truth or falsity of the defendants' faith healing claims. Here, the prosecution is entitled to prove that Butcher did not in fact believe his claims, but it is not clear that the prosecution should be entitled to show in detail that they were false, as a means of making a circumstantial case that Butcher believed his claims were false — a court might well conclude that, as in *Ballard*, the evidence as to truth or falsity was prejudicial, given that the only ultimate issue properly before the jury was the genuineness of Butcher's belief.

Exam Tips on
FREEDOM OF RELIGION

Issues involving freedom of religion are usually easy to spot: the fact pattern has to refer to religion, religious beliefs, church, parochial school, God, prayer, or some symbol commonly associated with religion (e.g., a creche, a Star of David, etc.). So the trick with freedom of religion issues is to analyze them correctly, not to spot them. Here's what to concentrate on:

☛ Of utmost importance: decide whether the issue poses an *Establishment* Clause or a *Free Exercise* Clause problem. A given governmental action will rarely pose the danger of both (though the government will often have a ***choice*** of two actions, each posing the risk of violating a different clause).

    ☞   Here's a tip for deciding which Clause is involved: if government seems to be *favoring* religion generally, or favoring a particular religion over the "rest of society," you probably have an Establishment Clause problem. If government seems to be *disfavoring* a particular person relative to the rest of society, in a way that is related to that person's religious beliefs, then you probably have a Free Exercise Clause problem. Classic illustration of Establishment Clause problem: school prayer. Classic illustration of Free Exercise Clause problem: P can't get unemployment benefits if she doesn't make herself available for Saturday work forbidden by her religion.

Establishment Clause Issues

☛ In analyzing an *Establishment Clause* problem, the first thing to do is to recite the three-part test (which you should cite as the *"Lemon v. Kurtzman"* test):

   ☞ First, the government action must have a *secular legislative purpose* (but it's OK if there is *also* a religious purpose);

   ☞ The act must have a *primary secular effect*; and

   ☞ The government action must not involve *undue entanglement* of government in religious affairs, or religion in government affairs.

      ☞ But you should note that (1) although the *Lemon v. Kurtzman* test is still officially good law, the Court often *fails to apply it*, and (2) some Justices have said that it should be *abandoned*.

      ☞ Also, you should note that this test officially *no longer applies* to cases involving the *display of religious symbols on public property.* (Cite to *American Legion v. Amer. Humanist Assoc.* on this point.)

☛ The most common type of Establishment Clause problem that you will see on an exam involves *religion in the public schools*. Typically, the state gives some sort of financial aid to religious schools or to students who attend religious schools. Here are some rules of thumb in analyzing these:

   ☞ If the program benefits *all students*, or even all *private-school* students (including non-parochial students), the fact that the biggest beneficiaries are religious students is not fatal. (*Example:* Tuition vouchers which can be used to send a student to any private school, religious or non-religious, are allowable — *Zelman v. Simmons-Harris*.)

   ☞ If the assistance is being rendered to a *college or university*, it's more likely to pass muster than where it is rendered to a secondary or elementary school.

   ☞ Loans of *tangible objects* (e.g., text books or school buses) are easier to justify than loans of *personnel*, since the loans of tangible objects involve fewer supervisory/entanglement problems for government. But even a loan of personnel to teach inside the religious school is OK, so long as the religious school authorities don't have any influence over the curriculum or the style of teaching.

☛ A common type of fact pattern involves a school district that makes school premises available *after hours* to various groups. The issue becomes, "Must religious groups be excluded?" The correct answer: religious groups typically need *not* be excluded, as long as the government does not get entangled with what the group is doing, as by having public officials co-sponsor the activity. In fact, exclusion of religious groups from a program open to other sorts of groups generally violates the religious groups' free exercise rights.

Example: A school district opens elementary school classrooms after hours to various community groups. If religious groups are allowed to participate (even if their programs are worship services), this is not an Establishment Clause program, because the religious groups are just getting equal treatment. (And if the religious groups were excluded, this would violate their free expression rights. *Good News Club.*)

☛ Another common fact pattern occurs where government *gives funds* to some religious organization for use in some theoretically non-religious "socially beneficial" charitable purpose. (*Example:* Government gives grants to religious and non-religious groups for use in running family planning clinics, legal services clinics, etc.) In this type of fact pattern, use the three-part *Lemon* test. Pay special attention to the risk of entanglement: how does government know that the particular religious organization isn't using the funds to advocate religious doctrine, or to favor its co-religionists? But say that the present Court seems inclined to find that there is no Establishment Clause violation in this type of fact pattern.

☛ A special type of Establishment Clause problem is posed where government *favors (or disfavors) one sect* or religion over another. (*Example:* Government gives tax breaks to certain religions, or gives certain sects free time on government-owned broadcast stations.) This kind of preference is *virtually per se violative* of the Establishment Clause.

   ☞ But in the area of *national security and immigration*, the Court gives great *deference* to the Executive Branch and Congress. As long as the government action is *rationally related* to achieving the government's stated non-religiously-oriented national-security objective, the Court will *uphold* the action, despite the existence of evidence that the main motive for the action was in fact bias against (or in favor of) a particular religious group. [Cite to *Trump v. Hawaii*]

Free Exercise Clause Issues

☛ In analyzing *Free Exercise* Clause problems, be on the lookout for three different kinds of scenarios:

   ☞ In one scenario, government provides some *generally-available program* of benefits, and intentionally *excludes* P from receiving the benefit solely on the grounds of his/its *religious identity* (e.g., because P is church).

   ☞ In another scenario, P wants to do something that is required by P's religion, and the government *blocks him* from doing so.

   ☞ In a last scenario, P doesn't want to do something that is forbidden by her religion, and the government *requires her to do so* (typically, as a condition to the receipt of some kind of government benefit).

☛ If government's interference with a religious practice or belief is *intentional* and motivated by government's *hostility* to that religion (or to all religions), the interference will be strictly scrutinized, and almost certainly struck down. This kind of fact pattern is rare on exams. One example: government bans animal sacrifices, in circumstances showing that government is acting out of dislike of an unpopular minority religion (*Lukumi*, the Santeria Case).

☛ Similarly, if government intentionally *excludes someone* from participating in a generally-applicable *benefit* program solely on the basis of that person's *religious identity*, here, too, strict scrutiny is probably required.

   Example: Suppose a state offers free public-bus passes to all private elementary schools for use by their students, but refuses to allow parochial schools to participate, because of a state policy of "separating church and state." It's very likely that this exclusion will be strictly scrutinized, and found to violate the parochial schools' (and their students') Free Exercise rights. Cite to *Espinoza v. Montana Dept. of Revenue* on this point.

☛ In the more usual free exercise case, the government's interference with religious practices or beliefs is *unintended* and *incidental*. Here's what to look for in this usual situation:

   ☞ The key rule is that where government enacts a *"valid and neutral law* of *general applicability,"* a person has *no* free exercise right to disobey the law, even if the law forbids (or requires) an action that the person's religion requires (or forbids). In other words, government does not have to give an exemption from the general rule.

   Example 1: Recall *Employment Div. v. Smith*: Oregon can make it a crime to possess or smoke peyote. Native Americans must obey the ban, even though smoking peyote is a core part of their religious rites.

   Example 2: Government bans all cruelty to animals, defined to include any death not administered in a painless manner. Assuming that there is no motive to disfavor particular religions, this ban may be applied to groups sacrificing animals as part of a religious ritual, since the ban is a rule of general applicability.

   ☞ Pay special attention to the requirement that the law be one of *"general applicability."* Most of the time on an exam, you'll probably see something that makes the law *not* generally applicable.

      ☞ There are *two main types of "defects"* that are mostly likely to prevent a law from being generally applicable:

      [1] First, where government gives an administrator discretion to allow *"individualized exemptions"* to the law's requirements, i.e., exemptions based on the circumstances of the particular person seeking the exemption; or

      [2] Second, where government has *exempted an entire category of secular activities* from the law's application, if that category is found to pose dangers or problems that are *"comparable"* to dangers/problems posed by the religious activity that has not been granted an exemption.

      If *either type* of defect is present, then *Employment Div. v. Smith won't apply.* Then, the court will *strictly scrutinize* the government's failure to give the religious plaintiff (P) an exemption from the law, and in all likelihood will find that that failure violated P's free-exercise rights.

      Example 1 (defect [1]): Muni, a city, tells all public school teachers that they must be vaccinated against COVID, and refuses to give an exemption to P, a teacher who says that her religion forbids her to receive a vaccine which was originally created from fetal cells (which is how all available vaccines for COVID were created). But Muni's written vaccination policy says that the Muni Schools Chancellor has "discretion to waive the vaccination requirement in a particular instance." This grant of discretion to the Chancellor will be enough to prevent the vaccine mandate from being a "generally-applicable law." Therefore, *Employment Div. v Smith* won't apply, and the court must strictly scrutinize (and likely invalidate) the mandate as to any teacher (including P) who asserts a genuine claim that receiving a vaccination would violate the teacher's religious beliefs. [Cite to *Fulton v. Philadelphia.*]

Example 2 (defect [2]): Same basic facts as Example 1: again, Muni requires all teachers to receive the COVID vaccine. However, the terms of Muni's written mandate policy give an automatic exemption to any teacher who submits a doctor's note stating that the teacher has a medical condition that would make the vaccine dangerous to them; an exempted teacher may teach, as long as she wears a mask and socially-distances herself from any students or adults at the school. P, who has a genuine religious objection to any vaccine, seeks an exemption and says that if she's given one, she'll be willing to wear a mask and socially-distance herself while teaching. Muni rejects P's request without even considering whether the risk that P will spread COVID while masked and socially-distancing is any greater than the risk that a teacher with a medical exemption (who follows the same masking and social-distancing precautions) would do so.

A court should find that unvaccinated-teaching-with-a-*medical*-objection and unvaccinated-teaching-with-a-*religious*-objection are **similar "categories"** (since Muni hasn't rebutted the presumption that the two activities involve similar risks of COVID-spreading when masking and social distancing are used). Again, therefore, the court must strictly scrutinize Muni's refusal to give P an exemption, and will in all likelihood strike down that refusal as a violation of P's free-exercise rights. [Cite to *Tandon v. Newsom.*]

☞   Be on the lookout for one special situation in which *Employment Div. v. Smith*'s rule that people aren't entitled to a free-exercise exemption from a generally-applicable law **won't apply**: religious groups *do* have a free exercise right not to have government interfere with the group's **choice of "ministers" and other employees** who **carry out the group's religious mission.** This may require government to grant an exemption from a generally-applicable and neutral rule, such as an **anti-discrimination law.**

☛ In any free exercise case, be on the lookout for an issue concerning, *"What is a religious belief?"* Here are the key aspects of this issue:

☞   The courts may insist that the belief be *"bona fide."* So the court is permitted to gauge the *"genuineness"* or *"sincerity"* of the individual's belief.

☞   But the court is *not* permitted to gauge the *"truthfulness"* or *"reasonableness"* of the belief. No matter how bizarre or out-of-the-ordinary the belief, only sincerity counts.

☞   Even *unorganized* beliefs, and beliefs practiced by just a *single person*, are protected. Thus the court may not consider that a particular practice is "not traditional" — if it's part of P's own practice of the religion, it doesn't matter that it's a deviation from the general practices of the sect to which P belongs.

JUSTICIABILITY

ChapterScope

In order for a case to be heard by the federal courts, the plaintiff must overcome a series of procedural obstacles that we collectively call the requirements of *"justiciability."* Here is an overview of each of these obstacles:

- **Advisory opinion:** The federal courts may not issue opinions based on **abstract** or **hypothetical** questions. This is known as the prohibition of *"advisory opinions."* It stems from the fact that the Constitution limits federal court jurisdiction only to "cases and controversies."

- **Standing:** The most important single justiciability requirement is that the federal courts may hear a case only when the plaintiff has *"standing"* to assert his claim. By this, we mean that the plaintiff must have a significant *stake* in the controversy.

    - ❏ **Requirement of "injury in fact":** That is, P must show that he has suffered an *"injury in fact."* That is, P must show that *he has himself been injured* in some way by the conduct that he complains of.

- **Mootness:** A case may not be heard by the federal courts if it is *"moot."* A case is moot if *events occurring after the filing* have deprived the litigant of an *ongoing stake* in the controversy.

- **Ripeness:** A case is not yet *"ripe,"* and therefore not yet decidable by a federal court, if it has *not yet become sufficiently concrete* to be easily adjudicated. For instance, if a criminal statute is almost never enforced, P's challenge to the constitutionality of the statute may be found not to be ripe if it is unlikely that the statute will be enforced against P.

- **The 11th Amendment and suits against the states:** The 11th Amendment bars certain types of suits against states. In particular, the amendment bars most types of *damage suits* against the state, including suits where the plaintiff is a citizen either of the defendant's state or some other state.

- **Political questions:** Certain issues are held to involve non-justiciable *"political questions."*

    - ❏ **Commitment to another branch:** For instance, a case will be found to pose a non-justiciable political question if it raises an issue whose determination is clearly committed by the Constitution to *another branch* of the federal government rather than the judiciary. Many issues concerning *impeachment* fall into this category.

    - ❏ **Lack of manageable standards:** Alternatively, an issue may be found to be a non-justiciable political one if there are *"no manageable standards"* to guide the judiciary in deciding that issue.

I. INTRODUCTION

    A. Scope: This chapter discusses preconditions which must be satisfied before a federal court will adjudicate a lawsuit, including a suit raising a constitutional claim.

1. **Source of preconditions:** Some of these preconditions come from Article III, §2's limitation of federal jurisdiction to "cases and controversies." Others come from non-constitutional discretionary policies implemented by the Supreme Court, sometimes called *"prudential"* considerations. Only if a case satisfies *all* of these preconditions will it be deemed *"justiciable,"* i.e., suitable for being disposed of on the merits.

2. **Summary of topics:** The preconditions discussed in this chapter include:

   a. that the suit involve a concrete controversy, so that the court will not be issuing an *"advisory opinion;"*

   b. that the plaintiff have *"standing,"* i.e., an appropriate interest or stake in the matters under suit;

   c. that the suit not be *"moot"* because of events which have occurred following institution of the action;

   d. that the suit be *"ripe,"* i.e., sufficiently well-developed and specific to merit adjudication;

   e. that the suit (or appeal to the Supreme Court) not be one from which the federal courts should *abstain* for the sake of certain discretionary policies (e.g., non-interference with state court proceedings in order to promote federalism); and

   f. that the case not present a non-justiciable *"political question."*

B. **Policies served:** Most of these requirements for justiciability further one or both of the following policies, implicit within the constitutional requirement of a "case or controversy":

   1. the limitation of federal court jurisdiction to issues presented in an *adversary context* and capable of being resolved by the judiciary; and

   2. the maintenance of the *separation of powers*, by assuring that the federal courts do not intrude into areas reserved for the two other branches of government. See Tribe, p. 67.

II. ADVISORY OPINIONS

A. **"Case or controversy" requirement:** Article III, §2 of the Constitution limits federal court jurisdiction to "cases" and "controversies." The federal courts are thus prevented from issuing opinions on *abstract* or *hypothetical* questions. An important consequence of this limitation is that federal courts *may not give "advisory opinions,"* that is, opinions which give advice about particular legislative or executive action, when no party is before the court who has suffered or imminently faces specific injury.

> **Example:** Secretary of State Jefferson, on behalf of President Washington, writes to the Supreme Court asking it to give informal advice on various legal issues, such as the rights and duties of the United States under a treaty with France during the 1793 European War.
>
> *Held* (in a return letter to the President), the Constitution's separation-of-powers principles limit the President, when he wants to solicit opinions, to calling on members of the Executive Branch. Therefore, the Court may not give the requested opinions. *Letter from the Justices to President Washington*, August 8, 1793 (reprinted in Hart and Wechsler, *Federal Courts*, 1973 Ed., pp. 64-66).

1. **Need for focused controversy:** In addition to the separation-of-powers rationale relied on by the Justices in response to Washington's request, the ban on advisory opinions is also frequently justified by the need to have the judiciary decide only *focused, specific conflicts*, in which adversaries *explore every aspect* of the situation. Otherwise, it is feared, the court will not be adequately briefed, and may make an unwise or unduly broad pronouncement which it will then have to revise when confronted with a specific, and real, conflict. (But this problem could probably be overcome if the Court were to assign "friends of the court" or other interested parties to brief and argue the issues, even in the absence of a concrete dispute. See Tribe, p. 74, n. 7.)

2. **"Strict necessity":** The ban on advisory opinions also reflects the general policy of *judicial restraint* in deciding constitutional issues; such issues will not be decided unless *"strictly necessary."* (Most of the other preconditions for justiciability, considered later in this chapter, similarly reflect this policy of avoiding constitutional adjudication whenever possible.)

B. **Declaratory judgments:** A *declaratory judgment* is one in which the court is not requested to award damages or an injunction, but rather, requested to state what the legal effect would be of proposed conduct by one or both of the parties.

1. **Some actions allowed:** The Court has permitted federal court decision or review of at least those declaratory judgment actions which are reasonably *concrete*.

2. **Insufficiently concrete:** But if a declaratory judgment action presents only questions which are unduly *hypothetical* or *abstract*, the federal court may conclude that it is being called upon to issue an illegal advisory opinion, not because the action is for a declaratory judgment, but simply because no specific, concrete controversy exists.

   a. **Criminal statutes:** A plaintiff seeking a declaratory judgment that a *criminal statute* is unconstitutional must generally show *either*: (1) a sometimes-enforced prohibition which *on its face clearly applies* to conduct in which the plaintiff has regularly engaged or will engage; or (2) an *actual threat* that the statute will be enforced *against the plaintiff* (in the case of a statute which on its face does *not* unambiguously cover the plaintiff's conduct). See Tribe, p. 78. If neither showing is made, the declaratory judgment action will be dismissed as being unduly hypothetical.

III. STANDING

A. **Nature of "standing" generally:** When we say that a litigant must have "standing" to assert his claim, we mean that he must have a significant *stake* in the controversy to merit his being the one to litigate it. Thus standing focuses mostly on the *party* asserting the claim, whereas most other elements of justiciability focus upon the nature of the *issue* being litigated. See Tribe, p. 107. The study of standing is thus the study of *what kind of interests in the outcome of a controversy* are sufficient.

1. **Policies behind doctrine:** The requirement of standing reflects principally the policy against allowing federal courts to act like a *"roving commission"* whose purpose is to enforce judges' own views of legality or the interests of "bystanders" in having constitutional or statutory principles adhered to.

2. **Special relevance to constitutional issues:** In most civil actions, the existence of standing is quite clear. The tort plaintiff who alleges personal injury, for instance, and the contract plaintiff who alleges economic damages from a breach, clearly have a sufficiently direct and personal stake in the suit's outcome that they should be permitted to litigate it. But in much *constitutional* litigation, where a plaintiff alleges that the government has acted in an unconstitutional manner, it will be much less clear that the governmental action has affected the plaintiff *more directly* than any other citizen, or that resolution of the dispute in his favor will be of special benefit to him.

   a. **No general interest in constitutional government:** The Court has never been willing to hold that the *generalized interest* of a *citizen* in having his government *behave constitutionally* is a sufficient "stake" to permit the litigation. Therefore, in most of the cases below, the plaintiff tries to show (sometimes successfully, often not) that his interest in the controversy is somehow *more direct* and *individualized* than that of the citizenry at large.

3. **Article III vs. prudential limitations:** The Supreme Court's rules on standing are a blend of: (1) requirements deemed to be imposed by the Article III "case or controversy" requirement; and (2) so-called *"prudential"* considerations, i.e., non-constitutional judgments about what constitutes wise policy in administering the judiciary. The principal consequence of the distinction is that Congress is *not free to override* the Supreme Court as to an element of standing found by the Court to fall within the "case or controversy" requirement, but it *is* free to override the prudential considerations.

4. **Two-part discussion:** Our discussion of standing is divided into two main parts: (1) cases brought by plaintiffs alleging that their rights as *taxpayers* or (less successfully) their rights as *"citizens"* have been infringed; and (2) cases claiming other, usually more individualized, types of injury. The Supreme Court has applied different rules in the two contexts; generally, but not always, the requirements are easier to fulfill for type (2) suits.

5. **Requirement of "injury in fact":** The standing doctrine boils down to just one requirement, in most instances: the requirement that the litigant have suffered an *"injury in fact."*

   a. **"Nexus" requirement in taxpayer cases:** In cases where the plaintiff sues *as a federal taxpayer*, claiming that his taxes are being spent in a way that violates the Constitution or a federal statute, the Court imposes an additional requirement: that there be a certain type of *"nexus"* between the taxpayer's status and the claim sought to be litigated. See *infra*, p. 733.

   b. **"Causation in fact" requirement:** In *non-taxpayer* cases, the modern Court has imposed what might be thought of as a corollary to the "injury in fact" requirement: the injury must be one which was *caused by the act being complained of* (typically a violation of the Constitution or of a federal statute), and there must be a significant possibility that this injury will be *redressed* by giving the litigant the relief he seeks. These two causal aspects may be summarized by saying that the asserted wrongdoing must be the *"cause in fact"* of the injury. See *infra*, p. 738.

6. **Significance:** The standing doctrine tends to keep out of the federal courts three main classes of suits:

   a. **Non-individuated harm:** Cases in which the harm complained of by the plaintiffs is *no different from that suffered by very large numbers of people* not before the court.

The prime example is the harm claimed to be suffered by *"citizens" at large* when government does not act according to constitutional or statutory dictates. See, e.g., *Schlesinger v. Reservists to Stop the War, infra,* p. 734.

b. **"Speculative" future harm:** Cases in which the plaintiff is trying to avoid *future* harm. Plaintiffs can have standing to try to prevent future harm, but the plaintiff must show that the threatened harm is *reasonably likely to occur* in the near future, not merely *"speculative."* This category includes cases in which people try to prevent harm that they fear will be inflicted on them by *government* (e.g., illegal eavesdropping). See, e.g., *Clapper v. Amnesty Int'l, infra,* p. 736.

c. **Third parties' rights:** Cases where the rights claimed to be violated are those of *third parties* not before the court. (But the general rule against assertion of third parties' rights has numerous exceptions; see *infra,* p. 741.)

B. **Federal taxpayer and citizen suits:** The assertion that the plaintiff's harm is no different from that suffered by lots of others arises most often where the plaintiff is claiming that his rights as a *federal taxpayer* or *federal citizen* have been abridged.

1. **Rule before 1968:** Until the late 1960's, the Supreme Court took a completely hostile view towards actions brought by plaintiffs claiming that their rights as federal *taxpayers* or as federal *citizens* had been abridged. A federal taxpayer could, of course, bring suit on a claim that *his own taxes* had been improperly assessed. But a taxpayer simply had no standing to assert that *taxpayers' funds in general* were being improperly collected or spent. See *Frothingham v. Mellon,* 262 U.S. 447 (1923), reasoning that the plaintiff-taxpayer's "interest in the moneys of the Treasury [is] shared with millions of others [and] is comparatively minute and indeterminable."

2. **Exception in *Flast*:** But in a 1968 case, the Court finally made an exception to *Frothingham*'s general rule that taxpayers do not have standing to attack the validity of government spending. In *Flast v. Cohen,* 392 U.S. 83 (1968), the Court held that a taxpayer may challenge the constitutionality of a federal taxing or spending program if there is a *"logical nexus* between the status [of taxpayer] and the claim."

a. **What "nexus" requires:** The requisite nexus will be found to exist, the Court held, only where two showings are made: (1) that the statute relies on Congress' power under the *Taxing and Spending Clause* of Article I, §8, rather than being merely "an incidental expenditure of tax funds in the administration of an essentially regulatory [law];" and (2) that the challenged law violates *"specific constitutional limitations"* imposed *on that taxing and spending power,* not simply that the statute is "generally beyond the powers delegated to Congress by Article 1, §8."

b. **Test satisfied in *Flast*:** The claim in *Flast,* the Court found, *passed* the two-part test. Mrs. Flast's claim was that a federal-aid-to-education act, by giving financial aid to religious schools, violated the First Amendment's Establishment Clause. This Clause, the Court held, operates as a *"specific constitutional limitation"* upon Congress' Taxing and Spending powers.

3. **Modern Court's view:** The Burger, Rehnquist and Roberts Courts have never overruled *Flast.* But they have stubbornly refused to allow any broadening whatsoever of the *Flast* exception to *Frothingham*'s general rule against taxpayer actions, and in fact *no case* after *Flast* has been able to come within that exception.

a. **Must be limit on "taxing and spending" power:** Thus the Court has continued to insist that, in a taxpayer action, only those constitutional provisions which act as *"specific"* limitations on the "taxing and spending" power of Congress may be relied upon. *U.S. v. Richardson*, 418 U.S. 166 (1974).

Example: President George W. Bush, by executive order, sets up the Faith-Based and Community Initiatives Program. Under that program, money supplied by the Executive Branch is used to fund conferences at which the merits of faith-based non-profit social-service programs are extolled by government speakers. The Ps are taxpayers who argue that the purpose and effect of the conferences is for the federal government to promote religion. Congress has not separately authorized any funds for the Faith-Based Program; any funds expended are spent by the Executive Branch from the general (non-earmarked) funds appropriated by Congress for the running of the Executive Branch.

Held, the *Flast* exception does not apply, and the Ps therefore do not have standing. The expenditures here were made by the Executive Branch, not by Congress. *Flast* allowed taxpayer standing to attack violations of the Establishment Clause that occur as the result of Congress' use of its Art. I § 8 power to tax and spend for the general welfare. Therefore, *Flast* will be confined to suits alleging Establishment Clause violations that are funded by a *"specific congressional appropriation* and undertaken pursuant to an express congressional mandate[.]" *Hein v. Freedom from Religion Foundation*, 551 U.S. 587 (2007).

b. **Tax credits:** Similarly, where a state gives taxpayers a *tax credit* that they can use to contribute to a religious school to cover tuition, a member of the public does ***not*** have taxpayer standing under the *Flast* exception, the Court held by a 5-4 vote. See *Arizona Christian School Tuition Organization v. Winn*, 131 S.Ct. 1436 (2011).

c. **Significance:** So today, only suits that are virtually ***identical*** to *Flast* — i.e., suits claiming that congressional action taken under the "taxing and spending" power violates the Establishment Clause — may be brought by taxpayers.

d. **Suits by state and local taxpayers:** What about federal suits by ***state*** and ***local*** taxpayers?

   i. **State taxpayers:** As to ***state taxpayers***, the same no-standing rule applies as to suits by federal taxpayers — "***state taxpayers have no standing*** ... to challenge state tax or spending decisions simply by virtue of their status as taxpayers." *DaimlerChrysler Corp. v. Cuno*, 547 U.S. 332 (2006).

   ii. **Municipal taxpayer:** M*unicipal* taxpayers, on the other hand, clearly *do* have federal-court standing to assert that their tax dollars are being improperly spent. A municipality is viewed as being sufficiently smaller than a state that a municipal taxpayer is deemed to be ***directly injured*** by an improper expenditure of the town's tax dollars.

4. **Citizenship suits:** The Court has ***never*** been willing to recognize standing on the part of individuals ***as citizens*** to object to unlawful or unconstitutional conduct. This refusal has been based upon the view that one citizen's interest in lawful government is no different from that of any other citizen, and that an individual litigant relying upon citizenship has

not shown the *"individualized"* injury-in-fact required for standing. *Schlesinger v. Reservists to Stop the War*, 418 U.S. 208 (1974).

C. Standing not based on taxpayer or citizen status: Somewhat different rules have evolved for actions in which the standing claim is *not* based on taxpayer or citizen status.

   1. Summary: The rules presently imposed may be summarized as follows:

   a. Injury in fact: The litigant must have suffered (or be likely to suffer) an *"injury in fact."*

   b. Must be "individuated":   The injury suffered must be concrete and *"individuated."* That is, it must not be precisely the same harm as is suffered by an extremely large group of others (so that harms suffered by every "citizen" as the result of, say, violation of the Establishment Clause do not qualify, as noted above). However, the injury in fact need not be *economic*; for instance, damage to environmental conditions where one lives or pursues recreation qualifies.

   c. Causation in fact: The action challenged must be the *"cause in fact"* of the injury. This means both that the challenged action was a "but for" cause of the injury, and that the relief being sought, if granted, has a reasonable likelihood of *redressing* the injury. (No comparable causation requirement is imposed in taxpayer suits.)

   d. No nexus requirement: No requirement of a "nexus" between the injury and the challenged action, comparable to that imposed in taxpayer suits (e.g., *Flast*) is imposed outside the taxpayer context.

   We consider each of the above aspects in sequence below: (a) injury in fact (Par. D); (b) "individuated" harm (Par. E); (c) causation in fact (Par. F); and (d) absence of a "nexus" requirement (Par. G).

D. The "injury in fact" requirement: The plaintiff must show that he has suffered or will probably suffer some concrete, "individuated," *"injury in fact."* The most important aspect of this requirement is that if the harm has not yet occurred, there must be a more-than-speculative chance that it will occur.

   1. Non-economic harms: The harm that the plaintiff complains of need not be *economic* in nature.

   > **Example:** An environmental group claims that construction of a recreation area in a national forest will violate federal laws. *Held*, injury to "aesthetic and environmental well-being" can constitute injury in fact. Therefore, the group (whose members use national forests) have standing. *Sierra Club v. Morton*, 405 U.S. 727 (1972).

   2. Must be "actual or imminent," not "speculative":   The "injury in fact" must be *"actual or imminent."* Thus if the threatened harm is too *far in the future*, or its eventual occurrence is too *"speculative,"* the "actual or imminent" element will not be satisfied, and standing will not be found.

   > **Example:** The Ps challenge certain federal agency action that, they say, will have the effect of endangering certain species abroad. D (the U.S. government) argues that the Ps do not have standing. The Ps retort that they have in the past, and will again, travel abroad to the habitats of the potentially affected species, in order to observe and study those species.

Held, for D. The Ps have not shown the requisite actual or imminent harm. "Such 'someday' intentions — without any description of concrete plans, or indeed any specification of *when* the someday will be — do not support a finding of the 'actual or imminent' injury that our cases require." *Lujan v. Defenders of Wildlife*, 504 U.S. 555 (1992).

Note: In at least one recent case, the Court has said that the threatened harm has to be *"certainly impending."* See *Clapper*, immediately *infra*. It's not clear whether this phrase means anything different than "imminent," but the Court's use of it in *Clapper* seems to mean that if the harm hasn't already occurred, its occurrence has to be not only imminent but highly probable.

a. **Government surveillance in the war on terror:** The principle that future harms must not be unduly speculative has made it hard for anyone to challenge *federal surveillance programs* enacted as part of the war on terror. For instance, in an important 2013 case involving a special statute allowing intelligence officials to eavesdrop on international phone calls and e-mails, the Court held, 5-4, that the plaintiffs lacked standing because they were unable to show the requisite likelihood that the statute would soon be used to eavesdrop on their own conversations. *Clapper v. Amnesty Int'l USA*, 133 S.Ct. 1138 (2013).

   i.   **The statute:** In 2008, Congress amended the Foreign Intelligence Surveillance Act of 1978 (FISA) to add a new section, §1881a, which permits federal intelligence authorities to conduct e-mail and telephone surveillance of *non-citizens* who are believed to be outside of the country, in order to obtain "foreign intelligence information." Congress mainly had in mind surveillance done for *counter-terrorism* purposes.

   ii. **The plaintiffs:** The plaintiffs were a loose collection of *U.S. citizens* — including attorneys, reporters, and human-rights workers — who alleged that their work required them to communicate with foreigners that the federal government suspected of having links to terrorist organizations. The plaintiffs said that they reasonably feared that §1881a would be used in the near future to eavesdrop on *conversations between the plaintiffs and these targeted foreigners.* (The plaintiffs conceded that they did not fear being themselves the targets of the surveillance; but they were concerned that the government would target the foreigners, and thereby intercept the plaintiffs' conversations with these foreigners.)

   iii. **Majority denies standing:** But the Court in *Clapper*, in an opinion by Justice Alito (joined by Roberts, Scalia, Thomas and Kennedy), rejected the plaintiffs' claim that they had standing.

      (1) **"Certainly impending":** Alito said that prior cases had required that the threatened injury be *"certainly impending."*

      (2) **"Speculative":** The plaintiffs failed to meet this "certainly impending" requirement, Alito concluded. Because the plaintiffs had *"no actual knowledge"* of what foreign targets the government would choose for surveillance, Alito said, their fear that their own communications would be captured through surveillance targeting others was "necessarily conjectural" and *"highly speculative."*

(3) Alternative statutory authority: Furthermore, Alito wrote, even if the plaintiffs' fears of having their communications intercepted *had* been sufficiently non-speculative, their worries that this interception would be accomplished by means of *the challenged statute* (§1881a), rather than by use of one of the other possibly-available sources of authority, magnified the speculative element.

(4) "Avoidance costs" argument rejected: Lastly, Alito rejected the plaintiffs' argument that they had standing because of the *costs they were incurring* in their efforts to *avoid the effects* of the challenged statute (e.g., the cost of traveling abroad for face-to-face meetings instead of telephone calls). The plaintiffs "cannot *manufacture standing* merely by *inflicting harm on themselves* based on their *fears of hypothetical future harm* that is not certainly impending."

iv. **Dissent:** Justice Breyer (joined by Ginsburg, Sotomayor and Kagan) *dissented*. Breyer rejected the majority's conclusion that the plaintiffs had shown only "speculative" future harm. He argued that prior case law merely required that there be a *"realistic danger"* that the relevant harm would occur, and that this test was met here.

v. **Significance:** *Clapper* may well mean that for many kinds of secret national security programs, *no one has standing* to challenge the program's legality.

b. **Individual threatened with enforcement of law:** A common issue is whether a person who *reasonably fears that a law will be enforced against him* if he takes a contemplated action has suffered an actual/imminent injury even though the individual hasn't yet *taken* that action. In this situation, the Supreme Court has been fairly generous to plaintiffs: the plaintiff meets the injury-in-fact requirement as long as:

[1] he alleges "an *intention to engage* in a course of conduct arguably affected with a constitutional interest, but proscribed by a statute" and

[2] there exists a *"credible threat of prosecution*[.]"

Susan B. Anthony List v. Driehaus, 134 S. Ct. 2334 (2014).

E. **Harm suffered by many:** As long as the litigant (or the group representing him) alleges the requisite "concrete" and "individuated" harm, standing will not be denied merely because there is a *large number* of people suffering the harm.

1. **Citizenship:** But there are limits on how widespread the class may be. Thus the interest of all "citizens" in having their government operate constitutionally and according to statute is so diffuse that actions based on citizenship will not be allowed. See *Schlesinger v. Reservists*, *supra*, p. 734.

a. **No interest in avoiding abstract "denigration":** Similarly, *members of a minority group* will not from that membership alone derive standing to litigate against governmental conduct which *denigrates* that minority group. For instance, in *Allen v. Wright*, 468 U.S. 737 (1984) (discussed more extensively *infra*, p. 739), parents of black public school children sued the IRS, claiming that the latter was not effectively carrying out its obligation to ensure that discriminatory private schools do not receive tax-exempt status. The parents' interest in avoiding the "stigmatizing injury" generally caused by racial discrimination was insufficient to establish standing — only those who were *"personally denied equal treatment"* by the challenged discriminatory conduct had standing.

2. **No interest in avoiding "institutional" loss of power:** Similarly, members of a *political body*, such as a *legislature*, do *not* have standing to litigate against an action that they say *takes away the political power of that body*. Thus members of Congress who unsuccessfully voted against a bill allowing line-item vetoes by the President were held not to have standing to litigate the constitutionality of the resulting statute, where their only claim was that the bill "causes a type of *institutional injury* (the diminution of legislative power), which necessarily damages all Members of Congress and both Houses of Congress equally." *Raines v. Byrd*, 117 S. Ct. 2312 (1997).

3. **Organizations and associations:** On the other hand, the Supreme Court is perfectly willing to grant standing to *associations* in some circumstances. An association has standing not only where its own interests are at stake, but in some cases where it is suing solely as a *representative* of its members. An association has standing to sue on behalf of its members if three conditions are met:

[1] its members would "otherwise have standing to sue *in their own right*";

[2] the interests the association seeks to protect are "germane to the organization's *purpose*"; and

[3] "neither the claim asserted nor the relief requested requires the participation of *individual members* in the lawsuit."

Hunt v. Washington Apple Advertising Comm., 432 U.S. 333 (1977).

F. **Causation:** Outside of the taxpayer-suit context, the Court has required that the litigant show that the challenged governmental action *"caused"* the injury of which he complains. This causation requirement has two components; the litigant must show that:

[1] the challenged action was a *"but for"* cause of the injury, in the sense that the injury *would not have occurred unless the challenged action had taken place*; and

[2] a favorable decision in the suit will *redress* the injury. (Requirement (2) is called the *"redressability"* requirement.)

1. **Confusion as to "redressability" standard:** It is not clear whether, to satisfy the redressability requirement, it is sufficient to show that a favorable decision will *probably* redress the harm. Sometimes, the Court has indicated that a *probability* of redress is sufficient; at other times, however, it has suggested that there must be a *virtual certainty* that redress will follow a favorable decision. See Tribe, pp. 129-30.

   a. **Potential easier standard:** But the 2007 decision in *Massachusetts v. EPA* (*infra*, p. 740) suggests that in some circumstances, even a *less-than-50/50 chance* that the sought-for relief will redress the problem may be enough, if the severity of the problem is great enough. In that case, Massachusetts tried to require the EPA to regulate U.S. automobile emissions so as to reduce global warming; the majority found that the redressability requirement was met, even though the harm feared by Massachusetts (flooding of its coastal lands) was nearly all yet-to-occur, and even though there was little concrete showing that if the requested relief were granted, the threatened harm would be averted. But *Mass. v. EPA* probably represents merely a weakening of the redressability requirement for the special case of *state-as-plaintiff*, not a general weakening for all plaintiffs.

b. *Warth v. Seldin:* A good case illustrating how the Court applies the two causation requirements — the "but for" requirement and "redressability" requirement — is *Warth v. Seldin*, 422 U.S. 490 (1975). The plaintiffs in *Warth* failed to satisfy *either* part of the causation test.

   i. Facts: The plaintiffs in *Warth* were a number of parties who claimed to have been injured by the zoning rules of Penfield, New York. They claimed that these rules had been imposed for the purpose of excluding the building of low- and moderate-income housing in the town.

   (1) Low-income seekers of housing: For instance, some plaintiffs were low- and moderate-income individuals who had never lived in Penfield, but who alleged that they had sought housing there and *would have moved there had affordable housing been available*; and

   ii. Standing rejected: The Supreme Court found that these individuals (like all of the plaintiffs in the case) *lacked standing*.

   (1) "But for" requirement: The individuals failed the *"but for"* requirement, because they were unable to show that, had the restrictive zoning practices not existed, there was a *"substantial probability* that they would have been able to purchase or lease in Penfield." Construction of the appropriate housing would require not merely removal of the zoning laws but also a *third party willing actually to build* the projects, and there was no showing that any third party would indeed have built projects which these particular individual plaintiffs could have afforded.

   (2) "Redressability" requirement: Similarly, these plaintiffs failed the *"redressability"* requirement: they couldn't show that if the court awarded the relief being sought — a striking down of the zoning rules — the desired moderate-income projects would in fact likely be built.

2. Article III basis for cause-in-fact rule: The requirements that the challenged action be the cause of the injury, and that the sought-for relief would remove that injury, are *imposed by Article III*. *Simon v. Eastern Ky. Welfare Rights Organization (EKWRO)*, 426 U.S. 26 (1976).

3. Government allows injury by third party: A plaintiff will generally find it hard to establish the cause-in-fact aspect of standing for a claim that *government action or inaction* has caused some *third party not before the court* to injure him. The difficulty of establishing standing for such a claim was illustrated when the Court found the cause-in-fact requirement unsatisfied in a case in which *parents* of black public school pupils attacked the IRS's *grant of tax-exempt status* to *discriminatory private schools. Allen v. Wright*, 468 U.S. 737 (1984).

a. Facts: In *Wright*, the parents claimed that the tax breaks enabled discriminatory private schools to offer cheaper tuition, thus inducing more parents of white students than would otherwise be the case to withdraw their children from the public schools to place them in these private schools. These withdrawals in turn deprived the black students of their constitutional right to attend integrated public schools, the parents claimed.

b. Holding: But the Court, by a 5-3 vote (with Justice Marshall not participating), concluded that the line of causation from the IRS's conduct to the continued segregation of the public schools was *so attenuated* that the latter was *not* "fairly traceable" to the former.

    i. Speculative elements: For there to have been standing, the majority indicated, the parents would have had to make three showings: (1) that "there were enough racially discriminatory private schools receiving tax exemptions in [plaintiffs'] communities for withdrawal of those exemptions to make an appreciable difference in public-school integration;" (2) that a significant number of schools would, if threatened with loss of the tax exemption, change their policies; and (3) that a significant number of parents of children attending such schools would transfer their children to public school if the exemption were withdrawn. According to the majority, plaintiffs had not alleged any of these three elements.

G. Special deference when plaintiff is a state acting for its citizens: When the plaintiff is a *state* acting on behalf of its citizens, the usual rules of standing will apparently be *relaxed*, as a result of a 5-4 decision by the Court in a case involving global warming. The case, *Massachusetts v. EPA*, 549 U.S. 497 (2007), seems to mean that the *individuated-harm* and *causation* requirements are especially likely to be relaxed where the plaintiff is a state suing in an ombudsman-like manner.

1. Facts: Massachusetts and ten other states sued the EPA, arguing that the agency was required under a congressional statute to issue regulations that would limit automobile emissions of carbon dioxide and thus reduce global warming. The agency, which under the George W. Bush administration did not want to (or believe that it had authority from Congress to) issue the regulations, argued that the states did not have standing to bring the suit, in part because they had not met the injury-in-fact or causation requirements.

2. Holding: The four liberal members of the court (Stevens, Ginsburg, Souter and Breyer) joined with Justice Kennedy to form a majority that concluded that Massachusetts, at least, *had the requisite standing* on account of the danger that *rising sea levels* would pose to its *coastal areas.* The opinion was by Justice Stevens.

    a. State as sovereign: Stevens seemed to be saying that Massachusetts' status in the suit as a *sovereign representing the interests of its citizens* justified some relaxation of the usual standing requirements imposed on private plaintiffs.

        i. Injury in fact: Stevens said that Massachusetts had met the *injury in fact* requirement because global warming had already caused a slight rise in sea level, and the rising seas "have already begun to swallow Massachusetts' coastal land."

        ii. Causation: As to the requirement of causation (that the relief sought might redress the claimed harm), Stevens said, the risk to Massachusetts would be "*reduced to some extent* if [Massachusetts] received the relief [it] seek[s]."

    b. Significance: *Massachusetts v. EPA* seems to mean that states will find it meaningfully easier than private parties to bring federal suits, especially in the environmental area. It is doubtful that a private citizen – even a coastal landowner – would have been found to have standing to attack the EPA's lack of steps to prevent global-warming.

H. Third-party standing: One of the principal functions of the standing doctrine is to implement the general rule that a litigant may normally *not assert the constitutional rights of persons not before the court.* This principle is also sometimes referred to as the rule against assertion of "constitutional *jus tertii*" ("rights of third persons" in Latin).

> **Example:** In *Warth v. Seldin*, 422 U.S. 490 (1975) (other parts of which are discussed *supra*, p. 739), one group of plaintiffs consisted of residents of Rochester who claimed that, because nearby Penfield had refused to allow low- and middle-income housing, their own taxes were higher since Rochester had had to grant tax abatements to encourage construction of more such housing than it otherwise would. The Rochester residents were denied standing; although their higher taxes constituted an "injury in fact," the zoning laws did not apply to them and thus did not violate *their* rights. Their claim thus fell within the general rule that one may not assert the rights of third persons (e.g., those who were excluded from Penfield by the zoning laws) except under special situations, none of which existed here.

1. Rule is prudential, not constitutional: The Court has held that the general rule against third-party standing is founded upon *discretionary* or *"prudential"* considerations, and is *not mandated by the Article III "case or controversy" requirement.*

a. Exceptions: Therefore, the Court has felt free to develop a set of judge-made *exceptions* to the no-third-party-standing rule. The Court has recognized *four major exceptions* to the rule:

[1] Third party unlikely to be able to sue: First, a person may assert the rights of a third-party not before the court *if the third party would face "substantial obstacles to ... asserting his or her own rights."* But the exception applies only if there is "reason to believe that the advocate will *effectively represent* the interests of the third-party." Chemerinsky Hnbk (6e), p. 90, § 2.5.4.

Example: D (Barrows) is a white homeowner who signed a covenant promising not to allow non-whites to occupy the property. P, the owner of a different property that benefits from the covenant, sues D under state contract law for damages for breaching the covenant; he says that D allowed (unnamed) Black persons to move into the property. D defends on the grounds that enforcement of the covenant would violate the constitutional rights of (unnamed) Black people residing in the community not to have the state enforce the covenant in a way that prevents them from being able to rent or occupy D's property. P counters by claiming that under the general rule disallowing third-party standing, D should not be able to assert the constitutional rights of these Black people since they are not before the court.

Held (by the Supreme Court), for D. In this situation, "it would be difficult if not impossible for the [Black] persons whose rights are asserted to present their grievance before any court." And D, as the property owner, is the only person who has the power to use the property to discriminate or not discriminate against the absent would-be renters; that makes D *"the only effective adversary"* of the discriminatory covenant. Therefore, the courts should decline to follow the usual rule against permitting a litigant to assert the constitutional rights of persons not before the court. *Barrows v. Jackson*, 346 U.S. 249 (1953).

[2] Close relationship between P and the third party: A second exception to the no-third-party-standing rule permits a litigant to assert the rights of someone not before the court where "there is a ***close relationship between the advocate and the third-party.***" Chemerinsky Hnbk (6e), p. 92, § 2.5.4. Generally, this happens because the litigant is ***"part of the third party's constitutionally protected activity.***" Id.

Example: Recall *Craig v. Boren* (*supra*, p. 321), where Oklahoma allowed women of age 18 to 21 to buy 3.2% beer, but forbade men under 21 from doing so. The party who challenged the statute was a bartender, whose own constitutional rights were not being violated, but who was asserting the rights of his potential 18-20-year-old male customers who were not parties to the suit.

Nonetheless, the Court granted standing to the bartender, saying that "vendors and those in like positions have been uniformly permitted to resist efforts at restricting their operations by acting as advocates of the rights of third parties who seek access to their market or function." *Craig v. Boren*, 429 U.S. 190 (1976).

i. **Access to abortions and contraceptives:** An important sub-group of cases recognizing this "close relationship" exception consists of cases in which ***doctors and clinics*** have been permitted to assert the rights of their ***absent patients who seek access to contraceptives or abortions.***

Example: Louisiana enacts a statute requiring abortion providers to have admitting privileges at local hospitals. The Ps, a group of clinics and doctors who provide abortions, sue the state in federal court, asserting that the law violates their patients' constitutional right to abortion. The state asserts that the proper parties to challenge the statute are the patients themselves, and that the Ps should not be allowed to assert the constitutional rights of these absent third-parties.

Held (by a 4-justice plurality on this point), for the Ps. The Court has "long permitted abortion providers to invoke the rights of their actual or potential patients in challenges to abortion -related regulations." Furthermore, the Court has generally permitted plaintiffs to assert third-party rights where the "enforcement of the challenged restriction *against the litigant* would result indirectly in the violation of third parties' rights" (emphasis in original), since in such cases "the obvious claimant" and the "least awkward challenger" is the "party upon whom the challenged statute imposes 'legal duties and disabilities.'" *June Medical Services v Russo*, 140 S.Ct. 2103 (2020). (The Court's decision on the merits is discussed *supra*, p. 188.)[1]

---

1. But the Court's continued willingness to allow abortion providers to assert the rights of their patients may be on thin ice. Only a four-justice plurality in *June Medical* thought the case was a suitable one for third-party standing; the fifth vote on the merits came from Chief Justice Roberts, concurring in result, who did not comment on the standing issue. At least three justices who dissented in *June Medical* (Thomas, Alito and Gorsuch) said they did not think third-party standing was appropriate. (The fourth dissenter, Kavanaugh, was silent on the standing issue.) But after *June Medical* was decided, one member of the plurality, Justice Ginsburg, was replaced by Justice Barrett, who appears generally hostile to abortion rights. Going forward, if two Justices out of the group of Roberts, Kavanaugh and Barrett adopt the standing approach of Thomas, Alito and Gorsuch in *June Services*, that would be five votes for reversing the standing ruling in that case, thus denying abortion providers standing to assert the rights of their patients.

[3] First Amendment "overbreadth" doctrine: What can be viewed as the third exception to the rule against third-party standing is the doctrine known as the *First Amendment "overbreadth" doctrine.* Recall (see *supra*, p. 498) that by the overbreadth doctrine, a party to whom a criminal statute clearly (and constitutionally) applies may be permitted to argue that the statute as drafted would criminalize some types of *expressive conduct* that, if engaged in by third parties not before the court, would be protected by those parties' First Amendment rights. In the overbreadth context, the defendant is thus allowed to assert the rights of hypothetical third parties, and to argue that he has his *own* constitutional right not to be convicted under a broadly-drawn statute that would *chill his (as well as the third parties') freedom of expression.* See Chemerinsky Hnbk (6e), p. 94, § 2.5.4.

[4] Standing for associations: Finally, the fourth major exception is that "an *association or organization* can sue ... *based on injuries to its members." Id.* at p. 95. We discuss this type of standing under "Organizations and associations" *supra*, p. 738.

I. **"Prudential" standing:** We just saw that the rule against third-party standing is not dictated by the Article III "case or controversy" requirement, and is instead the result of *"prudential"* considerations (i.e., considerations "dictated by prudence"). More generally, the federal courts retain the right refuse to hear *any* case on such prudential-standing grounds, even cases falling outside the pure third-party-standing area.

Example: P is an atheist whose daughter attends a public elementary school that conducts a group recitation of the Pledge of Allegiance. P contends that his First Amendment rights (not his daughter's) are violated by the Pledge, because the Pledge interferes with his right to inculcate in his daughter, free from government interference, his own atheistic beliefs. The case is complicated by the fact that P is divorced from the child's mother, who under California law has the right to make final legal decisions about the daughter's upbringing if the two parents disagree. The mother opposes P's suit.

Held (by a 5-3 Supreme Court vote), the prudential standing doctrine should be applied, so that the case will not be heard by the federal courts. The federal courts should generally "leave delicate issues of domestic relations to the state courts." Also, the decision here might have an adverse effect on the non-party daughter's own First Amendment rights; abstention is proper where "prosecution of the lawsuit may have an adverse effect on [a third] person who is the source of the plaintiff's claimed standing." *Elk Grove Unified School Dist. v. Newdow*, 542 U.S. 1 (2004).

IV. MOOTNESS

A. Mootness generally: A case is not justiciable if it is *"moot."* A case is moot if it raised a justiciable controversy at the time the complaint was filed, but *events occurring after the filing* have deprived the litigant of an ongoing stake in the controversy.

Example: P sues D, a state university, claiming that its law school admissions program is racially discriminatory. He is permitted to attend the law school while the case is being litigated. By the time the case arrives at the Supreme Court for review, P is in his final year of law school, and the university says that he will be allowed to graduate.

Held, the case is moot, and determination of the legal issues in the suit is no longer necessary. Therefore, the appeal will not be decided. *DeFunis v. Odegaard*, 416 U.S. 312 (1974).

B. Exceptions: There are a number of reasons for which a case which is ostensibly moot will nonetheless be heard. The main ones, each of which is discussed below, are: (1) that the issue is *"capable of repetition, yet evading review"*; (2) that the case seems moot only because the defendant has *voluntarily*, but not necessarily permanently, changed his conduct; and (3) that there are *collateral consequences* to the defendant's action which, when considered, prevent mootness. See Tribe, p. 84.

1. **"Capable of repetition, yet evading review":**   An issue will not be treated as moot if it is *"capable of repetition, yet evading review." Southern Pacific Terminal Co. v. ICC*, 219 U.S. 498 (1911).

   Example: P, a pregnant woman, attacks the constitutionality of state anti-abortion laws. She brings the suit as a class action, in which she is the named plaintiff and other pregnant women desiring abortions are unnamed members. By the time the case reaches the Supreme Court, P is no longer pregnant.

   Held, the case should not be dismissed as moot. Pregnancy will almost always be completed before the usual appellate process is complete. P herself may become pregnant again, but even if she does not, obviously other women will. The issue is thus "capable of repetition, yet evading review." *Roe v. Wade*, 410 U.S. 113 (1973).

2. **Voluntary cessation by defendant:**   If the defendant *voluntarily ceases* the conduct about which the plaintiff is complaining, this will normally *not* be enough to make the case moot. If the plaintiff seeks damages, the cessation will of course be irrelevant to the issue of mootness. But even if the plaintiff seeks an *injunction*, the cessation will not make the case moot, if there is any substantial chance that the defendant might "return to his old ways." See Tribe, p. 89.

3. **Collateral consequences:**   In determining whether the plaintiff continues to have a stake in the controversy, all *collateral consequences* of the challenged conduct must be examined. If any of these collateral consequences could be adverse to the plaintiff, the case is not moot. For instance, where a criminal defendant has already *served his sentence*, his attack on the constitutionality of his conviction will not be deemed moot, because of the likelihood of collateral consequences from the conviction, such as loss of the right to vote, and damage to reputation or to employability. See Tribe, p. 92.

V.   RIPENESS

A. Problem generally: The problem of *ripeness* may be regarded as the opposite of that of mootness. Whereas a case is moot (and therefore not justiciable) because it *no longer* involves an actual controversy, a case will be regarded as not yet ripe (and therefore not yet justiciable) if it has *not yet become sufficiently concrete* to be worthy of adjudication.

1. **Relation to ban on advisory opinions:**   The ban on adjudication of unripe matters is closely related to the ban on *advisory opinions (supra*, p. 730). Both doctrines reflect the view, based partly on the constitutional requirement of a "case or controversy," that the federal courts must not render opinions except in situations where there is a well-defined,

live controversy, with specific facts, and with either an allegation of past injury or a likelihood of future injury.

2. ***Mitchell* case:** The classic illustration of a matter not yet ripe for adjudication is *United Public Workers v. Mitchell*, 330 U.S. 75 (1947).

    a. **Facts:** The plaintiffs in *Mitchell* were federal civil servants who wished to attack the Hatch Act, which prohibits federal Executive-Branch employees from involvement in "political management or … political campaigns." The plaintiffs claimed, in essence, that they ***desired*** to engage in prohibited political activities; however, all but one conceded that they had ***not yet done so.***

    b. **Holding:** A majority of the Court held that the claims of those plaintiffs who had not yet violated the Act were ***not ripe.***

        i. **Rationale:** The Court reasoned that plaintiffs' claims were so general that they constituted "really an attack on the political expediency" of the statute, "not the presentation of legal issues." It was the province of the legislature, not the judiciary, to make such general determinations of political expediency.

        ii. **Specific conduct:** Thus the Court seems to have really been troubled not so much by the fact that the plaintiffs had not yet violated the statute and not yet been subjected to the prescribed punishment (discharge), but rather, by the fact that the plaintiffs were not ***adequately specific*** as to the precise acts which they wished to carry out. Had the plaintiffs set forth ***in detail*** what they wished to do, the ripeness doctrine might not have prevented their case from being adjudicated even though these acts had not yet been carried out. See Tribe, p. 79.

B. **Uncertain enforcement of criminal statute:** Ripeness problems also may arise where the plaintiff alleges that he has violated a statute whose constitutionality he attacks, but it is not clear that the statute is ***generally enforced***, or that it will be enforced in this particular case. In this situation, the Court has often been reluctant to allow the case to be adjudicated.

1. ***Poe v. Ullman:*** For instance, in *Poe v. Ullman*, 367 U.S. 497 (1961), two married couples and a physician challenged Connecticut's anti-contraception law. A majority of the Court refused to hear the case on appeal, on the grounds that the statute had been on the books for 80 years with only one reported prosecution and that there was thus not the requisite "clear" threat of prosecution.

2. **Willingness to hear evolution case:** But the Court has not always held that a rarely-enforced statute fails to present a ripe controversy. For instance, in *Epperson v. Arkansas, supra*, p. 665, the anti-evolution statute struck down by the Court had not been enforced in the 40 years of its history, nor was there any showing of a specific threat of enforcement against the plaintiff. See L,K&C, p. 1682, n. 2. The Court's willingness to adjudicate *Epperson* suggests that its refusal to hear *Poe* was an exercise of its ***discretion***, not the product of a lack of an Article III "case or controversy." See Hart and Wechsler, *Federal Courts*, p. 657.

C. **Requirement of specific threatened harm:** For a case to be ripe, it is not necessary that the litigant have already suffered harm; it is sufficient that there is a reasonable probability of harm. However, the anticipated harm must be ***reasonably specific***.

1. ***Laird v. Tatum:*** For instance, in *Laird v. Tatum*, 408 U.S. 1 (1972), plaintiffs attacked an Army Intelligence scheme for ***gathering data*** about persons and activities who had the

potential for "civil disorder." Plaintiffs claimed that this surveillance scheme had a "present inhibiting effect" on their activities, even though they had no idea what use, if any, the Army might make of the information being gathered. But the Court, by a 5-4 vote, found that a present "subjective chill" was not enough to make the case ripe; what had to be shown was a ***"specific present objective harm"*** or a ***"threat of specific future harm."***

VI. THE 11TH AMENDMENT, AND SUITS AGAINST STATES

A. The 11th Amendment: The 11th Amendment imposes limitations — increasingly important ones in the 1990s — on the jurisdiction of the federal courts.

1. **Text of the Amendment:** That Amendment provides:

> The Judicial power of the United States shall not be construed to extend to ***any suit in law or equity***, commenced or prosecuted ***against one of the United States*** by ***Citizens of another State***, or by Citizens or Subjects of any ***foreign*** state.

2. **Facial meaning:** So on its face, the 11th Amendment merely seems to say that one state can't be sued in federal court by a citizen of a different state, or by a foreigner. And in fact, if you were wearing your *Civil Procedure* hat, you might think that this Amendment was simply saying that suits based solely on diversity — rather than on a federal question — could not be brought against a state.

3. **Interpreted more broadly:** But over the years, the Amendment has been interpreted much more broadly than that. We don't have space for a long explication of the Amendment, but here are the highlights of how the Supreme Court has interpreted its scope:

    a. **Suits by citizens of the defendant state:** First, the Amendment is interpreted so as to bar suits by a citizen against his or her ***own state***. *Hans v. Louisiana*, 134 U.S. 1 (1890).

    b. **Suits involving federal question:** Second, the Amendment covers ***federal question suits***, not just diversity suits. Many scholars believe that the 11th Amendment was intended only to block diversity suits against states, not federal-question suits against them. But this view has not prevailed, and the 11th Amendment is interpreted to block all suits by private citizens against states, whether based on diversity, alienage, or federal question.

    c. **Constitutional embodiment of sovereign immunity:** Third, this broad reading of the limits on suits against states — that a state may not be sued even by its own citizens, and may not be sued even in a case raising a federal question — is now held to be a core ***constitutional limitation on federal judicial power***, not just an interpretation of broad "principles" surrounding the 11th Amendment itself. The most important consequence is that ***Congress generally cannot overrule this broad reading***, and cannot authorize a state to be sued by its own citizens in federal-question suits. This is the nub of the Court's 1996 ruling in *Seminole Tribe*, discussed in detail *infra*, p. 748.

    d. **Suits in equity:** Finally, the Amendment applies not only to suits "at law," but also to suits "at ***equity***." Thus a private citizen cannot sue to have a state enjoined or ordered to do something, any more than she can sue to recover damages. (But as we discuss immediately below, the Amendment does not bar suits against a state *official*, in his private capacity, seeking to enjoin him from violating federal law.)

4. **Exclusions:** There are a number of important exclusions from the coverage of the 11th Amendment:

a. **Suits against officials for injunctions:** Most important, the 11th Amendment does not prevent suits against *state officials* in which the relief sought is an *injunction* against the *violation of federal law*. This principle was established in *Ex parte Young*, 209 U.S. 123 (1908). The theory behind the principle is that when a state officer's official conduct violates the U.S. Constitution or a federal statute, he is acting without true authority, and his conduct is therefore not really "state conduct" for purposes of the 11th Amendment. See Chemerinsky Hbnk (5e), §7.5.1.

b. **Suits against official for money damages:** The Amendment also doesn't bar suits against a *state official* for *money damages*, as long as the damages are to be paid out of the official's own pocket. But where a suit would if successful lead to a state's being ordered to pay damages out of its own pocket, the suit is barred by the Amendment, even if the suit is nominally filed against the official rather than the state itself. Chemerinsky Hbnk (5e), §7.5.2.

c. **Suit for injunction against violation of state law:** The 11th Amendment *does* apply to bar injunctions prohibiting state officials from violating *state* (as opposed to federal) law. *Pennhurst State School Hosp. v. Halderman*, 465 U.S. 89 (1984).

d. **Suits by federal government:** The 11th Amendment does not bar suits *by the federal government* against a state.

e. **Suits against cities:** The Amendment does not bar suits against *cities*, or other political subdivisions of a state.

f. **State agencies and other entities:** The caselaw is unclear and inconsistent as to when the Amendment bars suits against state *agencies*, boards and other entities — such as state-owned universities — associated with state government.

g. **Suits by one state against another:** The Amendment does not bar suits by *one state against another* (as long as the plaintiff state is truly suing for itself rather than merely to protect private interests of individual citizens).

h. **Suits in state court:** The Amendment only applies in federal courts; it doesn't prevent a private individual from suing a state in *state court*, even to vindicate a federal right. (But, of course, the state court must have jurisdiction over the suit. Some state courts may not have jurisdiction because of the state's enabling statutes; also, some federal statutes that create rights provide for exclusive federal-court jurisdiction in proceedings to enforce those rights, in which case no state-court forum is available.)

    i. **Appellate jurisdiction:** Also, as long as the suit started in state court, nothing in the 11th Amendment prohibits the U.S. Supreme Court from using its *appellate jurisdiction* to review a state-court decision to see if it violates federal law. Chemerinsky Hbnk (5e), §7.4

i. **Waiver by state:** The protections of the 11th Amendment can be *waived* by a state — if the state consents to be sued in federal court, the 11th Amendment will no longer stand as a bar. Chemerinsky Hbnk (5e), §7.6.

j. **Suits under the post-Civil War Amendments:** If Congress passes a statute pursuant to its power to enforce the *post-Civil War Amendments* (13th, 14th and 15th), and that statute gives private citizens the right to sue a state in federal court, this statute will be enforced, and won't be deemed to violate the 11th Amendment.

5. **Congress' general power to allow suits against the states:** As just noted, where Congress is legislating pursuant to its special powers to enforce the post-Civil War amendments, it may abrogate the 11th Amendment and permit private citizens to sue the states in federal court. But outside this post-Civil War area, *Congress may not abrogate the 11th Amendment*, no matter how explicitly it tries to do so. This is the somewhat startling holding of *Seminole Tribe of Florida v. Florida*, 517 U.S. 44 (1996), a major case that significantly hampers Congress' ability to give private citizens the ability to sue states for violations of federal law.

    a. **Facts:** Congress passed a statute, the Indian Gaming Regulatory Act, to govern aspects of gambling operations run by Indian tribes. The IGRA provided that when a state allows non-Indian gambling, the state must also negotiate in good faith with any tribe located in the state to try to reach an agreement permitting the tribe to conduct comparable gambling operations. The statute also provided that if a tribe believed that the state was not negotiating in good faith, the tribe could sue the state in federal court for an order directing the state to negotiate in good faith.

    b. **Split:** The Court, by a 5-4 vote, held that this statute *violated the 11th Amendment*. The split was precisely the same as in *U.S. v. Lopez*, the case restricting Congress' Commerce Clause powers (see *supra*, p. 31).

    c. **Holding:** The majority opinion, by Chief Justice Rehnquist, held that "Even when the Constitution vests in Congress *complete law-making authority over a particular area*, . . . the Eleventh Amendment *restricts the judicial power under Article III*, and Article I cannot be used to circumvent the constitutional limitations placed upon federal jurisdiction." So even though Article I gives Congress full authority to "regulate commerce . . . with the Indian tribes," Congress cannot allow a tribe to sue a state in federal court.

        i. **Rationale:** The majority's rationale was that the 11th Amendment *embodies concepts of state sovereignty*. Furthermore, the principle of state sovereignty embodied in the 11th Amendment limits the Article III jurisdiction of the federal courts, and Congress cannot expand those limits just because it wants to.

        ii. **Suits based on Commerce Clause:** Even though *Seminole* itself involved congressional power based on the Indian Commerce Clause, the decision applies broadly to *all sources of congressional power other than the post-Civil War amendments*. For instance, it clearly applies to congressional action based on the *"regular" Commerce Clause*, a source that probably accounts for a majority of federal statutes enacted over the last 50 years.

    d. **Dissents:** There were two dissents, one by Stevens, the other by Souter (joined by Ginsburg and Breyer). Souter's dissent was the principal one; indeed, at 92 pages it was three times the length of Rehnquist's majority opinion.

        i. **Limited view of Amendment:** To Souter, all the drafters of the 11th Amendment ever meant to do, and all the Amendment had ever been interpreted as doing, was to prevent suits based *solely on diversity*, i.e. those brought by a state against a non-citizen of that state in circumstances under which no federal question was raised.

    ii. Destructive of ability to protect federal rights: The dissenters believed that the majority's view was not only wrong but ***highly destructive of federally-guaranteed rights***. As Stevens put it, the majority's holding ***"prevents Congress from providing a federal forum*** for a broad range of actions against States, from those sounding in **copyright** and **patent** law, to those concerning **bankruptcy**, **environmental law**, and the regulation of our vast national economy."

  e. Later illustration: A post-*Seminole* decision by the Supreme Court demonstrates the broad impact that *Seminole* is likely to have. In *Florida Prepaid Postsecondary Education Expense Board v. College Savings Bank*, 527 U.S. 627 (1999), the Court held that just as Congress may not abrogate the 11th Amendment when acting under authority of the *commerce* power (the point decided in *Seminole*), Congress may not do so when acting under its ***patent*** power. Therefore, Congress, no matter how explicitly it tries to do so, ***may not force the state to defend a private patent damage suit in federal court.***

  f. Broader significance: The greatest significance of *Seminole* and *Florida Prepaid* may turn out to be these cases' suggestion of a radically new — and restricted — view of federal power. These cases, taken together with *U.S. v. Lopez*'s limits on the Commerce power (*supra*, p. 31), *New York v. U.S.*'s resurrection of the Tenth Amendment (*supra*, p. 48), *Alden v. Maine*'s recognition of state immunity from state-court suits based on federal rights (*infra*, p. 749), and *Federal Maritime*'s prohibition on certain federal administrative proceedings involving state defendants (*infra*, p. 750), represent the view of a 5-Justice majority that federal power is ***far less extensive than had previously been thought***. As Prof. Tribe has said, "the Court's current dedication to a states' rights doctrine seems to be a rather free-floating cloud that can rain on almost any source of congressional power." *NY Times*, April 1, 1996, p. A1.

6. States' sovereign immunity from state-court suits based on federal rights: Just as *Seminole Tribe* says that Congress generally can't authorize federal-court suits against the States, so the doctrine of **sovereign immunity** generally prevents Congress from subjecting the states to private suits ***in their own courts, even where the right sued on is federal***. That is the startling result of a 1999 decision, ***Alden v. Maine***, 527 U.S. 706 (1999), decided three years after *Seminole* by the same 5-4 split as in *Seminole*.

  a. Facts of *Alden*: Congress had said that the Fair Labor Standards Act (FLSA), which governs overtime and other wage matters, applies to the states as employers, just as it does to private employers. Congress also said that a state's employees could bring FLSA suits against the state in the state's own courts. In *Alden*, workers employed by the state of Maine did just that, arguing in the Maine courts that they were entitled to certain extra pay for overtime.

  b. Struck down: But in an opinion by Justice Kennedy, the 5-member majority held that Congress had no constitutional authority to force the Maine courts to hear the workers' suit, ***even though that suit was based upon a federal right*** that (even the majority agreed) Congress had authority to confer upon the workers. For a state's immunity from private suits for money damages in the state's own courts was "a ***fun-***

damental aspect of the sovereignty which the states enjoyed before the ratification of the Constitution, and which they *retain today*."

    c. **Significance:**   *Alden* seems to mean that the states now have *full sovereign immunity from any private suit in the state's own courts seeking damages for the state's violation of federal law.* For instance, the states as employers are presumably immune to damage suits alleging that they committed *employment discrimination* (e.g., discrimination based on age or disability), and the states as market participants are apparently immune from state-court claims that they have violated federal laws governing commerce (e.g., *trademark* and *antitrust* laws). Coupled with the extensive federal-court 11th Amendment immunity recognized in *Seminole Tribe*, the states now seem to have a large zone in which, as a practical matter, they are completely insulated from congressional attempts to give private individuals a damages remedy for violations of federal rights.

  7. **Complaints before federal agencies:** The latest extension of the Court's tendency to limit federal-law-related actions against the states involves federal *administrative-agency* proceedings. In a 2002 decision, the Court held that the same principle of state sovereignty cited in *Alden* bars the federal government from *requiring that states defend* against private complaints in *proceedings brought before federal administrative agencies*. *Federal Maritime Comm. v. South Carolina State Ports Auth.*, 535 U.S. 743 (2002).

VII. POLITICAL QUESTIONS

  A. **Introduction:** The final aspect of justiciability is the requirement that the case not require decision of what is commonly called a *"political question."* The scope of the "political question" doctrine is even less well-defined than the other aspects of justiciability considered above. Also, the doctrine is less important today than it was in prior periods; in only a few cases since 1970 has the Court found an issue to be a non-justiciable political question.

    1. **Phrase a misnomer:** The phrase "political question" is something of a misnomer. The Court will not treat as a non-justiciable political question an issue which merely happens to *involve politics*, even if politically-related issues are at the very heart of the case. Rather, the political question doctrine seems to be a meshing of two sets of principles:

        a. **Separation of powers:** *Separation-of-powers* principles, by which, as a constitutional matter, the Court will not decide matters which it concludes are committed by the Constitution to other branches of government for decision; and

        b. **Prudential concerns:** various *"prudential"* considerations, because of which the Court concludes that it is unwise, even if not strictly unconstitutional, for it to decide the case.

    2. **General unifying principle:** The factors which lead a court to conclude that an issue is a political question, factors which are discussed in detail below, are not easily summarized into one overarching principle. Perhaps the most useful formulation is that proposed by Tribe; he asserts that in deciding whether an issue is a non-justiciable political question, the court is "determin[ing] whether constitutional provisions which litigants would have judges enforce do in fact *lend themselves to interpretation as guarantees of enforceable rights*." Tribe, p. 106. (But as Tribe himself concedes, the factors which the courts must

consider in making this determination are a diverse blend of constitutional and discretionary considerations. *Id.*)

B. *Baker v. Carr:* The modern Court's approach to political questions is set forth most notably in the well-known case of *Baker v. Carr*, 369 U.S. 186 (1962). That case, which held that the constitutionality of legislative apportionment schemes is not a political question, paved the way for the Court's "one person, one vote" ruling; therefore, the case is discussed more extensively in our treatment of reapportionment, *infra*, p. 754.

1. Factors: For now, what is significant is that the Court in *Baker* announced a series of *factors*, at least one of which (the Court asserted) *must be present* in order to make an issue a non-justiciable political question. Each of these factors, the *Baker* Court argued, relates in some way to the *separation of powers*. The Court listed the following factors:

a. Commitment to another branch: A "textually demonstrable constitutional *commitment of the issue* to a *coordinate political department*" (i.e., to Congress or to the President);

b. Lack of standards: A "lack of judicially discoverable and manageable *standards* for resolving" the issue;

c. Unsuitable policy determination: The "impossibility of deciding [the issue] without an initial *policy determination* of a kind clearly for non-judicial discretion";

d. Lack of respect for other branches: The "impossibility of a court's undertaking independent resolution without expressing *lack of the respect due co-ordinate branches of government*";

e. Political decision already made: An "unusual need for unquestioning adherence to a *political decision already made*"; and

f. Multiple pronouncements: The potential for "embarrassment from *multifarious pronouncements* by various departments on one question."

2. Most significant factors: Here, we will concern ourselves mainly with three of these factors: (1) the "commitment to other branches" factor; (2) the "lack of judicially discoverable and manageable standards" factor; and (3) the "need for a single pronouncement" factor. Additionally, we will consider the existence of a fourth factor not explicitly mentioned in *Baker*, the extent to which the issue raises a controversial question whose adjudication might lead to major, undesirable consequences. Finally, we give separate consideration to the reapportionment cases, which involve more than one of these factors.

C. The "commitment to other branches" strand: As *Baker v. Carr* suggested, the Court will regard as a non-justiciable political question any issue the determination of which is clearly committed by the Constitution to *another branch of government*. The cases decided under this strand have all involved decisions arguably committed to the President or Congress (not decisions arguably committed to the states).

1. Impeachment: A strong case can be made that the House of Representatives' decision whether to *impeach* the President or other federal officer, and the Senate's decision whether to convict, are *not judicially reviewable* because these decisions are committed to those bodies by the Constitution. If this view is accepted, the Court would not have jurisdiction even to determine whether the grounds upon which, say, the President was convicted fell within the constitutionally-defined category of "high Crimes and Misdemeanors." See *supra*, p. 143.

a. **Majority view:** Most commentators believe that impeachment decisions do indeed fall within the "committed to other branches" category, and are therefore non-justiciable political questions. One of the difficulties with a contrary view is that the legitimacy of Supreme Court review of an impeachment conviction might not be apparent to the nation. As one author has noted, if the Senate voted to convict, and the Supreme Court ordered reinstatement, "[o]ur military commanders would have to decide for themselves which President they were bound to obey, the reinstated one or his successor." Black, *Impeachment: A Handbook*, pp. 61-62 (quoted in L,K&C, p. 50).

b. **Senate has sole power to decide what constitutes a "trial":** The Court has never had to determine whether Congress' decision to impeach or convict a federal officer is judicially reviewable. But a recent case on a different aspect of impeachment law strongly indicates that most controversies relating to impeachment will be found to fall within the "committed to other branches" category and thus to be non-justiciable political questions. In *Nixon v. U.S.*, 506 U.S. 224 (1993), Walter Nixon, a federal judge whom the House had impeached and the Senate convicted based on bribery charges, challenged the ***procedures*** used by the Senate. The Senate ***delegated to a committee*** of senators the job of holding hearings on the accusations against Nixon. The committee then gave the full Senate a transcript of the proceedings, and the Senate voted by more than the required two-thirds majority to convict Nixon.

    i. **Argument:** Nixon argued that the Senate, by having a committee rather than the full Senate hear the evidence, violated the requirement of Article I, Section 3, Clause 6 that the Senate "try all impeachments."

    ii. **Held non-justiciable:** But the Supreme Court held that Nixon's argument presented a non-justiciable political question. The Court relied mainly on the plain text of the Senate Impeachment Clause, which provides that "the Senate shall have ***sole Power*** to try all Impeachments." The Court interpreted this reference to "sole Power," along with the history behind the provision, to mean that the Senate, nor the courts, should determine what procedures could validly constitute a "trial." (The Court also reasoned that a "lack of finality" problem dictated that the courts not hear Nixon's claim: "Opening the door of judicial review to the procedures used by the Senate in trying impeachments would 'expose the political life of the country to months, or perhaps years of chaos,'" especially if it were the President who was being impeached.)

2. **Amendment of Constitution:** The process by which ***constitutional amendments*** are adopted is probably also committed to Congress for final determination, and therefore presents a non-justiciable political question. Thus in *Coleman v. Miller*, 307 U.S. 433 (1939), four members of the Court, concurring, believed that only Congress could determine whether a particular state had ratified a constitutional amendment. (The case is discussed more extensively *infra*, p. 753, because of the Court's reliance on the "lack of judicially manageable standards" strand.)

3. ***Powell v. McCormack:*** The most famous case discussing the "commitment to other branches" strand was one in which the Court concluded that at most only a ***limited*** commitment of the decision-making authority in question to another branch (Congress) was

involved. In ***Powell v. McCormack***, 395 U.S. 486 (1969), Adam Clayton Powell, Jr., who had been elected to Congress from Harlem, successfully challenged the House's refusal to seat him.

    a. Facts: The House's refusal came after one of its committees found that Powell had dodged the process of the New York courts, had wrongfully diverted House funds, and had made false reports to a House committee. When Powell sued for a declaratory judgment that the refusal to seat him was unconstitutional, the House defended on the grounds that Article I, §5 (which provides that "[e]ach House shall be the Judge of the … Qualifications of its own Members") gave the House the sole right to determine what qualifications are necessary for membership. Powell, by contrast, argued that that clause merely gives the House the right to determine whether a person possesses the "standing qualifications" expressly set out in the Constitution (Article I, §2's age, citizenship and residence requirements).

    b. Victory for Powell: The Supreme Court agreed with Powell. Article I, §5 was at most a grant to Congress of the right to determine whether the three standing qualifications set forth in Article I, §2 were satisfied. Therefore, Congress had not been given the right to impose additional qualifications for membership.

        i. Standing qualifications: But, the Court noted, it was still possible that the decision about whether a member met the three standing qualifications *was* committed to Congress, so as to bar the federal courts from reviewing that determination. The Court noted that it was not deciding this issue, which remains undecided to this day. The issue did not arise in *Powell* itself because all parties conceded that Powell met these qualifications.

D. "Lack of judicially manageable standards" strand: A second major factor which may lead the Court to conclude that a case presents a non-justiciable question is that there is a "lack of *judicially discoverable* and *manageable standards* for resolving it."

    1. Guarantee of republican form of government: For instance, the Court has consistently held that claims based upon Article IV, §4 (which provides that "[t]he United States shall guarantee to every State in this Union a *Republican Form of Government*") are non-justiciable political questions.

        a. *Luther v. Borden:* The best-known case on this so-called *Guaranty Clause* is ***Luther v. Borden***, 7 How. 1 (1849). The case grew out of a rebellion by some dissatisfied Rhode Island citizens, and ultimately required the federal courts to decide which of two competing governments was the lawful government of the state. But the Supreme Court declined to make this determination, concluding that the case posed a political question. The decision seems to have been based in part upon the "lack of criteria by which a court could determine which form of government was republican" (as the decision was summarized in the later case of *Baker v. Carr, infra,* p. 754).

    2. War Powers disputes: If the federal courts were called upon to referee a dispute between the President and Congress concerning whether the President had *usurped Congress' war-making powers* by *committing our armed forces to combat* without congressional approval, the "lack of judicially manageable standards" strand might cause the case to be regarded as a political question.

E. The need for a unified voice (especially in foreign affairs):   The need for the federal government to speak with a ***single, unified voice*** has occasionally been a factor in the conclusion that an issue presents a political question. This is more likely to happen in the area of ***foreign affairs*** than in the domestic area.

    1. Treaty termination: For instance, the Court has refused to decide whether the President can ***terminate a treaty*** with Taiwan without congressional approval. *Goldwater v. Carter*, 444 U.S. 996 (1979). There was no majority in agreement on why the case was non-justiciable; the four-member plurality may have had the "single voice" rationale in mind when it remarked that the case posed a political question because "it involves the authority of the President in the conduct of our country's foreign relations."

F. Reapportionment -- The "one person, one vote" issue: Until 1962, the Court consistently refused to adjudicate claims concerning ***legislative apportionment***, on the grounds that they presented political questions. See, e.g., *Colegrove v. Green*, 328 U.S. 549 (1946), in which Justice Frankfurter's plurality opinion declared that "[i]t is hostile to a democratic system to involve the judiciary in the politics of the people. ... [C]ourts ought not to enter this political thicket."

    1. *Baker v. Carr:*   But in ***Baker v. Carr***, 369 U.S. 186 (1962), the Court reversed its course. The challenge in *Baker* was to the apportionment of the Tennessee Assembly, which had not been reapportioned in 60 years, despite a state constitutional requirement that representation be on the basis of population, and despite significant changes in population over the years. The Court concluded that the claim, which was that the malapportionment violated the ***Equal Protection Clause***, did ***not*** present a political question.

        a. Rationale: The Court reasoned that not all cases involving "politics" present non-justiciable "political questions." The Court listed a catalogue of factors, at least one of which, it asserted, had always been present in true political-question cases. (See *supra*, p. 750.) The equal protection claim here, the majority concluded, did not involve any of these factors. For instance, the issue had not been "textually ... commit[ted] by the Constitution to another branch of government"; nor were "judicially discoverable and manageable standards for resolving it" lacking.

    2. "One person, one vote" principle (*Reynolds v. Sims*):   The conclusion in *Baker* that apportionment claims do not necessarily present non-justiciable political questions opened the door for numerous challenges to the apportionment of state legislatures and federal congressional districts. In a series of decisions, the Court developed its famous, and simple, ***"one person, one vote"*** principle. The major case in this line was ***Reynolds v. Sims***, 377 U.S. 533 (1964).

        a. Facts: *Reynolds* was a challenge to the apportionment of the Alabama legislature. Therefore, it posed different problems from a case decided shortly before, *Wesberry v. Sanders*, 374 U.S. 1 (1964), a challenge to a state's apportionment of its ***federal congressional districts*** — in *Wesberry*, the Court had been able to dispose of the case by interpreting Article I, §2's requirement that representatives be chosen "by the People of the several States" as requiring that "as nearly as practicable one man's vote in a congressional election is to be worth as much as another's."

        b. Apportionment struck down: Nonetheless, the *Reynolds* Court struck down the Alabama apportionment (or rather, malapportionment) scheme. It did so upon an ***equal protection*** theory: the Equal Protection Clause "requires that the seats in ***both***

houses of a bicameral state legislature must be apportioned *on a population basis*. ... An individual's right to vote for state legislators is unconstitutionally impaired when its weight is in a *substantial fashion diluted* when compared with votes of citizens in other parts of the State."

    i. Rationale: The Court observed that equal protection generally requires "the uniform treatment of persons standing in the same relation to the governmental action questioned or challenged." Since "legislators represent people, not trees or acres," there was no apparent reason for making one person's vote worth more than another's in the election of those legislators.

    ii. Some deviations allowed: The Court in *Reynolds* did *not* require *strict mathematical equality*. "Some deviations" from the equal-population rule would be permissible, if they were directed towards the carrying out of a "rational state policy." But "neither history alone, nor economic or other sorts of group interests, are permissible factors. ... " Furthermore, even pursuit of a "clearly rational state policy" (e.g., "according some legislative representation to political subdivisions") by an apportionment scheme would *not* be valid if "population is submerged as the *controlling consideration.*."

  c. Disagreement: Three members of the Court disagreed with the majority's general approach in *Reynolds*.

    i. Harlan's dissent: Only Justice Harlan dissented from the result in *Reynolds*; he argued mainly that the framers of the Equal Protection Clause simply did not intend that Clause to be used to limit the power of the states to apportion their legislatures however they wished.

    ii. Stewart's concurrence: Justice Stewart (joined by Justice Clark) agreed that the Alabama scheme was "completely lacking in rationality." However, he disagreed with the majority's general approach. He did not think that the Equal Protection Clause barred a state's divergence from mathematical equality of votes if this was done for the purpose of providing "effective and balanced representation of all substantial interests." The only limitation imposed by that Clause, he believed, was that a plan "must be such as not to permit the *systematic frustration of the will of a majority* of the electorate of the State." That is, so long as a majority was not consistently blocked from electing a majority of the legislators, the scheme must merely be "rational." (For instance, Stewart believed that New York's scheme, reviewed in a companion case, met this standard even though it guaranteed at least one representative to each county, and gave fewer legislators to New York City than it would have been entitled to strictly on the basis of population; Stewart thought that this was a valid attempt to "protect against overcentralization of power.")

  d. Justiciability of "one person, one vote" rule: Observe that the existence of "judicially discoverable and manageable standards" for resolving apportionment questions was greatly aided by the Court's selection in *Reynolds* of the "one person, one vote" principle. For instance, had the Court accepted Justice Stewart's more limited rule that there must simply not be "systematic frustration of the will of a majority of the electorate," the Court might have been required to "canvass the actual workings of the floor leadership in the legislative branches, the mechanisms of party control not only over voters in the city government but also over elected representatives — in short, the details of the petty corruption and networks of personal influence that all too often constitute critical sources of power in municipal politics." 20 STAN. L. REV. 247 (quoted in Ely, p. 124). Thus it was "precisely because of considerations of administrability [that the Court] found itself with no perceived alternative but to move to a one person, one vote standard." Ely, p. 124.

3. **Other issues:** The companion cases to *Reynolds* settled some other issues, in addition to the basic "one person, one vote" principle. Most importantly, *Lucas v. Colorado General Assembly*, 377 U.S. 713 (1964) established that an apportionment scheme that violated the "one person, one vote" rule could not be saved by the fact that it had been ***approved by the voters of the state***. A "citizen's constitutional right can hardly be infringed simply because a majority of the people choose that it be." (Similarly, the fact that the state ***constitution*** apportions one of the two houses on a basis other than population will not make that apportionment valid.)

4. **Local government:** Subsequent cases applied the general "one person, one vote" rule to elections for ***local government*** bodies. After some initial confusion, the Court settled on the rule that the "one person, one vote" standard applies whenever persons are chosen by popular election to "perform ***governmental functions***," whether or not those governmental functions are ***"general"*** ones. Thus in *Hadley v. Junior College Dist.*, 397 U.S. 50 (1970), the case in which the Court articulated this rule, the Court required an attempt at equal-population apportionment for trustees of a junior college district, obviously not a body of general jurisdiction.

    a. **Special-purpose bodies:** However, the Court noted in *Hadley* that some bodies or officials may have "duties [that] are so far removed from normal governmental activities and [may] so disproportionately affect different groups that a popular election … might not be required." See *Ball v. James, supra*, p. 370, for an example of such a special-purpose body (a water district) not requiring application of the *Reynolds* principle.

5. **How much equality is required:** In cases following *Reynolds, supra*, the Court was required to decide ***how much*** deviation from strict mathematical equality is permissible. In doing so, it established a key distinction between ***congressional*** districting on the one hand, and districting for state and local governmental bodies on the other.

    a. **Congressional districting:** In ***congressional*** districting, the rule is that ***"as nearly as is practicable***, one man's vote in a congressional election is to be worth as much as another's." *Kirkpatrick v. Preisler*, 394 U.S. 526 (1969). States must make a "good-faith effort to achieve ***precise mathematical equality***." *Id.*

    b. **State and local apportionment:** By contrast, the Court has been willing to allow ***much greater deviation*** from mathematical equality in the apportionment of ***state legislatures*** or ***local governmental bodies***.

        i. ***"De minimus"* category:** First, the Court has established a ***"de minimus"*** category — deviations below a certain level ***need not be supported by any state objective at all***. This category covers ***"minor population variations,"*** and seems to include all deviations of ***less than 10%***.

        ii. **"Legitimate state considerations":** Second, even deviations above this roughly 10% threshold will not cause a state legislative or local governmental apportionment scheme to be invalidated, if the deviations are justified by ***"legitimate state considerations." Abate v. Mundt***, 403 U.S. 182 (1971). For instance, in *Mahan v. Howell*, 410 U.S. 315 (1973), the Court approved an apportionment of one house of the Virginia Legislature having a maximum variation of 16.4% from population equality; this deviation was justified by the state's policy of "maintaining the ***integrity of political subdivision lines***."

G. Reapportionment – partisan gerrymanders: The *Reynolds* "one person, one vote" formulation says nothing about ***how the district lines are to be drawn***; all that standard requires is that the districts end up with equal numbers of voters in each. But "one person, one vote" by itself leaves room for a maneuver which may have a dramatic ability to dilute some voters' strength: the ***gerrymander***. And as we'll see shortly below, gerrymanders enacted for ***partisan political purposes*** are ***non-justiciable***, as the result of the 2019 decision in ***Rucho v. Common Cause***, *infra*, p. 758.

1. **Gerrymander defined:** The gerrymander is a device by which the ***strength of a particular disfavored voting bloc*** is ***curtailed*** by restricting its members to carefully- and artificially-constructed districts. There are ***two quite different forms*** of gerrymandering, only one of which we'll be concerned with here in our discussion of justiciability.

   a. **Racial gerrymanders:** First, there are ***"racial gerrymanders,"*** in which the people drawing the district lines act with the predominant purpose of boosting or curtailing the voting strength of a ***particular racial group***. The Supreme Court has held that racial gerrymanders *are* justiciable, and they will often be struck down on equal protection grounds. See *supra*, p. 312, for our discussion of racial gerrymanders.

   b. **Partisan gerrymanders:** Second, there are ***"partisan gerrymanders,"*** in which district lines are drawn for the purpose of curtailing the voting strength of a ***particular political group***, typically members of a particular ***political party***. As we'll see shortly below, the Supreme Court has definitively held that suits attacking partisan gerrymanders are ***non-justiciable***.

2. **Illustration of a partisan gerrymander:** Here is a hypothetical, but fairly representative, example of how a partisan gerrymander for U.S. congressional districts might be enacted by the party that has control of a state legislature. The example assumes that, as is the case in most states, the boundary lines for congressional districts are ***drawn by the state legislature.***

   Example: Let's assume that in the year 2021 (just after the 2020 Census results have been released) the legislature of State X is controlled by Democrats, and that the state has 14 U.S. House of Representatives districts. Let's further assume that 50.1% of the state's registered voters are Democrats and 49.9% are Republicans. And let's also assume that during the most recent ten years since the prior (2010) redistricting, the district lines were drawn in a non-partisan and essentially random way, so that the state has usually elected seven Democrats and seven Republicans to Congress. Now, however, let's imagine that through some quirk of local politics the State X legislature has swung so completely in the Democrats' favor that the Democrats have the ability to cause the legislature to enact any districting plan the Democrats want, so long as the plan meets the requirement of mathematical equality (i.e., that all districts have virtually identical populations, in accordance with the Supreme Court's "one-person, one-vote" rule, described *supra*, p. 754.)

Now, when it's time in 2021 for the state legislature to redraw the congressional district boundaries to reflect the 2020 Census results, assume that the Democrats spring into action to enact whatever redistricting plan will maximize the number of seats in the State X congressional delegation held by Democrats. They start by hiring a consultant who uses a computer to draw thousands of semi-random alternative maps, many of which (1) create very oddly shaped districts, (2) ignore political subdivisions (e.g., by splitting a given city into multiple districts), and (3) ignore natural geographical features (e.g., by putting neighborhoods on opposite sides of a river into a single district while splitting a single neighborhood into two districts). From these thousands of possible plans, the Democrats choose the one that is likely to give them the highest possible number of congressional seats. The chosen plan does this by "*packing*" most Republican voters into four districts, in each of which Republicans are expected to win 75% of the votes; conversely, the plan engages in "*cracking*" the remaining 10 districts, i.e., spreading out the remaining Democratic and Republican voters so that Democrats will likely have a narrow but clear majority in these other districts. The Democrats use their majority in the state legislature to enact this chosen redistricting plan, over the fierce objection of the Republicans.

If voters in the next congressional election vote along party lines, the Democrats will end up with 10 of the 14 members of the state's congressional delegation, versus the seven seats that would likely be produced by a neutral plan given the nearly 50/50 split in the electorate. The Democratic redistricting plan, when put into law, is a classic "partisan gerrymander."

Note on "cracking" and "packing": Discussions of gerrymanders often use the terms "cracking" and "packing" to describe the main techniques that the gerrymanderers use to dilute the voting strength of the disfavored group (as I did in the above Example). As the Supreme Court explained in its 2019 decision on gerrymandering (the *Rucho* case, discussed *infra*):

> "A *"cracked"* district is one in which a [disfavored] party's supporters are *divided among multiple districts*, so that they *fall short of a majority in each*; a *"packed"* district is one in which [the disfavored] party's supporters are *highly concentrated*, so they *win that district by a large margin*, 'wasting' many votes that would improve their chances in others."

In our hypothetical Example above, the Democrats have "packed" most Republican voters into four districts where the Republicans will win 75% of the voters (thus wasting the 24.9% of the voters who are beyond the bare majority needed for victory in those districts), and have "cracked" the remaining Republican voters into 10 districts in each of which the Republicans will just fall short of a majority. This will create a congressional delegation of 10 Democrats and 4 Republicans, even though the state's voters are split virtually 50/50.

3. **Partisan gerrymanders held non-justiciable by a 5-4 vote (*Rucho*):** In a major 2019 decision, ***Rucho v. Common Cause***, 139 S.Ct. 2484 (2019), the Supreme Court held that partisan gerrymanders like the one in the above example are ***non-justiciable***. Consequently, no matter how severely (and intentionally) a gerrymandering scheme boosts the political power of one party at the expense of another, ***the federal courts may not hear a***

constitutional challenge to the scheme. In *Rucho*, the five conservative justices prevailed over the four liberal ones. The majority opinion was by Chief Justice Roberts.

    a. **The two gerrymanders at issue:** *Rucho* involved two gerrymanders (and two cases, joined only at the Supreme Court level), one from North Carolina that advantaged Republicans, and the other from Maryland that advantaged Democrats. In each instance, the gerrymandered plan was approved by a straight party-line vote of the legislature, with Republicans being in control of the North Carolina legislature and Democrats in control in Maryland.

    In each state, the controlling party made no secret of its intent to put through a plan that would maximize that party's control of the state's congressional delegation. And both plans were remarkably successful at this – each expanded the controlling party's dominance of the state's congressional delegation far beyond the proportion of votes that that party received in the congressional election following the plan's enactment.

    i. **North Carolina:** Thus in North Carolina, the Republican state legislator in charge of drafting that party's redistricting plan for the 2016 elections announced beforehand that whatever plan the party came up with would be drawn to give Republicans 10 of the state's 13 congressional districts, because "[I] d[o] not believe it's possible to draw a map with 11 Republicans and two Democrats." And the scheme worked exactly as intended: in 2016, Republican candidates won 10 of North Carolina's 13 congressional seats (77%), even though the party received only 53% of the statewide vote.[2]

    ii. **Maryland:** In Maryland, the Democratic party's 2012 redistricting plan was designed to bring one additional district under Democratic control, so that the Democrats would receive seven of the state congressional delegation's eight seats, versus the six or seven seats the party had controlled in prior elections. The plan did this by focusing on flipping the Sixth District from Republican to Democrat. Although the 2010 Census figures required moving only 10,000 residents out of the Sixth District (in order to comply with the one-person one-vote principle), the Democrats' plan moved about 360,000 voters out of the district (mostly Republicans) and another 350,000 voters in (mostly Democrats), in hopes of flipping the district from majority-Republican to majority-Democrat. The plan worked brilliantly: the Sixth District was indeed flipped to the Democrats, enabling the party to go on to win seven of the state's eight congressional seats in each of the four elections that followed, even though Democrats never got more than 65% of the statewide congressional vote.

4. **Nature of constitutional challenge:** The North Carolina plan was challenged as a violation of several federal constitutional grounds, including the ***Equal Protection Clause*** of the Fourteenth Amendment (for having devalued the votes of Democratic voters) and the ***First Amendment*** (for having infringed those voters' right to ***free speech*** and ***free association***). The Maryland plan was challenged, among other constitutional grounds, as a violation of Republicans' First Amendment rights. In each case, the federal district court hearing the case found the case to be justiciable, and the plan to be unconstitutional. Both

---

2. On this point, see Justice Kagan's dissent.

sets of defendants appealed, and the two cases were consolidated into a single proceeding in the Supreme Court.

5. **The majority opinion:**   Chief Justice Roberts' majority opinion was joined by the other four conservative members of the Court, Thomas, Alito, and the two recently-appointed Trump appointees, Gorsuch and Kavanaugh. Roberts came to a broad-sweeping conclusion: "We conclude that partisan gerrymandering claims *present political questions beyond the reach of the federal courts.*" Federal judges, he wrote "have *no license to reallocate political power between the two major political parties*, with no plausible grant of authority in the Constitution, and *no legal standards to limit and direct their decisions.*"

    a. **"Results that reasonably seem unjust":**   Roberts did not trivialize the dangers posed by extreme gerrymanders. He conceded that "excessive partisanship in districting leads to results that *reasonably seem unjust.*" But, he said, even though extreme gerrymandering is "incompatible with democratic principles," this did not mean that "the solution lies with the federal judiciary."

    b. **Roberts' view of the problem:**   In order for the federal courts to treat partisan gerrymandering claims as being justiciable, Roberts wrote, the Constitution required that they do so by applying standards that are "grounded in a *'limited and precise rationale'* " and that are *"clear, manageable, and politically neutral."* But since *some* degree of partisanship has always been regarded – even by the framers – as being acceptable in districting, the courts would have to *"provid[e] a standard for deciding how much partisan dominance is too much."* And, Roberts continued, such a standard would need to be "especially clear," one that can *"reliably differentiate unconstitutional from constitutional gerrymandering."*

    c. **No "clear, manageable and politically neutral" standards:**   But Roberts concluded that *no such standard could be found.* There are, he said, *"no legal standards discernible in the Constitution"* for making such judgments about how much partisan dominance is too much, let alone the "limited and precise standards" that would be *"clear, manageable and politically neutral"* as the Constitution required.

        i.   **Rejects claims sounding in "proportional representation":**   In explaining why this was so, Roberts began by asserting that partisan gerrymandering claims "invariably sound in a *desire for proportional representation."* That is, he said, plaintiffs "inevitably ask the courts to *make their own political judgment* about *how much representation* particular political parties *deserve* — based on the votes of their supporters — and to *rearrange the challenged districts to achieve that end."* But, Roberts continued, there are several intractable problems in trying to devise and implement a test for fairness.

        ii. **Competing visions of "fairness":**   First, he said, there are *multiple ways* even to plausibly *define "fairness."* "Fairness" might mean trying to achieve any one of the following *mutually-incompatible objectives*:

        [1] Fairness might mean *maximizing the number of competitive districts* "by undo[ing] packing and cracking so that supporters of the disadvantaged party have a better shot at electing their preferred candidates";

        [2] Fairness might mean *"yielding to the gravitational pull of proportionality"*

(by "engaging in cracking and packing, to ensure each party its 'appropriate' share of 'safe' seats"); or

[3] Fairness might mean "adher[ing] to *'traditional' districting criteria*" (by "maintaining political subdivisions, keeping communities of interest together, and protecting incumbents").

(1) No clear standards exist: Furthermore, Roberts said, there are *no "limited and precise standards* that are *clear, manageable, and politically neutral"* for choosing among these different definitions of fairness. Any choice of a definition would be an " 'unmoored determination' of the sort characteristic of a *political question beyond the competence of the federal courts. "*

iii. **"How much is too much?":** Even if courts *could* settle on a principled choice from among the above definitions of fairness, Roberts continued, they would still have trouble answering "the determinative question: *'How much is too much?' "* That is, there would be no principled way to say, "At what point does permissible partisanship become unconstitutional?" He gave the following example to illustrate the quandary:

"If a court ... focused on the respective *number of seats in the legislature*, it would have to *decide the ideal number of seats for each party* and determine at what point deviation from that balance went too far. If a *5-3 allocation* corresponds most closely to statewide vote totals, is a *6-2 allocation permissible*, given that legislatures have the authority to engage in a certain degree of partisan gerrymandering?"

d. **Rejection of standard based on "vote dilution that is likely to persist":** Roberts went on to consider – and reject – various legal standards proposed by the plaintiffs, the courts below and the dissent. He paid greatest attention to the test imposed by the district court in the North Carolina case, under which plaintiffs were required to show, in addition to the proposed plan's "predominant partisan intent," that the vote dilution created by the plan was " *'likely to persist'* to such a degree that the elected representative will *feel free to ignore the concerns of the supporters* of the minority party."

But, Roberts concluded, this test would not work, because it would invite courts to make findings "on matters as to which *neither judges nor anyone else can have any confidence."* That was so because the test would require judges to forecast not only "who would prevail in future political contests," but also "whether a prospective winner will have a *margin of victory sufficient to permit him to ignore the supporters* of his defeated opponent (whoever that may turn out to be)." In sum, he said, using the "is the dilution likely to persist?" standard would mean that "judges not only have to pick the winner – *they have to beat the point spread."*

e. **Other avenues of redress:** Roberts pointed out that even given the *Rucho* majority's stripping the federal courts of power to limit partisan gerrymandering, *other methods* might be available to constrain excessive partisanship in districting.

i. **Statutes or state-constitutional provisions:** For instance, states could enact *statutes or state-constitutional provisions* placing limits on partisan gerrymandering. Indeed, he said, a number of states had already done so; for instance, the Florida Constitution provides that "No apportionment plan or individual district shall be drawn with the *intent to favor or disfavor a political party* or an incumbent."

       ii. Redistricting commissions: Alternatively, Roberts noted, states are free to restrict partisanship in districting by "placing power to draw electoral districts in the hands of *independent commissions,"* as both Colorado and Michigan had recently done via state-constitutional amendments.[3]

6. The dissent in *Rucho*: Justice Kagan, joined by the Court's other three liberals (Ginsburg, Breyer and Sotomayor), *dissented* with what she described as *"deep sadness."*

   a. Abdication of responsibility: Kagan accused the majority of *abdicating its responsibility* to *remedy a major constitutional violation.* The partisan gerrymanders in *Rucho*, she said, "deprived citizens of the *most fundamental* of their constitutional rights: the rights to *participate equally in the political process*, to *join with others* to advance political beliefs, and to *choose their political representatives.*"

      i. "Not your grandfather's gerrymanders": She asserted that modern computer-assisted district-mapping techniques had made partisan gerrymanders *far more damaging to democracy* than they used to be. Mapmakers now "avail themselves of data sets providing wide-ranging information about even individual voters." And advances in computer technology now enable mapmakers to use this new information "with unprecedented efficiency and precision." She continued:

> "While bygone mapmakers may have drafted three or four alternative districting plans, today's mapmakers can *generate thousands of possibilities at the touch of a key* — and then choose the one giving their party maximum advantage (usually while still meeting traditional districting requirements). The effect is to make gerrymanders far more *effective and durable* than before, *insulating politicians against all but the most titanic shifts in the political tides. These are not your grandfather's — let alone the Framers' — gerrymanders."*

   b. Workable standards exist: Kagan asserted that extreme partisan gerrymandering violates both the Fourteenth Amendment's Equal Protection clause and the First Amendment. And she rejected the majority's conclusion that there were *no workable standards* for distinguishing between constitutional and unconstitutional partisan gerrymanders. She said that federal courts across the country – including but not limited to the two district courts whose decisions were under review in *Rucho* – had *"largely converged"* on a standard for adjudicating constitutional challenges to partisan gerrymandering schemes.

      i. The workable standard: This workable standard, she said, was the one applied by the district court in the North Carolina case. The standard has three steps:

---

3. But it's not clear that the present Court would find such independent-commission schemes valid under the federal Constitution. In *Arizona State Legislature v. Arizona Independent Redistricting Commission*, 135 S.Ct. 2652 (2015), discussed *supra*, p. 315, Roberts was one of four dissenters who believed that a state constitutional amendment in Arizona giving redistricting power to just such an independent commission violated the federal constitution's "Elections Clause." In the Arizona case, Justice Kennedy supplied the fifth vote to uphold the independent-commission structure. But since then, Kennedy has been replaced by the much more conservative Kavanaugh. And Justice Ginsburg has died, replaced by a conservative, Justice Amy Coney Barrett. Therefore, if an Elections Clause attack on a state's use of an independent redistricting commission were to come before the present Court, it seems likely that Kavanaugh and Barrett would join with the four conservatives who dissented in the Arizona case, thereby enabling the attack to succeed. So it's far from clear that the use of bipartisan commissions to carry out redistricting functions will prove constitutionally viable, despite Roberts' suggestion that the states are free to take this route.

[1] **Purpose to dilute:** First, the plaintiffs who are challenging a districting plan must prove that state officials' *"predominant purpose"* in drawing a district's lines was to *"entrench [their party] in power"* by *diluting the votes of citizens favoring its rival.*

[2] **Effect of dilution:** Second, the plaintiffs must "establish that the lines drawn in fact *have the intended effect* by *"substantially"* diluting* their votes."

[3] **State's justification:** Third, if the plaintiffs make these two showings, then "the State must *come up with a legitimate, non-partisan justification* to save its map."

ii. **Standard would reject only "extreme outliers":** Kagan rejected the majority's argument that there were no "discernible and manageable" standards available for deciding the key issues, including the issue of "how much [partisan gerrymandering] is too much?" She approved of the method used by the district court in the North Carolina case (and some other federal trial courts) to handle this issue, a method she characterized as the *"extreme outlier approach."* She described this approach, and its merits, as consisting of the following elements:

[1] **Invalidates only "the most extreme" gerrymanders:** The approach invalidates "only the *most extreme* partisan gerrymanders."

[2] **Uses state's own criteria of "fairness":** The approach *"does not use any judge-made conception* of *electoral fairness* — either proportional representation or any other[.]" Instead, "it takes as its baseline a *State's own criteria of fairness, apart from partisan gain."*

[3] **Uses state's own districting criteria:** In terms of mechanics, the approach takes as a given the state's *"physical and political geography,"* as well as *whatever the state says are its districting criteria* "except for partisan gain."

[4] **Generates many sample maps:** The approach then uses *"advanced computing technology"* to *"randomly generate a large collection* of districting plans"; each of these plans "incorporate[s] the state's *physical and political geography* and meet[s] [the state's] declared districting criteria, *except for* partisan gain."

[5] **Determines the outcome of each sample map:** Next, the approach, for each of the randomly-generated maps, "uses *actual precinct-level votes from past elections* to *determine a partisan outcome* (i.e., the number of Democratic and Republican seats that map produces)."

[6] **Lines the maps up on a continuum:** The approach then *"line[s] up those maps on a continuum* — the most favorable to Republicans on one end, the most favorable to Democrats on the other." And the *"median outcome"* — the "outcome smack dab in the center [ ] in a world with no partisan manipulation" — is identified.

[7] **Maps that are far out on the tail:** Finally comes the part of the approach that permits the court to see *where the state's actual plan fits* on this partisan-outcome continuum: "The *further out on the tail, the more extreme the partisan*

distortion and the ***more significant the vote dilution.***"

[8] **No standard for "excessively partisan"**: Kagan's description of her preferred method for determining how much partisanship is too much ended here. She did not explain ***how far*** "out on the tail" of the randomly-generated maps the state's actual map would have to be in order to be considered excessively partisan and thus unconstitutional. But she agreed with the conclusion of the district court in the North Carolina case who used this "extreme outlier" approach: the state's plan was so far out on the tail that it clearly had an excessively partisan effect.

c. **Application of Kagan's test to North Carolina plan:** Kagan then explained, approvingly and in detail, how the above multi-step approach was applied by the North Carolina trial court to the districting plan under challenge:

i. **A "boatload of plans":** The North Carolina plaintiffs had "offered a ***boatload of alternative districting plans,***" all of which showed that the state's actual plan was ***"an out-out-out-outlier."***

ii. **More extreme than all of the 3,000 plans:** For example, Kagan said, one of the plaintiffs' experts produced ***3,000*** computer-generated ***maps***, done by means of the above method and by use of the same districting criteria that the North Carolina Republicans had used except that the expert's plans didn't seek "partisan advantage." It turned out that the state's actual plan was more extreme than ***every single one*** of these 3,000 maps; each of the 3,000 "would have produced ***at least one more Democratic House Member*** than the State's actual map," and 77% of the maps would have produced three or four more Democratic members.

iii. **Court intervenes only in "worst partisan gerrymanders":** In sum, Kagan said, she approved the methodology used by, and the findings and conclusion made by, the North Carolina trial court (as well as those used by the Maryland trial court). The two courts had made findings that were "evidence-based, data-based, statistics-based." And both courts properly reached the inevitable conclusion that "[b]y substantially diluting the votes of citizens favoring their rivals, the politicians of one party had ***succeeded in entrenching themselves in office.***" The two trial courts had appropriately "set the bar high, so that courts could intervene ***in the worst partisan gerrymanders, but no others.***" And they had correctly concluded, she said, that the two districting plans were ***"constitutionally appalling"*** and ***"inordinately partisan."***

d. **Practices "imperil our system of government":** Kagan concluded by saying that "Of all times to abandon the Court's duty to declare the law, this was not the one." The practices in the two states ***"imperil our system of government."*** The Court's role, she said, was to "defend [the] foundations" of that system of government; and of those foundations, "None is more important than ***free and fair elections.***"

7. **Significance of case:** *Rucho* establishes a very clear, bright-line rule: Constitutional challenges to partisan gerrymanders are ***simply not justiciable***, and therefore ***cannot be heard by the federal courts.*** No matter how severely a gerrymander ***dilutes the effective voting power*** of members of a particular party, and no matter how clear it is that the party whose members have sponsored the plan in the state legislature acted with the ***primary***

intent of bringing about that dilution, there is *no possible federal-court remedy* available to anyone disadvantaged by the gerrymander.

Quiz Yourself on

JUSTICIABILITY (ENTIRE CHAPTER)

107. The President, in an attempt to restore democracy in Haiti, dispatched American troops to that island without a congressional declaration of war. The troops have now remained there for 60 days, still without a congressional declaration. Their expenses have been paid for out of the general Defense Department budget, appropriated by Congress before the troops were sent and without the expectation that they would be sent. Paul, a U.S. citizen and taxpayer, has sued the President seeking an injunction requiring the President to withdraw the troops. The substance of Paul's suit is that only Congress has the power to declare war, and that the President's action amounts to an illegal declaration of war. Paul further asserts that his federal tax dollars are being unconstitutionally spent to support this illegal action.

    (a) If you are the President's lawyer, what is the first defense you should assert? _____

    (b) Will this defense prevail? _____

108. Same basic facts as above question. Now, however, assume that Paul asserts that he has standing to pursue his claim in federal court, because he is a citizen of the United States, and his right to have his government not behave in an unconstitutional manner has been abridged. Is Paul correct? _____

109. A federal statute places restrictions on the extent to which private companies may be permitted by the U.S. government to engage in logging in national forests. Penzel, a private individual, sues the U.S. Secretary of the Interior. His suit contends that the Secretary has administered regulations on logging in a way that contravenes the statute. The suit contends that the effect will be to allow more logging in the forests than permitted by statute. Penzel asserts that he uses a particular national forest for a one-week hike twice per year, and that the unauthorized logging affects a part of the forest that he expects to hike in during the next year. At least four million hikers each year will cross through parts of federal forests that are likely to have been affected by the allegedly excessive logging. The Secretary asserts that Penzel lacks standing to make this claim. Does Penzel have standing? _____

110. Same facts as prior question. Now, however, assume that the plaintiff is Friends of the National Forests, Inc. (FNF), a non-profit corporation whose members are users and lovers of the national forests. No individual plaintiffs are named. Does FNF have standing to pursue the suit? _____

111. George Brensteiner was the owner of the New York Strikers of the National Soccer League. Brensteiner's existing stadium was about to be demolished, and he needed to pick a new site for a stadium that he would build. After some preliminary investigation, Brensteiner announced that there were three "finalist sites," of which one was Yonkers, New York. Brensteiner applied for clearances from the federal Environmental Protection Agency (EPA) for all three sites. He received quick clearances for the other two. As to Yonkers, the local EPA administrator covering Yonkers determined that the proposed stadium would be on a protected wetland, and that the stadium could not be built unless Brensteiner first filed an Environmental Impact Statement (EIS) showing that the wetlands would not be damaged. Brensteiner then announced, "Because of the expense of preparing an EIS for the Yonkers site, I have selected one of the other sites as the winner, namely, Rutherford, New Jersey." Brensteiner acquired land in Rutherford, and quickly completed about 10% of the construction. At that moment, Steve, a Yonkers resident, brought suit against the EPA. Steve's suit argued that the EPA's requirement of an EIS for the Yonkers site was in violation of federal statutes, and that the effect of this violation was to deprive him, Steve, of easy access to a soccer stadium (in Yonkers) in which to view Strikers games. Steve's suit asked for a declaratory judgment that an EIS was not required for the Yonkers site. The EPA has defended on the grounds that Steve lacks standing. Is the EPA's contention correct? _____

112. Fred, who is black, is a police officer on the force of the town of Suburbia. Suburbia's population is 30% black, but Fred is the only black out of 15 officers on the force. Fred has sued the department, arguing that the department's failure to hire more black patrol officers is intentional, and constitutes a violation of the Equal Protection Clause. Fred asserts that this failure to hire additional black officers harms him, by making him racially isolated on the force and leading to a department that is generally insensitive to the concerns of the minority community, thus making Fred's own working conditions less attractive. Does Fred have standing to bring this suit? _____

113. A local school district allows non-profit community groups to use classrooms at the district's public high school at night. The Old Christians Association (OCA), a group of senior citizens who want to pray together, applied for a room. The school district turned them down on the grounds that to allow them to use the room would constitute an unconstitutional establishment of religion. The OCA began a suit in federal district court against the school board, asserting that the denial of a room violated their free exercise rights. After the suit was begun, the school board issued a statement reversing its policy against allowing religious groups to use classrooms, and granted the OCA's permit request. The OCA would like to continue with the suit, so that they may obtain a judicial opinion in their favor that can be cited as precedent in other school districts.

 (a) What defense should the school board defendant raise? _____

 (b) Will this defense succeed? _____

114. Pintard is a 52-year-old trooper in the police department of the State of New Spain, and is a resident of that state. New Spain has fired him because, in the department's judgment, no one over the age of 50 is physically fit enough to carry out the duties of state trooper. A federal statute, the Federal Age Discrimination Act, applies to all employees and forbids firing on account of age. Pintard has sued the state of New Spain for damages. (He does not want to be reinstated, because he has found a new job.)

 (a) What defense should the state raise? _____

 (b) Will this defense succeed? _____

115. The state of Caledonia was running short of funds, due to a budget crisis. To save money, the Governor ordered that only one copy be purchased of any personal-computer software package needed by the state government, and that staff members make copies. A staffer made 2,000 copies of the "PC-Word" word-processing package (published by PC Word Corp., a Caledonia company), and distributed these to each state office, where they were used. The retail value of each copy of PC Word is $295. PC Word Corp. has sued the state in federal court for the district of Caledonia, alleging that the state has violated the federal copyright act and seeking money damages ($295 x 2,000). Assume that the federal copyright act expressly allows a state to be sued in federal court (whether by its own citizen or by a citizen of another state).

 (a) What defense should Caledonia raise? _____

 (b) Will this defense succeed? _____

116. Jose won a U.S. congressional seat from a district located in New York City, in a close race against Martin. The House routinely determined that Jose met the constitutional requirements to be seated (that he was at least 25 years old, a U.S. citizen, and a resident of the state from which he had been elected). Martin then brought a federal district court suit against the House of Representatives and Jose, seeking to have Jose ruled unqualified to sit in the House. The essence of Martin's suit was that Jose really "inhabits" (as that term is used in Art. I, §2, second sentence) not the state of New York but rather, the State of Pennsylvania. Martin has come forward with evidence from voting records, state income tax filings, and other documents strongly suggesting that Jose spends the vast bulk of his time in, and considers himself a resident of, Pennsylvania.

(a) What defense should Jose raise to these proceedings? _____

(b) Will this defense succeed? _____

117. In 2021, Republicans had narrow control of the State of Acme legislature and wanted to use that control to enact – against the will of the legislature's Democratic minority – a redistricting plan for the state to use in the upcoming 2022 elections for the state's 10 U.S. House seats. In the prior (2020) elections for the House seats, Republican candidates got 50.1% of the statewide votes and Democrats the remaining 49.1%. Experts now expect the same breakdown in the 2022 races.

To choose their redistricting plan, the Republicans in the legislature have just used a computer to test 10,000 randomly-generated statewide plans before picking the single one that they think gives them the chance to win the most congressional seats in the next election. The plan they have selected (the "Plan") accomplishes this by (1) "packing" as many likely-Democratic voters as possible into two bizarrely-shaped districts that will each probably vote 96% for the Democratic candidate and 4% for the Republican one; and (2) "cracking" the remaining likely-Democratic voters into eight equally bizarrely-shaped districts, in each of which the vote will probably be about 51% for the Republican candidate and 49% for the Democratic one. Thus if all goes as intended, the Republicans will capture eight of the ten seats while getting slightly more than 50% of the statewide vote.

You are counsel to a group of Democratic voters who want you to bring a federal-court suit on their behalf seeking an injunction against the use of the Plan for the 2022 congressional elections. Your potential clients have convinced you that the Plan, by packing and cracking Democratic voters, has grossly diluted the effective voting power of Democratic voters, compared with the voting power of Republicans. Is there a federal-constitutional claim that you can assert on these voters' behalf that will likely persuade the court to issue an injunction against the Plan? (And if there is, then for extra credit, on what constitutional provision should the claim be based?) _____

Answers

107. (a) That Paul lacks standing.

(b) Yes. As a general matter, federal taxpayers do not have standing to assert that taxpayers' funds in general are being improperly spent. There is an extremely narrow exception if plaintiff is able to show: (1) that the federal action complained of is an exercise of Congress' power under the Taxing and Spending Clause; and (2) that the challenged action violates some specific constitutional limitation imposed on the taxing and spending power. *Flast v. Cohen.* It is highly unlikely that Paul can satisfy either of these requirements for the exception. The President's dispatch of troops presumably relies upon his Commander in Chief powers, and certainly does not rely upon Congress' taxing and spending power. Furthermore, the requirement that only Congress may declare war is not a specific constitutional limitation on the taxing and spending power, merely an unrelated constitutional limit. Therefore, the general rule that there is no taxpayer standing would apply.

108. **No.** The Supreme Court has never been willing to recognize standing on the part of individuals *as citizens* to object to unlawful or unconstitutional conduct. This refusal is based on the view that one citizen's interest in lawful government is no different from that of any other citizen, and that an individual litigant relying upon citizenship has not shown the *"individualized"* injury-in-fact required for standing. See, e.g., *Schlesinger v. Reservists to Stop the War.*

109. **Yes, probably.** A federal-court plaintiff must show some concrete, *"individuated,"* "injury in fact." But this harm need *not* be *economic* in nature; harms to a person's esthetic enjoyment of nature, for example, will suffice. See, e.g., *Sierra Club v. Morton* (giving people who use national forests standing to protest construction of recreation area in the national forest). The threatened harm must be "actual or imminent." Since Penzel asserts that he will walk within one of the affected areas within the next year, the "imminence" requirement is probably satisfied. The fact that there are a large number of people suffering or likely to suffer the same harm as alleged by the plaintiff does not by itself remove standing from the plaintiff.

110. **Yes.** An association or organization has standing not only where its own interests are at stake, but in some cases where it is suing solely as a *representative* of its members. An association has standing to sue on behalf of its members if three conditions are met: (1) its members would otherwise have standing to sue *in their own right*; (2) the interests the association seeks to protect are *germane* to the organization's *purpose*; and (3) neither the claim asserted nor the relief requested requires the participation of *individual members* in the lawsuit. *Hunt v. Washington Apple Advertising Comm.* Here, all three of these requirements seem to be met: the prior question illustrates that individual forest-lovers would have standing; protection of the forests certainly is the core purpose of the organization; and there seems to be no reason why individuals rather than the organization need to participate in the lawsuit.

111. **Yes, probably.** One of the requirements for standing is that the challenged action must be the *"cause-in-fact"* of the injury. A sub-aspect of the "cause in fact" requirement is that the litigant must show that the relief being sought, if granted, has a reasonable likelihood of *redressing* the injury. The problem here is that even if the EPA was completely wrong in the first instance, it is far from clear that a victory by the plaintiff will result in the stadium being built in Yonkers rather than Rutherford. The ultimate decision is up to Brensteiner. Since Brensteiner has already bought the property in Rutherford and commenced construction, it is very unlikely that a declaratory judgment that the EPA should not have required an EIS for Yonkers will cause Brensteiner to stop construction and start it instead in Yonkers. Therefore, even though the other requirements of standing are met (Steve's loss of the ability to watch Strikers games near his house is certainly an "injury-in-fact" that is sufficiently concrete, individuated and imminent), the fact that victory in the suit will not redress the harm is fatal to Steve's standing. See, e.g., *Simon v. Eastern Ky. Welfare Rights Organization* (where IRS rules reduced the amount of free medical care that hospitals must donate to the poor in order to get tax breaks, a suit by poor people attacking those rules does not have standing, because the hospitals might not give the free medical care even if the rules were struck down).

112. **No, probably.** As a general rule, a litigant may normally not assert the constitutional rights of *third persons not now before the court*. This is the rule of constitutional *"jus tertii."* Fred may have been injured "in fact" by the absence of other blacks on the force. But the Equal Protection Clause protects only those applicants who would have been hired had there not been intentional discrimination. Since Fred was not part of this group, the fact that he may have suffered some incidental injury is not enough to give him

standing — he must assert that the challenged governmental action violates *his* rights, not the rights of some other person not now before the court. (There are some important exceptions to the rule against third-party standing, such as where there is some legal restriction preventing the third party from exercising his own constitutional rights. But here, black applicants whom the department intentionally declined to hire because of their race clearly could bring their own suit, so neither this nor any of the other exceptions to the rule against third-party standing applies.)

113. **(a) That the action is now moot.** A case is moot if it raised a justiciable controversy at the time the complaint was filed, but *events occurring after the filing* have deprived the litigant of an ongoing stake in the controversy.

(b) Yes. Where the intervening event is the defendant's *voluntary* cessation of the conduct complained of, this may or may not be enough to render the case moot. If the facts show that the conduct claimed to be illegal is *very unlikely* to recur, then the voluntary cessation usually *is* enough to make the case moot. That is probably what the court would find to be the situation here. Therefore, the OCA's desire to obtain a favorable decision that it may use as precedent elsewhere will not be enough to give it an ongoing stake in the controversy, and the action will be dismissed.

114. **(a) The Eleventh Amendment.** The Eleventh Amendment excludes from the federal judicial power any suit "against any one of the States by Citizens of another State or by Citizens or Subjects of any Foreign State."

(b) Yes. Although on its face the Eleventh Amendment does not seem to prohibit federal-court suits against a state by a citizen of that state, the amendment has been interpreted to ban these suits as well as those by a citizen of one state against another state. See *Hans v. Louisiana*. The Eleventh Amendment applies only to suits for damages (as opposed to suits for injunctions), but the facts make it clear that money damage relief is what is sought here. Therefore, the Eleventh Amendment defense will be successful.

115. **(a) The Eleventh Amendment.**

(b) Yes. *Seminole Tribe v. Florida* holds that except with respect to suits brought under federal statutes supported by Congress' power to enforce the post-Civil War Amendments, Congress cannot remove the state immunity provided by the Eleventh Amendment. Therefore, even though Congress has clearly said that a state may be sued for damages for violating the copyright act, this statement of congressional intent is without effect, and the Eleventh Amendment applies to bar the suit. (But PC Word Corp. could get an *injunction* against the governor prohibiting further violations, since the Eleventh Amendment does not apply to injunction suits against state officials; see *Ex parte Young*.)

116. **(a) That the issue posed here is a non-justiciable political question.**

(b) Yes, probably. The Court will regard as a non-justiciable political question any issue whose determination is committed by the Constitution to *another branch* of government (i.e., the Executive or the Legislative). There is an excellent chance that the Court will conclude that the decision about whether a person elected to Congress meets the three standing requirements is committed by the Constitution to the House itself. The Court would point to Art. I, §5, which provides that "each House shall be the Judge of the Elections, Returns and Qualifications of its own members. ... " In *Powell v. McCormack*, the Court held that the issue of whether the House could refuse to seat a Congressman who met the three standing requirements but who had, in the House's opinion, committed other infractions, was *not* committed by the Constitution to the House, and could be heard by the Court. But it seems probable that a suit involving the narrow issue of whether a person met all of the three requirements expressly listed in Art. I, §2 is committed to the House and is thus non-justiciable (though the Court has never explicitly decided that question).

117. **No, because any such claim would be non-justiciable.** In the major case of *Rucho v. Common Cause*, 588 U.S. __ (2019), the Supreme Court held by 5-4 that ***partisan-gerrymander claims,*** such as the one proposed in this question, are ***always non-justiciable***. Consequently, no matter how severely a gerrymandering scheme boosts the political power of one party at the expense of another – and no matter how clear it is that this was the sole intended effect of the gerrymander – the federal courts may not hear a constitutional challenge to the scheme. So there's no claim you can bring on behalf of the Democratic voters that the federal court can even entertain. (But if the plan were shown to have used voters' *race, religion* or *ethnicity* as a "predominant factor" in the drawing district lines – as opposed to voters' political-party membership, used in the present fact pattern – then a suit alleging an Equal Protection violation would not only be justiciable but would trigger strict scrutiny, and probably prevail. See *Miller v. Johnson*, 515 U.S. 900 (1995).)

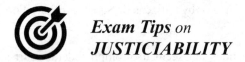

Exam Tips on
JUSTICIABILITY

Justiciability questions are pervasive and often hidden. Typically, your fact pattern will ***not*** contain the key words "standing," "ripe," "moot," "abstain," "political question," etc. — it will be up to you to spot these issues. Worse, these issues can be hidden in absolutely ***any type*** of fact pattern, so you can't let your guard down for a moment. Here are some specifics to watch for:

☛ Here's a brief checklist of justiciability issues:

    (1) ***advisory opinions;***

    (2) ***standing;***

    (3) ***mootness;***

    (4) ***ripeness;***

    (5) ***11th Amendment's*** ban on certain ***suits against the states;***

    (6) ***abstention;*** and

    (7) ***political questions***.

☛ "Advisory opinion" problems usually arise on exams where a ***state court*** issues an advisory opinion (as allowed by the procedures of most states), and the loser seeks review in the U.S. Supreme Court. Typically, you'll say that even if the state court advisory opinion is based on federal law, the Supreme Court cannot hear the issue because there is no true "case or controversy" as required by Article III.

☛ The overwhelmingly most important aspect of justiciability on exams is ***"standing."*** For ***every claim*** asserted anywhere on your exam, ask yourself, "Has P suffered, or is she about to suffer, a ***concrete, individualized harm***, that would be ***redressed*** by a favorable result in the lawsuit?" Unless the answer is "yes," there's probably no standing.

☞ Here's a checklist for standing, with the five individual elements broken out::

    ☞ P must have suffered an *"injury-in-fact,"* or be *likely* to suffer one reasonably *soon*;

    ☞ P's harm must be *concrete*, not abstract;

    ☞ P's harm must be *"individuated,"* i.e., not the same as that suffered by every other citizen or taxpayer;

    ☞ The action that P is complaining about must have been the *"but for" cause* of P's harm; and

    ☞ A favorable decision in the suit must be likely to *redress* the injury to P.

☞ One common fact pattern: P has a contract with the government, and some statute or rule would prevent (or dissuade) the government from honoring the contract. Here, there's usually standing because P is likely to suffer an "injury in fact" from losing the benefit of the contract. (*Example:* P has a contract to build a school for state X; a federal statute would withdraw funds that X was expecting to receive and pay over to P. In this situation, P has standing.)

☞ Remember that P need not have already suffered the harm. But if not, the threatened harm needs to be pretty *imminent* and pretty likely — some small chance of harm at some indefinite future time won't suffice. (*Example:* A first-year law student doesn't have standing to challenge a state's Continuing Legal Education requirement, because that requirement won't apply to her for several years.)

    ☞ Be on the lookout for a fact pattern where the plaintiff is contending that the *government* is likely to take some adverse action against him in the future. If the government's procedures are shrouded in *secrecy*, it will be difficult for the plaintiff to prove the *requisite likelihood* that the government will really take the feared action soon.

    Example: P has email contacts with two foreign terror suspects, X and Y, and is afraid that the National Security Agency will intercept these emails under a statute letting the agency do surveillance on terror-related emails. If P can't show how the NSA chooses its surveillance targets and thus whether X and Y have been targeted, P won't have standing to challenge the constitutionality of the surveillance. (Cite to *Clapper v. Amnesty Int'l.*)

☞ An *organization* will generally be allowed to sue *on behalf of its members*, if the members would individually have standing, and if the suit is *related* to the organization's *purposes*. Most organization-based suits you'll see on an exam will *satisfy* these conditions.

☞ If P is asserting rights as a *federal "taxpayer"* or as a *"citizen,"* and P is not part of the transaction in question, probably P does *not* have standing. Three special cases:

☞ If P is a *state* taxpayer challenging a state expenditure, then probably all that's required for standing is that there be a "direct expenditure of funds" by the state. Normally, this will be satisfied in your fact pattern.

☞ If P is a federal taxpayer who is challenging the *tax itself*, which P would have to pay unless the suit succeeds, P has standing.

☞ If P is a federal taxpayer or citizen challenging a federal expenditure that *directly violates some constitutional guarantee*, P may have standing. Probably, this exception only applies to federal expenditures that violate the First Amendment's *Establishment Clause* (e.g., the federal government pays money to private schools to be used in furthering their religious message).

☞ Regardless of whether P has standing on her own, P will *not* usually be allowed to assert the rights of *third persons* not then before the court. You can refer to this as the rule against *"jus tertii"* to sound erudite. There are three important exceptions:

☞ In free-expression cases, litigants get to use the First Amendment *overbreadth* doctrine. This lets P say, in effect, "This statute blocks expressive conduct of mine that may constitutionally be proscribed, but it also could be interpreted to block expressive conduct or speech on the part of others not present, for whom it would violate their free speech rights."

☞ The litigant can assert the third party's rights if these rights would be impaired, and it's legally or practically *difficult* for the third party to be present in the suit. (*Example:* Vendors are often permitted to assert the rights of their customers, who would each individually have too little at stake to sue.)

☞ Associations get to assert their members' rights, as noted above.

☛ You can spot a *mootness* problem by the fact that P "doesn't really seem to have a problem anymore." (*Example:* P has been kept out of a public university by an allegedly discriminatory policy; if the university then allows P to enroll, the case has become moot.)

☞ Before you conclude that P doesn't really have a problem anymore, look for *"collateral consequences."* Most common: the litigant (he can either be P or D) has been *convicted*, then paroled or discharged — there will still be collateral consequences to him from having a conviction on the books (e.g., job or voting problems), so the case is not moot.

☞ Look for issues that are "capable of *repetition*, yet evading review." This happens where P is one of a series of similarly-situated people, each of whom would face the same problem that would always turn out to be moot. Classic illustration: P is a pregnant woman seeking to overturn restrictions on abortion; she's no longer pregnant by the time the suit gets heard, but all other pregnant women similarly situated would have the same problem, so a court will hear the case now. Another illustration: a political group is prevented from doing something until "after the election"; the election is now over, but other political groups, or this very group, would be likely to face the same mootness problem in a future context.

☛ You can spot a *ripeness* problem by looking for a situation that's *"too early"* or *"not con-*

crete enough."

☞ Classic illustration of ripeness: there's a criminal statute on the books that P wants to violate or has violated, but there's very little risk that the statute will in fact be enforced against P. (In this scenario, P is generally seeking a declaratory judgment that the statute is unconstitutional.) This type of problem is especially acute where P *hasn't committed* the violation yet, and we're not sure that he will. (*Example:* A statute prevents people from distributing literature on private property, including shopping centers. P says he wants to do this kind of distribution, but hasn't done it yet, and it's not even clear that the owner will object or that the police will arrest. P's case is probably unripe.)

☞ Another type of scenario: the risk is too *abstract*. (*Example:* A state keeps a secret file on citizens; P, one of the monitored citizens, claims that his First Amendment rights are being "chilled." The Court will probably hold that any chilling problem is too speculative and abstract, and the case unripe, unless P can show what activity he is being dissuaded from engaging in.)

☛ Whenever a suit is brought in federal court by a *private citizen* against a *state*, there's a good chance that the suit is blocked by the *11th Amendment*. This is true whether P is a citizen of the defendant state or of some other state. (*Example:* P, a citizen of state D, is injured when a state D employee runs him over while the employee is on the job. P sues state D in federal court for damages. The suit will be blocked by the 11th Amendment.)

☞ Some *exceptions* to the 11th Amendment:

☞ Suits against a state by *another state* or by the *federal government*;

☞ Suits against *counties*, *cities*, or anything but the state itself.

☞ Suits for an *injunction* against state *officials* directing them to *cease violating federal law*. (But a suit to force a state official to obey *state* law *is* covered by the 11th Amendment and thus not allowed in federal court.)

☞ Keep in mind that *Congress generally can't change* this "no federal-court suits against the states" law, even if it wants to. Cite to the *Seminole Tribe* case on this point. (*Example:* Congress passes a statute saying any state can be sued by private citizens for violating federal environmental-protection laws. This statute won't have any effect, and the federal court won't be allowed to hear a private suit against a state for damages for environmental violations.)

☞ But also remember that Congress *can* provide for federal-court suits by private citizens when the right being sued on stems from Congress' power to enforce the *post-Civil War Amendments*. (*Example:* Congress passes a broad statute banning racial and gender discrimination in employment, and says that workers can sue states in federal court for violations. The 11th Amendment won't block such suits, because Congress has the power to say that the Amendment won't apply to suits brought under federal statutes passed under Congress' authority to enforce the 14th Amendment.)

☞ If the question involves a private damages suit brought on a congressionally-guaranteed right, but brought *against a state in its own courts*, remember that the newly-recognized constitutional doctrine of *sovereign immunity* (the *Alden v. Maine* case) means that the state *doesn't have to hear the case.*

☛ Be alert to possible non-justiciable *"political questions."* Remember that there are two different ways a question can become a non-justiciable political one:

  ☞ First, this can happen where, at least arguably, the Constitution gives the problem to the *Executive* or *Legislative* Branch to resolve, rather than to the judiciary. Classic illustration: anything to do with the procedures or grounds for *impeachment*. Another illustration: a federal court is asked to overrule Congress' decision that P doesn't satisfy the age, citizenship or residency requirement for Senators and Representatives.

  ☞ Second, a question can be a non-justiciable political one because there are *no "manageable standards"* to guide the judiciary in deciding. This type of fact pattern is relatively rare. (*Example:* P claims that a particular tax is so burdensome that it amounts to an uncompensated "taking" in violation of the Fifth Amendment. This issue is a nonjusticiable political one, because no standards exist to tell the Court how to decide.)

    ☞ Thus *"partisan gerrymander"* claims are *non-justiciable* because of the "lack of manageable standards" problem.

    Example: Suppose Democrats use their control of the State X legislature to cause the state to enact a redistricting plan for the state's 15 congressional seats that is, intentionally, highly favorable to the Democratic Party – by "packing" and "cracking," the plan causes 12 of the 15 seats to go to the Democratic candidate in the next election, even though the statewide vote is narrowly split 52% for the Democratic candidates and 48% to the Republican ones. Any federal-court constitutional attack on the plan will be thrown out as non-justiciable. [*Rucho v. Common Cause.*]

      ☞ On the other hand, cases attacking a redistricting plan for violating the *"one person, one vote"* principle *are* justiciable. The Court has decided that this principle applies to virtually all federal and state elections, and can be successfully interpreted by the federal judiciary.

      ☞ Similarly, cases attacking a redistricting plan for making *race* or ethnicity (as opposed to political affiliation) a *"predominant factor"* in the drawing of the district lines *will* be justiciable.

TABLE OF CASES

Principal discussion of a case
is indicated by page numbers in *italics*.

A. v. Hochul... 713
Abate v. Mundt.. *757*
Abington School District v. Schempp 660, *663*
Abrams v. U.S... 479, 490, *491*
ACLU v. Reno 551
Adarand Constructors, Inc. v. Pena *306–308*, 337, 392
Adkins v. Children's Hospital 170
Agency for Int'l Dev. v. Alliance for Open Soc'y
    Int'l, Inc.. *626*, 658
Agins v. Tiburon 402
Agostini v. Felton *679*
Akron v. Akron Center for Reproductive Health 193
Alaska Hire case 104
Alden v. Maine 48, *749*, 774
Allen v. Wright 737, *739*
Allgeyer v. Louisiana... 167
Allied Structural Steel Co. v. Spannaus...................... *415*
Alvarez, U.S. v. 486, *558–559*, 654
Ambach v. Norwick............................... 340, *342*, 351
Amer. Library Ass'n., Inc., U.S. v................................ 541
American Legion v. American Humanist Assoc. 661, 673,
    674–677, 725
American Party of Texas v. White 377
American Trucking Assoc. v. Scheiner 98
Americans for Prosperity Foundation v. Bonta ... *616–620*,
    647
Anderson v. Martin... 266
Arizona Christian School Tuition Organization v. Winn ...
    734
Arizona Free Enterprise Club's Freedom Club PAC v.
    Bennett 580
Arizona State Legislature v. Arizona Independent
    Redistricting Commission...................... *315*, 762
Arkansas Educational Television Comm'n v. Forbes . 537,
    539, 540
Arkansas Writer's Project, Inc. v. Ragland 628
Arlington Heights v. Metropolitan Housing Corp......... 259
Arnett v. Kennedy... 499
Arthrex, U.S. v. *128–130*, 133
Ashcroft v. ACLU *530–532*, 551, 655
Ashcroft v. Free Speech Coalition.............................. 563
Associated Press v. Walker... 554

Baird v. State Bar of Arizona 621
Baker v. Carr.. 751, 753, *754*
Bakke, Univ. of California v., see University of California
    Regents v. Bakke
Baldwin v. G.A.F. Selig, Inc. *81*

Baldwin v. Montana Fish and Game Comm'n 104
Ball v. James.. 370, 389, 756
Ballard, U.S. v.. 670, 716, 724
Barron v. The Mayor and City Council of Baltimore ... 163
Barrows v. Jackson 439, 741
Bartnicki v. Vopper... 637
Bates v. State Bar of Arizona....................................... *567*
Batson v. Kentucky... 261, 331
Belle Terre v. Borass 198
Bellotti v. Baird... 193
Bernal v. Fainter 342
Bethel School District No. 403 v. Fraser..................... 594
Bibb v. Navajo Freight Lines, Inc................................. 80
Blum v. Yaretsky 438, 441
BMW of North America v. Gore 225, 226
Board of Curators v. Horowitz 233
Board of Directors of Rotary Int'l v. Rotary Club
    of Duarte... 606
Board of Education of Kiryas Joel v. Grumet 662, *681–*
    682, 682
Board of Education v. Allen 678
Board of Education v. Dowell 271
Board of Education v. Pico.................................. 210, *592*
Board of Regents v. Roth........................... 213, *221–222*
Board of Trustees of SUNY v. Fox 572
Board of Trustees of Univ. of Alabama v. Garrett 468,
    469, 470, 471
Boddie v. Connecticut... 380
Boerne, City of v. Flores....... 459, *464–466*, 468, 473, 474
Bolger v. Youngs Drug Products Corp.......................... 573
Bolling v. Sharpe 243
Bond v. Floyd 496
Boos v. Barry 480–481
Bostock v. Clayton County............................... *363–363*
Boumediene v. Bush 122, *123–124*
Bowen v. Kendrick 668
Bowers v. Hardwick *202–204*, 367
Bowsher v. Synar 142–143, 157
Boy Scouts of America v. Dale *610–611*
Brandenburg v. Ohio.... 489, 492, 494, 495–496, 498, 505,
    518, 611
Branti v. Finkel 612
Branzburg v. Hayes............................ 627, *634–636*, 648
Brentwood Academy v. Tenn. Secondary School
    Athletic Assoc. *445*, 446
Broadrick v. Oklahoma... *500–501*
Brockett v. Spokane Arcades, Inc......................... 560, 561
Brown v. Board of Education *268–269*, 272, 274

Brown v. Board of Education (Brown II)..................... 269

Brown v. Entertainment Merchants Ass'n................... 563

Brown, U.S. v. 425, 429

Buck v. Bell 175

Buckley v. Valeo 128, 130, *131–132*, *576–579*, 644

Burdick v. Takushi.. 371, 373

Burton v. Wilmington Parking Authority.... 440, 442, 448, 450

Bush v. Gore... *373–374*

Bush v. Vera 314

Butler, U.S. v. *62*

C & A Carbone, Inc. v. Clarkstown.......................... 86, 87

Caban v. Mohammed.. 330

Cabell v. Chavez-Salido 341, 342

Calder v. Bull.. 423

Califano v. Webster 276, 323, 328

Caperton v. A.T. Massey Coal Co......................... *226–227*

Carey v. Population Services Int'l............... 176, 177, *196*

Carolene Products Co., U.S. v. 171, 262, 349

Carter v. Carter Coal Co.. *25*, 46

Castle Rock v. Gonzales...................................... *212–213*

Cedar Point Nursery v. Hassid.............................. *406–407*

Central Hudson Gas v. Public Service Commission ... 566, 568, 572, 575

Champion v. Ames 23

Chaplinsky v. New Hampshire............. *516*, 551, 552, 559

Christian Legal Society Chapter v. Martinez *538*, 540

Church of the Lukumi Babalu Aye, Inc. v. Hialeah *690–691*, 701, 722

Citizens United v. FEC... 645

Citizens United v. Federal Election Comm. 578, 582, 585, *586–587*

City of — see city name

Civil Rights Cases.. *432–434*

Clapper v. Amnesty Int'l USA 733, *736–737*, 771

Clark v. Community For Creative Non-Violence. 507, *544*

Clark v. Jeter.. 346

Cleburne, City of v. Cleburne Living Center......................... *252*, 252, 254, *347–349*

Cleveland Bd. of Ed. v. Loudermill...................... 225, *233*

Clinton v. Jones 147

Clinton v. New York.. *114–115*

Cohen v. California................... 478, *519*, 527, 551, 652

Cohen v. Cowles Media Co.................................... 627

Cohens v. Virginia.. 8

Cole v. Richardson.. 612, 646

Colegrove v. Green... 754

Coleman v. Court of Appeals of Maryland 329

Coleman v. Miller... 752

Collin v. Smith.. 522

Colorado Republican Federal Campaign Committee v. Federal Election Commission ("Colorado Republican I")... 588

Comstock, U.S. v. 19

Connally v. General Construction Co........................... 501

Connick v. Myers.. *613*, 646

Consolidated Edison v. Public Serv. Commission 485, 504

Cooley v. Bd. of Wardens of the Port of Philadelphia .. *76*, 84, 95

Cooper v. Aaron.. 269

Cornelius v. NAACP Legal Defense and Educational Fund.. 533, 539, 540

Cox Broadcasting Corp. v. Cohn............................... 636

Cox v. Louisiana.. 517, 551

Cox v. New Hampshire.. 512

Craig v. Boren....... 248, 275, 276, 277, 320, 321, 328, 742

Crawford v. Marion County Election Board *371–372*

Crist v. Bretz.. 165

Cruzan v. Missouri Department of Health.... *206–207*, 218

Curtis Pub. Co. v. Butts... 553

Curtiss-Wright Export Corp., U.S. v. 119

Cutter v. Wilkinson.. 668, *683*

DaimlerChrysler Corp. v. Cuno.................................. 734

Dames & Moore v. Regan 113, 158

Dandridge v. Williams.. 384, 389

Darby, U.S. v. *28–29*

Davis v. F.E.C. *580*

DeFunis v. Odegaard 744

Dean Milk Co. v. City of Madison 78, 82, 97

Debs v. U.S. 490

Dennis v. U.S. 494–495

District Attorney's Office for the Third Judicial District v. Osborne *229–230*

District of Columbia v. Heller *417–423*

Dobbs v. Jackson Women's Health Organization 189

Dolan v. City of Tigard................................ *409–410*, 411

Douglas v. California.. 379, 384

Duke Power v. Carolina Environmental Study Group, Inc. 172

Dun & Bradstreet, Inc. v. Greenmoss Builders, Inc. ... 555, *556–556*

Duncan v. Louisiana 164

Dunn v. Blumstein 370, 383

Edenfield v. Fane 567, 568, 572, 573

Edmonson v. Leesville Concrete Co............................ 445

Edwards v. Aguillard 666

Edwards v. California 84

Eichman, U.S. v. 546

Eisenstadt v. Baird 176

Elfbrandt v. Russell.. 611

Elk Grove Unified School Dist. v. Newdow 743

Employment Division v. Smith ... 465, *688*, 694, *700–701*, 701, 702, 703, 706, 707, 712, 713–715, 722, 723, 727

Energy Reserves Group, Inc. v. Kansas Power and Light Co... 416

Engel v. Vitale 663

Epperson v. Arkansas 592, *665–666*, 666, 745

Erie v. Pap's A.M. *528–529*, 561

Espinoza v. Montana Dep't. of Revenue, ... 680, *695–697*, 721, 727

Evans v. Abney 437, *440*

Evans v. Newton *437*, 440

Everson v. Board of Education 661, 678

Evitts v. Lucey 229

Ex parte — see name of party

Exxon Corp. v. Eagerton 428

Exxon Corp. v. Governor of Maryland *83–84*

Farber, In re 635

FCC v. League of Women Voters 625, 640

FCC v. Pacifica Foundation 530, 532, 640

Federal Election Comm. v. Wisconsin Right to Life... 582, *585–588*

Federal Maritime Comm. v. South Carolina State Ports Auth. 749, 750

Feiner v. New York 518

Fiallo v. Bell 125

First National Bank of Boston v. Bellotti 589

Fisher v. Univ. of Texas (Fisher I) 282, 284, 286, *286–289*, 300, 318, 338, 393

Fisher v. Univ. of Texas (Fisher II) 282, 286, *290–294*

Flagg Bros., Inc. v. Brooks 437, *438*, 444, 446

Flast v. Cohen 733, 767

Florida Lime & Avocado Growers v. Paul 94

Florida Prepaid Postsecondary Education Expense Board v. College Savings Bank *749*

Foley v. Connelie 342

Fordice, U.S. v. 274

Forsyth County v. The Nationalist Movement 511

44 Liquormart v. Rhode Island 570, *571*, 575

Frazee v. Illinois Dept. of Employment Security 716

Free Enterprise Fund v. Public Company Accounting Oversight Board *140–141*

Frisby v. Schultz 513, 534

Frohwerk v. U.S. 490

Frontiero v. Richardson 321, 344

Frothingham v. Mellon 733

Fulton v. City of Philadelphia *702–707*, 728

Gade v. National Solid Wastes Management 93

Gannett Co. v. DePasquale 633, *638*

Garcetti v. Ceballos 613, *614–615*, 646

Garcia v. San Antonio Metropolitan Transit Authority *47–48*, 52, 54, 103

Garner v. Louisiana 517

Geduldig v. Aiello 329–330

Gentile v. State Bar of Nevada 633, 648

Georgia v. McCollum 445

Georgia, U.S. v. 471

Gertz v. Robert Welch, Inc. 554, *555–556*, 575

Gibbons v. Ogden 22–23, *75*

Gillette v. U.S. 715

Gitlow v. New York 493, 494

Globe Newspapers v. Superior Court 639

Goesaert v. Cleary 320

Goldberg v. Kelly 221, 223, 224, 225, 385

Goldblatt v. Hempstead 428

Goldman v. Weinberger *700*

Goldwater v. Carter 754

Gonzales v. Carhart *194–196*

Gonzales v. Raich 28, 31, *35–37*, 44, 54, 55

Good News Club v. Milford Central School 662

Goss v. Board of Education 270

Goss v. Lopez 223, 233

Graham v. Richardson 341, 344

Gratz v. Bollinger 280, 281, 282, *285–286*, 338, 393

Graves v. New York ex rel. O'Keefe 102

Greater New Orleans Broadcasting Assoc., Inc. v. U.S. 573

Greece v. Galloway *671*

Green v. County School Board 270

Greenholtz v. Inmates 228

Greer v. Spock 540

Gregory v. Ashcroft 254

Griffin v. County School Board 270

Griffin v. Illinois *379–379*, 384

Griffiths, In re 341

Griswold v. Connecticut 174, *175–177*, 216

Grutter v. Bollinger 264, 278, 280, 281, *282–285*, 305, 306, 309, 318, 337, 338, 393

Guest, U.S. v. 433, 452, *454*, 458

Gundy v. U.S. *118–119*, 154, 155

H.L. v. Matheson 193

Hadley v. Junior College Dist. 756

Hague v. CIO 506, 534

Hamdi v. Rumsfeld *230–232*

Hamling v. U.S. 564, 565

Hammer v. Dagenhart *24*, 28

Hampton v. Mow Sun Wong 211, 343

Hans v. Louisiana 746, 769

Harlow v. Fitzgerald 147, 157

Harper v. Virginia Bd. of Elections 364, *369–369*

Harris v. McRae 194

Hawker v. New York 425

Hazelwood School District v. Kuhlmeier 594

Hein v. Freedom from Religion Foundation 734

Hernandez v. Texas 256

Hess v. Indiana 496

Hicklin v. Orbeck 104

Hill v. Colorado 513

Hines v. Davidowitz 93

Hipolite Egg Co. v. U.S. 24

Holder v. Humanitarian Law Project 497–498

Home Building & Loan Ass'n v. Blaisdell.................. 415

Hosanna-Tabor Evangelical Lutheran Church and
       School v. EEOC 669

Houston E. & W. Texas Railway Co. v. U.S.............. 23

Hudgens v. NLRB *436*, 541

Hughes v. Alexandria Scrap Corp. 89, 98

Hughes v. Oklahoma 85

Humphrey's Executor v. U.S....... *136–136*, 137, 138, 140,
       156, 159

Hunt v. Washington Apple Advertising
       Commission.............................. *83*, 738, 768

Hunter v. Erickson.. 266

Hunter v. Underwood 259

Hurley v. Irish-American Gay, Lesbian, and
       Bisexual Group of Boston 609, 610, 621

Hustler Magazine v. Falwell 557

Iancu v. Brunetti *482–483*

Immigration and Naturalization Service (INS) v.
       Chadha.................................. *115–116*, 154, 158

In re — see name of party

International Society for Krishna Consciousness v.
       Lee............................... 537, 539, 540, 551

J. W. Hampton, Jr. & Co., v. U.S. 118

J.E.B. v. Alabama 261, 331

Jackson v. Metropolitan Edison Co............. 437, *443*, 446

Jacobellis v. Ohio.. 560

Jacobsen v. Massachusetts.................................. 715

James v. Valtierra 383

Janus v. AFSCME *607–608*, 645, 657

Jenkins v. Georgia 564

Jenness v. Fortson.. 377

Johnson v. California................................ 266, *317–318*

Johnson v. Maryland... 103

Jones v. Alfred H. Mayer Co. 433, 452, *456–457*, 473

June Medical Services v. Russo................... *188–188*, 742

Kassel v. Consolidated Freightways Corp............... 80, 81

Katzenbach v. McClung 30, 33

Katzenbach v. Morgan....................................... 465

Kelley v. Johnson... 218

Kelo v. New London.................... 411, *412–413*

Keyes v. School District 1 .... *272–273*

Keystone Bituminous Coal Ass'n v. DeBenedictis...... 401

Kimel v. Florida Bd. of Regents................... *468–469*, 470

Kirkpatrick v. Preisler....................................... 756

Klein, U.S. v. 11

Koontz v. St. Johns River Water Mgmt.
       Dist. 408, *410*, 411

Korematsu v. U.S................................ 264, 686, 687

Kovacs v. Cooper.. 478, 512

Kramer v. Union Free School District No. 15 369

Kras, U.S. v.. 380

Ladue, City of, v. Gilleo 510

Laird v. Tatum 745

Landmark Communications, Inc. v. Virginia 636

Larkin v. Grendel's Den, Inc. 671

Larson v. Valente 681, 682, 720

Law Students Research Council v. Wadmond............. 621

Lawrence v. Texas 177, *202–205*, 216, 217,
       238, 353, 367

League of United Latin American Citizens v. Perry 314

Leathers v. Medlock 628

Lebron v. National Railroad Passenger Corp. 432

Lee v. Weisman *664*

Lehman v. Shaker Heights..................... 513, 541

Lemon v. Kurtzman..... 661, 663, 668, 674, 677, 678–679,
       687, 720, 725

Lindsey v. Normet 384

Linmark Associates, Inc., v. Willingboro.................. 566

Little v. Streater 378, 380

Lochner v. New York *167–170*, 211, 569, 623

Locke v. Davey................................... *694*, 697

Lopez, U.S. v. *31–34*, 44, 45, 56, 748, 749

Loretto v. Teleprompter Manhattan CATV
       Corp. 401, *405*

Lorillard Tobacco Co. v. Reilly 571, 573

Los Angeles v. Taxpayers For Vincent 541

Lovell v. Griffin 511, 550

Lovett, U.S. v. 425

Loving v. Virginia.................................... 265, 267

Lubin v. Panish 378

Lucas v. Colorado General Assembly 756

Lucas v. South Carolina Coastal Council..... *402–402*, 404

Lucia v. SEC.................................... *132*, 155, 159

Lugar v. Edmondson Oil Co. 444

Lujan v. Defenders of Wildlife 736

Luther v. Borden 753

Lynch v. Donnelly 664, 720

Lynch v. U.S. 413

Lyng v. Castillo... 263

Lyng v. Northwest Indian Cemetery Protective
       Ass'n... 700

M.L.B. v. S.L.J... 380

Mahan v. Howell... 757

Mahanoy Area School District v. B.L. . *595–599*, 645, 656

Maher v. Roe... 194

Malloy v. Hogan 165

Manhattan Community Access Corp. v. Halleck . *438–438*

Marbury v. Madison *5–7*, 150, 466

Marsh v. Alabama.................................... *436*, 438

Marsh v. Chambers 671

Marston v. Lewis 370

Martin v. Hunter's Lessee 8

Martin v. Struthers 514

Massachusetts Bd. of Retirement v.
       Murgia 246, *253*, 255, 469

Massachusetts v. EPA... 738, 740
Masses Publishing Co. v. Patten........................... 492, 495
Masterpiece Cakeshop, Ltd. v. Colorado
       Civ. Rights Comm'n 126, *691–694*
Matal v. Tam.. *481–483*, 522
Mathews v. Eldridge............................ 224–225, 230, 233
Matthews v. Diaz.. 343
McCardle, Ex parte.. 10–11
McConnell v. Federal Election Comm. *582–585*, 585, 587
McCreary County v. ACLU of
       Kentucky 673, *674–674*, 687
McCullen v. Coakley.... *487–488*, 508, 513, *515–516*, 533
McCulloch v. Maryland.............. *17–18*, 41, 101, 103, 454
McCutcheon v. FEC 577, 579, *580–582*, 644
McDermott v. Wisconsin.. 95
McDonald v. Board of Election..................................... 251
McDonald v. City of Chicago............................ *421*, 422
McGowan v. Maryland.. 667
McKane v. Durston... 229
Meachum v. Fano... 228
Memorial Hospital v. Maricopa County.............. 382, 389
Metro Broadcasting, Inc. v. FCC....................... 306, 307
Metromedia, Inc. v. San Diego.................... 507, 534, 541
Metropolitan Life Ins. Co. v. Ward 249
Meyer v. Nebraska...................... 174, 210, 220, 592
Michael H. v. Gerald D... 202
Michael M. v. Superior Court....................... 245, 276, 323
Milkovich v. Lorain Journal Co.................................... 556
Miller v. California............................ *561–562*, 564, 575
Miller v. Johnson *313–315*, 770
Miller v. Schoene... 404
Miller, U.S. v. 418
Milliken v. Bradley... 273
Minneapolis Star & Tribune Co. v. Minnesota
       Comm'r of Revenue 627
Minnesota v. Clover Leaf Creamery Co................ *89*, 253
Mississippi University for Women v. Hogan 322
Mistretta v. U.S... 117
Mitchell v. Helms.. *678*
Moore v. East Cleveland............................ *197*, 238, 404
Moose Lodge No. 107 v. Irvis.............................. 443, 450
Morrison v. Olson.. 138, 159
Morrison, U.S. v. 31, *34–35*, 44, 46, 56, *455*, 472
Morse v. Frederick... 595
Mugler v. Kansas.. 167
Muller v. Oregon 169
Munn v. Illinois 167
Murphy v. National Collegiate Athletic
       Ass'n...................................... *51–51*, 52, 56

NAACP v. Alabama ex rel. Patterson 606, 616
NAACP v. Button.. 567, *600*
National Bellas Hess, Inc. v. Dep't of Rev..................... 91
National Endowment for the Arts v. Finley................. 602

National Institute of Family and Life Advocates v.
       Becerra.. *621–623*, 657
National Labor Relations Board v. Noel
       Canning *134–135*
National League of Cities v. Usery..................... *46–47*, 54
Near v. Minnesota.. 511, *628*
Nebbia v. New York 170
Nebraska Press Association v. Stuart ... *632–633*, 638, 647
New York Times Co. v.
       Sullivan...................... *552–555*, 556, 566, 654
New York Times Co. v. U.S.. 629
New York v. Ferber 527, *563*, 563
New York v. U.S. (326 U.S. 572, 1946)...................... 102
New York v. U.S. (505 U.S. 144, 1992)............ 47,48–50,
       51, 54, 56, 749
N.F.I.B. v. Sebelius................. 31, *37–44*, 44, 46, 54, 55,
       56, 58, *59–62*, *63–67*, 72
Nguyen v. INS *323–324*, 330
Nixon v. Administrator of General Services 151
Nixon v. Fitzgerald 146–147, 157, 160
Nixon v. Shrink Missouri Government PAC.............. 588
Nixon v. U.S. 144, 752
Nixon, U.S. v. 145, *149–151*
NLRB v. Jones & Laughlin Steel Corp. 26–27
Nollan v. California Coastal Commission 408, 411

O'Brien, U.S. v. *542*, 544
Obergefell v. Hodges ... *199–201*, 205, 236, 237, 238, 252,
       353, *356–363*, 364, 367, 387, 395
Ogden v. Saunders 414
Ohralik v. Ohio State Bar Ass'n 567
Oregon Waste Systems, Inc. v. Dep't of
       Environmental Quality 88
Orr v. Orr 275
Ortwein v. Schwab.. 380
Osborne v. Ohio 562, 563, 575
Our Lady of Guadalupe School v.
       Morrissey-Berru 669, *669–670*, 713

Pacific Gas & Electric Co. v. State Energy
       Comm'n 94, 95
Packingham v. North Carolina............. *508–509*, *535–536*
Palazzolo v. Rhode Island... 407
Palmore v. Sidoti.. 266, 335
Parents Involved in Community Schools v. Seattle
       School District No. 1 ..... 264, 265, 274, *294–301*,
       338, 393
Paris Adult Theatre I v. Slaton............................ 561, 562
Paul v. Davis 222, *223*
Pavan v. Smith 360
Pell v. Procunier.. 638
Penn Central Transportation Co. v. New York City..... 404
Pennhurst State School Hosp. v. Halderman 747
Pennsylvania Coal Co. v. Mahon................................ 401
Pennsylvania v. Finley.. 229

Pentagon Papers Case 631
People v. (See opposing party)
Perry Education Ass'n v. Perry Local Educators'
    Ass'n 540
Perry v. Sindermann *221–222*, 234
Personnel Administrator of Massachusetts v.
    Feeney *260*, 329
Philadelphia Newspapers, Inc. v. Hepps 555
Philadelphia, City of, v. New Jersey *87–88*, 98
Philip Morris USA v. Williams 226
Pierce v. Society of Sisters *174*, 198, 217
Pike v. Bruce Church, Inc. 78, 86
Pittsburgh Press Co. v. Human Relations
    Commission 571
Planned Parenthood of Missouri v. Danforth 192
Planned Parenthood of Southeastern Pennsylvania
    v. Casey *179–182*, 184, 187, 192, 193
Playboy Entertainment Group, Inc., U.S. v. 641
Pleasant Grove City v. Summum 600, *603*, 604
Plessy v. Ferguson *267*
Plyler v. Doe 341, *343–346*, 351
Poe v. Ullman 176, 745
Powell v. McCormack 753, 769
Press Enterprise Co. v. Superior Court 639
Price, U.S. v. 456
Primus, In re *567*, 600
Printz v. U.S. 47, 48, *50–50*, 51, 52
Progressive, Inc., U.S. v. 631
Prudential Insurance Co. v. Benjamin 96
Prune Yard Shopping Center v. Robins 406–407, 542

Quilloin v. Walcott 201, 202

R.A.V. v. City of St. Paul 486, 523, *523–525*, 551
Railway Express Agency v. New York 247, 249
Raines v. Byrd 738
Ramos v. Louisiana 165
Randall v. Sorrell 579
Rankin v. McPherson 614, 646
Red Lion Broadcasting Co. v. FCC 640
Reed v. Reed 320
Reed v. Town of Gilbert *483–485*, 504
Reeves v. Stake 89, 98
Regents of Univ. of Calif. v. Bakke, see
    University of California Regents v. Bakke
Reid v. Covert 68
Reidel, U.S. v. 562
Reitman v. Mulkey 441
Rendell-Baker v. Kohn 438, 444, 448
Reno v. American Civil Liberties Union *529–530*
Reno v. Condon 45, 56
Republican Party of Minn. v. White 589
Reynolds v. Sims 374, *754–756*
Rice v. Cayetano 375
Richardson v. Ramirez 372

Richardson, U.S. v. 734
Richmond Newspapers, Inc. v. Virginia 638, *638–639*
Richmond v. J.A. Croson Co. 256, 275, 278–281, *301–306*,
    307, 312, 316, 336, 392
Roberts v. United States Jaycees 606, 611
Roe v. Wade .. 174, 175, *177–179*, 180, 187, 189, 196, 744
Rogers v. Lodge 258, 261
Roman Cath. Diocese of Brooklyn v. Cuomo 724
Rome, City of v. U.S. 459–460, 461
Romer v. Evans 252, 254, 353, *353–355*
Rosenberger v. University of Virginia 537, *538*, 601,
    602, *663*
Rosenbloom v. Metromedia, Inc. 555
Ross v. Moffitt 379
Rostker v. Goldberg *277*, 323
Roth v. U.S. 559–561
Rowan v. Post Office Dept. 513
Rubin v. Coors Brewing Co. 573
Rucho v. Common Cause 315, 757, *758–765*, 770, 774
Rumsfeld v. FAIR 68, *609*
Rust v. Sullivan 194, 601, *625*
Rutan v. Republican Party of Illinois 612

Saenz v. Roe 383, *399*, 427
St. Amant v. Thompson 553
Salerno, U.S. v. 244
San Antonio Ind. School Dist. v.
    Rodriguez 345, *365–367*, 384
Sandin v. Conner 228, 229
Santa Fe Independent School Dist. v. Doe *665*
Saxbe v. Washington Post Co. 638
Scales v. U.S. 497
Schaumburg v. Citizens For Better Environment 514
Schechter Poultry Corp. v. U.S. 25, *117*
Schenck v. U.S. 489
Schlesinger v. Reservists to Stop the
    War 733, 735, 737, 768
Schneider v. State 479, 507, 533
Schuette v. Coalition to Defend
    Affirmative Action (BAMN) *318–319*
Schware v. Board of Bar Examiners 211
Seila Law v. Consumer Fin. Prot. Bureau ... *136–139*, 141,
    142, 156, 159
Seminole Tribe of Florida v. Florida ... 467, 746, *748–749*,
    750, 769
Sessions v. Morales-Santana *326–328*
Shapiro v. Thompson 211, 364, *381–382*, 383
Sharpnack, U.S. v. 103
Shaw v. Hunt 312, 314
Shaw v. Reno *312*, 314
Shelby County v. Holder *461–464*
Shelley v. Kraemer *439–441*, 449
Sheppard v. Maxwell 632
Sherbert v. Verner *698–699*
Sierra Club v. Morton 735, 768

Simon v. Eastern Ky. Welfare Rights
  Organization 739, 768
Skinner v. Oklahoma *174*
Slaughterhouse Cases 166–167, *398–399*
Smith v. Allwright 435
Smith v. California 565
Smith v. Daily Mail Publishing Co. 636
Snyder v. Phelps 478, 505, *520–522*, 557, 649
Sorrell v. IMS Health Inc. 573
Sosna v. Iowa 382
South Carolina State Highway Dept. v. Barnwell
  Bros., Inc. 79
South Carolina v. Katzenbach 453, *460–461*
South Dakota v. Dole 55, 63, 65
South Dakota v. Wayfair, Inc. *92*
South-Central Timber Development, Inc. v.
  Wunnicke 90
Southeastern Promotions, Ltd. v. Conrad 535
Southern Pacific Terminal Co. v. ICC 744
Spence v. Washington 489
Stanley v. Georgia 210, *562, 563*, 575
State Farm Mut. Automobile Insur. Co. v.
  Campbell 226
Stenberg v. Carhart 195
Stevens, U.S. v. 486, *563*
Strauder v. West Virginia 257
Stromberg v. California 502, 542
Sugarman v. Dougall 341
Supreme Court of New Hampshire v. Piper 105, 108
Susan B. Anthony List v. Driehaus 737
Swann v. Charlotte-Mecklenburg Board of
  Education *270–271*, 280

Tahoe-Sierra Preservation Council, Inc. v. Tahoe
  Regional Planning Agency *403*
Tancil v. Woolls 266
Tandon v. Newsom 363, *707–711*, 712, 723, 724, 728
Tenn. Wine & Spirits Ret. Ass'n v. Thomas 77, 78, 81
Tennessee v. Lane *470*, 471
Terminiello v. Chicago 517
Terry v. Adams 435
Texas Monthly, Inc. v. Bullock 667
Texas v. Johnson *545*
Texas, U.S. v. 189
Thomas v. Review Bd. Ind. Empl. Sect. Div. 716
Thompson v. Western States Medical Center 572
Thornhill v. Alabama 498
Thornton v. Caldor, Inc. *667*
Timbs v. Indiana 165
Time, Inc. v. Firestone 554
Timmons v. Twin Cities Area New Party 377
Tinker v. Des Moines School District 592
Tinker v. Des Moines School District, *543–544*, 593, 594,
  595
Toomer v. Witsell 104

Torcaso v. Watkins 716
Town of — see town name
Trimble v. Gordon 350, 352
Troxel v. Granville *198*, 217
Trump v. Hawaii *124–126, 683–688*, 721, 726
Trump v. Mazars USA *148–149*, 150, 157
Trump v. Vance *145–146*, 157, 160
Turner Broadcasting System Inc. v. FCC (Turner II)... 641
Turner Broadcasting System, Inc. v. FCC (Turner I)... 640

U.S. Dep't of Agric. v. Moreno *251*, 252, 254
U.S. Postal Service v. Greenburgh Civic Assns. 514
U.S. R.R. Retirement Bd. v. Fritz *250–251*
U.S. Trust Co. v. New Jersey *413*, 416, 428
U.S. v. Windsor 252
United Building and Constr. Trades Council v.
  Camden 90, *105*
United Haulers Ass'n v. Oneida-Herkimer Solid
  Waste Management Auth. 86
United Public Workers v. Mitchell 745
United States v. — see opposing party
University of California Regents v. Bakke 262, 282

Van Orden v. Perry *673–674*
Virginia Board of Elections v. Hamm 266
Virginia Pharmacy Board v. Virginia Consumer
  Council 478, 480, *565–566*, 568
Virginia v. Black 523, *526–527*
Virginia v. Tennessee 107
Virginia, U.S. v. 277, 320, 322, *324–326*, 337, 394
Vitek v. Jones 228

Walker v. Birmingham 628
Walker v. Tex. Div., Sons of Confederate
  Veterans, Inc. *603–605*
Wallace v. Jaffree *663*, 667
Walz v. Tax Commission 667
Ward v. Rock Against Racism *509*, 512
Warth v. Seldin *739*, 741
Washington v. Davis *258*, 543
Washington v. Glucksberg 205, *207–209*, 218
Watchtower Bible and Tract Soc. of N.Y. v.
  Village of Stratton 550
Watts v. U.S. 496
Webster v. Reproductive Health Services 194
Wesberry v. Sanders 754
West Coast Hotel v. Parrish 170
West Virginia Bd. of Ed. v. Barnette 358
West Virginia State Bd. of Educ. v.
  Barnette 210, 592, 621
Whalen v. Roe 172
White Primary Cases *435*, 438
Whitney v. California *493–494*, 495–496
Whole Woman's Health v.
  Hellerstedt177, 179, 180, *183–188*, 188, 189, 193

Whole Woman's Health v. Jackson 189
Wickard v. Filburn.... *27–28*, 30, 32, 35, 37, 40, 42, 44, 54
Widmar v. Vincent 479, 504, 662
Wilkinson v. Austin 229
Williams v. Rhodes 376–377, 389
Williamson v. Lee Optical Co. 171, 391
Williams-Yulee v. Florida Bar 590–591
Windsor, U.S. v. 218, 252, 254, 353, *355–356*, 388
Wisconsin v. Mitchell 523, 526
Wisconsin v. Yoder 699, 722
Witters v. Washington Dep't of Services for the
　　Blind 680
Woods v. Miller Co. 68
Wooley v. Maynard 621

Wygant v. Jackson Bd. of Ed. 311

Yick Wo v. Hopkins 256, 257
Young v. American Mini Theatres 532
Young, Ex parte 747, 769
Youngberg v. Romeo *210*
Youngstown Sheet & Tube Co. v. Sawyer ... *112–113*, 119

Zablocki v. Redhail *199*, 367
Zelman v. Simmons-Harris 678, *679–680*, 725
Zivotofsky v. Kerry *120–121*
Zorach v. Clauson 662
Zurcher v. Stanford Daily 627, 636

SUBJECT MATTER INDEX

ABORTION
Consent to, 192
    By spouse, 192
Counseling, restrictions on, 194
Deference due to legislature's fact-finding, 188
Free speech concerning, 513
Hospital admitting privileges and, 183, 185-186, 188
Informed consent, 193
    Regulations discouraging abortion, 181
Legislature's motive in regulating, significance of, 187
Minors
    Immature, 193
    Mature or emancipated, 193
Notice and consultation, 181, 193
    By spouse, 181
    To parents, 193
Planned Parenthood v. Casey, 179
    Undue burden standard, 180
Procedures for, 194
Public funding of
    Counseling about abortions, 194
    Refusal of in non-therapeutic abortions, 194
Right to privacy rationale, 178-179
Roe v. Wade case
    First, second, third trimesters, 177, 178
    Holding, 177
    Planned Parenthood v. Casey, effect of, 179, 181
    Post-Roe developments, 179
    Rationale, 178
Scrutiny, degree of to be used by court, 187-188
Surgical-center rules and, 183, 186-187
Undue burden standard, 180, 181, 183-188, 192

ABORTION CLINICS
Speech outside, 487-488, 515-516

ADMINISTRATIVE LAW JUDGES
Appointment of, 128-130

ADMISSIONS
Use of race in, 281-294

ADVISORY OPINIONS
    Generally, 730-731

AFFIRMATIVE ACTION
See EQUAL PROTECTION

AFFORDABLE CARE ACT
Commerce power as basis for, 53-61
Taxing power as basis for, 24-25

AGENCIES
President's right to remove heads of, 135-139, 142

ALIENAGE
See EQUAL PROTECTION

ANCESTRY
As proxy for race under post-Civil War Amendments, 257

APPOINTMENTS CLAUSE
    Generally, 126-143
Officers of the U.S.
    Defined, 131
    Officers and non-officers distinguished, 128-130, 131-133
    Power to appoint, 16, 127-130, 131-133

Significant-authority standard for determining who
    is, 131, 132

"AS APPLIED" ATTACKS, 243-244

ASSOCIATION, FREEDOM OF
See FREEDOM OF ASSOCIATION

BILL OF RIGHTS
Application to states, 163-166
    Selective incorporation approach, 164
Total incorporation approach, 164

BILLS OF ATTAINDER
    Generally, 424-425
"Punishment" defined, 425
Rationale for ban on, 425

BIRTH CONTROL
    Generally, 175-177
Regulation of, following *Roe v. Wade*, 196-197
Use by minors, 197

CABLE TV
Free speech and, 529

CHILD PORNOGRAPHY, 562, 563

CHILD-REARING
Parent's substantive due process right to control, 198

CITIZENSHIP
Of child born to U.S. citizen parent living abroad, 326-328

CIVIL RIGHTS LAWS
"Color of law," actions taken under, 452
Commerce Clause as support for, 45-46
Congress' power to modify constitutional rights given
    by, 458, 464-466
Congressional enforcement of, 451-474
    Private conduct, Congress' power to reach, 453-458
Public accommodations, 453
Repeal of as state action, 441
Thirteenth Amendment, laws passed under authority of, 456-458
Voting rights, 453

COMA
Rights of patient in, 205-207

COMMANDEERING
Rule against imposed on Congress by Tenth Amendment, 64-68

COMMERCE CLAUSE
See INTERSTATE COMMERCE

COMMERCIAL SPEECH
See FREEDOM OF SPEECH

CONGRESS' POWERS
Appointment and removal of federal officers, 126-144
Commerce, *See* INTERSTATE COMMERCE
Commitment of the armed forces, 121-122
Enforcement of civil rights laws, 451-474
Enumerated powers of, 33-34
Executive officers, right to remove, 142-144
Legislative veto, 115-116
Modification of constitutional rights, 464-471
Removal of executive officers, 143-144
Removal of federal officers, 142-143

Specific powers of, 16
Substantive scope of constitutional rights, modification
　　　　of, 464-466
Use of "Necessary and Proper" Clause, 17-18

CONSCIENTIOUS OBJECTION
See FREE EXERCISE CLAUSE

CONTRACT CLAUSE
Generally, 413-417
Deferential standard, 416-417
Distinction between public and private contracts, 416
Private contracts, application to, 414-416
Public agreements, application to, 413-414

COVID-19
Free Exercise Clause and, 707-711

CROSS BURNING, 523-525

DECLARATORY JUDGMENT
As advisory opinion, 731

DEFAMATION
Generally, 552-557
Damages for, types of, 554
Falsity, burden of proving, 555
Non-media defendants, 555
Opinion, 556
"Private figures", 554
"Public figures", 553
Public interest, statements having no, 556

DEFENSE OF MARRIAGE ACT
Partial invalidation of, 355-356

DELEGATION
By Congress to the executive branch, 116-119
Delegation struck down, 117
Excessive delegation, prohibition of, 116-119
Intelligible principle required, 118, 155, 158
Modern view of limits on, 117
Nondelegation doctrine, 117

DISCLOSURE
Compelled by government, 615-620

DIVERSITY
As compelling governmental interest, 284

DNA TESTING
Prisoner's due process right to, 229-230

DORMANT COMMERCE CLAUSE
Generally, 74-92
Local processing requirements, 85
Modern test for, 76
State barriers to outgoing trade, 84

DUE PROCESS OF LAW
Generally, 161-233
Abortion, 177
　　See also ABORTION, 177
Child visitation, 198-199
Child-rearing, 198
Civil litigation, 225-227
Criminal defendant's right to, 227-230
DNA testing
　　Prisoner's right to, 229-230
Economic regulation, 170-172
　　Hypothesizing of legislative objectives, 171

Modern approach to, 170-172
Pre-1934 approach, 166-170
Summary of modern approach, 171-172
Enemy combatants, detention of, 230-233
Family relations, 197-202
　　Child-raising, 198
　　Marriage, 199-201
　　Zoning and the "non-nuclear" family, 197-198
Freedom of inquiry, 210
Fundamental rights, 173
Homosexuality, 205
Incorporation of Bill of Rights, 161-166
Judicial bias as violation of, 226-227
Marriage, right of, 199-201
Mentally retarded, rights of, 210
Motorcycle helmet rules, 210
Natural father, rights of, 201-202
Non-economic rights, 173-177
　　Birth control use, 175-177, 196-197
　　Early cases, 174-175
Occupation, right to engage in, 211
"Penumbra" theory, 175
Prisoners, rights of, 227-230
Privately-imposed harm, no right of protection, 211-213
Procedural due process, 219-233
　　Early view, 220
　　Governmental regularity *per se*, 219
　　Legislature's right to limit procedures, 233
　　"Liberty" definition narrowed, 223
　　Protection from third-party harm, as property
　　　　interest, 211-213
　　Reputation, interest in, 223
　　Students, rights of, 223, 233
　　Tenured employees, 221-222, 225
　　Welfare benefits, 221, 224
　　What process is due, 223-233
Punitive damages, 225
Purposeful discrimination, 257
　　In administration, 257
Reputation, no protected right in, 223
Right to die, 205-209
　　"Clear and convincing" standard, 206
　　Suicide, 207-209
Same-sex marriage, 199-201
Sexual privacy, 176-177
Sexuality, 202-205
Substantive due process, 166-213
　　Early history of, 166-170
　　Maximum-hour laws, 169
　　Minimum wage laws, 170
　　Protection of non-economic rights
　　　　Generally, 173-177
　　Same-sex marriage and, 202-205
Visitation rights, 198-199

ECONOMIC AND SOCIAL REGULATION
See EQUAL PROTECTION

EDUCATION
Denial of as equal protection violation, 365
Illegal aliens, 343

EIGHTH AMENDMENT
Incorporated into Fourteenth Amendment, 165

ELECTION DISTRICTS
See VOTING RIGHTS

ELEVENTH AMENDMENT
Generally, 746-749
Administrative agencies and, 750
Age discrimination and, 468-469
Broad interpretation of amendment, 746
Court access and, 470
Disability discrimination and, 469
Exclusions, 747-748
Facial meaning, 746
Heightened scrutiny and, 469
Patent suits, states' immunity from, 749
State-court suits and, 749-750
Suits against state official, 747
Suits against states, Congress' general power to allow, 748-749
Text of, 746
Three-step analysis for overcoming, 471

EQUAL PROTECTION
Generally, 243-385
Admissions, use of race in, 281-294
Adoption, 266-267
Affirmative action, 274-318
    Alimony, 275
    Attempt to remedy past discrimination, 276
    Congressionally imposed, 306-308
    Harm to members of minority from, 316
    Hiring, 308, 310
    Housing, 316
    Lay-offs, 311
    Minority set-asides, 301-306
        Congressionally imposed, 306-308
    Popular vote to repeal, 318-319
    Promotion preferences, 311
    Quotas, use of, 280, 305, 310, 316
    Racial classifications, benign use of, 278-281
    Separation desired by minorities, 316
    Sex discrimination remedied, 328-329
    Sex-based classes, 275, 319
        Intermediate scrutiny rigorously applied, 320
        Single-sex education, 324-326
        Stereotypes or generalizations, 324-328
    Standard of review for, 263
    Strict scrutiny, required, 263
    To cure racial discrimination generally, 278-318
    Voluntary plans by public employers, 311
Alienage, 340-346
    Education of illegal aliens, 343-346
    Exceptions to strict scrutiny of, 341-342
    Federal government's right to classify based on, 342-343
    Strict scrutiny applied, 341
Animus toward unpopular groups, 251-252
    Anti-gay laws, 252
    Out-of-staters, discrimination against, 252
Child custody, 266
Citizenship based on parent's gender, 326-328
Courts, access to, 378-380
    Civil litigation, 380-381
    Counsel during appeal, 379
    Transcripts on appeal, 379
Desegregation

As type of affirmative action, 281
    Busing to accomplish, 271
    Closing of public schools, 270
    De facto/de jure distinction, 258, 270, 272, 281
    Ending court supervision, 274
    "Freedom of choice", 270
    Harm to minority members from, 316
    In the North, 272
    Interdistrict remedies, 273-274
Diversity as compelling interest, 284
Economic and social regulation, 248-254
    Hypothetical legislative objectives, 251
    Means-end link, 253, 254
    Objective of legislature, 249
    "One step at a time", 249
Education, right to, 365-367
Federal government, application to, 243
Fundamental rights, 364-385
    Access to courts as, 378-380
    Ballot access as, 375-378
    Education as, 365-367
    Right to travel as, 381-383
    Voting rights as, 368-374
Hiring, 308-312, 317
Homosexuals, singling out of, 251-252
Illegitimacy, 346
Jury selection, 261
Mentally ill, discrimination against, 349
Mentally retarded, discrimination against, 252, 347
"Mere-rationality" standard, 247, 248-254
Middle-level review, 248, 349-350
    Close means-end fit required, 349
    General principles of, 349
    Hypothesizing of state purpose, 350
    Mental illness, 349
    Mental retardation, not applicable to, 347-349
Objective of legislature, significance of, 245-246
"One step at a time" reform, 249
Operation of the Clause, generally, 243-248
Over-inclusive classification, 246-247
Partisan gerrymanders, 312-316
Political process, race used in, 266
Poll tax as violation of, 369
Private conduct
    Congress' power to reach, 453-456
Public school admissions based on race, 294-301
Purposeful discrimination, 257-262
    Circumstantial evidence used to prove, 257
    Dual motives, 259
    Facially discriminatory statute, 257
    Must be cause of conduct, 260
    Passage of time, 260
    Proving, 258
    Sex discrimination, 330
    Statistics used to prove, 261-262
Racial discrimination, 256-274
    Adoption, 267
    Child custody, 267
    Establishment-of-religion defense against claim of, 688
    Law enforcement operations, 317
    Racially restrictive covenants, 439-440
    Voting, 368-374
Remedial powers of Congress, 459-471

Same-sex marriage, 355-364
Segregation, 267-274
    See also "Desegregation" under this main heading
    Prison-cell assignments, 317-318
    Remedies to combat, 267-274
    "Separate but equal" doctrine, 267-268
"Separate but equal" treatment, 265-266
Sex discrimination, 274-278, 319-331
    Alimony, 275
    Attempt to remedy past discrimination, 276
    Bathrooms and locker rooms, 330
    Child-rearing stereotypes, 326-328
    Citizenship based on parent's gender, 326-328
    Discriminatory purpose required, 329-330
    Draft registration, 277-278
    Gays and transgendered persons as victims of, 363
    Intermediate scrutiny of, 321-322
    Statutory rape, 276-277
    Veterans' preference as, 260
Special traits pertaining to one race, 265
States, violation of by, 467-471
Stereotypes, significance of, 262
Strict scrutiny, 248, 256-274
    How much, 267
    How strict, 263-267
    Immutability, significance of, 262
    Other requirements for, 262-263
    Purposeful discrimination required for, 257-262
    Stereotypes, significance, 262
    Surviving strict scrutiny, chances of, 264
Suspect classifications, 256-263
    See also SUSPECT CLASSIFICATIONS
Travel, right to, 381-383
    Medical benefits, residency requirements for, 382
    Welfare benefits, residency rules for, 381-382
Under-inclusive classification, 246
University admissions, use of race in, 281-294
Voting rights, 259, 368-375, 383
    Ballot access, 375-378
    Ballot counting procedures, 373-374
    Duration-of-residence requirements, 370
    Felons, denial of vote to, 372
    Partisan gerrymanders, 312-316
    Standards for judging cases involving, 312-316
Wealth, classifications based on, 257, 383-385
    Housing, 384
    Welfare benefits, 384
Welfare benefits, 384

ESTABLISHMENT CLAUSE
    Generally, 661-680
Ceremonies and displays, 671-677
Cross, display of, 677
Entanglement of church and state, 671
Free Exercise Clause, relation to, 660-661
Funding of student activities, 663
Graduation ceremony, 664
Holidays, celebration of, 672
Interdenominational preferences, 680-688
Legislative chaplain, 671
Military chaplains, 668
Ministerial exception from government regulation, 669-670
National security and the Clause, 683-688
Nativity scene, display of, 672

Parochial schools aid to, 677-680
    Equipment, 678
    Salary supplements, 678
    Scholarships for religious study, 680
    Services, furnishing of, 679
    Teachers, furnishing of, 679
    Textbooks and other materials, 678
    Three-prong test for, 677
    Transportation, 678
Pledge of Allegiance, 664, 672
Prayer-reading in public schools, 663-665
Prayers before town board meetings, 671
Preference among denominations, 680-688
Public schools, 662-667
    Anti-evolution laws, 665
    Facilities use by student groups, 662-663
    Graduation ceremony, 664
    Modification of curriculum, 665-667
    Moment of silence, 663
    Prayer reading, 663
    Religious instruction, 662-663
    Tuition vouchers, 679-680
Religious displays, 672-677
Sabbath, right not to work on, 667, 698-699
Secular purpose required, 667
Sincerity of religious belief, 670
Specific prohibitions, 661
Sunday closing laws, 667
Ten Commandments, display of, 673-674
Three-prong test for, 661
Tuition vouchers, 679-680

***EX POST FACTO* LAWS**, 423-424

EXCESSIVE FINES
Ban on incorporated into Fourteenth Amendment, 165

EXECUTIVE AGREEMENTS, 33, 120

EXECUTIVE POWERS
    See also IMMUNITIES
Appointment of officials by President, 126-130
Commitment of the armed forces, 121-122
Entry into U.S., 124-126
Executive privilege, 149-151
Immigration, 124-126
Legislative veto, 115-116
"Line item" veto, 114-115
National security, 124-126
No right to make laws, 112-113
Pocket veto, 114
Recess appointments, 133-135
Recognition of foreign governments, 120-121
Right to remove appointees, 135-142
    Heads of independent agencies, 135-139, 142, 156
Veto power, 113-116

EXECUTIVE PRIVILEGE, 149-151

FACIAL ATTACKS ON STATUTES, 243-244

FALSE STATEMENTS
Government power to ban, 557-559

FEDERAL COURTS
Powers of, 34

FEDERALISM, 15-17

FIFTEENTH AMENDMENT, 374

FIRST AMENDMENT
See FREEDOM OF SPEECH, FREEDOM OF
ASSOCIATION, FREEDOM OF EXPRESSION,
FREEDOM OF RELIGION

FOREIGN AFFAIRS
Commitment of the armed forces, 121-122
Federal government's power over, 16, 33
Recognition of foreign governments, 120-121

FOURTEENTH AMENDMENT
See DUE PROCESS OF LAW, EQUAL PROTECTION,
IMMUNITIES
Congress' remedial powers under, 458-471

FREE EXERCISE CLAUSE
Generally, 688-716
Categorical exemptions to a law, consequences of
granting, 707-711, 723-724
Centrality of belief, 716
Conflict with criminal statute, 700-701
Drugs, 700-701
Essentially-religious uses excluded from government
benefit, 694
Establishment Clause, relation to, 660-661
Generally-applicable laws, 701-713
Generally-available benefit from which religious groups are
excluded, 694-697, 721
Hostility to religion by government, 690-691
During adjudications, 691-694
Incidental burden on religion, 698-713
Individualized exemptions to a law, consequences of
granting, 702-707
Intent to disfavor religious practice, 688-697
Life-saving medical treatment, 715
Ministerial exception from regulation, 713
Most-favored-nation approach to granting exemptions, 712-
713
Nativity Scene, right to display, 672
Public health objectives as interference with, 715
Religious belief, definition of, 715-716
Sabbath, accommodation for, 698-699
Sincerity of belief, 716

FREEDOM OF ASSOCIATION
Generally, 605-626
Bar membership restrictions, 620-621
Campaign spending, compulsory disclosure of, 620
Compulsory disclosure of membership as violation of, 615-
620
Denial of public jobs or benefits, 611-615
Loyalty oaths, 612-613
Patronage dismissals and hirings, 612
Speech critical of superiors, 613-615
Illegal groups, 611
Legal services furnished by lay groups, 599-600
Loyalty oaths, 612-613
Membership, compulsory disclosure of as violation, 615-620
Membership, interference with, 610-611
Social association, no general right, 605
Strict scrutiny of interferences with, 605

FREEDOM OF EXPRESSION
See FREEDOM OF SPEECH, FREEDOM OF
ASSOCIATION

FREEDOM OF RELIGION
Generally, 659-716
Religious belief, definition of, 715-716
See also ESTABLISHMENT CLAUSE, FREE EXERCISE
CLAUSE

FREEDOM OF SPEECH
Abortion clinics, women visiting, 513, 515-516
Accountant, solicitation by as protected speech, 567
Advocacy of illegal acts, 489-502
"Clear and present danger" test for, 489-492
Incitement required, 495
Modern standard for, 495-498
Statutes directly proscribing speech, 492-494
Audience's right to information, 566
Broadcast ads, regulation of, 582-588
Broadcasting
See also "Media" under this main heading
Phone, cable and computer systems distinguished, 529-
532
Special rules applicable to, 529
Cable TV, 529
Campaign spending as
See "Political campaign spending" under this main
heading
Campus speech, regulation of, 527
Canvassing and soliciting, 513-514
Anonymously, 514
In public places, 514
Mailboxes, 513
Visits to home, 514
Captive audience, 513, 519
"Clear and present danger" test, 489-492
Commercial speech, 565-573
Current status of, 571-573
"For Sale" signs banned, 566
Harmful products, advertising of, 570-571
Constitutionally-protected products, 573
Vice products, 570-571
Internal consistency required in regulation of, 572
Lawyers, regulation of speech of, 567
Misleading statements, 571
Protection curtailed, 568-569
Protection first given to, 565
"Reasonably tailored means", 572
Viewpoint discrimination as to, 569-570
Computer-generated images, 563
Conduct distinguished from speech, 509
Confidential information, disclosure of, 636-638
Content-neutrality generally required, 483-485, 525, 537-538
Corporate political expression, 589
Crime, disclosure of information obtained by, 636-637
Criminal trials, access to, 638
Cross burning, 523-525
Defamation, 552-557
See also DEFAMATION
Draft resistance, 542-543
Draft-card burning, 542-543
Drug use, advocacy of in schools, 595
Emotional distress, intentional infliction of, 556

Fairgrounds, 514
False statements of fact
    Government's right to ban, 557-559
"Fighting words" doctrine, 516-519, 524, 525
Financial support, right not to be compelled to give, 607-608
Flag desecration and misuse, 545
    Constitutional amendment, need for, 547
    Federal statute, 546
Gag order to preserve fair trial, 631-633
Government as speaker or funder of speech, 600-602
    Display of privately-donated monument, 603
Government employees, speech by, 613-615
Hair and clothing regulation, 544
"Hate speech," regulation of, 481-483, 523-527
    Penalty-enhancement statutes, 525
Hostile audience, 516-518
    Anger by audience not sufficient, 517
    Crowd-control required, 517
Indecency, regulation of, 527-529, 529-532
    Internet, 529-532
    Secondary-effects doctrine, 527-529
Intentional infliction of emotional distress, 520-522, 556
Internet, 508-509, 529-532, 535-536
Internet connections in libraries, 541
Intimidation as non-protected activity, 526-527
Issue ads, 582-588
Jails, 540
Lawyers, comments by, 633
Lawyers, commercial speech by, 567
Legal services furnished by lay groups, 599-600
License plates, messages on, 603-605
Licensing requirements, 510-512
Loudspeakers, 512
Media, 626-641
    Access to jails, 638
    Access to pre-trial proceedings, 638
    Broadcast media, 639-641
    Criminal trials, right of access to, 638
    Editorializing by public broadcasters, 640
    Ex parte search warrants, 636
    Government demands for information held by, 633-635
    Grand jury subpoenas, 634
    Prior restraints, 628-633
    Right of access to government-held information, 638-639
    Shield laws, 635
    Special role for the press, 626
Mental anguish to listeners, 522
Military bases, 540
Military honors, lying about, 557-559
Minors, protection of, 571
Monument, government display of, 603
Non-communicative impact aimed at speech, 477, 488
Nude dancing, 528-529
Obscenity, 559-565
    See also OBSCENITY
Offensive words, 481-483, 519-523
Opinion, statements of, 556
Outside speeches and articles, ban on payment for, 615
Overbreadth
    See OVERBREADTH
Political campaign spending
    Aggregate donation limits, 580-582

Constitutional limits, 577
Contributions by individuals, 577, 580-582, 588
Contributions to and by Political Action
    Committees, 579
Corporate political expression, 589
Expenditures by individuals, 577
General rules governing, 576
Limits on total campaign spending, 578
Political parties, regulation of, 588
Soft-money donations, 582
Spending by millionaire's opponent, 579
Spending by political parties, 582, 588
Spending of candidate's own money, 578
Pornography
    Child pornography, 562-563
Pre-trial proceedings, access to, 638
Prior restraints, 511, 628-633
    Distinguished from subsequent punishment, 628, 633
    Gag orders to preserve fair trial, 631-633
    Receipt of stolen goods as exception to, 630
    Strict scrutiny of, 629
    Threat of H-bomb, 631
Private places, 488, 507, 534
    Right of access to, 541-542
Public forum, 488, 506, 532-541
    Designated public forum, 535-536
    Internet as, 535-536
    Jails, 540
    Military bases, 540
    Non-public forums, 536-541
    Schools
        School mail system, 540
    Semi-public forums, 532
    Significant state interest required for regulation, 533
    True public forums, 534
    Workplace, governmental, 540
Right not to speak, 621-623
School mail system, 540
Schools, 592-595
    Advocacy of illegal drue use by students, 595
    Disciplinary needs of, 593-595
    Off-campus speech, 595-599
    Protest in, 543
    Students, speech by, 593
    Teaching materials, choice of, 592-593
Secondary-effects doctrine, 528-529
Secret information, disclosure of, 636-638
Shopping centers, 541
Signs, regulation of, 483-485
Sleeping in park, 544
Sound equipment, regulation of, 512
Students, speech by, 593
Subject matter forbidden, 483-488
Subversive advocacy, 489-502
    See also "Advocacy of illegal acts" under this main
        heading
Symbolic expression, 542-547
"Time, place and manner" regulations, 506-542
    General test for validity, 507, 508
    Meaning of narrowly-tailored, 508-510
"Unprotected categories" approach, 486-487
Vagueness
    See VAGUENESS

Viewpoint neutrality, 480-483, 537
    Commercial speech and, 569-570
Workplace, 540

FUNDAMENTAL RIGHTS
See DUE PROCESS OF LAW

GAY MARRIAGE
Equal protection analysis of, 252, 355-356, 356-364
Substantive due process analysis of, 199-201, 205

GERRYMANDERING
Partisan gerrymanders, 757-765
Racial gerrymanders, 312-316
See also VOTING RIGHTS

GOVERNMENTAL MOTIVE
Commerce Clause cases, irrelevant in, 45
Discriminatory intent, 257-262
Generally not inquired into, 19
In freedom of speech cases, 488

HABEAS CORPUS, 122-124

"HATE SPEECH"
See also FREEDOM OF SPEECH
Regulation of as First Amendment violation, 523-527

HEALTH CARE ACT
Constitutionality of federal, 53-60

HIRING
Equal protection and, 308-312, 317

HOMOSEXUALITY
See also DUE PROCESS OF LAW, GAY MARRIAGE, and
      SEXUALITY
Animus toward unpopular groups, 251-252
Equal protection analysis of, 356-364
Fundamental right not found, 202
Gay marriage, 252
Substantive due process protection of, 202-205

ILLEGITIMACY
See also EQUAL PROTECTION
    Generally, 346

IMMIGRATION AND NATURALIZATION
President's powers concerning, 124-126

IMMUNITIES
Civil immunity of presidential assistants, 147
Civil liability of President for official acts, 146-147
Civil liability of President for unofficial acts, 147
Criminal prosecution of executive officials, 147
Federal immunity from state regulation, 103
From taxation, 101-102
    Federal immunity from state regulation, 101-102
    State immunity from federal taxation, 102
Of Congress, 145
Of executive, 145-148
Of President
    From subpoenas, 145-146, 148-149, 157

IMPEACHMENT
    Generally, 143-144
Congress' demand for materials pursuant to, 150
Criminal liability following, 144
"High crimes and misdemeanors," meaning of, 143
Reviewability of by the courts, 144, 752

INDEPENDENT AND ADEQUATE STATE GROUNDS
Supreme Court review obviated by, 8-10

INTERMEDIATE SCRUTINY
See EQUAL PROTECTION

INTERNET
Indecency on, regulation of, 529-532
Restrictions on use of, 508-509
Taxation by states of transactions on, 91-92

INTERSTATE COMMERCE
Channels of interstate commerce, 61
Congress' power over, 62-68
    "Activity" required for, 55
    Child labor, 40
    Civil rights legislation, 45-46
    "Cumulative effect" theory, 43-44
    "Current of commerce" theory, 41
    "Direct logical relationship" to required, 41
    Forced purchase of good or service, 53-60
    Insurance, forced purchase of, 53-60
    Intrastate activities, regulation of, 39, 42-43, 51-53
    Limits on, 47-61
    Marijuana cultivation, 51-53
    Modern trend, generally, 42-46
    Non-commercial activities, regulation of, 51-53, 60
    Police-power regulations, 39-40, 44-45
    "Substantial economic effect" on, 39, 42-43
    Tenth Amendment as limit on, 62-68
    Violence against women, 50-51
Instrumentalities of interstate commerce, 61
Outgoing trade, barriers to, 88
Relocation, pressures inducing, 85
State as purchaser or subsidizer, 89-90
State regulation of, 74-90
    Balancing test, 78-79
    Congress' power to reverse, 74
    Congress' silence, general effect of, 75
    Contradictory standards, 80
    Cumulative burdens, 80-81
    Discrimination, 77, 80, 81, 83-84, 85, 88
    Disproportionately burdensome to, 83, 90
    Environmental rules, 87-89
    Health objectives, 81, 82
    Incoming trade, barriers to, 81-84
    Less-restrictive alternatives, 78, 82
    Local matters, 76, 84-85
    Local-processing requirements, 85
    "Market participant," state as, 89-90, 105-106
    Means-end fit, 78
    Migration by individuals, 84
    Modern approach, 76
    Natural resources, embargo of, 85
    Need for "legitimate state end", 77
    Outgoing trade, barriers to, 84-85
    Protectionism, 81
    Purchaser or subsidizer, state acting as, 89-90
    Taxation, 90-92
    Transportation, 79-81
"Substantially affecting" commerce, 61

INTERSTATE COMPACTS, 106-107

JUDGES
Campaign fundraising by, 590-591

Campaign speech by, regulation of, 589, 590, 591

JUDICIAL BRANCH
Bias by judge as due process violation, 226-227
Congress' control of federal judicial power, 10-12
Speech by judges, regulation of, 589, 590, 591
Supreme Court's powers, 5-12

JUDICIAL REVIEW
Legitimacy of, 5-10

JUSTICIABILITY, 729-765
See also ADVISORY OPINIONS, ELEVENTH
           AMENDMENT, MOOTNESS, POLITICAL
           QUESTIONS, RIPENESS and STANDING

LEGISLATIVE VETO
Invalidated, 115-116

LESS RESTRICTIVE ALTERNATIVES
Access to criminal trials, 638
Interstate commerce, 78, 82-83
State regulation of commerce, 78, 82-83

LIBERTY OF CONTRACT, 167

LICENSE PLATES
Regulation of messages on, 603-605

"LINE ITEM" VETO
Invalidated, 114-115

MARRIAGE
As fundamental right, 199
By homosexuals, 205, 355-364
By persons owing child support, 199
Same-sex marriage, 199-201

MEDICAL TREATMENT
Right to refuse, 205-207

"MERE-RATIONALITY" TEST
See EQUAL PROTECTION

MIDDLE-LEVEL SCRUTINY
See EQUAL PROTECTION

MILITARY COMMISSIONS
President's power to establish, 122-124

MOOTNESS
Generally, 743-744
"Capable of repetition, yet evading review", 744
Class actions, 744
Collateral consequences, 744
Voluntary cessation by defendant, 744

MOTIVE
See GOVERNMENTAL MOTIVE

NARROW TAILORING
Compulsory disclosure of association's members as
           requiring, 615-618, 647
Content-based classifications as requiring, 484
Content-based regulation of speech as requiring, 551, 590
Requirement of, 617-618
           Race, use of, 284-285, 288-289, 294, 297-299, 299-300,
                      303, 305-306, 307
Time, place and manner regulations as requiring, 507, 508,
           516, 549-550
           Least-restrictive alternative not necessarily
                      required, 509-510
Viewpoint-based regulation of commercial speech as

requiring, 570

NATIONAL SECURITY
President's power regarding, 124-126

NECESSARY AND PROPER CLAUSE
Broad reading given to, 18
Must be incidental to enumerated power, 57

OBSCENITY
Generally, 559-565
Child pornography, possession of, 562, 563
Children as audience, 562
Children as photographic subjects, 563
Community standards, 561, 564
Pictures, book without, 564
Private possession by adults, 562, 563
Scienter required, 565

ONE PERSON, ONE VOTE PRINCIPLE, 754-757

OPINION
Statement of as defamation, 556

OVERBREADTH
Generally, 498-502
Canvassing and soliciting, 513
Communist-control statutes, 495
Defined, 498
Rationale for, 499
Substantial overbreadth now required, 500-501

PARADES
Government interference with participation in, 609

PERMIT
Requirement of as free-speech violation, 510-512

PLEDGE OF ALLEGIANCE
As violation of Establishment Clause, 672

POLITICAL QUESTIONS
Generally, 750-765
Commitment to other branches, 751-753
Factors giving rise to, 751
Impeachment, 751
Judicially manageable standards, lack of, 753
Reapportionment, 754-765
Republican form of government, guarantee of, 753
War Powers disputes, 753

PRAYERS
Sponsored by government, as Establishment Clause
           violation, 671

PREEMPTION
Generally, 92-96
Conflicts preemption, 94-95
Consent by Congress to state laws, 95-96
Express preemption, 93
Field preemption, 93
Implied preemption, 93-95

PRESIDENT
See EXECUTIVE POWERS

PRIVACY, RIGHT OF, 173
See also DUE PROCESS OF LAW

PRIVATE CONDUCT
Congress' power to reach under 14th Amendment, 453-456

PRIVILEGES AND IMMUNITIES
Of national citizenship (14th Amendment), 383, 398-400
    Recent expanded view of, 399
    Right to travel, 399
Of state citizenship (Art. IV), 104-107
    Discrimination, test for, 90, 104
    Equal protection, distinguished from, 106
    "Fundamental rights," limitation to, 104
    Market participant, no exception for, 105-106
    Municipal residence, discrimination based on, 106
Practice of law, right to, 105

PUBLIC FORUM
See FREEDOM OF SPEECH, Public forum

PUNITIVE DAMAGES
See DUE PROCESS OF LAW, Punitive damages

QUOTAS
Ban on in admissions, 284, 285
Defined, 280

RACIAL CLASSIFICATIONS AND QUOTAS
    See also EQUAL PROTECTION and QUOTAS
Minority set-asides by states and cities, 301-306

REAPPORTIONMENT
    Generally, 312-316, 754-765
Commission, use of to carry out, 315-316
Equality, permissible deviation from, 756-757
Gerrymandering, 757-765
Local government bodies, 756
"One person, one vote" principle, 754
Race-conscious grounds used in, 312-316
Redistricting process, 315-316

RECESS APPOINTMENTS
By President, 133-135

RECOGNITION OF FOREIGN GOVERNMENTS, 120-121

REDISTRICTING
Election Clause and, 312-316
Use of partisan criteria in, 757-765
Use of race-conscious criteria in, 312-316

RELIGION, FREEDOM OF
See ESTABLISHMENT CLAUSE and FREE EXERCISE
    CLAUSE

RETROACTIVITY
Contract Clause as restriction on, 413-416
Ex post facto rule as restriction on, 423-424
Taking Clause as restriction on, 400

RIGHT OF INTERSTATE MIGRATION
See RIGHT TO TRAVEL, EQUAL PROTECTION

RIGHT TO DIE
See also DUE PROCESS OF LAW, "Right to die"
    Generally, 205-209
"Clear and convincing" standard, 206
Suicide, 207-209

RIGHT TO TRAVEL
See also EQUAL PROTECTION
    Generally, 381-383
Protected under 14th Amendment Privileges or Immunities
    Clause, 383, 399

RIPENESS
    Generally, 744-746
Criminal statute, uncertain enforcement of, 745
Specific threatened harm, 745

SAME-SEX COUPLES
Discrimination against, 363-364

SAME-SEX MARRIAGE
Equal protection analysis of, 252, 355-364
Fundamental Right to, 367
Substantive due process analysis of, 199-201, 205

SECOND AMENDMENT, 417-423
Handgun ban and, 419, 422
Standard of review for, 422
Types of weapons covered, 422
Unloaded guns, requirement of, 419

SECONDARY-EFFECTS DOCTRINE
In free-speech cases, 528-529

SEGREGATION
See EQUAL PROTECTION

SELECTIVE INCORPORATION
Of Bill of Rights guarantees into Fourteenth Amendment due
    process, 164-166, 236

SEPARATION OF POWERS
    Generally, 111-151
Administrative law judges, 128-130
Appointment of federal officers, 126-130
    Officers and non-officers distinguished, 128-130, 131-
        133
Commitment of the armed forces, 121-122
Executive immunity, 145-148
Executive privilege, 149-151
Federal officers, 128-130
Habeas corpus and, 124
Impeachment, 143-144
President's power, *see* EXECUTIVE POWERS
President's veto power, 113-116
    Legislative veto, 115-116
    "Line item" veto, 114-115
    Pocket veto, 114
Recognition of foreign governments, 120-121
Removal of appointees, 135-144
    By Congress, 142-144
    By President, 135-142

SEX DISCRIMINATION
See also EQUAL PROTECTION
Affirmative action to cure, 275-278

SEXUALITY
Consensual sexual activity
    Homosexual conduct, change in Court attitude
        towards, 251-252
Equal protection and, 356-364, 367
Substantive due-process protection of, 202-205

SIGNS
Regulation of as First Amendment violation, 483-485

SOVEREIGN IMMUNITY
Of states before federal administrative agencies, 750
Of states in their own courts, 749-750

SPEECH AND DEBATE CLAUSE, 145

SPENDING POWER
Generally, 26-31
Coercion of states as limit on, 27-30
Conditions set on use of federal funds, 27-30
Distinct enumerated power, existence as, 26-31
"General welfare" requirement, 31
Regulation, attempt to use for, 26

STANDING
Generally, 731-743
"Actual or imminent harm" requirement, 735
   Threat of prosecution as satisfying, 737
Causation requirement, 738-740
   Constitutional basis for, 739
"Certainly impending" requirement, 736-737
Citizenship suits, 734
Constitutional vs. prudential limitations, 732
Federal taxpayer suits, 733-735
Harm suffered by many, 737
"Injury in fact" requirement, 735
Minorities, denigration of, 737
Nexus requirement for taxpayer suits, 733
Non-economic harms, 735
Organizations and associations, 738
Prudential standing, 743
Rationale behind doctrine, 731
State as plaintiff, 740
Suits not based on taxpayer or citizenship status, 735-740
Tax breaks for discriminatory private schools, 739
Taxpayers' standing, 733-734
Third-party standing, 741-743

STATE ACTION
Generally, 431-446
Acquiescence by state, 445
Civil rights laws, repeal of, 441
Commandment by state, 439-441
Company towns and shopping centers, 435
Electoral process as constituting, 435
Encouragement by state, 441
Entanglement by state, 443-446
Entwinement between state and private actor, 445
Final act, by state, 446
Funding by state, 444
"Government entity" defined, 431
Involvement of state, 438-446
Joint participation by state as private actor, 444-445
Licensing by state, 443
Modern approach to, 434
Monopoly, grant of by state, 443
"Nexus" doctrine, 438-446
Parks and recreation, operation of, 437
Private school, operation of, 438
"Public function" approach, 435-438
Racially-restrictive covenants, 439-440
Recognition by state of private actor's role, 446
State "exclusivity" requirement, 437
"Symbiosis" between state and private actor, 442
Utility, operation of, 437
Warehouseman's lien as, 437

STRICT SCRUTINY
See EQUAL PROTECTION

STUDENTS, FREE SPEECH OF
Advocacy of illegal drug use, 595
Disciplinary needs of school, 593-595
Off-campus speech, 595-599, 656
Student newspaper, 594

SUBSTANTIVE DUE PROCESS
See DUE PROCESS OF LAW

SUICIDE
See DUE PROCESS OF LAW, RIGHT TO DIE

SUPREMACY CLAUSE
See PREEMPTION

SUPREME COURT'S AUTHORITY
Generally, 5-13
Certiorari, 12-13
   Grounds for grant of, 12
Congress' control of, 10-12
Jurisdiction of Court today, 12-13
Review of state court decisions, 7-10
   Independent and adequate state grounds, 8-10
Right to judge statute's constitutionality, 6-7

SUSPECT CLASSIFICATIONS
Generally, 256-263
National origin, 256
Purposeful discrimination required, 257-262
Race, 256
Wealth as, 257, 383-385

TAKING CLAUSE
Generally, 400-413
Denial of all economically viable use, 402
Diminution in value, 401
Economic development as basis for taking, 411-413
Landmark preservation, 404
Moratorium on development as taking, 402
Notice, owner who takes with, 411
Physical occupation, 401
"Prevention of harm" or "noxious use" rationale, 403-404
"Public use" required, 411
Taking distinguished from regulation, 400-411
Temporary delay as taking, 402
Temporary occupation, 406-407
Zoning regulations, 404

TAXATION
Apportionment of direct taxes, 22
Cumulative burdens
   Based on content, 628
Exports not taxable, 22
Federal government's power of, 21-26
Immunities from, 101-102
Internet transactions and, 91-92
Penalty as falling within Congress' power to tax, 24-25
Regulatory effect of, 22-26
States, power of, 90-92
   Discrimination against commerce, 91
   Minimum contacts required, 90
   Taxation of Internet transactions, 91-92

TAXPAYERS
Standing of to bring federal suit, 733-734

TEN COMMANDMENTS
Display of as Establishment Clause violation, 673-674

TENTH AMENDMENT
Commandeering, rule against, 64-68
Impairment of state's essential functions, 62-68
    Law-making mechanisms, use of states', 64-68
Insignificant as general rule, 45, 62-63
Procedural safeguards protecting, 64
Prohibition by Congress on state's right to legislate, 67

THIRD-PARTY STANDING, 741-743

THIRTEENTH AMENDMENT
Congress' power to enforce, 456-458
Private conduct reachable under, 456-457
Purposeful discrimination required, 457
Self-executing scope of, 457

TRADEMARKS
Offensive trademarks and free speech, 481-483, 522

TRANSGENDERED PERSONS
Discrimination against, 363

TRAVEL BAN
President's power to implement, 124-126, 683-688

TREATY POWER
    Generally, 32-33
Executive agreements, 33, 120

TUITION VOUCHERS
Establishment Clause and, 679-680

UNIONS
Right of non-members to refuse to pay for costs of collective
    bargaining, 607-608

UNIVERSITIES
Race-conscious admissions to, 281-294

VACCINATIONS
Free Exercise Clause and vaccine mandates, 713, 715

VAGUENESS
    Generally, 501

Canvassing and soliciting, 513
Use of to invalidate denials of public jobs or benefits, 611

VOTING RIGHTS
See also FREEDOM OF SPEECH, "Political campaign
        spending," FIFTEENTH AMENDMENT, and
        VOTING RIGHTS ACT
As being fundamentally right, 368
Ballot access, 375-378
Candidate eligibility rules, 375
Discriminatory purpose required, 258-259
Drawing of election districts, 312-316, 757-765
Duration-of-residence requirements, 370
Election districts, drawing of, 312-316
Election districts, racially motivated, 312-316
Electoral process as state action, 435
Felons, denial of voting rights to, 372
Filing fees payable by candidates, 378
Gerrymandering, 312-316, 757-765
    Partisan gerrymanders, 757-765
    Racial gerrymanders, 312-316
Minor parties, 376-378
Partisan gerrymanders, 312-316
Poll tax, 369
Statutory protection of, 451-453
Voter identification requirements, 371-372
Voter qualifications, 369-373
Voting Rights Act, 264, 459-464

VOTING RIGHTS ACT
Congressional enforcement of voting rights in, 459, 460-464

WAR POWERS
    Generally, 31, 121
Commitment of the armed forces, 121-122
Power to establish military commissions, 122-124

WEALTH CLASSIFICATIONS
See EQUAL PROTECTION